W9-BZG-085

Based upon a thorough research of never-published documents housed in 14 European archives including those in Vienna, London, Berlin, Paris and Moscow, the book attempts to offer a new insight into the history of the Eastern Question during *Vormärz* from Austria's point of view and introduce the subject as a complex issue of not only diplomatic but also economic, military, religious and social history. As explained in the book, Austrian Chancellor Metternich was fully engaged in each of these spheres and deeply involved in solving various Ottoman affairs. The presented topics concerning the relations between the Ottoman Empire and European Powers should also serve as a platform for refuting the misinterpretations, deep-rooted myths and some prejudices concerning not only Metternich's diplomatic activities but also his personality.

METTERNICH, THE GREAT POWERS AND THE EASTERN QUESTION

METTERNICH,

THE GREAT POWERS AND THE EASTERN QUESTION

Miroslav Šedivý

Title: Metternich, the Great Powers and the Eastern Question
Author: Miroslav Šedivý

This book was written as part of the project "Metternich a Východní
otázka 1821–1841" (Metternich and the Eastern Question 1821–1841)
financed by the Czech Science Foundation (grant No. P410/10/P027).
This book can be downloaded free of charge from
http://metternich.zcu.cz.
Printed by TYPOS, tiskařské závody, s. r. o.,
Podnikatelská 1160/14, Pilsen, Czech Republic

Published by the University of West Bohemia
Univerzitní 8, 316 14 Pilsen, Czech Republic
Telephone number: 00420 377 631 951, e-mail: vydavatel@vyd.zcu.cz

Published 2013, first edition
Publication number: 2088, editorial number: 55-077-12
number of pages: 1033, impression: 220 copies

This publication underwent a review process and was approved by
the Academic Editorial Board of the University of West Bohemia in
Pilsen.

The book was reviewed by Professor Mag. Dr. Helmut Rumpler,
Professor Dr. Walter Sauer and Professor Dr. Karl Vocelka.

English revision by Helen Nathan.
The picture of Metternich on the front cover is a detail from his portrait painted by Sir Thomas Lawrence, now in possession of the Czech
foundation *Nadání Josefa, Marie a Zdeňky Hlávkových*.

Graphic design of the book jacket: Miroslava Wiejová, 2013
Typeset & Layout: Libor Benda, Marie Větrovcová, 2013

ISBN 978-80-261-0223-6 (hardcover)
ISBN 978-80-261-0224-3 (on-line version)

Contents

List of Abbreviations

Archives and Their Sections

ADA	Archives diplomatiques et africaines, Brussels
AMAE	Archives du Ministère des affaires étrangères, Paris
Arch. Nunz. Vienna	Archivio della Nunziature Apostolica in Vienna
ASV	Archivio Segreto Vaticano, Vatican City
AVPRI	Arkhiv vneshnei politiki Rossiiskoi Imperii, Moscow
BHStA	Bayerisches Hauptstaatsarchiv, Munich
CP	Correspondance politique/ Correspondances politiques
FO	Foreign Office
GStA PK	Geheimes Staatsarchiv Preussischer Kulturbesitz, Berlin
HD	Hauptstaatsarchiv, Dresden
HDA	Hrvatski državni arhiv, Zagreb
HHStA	Haus-, Hof- und Staatsarchiv, Vienna
MA	Ministerium des Äußern
MdA	Ministerium des Auswärtigen
NA	Národní archiv, Prague
OO	Obitelj Ottenfels
RA C-A	Rodinný archiv Clary-Aldringenů
RAM-A	Rodinný archiv Metternichů, Starý archiv
RAM-AC	Rodinný archiv Metternichů, Acta Clementina
SG	Sächsische Gesandschaften
SOA	Státní oblastní archiv, Litoměřice
SS	Sächsisches Staatsarchiv, Dresden
StA	Staatenabteilungen
StK	Staatskanzlei
TNA	The National Archives of the United Kingdom, London

Journals and Documentary Collections

AHR	*American Historical Review*
AHY	*Austrian History Yearbook*
CEH	*Central European History*
CHJ	*Cambridge Historical Journal*
DI	*Dépêches inédites du chevalier de Gentz aux hospodars de Valachie*
DWI	*Die Welt des Islams*
EEQ	*East European Quarterly*
EHR	*English Historical Review*
IHR	*International History Review*
IJMES	*International Journal of Middle East Studies*
JCEA	*Journal of Central European Affairs*
JMH	*Journal of Modern History*
MIÖG	*Mitteilungen des Instituts für Österreichische Geschichtsforschung*
MÖStA	*Mitteilungen des Österreichischen Staatsarchivs*
NP	*Aus Metternichs nachgelassenen Papieren*
ÖGL	*Österreich in Geschichte und Literatur*
RH	*Revue historique*
SEER	*Slavonic and East European Review*
SOF	*Südost-Forschungen*
SR	*Slavic Review*
WRP	*World Politics*

Introduction

The importance of Prince Klemens Wenzel Lothar Nepomuk von Metternich-Winneburg for 19th century European history can hardly be denied, and numerous books and articles dedicated to this man and his diplomatic career would seem to show that his significance has been given due attention. This appearance is, however, deceptive. A considerable number of these works are biographies of a merely popular nature or brief surveys offering but a superficial overview of the relevant topics, often based upon a rather limited number of sources and negatively influenced by the personal feelings of their authors towards Metternich, regardless of whether their biases were positive or negative. Despite the fact that Metternich played a significant role in European diplomacy from 1809 to 1848, some of his activities in international relations have been insufficiently researched, and this is particularly evident for the period after 1822 and especially after 1830. It is true that his influence decreased after the end of the congress era, but he undoubtedly remained an important player on the diplomatic chessboard. Consequently, more than 150 years after Metternich's death in 1859, thorough and impartial research on this statesman and his time is still needed. This book seeks to partly rectify this omission and, with an analysis of Metternich's Near Eastern policy, add more detail to the mosaic of the diplomatic history of his period. It attempts to present Metternich's policy within the broader scope of the Eastern Question and introduce the subject as a complex issue of not only diplomatic but also economic, military, religious and social history.

The Eastern Question, the question that can be briefly explained as what should become of the Ottoman Empire, was an important part of European politics from the late 18th to the early 20th century and it is also one of the crucial issues of Metternich's era. Although at that time no Great Power wanted to destroy the Ottoman Empire, their geopolitical, economic and even prestigious interests in south-eastern Europe, North Africa, the eastern Mediterranean and the Black Sea significantly shaped not only the development of these parts of the world but also strongly affected the relations among the Great Powers themselves, thus having a significant impact on the history of both European as well as non-European regions. The denomination of this important question as "Eastern" results from the fact that this term originated in Europe, more accurately in Western Europe, whose populations usually viewed the Ottoman Empire a remote – geographically as well as culturally – country in the East, consequently the Near East/Levant/Orient. Metternich also understood the Ottoman Empire with regard to the term "East" in this way, and the fact that he saw in this not only a geographical but also cultural boundary is very important because the term East/Levant/Orient was used by him for the whole of the Ottoman Empire, whose territory he never entered, including its Balkan domains, which were for him, a man born in the Rhineland deeply rooted in Western civilisation and 18th century enlightenment, as alien as those in Asia or Africa. This outlook is clearly evident not only from the studied documents but also from his often declared statement, probably not greatly exaggerated from his point of view, that he regarded the garden on the road leading from Vienna to Pressburg, owned by the House of Schwarzenberg and divided by the frontier between Austria and Hungary as "the place where Europe ends and Asia begins."[1] Consequently, when Metternich talked about affairs as Eastern/Oriental, he meant any of the affairs concerning the Ottoman Empire including, for example, the Algerian or Greek Questions as will be seen in this book.

The period covered in this book is from the beginning of the Greek insurrection against Ottoman rule in 1821 to the end of the second Turko-Egyptian crisis in 1841. These twenty years were chosen because the most important affairs of the Eastern Question in Metternich's era occurred during these two decades. The preceding Serbian uprising was undeniably of some importance to Austria, and it occupied Metternich after his accession to the helm of the Austrian foreign ministry in 1809, but first, it was a matter of far less significance for European politics than later incidents like the Greek

---

[1]   Langsdorff to Sainte-Aulaire, Vienna, 6 May 1836, AMAE, CP, Autriche 423. According to a similar story, Metternich was said to claim that the Orient began at the Landstrasse leading out from Vienna. L. Wolff, "'Kennst du das Land?' The Uncertainty of Galicia in the Age of Metternich and Fredro," *SR* 67, 2008, 2, p. 294.

uprising or two Turko-Egyptian crises, and second, Austria's policy towards the Serbian uprising has already been thoroughly researched by Ulrike Tischler.[2] The same applies for the period from 1841 to Metternich's political downfall seven years later when no incident in the Balkans or the Levant raised such serious issues for the Great Powers as those in the two preceding decades. Their involvement in the Mount Lebanon affairs launched in 1840 surely was of some importance but it has been adequately researched by Caesar E. Farah.[3]

This volume is strictly limited to the history of the Eastern Question from Austria's point of view, it does not examine the internal history of the Ottoman Empire or its relations with all European Powers, and although Austria's involvement in the Near Eastern affairs must naturally be put into the wider context of European history, this book is not and cannot be a comprehensive survey of Metternich's entire diplomacy, including his activities in Germany or Italy. The choice of the Near East does not imply that this area was of more significance than the two previously mentioned regions, which of course it was not, nor that Austria played the most important role of all the Great Powers in the Eastern Question, which it definitely did not, but it should prove that for the Danube Monarchy and Metternich himself the importance of the Ottoman Empire as well as the politics connected with its decay have generally been underestimated and that much remains to be discovered with regard to Metternich's character and activities in general. The appropriate question is not whether the areas of German Confederation and the Apennines were of greater importance for Metternich's Austria but whether the Ottoman Empire was actually of far less importance for the Central European Power. The significance of this question becomes apparent when one considers that Austria was connected to the Ottoman Empire by the longest frontier of all European countries and this border was also the longest of all Austria's neighbours. The book should thus also contribute to the research on Austrian as well as Central European history from the "south-eastern point of view."

---

[2] U. Tischler, *Die habsburgische Politik gegenüber den Serben und Montenegrinern 1791–1822*, München 2000.
[3] C. E. Farah, *The Politics of Interventionism in Ottoman Lebanon, 1830–1861*, London, New York 2000.

It is my intent to offer an in-depth analysis probably not entirely in compliance with the latest fashion of broad theorisation of diplomatic frameworks, standards and rules, as for example American historian Paul W. Schroeder or German historian Matthias Schulz did,[4] but perhaps making it possible to refute the misinterpretations, deep-rooted myths and some prejudices concerning not only Metternich's diplomacy but also his personality. This does not mean that my purpose is to glorify this man and repudiate all his critics. In contrast to Paul W. Schroeder, as he has mentioned in the introduction of his book on Metternich, I did not start my research with any supposition that the revisionist, meaning positive, views on Metternich are correct.[5] To be frank, my original interest focused on Austria's activities in the Levant and not at all on Metternich. I was not among his admirers then and I still do not consider myself one of them. In the course of time, however, through the study of relevant archival sources, I started to better understand this man and what motivated him, and I dare say that I gradually discovered a considerable number of incorrect statements and appraisals made by historians in the past. This particularly happened at the moment when I went through the documents covering a longer time span, which helped me to better, and I hope more correctly, evaluate Metternich's policy, its motivations and goals. For this reason, the characteristics of my findings approach more closely those of Alan J. Reinerman, Ulrike Tischler, and particularly Wolfram Siemann,[6] all of them having dealt with or still dealing with Metternich in a wider timeframe, than to the general views of Paul W. Schroeder, who focused intently on Metternich's diplomacy within only a short period.[7]

The picture of Metternich that materialised after the end of my research is a portrait of a man who was conservative, but this term, which is frequently used in the literature about him, does not ade-

---

[4]   P. W. Schroeder, *The Transformation of European Politics 1763–1848*, Oxford 1996; M. Schulz, *Normen und Praxis: Das Europäische Konzert der Großmächte als Sicherheitsrat, 1815–1860*, München 2009.

[5]   P. W. Schroeder, *Metternich's Diplomacy at Its Zenith, 1820–1823*, New York 1962, p. x.

[6]   A. J. Reinerman, "Metternich and Reform: The Case of the Papal State, 1814–1848," *JMH* 42, 1970, 4, pp. 526–527; W. Siemann, *Metternich: Staatsmann zwischen Restauration und Moderne*, München 2010.

[7]   Schroeder, *Metternich's Diplomacy*, p. 266.

quately explain his policy and leads to the assumption that his diplomacy was dogmatic and unrealistic. What I want to do with this book is to contribute to the re-evaluation of Metternich and his time; it is the fact that his policy, at least during the given period of 1821–1841 and in relation to the Eastern Question, was conservative as well as rather realistic and so to speak pragmatic, based upon his rational and usually unbelievably accurate analysis of events and his profound knowledge of facts and people; it is even possible to claim that in many respects his opinions relating to Near Eastern affairs were quite rational and his corresponding policy very consistent and actually not duplicitous – at least not to the degree generally attributed to him. Furthermore, the following chapters should demonstrate that the vast regions of the Ottoman Empire constituted a politically and economically important area for the Danube Monarchy; and although Metternich would definitely have liked to avoid dealing with Ottoman affairs, he was unable to do so and not only dealt with them but also paid remarkable attention to various problems resulting from the decay of the sultan's weak empire. I would dare to go so far as to claim that no other member of the European political and diplomatic elites of the period under research paid so much attention to the internal situation of the Ottoman Empire as Metternich did, but of course this is always hard to evaluate. Another objective of the presented study is to show that Metternich's views and steps in the Eastern Question in the 1830s were not actually anti-Russian but markedly anti-French and that Austria's relations with Russia in the Ottoman affairs during the same decade were surprisingly good because the two Powers' interests in the Ottoman Empire were identical, they needed each other's support in the West as well as in the East and it can be said that a specific sort of an "entente cordial" existed between them. And last but not at least, with this book I will attempt to refute the opinion advocated by the "apostles" of structural history in the last several decades that after 1815 an important transformation in European politics occurred and that the Great Powers limited their self-serving ambitions with their alleged sense of an all-European responsibility. I originally did not plan to deal with this subject, but since a correct assessment of European politics in the so-called Pre-March period (*Vormärz*) is naturally crucial for a correct evaluation of Metternich's role in it and because my own research and conclusions persuaded me that the "transformation theory" is for the most part entirely baseless and distorts the real image of European politics,

the character of which did not significantly differ from the periods before 1815 and after 1848, the Eastern Question will also serve in this
book as a model example for the re-evaluation of the motivations
behind the Great Powers' conduct and Metternich's position in the
diplomatic relations still mostly shaped by the egoistic interests of
their protagonists. Furthermore, if in this generally predatory world
someone was actually motivated by any principles surpassing simple
national or power-hungry interests in determining his policy, then it is
difficult to see a better candidate than Metternich. It does not mean
that I will try to enter into the dispute as to whether Metternich was
more an Austrian or a European statesman, in other words whether
his steps were directed more by Austrian or European interests, simply because it is impossible to find a definite answer when the crucial
question can never be clearly defined: what Europe's interest actually
was – the preservation of general peace, or the spread of liberalism,
or the establishment of national states? What I want to prove is the
fact that Metternich, more than any of his allies or opponents on the
diplomatic chessboard, not only wanted to maintain the existence of
the Ottoman Empire and never deviated from pursuing this goal, but
that he also maintained a highly consistent politico-legal strategy in
his Near Eastern policy with the aim of applying the rules shaping
the relations among the European countries, or at least the rules he
wished to apply to them, to their relations with the Ottoman Empire and through his willingness to observe these rules to ensure not
only the political status quo beyond Austria's south-eastern border
but also to prevent the rivalry between the European Powers in the
regions beyond it from destabilising their own relations and thereby
threatening the general peace of Europe.

   All of this should be proved in the following text, which is divided
into 31 sections and arranged thematically although not necessarily
chronologically. Altogether they should introduce the phenomenon of
the Eastern Question, as mentioned above, as a complex problem
covering various spheres of diplomatic, economic, military, religious
and even social history. Metternich was fully engaged in each of these
spheres and, consequently, none can be omitted if his Near Eastern
diplomacy is to be fully explained. His fundamental attitude towards
the importance of preserving the Ottoman Empire, his wish to anchor
its existence in the European state system as created at the Congress
of Vienna and his handling of the affairs beyond Austria's south-
eastern frontier until the outbreak of the Greek insurrection in 1821

are all dealt with in Chapter 1. Metternich's conduct in the conflict between the Greeks and the Ottomans from its very beginning to the death of Tsar Alexander I (1821–1825) is covered in the following two chapters (Chapters 2 and 3), which attempt to prove that Russia's policy followed more its own rather than European interests and that Metternich was more consistent in his policy and more sincere in his statements and less disingenuous in his dealings with the tsar than he has generally been accused of being. Chapter 4 focuses on the genesis of the St Petersburg Protocol in 1826 and the fact that British Foreign Secretary George Canning not only made a crucial mistake from the British as well as the Austrian point of view when he granted Tsar Nicholas I freedom of action towards the Ottoman Empire with this document but that he also did so unnecessarily; if anyone saved the peace between Russia and the Ottoman Empire in 1826, it was not Canning but Metternich. Metternich's reaction to the conditions of the Protocol as well as the Treaty of London (1826–1827) is explained in Chapter 5, and it is emphasised here that his criticism of these two documents resulted not from any blind irrational conservative dogmatism but his consistent respect for existing international law and his correct predictions of the consequences resulting from the conditions of the two documents. Chapter 6 reveals Metternich's attitude towards the Greek insurrection and his steps undertaken in favour of the sultan in the Near East during the period preceding the battle in Navarino Bay in 1827. Chapter 7 focuses on Metternich's considerable but unsuccessful efforts to save the peace between Russia and the Ottoman Empire after the Battle of Navarino. The complicated situation for Austria when a war between Russia and the Ottoman Empire was in progress in its immediate vicinity in 1828 and at a time when Metternich's options for action were severely restricted by Austria's internal weakness and the attitudes of other Great Powers is covered in Chapter 8. Metternich's attitude during the final phase of the Russo-Ottoman war in 1829 and towards the related peace treaty is analysed in Chapter 9. The Greek Question from the Battle of Navarino until the foundation of independent Greece in 1832 with relation to Metternich's diplomacy is examined in Chapter 10, where particularly Metternich's skill in coping with unfavourable and difficult circumstances is shown. His conduct in religious affairs is examined for the first time in Chapter 11 dealing with the Constantinople Armenian Catholic Affair from 1828 to 1831 and then in three later chapters covering, first, his attitudes towards Islam, his anti-Philhellenism, and his criticism of the one-sided and hypocritical views of some Europeans and their humanitarian projects concerning the religious situation of the Ottoman Empire; second, his effort to help the persecuted Jews during the Damascus Affair in 1840; and third, his plan for the provision of a favourable and safe future for the Christians, in particular the Catholics, in Syria in 1840–1841 (Chapters 12, 28 and 29). Chapter 13 explains Metternich's surprisingly deep involvement in the affair of the French expedition to Algeria in 1830. Chapter 14 covers his considerable interest in Austro-Ottoman commercial relations and tries to answer the question whether they had any impact on his diplomatic activities; this chapter also introduces the first Turko-Egyptian or so-called First Mohammed Ali Crisis whose early phase during 1831–1832 is analysed here in connection with Austria's economic interests in Egypt. The same crisis, in particular its final phase in 1833, is analysed from a wider European perspective in Chapter 15. This as well as the following chapter (Chapter 16) which explains the mission of Austrian diplomat Anton Prokesch von Osten to Alexandria in 1833 reveal the anti-French bias in Metternich's Near Eastern policy in the early 1830s. Chapter 17 deals with the well-known Russo-Ottoman Treaty of Unkiar-Skelessi and particularly with the meeting of the Austrian and Russian monarchs in Münchengrätz in September 1833 and attempts to re-evaluate its significance and particularly to refute the deep-rooted claim that Metternich yielded to Nicholas I's interests in the East in return for the tsar's support against the revolutions in the West. The British Russophobia in the mid 1830s that was as baseless as it was harmful to the Great Powers' relations within the Eastern Question and to Metternich's position together with his desire to overcome their mutual distrust are examined in Chapter 18. This is also partly reflected in Chapter 19, which covers Metternich's apprehensions and reaction to Russia's political penetration into the Danubian Principalities, Moldavia and Wallachia, ending in Russia's political predominance in the early 1830s, and his concern about commercial navigation on the Danube, whose delta was directly controlled by Russia from 1829. Since the Ottoman reform movement attracted the attention of the Great Powers and became an integral part of their contention for influence over the sultan's court, in other words it constituted an important component of the Eastern Question in the 1830s, and because Metternich was personally interested in this matter and took part in the competition for this influence, this topic receives considerable attention in the next two chapters (Chapters 20 and 21). It is also later analysed in Chapter 30, which seeks to explain Metternich's attitude towards the leading Ottoman reformer, Mustafa Reshid Pasha, and refute the allegation against the chancellor that he initiated Reshid's fall in March 1841. All of these three chapters should prove that Metternich not only did not oppose but in fact actually supported the effort for the regeneration of the Ottoman Empire during Mahmud II's reign as well as the early phase of the Tanzimat (a period of reforms from 1839 to 1876) although this support was naturally limited by his conservative thinking. Since in the mid 1830s, the Great Powers contended not for the Ottoman Empire's territories but for influence over the decisions made by its government, Chapter 22 therefore attempts to discover the level of Austria's influence in Constantinople and Metternich's attempts at increasing it. Chapter 23 covers Metternich's attitude towards Egyptian Governor Mohammed Ali and his personal ambitions destabilising the fragile peace in the Ottoman Empire after 1833; this chapter also examines Metternich's efforts to prevent the outbreak of war between Mohammed Ali and Sultan Mahmud II in the spring of 1839 and his diplomatic intervention leading to the internationalisation of the Second Mohammed Ali Crisis at the end of July 1839. Chapter 24 explains Metternich's attempts to deal with the crisis on the European stage and, by means of a convocation of a ministerial conference in Vienna in 1839 with the aim of forestalling the rupture among the Great Powers caused by the conflict in the Levant, to revive a part of his diminishing influence and step once more into the limelight. Chapters 25 and 26 outline Metternich's role in the further course of the Near Eastern Crisis after mid 1839 finally leading to the signing of the London Convention for the Pacification of the Levant in mid July 1840 and the eruption of the so-called Rhine Crisis in the late summer and autumn of the same year. The military intervention in Syria against Egyptian forces in late 1840 in which Austria's navy participated is outlined in Chapter 27. The history of the Second Mohammed Ali Crisis as well as Metternich's active involvement in the Eastern Question in 1841 is concluded in the final Chapter 31.

It is naturally impossible to analyse all the topics in all relevant details in one book. Consequently, it must be emphasised that all topics have been examined only to the extent necessary for the explanation of Metternich's policy. Inasmuch as this book is not a general survey of his diplomatic activities everywhere or the history of the Eastern Question in general, it is likewise not dedicated to Austria's presence in the Near East. It was necessary only to sketch the activities of its navy in the eastern Mediterranean or the presence of Ottoman students in Vienna, and themes without any significance for Metternich's involvement in the Eastern Question like the functioning of Austria's consular network in the Levant have even been entirely omitted.[8] An exception had to be made in the case of Austria's commerce with the Ottoman Empire because its extent and importance for the Danube Monarchy is generally unknown and must be presented in more detail for Metternich's role in this sphere to be correctly understood.

Although Austria's involvement in the Near East and its relations with the Ottoman Empire are more or less well researched for the periods before 1821 and after 1848, the years between have been considerably omitted by historians and only a few published and some unpublished studies exist, and mainly for the 1820s. The works of Anton Prokesch von Osten on the Greek insurrection and Mohammed Ali, published between the late 1860s and the early 1880s, long served as the only richer sources of information, even after the issue of the first survey of Austria's Near Eastern policy by Austrian historian Adolf Beer in 1883. This survey, however, for the period 1821–1841 was more or less based upon Prokesch's works.[9] The situation considerably improved in 1971 when Austrian historian Manfred Sauer finished (but unfortunately never published) his dissertation thesis *Österreich und die Levante 1814–1838* based upon thorough archival research. Although diplomacy forms only one of four main topics also including Austria's consular administration, navy and commerce, and even though Metternich's policy is analysed briefly, it is still the great-

---

[8] Fortunately, this topic has already been well researched. For more see R. Agstner, *Von k. k. Konsularagentie zum Österreichischen Generalkonsulat: Österreich (-Ungarn) und Alexandrien 1763–1993*, Kairo 1993; L. Kammerhofer, "Das Konsularwerk der Habsburgermonarchie (1752–1918): Ein Überblick mit Schwerpunkt auf Südosteuropa," H. Heppner (ed.), *Der Weg führt über Österreich ... Zur Geschichte des Verkehrs- und Nachrichtenwesens von und nach Südosteuropa*, Wien, Köln, Weimar 1996, pp. 7–31; M. Sauer, "Zur Reform der österreichischen Levante-Konsulate im Vormärz," *MÖStA* 27, 1974, pp. 195–237.

[9] A. von Prokesch-Osten, *Mehmed-Ali, Vize-König von Aegypten: Aus meinem Tagebuche 1826–1841*, Wien 1877, and *Geschichte des Abfalls der Griechen vom türkischen Reiche im Jahre 1821 und der Gründung des hellenischen Königreiches: Aus diplomatischem Standpuncte*, I–VI, Wien 1867–1880; A. Beer, *Die orientalische Politik Österreichs seit 1773*, Prag, Leipzig 1883.

est and by far the most comprehensive contribution to the research on Austro-Ottoman relations and is a necessary source of information for other authors like Bertrand Michael Buchmann and Robert-Tarek Fischer. The brief surveys from these two Austrian historians, however, contribute nothing really new to the state of research, the former's work being in fact a textbook for University students.[10]

Except for the already mentioned monograph by Ulrike Tischler covering the pre-1821 period, there is only one book fully aimed at Metternich's Near Eastern policy, *Die Orientpolitik des Fürsten Metternich, 1829–1833* by Ernst Molden published in 1913.[11] Molden spent some time in the Austrian State Archives and wrote a worthwhile but unfortunately rather short analysis. In the same year another Austrian historian, Josef Krauter, published his book on the Austrian internuncio in Constantinople, Franz von Ottenfels. His work focuses particularly on Ottenfels' career and on Friedrich von Gentz, but it is of course useful for the research on Metternich's diplomacy, and definitely more so than most biographies of Metternich, including the largest one written by Heinrich von Srbik, who did not use archival documents for this topic and compiled it predominantly from the published literature.[12] No subsequent author devoted more space in their Metternichian biographies to this particular question with the exception of Guillaume de Bertier de Sauvigny, the author of *Metternich: Staatsmann und Diplomat für Österreich und den Frieden* and the more important *Metternich et la France après le congrès de Vienne.* The latter is the best analysis of Metternich's foreign policy from 1815 to 1830 based upon thorough research in several European archives.[13] Of considerable importance is also Paul W. Schroeder's monograph

---

[10] M. Sauer, *Österreich und die Levante 1814–1838*, unpublished dissertation, Wien 1971; B. M. Buchmann, *Österreich und das Osmanische Reich: Eine bilaterale Geschichte*, Wien 1999; R.-T. Fischer, *Österreich im Nahen Osten: Die Großmachtpolitik der Habsburgermonarchie im Arabischen Orient 1633–1918*, Wien, Köln, Weimar 2006.

[11] E. Molden, *Die Orientpolitik des Fürsten Metternich, 1829–1833*, Wien, Leipzig 1913.

[12] J. Krauter, *Franz Freiherr von Ottenfels: Beiträge zur Politik Metternichs im griechischen Freiheitskampfe 1822–1832*, Salzburg 1913; H. von Srbik, *Metternich: Der Staatsmann und der Mensch*, I–II, München 1925.

[13] G. de B. de Sauvigny, *Metternich et la France après le congrès de Vienne*, II–III, Paris 1970, and *Metternich: Staatsmann und Diplomat für Österreich und den Frieden*, Gernsbach 1988.

Metternich's Diplomacy at Its Zenith, 1820–1823, which explains very well Metternich's conduct in the first phase of the Greek revolt, and this is by far the best researched topic of Metternich's entire policy in the Near East due largely to Schroeder's book and the works of Henry Kissinger, Irby C. Nichols, and finally Nazif Gürbüz's never published dissertation thesis based on Austrian as well as Turkish archival sources although this is unfortunately too descriptive and somewhat pro-Turkish.[14] Useful information can naturally be obtained from numerous books and articles on the history of Austria, European politics or the Eastern Question, but only some are of greater importance for the submitted project and they can hardly entirely fill the vacuum in the research on Metternich's diplomacy. For example, even his policy towards the Danubian Principalities, the regions of extraordinary geopolitical and economic importance for the Austrian Empire, remains more or less unresearched.[15]

The lack of relevant sources is not the only problem for a scholar dealing with the presented theme. False interpretations often transformed into automatically adopted myths are another and more serious issue, giving thus important impetus for research on Metternich. There are obviously two reasons for this. First, such errors can result from the biased attitudes of the authors against the man who, as for example Romanian historian Nicolae Ciachir wrote, "was hesitating at nothing."[16] It would be entirely senseless to recall in detail such historians as Heinrich von Treitschke or Victor Bibl because the motivation of their hostility towards Metternich is too well known and their works

---

[14] H. A. Kissinger, *A World Restored: Metternich, Castlereagh and the Problems of Peace 1812–22*, London 1957; I. C. Nichols, "The Eastern Question and the Vienna Conference, September 1822," *JCEA* 21, 1961, 1, pp. 53–66, and a book by the same author *The European Pentarchy and the Congress of Verona 1822*, The Hague 1971; N. Gürbüz, *Die österreichisch-türkischen Beziehungen vom Wiener Kongreß (1814–1815) bis zum Tod des Zaren Alexander I. (1825): Mit besonderen Beachtung der österreichischen Quellen*, unpublished dissertation, Wien 1983; Schroeder, *Metternich's Diplomacy.*

[15] The exception proving the rule is a paper by M. Sauer, "Österreich und die Sulina-Frage 1829–1854, Erster Teil," *MÖStA* 40, 1987, pp. 184–236; "Zweiter Teil," *MÖStA* 41, 1990, pp. 72–137. It is an excellent scholastic contribution, but it deals almost exclusively with the problem of shipping in the Danubian Delta.

[16] N. Ciachir, "The Adrianople Treaty (1829) and its European Implications," *Revue des études sud-est européennes* 17, 1979, p. 713.

are not of great importance for the topic.[17] In contrast is the case of a definitely fundamental book by the famous British historian, Sir Charles Kingsley Webster, *The Foreign Policy of Palmerston 1830– 1841: Britain, the Liberal Movement and the Eastern Question*, which undoubtedly contains a considerable number of correct assertions concerning the Austrian chancellor and is probably the most comprehensive contribution to his diplomatic activities within the Eastern Question in the 1830s.[18] Nevertheless, one also cannot overlook the fact that Webster uses Metternich as a negative contrast to British Foreign Secretary Henry John Temple 3rd Viscount Palmerston, who was highly praised for guarding the interests of the British Empire, which was crumbling at the moment when Webster was writing his book. It is hard to overlook the fact that some of Webster's criticism is the result of his personal attitude, to some extent probably caused by the fact that "the historian of the British Empire" could not or did not want to understand the man whose political views, principles and diplomatic behaviour were considerably different from those of the foreign secretary. Some of Webster's views have recently been challenged by another British historian, Alan Sked, in *Metternich and Austria: An Evaluation*, which has effectively shown that Metternich's personality and activities cannot be correctly understood without a thorough familiarisation with his period, which has so often been depicted in black and white, in particular by nationalist and liberal historians or later Marxist scholars.[19] The problem with Sked's evaluation lies in his lack of relevant archival sources. It cannot be regarded as a negative in itself because the character of the book did not require such a detailed background, but it nevertheless precluded the author from obtaining a more powerful weapon for challenging Webster's opinions based upon some Austrian official diplomatic correspondence exchanged between Metternich and his diplomats in London and the British envoy's reports from Vienna. The latter's letters serving as Webster's major source of information were, in my opinion, sometimes interpreted incorrectly and conformed with the predominantly

---

[17] H. von Treitschke, *Treitschke's History of Germany in the Nineteenth Century*, VI, London 1919; V. Bibl, *Metternich in neuer Beleuchtung*, Wien 1928.
[18] Sir C. K. Webster, *The Foreign Policy of Palmerston 1830–1841: Britain, the Liberal Movement and the Eastern Question*, I–II, London 1951.
[19] A. Sked, *Metternich and Austria: An Evaluation*, New York 2008.

negative picture of Metternich as drawn by the author. Some historians, however, interested in the diplomacies of Great Britain, France, Russia or Prussia made an even more serious scholarly mistake when they based their opinions on Metternich's policy only upon documents written by non-Austrian diplomats containing second-hand and often incorrect information.

The lack of ample documentary evidence in the case of numerous books and articles on Metternich is the second reason for various misinterpretations and legends. It is scarcely credible how far-reaching conclusions were often based upon a curiously low number of convincing primary sources, if any at all. If one examines the works written in the last 150 years or more, one cannot fail to be surprised how some generally accepted theses came into existence – a rumour or seemingly logical but actually unfounded presumption sufficed. What most probably contributed to this situation is the low number of relevant published documents. What has been hitherto issued is but a fragment of the volume of correspondence written by Metternich and it in no way suffices for a complete analysis either of his general politics and opinions or his diplomacy in the Near East. Some importance must be given to eight volumes containing especially Metternich's correspondence published by his son, Richard von Metternich-Winneburg, or several other collections containing the letters of Metternich, Friedrich von Gentz, Anton Prokesch von Osten or Ludwig von Lebzeltern.[20] Nevertheless, they offer but a small amount of these men's total correspondence and predominantly cover the period of the Greeks' struggle for independence.

One cannot avoid a feeling of astonishment owing to the immense disproportion in the editing and publishing of documents on Austria's history before and after 1848, where the former period remains almost absolutely neglected. As a consequence of the scant elaboration of the presented topic by scholars and the unsatisfactory number of published documents, this work is largely based on the manuscript collections of several European archives. The Austrian State Archives in Vienna were certainly the most useful. For our topic, the collections of all Austrian official correspondence, not merely of a diplomatic nature, dispatched between the Danube Monarchy and the Ot-

---

[20] For relevant volumes with published documents see the Bibliography at the end of the book.

toman Empire, France, Great Britain, Russia and Prussia were of
primary importance. For certain particular topics, some additional
research had to be carried out on correspondence between Metternich and his diplomats in less important diplomatic or consular posts
in Europe and the Levant. I found it necessary to visit other European archives because it would hardly be possible to arrive at correct conclusions in certain cases without the use of other manuscript
collections as the documents of Austrian provenance lack a considerable number of discussions between Metternich and foreign diplomats
and usually do not contain information concerning, for example, the
relations among the Austrian elites, the characters of Ottoman representatives, or the stay of Ottoman students in Vienna. The reason
for the choice of those archives preserving relevant diplomatic correspondence in London, Paris, Moscow and Berlin surely need not be
explained here in detail since all the Great Powers were involved in
the Eastern Question, including Prussia albeit to a rather limited extent. Their diplomats' reports from Vienna, Constantinople or some
other cities generally were of great use. A specific contribution came
from the study of Bavarian, Saxon and Belgian diplomatic correspondence: since the representatives of those courts in Vienna did not take
part in the most important diplomatic talks, they had time to observe the marginal events of the country and comment on them in
their reports, which consequently contain information that is of less
importance from the diplomatic point of view but sometimes adds
significant pieces to the puzzle which cannot be found in the letters
of the Great Powers' diplomats. In this respect the Bavarian State
Archives in Munich were very fertile, while the archives in Dresden
and Brussels were considerably less useful. The research carried out in
the Vatican Secret Archives helped to better clarify Metternich's conduct in the affairs concerning the Ottoman Christians and Jews. The
Czech National Archives in Prague could not be omitted for the fact
that Metternich's private manuscript collection (*Acta Clementina*)
forms a well-known, although hitherto scarcely exploited part of it.
Their importance for writing this book was, however, negligible, particularly in comparison with the Czech archives in Tetschen (Děčín)
in the north-west of Bohemia, which hold the private collection of
the Austrian ambassador in St Petersburg, Count Karl Ludwig von
Ficquelmont. Of particular significance was Metternich's library in
the Chateau of Königswart (Kynžvart) in western Bohemia because
the expectation that some of the books held there contain Metter-

nich's personal comments in their margins was correct, turning thus the relevant books into archival material and a part of the library into a record office. Consequently, the library in Königswart is listed in the Bibliography among archives. The last two in Ljubljana and Zagreb were of different importance. Whereas the former offered just one document for a marginal topic, the latter provided Franz von Ottenfels' private manuscript collection containing his correspondence with Metternich and a more useful manuscript of his never-published memoirs.[21] It is true that Josef Krauter based his above-mentioned monograph upon these memoirs, in some cases rather "literally," but the original version is still a considerably valuable and unexploited source of information on Austro-Ottoman relations.

The use of Turkish archives would undoubtedly have cleared up some matters like the impact of Metternich's advice on the Ottoman ruling class or the degree of his influence over it, but since I am dealing with Metternich's opinions and activities within the Eastern Question and not Austro-Ottoman relations, Turkish documents were not necessary for writing this book. Consequently, the present theme, like my sources and my opinions, is purely European in its perspective. When I more or less touch on Ottoman topics, I often have to remain on the threshold, but it must be emphasised that I have never had an ambition to go further. The monograph should be understood in such a way.

This book could have never been written without the courage and assistance of many people and organisations to whom I am deeply indebted and all of whom I unfortunately cannot mention here by name. In the first place I would like to express my deepest gratitude to Professor Aleš Skřivan, who supervised my research from the very beginning of my University studies and always readily offered his advice and assistance. My special thanks go to Professor Wolfram Siemann, who deals at the present time with Metternichian topics and whose opinions were always extremely helpful and inspiring. I would also like to thank Professor Ivo Budil, the director of the Department of Historical Studies at the University of West Bohemia in Pilsen, who enabled me to start my academic career and never was deaf to my often immodest wishes, to professors Arnold Suppan and Karl Vocelka for their helpful

---

[21] F. von Ottenfels, *Memoari Franze Ottenfelsa*, HDA, 750, OO 18. [hereafter: Ottenfels, *Memoari*]

advice and enabling me to carry out my research in Vienna, to professors Helmut Rumpler, Walter Sauer and Robert D. Billinger Jr. for their useful counsels, to Austrian historians Manfred Sauer and Marcel Chahrour for their valuable suggestions, to French historian Victor Demiaux for his help with the translations of some French diplomatic texts into English, to Barbora Szabová for her technical assistance in creating the graphs and to Howard Golden for his encouragement. I also cannot and do not want to omit the Czech foundation *Nadace Josefa, Marie a Zdeňky Hlávkových* for making available the free use of the painting of Metternich in its possession for the book jacket. I am grateful to the publishers of the journals *Austrian History Yearbook, British Journal of Middle Eastern Studies, Central European History, European Review of History/Revue européenne d'histoire, International History Review, Middle Eastern Studies* and *Slavonic and East European Review* for permission to reproduce material from my articles which appears in Chapters 11, 15, 17, 19, 20, 24 and 29.[22] A person who deserves a special mention is Helen Nathan, who played a key role in this project. She revised my text and my translations of the French and German diplomatic correspondence, thus enabling the publication of this book in English. I can hardly express my appreciation for her work as well as her enthusiasm and support during the eighteen months we collaborated on the text. Finally, I cannot fail to express my infinite gratitude to my family and my mother in particular, who were not directly involved in my scholarly work but all the time unselfishly and unequivocally supported it. It is probably not necessary to add that although many people contributed to this book with their advice, the responsibility for all eventual mistakes and imperfections ultimately rests with me.

---

[22] For relevant articles in these journals see the Bibliography at the end of the book.

1

The Ottoman Empire and the European State System

The significance which Metternich attributed to the existence of the Ottoman Empire for Austria's position as a Great Power and the stability of the European politics was revealed soon after his nomination to the Austrian foreign ministry. He tried to contribute to the solution of the Serbian uprising and attempted to introduce the sultan's state into the European state system created at the Congress of Vienna and guarantee thus its further political sovereignty and territorial integrity. These efforts resulted from Metternich's deep conviction that although the Ottoman Empire lay culturally outside Europe, politically it could not be excluded because it formed an important barrier against the nationalism of Balkan nations and Russian imperialism, making this country an important component of the balance of power in Europe and a useful and necessary ally to Austria.

The Ottoman Empire: The Barrier against Nationalism and Russian Imperialism

The arrival of Metternich at the head of the Austrian foreign ministry in October 1809 did not signal any turning point in Austro-Ottoman relations, which had already been significantly modified in the previous century. Even during the 1711–1740 reign of Emperor Charles VI, who waged two wars with the Ottomans, the Balkan territory was regarded in Vienna as economically and culturally backward and eventual gains in this part of Europe as exigent of vast investments and doubtful value. This opinion prevailed after his death, when his daughter Maria Theresa was forced to wage costly wars in the West, which precluded the seizure of regions also requiring considerable expenditure as well as any hostile policy in the south-east. The queen had to maintain good relations with the Sublime Porte, as both the sultan's court and the Ottoman Empire as a whole were referred to by European diplomats. Maria Theresa actually pursued a friendly policy towards Austria's south-eastern neighbour, and instead of territorial expansion she supported economic penetration into the Levant.[1]

Maria Theresa's attitude was also taken by her son Joseph II. The war with the Ottoman Empire, which he started in 1787,[2] was an unwilling deviation from the given political line, an anachronism that in fact reflected the emperor's political orientation to the West and in no way signified any nostalgia for Charles VI's warlike policy in the Balkans. Joseph II and his Chancellor Prince Wenzel Anton von Kaunitz-Rietberg reluctantly joined Russia in the conflict because they were obliged to maintain the alliance they had contracted in the event of an eventual war with Prussia. If they remained apart, Russia could discard the treaty of alliance and on its own obtain more territory at the expense of the Ottoman Empire than if it had to share any gains with its ally. For Kaunitz the participation in this involuntary conflict was "a diplomatic device both to preserve the Russian alliance and to limit Russian expansion,"[3] and Joseph II went to war with a similar disinclination and was already in late 1788 resolutely resolved to make peace. The protracted negotiations did not arrive at the desired result until 1791 when the Austro-Ottoman peace treaty signed at Sistova brought to an end centuries of wars between the two empires. The peace of Sistova occurred a year and half after Joseph II's death and two years after the outbreak of a revolution in France that definitely forestalled any serious thinking in Vienna of undertaking any projects hostile to the Ottoman Empire. During the revolutionary and Napoleonic Wars, when all the forces of the Habsburg Monarchy were deployed for its own survival in the West, not only any aggressive but even any active policy in the Balkans was completely out of the question. This was proved in 1804 during the uprising of the Ottoman

---

[1] K. A. Roider, *Austria's Eastern Question, 1700–1790*, Princeton 1982, pp. 194–195; Fischer, pp. 38–43.

[2] The year 1787 is generally stated for the outbreak of the war, but Austria's declaration was not delivered to the Turks until February 1788, the fighting itself started even considerably later. K. A. Roider, "Kaunitz, Joseph II and the Turkish War," *SEER* 54, 1976, 4, p. 545.

[3] Ibid.

Serbs, who were denied support from Emperor Francis I when they asked for it.[4]

It was during this difficult situation that Metternich was entrusted with the leadership of Austria's foreign policy. With ambitious Napoleon Bonaparte in the West and Tsar Alexander I waging war with the Ottoman Empire in the East since 1806, he was faced with the difficult task of guiding the monarchy through uneasy times and assuring not only its preservation but also that its further existence was based upon solid foundations, which, in the case of the Balkan Peninsula, meant that Russia's gains would be as few as possible. Under the given conditions, however, there was no way in which Metternich could influence the outcome of the Russo-Ottoman conflict. The only course of action open to him was to intervene in the Serbian Question and check the growth of Russia's influence in the western Balkans. The revolt of the Serbs had begun to attract more attention from the Viennese cabinet in 1806 when the war in the East broke out, and the Russians started to support the insurgents who declared their independence from the Ottoman Empire in the following year. In 1810, the Russian troops had arrived in the Pashalik of Belgrade and united with the Serbians in the field, and they even temporarily occupied Belgrade in January 1811.[5]

The Russians' actions in Serbia greatly alarmed the cabinet in Vienna where the Serbian Question had constituted an important part of Metternich's agenda since the beginning of his ministry. What he wished to achieve in this affair was a quick restoration of peace between the Serbs and Ottomans under the condition that the province remained under the sultan's rule but the administration would be improved. Such an outcome was intended to prevent Russia's direct or indirect dominion over this region of great strategic importance for Austria. To assure this, Metternich advised Francis I in 1810 to pursue a more active policy. Austria was to assume a role of mediator between the Porte and the Serbs, of course with the consent of the former. Moreover, Metternich advised that the Austrian army should temporarily seize Belgrade to preclude a similar step by the Russians.

---

[4] Beer, *Die orientalische Politik*, p. 162; Buchmann, *Österreich und das Osmanische Reich*, p. 187.
[5] L. P. Meriage, "The First Serbian Uprising (1804–1813) and the Nineteenth-Century Origins of the Eastern Question," *SR* 37, 1978, 3, pp. 425–430.

The Porte was to be informed that this measure had been done with the aim of coercing the Serbs to yield. The suggested course of action was a compromise between a policy of an absolute passivity advocated by Francis I and Klemens' father and Austrian diplomat, Franz Georg Karl von Metternich, and the warlike demands of Austrian military elites like Count Josef Wenzel Radetzky von Radetz and Archduke Charles, who disliked the neutrality course and considered the western Balkans to be an area where Austria was to compensate for its losses in the West, or who at least wished to help the Serbs. Metternich was not willing to aggravate the relations with the Porte and in no way desired to become involved in a conflict, but he also took the Russian threat seriously and was of the opinion that something needed to be done. Metternich senior, a strong Turkophile, came out against his son's proposal in which he saw many problems and a source of a serious aggravation in relations with its Ottoman neighbour. Moreover, he did not believe that the Porte would allow Austria to mediate peace, which was not an unfounded argument because such a proposal had already been made by the emperor and firmly rejected in Constantinople in 1806. Francis I finally agreed with Georg Metternich, and the foreign minister had to compromise with the temporisation in the Serbian affairs. Consequently, when the Serbs made an attempt to win Francis I's support for their autonomy at the end of 1810, Metternich merely advised them to negotiate with Sultan Mahmud II. They finally obtained autonomy after several uneasy years and without the participation of Austria, whose priority was to maintain friendly relations with the Porte.[6]

The Serbian uprising strengthened the belief in Vienna that the maintenance of the sultan's empire was of vital interest to Austria. The Ottoman domination in the Balkans formed a barrier against the Russian expansion to the south as well as the nationalism of local nations. As for the former, any Russian territorial progress into the heart of the Balkans would have had disastrous consequences for the Danube Monarchy, which could become hemmed in by the tsar's em-

---

[6]   F. von Demelitsch, *Metternich und seine auswärtige Politik*, Stuttgart 1898, pp. 122–145, 251–304, 451–478; I. J. Dostjan, "Rußland, Österreich und der erste serbische Aufstand 1804–1813," A. M. Drabek, R. G. Plaschka (eds.), *Rußland und Österreich zur Zeit der Napoleonischen Kriege*, Wien 1989, pp. 95–111; M. B. Petrovich, *A History of Modern Serbia 1804–1918*, I, New York, London 1976, p. 68; Tischler, pp. 87–130.

pire from the north, east and even south. It would have been a tragedy from the geopolitical point of view, essentially undermining Austria's ability to defend itself against its powerful eastern neighbour. Alan Sked is entirely right when he claims that in such a situation Austria would have become Russia's satellite.[7] The economic consequences of Russian domination over the Balkans would also be serious. Furthermore, Russia was becoming an increasingly dangerous factor in Balkan politics due to the growing nationalism in the Balkan regions which could be easily exploited by the tsar to increase his own power in south-eastern Europe. Russia's interference in the Serbian uprising and its close contacts with the Montenegrins considerably disquited Metternich and shaped his pro-Ottoman policy.

The looming rebirth of the Balkan nations in the early 19th century did not escape Metternich's attention. He was well aware of this transformation process, and although he had nothing against the cultural aspect of this transformation, he was concerned about the consequences of related power ambitions, the logical outcome of which had to be efforts at political emancipation. The eventual success of such efforts would necessarily bring an end to the Ottoman dominion in Europe and could also give impetus to a process leading to its general collapse. The formation of Balkan nation states would definitely be rather disadvantageous for the multinational Austrian Empire, in particular when some of its citizens were of the same nationality as those beyond its south-eastern frontier, like the Serbs or the Rumanians. The expected effect on other nationalities, particularly those of Slavic origin, living in the monarchy would most probably be of a kind viewed as undesirable by Metternich, who, as a keen and dispassionate observer, well understood the dangerous potential of nationalism and his views in this respect were quite far-sighted. He particularly feared the influence of Russia on the southern Slavs, naturally those belonging to the Orthodox Church above all, and the spread of a pro-Russian oriented Slavism among them. Their cooperation with the Orthodox tsar could lead to a considerable increase of Russia's influence over south-eastern Europe and, in the worst case, it could have a devastating effect on the very existence of not only the Ottoman but also the Austrian Empires. Consequently, together with geopolitics, the national factor played a crucial role in Metternich's belief that

---

[7]   Sked, *Metternich*, p. 82.

the Ottoman Empire had to continue to exist for as long as possible and attracted his interest following his accession to the ministry.[8]

It is true that the barrier that the Ottoman Empire constituted was in both cases, against Russian expansion and the nationalism of Balkan nations, somewhat weak, but at the given moment it was the best option and, consequently, Metternich had no reason to change in any way the opinion he had held since before 1809 that the Ottoman Empire had to be preserved. If it had collapsed, "the vast areas where the Sultan's name still has power, perhaps more as a figurehead than as a real power would inevitably become ... a theatre of a terrible anarchy or a looting opportunity for a foreign invasion."[9] In such a case, the European Powers would most likely attempt to acquire the utmost territorial gain, and since their interests would be so contradictory that they could not be settled by their diplomats, their inevitable quarrel would be, as Metternich claimed, "the cause of protracted wars which would end only by turning all Europe into a pile of rubble."[10] As for Austria, eventual gains would in fact be unwanted, of questionable value and could never outweigh the negatives resulting from the fall of the Ottoman Empire, the integrity of which, as the prince was completely convinced, was "the *condicio sine qua non* of the maintenance of peace in Europe."[11]

---

[8] A. G. Haas, "Metternich and the Slavs," *AHY* 4/5, 1968–1969, pp. 134–136; G. Roloff, "Fürst Metternich über die slavische und magyarische Gefahr im Jahre 1839," *MIÖG* 52, 1938, pp. 69–70; Siemann, pp. 103–108; Tischler, pp. 377–378.

[9] Metternich to Neumann, Vienna, 15 Feb. 1833, HHStA, StA, England 204, see also *NP*, III, p. 476.

[10] Rayneval to Polignac, Vienna, 25 Jan. 1830, AMAE, CP, Autriche 412.

[11] Sainte-Aulaire to Thiers, Vienna, 16 June 1836, AMAE, CP, Autriche 423. Several brief quotations with Metternich's expressions on the importance of the preservation of the Ottoman Empire and the extreme dangers for Austria resulting from its eventual fall represent here just a fragment of the hundreds of archival documents containing the same information and housed throughout Europe. Since this attitude of Metternich is generally well known it is not necessary to offer other evidence. It suffices to emphasise the fact that the maintenance of the status quo in the Balkans and the Near East as far as it was possible was one of the fundamental imperatives of Metternich's diplomacy and from which he never deviated.

The Congress of Vienna

Metternich included the Ottoman Empire in his political-philosophical *Weltanschauung* containing the strong belief that the fundamental premise for good relations among countries is the preservation of the balance of power. If this is compromised and an hegemony arises among them, as for example Napoleonic France, the peaceable coexistence according to the standards of international law is impossible and war inevitable. Since Alexander I's power in Europe could considerably increase in particular at the expense of the Ottoman Empire, which was exactly what the cabinet in Vienna greatly feared, Metternich needed to rein in Russia's ambitions with some restrictions. However, for Metternich this goal could not be achieved by mere observance of the balance of power in European politics because he regarded it as an insufficient guarantor of stable peace. It did not prevent the outbreak of numerous wars in the 18th century when the idea of a balance of power guided international relations and it also in no way prevented Russia from pursuing an expansionist anti-Ottoman policy. Consequently, for Metternich the balance of power was not a goal in itself but a mere premise for achieving it: the creation of political equilibrium based upon a more solid footing – legal norms regulating the relations among the countries and restraining their egoistic ambitions. Today one would call this goal a collective security system.[12]

The creation of a functioning system of international relations, of which the most important aim was the preservation of peace, became an important new task for the participants of the Congress of Vienna summoned for late 1814. Metternich, in accordance with his philosophical dogma as well as for geopolitical reasons, strongly desired to include the sultan's state in the peace settlement that was to be arranged at the congress. If the Ottoman Empire were to become

---

[12] J. Droz, *Histoire diplomatique de 1648 à 1919*, Paris 2005, p. 291; H. Rieben, *Prinzipiengrundlage und Diplomatie in Metternichs Europapolitik, 1815–1848*, Bern 1942, p. 10; J. R. Sofka, "Metternich's Theory of European Order: A Political Agenda for 'Perpetual Peace'," *The Review of Politics* 60, 1998, 1, pp. 121–132; H. von Srbik, "Statesman of Philosophical Principles," E. E. Kraehe (ed.), *The Metternich Controversy*, New York, Chicago, San Francisco, Atlanta, Dallas, Montreal, Toronto, London, Sydney 1971, pp. 34–39; E. L. Woodward, *Three Studies in European Conservatism: Metternich, Guizot, the Catholic Church in the Nineteenth Century*, London 1963, pp. 38–52.

subject to the international law guaranteeing peaceful relations between the participating states, it would be more difficult for a Russian monarch to provoke new wars with its southern neighbour. Metternich's attitude can be succinctly explained by Friedrich von Gentz's words of 5 February 1814 that the prince "regards today and more than ever before the Ottoman Porte to be one of the most essential counterweights in the general equilibrium of Europe."[13]

The idea of a written assurance of the Ottoman Empire's integrity that would establish a barrier to Russia's expansion to the south was first mentioned by Metternich in January 1806 and he did not hesitate to revive it in the summer of 1814.[14] He wanted to bring the Ottoman Empire into the European state system at the forthcoming congress and ensure as well as the general peace and tranquillity for all of Europe by "placing its territorial possessions under the general guarantee of the new order,"[15] which meant that European countries were to recognise the sultan's sovereignty and the integrity of his empire. Metternich attributed a great deal of importance to the fulfilment of this plan because if the peaceful relations between the Ottoman Empire and Russia were not based upon a more solid basis of international law, the chance of a long-lasting European peace would be weakened and Austria's position in the middle of the Continent would be less secure. Consequently, in July 1814 the prince tried to persuade Mahmud II and his advisors to send a senior diplomatic representative to Vienna, where none was posted at that time, and to request an extension of the general guarantee to the Ottoman Empire. Metternich even suggested that a reis effendi (Ottoman foreign minister) should come to the Austrian capital and personally represent his monarch there in this matter. The reaction of the Porte was, however, rather lukewarm because it did not attribute much significance to the question of the guarantee and regarded it as considerably less important than the requested evacuation of the Russian troops from several places on the Russo-Ottoman Caucasus border which had been under dispute since the Russo-Ottoman Treaty of Bucharest concluded in 1812.[16] The reis

---

[13] Gentz to Ioan Gheorghe Caradja, Vienna, 5 Feb. 1814, *DI*, I, p. 55.

[14] Tischler, pp. 41–42.

[15] Metternich to Stürmer, Vienna, 6 Oct. 1814, HHStA, StA, Türkei VI, 10.

[16] For more on the origin of the dispute see A. Bitis, *Russia and the Eastern Question: Army, Government, and Society 1815–1833*, Oxford, New York 2006, pp. 30–31.

effendi declared that the condition for the Porte's participation in the congress was the negotiations concerning the Caucasus border with Austria as an intermediary. The Porte's reticence was a result of its distrust of European politics and even its confidence in Metternich was rather limited, especially when he met with silence its wish to discuss the border at the congress; his mediation was not possible because he was not interested in this problematic issue and did not want to aggravate his relations with Tsar Alexander I, in particular after the opening of the congress and the stormy negotiations among the Great Powers concerning the Polish and Saxon Questions. Nevertheless, Metternich did not give up his plan and although he did not wish to interfere in the affairs between the sultan and the tsar concerning a distant and for Austria unimportant area on the eastern coast of the Black Sea, he did not stop trying to persuade the former to take part in the congress. He tried to utilise the Porte's fear of Russia and persuade it that Alexander I would be able to carry out his plans in the Balkans whenever he pleased and the only way to prevent him from doing so would be to sign the general treaty guaranteeing the status quo of Europe.[17]

The answers from Constantinople to Metternich's proposals in the late autumn of 1814 were, however, negative. Their strong distrust of European countries, the question of Caucasus border and a rumour that Russia would like to raise the Serbian Question as a part of the talks at the congress moved the Ottomans to withhold their participation. Metternich did not abandon his cause but changed his strategy at the end of the year; he did not demand the Porte's direct attendance but that it charged Austria with defence of its rights. Without this commission, the issue could not officially be put on the agenda of the congress talks. When Mahmud II seemed to be compliant to this suggestion, Metternich turned his attention to Alexander I, who in no way inclined towards the idea of extending the guarantee on the Ottoman Empire.[18]

Some scholars dealing with the history of the Congress of Vienna omit to mention Metternich and instead present British Foreign Secretary Robert Stewart Viscount Castlereagh, generally known as Lord Castlereagh, as the author of the plan for the inclusion of the Ottoman

---

[17] Gürbüz, pp. 4–17.
[18] Ibid., pp. 21–22; Tischler, p. 164.

Empire into the European state system.[19] It is true that Castlereagh shared Metternich's attitude towards the question, but he only took the baton when the latter ascertained that the tsar was not inclined to guarantee the Ottoman Empire's integrity and did not want to bargain with the tsar personally; in fact Metternich most likely had never spoken with Alexander I about the issue at the congress. Castlereagh opened negotiations with the tsar that ended with the latter's declaration that he was prepared to extend the general guarantee on the Ottoman Empire in exchange for the inclusion of negotiations on the Caucasus border under the mediation of Austria, France and Great Britain which, under the given political constellation and the significance of Russia for European politics, would most likely have led to a settlement favourable to Russia. It is not clear whether Alexander I planned to thwart the project with a condition hardly acceptable for the Porte or whether he really was prepared to agree with it in order to gain Asiatic territories with 30,000 inhabitants as he told French diplomat Charles Maurice de Talleyrand-Périgord; it can be taken for granted that he truly did not become a supporter of Metternich's plan. His ostensibly compliant attitude, however, sufficed to invoke optimism of the Viennese cabinet, with Gentz seriously contemplating a special mention about the Ottoman Empire in the Final Act of the congress.[20]

For such an outcome it was still necessary to persuade the Porte to agree. Castlereagh undertook the necessary steps in February 1815 when he sent the pertinent instructions to Constantinople. He was of the opinion that Mahmud II should sacrifice the Asiatic places in return for the guarantee, and, even though no written proof exists, Metternich most likely entirely shared this view and definitely supported Castlereagh's attempts to gain the Porte's agreement with a note inviting it to accept the three Powers' mediation, which he considered a necessary condition for opening formal talks. Since he wanted to maintain a strong influence over its decision-making in this question, he did not want to let the Porte forget that "the original

---

[19] I. Rautsi, *The Eastern Question Revisited: Case Studies in Ottoman Balance of Power*, Helsinki 1993, p. 54; J.-A. de Sédouy, *Le congrès de Vienne: L'Europe contre la France 1812–1815*, Paris 2003, p. 254; Sir C. K. Webster, *The Foreign Policy of Castlereagh, 1815–1822: Britain and the European Alliance*, London 1947, p. 349.

[20] Gürbüz, pp. 25–33.

idea of imposing an agreement on Russia to suppress its plans of conquests in the Levant is entirely ours."[21] All his efforts turned out to be completely futile because Mahmud II promptly rejected the offer under the pretext that there were no unresolved questions between him and the tsar that would necessitate foreign mediation. The real reason for his rejection was the suspicion that the European mediators would not proceed in the Caucasus affair in his favour and would force him to recognise some of Russia's most recent gains on the eastern Black Sea coast as permanent, which was exactly what he was not willing to do. His negative answer arrived in Vienna at the same time as Napoleon's escape from Elba was made known and therefore did not receive much attention.[22]

The question of the Ottoman Empire's entrance into the European state system was never further discussed at the Congress of Vienna. Mahmud II's apprehension about a one-sided mediation was definitely well founded but, on the other hand, with his refusal he lost an opportune occasion for the Ottoman Empire to become an integral part of the European state system after 1815, and despite its previous treaties with European countries, it was not generally regarded as a member – a fact of which Metternich was well aware.[23] Besides obtaining a guarantee of its territorial integrity, membership could also have solved its problems with Russia. It is naturally not certain whether such an outcome, if realised according to Metternich's plan, would really have hindered or at least made awkward any foreign interference in Ottoman affairs; what is certain, however, is the conviction of the cabinet in Vienna about the usefulness of the system created at the congress for the Ottoman Empire, as, for example, Gentz wrote three years later: "The present system, even though the Porte is not

---

[21] Metternich to Stürmer, Vienna, 18 Feb. 1815, HHStA, StA, Türkei VI, 10.

[22] A. Kargl, *Studien zur österreichischen Internuntiatur in Konstantinopel 1802–1818*, unpublished dissertation, Wien 1974, p. 357; A. Zamoyski, *Rites of Peace: The Fall of Napoleon and the Congress of Vienna*, London 2007, p. 415; Gürbüz, pp. 31–40.

[23] Metternich to Ficquelmont, Vienna, 1 Nov. 1828, SOA, RA C-A 382; Metternich to Gentz, Ischl, 1 Aug. 1825, G. Kronenbitter (ed.), *Friedrich Gentz: Gesammelte Schriften, Band XI.4: Briefe von und an Friedrich von Gentz: Schriftwechsel mit Metternich. Zweiter Teil: 1820–1832*, Hildesheim, Zürich, New York 2002, p. 223; A. Sked, *Europe's Balance of Power, 1815–1848*, London 1979, p. 7.

included in it, is one of the strongest guarantees of its security and its rights."[24]

The Question of the Ottoman Empire's Guarantee after 1815

The Final Act of the Congress of Vienna constituted the foundation-stone of the new international legal order offering to its signatories solid guarantees of security and stability,[25] which was exactly what the Ottoman Empire lacked in the 1820s and 1830s. Consequently, Metternich still regretted many years later that he had not succeeded in bringing it into "the great European family."[26] Although he never revived the idea with the same intensity as he had in 1814–1815, it had a life of its own and he was later faced with this question a few times. The first attempt occurred in late 1828 when the Porte was at war with Russia and informed the cabinet in Vienna about its wish to arrange its relations with its powerful northern neighbour in a European congress where, moreover, the legal basis of its future existence was to be determined; in other words "where Turkey would be approved and recognised as an integral part of the European political system."[27] Mahmud II turned to Metternich with a formal request for advice – in reality a plea for assistance – in this project, but the prince remained passive because the sultan's plan was unfeasible

---

[24] F. von Gentz, "Considerations on the Political System Now Existing in Europe, 1818," M. Walker (ed.), *Metternich's Europe*, New York 1968, p. 83.
[25] A. Doering-Manteuffel, *Vom Wiener Kongreß zur Pariser Konferenz: England, die deutsche Frage und das Mächtesystem 1815–1856*, Göttingen 1991, p. 35; W. Baumgart, *Europäisches Konzert und nationale Bewegung: Internationale Beziehungen 1830–1878*, München, Wien, Zürich 1999, p. 148.
[26] Tatishchev to Nesselrode, Vienna, 8 Sept. 1839, AVPRI, fond 133, Kantseliariia, opis 469, 1839/214. See also Metternich's Observations on Ficquelmont's letter written in Baden on 29 July 1835, HHStA, StA, Russland III, 104; Metternich to Stürmer, Vienna, 24 Dec. 1839, HHStA, StA, Türkei VI, 72; Struve to Nesselrode, Vienna, 2 Aug. 1839, AVPRI, fond 133, Kantseliariia, opis, 469, 1839/214.
[27] Ottenfels to Metternich, Constantinople, 10 Dec. 1828, HHStA, StA, Türkei VI, 34.

due to the expected opposition of Russia.[28] A year later, when the Russo-Ottoman war was over, the idea of a guarantee of the Ottoman Empire's integrity on the part of all the Great Powers came to Vienna from London. At this time, Metternich agreed that any general guarantee would be useful and pointed out that if further existence was guaranteed to Greece, it could also be bestowed upon the sultan's state. Nevertheless, this tentative discussion did not survive the year's end, and no new impulse for any deliberation on this issue came from London or Vienna.[29] It thus remained unaddressed for a decade. It is true that in October 1836, British ambassador in Constantinople, John Lord Ponsonby, rejected Metternich's alleged "proposal to unite England and Russia in a Guarantee of the Integrity and Independence of Turkey,"[30] but in fact no studied correspondence contains such a plan.

A real proposal for the guarantee did not appear again until the autumn of 1839 when Europe was witness to a conflict between the sultan and his powerful governor of Egypt. The French government raised this issue and suggested that the integrity of the Ottoman Empire should be placed under the guarantee of the Great Powers. A reformatory and towards Europe well-disposed Ottoman foreign minister, Mustafa Reshid Pasha, welcomed this project and added that the Porte would actually want to become a part of "the European confederation,"[31] but Metternich's attitude was rather reserved. He disagreed with the idea because it was suggested by France with an obvious aim to increase its own influence in Constantinople and hamper the British-Russian rapprochement under way in the affairs of the Near East, where the views of France on the one hand and those of Austria, Great Britain, Russia and Prussia on the other strongly differed.[32] Metternich particularly denounced the Parisian cabinet for

---

[28] Ottenfels to Metternich, Constantinople, 10 Nov. and 10 Dec. 1828, HHStA, StA, Türkei VI, 34.
[29] Metternich to Esterházy, Vienna, 24 Nov. and 16 Dec. 1829, HHStA, StA, England 188; Esterházy to Metternich, London, 12 Oct. and 26 Dec. 1829, HHStA, StA, England 186.
[30] Ponsonby to Palmerston, Therapia, 19 Oct. 1836, TNA, FO 78/277.
[31] Stürmer to Metternich, Constantinople, 6 Nov. 1839, HHStA, StA, Türkei VI, 71.
[32] For more on this divergence in views between France and other Great Powers in late 1839 see Chapter 25.

talking about the integrity and independence of the sultan's state while simultaneously supporting the Egyptian governor, which could seriously weaken the already fragile edifice of the Ottoman Empire. He suspected the French wanted to offer to exchange their guarantee for the Porte's compliance in the Egyptian Question.[33] He naturally could not fail to see the anti-Russian target of the French proposal: "The idea of a guarantee on the part of the Great Powers for the sovereignty of the Ottoman Empire has germinated for some years in France. It has its origin in the desire to counterbalance the predominance of the Russian court in Constantinople."[34] At the moment when Russia sincerely wished to preserve the existence of the Ottoman Empire and cooperated in this sense with other Powers, Metternich had no reason to support a plan hostile to the tsar, which was, in his opinion, not entirely necessary at that point when the Russian monarch sincerely wished the preservation of the Ottoman Empire. Moreover, Metternich was well aware of the fact that even though Russia had renounced projects of conquest against its southern neighbour, he also was right in the assumption that it did not want to give up the possibility of changing this position and gaining a part of the Ottoman territory if such a goal was profitable and easy to achieve. He understood that for this reason a tsar would always reject the idea of a guarantee, and the expressions of Russian diplomats clearly proved it. He soon received from St Petersburg their appreciation of the fact that the cabinet in Vienna had abandoned the idea of the Parisian cabinet.[35]

Metternich reacted with disapproval towards the Russian statement, claiming: "We cannot abandon something we neither proposed nor wanted!"[36] This is definitely a surprising and not really trustworthy claim at first sight from the man who wished to guarantee the Ottoman Empire's future at the Congress of Vienna, but not entirely so when considered more carefully. Another reason for the prince's

---

[33] Metternich to Kaisersfeld, Vienna, 2 Jan. 1840, HHStA, StA, Russland III, 120; Metternich to Neumann, Vienna, 1 Jan. and 7 Feb. 1840, HHStA, StA, England 230.

[34] Metternich to Stürmer, Vienna, 24 Dec. 1839, HHStA, StA, Türkei VI, 72.

[35] Ibid.; Maltzan to Frederick William III, Vienna, 12 Dec. 1839, GStA PK, HA III, MdA I, 7350.

[36] Metternich to Neumann, Vienna, 1 Jan. 1840, HHStA, StA, England 230. See also Metternich to Kaisersfeld, Vienna, 2 Jan. 1840, HHStA, StA, Russland III, 120.

rejection of the French proposal was the fact that it differed from his original plan also advocated in 1839 with which he wanted to provide "the accession of the Porte according to the terms of the Congress of Vienna,"[37] in other words to "extend to this Power the sort of general and reciprocal guarantee that ensued from this transaction."[38] In mid November, the British ambassador in Vienna reported that Metternich was asked "whether he should not consider it desirable even at this late period to obtain the accession of Turkey to the acts of the Congress of Vienna (which at the time was successfully resisted by the Emperor Alexander) thereby associating her to the whole body of European international law. He answered that it ought to be done, that the proper time would be at the close of the present negotiations and it would be far preferable to a guarantee of the Turkish dominion which Austria could not undertake."[39] According to the French proposal, all the territory of the Ottoman Empire was to be placed "under the protection of the European nations' rights and under the guarantee of the Great Powers."[40] Metternich found the idea too vague and impracticable,[41] but what he objected to most of all was that it would limit the Porte's independence: "A European guarantee of the Ottoman Power is a word devoid of sense ... The Ottoman Porte placed under the burden of a European guarantee will acquire no more guarantee of continued existence than it already has but it will lose its political independence ... A power that relies on a foreign guarantee for its existence ceases to be politically viable because it ceases to be independent."[42] In September 1840, he touched on the problem again: "The word 'guarantee' applied to the independence of an empire is essentially a misnomer because there is a contradiction between what the word implies and the independence to which one wants to apply it. Any state whose existence is placed under a foreign

---

[37] Metternich to Stürmer, Vienna, 24 Dec. 1839, HHStA, StA, Türkei VI, 72.
[38] Ibid.
[39] Beauvale to Palmerston, Vienna, 16 Nov. 1839, TNA, FO 120/180.
[40] Maltzan to Frederick William III, Vienna, 25 Dec. 1839, GStA PK, HA III, MdA I, 7351.
[41] Metternich to Esterházy, Johannisberg, 21 Oct. 1839, HHStA, StA, England 225; Esterházy to Metternich, London, 1 Oct. 1839, HHStA, StA, England 223; Maltzan to Frederick William III, Vienna, 16 Oct. 1839, GStA PK, HA III, MdA I, 7349.
[42] Metternich to Stürmer, Vienna, 24 Dec. 1839, HHStA, StA, Türkei VI, 72.

guarantee is simultaneously a state voluntarily or involuntarily deprived of its independence. It has, in a word, lost its sovereign rights, it is subordinated."[43] When he read an article in the French newspaper *Journal des débats* in early December 1840 about the necessity of replacing Russia's exclusive protectorate of the Ottoman Empire with the protectorate of Europe, Metternich reacted negatively to this proposal, saying: "This manner of expressing oneself distorts the real sense of what the cabinets are trying to achieve in the Levant. The word *protectorate* should not be used to refer to what they want because, in agreement with the terms adopted and pronounced by all the Great Powers including France, it clearly is a question of *maintaining the independence and integrity of the Ottoman Empire*. The difference between these two perspectives is significant. It is the independence of a country that guarantees its existence, provided that this country does not want to place itself beyond the principle of the law of nations. Every country that does not want to do that enjoys the most effective protection, that of the law of nations. In this respect it is placed on the same level as all other countries, large as well as small: because in the eyes of a judge, the law cannot be modified according to the smaller or greater territorial extent of this or that Great Power. *Protection* is a dominant idea in the heads of the French pamphleteers, and in essence it is nothing other than a mask concealing the *principle of mediation* ... The president of the council [of ministers], Mr Soult, expressed himself much more correctly in his speech of 25 November, saying: 'France wants the Levant to be protected from war and the Ottoman Empire, instead of being placed under the protection of the only one Great Power, to assume its place in the law of European nations and to find itself thus protected by the agreement of all the Great Powers.'"[44]

Although it might appear so, it was not merely a theorisation but a keen reaction to the content of the French proposal as well as the affairs in the eastern Mediterranean during the previous decade. The egoistic ambitions of France, Russia and Great Britain led to the struggle for influence over the sultan's court, which was proble-

---

[43] Metternich to Apponyi, Königswart, 1 Sept. 1840, HHStA, StA, Frankreich 319.
[44] Tatishchev to Nesselrode, Vienna, 19 Dec. 1840, AVPRI, fond 133, Kantseliariia, opis 469, 1840/178.

matic for the internal situation of the empire. If the French proposal for the guarantee had been accepted, it could have opened a door to much greater interference on the part of the European Powers into Ottoman affairs. Greece, whose existence was guaranteed by Great Britain, France and Russia, suffered from the three Powers' struggle for influence in Athens and, without much exaggeration, in the 1830's exchanged Ottoman control for the supremacy of these European countries.[45] If the Greeks' independence of action was not limited *de jure*, it was definitely limited *de facto*. When the British foreign secretary, Henry John Temple 3rd Viscount Palmerston, generally known as Lord Palmerston, used their example in 1841 to counter Metternich's opinion that a country placed under a guarantee of other states loses its independence, the prince replied with these words, and it must be admitted that truth was on his side: "Lord Palmerston challenges my thesis that a state that accepts a foreign guarantee without being able to grant another in exchange loses its independence. To prove the contrary, he refers to the example of Greece. If I am not entirely mistaken, Lord Palmerston has chosen a bad example and in his desire to destroy my thesis, he has, on the contrary, reinforced it with an example [of his own]."[46] Metternich's words about limited independence were not at all idle. He realised the danger of a state being placed under the guarantee – protection – of another one. The imperialism of the World Powers later proved that such protectorates ended with the submission of protected, weaker, countries and their being put into a submissive – colonial – status. Against this form of guarantee Metternich always advocated his own version of the Ottoman Empire's admission into the European state system under the principle of equality, which meant its accession to the settlement of the Congress of Vienna with the same rights as well as duties.[47] In any case, with or without this outcome, another contribution to the Ottoman Empire's internal stability was to be the European coun-

---

[45] B. Jelavich, C. Jelavich, *The Establishment of the Balkan National States 1804–1920*, Seattle, London 1977, p. 51.

[46] Metternich to Esterházy, Vienna, 26 May 1841, HHStA, StA, England 237.

[47] Metternich to Apponyi, Königswart, 1 Sept. 1840, HHStA, StA, Frankreich 319; Metternich to Neumann, Königswart, 2 Sept. 1840, HHStA, StA, England 231.

tries' abandonment of imperialistic policy according to Metternich's
motto: "If we want the Porte to survive, we should let it be."[48]
Metternich left the representatives of the Great Powers in no
doubt that he was against the French method of guarantee and he
did his best to persuade the Porte of its unsuitability and futility. He
even voiced the opinion that the Ottoman Empire was no longer in
isolation, that it had *de facto* recently entered "the great European
family" and called to mind that the Great Powers had already expressed their desire to maintain the independence and integrity of the
Ottoman Empire under its ruling dynasty. In the eyes of Europe the
Ottoman Empire was thus placed into the system of European public
law and nothing else was really necessary to be done for the Porte:
"To enter into the so-called association of Europe, the Porte has to
do nothing because it is already *de facto* in the association."[49] In
fact considerable significance must be ascribed to the expression "de
facto" because with regard to the relationship between the Ottoman
Empire and the European countries in the preceding years, it could
actually have been the case as Metternich declared. However, his own
statements mentioned above prove that he was well aware that the
sultan's empire formally continued to exist outside the area protected
by the Viennese settlement. In this case the arguments used towards
the Ottomans were decidedly more pragmatic than sincere and their
only aim was to persuade the Ottomans to let the French guarantee fall by the wayside. This happened in early 1840, and since the
Parisian cabinet did not continue to press the issue and the Ottomans
remained silent, it ceased to constitute a part of diplomatic agenda.[50]
The hiatus did not last long because in February 1841 the French
government revived its project and this time the Ottomans reacted
with much more enthusiasm. Metternich again sharply denounced the
plan to place the Ottoman Empire under the guarantee of the European Powers using the same arguments as he had in the two previous
years,[51] in particular forestalling the restriction of the Porte's inde-

---

[48] Esterházy to Metternich, London, 1 Oct. 1839, HHStA, StA, England 223.
[49] Metternich to Stürmer, Vienna, 24 Dec. 1839, HHStA, StA, Türkei VI, 72. See
also Maltzan to Frederick William III, Vienna, 5 Dec. 1839, GStA PK, HA III,
MdA I, 7350.
[50] Metternich to Stürmer, Vienna, 24 Dec. 1839, HHStA, StA, Türkei VI, 72;
Stürmer to Metternich, Constantinople, 8 Jan. 1840, HHStA, StA, Türkei VI, 73.
[51] Metternich to Esterházy, Vienna, 23 April and 26 May 1841, HHStA, StA,

pendence: "A state placed under a guarantee becomes a state that has been subordinated because for a guarantee to be granted, it is necessary for the state that requests [such a guarantee] to submit to the will of the state that will be charged with defending it. The guarantor, to be of any use, must assume the role of protector, and if one protector is at the very least an inconvenience, several protectors would become an unsustainable burden."[52] He also added a new argument against the project: the French and the Ottomans would have to settle their dispute over Algeria, which had been occupied by the former since 1830 but never formally surrendered by the latter. He presumed that France would not give up this North African possession and the Porte would not surrender its province, thus rendering the entire question moot, and in both cases his supposition seemed more than justified.[53] He wrote in May: "How could the Divan accept a guarantee of the integrity of the Empire from France without releasing this Power at once from an act of usurpation with respect to that Empire, which from that moment on would not be able to depend any longer upon the guarantor? France will certainly not allow Algeria to become a domain of the Ottoman Empire ... We cannot view this as anything other than clearing the way of everything of secondary importance because it is clear that we could not possibly guarantee the return of Algeria to the sultan."[54] Since the French and Ottomans found no echo among the other Powers, the proposal for the guarantee was abandoned once again.[55]

England 237; Stürmer to Metternich, Constantinople, 12 May 1841, HHStA, StA, Türkei VI, 81; Beauvale to Palmerston, Vienna, 22 April 1841, TNA, FO 120/197; Struve to Nesselrode, Vienna, 28 April and 7 May 1841, AVPRI, fond 133, Kantseliariia, opis 469, 1841/191; Webster, *Palmerston*, II, p. 759.
[52] Metternich to Stürmer, Vienna, 20 April 1841, HHStA, StA, Türkei VI, 83.
[53] Ibid.; Struve to Nesselrode, Vienna, 7 May 1841, AVPRI, fond 133, Kantseliariia, opis 469, 1841/191.
[54] Metternich to Esterházy, Vienna, 26 May 1841, HHStA, StA, England 237.
[55] F. S. Rodkey, *The Turko-Egyptian Question in the Relations of England, France and Russia 1832–1841*, Urbana 1924, p. 227.

The Holy Alliance

Metternich regretted that the Ottoman Empire remained outside the European state system in 1815 and also that the Holy Alliance was created in the same year – a product of little practical value but a much-favoured theme for historians. The Proclamation of the Holy Alliance, Alexander I's attempt to instill Christian principles into European political life to defend the conservative order, was signed by the monarchs of Russia, Austria and Prussia in Paris on 26 September and later signatures were added by almost all European rulers except the British king, the pope and the Ottoman sultan. Although Metternich was often associated with this, in his words, "a loud sounding nothing"[56] or "a kind of delusion,"[57] in fact he tried to prevent its creation and he never liked it. In January 1837, he wrote: "The Holy Alliance has never played any role in any affair and has never been in a position to be able to play any for the simple reason that what is nothing in reality can produce nothing."[58] Not only these contemptuous words but Metternich's practical behaviour in particular proved that he actually attributed no significance to the Holy Alliance, which was too vague and too impracticable in his eyes. The Alliance which he considered to be of any practical value and which he often referred to in collocations like "the ancient and salutary Alliance,"[59] "the great Alliance,"[60] "the ancient and veritable Alliance,"[61] "the glorious Alliance,"[62] or "the European Alliance,"[63] was the Alliance of the Great Powers, "the guardians of the common peace of Europe,"[64] which before 1818 were the Quadruple Alliance and afterwards the Quintuple

---

[56] T. Chapman, *The Congress of Vienna: Origins, Processes and Results*, London, New York 1998, p. 61.

[57] Rayneval to Polignac, Vienna, 27 April 1830, AMAE, CP, Autriche 412.

[58] G. de B. de Sauvigny, "Sainte Alliance et Alliance dans les conceptions de Metternich," *RH* 223, 1960, p. 256.

[59] Metternich to Lebzeltern, Vienna, 16 May 1826, HHStA, StA, Russland III, 75.

[60] Metternich to Trauttmannsdorff, Vienna, 12 Oct. 1829, HHStA, StK, Preussen 132.

[61] Metternich to Apponyi, Vienna, 1 Dec. 1834, HHStA, StA, Frankreich 294.

[62] Metternich to Lebzeltern, Vienna, 24 Nov. 1823, HHStA, StA, Russland III, 60.

[63] Metternich to Vincent, Vienna, 8 Oct. 1824, HHStA, StA, Frankreich 254.

[64] Metternich to Lebzeltern, Ischl, 13 Aug. 1825, HHStA, StA, Russland III, 71.

Alliance, those states destined to solve various issues of European politics. Metternich's Alliance was the practical collective security system that was the expression of the idea of equilibrium.[65] If a historian reads the prince's instructions and recorded discussions, he or she realises that he did not make use of the term "Holy Alliance" and even in contact with Russian diplomats he generally used the term "Alliance," apparently leaving Tsar Alexander I to make his own interpretation.

Metternich was considerably annoyed when the term Holy Alliance was used in diplomatic practice. For example, he considered it inappropriate when a French foreign minister addressed the representatives of the Great Powers and Spain in Paris on 31 August 1824, as "the ambassadors and *ministers of the Holy Alliance.*"[66] Metternich promptly reacted with these words: "The Alliance is one ... As often as the representatives of the courts assemble in Paris to consider the affairs of European interest, they come together united in the name of the Alliance founded in Töplitz in 1813, confirmed in Chaumont in 1814, sanctioned anew and published in Paris in 1815, consolidated by the accession of France in Aix-la-Chapelle in 1818 and subsequently applied in Ljubljana in 1821 and in Verona in 1822. To admit into this state of affairs a subordination of the ministers to the Holy Alliance would in a way permit an act of defection or disunion within the great Alliance ... We do not know and we will never recognise in our diplomatic language anything other than the Alliance, its spirit, its precepts and its stipulations as they are found included with the diplomatic acts mentioned above."[67] The "act of disunion" signified an important reason for Metternich's outbursts of displeasure whenever he made a comment about the Holy Alliance – Great Britain was not a member and the cooperation of the five Great Powers in European as well as Near Eastern affairs to which Metternich attached great importance was thus attacked.[68] It is true that the Holy Alliance became an important symbol of the period, but in fact it had little impact on diplomatic practice[69] and it must be added that giving it undue at-

---

[65] Sofka, p. 137. A fitting example clearly illustrating Metternich's more practical outlook than that contained in the Proclamation of the Holy Alliance can be found in his project for the league to preserve peace from 1840. For more see Chapter 26.
[66] Metternich to Vincent, Vienna, 8 Oct. 1824, HHStA, StA, Frankreich 254.
[67] Ibid.
[68] Ibid.
[69] R. B. Elrod, "The Concert of Europe: A Fresh Look at an International Sys-

tention in connection with Metternich reflects a distorted reality and
leads to simplifications and misinterpretations. Unfortunately, historians have often added the word "Holy" to the word "Alliance" uttered
by Metternich, thereby changing the real sense of the term as used by
him. Consequently, it must be emphasised that in this book the term
Alliance does not mean the "Holy Alliance," which term is always
mentioned explicitly in its full length if necessary.

It is a certain paradox that although the Holy Alliance had little
value with regard to practical politics, its creation caused problems
in the relations between Europe and the Ottoman Empire after 1815.
Mahmud II was not invited to add his signature to the charter that
was, contrary to the promise made by Alexander I to Metternich, made
public during the Christmas of 1815. The Porte learnt in this way of
the declaration of the Holy Alliance and started to fear that its main
goal was a new holy war of the Christians against Moslems, in other
words a new crusade against the Turks, but Metternich saw no reason
why Alexander I would wish to attack the Ottomans; he had faith in
the tsar's peaceful intentions and did not share the Porte's suspicions
of the anti-Ottoman prejudice at the core of the Holy Alliance. He
also tried to dispel anxieties in Constantinople, and for that purpose
in early 1816 he sent to Constantinople a declaration designed to reassure the sultan that no country in Europe desired to wage war in
the Levant and that the Holy Alliance contained nothing threatening
to the existence of the sultan's empire. This protestation actually had
no success and the Porte's fear of a war with Russia was so acute that
when the friendly Viennese cabinet moved 20,000 soldiers to Transylvania on the Ottoman frontier in 1816, Mahmud II and his advisors
regarded it as a sign of a forthcoming attack from the alleged Russo-
Austrian alliance. Even Lord Exmouth's naval assault against Algeria
in the spring of the same year intensified this fear of the Holy Alliance
despite the fact that Great Britain was not a member. The hysteria
among the Ottomans reached such proportions that they undertook
measures for defence in 1817–1818. Their concern regarding the aim of
the Holy Alliance was naturally further intensified with the outbreak
of the Greek insurrection in the spring of 1821.[70] At the end of the

---

tem," *WRP* 28, 1976, 2, p. 171.
[70] Lützow to Metternich, Constantinople, 10 Dec. 1821, HHStA, StA, Türkei VI,
12; Gürbüz, pp. 78–107; Kargl, p. 361; Webster, *Castlereagh*, p. 372.

same year, Metternich felt obliged to calm the Porte once again: "It is true that the Holy Alliance in no way affects the relations between the Christian Powers and the Ottoman Empire ... We do not see in the Holy Alliance a religious war of Christianity against Islam."[71] Together with the British government, he finally succeeded in dispelling the Ottomans' apprehensions later in 1822.[72]

The Porte's fear of the Holy Alliance was intensified by difficult negotiations with Russia about the Caucasus and Danubian borders and the Serbian Question. Whereas the frontier in Europe was settled in September 1817 to the benefit of Russia, the two other issues were more difficult to solve, and in the summer of 1820 the negotiations were interrupted. Metternich remained passive and did not interfere in the discussions because he wanted to preserve good relations with both countries and was occupied with other affairs in Europe. As for the Caucasus border, he was as uninterested in this issue as at the Congress of Vienna. Although the Russian pretension to several places on the eastern Black Sea coast was rather ambiguous, any eventual fulfilment of Russia's schemes to annex those areas would have no negative impact on Austria and, therefore, Metternich was an entirely disinterested observer in this dispute. His only concern during these years was that the Russo-Ottoman negotiations did not break out into war, which was an outcome that could not be entirely excluded owing to the strained relations between St Petersburg and Constantinople.[73]

*   *   *

Metternich's conduct in Near Eastern affairs until the early 1820s shows that he considered the preservation of the Ottoman Empire to be of vital significance for Austria. The Ottoman regions in the Balkans were of particular importance for him, not because he and "his" monarchy could gain much there but because they could lose a great deal. Metternich was firmly convinced that Austria would gain

---

[71] Metternich to Lützow, Vienna, 17 Nov. 1821, HHStA, StA, Türkei VI, 11.
[72] Metternich to Esterházy, Vienna, 14 June 1821, HHStA, StA, England 166; Lützow to Metternich, Constantinople, 25 Sept. 1822, HHStA, StA, Türkei VI, 13.
[73] Metternich to Stürmer, Milan, 13 Feb. 1816, HHStA, StA, Türkei VI, 10; Gürbüz, pp. 106–132.

nothing from expansion at the expense of its weak neighbour, and he
once told Radetzky: "For Austria there are no edible fruits growing
in the fields of the Levant."[74] However, the destruction of Ottoman
domain in the Balkans could result in the rise of nation states with expected leanings towards Russia as well as direct territorial conquests
by this Great Power, both increasing Russia's influence over regions
with great strategic and economic importance for the Danube Monarchy. Consequently, Metternich occupied himself with the possibility
of laying a more solid foundation for the Ottoman Empire's further
existence and for this reason he proposed the political incorporation
of its whole body into the family of European countries, which would
provide it with legal protection of its sovereignty and independence.
The failure of this plan later facilitated what Metternich had feared
from the beginning: the pursuance of ambitious policies of some Great
Powers at the expense of the Ottoman Empire with a disturbing impact not only on the situation in the Near East but also on their
mutual relations.

The preservation of the Ottoman Empire definitely became the
cornerstone of Austrian Near Eastern policy at the end of the Napoleonic era, and although the sultan's state did not become a part of the
system created at the Congress of Vienna, Metternich completely acknowledged its territorial integrity and the legitimacy of its ruler as
an important component of international law. Francis I, who had no
ambitions for imperial expansion or glory[75] and regarded the culti-
vation of amicable relations with the Ottoman Empire as one of the
principal aims of Austria's foreign policy, maintained the same attitude and saw no reason to alter anything in this political line, in
particular when the dearly won victory over France against which he
fought intermittently for more than two decades was also made possible by the peace in the East. He told the Russian ambassador in
December 1827 that "he felt a deep gratitude towards the Turks for
the discretion they had shown him during his [military] difficulties;
that if they had attacked him while he had Bonaparte at his throat,

---

[74] Gürbüz, p. 56.
[75] B. Jelavich, *Modern Austria: Empire and Republic, 1815–1986*, London, New
York 1987, p. 31.

they would have plunged him into the utmost peril."[76] These words were, of course, uttered at a specific time and with a specific aim, but there is no reason not to take them at face value. Francis I's considerably friendly behaviour towards the Ottoman Empire until his death in 1835 proved their validity.

For several years after the Congress of Vienna, Metternich pursued a markedly passive policy towards the Ottoman Empire, mainly for two reasons: first, he had nothing to gain in the Near East except an economic benefit; second, he had no reason to pay much attention to the affairs in the Levant. Fortunately for him, Alexander I actually did not have hostile plans against the Ottoman Empire. For the sultan, serious difficulties were not to come initially from abroad but from his own subjects. When these problems began to attract the attention of Europe, Metternich had to turn his attention to the East and participate in managing Near Eastern affairs, which was not a task he welcomed but undoubtedly one that was necessary for the Austrian Empire. As he wrote in 1854: "In every struggle between the West and the Levant, Austria cannot remain outside; it is at the head of the issue where it [Austria] takes its place."[77] This may be a somewhat exaggerated statement, but the fact remains that peace and stability in the Near East were extremely important for the central European Power, and Metternich's further steps entirely reflected this situation.

---

[76] Tatishchev to Nesselrode, Vienna, 28 Dec. 1827, AVPRI, fond 133, Kantseliariia, opis 468, 11874.
[77] Tischler, p. 227.

2

The Beginning of the Greek Insurrection

The event that moved Metternich to turn his attention to the Ottoman Empire was the Greeks' struggle for independence that erupted in the spring of 1821. It contained the two principal dangers which Metternich immediately recognised and feared: nationalism disturbing the political status quo and an opportunity for Russia's active interference into Ottoman affairs that could easily develop into a war in which the Ottoman Empire would have considerably fewer prospects for success than its powerful northern neighbour. Consequently, Metternich exerted a great deal of effort from the very beginning to prevent an open rupture between the sultan and the tsar and tried thus to offer to the former the time necessary to crush the insurrection.

The Greek Uprising and the Congress of Ljubljana

Neither Metternich's considerable interest nor his knowledge of some nationalistic and conspiratorial tensions among the Greeks prepared him for the events of 1821, when a Russian general of Greek origin and the leader of a Greek secret revolutionary organisation Society of Friends (*Filiki Eteria*), Alexander Ypsilantis, crossed the Pruth River on 6 March and invited the Christians in the Ottoman Empire to throw off the sultan's yoke.[1] Metternich was taken by surprise because first, the reports with news of a Greek plot that he had obtained and forwarded to the Porte contained little really useful information, second, he had been fully engaged with revolutions in Spain and Naples since the previous year and third, he regarded as the most immediate

---

[1] D. Brewer, *The Greek War of Independence: The Struggle for Freedom from Ottoman Oppression and the Birth of the Modern Greek Nation*, Woodstock, New York 2003, p. 53.

threat in the Balkans an ambitious and powerful Ottoman governor
in western Greece and southern Albania, Ali Pasha of Yannina, who
controlled the regions entrusted to his administration almost like an
independent ruler. Ali's power was so considerable that he maintained
direct contact with some European Powers. In 1814, he also found it
useful to approach Austria. This attempt met with some success because the Viennese cabinet wished to know more about his plans and,
therefore, it allowed its consul in Patras to hand over news about
political affairs to the pasha and provided a physician when it was
asked. This generosity was in no way the result of a friendly attitude
but rather due to the fear that Ali could unite with Russia. When Ali
asked the Austrian consul in 1820 about the emperor's eventual support in a war against the sultan, the answer was, of course, negative.
In the same year, he had to face alone the attack of a Turkish army
sent by Mahmud II against him, and he was besieged in Yannina and
killed in February 1822.[2]

The news of Ypsilantis' actions raised the question about the
tsar's attitude. Metternich feared his intervention on behalf of his Orthodox co-religionists, which was exactly what Ypsilantis had counted
on; he addressed a request to Alexander I for assistance in the fight
against the Ottomans. His hopes were frustrated by the fact that at
the same moment when he was stoking the flames of rebellion in the
Danubian Principalities, Alexander I was at the Congress of Ljubljana.
It was here and from Metternich himself that he learnt on 19 March
about Ypsilantis' exploits. Alexander I was easily persuaded by Francis I and his foreign minister that the enterprise was the result of a
long prepared plan, which was entirely correct, and that the secret
society responsible for the action was basically the same as the Italian Carbonari, which was basically true since the Carbonari served
as a model for the Greek conspirators. Hostile to revolutions, the tsar
reached a decision on the same morning that the insurrection would be
left to its own fate and promised to discharge all the officers involved
including Alexander Ypsilantis from his service, a promise which he

---

[2]   J. W. Baggally, *Ali Pasha and Great Britain*, Oxford 1938, p. 91; D. N. Skiotis,
"The Greek Revolution: Ali Pasha's Last Gamble," N. P. Diamandouros, J. P. An-
ton, J. A. Petropulos, P. Topping (eds.), *Hellenism and the First Greek War of
Liberation (1821–1830): Continuity and Change*, Thessaloniki 1976, pp. 97–109;
Gürbüz, pp. 280–287.

fulfilled. He also condemned the action and professed not to offer his assistance, which was the kiss of death for Ypsilantis because the support he obtained in the Principalities where the Greeks were generally unpopular was chiefly a result of the local inhabitants' faith in a Russian military intervention. Now, the tsar's assistance of which the people had been constantly assured became an illusion. Even worse for the Greeks, Alexander I allowed the Turks to send their troops into the Principalities to crush the revolt, which was the consent that Sultan Mahmud II needed according to Russo-Ottoman treaty stipulations. The tsar's response filled Metternich with optimism as he believed in the prompt defeat of "that madman, that masked liberal, that ill-advised Hellenist."[3] This desire was soon satisfied. In early May, Turkish soldiers entered the Principalities and seized Bucharest before the month passed. Ypsilantis fled to Austrian soil in late June and the rest of his companions fighting in the Danubian Principalities were sent fleeing during the summer.[4]

The defeat of the Eterists in the Principalities was, however, only a partial success for the Turks. One rebellion kindled by *Filiki Eteria* burnt out but another one started by the same society flared up with full strength in the Peloponnese, some regions above the Gulf of Corinth and in the adjacent islands in early April 1821. The Greeks, dissatisfied with the corrupt and inept Ottoman government and motivated by their religious, nationalistic and economic ambitions, started a struggle for independence that was much more difficult to suppress.[5] Already in mid May, Metternich realised its importance and considered the war in the southern Balkans as much more serious than Ypsi-

---

[3] Metternich to Princess Lieven, Ljubljana, 6 May 1821, NA, RAM-AC 6, 1.
[4] Metternich to Esterházy, Ljubljana, 19 and 28 March 1821, HHStA, StA, England 166; Nesselrode to Stroganov, Ljubljana, 26 March 1821, Prokesch-Osten, *Griechen*, III, pp. 68–70; V. Roman, *Rumänien im Spannungsfeld der Grossmächte 1774–1878: Die Donaufürstertümer vom osmanischen Vasallentum zur europäischen Peripherie*, Offenbach 1987, p. 30; E. D. Tappe, "The 1821 Revolution in the Rumanian Principalities," R. Clogg (ed.), *The Struggle for Greek Independence: Essays to Mark the 150th Anniversary of the Greek War of Independence*, London, Basingstoke 1973, p. 149.
[5] D. Dakin, *The Greek Struggle for Independence, 1821–1833*, London 1973, pp. 65–69; W. W. McGrew, "The Land Issue in the Greek War of Independence," N. P. Diamandouros, J. P. Anton, J. A. Petropulos, P. Topping (eds.), *Hellenism and the First Greek War of Liberation (1821–1830): Continuity and Change*, Thessaloniki 1976, pp. 111–129.

lantis' activities in the Principalities. He had thus another and greater reason to be concerned about the tsar's attitude, but fortunately for him, Alexander I was still under his influence at the Congress of Ljubljana. The monarch again learnt about the insurrection in Greece from Metternich, and in the prince's words he "was like a man struck by a thunderbolt."[6] The tsar was met with the same monarchical and anti-revolutionary arguments that Metternich had already used against Ypsilantis' enterprise, depicting the Greek uprising as the same threat as the revolutions in Spain and the Apennines. While Ypsilantis was presented to Alexander I as a mere criminal, the Greeks were depicted by Metternich as being like the Italian Carbonaris, infected by liberal ideas and allegedly directed from Paris not only against the sultan but also against the union of the two conservative Powers.[7] Metternich wrote to Alexander I on 7 May that the Greek revolution was "a torch thrown between Austria and Russia, an instrument for keeping the fire burning, for stoking the liberal conflagration ... for breaking the bonds that unite the two emperors."[8] He asked him in the same letter to continue in his actual neutral policy, to trust in his conservative principles, to support the legitimate power of the sultan, which meant not to interfere in the civil war and not to stray from the course already taken because, according to the chancellor, the tsar was the only one who could "strangle the revolutionary hydra."[9]

Metternich's verbal offensive continued and finally met with success during another personal meeting on 13 May when Alexander I agreed to the opinion that the Great Powers had to oppose the uprising in the Near East and promised to abstain from taking any separate action in the Greek affairs; according to some witnesses he even promised not to act without consulting with Francis I first. He instructed Russian diplomats and consuls accordingly and openly showed in this way that Russia would remain passive and would take no steps without the consent of its allies. It must be admitted that this victory was not very difficult to achieve because after the outbreak of revolutions in Europe in 1820 the tsar disliked them to the

6   Stewart to Londonderry, Vienna, 31 May 1821, TNA, FO 120/47.
7   Metternich to Lützow, Ljubljana, 26 March and 29 April 1821, HHStA, StA, Türkei VI, 11; Metternich to Esterházy, Ljubljana, 9 and 14 May 1821, HHStA, StA, England 166.
8   Metternich to Esterházy, Ljubljana, 14 May 1821, HHStA, StA, England 166.
9   Ibid.

same extent as did Metternich and, consequently, was strongly attached to the Alliance. Moreover, he had no hostile designs against
the Ottoman Empire; he in no way wished to continue in the policy of
his grandmother Catherine the Great, who had wanted to overthrow
the sultan's power and re-establish a Byzantine Empire in its place.
On leaving Ljubljana in May, Alexander I's declarations supporting
opposition to the Greek rebellion were undoubtedly sincere, and when
he returned in mid June to St Petersburg, he continued to repeat his
assurances of loyalty to the Alliance and his unwillingness to support
the rebellious Greeks. Then, however, under the influence of the news
coming from the Ottoman Empire, he started to vacillate between the
interests of Europe and those of Russia.[10]

The Deterioration of Russo-Ottoman Relations

After the termination of the congress, on the way to Vienna, Metternich was acquainted with his appointment as the court and state
chancellor. This was the emperor's reward for his diplomatic achievements, but his accomplishments concerning the Near East started to
be more and more uncertain. Metternich hoped that the Turks would
quickly suppress the revolt and do nothing to upset Russia, but they
started to do exactly the opposite. They were unable to defeat the
Greeks and began to irritate the tsar in two ways. First, the atrocities
towards the Orthodox Christians spread through the capital and other
parts of the empire. The most visible crimes were committed against
a Greek dragoman of the Porte, who was executed shortly before the
planned interview with the Austrian representative in Constantinople,
Internuncio Count Rudolf von Lützow,[11] and particularly against old

---

[10] Ibid.; Gordon to Londonderry, Ljubljana, 13 May 1821, TNA, FO 120/47; Caraman to Pasquier, Vienna, 1 June 1821, AMAE, CP, Autriche 402; Bitis, pp. 26–
28; Nichols, "The Eastern Question," p. 55; Schroeder, *Metternich's Diplomacy*,
p. 171. For more on Catherine's so-called Greek Project D. L. Ransel, *The Politics
of Catherinian Russia: The Panin Party*, New Haven, London 1975, p. 252.
[11] The rank of internuncio was used by a representative of the Habsburg monarch
in Constantinople for the first time in 1627, but it was continually used from 1779.
After the Congress of Vienna, the title of a Minister Plenipotentiary was added.
Austria's representative was thus the first in the ranks of diplomats of the second
class immediately following ambassadors. Kargl, p. 84; Sauer, *Österreich und die*

Greek Patriarch Gregorios V, who was hanged on the gate of his office on Easter Sunday. The persecution of these Christians accompanied by the damage to churches naturally displeased the Russian orthodox monarch, and the fact that a considerable number of these killings were not ordered by the Ottoman government but were carried out by the excited population could scarcely diminish his outrage. Second, the Porte took economic measures against the Greeks simultaneously harming Russian trade. In May, Mahmud II ordered an obligatory sale of cargoes transported from the Black Sea through the Straits to assure food, in particular grain, for the capital and to prevent the import of this commodity into the areas controlled by the insurgents. This measure damaged Russian export trade from the Black Sea, especially Odessa, and affected relevant Russo-Ottoman treaty stipulations. In the Danubian Principalities, the Turks not only intervened but also dismissed their princes (hospodars, one representing the sultan in each Principality) and imposed taxes without the tsar's obligatory consent.[12]

The Russian ambassador in Constantinople, Baron Gregory Alexandrovitch Stroganov, acted from the very beginning according to his instructions and protested against Ypsilantis and the rebellious Greeks, but the massacre of large numbers of them and his personal sympathies for their cause led him to raise official protests against the mass slaughter, destruction of churches and other inhumane measures perpetrated by the Turks, and he acted in the same way when the Porte harmed Russian trade with its measures. The Turks, who were angered by the murder of thousands of Moslems by the Greeks and suspected Russia's government of standing behind the revolt, secretly supporting it and trying to prevent its suppression by its protests, ignored Stroganov's grievances. Alexander I's condemnation of Ypsilantis' action did nothing to lessen their distrust because they could hardly believe him when they knew that some Russian consuls and agents in the Ottoman Empire had helped the Greeks to plan the uprising and, at variance with the tsar's instructions, continued to support it after its outbreak, when Stroganov was seldom cordial in his declarations, when Russia's commerce was carried out by the Greeks, and finally when all the world was claiming that the Russians stood

---

Levante, p. 42.
[12] Bitis, pp. 108–109; Prokesch-Osten, *Griechen*, I, p. 43.

behind the insurgents. Metternich pointedly commented on this at the end of the year: "Prince Ypsilantis suddenly appeared in Moldavia. He presented himself there wearing a Russian uniform, followed by Russian officers, arriving from a Russian territory, boldly proclaiming the alleged support of H. I. M. [His Imperial Majesty] of all the Russias, and announcing the protection of the monarch on behalf of a general liberation of the Greek nation."[13] Consequently, the Turks accused Alexander I of supporting the rebellious Greeks, which he actually did not, and they did not care that their actions offended his feelings or interests. The only possible outcome of their attitude was the considerable chilling of relations between them and Stroganov, which already happened in late May.[14]

In the early summer of 1821, the Turks found themselves in the situation where they were unable to suppress the insurrection and hardly able to maintain peace with Russia. This forced Metternich to do something to prevent an eventual outbreak of war, which was, however, a rather difficult task. On the one hand, he personally sided with the Turks and strongly disapproved of the pro-Greek activities of some Russian agents and consuls but, on the other hand, Russia was an essential ally of Austria. To be openly friendly to the Turks meant he could lose his influence with the tsar; to side decisively with the Russians meant he could lose his influence in Constantinople. In both cases he would have been deprived of the weapons with which he wanted to work upon the two monarchs: on Alexander I with the aim of preventing him from declaring war and on Mahmud II, whom he wanted to persuade to give in to some of Russia's demands. He had to exert great effort and tact on both sides in order to urge them to moderation and to overcome the "radical parties" existing at the two courts.[15]

In Constantinople, Lützow was instructed in March to give the Porte confidence in Austria's and Russia's support and later to mitigate its fury. Metternich strongly criticised needless complications resulting from the "imprudent blindness"[16] of the Divan and warned

---

[13] Metternich to Lebzeltern, Vienna, 23 Dec. 1821, HHStA, StA, Russland III, 45.
[14] Lützow to Metternich, Constantinople, 24 March, 10 April, 10 and 25 May 1821, HHStA, StA, Türkei VI, 11.
[15] Schroeder, *Metternich's Diplomacy*, p. 173.
[16] Metternich to Esterházy, Vienna, 30 May 1821, HHStA, StA, England 166.

it against excessive brutality, urged it to justice and condemned the murder of the patriarch and prominent clergymen; he insisted that the killing of orthodox Christians was to be stopped. He regarded the fanaticism of some Ottoman Moslems as not only inhumane but also as highly imprudent and advised clemency, justice and particularly regard for Russia. Lützow actually did his best to satisfy Metternich's wishes. He was truly personally horrified by the massacre of the Greeks and for personal as well as political reasons he disapproved of such behaviour against people who had nothing in common with the rebellion, including two Austrian sailors who were murdered while they were working on board their ship and some employees of the internunciature who were insulted by a mob. Lützow also formally came out against the prohibition of the grain export on 20 May for its negative impact on Russo-Ottoman relations as well as Austria's commerce, and when nothing happened, he repeated his complaint against the embargo on ships carrying grain in mid July. Nevertheless, it was impossible to change the Porte's actions against the Greeks as well as its attitude towards Russia because its obstinacy was too determined and its confidence in Lützow too low – he was a representative of a member country of the Holy Alliance. Additionally, as in 1816, the presence of Austrian troops on the eastern rim of the Military Frontier, where they were to prevent the insurgents in the Principalities from fleeing to Austria at this time, further invoked the Porte's distrust. It also was not pleased with Lützow's cooperation with Stroganov as instructed by Metternich. This Austro-Russian intimacy weakened Lützow's position in Constantinople not only with the Turks but also with the new British ambassador, Percy Clinton Sydney Smythe Lord Strangford, a man with strong pro-Turkish sentiments and insatiable ambitions. He deeply distrusted Russia and disliked Stroganov. He also suspected Austria of submitting to Russia's interests and acting with it on a premeditated plan directed against the Ottoman Empire. Consequently, when on the day of the patriarch's arrest Lützow wanted to arrange a collective diplomatic advance towards the Porte against the excessive violence, Strangford refused, which further deepened the distrust between the two men despite the fact that their interests were identical.[17]

---

[17] Metternich to Lützow, Ljubljana, 26 March, 12 and 29 April, 17 May, 3 June and 3 July 1821, HHStA, StA, Türkei VI, 11; Metternich to Esterházy, Ljubljana,

Strangford's conduct was based upon an incorrect assessment of Austria's policy but was not entirely illogical because his forbearance ensured him considerable influence over the Ottoman government. The more hostile Stroganov was to the Turks, the more influence the benevolent British ambassador possessed. Metternich was well aware of the value of Strangford's eventual support, which he urgently needed because the chancellor himself "saw no direct means that he could employ for opening the eyes of the Turkish government and for inducing it to follow a course less harmful to its real interests."[18] Metternich would have liked Strangford to cooperate with Lützow and be on more friendly terms with Stroganov. He instructed the internuncio in this sense but any cooperation proved to be impossible due to Strangford's aloofness, which led to Metternich's strong criticism and the accusation against Strangford that he did not serve the peace with his behaviour and that he let himself be influenced by the "false appearances"[19] of Austria's complicity with Russia at the moment when Austria and Great Britain had to proceed in Constantinople in unity. He demanded from the British cabinet a joint action in Constantinople but nothing changed in the ambassador's attitude during the summer; his relations with Lützow did not improve and those with Stroganov became even worse.[20]

In St Petersburg, the Austrian ambassador, Count Ludwig von Lebzeltern, was instructed to praise Alexander I for his conservative principles and loyalty to the Alliance and peace. He was to terrify

---

28 March 1821, Vienna, 14 June 1821, HHStA, StA, England 166; Metternich to Zichy, Vienna, 15 Aug. 1821, HHStA, StK, Preussen 113; Lützow to Metternich, Constantinople, 31 March, 10, 20 and 25 April, 2, 18 and 25 May, 25 July 1821, Lützow's notes to the Porte, Constantinople, 20 May and 16 July, HHStA, StA, Türkei VI, 11; Strangford to Londonderry, Constantinople, 25 July 1821, attached to Metternich to Esterházy, Vienna, 15 Aug. 1821, HHStA, StA, England 166; Gürbüz, pp. 305–309; Prokesch-Osten, *Griechen*, I, p. 47; Webster, *Castlereagh*, p. 355.

[18] Krusemark to Frederick William III, Vienna, 13 June 1821, GStA PK, HA III, MdA I, 5995.

[19] Metternich to Esterházy, Vienna, 14 June 1821, HHStA, StA, England 166.

[20] Metternich to Lützow, Ljubljana, 29 April 1821, HHStA, StA, Türkei VI, 11; Metternich to Esterházy, Ljubljana, 21 May 1821, Vienna, 14 June, 18 and 20 July 1821, HHStA, StA, England 166; Metternich to Zichy, Vienna, 15 Aug. 1821, HHStA, StK, Preussen 113; Lützow to Metternich, Constantinople, 25 July 1821, HHStA, StA, Türkei VI, 11; Krusemark to Frederick William III, Vienna, 27 June 1821, GStA PK, HA III, MdA I, 5995.

the tsar with the vision of a widespread revolution if Russia were to support the Greeks' cause. Lebzeltern was a skilful diplomat, but the task was becoming more and more difficult as Stroganov's distressing reports about the Turks' war not merely against the Greeks but Christianity as a whole started to arrive in the Russian capital. Alexander I found himself under pressure from the "war faction" dreaming about the expulsion of the Turks from Europe or even the destruction of the Ottoman Empire and trying to persuade the tsar to take advantage of the situation and go to war. The group of Russian hawks was composed of military officers like generals Aleksey Petrovich Ermolov and Pavel Dmitrievich Kiselev, diplomats like Stroganov, Ambassador in Vienna Yurii Alexandrovich Golovkin, Ambassador in Paris Pozzo di Borgo and some members of social elite like Baroness Barbara Juliane von Krudener, the spiritual "mother" of the Holy Alliance, now preaching a crusade against the Turks.[21]

The most influential man with considerably hostile designs towards the Ottoman Empire but with more pro-Greek than pro-Russian goals was the Russian vice-chancellor, Count Ioannis Antonios Capodistrias, together with Count Karl Robert von Nesselrode leading the portfolio of foreign affairs. Capodistrias was one of five main European statesmen with whom Metternich crossed swords in Near Eastern affairs between 1821 and 1841. The others were George Canning, Nesselrode, Palmerston and Adolphe Thiers. None of these four, however, advocated the expulsion of Ottoman power from Europe or maintained such diametrically opposite attitudes towards the sultan's empire to Metternich as did Capodistrias, who longed for an independent and constitutional Greece under Russian protection, a goal that was to be reached by means of a Russo-Ottoman war. When one finally broke out in 1828, he desired the destruction of the Ottoman dominion in Europe and the creation of a pro-Russian Balkan confederation.[22] In other words, Capodistrias wanted in the Balkans precisely what Metternich did not, and his wishes directly threatened

---

[21]   M. Rendall, "Cosmopolitanism and Russian Near Eastern Policy, 1821–41: Debunking a Historical Canard," W. Pyta (ed.), *Das europäische Mächtekonzert: Friedens- und Sicherheitspolitik vom Wiener Kongreß 1815 bis zum Krimkrieg 1853*, Köln, Weimar, Wien 2009, p. 240; C. W. Crawley, *The Question of Greek Independence: A Study of British Policy in the Near East, 1821–1833*, Cambridge 1930, p. 18; Bitis, pp. 30–34, 110.
[22]   Bitis, p. 33.

Austria's interests in the Near East as well as the European balance of power.

Metternich was well aware of the situation existing in St Petersburg. He was of the correct opinion that Alexander I's policy towards the Ottoman Empire was ambitious in the sense of wanting to maintain Russia's influence, in particular over the Principalities, but without a desire for conquest, and that the tsar wanted to preserve the peace. The chancellor also knew the tsar's character and believed that if the monarch once yielded to the war faction and decided to consider the affairs in the Near East as solely Russian affairs, it would be almost impossible to get him back to the idea of peace: "If one cannon is fired, *Alexander will escape us at the head of his retinue* and then there will be no limit any longer to what he will consider his divinely ordained laws."[23] Consequently, he had no other option than to continue his efforts to prevent the tsar from going beyond the point of no return. The fight for the tsar's heart and soul was to be a match between him and Capodistrias, with whom he had already had rather reserved relations before the outbreak of the Greek insurrection, and which now became even colder. Metternich suspected him of complicity in the Greek revolt, although indirect, and sent some intercepted letters to the tsar that were to prove it, but the evidence was extremely weak and the chancellor was therefore logically unable to provide a convincing argument. This attempt well reflected Metternich's desire to undermine Capodistrias' influence over the tsar and, at best, to get rid of him. Another weapon at Metternich's disposal was his anti-revolutionary rhetoric, now even more strongly depicting the Greeks' insurrection as a part of a wider plot allegedly directed from Paris: "It is in Paris, Sire, where the main source [of the rebellion] exists; it is there where the greatest conspiracy that ever threatened our entire society is to be found. Every day further proves this sad truth and every hour provides us with new evidence."[24] Metternich was also trying to persuade the tsar of the necessity to maintain peace and good relations between the Great Powers. Both these tactics seemed to have some effect; Alexander I believed the baseless warnings against the threat of revolution directed from Paris and, although upset by the

---

[23] Kissinger, p. 293.
[24] Sauvigny, *Metternich et la France*, II, p. 514.

Turks' behaviour, did not wish to wage war and undertake a unilateral action without his allies.[25]

In the midsummer of 1821, however, Alexander I's patience with the behaviour of the Turks was severely weakened and the war party seemed to gain predominance. Capodistrias' hostile attitude towards the Porte could thus be expressed in a note presented by Stroganov on 18 July in which Russia demanded the withdrawal of the Turkish army from the Principalities, the guarantee for the lives of the Christians in the Ottoman Empire, the restoration of churches destroyed during the riots and for the distinction to be made between innocent Greeks and the rebels. If the Porte did not consent within eight days, Stroganov was entitled to leave Constantinople. Reis Effendi Hamid Bey's written answer came too late and was negative. Moreover, the Porte added fuel to the fire when it publicly declared that Russia was responsible for the Greek insurrection and it even seemed to contemplate Stroganov's imprisonment, which would inevitably have led to war. This was finally prevented by the intervention of Lützow and Strangford, but since they failed to persuade their Russian colleague to stay, Stroganov departed to Odessa on 10 August. Lützow assumed the responsibility for the protection of Russian citizens, which again made his position vis-à-vis the Turks more difficult. The war did not come, but Russo-Ottoman diplomatic relations were suspended.[26]

[25] Metternich to Esterházy, Ljubljana, 14 May 1821, Vienna, 16 July 1821, HHStA, StA, England 166; Metternich to Zichy, Vienna, 1 June 1821, HHStA, StK, Preussen 113; Stewart to Londonderry, Vienna, 31 May 1821, TNA, FO 120/47; Lebzeltern to Metternich, St Petersburg, 3 July 1821, E. de L.-M. de Robech (ed.), *Un collaborateur de Metternich: Mémoires et papiers de Lebzeltern*, Paris 1949, p. 412; P. K. Grimsted, *The Foreign Ministers of Alexander I: Political Attitudes and the Conduct of Russian Diplomacy, 1801–1825*, Berkeley 1969, pp. 253–254; C. M. Woodhouse, "Kapodistrias and the Philiki Etairia, 1814–21," R. Clogg (ed.), *The Struggle for Greek Independence: Essays to Mark the 150th Anniversary of the Greek War of Independence*, London, Basingstoke 1973, pp. 104–134; Bitis, p. 112; Sauvigny, *Staatsmann und Diplomat*, p. 382.

[26] Lützow to Metternich, Constantinople, 25, 26 and 30 July 1821, HHStA, StA, Türkei VI, 11; Lützow to Metternich, Constantinople, 10 and 18 August 1821, HHStA, StA, Türkei VI, 12; M. Bayrak, "The Attitude of the European States during the Greek (Rum) Revolt," K. Çiçek (ed.), *The Great Ottoman-Turkish Civilisation, Vol. 1: Politics*, Ankara 2000, p. 443; Prokesch-Osten, *Griechen*, I, p. 81.

The Austro-British Cooperation

Stroganov's departure was an important incident indicating a new phase in Russo-Ottoman relations, but even though Metternich understood the seriousness of the situation, he was not frightened by it. The closure of the Russian embassy did not automatically mean the declaration of war, and at least the diplomat with strong pro-Greek sentiments had left the main stage. Metternich still counted on Alexander I's promise given in Ljubljana and believed that he did not desire war, and he was not mistaken because the tsar actually did not want to go further; the break of relations with the sultan was the maximum he was willing to undertake at that moment. This, however, could change if the war faction was able to bring the tsar under its control or the Turks remained deaf to the Russian requests. Metternich had to do something on both fronts if he wanted to preserve peace. In Constantinople, Austria actually assumed the protection not only of Russian citizens but also of Alexander I's interests. Metternich supported the ultimatum, the existence of which he had already learnt from St Petersburg. A day before Stroganov's presentation of the note to the Porte, the chancellor dispatched his instructions to Lützow in which he advised the Porte to accept the ultimatum and promptly suppress the insurrection. He regarded the requests as acceptable and although he secretly complained that Russia "opened a vast range of squabbles and claims"[27] and considered Stroganov's behaviour as anything but ideal, placing himself on "the sharpest line possible,"[28] the Porte could hardly refuse to yield under the given conditions. According to Metternich, the tsar's further attitude primarily depended on the decisions made in Constantinople.[29]

In the Ottoman capital Lützow in vain tried to obtain some concessions that would satisfy the tsar. The Porte responded in a con-

---

[27] Metternich to Lützow, Vienna, 5 Oct. 1821, Prokesch-Osten, *Griechen*, III, pp. 209–210.

[28] Metternich to Zichy, Vienna, 14 Aug. 1821, HHStA, StK, Preussen 113.

[29] Metternich to Lützow, Vienna, 17 July, 3 and 19 Aug. 1821, HHStA, StA, Türkei VI, 11; Metternich to Esterházy, Vienna, 15 Aug. 1821, HHStA, StA, England 166; Metternich to Zichy, Vienna, 15 Aug. 1821, HHStA, StK, Preussen 113; Metternich to Vincent, Vienna, 20 July and 17 Aug. 1821, HHStA, StA, Frankreich 244; Miltitz to Frederick William III, Pera, 10 Aug. 1821, GStA PK, HA III, MdA I, 7255; Gordon to Londonderry, Vienna, 16 Aug. 1821, TNA, FO 120/48; Grimsted, p. 261.

ciliatory manner to the questions of the amnesty or the restoration
of the churches, but in fact it offered mere promises and refused to
withdraw its troops from Moldavia and Wallachia. It maintained that
the Principalities required the military regime and the presence of the
Turkish army until the full suppression of the revolution, especially
when some Greek rebels who had fled to Russian soil were allegedly
waiting close to the Ottoman border prepared to return and renew
their fight. Mahmud II was so irritated by their seeking refuge in Russia that he requested their extradition in early August. Metternich did
his best to persuade him to drop this demand despite the fact that
in this case right was on the sultan's side; the chancellor knew that
but considered it as politically unfeasible and another complication
threatening peace. The tsar could hardly send the Christians to their
deaths at the hands of the Turks, and Metternich argued that Mahmud II would have behaved in the same way if, being simultaneously
not only a sultan but also a khalif, he had been asked to extradite
Moslem fugitives to his dominions. The persuasion had no positive
effect, and the animosity against Russia and distrust of Austria continued to prevail among the Turks. Their distrust increased even more
when the Porte learnt that Alexander Ypsilantis had saved his life by
escaping to Austrian territory. The Porte demanded his extradition
into Turkish hands, but the Viennese government refused and justly
argued that all Austro-Ottoman treaties contained clauses forbidding
the extradition of fugitives. Both countries were only obliged to withdraw them further from the frontier from where they could harm the
affairs in their native lands. This obligation was entirely fulfilled when
Ypsilantis was arrested and kept in prison. In conformity with this
ruling, Imre Thököly or Francis II Rákóczi had been "saved" by the
Porte and recently the Serbian leader, George Petrovich, by Austria.
The fact that right was entirely on Austria's side helped to end the
dispute with the Turks but could hardly improve Lützow's position
in Constantinople. The only success that was achieved, and the merit
was particularly Strangford's, was the termination of restrictions on
the grain commerce on 9 August 1821.[30]

---

[30] Metternich to Lützow, Vienna, 5 and 10 Sept. 1821, HHStA, StA, Türkei VI,
11; Metternich to Lebzeltern, Vienna, 1 Sept. 1821, HHStA, StA, Russland III,
45; Lützow to Metternich, Constantinople, 18 and 25 Aug. 1821, HHStA, StA,
Türkei VI, 12; Miltitz to Frederick William III, Pera, 25 Aug. 1821, GStA PK,

In St Petersburg the diplomatic and personal war between Capo-distrias and Metternich continued, with the former longing for war and advocating the right of a foreign intervention into Ottoman internal affairs and the latter desiring peace and strictly rejecting such a claim. In this respect a danger had arisen for Metternich in June 1821 when the director of the Political Division of the Prussian Foreign Ministry, Johann Peter Friedrich Ancillon, wrote a memorandum closely echo-ing the views of Capodistrias in which the legitimacy of the Ottoman rule in Europe was refuted, war was advocated and the replacement of the Ottoman Empire with an independent Greece under European protection was proposed. Ancillon also suggested that Russia's and Austria's armies were entrusted with this task in the interest of the Alliance. This document was presented to the Russian ambassador in Berlin, who sent it forward on 9 July to St Petersburg. At the moment when the threat of war was in the air, Metternich worried about the eventual impact of its content on Alexander I and moved the Prus-sian foreign minister, Count Christian Günther von Bernstorff, to call Ancillon's memorandum a mere expression of a private opinion. This incident led Metternich to be dissatisfied with the attitude of the cab-inet in Berlin, and he criticised the inexplicit and passive conduct of the government in Paris even more: "This government actually does not know what it could want and, consequently, it is not surprising that it ignores to the same extent what it should want."[31] Metternich would definitely have felt less secure if he had known that in a case of a war in the Near East, the French cabinet most likely would not have opposed Russia's designs and would have wished to conclude an alliance, a possibility that Capodistrias examined in Paris in July and that was strongly supported by Pozzo di Borgo, but refused by the French prime minister, Duke Armand-Emmanuel du Plessis de Riche-lieu, for the moment owing to the peaceful attitudes of Austria and Great Britain.[32]

HA III, MdA I, 7255; Gürbüz, pp. 324–330.

[31] Metternich to Vincent, Vienna, 20 July 1821, HHStA, StA, Frankreich 244.

[32] Metternich to Lebzeltern, Vienna, 3 Aug. 1821, HHStA, StA, Russland III, 45; Metternich to Vincent, Vienna, 7 Sept. 1821, HHStA, StA, Frankreich 244; Metternich to Esterházy, Vienna, 7 Sept. 1821, HHStA, StA, England 166; Cara-man to Montmorency, Vienna, 1 June 1822, AMAE, CP, Autriche 403; *Mémoire Confidentiel de Mr. Ancillon à Berlin*, late June 1821, Prokesch-Osten, *Griechen*, III, pp. 336–346; E. Schütz, *Die europäische Allianzpolitik Alexanders I. und der*

The not entirely clear attitudes of some European Powers were highly inopportune for Metternich trying to influence Alexander I not only with the warnings of revolution but also with the assurance of other Great Powers' support in Constantinople. The subordination of Russia to the Alliance was rather difficult when Metternich could only rely on Castlereagh, whose views concerning the Near Eastern affairs were identical and well known to the chancellor. In St Petersburg, Lebzeltern closely cooperated with British Ambassador Sir Charles Bagot and, at Metternich's urgence, new instructions for Strangford to move the Porte to more humane conduct and cooperate with the Austrian and Russian representatives were dispatched from London in mid July. Nevertheless, in neither instance was the British assistance without problems. First, Strangford was not an easily controllable instrument as was proved when he wanted to make a proclamation on behalf of the Great Powers to the rebellious Greeks with the aim of persuading them to end the insurrection in exchange for an amnesty. Metternich sharply denounced this plan as unacceptable interference into Ottoman internal affairs and with little hope for success. Second, Castlereagh's support of Metternich's steps within the Eastern Question was not absolute. When on 23 August in reaction to Stroganov's departure the prince proposed a ministerial conference in Vienna, a plan he had contemplated since mid July, where the Great Power's representatives were to obtain from their relative governments title to negotiate over the Near Eastern affairs, only Prussia consented. According to Sir Charles Kingsley Webster, Castlereagh's refusal was caused by the difference in the two statesmen's policies, leading Castlereagh to the refusal to "discuss any possibility of change in the Ottoman dominion ... He could not follow Metternich therefore into a discussion of eventualities."[33] The problem consists in the fact that Webster neither says which eventualities the latter wanted to discuss nor offers any relevant references. In fact no evidence was found for Metternich's desire to discuss any "eventuality" or for any divergence in the two men's opinions concerning the Russo-Ottoman relations in the summer of 1821. The primary aim of the conference was definitely quite practical: Metternich wanted the four Powers'

---

griechische Unabhängigkeitskampf 1820–1830, Wiesbaden 1975, pp. 68–71; Bitis, p. 112; Kissinger, p. 296; Sauvigny, *Metternich et la France*, II, pp. 514–522.
[33] Webster, *Castlereagh*, p. 361.

representatives in Vienna to be entitled to instruct their colleagues in Constantinople, which would have increased his own influence over the relations between Europe and the Ottoman Empire, provided Lützow with the cooperation of his colleagues and thus more easily persuaded the Porte to comply with the Russian ultimatum.[34]

In the early autumn, Metternich could be sure of British and even Prussian support and although he still did not know the attitude of France, at least in Constantinople the French ambassador supported the effort of his Austrian, British and Prussian colleagues to preserve peace. Metternich's position was, however, still difficult: despite the persuasive efforts of the four Powers, Mahmud II did not change his mind, and although Metternich strongly believed that "the tsar and his minister are more further apart than ever in their principles, their opinions and their intentions,"[35] his war with Capodistrias was far from over and the reports from the Russian capital were not very optimistic. All the more pleased was Metternich with Castlereagh's invitation to Hanover where the foreign secretary was about to accompany King Georg IV. Always of the opinion of the usefulness of personal meetings, the chancellor wrote to Lebzeltern: "I am entirely of the conviction that by my interview with Lord Castlereagh ... I shall achieve more in a few days to settle the general question, to strengthen the present and to save the future, than in six months of writing. It is also necessary that I know a little about the English; their role is extremely influential in the European-Russo-Turko-Greek affair. Only this conviction could induce me to travel 500 leagues in the space of four weeks at the most."[36] He also went to the German town with the hope for the realisation of the conference he had planned in August, but in this he was again unsuccessful. The French

---

[34] Metternich to Lützow, Vienna, 31 July 1821, HHStA, StA, Türkei VI, 11; Metternich to Vincent, Vienna, 23 Aug. 1821, HHStA, StA, Frankreich 244; Metternich to Zichy, Vienna, 8 and 24 Aug. 1821, HHStA, StK, Preussen 113; Metternich to Esterházy, Vienna, 18 July, 14 and 24 Aug., 2 and 9 Oct. 1821, HHStA, StA, England 166; Metternich to Lebzeltern, Vienna, 24 Aug. 1821, HHStA, StA, Russland III, 45; Krusemark to Frederick William III, Vienna, 5 Aug. 1821, GStA PK, HA III, MdA I, 5995; Gordon to Londonderry, Vienna, 8 and 23 Aug. 1821, TNA, FO 120/48; Francis I to Alexander I, Salzburg, 22 Aug. 1821, Prokesch-Osten, *Griechen*, III, pp. 156–161; Sauvigny, *Metternich et la France*, II, pp. 519–521; Schroeder, *Metternich's Diplomacy*, p. 175; Webster, *Castlereagh*, pp. 360–362.
[35] Metternich to Esterházy, Vienna, 2 Oct. 1821, HHStA, StA, England 166.
[36] Nichols, "The Eastern Question," p. 56.

foreign minister, Baron Étienne Denis Pasquier, refused to come and France was represented by a diplomat of lesser rank, Marquis Clément Edouard Moustier. Bernstorff could not go to Hanover even though he wanted to, and Baron Heinrich von Bülow, whom he sent, did not take part in the negotiations. The Russian ambassador in London, Prince Christophe Andreievich von Lieven, did not arrive until 28 October. The talks between Metternich and Castlereagh from October 20 to 29 were thus almost exclusively bilateral, but they finally served their purpose and Metternich was able to return to Vienna satisfied. The two statesmen were reassured in their opinions that the tsar did not desire a war in the Levant, and not at all simply because of the Greeks, and they agreed to cooperate in St Petersburg and Constantinople, supporting Alexander I's wishes to maintain peace by obtaining concessions from Mahmud II, who had to accept the Russian four points, in particular that requesting the withdrawal of Turkish troops from the Principalities. In St Petersburg, they were to weaken the position of the war faction and Capodistrias in particular by persuading the tsar of the necessity to act within the Alliance. Their position improved in December when Richelieu's cabinet fell and the new French government led by Baron Joseph de Villèle and with Viscount Mathieu Jean Felicité de Montmorency-Laval as foreign minister was more willing to cooperate with Austria and Great Britain.[37]

Success in St Petersburg greatly depended on the success of efforts in Constantinople because if Metternich and Castlereagh failed with the Turks, they would have offered the Russians a pretext for war. Nevertheless, even the concentrated British-Austrian pressure supported by France and Prussia did not lead to success in the Ot-

---

[37] Metternich to Lützow, Vienna, 19 Sept., 5, 13 and 14 Oct. 1821, HHStA, StA, Türkei VI, 11; Metternich to Zichy, Vienna, 26 Sept. 1821, Hanover, 31 Oct. 1821, HHStA, StK, Preussen 113; Metternich to Lebzeltern, Vienna, 6 and 8 Oct. 1821, HHStA, StA, Russland III, 45; Metternich to Vincent, Vienna, 1 Oct. 1821, Frankfurt am Main, 9 Nov. 1821, HHStA, StA, Frankreich 244; Lützow to Metternich, Constantinople, 10 and 25 Sept., 25 Oct. 1821, HHStA, StA, Türkei VI, 12; Krusemark to Frederick William III, Vienna, 26 Sept., 6 and 23 Oct. 1821, GStA PK, HA III, MdA I, 5995; Piquot to Frederick William III, Vienna, 19 Sept. 1821, GStA PK, HA III, MdA I, 5996; L. J. Baack, *Christian Bernstorff and Prussia: Diplomacy and Reform Conservatism 1818–1832*, New Jersey 1980, p. 85; C. M. Woodhouse, *Capodistria: The Founder of Greek Independence*, London 1973, pp. 273–275; Nichols, *The European Pentarchy*, pp. 9–12; Sauvigny, *Metternich et la France*, II, pp. 524–527, 551; Schütz, pp. 58–61; Webster, *Castlereagh*, pp. 378–379.

toman capital where, while Metternich had been to Hanover, new atrocities against the Greeks occurred. Furthermore, in early November, Hamid Bey was replaced by Sadık Effendi, a Turk more hostile to the Christians. The logical outcome of the latest development of affairs in the Ottoman Empire was the continuation of a policy of intransigence. The Porte's declarations on the four points left little hope for whose warnings against a war with Russia fell on deaf ears. When, for example, Metternich supported the withdrawal of Turkish troops from the Principalities and the nomination of hospodars quoting Russia's rights given by various treaties concluded with the Ottoman Empire, the answer was that the extradition of fugitives was also entitled by these treaties, which was a legitimate but under the given conditions a not very prudent argument.[38]

With the aim of simplifying the whole affair and making the Porte more pliable, Metternich made a far-sighted diplomatic manoeuvre in late December 1821 and January 1822 when he suggested the separation of the Greek affairs from Turkish infractions of the treaties with Russia, which was a difference he had already pointed out in July 1821: "In order not to make a mistake, it is necessary to make an essential distinction between the two sorts of complications that threaten the general peace of the Levant: the Greek revolt and the political complication between the Porte and Russia."[39] He created thus two questions: Russian and Greek, the former connected with Russia's direct interests in the Principalities, the latter concerning the churches, the protection of Ottoman Christians and the distinction between those innocent of crimes and those who committed atrocities during the uprising. The Russian Question was to be solved between Russia and the Ottoman Empire with the assistance of other Great Powers without delay; the Turks were to withdraw their troops from the Principalities, which would have two beneficial effects: they could use the released forces against the Greeks and the diplomatic relations between the sultan and the tsar would be restored. The Greek

---

[38] Metternich to Lützow, Vienna, 6 Dec. 1821, HHStA, StA, Türkei VI, 11; Metternich to Esterházy, Vienna, 5 Dec. 1821, HHStA, StA, England 166; Lützow to Metternich, Constantinople, 10 and 26 Nov., 8 Dec. 1821, HHStA, StA, Türkei VI, 12; Krusemark to Frederick William III, Vienna, 6 Nov., 23 and 24 Dec. 1821, GStA PK, HA III, MdA I, 5995.

[39] Metternich to Esterházy, Vienna, 16 July 1821, HHStA, StA, England 166.

Question could be left to the discussion of the European concert and preferably after the fulfilment of purely Russian grievances.[40]

This split of the Russo-Ottoman dispute later contributed to the relaxing of the mutual tensions, but in early 1822, neither this measure nor the removal of the fugitives away from the Turkish frontier further into Russia's interior helped to overcome the Porte's intransigence. On the contrary, Metternich was rewarded by the Porte's note delivered to Lützow on 28 February in which Austria was accused of showing a pro-Russian bias and ignoring the Turkish "just" claims and arguments. The Turks defended the presence of their army in the Principalities with the necessity to maintain order and peace, and the only way Austria could achieve their withdrawal was to persuade Russia to extradite the fugitives and settle the dispute over the Caucasus border, which was a new requirement that, according to Metternich, added to the confusion and made the solution more difficult. He had not wanted to deal with this question before 1821 and was even less willing to interfere in it after the outbreak of the Greek insurrection. He knew that the Russians did not always behave strictly according to the treaty stipulations, but he realised only too well that any remonstration in this sense would strongly strengthen the war faction. He did not want to investigate the virtues and vices of the contending parties, and he supported Russia's demands not because he believed they were absolutely warranted but because "they are the same as the conditions for the preservation of peace, this noble outcome that we regard as the most important of all; we never pursue our search for peace to the point of having to decide whether the Russians are more worthy of our solicitude than the Ottomans."[41] Consequently, the Porte was to forget the past and concentrate on the present not to endanger its future, which meant achieving the re-establishment of its relations with Russia by means of a prompt withdrawal of its troops from the Principalities, the nomination of hospodars and the end of the dangerous dispute with its powerful northern neighbour: "Our

---

[40] Metternich to Lützow, Vienna, 19 Jan. 1822, HHStA, StA, Türkei VI, 14; Metternich to Lebzeltern, Vienna, 23 Dec. 1821, HHStA, StA, Russland III, 45; Metternich to Esterházy, Vienna, 31 Jan. and 3 Feb. 1822, HHStA, StA, England 166; Krusemark to Frederick William III, Vienna, 31 Jan. and 18 Feb. 1822, GStA PK, HA III, MdA I, 5997; Gordon to Londonderry, Vienna, 3 Feb. 1822, TNA, FO 120/51; Kissinger, p. 301; Schroeder, *Metternich's Diplomacy*, p. 182.

[41] Metternich to Lützow, Vienna, 4 Jan. 1822, HHStA, StA, Türkei VI, 14.

reasoning is with St Petersburg and our demands for Constantinople very simple ... Do you want war? So wage one. Do you not want one? In that case, do not play the game of your adversaries."[42] But nothing changed until late April despite Metternich's effort to explain to the Turks that at the given moment the political aspect of the problem outweighed the legal one if they really wanted to avoid war.[43]

At the same time, reports offering little promise were also arriving during the winter from St Petersburg where the duel between Metternich and Capodistrias continued, the latter wanting the Great Powers to leave the Ottoman Empire to Russia's mercy. Whereas Metternich tried to persuade the Porte to comply with Russia's demands, in the Russian capital he appealed to a sense of moderation that could be expected from Alexander I but never from his warlike minister.[44] At the end of October 1821, Metternich wrote to Lebzeltern: "When we speak about our confidence in the *moderation* of H. I. M. of A. T. R. [His Imperial Majesty of all the Russias], the cabinet says: '*Moderation?* That means that they would like to force us to give up our 4 demands!' – Eh! O God, no, messieurs, hold firmly onto your four wretched points. But be moderate in every preposterous claim you shall be asked to make. Abandon the position that is neither peace nor war and be strong. You will be [strong] upon the day when you want to live in peace with your neighbour and not in intrigues with his subjects!"[45] The situation for the chancellor was not the most desirable, and in particular in early 1822 his voice seemed to lose

---

[42] Metternich to Lützow, Vienna, 20 Feb. 1822, HHStA, StA, Türkei VI, 14.

[43] Metternich to Lützow, Vienna, 2 and 20 March 1822, HHStA, StA, Türkei VI, 14; Lützow to Metternich, Constantinople, 24 Dec. 1821, HHStA, StA, Türkei VI, 12; Lützow to Metternich, Constantinople, 25 Feb., 5, 11 and 23 March, 10 April 1822, the Porte's note to Lützow, 28 Feb. 1822, HHStA, StA, Türkei VI, 13; Miltitz to Frederick William III, Pera, 25 Jan. 1822, GStA PK, HA III, MdA I, 7256; Krusemark to Frederick William III, Vienna, 28 Jan., 21 and 6 Feb., 3 March 1822, GStA PK, HA III, MdA I, 5997.

[44] Metternich to Lebzeltern, Vienna, 3 Dec. 1821, HHStA, StA, Russland III, 45; Metternich to Vincent, Vienna, 5 Dec. 1821, HHStA, StA, Frankreich 244; Metternich to Vincent, Vienna, 16 Feb. 1822, HHStA, StA, Frankreich 247; Metternich to Esterházy, Vienna, 18 Feb. 1822, HHStA, StA, England 166; Metternich to Zichy, Vienna, 11 Jan. 1822, HHStA, StK, Preussen 115; Krusemark to Frederick William III, Vienna, 14 Jan., 18 Feb. and 3 March 1822, GStA PK, HA III, MdA I, 5997.

[45] Metternich to Lebzeltern, Hanover, 31 Oct. 1821, HHStA, StA, Russland III, 45.

its strength. It is true that the tsar withdrew the Greek refugees
from the border with the Ottoman Empire probably upon Metternich's proposal, but it was Austria's only success for a long time.
The defamation of Capodistrias, the anti-revolutionary rhetoric and
Castlereagh's support all had negligible success, Metternich's proposal
on the division of the questions was met with silence and the fact that
the Porte did not accept the four points did not make the situation
better – the language used by the Viennese cabinet towards the Turks
was regarded by the tsar as much too conciliatory and not decisive
enough.[46] Golovkin greatly contributed to this opinion, being personally one of Capodistrias' supporters and having a poor relationship
with Metternich, who considered the ambassador hawkish and complained that "while I devoted myself to a line of confidence in the
preservation of peace, Mr Golovkin was indulging himself in theatrics
on the probabilities of war."[47] In his animosity Metternich labelled
Golovkin as inept; when in early January 1822 the latter was said to
declare that he did not understand what his court actually wanted,
Metternich "stopped him at that word and assured him that it was
precisely evil."[48] The chancellor suspected Golovkin of misinforming
the Russian court and stayed in contact with him only to reduce the
misinterpretations allegedly sent by the ambassador to St Petersburg.
At the end of January, Metternich openly asked Nesselrode to replace Golovkin because he wanted to work with someone whom he
could trust.[49] He supported this request with his typical sarcasm: "It
was at the beginning of December when Mr Golovkin declared war
between Russia and the Porte, and since that moment he ceased to
understand me because he translated my language into a dialect that
I do not understand myself."[50]

---

[46] Metternich to Lebzeltern, Vienna, 23 Dec. 1821, HHStA, StA, Russland III, 45;
Metternich to Lützow, Vienna, 28 Jan. 1822, HHStA, StA, Türkei VI, 14; Metternich to Esterházy, Vienna, 5 March 1822, HHStA, StA, England 166; Krusemark
to Frederick William III, Vienna, 29 Nov. 1821, GStA PK, HA III, MdA I, 5995;
Krusemark to Frederick William III, Vienna, 21 Feb. 1822, GStA PK, HA III,
MdA I, 5997; Grimsted, pp. 252–256.
[47] Metternich to Lebzeltern, Vienna, 31 Dec. 1821, HHStA, StA, Russland III,
45.
[48] Metternich to Esterházy, Vienna, 4 Jan. 1822, HHStA, StA, England 166.
[49] Caraman to Montmorency, Vienna, 28 Feb. 1822, AMAE, CP, Autriche 403.
[50] Metternich to Lebzeltern, Vienna, 28 Jan. 1822, HHStA, StA, Russland III, 54.

Negotiations with Tatishchev

Fortunately for Metternich, the decision about war or peace was the prerogative of the tsar and not the Russian hawks, and despite the Turks' obstinacy Alexander I continued to disagree with Capodistrias' warmongering and pro-Greek sentiments. On the other hand, he also wanted to keep his minister and find an honourable way out that would save his face. For the latter purpose, in February 1822 he decided to find support in Vienna and to send a diplomat to negotiate with Metternich there. This step in itself was clearly a sign that he wanted to maintain peace and not to act separately in Near Eastern affairs. It was a blow for Capodistrias, who in vain tried to thwart the mission, and once it was decided, he was also unable to put forward his own supporter for the task, Peter Tolstoy, because Alexander I chose Nesselrode's candidate Dmitrii Pavlovic Tatishchev. Consequently, Metternich was very pleased with the mission because he immediately understood its real purpose and the chances that it offered, and he was also greatly satisfied with the diplomat sent by Alexander I. After Tatishchev's arrival in Vienna on 5 March, this optimism proved to be well founded. During the negotiations that started on the following day and lasted till the Russian diplomat's departure on 19 April, Metternich was able to demonstrate his diplomatic talent and take full advantage of the fact that Alexander I desired peace and Tatishchev did not belong to the war faction. The first indication that the tsar desired peace materialised in the tsar's instructions for Tatishchev in addition to those of Capodistrias, which enabled Metternich to better manouevre. The prince persuaded the Russian diplomat to act according to the tsar's wishes, which meant strictly within the Alliance and for peace. Metternich thus obtained a veto power and was able to act as a judge deciding on the legitimacy of Russia's requests. This resulted in Tatishchev's restrained behaviour when he did not press very hard for the prescribed requests and his willingness to exclude Golovkin from the negotiations; the Russian ambassador was practically ignored not only by the chancellor but also by his own colleague and did not take part in the important meetings from 8 March onwards.[51]

---

[51] Metternich to Esterházy, Vienna, 6 and 17 March, 24 April 1822, HHStA, StA, England 166; Metternich to Lebzeltern, Vienna, 31 March 1822, HHStA, StA,

The process of the talks lasting little longer than six weeks went in a simple way: Tatishchev gradually presented new demands and Metternich refused them. Besides the four points of the July ultimatum, the former requested the consent to Russia's temporary occupation of the Danubian Principalities as a coercive measure that was to lead to the Porte's compliance, he presented plans for the settlement of the Greek Question that would, however, have made Greece another autonomous principality under Russia's influence, and he advocated Russia's interference in Greek affairs with its alleged right of the guardianship over the Christians in the Ottoman provinces "which the treaties placed under the protection of His Imperial Majesty [Alexander I] and which deplorable events are dragging into the abyss of revolutions."[52]

Metternich basically did not want to go beyond the four points or agree with anything that could be used in St Petersburg as a declaration of war. Therefore, he refused to consent to a temporary Russian occupation of the Principalities as a measure incompatible with the preservation of peace. It was no accident that this was Capodistrias' idea earlier communicated to Lebzeltern, and Metternich believed that such a measure would not force the Porte to yield but would result in its declaration of war, an opinion which was validated by the events of 1806 as well as later with the beginning of the Crimean War.[53] He told Tatishchev in this respect: "To give the slightest credence to the idea, [the temporary occupation of the Principalities by Russian troops] would be to deceive oneself with regard to its intentions; the first Russian soldier who would cross your borders would lead *you to war and never to reconciliation*; on the contrary, it is necessary to carefully repel within the limits of war what belongs there and within those of peace what does not exceed those limits."[54] Tatishchev tried to save the situation by comparing Russia's eventual occupation of

---

Russland III, 54; Grimsted, p. 283; Kissinger, pp. 302–303; Schroeder, *Metternich's Diplomacy*, pp. 185–190; Woodhouse, *Capodistria*, p. 283.

[52] Tatishchev's verbal note to Metternich, Vienna, 8 March 1822, Prokesch-Osten, *Griechen*, III, p. 311.

[53] Metternich to Esterházy, Vienna, 17 March, 4 April and 16 May 1822, HHStA, StA, England 166; Gordon to Londonderry, Vienna, 17 and 25 March 1822, TNA, FO 120/51.

[54] Metternich to Lebzeltern, Vienna, 31 March 1822, HHStA, StA, Russland III, 54.

the Principalities with Austria's military intervention in Naples and Piedmont in 1821, but Metternich sharply rejected any comparison and argued with "the *total* dissimilarity: A certain number of Austrian troops garrisoned in the two countries *in the name of the Allies* and *on the basis of an invitation and under the guarantee of a formal treaty concluded between the two kings and the same Great Power.* – An act of the occupation of the two Principalities on the Danube *would be*, totally on the contrary, *accompanied by the protestations of the legitimate sovereign.* How was it possible to compare two situations so contrastingly different?"[55]

The plan for the occupation of the Principalities was also challenged by Metternich's argument that the Porte would meet the tsar's four requests and, therefore, additional threats, as well as demands, were counterproductive. Moreover, he pointed out that Alexander I's wishes and the law were different things, and for this reason he rejected the plans that could deprive the sultan of sovereignty over the Greeks, particularly the claim to the protection of all Ottoman Christians. From the beginning of the insurrection, the Russians tried to impose on Europe the view that articles 7 and 14 of the Russo-Ottoman Treaty of Kuchuk-Kainardji concluded in 1774 gave them right to make representations in favour of the Christians in the whole of the Ottoman Empire including the Peloponnese, the core of the Greek rising, and this myth lived long into the late 20th century.[56] Metternich was not among those who supported this interpretation of the treaty and revealed its lack of sustainability in 1822. In this matter he did something typical of him: he thoroughly analysed relevant documents from a legal point of view, in this case several Russo-Ottoman treaties with that of 1774 being the most important among them, and discovered "the chimera of this right to protection."[57] He correctly pointed out that such a right was limited to Moldavia and Wallachia and could not be applied in other parts of the Ottoman Empire includ-

---

[55] Ibid.

[56] A perfect analysis of the relevant articles of the Treaty of Kuchuk-Kainardji supporting Metternich's opinion can be found in R. H. Davison, "Russian Skill and Turkish Imbecility: The Treaty of Kuchuk Kainardji Reconsidered," *SR* 35, 1976, 3, pp. 463–483; R. H. Davison, "The 'Dosografa' Church in the Treaty of Küçük Kaynarca," R. H. Davison (ed.), *Essays in Ottoman and Turkish History, 1774–1923: The Impact of the West*, Austin 1990, pp. 51–59.

[57] Metternich to Zichy, Vienna, 25 March 1822, HHStA, StK, Preussen 115.

ing the Peloponnese. His analysis clearly revealed that the sultan and
not the tsar was the protector of the Christians in the major part of
the Ottoman Empire. Consequently, Metternich did not acknowledge
Russia's right to protect all Ottoman Christians and therefore refused
its special right to interfere in the Greek Question. He acknowledged
that the Greeks needed to obtain guarantees of a safe and peaceful
existence, but it had to be done by the sultan and the European Powers could merely put in a good word to this end. When he supported
the Russian requests concerning the reconstruction of churches, the
guarantees of the Christians and the necessary distinction to be made
between innocent civilians and participants in the revolt, it was not for
the reason that these demands would have been authorised by treaty
stipulations but because their fulfilment was fair, they were not difficult for the Porte to meet and they were necessary for preventing
the outbreak of war; it could be at best "an intervention of benevolence."[58] He was all the more enraged when he learnt of a Prussian
protocol of 14 March 1822 in which Bernstorff pronounced the right
of protection of all Ottoman Christians to Russia.[59] Metternich decidedly expressed his disagreement: "One of the phrases that I most
regret to see admitted in the protocol of Berlin is that concerning the
rights to protection that the treaties accord to Russia on behalf of the
Greeks. Since the beginning of the current dilemma, the cabinet of
St Petersburg has been promoting these rights to protection but almost always in terms so ambiguous that it was difficult to understand
whether it has only insisted on the full execution of certain rights stipulated in the treaties on behalf of inhabitants of certain provinces or
whether it indeed demanded a general right to protection of all Greek
subjects of the Porte in its European provinces. In the protocol signed
in Berlin this right to protection is cited in three different places; once

---

[58] Caraman to Montmorency, Vienna, 19 March 1822, AMAE, CP, Autriche 403.
[59] Metternich to Lebzeltern, Vienna, 16 March 1822, HHStA, StA, Russland III,
54; Metternich to Zichy, Vienna, 16 March 1822, HHStA, StK, Preussen 115; *Dispo-
sitions des Traités entre la Rusie et la Porte, relativement aux Chrétiens /:Grecs:/
habitans des Provinces Européennes de l'Empire Ottoman* attached to Metternich
to Esterházy, Vienna, 17 March 1822, HHStA, StA, England 166; Caraman to
Montmorency, Vienna, 13 March 1822, AMAE, CP, Autriche 403; Tatishchev to
Nesselrode, Vienna, 22 March 1822, T. Schiemann, *Geschichte Russlands unter
Nikolaus I.*, I, Berlin 1904, p. 574; *Observation sur la Note verbale du 8 Mars*,
Prokesch-Osten, *Griechen*, III, p. 316; Davison, "Russian Skill," pp. 480–481;
Schütz, p. 90.

in a sense that it could be limited to several provinces, but twice in terms which seem to embrace all of the Greeks in the European part of Turkey. It is also in this latest sense that Mr Tatishchev expressed himself during our first conference ... No treaty nor any particular convention ever accorded to Russia a general right of protection in favour of the Greek subjects of the Porte."[60]

Successively conceding to Metternich's arguments, Tatishchev finally found himself in complete retreat and without any significant success. To save the situation and obtain something with which he could return to St Petersburg, he came up with a request that Austria should break off its diplomatic relations with the Ottoman Empire if the latter's refusal to yield were to force the tsar to go to war. It was difficult for Metternich to flatly refuse this request because his position was again made more difficult by Prussian ineptitude. In the March protocol Bernstorff had made such a promise and it was now impossible for Austria, Russia's close ally, to withdraw something that had already been promised by Prussia. Fortunately for Metternich, Bernstorff stipulated a condition that this pledge was valid only under the condition that other Great Powers would agree to undertake the same measure. Metternich agreed but, like the Prussian minister, he promised that his country would break relations with the Porte only if all the Great Powers consented – and he rightly presumed that the British cabinet would refuse to bind itself to such a pledge. Since this concession was Tatishchev's best achievement, he virtually obtained from Austria no effective assistance that Russia had not actually possessed before his arrival in Vienna. Metternich repeated the old thesis about the division of the problems into two questions, Russian and Greek, expressing his willingness to support the demand for the Turkish withdrawal from the Principalities, which in fact he had been doing for many months, and refusing Russia's demand for exclusiveness in Greek affairs, which could be addressed only by all of the Great Powers but preferably after the solution of the Russian Question and never at the expense of Turkish sovereignty. Any discussion, as Metternich suggested, could take place in a conference in Vienna or at the forthcoming congress in Italy in the autumn, which was an idea earlier discussed and settled between Metternich and Castlereagh. Consequently, the Russian diplomat departed for St Petersburg with

---

[60] Metternich to Zichy, Vienna, 25 March 1822, HHStA, StK, Preussen 115.

no practical gains but he took with him a lifeboat for Alexander I, who had to decide whether he would accept it and with Metternich's help escape the troubled waters leading to the rapids or if he would drift along to the waterfall desired by Capodistrias. The choice between these courses offered by the two diplomats was the same as the option between peace and war.[61]

Metternich Wins the Battle

Metternich was completely satisfied with this result and believed that it would please the tsar and lessen the influence of the triumvirate of Pozzo di Borgo, Stroganov and Capodistrias. He did not consider the whole affair terminated but he hoped he had saved the peace. This prospect was increased by the change in the Porte's attitude. The Turks did not facilitate his negotiations with Tatishchev with their stubbornness, and in particular the note of 28 February containing not only complaints of Austria's partiality but also Russia's behaviour could have furnished Capodistrias with a pretext for war if Metternich had not persuaded Tatishchev not to mail it forward to St Petersburg. But on 25 April 1822, after the long pressure of European diplomats led by Strangford, Mahmud II agreed to withdraw his troops from the Principalities, and they actually started to leave on 13 May. Precisely two months later, the sultan named new hospodars. These compromise steps and the not ideal situation of the Russian army definitely contributed to Alexander I's decision for peace; he accepted the idea of a conference and sent Tatishchev back to Vienna to continue in the talks on Near Eastern affairs with Metternich and without Golovkin[62] and to communicate the promise that

---

[61] Metternich to Zichy, Vienna, 2 April and 11 May 1822, HHStA, StK, Preussen 115; Metternich to Vincent, Vienna, 4 April 1822, HHStA, StA, Frankreich 247; Metternich to Lebzeltern, Vienna, 22 April 1822, HHStA, StA, Russland III, 54; Gordon to Londonderry, Vienna, 3 April 1822, TNA, FO 120/52; Kissinger, p. 305; Schroeder, *Metternich's Diplomacy*, pp. 189–190.

[62] Tatishchev's second mission actually led to his permanent residence in Vienna and the substitution of Golovkin in the representation of the tsar's interests in Austria though he was not named an ambassador until the autumn of 1826 and therefore possessed no official rank in the diplomatic corps for more than four years; despite this, he practically fulfilled the task of a permanent and accred-

the Russian army would not cross the Pruth River in the summer, which meant that he gave up the claim to Russia's independent solution of the Greek Question and agreed with Russia's subordination to the European concert. Capodistrias was of course against the tsar's compliance and Metternich was not far from the truth when he wrote to his mistress and the wife of the Russian ambassador in London, Princess Dorothea von Lieven, that the Russian minister "is raving like a devil in a font,"[63] but nothing could help Capodistrias to change his monarch's wishes. His duel with Metternich was over and he was ousted, as Metternich well knew: "The Tsar has accepted all my proposals. It's all over with Capodistrias."[64] Since Capodistrias could not cope with this defeat, he retired to an unspecified vacation on 25 June 1822 that in effect meant the same as his demise and settled in Switzerland from where he supported the Greeks' cause. Metternich was extremely pleased by his fallen opponent's decision: "The fatal element of eternal discord has finished his career, and with him a thousand embarrassments disappear."[65] From this moment on the Austrian chancellor only had to deal with Nesselrode, which was for him a much easier and more pleasant business.[66]

Metternich congratulated himself on a diplomatic triumph, which he labelled as "the most total victory that any cabinet ever achieved over another."[67] What he actually obtained was definitely respectable,

---

ited representative, which was entirely tolerated by Metternich who accorded him considerable distinction. Caraman to Damas, Vienna, 11 Nov. 1824, AMAE, CP, Autriche 405; Schwebel to Damas, Vienna, 17 Sept. 1826, Caraman to Damas, Vienna, 6 Nov. 1826, AMAE, CP, Autriche 407.

[63] Metternich to Princess Lieven, 24 May 1822, NA, RAM-AC 6, 1.

[64] *NP*, III, p. 515.

[65] Gürbüz, p. 369.

[66] Metternich to Lützow, Vienna, 27 March and 3 June 1822, HHStA, StA, Türkei VI, 14; Metternich to Esterházy, Vienna, 24 April 1822, HHStA, StA, England 166; Metternich to Vincent, Vienna, 24 April 1822, HHStA, StA, Frankreich 247; Metternich to Princess Lieven, 29 April 1822, NA, RAM-AC 6, 1; Lützow to Metternich, Constantinople, 25 April, 10 May, 10 June and 18 July 1822, HHStA, StA, Türkei VI, 13; Miltitz to Frederick William III, Pera, 25 May and 18 July 1822, GStA PK, HA III, MdA I, 7256; Piquot to Frederick William III, Vienna, 13 May 1822, GStA PK, HA III, MdA I, 5998; Gordon to Londonderry, Vienna, 25 March 1822, TNA, FO 120/51; Caraman to Montmorency, Vienna, 13 June 1822, AMAE, CP, Autriche 403; Bitis, p. 115; Grimsted, pp. 270–271; Gürbüz, p. 358; Schroeder, *Metternich's Diplomacy*, pp. 187–191.

[67] Sauvigny, *Staatsmann und Diplomat*, p. 389.

but in reality he merely won a battle in the war that continued. The renewed negotiations with Tatishchev, who arrived in Vienna on 11 June, confirmed the peaceful intentions of the tsar and strengthened Metternich's satisfaction and faith in his influence over Alexander I, as he boasted in a letter to Princess Lieven: "The tsar is pleased with everything that Metternich does and says. He has only praise for him and assurances of confidence."[68] Nevertheless, the withdrawal of the Turkish army from the Principalities proceeded slowly, and in the summer the Porte forbade ships with borrowed Russian flags to sail to the Black Sea: in other words it refused to admit the Russian flag on Greek merchant vessels, consequently affecting Russian grain commerce, and again complained about Russia's occupation of the disputed places on the Caucasus border. None of this could please Russia, and diplomatic relations between the two countries were still suspended, which was exactly what Metternich sought to change. As for the Greek insurgents, they not only continued to fight but they also stabilised their positions and declared independence in January 1822. In vain Metternich urged the Porte to give up measures affecting Russia and to offer an amnesty to the Greeks that would please the tsar and, if supported by the Great Powers, could have some chance of success.[69] If such an amnesty later proved to be unsuccessful, at least the Porte would be able to improve its position in the eyes of Europe: "We are convinced that a wise and acceptable amnesty would be the only means to better deal with the questions for the Porte."[70]

The optimism after Capodistrias' retirement was soon dampened by Castlereagh's suicide on 12 August 1822, three days before his planned departure for Vienna. Metternich regarded this as a catastrophe because he lost not only a man with whom he was connected by the tie of close friendship but also one whose support in Near

---

[68] Metternich to Princess Lieven, 1 Aug. 1822, NA, RAM-AC 6, 1.
[69] Metternich to Lützow, Vienna, 3 and 19 June, 5 and 31 July 1822, Metternich to Strangford, Vienna, 31 July and 9 Aug. 1822, HHStA, StA, Türkei VI, 14; Metternich to Lebzeltern, Vienna, 5 and 11 June, 4, 15 and 31 July 1822, HHStA, StA, Russland III, 54; Metternich to Esterházy, Vienna, 13 and 6 June, 9 July 1822, HHStA, StA, England 166; Metternich to Binder, Vienna, 8 June 1822, HHStA, StA, Frankreich 247; Lützow to Metternich, Constantinople, 25 June, 10 July, 10 and 26 Aug. 1822, HHStA, StA, Türkei VI, 13; Hatzfeldt to Frederick William III, Vienna, 28 Aug. 1822, GStA PK, HA III, MdA I, 6000.
[70] Metternich to Lützow, Vienna, 7 Aug. 1822, HHStA, StA, Türkei VI, 14.

Eastern affairs was invaluable: "This event, cruel for the whole of Europe, is even more particularly painful for me personally. Bound with Mr Londonderry in friendship for many years, accustomed to being perfectly understood by him and perfectly comprehending him, certain of possessing all his confidence, I am losing in him an enlightened colleague and a reliable support."[71] The tragedy of Castlereagh's death was heightened by the arrival of George Canning, the most liberal of Tories, to the head of the Foreign Office. At first, however, nothing seemed to be ominous in this ministerial change for Metternich. Castlereagh promised before his death to take part in the Viennese conference as well as the congress in Verona, and the British government kept its word and participated in the meetings, sending the Duke of Wellington to the Continent with their original instructions the primary aim of which was to support Austria, Prussia and France in the negotiations with Russia.[72]

The conference in Vienna took place in late September 1822 with Alexander I's personal attendance. The tsar manifested as much hostility towards the Greeks' insurrection as in Ljubljana and the Greek Question did not become an important issue, in contrast to the Russian Question where Nesselrode complained about the slowness of the Turkish withdrawal from the Principalities, the nomination of hospodars without Russian consent and the measures harming Russian trade. On 26 September, he even attacked Strangford personally participating in the conference for his excessive Turkophilism and complained that Russia's requests had received little support. Metternich saved the situation, repaired the cold relations between the Russians and Strangford and placated the tsar with the promise that the Great Powers would support his claims against the Porte, which the representatives of France, Great Britain and Prussia acknowledged. In return, the tsar satisfied Metternich's wish for the removal of overly pro-Greek Russian consuls from Bucharest and Jassy. On 2 October 1822, the participants of the conference started to move to Verona where Near Eastern affairs did not constitute part of the official agenda of the congress and were merely discussed unofficially.

---

[71] Metternich to Lützow, Vienna, 27 Aug. 1822, HHStA, StA, Türkei VI, 14.
[72] Metternich to Esterházy, Vienna, 26 Aug. 1822, HHStA, StA, England 166; Hatzfeldt to Frederick William III, Vienna, 21 Aug. 1822, GStA PK, HA III, MdA I, 6000; Nichols, "The Eastern Question," p. 59.

The Greeks were in practice ignored and, as Gentz stated, "it was a matter of courtesy not to mention Turkish difficulties at Verona."[73] Metternich considerably contributed to this by preventing the participation of two Greek deputies sent by the Greek government to the congress with the goal of obtaining the recognition of Greece's independence and the tsar's support. Their eventual acceptance at the congress could have attracted the attention of the tsar, which Metternich wanted to prevent and, consequently, they did not get closer than Ancona, where they were stopped at the end of October owing to Metternich's intervention at the Holy See, giving the chancellor enough time to persuade the other Powers to prohibit them from continuing to the north.[74]

The debated topics in Verona dealt mainly with the Russian Question, and Alexander I's main interest was not the Greeks but the obstruction of the shipping in the Straits. He complained about the prohibition against the use of the Russian flag on the Greek ships, but he was actually more eager to arrange for the permission for ships of other nations to sail through the Straits, which would have a beneficial effect on Russian trade. He declared that he would not restore diplomatic relations with the Ottoman Empire as long as this matter was not settled. Since the restoration of diplomatic relations was exactly what Metternich most desired at that moment, he promised to support this demand despite the fact that the Turkish measure directed against the use of a Russian flag on Greek vessels did not always violate treaty stipulations. The baselessness or exorbitance of Russia's grievances were well known to the participants of the congress including the tsar, and were confirmed by the internuncio in Constantinople who, as a protector of Russian citizens after Stroganov's departure, was directly involved in the solution of disputes between the Porte and the ships sailing under the Russian flag. In the beginning, it was Wellington who refused to support Russia's demand but again, owing to Metternich's placating intervention, a breakdown in negotiations was avoided and the final talks on this issue in late November were

---

[73] Nichols, *The European Pentarchy*, p. 254.
[74] Hatzfeldt to Frederick William III, Vienna, 14 Sept. 1822, GStA PK, HA III, MdA I, 6000; A. J. Reinerman, "Metternich, the Papacy and the Greek Revolution," *EEQ* 12, 1978, 2, p. 183; Nichols, "The Eastern Question," pp. 61–64; Nichols, *The European Pentarchy*, pp. 253–255.

conducted in a friendly atmosphere when Austria and Great Britain assumed responsibility for the defence of Alexander I's interests in Constantinople. The danger of his hostile action against the Ottoman Empire was thus avoided, and Metternich obtained time for the Great Powers to help settle the Russian Question and for the Turks to solve the Greek one in their own way.[75]

Strangford's presence in Vienna and Verona well attested the significant role he played in Constantinople. His influence increased after 1821, whereas Lützow's position considerably deteriorated during 1822. The distrust towards the internuncio prevailed among the Turks, the affair surrounding Ypsilantis' escape to Austria constituted an important role in their dislike of him, and in late 1822 it was even a problem for Lützow to gain an audience with the Turks on political affairs. Consequently, Metternich's most important advocate for peace was Strangford, whom he instructed during 1822 with the consent of Castlereagh, who relinquished to the chancellor the management of affairs in Constantinople. Strangford largely proceeded in the Russo-Ottoman dispute under Metternich's instruction and he also was in close contact with Gentz. This situation of course was not ideal for Metternich, who needed to keep Austria's influence at the highest level, and he finally reacted to Lützow's troubled situation by replacing him with Baron Franz Xaver von Ottenfels, who had been educated at the Oriental Academy, had spent 13 years in his youth in Constantinople and in 1822 was functioning as a secretary of the Political Department of the Viennese Chancellery. His experience and knowledge of the Levant offered a prospect for better treatment in Constantinople. He was appointed as an internuncio and plenipotentiary minister on 30 July 1822 and relieved Lützow in mid October. His first instructions were to persuade the Porte that the tsar desired peace and Austria wanted what the sultan himself desired.[76]

---

[75] Ottenfels to Metternich, Constantinople, 24 Dec. 1822, HHStA, StA, Türkei VI, 13; Nichols, *The European Pentarchy*, pp. 245–251.

[76] Metternich to Ottenfels, undated, HHStA, StA, Türkei VI, 13; Lützow to Metternich, Constantinople, 25 Sept. 1822, HHStA, StA, Türkei VI, 13; Crawley, *Greek Independence*, p. 25; Gürbüz, pp. 366–368; Krauter, pp. 98–106; Prokesch-Osten, *Griechen*, I, p. 163. Romanian historian Radu Florescu claimed that Strangford's representations of Metternich in Constantinople irritated Lützow and Ottenfels. R. R. Florescu, "Lord Strangford and the Problem of the Danubian Principalities, 1821–24," *SEER* 39, 1961, 93, p. 476. Nothing proves this supposition. In partic-

*   *   *

In the first two years of the Greek insurrection, Metternich was able
to manage the crisis according to Austria's wishes: he prevented the
outbreak of war between Russia and the Ottoman Empire and the interference of European Powers into the Greek affairs. He owed much
to his own diplomatic talent, Alexander I's desire to preserve peace
and the close cooperation with Castlereagh. Nazif Gürbüz pointed out
that this success was achieved by sacrificing the Porte's interests when
the chancellor acquiesced to Russian demands regardless of their validity.[77] One must agree that Metternich's policy was in the first place,
not surprisingly, Austrian and its primary aim was the preservation
of peace, but no one can deny that his conduct was considerably in
the Turks' favour. The prince skilfully analysed the situation at the
beginning of the uprising and reached the correct conclusions concerning the strengths and possibilities of Russia and the Ottoman Empire.
He understood that Alexander I did not want war but some of his requests had to be met so that he would not lose face and would continue
to maintain the peace. He also knew that Mahmud II did not desire
and could not make war with Russia. Greater compliancy from the
sultan's side was the only way to preserve peace and, therefore, Metternich defended the tsar's demands even if he did not think they were
justified, and they actually often were not. Two important aspects of
his actions, however, cannot be overlooked. First, he did not meet all
Alexander I's or, more correctly speaking, "Russian" demands and
he did not hesitate to reject, for example, the claim for the protection of all Ottoman Christians or the idea of a temporary occupation
of the Principalities by the Russian army. He clearly saw that such
plans endangered both the sultan's sovereignty and the existing peace
too much and increased Russia's influence over Ottoman Empire thus
threatening Austria's interests. He clarified and reduced Russia's demands on the Porte as much as he was able, thereby making eventual
agreements between the two Powers more possible. Second, a war definitely was not in the Porte's interest at the moment it was fighting in

---

ular Lützow wished only one thing – to leave Constantinople as soon as possible,
and he did not mind playing a secondary role in the affairs. As for Ottenfels, he
was well known for his amiability, and his official as well as private correspondence
contains no indication whatsoever of any envy towards Strangford.
[77] Gürbüz, p. 334.

the first year of the Greek uprising not only with the Greeks but also with Ali Pasha of Yannina and Persia. Another conflict in the North against a formidable enemy would most probably be disastrous for the Turks.[78] In the Greek Question, Metternich's actions were even more pro-Turkish when he did his best to keep the insurrection from the agenda of European Powers' talks, giving Mahmud II time to solve it alone, and even Gürbüz admits that the period won from 1821 to 1827 could have been sufficient for defeating the Greeks and that the blame for the inability to take full advantage of it falls on the sultan's head.[79]

Nevertheless, two related deficiencies in Metternich's actions later became apparent. First, the sultan proved unable to quickly pacify the rebellious regions. Second, the prince had underestimated Alexander I's interest in the Greek Question and incorrectly presumed that the Russian monarch would abandon it if his demands were met.[80] After the victory over Capodistrias, Metternich even considered "the Greeks' affair with regard to its eventual influence over Europe as entirely finished."[81] The tsar, it is true, often declared his dislike of the insurgents but he never entirely forsook them. What Alexander I did in 1822 was to put his direct interests in first place and he turned his main focus on the unsettled situation in Spain caused by the revolution of 1820, leaving the Greek Question for the future. Metternich's policy was correct merely to the point that the appeasement of the Porte was necessary for forestalling a war with Russia, but in fact it could not prevent Russia's intervention into the Greek Question indefinitely, in particular when this second problem continued unresolved owing to the inability of Turkish forces to crush the revolt. Moreover, Metternich's pressure on the Porte to promptly meet just Russia's requests was drawing nearer the moment when the Greek Question was put on the agenda. And the not too distant future was to show that Alexander I was eager to discuss the Greek affairs even before all his demands concerning the Principalities and navigation in the Straits were met.

---

[78] C. M. Woodhouse, *The Greek War of Independence*, London 1952, p. 58.
[79] Gürbüz, p. 421.
[80] Hatzfeldt to Frederick William III, Vienna, 15 July 1822, GStA PK, HA III, MdA I, 6000; Gürbüz, p. 360.
[81] Hatzfeldt to Frederick William III, Vienna, 29 Aug. 1822, GStA PK, HA III, MdA I, 6000.

3

The Eastern Question in the Last Years of Alexander I's Reign

After his success in 1822, Metternich had to continue paying considerable attention to affairs in the Near East. His effort to avoid further deterioration in Russo-Ottoman relations was continually complicated by the Porte's disclination to meet some Russian requests concerning the Straits and the Principalities and particularly by Alexander I's increasing desire to solve the Greek Question, which resulted in the Russian plan of settlement in January 1824. From that moment it became more and more difficult for Metternich to maintain close cooperation with the tsar, whose designs had considerably changed since 1821 and had become detrimental to Austria's interests. The rupture in the relations between the two Great Powers that Metternich had feared finally became a reality in the summer of 1825. Historians often blamed the Austrian chancellor for this outcome and pointed out his inconsistent and deceitful behaviour towards Alexander I, who was said to sacrifice his own interests due to his pro-European stance when for a long time he withheld his support to the Greeks. In fact Metternich was very consistent in his Greek policy and more frank in his statements to the tsar, and Alexander I was considerably less consistent in his approach towards the Greek uprising and much less so in his pro-European attitude than has generally been presumed.

The Russo-Ottoman Disputes

After the Congress of Verona, Alexander I's attention turned to Spanish affairs, and therefore Austria together with Great Britain had some time to focus on the concessions desired by the tsar in Constantinople. Ottenfels and Strangford were instructed to support unrestricted

commercial navigation through the Straits and the extension of the
rights to other European nations that did not have them. They were
also to ask the Porte to officially inform Russia that it had removed its
troops from the Principalities and had named the hospodars. Metternich continued in his policy of requesting Mahmud II to yield because,
as he wrote to the internuncio, "he must be shown that it is only in
such ways that he will be able to reinforce his existence."[1] The restoration of diplomatic relations between Russia and the Ottoman Empire
was still Metternich's primary aim since its achievement would not
only normalise the two countries' relations and reduce the risk of war
but would also demoralise the rebellious Greeks who, as Metternich
and Ottenfels hoped, would be more willing to end their struggle for
independence in exchange for an amnesty and some administrative
improvements. Consequently, Metternich let the Turks know that it
was worth it for them to sacrifice something for the reestablishment
of the Russian diplomatic representation. He did so primarily through
Strangford, who was known for his extreme vanity and desire to take a
lead in affairs; the British ambassador consequently remained Metternich's primary negotiator with the more modest Ottenfels zealously
assisting him. The negotiations in Constantinople, however, proved
to be just as difficult as they had been since the beginning of the
Greek insurrection. The Porte was only willing to yield in part and,
worse, it raised some new obstacles that could further damage its
relations with Russia instead of improving them considerably. First,
Mahmud II decided not to withdraw all his troops from Moldavia and
Wallachia but to keep 1,000 of them in the former and 2,000 in the
latter, which exceeded the stipulated limits. However, this was not to
become a matter of controversy until the autumn of 1823. Second,
Sadık Effendi sent a letter to Nesselrode in which he informed him
about the withdrawal of troops from the Principalities, the nomination of the hospodars and the sultan's desire for the renewal of good
relations with Russia, but in private conversations with Ottenfels and
Strangford he again started to express his dismay about the unsettled
Caucasus border. The internuncio and the British ambassador had
been able to persuade Sadık not to mention this topic in his letter
to Nesselrode and later it was not raised by the Porte as a *condicio sine qua non* of the settlement with Russia, but the problem re-

---

[1]   Metternich to Ottenfels, Vienna, 5 Feb. 1823, HHStA, StA, Türkei VI, 19.

mained unresolved and continued to complicate the relations between the two empires. Third, Sadık also revived the problem of the Christian refugees involved in the uprising in the Principalities; this issue was included in his letter to Nesselrode and he privately continued to express the wish for their extradition into Ottoman hands. Fourth, in the question of navigation in the Straits, the Turks did exactly the opposite of what they were asked to do by Ottenfels and Strangford; they took measures compromising the European grain trade in the Dardanelles and were unwilling to negotiate with new countries terms for their admittance into the Black Sea, in particular with Tuscany whose trade was dependent on obtaining such permission, but which had rather displeased the Porte with the support Tuscany had given to the Greeks in Leghorn (Livorno).[2]

In addition to the above-mentioned obstacles interposed by the Turks, Ottenfels and Strangford were obliged to solve some additional problems of lesser significance but with a dangerous potential for the Russo-Ottoman relations. In May 1823, the Turks stopped in the Bosphorus and towed away to the arsenal three ships sailing under the Russian flag but according to the Turkish officials belonging to the Greek insurgents. Ottenfels assured Metternich that this measure did not signify any attempt to trick the Russians since it was sometimes used against the vessels of other nations: "Ships carrying the Russian flag are the most numerous and often carry irregular cargo, so it is logical that they are the most exposed to the results of these severe measures. When one knows the elements of which the Russian merchant navy is composed, one cannot be surprised by this. Nevertheless, I would believe I would be negligent in my duty and would misrepresent the truth if I did not recognise the right of the Ottoman government to say that the Russian subjects and merchants settled in this capital are in no way molested by the Turkish authorities, that they go about their affairs in peace and in complete safety, and that the Russian ships whose documents are in order and whose

---

[2] Ottenfels to Metternich, Silistra, 22 Sept. 1822, HHStA, StA, Türkei VI, 13; Ottenfels to Metternich, Constantinople, 25 Jan., 10, 25 and 28 Feb., 10 and 26 March, 10 April 1823, the Porte's note to Ottenfels, 25 Feb. 1823, HHStA, StA, Türkei VI, 18; Ottenfels to Metternich, Constantinople, 16 July 1823, HHStA, StA, Türkei VI, 19; Miltitz to Frederick William III, Pera, 25 Jan. and 10 Feb. 1823, GStA PK, HA III, MdA I, 7257; Gürbüz, p. 382; Prokesch-Osten, *Griechen*, I, p. 202.

origin and property are not suspect do not experience the slightest
difficulty in their passage to Constantinople; their cargoes are delivered to them with the same regularity as those of Austrian, British
or French ships; a day does not pass when I am not reminded about
it ... Consequently, it is only rarely and in very exceptional cases to
the general order of things that the Russian government can make
representations against the procedures of the Porte."[3] Nevertheless,
it was hardly likely that such reasoning would have any positive response in St Petersburg, and Ottenfels, who was still responsible for
the protection of Russian subjects and commercial activities, immediately and without waiting for instructions attempted to reverse the
decision. The reaction of the Porte was at first negative but by the
end of July all of the ships stopped could continue on their way owing to the internuncio's intervention.[4] Another incident with greater
publicity and which took a longer time to resolve occurred in April
when a prominent Wallachian boyar, Alexander Villara, was arrested
in Bucharest. This was also not a result of the Porte's anti-Russian
conduct, and in fact the Turks were innocent in this affair. The arrest
was ordered by Wallachian Hospodar Grigore IV Ghica and the reason
was purely financial. Nevertheless, in July, Nesselrode complained of
the arrest, he argued that this was a violation of the amnesty in the
Principalities promised by the Porte and labelled it as another obstacle in the Russo-Ottoman relations although the real reason for his
discontent was presumably Villara's pro-Russian attitude. In fact the
whole affair was nothing but "a tempest in a teacup,"[5] but Austria
and Great Britain were forced to react and their intervention finally
led to Villara's release in April 1824.[6]

   The situation forced Metternich to pursue the same policy as
he had been doing since 1821: taking advantage of every sign of the

---

[3] Ottenfels to Metternich, Constantinople, 10 June 1823, HHStA, StA, Türkei
VI, 18.
[4] Ottenfels to Metternich, Constantinople, 26 May, 10 and 25 June 1823, Ottenfels to the Porte, Constantinople, 16 May 1823, Testa to Ottenfels, 17 and 31
May 1823, HHStA, StA, Türkei VI, 18; Ottenfels to Metternich, Constantinople,
25 July 1823, HHStA, StA, Türkei VI, 19.
[5] Florescu, "Lord Strangford," p. 481.
[6] Ibid., p. 482; Metternich to Lebzeltern, Vienna, 28 June 1823, HHStA, StA,
Russland III, 60; Ottenfels to Metternich, Constantinople, 25 April 1823, HHStA,
StA, Türkei VI, 18.

Porte's compliance to appease the tsar and overcome the obstinacy in Constantinople that so dissatisfied him and made him complain of "errors that we see committed almost continually by the Ottoman government"[7] and denounce its behaviour: "The Ottoman Empire seems to me to follow at this moment a line of action to which bankrupts resort only too often; not knowing how to continue to sustain their fortune, they are seen to indulge in partial speculations that, even if they are successful, do not save them from ruin!"[8] He had little understanding of measures without real profit and only connected with dangers for the sultan. The prince sharply criticised the seizure of the ships because although they could be prohibited from sailing through the Dardanelles, he saw no reason for them to sail to the arsenal. If they actually belonged to the rebellious Greeks as the Porte claimed, it had to offer proof to the internunciature. This irregular behaviour was neither well-considered nor wise. The arrest of Villara was also regarded in Vienna as an entirely needless affair. Consequently, the ships and the boyar had to be released and other obstacles put in the way of preventing the regularisation of Russo-Ottoman relations had to be removed, regardless of the extent to which either of the parties had the law on their side because it was more important who had the military force. In legal disputes Metternich often attributed more right to the Porte but military power was more advantageous to Russia: "The discussion pertains, on the one hand, to Russia's claims that justice cannot be regarded as anything other than a form of subterfuge and on the other hand to the predicament and all the consequences inherent in the whole situation such as the one in which the Ottoman government finds itself."[9] Consequently, the concessions had to be made by the Porte, and Metternich did not see them as so monstrous – not at all in comparison with what would have followed if they had not been made. The opinion of the Porte, however, was different, and neither Metternich's warning that without a more subtle and cautious approach towards Russia the sultan could quickly lose his domain in Europe, nor his advice that a prompt settlement of the dispute was needed before the tsar turned his attention to the East again changed much in this state of affairs.[10]

---

[7] Metternich to Ottenfels, Vienna, 4 May 1823, HHStA, StA, Türkei VI, 19.
[8] Metternich to Ottenfels, Vienna, 21 June 1823, HHStA, StA, Türkei VI, 19.
[9] Metternich to Lebzeltern, Vienna, 7 Aug. 1823, HHStA, StA, Russland III, 60.

Metternich's cautionary advice addressed to Constantinople was not insubstantial because when the Spanish affair was settled in the spring of 1823, Alexander I turned his attention back to the Near East and what he saw considerably increased his animosity. The situation was serious and the anxiety in Vienna about the outbreak of war between Russia and the Ottoman Empire was similar to their apprehension two years earlier, with the same belief in the tsar's wish to maintain peace, but not at any price, and with the same distrust of the Russian elites. Metternich warned Alexander I of the terrible results of a war that would support the spirit of revolution and lead to the suffering of Ottoman Christians, and he conveyed every piece of information from Ottenfels that could find favour with the Russian cabinet, like the fact that most of the Russian ships were sailing through the Straits unmolested, but the positive effect was doubtful. Metternich needed more concessions from the Porte, on which depended the result of the meeting in Galicia suggested to him and Francis I by Alexander I for October 1823; the Austrian emperor and his chancellor had no option other than to accept the invitation and work for peace in the Galician town chosen for that purpose, Czernowitz. If they were found inadequate there by the tsar, Metternich worried that Russia and the Ottoman Empire would "arrive at open hostility before the end of the year."[11] Consequently, he wanted to obtain those concessions before the start of negotiations with Alexander I and his retinue.[12] It was important to have a trump card because, as he declared, "peace or war will come out of Czernowitz."[13]

---

[10] Metternich to Ottenfels, Vienna, 12 and 18 April, 4 May, 21 June 1823, HHStA, StA, Türkei VI, 19; Metternich to Ottenfels, Vienna, 2 July and 13 Sept. 1823, HHStA, StA, Türkei VI, 20; Metternich to Ottenfels, Vienna, 20 April 1823, HDA, 750, OO 37; Metternich to Lebzeltern, Vienna, 30 March 1823, HHStA, StA, Russland III, 60; Metternich to Neumann, Vienna, 1 and 5 Sept. 1823, Witzomierziz, 21 July 1823, HHStA, StA, England 169; Hatzfeldt to Frederick William III, Vienna, 5, 19 and 24 June 1823, GStA PK, HA III, MdA I, 6001; Hatzfeldt to Frederick William III, Vienna, 1 and 6 July 1823, GStA PK, HA III, MdA I, 6002.

[11] Metternich to Ottenfels, Vienna, 19 July 1823, HHStA, StA, Türkei VI, 20.

[12] Metternich to Ottenfels, Vienna, 21 June, 2 July and 1 Sept. 1823, HHStA, StA, Türkei VI, 20; Metternich to Lebzeltern, Vienna, 7 Aug. 1823, HHStA, StA, Russland III, 60; Metternich to Vincent, Vienna, 11 Aug. 1823, HHStA, StA, Frankreich 250; Hatzfeldt to Frederick William III, Vienna, 9 July 1823, GStA PK, HA III, MdA I, 6002.

[13] Metternich to Lebzeltern, Vienna, 7 Aug. 1823, HHStA, StA, Russland III, 60.

In Constantinople, the Austro-British diplomatic pressure in the summer of 1823 came up against a wall of dissent from the Ottoman dignitaries dissatisfied with the fact that after concessions from their part relations between their own and the Russian Empire were still suspended. When on 7 August Ottenfels visited Ghanib Effendi, an influential Ottoman dignitary, and complained that if Sadık Effendi had listened to Austria's friendly advice, relations would have been restored, Ghanib pleaded for his colleague: "In what way have we profited until now with our compliance in following your advice? You told us a year ago to grant an amnesty, withdraw from the Principalities, name the hospodars, [and] transfer the administration of these provinces to them. We have done all of that. What has been the result of our compliance with what you were pleased to call the ultimatum of the Russian court? You told us six months ago that before witnessing the arrival of a Russian minister in Constantinople, it was necessary that we addressed a letter to the Russian cabinet informing them about the steps undertaken and executed with regard to the Principalities. We wrote that letter in which, however, you prevented us from reminding them of grievances against Russia and mentioning our most sacred rights based upon the unequivocal treaty stipulations. What was the result? That we are told that the Russian court still has other demands and that we must first satisfy these requests before Russia could decide to restore its diplomatic mission. Do you think then that Sadık Effendi, that I, that any other member of the Divan, being the guarantors of the next arrival of a Russian minister, dare to take it upon ourselves to propose new concessions, new sacrifices to His Highness?"[14] Ghanib's protestation was probably the result of the general atmosphere existing in the Divan and definitely of his personal antipathy towards concessions. It was not until Sadık's fall later in August when the chance for a turn of events occurred. Afterwards, Ottenfels and Strangford quickly brought about a change in the Porte's attitude during a meeting on 30 August 1823. The Turks promised to revoke the measures hampering European trade in the Straits, to conclude the treaty enabling Sardinian ships to enter the Black Sea and to negotiate with other European countries on the same subject. Some of the promises were quickly put into effect

---

[14] Ottenfels to Metternich, Constantinople, 11 Aug. 1823, HHStA, StA, Türkei VI, 19.

and the problems of the Caucasus border and the fugitives were not mentioned.[15]

These promises improved Metternich's position for negotiations. Dealing with Francis I in Czernowitz in October 1823, Alexander I expressed satisfaction with the results concerning commerce and navigation. Metternich, who fell ill on the way and could not continue to Czernowitz, negotiated with Nesselrode in Lemberg with the same cordiality. The tsar also promised to send a commercial agent to Constantinople, Matvei Lvovici Minciaky, as a forerunner to an ambassador who, however, could not arrive on the Bosporus until the fulfilment of all of Russia's requests, one of them being the complete removal of Turkish troops from the Principalities, a topic that had been now resuscitated after several months of silence. Metternich, who had already advised the Porte on 13 September to effect the withdrawal as soon as possible, had no problem in forcefully supporting this request after the meeting in Galicia; if some soldiers were the only obstacle to the appeasement of Russia, the Porte had to remove them. On the other hand, he contributed to a greater chance of a positive reaction in Constantinople by persuading Alexander I not to demand an absolute withdrawal but only the return to the state of affairs before 1821 that would enable some Turkish soldiers to remain.[16]

Ottenfels continued therefore to persuade the Porte to comply with this one wish of the Russian cabinet. The withdrawal of other Turkish soldiers, however, was an insuperable problem. For a long time, the answers from the Porte were negative, although in accordance with the status before 1821 as permitted by Russo-Ottoman

---

[15]   Ottenfels to Metternich, Constantinople, 25 July, 11 and 25 Aug., 7, 11 and 23 Sept., 10 and 25 Oct. 1823, Ottenfels to Stürmer, Constantinople, 23 Sept. 1823, HHStA, StA, Türkei VI, 19; Strangford to Metternich, Constantinople, 23 Sept. 1823, GStA PK, HA III, MdA I, 7257.

[16]   Metternich to Ottenfels, Vienna, 1 and 13 Sept., 6 and 19 Nov., 3 Dec. 1823, Lemberg, 16 Oct. 1823, Nesselrode to Tatishchev, St Petersburg, 18 Aug. 1823, HHStA, StA, Türkei VI, 20; Metternich to Lebzeltern, Vienna, 7 Aug. 1823, HHStA, StA, Russland III, 60; Metternich to Zichy, Vienna, 13 Nov. 1823, HHStA, StK, Preussen 117; Metternich to Strangford, Lemberg, 16 Oct. 1823, GStA PK, HA III, MdA I, 7257; Piquot to Frederick William III, Vienna, 23 Oct. 1823, Hatzfeldt to Frederick William III, Vienna, 24 and 30 Oct. 1823, GStA PK, HA III, MdA I, 6002; Hatzfeldt to Frederick William III, Vienna, 14 Jan. and 8 April 1824, GStA PK, HA III, MdA I, 6003; Wellesley to Canning, Vienna, 11 Nov. 1823, TNA, FO 120/60; Metternich to Gentz, Johannisberg, 7 June 1824, Kronenbitter, p. 104.

treaties a small number of troops could be retained. The Turks firmly insisted on maintaining the garrisons in the Principalities and argued that the number of the soldiers was not considerable and that their presence in Moldavia and Wallachia was not a nuisance for the local inhabitants and was necessary to preserve order. They were also of the opinion that they had already relinquished too much to be able to go any further. The maximum Ottenfels achieved in the autumn was a statement from a new reis effendi, Seida, that the situation could change after the Russian agent's arrival in the Ottoman capital: "We are aggrieved that we could not satisfy our friend, monsieur the internuncio, but having thoroughly considered the question, we are resolved to being unable to answer otherwise; when Monsieur Minciaky arrives, we will reduce the number of our troops, we will even withdraw from the Principalities."[17] This led Ottenfels to hope that the Porte would yield after Minciaky's arrival. However, when the Russian agent appeared in Constantinople on 22 January 1824 and even though his presence helped to solve some commercial issues between Russia and the Ottoman Empire, it had no positive impact on the matter concerning the Principalities. Consequently, Minciaky refused to hand over his credentials as a chargé d'affaires until the troops had been withdrawn, and the arrival of the Russian ambassador, Count Alexander Ivanovich Ribeaupierre, was also postponed.[18]

Metternich became increasingly tired of this continuing obstinacy, but the only thing he could do in this situation was not give up. He continued to repeat that "the state of affairs in the Principalities must be restored to the status quo before the events of 1821. The right of Russia to insist on this action is obvious; the obligation of the Porte to fulfil it is no less evident. The Divan has finally made the commitment to do so; it is necessary that it carries it out."[19] But the months went

---

[17] Miltitz to Frederick William III, Pera, 10 Nov. 1823, GStA PK, HA III, MdA I, 7257.

[18] Ottenfels' note to the Porte, 28 Oct. 1823, the Porte's note to Ottenfels, 8 Nov. 1823, Ottenfels to Metternich, Constantinople, 10 and 25 Oct., 6 and 26 Nov., 10 and 24 Dec. 1823, HHStA, StA, Türkei VI, 19; Ottenfels to Metternich, Constantinople, 25 Feb. and 10 March 1824, HHStA, StA, Türkei VI, 20; Miltitz to Frederick William III, Pera, 10. Oct and 6 Nov. 1823, GStA PK, HA III, MdA I, 7257.

[19] Metternich to Ottenfels, Johannisberg, 20 June 1824, HHStA, StA, Türkei VI, 22.

by after the beginning of 1824 and no progress was actually made despite the cooperation of Austrian, British and French representatives in Constantinople, led again by Strangford. The Porte repeated the already raised arguments and claimed it had nothing to change in this matter, and it was not until June that it ordered the reduction of its forces in the Principalities – but from the first this victory was flawed. What somehow complicated the situation was Strangford's intention not to depart in October without achieving some sort of diplomatic victory. Consequently, the withdrawal of troops from the Principalities became his personal farewell challenge, and to achieve it, he joined two different issues – the Principalities and the Caucasus border – into one when he promised that Russia would be more compliant in the latter if the Porte would yield in the former. This move could not be successful for long because sooner or later it had to become clear that the tsar had no wish to do what Strangford promised. Moreover, it raised the topic that Metternich wished to avoid because the recriminations of the Porte against Russia's tenure of some Caucasus territories could only make the situation worse: "The idea of combining Asian issues with those which are foreign to them is Turkish. It is mistaken in all its points. It is so because it tends to confuse questions of a different nature, because it is only a weapon exploited by a fear of everything [and] because in the end the claim on which it is based is inadmissible. The Divan requests that the same solicitude that the European courts have devoted since 1821 to the interests of Russia should be shown today equally in favour of the Porte. Well, we admit in all conscience that, if we have the feeling of having done much on our part for the preservation of political peace in Europe, we have not done it any more *for Russia* than for ourselves, and we have done it even less *for the Porte*."[20] If war broke out, it would place the Porte "between the fire of the Russian cannon and that of the Greek insurrection. To call the maintenance of peace a service rendered *to Russia* would simultaneously be a mistake and a laughing matter."[21] Consequently, Metternich denounced this new complication and prohibited Ottenfels from discussing the disputed places on the Caucasus border; this matter was finally set aside once more. Another problem with the June achievement was the fact that the withdrawal only oc-

---

[20] Metternich to Vincent, Vienna, 17 Oct. 1824, HHStA, StA, Frankreich 254.
[21] Ibid.

curred in Wallachia; in Moldavia it failed owing to the opposition of Hospodar Ioan Sandu Sturdza, whose attitude was finally overcome by the intervention of an Austrian agent in Bucharest. It was not before November 1824 that Ottenfels could inform Metternich about the withdrawal of troops from Moldavia and December about Minciaky's presentation of his letters of credential as chargé d'affaires; the diplomatic relations were thus restored. And although several days later Minciaky made demands for Russia's other requests to be satisfied – in particular for the removal of the Beshli-Agas, the commanders of the Turkish police for the affairs of the Moslems from the Principalities, which was to form a new dispute in 1825 with a similar history to the one recently settled – another chapter of the Russian Question was solved and an eventual deterioration in the relations between Russia and the Ottoman Empire was prevented for the time being.[22]

Alexander I Raises the Greek Question: The January Mémoire and the St Petersburg Conferences

The withdrawal of most of the Turkish troops from Moldavia and Wallachia in no way meant the end of the "diabolical complication"[23] that emerged in early 1821. When Metternich left Lemberg in October

---

[22] Metternich to Ottenfels, Vienna, 17 Dec. 1823, HHStA, StA, Türkei VI, 20; Metternich to Ottenfels, Vienna, 17 Jan., 17 March, 4 April, 3 Oct., 17 Nov. and 4 Dec. 1824, Johannisberg, 20 June and 15 July 1824, HHStA, StA, Türkei VI, 22; Metternich to Esterházy, Vienna, 17 Oct. 1824, HHStA, StA, England 169; Ottenfels to Metternich, Constantinople, 26 Jan., 26 March, 10, 26 and 27 April, 17 May 1824, HHStA, StA, Türkei VI, 20; Ottenfels to Metternich, Constantinople, 21 June, 2 and 17 Sept., 11, 14 a 25 Oct., 11 and 26 Nov., 10, 14 and 24 Dec. 1824, HHStA, StA, Türkei VI, 21; Miltitz to Frederick William III, Pera, 26 Jan. and 19 March 1824, GStA PK, HA III, MdA I, 7258; Miltitz to Frederick William III, Pera, 5 July, 11 and 24 Dec. 1824, GStA PK, HA III, MdA I, 7259; Hatzfeldt to Frederick William III, Vienna, 13 Dec. 1823, GStA PK, HA III, MdA I, 6002; Hatzfeldt to Frederick William III, Vienna, 12 May 1824, GStA PK, HA III, MdA I, 6003; Hatzfeldt to Frederick William III, Vienna, 7 Sept. and 4 Dec. 1824, GStA PK, HA III, MdA I, 6004; Schwebel to Chateaubriand, Vienna, 12 May 1824, AMAE, CP, Autriche 405; Florescu, "Lord Strangford," p. 486.
[23] Metternich to Princess Lieven, 14 Oct. 1824, NA, RAM-AC 6, 1.

1823, he was full of optimism due to having avoided war and having made progress towards the restoration of Russo-Ottoman diplomatic relations. He was also greatly satisfied with the tsar's attitude: "The triumph of the Russian emperor's moderation is complete; and this triumph, thanks to our tenacity, is at the same time ours."[24] Nevertheless, this triumph, if it really was a triumph, was far from being absolute as Metternich claimed. It is true that peace was maintained and the tsar's promise to send Minciaky to Constantinople was an important step to the normalisation of relations, but there was another, and as the future would prove, much more ominous problem for Austria concerning not the Russian but the Greek Question. The latter became considerably more important for Alexander I during 1823, and in Czernowitz he requested its prompt settlement with the help of the Alliance. This was exactly what Metternich had wished to avoid since the very beginning of the Greek insurrection, and he always had done his best to sweep away this problem in dealing with the tsar and the Porte, even instructing Ottenfels shortly before the meeting in Czernowitz to consider it as "non-existent."[25] Nevertheless, he could not risk displeasing the tsar with a refusal because in such a case he would risk the loss of his influence over Russia in all Near Eastern affairs. What relieved him of his decision-making was the fact that Alexander I did not want to proceed in the Greek affairs alone but to submit them to the consideration of the allied cabinets and reach some sort of settlement at a ministerial conference in St Petersburg where the topic was to be discussed with Nesselrode and the representatives of the Great Powers. Consequently, the Austrian chancellor agreed to the conference and promptly authorised Lebzeltern to take part in it.[26]

Metternich definitely welcomed the conference as an opportunity to temporise, and he actually believed that no solution harmful to

[24] Metternich to Ottenfels, Lemberg, 16 Oct. 1823, HHStA, StA, Türkei VI, 20.
[25] Krauter, p. 131.
[26] Metternich to Zichy, Vienna, 13 Nov. 1823, HHStA, StK, Preussen 117; Metternich to Lebzeltern, Vienna, 30 Nov. 1823, HHStA, StA, Russland III, 60; Metternich to Ottenfels, Vienna, 18 Feb. 1824, HHStA, StA, Türkei VI, 22; Hatzfeldt to Frederick William III, Vienna, 30 Oct., 3, 10 and 12 Nov. 1823, GStA PK, HA III, MdA I, 6002; Hatzfeldt to Frederick William III, Vienna, 14 Jan. 1824, GStA PK, HA III, MdA I, 6003; Caraman to Chateaubriand, Vienna, 11 Nov. 1823, AMAE, CP, Autriche 404; Sauvigny, *Staatsmann und Diplomat*, p. 408.

the Porte owing to the attitudes of other Great Powers would be accepted there.[27] The French ambassador in Vienna, Marquis Victor Louis Charles de Riquet de Caraman, was right when he wrote that Metternich "desires that it is Russia itself that would be forced to reach a decision of its own conviction on the obstacles which oppose the advancement of any acceptable means. He also believes that it is a question on which one becomes exhausted trying to resolve without arriving at any result."[28] The illness from which Metternich suffered in Lemberg was his pretext for postponing having to deal with the Greek Question from the very beginning. He withdrew from the discussions on the Greek affairs and merely asked Nesselrode to prepare a plan for the Greeks, which the Russian vice-chancellor promised to do, and on 21 January 1824 the Russian cabinet presented a proposal, the *Mémoire sur la pacification de la Grèce*, for the creation of three autonomous Greek Principalities: (1) the Peloponnese; (2) Eastern Rumelia with Thessaly; (3) Western Rumelia with a part of Epirus. These autonomous regions were to have their own administration, their own flags and their ties with the Ottoman ruler were to be more illusory than real: the presence of a few small Ottoman garrisons in designated forts and an annual payment of a tribute. Moreover, the islands of the Archipelago were to be granted autonomy. The territory which would belong to the Greeks was to be far more extensive than they finally obtained in 1832. The primary aim of the plan obviously was to create new zones of Russian influence in the Balkans at the expense of the sultan's sovereignty, and if realised, together with Serbia, Moldavia and Wallachia, Russia would have had six satellites in the Balkans.[29]

Metternich's opinion was completely negative: "The plan put forward for the purpose [of the pacification of the Greeks], judged as it is, and leaving aside the methods for executing it, offers nothing that seems acceptable to us for the restoration for the internal peace of the

---

[27] Krauter, p. 121.
[28] Caraman to Chateaubriand, Vienna, 18 Dec. 1823, AMAE, CP, Autriche 404.
[29] Wellesley to Canning, Vienna, 11 Nov. 1823, TNA, FO 120/60; *Mémoire du cabinet de Russie sur la pacification de la Grèce*, 9 Jan. 1824, Prokesch-Osten, *Griechen*, IV, pp. 62–73; A. L. Narotchnitzki, "La diplomatie russe et la préparation de la conférance de Saint-Pétersbourg sur la Grèce en 1824," *Les relations gréco-russes pendant la domination turque et la guerre d'indépendance grecque*, Thessaloniki 1983, pp. 87–97.

Ottoman Empire on bases in accordance with the sovereign rights of the sultan."[30] Moreover, he was convinced, and the past statements of the two quarrelling parties as well as future events entirely proved the correctness of the opinion, that neither the Turks nor the Greeks would accept the Russian plan. This became evident soon after the publication of the January *Mémoire* in *Le Constitutionnel* in Paris on 31 May 1824; both parties reacted negatively.[31] According to the chancellor, the only real solution could be either the restoration of Turkish rule, albeit with some administrative changes on behalf of the Greeks, or the complete independence of Greece. The Russian plan, however, assured neither of these results. Metternich, who desired neither the increase of Russia's power in the Balkans nor the Greeks' autonomy or independence, regarded the plan as dangerous from the geopolitical point of view, attacking Ottoman independence and impractical as a means of solving the Greek Question.[32]

It was, however, impossible for Metternich to reject explicitly what Gentz labelled as "a hopeless piece inspired by the devil"[33] for the same reasons the chancellor could not oppose the idea of the conference in St Petersburg. They forced him to be rather circumspect and careful in his comments. He finally did not accept the plan but instead made a rather diplomatic speech praising Alexander I for his moderation, by which he meant the tsar's willingness not to go to war because of the Greeks. Metternich expressed his satisfaction with the tsar's intent to settle the Greek Question. He agreed with the opinion that for a durable pacification of the Greeks the Ottoman administration could not remain the same as it had been before the outbreak of the insurrection and had to be somehow modified – which actually was Metternich's own opinion although he differed with regard to the

[30] Metternich to Ottenfels, Vienna, 18 Feb. 1824, HHStA, StA, Türkei VI, 22.
[31] Brewer, p. 250; Crawley, *Greek Independence*, p. 36; Schiemann, I, p. 336; Woodhouse, *The Greek War*, p. 104. According to German historian Theodor Schiemann, it was quite possible that Metternich was the author of this indiscretion, but it is impossible to agree with this presupposition because, first, Metternich wanted to conciliate the Ottoman Empire and Russia and this disclosure was rather contradictory, and second, Gentz expressed his displeasure with the publication of the *Mémoire* in a private letter to Ottenfels. Krauter, p. 144.
[32] Metternich to Ottenfels, Vienna, 18 Feb. 1824, HHStA, StA, Türkei VI, 22; Hatzfeldt to Frederick William III, Vienna, 9 Feb. 1824, GStA PK, HA III, MdA I, 6003; Prokesch-Osten, *Griechen*, I, p. 311.
[33] Krauter, p. 145.

extent of the modification. He stated his willingness to negotiate over its principles with the other Great Powers but made careful reference to the difficulties connected with its implementation.

By discreetly expressing doubt about the possible obstacles, Metternich prepared a platform for future controversy over the plan.[34] He let the British ambassador in Vienna, Sir Henry Wellesley, know that he did not believe that "either party could be brought to acquiesce in it, but for his part, he would willingly concur in this, or in any other plan, which should offer a prospect of a termination of the distressing events, which are daily passing in Greece, and afford some hope of securing the future tranquillity of that Country."[35] Wellesley heard similar statements from Gentz, who told the ambassador that it was possible to say that the Austrian cabinet "felt no objection to the plan, provided it were practicable, or could be rendered palatable to the parties concerned ... [but] this Government was led to doubt the practicability of the plan."[36] Metternich's declarations sometimes came close to recognising the plan, as for example when he told the French chargé d'affaires in Vienna that he "did not disapprove of the principles and the propositions contained in the *Mémoire* of the cabinet in St Petersburg ... that he found it reflected the views of moderation and wisdom that Emperor Alexander always manifested, and that he wrote to Mr Lebzeltern to express himself accordingly in this sense at the conference. He [Metternich] added that he in no way doubted that the tsar's agreement to the substance, and the principles would be promptly attained, but that the discussion over the application of these same principles, the period for their execution and the means for the acceptance of the intervention presented difficulties which would not be easy to resolve."[37]

Metternich's strategy for 1824 was thus the same as in the previous years: not to mix the Russian and Greek Questions, to promptly solve the former and draw out the European settlement of the latter. At first this strategy seemed to be successful because the conference could not meet before the summer, and Metternich succeeded in per-

---

[34] Metternich to Lebzeltern, Vienna, 17 April 1824, HHStA, StA, Russland III, 64.
[35] Wellesley to Canning, Vienna, 29 Feb. 1824, TNA, FO 120/62.
[36] Wellesley to Canning, Vienna, 6 April 1824, TNA, FO 120/63.
[37] Schwebel to Caraman, Vienna, 22 Feb. 1824, AMAE, CP, Autriche 405.

suading the Prussian and French cabinets not to instruct their ambassadors with anything other than registering the Russian proposals and submitting them to their respective governments' review.[38] But later it was shown that he underestimated the attention paid by Alexander I to the war between the Greeks and the Turks. The chancellor seemed to hope that the Russian monarch would lose interest in the fate of the Greeks after the settlement of Russo-Ottoman dispute, but such a hope was in vain because Alexander I did not want to give up the Greek Question. The path to the deterioration of relations between Austria and Russia was laid in Czernowitz. However, it is difficult to agree with Anton Prokesch von Osten, who claimed that Austria recognised there the Great Powers' right to interfere into Greek affairs.[39] This statement goes too far although Alexander I most likely understood the outcome in this way, but Metternich did not and he merely recognised the right of the Alliance to discuss it and suggest a solution to the Porte. The same argument can be applied to Eberhard Schütz's statement that what Prokesch regarded as acknowledged in Czernowitz had already been done in principle in Verona on 9 November 1822 when the Great Powers agreed with the Russian memorandum inviting the Porte to discuss the Greek affairs with the members of the Alliance if the Turkish troops were unable to suppress the revolt.[40] Again, the vague text of the memorandum approved at the congress can hardly be considered as the recognition of Russia's request for a collective intervention into the internal crisis of the Ottoman Empire. The deciding moment occurred in Czernowitz and not in Verona, and not because Metternich would have agreed with the intervention but because he allowed the opening of the discussions on the Greek Question in which the goals of Austria and Russia differed.

The conference in St Petersburg took place for the first time in two sessions in the summer of 1824, the first on 17 June, the second on 2 July. Nesselrode presented the January *Mémoire* as the basis for the solution of the Greek Question and asked the attendant diplo-

---

[38] Metternich to Ottenfels, Vienna, 18 Feb. 1824, HHStA, StA, Türkei VI, 22; Metternich to Lebzeltern, Vienna, 17 April 1824, HHStA, StA, Russland III, 64; Sauvigny, *Metternich et la France*, II, pp. 850–851.

[39] Prokesch-Osten, *Griechen*, I, p. 227.

[40] Schütz, p. 94.

mats for their opinions, but since they had no instructions for the negotiations about the plan, the discussions were suspended for several months. From the short summer conference the most interesting incident was Lebzeltern's objection to the record of the first meeting in which his answer to the Russian project was written: "The Viennese cabinet gave its full assent to the plan for pacification described in the *Mémoire* of the Russian cabinet."[41] The Austrian ambassador asked Nesselrode to change the sentence because in fact he had said more about the general character of the plan than about the details of its content. The vice-chancellor met this request and the disputed part of the text was finally worded in this way: "The Viennese cabinet has completely done justice to the generous views which dictated the plan of the pacification outlined in the *Mémoire* of the Russian cabinet [and Lebzeltern] expresses the complete support of its court to the general basis of the plan and the desire to aid its execution."[42] Lebzeltern's conduct entirely reflected Metternich's emphasis on not accepting the plan while simultaneously avoiding actual disavowal of the plan.

Metternich won the first round but he knew that another would come. He postponed the discussion over the Russian proposals for the settlement for another half year, and he persuaded the tsar that the Greek Question was not to be mentioned in Constantinople before the solution of the dispute concerning the Principalities because it could impede the progress of the latter. However, Austria was bound to express some attitude towards the plan at the next meeting in St Petersburg, and what Metternich knew in the autumn was that his statement would in no way be sympathetic. He still found the plan impracticable because neither the Turks nor the Greeks were willing to accept it, the former refusing any intervention or advice, the latter wanting nothing less than complete independence: "The Porte as well as the Greeks will not listen to the propositions regardless of how just and how wise they may be; the Divan will refuse them because it is customary for it to do so, because of its stubborn pride [and] because of the spirit of jealousy that is inherent in it and that will constantly

---

[41] Lebzeltern to Metternich, St Petersburg, 3 July 1824, Prokesch-Osten, *Griechen*, IV, p. 84.
[42] *Protocole de la conférence du 17. Juin 1824*, Prokesch-Osten, *Griechen*, IV, p. 87.

prevent it from regarding even the services which the Great Powers would like to render it other than as a claim on their part to dictate to it the laws for the administration of its internal affairs or as a subterfuge masking secret and ambitious designs. The Turks, in a word, will always see in the affair what is not there and never what is to be found in it in reality. The Greeks, on the other hand, will not listen to a proposition that will not assist them in the achievement of their political independence or, which is the same, that does not come from the determination of the Great Powers to regard the Ottoman Empire as eliminated from Europe."[43] The plan, according to Metternich, was also inadmissible because it would impose an unwanted solution on a legitimate ruler, with most probability by force because the possibility of the Turks' withdrawal without a war was unrealistic; on the other hand, the plan envisaged negotiations with the Greeks, which meant the same as their factual political recognition. The Great Powers had thus no right to interfere in Ottoman internal affairs, and Russia had no exclusive right to do so. In the autumn of 1824 as well as in the spring of 1822, Metternich refuted Russia's alleged right to protect the Christians in Greece: "No stipulation could ever authorise Russia to support the cause of the Greeks in a complete revolt against the authority of the Porte."[44] He also rejected the arguments of the Russian cabinet raised to support Russia's intervention, for example, the fact that Russia was the Ottoman Empire's neighbour or that the uprising damaged its commerce. In both cases Austria would have had the same right because it also bordered the sultan's empire, its frontier being even longer than Russia's, and Austria's commerce was damaged as well.[45]

In the autumn of 1824, Metternich was searching for a suitable countermove to the January plan which he wanted to reject, but not at the cost of the loss of good relations with the tsar. A failure to come up with such a countermove could open the door to a Russo-Ottoman war. However, his means were considerably limited by Alexander I's determination to act decisively and by the lack of British support; Canning refused to participate in the conferences. The solution sug-

---

[43] Metternich to Esterházy, Vienna, 17 Oct. 1824, HHStA, StA, England 169.
[44] Ibid.
[45] Ibid.; Metternich to Lebzeltern, Ischl, 11 Aug. 1824, HHStA, StA, Russland III, 65; Prokesch-Osten, *Griechen*, I, p. 340.

gested by Gentz and sent by Metternich to Lebzeltern on 15 January 1825 contained a proposal for the recognition of Greek independence – in the Peloponnese and the islands of the Archipelago – if the Porte would not listen to the advice of the Great Powers.[46] It was argued that the Greeks' situation could be improved only through negotiations between the Great Powers and the Porte as the legitimate authority, and if the latter did not want to accept their proposals on behalf of the Greeks, the sultan could be encouraged to moderation by means of a threat: "This instrument would be *the eventual acceptance of the independence of the Greeks*, not as a recognition *of right* but as a measure of *fact* and *necessity* directed in the form of a threat against an otherwise insuperable opposition."[47] This in no way signified that Metternich had altered his opinion and had started to seriously contemplate Greek independence, nor, as British historian Alexander Bitis claims, that he proposed it because he preferred it to the autonomy as suggested in the Russian *Mémoire*.[48] It is true that in the late 1820s Metternich really prioritised the absolute independence of Greece, but such a consideration played no role in the middle of the decade. He was simply sure, and this presumption proved to be entirely correct, that the tsar would never accept the possibility of the Greeks' independence because it did not serve Russia's interest. The proposal was a mere diplomatic manoeuvre with the aim of drawing out the negotiations in St Petersburg for as long as possible without reaching a decision hostile to the sultan.

The second round of conferences in St Petersburg took place from 24 February to 8 April 1825. The Prussian and French representatives were instructed to support the Austrian ambassador, but they actually remained passive and the negotiations were a duel between

---

[46] Metternich to Ottenfels, Vienna, 3 Oct. 1824, HHStA, StA, Türkei VI, 22; Metternich to Vincent, Vienna, 17 Oct. 1824, HHStA, StA, Frankreich 254; Caraman to Damas, Vienna, 13 Dec. 1824, AMAE, CP, Autriche 405; Wellesley to Canning, Vienna, 4 Oct. 1824, TNA, FO 120/66; Wellesley to Canning, Vienna, 17 Jan. 1825, TNA, FO 120/68; P. R. Sweet, *Friedrich von Gentz: Defender of the Old Order*, Madison 1941, p. 258; Krauter, p. 148. According to British historian Douglas Dakin, this plan was inspired by Alexandros Mavrokordatos' letters to Gentz in which the Greek leader claimed that an independent Greece would be anti-Russian. However, no proof for Dakin's theory has been found in the studied documents. Dakin, p. 155.

[47] Metternich to Lebzeltern, Vienna, 15 Jan. 1825, HHStA, StA, Russland III, 70.

[48] Bitis, p. 163.

Lebzeltern and Nesselrode. When the vice-chancellor suggested at the first meeting on 24 February the solution of the Greek affairs according to the January plan and that they should contact the provisional Greek government and break diplomatic relations with the Porte if the sultan refused to agree with the cessation of hostilities, Lebzeltern was forced to present the Austrian counterproposal. Nesselrode was initially speechless then expressed his surprise that *"such an idea was born on Austrian soil and that it could be accepted in a moment by a cabinet that has always declared itself to be the defender of reasonable principles, the enemy of revolutions* and of their dangerous triumph."[49] Lebzeltern answered that one could not forget that "we have not at all presented this idea as something we would desire to undertake but as an appropriate instrument for inspiring terror into the Divan for a worthy purpose, actually as a powerfully coercive measure against it *without the use of arms.* If I admitted the possibility of its execution, it only was in the hypothetical sense of being brought to it by a *necessity,* just as the Russian cabinet allowed the hypothesis of a similar *necessity* that would lead the emperor to use methods with an extremely dangerous consequence and that would horrify his generous spirit as well as his just and gracious policy."[50] Then Lebzeltern explained that whereas Russia saw beyond the failure of the negotiations in Constantinople coercive measures, which most probably meant the same as a war with the Ottoman Empire, Austria still saw a chance to avoid such a war with the threat of Greek independence – an outcome definitely not welcome in Vienna but surely more acceptable than a breakdown in the relations between St Petersburg and Constantinople. He introduced the advantages of Austria's proposal: (1) The Great Powers would avoid direct negotiations with the Greek rebels; (2) the threat of war could move the Turks to make a greater effort to suppress the revolt, and they possessed the best means to reach this goal; (3) Austria's methods would be less dangerous for general peace than a military intervention; (4) the war with the Porte would be avoided. This reasoning as well as Lebzeltern's conduct at the conference had Metternich's full support, in particular when the chancellor learnt about Russia's sudden proposal for the use of co-

---

[49] Lebzeltern to Metternich, St Petersburg, undated, Prokesch-Osten, *Griechen,* IV, p. 158.
[50] Ibid.

ercive measures. He absolutely agreed with the argument presented by Lebzeltern that "the Great Powers can in no way employ coercive measures because they could not refer to a single right that could justify the employment of force to pacify the disputing parties."[51] Such measures were not only contradictory to international law but also illogical: if the Greeks and the Turks accepted the intervention, the coercive measures would not have to be applied. But would the Great Powers be willing to enforce their will, in other words wage war, not only against the Turks if they refused to comply but also against the Greeks if they did the same, or against both if neither wanted to yield? Metternich could merely answer for Austria and in all cases the answer was negative.[52]

The unyielding opposition of the other three Powers to the coercive measures finally moved Russia to withdraw its demands. Consequently, the only result of the conference was a note agreed by its participants on 8 April 1825 inviting the Porte to request the intervention of Austria, France, Prussia and Russia. This polite offer was not accompanied by a threat of force and it thus had little practical value. Ottenfels, who had been instructed to negotiate in compliance with the decision of the conference that he obtained on 13 May, persuaded his colleagues, with the aim of increasing the chance for the acceptance of the proposal, to use the expression "conciliation" (*bons offices*) instead of "intervention" because the only Turkish equivalent to the latter was "mediation," an expression entirely inadmissible for the Porte. This stylistic modification, however, did not contribute to a more positive answer. As had generally been expected, the sultan refused the Great Powers' interference as incompatible with his sovereignty, independence and dignity and unnecessary at the time when he believed in a quick final victory over the insurgents. The reis effendi told the Austrian dragoman, Baron Karl von Testa: "You can believe me that the affair is finished and I ask monsieur the internun-

---

[51] Metternich to Lebzeltern, Paris, 11 April 1825, HHStA, StA, Russland III, 70.
[52] Ibid.; Metternich to Zichy, Vienna, 18 Jan. 1825, HHStA, StK, Preussen 121; Wellesley to Canning, Vienna, 21 Jan. 1825, TNA, FO 120/68; Hatzfeldt to Frederick William III, Vienna, 17 Feb. and 21 March 1825, GStA PK, HA III, MdA I, 6005; Caraman to Damas, Vienna, 28 Feb. 1825, AMAE, CP, Autriche 406; *Feuille volante de Mr. le Comte de Lebzeltern sur les moyens d'arriver à la pacification de la Grèce*, Prokesch-Osten, *Griechen*, IV, p. 160.

cio to inform his court of this."⁵³ This answer invoked Metternich's
displeasure, actually not so much for its content as for its form that
was too conclusive and left no room for further discussions that could
keep Russia in the game, but generally the chancellor was satisfied
with the outcome of the conference and was glad not to have to deal
with the Greek Question in the following months.⁵⁴

The Austro-Russian Rupture

Alexander I and Nesselrode were highly dissatisfied with this outcome. They felt betrayed by their allies, and above all by Metternich.
The negotiations in St Petersburg were terminated and in a circular
dispatch in August, Nesselrode informed Austria, France and Prussia
that further discussions on the Greek Question were pointless and all
relevant proposals on their part were to be taken by Russian representatives ad referendum; the point of this message was clearly directed
against Metternich. The tsar's annoyance was so considerable that he
did not even send the chancellor a letter of sympathy on the death of
his wife. Nesselrode, a well-known Austrophile before the mid 1820s,
changed his attitude and became an advocate of a more vigorous policy towards the Ottoman Empire and thereby Metternich's opponent.
This was a well-known fact in Vienna; already in March 1825 when
Gentz called the Russian vice-chancellor "our friend," he did so "in
the sense of an English minister calling certain opposition members
[of the British Parliament] his right honourable friend"⁵⁵ and the dis-

⁵³ Ottenfels to Metternich, Constantinople, 11 July 1825, HHStA, StA, Türkei
VI, 23.
⁵⁴ Metternich to Ottenfels, Paris, 1 April 1825, Milan, 26 May 1825, Vienna, 4
Sept. 1825, HHStA, StA, Türkei VI, 24; Ottenfels to Metternich, Constantinople, 4
March, 25 April, 10 and 25 May, 10 and 17 June, 21 July and 10 Aug. 1825, Testa
to Ottenfels, 26 April, 7 and 16 June 1825, HHStA, StA, Türkei VI, 23; Maltzan
to Frederick William III, Vienna, 16 April 1825, GStA PK, HA III, MdA I, 6005;
Ottenfels, *Memoari*, p. 151; Lebzeltern to Ottenfels, St Petersburg, 18 April 1825,
Prokesch-Osten, *Griechen*, IV, pp. 163–170; Dakin, p. 155; Gürbüz, p. 413.
⁵⁵ Gentz to Metternich, [?] March 1825, A. von Prokesch-Osten (ed.), *Zur Geschichte der orientalischen Frage: Briefe aus dem Nachlasse Friedrichs von Gentz
1823–1829*, Wien 1877, p. 46.

trust naturally increased in the following years. The cordial relations with Metternich were interrupted until the end of the 1820s.[56]

The rest of 1825 was characterised by Russian embitterment manifested in anti-Austrian declarations full of accusations of its disloyalty and betrayal of the tsar's interests, of which the most important were frequently expressed by Princess Lieven, at that time Metternich's former mistress, and Nesselrode. The princess told Lebzeltern in July that "Austria did not at all consider the real interests of Russia as a good friend and ally and it did not appreciate enough the nobility and generosity of Emperor Alexander during three years of ordeal and of patience."[57] In September she added: "However, the emperor is profoundly offended, he feels abandoned by you, deceived by everyone."[58] Nesselrode told Lebzeltern in late July 1825: "See here what you have proved to us with your latest dispatches, which do not satisfy our demands at all and which, on the contrary, tend to throw us off course, and this due to your distrust and jealousy of Russia, of a Great Power that has acted at every opportunity to your benefit with so much loyalty and friendship."[59] The favourite topic of the Russian vice-chancellor was the comparison of the uprisings in the Appenines with the rebellion in Greece when he occasionally complained that whereas Russia gave permission to Austria to intervene in Naples and Piedmont in 1821, the Viennese cabinet refused to allow Russia's intervention in the Ottoman Empire. It accused Austria of inconsistency in its policy when it refused to support the Russian plan for the solution.

Metternich was not deaf to these accusations. First of all he pointed out that it was not Austria which had altered its policy and insisted that its attitude to the Near Eastern affairs was consistent: "We want the same today as we have wanted since the beginning of the

---

[56] Metternich to Esterházy, 29 April 1826, HHStA, StA, England, 175; L. Cowles, "The Failure to Restrain Russia: Canning, Nesselrode, and the Greek Question, 1825–27," *IHR* 12, 1990, 4, pp. 701–702; Bitis, p. 168; Robech, p. 453; Schütz, p. 121.

[57] Lebzeltern to Metternich, St Petersburg, 31 July 1825, NA, RAM-AC 2, 4.

[58] Lebzeltern to Metternich, St Petersburg, 13 Sept. 1825, NA, RAM-AC 2, 4.

[59] Lebzeltern to Metternich, St Petersburg, 31 July 1825, N. Mikhaïlowitch (ed.), *Les rapports diplomatiques de Lebzeltern, ministre d'Autriche à la cour de Russie (1816–1826)*, St. Petersburg 1913, pp. 183–184.

Greek insurrection."[60] He wrote to Lebzeltern in August 1825: "We have not deviated for a single moment from the principle which has served as a point of departure in the Greek affair since Ljubljana, and we have not uttered a word in our proceedings that we would wish to take back and, consequently, that we would regret."[61] He also sharply disagreed with the opinion that Austria had behaved according to different principles in the Greek Question as in the Apennines but, contrary to the Russian cabinet, he believed that to act in the same way meant to act on behalf of the ruler and against the insurgents: "Here the monarch is the sultan and any consequent action must be the use of material force against the Greeks."[62] The main difference between these affairs was that the interventions in the Apennines were welcomed and even requested by the monarchs, whereas the sultan refused foreign intervention in his own affairs. The chancellor's thoughts were clearly presented by Lebzeltern who told Nesselrode: "If we had asked you in Naples to march against the legitimate authority, you would not have consented!"[63] Metternich repeated that since the Porte violated no international treaty with its measures in the Greek Question, the Great Powers had no right to threaten it with force; their possibilities were in fact extremely limited. He wrote to Lebzeltern: "What everyone in St Petersburg was recently pleased to refer to under the misleading term *coercive measures* to be employed against the Turks is nothing other than *war* according to the judgement of your court. Austria has decided not to compromise itself with the Turks; it does not recognise the right to do so, and it also would have no justifiable motive for such a determination ... Every military operation on the part of Russia against the possessions of the Porte under whatever pretext that it would like to make would be regarded by us as a positive act of war."[64] Gentz, who was personally more hostile to Russia, agreed with the chancellor: "The Russians care little whether we stand by them or not in matters in which they have or think they have the stipulated legal right on their side; such questions, they think, will possibly be achieved without foreign assistance and

---

[60] Metternich to Zichy, Vienna, 21 Sept. 1825, HHStA, StK, Preussen 121.
[61] Metternich to Lebzeltern, Ischl, 13 Aug. 1825, HHStA, StA, Russland III, 71.
[62] Metternich to Lebzeltern, Milan, 18 June 1825, HHStA, StA, Russland III, 71.
[63] Lebzeltern to Metternich, St Petersburg, 13 Sept. 1825, Mikhaïlowitch, p. 185.
[64] Metternich to Lebzeltern, Ischl, 13 Aug. 1825, HHStA, StA, Russland III, 71.

the clamour that they raise from time to time is nothing other than harassment and a poor sense of fair play. The only thing they demand of us, either longingly or vehemently, is our participation in an enterprise that lies totally outside the extent of their rights and likewise certainly also outside the extent of ours and in which we neither want nor are able to participate for reasons of vital importance, and which no one should expect of us."[65]

Metternich rejected the use of coercive measures because they were equivalent to "the intervention of an armed force."[66] The rejection of the plan for Greek autonomy was advocated by the prince because of its unfeasibility by peaceful means; if it had been accepted at the conference, a war would have been inevitable, and a conflict between Europe and the Ottoman Empire would have strengthened the position of the Greeks and contributed to their independence, something that Russia officially opposed. When Tatishchev, echoing Nesselrode's displeasure in Vienna, asked Metternich in June 1825 for his comments on Russia's attitude, Metternich replied: "I found myself completely incapable of replying to something that offers me no clear idea! The emperor does not want a war with the Turks; he also does not want the political emancipation of the Greeks; no one talks to us about anything other than coercive measures against the former. These measures, which at the same time [would lead to] neither war nor the liberation of the Greeks – measures that would be pointless, should they be separated from each other – are for me an irresolvable problem."[67] Finally, Metternich expressed his conviction that it was not Austria but Russia which decided to act contrary to its long declared opinions and that the solution of the whole affair was to be sought more in Greece than in Constantinople because "only two objectives could be achieved in Constantinople: an act of amnesty with a clause containing an absolutely stipulated period of submission; an act of insurance relating to the future civil existence of the Greeks, who would use this guarantee to their benefit. Everything that is outside these acts would be incompatible with our principles of public law [and] with those same principles by which Emperor Alexander lives

---

[65]   Gentz to Metternich, Vienna, 3 July 1825, Kronenbitter, p. 187.
[66]   Metternich to Vincent, Milan, 20 May 1825, HHStA, StA, Frankreich 257.
[67]   Metternich to Lebzeltern, Milan, 18 June 1825, HHStA, StA, Russland III, 71.

and has proclaimed in all the great events of our time."[68] Even though
the prince considered the Russian designs to be ambitious and hardly
sincere, his arguments lacked the bitter incriminations peculiar to the
declarations of his Russian counterparts. He wished to restore good relations with Alexander I and Nesselrode, but this was an unattainable
goal.[69]

The Legend of the Chancellor's Parisian Boast

The tsar no longer had any desire to cooperate with Austria, and
this attitude was hardened with the news of Metternich's visit from
14 March to 21 April 1825 to Paris, where the chancellor hurried
to see his dying wife. Metternich, of course, made good use of his
stay in the French capital to discuss the current political affairs and
strengthen Austro-French relations. Since his journey coincided with
the failure of the conference in St Petersburg, the Russian cabinet
believed that he persuaded the French cabinet to oppose Russia's
January plan at the conference. However, although Metternich's visit
definitely reinforced the cordiality between the courts in Paris and
in Vienna, it predated Metternich's sojourn in Paris, and the French
cabinet had supported Austria in the Greek Question at least since
early 1825, which was entirely proved by the conduct of the French
ambassador in St Petersburg, Count Pierre Louis Auguste Ferron La
Ferronnays, in January, long before Metternich's arrival in the city on
the Seine.[70] What offended Alexander I even more was the chancellor's

---

[68] Metternich to Lebzeltern, Pressburg, 28 Sept. 1825, HHStA, StA, Russland III,
71.
[69] Metternich to Lebzeltern, Milan, 18 June 1825, Ischl, 15 Aug. 1825, Pressburg,
28 Sept. 1825, HHStA, StA, Russland III, 71; *Observations sur la pièce transmise
par Mr. de Tatischeff relativement aux négociations entamées à Constantinople*,
Milan, 15 May 1825, attached to Metternich to Vincent, Milan, 26 June 1825,
Metternich to Vincent, Vienna, 2 Sept. 1825, HHStA, StA, Frankreich 257; Caraman to Damas, Milan, 17 June 1825, Vienna, 2 Sept. and 6 Oct. 1825, AMAE,
CP, Autriche 406; Hatzfeldt to Frederick William III, Vienna, 7 July 1825, GStA
PK, HA III, MdA I, 6005; Wellesley to Canning, Vienna, 1 Sept. 1825, TNA, FO
120/71; Metternich to Francis I, Paris, 1 April 1825, *NP*, IV, p. 166.
[70] Wellesley to Granville, Vienna, 3 March 1825, TNA, FO 120/69; Werther to
Frederick William III, Paris, 27 March 1825, GStA PK, HA III, MdA I, 4906;
Sauvigny, *Metternich et la France*, II, p. 852.

alleged boasting of his ascendancy and leadership over the tsar, which allowed him to prevent the Russian monarch from declaring war on the Ottoman Empire, a conflict that, as Metternich was said to declare, the tsar desired. According to Princess Lieven, Metternich behaved in this way owing to his distress over his wife's death. It was said to have happened when he visited Princess Bagration's salon in Paris and heard sad music; the result was his lapse from discretion and his boastful speech so humiliating for the tsar.[71]

This construct was uncritically accepted by historians despite its evident weakness.[72] The number of eye-witnesses was extremely low, and the original source of the rumour was really Pozzo di Borgo alone; Princess Lieven, who personally was not in Paris, only received the relevant information from him. The lack of primary sources is not the only problem; another concerns the credibility of Pozzo, who was not only a wily and intriguing diplomat and,[73] according to American historian Patricia Kennedy Grimsted, "a master of political intrigue,"[74] but also an exponent of the hawkish Russian party and after Capodistrias' retirement the most prominent advocate of pro-war policy among the Russian diplomatic elites. His attitude towards Metternich, and not only owing to their different views of the Near Eastern affairs, was extremely hostile. In Vienna the antagonistic attitude of the Russian ambassador in Paris was no secret. Already in April 1822 Tatishchev warned Metternich that Pozzo was a supporter of Capodistrias' party, with which Metternich agreed and considered the Russian ambassador in Paris at that time as well as later to be his arch enemy, an "infernal intriguer."[75] In August 1825, the prince concurred with Gentz's description of Pozzo as the only man who could completely destroy the Austro-Russian relations and as "a real European plague against which quarantine measures should be arranged from all sides."[76] Since in March 1825 Pozzo no longer exerted his

---

[71] H. Temperley (ed.), *Das Tagebuch der Fürstin Lieven: Mit politischen Skizzen und einigen Briefen*, Berlin 1926, p. 86.

[72] F. R. Bridge, *The Habsburg Monarchy among the Great Powers, 1815–1918*, New York, Oxford, Munich 1990, p. 33; H. Temperley, "Princess Lieven and the Protocol of 4 April 1826," *EHR* 39, 1924, p. 57.

[73] Crawley, *Greek Independence*, p. 4.

[74] Grimsted, p. 281.

[75] Metternich to Lebzeltern, Vienna, 7 Feb. 1824, Mikhaïlowitch, p. 374.

[76] Gentz to Metternich, Vienna, 12 Aug. 1825, Kronenbitter, p. 238.

earlier strong influence over the French government, Metternich logically did his best to preserve this situation – something which could
not please the ambassador. Consequently, it is hard to believe how
Metternich, well known and generally admired for his perfect self-
control, could say in Pozzo's presence anything that could insult the
tsar.[77] During the 20 years covered by this book he never made such
an error of judgement and he was extremely, according to some foreign diplomats even pitifully cautious in his expressions on Russia.[78]
The alleged suffering caused by his wife's death, a woman whom he
respected and liked but never loved, could hardly provoke such an
indiscretion or mental disorder such as described by Princess Lieven.

   Consequently, some contemporaries had problems believing the
rumour. Tatishchev, for example, doubted this version in a report to
Nesselrode: "I doubt that he [Metternich] expressed any sentiments
in Paris which could have displeased you ... he is too experienced
a man to risk of the displeasure of cabinets. Has he been indiscrete?
That is not like him. Since his return he has continually praised the
emperor, repeating to everybody that in the affair of the Levant the
Viennese cabinet's procedures were based upon certainty that the emperor wanted to avoid war. If during his visit to Paris he gave you
some reasons to be dissatisfied with him, I assure you that I cannot
guess the motives which provoked him to act in such a way."[79] A sim-

---

[77] Metternich to Lebzeltern, Vienna, 22 April 1822, HHStA, StA, Russland III,
78; Metternich to Lebzeltern, Milan, 18 June 1825, HHStA, StA, Russland III, 71;
Hatzfeldt to Frederick William III, Vienna, 29 July 1822, GStA PK, HA III, MdA
I, 6000; Hatzfeldt to Frederick William III, Vienna, 1 March 1823, GStA PK, HA
III, MdA I, 6001; Wellesley to Canning, Vienna, 6 April 1824, TNA, FO 120/63;
Metternich to Gentz, Ischl, 5 and 16 Aug. 1825, Prokesch-Osten, *Zur Geschichte
der orientalischen Frage*, pp. 80–83; Sauvigny, *Metternich et la France*, III, p. 978.
[78] French historian Guillaume de Bertier de Sauvigny referred to Pozzo's report
based upon information from French Minister of Foreign Affairs Baron Ange Hyacinthe Maxence de Damas, whom Metternich told during their last Parisian meeting that Austria would never consent to coercive measures against the Turks and
would not support the tsar if he decided to wage war. According to Sauvigny, its
accuracy has been proved by Damas' memoirs. Sauvigny, *Metternich et la France*,
III, p. 979. Nevertheless, this was not a new and scandalous claim, and the relevant
parts from neither Pozzo's report nor Damas' memoir, both quoted by Sauvigny,
contain anything for which Metternich was blamed by the Russian cabinet or by
historians in particular: his alleged declarations of his ascendency over the tsar and
the latter's hunger for war with the Ottoman Empire.
[79] Tatishchev to Nesselrode, Milan, 28 May 1825, Schiemann, I, p. 606.

ilar attitude was assumed by Bernstorff, who contemplated "whether Prince Metternich really dared to make such statements or whether they were merely ascribed to him by the Russian ambassador in Paris with whom, as it is well known, he is on inimical terms."[80] Bernstorff expressed the suspicion that it was all a plot on the part of Pozzo, which is not at all improbable since the Russian ambassador surely wished to see the deterioration of the Austro-Russian relations and contribute to the tsar's more independent policy in the Near East and the outbreak of war with the Ottoman Empire. The most persuasive proof against the "boasting theory" can be found in a secret report of a Prussian envoy in Paris, Baron Heinrich von Werther, who resolutely denied that Metternich had talked about Alexander I in a negative way and, to the contrary, his comments concerning the tsar's goals had been very positive and entirely denying any desire on the tsar's part for war. Here one must support the credibility of Werther's statements with the fact that Metternich always expressed this opinion about the tsar's opposition to war at meetings with foreign diplomats from the outbreak of the Greek insurrection until Alexander I's death. Werther also confirmed that Metternich had not influenced the French policy in the Near East because it had been the same before as well as after his stay in Paris. The report ended with the acknowledgement that Metternich's words transmitted to the tsar were "perhaps misrepresented,"[81] obliquely ascribing the guilt to Pozzo di Borgo.

Metternich knew the rumours including the most serious accusation raised against him and he naturally knew their source: "I admit that General Pozzo did all he could to misrepresent all my actions in Paris [and] that he tried to distort my words and to even interpret my silence the same way. I will go even further; I know that he did; that, for example, he reported to his court that I had taken great pains to raise alarm in the French cabinet about the hidden warlike intentions of Emperor Alexander."[82] Despite their seriously negative influence, Metternich assumed a disdainful attitude towards these insinuations.[83] He shrugged them off with a moralising sarcasm peculiar

---

[80] Bernstorff to Frederick William III, 15 June 1825, Ringhoffer, p. 254.
[81] Werther to Frederick William III, Paris, 24 May 1825, GStA PK, HA III, MdA I, 4906.
[82] Metternich to Lebzeltern, Milan, 18 June 1825, HHStA, StA, Russland III, 71
[83] Metternich to Lebzeltern, Paris, 26 March and 12 April 1825, HHStA, StA, Russland III, 70; Metternich to Lebzeltern, Ischl, 15 Aug. 1825, Pressburg, 28

to him in his instructions to Lebzeltern that in St Petersburg *"one does not know what he* [Alexander I] *wants in the Eastern Question and the more it develops, the less the Russian cabinet knows how to recover itself.* In a moral situation like this, courts as well as individuals indulge in the mistrust of everyone."[84]

Alexander I: A Pro-European and Self-Restrained Monarch?

As well as in the case of the accusation of his boasting in Paris, historians have generally accepted the complaints of the Russian cabinet raised against Metternich for his conduct in the Near Eastern affairs, particularly in the Greek Question. For example, British historian Janet M. Hartley claims that Alexander I, with his emphasis on European cooperation, proved a greater "consistency in his principles on the subject of revolts and held a more genuinely 'European' view about the obligations of the great powers in these circumstances than Metternich, whose attitude was always determined by the particular interests of Austria," and she added: "Yet again but Metternich's negative response exposed his contradictory position of supporting armed suppression of revolts when they threatened Austria but opposing both unilateral and collective military action by the powers in Greece."[85] The pro-Alliance, in other words pro-European attitude of the tsar is also emphasised by Paul W. Schroeder, who regards it as the main reason for Alexander I's restraint in the Near East, in other words for his willingness "to forego the likely gains of a legally justified war."[86] German historian Wolfram Pyta shares Schroeder's opinion about Alexander I's "self-restraint"[87] in the Greek Question

---

Sept. 1825, HHStA, StA, Russland III, 71; Metternich to Vincent, Ischl, 17 Aug. 1825, Vienna, 2 Sept. 1825, HHStA, StA, Frankreich 257; Schwebel to Damas, Vienna, 21 Aug. 1825, AMAE, CP, Autriche 406.

[84] Metternich to Lebzeltern, Milan, 18 June 1825, HHStA, StA, Russland III, 71.

[85] J. M. Hartley, *Alexander I*, London 1994, p. 156.

[86] Schroeder, *Transformation*, p. 621.

[87] W. Pyta, "Idee und Wirklichkeit der "Heilige Allianz"," F.-L. Kroll (ed.), *Neue Wege der Ideengeschichte: Festschrift für Kurt Kluxen zum 85. Geburtstag*, Paderborn, München, Wien, Zürich 1996, p. 335.

and regards Alexander I's decision not to wage war on behalf of the Greeks as a sacrifice to the Alliance of Europe because the tsar was allegedly entitled to wage such a war: "When the Greeks rebelled in the spring of 1821 against Ottoman rule and the Ottoman Empire obviously violated treaties concluded with Russia in the wake of bloody conflicts with the risen Greeks, it directly invited the tsar's empire to a military enterprise against the Turks."[88] Alexander Bitis also praises Alexander I for his moderation and accuses Metternich of deceiving the tsar.[89] Eberhard Schütz was of the opinion that Metternich's conduct was disloyal and in conflict with the agreement from Czernowitz.[90]

No one ever raised the question whether this one-sided view is tenable. To be able to do so, it is necessary to summarise the Russian policy in brief. Alexander I was moderate in his policy towards the Ottoman Empire simply for the reason that he did not want to destroy it and wished to avoid war. When the Greeks revolted, the tsar denounced this act of insubordination and declared his support for the legitimate monarch, but he later proposed a plan that was advantageous to the Greeks and affected the rights of the sultan. This was not primarily done for European or Greek but for Russian interests, and even though Alexander I did not want to take the Ottoman Empire by storm, he wanted to undermine it when he proposed the creation of new autonomous principalities in the Balkans. This assistance to the Greeks was hardly due to philanthropy but rather to a desire to extend his influence over south-eastern Europe. Nevertheless, and in this Metternich was right in his arguments, the Turks' actions against the insurgents in the southern Balkans in no way violated the Russo-Ottoman treaties and even the massacres of the Christians in the areas outside the Danubian Principalities did not authorise the tsar to begin an armed conflict against the sultan. Consequently, Alexander I had no right to wage war against the Ottoman Empire because of the Greek insurrection. He was entitled to do so only owing to the infractions of the Russo-Ottoman treaties by the Porte but also in this case his alleged restraint was more than problematic: first, not all his complaints of the Turks' infringement of the treaties were justified

---

[88] Ibid., pp. 334–335.
[89] Bitis, pp. 114–115.
[90] Schütz, pp. 105–108.

and some of his complaints were merely pretexts, and second, he too
was far from observing the terms of the treaties. In brief, Alexander I
wanted to exploit both the Greek and Russian Questions for his own
– Russia's – profit and he proceeded as far as it was safe for him to
do so; the main reason he did not start a war was not his attachment
to Europe and the Alliance but as Korina Kagan correctly empha-
sises, his fear of revolution,[91] and in particular his apprehension of
the hostile reaction of other Great Powers to Russia's eventual unilateral warlike measures against the Ottoman Empire, in other words
his fear of the creation of a powerful anti-Russian coalition difficult to
beat. Knowledge of the problems in his own army[92] and the expected
resistance of some members of the Alliance to Russia's belligerence
seemed to be the main reasons for his "discreet imperialism" in the
Near East that still destabilised peace in that region as well as the
functioning of the Alliance.

Since Metternich above all wanted to preserve peace, he emphatically supported the tsar in his demands concerning the Turks' violation of Russo-Ottoman treaties and, for the sake of peace, he was
even prepared to support the Russian point of view when it was in
contravention of treaty stipulations. This support was carried out at
the cost of Austria's influence in Constantinople in the early 1820s,
and Metternich can hardly be held responsible for the length of time
it took for the Russian demands to be accepted by the Turks. In the
Greek Question he actually did not change his fundamental attitude
towards insurrections anywhere: he always sided with the legitimate
ruler and denounced the activities of the insurgents. He never ceased
to declare that respect for the sultan's sovereignty was a basis of Austria's foreign policy and that the empire would never participate in a
move containing coercive measures against the Ottoman ruler. He was
not an advocate of intervention in and of itself, but he approved of
intervention in support of a legitimate power and with its consent as
was done in the Apennines. Consequently, it is impossible to see any
change in his attitudes towards revolutions when he was not willing to
intervene in Greece against Mahmud II's will. He would have agreed if

---

[91] K. Kagan, "The Myth of the European Concert: The Realist-Institutionalist
Debate and Great Power Behaviour in the Eastern Question, 1821–41," *Security
Studies* 7, 1997/98, 2, p. 27.
[92] Bitis, p. 115.

the intervention had been requested by the sultan and aimed against the insurgents.

Eberhard Schütz unfortunately did not clearly state which part of the Czernowitz gentlemen's agreement Metternich violated with his conduct. Metternich promised to negotiate, and he did so. He declared that he sought a prompt solution of the Greek affairs, and it was true, but he in no way desired the Russian method of settlement, which was also rejected by the other European Powers. He wanted to use the conference in St Petersburg to defend the attitude not only of Austria but also of the other Great Powers – all of them disagreed with the January *Mémoire*, whereas Alexander I wanted to force through his own plan corresponding to purely Russia's interests. Metternich was definitely guilty of using delaying tactics and expressing opinions that gave the impression that Austria might accept the settlement according to this *Mémoire*, but it is a question whether or not this was a form of deception or mere diplomacy. Moreover, even after January 1824 Metternich continued to state that the use of coercive measures and actions violating Ottoman sovereignty were inadmissible for him. The Russo-Austrian conflict thus resembled a collision of two ships whose captains first sail in the same direction but then one of them suddenly changes course, crossing the path of the second ship with the tragic but inevitable consequence. The captain of the second vessel is merely responsible for not changing from the original course and for not blowing the ship's horn loudly enough. Metternich was the latter. In conclusion, the accusations raised against his conduct towards Russia in the Near East from 1821 to 1825 were often excessive or entirely unsubstantial, and the arguments used by Metternich against those charges must be regarded as more reasonable and of course more well founded than the grievances of the Russians, including Alexander I and Nesselrode, who often desired to increase their own influence over the Ottoman Empire regardless of the justification of their wishes.

The War Scare in the Last Days of Alexander I's Reign

The disaffection of the Russian cabinet after the failure of the trilateral negotiations prevented Metternich from influencing them further. What remained to him was to show his goodwill by supporting Russia in Constantinople, where his influence was considerably greater. In the early summer of 1825, the Greek Question was put aside and the Russian Question gained importance again, namely the problem of the Beshli-Agas in the Principalities. Since their powers had increased and the method of their selection had changed since 1821, Alexander I argued that the status quo in Moldavia and Wallachia was not restored and requested their removal. Metternich promptly realised that a refusal could serve as a pretext for war more easily than ever before and pressed upon the Porte to comply with the tsar's wish; he considered this concession as insignificant for the Porte but very important for saving peace and he tried to frighten the Turks into compliance with the eventuality of war: "The personal situation of the [Russian] monarch is pitiable; for more than four years he has been struggling with Russian national sentiment that, rightly or wrongly – the fact changes nothing in the matter – is decidedly anti-Ottoman. Even a powerful prince can finally become weary of a struggle that is definitely honourable, but also exhausting if protracted. Everything consequently points towards a rupture with the Porte; this can be based on Russian matters. Does the Porte want to argue about the legality of its refusals? Cannon could be the response to this discussion."[93] In a secret addendum for Ottenfels Metternich merely added: "Unless the Divan has been reduced to absolute stupidity, it must understand us! What is necessary to achieve is to deprive the Russian faction of a means that it often uses itself: to represent to the emperor his own situation as humiliating. Are the Beshli-Agas worth the survival of the Ottoman power in Europe?"[94] The subsequent manoeuvring in Constantinople followed the same pattern as in the preceding years: the internuncio urging and arguing and the Porte strictly refusing to comply for several months, but finally yielding after Ottenfels' categorical note from 26 September in which he exhorted the Porte to comply with the request because the Austrian emperor would consider it as a proof of friendship towards him. This move prepared by Metternich with the aim of saving the sultan's face met with success on 4 October when Ottenfels was informed about the withdrawal of the Beshli-Agas; it did not take a long time to carry out.[95]

---

[93] Metternich to Ottenfels, Pressburg, 30 Sept. 1825, HHStA, StA, Türkei VI, 24.
[94] Ibid.
[95] Ottenfels to Metternich, Constantinople, 25 June, 10 Aug., 10 and 30 Sept., 5,

This achievement arrived at the moment when the European cabinets were occupied with the dilemma of the tsar's further behaviour towards the Ottoman Empire; to many the war in the Near East seemed to be imminent once again. A considerable number of historians have been of the opinion that Alexander I decided to go to war in the spring of 1826, but they have only offered theories instead of convincing evidence, and even that presented by Alexander Bitis in his fundamental book is far from persuasive.[96] On the other hand, the authoritative scholar on the topic, German historian Theodor Schiemann, frankly stated that he did not know whether Alexander I decided on war towards the end of his life, and American historian Irby C. Nichols has presented reasonable arguments against the theory of the tsar's alleged belligerency.[97] Metternich shared these doubts. He agreed that some danger existed but he found its source in the warlike sentiments of the Russian society and not in the tsar himself in whose moderation he always trusted. Just on the turn of September and October Metternich's peace of mind somehow diminished and he declared to Lebzeltern that "we have finally arrived at a period of crisis."[98] The reason was the Porte's determination in the Beshli-Agas' affair, but even at that time he did not abandon himself to the general panic, and the words uttered to Lebzeltern were the most far-reaching expression of concern in 1825 he ever spoke; the warnings sent to Constantinople and quoted above were intentionally exaggerated with the aim of encouraging the Turks to retreat. When this happened and the reassuring reports from Lebzeltern arrived in Vienna, Metternich's

---

11 and 25 Oct., 17. Dec. 1825, Ottenfels' note to the Porte, 26 Sept. 1825, Ottenfels to Lebzeltern, 5 Oct. 1825, HHStA, StA, Türkei VI, 23; Metternich to Ottenfels, Milan, 26 May 1825, Vienna, 4 and 15 Sept., 19 Oct. 1825, Pressburg, 2 Nov. 1825, HHStA, StA, Türkei VI, 24; Metternich to Vincent, Vienna, 2 Sept. and 20 Oct. 1825, HHStA, StA, Frankreich 257; Miltitz to Frederick William III, 5 and 25 Oct. 1825, GStA PK, HA III, MdA I, 7261; Maltzan to Frederick William III, Vienna, 18 Oct. 1825, GStA PK, HA III, MdA I, 6005; Wellesley to Canning, Vienna, 10 Aug. 1825, TNA, FO 120/70; Caraman to Damas, Vienna, 5 Sept. 1825, AMAE, CP, Autriche 406.

[96] Bitis, pp. 164–165; see also H. Temperley, *The Foreign Policy of Canning, 1822–27: England, the Neo-Holy Alliance, and the New World*, London 1966, p. 348.

[97] I. C. Nichols, "Tsar Alexander I: Pacifist, Aggressor, or Vacillator?," *EEQ* 16, 1982, 1, pp. 33–44; Schiemann, I, pp. 350–351.

[98] Metternich to Lebzeltern, Vienna, 6 Oct. 1825, Mikhaïlowitch, p. 312.

confidence constantly increased. Consequently, his convincing declarations about the preservation of peace – rather surprising and hard
to believe for the French, British and Prussian diplomats – were not
that far from his personal opinions.[99] One of the foreign diplomats,
an experienced Prussian envoy, Prince Franz Ludwig von Hatzfeldt-
Trachenberg, wrote to his king in late October: "The prince knows
how much the Russian emperor is personally dissatisfied with him at
this moment and that it is the Austrian cabinet that he particularly
accuses of having influenced Prussia and France to its opinion; he
is aware how much the Russian party [the Russians advocating the
war with the Porte as Russia's interest], inspired by an ill-intentioned
honour, seeks war and seeks to harm him by convincing the emperor
that the prince assures all cabinets that he [Alexander I] will never
have the courage to make the smallest demonstration of opposition,
but I did not find him [Metternich] to be either more alarmed or more
affected by this."[100]

*   *   *

The definite answer to Alexander I's real goals was never given because he suddenly died in Taganrog on 1 December 1825. For Metternich, who continued to ponder over the deceased monarch's designs
and believe that they were peaceful, there now arose a new problem
concerning the intentions of his successor's views, and what made
forming an opinion more difficult was the uncertainty over which of
Alexander I's brothers would succeed to the throne, the elder Constantine or the younger Nicholas. Metternich significantly preferred

[99] Metternich to Vincent, Ischl, 17 Aug. 1825, Vienna, 2 and 12 Sept., 10 Dec.
1825, HHStA, StA, Frankreich 257; Metternich to Ottenfels, Vienna, 11 Dec. 1825,
HHStA, StA, Türkei VI, 24; Schwebel to Damas, Vienna, 21 Aug. 1825, Caraman
to Damas, Vienna, 2, 12 and 23 Sept., 6 Oct., 15 Nov. and 12 Dec. 1825, AMAE,
CP, Autriche 406; Maltzan to Frederick William III, Vienna, 25 Aug. 1825, GStA
PK, HA III, MdA I, 6005; Wellesley to Canning, Vienna, 22 Nov. 1825, TNA, FO
120/72; Wellesley to Canning, Vienna, 5 Dec. 1825, TNA, FO 120/73; Gentz to
Ghica, Vienna, 28 Aug. 1825, DI, III, p. 26; Metternich to Gentz, Ischl, 13 July
1825, Prokesch-Osten, Zur Geschichte der orientalischen Frage, p. 72.
[100] Hatzfeldt to Frederick William III, Vienna, 25 Oct. 1825, GStA PK, HA III,
MdA I, 6005.

the former because he was convinced of Constantine's anti-Greek and peaceful sentiments and pro-Austrian sympathies. Although the last assumption is hard to prove, the others were entirely well founded and it is certain that Grand Duke Constantine Pavlovich did not favour war with the Ottoman Empire. With regard to Nicholas, the chancellor was unable to come to any conclusion because he did not know the views of the young czarevich who was at that time 29 years old. In the event of Nicholas' accession to power it was, as Metternich wrote to Ottenfels, "impossible to make any predictions about the new reign."[101] Moreover, Metternich worried that Nicholas could be influenced by his youth to go to war.[102] He was convinced regardless of the name of the new Russian monarch that, first, the Porte had to be prepared to please any tsar because otherwise it would be "Goodbye to the Alliance!"[103] and, second, that Austria's policy would be the same, unchanged by Alexander I's death: "What we thought or wanted yesterday we think and want today and we will want it tomorrow."[104]

---

[101] Metternich to Ottenfels, Vienna, 18 Dec. 1825, HHStA, StA, Türkei VI, 24.
[102] Ibid.; Metternich to Zichy, Vienna, 31 Dec. 1825, HHStA, StK, Preussen 121; Caraman to Damas, Vienna, 14 and 20 Dec. 1825, AMAE, CP, Autriche 406; Wellesley to Canning, Vienna, 17 Dec. 1825, TNA, FO 120/73; Wellesley to Canning, Vienna, 1 Jan. 1826, TNA, FO 120/75; Tatishchev to Nesselrode, Vienna, 12 Jan. 1826, AVPRI, fond 133, Kantseliariia, opis 468, 11870; Rendall, "Cosmopolitanism," p. 241.
[103] Krauter, p. 156.
[104] Metternich to Vincent, Vienna, 23 Dec. 1825, HHStA, StA, Frankreich 257.

4

George Canning and the St Petersburg Protocol

One of the reasons for the deterioration in Russo-Austrian relations in mid 1825 was the fact that Metternich could not count on British assistance. With Castlereagh's death, the close Austro-British relationship in Near Eastern affairs was gone. The new foreign secretary, George Canning, separated Great Britain from Austria and although he also wished to prevent a Russo-Ottoman war, he decided to achieve this goal in his own way corresponding more with his personal views and interests. He finally achieved both a great victory and a crushing defeat, the former when Alexander I repudiated Metternich, the latter when the St Petersburg Protocol was concluded. Historians have often claimed that the Protocol was not perfect but under the given conditions was the only means for preventing the outbreak of war in 1826. In reality it was Metternich's pressure in Constantinople and not Canning's blunder in St Petersburg that prevented it.

The Change in the British Greek Policy

George Canning was anything but an admirer of Metternich, whose role as the coachman of Europe he envied; he strongly disliked the chancellor and had no desire to cooperate with him. A strong personal animosity also existed on the side of Metternich. The affairs occupying the European cabinets after 1822 soon showed the differences in their opinions and increased their mutual distrust that with time developed into undisguised antipathy. Since the two men were united in the Near East with the wish to restrain Russia, Strangford was still instructed to cooperate with Ottenfels in persuading the Porte to accept Alexander I's requests resulting from the Russo-Ottoman treaty stipulations. In the Greek Question, however, the British and Austrian policies started to diverge early on. Contrary to Metternich's strict pro-Ottoman line, Canning began to adopt pro-Greek measures infringing the sultan's sovereign rights: he did not oppose the participation of British Philhellenes in the war on the Greeks' side, he supported the arrangement of the British loan to the Greek government in early 1824, and on 25 March of the previous year he acknowledged the Greek naval blockade of a part of the Turkish coast, which in effect meant a recognition of the insurgent Greeks as combatants. These actions were not the result of any exalted Philhellenism because Canning was not especially sympathetic to the Greeks, whom he even called "the most rascally set."[1] He did so to score political points in the British Isles where the pro-Greek sentiments were, as in Europe and the United States in general, on a high level and for the protection of British trade: the principle aim of the acknowledgement of the Greek blockade was to avert the attacks of the Greek pirates against British merchant vessels.[2]

Regardless of Canning's real motivation, these measures were highly deplored in Vienna where his Greek policy was regarded as entirely incalculable, bizarre and dangerous. Metternich would have liked the British government to take up the policy of Castlereagh, but this proved to be impossible because, as he wrote, "we unexpectedly find Mr Canning everywhere and ready to destroy everything!"[3] He blamed the foreign secretary for giving favours to the Philhellenes and thus the Greeks; the step he deplored most of all was the acknowledgement of the Greek blockade from March 1823. Nevertheless, the British attitude towards the insurgents did not become a serious topic of dispute between the two Great Powers until late 1824 when the administration of the Ionian Islands, at that time under British rule, started to manifest a strong pro-Greek bias. When, for example, the Greeks declared a blockade of the ports of Patras and Lepanto, the Lord High Commissioner of the Ionian Islands, Sir Frederick Adam, acknowledged the blockade as well as the right of Greek ships permitted by the provisional Greek government to search through cargoes of neutral merchant vessels and confiscate not only war contraband

---

[1]   Brewer, p. 252.
[2]   Ibid., p. 251; Bridge, p. 33; Cowles, p. 696; Crawley, *Greek Independence*, p. 27; Schroeder, *Transformation*, p. 639; Temperley, *Canning*, p. 326; Woodhouse, *The Greek War*, p. 103.
[3]   Metternich to Esterházy, Vienna, 7 July 1823, HHStA, StA, England 169.

but also other items belonging to the Turks. Metternich was against this measure because it was a further recognition of the Greek government and it relaxed the situation of the Greek pirates attacking Austrian merchant vessels. Austria could only acknowledge a blockade declared by the Porte, in other words by a legitimate authority. Consequently, Metternich formally protested against Adam's decision, which he found illogical not only from the point of view of international law but also from the point of view of common sense because Adam agreed with a blockade that the Greeks were unable to enforce in practice. The prince also remembered other examples of Adam's behaviour contradictory to both common practice and Austria's interests: on 17 September 1824, several Greek pirates were sentenced to prison but were released on 18 November and transported with their ship under the protection of a British corvette to Missolonghi; at the same time, a Greek ship that arrived at Corfu was suspected of an attack against an Austrian merchant vessel but was sent home on Adam's order under British protection.[4] In the second case an Austrian agent was given the unsatisfactory explanation that the administration of the Ionian Islands "had recommended to the Greek government to examine the affair and decide who was in the right."[5]

These incidents moved Metternich to lodge complaints and demand further explanations from the British cabinet, and some were offered. Adam's conduct was explained by the principle of neutrality maintained by Great Britain as a basis of its attitude towards the war between the Greeks and the Turks. Metternich was not at all satisfied with this reply and he answered that "it was the principle itself that was to blame because neutrality was only possible in the face of two warring parties having equal rights and that in a conflict between a sovereign authority and insurgent subjects one could be passive but

---

[4] Metternich to Esterházy, Vienna, 15 April, 7 and 8 July 1823, HHStA, StA, England 169; Metternich to Ottenfels, Vienna, 4 May 1823, HHStA, StA, Türkei VI, 19; Metternich to Ottenfels, Vienna, 19 July 1823, HHStA, StA, Türkei VI, 20; Metternich to Ottenfels, Vienna, 18 April and 18 Dec. 1824, HHStA, StA, Türkei VI, 22; Caraman to Damas, Vienna, 14 Dec. 1824, AMAE, CP, Autriche 405; Wellesley to Canning, Vienna, 16 Dec. 1824, TNA, FO 120/67; Gentz to Ottenfels, Vienna, 4 March 1823, Prokesch-Osten, *Zur Geschichte der orientalischen Frage*, p. 5; H. Schamesberger, *Canning und die Politik Metternichs*, unpublished dissertation, Wien 1972, pp. 29–40; Woodhouse, *Capodistria*, p. 297.
[5] Metternich to Lebzeltern, Vienna, 20 Dec. 1824, HHStA, StA, Russland III, 65.

not neutral."[6] Consequently, the only "neutrality" acknowledged by Austria was the abstention from any activities compromising international law: "If the leaders of an insurrection resort to acts which harm us but which we cannot prevent without resorting to conflict ourselves, prudence dictates that we should in no way answer them in a positive manner; but we will never condescend to legalise them with proclamations and decrees."[7] Metternich was particularly irritated because of Canning's remark that Adam's measures were necessary for the system of British neutrality from the period when the conflict between the Greeks and the Turks took on the form of a real war: "But who would dare to determine that point in time? What is the precise moment when the enterprises of an armed nation against its government acquire the status of a legal war? The Greek insurrection began with the wholesale massacre of Turks, the victims of its first fury. After this brutal start, it is true that it created voluntary units, flotillas and fire ships, that it organised the pillage of properties, the devastation of the coasts and all kinds of acts of piracy. But has it changed its nature? If it depended on a foreign power to determine the passage from a state of fury and violence to the state of a regular war, the most criminal insurrection would only have to put on some diplomatic and military forms for it to be able to count on protectors and allies. This would be to privilege in advance all the revolutions that these turbulent times can produce; because if soldiers and warships suffice for the establishment of revolutionary power equal in rights with that of the authority that has been rejected, there is no more stability for any government in the world, and social order everywhere will fall prey to the first rebel lucky enough to gather whatever support to usurp the title of a belligerent power!"[8]

The arguments sent from Vienna to London had no impact on the British conduct in the Greek Question. Despite this, Metternich raised them time to time in the following months, particularly in the autumn of 1825 when he again called to question the partiality of the administration of the Ionian Islands and the activities of the British

---

[6]   Caraman to Damas, Vienna, 12 Jan. 1825, AMAE, CP, Autriche 406.
[7]   *Les observations sur la dépêche de Mr. Canning à S. H. Wellesley du 31. décembre 1824, relative aux droits de guerre reconnus aux Grecs*, attached to Metternich to Lebzeltern, Vienna, 18 Feb. 1825, HHStA, StA, Russland III, 70.
[8]   Ibid.

Philhellenes in Greece, both negatively affecting Austrian commerce: "Seeing the damage to our trade, we thought it necessary to ask for the protection of different royal navies; that of Great Britain was denied to us in the name of neutrality and yet the captains of our merchant fleet meet so-called English agents who direct the pirates towards our vessels."[9] Nevertheless, all that he obtained from Canning were for Austria futile answers which finally moved him to end these pointless discussions.[10] He closed it with a complaint about the foreign secretary's sarcastic expression of satisfaction with the tone of Metternich's dispatches containing the objections: "I must declare that I believe that during the last years I have never written a paper more severe and less considered than our last intercession to the British cabinet."[11]

Another reason for Metternich's attack against the support granted to the Greeks by the British officials or individuals was its negative impact on Strangford's position in Constantinople, which became more and more precarious. This support or the mere toleration of the Greek uprising by the British government evoked the Porte's resentment and undermined the efforts of Strangford and Ottenfels to overcome the Turks' reluctance in the affairs directly touching Russia's interests. Consequently, Strangford's influence over the Turks was decreasing but despite his precarious position in Constantinople and the worsening in Austro-British relations, his relations with Metternich continued to be good and he remained the chancellor's useful ally. He was united with the prince by their joint opposition to Canning's conduct in the Greek affairs, and when he left his post in the autumn of 1824, it was to the dismay of the chancellor, which is clearly evident from Metternich's reaction to the replacement of Strangford by Canning's cousin, Stratford Canning. Ottenfels was instructed to behave cordially towards Stratford but not on terms of intimacy because "on the day when the new British ambassador arrives in Constantinople, there will be an Englishman there but no longer an ally."[12]

---

[9]   Metternich to Esterházy, Vienna, 8 Sept. 1825, HHStA, StA, England 173.
[10]   Metternich to Ottenfels, Vienna, 29 Jan. and 3 Dec. 1825, HHStA, StA, Türkei VI, 24; Wellesley to Canning, Vienna, 1 Sept. 1825, TNA, FO 120/71.
[11]   Metternich to Vincent, Vienna, 20 Oct. 1825, HHStA, StA, Frankreich 257.
[12]   Metternich to Ottenfels, Vienna, 3 Dec. 1825, HHStA, StA, Türkei VI, 24.

Canning's Contribution to the
Destruction of the Austro-Russian Alliance

Neither the general disagreement between Vienna and London nor their different conduct towards the insurgent Greeks changed anything in Metternich's belief in the necessity to proceed together for the preservation of peace in the Near East. He wished to cooperate with Canning and in August 1823 wrote to the Austrian ambassador in London, Prince Paul Anton Esterházy von Galantha: "The only issue on which it is important for us to frankly settle with England is the Near Eastern affair. It is at least fortunate that the conditions for attaining this goal seem to exist. It will thus be only these affairs into which Y[our] H[ighness] will enter discussions with Mr Canning."[13] Nevertheless, Canning firmly declined to cooperate with the continental Powers. For some time this aloofness had no serious consequences for Austria, but when it became evident in the autumn of 1824 that Metternich would soon have to declare his opinion on the Russian January *Mémoire*, British assistance was regarded in Vienna as necessary. What the chancellor actually wanted was Austro-British cooperation as practiced in 1821 and 1822 by himself and Castlereagh leading to Capodistria's fall and the restraint of Russia. Unfortunately for him, it was exactly what Canning did not want and why he remained apart from the negotiations in St Petersburg in the summer of 1824. Despite this "isolationism," Metternich hoped that the foreign secretary would change his negative attitude for the second round of the talks in the Russian capital; he stated to Wellesley that he found the Russian January plan impracticable but he did not want to directly oppose it because he would thus strengthen the war party that could be held in check only by the union of Austria and Great Britain. He pointed out that the interests of Austria and Great Britain with respect to Russia were identical and that the latter had no reason to be suspicious of the former's intentions. If the British cabinet refused, Metternich warned, the position of the war party would be strengthened.[14] The

---

[13] Metternich to Esterházy, Vienna, 11 Aug. 1823, HHStA, StA, England 169.
[14] Metternich to Esterházy, Vienna, 17 Oct. 1824, HHStA, StA, England 169; Wellesley to Canning, Vienna, 4 Oct. 1824, TNA, FO 120/66; Wellesley to Canning, Vienna, 3 and 16 Dec. 1824, TNA, FO 120/67; Hatzfeldt to Frederick William III, Vienna, 20 Oct. 1824, GStA PK, HA III, MdA I, 6004; Caraman to Damas, Vienna, 11 Nov. and 1 Dec. 1824, AMAE, CP, Autriche 405; Metternich to Werner, Vienna,

two Powers were to forget all their differences of opinion and cooperate to save the peace in the Levant: "We have consistently considered the matter of the pacification of the Levant in relation to its principal goal, that of maintaining the political peace in Europe needed by all governments and all nations. We regard every other consideration as secondary in comparison with so noble aim."[15]

These statements found no echo in London during late 1824, but Metternich did not give up and hoped to alter Canning's attitude through Stratford Canning, who was sent via Vienna to St Petersburg to observe the negotiations on the Greek Question without taking part in them. Canning's cousin arrived in Vienna on 22 December 1824 and met several times with Metternich, who strengthened his own opinion that "Canning wants the same thing that all of us want – to pacify Greece and prevent a war between Russia and the Turks, but he is not in agreement with the means."[16] He expressed his regret that Canning refused to take part in the conference and his wish that the minister would change his mind and authorise Stratford to participate. During their last meeting, Stratford asked Metternich what he considered possible to do for the Greeks, and the chancellor answered that "everything that will be able to assure their civil existence without attacking the principle of sovereignty."[17] When Stratford reacted with the statement that this was the same view of his government, Metternich immediately asked him if this was so, why it still refused to take part in the conference that had no other goal than this one, which was true from Austria's point of view because Metternich actually was not prepared to do more for the insurgents.[18] These talks led to no worthwhile conclusion, and none was possible since Stratford was not instructed to settle anything with the Viennese cabinet, something about which Metternich bitterly complained: "Mr Stratford Canning has failed here in all his objectives; he was not able to attain a single one of the goals which probably motivated his mission.

---

23 Oct. 1824, *NP*, IV, p. 140.

[15] Metternich to Esterházy, Vienna, 5 Dec. 1824, HHStA, StA, England 169.

[16] Caraman to Damas, Vienna, 22 Dec. 1824, AMAE, CP, Autriche 405.

[17] Caraman to Damas, Vienna, 31 Dec. 1824, AMAE, CP, Autriche 405.

[18] Hatzfeldt to Frederick William III, Vienna, 23 Dec. 1824, GStA PK, HA III, MdA I, 6004; Caraman to Damas, Vienna, 31 Dec. 1824, AMAE, CP, Autriche 405.

He failed because he had nothing reasonable to demand from or even
to object to in our decision-making. Why then was he sent to us?"[19]

How much Metternich desired a change in Canning's attitude is
proved by the fact that he continually asked Wellesley in the last
days of 1824 whether his arguments had managed to alter it in any
way.[20] Wellesley always replied to this question in the negative because despite the similarity of their aims in the Near East concerning Russia, Canning did not change his opinion. This naturally led
to Metternich's considerable displeasure.[21] He complained that Canning, "a scourge,"[22] wanted neither to cooperate nor to say what he
actually wanted and inveighed against him with his favourite verdict
that "indeed he does not know what he wants."[23] Nevertheless, in this
Metternich was mistaken because the foreign secretary was well aware
of his main desire: the destruction of the Russo-Austrian entente and
its replacement with an exclusive cooperation between Great Britain
and Russia. He was motivated by his hatred of the chancellor and his
desire to increase his own reputation and not remain apart from Greek
affairs. Therefore, he was not willing to participate in the St Petersburg conference because he presumed that if Austria was left alone
to face Russia, it would necessarily lead to a rift in their relations
and the conference would fail. He decided to use the Greek Question
for the destruction of the Alliance. As he later wrote: "By simply
keeping away [from the conference] we have left them to deal with
each other, and the consequence has been a collision which Metternich wished to avoid."[24] Stratford's presence in St Petersburg was an
important part of this game: it was to demonstrate to Alexander I
that he had an alternative to cooperation with the continental Powers. Although Stratford had to strictly avoid any participation in the
conference talks, he could bilaterally negotiate with the Russian cabinet. In March 1825, he asked Nesselrode to replace the conference on

---

[19] Metternich to Esterházy, Vienna, 10 Feb. 1825, HHStA, StA, England 173.
[20] Wellesley to Canning, Vienna, 29 Dec. 1824, TNA, FO 120/67.
[21] Metternich to Esterházy, Vienna, 1 Jan. 1825, HHStA, StA, England 173; Metternich to Ottenfels, Vienna, 6 Jan. 1825, HDA, 750, OO 37; Metternich to Ottenfels, Vienna, 29 Jan. 1825, HHStA, StA, Türkei VI, 24.
[22] Metternich to Esterházy, Vienna, 10 Feb. 1825, HHStA, StA, England 173.
[23] Hatzfeldt to Frederick William III, Vienna, 23 Dec. 1824, GStA PK, HA III,
MdA I, 6004.
[24] Dakin, p. 154.

Greece with a "frank and unreserved discussion"[25] with Great Britain only and declared that the government in London was prepared to diplomatically intervene in the Greek-Turkish contention; he did not stop trying to entice the Russians in the following months.[26]

At that very first moment, Alexander I had reservations about such an option, but after the failure of the conference he decided to take advantage of the hand offered by Canning and instructed Prince Lieven to probe into the British attitude towards the Greek Question. The answer was positive since the Russian ambassador reported in mid July that a British-Russian rapprochement on this issue was possible. Consequently, slightly later Princess Lieven left St Petersburg with secret information for Canning that the tsar was prepared to leave the continental Powers and cooperate with Great Britain. When Alexander I died, the discussions were already in progress in London. Nesselrode, Lieven and Pozzo planned on getting the British cabinet on their side and assuring its support for their policy in the Near East or at least its neutrality in the event of Russia's war with the Ottoman Empire.[27] Therefore, they had no reason to reconcile with Metternich, who was thus forced to react towards the rift between Austria and Russia with attempts to reach an understanding with Canning during the second half of 1825. He sent tentative suggestions to London about the Austro-British cooperation in Near Eastern affairs as well as warnings against their disunion, but again these offers were fruitless despite the fact that Canning's aim was exactly the same as Metternich's: to protract negotiations with the Russian cabinet and prevent the outbreak of a Russo-Ottoman war.[28] In March 1826 Canning wrote to Wellesley: "We are working in the sense of Austria – though not in concert with her – and if not in concert, only because we had reason to believe ... that our best chance of success

---

[25]   Bitis, p. 171.
[26]   Cowles, pp. 697–698; Nichols, *The European Pentarchy*, p. 257; Temperley, *Canning*, p. 335.
[27]   Bitis, p. 172; Brewer, pp. 253–254; Schroeder, *Transformation*, pp. 640–643; Schütz, pp. 115–120; Temperley, *Canning*, p. 351.
[28]   Metternich to Esterházy, Ischl, 7 Aug. 1825, HHStA, StA, England 173; Wellesley to Canning, Vienna, 19 Oct. 1825, TNA, FO 120/72; Caraman to Damas, Vienna, 19 Oct. and 15 Nov. 1825, AMAE, CP, Autriche 406; M. Günther, *Das Verhalten Englands und Österreichs zum griechischen Aufstand in den Jahren 1821–1827*, unpublished dissertation, Wien 1957, p. 84.

in pursuit of a common object, was to pursue alone ... Our object, however, is, you may assure Prince Metternich, a common object."[29]

The Accession of Nicholas I and the Origins of the St Petersburg Protocol

The news of Alexander I's death posed in European cabinets an important question on the further direction of Russia's policy. The first news from St Petersburg was not pleasant for Austria: the Decembrist Revolt, the accession of Nicholas I being a less welcome possibility for Metternich and the untenable position of Lebzeltern owing to the latest events. The short episode of the Decembrist uprising fatally touched the Austrian ambassador when one of its leaders and Lebzeltern's brother-in-law, Prince Sergei Trubetzkoi, fled after the defeat to the Austrian embassy. Although he was released and Lebzeltern had nothing to do with the plot, his situation became highly precarious. Metternich trusted him and his qualities, but he was finally moved to recall him because Lebzeltern essentially became a persona non grata. He left St Petersburg in June 1826. His worsening situation within Russian high society and his departure occurred at a rather critical moment for Austria's diplomacy and had a negative impact on it in the future. Metternich lacked a skilled diplomat and excellent observer, something for which the chancellor became responsible himself since he was unable or unwilling to find a suitable candidate for this post until 1829.[30]

On the other hand, the Decembrist Revolt raised Metternich's hopes that after the turbulent events at the beginning of his reign, Nicholas I would be considerably hostile to conspiracies and revolutions including those in Greece. The chancellor wrote in this sense to Esterházy in early 1826: "Emperor Nicholas has just received a lesson that he will not be able to forget."[31] He claimed that it was absolutely impossible that Nicholas I would wage a war "in the interest

---

[29] Bitis, p. 171.

[30] Metternich to Victor, Vienna, 27 Jan. 1826, NA, RAM-AC 12, 2; Robech, pp. 467–468; Sauvigny, *Staatsmann und Diplomat*, p. 426.

[31] Metternich to Esterházy, Vienna, 8 Jan. 1826, HHStA, StA, England 175.

of the insurgent Greeks; such a war, an enterprise for a revolutionary principle by an army so infected with a revolutionary spirit as the Russian army unfortunately has been for some time, could have at the moment of peace no other result than a revolution at home."[32] The tsar's unconcern for the Greeks' fate was soon proved to Metternich through two main information channels. The first one was Ribeaupierre, still absent from Constantinople where he was destined to assume the directorship of the embassy. Instead of the Ottoman capital, he was sent by the new Russian monarch for a brief visit to Vienna, where he stayed from 17 January to 12 February 1826. He had several long conferences with Metternich and an audience with the emperor in which he was assured of their assistance to the tsar with whatever he needed for the pacification of Greece except war or anything that could lead to it, which meant coercive measures. They insisted on the preservation of the sultan's sovereignty, the improvement of the Greeks' situation within the legal system and the strict separation of the Greek from the Russian Question. The objections to the plan of 21 January 1824 were repeated. Metternich explained that they had refused what Alexander I had suggested to them in the St Petersburg conference because "what was proposed to us legalised war and emancipation."[33] Although nothing had changed in the attitude of Austria since the St Petersburg conference, Ribeaupierre was content with the communications of the Viennese cabinet, and Metternich felt the same satisfaction.[34] Already after the first several meetings in January, the chancellor came to these conclusions: "(1) It was demonstrated to me that Emperor Nicholas feels an urgent necessity to terminate the odious affair of the Levant; (2) He in no way regards the chance to interfere with the affair as a course admissible for him; (3) He desires to hold firm to the principles which since their origin have served as the point of departure and arrival to the courts, desiring the maintenance of peace and the submission of the Greeks to

[32] Hatzfeldt to Frederick William III, Vienna, 25 Jan. 1826, GStA PK, HA III, MdA I, 6006.

[33] Metternich to Lebzeltern, Vienna, 14 Feb. 1826, HHStA, StA, Russland III, 75.

[34] Tatishchev to Nesselrode, Vienna, 12 and 18 Jan., 6 Feb. 1826, AVPRI, fond 133, Kantseliariia, opis 468, 11870; Hatzfeldt to Frederick William III, Vienna, 15 Jan. and 11 Feb. 1826, GStA PK, HA III, MdA I, 6006; Caraman to Damas, Vienna, 26 Jan. and 11 Feb. 1826, AMAE, CP, Autriche 407.

the regime capable of assuring their civil existence and not infringing upon the sovereign rights of the Porte."[35]

The second and more significant source of information was Archduke Ferdinand d'Este, the son of Archduchess Beatrix, who was sent by Francis I to St Petersburg to congratulate the new tsar on his accession to power and naturally on the suppression of the Decembrist Revolt.[36] Ferdinand stayed in St Petersburg from 30 January to 2 March and he was treated cordially. Since the very beginning, what Nicholas I told him was entirely in line with the statements made by Ribeaupierre in Vienna and completely compatible with the views of the Viennese cabinet. The tsar assured the archduke of his determination to adhere strictly to the principles of the Alliance and proceed with its members. When Ferdinand asked him about the Greeks, Nicholas I answered that they were for him mere rebels and he felt in no way inclined to wage a war on their behalf because he had to pay too much attention to his own affairs and, calling upon God as his witness, that he did not want to wage war at all. He made several statements to Ferdinand in this sense: "I am offered projects for conquest, but I have more than enough to do within my own borders without having to think about what to do outside them."[37] In the early phase of Ferdinand's visit, however, Nicholas added to his pledge to act in union with other Great Powers that if it did not work, he was prepared to act alone: "It is necessary to settle the matter. If agreement cannot be reached on the subject, let me deal with it alone; I have sufficient means and I will be well able to finish it with those rogues [the Turks]."[38] But after Ribeaupierre's return from Vienna this statement was never mentioned again and it can be assumed that what Metternich and Francis I told the Russian diplomat satisfied the young tsar.[39] Nicholas I told a French ambassador that he would not

---

[35] Metternich to Apponyi, Vienna, 27 Jan. 1826, HHStA, StA, Frankreich 260.
[36] As for Lebzeltern, his personally difficult position in St Petersburg prevented him from being a direct information channel for the tsar's opinions. His information about the Russian monarch's desire for peace was only second hand. Lebzeltern to Metternich, St Petersburg, 4 Feb. 1826, HHStA, StA, Russland III, 73.
[37] Caraman to Damas, Vienna, 13 March 1826, AMAE, CP, Autriche 407.
[38] Lebzeltern to Metternich, St Petersburg, 2 March 1826, HHStA, StA, Russland III, 73.
[39] Metternich to Zichy, Vienna, 24 and 31 Dec. 1825, HHStA, StK, Preussen 121; Metternich to Ottenfels, Vienna, 4 Jan. 1826, HHStA, StA, Türkei VI, 24; Metternich to Apponyi, Vienna, 20 Feb. 1826, HHStA, StA, Frankreich 260; Metternich

act until previous agreement was reached with his allies and said to Ferdinand: "I myself do not call them Greeks – I call them rebels, and I would never lend assistance to such as them; I have no right to do that. I have Moslem subjects, much like Your Emperor has Greek subjects; if my Turkish subjects were to revolt and the Porte wanted to prevent me from bringing them to justice, I would definitely be as angry and with as much justification as Your Emperor would be if I wanted to ally myself similarly with his Greek subjects."[40] And he added his desire to settle the matter of the disputes directly affecting Russo-Ottoman relations, peaceably if possible, but "if against my wishes this goes to extremes, *the issue of the insurgents will never interfere with my transactions with the Ottoman Porte.*"[41] One of the archduke's companions came to the logical conclusion that the young tsar "seemed to want to entirely *put aside the Greeks, who are nothing other than rebels*; he seemed to want to restrict the question *to the Russo-Turkish* matter and make a point of settling his disputes with the Porte without confusing it with the Greek cause."[42]

The long and intimate discussions between Nicholas I and Ferdinand in St Petersburg as well as those with Ribeaupierre in Vienna led Metternich to the belief that Nicholas I had no sympathy for the Greeks, did not want to support them, and did not wish to wage war with the Ottoman Empire. The prince already shared this confidence with Francis I in early March. The former declared that "everything seems to prove that the young monarch combines great intellect, a degree of wisdom and strong determination ... Everything in the personality of the monarch satisfies us."[43] Francis I proclaimed the happy and indestructible union of the two conservative Powers. This optimism increased when the news of the positive impact of Ribeaupierre's mission in Vienna as well as of Archduke Ferdinand's stay in St Peters-

---

to Lebzeltern, Vienna, 22 Feb. 1826, HHStA, StA, Russland III, 75; Wellesley to Canning, Vienna, 1 Jan. and 24 Feb. 1826, TNA, FO 120/75; Gise to Ludwig I of Bavaria, St Petersburg, 8 and 20 March 1826, BHStA, MA, Petersburg 2714; Gentz to Ghica, Vienna, 16 March 1826, *DI*, III, p. 102; Lebzeltern to Metternich, 11 Feb. 1826, Prokesch-Osten, *Griechen*, IV, p. 216; Schiemann, II, pp. 111–112.

[40] Lebzeltern to Metternich, St Petersburg, 2 March 1826, HHStA, StA, Russland III, 73.

[41] Ibid.

[42] Clam to Metternich, St Petersburg, 2 March 1826, Prokesch-Osten, *Griechen*, IV, p. 219.

[43] Metternich to Esterházy, Vienna, 2 March 1826, HHStA, StA, England 175.

burg on the tsar reached Vienna. Metternich felt much more confident
now that Nicholas I wanted to solve his own affairs with the sultan
alone but the Greek insurrection with his allies: "It appears to us to
have been proved that Emperor N[icholas] is endowed with a positive
outlook, and future experience will show us whether the spirit of his
character will live up to this first and fortunate impression. Supposing that this is effectively the case, the emperor will have to rid the
Eastern affair of a host of misconceptions, erroneous and groundless
assumptions, pretexts directed to the support of interests which are
alien to it and which, for six years have done nothing but complicate
the issue ... From this moment Emp[eror] N[icholas] has found himself in a position that our thoughts have occupied since the beginning
of this matter, a position that we have never abandoned but that we
could in no way cultivate alone or according to our will."[44] Metternich
was so optimistic that he even expected that the first messenger from
St Petersburg would bring news of the revival of the conference on
the Greek Question.[45]

Metternich's optimism after Ribeaupierre's and Ferdinand's missions was quite well founded. Nicholas I was actually greatly affected
by the Decembrist Revolt that haunted him for the rest of his life. He
also disliked the insurgent Greeks and did not want to wage war on
behalf of their interests because he worried about the eventual negative consequences for his army and his regime. Moreover, he did not
desire their independence, which would be almost certainly the logical
outcome of a Russo-Ottoman conflict. His primary interest did not lie
in Greece but, as in the case of his predecessor, in the Principalities,
Serbia and the Caucasus. Consequently, on 17 March 1826 Nicholas I
dispatched an ultimatum to Constantinople with the demands concerning Serbia, the Principalities and the Treaty of Bucharest, the

---

[44] Metternich to Lebzeltern, Vienna, 27 March 1826, HHStA, StA, Russland III,
75.
[45] Metternich to Apponyi, Vienna, 27 March 1826, HHStA, StA, Frankreich 260;
Metternich to Tatishchev, Vienna, 2 March 1826, Tatishchev to Nesselrode, Vienna,
4 and 26 March 1826, AVPRI, fond 133, Kantseliariia, opis 468, 11870; Caraman
to Damas, Vienna, 19 Feb., 7 and 22 March, 2 April 1826, AMAE, CP, Autriche
407; Wellesley to Canning, Vienna, 16 March 1826, TNA, FO 120/76; Hatzfeldt to
Frederick William III, Vienna, 3 and 5 April 1826, GStA PK, HA III, MdA I, 6006;
Gentz, *Tableau politique de la Russie relativement aux affaires de la Turquie et de
la Grèce*, 4 March 1826, NA, RAM-AC 5, 3; Gentz to Ghica, Vienna, 26 March
1826, *DI*, III, p. 108.

conditions of which were to be discussed on Russian soil where Turk-ish negotiators were to be sent. Mahmud II had six weeks to accept it, otherwise Minciaky and the whole Russian legation was to leave Con-stantinople.[46] The ultimatum was presented to the Porte on 5 April and Ottenfels did not hide his alarm about the Ottoman government's reluctance to comply: "Ottoman pride and tenacity will firmly with-stand all attacks which will be made simultaneously from all sides, and it can be foreseen that far from submitting out of necessity, the Divan will find it difficult to submit to any steps to comply in the foolish belief that what it calls its right must be the general rule for all European cabinets; it will keep up its opposition to such an extent that it will become necessary to use much more vigorous language than for giving mere advice in order to obtain from them anything more than illusory concessions."[47]

The existence of the ultimatum raised Metternich's concerns, but they did not arise from the tsar's designs but from the ominous con-sequences should the sultan refuse. The chancellor expressed his sat-isfaction with the measure undertaken by the Russian monarch, and he was quite sincere in this statement since he was pleased that the ultimatum dealt with only the Russian Question leaving the Greeks unmentioned. Although the chancellor was not informed about its existence in advance, he could hardly be entirely surprised by the step since Nicholas I had told Archduke Ferdinand that he was go-ing to focus on the settlement of the affairs directly affecting Russo-Ottoman interests. The ultimatum strengthened Metternich's earlier strong conviction that the tsar actually saw the two questions as two separate issues and had no desire to interfere with Greek affairs, and the chancellor understood the measure as a desire to get out of the difficult situation that the tsar had inherited from his predecessor. What the Viennese cabinet had learnt of Nicholas I's personal views from St Petersburg in previous weeks seemed to be confirmed by his actions and Metternich had thus no reason to change his opinion that

---

[46] B. Kondis, "Aspects of Anglo-Russian Rivalry during the Greek Revolution," *Les relations gréco-russes pendant la domination turque et la guerre d'indépendance grecque*, Thessaloniki 1983, pp. 115–116; Cowles, p. 700; Crawley, *Greek Indepen-dence*, p. 58; Dakin, p. 178; Nichols, "Tsar Alexander I," p. 40; Schroeder, *Trans-formation*, pp. 644–645.

[47] Ottenfels to Metternich, Constantinople, 7 April 1826, HHStA, StA, Türkei VI, 25.

the tsar was anxious to preserve peace: "Does the emperor believe that he would serve his position and his interests by throwing himself into the problems of war? We frankly declare that we do not believe that this would be his intention and we even consider ourselves authorised to call into doubt every such supposition because his explanations to us (and until now they have not deviated at all) have furnished us with nothing other than proof of his wisdom and judgement as correct as it is reasonable."[48] Consequently, the chancellor did not hesitate to support the acceptance of the ultimatum, the conditions of which he found acceptable and, moreover, the non-acceptance of which would undoubtedly result in war.[49]

Austria continued in the policy that it had pursued since 1821 despite Alexander I's death which, as Ottenfels warned the Porte, changed nothing in its situation as it was vitally important for the sultan to satisfy either of the Russian monarchs. In late March 1826, Metternich confirmed this policy: "As far as our present action is concerned, it is restricted to advising the Porte to comply to the utmost with its powerful neighbour."[50] The instructions to Ottenfels from 14 April were arranged in the same sense and the internuncio was to convey Francis I's recommendation to the reis effendi to accept the ultimatum: "Having carefully considered the initiative that the Imperial Majesty of All the Russias has made to the Porte, the evident advantages which are offered to the Ottoman government under its terms, and the serious dangers which would immediately result from a refusal given in the present circumstances, His Majesty Emperor [Francis I] believes he is fulfilling one of the primary duties of friendship and good neighbourliness to the sultan by giving to His Highness in his full and entire conviction the counsel to satisfy the proposals of His Majesty the Emperor of Russia and to nominate the plenipotentiaries charged with dealing and settling with those of the Russian court all the direct

---

[48] Metternich to Ottenfels, Vienna, 14 April 1826, HHStA, StA, Türkei VI, 24.
[49] Metternich to Lebzeltern, Vienna, 17 April 1826, HHStA, StA, Russland III, 75; Metternich to Esterházy, Vienna, 21 April 1826, HHStA, StA, England 175; Metternich to Apponyi, Vienna, 21 April 1826, HHStA, StA, Frankreich 260; Hatzfeldt to Frederick William III, Vienna, 15 and 22 April 1826, GStA PK, HA III, MdA I, 6006; Tatishchev to Nesselrode, Vienna, 15 April 1826, AVPRI, fond 133, Kantseliariia, opis 468, 11870; Wellesley to Canning, Vienna, 18 April 1826, TNA, FO 120/76.
[50] Metternich to Apponyi, Vienna, 27 March 1826, HHStA, StA, Frankreich 260.

controversies [existing] between the two empires since 1812."[51] Such
an outcome could lay the basis for stable and peaceful relations, and
the Viennese cabinet therefore hoped that Mahmud II would not hesitate to make the best of the given situation, in particular when only
a positive answer from the Porte could avoid war: "War with Russia
will be inevitable if it refuses the proposals which it [Russia] has addressed to it. This Great Power is prepared for war, the Porte is not;
the generals commanding the southern armies have been summoned
to St Petersburg, [and] once the Russian army is on the move, who
will prevent it from taking possession of the bank of the Danube and
who will expel it afterwards from the Principalities, who will prevent
the immediate Serbian insurrection, the repetition of the revolution
in the Morea [the Peloponnese] with an entirely new force, the arrival
of a host of adventurers and assistance of all kinds in these desolate
lands?"[52] Metternich summarised the sentiment of the day in several
words: "In Constantinople today it is not a matter of objections, it is
a matter of survival."[53] Furthermore, Metternich assured the Porte of
the tsar's peaceful designs, and he did so again five days later when
he personally guaranteed "that the most resolute opinions and intentions in favour of not only maintaining peace with the Porte but
also establishing better neighbourly relations with it are what drives
Emperor Nicholas, and that the plan for an agreement drafted by this
monarch and proposed by Mr Minciaky and supported by us is the result of these two desires so fortunately found in the Russian monarch.
I would even go so far as to say that war will inevitably take place if
the sultan refuses the demands of H[is] I[mperial] M[ajesty] of Russia,
that nothing will be able to prevent it."[54] Ottenfels did his best to
fulfil Metternich's instructions and the sultan, after some hesitation,
finally gave in and accepted the ultimatum in early May. According
to Ottenfels, this decision was a direct result of Austria's diplomatic
pressure, as he wrote to Metternich: "Once Austria raised its voice,
the Porte immediately ceded. It is Your Highness who has decided the
victory and the world will acknowledge it."[55] And he confirmed this

---

[51] Metternich to Ottenfels, Vienna, 14 April 1826, HHStA, StA, Türkei VI, 24.
[52] Ibid.
[53] Ibid.
[54] Metternich to Ottenfels, Vienna, 19 April 1826, HHStA, StA, Türkei VI, 24.
[55] Ottenfels to Metternich, Constantinople, 5 May 1826, HHStA, StA, Türkei VI,
25.

in his letter to Gentz: "As long as Prince Metternich did not speak, the Porte did not move a finger or open its mouth. As soon as I presented a note in the name of our court, a consultation took place with the mufti the same evening and the decision was made to consent to the Russian demands."[56] Ottenfels still held this opinion many years later when he repeated it in his memoirs and although it is difficult to confirm this somewhat boastful claim, the positive impact of Austria's diplomacy is quite probable and Metternich actually seemed to contribute to preventing war.[57]

Metternich's satisfaction with the news from Constantinople was overshadowed by the account from St Petersburg concerning an event that occurred in early April, and it actually was Canning who was responsible for it.[58] Whereas the Austrian chancellor was fairly confident on the turn of 1825 and 1826 that Russia would not go to war, and almost entirely sure in the early spring of 1826, Canning's fear that Alexander I or his successor were willing to wage war against the Ottoman Empire was more significant. This was partly due to the Lievens' deliberate warnings of open hostility. To ascertain the plans of Nicholas I and confirm or refute his willingness to go to war, Canning sent the Duke of Wellington to St Petersburg in February 1826 under the same pretext as Archduke Ferdinand had been sent earlier in the year by Francis I: to congratulate the new tsar on his accession to the throne. The duke arrived in St Petersburg on the day of Ferdinand's departure on 2 March, but in contrast to the archduke, he was instructed to go much further and coordinate the united British-Russian intervention into Greek affairs and settle them with the creation of a Greek autonomous state within the sultan's suzerainty. The principal goal of this manoeuvre was to restrain Nicholas I from going to war. The negotiations between Canning and Lieven were thus to be transferred from London to St Petersburg, but at their beginning, Wellington, expecting that the pacification of the Greeks was of the

---

[56] Ottenfels to Gentz, Constantinople, 10 May 1826, Prokesch-Osten, *Zur Geschichte der orientalischen Frage*, p. 131.

[57] Ottenfels to Metternich, Constantinople, 25 April, 5, 10, 17 and 26 May 1826, Ottenfels' note to the Porte, 28 April 1826, Klezl to Ottenfels, 5 May 1826, HHStA, StA, Türkei VI, 25; Miltitz to Frederick William III, Pera, 5, 17 and 26 May 1826, GStA PK, HA III, MdA I, 7262; Ottenfels, *Memoari*, p. 161.

[58] See the quotation at the beginning of this chapter, Metternich to Esterházy, Vienna, 7 July 1823, HHStA, StA, England 169.

utmost importance for the tsar, was surprised that they were not at all a topic of discussion. Nicholas I expressed himself towards the duke in much the same way as to Archduke Ferdinand: he in no way cared about their fate and declared that he had as much right to intervene in the fight between the Turks and the Greeks as the sultan was entitled to interfere with the tsar's relations with his Moslem subjects. Nicholas I clearly conveyed that what he actually wanted was to solve the Russo-Ottoman issues affecting the two countries' relations since 1812. Metternich, who knew about these statements to the duke, was greatly satisfied and reinforced in his belief that the young tsar did not want to concern himself with the Greeks' fate nor, above all, to wage war on behalf of their interests.[59]

Nicholas I did not talk about the Greek Question until the arrival of Prince Lieven from London on 21 March. Afterwards, he suddenly raised the topic. According to British historian Harold Temperley, this was all planned by the tsar, and before Lieven's arrival he merely "pretended that he was, for the moment, not occupied with Greece, as he regarded them as rebels."[60] Alexander Bitis is somehow critical of this version and offers another explanation that supports the evolution of events perceived from Austria's point of view. The reason for Nicholas I's previous silence was, according to Bitis, his shock at the Decembrist Revolt and his consequent unwillingness to support another rebellion, his lack of sympathy for the Greeks, and the fact that in early 1826 he was under the influence of his brother Constantine, who, as Metternich had well predicted, expressed pro-Turkish sentiments. The crucial moment occurred with the arrival of Prince Lieven, who started to explain to Nicholas I the advantages of an eventual rapprochement with Great Britain over the Greek Question. In this political orientation Lieven had an influential supporter in the Russian capital: Nesselrode, who in keeping with his office under the new tsar supported this union since the change on the Russian throne altered nothing in his reserved attitude towards Metternich and further Russo-Austrian cooperation,[61] something which Metternich was

---

[59] Lebzeltern to Metternich, St Petersburg, 6, 9 and 23 March 1826, HHStA, StA, Russland III, 73; Hatzfeldt to Frederick William III, Vienna, 10 April 1826, GStA PK, HA III, MdA I, 6006; Bitis, pp. 173–174; Cowles, p. 703; Crawley, *Greek Independence*, p. 54; Prokesch-Osten, *Griechen*, II, p. 13.

[60] Temperley, *Canning*, p. 354.

[61] Bitis, pp. 168–174.

well aware of. Although the prince was satisfied with Nicholas I's declarations on the Eastern Question, "it is entirely otherwise with those
of Count Nesselrode. We find him in 1826 once again in the same position with the same misconceptions and all the errors which poisoned
the last days of the late emperor."[62] And Metternich made no secret of
this sentiment during a meeting with Ribeaupierre: "I asked him not
to conceal at all from Count Nesselrode the fact that I do not understand him any more, seeing that he has ceased to understand me, and
that from my deep experience and long practice I count him among
our adversaries, and that this will be the case until the day when he
proves to me that he has regained his balanced view of things."[63] Nesselrode, who at the beginning of 1826 was openly advocating the right
of Russia to intervene in the Greek affairs, repeated to Lebzeltern the
opinion that "the only important matter, the only one with which
Russia wanted to occupy itself, was the pacification of Greece,"[64] and
was irritated by Nicholas I's preference for the Russian Question.[65]

Nesselrode continued to hope for a change in the tsar's attitude
and, together with Lieven, he finally succeeded in bringing Nicholas I
back to the Greek matter. The young tsar took up Alexander I's cause
from 1825 and started to negotiate with Wellington in late March
on the future of the Greeks. The talks finally led to the signature
of the Protocol of 4 April 1826, in which Great Britain and Russia
committed to mediate between the Greeks and the Turks with the
aim of pacifying the Levant. This was to be achieved by the creation
of a semi-autonomous Greek province bound to the Ottoman ruler
with rather weak ties, the most important of them being the annual
payment of a tribute by the Greeks. The territorial boundaries of
Greece, as well as other details of its creation, were to be negotiated
later. The St Petersburg Protocol contained no coercive measures,
but in the third article it was stipulated that if the sultan did not
accept the mediation of the two Powers, they would continue "whether
in concert or separately"[66] to seek reconciliation between the hostile

[62] Metternich to Lebzeltern, Vienna, 22 Feb. 1826, HHStA, StA, Russland III, 75.
[63] Metternich to Lebzeltern, Vienna, 14 Feb. 1826, HHStA, StA, Russland III, 75.
[64] Lebzeltern to Metternich, St Petersburg, 23 March 1826, HHStA, StA, Russland III, 73.
[65] Lebzeltern to Metternich, St Petersburg, 6, 9 and 23 March, 7 April 1826,
HHStA, StA, Russland III, 73.
[66] The Anglo-Russian Protocol of 4 April 1826, M. S. Anderson, *The Great Powers*

parties. This meant that if Great Britain hesitated to act according to the stipulations of the Protocol, Russia could proceed independently and even declare war on the Ottoman Empire, but the agreement would remain in force and the British cabinet would have no argument for declaring war on its ally. Consequently, the Russians achieved a great diplomatic victory: they obtained an important concession from Wellington without having to give anything in return for this "favour." The duke signed a document providing Russia with freedom of action, which meant exactly the opposite of what he had actually been sent to achieve, but this was not merely his fault; Canning in charging him with this mission must be blamed in particular.[67]

* * *

According to British historian Charles W. Crawley, Canning longed for success in the field where his rival, Metternich, failed.[68] The same opinion was also expressed by Harold Temperley: "Russia was likely to make war on her own account. It was better for England to act with her than to remain isolated and powerless. Metternich had failed to restrain Russia by a policy of doing nothing; Canning, therefore, could only restrain her by doing 'something' ... He averted war in the East for a time."[69] Alexander Bitis claims that although Canning legitimised an eventual Russo-Ottoman war and paralysed an eventual British opposition, he at least "secured a suspension of war."[70] The documents studied for the clarification of the whole history of the affair from Austria's point of view as well as some details offered by Bitis, however, offer a rather different picture of events from how they were presented, for example, by Crawley or Temperley and significantly prove the validity of the interpretation of the events put forward by Loyal Cowles, being rather critical of Canning's Near Eastern policy and regarding it as weak and unsuccessful.[71]

---

and the Near East 1774–1923, London 1970, p. 32.
[67] Bitis, p. 175; Brewer, p. 256; Schroeder, *Transformation*, p. 646.
[68] Crawley, *Greek Independence*, p. 50.
[69] Temperley, "Princess Lieven," pp. 74–75.
[70] Bitis, p. 176.

There are two principal problems that prevent agreement with the accolade of the foreign secretary: (1) that Metternich failed; (2) that Canning preserved the peace. Both of them are closely connected with the presumption that peace was at risk, but this claim is hardly provable for the end of Alexander I's reign and it can be successfully ruled out for the beginning of Nicholas I's rule. And if peace was indeed at risk, then it was owing to Russian and not Greek interests. As for Alexander I, Temperley admits that war in the spring of 1826 would have broken out "if he did not obtain satisfaction from the Turks on the question of the Principalities."[72] The same can be said about his successor: Nicholas I would most probably have waged war if Mahmud II had refused his ultimatum of 17 March, but nothing indicates that he was prepared to get into a conflict for the Greeks.[73] Since the Protocol of 4 April was signed in favour of the Greeks, how could it then preserve the peace? It was entirely unnecessary because when Mahmud II accepted the March ultimatum, the tsar could hardly continue to press the Porte on the Greek Question. If he had, he would have risked the outcome of his negotiations on purely Russian issues, which is therefore the main reason why he later did not press the Greek Question until the settlement of those issues. On the other hand, if the sultan had refused the ultimatum, the Protocol could in no way have saved the peace.[74] In fact it was not Canning with his negotiations in St Petersburg but Metternich who, with his vigorous diplomatic pressure in Constantinople, helped to prevent the outbreak of war. Considering this, it is difficult to claim unambiguously that Metternich failed in restraining Russia. The main goals of Austria's policy, the preservation of peace and the constraint of Russia's intervention in the Greek Question, were not at all lost in early 1826.

---

[71] For details see Cowles' paper already mentioned several times in the footnotes above "The Failure to Restrain Russia: Canning, Nesselrode, and the Greek Question, 1825–27," *IHR* 12, 1990, 4, pp. 688–720.

[72] Temperley, *Canning*, p. 348.

[73] Nicholas I himself, when facing Lebzeltern's criticism for his denouncement of the Greek revolt in March and his agreement with the intervention in early April, did not argue with the Austrian ambassador and plainly put Wellington in the wrong for promoting the negotiations on the Greek Question. Lebzeltern to Metternich, St Petersburg, 7 June 1826, Prokesch-Osten, *Griechen*, IV, pp. 270–271.

[74] Kondis, p. 114.

Where Metternich suffered heavy defeat was in losing his influence over the Russian cabinet in 1825, and this influence was not restored in any way with the accession of Nicholas I. The main credit for this must of course be ascribed to Canning and his decision not to cooperate with Austria and not to participate in the St Petersburg conference. This led to his desired victory over Metternich but it also "obviously damaged the process by which Russia had previously been restrained."[75] Metternich needed Canning's assistance in early 1825 in paralysing Russia's policy in the Greek Question and when he did not get it, he inevitably failed. Metternich had understood the dilemma and, therefore, he asked Canning for help which was refused. He suggested they should cooperate again in late 1825, but the answer from London was no different because Canning was going his own way. Metternich disagreed with this since he believed that the cooperation of Austria, Great Britain and Prussia was necessary and it sufficed for restraining Russia in the Greek affairs, and he also tried to persuade Canning about this in early 1826: "Let the Great Powers come together on the same issue of conservation and peace, and the world will be saved!"[76] This proposition was fairly well founded because Russia hesitated to act alone and risk the creation of a powerful anti-Russian alliance due to its unilateral intervention in the Ottoman Empire. Alexander I agreed to start the negotiations with Great Britain to obtain a measure of certainty that in the event of Russia's independent action against the Ottoman Empire he would not have to face British resistance. When this freedom of action became possible to obtain in March 1826, Nicholas I was persuaded by his diplomats to take the opportunity despite his previous total lack of interest in the Greeks' struggle.

Metternich labelled Canning in 1825 as "a man guided only by circumstance,"[77] and Prince Lieven's assessment from the same year entirely supported this view: "Having no system, nor principles determined in advance, it is only in the circumstances alone that he will find the compass of his policy."[78] Cowles offers the same judgement saying that Canning's Greek policy was "a quagmire of vague

---

[75] Cowles, p. 699.
[76] Metternich to Esterházy, Vienna, 8 Jan. 1826, HHStA, StA, England 175.
[77] Metternich to Ottenfels, Vienna, 4 Sept. 1825, HHStA, StA, Türkei VI, 24.
[78] Cowles, p. 702.

and contradictory statements and rationalizations; no principle can
be shown to have guided it."[79] Canning actually had no strategy, no
long-term plan and his policy was thus weak, which was utilised by the
Russians for their own interests. Instead of restraining them, he lost
control over events and presented Russia with a great deal of freedom
to act independently.[80] According to Paul W. Schroeder, Metternich's
victories over Russia from the early 1820s were nothing other "than
crisis management and buying time."[81] This is true but one must admit that this tactic was effective, especially when comparing it with
Canning's policy. With the Protocol of 4 April, the British foreign
secretary opened Pandora's box, and there is much evidence to prove
that he did so absolutely unnecessarily.

[79] Ibid., p. 719.
[80] Schroeder, *Transformation*, p. 647; Cowles, p. 691.
[81] Schroeder, *Transformation*, p. 621.

5

From the St Petersburg Protocol to the Treaty of London

British diplomacy opened a floodgate on 4 April 1826 but the resulting wave got out of its control and rushed in a direction desired more
by Nicholas I than Canning. Metternich was unable to thwart the
pro-Greek policy of Russia and Great Britain and finally also joined
by France and found himself in isolation in July 1827 when the three
Powers signed a treaty in London. He was completely defeated in his
desire to see the Greek Question left untouched by the Great Powers
and solved by the sultan alone. Where, however, he showed remarkable
superiority over his political opponents was with his keen foresight of
the goal to which the policy shielded by the Treaty of London would
lead. His criticism of the conditions under which the three Powers
wanted to pacify the Levant cannot be judged as a mere manifestation of his displeasure over the course of events but must be viewed
as a result of, first, his great analytical skills and, second, the application of the chancellor's own politico-legal views of the organisation
of international relations.

Metternich's Criticism of the St Petersburg Protocol

It would be an understatement to say that upon hearing the news
of the St Petersburg Protocol Metternich reacted merely with surprise and disapproval; he was in fact completely shocked and horrified. Hatzfeldt reported to Berlin that he had not seen him so greatly
affected and pessimistic for a long time.[1] The reasons for the chancel-

---

[1] Hatzfeldt to Frederick William III, Vienna, 26 April 1826, GStA PK, HA III,
MdA I, 6006.

lor's attitude were obvious and can be summarised in two words: the conditions and unexpectedness of the Protocol. Regarding the former, he considered the Protocol to be a "great evil"[2] and a "monstrosity"[3] because, first, the Greek Question was revived at the cost of Ottoman independence; second, the pacification according to the Protocol was hardly feasible due to the expected refusals of the two quarrelling parties, both of whom considered Greek autonomy unacceptable, although for exactly the opposite reasons; and third, it could provoke a Russo-Ottoman war, either owing to the Turks' rejection of the ultimatum of 17 March as soon as they learnt about the Protocol of 4 April or because of their simple refusal to agree with the conditions of the latter.[4] Metternich regarded the success of the mediation on the basis of the Protocol as impossible and Russia's consequent actions, allowed by the same document, as predictable: "The Duke of Wellington based the agreement contracted between him and the Russian cabinet upon two expressed conditions: first, that the English mediation would be accepted by the Porte and, second, on the non-use of coercive measures by England. But each of these two conditions excludes the success of the other. The sultan will never accept the mediation of England or any other Great Power between him and his Greek subjects of his own accord and without being forced to do so; in such a case – and how the court of London could be so blind as not to see it as a certainty – would it be Russia who would have to be called upon to use the coercive measures that would not be used by the Great Power that, in the act of 4 April, assumed the role of intermediary? Russia would then arrive again at war and in the combination of events resulting from 4 April would be dragged into one by England."[5]

Metternich could hardly overlook the glaring mistake that Wellington, wishing to avoid a war, made in the third article with the wording "whether in concert or separately," which in no way pre-

---

[2]   Metternich to Esterházy, Vienna, 29 April 1826, HHStA, StA, England 175.
[3]   Metternich to Ottenfels, Vienna, 24 April 1826, HHStA, StA, Türkei VI, 24.
[4]   Metternich to Apponyi, Vienna, 14 May 1826, HHStA, StA, Frankreich 260; Metternich to Esterházy, Vienna, 4 June 1826, HHStA, StA, England 175; Wellesley to Canning, Vienna, 29 April 1826, TNA, FO 120/76; Hatzfeldt to Frederick William III, Vienna, 10 and 15 May 1826, GStA PK, HA III, MdA I, 6006; Metternich to Neumann, Vienna, 12 May 1826, *NP*, IV, p. 274.
[5]   Metternich to Esterházy, Vienna, 4 June 1826, HHStA, StA, England 175.

vented a Russian attack upon the Porte: "It naturally ties England to the Russian chariot and it demotes its influence to second place. In the event of a rupture between Russia and the Porte, the role of England will in no way be that of a mediator between the Greeks and the Turks. The Greeks will only focus their attention on the Great Power in conflict with their own enemies, and it will be Russia at war, not England at peace, who will decide on the fate of the insurrection and the future of the Greeks. This is a position of weakness for England in every regard."[6] Metternich saw behind this mistake, first, Wellington's diplomatic inexperience which had led to this serious oversight: "The Duke of Wellington did wrong where, motivated by the least questionable intentions, he had wanted to do good,"[7] and second, his erroneous view that the tsar desired an open rupture with the Porte: "The Duke of Wellington wanted to prevent a war, and he has given rein to one; he saw a Russian war in the Greek affair, and one was never to be found and will never be found in any affair other than the Turkish affair; he wanted to arrest any plans for territorial extension, and he was searching for them again where they could not be found. He was keen to obtain on this last subject diplomatic and formal engagements, [but all] he gained [was] phrases."[8] The tsar's alleged belligerency was used as an argument by George Canning, who wrote to Sir Henry Wellesley on 4 May that when Wellington was departing for St Petersburg, the allies worried that, first, the European peace was at risk owing to the Greek Question and, second, Russia could use this issue for its expansion. Metternich sharply disagreed with these theories: "The Protocol is irrelevant with regard to the first as well as to the second of these dangers. As for the former, the allies have never feared it and, if it really existed, it would also exist in spite of the Protocol. As for the second, no one has attached fear of Russian expansion to the question of the pacification of the Greeks. The only danger that has existed still exists and will exist for as long as Russia does not feel satisfied as to its particular grievances against the Porte of which the Protocol did not make the least mention."[9]

[6]   Remarks to the Protocol of 4 April 1826, attached to Metternich to Esterházy, Vienna, 4 June 1826, HHStA, StA, England 175. For the same opinion see also Wellesley to Canning, Vienna, 29 April 1826, TNA, FO 120/76.
[7]   Metternich to Esterházy, Vienna, 4 June 1826, HHStA, StA, England 175.
[8]   Metternich to Apponyi, Vienna, 31 May 1826, HHStA, StA, Frankreich 260.
[9]   Metternich to Esterházy, Vienna, 4 June 1826, HHStA, StA, England 175.

The second reason for Metternich's anger was the surprising, and therefore all the more shocking origin of the Protocol. He had in no way anticipated the British-Russian rapprochement which he had considered to be absolutely impossible for months and, consequently, he had expected no result from Wellington's mission, in particular when Nicholas I had seemed to entirely abandon the Greeks and merely promote Russia's direct interests, an attitude which Metternich had always advocated: "Separate these two affairs, be as firm as possible on matters based upon law, and treat separately what is only discretional. The initiative of 17 March is based on this line of separation. It was supported without delay and in the first place by Austria."[10] Consequently, Metternich greatly resented the tsar's shift of allegiance from 17 March to 4 April opening thus "the second and new phase of the affair"[11] and accentuating the rift between Austria and Russia; their previous close relations had definitely broken down and been replaced by the British-Russian cooperation in the Near East.[12] Metternich's position was considerably weakened and, due to the tsar's preference for Canning,[13] he logically regretted finding himself defeated by his mortal enemy and Austria, with its long Ottoman frontier and vast economic interests in the Near East, excluded from the Russo-British negotiations and completely cut off from Russia: "I believe that in the arrangement signed in St Petersburg the Russian cabinet was completely hoodwinked by Mr Canning; England has made Russia a present of war, which will be able to lead it further than it perhaps wants to go, and Russia without intending to (or so I like to believe) has given England in return the sacrifice of the Alliance which Emperor Alexander himself established, and which was his as well as our safeguard in the most critical moments during the

---

[10] Metternich to Lebzeltern, Vienna, 16 May 1826, HHStA, StA, Russland III, 75.
[11] Metternich to Apponyi, Vienna, 24 April 1826, HHStA, StA, Frankreich 260.
[12] Metternich to Apponyi, Vienna, 20 Feb. 1826, HHStA, StA, Frankreich 260; Metternich to Lebzeltern, Vienna, 22 Feb. 1826, HHStA, StA, Russland III, 75; Metternich to Ottenfels, Vienna, 24 April 1826, HHStA, StA, Türkei VI, 24; Caraman to Damas, Vienna, 2 Sept. 1825, AMAE, CP, Autriche 406; Wellesley to Canning, Vienna, 29 April 1826, TNA, FO 120/76.
[13] Metternich to Lebzeltern, Vienna, 16 May 1826, HHStA, StA, Russland III, 75; Tatishchev to Nesselrode, Vienna, 29 April 1826, AVPRI, fond 133, Kantseliariia, opis 468, 11870; Hatzfeldt to Frederick William III, Vienna, 10 May 1826, GStA PK, HA III, MdA I, 6006.

last several years."[14] However, since this conduct from the British foreign secretary was expected, Metternich was more surprised with the tsar's behaviour, and it was thus all the more painful: "Russia has clearly detached itself from its former allies; in less than a week it reversed all its positions towards them to ally itself with a cabinet guided by a statesman who constantly pursues a line of self-interest and who, therefore, is the least predictable and controllable. Emperor Nicholas has strayed from his first resolutions, he has reversed the principles proclaimed by himself and especially recorded in an explicit diplomatic agreement ... He has harmed these principles and not only by sanctioning with his ministers' signature his reprehensible remarks, like that of freeing the Greeks of the Porte (which is equal to real emancipation) [or] like that of mediating (between insurgent subjects and their sovereign). He contradicted himself by declaring after eight days as only being the domain of Russia and Great Britain what eight days earlier he had explicitly recognised and announced that he regarded as a common interest for all the Allies."[15] Metternich bitterly wrote to Princess Lieven: "Everything has changed as if by the stroke of a wand. The strong emperor has become weak: his once so correct political attitude has changed; I was boasting about having cooperated on the March agreement; I would not want to be responsible for the one of April. If Russia were a frivolous country, I would say that the ministers have turned the prince's mind."[16] By "the ministers" Metternich meant the two principal instigators of the Protocol, Lieven and Nesselrode: "The fact is that the agreement of 4 April is full of error and weakness. It carries the character of its negotiators. The Duke of Wellington, who arrived in St Petersburg with the double misconception that the principle matter was the Greek affair and that Emperor Nicholas was looking for pretexts for going to war, immediately ascertained that this monarch had sincerely declared against the insurrection, and the initiative of 17 March, drafted and written without the knowledge of the Duke of Wellington, provided him with proof of this fact. Since that moment the duke wanted to save the English mediation in which Mr Stratford Canning had

---

[14] Hatzfeldt to Frederick William III, Vienna, 10 May 1826, GStA PK, HA III, MdA I, 6006.
[15] Metternich to Esterházy, Vienna, 29 April 1826, HHStA, StA, England 175.
[16] Metternich to Princess Lieven, 28 April 1826, NA, RAM-AC 6, 1.

already undertaken steps. Here he met with messieurs Nesselrode and Lieven; both of them alarmed at seeing their new master abandoning the holy cause of the Greeks and both desiring to save it, they exerted all their efforts to combine the English affair with the Russian one. On one side, Emperor Nicholas' fear of seeing the English perhaps seizing for themselves the permanent protection of the Peloponnese and the Islands and, from the other side, his understandably natural inexperience in diplomatic affairs influenced the concoction of an undertaking full of weakness and stupidity."[17]

The omission of Austria and the unwelcome pro-Greek conditions threatening peace as well as the sultan's sovereignty led Metternich to the firm resolution, entirely seconded by Francis I, not to follow the course marked out by Russia and Great Britain in the Protocol: "What undoubtedly arises from the arrangement from the beginning of April between Russia and England is our absolute freedom to proceed according to our own evaluation of necessity or propriety."[18] This grandiose declaration, however, could not hide the fact that he greatly hoped that Austria would not have to act independently for long and that the British-Russian alliance would not come into force owing to the expected opposition from Canning to the text with the dangerous third article: "What I have absolutely no doubts about at all is that what the Duke of Wellington has done in no way conforms to what his superior wanted to achieve."[19] Therefore, he nurtured the hope that His Majesty's government would refuse to ratify the Protocol: "The British cabinet will, according to our belief, pay Russia with the same coin. The act of 4 April will therefore rest on its signature and it will not go further than that."[20] However, this was an idle hope because Canning decided to agree with what Wellington brought him from St Petersburg despite an awareness of the danger hidden in the document.[21]

[17] Metternich to Ottenfels, Vienna, 19 May 1826, HHStA, StA, Türkei VI, 24.
[18] Ibid.
[19] Metternich to Esterházy, Vienna, 29 April 1826, HHStA, StA, England 175.
[20] Metternich to Apponyi, Vienna, 31 May 1826, HHStA, StA, Frankreich 260.
[21] Metternich to Apponyi, Vienna, 3 May 1826, HHStA, StA, Frankreich 260; Tatishchev to Nesselrode, Vienna, 29 April and 17 May 1826, AVPRI, fond 133, Kantseliariia, opis 468, 11870; Hatzfeldt to Frederick William III, Vienna, 10 May 1826, GStA PK, HA III, MdA I, 6006; Caraman to Damas, Vienna, 14 May 1826, AMAE, CP, Autriche 407; Cowles, p. 710; Temperley, *Canning*, pp. 391–393.

The Origins of the Treaty of London

Although Metternich refused to go along with Russia in the Greek Question, he continued to support the acceptance of its March ultimatum in Constantinople: "The most important question for us is that of peace and this is in the hands of the Porte. This Great Power should consent without delay to the negotiation requested by the Russian court; and by this single action it will efficiently thwart and extinguish all schemes which would present it with new problems."[22] Since Metternich feared that the news of the Protocol before the expiration time of the ultimatum could result in Mahmud II's non-compliance, he instructed Ottenfels not to reveal its existence. When the ultimatum was accepted, he continued to advise the Turks of "prudence, moderation and resignation"[23] towards their powerful northern neighbour, who, instead of Great Britain, could wage an effective war against them, and Metternich did not doubt that the tsar would do so if the negotiations finally opened in Akkerman were to fail. It was also with the threat of such a war that the Russian negotiators were able to finally persuade the Turks to yield and sign the Akkerman Convention on 7 October 1826. Its conditions weakened the Porte's position in the Principalities and Serbia and resolved the issues concerning shipping through the Straits as well as the Caucasus border in favour of Russia.[24]

The Akkerman Convention was hardly likely to find favour with the Viennese cabinet, and neither Gentz nor the former internuncio in Constantinople, Baron Ignaz von Stürmer, concealed their opinion that the articles were "thoroughly arbitrary, unjust, hostile and, what

---

[22] Metternich to Ottenfels, Vienna, 24 April 1826, HHStA, StA, Türkei VI, 24.
[23] Ottenfels to Metternich, Constantinople, 10 Oct. 1826, HHStA, StA, Türkei VI, 26.
[24] Metternich to Ottenfels, Vienna, 25 April and 12 June 1826, HHStA, StA, Türkei VI, 24; Metternich to Apponyi, Vienna, 3 May 1826, HHStA, StA, Frankreich 260; Metternich to Lebzeltern, Vienna, 19 May and 2 June 1826, HHStA, StA, Russland III, 75; Metternich to Esterházy, Vienna, 2 Sept. 1826, HHStA, StA, England 175; Ottenfels to Metternich, Constantinople, 10 and 16 Oct. 1826, HHStA, StA, Türkei VI, 26; Tatishchev to Nesselrode, Vienna, 17 June, 23 Sept. and 11 Oct. 1826, Carlsbad, 17 and 24 July, 3 Aug. 1826, AVPRI, fond 133, Kantseliariia, opis 468, 11870; Maltzan to Frederick William III, Vienna, 22 Sept. 1826, GStA PK, HA III, MdA I, 6007; Crawley, *Greek Independence*, p. 65.

is worst of all, sow the seeds of future resentment and hostility."[25] Metternich's statements were as diplomatic as ever. He received the news with stoic calm: "The first period of the drama that we have seen presented for more than 5 years is thus closed. It was characterised by Ottoman ineptitude, Greek deceit and jugglery, and Russian preponderance."[26] He instructed Ottenfels to convey to the reis effendi "that we congratulate the Porte on having made its arrangement with Russia; that it need not regret the sacrifices that this made necessary; that this was the only means it possessed for its salvation."[27] One can hardly doubt that he was extremely displeased with the conditions strengthening Russia's influence over the Balkans, but what mitigated this was the fact that the Russo-Ottoman dispute did not lead to war and Ribeaupierre finally departed for Constantinople: "The end of the conferences in Akkerman thwarts any expectations and speculations about revolution. The Philhellenes are extremely dissatisfied. This seems to me proved by the fact that the Porte in no way paid too high a price for this control of what is good or bad."[28]

Metternich further hoped that the conciliatory result of the negotiations would finally please Nicholas I enough that the Protocol would be forgotten in St Petersburg or, at least, that the tsar would respond to the Akkerman settlement by proceeding in a more restrained way in the Greek Question. This hope was strengthened by Metternich's personal conviction that the British-Russian cooperation would break down owing to the different goals of Nicholas I and Canning in European politics, and he tried to further this process by warning the former, whose conservatism he still trusted, about the ambitions of the latter: "Russia must be evaluated upon the character of the emperor and on the greater or lesser influence that his cabinet can exert on him. All this allows us to admit that the fundamental views of this monarch are pure and conform to our own principles. We are convinced he is positively motivated by a desire to preserve peace and we also have every reason to believe that he judges in an enlightened manner the moral conduct of Canning and the moral and

---

[25] Maltzan to Frederick William III, Vienna, 19 Oct. 1826, GStA PK, HA III, MdA I, 6007.
[26] Metternich to Ottenfels, Vienna, 18 Oct. 1826, HHStA, StA, Türkei VI, 24. See also Metternich to Apponyi, Vienna, 17 Oct. 1826, HHStA, StA, Frankreich 261.
[27] Metternich to Ottenfels, Vienna, 18 Oct. 1826, HHStA, StA, Türkei VI, 24.
[28] Metternich to Ottenfels, Vienna, 4 Nov. 1826, HHStA, StA, Türkei VI, 24.

physical state of England ... England's conduct is haughty, arrogant and full of audacious turns of events."[29] Metternich still believed that he would be able to change the attitude of the young monarch whom he found to be misled by his ministers to signing the Protocol: "It was known to us at the time that the Protocol was only authorised by His Imperial Majesty with great reluctance and that it was nothing other than an undertaking of circumstance and weakness on the part of the three negotiators [Lieven, Nesselrode, Wellington]."[30] At the same time, the chancellor strongly disagreed with the opinion spread in diplomatic circles that Nicholas I desired war with the Ottoman Empire and was merely seeking a pretext to declare it: "We believe that Emperor Nicholas is prepared to not refuse to go to war but we do not believe that he desires to do so. Confronting the realities, I would go even further. I do not believe the possibility that the Russian emperor could wage war on the Turks without being led by this to consequences diametrally opposed to those he would wish or could even want to achieve. He wants the end of the current problems, and war would be the beginning of an entirely new order of things, and with much more serious consequences."[31] One of his arguments, which was conveyed of course to the St Petersburg cabinet with the aim of setting it against the British government but which was, as the future proved, not unfounded, was that the first cannon shot would lead to the absolute political emancipation of the Peloponnese and the adjacent islands and place these regions under British protection, not Russia's. For this reason, according to Metternich, Nicholas I "cannot want the political emancipation of the Greeks because this emancipation would be the loss of Russian influence over the liberated Greeks and the inevitable extension of influence and power for England; their emancipation, in one word, would be to the direct detriment of the political as well as administrative interests of his crown as well as his empire."[32] Although this faith in the tsar's designs, still more or less in compliance with Austria's interests, was weakened in early 1827, it was not completely destroyed at this stage, the chancellor maintain-

---

[29] Metternich to Ottenfels, Vienna, 30 Dec. 1826, HHStA, StA, Türkei VI, 29.
[30] Metternich to Ottenfels, Vienna, 1 Dec. 1826, HHStA, StA, Türkei VI, 24.
[31] Metternich to Esterházy, Vienna, 26 March 1827, HHStA, StA, England 178.
[32] Metternich to Ottenfels, Vienna, 13 April 1827, HHStA, StA, Türkei VI, 29.

ing then as he did even later that Nicholas I's main objective was not war.[33]

Metternich's most serious mistake during that period was precisely this underestimation of Nicholas I's role in the whole affair. He generally considered the Russian monarch to be a victim of Canning, whereas it was actually the tsar who dictated the political course aimed at increasing Russia's influence over the Ottoman Empire, in particular its Balkan dominions. The reason for this error was exactly the same as that leading Canning to the Protocol: the desire to outmanoeuvre his rival. For both these men, the most hated opponent was the other. Metternich, seeing the main threat in the West, forgot to observe with the same vigilance the East, where Lebzeltern's absence now proved to be a serious loss. This tolerant attitude was not maintained by all in the Viennese Chancellery, but even Gentz was unable to diminish the chancellor's favourable attitude towards Russia with which he sharply disagreed: "Nothing would be more welcome for him [Metternich] than to be able to establish the closest understanding with Russia just in order to topple Canning whom he hates more than anyone else in the world ... Because of this attitude, he constantly has a certain hidden tendency to interpret Russia's steps favourably."[34]

Consequently, Metternich's attempts to break the British-Russian alliance with warnings against an eventual British predominance over Greece or by divulging Canning's comment about the real reason for his cooperation with Russia – not to allow it to finish the affair alone – found no echo in St Petersburg. Nor did the chancellor's hopes of the tsar abandoning the Greek Question prove to be well founded. The only positive outcome of the Akkerman negotiations for Austria was that Russia did not touch upon the Greek Question until the

---

[33] Metternich to Ottenfels, Vienna, 19 May, 18 June and 30 Dec. 1826, HHStA, StA, Türkei VI, 24; Metternich to Apponyi, Vienna, 29 Jan. and 12 Feb. 1827, HHStA, StA, Frankreich 264; Metternich to Esterházy, Vienna, 20 Feb. and 26 March 1827, HHStA, StA, England 178; Metternich to Bombelles, Vienna, 27 March 1827, HHStA, StA, Russland III, 81; Metternich to Zichy, Vienna, 30 April 1827, HHStA, StK, Preussen 125; Hatzfeldt to Frederick William III, Vienna, 9 Nov., 17 and 19 Dec. 1826, GStA PK, HA III, MdA I, 6007; Hatzfeldt to Frederick William III, Vienna, 6 Jan. 1827, Maltzan to Frederick William III, Vienna, 14 and 17 Feb., 12 March 1827, GStA PK, HA III, MdA I, 6008; Caraman to Damas, Vienna, 10 June 1827, AMAE, CP, Autriche 408.
[34] Krauter, p. 206.

conclusion of the talks because it did not want to endanger their success. The signing of the Convention had exactly the opposite effect on Nicholas I's actions to what Metternich had desired: the Greek Question was revived with full force because the tsar wanted to exploit it for the growth of his power and prestige with Canning's assistance and therefore sought its resolution, and the Lievens pressured Canning from August to December 1826 to accept the possibility of the use of coercive measures against the Porte if necessary.[35]

The activity of Russian diplomacy in the Greek Question after October 1826 was in sharp contrast to the British foreign secretary's previous passivity. After the ratification of the Protocol, Canning left the Greeks and turned to other affairs. His conduct in the issue that he had helped to bring out into the open was totally passive, influenced by an unreasonable optimism that the Porte would accept the Protocol without the threat of war. To his cousin advocating the British interests in Constantinople and requesting further instructions he merely wrote in early July 1826 that he had "nothing yet to say,"[36] and he paid attention to different political affairs. He was awakened from lethargy only when the demand for the use of force against the sultan came from St Petersburg since it was exactly what Canning did not wish. He would have liked to limit himself to the threat of the withdrawal of the five Powers' representatives from Constantinople and, if this step proved to be insufficient, to the threat of the Greek independence, which is surprisingly what Metternich had suggested in early 1825 and not surprisingly still unacceptable for Nicholas I, who firmly insisted on the use of coercive measures. The tsar started to press Canning to accept this option referring to the ominous phrase in the Protocol "whether in concert or separately," first quite diplomatically but after the Porte's formal refusal of the Protocol in early February 1827 without reserve when Lieven openly warned Canning of the possibility of Russia's unilateral action. The British minister was finally forced to agree and go much further than he had originally wanted, and instead of controlling Russia in Near Eastern affairs he became

---

[35] Tatishchev to Nesselrode, Vienna, 9 Feb. 1827, AVPRI, fond 133, Kantseliariia, opis 468, 11873; Schroeder, *Transformation*, p. 648.
[36] Cowles, p. 710.

its servant.[37] His position can be well explained by the claim of the
diplomat serving earlier at the British embassy in Vienna, Sir Robert
Gordon, to Gentz from early July 1826: "We have proceeded upon a
wrong conviction that war was inevitable between Russia and Turkey;
and to save ourselves from this, I question if we have not plunged into
more inextricable difficulties. Be that as it may, the protocol exists ⌐
and I suppose we are bound to proceed with our mediation."[38]

Divided by their different views of the coercive measures in the
autumn of 1826, Russia and Great Britain were joined at the same
time by their impatience concerning Austria's official answer to the
Protocol, the text of which had not been officially communicated in
Vienna before late September due to Metternich's absence. When he
was formally acquainted with it, his only immediate reaction was, however, the acceptance of the Protocol ad referendum. He explained this
proceeding to Tatishchev and Wellesley with the argument that the
Viennese cabinet needed time for reflection, something scarcely credible since the text had been well known for months. But despite these
protractions lasting another three months, Metternich's frank negative
statements to the foreign diplomats including the British and Russian
ambassadors obviously gave them no hope for Austria's consent and
its support of the two contracting parties' proposals for pacification.
The chancellor repeated the objections he had raised to the Protocol
immediately after its signature: its conditions were incompatible with
the principles of his emperor and impracticable in practice without
the use of coercive measures. He unofficially repeated that Austria
could not cooperate upon the basis of the document of 4 April, it
would always regard the insurgent Greeks as rebels and it would not
infringe upon the sultan's sovereignty. The character of the official
answer was also anticipated by his instructions to Ottenfels of 18 October: the internuncio was forbidden to offer any support to the joint
action of Minciaky and Stratford Canning in the Greek Question.[39]

---

[37] Ibid., pp. 711–715; Crawley, *Greek Independence*, p. 73; Schroeder, *Transformation*, p. 649; Temperley, *Canning*, p. 295.
[38] Gordon to Gentz, London, 4 July 1826, Prokesch-Osten, *Zur Geschichte der
orientalischen Frage*, p. 136.
[39] Metternich to Ottenfels, Vienna, 18 Oct. 1826, HHStA, StA, Türkei VI, 24;
Tatishchev to Nesselrode, Vienna, 23 Sept. 1826, AVPRI, fond 133, Kantseliariia,
opis 468, 11870; Hatzfeldt to Frederick William III, Vienna, 8 Nov. and 9 Dec.
1826, GStA PK, HA III, MdA I, 6007; Caraman to Damas, Vienna, 7 Dec. 1826,

It was clear that Austria would be willing to assist Great Britain and Russia only if some modifications were made, and this finally became certain on 22 December when Metternich communicated to Wellesley and Tatishchev a formal answer: Austria was willing to participate in the pacification of the Levant but refused to recognise the right to force the Porte to reduce its sovereignty to suzerainty and impose any mediation between the sovereign and his insurgent subjects. Francis I personally informed the British and Russian ambassadors that he could not apply the Protocol's conditions against an independent country, and particularly not coercive measures, whether the milder forms suggested by Canning or the stronger ones advocated by Russia. As Metternich wrote in a note to Tatishchev, "the emperor would actually assume in these two cases neither the right to employ such measures against the Porte nor even to threaten it with them."[40] This official answer was also sent to St Petersburg on 24, Paris on 25 and London on 26 December.[41]

The gap that widened between Austria and the other signatories of the Protocol now grew between Austria and France, which had defected to the latter camp. Until the late autumn of 1826, Metternich thought that Prussia and France would take the same attitude as Austria, something which could limit the activities of the British-Russian partnership, but just Prussia met this expectation. The good Austro-French relations reinforced during Metternich's Parisian visit in 1825 now gradually disengaged, a fact he was well aware of, and this increased his desire for the restoration of his good relations with Russia. Nevertheless, whereas Lieven was working zealously in London

---

AMAE, CP, Autriche 407; Wellesley to Canning, Vienna, 12 Dec. 1826, TNA, FO 120/83.

[40] Metternich's note to Tatishchev and Wellesley, Vienna, 22 Dec. 1826, HHStA, StA, England 175.

[41] Metternich to Bombelles, Vienna, 24 Dec. 1826, HHStA, StA, Russland III, 75; Metternich to Apponyi, Vienna, 25 Dec. 1826, HHStA, StA, Frankreich 261; Metternich to Esterházy, Vienna, 26 Dec. 1826, HHStA, StA, England 175; Hatzfeldt to Frederick William III, Vienna, 19 and 25 Dec. 1826, GStA PK, HA III, MdA I, 6007; Hatzfeldt to Frederick William III, Vienna, 6 Jan. 1827, GStA PK, HA III, MdA I, 6008; Caraman to Damas, Vienna, 21 and 22 Dec. 1826, AMAE, CP, Autriche 407; Caraman to Damas, Vienna, 3 Jan. 1827, AMAE, CP, Autriche 408; Tatishchev to Lieven, Vienna, 17 Dec. 1826, Tatishchev to Nesselrode, Vienna, 22 Dec. 1826, AVPRI, fond 133, Kantseliariia, opis 468, 11870; Tatishchev to Nesselrode, Vienna, 9 Feb. 1827, AVPRI, fond 133, Kantseliariia, opis 468, 11873.

on the Russo-British union, Pozzo was aiming equally vigourously at the destruction of Austro-French intimacy in Paris, and Metternich's attempts to forestall the process were successful neither in St Petersburg, where his warnings against the alleged link between the Decembrist Revolt and the revolutionary danger threatening Europe from Paris met with no success, nor in Paris, where the cabinet, willing to pursue a more active policy and to placate the strong pro-Greek opinion among the French public, paid more and more attention to the Russian ambassador's insinuations. The final blow to Metternich's efforts to keep the French cabinet on his side was Canning's six-week-long visit to Paris in September and October 1826, during which Charles X and his first minister consented to join Great Britain and Russia in the pacification of the Levant. They agreed with Greek autonomy and settled with the foreign secretary the extension of the Protocol into a treaty containing the measures which the Great Powers would jointly undertake for the termination of the whole affair. As well as Canning, French Minister of Foreign Affairs Baron Ange Hyacinthe Maxence de Damas advocated milder coercive measures than Russia but under pressure from Nicholas I he also finally gave way.[42]

The French defection to the British-Russian camp was another serious blow to Metternich who naturally greatly regretted France's decision and denounced its willingness to be active at any price: "The progress of the French cabinet continues to be pitiable. Nothing matches the ease with which it enters into all propositions. It does not care whether directed to the right or to the left, to the good or to the bad; it needs to act and to be able to boast of not being left behind England in any way."[43] He could only count on Prussia, but this was small compensation since Bernstorff was more neutral than pro-Austrian and Metternich could not expect any useful support from him in preventing the creation of the trilateral alliance. Nevertheless, since Metternich believed that Mahmud II's victory over the Greeks was a question of only a few months, he decided at least to buy more

---

[42] Metternich to Ottenfels, Vienna, 17 Nov. 1826, HHStA, StA, Türkei VI, 24; Tatishchev to Nesselrode, Vienna, 13 and 18 Jan, 6 and 12 Feb. 1826, AVPRI, fond 133, Kantseliariia, opis 468, 11870; Cetto to Ludwig I of Bavaria, London, 17 Nov. 1826, BHStA, MA, London 2221; Hatzfeldt to Frederick William III, Vienna, 18 Nov. 1826, GStA PK, HA III, MdA I, 6007; Brewer, p. 317; Sauvigny, *Metternich et la France*, III, pp. 1072–1087.

[43] Metternich to Zichy, Vienna, 15 April 1827, HHStA, StK, Preussen 125.

time for the Turks to finish the war before the European intervention could take place. What he was left with was France's desire for all the five Powers to cooperate together instead of only three of them acting in concert and Nicholas I's call for the five Powers to negotiate the treaty in London; both were to serve Metternich in drawing out these negotiations. He probably also hoped that the hidden distrust and suspicion held by the cabinet ministers in France, Great Britain and Russia towards each other would enable him to inject some dissension among them. If he succeeded in this, then, according to him, there was some chance to significantly modify the text of the treaty, of which the two versions proposed by Russia and France were equally unacceptable to him: "In firmly rejecting the bases on which the Protocol explicitly stands, it is clear that we are equally unlikely to accept them refashioned in another form."[44] He informed the other Great Powers that for Austria's participation the treaty had to differ from the Protocol in certain points, in particular the words "suzerainty" and "mediation" and the forced mediation had to be omitted. In late March 1827, he instructed Esterházy to take part in the London conference and negotiate upon these principles.[45]

This attempt was doomed to fail because although France desired to see Austria in the entente, it was more determined to follow its new partners. Canning was under Russia's influence and Nicholas I together with Nesselrode were not willing to make any important concessions to Metternich. It was Russia on which Metternich particularly counted in his manouevre because he thought that the tsar wanted to come closer to the Alliance at the London conference, but it was this Great Power which most resolutely opposed his attempt to delay signing the treaty and, consequently, it flatly refused to deviate from

---

[44] Metternich to Apponyi, Vienna, 3 Jan. 1827, HHStA, StA, Frankreich 264.

[45] Metternich to Apponyi, Vienna, 29 Jan., 12 and 27 Feb., 19 March 1827, HHStA, StA, Frankreich 264; Metternich to Esterházy, Vienna, 14 Feb., 25 and 26 March 1827, HHStA, StA, England 178; Metternich to Bombelles, Vienna, 27 March 1827, HHStA, StA, Russland III, 81; Hatzfeldt to Frederick William III, Vienna, 18 Dec. 1826, GStA PK, HA III, MdA I, 6007; Hatzfeldt to Frederick William III, Vienna, 25 Jan. 1827, GStA PK, HA III, MdA I, 6008; Caraman to Damas, Vienna, 18 Dec. 1826, AMAE, CP, Autriche 407; Caraman to Damas, Vienna, 2 and 29 March 1827, AMAE, CP, Autriche 408; Wellesley to Canning, Vienna, 19 Feb. 1827, TNA, FO 120/84; Tatishchev to Nesselrode, Vienna, 19 March 1827, AVPRI, fond 133, Kantseliariia, opis 468, 11873; Baack, pp. 150–153; Krauter, p. 211.

the conditions of the Protocol and give up the right to use coercive measures. When Esterházy obtained the March instructions, Canning and especially Lieven informed him that Great Britain, Russia and France would proceed in an alliance of three, which sufficed for the pacification of the Levant, and there was thus no reason for all five Great Powers to proceed together. This statement was soon confirmed by the Russian cabinet, which was not willing to repeat Alexander I's mistake and remain in long discussions with Metternich that would lead nowhere. It was a bitter disappointment for the chancellor who had expected no sympathy for his plan in London but some in St Petersburg. He reproached Tatishchev: "Did You not assure me that the emperor Your Noble Master would consider an agreement among the five Great Powers to work together on the pacification of the Levant as a way of bringing England back into the quintuple Alliance? Though in no way hoping for such a result, we are prepared to double our efforts to achieve it, and yet from the first step that we make in London, it is Russia which rejects us."[46] It was only now when Metternich stopped perceiving Nicholas I in such a favourable light that he lost his last illusions about the tsar's wish to proceed according to the chancellor's conservative principles; for him the tsar was no longer a mere victim of Canning. Metternich refused Russia's offer to accept the treaty as it was and with the acceptance of a fait accompli to join the "monstrous alliance."[47] In late May he recalled his previous instructions to Esterházy from late March and returned to his previous defensive position officially assumed in late December 1826. Austria's separation from the three Great Powers became thus complete.[48]

From late May 1827 Metternich was condemned to observe from the sidelines the trilateral negotiations over the treaty with an evident pro-Greek bias that was finally signed in London on 6 July 1827.

---

[46] Tatishchev to Nesselrode, Vienna, 13 April 1827, AVPRI, fond 133, Kantseliariia, opis 468, 11873.

[47] Metternich to Apponyi, Vienna, 31 May 1827, HHStA, StA, Frankreich 264.

[48] Metternich to Apponyi, Vienna, 31 March, 21 and 31 May 1827, HHStA, StA, Frankreich 264; Metternich to Esterházy, Vienna, 14 and 26 May 1827, HHStA, StA, England 178; Metternich to Bombelles, Vienna, 17 June 1827, HHStA, StA, Russland III, 81; Wellesley to Dudley, Vienna, 22 May 1827, TNA, FO 120/86; Maltzan to Frederick William III, Vienna, 25 May 1827, GStA PK, HA III, MdA I, 6008; Caraman to Damas, Vienna, 26 May 1827, AMAE, CP, Autriche 408; Sauvigny, *Metternich et la France*, III, p. 1092.

The document was composed of public and secret parts; the former contained the articles more or less identical to those of the Protocol – the contracting parties professed to mediate with the aim of assuring autonomy for Greece; the latter, disclosed by *The Times* a week after signing, contained the explanation of the coercive measures to be taken in the event that the Porte refused to accept the mediation: the signatories committed themselves to establishing commercial relations with the Greeks and ensuring an armistice by interrupting the supply of the sultan's forces in the Peloponnese by sea and terminating his naval and military operations against the Greeks. The allied fleets were to achieve these goals, however, without doing anything that could provoke a fight – as the relevant article was worded, without "taking any part in the hostilities between the two contending parties."[49] The admirals could defend themselves only if, for example, the sultan's battleships wanted to enforce the passage through the "peace blockade" by force.[50]

Metternich's Perceptive Criticism of the Treaty of London

With the conclusion of the Treaty of London of 6 July 1827, the first phase of the process started on 4 April 1826 was completed. During this period, Russia and not Canning was in the centre of affairs, directing the British and later also the French leaders in the desired direction. Even though Metternich was prevented by his hatred of Canning from seeing this for most of the given period, he otherwise demonstrated two things: his analytical skills in correctly foreseeing the inevitable outcome of the coercive measures as settled by Great Britain, France and Russia and the consistency of his views on the functioning of the European state system, both often being misinterpreted or scorned by historians as simply dogmatic, inconsistent, arti-

---

[49] T. E. Holland (ed.), *The European Concert in the Eastern Question: A Collection of Treaties and Other Public Acts Edited with Introduction and Notes*, Aalen 1979, p. 10.
[50] Woodhouse, *The Greek War*, pp. 122–123.

ficial and much-vaunted.[51] For example, Canning's advocate, British historian Harold Temperley, used sarcasm in his analysis of Metternich's arguments concerning the illegal aspects of the Protocol and the Treaty; the title of a subchapter "Metternich Moralises" in Temperley's monograph on the British statesman is more than eloquent.[52]

These examples well represent the scant attention paid to the rational background of Metternich's criticism of the legal character of the two international documents. In fact, his arguments were highly reasonable and touched more upon the questions of European law than philosophical dogmas. The arguments were based upon his firm belief that the independence of states was inviolable, with the exception of situations when they were threatened with revolutions. In such cases, nevertheless, the Great Powers could intervene for the sake of the legitimate ruler, not necessarily an absolute one, as German historian Matthias Schulz incorrectly explains Metternich's views,[53] but they could in no way represent a nation in uprising against the established authority. The legitimate authority's request for help was, moreover, needed for any foreign interference. Consequently, Metternich could never agree with an intervention without the formal consent of the legitimate ruler, and never against his will and interests or on behalf of the insurgents. Exactly this lack of respect for the territorial integrity of an independent country was included in the Protocol and the Treaty, attacking the sultan's sovereignty in the manner "scarcely justifiable according to the simplest principles of the respect to the independence of countries."[54] Metternich pointed out in early June 1826 the hypocrisy of the Protocol's authors, who planned to interfere in the internal affairs of an independent country but were hardly willing to admit the same right to other countries to proceed in the same way against them: "Upon what law could the two courts base the agreement that they have just concluded, an agreement whose purpose is the settlement of the internal relations of a third country? Is not the sultan within his rights to refuse with complete justification any offer of mediation? On the other hand the Greeks are regarded by

---

[51] Crawley, *Greek Independence*, p. 64; Schulz, *Normen und Praxis*, p. 93.
[52] Temperley, *Canning*, pp. 360–362.
[53] Schulz, *Normen und Praxis*, p. 585.
[54] Remarks to the Protocol of 4 April 1826, attached to Metternich to Esterházy, Vienna, 4 June 1826, HHStA, StA, England 175.

the two Great Powers who arranged the Protocol of 4 April either as the subjects of the Porte or as an established state. In the first case, upon what can the two courts base the principle of mediation? What would England or Russia say to an agreement strictly conforming to the text of the afore-mentioned Protocol which would take place between France and Austria and which would basically establish that His British Majesty or the Russian emperor would be deprived of an insurgent Ireland or Finland?"[55] Later in the year, the chancellor repeated this objection in his instructions to the Austrian ambassador in Paris, Count Anton Apponyi: "It is a question neither more nor less of the foundations of the law of nations recognised up to this hour. What would be the fate of Europe – that of civilisation if the doctrine of *dédoublement des États* were ever admitted by the last supporters of the peace of nations? How can a man of sense advance so subversive a contention, or at least permit himself the attempt to advance it? Is England then ready to *regard as a Power equal in rights to that of the [British] King* the first Irish Club which declares itself the *Insurgent Government of Ireland*? To regard as fondée *dans son droit* the French Power which would accept the office of mediator, by reason of the sole fact that the invitation had been addressed to it by *the Irish Government* – to regard finally as conformable to the law of nations, the menace of compulsory measures, or even of those furnished by France, or of those she should find means to combine with other Powers?"[56] It is actually very difficult to reject these arguments as merely artificial, irrational or dogmatic because they definitely formed the relations among the five Great Powers in the 1820s. Metternich believed that these arguments should also be applied to countries of the second rank, which in his opinion of course meant their legitimate governments. The cabinets in London, Paris and St Petersburg opposed this attitude in relation to the Ottoman Empire despite the fact that they would hardly allow a similar interference into their own affairs. The near future proved this at least in the case of Russia when Nicholas I refused with indignation the British and French offer

[55] Ibid. The comparison of Greece to Ireland in this way was already made by Francis I towards Stratford Canning during the British diplomat's short stay in Vienna at the end of 1824. Caraman to Damas, Vienna, 29 Dec. 1824, AMAE, CP, Autriche 405.
[56] Temperley, *Canning*, p. 361.

of mediation in the Polish November Uprising, something which he had pressed for in the Greek one. A British reaction in the event of any eventual foreign interference in its own Irish affairs could also be hardly different. This proves that although Metternich's rejection of the idea of managing international relations upon national principles did not correspond with the general development of the 19th century, one cannot say that during the Greek uprising any other Great Power actually held more progressive views in this sense. The diplomacy of Nicholas I or Canning in the Greek Question was definitely pursued in their own countries' interests and was not motivated by the welfare of the insurgents.[57]

Harold Temperley confined himself to a theory, never more closely explained, that Metternich's reasoning could not be applied to Great Britain because this country was not the Ottoman Empire and Greece was not Ireland.[58] This argument, if it can be called one, well characterises the attitudes of Canning and those Europeans desiring to pursue an active Greek policy at the expense of the Ottoman Empire whose rights they infringed. This imperialistic policy was made easier by the fact that the sultan's country lay outside the European state system, but Metternich argued that this in reality meant little since its existence was important for the maintenance of Europe's stability and tranquillity, something which was generally agreed among the members of the pentarchy. Furthemore, he considered the betrayal of the European Alliance's rules as the way to its dissolution and, consequently, the policy of the Great Powers involved in the resolutions of 4 April 1826 and 6 July 1827 "as corrupting the aims of the European alliance."[59] In support of Austria's refusal to conclude the Treaty of London, he cited the 4th article of the Protocol signed by all

---

[57] For more on Metternich's interpretation of the law see Metternich to Bombelles, Vienna, 13 Nov. 1826, HHStA, StA, Russland III, 75; Metternich to Apponyi, Vienna, 25 Sept. and 30 Oct. 1826, HHStA, StA, Frankreich 261; Metternich to Apponyi, Vienna, 31 March and 11 June 1827, HHStA, StA, Frankreich 264; Metternich to Zichy, Vienna, 14 June 1827, HHStA, StK, Preussen 125; Caraman to Damas, Vienna, 1 April 1827, AMAE, CP, Autriche 408; Wellesley to Canning, Vienna, 1 Nov. 1826, TNA, FO 120/82; Wellesley to Canning, Vienna, 30 April 1827, TNA, FO 120/85; Wellesley to Dudley, Vienna, 14 June 1827, TNA, FO 120/86; Tatishchev to Nesselrode, Vienna, 11 June 1827, AVPRI, fond 133, Kantseliariia, opis 468, 11873; Sauvigny, *Metternich et la France*, III, pp. 1097–1098.
[58] Temperley, *Canning*, p. 361.
[59] Sked, *Metternich*, p. 85.

the Great Powers at the Congress at Aix-la-Chapelle on 15 November 1818. This article contained the rule that the interests of a third country, and no restriction excluded the Ottoman Empire from being such a country, could not be discussed at a conference or congress without the formal invitation to that party to participate in such a meeting.[60] Metternich returned to this stipulation in January 1827: "We would not hesitate on our part to regard a treaty arranged among the five Great Powers concerning the settlement of the internal affairs of a sixth country, without a previous request and the cooperation of that country, as an irregular, dangerous and inadmissible form of proceeding ... I have every reason to suppose that in Paris they keep the quintuple Alliance in mind [and] if they want to proceed in compliance with it, it is necessary not to distort it, and the ways in which it should operate are at one time so simple, beneficial and regulated by the Aix-la-Chapelle Protocol that it must suffice us to refer to this act for support in formulating the refusals which we might see ourselves compelled to make."[61] In his opinion, the fact that the Ottoman Empire was not one of the signatories to this article in the Protocol of 1818 made it no less valid, and the Great Powers were obliged to act in accordance with its stipulations towards any country, in particular if they expected that country to act according to the law in return. The new Prussian envoy in Vienna, Baron Bogislaw von Maltzan, reported to Berlin: "Metternich strongly opposes the principle introduced by the French government that, in the matter of the distinction between suzerainty and sovereignty, it is not necessary to define them so precisely with the Turks who do not understand the difference themselves; he thinks that if one believes one can deviate from the treaties and from the principles of law with regard to the Turks, one no longer has the right to demand of the Porte that it observes them on its part."[62]

Even in this legal dispute Metternich's crucial enemy was Canning, not for the reason, as Harold Temperley claims, that the chancellor "was conscious that Canning, and not he, was at last dominating,

---

[60] L. von Neumann (ed.), *Recueil des traités et conventions conclus par l'Autriche avec les Puissances étrangères 1763–1856*, III, Leipzig 1857, pp. 441–442.
[61] Metternich to Zichy, Vienna, 31 Jan. 1827, HHStA, StK, Preussen 125.
[62] Maltzan to Frederick William III, Vienna, 10 June 1827, GStA PK, HA III, MdA I, 6008.

not only Russia but Europe,"[63] but because the foreign secretary's policy in the matter of non-intervention and intervention, the former advocated in Latin America and the latter in Greece, in both cases on behalf of the insurgents, constituted for the chancellor a "Bill of new political rights"[64] in exact opposition to his own precepts and detrimental for the empire whose interests he advocated: "Austria and England – two Great Powers which should always be closely bound together by permanent and indelible practical interests – are absolutely divided in the moral sphere. We represent the principle of conservation, and the new England has declared its support for the revolutionary principle."[65] For Austria these principles were needed: "Respect for all existing laws, the liberty and independence of each country, the inviolability of the principle of the union among the Great Powers, assistance for the oppressed legitimate authority when it requests this support; absolute respect for the independence of an established authority."[66] For Metternich, the bases of Canning's new legal code were: "The individual self-interest of each country placed in opposition to that of any another country. The right of intervention into every internal quarrel in a foreign country, provided that any appeal is made by the party in rebelling against the legitimate government, and under the explicit condition that this party has acquired enough power to establish itself into a form of government."[67] Metternich and Francis I refused to act according to this last point because they were not willing to create a new precedent in international law which could be repeated later in other affairs like national revolts against legitimate authorities. Since the multinational composition of the Austrian Empire greatly resembled the situation in the Ottoman Empire, Francis I and his chancellor were naturally very sensitive to such a danger. What was about to happen to the sultan with regard to his rebellious subjects could happen in the future to Francis I in his multinational empire.[68]

---

[63] Temperley, *Canning*, p. 362.

[64] Tatishchev to Nesselrode, Vienna, 25 Oct. 1826, AVPRI, fond 133, Kantseliariia, opis 468, 11870.

[65] Metternich to Zichy, Vienna, 10 June 1827, HHStA, StA, Russland III, 81.

[66] Tatishchev to Nesselrode, Vienna, 25 Oct. 1826, AVPRI, fond 133, Kantseliariia, opis 468, 11870.

[67] Ibid.

[68] Schroeder, *Transformation*, p. 650.

The second crucial argument raised by Metternich against the St Petersburg Protocol and the Treaty of London stipulations concerned their unfeasibility. Canning was in this respect extremely optimistic, both after the Protocol and the Treaty. When Mahmud II did not accept the former containing no coercive measures, Canning started to believe that it would be possible to succeed with just some. He was greatly influenced in this optimism by a British military intervention in Portugal during the winter of 1826–1827 that succeeded without a single shot. This made the foreign secretary, since 10 April 1827 the prime minister, believe that something similar could be achieved in Greece. He closed his eyes to the reality and hoped that Mahmud II would accept the Treaty conditions despite the diplomatic reports clearly stating the unlikely success of this option, and the near future proved how very wrong he was.[69]

Douglas Dakin attempted to defend Canning when he wrote: "Wellington later said that Canning's whole policy in the Greek Question ought to have been stopped in its early stages, and most Tories came to share this view; but at the time criticism of Canning's policy had been vague, deriving from a feeling of uneasiness rather than from a confident desire to substitute an alternative. It was only after Navarino that Canning's detractors began to look upon the hostilities as the inevitable result of his policy."[70] Nevertheless, Dakin forgot that Canning's most ardent enemy at the Viennese Chancellery had long clearly predicted its inevitable consequences. Metternich knew very well that the sultan was resolutely opposed to foreign intervention in "his" Greek Question, and he was convinced that not two, three nor five Great Powers would be able to persuade the Ottoman monarch to yield either without coercive measures or with those contained in the Treaty of London, the text of which he already knew since early June thanks to Damas. He supposed that the threat of a war with all the Great Powers could motivate Mahmud II to enter into the negotiations and declare a cease-fire but the Treaty did not, according to his opinion, contain any effective measure of this kind. So Mahmud II would refuse and the answer of the three Great Powers – mere demonstrations of their naval power – could never force him to surrender but had to provoke a war, which was exactly the opposite

---

[69] Brewer, p. 318.
[70] Dakin, *The Greek Struggle*, p. 228.

of their principal goals: to persuade the sultan to accept their method
of pacification and preserve peace. Metternich attacked the plan for
interposing their maritime forces between the two quarrelling parties
and for preventing the sultan's navy from supplying his troops fighting in the Peloponnese. For him this was no peaceful step but an act
of war without its formal declaration, and he did not doubt that Mahmud II would answer this hostile behaviour with the use of force. If
the Ottoman captains refused to obey the orders of the European admirals, they could be never made to comply except by force, and since
it could be presumed that the sultan's officers would indeed oppose
such orders, Metternich regarded an armed collision in consequence
of the trilateral intervention as a certainty: "It is impossible not to
consider [the plan] as an act of open hostility ... What we do not understand is how it [the naval blockade] could take place without those
in command taking part in the hostilities between the belligerent parties. The same holds for the stipulation by which the Great Powers
commit themselves to guarding the armistice if it is violated by the
parties that would have underwritten it. And again this 'without taking part in the hostilities.'"[71] Metternich of course did not refrain from
attacking the plan from the point of international law that he found
to be violated by this conduct. Maltzan reported after a meeting with
him: "The sending of squadrons to intercept the communications between Egypt and Greece seems to Prince Metternich to be a measure
as inadmissible as the right that England wanted to assume several
years ago to prevent Spain from making similar efforts to reconquer
its insurgent [American] colonies. He cannot understand how Russia,
which protested at that time against this claim of England's, could
sanction the principle with the measure it [Russia] has just joined."[72]
Furthermore, according to Metternich, this conduct had to create an
independent and not autonomous Greece, again the exact opposite to
what the trilateral alliance stated it wanted to achieve. The Greeks
desiring the former could hardly be compelled to accept the latter at
the very moment when they received diplomatic and military support
against the Turks: "Much like the political independence of Greece is
assured on the day when direct relations with Greece are established,

---

[71] Metternich to Ottenfels, Vienna, 20 June 1827, HHStA, StA, Türkei VI, 29.
[72] Maltzan to Frederick William III, Vienna, 10 June 1827, GStA PK, HA III,
MdA I, 6008.

so is war with the Porte declared on the day when squadrons are deployed."[73] Every war "that Europe would wage against the Porte would be a war of expulsion, and not an enterprise which could ever hope to bring the insurgent Greeks back under the Ottoman domination."[74]

Metternich's criticism of the trilateral alliance contained one more important aspect: the fact that each member signed the Treaty of London with the aim of holding the others in check. The motivation behind their behaviour was their distrust of one another, not their love for the Greeks.[75] Metternich of course knew that, particularly when the British and French did not make any secret of it with Austrian diplomats: "A union that has no other basis than great distrust between the contracting parties, that has no other goal than a mutual desire to control and that not only rests upon no justifiable principle but also infringes upon the least indisputable bases of common rights; only such a union could give birth to a monster like the proposal of the trilateral Treaty."[76] When he heard the explanation of the Parisian cabinet that France intended with the signature of the Treaty to check both England and Russia and prevent a war in the Levant, he merely answered: "You are bound and war will follow."[77]

In conclusion, Metternich was firmly convinced that the whole trilateral project was as unrealisable as it was illegal: "There is nothing useful in the wording that was chosen unless one wants to allow that the ridiculousness involved in stipulations devoid of every means of reasonable execution would be a good thing."[78] The cabinets in London, Paris and St Petersburg were simply and fundamentally mistaken if they thought that Mahmud II would "grow wise," as he had not wanted to yield before the Treaty and would not do so afterwards. In Metternich's opinion, the Treaty of London inevitably had to lead to war, Greek independence, the greater influence of Great Britain over the eastern Mediterranean owing to this independence and Rus-

---

[73] Metternich to Zichy, Vienna, 29 March 1827, HHStA, StK, Preussen 125.
[74] Metternich to Bombelles, Vienna, 27 March 1827, HHStA, StA, Russland III, 81.
[75] Crawley, *Greek Independence*, p. 77.
[76] Metternich to Ottenfels, Vienna, 4 July 1827, HHStA, StA, Türkei VI, 29.
[77] A. von Prokesch-Osten, *Mehmed-Ali, Vize-König von Aegypten: Aus meinem Tagebuche 1826–1841*, Wien 1877, p. 13.
[78] Metternich to Esterházy, Vienna, 16 June 1827, HHStA, StA, England 178.

sia's greater influence over the Balkans owing to the fact that such a war against the Ottoman Empire had to principally be fought out by this continental Power and not the two maritime ones: "It can lead to anything, only not to that for which it was intended. Where it will certainly lead is to a war of Russia against the Porte. England will assist in it without actually going to war herself. France will be the plaything of its own allies and its own miscalculations."[79] Even though he still believed that Nicholas I did not want an armed conflict, he presumed that the tsar would start one if the goals of the Treaty were not achieved by negotiations.[80]

$$* \quad * \quad *$$

Metternich's predictions were in many respects accurate, and his criticism of the St Petersburg Protocol and the Treaty of London was in certain points well founded. Another extoller of Canning's diplomacy, British historian Charles W. Crawley, reacted with this argument: "It was easy for unfriendly critics to attack the treaty point by point and to accuse it of uncertainty, inconsistency, and even of partiality: but the alternative offered by Metternich was not a better treaty, but no treaty, nor any other useful suggestion to end the six years' misery."[81] In fact Metternich did have a suggestion, which may not have been more moral or better for the Greeks, but from the general desire to end the war in Greece it is also difficult to label it as worse. The idea was not new, in fact it had been maintained and advocated by Metternich since the very beginning: to let Mahmud II pacify the Greeks with his own resources and persuade him to improve their future by

---

[79] Metternich to Ottenfels, Vienna, 4 July 1827, HHStA, StA, Türkei VI, 29.
[80] Metternich to Zichy, Vienna, 29 March and 24 June 1827, HHStA, StK, Preussen 125; Metternich to Esterházy, Vienna, 14 May 1827, HHStA, StA, England 178; Metternich to Apponyi, Vienna, 31 May, 11 and 16 June, 31 July 1827, HHStA, StA, Frankreich 264; Metternich to Bombelles, Vienna, 17 June 1827, HHStA, StA, Russland III, 81; Caraman to Damas, Vienna, 24 April and 24 July 1827, AMAE, CP, Autriche 408; Tatishchev to Nesselrode, Vienna, 25 April 1827, AVPRI, fond 133, Kantseliariia, opis 468, 11873; Maltzan to Frederick William III, Vienna, 10 and 23 June 1827, GStA PK, HA III, MdA I, 6008; Sauvigny, *Metternich et la France*, III, p. 1097.
[81] Crawley, *Greek Independence*, p. 78.

some administrative concessions; the final settlement would not have been very different from that offered by the signatories of the Treaty of London. Although its durability from the long-term point of view was more than doubtful, Metternich's solution was superior to that of the trilateral alliance in one important aspect: it could be quickly achieved because in the summer of 1827, exactly at the moment when the Treaty of London was signed with this aim, the Greek insurrection was on the verge of complete collapse and the sultan's victory seemed to be close at hand and certain.

6

The Eastern Mediterranean at the Time of the Battle of Navarino

Metternich criticised not only the trilateral alliance for its illegal policy with little hope for the expected success but also the Turks for their inability to crush the Greek revolt for many years. Since he was no blind reactionary statesman, he well understood that the sultan could win the war with the insurgents only at the moment when vigorous military operations were combined with a willingness to ensure the Greeks a prospect for their better future. When foreign intervention into the Greek Question became imminent, he intensified his advice that the sultan should proceed in a more diplomatic way towards the Greeks as well as the Great Powers, but this counsel went unheeded in Constantinople. The Porte's refusal to allow any foreign interference into its affairs deteriorated not only its relations with the allied Powers but also their relations with Austria, which they regarded as the main culprit of the sultan's intransigence. George Canning's death in August 1827 gave Metternich hope for the reversal of the situation, but such an option was soon thwarted by an encounter between the allied and the sultan's fleets in Navarino Bay.

The Egyptian Intervention in Greece and Anton Prokesch's First Mission to Alexandria

The more than six years that passed between the outbreak of the Greek insurrection and the signature of the Treaty of London were filled with Metternich's urgent appeals to the Porte for a prompt suppression of the Greek uprising, which Mahmud II was unable to satisfy, not because he did not want to but because the decay of his empire showed itself in the weakness of its military as well as its naval

forces, which were unable to destroy the hotbeds of the Greek resistance: the Peloponnese and some of the islands in the Aegean Sea, the
so-called Archipelago. The news of repeated Turkish defeats greatly
displeased Metternich and in the early years of the uprising made him
rather sceptical about a quick victory for the sultan.[1] He had to come
to terms with how the precious time gained in his negotiations with
Alexander I was lost in the sultan's never-ending conflict against an
enemy who had no strong, regular and centrally commanded army or
navy and was weakened by squabbles in its own camp, which finally
led to a series of civil wars among the Greeks who, according to the
Austrian chancellor, were still alive and "strong due to the stupidity
of the Turks."[2]

Mahmud II was equally dissatisfied with the development of the
war, and in early 1824 he asked his powerful Egyptian governor, Mohammed Ali Pasha, for help. Mohammed Ali was not a native Egyptian; he was born in the Thrakian town of Kavala, and he had come
to the land on the Nile at the beginning of the century to expel the
French army brought there earlier by Napoleon Bonaparte. When the
French were expelled, he seized power in 1805 and proclaimed himself governor of this Ottoman province, a fact that a weak government in Constantinople had to recognise. In the following years, he
eliminated all the opposition and became effectively the only man
in his own house, which is a perfect analogy of the given situation
because he had absolute control of not only the country but also of
the agricultural land and its revenues. With the same Albanian origins and far-reaching ambitions, he resembled Ali Pasha of Yannina,
but he considerably exceeded Ali Pasha in the administrative, economic, military and other reforms that he soon began to implement
and which were entirely unprecedented in the Levant. Consequently, in
the early 1820s, Mohammed Ali disposed of high revenues from farm-
ing, manufacturing and commerce. The money collected was mainly
used for the creation of a strong army and navy, which were gradually
transformed upon a European-French military model. The reforms in

---

[1]   Metternich to Ottenfels, Venice, 21 Dec. 1822, HHStA, StA, Türkei VI, 14;
Ottenfels to Metternich, Constantinople, 17 Sept. 1824, HHStA, StA, Türkei VI,
21; Caraman to Damas, Vienna, 3 Nov. 1824, AMAE, CP, Autriche 405.
[2]   Hatzfeldt to Frederick William III, Vienna, 1 Nov. 1824, GStA PK, HA III,
MdA I, 6004. For more on the evolution of the war in the early 1820s see Brewer,
pp. 226–232; Dakin, pp. 71–130; Woodhouse, *The Greek War*, pp. 59–101.

Egypt were accompanied by a territorial expansion particularly motivated by economic interests, so at the time when Mohammed Ali was asked by Mahmud II for help against the Greeks, he administrated not only Egypt but also the Sudan and a considerable part of the Arabian Peninsula with Mecca and Medina as well. Although he was not personally hostile to the Greeks and never allowed them to be persecuted in "his" lands as was so often seen in other parts of the Ottoman Empire after 1821, he agreed to intervene against them because the prospect of increasing his own political as well as economic power in the eastern Mediterranean by gaining Crete and the Peloponnese under his administration should he be successful was too tempting for him to refuse.[3]

The Viennese cabinet did not have a hand in Mahmud II's request as French historian Gaston Isambert claimed,[4] but it was actually extremely pleased when Mohammed Ali agreed since it realised only too well that this pasha could offer something that the sultan lacked: a considerable amount of money and a fighting-fit army. Mohammed Ali was considered by Metternich as the only pasha able to change the course of affairs in Greece, and this opinion was strengthened during the spring of 1824 by the reports from Ottenfels and the Prussian envoy in Constantinople, Baron Alexander von Miltitz, on the superior quality of the Egyptian armed forces. These two men paid particular attention to the military commander of these forces, Ibrahim Pasha, the eldest son of Mohammed Ali. What the father, compared by contemporaries to a fox, achieved in the administration of Egypt, his son, compared to a lion, was predestined to achieve in the battlefields as a great military leader. His intelligence, military skills, ability and willingness to learn from French officers employed in the Egyptian army, together with his modesty during the campaigns and loyalty to his father made him an effective tool in Mohammed Ali's hands.[5] Al-

---

[3]   For more on Mohammed Ali's early reign and territorial expansion see A. Lufti al-Sayyid Marsot, *Egypt in the Reign of Muhammad Ali*, Cambridge 1984, pp. 24–205; K. Fahmy, *Mehmed Ali: From Ottoman Governor to Ruler of Egypt*, Oxford 2009, pp. 27–68. For more on his attitude towards the Greeks see A. G. Politis, *L'Hellénisme et l'Égypte moderne*, I, Paris 1929, pp. 176–198.

[4]   G. Isambert, *L'indépendence grecque et l'Europe*, Paris 1900, p. 176.

[5]   Ottenfels to Metternich, Constantinople, 10 and 21 March 1824, HHStA, StA, Türkei VI, 20; Miltitz to Frederick William III, Pera, 15 April 1824, GStA PK, HA III, MdA I, 7258; Buccianti to Miltitz, Alexandria, 21 June 1824, Miltitz to Frederick William III, Pera, 10 Aug. 1824, GStA PK, HA III, MdA I, 7259; Piquot

though Miltitz in particular somewhat exaggerated the fighting spirit of the Egyptian troops, the reports which Metternich obtained were basically well founded and it was soon proved that Mohammed Ali's army was by far the best military corps in the Near East and a hard nut for the Greeks to crack.[6] When the first Egyptian landing force under Ibrahim's command reached the Peloponnese on 24 February 1825, the same day on which the second round of the St Petersburg conferences was opened, a new phase in the history of the Greek insurrection started. It was difficult for the insurgents to check the Egyptians' advance, and before the year ended, Ibrahim Pasha controlled most of strategic points in the peninsula. In 1826, the Egyptians and the Turks captured Missolonghi and Athens leaving just the Acropolis on the mainland, the town of Nafplion and some of its surrounding area in the Peloponnese and some islands in Greek hands.[7]

Despite their serious defeats, the Greeks continued to fight and their dream of freedom still lived on at the end of 1826. The preceding two years represented thus for Metternich a series of expectations and disillusionment. In the late summer of 1825, he wrote to his diplomats that the insurrection was coming to its end, and he then had to face the hard reality during the autumn. After the fall of Missolonghi in May 1826 and with news of the increasingly precarious situation of the Greeks, his optimism was revived only to be quashed again in the following months, this time with more regrets owing to the existence of the St Petersburg protocol and the forthcoming European interference into Greek affairs.[8] Consequently, he was more hopeful than ever

---

to Frederick William III, Vienna, 17 May 1824, GStA PK, HA III, MdA I, 6003.

[6] An excellent survey on Mohammed Ali's army is offered by K. Fahmy, *All the Pasha's Men: Mehmed Ali, His Army and the Making of Modern Egypt*, Cambridge 1997.

[7] V. H. Aksan, *Ottoman Wars 1700–1870: An Empire Besieged*, Harlow 2007, p. 294; P. Crabitès, *Ibrahim of Egypt*, London 1935, pp. 65–70; G. Sinoué, *Le dernier Pharaon: Méhémet Ali (1770–1849)*, Paris 1997, pp. 254–259; Brewer, pp. 234–237, 283–309.

[8] Metternich to Esterházy, Ischl, 7 Aug. 1825, HHStA, StA, England 173; Metternich to Lebzeltern, Ischl, 13 Aug. 1825, HHStA, StA, Russland III, 71; Metternich to Vincent, Vienna, 5 Dec. 1825, HHStA, StA, Frankreich 257; Metternich to Lebzeltern, Vienna, 19 May and 2 June 1826, HHStA, StA, Russland III, 75; Metternich to Apponyi, Vienna, 14 June 1826, HHStA, StA, Frankreich 260; Metternich to Ottenfels, Vienna, 1 Dec. 1826, HHStA, StA, Türkei VI, 24; Maltzan to Frederick William III, Vienna, 13 and 17 June 1826, GStA PK, HA III, MdA I, 6006.

to see the Greeks defeated, but one problem that could frustrate such an outcome arose during 1826: Mohammed Ali was irritated by the inept conduct of Kapudan (Grand Admiral) Husrev Pasha whom he blamed for undermining the joint Turko-Egyptian operations; Husrev's conduct destroying the joint Turko-Egyptian war effort was a result not only of his inability – he was in fact no sailor – but also his personal hostility towards Mohammed Ali with whom he had originally struggled unsuccessfully for rule over Egypt, from which he was finally expelled in 1805. Mohammed Ali requested now the removal of his mortal enemy from his post and threatened to withdraw his forces from Greece if this request was denied.[9]

Despite its diplomatic support of the sultan in the West, Austria did not till then actively intervene in his conflict with the Greeks in the East. Austrians were forbidden to fight with the Greeks and none fought against them on the sultan's side; they were to abstain from any political conduct towards the rebels since doing so could be taken for a recognition of their independence; the emperor's navy assisted the sultan only in so far that it protected Austrian commercial vessels, often loaded with goods for the Turks, against Greek pirates and undertook military operations against them, but only with the aim of releasing captured vessels or obtaining financial satisfaction for losses suffered by their attacks.[10] Nevertheless, when the continuation of the Turko-Egyptian joint operations was threatened by the animosity between Mohammed Ali and Husrev Pasha, Austrian diplomacy intervened. The main protagonist of this intervention from late 1826 was Anton Prokesch, later receiving the predicate "von Osten," a young Austrian officer active in the eastern Mediterranean since 1824. He won the respect of Ottenfels, Gentz and Metternich himself during 1825 with his informative reports on the situation in Greece that were by far the best source of information on the insurrection at that time since the Austrian consuls were not able to offer reliable accounts; Metternich labelled him as one of "our most reliable and intelligent correspondents."[11] Since Prokesch's accounts received not only recognition at the Viennese Chancellery but were also highly valued by the

---

[9]   Sauer, *Österreich und die Levante*, p. 175.

[10] For more on the activities of Austria's navy in the Eastern Mediterranean see Chapter 14.

[11] Metternich to Esterházy, Vienna, 8 Sept. 1825, HHStA, StA, England 173.

foreign diplomats to whom they were given,[12] he became an important reporter on Greek military as well as political affairs not only from the purely Austrian but also the wider European perspective.[13] The Prussian envoy in Vienna wrote to his king in early 1827: "This naval officer has demonstrated a rare intelligence and service in getting himself to all the places where he could be a spectator of the most interesting events and obtain thus prompt and direct news of them. Although the present report of Baron Miltitz is essentially drafted upon those of Mr Prokesch of whom I am speaking, these [Prokesch's] contain more details and more precise information, which make me wish I could mail them in their entirety to Your Majesty."[14]

When the problem with Husrev Pasha arose, Prokesch got the opportunity to prove that he possessed talent not only as an observer but also as a diplomat. He had wanted for a while to visit Egypt, and in September 1826 he was encouraged to undertake this journey by Ottenfels, who for some time had not been receiving reports from the Austrian consulate where the consuls were changing right at that

---

[12] Despite the high evaluation of Prokesch's messages and memoirs by foreign diplomats it was quite difficult for some of them to remember the author's name. Consequently, a Prussian agent in Vienna named him in the beginning as "Prohaska," his British colleague simultaneously as "Prokisk" and "Prokesen," later writing just "P." to avoid another mistake. Maltzan to Frederick William III, Vienna, 27 April 1825, GStA PK, HA III, MdA I, 6005; Cowley to Dudley, Vienna, 16 April and 17 May 1828, TNA, FO 120/91.

[13] Metternich to Ottenfels, Vienna, 19 April. 1828, HHStA, StA, Türkei VI, 35; Ottenfels to Metternich, Constantinople, 25 Feb. 1824, HHStA, StA, Türkei VI, 20; Ottenfels to Metternich, Constantinople, 11 Nov. 1824, HHStA, StA, Türkei VI, 21; Ottenfels to Metternich, Constantinople, 11 April and 10 June 1825, HHStA, StA, Türkei VI, 23; Ottenfels to Metternich, Constantinople, 10 Aug. 1827, HHStA, StA, Türkei VII, 25; Maltzan to Frederick William III, Vienna, 4 May, 30 July and 19 Oct. 1825, GStA PK, HA III, MdA I, 6005; Hatzfeldt to Frederick William III, Vienna, 25 Jan. 1827, GStA PK, HA III, MdA I, 6008; Caraman to Damas, Vienna, 6 Oct. 1825, AMAE, CP, Autriche 406; Miltitz to Frederick William III, Pera, 26 March 1825, GStA PK, HA III, MdA I, 7260; Ottenfels, Memoari, pp. 147–149; Ottenfels to Gentz, Constantinople, 10 March 1825, Prokesch-Osten, Zur Geschichte der orientalischen Frage, p. 51; Metternich to Gentz, Ischl, 13 July 1825, Prokesch-Osten, Zur Geschichte der orientalischen Frage, p. 75; D. Bertsch, Anton Prokesch von Osten (1795–1876): Ein Diplomat Österreichs in Athen und an der Hohen Pforte. Beiträge zur Wahrnehmung des Orients im Europa des 19. Jahrhunderts, München 2005, pp. 88–91.

[14] Maltzan to Frederick William III, Vienna, 3 Aug. 1825, GStA PK, HA III, MdA I, 6005.

time. So although Prokesch sailed at the end of September to Egypt as a private citizen without any formal delegation from his government, he was privately charged by Ottenfels to ascertain Mohammed Ali's plans and persuade him to continue in the war. Therefore, after his arrival in Alexandria on 5 October, Prokesch met several times with Mohammed Ali and his advisor for foreign affairs generally regarded as an Egyptian foreign minister, Yusuf Boghos Bey, and learnt that the pasha's willingness to fight was limited by his fear of European military intervention on behalf of the Greeks and Husrev's presence at the head of Ottoman navy. Prokesch advised Ottenfels first, to try to dispel Mohammed Ali's concerns about a European incursion and, second, to persuade the Porte to remove Husrev. Mohammed Ali told Prokesch that if he could obtain control over the sultan's navy, he would not only keep Ibrahim Pasha in the Peloponnese but also send him reinforcements and money to maintain the sultan's fleet. The reaction of the Austrian diplomacy was immediate: Prokesch personally tried to persuade Mohammed Ali that there was time for a decisive attack against the Greeks, and Ottenfels instructed the new Austrian consul general in Alexandria, Joseph von Acerbi, to relieve Mohammed Ali's anxiety about a European intervention. Since the internuncio shared the view of Husrev's ineptness and held him responsible for the failures in war, he had no problem advising the Porte to depose Husrev, which the Porte finally did at the end of the winter, and the Turkish fleet was actually put under Mohammed Ali's command. It goes without saying that Prokesch's mission as well as the subsequent action taken by Ottenfels met entirely with Metternich's approval.[15]

The placated Mohammed Ali honoured his promise: he started a new campaign in 1827, supplied Turkish ships himself and significantly augmented the Egyptian naval and land forces fighting in Greece. A huge convoy with reinforcements left Alexandria on 6 August, just two days before the arrival of British Major J. H. Cradock, who had

---

[15] Ottenfels to Metternich, Constantinople, 10 Sept. 1825, HHStA, StA, Türkei VI, 23; Ottenfels to Acerbi, Constantinople, 7 Dec. 1826, Ottenfels to Metternich, Constantinople, 10 Oct., 25 Nov., 11 and 15 Dec. 1826, 10 Feb. and 31 March 1827, HHStA, StA, Türkei VI, 26; Ottenfels to Metternich, Constantinople, 25 April 1827, HHStA, StA, Türkei VI, 27; Miltitz to Frederick William III, Pera, 10 Feb. 1827, GStA PK, HA III, MdA I, 7264; Prokesch-Osten, *Mehmed Ali*, pp. 5–10; Sauer, *Österreich und die Levante*, pp. 175–181.

been sent to Egypt by George Canning with exactly the opposite aim
to that with which Prokesch had sailed in the same direction the previous year. Cradock was to induce the pasha to withdraw all his forces
from the war arena, but he arrived too late to be able to persuade
Mohammed Ali to alter his decision which had been influenced by
Austria and which definitely contributed to the continuation of the
Egyptian presence in the war offering prospects of the sultan's final
victory in mid 1827. With the fall of the Acropolis of Athens on 5 June,
the Greeks lost their last stronghold north of the Gulf of Corinth and
in the Peloponnese they controlled only their capital Nafplion with
the adjacent tiny northeast region of the peninsula. Their government
lacked almost everything needed to be able to continue fighting and
pursuing any further active operations was out of question. There were
seven different civil wars among the Greeks in the summer of 1827,
and an Orthodox patriarch was seen in Constantinople pleading with
Mahmud II for pardons and amnesties on behalf of his own congregants from different parts of Greece. Ibrahim Pasha was commanding
the joint Turko-Egyptian fleet and just waiting for his reinforcements
for the attack on Nafplion while the last important Greek islands were
still fighting.[16] Ottenfels reported in August with good reason that despite the existence of some armed bands "according to Mr Prokesch's
reports, there is today no Greek army, no government, no moral force
sufficient to give new life to the insurrection that is kept afloat only
owing to the prospect of relief that will be promptly given to it by
the foreign Great Powers."[17] For the first time, Metternich's statements that the insurrection was at its end and no foreign intervention
needed were well founded. At the moment of the signing of the Treaty
of London, Canning ascertained this from his cousin in Constantinople, who announced that the insurrection was on the verge of collapse
and could only be saved by prompt foreign intervention.[18]

---

[16] H. Dodwell, *The Founder of Modern Egypt: A Study of Muhammad Ali*, London
1931, pp. 87–89; G. Fargette, *Mehemet Ali: Le fondateur de l'Égypte moderne*,
Paris 1996, p. 80; Aksan, pp. 296–297; Crawley, *Greek Independence*, pp. 80–81;
Woodhouse, *The Greek War*, p. 121.
[17] Ottenfels to Metternich, Constantinople, 22 Aug. 1827, HHStA, StA, Türkei
VI, 27.
[18] Metternich to Apponyi, Vienna, 11 June 1827, HHStA, StA, Frankreich 264;
Caraman to Damas, Vienna, 16 July 1827, AMAE, CP, Autriche 408; Temperley,
Canning, p. 401.

Metternich Warns the Sultan

Despite his increasing optimism during early 1827, Metternich was not blind to the danger originating for Mahmud II in London and, therefore, he advised him to proceed against the insurgents not only with arms but also with an olive branch. Metternich had been convinced for a long time that a military victory over the insurgents in no way meant a real and durable settlement of the Greek Question and that some administrative changes on behalf of the Greeks had to be made as well. Any real pacification should be achieved not only by arms but also by a conciliation that could facilitate the settlement with the Greeks and create a good impression in Western society rather hostile to the Turks. The sultan should ensure them the freedom of faith, person and property together with a just and functional administration, and he should show this conciliatory attitude first by the offer of amnesty and pardon. It was the same attitude as Metternich had maintained during the Serbian uprising, but it must be stated that during the Greek rebellion this opinion, which he openly propounded, first, increased as the sultan's difficulties with suppressing the rebellion grew and, second, was to all appearance considerably shaped by Gentz.[19] Nevertheless, it was impossible to achieve any solution at the negotiating table. The Greeks were not willing to give up their dream of independence, and since the sultan was unable to reach any great victory in the early phase of war, there was nothing to force them to do so and accept any different solution. On the other side, Mahmud II was willing to offer pardons but was in no way inclined to undertake any administrative changes which would weaken his power over Greece, and when the scales of the war tipped in his favour after the Egyptian intervention, his willingness to negotiate was as weak as his belief in the achievement of the victory by arms was strong, and he let Ottenfels be informed that any concession to the insurgents from his side was out of question.[20]

---

[19] Metternich to Ottenfels, Ischl, 1 Aug. 1824, HHStA, StA, Türkei VI, 22; Metternich to Ottenfels, Vienna, 6 Jan. and 18 Dec. 1825, 4 Jan. 1826, HHStA, StA, Türkei VI, 24; Metternich to Lebzeltern, Paris, 11 April 1825, HHStA, StA, Russland III, 70; Krauter, pp. 135–138.

[20] Ottenfels to Metternich, Constantinople, 25 Feb. 1826, HHStA, StA, Türkei VI, 25; Gürbüz, pp. 379 and 385.

Metternich attempted to change the sultan's uncompromising attitude during 1826, but all his warnings against the impossibility of returning to the state of things in Greece before 1821 were in vain.[21] At the end of December 1826, at the same moment when the three Great Powers were officially informed about Francis I's firm decision not to join in the pacification as proposed by them, the chancellor drafted important instructions for Ottenfels. These contained warnings to the Porte that time was not on its side and that it was necessary to pacify the Greeks as soon as possible and this was to be achieved by force as well as by moderation, which was particularly needed owing to the Great Powers determination to intervene in the Greek affairs. Metternich believed that Mahmud II could not and would not accept the requested mediation but he also could not flatly refuse the intervention because if their diplomatic notes were sharply rejected, then he would have to face their armed forces. Consequently, Metternich advised Mahmud II to do himself what he was soon to be requested to do and undoubtedly compelled to do by force if he refused. The sultan was to continue negotiating with the Great Powers but was not to accept their mediation and should pacify the Greeks alone. His efforts to achieve a complete military victory were to be accompanied by his conciliatory statements towards the Great Powers as well as his moderate behaviour towards the Greeks like offers of a cease-fire and amnesty, and Metternich strongly urged the sultan to take these steps himself and thus placate the Great Powers, who would have no reasons to raise these issues themselves. The regions where the suspension of hostilities were to be applied should not exceed the Peloponnese and some adjacent islands of the Archipelago, which Metternich considered as areas where some rights had to be accorded to the Greeks. Since Russia and Great Britain had not yet officially presented the St Petersburg Protocol to the sultan, Metternich advised him to give them this negative but highly conciliatory answer: "You want what I want, but you do not seem to want it as only I could ever want it. You want my insurgent provinces to be pacified. It is something to which I have been directing my efforts for several years, indeed rendered useless for reasons that with your kind permission I do not have

---

[21] Metternich to Ottenfels, Vienna, 18 March and 18 June 1826, HHStA, StA, Türkei VI, 24; Gentz to Ottenfels, [?] April 1826, Prokesch-Osten, *Zur Geschichte der orientalischen Frage*, p. 123; Sweet, p. 262.

to enumerate and qualify. I do not have other desire today; I am even impatient to arrive at the goal. Assist me because you can do it. I will never grant to any Great Power the right of intervention and even less to act as mediator between me and my insurgent subjects. To justify this frank and categorical declaration, I would confine myself to ask you the question whether anyone among you would permit for his part what I refuse to do? What you would not accept and what you would have the complete right to refuse, I would not accept or tolerate either. I want to pacify and not destroy, pardon those who have seriously offended me, and not wipe them out. [I want] my subjects to obey me again and I will grant them what could serve their future prosperity and happiness because I want a real and durable peace and not an illusory pacification. Assist me in the only forms and in the only ways in which I can accept your support, in which I even dare to demand it. Make it clear to the insurgents that they have nothing to expect from you if they do not submit to the conditions under which I am prepared to pardon them."[22] On 1 January 1827, Metternich summarised the content of his previous instructions into one piece of advice for Ottenfels: "Always remain true to the idea that it should be the sultan who does what others would like to do for him and in spite of him. The whole affair depends on this."[23] He hoped that with such an approach Mahmud II could obtain a better starting position for further negotiations on the Greek Question or, in a better case, completely break up the Russo-British alliance.[24] He based this latter belief upon his personal overconfidence in Nicholas I's restraint as explained in the previous chapter: "This goal must be attained if the Divan is able to understand us and if it knows how to serve itself in enlightened ways and in the only ways at its disposal. England cannot wage war against the Turks. It can threaten them, [it can] even apply more than one moral torture. It cannot attack them, and Russia, which could do the latter, does not want to. That is the whole secret right there!"[25]

---

[22] Metternich to Ottenfels, Vienna, 30 Dec. 1826, HHStA, StA, Türkei VI, 29.
[23] Metternich to Ottenfels, Vienna, 1 Jan. 1827, HHStA, StA, Türkei VI, 29.
[24] See also Metternich to Apponyi, Vienna, 3 Jan. 1827, HHStA, StA, Frankreich 264; Metternich to Esterházy, Vienna, 3 Jan. 1827, HHStA, StA, England 178.
[25] Metternich to Ottenfels, Vienna, 1 Jan. 1827, HHStA, StA, Türkei VI, 29. For the same view see also Metternich to Ottenfels, Vienna, 19 April 1826, HHStA, StA, Türkei VI, 24.

The belief that the Porte should take the wind out of the three Great Powers' sails with a quick defeat of the insurrection as well as with moderation on its own was also the impetus of Metternich's instructions for Ottenfels in the following months.[26] In mid April 1827, he made his proposal more elaborate. As for the pacification itself, it was based upon the separation of the Moslems from the Christians, which would be limited to the Peloponnese, something easy to achieve because the former were mostly slaughtered by the latter during the insurrection, and some adjacent islands. In the peninsula the Greeks were to enjoy considerable independence in their administration with the right to elect their leaders, the sultan keeping the right of their confirmation. An annual tribute would be fixed for eternity or for at least 20 years. In the islands the old method of administration was to be confirmed and the tribute fixed in the same way. The Great Powers were to be asked for advice and assistance in overcoming the expected resistance of the insurgents against this plan for pacification, and, as an expression of generosity, an armistice was to be proposed and an amnesty was to be granted to those who would submit.[27] This plan did not differ all that much from that proposed by France, Great Britain and Russia, since the Greeks would have received a sort of autonomy. The main difference, as Metternich wrote to Esterházy on 25 March 1827, was that Austria suggested they "demonstrate to the sultan the necessity of pacifying his insurgent provinces," whereas the three Great Powers proposed to "demonstrate to the sultan the necessity of *allowing* these same provinces *to be pacified.*"[28] A day later, he added: "We also want an end to this terrible situation; we call for it loud and clear ... If England wants what we want and does not want anything we do not want, then we understand each other. We want the return of the insurgent people to the sovereign authority of the sultan, we do not want to lead them to slaughter. We see an advantage for the Porte, combined with that of these same peoples, in certain concessions that the sovereign authority would accord them and in certain conditions that would ensure the sultan the submission

---

[26] Metternich to Ottenfels, Vienna, 18 Feb., 21 March and 4 April 1827, HHStA, StA, Türkei VI, 29; Maltzan to Frederick William III, Vienna, 31 March and 1 May 1827, GSt.A PK, HA III, MdA I, 6008.
[27] Metternich to Ottenfels, Vienna, 13 and 14 April 1827, HHStA, StA, Türkei VI, 29.
[28] Metternich to Esterházy, Vienna, 25 March 1827, HHStA, StA, England 178.

of his rebellious subjects for the present and for the future, and in these precautions the guarantee of present and future peace."[29]

It is difficult to guess whether Metternich's plan, which was shaped between December and April, could change the course of events because it was never accepted in Constantinople for one simple reason: the acceptance of the chancellor's advice required the concessions that were regarded by Mahmud II as unnecessary at the moment when his complete victory over the Greeks seemed to be very close. Ottenfels in vain advocated the plan and warned against the unfortunate consequences that would befall the sultan if he refused to accept it. Seida Effendi told him that if the Great Powers were allowed to interfere with Ottoman internal affairs because of the Greeks, they could later do so again because of the Ottoman Jews. Soon after this statement, in March 1827, Seida was removed from office, but this in no way implied the Porte's shift to a more moderate attitude. To the contrary, the new reis effendi, Mohammed Sayd Pertev, was well known for his strong attachment to Islam, as Ottenfels wrote in his memoirs: "His mind was affected by blind fanaticism and stubborn attachment to his religious principles to such a level that it often was impossible to convert it to reasonable ideas as soon as these ideas seemed in the least contrary to the precepts of the Mohammedan faith."[30] To yield now, to surrender willingly direct control over a part of the Ottoman Empire was equally as unthinkable for Pertev as for his master, but it was much more difficult for Ottenfels to hold a discussion on this issue with him than with other Ottoman dignitaries, like his predecessor Seida.[31] First of all, there were no negotiations for several weeks after Pertev's accession to office, and when he finally asked the internuncio for Austria's opinion on the Greek Question, which was promptly answered in a letter, it took several more weeks until Ottenfels could personally visit Pertev on 11 May only to ascertain that the sacred law of the Ottoman Empire prohibited any foreign interference in its own affairs, refusing with this statement to accept not only the mediation but also Metternich's more modest solution, which prompted

---

[29] Metternich to Esterházy, Vienna, 26 March 1827, HHStA, StA, England 178.
[30] Ottenfels, *Memoari*, p. 183.
[31] Ottenfels to Metternich, Constantinople, 25 Jan. and 23 March 1827, HHStA, StA, Türkei VI, 26; Ottenfels to Metternich, Constantinople, 25 April 1827, HHStA, StA, Türkei VI, 27.

Ottenfels' reaction: "I recognised this law but I drew his attention to the fact that politics was not a court of law where the one who had good reason on his side always won out."[32]

The Porte's uncompromising attitude was strengthened by its army's success in Attica, the arrival of Egyptian reinforcements and the desperate situation of the Greeks on the one hand, and the activities of Stratford Canning in Constantinople and some prominent British Philhellenes in Greece on the other hand. Mahmud II was simultaneously becoming increasingly satisfied with the progress of the war and outraged at the conduct of the Great Powers and was not prepared to yield to any pressure from them. Ottenfels was unable to appease the sultan and he at least tried to persuade the Porte to be as diplomatic as possible. When the Porte finally issued a statement concerning foreign intervention on 9 June, it was actually not entirely offensive to the Great Powers willing to mediate, but it was completely negative towards their eventual mediation and in no way compatible with what Metternich wished to achieve by placating them. This note symbolised the full stop to the Porte's negotiations with the Great Powers including Austria. When Ottenfels tried to raise the issue once more, Pertev merely answered that everything necessary had already been incorporated into this document and declared: "We are prepared for everything, nothing will surprise us, nothing will make us change our resolve."[33] At the end of July Ottenfels maintained that the Porte's resolution not to yield was irrevocable, an opinion entirely shared by Miltitz, and the internuncio stopped endeavouring to change it.[34]

This obstinacy exasperated Metternich who, still without any knowledge of the note from 9 June, warned the Porte against regarding "the proposals of which the intervening courts are going to inform it as the maximum embarrassment awaiting it. It can pride itself, and not

---

[32] Ottenfels to Metternich, Constantinople, 17 May 1827, HHStA, StA, Türkei VI, 27.

[33] Ottenfels to Metternich, Constantinople, 10 July 1827, HHStA, StA, Türkei VI, 27.

[34] Ottenfels to Metternich, Constantinople, 17 and 25 May, 25 July 1827, Ottenfels to Huszár, 14 May 1827, the declaration of the Sublime Porte to the internuncio, 9 June 1827, attached to Ottenfels to Metternich, Constantinople, 14 June 1827, HHStA, StA, Türkei VI, 27; Miltitz to Frederick William III, Pera, 11 June and 25 July 1827, GStA PK, HA III, MdA I, 7264.

without reason, at resisting threats, in part inexecutable, in part so badly calculated and arranged that they will have to self-destruct. But it must not forget that behind these threats a completely different kind of danger to defy with impunity is being prepared for the Ottoman Empire. Nobody is more convinced than I that Emperor Nicholas does not desire a war, and my opinion on this subject has never wavered, but [I] also do not doubt that forced by circumstances he will wage one, and which circumstance more pressing is it possible to imagine in evaluating with impartiality his position, than for the whole world to see his plans imperilled, plans which his infatuated and passionate advisors had presented to him as certain to succeed."[35] He advised the Porte to talk to the three Great Powers because "in the obstinate silence of the Porte lies its ruin."[36] But the June note was not at all the style of communication that he had had in mind.[37] As well as Ottenfels, Metternich also ceased trying to achieve anything in Constantinople in July with these prophetic words: "I accept that the sultan will not be able to give in to the requirements certainly rather badly motivated which the three courts will put to him. From that moment on he will have to regard war as certain. This war, we believe, will fall on the shoulders of Russia."[38]

Ottenfels' Humiliation

The Porte's refusal to allow foreign mediation also damaged the re-lations between Ottenfels and his British, Russian and French col-leagues. Because the ambassadors were unable to obtain a positive answer from the Turks in this respect, they asked the internuncio for assistance more than once. Since his instructions forbade it, Ot-tenfels always had to refuse to join his colleagues in their pressure on the Porte. The most affected was Stratford Canning, whose anger reached such an extent that he scandalously scolded the internuncio on 29 March when the latter refused the demand for the official back-ing of the St Petersburg Protocol before the Porte. When Ottenfels,

---

[35] Metternich to Ottenfels, Vienna, 20 June 1827, HHStA, StA, Türkei VI, 29.
[36] Ibid.
[37] Wellesley to Dudley, Vienna, 29 June 1827, TNA, FO 120/86.
[38] Metternich to Ottenfels, Vienna, 4 July 1827, HHStA, StA, Türkei VI, 29.

a man generally estimated more for his clemency than diplomatic talent, tried to explain that he simply could not do so because his instructions did not allow him to go so far, Stratford started to shout angrily that he regarded this answer as a personal offence and that "he would no longer have diplomatic relations with him if he did not apologise for what he [Stratford] took to be an offence."[39] These poor mutual relations deteriorated even more on 16 August when the three ambassadors presented to Pertev Effendi their notes based upon the Treaty of London and demanding the acceptance of its conditions. The Porte had a fifteen day deadline to give an answer to this ultimatum. At the same moment they asked Ottenfels for his support of their measures, but he refused to do so again for two reasons: first, he had no instructions allowing such a step, and second, nothing during the several previous weeks had made him believe that the Porte had changed its reluctant attitude and would accept the demands even if he joined his colleagues' action. He believed that the only results would have been a deterioration of Austro-Ottoman relations and the weakening of his influence over the Porte. The sultan's answer entirely corresponded with Ottenfels' expectation. On 30 August, Pertev told the three Great Powers' dragomans coming to ask him about the outcome of the ultimatum: "If you mean by that the document there which was put on my sofa fifteen days ago, the document that I neither accepted nor read and which has not even been translated yet, I must tell you by the order of my superiors that the Porte has no response to make to it and that it will never provide one; it refers all in all to its declaration of 9 June that contains its last word [on the subject] saying that His Highness will never permit any mediation or foreign interference into his internal affairs."[40] He also expressed himself in the same sense towards the dragoman of the internunciature, Valentin von Huszár.[41]

---

[39] Caraman to Damas, Vienna, 30 April 1827, AMAE, CP, Autriche 408.

[40] Ottenfels to Metternich, Constantinople, 31 Aug. 1827, HHStA, StA, Türkei VI, 27.

[41] Metternich to Ottenfels, Vienna, 18 Feb. 1827, HHStA, StA, Türkei VI, 29; Metternich to Esterházy, Vienna, 1 April 1827, HHStA, StA, England 178; Ottenfels to Metternich, Constantinople, 24 Feb. 1827, HHStA, StA, Türkei VI, 26; Ottenfels to Metternich, Constantinople, 10 and 25 April, 10, 25, 22 and 31 Aug. 1827, HHStA, StA, Türkei VI, 27; Miltitz to Frederick William III, Pera, 7 Feb. 1827, GStA PK, HA III, MdA I, 7264; Miltitz to Frederick William III, Pera, 22 and 31 Aug. 1827, GStA PK, HA III, MdA I, 7265; Tatishchev to Nesselrode,

Ottenfels' conduct angered Stratford as much as Ribeaupierre and his French colleague, French Ambassador Count Armand Charles de Guilleminot, who had been informed by the British, French and Russian representatives in Vienna that Metternich had promised to instruct the internuncio to support their conduct, and they bitterly complained that this promise had not been fulfilled. The ambassadors in the Austrian capital took this even more personally, Tatishchev now complaining to Metternich first and foremost and personally accusing the chancellor of thwarting his own promise by giving additional instructions to Ottenfels. Metternich accepted these complaints, denied that Ottenfels had been ordered not to act, expressed his own displeasure with him and rebuked him for his conduct of 16 August. On the other hand, he tried to defend his subordinate's action by confirming the latter's view that even Austria's support would not have changed anything in the Porte's attitude.[42] Of Ottenfels' conduct he told Tatishchev: "He saw only Constantinople and he forgot that Austria has relations with the whole of Europe. Believing he would receive a refusal, he thought he would be doing us an ultimate service by avoiding this problem, whereas I wanted him to obtain the same response himself that would be given to the representatives of the signatory Powers of the Treaty."[43]

In reality what Metternich told the foreign diplomats about the instructions was definitely not true because he had never instructed Ottenfels to support the actions of his three colleagues in Constantinople aimed at mediation. The internuncio had lacked instructions for the moment when his colleagues, also supported by Baron Miltitz, made their official approach based upon the Treaty of London. He merely received, and after 16 August, these plain words from Metter-

---

Vienna, 28 Feb. 1827, AVPRI, fond 133, Kantseliariia, opis 468, 11873; Ottenfels, *Memoari*, p. 180.
[42] Metternich to Zichy, Königswart, 15 Sept. 1827, HHStA, StA, Russland III, 81; Metternich to Ottenfels, Vienna, 19 Sept. 1827, HDA, 750, OO 37; Metternich to Apponyi, Vienna, 28 Sept. 1827, HHStA, StA, Frankreich 265; Guilleminot to Damas, Therapia, 19 and 22 Aug. 1827, AMAE, CP, Autriche 247; Schwebel to Damas, Vienna, 6, 20 and 27 Sept. 1827, AMAE, CP, Autriche 408; Wellesley to Dudley, Vienna, 7 and 29 Sept. 1827, TNA, FO 120/87; Tatishchev to Nesselrode, Töplitz, 10 and 16 Sept., Vienna, 26 Sept. 1827, AVPRI, fond 133, Kantseliariia, opis 468, 11874.
[43] Tatishchev to Nesselrode, Töplitz, 16 Sept. 1827, AVPRI, fond 133, Kantseliariia, opis 468, 11874.

nich: "You have nothing better to do, Baron, than to speak frankly
to everybody. Tell the Turks what you think; in the same way, do not
hold back your thoughts from your colleagues. Justice supported by
sound reasoning does not need a mask. Our role at this moment is that
of spectators clearly interested in the forthcoming solutions. Our eyes
are open and we are on an absolutely free ground."[44] Where Ottenfels could actually be criticised and what most probably aroused some
displeasure at the Chancellery was that he did not act more diplomatically towards his colleagues and did not support the pacification in
general without, however, advocating the mediation.[45] Maltzan quite
correctly perceived this after a discussion with the ex-internuncio,
Baron Ignaz von Stürmer, functioning in the Chancellery: "There is
a pretence that Metternich did not approve of the manner in which
Ottenfels replied to the note that the representatives of the signatory
courts of the Treaty of London had addressed to him on 16 August.
Stürmer only told me that it had appeared to him more desirable that
the response of the internuncio had been less severe, but I observed
nothing in the words that he used when speaking to me on the subject that would have indicated that there is any disapproval of the
determination on the part of the internuncio not to support the note
collectively addressed on 16 August to the reis effendi by virtue of the
Treaty of London."[46]

There is no doubt that Ottenfels was used as a scapegoat, and
in mid September Gentz explained to him the reason – Metternich
decided to do so with the aim of mitigating the anger of the Russian
cabinet, terminating his letter with these words: "I tell you without
hesitation, you have done a service to the dignity of our court to which
all the just world and history will do homage."[47] Ottenfels accepted
this role without reserve and assumed the responsibility to save his
government's "dignity" despite the personal humiliation which he suffered not only from the rebuke given to him by Metternich but also
from the personal excuses he was ordered to make to the three allied ambassadors whom he had to visit and inform of his mistake.

[44] Metternich to Ottenfels, Vienna, 4 Aug. 1827, HHStA, StA, Türkei VI, 29.
[45] Metternich to Esterházy, Königswart, 15 Sept. 1827, HHStA, StA, England
178.
[46] Maltzan to Frederick William III, Vienna, 18 Sept. 1827, GStA PK, HA III,
MdA I, 6009.
[47] Krauter, p. 199.

Whereas Guilleminot and Ribeaupierre tried to relieve him of his embarrassment, Stratford got great pleasure out of it, obtaining thus his satisfaction for the alleged personal insult from late March.[48] Ottenfels himself was in December rewarded for the humiliation he had suffered by his appointment as a secret councillor of the state, officially for his conciliatory conduct after the Battle of Navarino but in reality for his earlier personal sacrifice.[49]

Metternich's Hope and Frustration: George Canning's Death and the Battle of Navarino

What is actually difficult to understand in this whole affair is how such an experienced diplomat as Metternich could make such a mistake. By promising to do something that he did not intend to do from the very beginning he set a trap for himself and then stepped into it. Nothing indicates that he would have supposed that the Greeks would be pacified before the intervention of the three Great Powers, which would have relieved him of keeping the promise so unwisely made. The answer to this puzzle seems to lie in, first, the real content of Metternich's promise and, second, Canning's death on 8 August. As for the former, the dispatches of British, French and Russian ambassadors in Vienna from May to June prove that Metternich expressed himself in his usual diplomatic, or more correctly, his rather sophisticated language, by which he in no way promised to support the request for mediation but merely the effort for pacification, and he in no way urged the Porte to accept the propositions but only to continue to listen and negotiate.[50] For example, Caraman wrote on 10 June that after a consultation with his collaborators, Metternich promised him to "support in Constantinople those approaches which the courts' sig-

---

[48] Miltitz to Frederick William III, Pera, 10 Oct. 1827, GStA PK, HA III, MdA I, 7265; Ottenfels, *Memoari*, p. 189; the extract from Stratford Canning's report from 11 October 1827, TNA, FO 352/59.
[49] Metternich to Francis I, Vienna, 28 Nov. 1827, HHStA, StK, Vorträge 252; Ottenfels, *Memoari*, p. 195.
[50] Wellesley to Dudley, Vienna, 29 May 1827, TNA, FO 120/86; Caraman to Damas, Vienna, 10 and 21 June 1827, AMAE, CP, Autriche 408; Tatishchev to Nesselrode, Vienna, 11 June 1827, AVPRI, fond 133, Kantseliariia, opis 468, 11873.

natories of the Treaty will in this case undertake to achieve the goal of pacification and to assist them in pressing the Porte to answer to their intentions."[51] Later the chancellor promised to instruct the internuncio to "press the Divan to listen to the propositions which will be made to it in order to arrive at the pacification of Greece and to instruct him to firmly explain to the reis effendi again that it still depends upon the present moment to prevent the incalculable and dangerous ways in which it [the Porte] can be threatened if it persists in rejecting the intervention of the courts which present themselves as allies, and to draw his attention to the fact that in a short while there will perhaps be no more time to avoid the consequences which its obstinacy could bring about."[52] These expressions conformed to Metternich's instructions to Ottenfels from the end of December 1826, in which the chancellor had been warning the Porte against its reluctance to offer an armistice and amnesty and against a peremptory refusal of the allied mediation. What he actually intended to do and actually did, is described above as well as explained at the end of July in his instructions to London as well as Paris: "We have judged the moment to be opportune for ordering the representative of H. I. M. [His Imperial Majesty] to once more draw the attention of the Porte to the perilous situation in which it would find itself and for expressing our concern in favour of a sane and conciliatory conduct on its part."[53] In fact, this was exactly what Ottenfels had been pursuing for a long time.

The foreign ambassadors were easily confused by this sophistry and expected from the internuncio more than Metternich was either willing or able to offer owing to his principles (read: attachment to the existing international law system) as well as the attitude of Francis I who openly declared in late May that he was prepared "to support his allies in their negotiations in Constantinople, as far as he can do so consistently with the aforesaid principles."[54] Nevertheless, this ex-

---

[51] Caraman to Damas, Vienna, 10 June 1827, AMAE, CP, Autriche 408.
[52] Caraman to Damas, Vienna, 21 June 1827, AMAE, CP, Autriche 408.
[53] Metternich to Apponyi, Vienna, 31 July 1827, HHStA, StA, Frankreich 264. The same statement can be found in Metternich to Esterházy, Vienna, 31 July 1827, HHStA, StA, England 178.
[54] Wellesley to Dudley, Vienna, 29 May 1827, TNA, FO 120/86. Francis I also repeated this declaration later, see Wellesley to Dudley, Vienna, 14 June 1827, TNA, FO 120/86.

planation of the whole confusion in no way intends to put only the ambassadors in the wrong. Some responsibility must also be ascribed to Metternich who deliberately chose such ambiguous expressions simply to placate the authors of the trilateral Treaty and to remain in the game as much as it was possible. This was also the reason why he not only did not simply oppose the complaints raised against Ottenfels' conduct but also censured it, not wanting to damage any further Austria's relations with the three allied Powers at the moment when an important incident gave him hope for a turn in the course of events: George Canning's death on 8 August, which pleased him as much as the death of Castlereagh had chagrined him almost to the day five years earlier.[55] He was in his West Bohemian chateau in Königswart when he learnt of Canning's death on 13 August, and immediately wrote to Tatishchev residing in nearby Carlsbad: "I very much want to see you ... If something prevents you from coming here, I will send one of my gentlemen to you. I do not want to go myself to Carlsbad because I would be taken for the messenger of the death of the man who – the fact being beyond all doubts – was of an altogether different stock."[56] He was very happy that Canning's premiership, which he compared to Napoleon's hundred days, had ended: "Mr Canning began many enterprises but he finished none. He destroyed and ruined a great deal but he achieved nothing. His ministry of 3 months will assume in the annals of history a place next to those other 100 famous days! ... I do not doubt that in Paris and in St Petersburg they will feel as though freed from a burden; in the first of these places, they will feel stronger, in the second they will regard themselves as though emancipated."[57]

Metternich immediately concluded that the new prime minister, Lord Goderich, and even Lord Dudley, his foreign secretary inherited from his predecessor, could not pursue the same policy and would be willing to modify it. He also believed in some changes in the attitudes of the French and Russian cabinets. To increase Austria's chances of

---

[55] Metternich to Apponyi, Königswart, 19 Aug. 1827, HHStA, StA, Frankreich 265; Tatishchev to Nesselrode, Carlsbad, 16 Aug. 1827, AVPRI, fond 133, Kantseliariia, opis 468, 11873.

[56] Metternich to Tatishchev, Königswart, 13 Aug. 1827, attached to Tatishchev to Nesselrode, Carlsbad, 16 Aug. 1827, AVPRI, fond 133, Kantseliariia, opis 468, 11873.

[57] Metternich to Werner, Königswart, 14 Aug. 1827, HHStA, StK, Preussen 125.

becoming involved and acting in the larger union of five instead of leaving the others to act as a group of three, he tried in August and September to persuade the quarrelling parties to adopt a more conciliatory attitude to each other: in Constantinople by attempts to dispel any hopes for a change in the trilateral alliance's approach to the Greek Question, and with the cabinets in London, Paris and St Petersburg by warnings that there was never a chance that the sultan would agree to their mediation and if they did not amend their approach, war would be the inevitable result. In brief, he wanted to persuade the Turks to negotiate and agree with the amnesty, the armistice and some administrative modifications in Greece, and the British, French and Russians to give up the mediation that was considered unacceptable not only for Mahmud II but also Francis I. In October Metternich explained this goal to Esterházy: "It is now a question of preparing above all a breathing space by offering the government that considers its very existence attacked and the cabinets bound by the Treaty of London at one and the same time a situation more favourable for a rapprochement than the current one. It is towards this goal that we direct our efforts."[58] To increase his chances to obtain a positive response to his proposals, he quickly followed up with assurances of Austria's desire to aid in achieving the pacification and to contribute to it by all possible means.[59]

The indications that this approach could meet with some success soon started to arrive in Vienna. At the end of August, Villèle told Apponyi that France wished to preserve the Ottoman Empire, prevent a war and that "we hope to succeed in this endeavour and look forward to the moment when the intervention of Austria ensures the complete success of the peace task to which we are directing our

---

[58] Metternich to Esterházy, Vienna, 8 Oct. 1827, HHStA, StA, England 179.
[59] Metternich to Ottenfels, Königswart, 13 Aug. 1827, HHStA, StA, Türkei VI, 29; Metternich to Werner, Königswart, 14 Aug. 1827, HHStA, StK, Preussen 125; Metternich to Apponyi, Königswart, 19 Aug., 15 and 28 Sept. 1827, HHStA, StA, Frankreich 265; Metternich to Zichy, Königswart, 2 and 15 Sept. 1827, HHStA, StA, Russland III, 81; Metternich to Esterházy, Königswart, 15 Sept. 1827, HHStA, StA, England 178; Ottenfels to Metternich, Constantinople, 10 Sept. 1827, HHStA, StA, Türkei VI, 27; Ottenfels to Huszár, Büyükdere, 8 Oct. 1827, Ottenfels to Metternich, Constantinople, 15 Oct. 1827, HHStA, StA, Türkei VI, 28; Maltzan to Frederick William III, Vienna, 29 Sept. and 2 Oct. 1827, GStA PK, HA III, MdA I, 6009; Schwebel to Damas, Vienna, 30 Sept. 1827, AMAE, CP, Autriche 408; Sauvigny, *Metternich et la France*, III, p. 1106.

efforts."[60] But considerably greater prospects were contained in the reports from London. Esterházy wrote on 14 September that Lord Dudley wished to cooperate with Metternich on the Portuguese affairs, which was the first hint of the British cabinet's desire to come closer to Austria, and the evidence was that whereas Dudley discussed this question with Esterházy he omitted to do so with Lieven.[61] Just four days later, Esterházy reported that the majority of the cabinet desired to cooperate with Austria not only in the Portuguese but also Near Eastern affairs and that Dudley had confidentially conveyed this wish to him so that Austria could moderate the Porte's intransigent attitude and obtain some reasonable concession from its part. Dudley told to him: "It is easier to define the goal than to determine the means for its attainment. We desire, through your intervention and your assistance at the Porte, that instead of adding insult to injury by a stubborn refusal on its part, running the risk of forcing us, against our will, to resort to the extremes which we desire to avoid, it [the Porte] makes this task possible for us by a reasonable concession on which we can count. We can content ourselves with little but we need something, for example: that the Porte of its own accord allocates a territory where the stipulations of the Protocol could be applied but, above all, that it consents to an armistice with the aim of putting a stop to the scenes of slaughter which are becoming intolerable, in a word, that we are given the means to proceed no further with honour, and we will proceed no further immediately after having carried out, with good will, the stipulations of the Protocol. If Russia does not consent with this, it is its affair; our engagements are over and we find ourselves completely freed from [our obligations]."[62]

This was exactly what Metternich needed and wished to obtain because it opened, or at least it so seemed to the chancellor, the door for his entrance into the affair. Having received Esterházy's report of 18 September, Metternich immediately prepared in early October secret instructions for Ottenfels based upon Dudley's request. The internuncio was ordered to persuade the Porte to act in a more conciliatory manner and make it aware that its complaints against the trilateral alliance could in no way facilitate its own situation: "Is sending us

---

[60] Sauvigny, *Metternich et la France*, III, p. 1102.
[61] Esterházy to Metternich, London, 14 Sept. 1827, HHStA, StA, England 177.
[62] Esterházy to Metternich, London, 18 Sept. 1827, HHStA, StA, England 177.

its futile regrets going to make us change the results? The trilateral alliance exists, the ultimatum of the three courts has been given, and the Porte, trying as it might to loudly remonstrate against these measures, will suffer tragic consequences if it does not find a way to disarm them."[63] Consequently, the Porte was to express its wish to reach a settlement with the Great Powers on the pacification and agree with the armistice as proof of its goodwill, and it was to acquaint the Viennese cabinet of this as though it had arrived at these decisions on its own, and this communication would be mailed forward to the three allied courts, "in a word, that it talks to us to provide us the means that we can talk to our allies."[64] When Dudley was confidentially informed by Esterházy about these instructions, he expressed his satisfaction, telling the ambassador: "Your Highness perfectly satisfied our expectation with his words in Constantinople."[65] This positive answer made Metternich believe that the British-Austrian intimacy was restored but the near future was to prove how very mistaken he was.[66]

The fundamental premise for Metternich's success lay in the Porte's willingness to accept his advice, and it also was in Constantinople where the seed of his failure was sown. Although Ottenfels obtained on 24 October a letter for Metternich from the grand vizier, Mehmed Selim Pasha, with a request for Austria's intercession, it did not contain the promise of an armistice. This was Ottenfels' fault because he had not even raised this issue in the negotiations with Pertev, believing firmly that it would not be accepted by the sultan. However, this was exactly what Metternich needed so much and why he urged Ottenfels in the instructions of 3 October to press the Porte to agree to an armistice regardless of whatever reluctance it might express.

---

[63] Metternich to Ottenfels, Vienna, 3 Oct. 1827, Prokesch-Osten, *Griechen*, V, p. 122. These instructions are missing in the Austrian State Archives but were published by Anton Prokesch von Osten in his history of the Greek insurrection and Richard von Metternich-Winneburg in the *NP*. See Prokesch-Osten, *Griechen*, V, pp. 118–124, and *NP*, IV, pp. 379–387.

[64] Metternich to Ottenfels, Vienna, 3 Oct. 1827, Prokesch-Osten, *Griechen*, V, p. 121.

[65] Esterházy to Metternich, London, 30 Oct. 1827, HHStA, StA, England 177.

[66] Metternich to Ottenfels, Vienna, 4 Nov. 1827, HHStA, StA, Türkei VI, 29; Metternich to Esterházy, Vienna, 4 Nov. 1827, HHStA, StA, England 179; Esterházy to Metternich, London, 19 and 28 Oct. 1827, HHStA, StA, England 177; Wellesley to Dudley, Vienna, 29 Sept. 1827, TNA, FO 120/87.

The chancellor repeated in a letter to the internuncio of 17 October (of course delivered to Constantinople long after the 24th) how essential a truce was for the preservation of peace: "If it [the Porte] refuses, notify it that we foresee for it a war with all its possible consequences."[67] Furthermore, the Porte's wish to attain better relations with the three Great Powers expressed in the same letter of 24 October was accompanied by lengthy and undiplomatic criticism of their actions hitherto together with its request that they terminate their interference with its internal affairs: "[The Porte hopes] that Austria as a sincere and real friend of all the other courts will employ its good will and kind solicitude for putting an end to this crisis instead of letting it take place, without any provocation on the part of the Sub-lime Porte, between it and its friends, by their unjust interference in its internal affairs, so that they entirely abstain from every irreconcilable proceeding and approach, and that everything that took place in the past is regarded as forgotten, and that the ties of friendship and understanding of the Porte with all these courts are restored as they were in the past and without any change."[68] Although Ottenfels regarded the letter as a success, in fact there was nothing in it that enabled Metternich to advance in the affair.[69]

The grand vizier's letter was received by Metternich in the morning of 5 November, on the day of his marriage in Hetzendorf. Just several hours later on the same day, after the wedding ceremony, another important piece of news was delivered to him from the Ottoman Empire: on 20 October, the united British, French and Russian fleets had destroyed most of the Turko-Egyptian warships in Navarino Bay. If the first news did not offer any material for Austria's diplomatic approach towards the allied courts, the second one completely destroyed any such a possibility. The Battle of Navarino was shocking for Metternich and Francis I, the former calling it a "holocaust," the second an "assassination."[70] The generally calm emperor did not hide his indignation, as Metternich informed Apponyi: "The event of Navarino, its causes and its probable consequences, all place His Imperial Majesty

---

[67] Metternich to Ottenfels, Vienna, 17 Oct. 1827, HHStA, StA, Türkei VI, 29.

[68] Mehmed Selim Pasha to Metternich, 24 Oct. 1827, HHStA, StA, Türkei VI, 28.

[69] Ottenfels to Metternich, Constantinople, 25 Oct. 1827, HHStA, StA, Türkei VI, 28.

[70] Metternich to Werner, Vienna, 16 Nov. 1827, HHStA, StK, Preussen 125.

in the most painful moral situation. I even declare to you that in the course of the more than 18 years that I have occupied a place that put me in the daily contact with His person, I have never seen our Noble Master more sorely affected or more actively alarmed."[71] Tatishchev reported that Francis I was heard to say that "if he followed his feelings, he would immediately have summoned an army of hundred thousand men, he would have sent fifty thousand to the Morea to deliver this region from the fighting that devastates it and to put it beyond reach."[72]

Metternich was indignant because this battle not only disrupted his diplomatic plans and made the present more precarious and the future more uncertain, but also because there was no justifiable reason for the fighting. In the general surveys of the period, attention is generally paid to the question of which side shot the first cannon, and the answer is that with the most probability the sultan's sailors were responsible. Nevertheless, as for the origin of the battle, the question of the first cannon shot is quite unimportant for seeing the whole affair in detail. Although it is impossible to do so here, to fully understand the reasons for Metternich's anger the battle must be explained in brief. The three allied squadrons led by admirals Sir Edward Codrington, Marie Henri Daniel Gauthier de Rigny and Lodewijk Sigismund Vincent van Heyden were instructed by their respective ambassadors in Constantinople in early September, in compliance with the Treaty of London, to "peacefully" blockade the Peloponnese and some regions north from the Isthmus and protect the Greeks who had formally accepted the armistice but in fact continued fighting.[73] Soon afterwards they made a certain agreement with Ibrahim Pasha – unfortunately for historians only a verbal one – that each party understood in a different way. When the admirals came to the conclusion that Ibrahim had broken the commitment, which he most likely had not, and de-

---

[71] Metternich to Apponyi, Vienna, 13 Nov. 1827, HHStA, StA, Frankreich 265. For a similar statement see also Maltzan to Frederick William III, Vienna, 9 Nov. 1827, GStA PK, HA III, MdA I, 6009.

[72] Tatishchev to Nesselrode, Vienna, 9 Nov. 1827, AVPRI, fond 133, Kantseliariia, opis 468, 11874. Historian Lawrence J. Baack claimed that Francis I contemplated the use of 100,000 Austrian soldiers to aid the Turks. Baack, p. 154. However, to attribute such a plan, never considered either by the emperor or by his chancellor, to one embittered exclamation is absurd.

[73] Crawley, *Greek Independence*, p. 85.

spite the fact that the blockade of the designated area was successfully under way, on 20 October they entered the bay where the Egyptian, Turkish and several Tunisian ships anchored. The correspondence of the pro-Greek Codrington on the eve of the battle, the preparations on the allied decks for battle and the order given by Rigny to the French naval officers serving on the Egyptian ships to desert their posts offer evidence that the real aim of the admirals was nothing less than a battle.[74] Metternich ascertained Codrington's belligerency from the admiral's own account of the battle obtained by an Austrian representative from a British envoy in Florence in which Codrington justified his conduct with the alleged necessity to fulfil the goals of the trilateral Treaty and "punish Ibrahim Pasha for his alleged insolence and the lack of faith."[75] Tatishchev obtained this copy with Metternich's pen strokes underlining the admiral's expressions that particularly annoyed the prince like "an enemy," "the measure of which the battle was the consequence was absolutely necessary for not making the Treaty an illusion," "I declare that I felt a desire to punish serious offences," or "a scene of horror and devastation probably without example."[76] Metternich also criticised the way the battle was fought: "If the action had taken place on the open sea, occurring after seeing how the [Turko-Egyptian] fleet had attempted to leave the harbour, or while it was still passing [the inlet], it would have been a battle, but inside the harbour, and in the way that it happened, it was an assassination, a real assassination."[77] In brief, Metternich regarded the admiral's step as needless and as a breach of international law and against humanity.[78]

---

[74] G. Douin, *Navarin, 6 Juillet – 20 Octobre 1827*, Caire 1927, pp. 94–97, 225–281; C. M. Woodhouse, *The Battle of Navarino*, London 1965, pp. 75–111; Crawley, *Greek Independence*, pp. 90–91; Dakin, pp. 229–230.

[75] Codrington's report, Navarino, 21 Oct. 1827, attached to Tatishchev to Nesselrode, Vienna, 10 Nov. 1827, AVPRI, fond 133, Kantseliariia, opis 468, 11874.

[76] Ibid.

[77] Schwebel to Damas, Vienna, 12 Nov. 1827, AMAE, CP, Autriche 408. Stratford Canning expressed a similar opinion: "It might fairly be said that to take so large a force without previous agreement to a port which, belonging to a friendly government, was already occupied by a numerous fleet bearing that government's flag, was in the first place a flagrant breach of courtesy, and in the second a provocation." J. Marlowe, *Perfidious Albion: The Origins of Anglo-French Rivalry in the Levant*, London 1971, p. 162.

[78] Metternich to Ottenfels, Königswart, 2 Sept. 1827, HHStA, StA, Türkei VI,

Metternich's wedding was thus spoiled by these two pieces of news making the success of Austria's eventual diplomatic intervention impossible. The grand vizier's letter did not correspond with the chancellor's expectations since it lacked any tangible concession that could persuade the three Great Powers to modify their attitude towards the sultan.[79] Metternich compared it to "a thread for halting a chariot down a steep slope"[80] and regretted the Porte's unsatisfactory actions: "It negotiates neither with the Greeks nor with the Great Powers. Finally it addresses itself to us and what does it say to us? That it prefers peace to war."[81] The news of the battle definitely gave no hope that the Porte's intransigence could be diminished. This led Francis I to the firm decision to remain neutral and not go rushing into the "brawl,"[82] saying to Metternich: "If yesterday I was still satisfied to see myself faced with a real chance to contribute to the accommodation of a political dilemma full of embarrassment and danger by means of honest counsel, I do not nurture the same hope today."[83] Metternich told to the French chargé d'affaires in Vienna, Ludwig Schwebel, that the emperor "is so irritated and bad-tempered by the turn of events that have taken place in the affair of the Levant that he no longer wants to hear speak of any cooperation from his part. For the rest he regards the war as decided."[84] Francis I even hesitated to forward the grand vizier's letter, but when Metternich persuaded him that its existence could be hardly kept secret and that concealing it could have more serious consequences, he finally agreed to dispatch it to London, Paris and St Petersburg, but without any offer of support. Moreover, the foreign diplomats were informed that passing on the grand vizier's letter was the maximum which the emperor was willing to do and that no one could expect that he would agree for Austria

29; Metternich to Esterházy, Vienna, 29 Sept. 1827, HHStA, StA, England 178; Maltzan to Frederick William III, Vienna, 6 Nov. 1827, GStA PK, HA III, MdA I, 6009.

[79] Wellesley to Dudley, Vienna, 13 Nov. 1827, TNA, FO 120/88; Metternich to Francis I, Vienna, 9 Dec. 1827, *NP*, IV, p. 407.

[80] Metternich to Werner, Vienna, 16 Nov. 1827, HHStA, StK, Preussen 125.

[81] Metternich to Ottenfels, Vienna, 6 Jan. 1828, HHStA, StA, Türkei VI, 35.

[82] Bray to Ludwig I of Bavaria, Vienna, 25 Nov. 1827, BHStA, MA, Wien 2401.

[83] Metternich to Esterházy, Vienna, 9 Nov. 1827, HHStA, StA, England 179.

[84] Schwebel to Damas, Vienna, 13 Nov. 1827, AMAE, CP, Autriche 408.

to participate in the mediation between the Ottoman Empire and the three Great Powers, as requested by the grand vizier.[85]

Metternich explained Austria's given position to an employee of Austria's mission in Berlin, Baron Joseph von Werner: "It does not seem at all to us that the moment has arrived where third parties would make good by directly interfering in an affair which, seeing the stage it has reached at present, has first of all turned into an entirely new affair for the allies themselves. It is above all completely up to them to familiarise themselves with the serious consequences of their efforts in which they now find themselves involved. The diverse and often contradictory interests which are meshed in the formless thing exalted by the name of trilateral treaty will have to be evaluated by the indubitable force of time. United by a specific common goal, but this goal lacking, the hour of reflection for the three compromised Great Powers, or at least one or two of them, must come to pass. To offer mediation at the moment of confusion and trouble as it is at present would be to expose oneself to more than a defeat. Our role had to confine itself in the first instance to the transmission of the grand vizier's letter, giving it no other character than that of a communication of news; we must wait for the effect that this will produce in the different places towards which it has been directed. If the three courts, or one or two of them, will believe they must or can take advantage of the first evidence of a more conciliatory attitude on the part of the Divan, the courts, or the court, will not keep us in ignorance of it."[86] This as well as Metternich's other statements on the subject indicate that despite its little value he hoped that the letter would evoke some positive reaction from the signatory Powers, or any one of them. But he could hardly have many illusions and the negative answers from London as well as Paris and St Petersburg

---

[85] Metternich to Esterházy, Vienna, 9 and 10 Nov. 1827, HHStA, StA, England 179; Metternich to Apponyi, Vienna, 13 Nov. 1827, HHStA, StA, Frankreich 265; Metternich to Werner, Vienna, 16 Nov. 1827, HHStA, StK, Preussen 125; Metternich to Tatishchev, Vienna, 12 Nov. 1827, Tatishchev to Metternich, Vienna, 13 Nov. 1827, Tatishchev to Nesselrode, Vienna, 13 and 24 Nov. 1827, AVPRI, fond 133, Kantseliariia, opis 468, 11874; Wellesley to Dudley, Vienna, 10 Nov. 1827, TNA, FO 120/88; Maltzan to Frederick William III, Vienna, 13 and 23 Nov. 1827, GStA PK, HA III, MdA I, 6009.

[86] Metternich to Werner, Vienna, 27 Nov. 1827, HHStA, StK, Preussen 125.

proved the correctness of his own opinion that the grand vizier's letter without any practical use was a "still-born child."[87]

According to Crawley, Metternich "misunderstood Dudley's suggestion as an offer for Austria's mediation and persuaded the Grand Vizier to ask for it."[88] Nevertheless, Metternich perceived it quite correctly and knew very well what he had to request from the Porte, but he simply did not get it. As for the "mediation," it definitely was the best position for leading the negotiations on the Greek affairs if he succeeded in restoring the alliance from three Powers to five, including Prussia sharing Austria's basic views; and he probably hoped to play this role, although informally. However, it also must be added that from the very beginning he fought hard against the use of the term "mediation," denied that it was his goal owing to Russia's expected opposition and, above all, he did not request it in his early October instructions to Ottenfels. It was the Porte which pressed for Austria's mediation between itself and the three allied Powers, in particular in its note for Ottenfels from 9 November. In any case this explicit mention of the mediation made the Great Powers, in particular Russia, more hostile to Austria. Their refusal as well as Francis I's calculated – and sincere – passivity totally destroyed Metternich's plans of whatever nature. He definitely hoped until the last moment for the smallest success of his diplomatic move and it was not until the receipt of the refusal from London that he instructed Ottenfels to inform the Porte about the failure of grand vizier's letter and the impossibility of any support for it from Austria, thereby terminating the whole affair in December.[89]

---

[87] Metternich to Ottenfels, Vienna, 6 Dec. 1827, HHStA, StA, Türkei VI, 29.

[88] Crawley, *Greek Independence*, p. 94.

[89] Metternich to Werner, Vienna, 29 Nov. 1827, HHStA, StK, Preussen 125; Metternich to Ottenfels, Vienna, 6 Dec. 1827, HHStA, StA, Türkei VI, 29; the Porte's note to Ottenfels, 9 Nov. 1827, Ottenfels to Metternich, Constantinople, 10 Nov. 1827, HHStA, StA, Türkei VI, 28; Esterházy to Metternich, London, 20 and 26 Nov., 1 Dec. 1827, HHStA, StA, England 177; Dudley to Wellesley, London, 1 and 20 Nov. 1827, TNA, FO 120/88; Schwebel to Damas, Vienna, 29 Nov. 1827, AMAE, CP, Autriche 408; Tatishchev to Nesselrode, Vienna, 1 Dec. 1827, AVPRI, fond 133, Kantseliariia, opis 468, 11874.

*   *   *

Metternich's hopes for a change in the development of the trilateral affair evoked by Dudley's September statements to Esterházy were turned into even greater pessimism due to his failure to get the Porte to act in a more conciliatory manner and particularly because of the events of 20 October that, according to him, opened "a new era for Europe."[90] Although this statement was exaggerated, the battle proved that the chancellor's warnings against the consequences of the Treaty of London and the unfeasibility of a peaceful blockade in practice were well founded and quite correct. Whereas the attitude of Canning, who wrote shortly after the signing of the Treaty to Stratford that the "spirit of that agreement was peaceful interference, recommended by a friendly demonstration of force"[91] cannot be seen as anything other than imprudent optimism, then Metternich's attitude must be regarded not as pessimistic but highly realistic. One did not need great analytical skills to see the probable consequences of the Treaty stipulations, but the Austrian chancellor definitely proved to have better skills than his British counterpart.

Metternich's attitude was essentially based upon the conviction that Mahmud II would never agree to either the mediation or to the allied naval blockade, both confirmed by the sultan's statements communicated to the foreign diplomats through his advisors as well as his instructions to Ibrahim Pasha. Some historians accredited partial responsibility of the sultan's persistent obstinacy in 1827 to Austria's unconcealed opposition to the mediation.[92] Nevertheless, in this case Paul W. Schroeder is absolutely right when he claims that the allies had no hope in persuading the Porte to accept their demands.[93] The reports from Ottenfels and Miltitz – and there is no doubt that they contained the real opinions of their authors – were full of proof that the Great Powers whether in an alliance of three or five had no chance of persuading the Ottoman monarch to yield. Some rather persuasive evidence can be found in the fact that Mahmud II constantly rejected Metternich's less radical proposals for more moderate measures con-

---

[90] Metternich to Apponyi, Vienna, 13 Nov. 1827, HHStA, StA, Frankreich 265.
[91] Temperley, *Canning*, p. 403.
[92] Crawley, *Greek Independence*, p. 94; Douin, *Navarin*, pp. 120–121.
[93] Schroeder, *Transformation*, p. 652.

taining some concessions like the armistice and amnesty; if the sultan would not yield in the case of this more compromising plan, how could he be expected to yield to the much more dangerous conditions of the trilateral alliance supported on 16 August not by three but four representatives, Baron Miltitz being among them? There was no chance of changing his obstinate attitude, as well as no need for the chancellor to persuade Mahmud II to reject the foreign mediation because there was nothing less acceptable to the sultan at that moment.

Sauvigny asked an important question regarding whether Metternich's respect for Mahmud II's sovereignty leading to, as the French historian says, "absurdity" did not merely reflect the uncompromising attitude of the Austrian emperor.[94] The answer is more simple than might be presumed: Metternich's attitude towards the sultan's sovereignty was his own, resulting, as shown in the previous chapter, from his perception of the fundamental rules of the European system of law, the observance of which was much needed for Austria placed as it was in the middle of Europe and being the least powerful among the four Powers directly involved in the Near East. His steps in the discussions with the European cabinets as well as the Porte on the Greek Question reflected his own politico-legal ideas. Nothing in his official as well as his personal correspondence from this or the other years covered by this book indicates any divergence in his and Francis I's opinions in this respect; as for late 1827, some signs merely indicate Metternich's greater willingness to pursue more active steps after the Battle of Navarino in connection with the grand vizier's letter. Despite the lack of success, he did not remain passive and continued in his efforts to save the peace that was becoming more and more uncertain in the following months.

---

[94] Sauvigny, *Metternich et la France*, III, p. 1111.

7

The Outbreak of the Russo-Ottoman War

The Battle of Navarino led to the suspension of diplomatic relations between the Ottoman Empire and the signatory Powers of the Treaty of London and significantly increased the prospect for war between the sultan and the tsar, an outcome which had been a real nightmare for Metternich since the beginning of the Greek insurrection. The Austrian chancellor therefore strived in the months following the battle for the preservation of peace, but his consummate efforts clashed with the Porte's intransigence, Russia's belligerency, France's pro-Russian inclination, British indifference and Prussia's passivity.

The War in Sight

The Navarino graveyard of most of the Ottoman fleet and 6,000–8,000 sailors raised concerns in the West about how Mahmud II as well as his Moslem subjects would react. What Metternich feared most were massacres of the Ottoman Christians that would have been as inhumane as politically imprudent but, according to the chancellor, not entirely incomprehensible. He also feared that the Turks did not consider the disaster as a punishment from the heavens and, consequently, did not direct their anger against their monarch and his reforms.[1] Fortunately for Mahmud II, his reforms and his Christian subjects, the empire did not experience any outburst of visible hatred and Ottenfels could report from Constantinople that "the most perfect tranquillity reigns once again in this capital, even though the cries of the widows and orphans of the victims of the disaster from Navarino resound in

---

[1]   Metternich to Werner, Vienna, 27 Nov. 1827, HHStA, StK, Preussen, 125; Schwebel to Damas, Vienna, 12 Nov. 1827, AMAE, CP, Autriche 408.

the neighbourhoods inhabited by the families of the sailors."[2] This news was welcomed by Metternich with great relief: "We still maintain that we were surprised by the moderation with which the Porte conducted itself until the moment when it stated its course of action and particularly by the calm of the large Moslem population. Indeed, we do not know of a Christian capital which, under the same circumstances, would show the unshakeable calm which Constantinople has just exhibited."[3]

The behaviour of the Porte towards the three Great Powers responsible for the battle was significantly different. It requested their apology for the committed crime, financial compensation for the lost ships and the end to their interference into the Greek affairs. Their ambassadors, on the other hand, sharply rejected these demands and insisted on the armistice and the concessions for the Greeks according to the stipulations of the Treaty of London. Ottenfels did his best for weeks to reduce the anger felt by both parties, and what Metternich was trying to attempt on a large scale among the cabinets, the internuncio was now doing on the small stage of the Constantinople theatre. However, the two parties were irreconcilable. The Turkish dignitaries seen in their military uniforms with pistols, daggers and sabres and talking about dignity and holy law refused to make any concessions except the one ensured by Ottenfels: the Porte's relations with the ambassadors were not broken but merely suspended when the news of the battle arrived, and even this measure was soon recalled. The attitude of the ambassadors was identical with no willingness on their part to yield, all of them considerably distrustful of the internuncio, Ribeaupierre desiring war and Stratford Canning pointedly assertive as usual. Ottenfels reported about Stratford: "He was a tiger which had tasted blood and longed to kill again. He is speaking of nothing else than of bombarding all the Turkish ports, the destruction of all Ottoman ships which could sail on the open sea, the extermination of the Moslems to create a free and independent Greece required by the progress of civilisation, the entrance of the Russian armies into the Principalities, the discontent of the nation and the

---

[2]   Ottenfels to Metternich, Constantinople, 5 Nov. 1827, HHStA, StA, Türkei VI, 28. On the unchanged situation in Constantinople also see Ottenfels to Metternich, Constantinople, 10 and 26 Nov., 10 Dec. 1827, HHStA, StA, Türkei VI, 28.
[3]   Metternich to Werner, Vienna, 27 Nov. 1827, HHStA, StK, Preussen 125.

Ulemas who will force the sultan to yield."[4] Consequently, when Ottenfels attempted to improve the situation with the revival of his idea from the spring of 1825 to replace the word "mediation" with "intercession," he met with resolute refusals from both sides. Their rigidity finally ended with the ambassadors' departure from Constantinople on 8 December, something which Ottenfels also tried to prevent till the very end.[5] Frustrated and ill, he then expressed the opinion that if he had known of the emperor's decision not to meet the grand vizier's request earlier, the Divan, losing all hope of Austria's help, would have agreed with the concessions to the Greeks as demanded by the united Powers. Nevertheless, the present state of research agrees with Metternich, who wrote in the margin: "False."[6]

The Austrian chancellor entirely approved of his internuncio's conduct and effort to forestall the ambassadors' departure, which he deeply regretted since it made a war more probable. He believed, as always before, that it would not be a conflict between three and one but only between Russia and the Ottoman Empire, and it was the conduct of the cabinet in St Petersburg that Metternich feared most since it was the only one of the trilateral alliance possessing the means, as he declared, to "entirely change the face of the Levant."[7] And although he was still convinced that Nicholas I did not long for war, he also expected that the tsar would not hesitate to take up arms if he found himself to be forced to do so: "We are still convinced that the Russian emperor does not desire war, but we also believe that he will wage one, either together with his allies or alone, if he does not succeed in moving the Porte to an arrangement that would be equal to the most

[4] Ottenfels to Metternich, Constantinople, 5 Nov. 1827, HHStA, StA, Türkei VI, 28.

[5] Ottenfels to Huszár, 2 Nov. 1827, Huszár to Ottenfels, 2, 3 and 4 Nov. 1827, Ottenfels to Metternich, Constantinople, 5, 10 and 25 Nov., 11 and 31 Dec. 1827, HHStA, StA, Türkei VI, 28; Miltitz to Frederick William III, Pera, 5, 10 and 26 Nov. 1827, GStA PK, HA III, MdA I, 7265; Guilleminot to Damas, Constantinople, 6, 15, 19 and 21 Nov. 1827, AMAE, CP, Turquie 248; Schwebel to Damas, Vienna, 13, 20 and 25 Nov., 8 Dec. 1827, AMAE, CP, Autriche 408; Tatishchev to Nesselrode, Vienna, 20 Nov. and 11 Dec. 1827, AVPRI, fond 133, Kantseliariia, opis 468, 11874; Bray to Ludwig I of Bavaria, Vienna, 27 Nov. 1827, BHStA, MA, Wien 2401.

[6] Ottenfels to Metternich, Constantinople, 11 Dec. 1827, HHStA, StA, Türkei VI, 28.

[7] Bray to Ludwig I of Bavaria, Vienna, 27 Nov. 1827, BHStA, MA, Wien 2401.

moderate conditions of the Treaty of London."[8] Metternich naturally greatly feared such a conflict although he never, neither earlier nor later, believed that Nicholas I wished to destroy the Ottoman Empire: "What the Russian court wants is a Turkey materially weak, a Turkey disarmed and morally vilified; what it also wants is a Greece that nominally exists but is in reality nothing, a dual purpose creation whose existence would offer it the double advantage of being a source of disagreements, disasters and further weakening for the Porte, while at the same time offering the means to Russia for spreading its system of protection to the other parts of the Ottoman Empire."[9] However, Metternich also knew that once war commenced, its consequences could hardly be predicted: "Emperor Nicholas assures us that he does not want to conquer anything, overthrow anyone, but by shaking an old and dilapidated edifice, who can rest assured that this edifice will not collapse? War spares no one, it almost always overturns and confounds all calculations. With the current position of the Russian armies in Asia, if peace with Persia is once concluded, Trabzon and Erzurum are within marching distance and the Ottoman Empire can be attacked at its heart; where all this will lead? It is impossible to say that yet!"[10] There were also the problems concerning Russia's eventual territorial gains in the event of its victory and the preservation of the Ottoman Empire. Nicholas I assured foreign governments many times that he did not want and actually would not seize any Ottoman territory in Europe and he conveyed this promise in Vienna not only through Tatishchev but also a personal letter to Francis I.[11] However, Metternich was rather sceptical towards this claim because, first, if the war became expensive and cost many lives, Nicholas I could change his mind, second, the tsar did not say that he would not demand a war indemnity, and Metternich worried that under the pretext of an indemnity impossible for the Porte to repay the Russian monarch would ask for territory: "The Russian emperor pretends and assures [us] that he does not want to expand his territory, that he does not dream of any conquest. All of this is easy to

---

[8] Metternich to Ottenfels, Vienna, 6 Jan. 1828, HHStA, StA, Türkei VI, 35.
[9] Metternich to Esterházy, Vienna, 12 Feb. 1828, HHStA, StA, England 182.
[10] Bray to Ludwig I of Bavaria, Vienna, 30 March 1828, BHStA, MA, Wien 2402.
[11] Nicholas I to Francis I, St Petersburg, 19 Jan. 1828, attached to Metternich to Ottenfels, Vienna, 2 Feb. 1828, HHStA, StA, Türkei VI, 35; Tatishchev to Nesselrode, Vienna, 15 Jan. 1828, AVPRI, fond 133, Kantseliariia, opis 468, 11877.

say, but once war begins, it would be necessary for Russia to spend 200 to 300 million; these Oriental wars are fought on gold bullion. The regions to be crossed offer nothing, or very little; it is therefore necessary [for the troops] to carry with them all supplies; battles and disease will bring down 200 to 300 thousand men – frightened by so many losses, Russia will not make conquests but will demand security, and like it did in Persia it will demand money for paying expenses and since the Porte has none, it will take land as collateral."[12] The thought of Russia's eventual seizure of the Danubian Principalities or even the extension of its influence over them and Serbia was always a nightmare for the Viennese diplomatic as well as the military elite. Consequently, Metternich had more than one serious reason to prevent war and, therefore, the preservation of peace entirely absorbed his attention in late 1827 and early 1828.[13]

Metternich's Last Attempts to Preserve the Peace

The problem lay in the fact that Metternich's means to influence events were rather limited. The Porte had not wanted to listen to his counsels for moderation before the battle and did not become more willing to do so afterwards; preparations for war were in progress in the Ottoman capital, and the sultan made it clear that any negotiation with the insurgents on issues such as an armistice or amnesty could not be opened before their submission. Moreover, Francis I's refusal to intervene in the Porte's dispute with the allied Powers on the basis of the grand vizier's letter considerably reduced Austria's influence in Constantinople because the Turks' disillusion was as great as their previous expectations of its assistance had been. Despite the aggravated position in Constantinople and the little prospect for any

---

[12] Bray to Ludwig I of Bavaria, Vienna, 5 Feb. 1828, BHStA, MA, Wien 2402.

[13] Metternich to Trauttmannsdorff, Vienna, 15 Jan. 1828, HHStA, StK, Preussen 128; Metternich to Apponyi, Vienna, 24 Jan. 1828, HHStA, StA, Frankreich 267; Metternich to Esterházy, Vienna, 7 March 1828, HHStA, StA, England 182; Schwebel to Damas, Vienna, 26 Dec. 1827, AMAE, CP, Autriche 408; Tatishchev to Nesselrode, Vienna, 4 Dec. 1827, AVPRI, fond 133, Kantseliariia, opis 468, 11874; Maltzan to Frederick William III, Vienna, 18 March 1828, GStA PK, HA III, MdA I, 6010.

success, the imminence of war moved Metternich to continue in attempts to persuade Mahmud II to moderation. In January 1828, the chancellor started a new diplomatic offensive, the principal aim of which can be summarised again as "to induce the sultan to yield to the force of circumstances."[14] Metternich was convinced that in the given situation, it only was Mahmud II who could save himself as well as the allied Great Powers from the precarious situation.[15] The sultan could not count on the disintegration of the trilateral alliance or on Austria's mediation, he could only save himself if he wanted to avoid war by making some concessions which would enable the trilateral alliance to enter into negotiations with him. Metternich did not request the mediation but he repeated his old counsel: "That it [the Ottoman Empire] declares by means of a manifest what it will grant to its insurgent subjects under the condition of their submission. That it particularly declares a suspension of all hostilities if the allies on their part are prepared to do the same thing. We made this demand to the Porte before the Battle of Navarino. Agreeing to it would have saved the Turko-Egyptian fleet. We are making it again on the eve of the [Russian] occupation of the Danubian Principalities. If the sultan wants war, he will have it. If he does not want it, he can prevent it with the measures, belated though they may be, which we are advising him to take."[16] In Metternich's opinion, these concessions could place the Porte in a better situation in face of the three allied Powers and save the peace that was becoming more uncertain with every day the sultan hesitated to meet the counsel coming from Vienna; the chancellor went so far that he even sent a personal letter to the grand vizier setting out all the dangers facing the sultan and once again advising him of the necessity to yield.[17]

---

[14] Metternich to Apponyi, Königswart, 31 Dec. 1827, HHStA, StA, Frankreich 265.
[15] Metternich to Trauttmannsdorff, Vienna, 15 Jan. 1828, HHStA, StK, Preussen 128.
[16] Metternich to Ottenfels, Vienna, 6 Jan. 1828, HHStA, StA, Türkei VI, 35.
[17] Metternich to Ottenfels, Vienna, 19 Dec. 1827, HHStA, StA, Türkei VI, 29; Metternich to Mehmed Selim Pasha, Vienna, 6 Jan. 1828, attached to Metternich to Ottenfels, Vienna, 6 Jan. 1828, HHStA, StA, Türkei VI, 35; Ottenfels to Metternich, Constantinople, 31 Dec. 1827, HHStA, StA, Türkei VI, 28; Ottenfels to Metternich, Constantinople, 10 Jan. 1828, HHStA, StA, Türkei VI, 32; Miltitz to Frederick William III, Pera, 10 Nov. and 10 Dec. 1827, GStA PK, HA III, MdA I, 7265; Ottenfels, *Memoari*, p. 195.

According to Metternich, a reasonable and moderate vision of a settlement of the Greeks' future was necessary for reconciliation between the Porte and the Powers. Therefore, he advised Mahmud II of a plan consisting of six points for the solution that he regarded as acceptable in Constantinople: (1) The Peloponnese should be governed by a Christian prince and its territorial units should also be administrated by Christians; (2) this prince (or princes) should be hereditary, but in any case nominated and confirmed by the sultan; (3) the Peloponnese should pay an annual tribute to the Ottoman treasury; (4) the forts in the Peloponnese should be garrisoned by only Ottoman (Moslem) troops; (5) the islands should enjoy their ancient rights and privileges and also pay an annual tribute to the Ottoman treasury; (6) the earlier tributes unpaid owing to the insurrection should be excused as an expression of the sultan's graciousness. These six points were prepared upon the Austrian, Prussian and Sardinian December reports from Constantinople in which Metternich found some indications that the sultan could accept them. If he did not do so willingly and of his own accord, he would undoubtedly be forced by a foreign intervention to adopt not only these or even more stringent measures but probably foreign guarantees as well: "In this manner this Great Power would avoid with much greater ease the regime of foreign guarantees which would become an inevitable consequence of the concessions enforced by the Great Powers. The sultan must know well enough on account of the foreign guarantees and foreign protectorates over the parts of his empire that this proposal seems to me to hardly need any more specific explanation."[18] In short, what Metternich advised was not a pleasure but a necessity for the sultan to avoid even more serious problems. Unfortunately for this peace endeavour, the situation in Constantinople was anything but favourable to concessions and Metternich's reliance on the sultan's certain moderation as contained in the Austrian, Prussian and Sardinian reports proved to be totally wrong. If Mahmud II perhaps inclined to some concessions in late 1827, he definitely did not in early 1828. His attitude towards the allied Powers, and in particular Russia, was gradually deteriorating, which, for example, led to the embargo on the shipping in the Straits.[19] Ottenfels' despair was so great that

---

[18] Metternich to Ottenfels, Vienna, 21 Jan. 1828, HHStA, StA, Türkei VI, 35.

[19] Ibid.; Ottenfels to Metternich, Constantinople, 2 Feb. 1828, HHStA, StA,

he seriously contemplated leaving Constantinople in mid February: "I must leave it to the superior judgement of Your Highness to decide if maintaining an internuncio of His Majesty at a government which does not want to listen to us any more could henceforth be useful or convenient. Perhaps the declaration to recall His Majesty's minister, if the Porte persists in refusing a suspension of hostilities, could produce some effect, but I would not dare to answer to the result."[20] Although Ottenfels' departure was out of question, Metternich himself had to admit at the end of March that "the Divan lives in abstractions and it does not see the abyss to which it is advancing."[21]

The failure in Constantinople considerably weakened Metternich's position in dealing with the other Powers. He had no means at his disposal which could make their attitudes towards the Porte more conciliatory, or at least those of Great Britain and France, which would make Russia's position vis-à-vis the Ottoman Empire more difficult and perhaps move the tsar to more cautious conduct. Moreover, the allied courts were joined not only by the Treaty of London but also by their more or less mistrust of Metternich's policy for three principal reasons: (1) Austria's conduct and in particular that of Ottenfels on 16 August in Constantinople contrary to their wishes; (2) the grand vizier's letter, which all of them correctly assumed was provoked by Metternich, the British cabinet of course knowing that from him, and they presumed that he wanted to assume the role of a mediator between them and the Ottoman Empire; (3) the transport of Turkish and Egyptian supplies and ammunitions, even to Ibrahim Pasha's fleet anchoring in Navarino Bay, by Austrian commercial vessels.[22]

Türkei VI, 32; Miltitz to Frederick William III, Pera, 15 Feb. 1828, GStA PK, HA III, MdA I, 7266.
[20] Ottenfels to Metternich, Constantinople, 15 Feb. 1828, HHStA, StA, Türkei VI, 32.
[21] Metternich to Ottenfels, Vienna, 20 March 1828, HHStA, StA, Türkei VI, 35.
[22] There was much dissatisfaction among the allied cabinets and admirals owing to this service rendered by Austrian ships to the sultan's armed forces, but they themselves had to admit that nothing was illegal in this proceeding. Even the blockade ordered after the Porte's refusal to submit to the Treaty of London was not acknowledged by Austria, and Lord Dudley could do nothing since British lawyers found no legitimate way to justify the seizure of neutral ships if Great Britain was not in a state of war with the Ottoman Empire. Codrington's imputation raised in early October that Austrian war vessels joined the Turko-Egyptian fleet in its operations against the Greeks was entirely unfounded and easily refutable

Metternich had no other option than to try to influence the steps of the British and French cabinets by warning them against the imminent danger of the outbreak of a Russo-Ottoman war. Shortly after the Battle of Navarino he had already declared it as inevitable and openly accused the two Maritime Powers of playing Russia's game, which could lead to the increase of its territory at the expense of the Ottoman Empire and its greater influence over Ottoman provinces in Europe as well as in Asia. With their policy, they enabled the tsar to do what he wanted, and with the battle weakening the sultan's striking power they did him a great service should he decide to start a war: "The total destruction of all maritime forces of the Ottoman Porte exposes this Great Power to the mercy of Russia. That this is what the latter Great Power wants above all is the secret of the whole world."[23] Metternich wanted their conduct to be less benevolent towards Russia and more placable towards the Ottoman Empire, or at least that there should be some change in their Greek policy since the latest events had proved its inefficiency.[24] Metternich later did not refrain from making this sarcastic remark: "The approaches made in Constantinople in consequence of the Treaty of London failed; the operations of the admirals, although more brilliant than those of the negotiators, were no more effective."[25]

Great Britain and France, bound by the Treaty of London, made no positive response to Austria's insinuations, but whereas Great Britain sincerely did not want the opening of a Russian campaign

---

for the Austrians. Metternich to Esterházy, Vienna, 31 Oct. and 4 Nov. 1827, HHStA, StA, England 179; Esterházy to Metternich, London, 5 Oct. 1827, HHStA, StA, England 177; Dandolo to Codrington, Smyrna, 4 Oct. 1827, Ottenfels to Metternich, Constantinople, 10 Oct. 1827, HHStA, StA, Türkei VI, 28; Guilleminot to Damas, Therapia, 19 Aug. 1827, AMAE, CP, Turquie 247; Schwebel to Damas, Vienna, 18 Oct. 1827, AMAE, CP, Autriche 408; Tatishchev to Nesselrode, Vienna, 31 Oct. 1827, AVPRI, fond 133, Kantseliariia, opis 468, 11874; Cowley to Dudley, Vienna, 5 Feb. 1828, TNA, FO 120/90; Crawley, *Greek Independence*, p. 84.
[23] Metternich to Esterházy, Vienna, 9 Nov. 1827, HHStA, StA, England 179.
[24] Metternich to Esterházy, Vienna, 9 and 19 Nov., 3 Dec. 1827, HHStA, StA, England 179; Metternich to Esterházy, Vienna, 4 Feb. 1828, HHStA, StA, England 182; Metternich to Ottenfels, Vienna, 6 Dec. 1827, HHStA, StA, Türkei VI, 29; Metternich to Ottenfels, Vienna, 6 Jan. 1828, HHStA, StA, Türkei VI, 35; Schwebel to Damas, Vienna, 15 Dec. 1827, AMAE, CP, Autriche 408; Wellesley to Dudley, Vienna, 16 Dec. 1827, TNA, FO 120/88.
[25] Metternich's memorandum attached to Metternich to Esterházy, Vienna, 15 March 1828, HHStA, StA, England 182.

and was dissatisfied with the development of events, France inclined towards Russia and showed greater satisfaction with the hostile measures undertaken against the Ottoman Empire. This difference in opinions clearly showed in their reactions to the Battle of Navarino: whereas it was generally regretted in London, in Paris its outcome was celebrated as a great victory for the French, in other words it resembled the deep satisfaction which the tsar had displayed when he learnt of the destruction of the sultan's fleet.[26] Metternich not only could not fail to notice these different assessments of the unfortunate event, but he had also predicted them: "The greatest evil is no longer to be found in London; it must be sought in Paris. It is there where errors and faults of all kinds seek to cover themselves with the colours of force and where they would also like to deck themselves in those of glory. It is impossible that the calamity of Navarino is not seen in England as a political disaster; we will see the French ministers publish apologies and their newspapers proclaim the glory of France. Navarino will replace Trocadéro."[27] Consequently, Metternich held higher hopes for Great Britain whose attitude he believed he might be able to change. He also hoped in November and December 1827 to be able to modify the conduct of the cabinet in St Petersburg with Prussia's assistance; on 16 November, he asked Bernstorff to influence the attitude of Nicholas I, who was a son-in-law of Frederick William III. On 27 November Metternich dispatched new instructions to Berlin with the proposal for some common understanding and joint language towards the Great Powers as well as the Porte. Some historians later considered this as an offer for an alliance and a joint active policy. Historian Lawrence J. Baack claims that its aim was the restoration of order in Greece and the obstruction of the triple alliance's military action against Turkey.[28] Metternich's real aim was less adventurous, and the attitude of his emperor did not allow a different one. The careful study of his instructions to Berlin and the reports sent from Berlin back to Vienna with Metternich's added notes in the

---

[26] Metternich to Ottenfels, Vienna, 6 Jan. 1828, HHStA, StA, Türkei VI, 35; Schwebel to Damas, Vienna, 27 Oct. 1827, AMAE, CP, Autriche 408; Crawley, *Greek Independence*, p. 95; Fargette, p. 82.

[27] Metternich to Apponyi, Vienna, 13 Nov. 1827, HHStA, StA, Frankreich 265.

[28] Baack, p. 154. A similarly radical attitude was maintained by Crawley, *Greek Independence*, p. 93, a less radical one by Schiemann, II, p. 210 and Ringhofer, pp. 85–86.

margins reveal that the Prussian backing was to be particularly used to add strength to his arguments for persuading the allied Powers as well as the Porte to yield, in other words to increase the prospect for the success of the chancellor's actual efforts, while not making any radical new steps towards either of the quarrelling parties. However, Bernstorff refused to move from Prussia's position of absolute passivity or raise discussion on the topic with Nicholas I, arguing that there was no chance for any success since the tsar had not discussed the Eastern Question with Prussia since the moment it had stayed apart from the trilateral Treaty.[29]

What enabled Metternich to be optimistic for some time were the governmental changes during the winter in France and Great Britain. The first occurred in France where Count La Ferronnays became the new foreign minister. The fact that he had served for several years as an ambassador in St Petersburg did not change Metternich's belief that this Frenchman shared his view, which was an opinion based upon personal meetings but was soon to be shown to be entirely mistaken since La Ferronnays maintained a considerably pro-Russian bias.[30] Metternich was to realise his mistake soon enough when he proposed to Paris that the allied Powers make a concession from their side and request an armistice and amnesty without using the term "mediation," which was to make the solution to the problem more possible: "If they want the Porte to agree to the pacification, they will have it; if they want the mediation, there will be no pacification, there will be war."[31] This proposal made on 24 January 1828 to the French government first since the British government was still not formed was accompanied by Metternich's personal letter for La Ferronnays in which he pledged himself to attempt to obtain some concessions from the sultan: "The question is to know whether you will content yourselves with the concessions considered by the sultan? We will do what we can to provide them without being able to guarantee success."[32] Nevertheless, La Ferronnays had no desire to cooperate with Austria and he even conveyed Metternich's personal letter to Pozzo

---

[29] Metternich to Werner, Vienna, 16 and 27 Nov. 1827, Werner to Metternich, Berlin, 21 and 22 Nov., 8 Dec. 1827, HHStA, StK, Preussen 125.

[30] Sauvigny, *Metternich et la France*, III, p. 1194.

[31] Bray to Ludwig I of Bavaria, Vienna, 5 Feb. 1828, BHStA, MA, Wien 2402.

[32] Metternich to La Ferronnays, Vienna, 24 Jan. 1828, HHStA, StA, Frankreich 267.

di Borgo and informed London of the chancellor's alleged proposal for mediation. Metternich learnt this as well as La Ferronnays' public statement that "the cannon from Navarino caused an explosion of glory and not of war,"[33] both making him aware of his misplaced optimism towards France. The pro-Russian attitude of the new French cabinet became entirely evident when on the turn of January and February La Ferronnays agreed with Russia's eventual occupation of the Danubian Principalities planned as a coercive measure against the Porte, something which Metternich still regarded not as a measure of coercion but as a trigger to start a war.[34] The new British government was more pro-Austrian, which was due to the fact that the new prime minister, the Duke of Wellington, was on friendly terms with Metternich and Esterházy. Nevertheless, Metternich, who since Canning's death had always had more hopes for a change in the British rather than French Near Eastern policy, could not be satisfied with Wellington. Despite his rejection of any question of Russia's temporary occupation of the Danubian Principalities, Wellington preferred to maintain a passive attitude and he saw no chance to abandon it without a concrete concession from the Porte; he hoped that Austria would obtain one, something which Metternich naturally desired but was unable to achieve.[35]

Under the given conditions, when it was impossible to appease either of the two quarrelling parties, Metternich made a new attempt in mid March to save the peace that seemed to be almost lost at that time by reviving his idea from early 1825: the threat of the recognition of the Greek independence. If Mahmud II did not agree to the Greeks' autonomy after the receipt of this threat, then the Great Powers were to declare Greece's independence. Metternich promised that if the plan were accepted by the allies, Austria would support the

---

[33] Metternich to Trauttmannsdorff, Vienna, 3 March 1828, HHStA, StK, Preussen 128.
[34] Metternich to Ottenfels, Vienna, 6 Jan. 1828, HHStA, StA, Türkei VI, 35; Metternich to Apponyi, Vienna, 24 Jan. 1828, HHStA, StA, Frankreich 267; Metternich to Trauttmannsdorff, Vienna, 22 Feb. 1828, HHStA, StK, Preussen 128; Metternich to Esterházy, Vienna, 15 March 1828, HHStA, StA, England 182; Bray to Ludwig I of Bavaria, Vienna, 19 Jan. 1828, BHStA, MA, Wien 2402; Schroeder, *Transformation*, p. 654.
[35] Metternich to Ottenfels, Vienna, 2 Feb. 1828, HHStA, StA, Türkei VI, 35; Metternich to Esterházy, Vienna, 7 April 1828, HHStA, StA, England 182; Maltzan to Frederick William III, Vienna, 18 Dec. 1827, GStA PK, HA III, MdA I, 6009.

threat and, in the event of its failure, would also recognise the Greeks' independence. He pointed out that the prospect of success would be increased by the clear territorial restriction of an autonomous Greece, which he suggested should be limited to the Peloponnese and some islands of the Archipelago. Any territory too extensive or not specified could lead to the sultan's refusal. If the Porte submitted to this dictate and agreed to an autonomous Greece, then the crisis would be terminated. If not, they would create an independent Greece and limit its military operations to its defence, which would be advantageous since no other regions of the Ottoman Empire could be attacked if the sultan did not declare war on any of the European countries. As for the Egyptian forces in the peninsula, the chancellor was of the opinion that Mohammed Ali and his son would not want to face the displeasure of the European Powers and would agree to the withdrawal of their forces. Metternich was well aware of the fact that the sultan could also choose to fight instead of yielding when confronted with the threat, but, according to him, if Mahmud II did not abandon his present stubborn attitude, war would be inevitable anyway. Compared to 1825, in March 1828 Metternich sincerely hoped that this proposal would be accepted by the Great Powers, or at least by Great Britain, which would cause a rupture among the members of the trilateral alliance. Nevertheless, as he had in 1825, he also hoped that the threat of independence would suffice, that the Porte would yield and the recognition of an independent Greece by the Great Powers would not be necessary; it was in no way, as Paul W. Schroeder claims, a "plan of immediately recognizing an independent Greek state."[36] Nevertheless, Wellington rejected Metternich's proposal with the explanation that an independent Greece was inadmissible for him, not because he did not want to prevent a war but because he "was slower than Metternich to see how far the pursuit of reality would have to go."[37] Negative reactions also came from Paris and St Petersburg where the same proposal had also been addressed.[38]

---

[36] Schroeder, *Transformation*, p. 653.

[37] Woodhouse, *Capodistria*, p. 363.

[38] Metternich's memorandum attached to Metternich to Esterházy, Vienna, 15 March 1828, HHStA, StA, England 182; Tatishchev to Nesselrode, Vienna, 12 April 1828, AVPRI, fond 133, Kantseliariia, opis 468, 11877; Esterházy to Metternich, London, 28 March 1828, Prokesch-Osten, *Griechen*, V, pp. 187–189; Crawley, *Greek Independence*, p. 104.

The Outbreak of War

Nicholas I's refusal was motivated by different reasons from those of Wellington. Since the Battle of Navarino, the tsar and his ministers had aimed at the armed solution and what they feared was not an outbreak of war but the maintenance of peace.[39] Metternich's activities seeking to avert the conflict were thorns in their flesh. Consequently, when news of the Porte's request for Austria's mediation arrived at St Petersburg, its cabinet accused Metternich of making an offer of mediation to London and Paris, which forced Metternich to ask the two relative governments for formal denial. Furthermore, Tatishchev was instructed to obtain an unequivocal promise from Francis I that he would neither assume the role of a mediator nor help the Ottoman Empire in other ways. When on 27 December 1827 Tatishchev asked the emperor for this declaration, he obtained this satisfactory answer: "I agree to it. Prince Metternich will reply to the grand vizier and he will tell him that I do not want the mediation and that in no case can the Porte, if it persists in its refusal, expect any assistance from my part, that it has been warned against the perils which are threatening it and that it will have to endure them alone if they come to pass."[40] However, Tatishchev so greatly feared Austria's interference in the Greek Question and an Austro-British rapprochement after the formation of Wellington's cabinet that he wanted to hear the emperor state his promise again and, consequently, a new audience took place on 1 February 1828 where, despite the irritating manner of the ambassador's conduct, Francis I willingly repeated it.[41]

The Porte's position towards Russia considerably deteriorated when on 20 December 1827, despite Ottenfels' effort to persuade the Turks to avoid doing anything that could displease their powerful northern neighbour, Mahmud II addressed a proclamation of

---

[39] Bitis, pp. 179–188.

[40] Tatishchev to Nesselrode, Vienna, 28 Dec. 1827, AVPRI, fond 133, Kantseliariia, opis 468, 11874. The promise was fulfilled in Metternich's abovementioned letter to Mehmed Selim Pasha of 6 Jan. 1828, HHStA, StA, Türkei VI, 35.

[41] Nesselrode to Tatishchev, St Petersburg, 2 Dec. 1827, attached to Metternich to Apponyi, Vienna, 31 Dec. 1827, HHStA, StA, Frankreich 265; Metternich to Tatishchev, Vienna, 24 Dec. 1827, Metternich to Esterházy, Vienna, 31 Dec. 1827, HHStA, StA, England 179; Tatishchev to Nesselrode, Vienna, 10 Feb. 1828, AVPRI, fond 133, Kantseliariia, opis 468, 11877.

extreme anti-Russian bias to Ottoman high dignitaries from Anatolia and Rumelia. Russia was accused of being the instigator of the Greek revolt and the mortal and implacable enemy of the Ottoman Empire and Islam, and the Akkerman Convention was said to be regarded by him as null and void.[42] Although this was a mere circular for local governors and in no way a declaration of war as some historians claim,[43] it was soon revealed to the public and it was evident that the reaction in St Petersburg would be negative. Moreover, its existence and the sultan's other steps like the embargo on the shipping in the Straits could well serve as a pretext for as well as the legitimisation of Russia's declaration of war.[44] Metternich sharply criticised this declaration as entirely needless, irrational and provocative,[45] being well aware of its disastrous effect on the tsar's attitude: "The declaration to the pashas has furnished Russia with pretexts from which it now knows only too well how to profit. It claims to have been attacked and turns its demands to the dual goal of the trilateral Treaty and the execution of the Akkerman stipulations. With an unprecedented folly, the Porte has returned itself to the situation in which it was at the beginning of 1825 ... If anyone asks you what I predict about the future, say that I see the Porte reduced to its death throes. It will consent to everything that Russia will demand from it when its armies approach the capital, and what Russia will demand from it will be a hundredfold of what we have advised the sultan to agree to in the form of honourable spontaneity."[46] The declaration greatly annoyed the chancellor, who was unable to see any point in the Turks' actions: "They are incapable of rising to the necessary level to confront the truth, and this truth is that however unjust the actions of the three

---

[42] Hatt-i sharif issued by the Porte to the pashas and governors of the Ottoman Empire, 20 Dec. 1827, attached to Ottenfels to Metternich, Constantinople, 10 Jan. 1828, HHStA, StA, Türkei VI, 32.
[43] For this opinion see for example Aksan, pp. 299 and 343.
[44] Ottenfels to Metternich, Constantinople, 10 Jan. 1828, HHStA, StA, Türkei VI, 32; Bitis, p. 179.
[45] Metternich to Esterházy, Vienna, 12 Feb. 1828, HHStA, StA, England 182; Maltzan to Frederick William III, Vienna, 9 Feb. 1828, GStA PK, HA III, MdA I, 6010; Caraman to La Ferronnays, Vienna, 9 Feb. 1828, AMAE, CP, Autriche 409; Tatishchev to Nesselrode, Vienna, 10 Feb. 1828, AVPRI, fond 133, Kantseliariia, opis 468, 11877; Bray to Ludwig I of Bavaria, Vienna, 12 Feb. 1828, BHStA, MA, Wien 2402; Gentz to Neumann, Vienna, 15 March 1828, NA, RAM-AC 5, 3.
[46] Metternich to Ottenfels, Vienna, 20 March 1828, HHStA, StA, Türkei VI, 35.

allied courts may be, this conduct and the injustice are facts and the sultan no longer has a choice between right and wrong but actually finds himself reduced to one of those extreme situations where there is only a choice between two evils. What is most dangerous in such situations is the extreme proclivity of people towards a call to arms as a last resort."[47] He briefly characterised the Porte's diplomacy with this harsh criticism: "The Ottoman government is not malicious, it is inept; it is not savage, it is stupid."[48]

Irrespective of how offending the manifest was, Metternich was also of the opinion in late March that the decision for war had already been made in St Petersburg before the sultan's manifest became known. The hostile reaction to the document in a special 11 March issue of the French language Russian governmental newspaper *Journal de St.-Pétersbourg politique et littéraire* in his opinion exaggerated complaints of the losses suffered owing to the Turkish obstacles laid to the shipping in the Straits. Russia's intensive preparations for war and its reluctance to compromise, clearly evident from its diplomatic activities, convinced him that Nicholas I wanted to march and not to negotiate.[49] Despite the Porte's ill-favoured and inept steps, Metternich considered the reasons for war to be insufficient and, consequently, an eventual armed conflict as unfounded, seeing much hypocrisy in the Russian explanations and declarations: "Russia begins by invading the provinces all the while declaring that it does not want to seek guarantees and indemnities. The same language was used in the manifests of Napoleon and it is unfortunate for the world that the mould was not destroyed with its first cast!"[50] He elaborated this comparison in other instructions: "If I had not already made a comparison with the system of Bonaparte, I would see myself forced to make one following the new Russian publications. Everything in them is modelled on the manifests of the French Empire. It is not only the basic thinking which

---

[47] Metternich to Ottenfels, Vienna, 2 March 1828, HHStA, StA, Türkei VI, 35.
[48] Metternich to Trauttmannsdorff, Vienna, 17 Feb. 1828, HHStA, StK, Preussen 128.
[49] Metternich to Trauttmannsdorff, Vienna, 18 March 1828, HHStA, StK, Preussen 128; Metternich to Apponyi, Vienna, 26 March 1828, HHStA, StA, Frankreich 267; H. Jahn, *Das „Journal de St.-Pétersbourg politique et littéraire"* und *„The Courier": Die Berichterstattung zweier offiziöser Zeitungen zur „Orientalischen Frage" in den Jahren 1827–1833*, München 1984, p. 35.
[50] Metternich to Apponyi, Vienna, 26 March 1828, HHStA, StA, Frankreich 267.

is identical but the manner of expressing it, masking it, structuring it effectively; everything in it echoes the style. Is it not said that the emperor of the North has been awoken by a sudden attack from the sultan, that Emperor Nicholas has been disturbed from a just sleep, from a sleep not troubled by the slightest memory or even the noise of the cannon from Navarino? It is the Great Power, inoffensive and entirely confident, which sees itself attacked, taken unawares, by a neighbour who is always oppressive and what is more, constantly ungrateful and forgetting the numerous demonstrations of a tried and tested friendship. It is the sultan, it seems, who, by talking in Turkish to his people, has declared war on the Russian Empire; it is also he who with his manifest *made an appeal to the allies of Russia*; it is he who is interfering with the commerce of his peaceful neighbour, he who has none of the required respect for nationals abandoned by their natural protector; finally with the war already started it is the court which has been attacked, however, which still does not give up hope of seeing the peace restored but which, meanwhile, carefully paves the way for large indemnities [etc.]."[51]

These statements were pronounced in late March when the black clouds gathering on the horizon were clearly visible. In the same month, Austria's diplomacy in Constantinople undertook the last steps to dispel them. The first step was taken by Ottenfels, who learnt that Mahmud II, having seen little enthusiasm among the Ottomans for war and Mohammed Ali's unwillingness to help him against Russia, expressed his intent to grant the insurgents a three-month-long armistice and amnesty. The internuncio did not want to let this opportunity go to waste and together with the Prussian envoy in early March asked Admiral Rigny to inform the Greeks of the sultan's offer and persuade them to accept it. Rigny agreed to make this communication to the Greek provisional government, but when he learnt of a Turkish expedition against the Island of Chios where the Greeks led by a French Philhellene, Charles Nicolas Fabvier, had landed, he denounced the Turks' step as a violation of the armistice despite the fact that it had not yet been accepted by the Greeks and he refused to complete the task agreed with Ottenfels and Miltitz.[52] The second

---

[51] Metternich to Esterházy, Vienna, 24 March 1828, HHStA, StA, England 182.
[52] Ottenfels to Metternich, Constantinople, 23 Feb. 1828, HHStA, StA, Türkei VI, 32; Ottenfels to Rigny, Constantinople, 1 March 1828, Miltitz to Rigny, Con-

step was made by Metternich who, with little faith in any change in either the sultan's or the tsar's attitudes but urged by Francis I, instructed the internuncio at the end of March to request from the sultan in the name of the emperor the immediate withdrawal of all the measures that could be represented by Russia as being in conflict with its treaties with the Ottoman Empire; in particular the sultan was to reopen the Straits and dispatch to St Petersburg a letter confirming his willingness to fulfil all conditions of the Akkerman Convention. This step seemed to be made by the chancellor more with the intention of obtaining something that would have deprived Russia of a justifiable pretext for war in the eyes of his allies than with any real expectation that the tsar could be influenced by it, but in any case there was no chance to reach any of these goals. At the moment he dispatched his instructions, Pertev told Ottenfels under the influence of the declarations in the *Journal de St.-Pétersbourg* that since the Akkerman Convention contained the seed of the destruction of the Ottoman Empire, it could not be executed. When Francis I's recommendation that the sultan comply with Russia's demands together with his statement that he recognised the tsar's right to demand the fulfilment of his treaties arrived in Constantinople, Pertev merely "abandoned himself to reproaches that we [the Austrians] were making such humiliating proposals to him adding that even if the land and naval forces of all the Great Powers were approaching Constantinople, even if Austria, God forbid, were to change its attitude and wage war with the Porte, it still would not yield at all."[53] In brief, the Porte seemed reconciled to the prospect of a war with Russia.[54]

---

stantinople, 1 March 1828, Rigny to Ottenfels, Smyrna, 8 March 1828, Rigny to Ottenfels, 5 April 1828, Ottenfels to Metternich, Constantinople, 1, 3 and 19 March, 25 April 1828, HHStA, StA, Türkei VI, 33; Ottenfels, *Memoari*, p. 198.

[53] Ottenfels to Metternich, Constantinople, 15 April 1828, HHStA, StA, Türkei VI, 33.

[54] Metternich to Esterházy, Vienna, 19 and 29 March 1828, HHStA, StA, England 182; Metternich to Apponyi, Vienna, 26 and 29 March 1828, HHStA, StA, Frankreich 267; Metternich to Ottenfels, Vienna, 28 March 1828, HHStA, StA, Türkei VI, 35; Metternich to Trauttmannsdorff, Vienna, 30 March 1828, HHStA, StK, Preussen 128; Ottenfels' note to the Porte, 10 April 1828, Huszár to Ottenfels, 10, 12, 13 and 28 April 1828, Ottenfels to Metternich, Constantinople, 29 March, 15 and 25 April 1828, HHStA, StA, Türkei VI, 33; Cowley to Dudley, Vienna, 27 March 1828, TNA, FO 120/90; Tatishchev to Nesselrode, Vienna, 29 March 1828, AVPRI, fond 133, Kantseliariia, opis 468, 11877. The gathering of Russia's

The last desperate attempt to save the peace was made during April when Francis I suggested a personal meeting with Nicholas I anywhere, even in Poland or Podolia (south-western Ukraine). The emperor told Tatishchev: "I am absolutely prepared to go anywhere the emperor [the tsar] desires."[55] But neither this offer, nor Francis I's personal letter nor his attempt to frighten the tsar with reference to the increasing liberalism in France could change Nicholas I's decision to wage war, which was finally declared by the tsar on 26 April 1828.[56] The official reasons merely concerned the Russian Question, like the infraction of the treaties, the obstruction of Russian ships in the Straits, the nullification of the Akkerman Convention, and not the Greek Question, but it was evident that the war would solve not only Russo-Ottoman disputes but also Greek affairs. On 7 May, the Russian army crossed the Pruth river.[57] Since the Turks' conduct actually infringed the Russo-Ottoman treaties, Metternich had to admit that the declaration of war was legitimate and there could be no objections to it from the legal point of view. This, however, enabled the Austrian emperor to easily give reasons for his strict neutrality, which he declared soon after the receipt of the news of the declaration of war.[58]

---

forces beyond the Moldavian frontier finally persuaded the Porte in early May to yield; it announced on 7 May its recognition of the Akkerman Convention and two days later it promised to fulfil its conditions as well as meet Russia's other requests concerning the shipping in the Straits, compensation for Russian merchants or mutual negotiations on the Serbian affairs. There is no evidence that it might have been caused by Austria's diplomacy but, in any case, this conciliation came too late. Metternich regretted the fact that an ultimatum had not preceded the declaration of war since he was convinced that it would have been accepted. Canitz to Frederick William III, Pera, 19 May 1828, GStA PK, HA III, MdA I, 7266; Schwebel to La Ferronnays, Vienna, 29 May 1828, AMAE, CP, Autriche 409; Ottenfels, *Memoari*, p. 201.

[55] Tatishchev to Nesselrode, Vienna, 30 April 1828, AVPRI, fond 133, Kantseliariia, opis 468, 11877.

[56] Francis I to Nicholas I, 5 April 1828, attached to Metternich to Zichy, Vienna, 5 April 1828, HHStA, StA, Russland III, 84; Metternich to Esterházy, Vienna, 7 April 1828, HHStA, StA, England 182; Tatishchev to Nesselrode, Vienna, 6 and 30 April 1828, AVPRI, fond 133, Kantseliariia, opis 468, 11877.

[57] Bitis, pp. 186–187.

[58] Metternich to Ottenfels, Vienna, 18 May and 4 June 1828, HHStA, StA, Türkei VI, 35; Metternich to Trauttmannsdorff, Vienna, 2 June 1828, HHStA, StK, Preussen 129; The record of Francis I's declaration to Tatishchev of 13 May 1828, HHStA, StA, Russland III, 84; Metternich's note to Tatishchev, Vienna,

* * *

George Canning has often been praised by historians for his outstanding Greek policy and the Treaty of London was regarded as his masterpiece. He was in no way blamed for the Battle of Navarino and the outbreak of the Russo-Ottoman war. The responsibility for these events was ascribed to the British ministers and diplomats who, after Canning's death, "proved unable or unwilling to understand it or to see it carried through."[59] It took a long time for the increasing criticism of this too positive assessment to reveal that in reality his Near Eastern policy in relation to Russia was extremely weak and inconsistent and generally outmanoeuvred by Russia's well-considered diplomacy. The Treaty of London enabled Nicholas I to commence the war without fear of British-French opposition. Moreover, according to Loyal Cowles, nothing merits the view that if Canning had not died in August 1827, he could have restrained Russia, to which he was bound by a partnership that he could have abandoned only at the cost of his prestige.[60] Canning was thus significantly responsible not only for the battle which took place on 20 October but also for the declaration of war of 26 April. This was the price he paid for the destruction of the Austro-Russian alliance which Metternich used to try to restrain Russia from going to war. Shortly before the outbreak of the war the prince had to admit the superiority of Russia's diplomacy in the Eastern Question since 1826: "I see in all of this only one cabinet that has proceeded with a skill of which I did not believe it to be capable; it is the Russian cabinet. Finally, it has arrived at what it wanted and all the advantages of the position are on its side."[61] At the same time he made this quip briefly but fittingly characterising Canning's role in the whole performance: "I see that the friends of Mr Canning want to have a statue erected for him. It would be fair if the Russian emperor were to meet all the expenses of the monument himself."[62]

---

24 May 1828, attached to Tatishchev to Nesselrode, Vienna, 25 May 1828, AVPRI, fond 133, Kantseliariia, opis 468, 11879; Caraman to La Ferronnays, Vienna, 1 May 1828, Schwebel to La Ferronnays, Vienna, 24 May 1828, AMAE, CP, Autriche 409; Bray to Ludwig I of Bavaria, Vienna, 7 April and 10 May 1828, BHStA, MA, Wien 2402.

[59] Florescu, "Lord Strangford," p. 476.
[60] Cowles, p. 717.
[61] Caraman to La Ferronnays, Vienna, 3 April 1828, AMAE, CP, Autriche 409.
[62] Metternich to Esterházy, Vienna, 7 April 1828, HHStA, StA, England 182.

8

The Russo-Ottoman War: The First Campaign

The Russian military operations in the Balkans and the Caucasus did not, to the surprise of many, end with a crushing defeat of the enemy. When the winter arrived, the tsar's soldiers could claim very few victories, none of them decisive for the outcome of the war. For Metternich, his diplomatic failures did not end with the outbreak of the Russo-Ottoman war but continued during the whole of 1828 when in vain he tried to expedite the solution of the Greek Question and bring the two empires at war on the way to conciliation. The only result of his diplomatic effort was the deep animosity of a considerable number of the Russians including Nicholas I and Nesselrode, who suspected the Austrian chancellor of the most devilish anti-Russian designs. The most well-known of them was Metternich's alleged plan for the creation of an anti-Russian coalition that would force the tsar to conclude peace under very disadvantageous conditions. Although most of the accusations raised against Metternich in 1828 were baseless or doubtful, the fact remains that the relations between Austria and Russia ominously reached freezing point.

Austria's Neutrality

When the Russo-Ottoman war began, Metternich shared the generally widespread belief in Nicholas I's quick victory and he saw no prospect for the sultan's success in the forthcoming conflict.[1] The Porte's in-

---

[1] Metternich to Esterházy, Vienna, 30 April and 17 May 1828, HHStA, StA, England 182; Metternich to Ottenfels, Vienna, 3 May 1828, HHStA, StA, Türkei VI, 35; Metternich to Apponyi, Vienna, 9 May 1828, HHStA, StA, Frankreich 268; Cowley to Dudley, Vienna, 30 April 1828, TNA, FO 120/91; Schwebel to La Ferronnays, Vienna, 11 May 1828, AMAE, CP, Autriche 409.

ability to crush the Greek revolt led to the general expectation in Europe that the tsarist army would go through the Balkans like a knife through butter and that Nicholas I, personally present at his army's headquarters, would soon dictate the peace conditions to Mahmud II from a military camp before the Constantinople walls. Metternich had good reason to hold this belief since the Turkish preparations for war were actually slow and insufficient, which forced Ottenfels to make this ironic remark at the end of May 1828: "Having shown us for seven years that it does not know how to make peace when it has needs to, it will prove to us that it also does not know how to wage war when the force of circumstances oblige it to do so."[2] The chancellor commented on the Turkish mobilisation in the same way when he learnt that in Adrianople and its surroundings "until recently there did not exist the slightest trace of armaments, nor even preparations for defensive measures. The saying that the sultan seemed to have taken as his motto is that of 'God and my right.' I fear that he forgot that God only helps those who help themselves."[3] To the surprise of many, Metternich and his internuncio not excluded, instead of a quick triumph the Russian offensive soon deadlocked. The reason for this situation was not the superior quality of the Ottoman armed forces but a lack of it on both sides. The campaign of 1828 was characterised by the Turks defending their fortresses and the Russians attempting with little success to capture them and destroy the core of the sultan's land forces in the Balkans. Definitely the most significant victory of the tsarist army was the capture of Varna on 10 October 1828, which actually terminated the fighting in that year; the Caucasian front also did not bring a decisive victory.[4] This development of the conflict evoking a duel between the one-eyed and the blind surprised Metternich, who reacted with his typical irony used earlier to criticise the sultan's insufficient preparations for war: "The mistaken belief with which the young Russian monarch was deluded that merely his voice and appearance at the head of his army would suffice to disarm the

---

[2] Ottenfels to Metternich, Constantinople, 31 May 1828, HHStA, StA, Türkei VI, 33.
[3] Metternich to Ottenfels, Vienna, 18 May 1828, HHStA, StA, Türkei VI, 35.
[4] B. Jelavich, *St. Petersburg and Moscow: Tsarist and Soviet Foreign Policy, 1814–1974*, Bloomington, London 1974, p. 75; Aksan, pp. 345–351; Bitis, pp. 274–303; Prokesch-Osten, *Griechen*, II, pp. 257–258.

sultan and his nation has not yet been justified in any way by the course of events."[5]

Already during the planning stages of the war, Nicholas I and his military as well as diplomatic advisors worried about Austria's attitude. Consequently, when in early February 1828 Tatishchev urged Francis I to refuse any mediation between the trilateral alliance and the Ottoman Empire, he also asked him whether the sultan could expect Austria's direct assistance against Russia, which evoked the emperor's embittered answer: "Am I then regarded to be so insane as to go to attack Russia? I attack Russia? Never has such a thought entered my head. Cetainly if it attacks me, I will have to defend myself, but it is only in this case that war could take place between us. That I should start the hostilities, how I could possibly consider it for a single moment!"[6] When on 13 May Tatishchev informed Francis I about the tsar's decision to wage war and asked him about Austria's neutrality again, the emperor simply answered: "I ask you not to question me any longer. You have my declaration of neutrality, you can count upon it."[7] This promise of Austria's neutrality in the war against the Turks was repeated on 22 May and accompanied with the assurance that if the Poles rose against the tsar during the war while the Russian troops were engaged in fighting the Turks, Austrian forces would help him.[8] Nevertheless, with the growing failures of the Russian armies, the tsar's apprehensions of Francis I's conduct increased despite the latter's formal declaration of neutrality and the fact there was nothing from the military point of view that would have justified such fears. In 1827, the state of the Austrian armed forces reached its lowest level during the period from 1815 to 1848, with 375,586 men only, and it entirely lacked reserves. Its material availability also was rather poor; for example in the previous year, it went short of horses, uniforms, rifles and other arms at the overall cost of 14.6 million gulden. The opinion generally maintained by the emperor's advisors and the army commandants was that the forces had to be increased at least to the peacetime level, and some effort was made towards this goal during

[5]   Metternich to Esterházy, Vienna, 9 July 1828, HHStA, StA, England 183.
[6]   Tatishchev to Nesselrode, Vienna, 10 Feb. 1828, AVPRI, fond 133, Kantseliariia, opis 468, 11877.
[7]   Tatishchev to Nesselrode, Vienna, 25 May 1828, AVPRI, fond 133, Kantseliariia, opis 468, 11879.
[8]   Ibid.

1828, but although a considerable recruitment of 74,831 men was carried out during the year, the total number of Austria's armed forces increased to only 418,415 by the end of the year due to a considerable number of men being on leave. The actual number of soldiers who could be deployed in a campaign increased by an even smaller percentage from 191,552 in 1827 to 195,133 in 1828.[9] From Tatishchev's reports Nicholas I was well aware of the insufficient state of the Austrian army and its very limited increase in power in 1828.[10]

The movements of the land forces within the Danube Monarchy were of little concern to Russia with their slow and limited increase and posed no real threat. No significant concentration of the army took place on Austria's eastern frontier and no important movements of troops to its proximity were undertaken. Already in the autumn of 1827, the Court Council of War (*Hofkriegsrat*) discussed the possibility of the displacement of 60,000 soldiers from the Adriatic Sea to the Wallachian border, in particular as a quarantine line, but this measure was never realised in full; moreover, the soldiers were scattered in small units and, consequently, they could not cause any legitimate uneasiness at the Russian headquarters. A similar idea for the creation of an observation unit in Transylvania was also never realised. The only

---

[9] B. M. Buchmann, *Militär – Diplomatie – Politik: Österreich und Europa von 1815 bis 1835*, Frankfurt am Main, Bern, New York, Paris 1991, pp. 67–68 and 335.

[10] Tatishchev, who usually obtained the numbers of the Austrian army from the President of the Court Council of War, Prince Friedrich Franz Xaver von Hohenzollern-Hechingen, reported that, owing to the earlier economisation of the military forces, the size of the Austrian land forces was approximately 291,378 men and 24,834 horses at the beginning of 1828, which was fewer than the peace establishment as settled in 1816: 334,685 men and 33,375 horses. Moreover, from this number only 191,389 men were battle ready, another 92,503 were on leave and 7,486 were ill; almost all the infantry troops had less than 50 percent of the soldiers in active service. When the year passed, the army still had fewer men and horses than it should have had according to the 1816 resolution: 320,095 men and 28,303 horses. Furthermore, only 194,459 men were battle ready, while 117,004 were on leave and 8,632 were ill. Similar numbers can be found in the reports of other diplomats residing in Vienna. Tatishchev to Nesselrode, Vienna, 3 Oct. 1827, AVPRI, fond 133, Kantseliariia, opis 468, 11874; Tatishchev to Nesselrode, Vienna, 7 Jan 1829, AVPRI, fond 133, Kantseliariia, opis 468, 11881. Schwebel to Damas, Vienna, 26 Aug. 1827, AMAE, CP, Autriche 408; Cowley to Dudley, Vienna, 16 April 1828, TNA, FO 120/91. According to Austria's official statistics, the number of horses in the army increased from 36,072 in 1827 to 41,617 in 1828. Buchmann, *Militär – Diplomatie – Politik*, p. 136.

significant army movement was a military exercise on 22 September 1828 of approximately 29,000 men in the proximity of Vienna between Laxenburg and Baden, but there was nothing in this event that could offer any reason for apprehension either, in particular when the exercising soldiers made little impression. Francis I himself admitted the imperfections during the exercises, which were due to the participation of fresh recruits. The principle cause for the inactivity of Austria's army during 1828 was, in addition to the declared neutrality, the lack of money. Any additional conscriptions or concentration of armed forces on the eastern border were quite expensive: the expected costs just for these limited measures were estimated not in the millions but in the tens of millions of florins, something that the state treasury could not afford. The provision of a loan in the substantial amount needed for the entire restoration of Austrian land forces to the peace level was unfeasible under the given conditions. Consequently, a cautious reinforcement of manpower and completion of war material was all that was done during the entire war because the poor financial situation of the Austrian Empire precluded any stronger military measures. When Metternich wrote to the Austrian envoy to Prussia, Count Joseph von Trauttmannsdorff-Weinsberg, that "Austria is not arming; what we are doing is calculating the forces we have at our disposal and those which we do not,"[11] he quite pointedly characterised the situation where Austria lacked a sufficient army for waging war against Russia without allies.[12]

---

[11] Metternich to Trauttmannsdorff, Vienna, 13 Aug. 1828, HHStA, StK, Preussen 129.

[12] Metternich to Bernstorff, Vienna, 10 Jan. 1829, HHStA, StK, Preussen 132; Tatishchev to Nesselrode, Vienna, 5 and 16 Oct., 6 and 28 Dec. 1827, AVPRI, fond 133, Kantseliariia, opis 468, 11874; Tatishchev to Wittgenstein, Vienna, 1 April 1828, Tatishchev to Nesselrode, Vienna, 10 Feb., 10 March, 1 and 12 April, 3 May, 20 Dec. 1828, AVPRI, fond 133, Kantseliariia, opis 468, 11877; Tatishchev to Nesselrode, Vienna, 12 June, 9, 18, 23 and 31 July, 4 and 19 Aug., 13 and 28 Sept., 12 Oct. 1828, AVPRI, fond 133, Kantseliariia, opis 468, 11879; Tatishchev to Nesselrode, Vienna, 1 and 17 Feb. 1829, AVPRI, fond 133, Kantseliariia, opis 468, 11881; Maltzan to Frederick William III, Vienna, 11 Dec. 1827, GStA PK, HA III, MdA I, 6009; Brockhausen to Frederick William III, Vienna, 10, 16, 17 and 24 Sept. 1828, GStA PK, HA III, MdA I, 6011; Bray to Ludwig I of Bavaria, Vienna, 9 Nov. 1828, BHStA, MA, Wien 2402; Schwebel to La Ferronnays, Vienna, 11 May 1828, AMAE, CP, Autriche 409; Cowley to Dudley, Vienna, 16, 25 and 30 April 1828, TNA, FO 120/91; Report upon the state of Austrian army (undated), TNA, FO 120/97, originally attached to Cowley to Aberdeen, Vienna, 19 Aug. 1828,

Despite the fact that such a war never seriously occupied his mind, Metternich was dissatisfied with the weakness of the Austrian army because it undermined his position in diplomatic affairs. He believed at the beginning as well as after the end of the war that if Austria had merited more respect on the international scene, the affair could have developed differently. This belief led him in October 1829 to an attempt to call the emperor's attention to the necessity of administrative, financial and military reforms necessary for strengthening Austria's position.[13] During the war, however, he had to accept reality and assume a considerably restrained attitude in the military affairs which he could influence from his significant office. When he was asked by the emperor in October 1827 whether the country should not react to the Russian as well as the Ottoman preparations for war, he refused to consider anything that could harm their diplomatic relations with either empire and merely suggested to cautiously observe their behaviour. On 21 December, Metternich reacted to the emperor's other question concerning what Austria was to do in the event of an open rupture between Russia and the Ottoman Empire with the suggestion that Austria should repeat the measures undertaken during previous Russo-Ottoman wars, which meant to assume a strict neutrality, maintain friendly relations with both and observe their military operations; as he declared, there was no need to worry about a hostile attack from either of them. At the moment when Austria could not and did not want to commit itself in the conflict, it had to avoid every measure with questionable usefulness and probable negative impact on its relations with Russia.[14] He even regarded any contemplation of them as dangerous. For example, when in March 1828 the Court Council of War discussed an eventual Austrian occupation of Serbia in the event of a Russian invasion in the Danubian Principalities, Metternich was considerably irritated because, first, he strongly disagreed with such an action and, second, any discussion about it could adversely affect Austria's relations with both Russia as

---

Cowley to Aberdeen, Vienna, 14 Aug. 1828, TNA, FO 120/93; Cowley to Aberdeen, Vienna, 4 Oct. 1828, TNA, FO 120/94; Spinola to Bernetti, Vienna, 10 Dec. 1828, ASV, Arch. Nunz. Vienna 256; Krauter, p. 223.

[13] Metternich to Francis I, Vienna, 18 May 1828, HHStA, StK, Vorträge 254; Metternich to Francis I, Vienna, 9 Oct. 1829, *NP*, IV, pp. 598–605.

[14] In both cases Francis I agreed. Metternich to Francis I, Vienna, 15 Oct. and 21 Dec. 1827, HHStA, StK, Vorträge 252.

well as the Ottoman Empire. Despite the fact that on 18 May 1828 he suggested to the emperor a meeting of the state advisors to deliberate the measures with the unspoken but obvious aim of increasing Austria's land forces, he never seemed to advocate anything other than to increase them to the peace level and he always opposed the idea – widespread among the high-ranking army officers – of an occupation of Serbia and Bosnia; the discreet steps undertaken for the reinforcement of the army were to strengthen his position on the diplomatic chessboard, but he would never agree to anything that could compromise Austria's strict neutrality that he so strongly advocated. This deliberate attitude caused a certain discontent among the Austrian elites considering the position of Austria in the conflict as scarcely corresponding to its dignity, but the restraint advocated by Metternich was entirely shared by Francis I. The emperor was well aware of the real strength of his armed forces as well as being personally unwilling to wage war. Consequently, Metternich's explanations of the moves in the Austrian army as merely an effort to remedy deficiencies were true and fitting. When Tatishchev in November 1828 informed him that Russia would maintain its army corps in sight of the Austrian frontier, he answered: "It will be as you wish, but I tell you that even if you assemble one hundred thousand men on the frontier, we will not march a single drummerboy; war between the two empires is impossible."[15] This as well as other assurances about Austria's nonaggression were absolutely sincere simply because Metternich knew well that there was no other option.[16]

Since Austria's military position is important for the full understanding of Metternich's diplomacy during the given period, it also is necessary to point out the fact that the effort for its improvement cannot just be explained as a simple reaction to Russia's campaign in

---

[15] Tatishchev to Nesselrode, Vienna, 21 Nov. 1828, AVPRI, fond 133, Kantseliariia, opis 468, 11877.

[16] Metternich to Francis I, Vienna, 18 May 1828, HHStA, StK, Vorträge 254; Maltzan to Frederick William III, Vienna, 11 Dec. 1827, GStA PK, HA III, MdA I, 6009; Maltzan to Frederick William III, Vienna, 18 March and 1 June 1828, GStA PK, HA III, MdA I, 6010; Maltzan to Frederick William III, Vienna, 23 Nov. 1828, GStA PK, HA III, MdA I, 6011; Tatishchev to Nesselrode, Vienna, 10 Feb. and 29 March 1828, AVPRI, fond 133, Kantseliariia, opis 468, 11877; Tatishchev to Nesselrode, Vienna, 25 May 1828, AVPRI, fond 133, Kantseliariia, opis 468, 11879.

the East; Austria's cautious armament was also undertaken owing to the augmentation of the army in France. Metternich did not accept La Ferronnays' explanation that this step undertaken by the Parisian cabinet was simply an administrative measure and he also saw no reason for it: "France is not threatened by any political danger. It is not only far from every line of attack but it is also considerably distant from the field on which will be decided some grave issues, of which practically each one is of a nature to compromise the fate of one or more empires!"[17] The uneasiness concerning the French armament was more serious due to the two Powers' tensions in the Apennines where the Parisian cabinet feared an increase of Austria's influence. Nevertheless, some of the rumours on this issue, as for example the one concerning Austria's design to conquer Piedmont, were baseless. Furthermore, Metternich's real apprehension of France's further steps was intensified by its pro-Russian attitude as well as the increase of a pro-Greek bias in French society to which the government replied in the spring of 1828 with the plan of a French military expedition to the Peloponnese. In any case, the chancellor's explanation that Austria had to assume some measures for the improvement of its land forces owing to the similar proceeding in the French army was true, although of course this was not the only reason as Metternich tried to persuade Nicholas I in early 1829. The full explanation for the reason for Austria's armament was because of the dual threats from France as well as Russia; but in both cases the armament was insignificant.[18]

---

[17] Metternich to Trauttmannsdorff, Vienna, 4 May 1828, HHStA, StK, Preussen 129.

[18] La Ferronnays to Caraman, Paris, 17 April 1828, attached to Metternich to Esterházy, Vienna, 25 April 1828, HHStA, StA, England 182; Metternich to Apponyi, Vienna, 9 May 1828, HHStA, StA, Frankreich 268; Metternich to Trauttmannsdorff, Vienna, 13 and 18 Aug. 1828, HHStA, StK, Preussen 129; Metternich to Ficquelmont, Vienna, 17 Jan. 1829, HHStA, StA, Russland III, 88; Tatishchev to Nesselrode, Vienna, 12 April 1828, AVPRI, fond 133, Kantseliariia, opis 468, 11877; Tatishchev to Nesselrode, Vienna, 4 and 19 Aug., 13 Sept. 1828, AVPRI, fond 133, Kantseliariia, opis 468, 11879; Cowley to Dudley, Vienna, 25 and 30 April 1828, TNA, FO 120/91; Maltzan to Frederick William III, Vienna, 25 April 1828, GStA PK, HA III, MdA I, 6010; Spinola to Bernetti, Vienna, 25 Aug. 1828, ASV, Arch. Nunz. Vienna 256.

Russo-Austrian Enmity

The military measures of mere precaution were not worthy of any serious attention and even though Austria's army was in a better situation
at the end of 1828 than at the beginning of the year, it absolutely did
not cause alarm among foreign diplomats including Tatishchev who,
however, complained to Austria that its armament made the Turks
more persistent in their defence against Russia and therefore forced
Nicholas I to prepare for a second campaign.[19] This accusation actually did not reflect the reality of the situation but rather Russia's
apprehensions of Austria's designs in 1828. Already in 1827, the rumour circulated in St Petersburg that the Viennese cabinet wanted
to set the Poles against the tsar's rule by nurturing their sympathies
towards Napoleon's son, Duke Francis of Reichstadt, who could become the new ruler of an independent Poland. This rumour persisted
despite the fact that its absurdity was entirely refuted by the advisor
of the Russian embassy in Vienna, Baron Peter von Meyendorff, in the
summer of 1827.[20] It was difficult for the Russians to give up their
concerns during 1828 when their reverses in the campaign against the
Turks made them more sensitive to rumours than ever and when the
number of the rumours concerning Metternich's anti-Russian plotting
considerably increased. Consequently, in the autumn of the same year,
Nicholas I and Nesselrode almost believed that Austria was Turkey's
secret ally, that it even prepared and sent to Constantinople the plan
for the campaign of the following year, that Austrian officers advised
the Turkish commanders in the field and that the army on Austria's
eastern frontier was strengthened to 160,000 men which, moreover,
were gathering into one military unit. Under such a situation everything, even the least dangerous steps like the September military
exercise between Laxenburg and Baden, aroused the suspicions and
concerns of Nicholas I and Nesselrode who, together with high military officers, even feared Austria's occupation of the Principalities,
which they would have considered a casus belli. This anxiety con-

---

[19] Maltzan to Frederick William III, Vienna, 21 Nov. 1828, GStA PK, HA III,
MdA I, 6011.
[20] Meyendorff to Nesselrode, Carlsbad, 22 July 1827, O. Hoetzsch (ed.), *Peter
von Meyendorff: Ein russischer Diplomat an den Höfen von Berlin und Wien.
Politischer und privater Briefwechsel, 1826–1863*, I, Berlin 1923, p. 3; Ringhoffer,
p. 136.

cerning Austria's eventual hostile actions was so considerable that it influenced Nicholas I's decision-making during the first campaign and prevented him from using the Serbian forces against the sultan.[21]

The apprehension existing at the Russian court as well as the incoming rumours concerning Austria's plots were, as Theodor Schiemann also emphasised, unfounded.[22] On a practical level there was little that Russia could fear from Austria. According to British historian Alan Sked, the "documents in the Vienna archives show that Metternich was indeed allowing the Turks to import arms secretly from Austria."[23] The problem lies in the fact that Sked offers no evidence for this claim and that no relevant note was found by this book's author in the Austrian and European archives visited during the research on this monograph, including the dispatches of the rather vigilant Tatishchev, who did not omit any real or pretended evil caused by Austria to Russia during that period. It is true that the Russian ambassador complained of the sale of rifles and pistols to the Turks and Egyptians with the emperor's permission, but during 1827 and not 1828. Although the Austrians actually wished to gain a share in this trade controlled by the French in Constantinople and by the French and the British in Alexandria, no proof that this occurred in either of the years was found although despite Metternich's persistent denial of its existence, such a possibility cannot be excluded at least for 1827.[24] What, however, definitely occurred was the sale of Hungarian cereals to the starving Turkish garrisons in the fortresses on the Danube during the winter of 1828–1829, which probably led some historians to the supposition that the arms were sold to the Turks during the war.[25]

---

[21] Bitis, pp. 178–185, 327–348; Sauvigny, *Staatsmann und Diplomat*, p. 440.
[22] Schiemann, II, pp. 257–258.
[23] Sked, *Metternich*, p. 71.
[24] Metternich to Tatishchev, Vienna, 11 June 1827, Tatishchev to Nesselrode, Vienna, 13 April, 11 and 30 June 1827, AVPRI, fond 133, Kantseliariia, opis 468, 11873; Tatishchev to Nesselrode, Vienna, 26 Sept., 31 Oct. and 16 Nov. 1827, AVPRI, fond 133, Kantseliariia, opis 468, 11874; Wellesley to Canning, Vienna, 30 April 1827, TNA, FO 120/85; Sauer, *Österreich und die Levante*, p. 94.
[25] Though Betrand Michael Buchmann claims that the sale of cereals did not take place owing to their high price, the contrary was the case, and the whole affair had negative consequences for the Austrian financiers involved and occupied Austrian diplomacy until the late 1830s. For more details see Chapter 22. Buchmann, *Militär – Diplomatie – Politik*, p. 350.

Although the sale of Hungarian cereals remained unnoticed by Tatishchev, the Russians found other grounds for complaint in 1828. For example, Nicholas I was not pleased when he learnt of the presence of two Austrian officers in Constantinople, believing that they were in the sultan's service. The rumour spread that they directed the fortification works in the Ottoman capital and the Danish chargé d'affaires, Mr Hübsch, even claimed that the city was fortified upon the plans sent from Vienna. The truth was that two Austrian officers actually resided in Constantinople in 1828, Lieutenant Philippovich and Captain Franz von Hauslab.[26] They had been sent by Francis I before the war, the former with the task of arranging a new postal route between Vienna and Constantinople, the latter to maintain correspondence with the Austrian navy. Both were assigned to the internunciature and did not enter the sultan's service. Metternich denied the assumption that they were charged with the fortification works and just admitted that one of them had sent a report on the state of the fortification. This was true but the information was incomplete. Although neither of these officers really took part in the fortification works, their presence in Constantinople did not escape the Porte's attention, and Pertev asked Ottenfels for their views of the city's preparedness for defence against an attack from the mainland. The internuncio instructed Hauslab to prepare an appropriate analysis, which was not a difficult task for this officer who had been travelling around the city in previous months. The analysis was handed over to the Turks, who, however, pigeonholed it and made no use of it. Unfortunately for Metternich, Tatishchev later obtained a copy of it, which strengthened Russia's distrust of Austria.[27]

---

[26] For more on Franz von Hauslab see Chapter 21.

[27] Hübsch's report, Constantinople, 26 Aug. 1828, attached to Metternich to Ottenfels, Vienna, 17 Sept. 1828, HHStA, StA, Türkei VI, 35; Metternich to Esterházy, Vienna, 28 Sept. 1828, HHStA, StA, England 183; Metternich to Trauttmannsdorff, Vienna, 19 Oct. 1828, HHStA, StK, Preussen 129; Trauttmannsdorff to Metternich, Berlin, 13 Oct. 1828, HHStA, StK, Preussen 128; Maltzan to Frederick William III, Vienna, 10 May 1828, GStA PK, HA III, MdA I, 6010; Maltzan to Frederick William III, Vienna, 19 Oct. 1828, GStA PK, HA III, MdA I, 6011; Tatishchev to Nesselrode, Vienna, 3 Nov. 1828, AVPRI, fond 133, Kantseliariia, opis 468, 11877; Tatishchev to Nesselrode, Vienna, 27 Sept. 1828, AVPRI, fond 133, Kantseliariia, opis 468, 11879; Tatishchev to Nesselrode, Vienna, 1 Feb. 1829, AVPRI, fond 133, Kantseliariia, opis 468, 11881; Ottenfels, *Memoari*, pp. 205–206.

In St Petersburg, a considerable hatred existed towards Austria, and Metternich himself "was hated more than the Sultan himself by almost every Russian who had heard of him."[28] The Belgian representative in Vienna after December 1833, Count Alphonse O'Sullivan de Grass de Seovaud, resided in St Petersburg in the autumn of 1828 and said later in retrospect that the hostility against Austria, the imperial family and particularly Metternich was so astounding that "one could believe that a violent encounter had taken place the previous day."[29] Metternich was well aware of the Austrophobia existing among the Russians but did nothing in 1828 to lessen it.[30] His indifference in his instructions to Esterházy from 8 October is symptomatic: "Many of our friends among the people in the salons in St Petersburg pretend today that it is we who would have dragged the emperor into the war and, at the same time, we who would have drafted and directed the plan of the Turks' campaign. All of this is in the natural order of things and merits no attention."[31]

Similar ill-feeling also existed in Austrian high society against the Russians. The Austrians manifested their satisfaction with the tsar's military failures and moved Tatishchev to complain that this Russophobia was unconcealed in the Viennese salons.[32] This anti-Russian sentiment also seemed to exist beyond the Viennese walls. The new French ambassador to Austria, Duke Adrien Pierre de Montmorency-Laval, remarked this on the way to his new post in early October: "From the banks of the Rhine to Vienna, despite the speed of our voyage, we could hardly fail to notice a national sentiment unanimous in its satisfaction and eagerness to hear news unfavourable to the Russian armies."[33] As for Metternich himself, his complicity in this antipathy was strongly suspected by Tatishchev, who reported that although the chancellor expressed himself in polite terms towards Russia, the sincerity of his expressions was hardly believable since the general ill-feeling

---

[28] Bitis, p. 393.
[29] O'Sullivan to Meulenaer, Vienna, 27 Sept. 1834, ADA, CP, Autriche 2.
[30] Metternich to Trauttmannsdorff, Vienna, 29 Oct. 1828, HHStA, StK, Preussen 129.
[31] Metternich to Esterházy, Vienna, 8 Oct. 1828, HHStA, StA, England 183.
[32] Tatishchev to Nesselrode, Vienna, 9 July 1828, AVPRI, fond 133, Kantseliariia, opis 468, 11879; Tatishchev to Nesselrode, Vienna, 21 Nov. 1828, AVPRI, fond 133, Kantseliariia, opis 468, 11877.
[33] Laval to La Ferronnays, Vienna, 9 Oct. 1828, AMAE, CP, Autriche 409.

in society was tolerated by the government, which the ambassador accused of exciting the anti-Russian bias.[34] Tatishchev believed that "it is often in the offices of the highest authorities that the most absurd and for us the most unfavourable rumours start."[35] Having arrived in Vienna, Laval also considered Metternich felt the same hatred: "The thoroughly hostile sentiment which incites the Austrians against the Russians has definitely taken on the character of a real national antipathy during the last several months. It is no longer a feeling of spite and jealousy towards the preponderance of a too powerful neighbour; it is an animosity without constraint that manifests itself in the least equivocal manner when receiving all the news unfavourable to the Russian army. It is a kind of merciless joy for which there are not enough deaths on the battlefield, not enough victims in the hospitals. This exulted mood breaks out in the same way in the public, in the upper classes, in the government. The head of the cabinet takes a share in it as much as anyone else. He is not successful in concealing it, and after the most recent defeats he did not even seem to show much concern that he does not. Even though Mr Metternich said affectedly that he would embrace the messenger who informed him about the capture of Varna, it is evident to me that he was disappointed by the news of this."[36] Laval found the evidence for his opinion in Metternich's scarcely hidden dismay at the capture of Varna by the Russians and his joy when they terminated the siege of the fortress Silistria, an event which the chancellor compared to Napoleon's withdrawal from Moscow.[37]

Metternich was undoubtedly satisfied with the fact that the tsarist army did not stand at the gates of Constantinople after the first campaign and its setback could hardly cause him displeasure. Even the considerably pro-Austrian Wellesley, now Lord Cowley, admitted

---

[34] Maltzan to Frederick William III, Vienna, 21 Nov. 1828, GStA PK, HA III, MdA I, 6011.

[35] Tatishchev to Nesselrode, Vienna, 12 Oct. 1828, AVPRI, fond 133, Kantseliariia, opis 468, 11879; K. Hammer, *Die französische Diplomatie der Restauration und Deutschland 1814–1830*, Stuttgart 1963, p. 137.

[36] Laval to La Ferronnays, Vienna, 30 Oct. 1828, AMAE, CP, Autriche 409.

[37] Laval to La Ferronnays, Vienna, 25 and 30 Oct. 1828, AMAE, CP, Autriche 409; Laval to La Ferronnays, Vienna, 27 Nov. 1828, AMAE, CP, Autriche 410. The opinion that Metternich kindled anti-Russian moods is also shared by some historians, see for example Hammer, p. 137.

that although "the Russian Cabinet had certainly no just grounds of complaint against Austria . . . it cannot be matter of surprize [sic] that she should be cautious of giving offence to the former Power. No one is more alive to the danger of offending Russia than Prince Metternich himself and yet no one exults more openly in the reverses sustained by that Power during the last campaign, or draws a more exaggerated picture of the sufferings and losses of the Russian army . . . It must be confessed that as far as relates to Prince Metternich's display of his feelings, the Russian ambassador has cause for complaint, and all His Highness's confidential friends lament that he is not more guarded in his language when speaking of disasters of the campaign, but would wish him at the same time to adopt a more firm and decided tone in repelling the unjust suspicions entertained by Emperor Nicholas respecting the conduct of Austria."[38] Nevertheless, one must be careful in exaggerating the chancellor's satisfaction and ostentatious displays of exultation. First, Laval often based his conclusions upon mere assumptions, and as thus they were reported to Paris. Some of them were definitely mistaken and it is highly likely that he exaggerated Metternich's remarks, which was not so implausible owing to the principal aim of Laval's mission corresponding with his government's wish to forestall any improvement in the relations between Austria and Russia and prevent the former from profiting from the problems of the latter.[39] Metternich's own diplomatic as well as personal correspondence lacks any remarkable anti-Russian comments. Second, the content of the chancellor's letters and discussions prove that he was well aware of the sufferings in the regions affected by the war, in particular by the epidemics decimating not only the Russian troops but also the inhabitants in the Danubian Principalities, the latter fleeing to Austrian territory. When, for example, he asked a banker from Odessa whether the news of 20,000 ill Russian soldiers was not exaggerated, the answer was that the actual number of sick and wounded reached 50,000.[40] Metternich did not hide from his own staff as well as from foreign diplomats his disgust at the dark side of the war and he was definitely not exaggerating at all in considering the actual number

---

[38] Cowley to Aberdeen, Vienna, 11 Dec. 1828, TNA, FO 120/95.
[39] Hammer, pp. 136–137.
[40] Metternich's meeting with Mr Risnisch, 1 Oct. 1828, attached to Metternich to Esterházy, Vienna, 8 Oct. 1828, HHStA, StA, England 183.

of casualties and general suffering.[41] Historians later confirmed that most of the 40,000 Russian soldiers who died in the first campaign were victims of diseases like typhus, fevers, dysentery, scurvy or inflammatory disorders, and from May 1828 to February 1829 210,108 soldiers, twice as many as actually employed in the first Balkan campaign, were treated in Russian hospitals with more or less serious illnesses.[42] Third, as well as in the preceding years, anti-Russian sentiment was now more common among Metternich's advisors but he himself remained more restrained. It was Gentz again who was unable to hide his anti-Russian feelings, the existence of which is evident from his correspondence. Laval justly wrote about him: "I have never seen a more strongly pronounced antipathy against someone's neighbours, a joy more sincere at their reverses and less troubled by the future that could result from them."[43] Fourth, anti-Russian feeling actually existed in Austrian society and Metternich acknowledged this fact, but there is no proof that he supported it. In comparison with the moods of the public, the government was definitely more reserved.[44] Fifth, Tatishchev's complaints must be regarded as exaggerated. For example, he felt insulted by the way Austria informed the public about the war in the *Österreichischer Beobachter* as well as in the newspapers in other parts of Europe allegedly trying to provoke hatred against Russia and sympathy towards the Turks.[45] In fact the *Österreichischer Beobachter* tried to be very discreet in its articles on the war[46] and the problem lay not in informing about Russia in a negative way but actually in describing its defeats at all, which, however, sufficed to offend Tatishchev's sensitive Russian soul. One can

---

[41] Metternich to Esterházy, Vienna, 2 Dec. 1828, HHStA, StA, England 184; Metternich to Ottenfels, Vienna, 10 Dec. 1828, HHStA, StA, Türkei VI, 35; Laval to La Ferronnays, Vienna, 23 Oct. 1828, AMAE, CP, Autriche 409.

[42] Aksan, pp. 351–352; Bitis, p. 300.

[43] Laval to La Ferronnays, Vienna, 26 Nov. 1828, AMAE, CP, Autriche 410.

[44] Metternich to Trauttmannsdorff, Vienna, 11 Jan. 1829, HHStA, StK, Preussen 132; F. Lorenz, *Karl Ludwig Graf Ficquelmont als Diplomat und Staatsmann*, unpublished dissertation, Wien 1966, p. 82.

[45] Tatishchev to Nesselrode, Vienna, 14 March 1828, AVPRI, fond 133, Kantseliariia, opis 468, 11877; Tatishchev to Nesselrode, Vienna, 12 June 1828, AVPRI, fond 133, Kantseliariia, opis 468, 11879.

[46] J. Mühlhauser, *Die Geschichte des "Österreichischer Beobachter" von der Gründung bis zum Tode Friedrich von Gentz 1810–1832*, unpublished dissertation, Wien 1948, p. 113.

understand this better when reading the report of a Bavarian envoy in
St Petersburg where, owing to the Russian failures, the officials tried
to prevent "the unfavourable news from circulating in public. Foreign
newspapers which mention the slightest set-back have been suppressed
by the censors ... Even the official bulletins have also begun to be
very incomplete and offer visible indications that one event or another has been concealed, or that an attempt has been made to give
it a different kind of interpretation, one that is clearly fabricated."[47]
Tatishchev's hypersensitivity as well as a sort of naivety is evident in
his complaint that Austrian General Prince Philip August Frederick
of Hesse-Homburg, who had been sent by Francis I to the Russian
headquarters in the early summer of 1828 as an Austrian observer,
was not deferential enough to the tsar in his reports: "I was offended
to find in them, next to the numerous proofs of the confidence with
which Our August Master honours him, no expression that demonstrates that the prince is sensitive to the goodwill of the emperor and
that he acknowledges His noble determination and the courage of our
troops."[48] The reports of Maltzan and his Bavarian and Papal colleagues, Envoy Count Franz Gabriel von Bray-Steinburg and Nuncio
Ugo Pietro Spinola, entirely confirm that Tatishchev's complaints of
Metternich in this respect were exaggerated.[49]

Further proof for the exaggeration of Metternich's alleged danc-
ing with joy on Russian graves can be found in Metternich's diplomacy
in general. When Metternich reacted to the fall of Varna with a remark that this defeat could be the motivation he desired for opening
the door to the peace negotiations between the Ottoman Empire and
Russia, Laval labelled this statement in his report as lacking sincerity
and just masking the chancellor's real anti-Russian aims.[50] Nevertheless, what Metternich told the French ambassador was true. Laval's

---

[47] Lerchenfeld to Ludwig I of Bavaria, St Petersburg, 12 Oct. 1828, BHStA, MA,
Petersburg 2716.
[48] Tatishchev to Nesselrode, Vienna, 3 Nov. 1828, AVPRI, fond 133, Kantseliariia,
opis 468, 11877.
[49] Maltzan to Frederick William III, Vienna, 18 Oct. 1828, GStA PK, HA III,
MdA I, 6011; Bray to Ludwig I of Bavaria, Vienna, 19 Oct., 5 and 7 Nov., 9 Dec.
1828, BHStA, MA, Wien 2402; Spinola to Bernetti, Vienna, 10 Dec. 1828, ASV,
Arch. Nunz. Vienna 256.
[50] Laval to La Ferronnays, Vienna, 25 and 30 Oct. 1828, AMAE, CP, Autriche
409.

erroneous assessment is, on the other hand, understandable because even with the volume of Metternich's correspondence it is difficult to ascertain his real diplomatic designs during 1828. It can be taken for granted that Metternich never at that time intended to leave the sphere of diplomacy, in other words he in no way contemplated war with Russia as British historian Alan John Percivale Taylor incorrectly claimed[51] since the above-stated weakness of Austria's army did not permit it to consider waging a war, in particular when the trilateral alliance continued to exist: "Austria is a central Power. Consequently, it needs to protect one or the other of its flanks. And it is not when Russia, France and Great Britain are united that Austria could make a move without imminent risks to itself."[52] He naturally did not fear a hostile reaction from Great Britain where Wellington was as indisposed to Russia as the chancellor was, but the French government's pro-Russian bias was too well known for Austria to risk a war on two fronts. Therefore, Austria had to maintain its neutrality in the Russo-Ottoman war: "It will not deviate from this system because it is the only one which is appropriate to the position of our empire."[53] On the other hand, it also could not remain entirely passive because the earliest end to the war was in its interest. Therefore, Metternich was compelled to continue to be active in the diplomatic field.[54]

Metternich's Attempts to End the Greek Question

The restoration of peace was an aim as optimistic as it was difficult to achieve since Metternich's possibilities were rather limited. What he wanted was to simplify the whole situation consisting of two problems, the Greek Question and the Russo-Ottoman war, by the prompt solution of the former. He hoped that this would end the existence

[51] A. J. P. Taylor, "Perceptive but Superficial Tinkerer," E. E. Kraehe (ed.), *The Metternich Controversy*, New York, Chicago, San Francisco, Atlanta, Dallas, Montreal, Toronto, London, Sydney 1971, p. 107.
[52] Metternich to Esterházy, Vienna, 31 May 1828, HHStA, StA, England 182.
[53] Metternich to Ottenfels, Vienna, 4 June 1828, HHStA, StA, Türkei VI, 35.
[54] Metternich to Francis I, Vienna, 18 May 1828, HHStA, StK, Vorträge 254; Metternich to Ottenfels, Vienna, 4 June and 3 July 1828, HHStA, StA, Türkei VI, 35; Maltzan to Frederick William III, Vienna, 13 June 1828, GStA PK, HA III, MdA I, 6011.

of the trilateral alliance and improve the sultan's relations with the two Maritime Powers. Although he did not conceal this plan from Tatishchev,[55] it is obvious that its eventual success could not find favour with the tsar since France and Great Britain would have been freed from the alliance with Russia and able to act more independently. What is unclear in Metternich's plan is the extent of the two Maritime Powers' anti-Russian activities desired by him. The solution of the Greek Question as an impulse for any bold or even hostile measures towards Russia on the part of Britain was particularly desired by Gentz, who wanted to gain the active support of Great Britain and Prussia against Russia, whom he accused of waging an "atrocious and infernal war."[56] Metternich definitely shared Gentz's desire that Wellington pursue a more decisive policy in Near Eastern affairs, but he was more sceptical in this respect and doubted that a decisive British opposition to Russia could result from the solution of Greek affairs. For him its settlement was in the first place a significant step to opening peace negotiations between Nicholas I and Mahmud II. Since among the reasons why the sultan did not want to start negotiations was his fear of the consequences of a peace settlement for his rule over Greece, Metternich hoped that by ending the Greek Question Mahmud II would become more willing to negotiate and, it is true, that the Maritime Powers would become less hostile to him. If Metternich maintained any belief that, having settled the Greek issue, France and Great Britain could exert any pressure on the tsar, this hope seemed to disappear during the summer months.[57]

The quick settlement of the Greek issue was, according to Metternich, possible with the fulfilment of several conditions. The first and most important was Mahmud II's acceptance of the conditions of the Treaty of London since merely this step could open the way

---

[55] Tatishchev to Nesselrode, Vienna, 9 July 1828, AVPRI, fond 133, Kantseliariia, opis 468, 11879.

[56] Gentz to Neumann, Vienna, 12 June 1828, NA, RAM-AC 5, 3; see also Gentz to Neumann, Vienna, 11 June 1828, NA, RAM-AC 5, 3; Bray, *Mémoire sur la politique générale des puissances européennes sur les affaires du Levant et sur le direction qu'il parait le plus convenables de donner à la politique de la Bavière*, Irlbach, 31 July 1828, BHStA, MA, Wien 2402.

[57] Metternich to Esterházy, Vienna, 9 July 1828, HHStA, StA, England 183; Gentz to Metternich, Vienna, 10 July 1828, Kronenbitter, p. 317; Gentz to Metternich, Vienna, 28 Aug. 1828, Kronenbitter, p. 326.

to the relevant negotiations and improve his relations with France and Great Britain. This did not signify any change in Metternich's conservative *Weltanschauung* but his submission to the force of circumstances – no forces at the sultan's disposal for his reconquest of the Peloponnese, Ibrahim Pasha's hopeless situation in this peninsula, the Russo-Ottoman war – all of them forcing the chancellor to "stop regretting what is past in order to place ourselves in a much more practical position to face the needs created by the current circumstances."[58] Since he well realised that the clock could not be turned back and the Ottoman direct rule over the Peloponnese was lost, he advised Mahmud II to do the only reasonable thing: acknowledge this fact and settle the Greek Question according to the stipulations of 6 July 1827 because, as he wrote to Ottenfels in early August 1828, the Peloponnese "is lost for the Porte, either within the limits of the arrangements anticipated by the Treaty of London, or by a complete emancipation. Would not this indisputable fact against which a remedy no longer exists compel the Divan to look for its course of direction from the point of view contained in my last dispatch to Y[our] E[xcellence]? In a word, would the sultan not do better to offer on his own initiative what he will no longer be able to avoid having to concede?"[59] Nevertheless, Mahmud II was not willing to demonstrate such realism and although he also wanted the end of the trilateral alliance, he hoped to achieve it without his agreement to the allies' conditions. Ottenfels' attempts to overcome this attitude during the summer were in vain.[60] The second condition of the settlement was the return of the British and French ambassadors to Constantinople to discuss the Greek affairs with the Turks, being in this way an extension of the main conference centre in London. Nevertheless, this was impossible to achieve owing to Russia's antagonism. To prolong the entire negotiations on the Greek issue, Nesselrode proposed in early 1828 that appropriate negotiations were held not in London but on one of the Greek Islands and among the three ambassadors who had left the Ottoman capital, with which the French and British cab-

---

[58] Metternich to Apponyi, Vienna, 15 June 1828, HHStA, StA, Frankreich 268.
[59] Metternich to Ottenfels, Vienna, 4 Aug. 1828, HHStA, StA, Türkei VI, 35.
[60] Metternich to Ottenfels, Vienna, 4 June and 4 Sept. 1828, HHStA, StA, Türkei VI, 35; Huszár to Ottenfels, 19 and 20 June 1828, Ottenfels to Metternich, Constantinople, 10 and 25 June 1828, HHStA, StA, Türkei VI, 33.

inets agreed. The ambassadors discussed the future territorial extent of Greece in Corfu during August and from September to October on the island of Poros.[61] The third condition necessary for the assurance of the sultan's willingness to end the Greek Question according to the wishes of the trilateral alliance was some placability on the part of the alliance, for example not using the word "mediation" or avoiding any hostile step against the Porte. However, exactly the opposite occurred, in particular when the French government put to its allies the idea of its own military expedition to the Peloponnese with the aim of expelling Ibrahim Pasha's forces condemned to stagnate in the peninsula since the Battle of Navarino.[62]

Consequently, from the summer of 1828, Metternich had to try to overcome obstacles that finally proved to be insuperable. As for the desired compliance of the Porte, in May Pertev addressed a letter to Guilleminot and Stratford containing the invitation for their return to Constantinople but promising nothing concerning the Greek Question. Ottenfels, who was not directly involved in this move but knew about it, tried in vain to persuade the reis effendi to write the letter in more compliant terms and, therefore, the two ambassadors refused to meet the Porte's wish. Metternich criticised the Porte for its attempts to cause the breakup of the trilateral alliance by having only negotiations with the two Maritime Powers without accepting the requested concessions since he believed that without agreeing to them there was no prospect for success.[63] When Pertev Effendi addressed a letter to Wellington in early July, Metternich was more satisfied with its content effectively summarised by Ottenfels in this way: "We want to agree with you on the manner of quickly ending [the insurrection] to our mutual satisfaction by resuming the negotiations interrupted by the departure of your representatives on the basis of the propositions which were made to us during the conferences which preceded

---

[61] Metternich to Ottenfels, Vienna, 4 June 1828, HHStA, StA, Türkei VI, 35; Crawley, *Greek Independence*, pp. 107–111; Dakin, p. 257.

[62] Metternich to Esterházy, Vienna, 17 May and 12 June 1828, HHStA, StA, England 182; Metternich to Ottenfels, Vienna, 3 July 1828, HHStA, StA, Türkei VI, 35; Sauvigny, *Metternich et la France*, III, p. 1200.

[63] Metternich to Apponyi, Vienna, 15 June 1828, HHStA, StA, Frankreich 268; Guilleminot to Pertev, Corfu, 14 June 1828, Ottenfels to Metternich, Constantinople, 8 July 1828, HHStA, StA, Türkei VI, 34; Tatishchev to Nesselrode, Vienna, 15 July 1828, AVPRI, fond 133, Kantseliariia, opis 468, 11879.

their departure."[64] Ottenfels, who was accredited with the more compliant tone of the content, did not initiate the writing of the letter as
Tatishchev wrongly presumed,[65] but when he saw its original version
every bit as vague as the letters sent earlier to the ambassadors, he
intervened and assisted in the composition of the final version. However, since he could only go so far as the Turks allowed, even the
second version was not ideal. Metternich welcomed the more precise
expressions concerning the Porte's willingness to conciliation and the
factual recognition of the British right to intervene on behalf of the
Greeks contained in the letter, but he still saw little prospect for this
attempt to break up the trilateral alliance since the Porte again did
not explicitly accept the conditions of the Treaty of London, which
was exactly the reason why Wellington refused to send his ambassador
back to Constantinople despite Metternich's reserved recommendation
to accept this offer.[66]

Metternich saw no way out of the deadlock other than changing the Porte's attitude and persuading it to abandon its principles
and accept the foreign intervention into Greek affairs due to the seriousness of the situation: "To stop at questions of this nature [of
principles] would be to lose precious time for nothing. The course of
events would take no consideration of it and would proceed in spite
of all our reasoning with irresistible force towards a solution of fact.
The Porte itself already has offered proof that it knows how to tell
the difference between the issues. It tacitly admitted that its fleet
could be fired on and destroyed by the Great Powers which called
themselves its friends."[67] This advice was contained in his instructions for Ottenfels of 22 July which formed an important basis for the

---

[64] Ottenfels to Metternich, Constantinople, 8 July 1828, HHStA, StA, Türkei VI,
34.
[65] Tatishchev to Nesselrode, Vienna, 31 July 1828, AVPRI, fond 133,
Kantseliariia, opis 468, 11879.
[66] Metternich to Apponyi, Vienna, 15 June 1828, HHStA, StA, Frankreich 268;
Metternich to Esterházy, Vienna, 24 July 1828, HHStA, StA, England 183; Wellington to Pertev, London, 6 Aug. 1828, Metternich to Ottenfels, Vienna, 22 July,
4 and 20 Aug. 1828, HHStA, StA, Türkei VI, 35; Pertev to Wellington, 6 July
1828, Ottenfels to Metternich, Constantinople, 8 July 1828, HHStA, StA, Türkei
VI, 34; Tatishchev to Nesselrode, Vienna, 23 and 25 July 1828, AVPRI, fond 133,
Kantseliariia, opis 468, 11879; Gentz to Neumann, Vienna, 24 July 1828, NA,
RAM-AC 5, 3.
[67] Metternich to Ottenfels, Vienna, 22 July 1828, HHStA, StA, Türkei VI, 35.

internuncio's further proceeding. Ottenfels was to declare that, first, some parts of Greece could never be returned to the former rule by the Ottoman government and Mahmud II was to give up all hope of being able to change anything in this state of affairs. Second, that the sultan's attempts to break up the trilateral alliance without meeting its members' requests could never meet with success and could only lead to a waste of time. Third, although Wellington's government was not satisfied with the existence of the Treaty of London, it inherited this agreement and, consequently, any attempt of the Porte to remove it from the trilateral alliance was pointless, like Pertev's letter for Wellington. Fourth, the Porte faced two difficulties, the war with Russia and the Greek insurrection, both embarrassing and desirable to be resolved. Since at the given moment at least the latter could be ended by negotiations, the sultan was to facilitate his own position by doing so.[68] The character of Metternich's counsel was summarised in his instructions to Trauttmannsdorff: "You would do better, you will not bring back the lands under insurrection to their former status with you; anything that you will still obtain from them will be at the most very little. Act in the spirit of your law, submit to an unavoidable necessity, and direct the efforts of your policy not to the impracticable goal of splitting up the trilateral alliance but fully to the entirely practical task of terminating one of the two affairs placing you in such obvious danger! Will your position not be clearly improved the day you would only have to solve with Russia its own affairs? On the day when the two Great Powers which are bound to [Russia] by the ties of the Treaty of London would find themselves freed? Confront these truths directly and firmly, and the Great Powers which declared their absolute neutrality will themselves be able to serve you better with the goal of contributing to a prompt pacification between you and your formidable neighbour!"[69]

As for the talks in Corfu and Poros, Metternich sharply criticised this measure as absurd and necessarily protracting the negotiations owing to the distances between the islands and the capitals of the trilateral Powers. Moreover, he disagreed that the negotiations over Greece were to be left in hands of the ambassadors who could be

---

[68] Ibid.
[69] Metternich to Trauttmannsdorff, Vienna, 16 July 1828, HHStA, StK, Preussen 129.

led "by their passions or calculations,"[70] which was a legitimate concern as the pro-Greek result of the talks proved. Metternich believed that the negotiations were to continue in the centre of the trilateral alliance, London, and could be accompanied by discussions in Constantinople where, however, Russia could hardly be represented. He was also dissatisfied with the fact that the three Great Powers had for a long time been unable to make clear conditions concerning the future political and territorial concept of Greece which could be presented in Constantinople for acceptance. These details, in his opinion, were to be settled in London and he did not see any advantage to discussions on the matter among the ambassadors on any island. His dissatisfaction further increased when he learnt of the three Powers' invitation to the Turks to send their own representatives to this insular, secondary conference, a step that was condemned to failure owing to the Porte's inevitable refusal to sit down at a table to discuss the Greek affairs face-to-face with a Russian diplomat as well as the Greeks also invited to participate.[71] He summarised his displeasure in his instructions for Ottenfels of 22 July: "To agree to participate at a secondary conference and to negotiations with the Greeks over decisions of vital importance which in the last instance could never be taken except by the cabinets themselves; to insist that the Divan recognise the fact or (what in the present circumstances is the equivalent) the right requested by three courts to impose on an independent power their mediation between a prince and his rebellious subjects; to not realise at all how such a demand becomes even more unusual when one of the Great Powers which wants to impose its mediation is at the same moment a belligerent power; finally to demand from the Turks that they have their plenipotentiaries sit the same conference table with a Russian plenipotentiary and a Greek plenipotentiary when the Rus-

---

[70] Metternich to Esterházy, Vienna, 8 Nov. 1828, HHStA, StA, England 184.
[71] Metternich to Esterházy, Vienna, 17 May and 12 June 1828, HHStA, StA, England 182; Metternich to Esterházy, Vienna, 9 and 24 July, 22 Aug. 1828, HHStA, StA, England 183; Metternich to Apponyi, Vienna, 15 June 1828, HHStA, StA, Frankreich 268; Metternich to Ottenfels, Vienna, 3 and 22 July 1828, HHStA, StA, Türkei VI, 35; Cowley to Aberdeen, Vienna, 12 July 1828, TNA, FO 120/93; Laval to La Ferronnays, Vienna, 17 Nov. 1828, AMAE, CP, Autriche 410; Brockhausen to Frederick William III, Vienna, 4 and 15 July, 5 Aug. 1828, GStA PK, HA III, MdA I, 6011; Maltzan to Frederick William III, Vienna, 3 Dec. 1828, GStA PK, HA III, MdA I, 6011.

sian mediator is at the same moment the representative of an enemy Power and when there is no Greece yet and that before the sultan's acknowledgement there would not be any; to do and demand all this with deliberate intention and after long and grave pauses taken for consideration; it is indisputably a way to a rather deplorable result. Consequently, it is not in London, Corfu, Aegina, or on any island of the Archipelago where such an extraordinary assembly of negotiators would meet where the Greek affair will be decided. It will be concluded at the point of a Russian sword and it will obtain its sanction in the place where peace between the two Powers at war will be made."[72] Metternich was naturally too experienced not to see for which of the allies this proceeding was advantageous and could hardly understand how Great Britain, particularly interested in the prompt settlement of the Greek Question, could pursue so condescending a policy towards Russia.[73] He wrote to Trauttmannsdorff: "If these conditions and this approach are arranged in London, from that time on the affair will be delayed more than ever and its resolution will necessarily be abandoned to the fate of the armies between the two Powers at war. That such an end to the deliberations of the trilateral conference can satisfy one of the allied parties is absolutely clear to us; but that it could satisfy the other two parties, that is what surprises us, if anything in the trilateral affair can still surprise us."[74]

Metternich considered the secondary conference to be a mistake because it simply postponed the final settlement of the Greek issue. From his point of view the trilateral alliance made more mistakes in late 1828. Another was its insistence on the use of the word "mediation" still unacceptable for the Porte. Metternich also regarded it as ridiculous because Russia could never be a mediating Power when it was at war with the state on which the mediation was to be imposed. Consequently, he believed that this term was to be avoided in dealing with the Porte, making thus the attainment of an understanding more feasible, but his counsel on the matter remained unanswered by the three Great Powers.[75] Another measure of the trilateral alliance

---

[72] Metternich to Ottenfels, Vienna, 22 July 1828, HHStA, StA, Türkei VI, 35.
[73] Ibid.
[74] Metternich to Trauttmannsdorff, Vienna, 16 July 1828, HHStA, StK, Preussen 129.
[75] Metternich to Esterházy, Vienna, 12 June 1828, HHStA, StA, England 182; Metternich to Apponyi, Vienna, 15 June 1828, HHStA, StA, Frankreich 268; Met-

which could hardly please the sultan was, in Metternich's opinion, the French military expedition to the Peloponnese. Although he welcomed this idea before the outbreak of the Russo-Ottoman war as a means of forcing the sultan to yield, something he himself wanted to achieve with the threat of Greek independence, he regarded it as absolutely unnecessary when the conflict was in progress. The Egyptian army cut off from supplies by the vigorous allied naval blockade was passive and suffering from disease and a lack of provisions, and Ibrahim Pasha was in fact merely waiting for the consent either of Mahmud II or of Mohammed Ali for his army's return to Egypt. Their departure, according to Metternich, was just a matter of time; their expulsion by force and the French occupation of the Peloponnese would not force Mahmud II to yield on the Greek Question. To the contrary, this attack, which could hardly be understood by the sultan as anything other than an act of war and which was in contradiction with the Treaty of London laying out the terms for the pacification by peaceful means, could make him more stubborn. In brief, the expedition could achieve nothing really useful at the given moment and only make the situation worse.[76] Therefore, Metternich refused to offer the diplomatic support in London requested by the French cabinet and, on the contrary, he tried to persuade both the French and the British to abandon this "insane act."[77] He told Cara-

---

ternich to Ottenfels, Vienna, 20 Aug. 1828, HHStA, StA, Türkei VI, 35.

[76] Metternich to Ottenfels, Vienna, 19 April and 4 Aug. 1828, HHStA, StA, Türkei VI, 35; Metternich to Apponyi, Vienna, 24 July 1828, HHStA, StA, Frankreich 268; Metternich to Trauttmannsdorff, Vienna, 5, 8, 13 and 18 Aug., 19 Sept. 1828, HHStA, StK, Preussen 129; Prokesch to Ottenfels, Smyrna, 18 June 1828, Ottenfels to Metternich, Constantinople, 30 May and 25 June 1828, HHStA, StA, Türkei VI, 33; Ottenfels to Metternich, Constantinople, 10 and 25 July, 11 Aug. 1828, HHStA, StA, Türkei VI, 34; Cowley to Aberdeen, Vienna, 12 July 1828, TNA, FO 120/93; Brockhausen to Frederick William III, Vienna, 16 Aug. and 3 Sept. 1828, GStA PK, HA III, MdA I, 6011; Lufti al-Sayyid Marsot, *Muhammad Ali*, p. 217.

[77] Metternich to Apponyi, Vienna, 22 Aug. 1828, HHStA, StA, Frankreich 268. Sauvigny pointed out the total difference in Metternich's expressions on this issue to Caraman and Cowley, quoting a long part of the former's report in which the French cabinet was informed about Metternich's support of the French expedition. Sauvigny was quite surprised by this and offered several explanations favourable to Metternich. In fact, the explanation for this alleged difference seems to be simpler: Neither the relevant nor other reports of the French ambassador studied by me actually contain Metternich's agreement to the expedition, even anything that

man in early July: "If you want to follow my advice, redirect your attention and your action to another area. Concentrate your activity to the conference in London. Try to use the opportunity to expedite the great number of decisions that urgently need to be made on all the points still to be decided. An action in Morea will not advance you in the affair. Greece or what the allies understand as Greece must be [diplomatically] conquered in Constantinople and not in situ."[78] When the probability of Ibrahim Pasha's withdrawal increased and was even recognised by La Ferronnays who, however, did not recall the expedition, Metternich met with the French chargé d'affaires in Vienna, Ludwig Schwebel: "I could not help addressing a question to the chargé d'affaires of France: To what end, in the case of the evacuation of Morea, would the expedition serve? He replied to me with his own words recorded in the dispatch which he had finished reading to me. Mr La Ferronnays says 'that then the expeditionary army will return.' It seems to me that France is preparing here to incur great expenses which, in the happiest circumstance, will only lead to the even greater embarrassment of the political attitude of the French government towards the Porte than already exists and to the glorification of the adventurous spirit and the conceit which predominate in the kingdom. The king evidently conforms to the same spirit, and by following his blind instinct, will he find the means for stopping himself in his course? And the French flag that will fly on the Acropolis, will they not want to hoist it over several other Christian places more coveted by the public spirit in France than over such distant places which they will not be able to maintain in any way?"[79] To Metternich's displeasure, Russia expectably and Great Britain unexpectedly for him agreed on 19 July with the expedition of the French forces, which arrived in the Peloponnese at the end of August. Nevertheless, earlier in the same month, Mohammed Ali had signed with Codrington a convention in Alexandria, in which he had pledged to withdraw his forces from the peninsula, and Ibrahim Pasha's remaining troops in a deplorable state were transported to Egypt during September and

---

could serve as consent; what the report quoted by Sauvigny actually contains is Metternich's support of the more deliberated and decisive conduct of the trilateral alliance in the Greek Question, which had nothing to do with the expedition. Sauvigny, *Metternich et la France*, III, pp. 1201–1202.

[78] Metternich to Esterházy, Vienna, 9 July 1828, HHStA, StA, England 183.
[79] Metternich to Esterházy, Vienna, 11 Aug. 1828, HHStA, StA, England 183.

October. The French expeditionary forces therefore arrived too late, but since their commander wanted to show some action, he ordered the capture of five fortresses left in the Peloponnese in the hands of sultan's soldiers by the Alexandrian Convention. To Metternich's relief, Mahmud II acted with great resignation and did nothing that could endanger the peace existing between Constantinople and Paris. On the other hand, the French expedition made him more opposed to any negotiations over Greece or peace with Russia. As Metternich had expected, the whole useless adventure did not accelerate the settlement of the Greek Question.[80]

Metternich's Plan to Use the Winter to Bring an End to the Russo-Ottoman War

In the late summer of 1828, the prospect for a quick settlement of the Greek Question was essentially nil. This forced Metternich to change his tactics and he openly advised Mahmud II to open peace negotiations with Russia. This advice was the result of his deeply held opinion since the beginning of the war that the Ottoman Empire had absolutely no prospect for any real victory. In successfully defending itself, it could prolong the conflict, but it could never bring about a reversal in the course of the war since Nicholas I was too strong. For this reason, according to Metternich, the more the tsar lost, the more he would demand at the end, and the peace agreement would be much worse for the sultan if the war lasted too long. Therefore, the Russian failures in 1828 did not change his opinion since first of all the Turks were also not the victors of the first campaign: "The Russian campaign failed without the Turks being victorious."[81] Second, he expected that

---

[80] Metternich to Esterházy, Vienna, 9 and 22 Aug., 1 Nov. 1828, HHStA, StA, England 183; Acerbi to Metternich, Alexandria, 27 Sept. 1828, NA, RAM-AC 5, 3; Esterházy to Metternich, London, 25 July and 15 Aug. 1828, HHStA, StA, England 181; Ottenfels to Metternich, Constantinople, 12 Sept., 10 and 25 Nov. 1828, HHStA, StA, Türkei VI, 34; Laval to La Ferronnays, Vienna, 1 Dec. 1828, AMAE, CP, Autriche, 410; V. J. Puryear, *France and the Levant from the Bourbon Restoration to the Peace of Kutiah*, Berkeley 1941, pp. 56–58; Crawley, *Greek Independence*, pp. 112 and 143; Dakin, p. 258; Dodwell, p. 92.
[81] Metternich to Apponyi, Vienna, 27 Oct. 1828, HHStA, StA, Frankreich 268.

Nicholas I would prepare himself much better for the second round, which the sultan could not survive without foreign assistance, which, however, the Maritime Powers would never grant him. Consequently, what Metternich feared from the late summer 1828 almost as much as a decisive Russian victory was the protraction of war into the following year, and what he advised the Porte despite the increasingly obvious problems in the field for Russia was that the Turks undertook steps not only with the aim of a prompt solution of the Greek Question but also restoration of peace with Russia. On 20 August, he informed Ottenfels that they could not expect any support from Great Britain and France and were to start to deal directly with Russia.[82] In Metternich's opinion, Mahmud II had a simple choice under the given conditions – to do nothing or to act according to his advice: "The first of these possibilities corresponds most to the customary approach of the Turkish mentality. It does not offer anything else for the Porte other than the possibility of disaster, the possible extent of which one cannot estimate in advance. If the present campaign should turn bad for the Russian forces – and it is permissible to admit such an eventuality or, what is the same, if Russia should not finish the war, it will be a justification for the Russian emperor to make up for the mistakes he made in 1828 with efforts equally serious in 1829. [With] the spirit that predominates in France and the presence of a French armed force in the southern provinces of the Ottoman Empire on the one side, and the extreme weakness that, from the other side, the English government displays, to what horrifying crisis could the repetition of the affair next spring not expose the existence of the European Turkey and the whole of Europe! The second possibility would be that which would certainly offer the greatest advantages to the Porte and would in no way compromise its existence or its honour."[83]

Metternich repeatedly suggested that the Porte extend an invitation to peace negotiations directly to the tsar's headquarters and that

---

[82] Metternich to Ottenfels, Vienna, 4 and 20 Aug. 1828, HHStA, StA, Türkei VI, 35; Metternich to Trauttmannsdorff, Vienna, 23 Aug. 1828, HHStA, StK, Preussen 129; Maltzan to Frederick William III, Vienna, 30 April 1828, GStA PK, HA III, MdA I, 6010; Brockhausen to Frederick William III, Vienna, 17 Sept. 1828, GStA PK, HA III, MdA I, 6011; Laval to La Ferronnays, Vienna, 7 Nov. 1828, AMAE, CP, Autriche 410; Bray to Ludwig I of Bavaria, Vienna, 29 Nov. 1828, BHStA, MA, Wien 2402.
[83] Metternich to Ottenfels, Vienna, 20 Aug. 1828, HHStA, StA, Türkei VI, 35.

it could be done through Ottenfels, who was in direct contact with the Prince of Hesse-Homburg, whose dispatch to Nicholas I was also undertaken for such a purpose; he was to serve as an instrument for the achievement of a quick peace settlement if possible. Since Pertev's letter for Wellington was also delivered by Austria, Metternich argued that there would be nothing new in the method for the Porte. Furthermore, the chancellor tried to reduce the animosity existing between the two parties at war. Whenever he saw even the slightest sign of the sultan's desire to yield, he did not hesitate to convey it to Nicholas I. When, for example, Ottenfels succeeded in persuading Mahmud II to treat the Russian war prisoners better, the tsar was immediately informed about this by the Prince of Hesse-Homburg. How greatly Metternich hoped for any improvement of the relations between the two empires at war is evident from his considerable expectations brought about by the news that Nicholas I had allegedly sent a captured pasha to the sultan with a verbal message that he "was prepared to come to an agreement with him and that it would not be as difficult as seemed to be believed to bring about peace between the two empires."[84] Nevertheless, the satisfaction with the progress of war and dissatisfaction with the proceeding of the trilateral alliance in the Greek Question, in particular the French landing in the Peloponnese, made Mahmud II deaf to conciliatory overtures. Metternich learnt from the reports he was receiving from Ottenfels in the late summer that the Porte was as far as ever from the idea of negotiating either with Russia about peace without the previous abolishment of the Akkerman Convention or with the two Maritime Powers about the Greeks upon the basis of the Treaty of London. Ottenfels, who in vain tried to persuade Mahmud II to send his agents to the Russian general staff, saw the only chance that the sultan would agree to the negotiations in the tsar making the first conciliatory step and, moreover, if this step followed any serious defeat of Ottoman army.[85]

---

[84] Metternich to Ottenfels, Vienna, 4 Sept. 1828, HHStA, StA, Türkei VI, 35.
[85] Metternich to Esterházy, Vienna, 12 June 1828, HHStA, StA, England 182; Metternich to Ottenfels, Vienna, 3 July, 4 Aug. and 4 Sept. 1828, HHStA, StA, Türkei VI, 35; Ottenfels to Thom, Constantinople, 18 Aug. 1828, Ottenfels to Metternich, Constantinople, 8 and 25 July, 6, 11 and 29 Aug., 12 and 25 Sept. 1828, HHStA, StA, Türkei VI, 34; Cowley to Aberdeen, Vienna, 10 and 11 Sept. 1828, TNA, FO 120/94; Tatishchev to Nesselrode, Vienna, 12 June, 13 and 27 Sept. 1828, AVPRI, fond 133, Kantseliariia, opis 468, 11879; Schwebel to La Ferronnays,

In mid September 1828, Metternich witnessed the situation where
the two belligerent monarchs were reluctant to start peace negotiations, neither willing to lose honour by yielding first: Mahmud II because he regarded such a step as humiliating when he was celebrating
accomplishments in the war, which in fact only meant that he did
not have to look down upon the Russian army from the Constantinople walls, and Nicholas I because he had suffered some defeats and
a peace offer could be regarded as a sign of weakness. It was thus
evident that although the military campaign of 1828 was almost at
an end owing to the forthcoming winter, the war was far from over.
What gave Metternich some hope for the future was the suspension
of hostilities during the winter, which he wanted to use for promoting the peace negotiations between Russia and the Ottoman Empire.
Metternich wrote on 11 September to Gentz: "Winter is coming soon.
If it is not utilised for serious negotiations, then the courts will go
on as before in the most miserable ways possible. In such a case the
year 1829 will bring complications which are bound to lead to the
overturning of all the present political conditions. We can then count
on more years of war."[86] Three days later, he sent his instructions to
Esterházy in which he warned Wellington against the possibility of
a second campaign in which Nicholas I could not allow Russia to be
defeated. Consequently, the campaign of 1829 would probably bear
little resemblance to that of the preceding year owing to the tsar's determination to bring it to a triumphant end. In such a case, however,
the peace conditions would have to be harsher for the sultan who, on
the other hand, would have more reasons not to yield and would be
destined to continue fighting to the last man. To prevent this, "the
winter will have to be devoted to reaching a firm agreement among
the leading courts. If the spring of year 1829 sees the war renewed
and if the same lack of agreement among the leading courts extends
into the same period, Europe will find itself confronted with a hor-
rible perspective of evil and upheaval."[87] Metternich mentioned his
hitherto unsuccessful attempts to persuade Mahmud II to talk with
Russia and posed the question concerning the British proceeding in

---

Vienna, 10 and 15 Sept. 1828, AMAE, CP, Autriche 409.

[86] Metternich to Gentz, Vienna, 11 Sept. 1828, Prokesch-Osten, *Zur Geschichte
der orientalischen Frage*, p. 185.

[87] Metternich to Esterházy, Vienna, 14 Sept. 1828, HHStA, StA, England 183.

this respect. In a secret part of his instructions he expressed his hope that Great Britain would not continue to agree with everything that its two allies suggested beyond the terms of the Treaty of London and that the British government would try to take advantage of the forthcoming winter to reach a peace settlement. It was to agree with its two allies on their further steps and invite Austria and Prussia to collaborate. Austria was prepared to meet the British proposals that could ensure the peace in the Near East.[88] On the same day Metternich expressed himself to Apponyi in the same sense that the winter was to be used for arranging unity among the Great Powers "to bring about a rapprochement between Russia and the Porte that could lead to a solid and stable peace before the start of the next campaign."[89]

The instructions to London of 14 September were of extraordinary importance, not so much for their content but for the consequences of their ambiguity. They gave rise to a legend that Metternich wanted to create a coalition of Austria, France, Great Britain and Prussia with the aim of mediating between the Ottoman Empire and Russia and forcing the latter to a peace settlement under unfavourable conditions. It should be mentioned that two important scholars already refuted this allegation: Sauvigny found no reliable evidence after a vast archival research and Schroeder drew a conclusion that Metternich would not have dared to go so far.[90] They both are right in the evaluation of the affair representing one of the greatest mysteries of Metternich's foreign policy in general and still deserving considerable attention. Before the explanation of what Metternich actually wanted and how the rumour originated, three facts must be emphasised. First, as Schroeder correctly claims, Metternich could never have dared go so far against Russia because he needed Russia as a conservative ally in the future. Francis I was also well aware of this, and he could hardly have allowed Metternich to pursue such a hostile and also overly active policy against Russia; both were too risky for a country in need of a larger army and, above all, a larger treasury. Second, it was Gentz who again maintained a rather hostile anti-Russian attitude, as he had done in the previous years.

---

[88]   Ibid.
[89]   Metternich to Apponyi, Vienna, 14 Sept. 1828, HHStA, StA, Frankreich 268.
[90]   Sauvigny, *Metternich et la France*, III, p. 1219; Schroeder, *Transformation*, p. 656.

He revealed in his letter to the Austrian diplomat, Baron Philipp von Neumann, on 28 November that the way in which he differed with Metternich was that he, Gentz, did not believe that the solution of the Greek affairs could appease the tsar and that he wanted the settlement of the Greek Question to be used for the creation of a coalition between the four Powers, which would assume an imposing attitude against Russia with the aim of forcing the tsar to proceed in a much more moderate way. Gentz added that these plans were entirely *"his* projects."[91] Third, Metternich must have known that he could hardly obtain any support for such an adventurous plan as was later ascribed to him. He was well aware that the French government maintained its pro-Russian attitude during the summer 1828, the Prussian cabinet wanted above all to remain neutral in the whole affair and the British government was also passive and merely attempted to ensure the activities of Russia as well as the trilateral alliance did not surpass certain limits. He did not write to Wellington on 14 September because of the British prime minister's courage and zeal in the diplomatic field but owing to the two men's friendship that made Great Britain the only Power which Metternich could approach and, at the same moment, the only Power that the tsar could fear. He definitely wished that Wellington would pursue a more active policy and not yield to Russia in all matters; at that time it was particularly the Russian blockade of the Dardannelles that Metternich sharply denounced in his 14 September instructions and which seemed to motivate their sharp tone, but the prince also actually did not expect much from his British friend.[92] He wrote to Apponyi on the same day that "all the evil of the day has come from London and the men who are found there at the head of affairs are rather weak to repair it."[93]

Although Metternich's insinuations directed to London on 14 September had a certain anti-Russian bias, his diplomatic effort was basically directed more against Constantinople than St Petersburg. The unified approach of the Great Powers was not aimed against Russia but the Porte, and it was intended to move the sultan to yield.

---

[91] The word "his" is underlined in the letter. Gentz to Neumann, Vienna, 28 Nov. 1828, NA, RAM-AC 5, 3.

[92] Metternich to Ottenfels, Vienna, 4 Aug. 1828, HHStA, StA, Türkei VI, 35; Esterházy to Metternich, London, 15 July and 8 Aug. 1828, HHStA, StA, England 181.

[93] Metternich to Apponyi, Vienna, 14 Sept. 1828, HHStA, StA, Frankreich 268.

Cowley reported in early October that "a reunion of five Powers in conference, and a strong representation from them to the Porte, might, in His Highness's opinion, lead to the accomplishment of the aforesaid objects."[94] What Metternich actually continued to propose from mid September was that the three allies should agree on restricting the territorial and political shape of Greece, the settlement of which was, in his opinion, directly connected with the attainment of Russo-Ottoman peace, and send their ambassadors, logically the two of France and Great Britain, to Constantinople to settle this affair with the Porte and, simultaneously, persuade it to enter into peace negotiations with Russia. Austria and Prussia would cooperate and support both steps. But, and this was the crux of Metternich's proposal, the members of the trilateral alliance had to stipulate what they actually wanted themselves. Metternich was firmly persuaded by the Prince of Hesse-Homburg's reports and the communications made in St Petersburg by various diplomats and mostly delivered to Vienna through Berlin that a considerable number of Russians were dissatisfied with the war and that Nicholas I desired peace and would not refuse to agree with the negotiations with the Porte after some tangible success.[95] When Wellington reacted on the instructions of 14 September with the idea of an entente among Austria, Great Britain, France and probably Prussia, Metternich rejected this and declared on 8 November that what he had actually wanted was that "it would be for the English cabinet to take the initiative towards its allies [France and Russia] in the discussion on what the court of London would regard within its power in the accomplishment of the stipulations of the trilateral Treaty or as exceeding its power ... The Treaty must not be interpreted, discussed or limited other than by the contracting parties, every discussion and agreement on this subject with a third party

---

[94] Cowley to Aberdeen, Vienna, 6 Oct. 1828, TNA, FO 120/94.
[95] Metternich to Trauttmannsdorff, Vienna, 11 and 29 Oct., 14 Dec. 1828, HHStA, StK, Preussen 129; Metternich to Apponyi, Vienna, 27 Oct., 12 Nov., 2 and 12 Dec. 1828, HHStA, StA, Frankreich 268; Metternich to Esterházy, Vienna, 8 and 20 Nov. 1828, HHStA, StA, England 184; Trauttmannsdorff to Metternich, Berlin, 13 and 17 Nov. 1828, HHStA, StK, Preussen 128; Maltzan to Frederick William III, Vienna, 24 and 29 Oct., 4 and 11 Nov. 1828, GStA PK, HA III, MdA I, 6011; Laval to La Ferronnays, Vienna, 3 Nov. 1828, AMAE, CP, Autriche 410; Cowley to Aberdeen, Vienna, 12 Nov. 1828, TNA, FO 120/95; Tatishchev to Nesselrode, Vienna, 13 Sept. and 12 Oct. 1828, AVPRI, fond 133, Kantseliariia, opis 468, 11879; Crawley, *Greek Independence*, p. 114.

would turn it very shortly into another affair."[96] Metternich repeated that his aim was to facilitate the way to peace, which was to be achieved by negotiations, but for this purpose the three allied courts had to first settle their conditions: "Once the action of the [trilateral] alliance has been precisely determined, the neutral courts will be able to come forward and use their salutary influence on what, without this preliminary work, could offer no chance for success."[97] Four days later he explained in the same sense in his instructions to Apponyi "that we recognise the great difficulties that exist in arriving at the restoration of peace, but that we are convinced of the absolute necessity of a peace settlement to prevent the renewal of the campaign in 1829. That we do not see any real chances for salvation other than in a peace that itself cannot be ensured except by the following measures: (1) Agreement between the courts of France and England; (2) Agreement between these two Powers and that of Russia; (3) Agreement between these three allies and the two neutral Great Powers on the moral support that these could lend to the negotiations that should open in Constantinople."[98]

This assistance was not naturally offered by Metternich without an ulterior motive: Austria's rapprochement with the trilateral alliance, which could enable him to exert more influence over the course of affairs. Nevertheless, to succeed he needed the three allied Powers to make the first step and, to achieve this, he tried to provoke Wellington to take the initiative that was not permissible for Austria because any proposal on its part would definitely have been rejected by Russia and with most probability also by France: "It is no longer from our side that in the present combination of things an initiative for the restoration of peace in the Levant could come."[99] Nevertheless, all that he received from the three capitals were mere assurances about their sincere desires to see peace restored during the winter and their general passivity. Great Britain and France did not want to do anything without the consent of Russia, for example send their representatives to Constantinople, and Bernstorff refused Metternich's request that Prussia support Austria's plan in St Petersburg

[96] Metternich to Esterházy, Vienna, 8 Nov. 1828, HHStA, StA, England 184.
[97] Ibid.
[98] Metternich to Apponyi, Vienna, 12 Nov. 1828, HHStA, StA, Frankreich 268.
[99] Ibid.

with the explanation that he saw no prospect for success. Since no Great Power did anything that Metternich could use to improve his own position in the diplomatic concert or to support his peace diplomacy in Constantinople, he assumed a more passive attitude towards them in early December.[100] However, he continued to warn the members of the trilateral alliance against the continuation of war in 1829 and repeated his complaint often stated during the previous months: "I do not know what you want, you do not know it well yourselves, and I cannot serve you if you do not clarify your intentions."[101]

Concurrently with his unsuccessful effort in the West to ensure the joint approach in the East, Metternich continued in Constantinople with his separate attempts to make Mahmud II more conciliatory. On 17 September, three days after the dispatch of the instructions to London, he instructed Ottenfels to persuade the Porte of the tsar's desire for peace and the necessity to use the winter to achieve it. He repeated the statement he had already made several times that the Peloponnese and adjacent islands were lost for Mahmud II, who was to forget Turkey's previous domination over them, and that no prospect for the sultan's victory in the war with Russia existed. Nevertheless, despite Ottenfels' considerable effort, nothing could change the situation existing in Constantinople where even Pertev did not dare mention "the word peace at the moment when the entire thinking of this monarch was directed to war."[102] Ottenfels' attempts to persuade the Porte to send peace proposals to Russia were absolutely fruitless, and the only answer he obtained was that the sultan could accept a proposal for peace negotiations from the tsar but he could never undertake the first step himself and he also requested the modifica-

---

[100] Metternich to Apponyi, Vienna, 18 Dec. 1828, HHStA, StA, Frankreich 268; Metternich to Trauttmannsdorff, Vienna, 20 Dec. 1828, HHStA, StK, Preussen 129; Metternich to Esterházy, Vienna, 2 Dec. 1828, HHStA, StA, England 184; Esterházy to Metternich, London, 27 Sept., 8 Oct., 9 and 21 Nov., 17 and 29 Dec. 1828, HHStA, StA, England 181; Apponyi to Metternich, Paris, 17, 28 and 31 Oct., 6, 11 and 20 Nov., 2, 19 and 27 Dec. 1828, HHStA, StA, Frankreich 267; Trauttmannsdorff to Metternich, Berlin, 24 Nov. and 18 Dec. 1828, HHStA, StK, Preussen 128; Maltzan to Frederick William III, Vienna, 18 Nov. 1828, GStA PK, HA III, MdA I, 6011; Bray to Ludwig I of Bavaria, Vienna, 13 Dec. 1828, BHStA, MA, Wien 2402.
[101] Laval to La Ferronnays, Vienna, 12 Dec. 1828, AMAE, CP, Autriche 410.
[102] Ottenfels to Metternich, Constantinople, 25 Sept. 1828, HHStA, StA, Türkei VI, 34.

tion of the Akkerman Convention and the end of Russia's interference
into Greek affairs. This failure to gain any influence over the Porte
proves the baselessness of the opinion widespread in Constantinople
that "the Austrian internuncio exerts a major and decisive influence
over the Porte at this moment. It decides nothing important without
consulting him and his advice is almost always taken."[103] In fact Metternich had almost no real influence over the Porte's decision-making
and, therefore, he reached the conclusion later in October that nothing useful could be achieved in Constantinople for the time being and
ordered Ottenfels to suspend all attempts because "it would be impossible for the Divan to be able to understand us and, consequently,
it is useless to talk to it."[104] The internuncio took advantange of every
opportunity to counsel peace, and Huszár actually talked about peace
whenever he had the opportunity, but all without success.[105]

Seeing the absurdity of the situation, Metternich had a certain
understanding for Mahmud II's attitude: "One Great Power openly
at war with the Porte but still continuing to behave as a mediator;
one Great Power, occupying the soil of Morea after having expelled
the Ottoman troops from it, at the same time behaving as a friend
and mediator; a third Great Power friendly, mediating, neutral and
at the same time allied with the Great Power openly at war with
the Porte and with the one that occupies Greece. What a Christian

[103] Blome to Schimmelmann, Odessa, 19 Sept. 1828, attached to Metternich to
Ottenfels, Vienna, 3 Oct. 1828, HHStA, StA, Türkei VI, 35. Even more absurd
is Douglas Dakin's claim that in the second half of 1828 Metternich "constantly
encouraged the Turks to resist all allied proposals." Dakin, p. 263. In fact the
Austrian chancellor advised them to compromise with most of the allied requests
and even in the case of those he disagreed with, like the secondary conference on a
Greek Island, Ottenfels did not advise against sending the Turkish negotiators but
he simply kept silent – in particular because he believed that Mahmud II could not
be persuaded to agree. Ottenfels to Metternich, Constantinople, 12 and 25 Sept.,
10 Oct., 10 and 13 Nov. 1828, HHStA, StA, Türkei VI, 34.
[104] Metternich to Ottenfels, Vienna, 19 Oct. 1828, HHStA, StA, Türkei VI, 35.
[105] Metternich to Ottenfels, Vienna, 17 Sept., 13, 17 and 19 Oct., 20 Nov., 3 Dec.
1828, HHStA, StA, Türkei VI, 35; Metternich to Esterházy, Vienna, 8 Oct. 1828,
HHStA, StA, England 183; Huszár to Ottenfels, 18 and 23 Sept. 1828, Ottenfels to
Pertev, 20 Sept., Ottenfels to Metternich, Constantinople, 25 Sept., 10 Oct.,
10, 13, 25 and 27 Nov., 10 Dec. 1828, HHStA, StA, Türkei VI, 34; Maltzan to
Frederick William III, Vienna, 8 Oct. 1828, GStA PK, HA III, MdA I, 6011; Laval
to La Ferronnays, Vienna, 11 Oct. 1828, AMAE, CP, Autriche 409; Cowley to
Aberdeen, Vienna, 11 and 17 Oct. 1828, TNA, FO 120/94.

cabinet has difficulty understanding, how could the sultan and his counsel themselves possibly make sense of it?"[106] On the other hand, the chancellor so wanted Mahmud II to make some concessions that he sincerely regretted the achievements of the Turks in the war because they, in his opinion, made the sultan blind to the dangers that still threatened him and made him averse to the possibility of terminating the conflict by negotiation. As for the further development of the war, despite some limited successes on the part of the Turks, Metternich predicted correctly that they would not be able to take advantage of the given situation, and he wrote to Ottenfels shortly before the fall of Varna: "If the Moslem nation is brave, its army lacks generals. The Russians have made enormous military mistakes; the Ottomans did not know how to profit from any of them. Their manner of waging war is negative [read: passive], and even if the campaign were to lead to an outcome materially more compromising for the Russians than it has been during their proceedings from the beginning until this moment, it would bring no other remedy to the Turks than [that they would be strengthened in their persuasion] that they knew how to defend their ramparts effectively."[107] Consequently, considering this and the fact that no European country would come to their aid in the war, in late summer Metternich started to regard any serious defeat of the Turkish army as a welcome means for opening the sultan's eyes to reality. Exactly for this reason he welcomed the fall of Varna because he considered this event as the desired way out of the impasse. Nicholas I could interpret an eventual offer for peace negotiations after this victory as an act of clemency on his part, and Mahmud II could do the same thing with the excuse to his people that it was in their best interests after the loss of the city. In brief, the capture of Varna by the Russian army strengthened his hope in the restoration of peace during the winter because the fall of this city "presents itself in this light as a fortunate turn of events. Without a notable success, the Russian emperor could hardly look favourably upon a conciliatory approach towards the Porte. The sultan for his part finds himself to be placed in a rather different position than if Varna had resisted all efforts of

---

[106] Metternich to Apponyi, Vienna, 27 Oct. 1828, HHStA, StA, Frankreich 268. For an almost identical expression see Metternich to Ottenfels, Vienna, 13 Oct. 1828, HHStA, StA, Türkei VI, 35.
[107] Metternich to Ottenfels, Vienna, 3 Oct. 1828, HHStA, StA, Türkei VI, 35.

the besiegers."[108] He used this event as a new attempt to persuade the Turks to replace fighting with negotiations because passing up the opportunity that the forthcoming winter offered would definitely have negative consequences for them: "What is an undeniable truth is that if peace is not restored during this coming winter, then according to all probability next year will see the Porte in a considerably worse situation than it is today."[109] Nevertheless, Mahmud II did not comply with Metternich's wish that he send a Turkish negotiator to the tsar and with the appointment of the brave defender of Varna, Izzet Mehmed Pasha, as grand vizier, clearly demonstrated his determination to continue at war.[110] Under the above-stated circumstances one must regard Metternich's statement made during the Christmas of that year as fairly sincere: "The Russian and Turkish war is not popular in Austria and the reason is too obvious for it to be necessary to explain it; Our public was far from desiring Russian successes but ... if certain persons say that the actual state of affairs must please us, tell them that we are not mad."[111]

A Historical Fabrication: Metternich's Plan for an anti-Russian Alliance

The question that remains to be answered is how the accusation that Metternich planned an anti-Russian coalition originated.[112] Before do-

---

[108] Metternich to Apponyi, Vienna, 27 Oct. 1828, HHStA, StA, Frankreich 268.
[109] Metternich to Ottenfels, Vienna, 5 Nov. 1828, HHStA, StA, Türkei VI, 35.
[110] Metternich to Ottenfels, Vienna, 3 and 13 Oct., 5 Nov. 1828, HHStA, StA, Türkei VI, 35; Metternich to Esterházy, Vienna, 8 Oct. 1828, HHStA, StA, England 183; Ottenfels to Metternich, Constantinople, 29 Oct. 1828, HHStA, StA, Türkei VI, 34; Bray to Ludwig I of Bavaria, Vienna, 10 May, 25, 19 and 28 Oct., 20 Nov. 1828, BHStA, MA, Wien 2402; Brockhausen to Frederick William III, Vienna, 27 Sept. 1828, GStA PK, HA III, MdA I, 6011; Canitz to Stiepovich, Pera, 10 Nov. 1828, Canitz to Frederick William III, Pera, 11 Nov. 1828, GStA PK, HA III, MdA I, 7266; Schwebel to La Ferronnays, Vienna, 3 Aug. 1828, Laval to La Ferronnays, Vienna, 25 and 30 Oct. 1828, AMAE, CP, Autriche 409; Tatishchev to Nesselrode, Vienna, 18 Oct. 1828, AVPRI, fond 133, Kantseliariia, opis 468, 11879.
[111] Metternich to Apponyi, Vienna, 25 Dec. 1828, HHStA, StA, Frankreich 268.
[112] Those who believed this accusation were, for example, Crawley, *Greek Independence*, p. 123, Ringhoffer, pp. 138–139, and Baack, pp. 156–158.

ing so, it is necessary to recall the atmosphere of distrust and suspicions of the aims of the Viennese cabinet since the outbreak of
the war. Already at the beginning of the war this atmosphere gave
rise to the rumour of Austria's proposal for an alliance with Great
Britain allegedly made by Esterházy in London. The inclination of
some people to believe it most likely increased with the change of the
foreign secretary when Dudley was replaced in June 1828 by George
Hamilton Gordon Lord Aberdeen, a man of pro-Greek sympathies but
also on good terms with the cabinet in Vienna, where he had represented his native country at the close of the Napoleonic Wars. His
personal relations with Metternich were almost as friendly as those of
the chancellor with Wellington. Nevertheless, the rumour was absolutely unfounded and even Tatishchev refused to believe it. The rest of
the year was rich with similar stories, for example, the rumour about
the Austro-Swedish anti-Russian offensive alliance from November, as
equally absurd as the previous one.[113]

As for the origin of the rumour concerning the plan for the four
Power's anti-Russian alliance, Metternich later explained it in this
way: "The primary source of the whole rumour is in Berlin. When
last September [1828] I exhorted the British cabinet to put to good
use the coming winter to restore peace between Russia and the Porte,
Count Bernstorff, at that time ill and almost unable to apply himself to serious affairs, was afraid of every idea that could stir up the
issues. After a while he arrived at sounder insights and made honourable amends for his mistake. Inbetween, he had written, no less, to
Mr Bülow in a sense that could only have been interpreted by Prince
Lieven in ways most opposed to our ideas and presented as such to
his cabinet. Since then a series of stories, in which General Pozzo has
not played a secondary role, has gained impetus."[114] What is most
important in this at first sight scarely trustworthy explanation is its
real core as proved by the researched documents. They show that on

---

[113] Cetto to Ludwig I of Bavaria, London, 16 May and 2 June 1828, BHStA, MA,
London 2223; Tatishchev to Nesselrode, Vienna, 25 June and 9 July 1828, AVPRI,
fond 133, Kantseliariia, opis 468, 11879; Maltzan to Frederick William III, Vienna,
25 Nov. 1828, GStA PK, HA III, MdA I, 6011.

[114] Metternich to Apponyi, Vienna, 25 Feb. 1829, HHStA, StA, Frankreich 271.
Metternich's identical explanation can also be found in Tatishchev to Nesselrode,
Vienna, 7 Jan. 1829, AVPRI, fond 133, Kantseliariia, opis 468, 11881; Laval to
Portalis, Vienna, 30 March 1829, AMAE, CP, Autriche 410.

19 September 1828 Metternich communicated to Berlin his instructions to Esterházy of the 14th of the month. Following these instructions, Trauttmannsdorff conveyed to Bernstorff Metternich's desire to
take advantage of the winter pause in the war to restore the peace and
persuade the British cabinet to undertake any steps in this respect.
The Prussian minister agreed and expressed his willingness to act in
this sense, emphasising though that Prussia would never give up its
neutrality. However, Bernstorff clearly misunderstood the real aim of
Metternich's instructions to London – to open the door to a peace settlement by joining forces in persuading the Porte to make concessions
and start negotiations with the Great Powers – and assumed that the
chancellor wanted to go much further in his policy towards Russia.
Bernstorff's illness claimed by Metternich cannot be proved, but it is
certain that when Trauttmannsdorff realised this misinterpretation in
early October, he immediately met the minister again and explained
Austria's main goal to him, which was, as Bernstorff now recognised,
to utilise the winter break "to reach an agreement on a method of
dealing with the Porte."[115] Nevertheless, before this second meeting
Bernstorff sent instructions to London with his own incorrect assumptions which were learnt by Prince Lieven. The Russian ambassador,
who seemed to add some dark interpretations of his own, informed not
only his own court about Metternich's alleged hostile designs against
Russia contained in the memorandum but also his Russian colleague
in Paris. Pozzo di Borgo, whose hatred of Metternich increased due to
the news of the anti-Russian sentiments in Austrian society to such
a level that he was said to deplore them to everybody he met, welcomed the accusation that the Viennese cabinet desired to dictate
with other Great Powers the peace terms to the tsar during the winter, and he informed La Ferronnays and also added in his report for
the tsar some slanderous statements about Apponyi's anti-Russian
memorandum read to the French foreign minister. Tatishchev, blaming Metternich for plotting against Russia and not pressing the Turks
enough to yield, contributed to this rumour with his own opinion
that Austria wanted to use Great Britain against Russia and even by
means of an armed intervention of the four Powers to force Russia to
be more moderate in its peace conditions. In St Petersburg the atmo-

---

[115] Trauttmannsdorff to Metternich, Berlin, 9 Oct. 1828, HHStA, StK, Preussen
128.

sphere of apprehension concerning Austria's designs made Nicholas I and Nesselrode easily disposed to believe the rumour. They addressed bitter complaints to the governments in Berlin, London and Paris of Austria's unfriendly and treacherous conduct with the principal aim of learning more about it.[116]

This led to a rather absurd situation where the cabinets in Berlin, London and Paris were unable to confirm the accusation since none of them had any written evidence nor were verbally addressed by Austrian representatives in this respect. Metternich's diplomats in these cities were extremely surprised and all of them declared that they knew nothing about "a *so-called memorandum written by our cabinet to be presented to those of Europe and that is related to the means of bringing peace to the Levant, that it was from Berlin where the existence of this memorandum was announced* and that not having mentioned its existence to the Russian court was regarded in St Petersburg as a lack of consideration for it."[117] Metternich of course firmly denied the accusation and officially asked the three cabinets for their formal repudiation; they were to declare that such a plan, verbal or written, on the restoration of peace, interference in the war and dictating the peace conditions to Russia had never been presented to them by Austria. Since the plan allegedly had been communicated in Berlin, Metternich personally wrote to Bernstorff on 10 January 1829: "We have learnt – and almost simultaneously – that in St Petersburg, London and Paris there is talk about the peace plan that the Viennese cabinet [is alleged to have] presented to the allies of Rus-

---

[116] Trauttmannsdorff to Metternich, Berlin, 27 Sept. and 9 Oct. 1828, HHStA, StK, Preussen 128; Apponyi to Metternich, Paris, 18 Dec. 1828, HHStA, StA, Frankreich 267; Nesselrode's instructions to Tatishchev conveyed to Metternich on 21 Jan. 1829, attached to Metternich to Ficquelmont, Vienna, 23 Jan. 1829, HHStA, StA, Russland III, 88; Maltzan to Frederick William III, Vienna, 24 Oct. 1828, GStA PK, HA III, MdA I, 6011; Tatishchev to Nesselrode, Vienna, 21 Nov. 1828, AVPRI, fond 133, Kantseliariia, opis 468, 11877; Tatishchev to Nesselrode, Vienna, 7 Jan. 1829, AVPRI, fond 133, Kantseliariia, opis 468, 11881; Agoult to La Ferronnays, Berlin, 10 Nov. 1828, AMAE, CP, Prusse 271; Agoult to La Ferronnays, Berlin, 8 Jan. 1829, Agoult to Portalis, Berlin, 4 Feb. 1829, AMAE, CP, Prusse 272; Bray to Ludwig I of Bavaria, Vienna, 18 March 1829, BHStA, MA, Wien 2402; Bernstorff to Maltzan, Berlin, 22 Dec. 1828, Ringhoffer, p. 388; Ringhoffer, pp. 142–143.

[117] Esterházy to Metternich, London, 17 Dec. 1828, HHStA, StA, England 181; see also Apponyi to Metternich, Paris, 27 Dec. 1828, HHStA, StA, Frankreich 267.

sia and of which the means and goal would be a forced intervention by the courts between Russia and the Porte. In St Petersburg we are accused of this act, in Paris and London one wonders where is then the plan? It is said in these three places that it was the Prussian court which informed them about its existence. It seems that I must inform you of this fact and I am charged at the same time with our response that cannot be anything other than a simple denial. It is thus a rather bad game, but it is not in the corridors of Vienna where the culprits must be sought."[118] In thirteen days he was forced to repeat this answer to Berlin after the arrival of a Russian messenger to Vienna with the instructions for Tatishchev, who had been ordered to inform the chancellor that Russia possessed incontestable proof of Austria's plan to create a coalition of four Great Powers for negotiating the peace conditions and dictating them to Russia. Metternich reacted to this accusation in his second letter to the Prussian minister with the ironic remark that Russia was assigning roles to the surprised actors but in fact no one knew anything about the alleged plan. Therefore, he urged Bernstorff again to say whether such a plan had ever been communicated to him.[119]

Whereas the answers of the governments in London and Paris to Metternich's request were entirely satisfactory for him, this could not be said about Bernstorff's reply which was rather evasive.[120] Historians Karl Ringhoffer and Lawrence J. Baack, believing that the Austrian chancellor wanted to create an anti-Russian coalition of Powers, praised Bernstorff for making a discreet response that was a com-

---

[118] Metternich to Bernstorff, Vienna, 10 Jan. 1829, HHStA, StK, Preussen 132.

[119] Metternich to Bernstorff, Vienna, 23 Jan. 1829, HHStA, StK, Preussen 132; Metternich to Esterházy, Vienna, 5 and 24 Jan. 1829, HHStA, StA, England 187; Metternich to Trauttmannsdorff, Vienna, 11 Jan. 1829, HHStA, StK, Preussen 132; Metternich to Apponyi, Vienna, 25 Feb. 1829, HHStA, StA, Frankreich 271; Maltzan to Frederick William III, Vienna, 31 Dec. 1828, GStA PK, HA III, MdA I, 6011; Tatishchev to Nesselrode, Vienna, 7 Jan. and 1 Feb. 1829, AVPRI, fond 133, Kantseliariia, opis 468, 11881; Cowley to Aberdeen, Vienna, 13 and 24 Jan. 1829, TNA, FO 120/98; Bray to Ludwig I of Bavaria, Vienna, 28 Jan. 1829, BHStA, MA, Wien 2402.

[120] Tatishchev to Nesselrode, Vienna, 17 Feb. 1829, AVPRI, fond 133, Kantseliariia, opis 468, 11881; Laval to Portalis, Vienna, 27 Feb. 1829, AMAE, CP, Autriche 410; Bernstorff to Metternich, Berlin, 3 Jan. and 1 Feb. 1829, HHStA, StK, Preussen 132. The correspondence between Metternich and Bernstorff on this topic from January and February 1829 is also housed in GStA PK, HA III, MdA I, 6093.

promise offending neither Russia nor Austria but also maintaining Prussian honour at the moment when Bernstorff reputedly was well informed about Metternich's hints of the British and French cabinets' acceptance of his plan.[121] Nevertheless, considering the facts, the Prussian minister simply did not want to acknowledge his own mistake that had incited the whole affair.[122] Metternich also understood the answer in this way and decided not to prolong the issue by addressing Bernstorff with a request for a more precise answer: "The explanations given to us by the English and French ministers are as precise as complete, you [Count Ficquelmont, see next chapter] cannot fail to see that Count Bernstorff's answer contains a certain ambiguity or, more correctly a kind of constraint regarding an alleged overture that had been made to him but on which the subject would have been exhausted at the time by means of conclusive debate between our two cabinets. As you fully know to which causes it is necessary to attribute this embarrassment of the Prussian cabinet, I believe it to be more convenient to avoid repeating to you here the tedious details. In Berlin what was not written in ambiguous terms was nonetheless misunderstood. Count Bernstorff hastened at the time to admit with all frankness to a misunderstanding the true sense of which has since that time been regarded as re-established. Now this minister seemed not at all to want to think back to a circumstance painful for his cabinet, and with regard to ourselves, we no longer see any reasonable motive for burdening ourselves in Berlin with a discussion that would soon be more pointless than it is now [and] that in the terms it presents makes no mention of the imputation that has been made on our honour."[123]

---

[121] Baack, pp. 156–158; Ringhoffer, p. 141.

[122] The conversations between the French ambassador in Berlin, Count Hector Philippe d'Agoult, and Bernstorff prove that the minister actually knew nothing about the plan. When in November Bernstorff was asked about the existence of the quadruple alliance allegedly suggested by Metternich, he declared that in late September Metternich's instructions to Esterházy were conveyed to him by Trauttmannsdorff but their content was so ambiguous that he was unable to say any more on the subject. In early 1829, Bernstorff told Agoult that he had no direct knowledge of the alleged Austrian plan and he only knew that this rumour had spread in Paris and London. Agoult to La Ferronnays, Berlin, 10 Nov. 1828, AMAE, CP, Prusse 271; Agoult to Portalis, Berlin, 4 Feb. 1829, AMAE, CP, Prusse 272.

[123] Metternich to Ficquelmont, Vienna, 28 March 1829, HHStA, StA, Russland

On behalf of objectiveness it must be added that informed rumours behind the accusation stemmed from more sources but they
are not very credible and the information is often only second hand.
What is quite surprising is the fact that they were mainly of French
origin. Besides Laval, it was the French ambassador in St Petersburg,
Duke Casimir Rochechouart de Mortemart, visiting Vienna on his way
to Paris, and Orientalist Pierre Amédée Jaubert travelling to Constantinople as an advisor of the resident Dutch representative, Baron
Hugo van Zuylen van Nijevelt. As for Mortemart, he offered rather obscure information that is, moreover, only known from Pozzo to whom
he addressed his letter, and thus not very trustworthy. Jaubert only
reported that Metternich openly told him about the congress where
Russia was to be obliged to accept the conditions of the four Great
Powers. Sauvigny himself did not attribute much credibility to them
and important questions put the truth on his side.[124] First, why would
Metternich, who distrusted and disliked Zuylen so much, talk without
restraint with his advisor and tell him what he did not say to Laval?[125]
Second, why are his alleged anti-Russian proposals contained neither
in his correspondence with Austrian diplomats nor in the dispatches
of his admirer and friend, Lord Cowley, whom he could trust considerably more than either of the Frenchmen and who would be a logical
bearer of Metternich's proposal to the British government?

Essentially the same questions arise in connection with Metternich's alleged talks about a conference or congress from late 1828.
According to Crawley, Metternich proposed a congress with the aim
of forcing Russia to make peace, and Baack mentioned a conference
in this respect.[126] Schroeder claims that Metternich wanted the Maritime Powers to mediate the peace between Russia and the Ottoman
Empire at a congress in Constantinople.[127] The principal source of
this opinion was the Porte's proposal of early November 1828 for a
congress under the auspices of Austria and Prussia where the peace
between the Ottoman Empire and Russia and its guarantee by the
two German Powers was to be discussed.[128] Ottenfels summarised

---

III, 88.

[124] Sauvigny, *Metternich et la France*, III, pp. 1214–1219.

[125] Metternich to Ottenfels, Vienna, 20 Aug. 1828, HHStA, StA, Türkei VI, 35.

[126] Crawley, *Greek Independence*, p. 123; Baack, p. 156.

[127] Schroeder, *Transformation*, p. 656.

[128] Ottenfels to Metternich, Constantinople, 10 Nov. and 10 Dec. 1828, HHStA,

the Porte's wish on 12 December: "A congress that would determine what the Treaty of 6 July left unresolved and vague, a congress that would guarantee to the Porte the stability and its peace with Russia, finally a congress where Turkey would be accepted and recognised as an integral party of the European political system, such is the desire of Sultan Mahmud. If his ministry did not convey till this time this intention to anyone other than the representative of the Austrian court, it is because the Viennese cabinet is the only one in which he has unlimited confidence, [and] it is because he expects from only you, my Prince, a frank and impartial discussion on the possibility and the means of execution of a proposition like this."[129] It was presumed by Metternich's contemporaries or later by Douglas Dakin that this proposal had been secretly advised by Metternich,[130] definitely quite a logical assumption, but the studied documents do not contain even the slightest hint of it from Metternich to the Turks. The idea actually originated in Constantinople without any suggestion on the part of Austria. Maltzan even reported that Metternich opposed the Porte's idea of the congress,[131] and to Laval Metternich expressed the unfeasibility of the plan: "The congress is impossible, Russia will never submit to this condition."[132] On the other hand, Laval reported on 19 November that Metternich indirectly and in a vague way mentioned a congress and the French ambassador was convinced that Metternich wanted to use it against Russia.[133] Tatishchev also wrote to Nesselrode that Metternich joined the proposal of sending French and British representatives to Constantinople with the often repeated idea of the congress of five Great Powers. As well as Laval, Tatishchev supposed that at such a congress Metternich wanted to submit the Turko-Russian conflict to international arbitration. He was led to this opinion by the fact that the Porte joined its idea of a congress with the desire to place the peace under the Great Powers' guarantee.[134]

StA, Türkei VI, 34.

[129] Ottenfels to Metternich, Constantinople, 10 Dec. 1828, HHStA, StA, Türkei VI, 34.

[130] Dakin, p. 263.

[131] Maltzan to Frederick William III, Vienna, 2 Dec. 1828, GStA PK, HA III, MdA I, 6011.

[132] Laval to La Ferronnays, Vienna, 12 Dec. 1828, AMAE, CP, Autriche 410.

[133] Laval to La Ferronnays, Vienna, 19 Nov. and 1 Dec. 1828, AMAE, CP, Autriche 410.

[134] Tatishchev to Nesselrode, Vienna, 21 and 30 Nov. 1828, AVPRI, fond 133,

However, it is difficult to attach much importance to Metternich's alleged suggestion concerning the congress. First, this idea is missing in his correspondence. Second, Cowley's reports kept silent in this respect and the conference mentioned by him and quoted earlier in the chapter was not to be held in Constantinople but London and its aim was not a union of four Powers to discuss measures to be taken against Russia with the aim of forcing the tsar to agree with disadvantagous peace conditons but the agreement of five Powers for their proceeding towards the Porte with the aim of compelling it to yield.

*   *   *

A considerable number of evidently false accusations made against Metternich during 1828 compel a historian to much vigilance in the case of others which seem to be also false or, at least, generally exaggerated. The main problem in deciphering his real aims is not whether they were directed against Russia, they definitely were, but how far he was willing to go in this respect and what he actually was suggesting to the other Powers in September and October. What was anti-Russian in his goals was that he wished a prompt peace settlement with mild conditions for the Porte. In the summer of 1828, he definitely hoped that the position of the sultan would be improved by a quick settlement of the Greek Question and the consequent improvement of relations between him and the Maritime Powers, in particular Great Britain. Although with most probability he did not intend to go as far as Gentz dreamed, he wanted to see Wellington's ministry forcing the tsar to restraint by more expressed firmness and he would have definitely welcomed Great Britain – and also France although it was much less probable – urging both parties at war to peace, even with some sort of mediation as Schroeder claims. Nevertheless, in mid September when the composition of the well-known anti-Russian plan was generally attributed to him, he lost most of his faith in Britain's policy and he was strongly dissatisfied with Wellington's passivity that dispelled his hopes in the prime minister's more decisive conduct against Russia. Consequently, if he had still possessed some faith in any change, and

Kantseliariia, opis 468, 11877.

he had hidden some suggestions in this respect in his instructions to London or Paris, his practical steps were actually aimed at persuading Mahmud II – with the help of other Powers staying out of the war – to open peace negotiations and make some concessions, both regarded by the prince as entirely necessary for the attainment of peace during the winter months. One can never forget that Metternich's caution resulted from not only the disclination of France, Great Britain and Prussia to follow a more active course towards Russia but also from his knowledge of Austria's internal weakness, its need of good relations with Russia in the future and Francis I's strong inclination to neutrality.

Whatever goal Metternich pursued in late 1828, he completely failed to achieve it. Neither the war nor the Greek insurrection was settled and Austria's relations with Russia reached freezing-point. Nicholas I and Nesselrode were dissatisfied not only with the rumours of various anti-Russian measures on the parts of the chancellor but also his attempts to contribute to the settlement of the Greek Question and the sending of the British and French ambassadors to Constantinople. They feared considerably the creation of an Austro-British alliance[135] and their strong disapproval of Metternich's behaviour seemed to be expressed with the aim of intimidating him and making him passive. If this really was their goal, they were entirely successful because their strong criticism directed to Vienna together with the British and French inaction persuaded Metternich on the turn of 1828 and 1829 to assume the attitude of a mere observer in both the Greek Question as well as the Russo-Ottoman conflict, and his passivity was characteristic for his conduct until the end of the war, the outcome of which he predicted quite well: "Little accustomed to indulging ourselves in illusions, we accept as entirely consistent with the nature of things the arrival of the Russian armies beneath the walls of Constantinople as the certain consequence of the renewal of the offensive by these armies in 1829."[136]

---

[135] Bitis, pp. 303–304.
[136] Metternich to Ottenfels, Vienna, 20 Nov. 1828, HHStA, StA, Türkei VI, 35.

9

The Russo-Ottoman War: The Second Campaign and the Treaty of Adrianople

With the arrival of the year 1829 Metternich became particularly anxious to improve Austria's relations with Russia and considerably passive in his activities regarding the Eastern Question. He made no significant contribution to Ottoman affairs until the end of the war in September. He regarded the peace conditions imposed by the tsar on the sultan as severe but could cope with them since above all he welcomed the restoration of peace. As in the previous year, he again became the victim of unfounded rumours, now accusing him of proposing to the tsar the partition of the Ottoman Empire. To believe this allegation, as some historians have, would be to totally misunderstand Metternich's maxims in his Near Eastern policy.

Metternich Strives for More Cordial Relations with Russia

Metternich's restrained attitude towards the war assumed on the turn of 1828 and 1829 also resulted from his awareness that neither the Great Powers nor the Ottoman Empire were willing to proceed according to his counsel for peace. The French government continued to be considerably pro-Russian and together with the British cabinet distrusted Metternich from whom they both expected the achievement of some concessions in Constantinople. The sultan, however, firmly refused to make any. The court in Berlin did not want to do anything that could harm its neutrality, and the affair with Metternich's alleged anti-Russian plan and the following dispute between him and Bernstorff naturally did not help to overcome Prussia's passivity in any way; even though the relations between the two German

Powers were generally good, they were far from being cordial. Under these circumstances, Metternich began to search for a return to better relations with Russia, whose governmental and military elites considerably disapproved of his actions in the preceding year. Consequently, from early 1829, Metternich's priorities were, first, the improvement of Austro-Russian relations and, second, the restoration of peace in the Near East to which he was willing to contribute if asked to do so, but he resigned himself to being active independently.

The chill existing between the courts in Vienna and St Petersburg had its roots in 1825 and it reached its climax on the turn of 1828 and 1829. A factor which considerably contributed to this situation was the absence of a skilled and active representative in St Petersburg after Lebzeltern's departure in mid 1826. His successors played no important role in local society and none in Austro-Russian relations at all. Chargé d'Affaires Count Heinrich von Bombelles and Ambassador Count Stephan von Zichy representing Francis I from 1826 to 1828 were only transitory figures without any influence. In particular Zichy's lack of skill and considerable inactivity in early 1828 deprived Metternich of any means of influencing the Russian cabinet's decision-making on the eve of war – although it must be recognised that even with Lebzeltern it would have been an impossible task to change Nicholas I's attitude. Zichy, labouring with illness and avoiding contact with the Russians as well as foreigners as much as he could, ceased to inform Metternich from early 1828 and consequently all important communications to St Petersburg had to be made through letters directly sent to the tsar and his vice-chancellor or through Tatishchev. After Zichy's departure in early July 1828, Austria was officially represented by the chargé d'affaires, Maximilian von Kaisersfeld, but a more important role was performed in this respect by the Prince of Hesse-Homburg, functioning in the tsar's headquarters as a link between the two emperors. The prince had already been sent by Francis I to St Petersburg on the occasion of Nicholas I's coronation in 1826, and he was treated by the tsar and his wife in a most friendly manner despite the deterioration in relations of the two countries. In early 1828, when Metternich wanted to be well informed about the campaign and did not want to offend the tsar by not sending a high military officer when Prussia had decided to do so, the Prince of Hesse-Homburg was a logical choice. He arrived in Odessa in August and spent considerable time with the tsar, who also invited him to the Russian capital when the first campaign was over. There, the prince was accommodated in the imperial palace and enjoyed the same favours as two years earlier. The Bavarian envoy in St Petersburg reported to his king in December that "the Prince of Hesse-Homburg is still here. He enjoys the privilege of being welcomed daily in the society of their majesties and of accompanying the emperor on parade every morning. The officers from his retinue also always assist in the military inspections and generally participate in the distinguished receptions with which the prince is favoured. The emperor ordered that all public establishments and interesting places in the capital are shown to these gentlemen, he appointed an officer to accompany them, and having remarked on one of the last days that they seemed to be sensitive to the extreme cold weather, he sent them beautiful furs."[1] Unsurprisingly, shortly before the prince's departure in early March 1829 a large military parade took place in his honour.[2]

Nevertheless, the Prince of Hesse-Homburg was not a diplomat in the classic sense of the word and he also did not assume the role of an ordinary representative. His mission to the tsar merely was a temporary solution and it was shown to be insufficient when Austro-Russian relations reached their lowest level. Consequently, in early January 1829, Metternich informed Francis I that he had decided to send the Austrian major general, Count Karl Ludwig von Ficquel-mont, who was at the time the envoy in Naples, to St Petersburg as a special envoy. As in the Prince of Hesse-Homburg's case, this choice was also not surprising since Ficquelmont had been a serious candidate for representing the Austrian emperor in Russia in 1826, but his plotting and garrulous Russian mother-in-law Princess Elisabeth Kutuzov had proved to be an insuperable problem; Metternich had written to Lebzeltern that he would like to replace him with Ficquelmont, who was very suitable for the diplomatic post in St Petersburg but that

---

[1]   Lerchenfeld to Ludwig I of Bavaria, St Petersburg, 6 Dec. 1828, BHStA, MA, Petersburg 2716.
[2]   Gise to Ludwig I of Bavaria, St Petersburg, 28 Feb., 12 April, 21 June and 17 Oct. 1828, Lerchenfeld to Ludwig I of Bavaria, St Petersburg, 5 July, 27 Aug., 1 and 19 Nov., 6 Dec. 1828, BHStA, MA, Petersburg 2716; Lerchenfeld to Ludwig I of Bavaria, St Petersburg, 21 Feb. and 7 March 1829, BHStA, MA, Petersburg 2717; Tatishchev to Nesselrode, Vienna, 25 May, 4 and 25 June 1828, AVPRI, fond 133, Kantseliariia, opis 468, 11879; Maltzan to Frederick William III, Vienna, 10 June 1828, GStA PK, HA III, MdA I, 6011; Cowley to Dudley, Vienna, 10 and 13 June 1828, TNA, FO 120/92; Krauter, p. 216.

he had been unable to "entrust madam Hitroff with the mission!"[3] In 1829, when a skilled representative in the proximity of the tsar was much needed, the choice finally fell on Ficquelmont, who was generally highly regarded for his diplomatic talent, intelligence, moderation, honesty and conciliatory and friendly demeanour. Moreover, he was a soldier, which was supposed would please the tsar; Tatishchev sharing the generally positive estimation labelled him a "military diplomat."[4] Ficquelmont was instructed by Metternich with the task of improving the two Powers' relations, dispelling the concerns existing in St Petersburg with regard to Austria's designs and armaments and discovering anti-Austrian intrigues. The chancellor also expressed his recognition of Russia as the only trilateral Power clear about its own aims and successfully pursuing them, his regret that Nesselrode had become as much anti-Austrian as he had been earlier pro-Austrian and his belief that Nicholas I sincerely wished peace. After his arrival in St Petersburg on 9 February 1829, Ficquelmont soon gained the tsar's trust and enjoyed a similar favour as had the Prince of Hesse-Homburg, and he actually succeeded in lessening tensions between the two courts and ending the discussion about the alleged anti-Russian plan. Nevertheless, the hatred and distrust spread among the Russians against Metternich was still on a very high level and whereas Nicholas I praised Francis I, his expressions concerning the chancellor were still of quite a different nature. As Tatishchev told Laval: "The latest discussions in which this [Austrian] cabinet deigned [to participate] with the aim of exonerating itself from its despicable conduct last year had no other effect than to make our relations easier, without making them more sincere."[5] There still was a long way to go to a full understanding, and Meyendorff's words conveyed to Bray that the friction between the two countries had eased considerably "but one cannot count on any true rapport as long as the war with the Porte lasts"[6] later proved to be prophetic. Until the end of the Russo-Ottoman conflict nothing considerably changed in the two countries' relations but the foundation stone of the process later leading to the

---

[3] Metternich to Lebzeltern, Vienna, 2 Feb. 1826, Mikhaïlowitch, p. 320.
[4] Tatishchev to Nesselrode, Vienna, 3 Nov. 1828, AVPRI, fond 133, Kantseliariia, opis 468, 11877.
[5] Laval to Portalis, Vienna, 11 May 1829, AMAE, CP, Autriche 410.
[6] Bray to Ludwig I of Bavaria, Vienna, 8 April 1829, BHStA, MA, Wien 2402.

restoration of their friendly relations was laid and Metternich, satisfied with Ficquelmont's proceeding, ensured his appointment as an ordinary ambassador in June 1829.[7]

What also contributed to allay the tsar's exasperation caused by various anti-Austrian rumours in late 1828 was the certainty in early 1829 that Austria would not undertake any hostile military measure against Russia's second campaign. The Russian general, Count Alexander Stroganov, leaving Vienna on 29 January, brought to Nicholas I the assurances of Francis I and Metternich that they had not had and did not have any hostile intentions against Russia, which was also proved by the unchanged situation in the Austrian army that, as Stroganov informed the tsar, represented no danger for the Russians.[8] Metternich also frequently assured Tatishchev in this respect: "I repeat to you that I do not accept the possibility of war between Russia and us – the Oriental affair appears to me of a secondary interest in comparison with the dangers which threaten us in Western Europe and which will occupy our all attention while you continue

---

[7] Metternich to Francis I, Vienna, 9 Jan. 1829, HHStA, StK, Vorträge 257; Metternich to Francis I, Vienna, 16 and 19 June 1829, HHStA, StK, Vorträge 258; Metternich to Bernstorff, Vienna, 10 Jan. 1829, HHStA, StK, Preussen 132; Metternich to Ficquelmont, Vienna, 17 Jan. and 28 March 1829, HHStA, StA, Russland III, 88; Tatishchev to Nesselrode, Vienna, 31 Jan. 1826, AVPRI, fond 133, Kantseliariia, opis 468, 11870; Tatishchev to Nesselrode, Vienna, 7 Jan. and 26 Feb. 1829, AVPRI, fond 133, Kantseliariia, opis 468, 11881; Lerchenfeld to Ludwig I of Bavaria, St Petersburg, 11 and 12 Feb., 17 March, 22 April and 8 July 1829, BHStA, MA, Petersburg 2717; Bray to Ludwig I of Bavaria, Vienna, 14 Jan., 8 and 18 March 1829, BHStA, MA, Wien 2402; Bourgoing to Portalis, St Petersburg, 10 and 23 Feb. 1829, AMAE, CP, Russie 177; Caraman to Damas, Vienna, 26 Jan. 1826, AMAE, CP, Autriche 407; Caraman to Damas, Vienna, 7 March 1827, AMAE, CP, Autriche 408; Laval to Portalis, Vienna, 28 May 1829, AMAE, CP, Autriche 410; Nesselrode to Tatishchev, St Petersburg, 12 March 1829, Prokesch-Osten, *Griechen*, VI, pp. 40–41.

[8] Bitis, p. 305. According to the reports of foreign representatives in Vienna, the changes in the Austrian army in 1829 were insignificant and though it gradually continued to be increased to the peace-time level, this state had not been achieved when the war was over. Tatishchev to Nesselrode, Vienna, 1 Feb., 8 March and 17 April 1829, AVPRI, fond 133, Kantseliariia, opis 468, 11881; Tatishchev to Nesselrode, Vienna, 18 Oct. 1829, AVPRI, fond 133, Kantseliariia, opis 468, 11885; Bray to Ludwig I of Bavaria, Vienna, 18 March and 27 April 1829, BHStA, MA, Wien 2402. According to Bertrand Michael Buchmann, the number of soldiers who could be employed in a campaign even decreased from 195,133 in 1828 to 194,367 in 1829. Buchmann, *Militär – Diplomatie – Politik*, p. 68.

your quarrels with the Turks in the second *campaign during which you can rest assured that we will remain neutral and peaceful spectators as in the past.*[9] Tatishchev believed this assurance because he could not fail to notice Metternich's effort to improve relations with Russia and not to "lose any occasion to demonstrate to me his desire of the rapprochement of the two empires' policies. He bases the necessity of this rapprochement upon the need of order and tranquillity in Europe."[10] Tatishchev also regarded as proof of the Viennese cabinet's restraint the fact that the *Österreichischer Beobachter* had not published any information offending Russia for a long time. In reality, as explained in the previous chapter, these newspapers had not actually issued any anti-Russian articles earlier. Tatishchev's satisfaction was caused in reality by an interval in reports about the events in the theatre of operations simply because the war was interrupted during the winter. What, on the other hand, really proved Austria's desire to improve its relations with Russia was Francis I's consent to the sale of Hungarian grain to the Russian troops. Grain was also being supplied to the Turkish soldiers, however, and Austria was thus secretly selling this commodity to the two parties at war in order to maintain good relations with both.[11]

Metternich Walks a Tightrope between St Petersburg and Constantinople

This goal was difficult to achieve since the conflict in the East still was in progress and Metternich found himself in a compromised situation with his desire to be on more or less good terms with both countries with contradictory interests and requests. Austria's delicate position can be well characterised, for example, with Metternich's re-

---

[9]   The last part of the text was twice underlined by Nesselrode. Tatishchev to Nesselrode, Vienna, 17 Feb. 1829, AVPRI, fond 133, Kantseliariia, opis 468, 11881.
[10]   Tatishchev to Nesselrode, Vienna, 26 Feb. 1829, AVPRI, fond 133, Kantseliariia, opis 468, 11881.
[11]   Francis I to the governor of Transylvania, 8 May 1829, Tatishchev to Nesselrode, Vienna, 26 Feb. 1829, AVPRI, fond 133, Kantseliariia, opis 468, 11881; Laval to La Ferronnays, Vienna, 23 Dec. 1828, AMAE, CP, Autriche 410; Stiepovich [?] to Royer, Pera, 22 June 1829, GStA PK, HA III, MdA I, 7267.

fusal to agree to the marriage of an employee of the internunciature to a daughter of a man earlier serving as the first dragoman of the Russian embassy. Since this marriage could cause the Porte's displeasure and affect its relations with Austria, the wedding had to be postponed until Russia and Turkey were at peace when it was actually permitted by Metternich. Nevertheless, a sacrifice of a personal happiness finally did not save Austria's position in Constantinople because by far the most serious measure considerably affecting Austria's commerce, the Russian blockade of the Dardanelles, had a negative impact on its relations with not only the perpetrator of the blockade but also the Ottoman Empire. Since the Black Sea was an important trade route for the Austrians and, moreover, because they were the most important shippers of grain from Egypt to Constantinople since the beginning of the war, Metternich was greatly embarrassed when he learnt in late 1828 that the Russian fleet operating in the Mediterranean would soon begin the blockade of the Dardanelles. His resentment was all the greater owing to Nicholas I's previous pledge that the Russians would not harm European trade in the Levant. The chancellor bitterly complained to Tatishchev that the intended blockade would be "ruinous for the Austrian commerce in the Mediterranean,"[12] he addressed protests to St Petersburg and hoped that the two Maritime Powers would not recognise it, but all in vain. Nicholas I had no reason to grant Austria's requests and since the British and French governments were reconciled to the blockade, nothing could prevent the Russian squadron from closing the Hellespont on 19 November 1828 to all ships carrying food or war material. What further deepened the indignation of the Austrians was, first, that the period of six weeks between its announcement and the blockade was not maintained as was a general custom and also settled between Heyden and the Austrian commander of the Levant squadron, Admiral Silvestro Dandolo, on 30 May 1828 and, second, that Austrian ships were exempted from Nesselrode's concession of 7 November 1828 that all British and French ships with whatsoever cargo leaving the Mediterranean ports for Constantinople before the end of October would be permitted to sail through the Dardanelles. Dandolo and Metternich tried in vain to obtain the same concession for Austria that had been accorded

---

[12] Tatishchev to Nesselrode, Vienna, 21 Nov. 1828, AVPRI, fond 133, Kantseliariia, opis 468, 11877.

to the Maritime Powers and the six-week interim period between the announcement and the commencement of the blockade.[13]

The closure of the sea passage from the Mediterranean to the Sea of Marmara caused serious problems with the food supply to Constantinople, where the lack of staples increased to such an extent that even the highest Ottoman dignitaries including the sultan, who had forgotten to make sufficient reserves of grain, daily sent their servants for fresh white bread to Ottenfels, who had not made a similar mistake and had ensured that the internunciature had been sufficiently supplied with flour. Nevertheless, as Ottenfels had rightly presumed, the main goal of the blockade, the starvation of the capital, was not achieved because its supply from the Black Sea (the Bosphorus remained unwatched by the Russians) and by land progressively replaced the deficiency caused by the blockade. Those who finally suffered the most were the merchant ships from neutral countries, above all the Austrians, which were harmed not only in the Mediterranean but also, and in particular, in the Black Sea where a considerable number of their captains were closed in with their ships. The need to feed the garrisons led around 70 of them to enter Russia's service and agree to the transportation of grain for the tsarist army fighting in Bulgaria. The Russian officials, however, misused them for the transport of weapons and troops as well. The Austrian consul general in Odessa, Karl von Thom, forbade the captains to enter Russian ser-

---

[13] Metternich to Esterházy, Vienna, 14 Sept. 1828, HHStA, StA, England 183; Metternich to Francis I, Vienna, 8 March 1829, HHStA, StK, Vorträge 257; Metternich to Ottenfels, Vienna, 13 Oct. 1828, HHStA, StA, Türkei VI, 35; Metternich to Ottenfels, Vienna, 17 Nov. 1829, HHStA, StA, Türkei VIII, 24; Heyden to Dandolo, Malta, 18 Oct. 1828, Dandolo to Heyden, Smyrna, 16 Nov. 1828, Ricord to Dandolo, the Dardanelles, 21 Nov. 1828, Ottenfels to Metternich, Constantinople, 10 and 25 Oct., 25 Nov. and 10 Dec. 1828, HHStA, StA, Türkei VI, 34; Dandolo to Heyden, Smyrna, 2 Feb. 1829, Ottenfels to Metternich, Constantinople, 25 Feb. 1829, HHStA, StA, Türkei VI, 36; Ottenfels to Metternich, Constantinople, 28 April 1829, HHStA, StA, Türkei VI, 37; Maltzan to Frederick William III, Vienna, 21 Nov. 1828, GStA PK, HA III, MdA I, 6011; Cowley to Aberdeen, Vienna, 19 Oct. 1828, TNA, FO 120/94; Cowley to Aberdeen, Vienna, 31 March 1829, TNA, FO 120/99; Tatishchev to Nesselrode, Vienna, 20 Dec. 1828, AVPRI, fond 133, Kantseliariia, opis 468, 11877; Tatishchev to Nesselrode, Vienna, 7 Jan. 1829, AVPRI, fond 133, Kantseliariia, opis 468, 11881; Laval to La Ferronnays, Vienna, 22 Dec. 1828, AMAE, CP, Autriche 410; Laval to Portalis, Vienna, 26 June 1829, AMAE, CP, Autriche 411; Prokesch-Osten, *Griechen*, II, p. 306; Schiemann, II, p. 231.

vice in December 1828 but they did not obey this order. If they had done so, the loss of their service would have caused serious logistic problems to the Russians. Consequently, the St Petersburg cabinet became nervous of such an eventuality and to forestall it Tatishchev raised protests against Thom's order in early January 1829. Metternich, finding himself in a difficult situation, answered that the cabinet had merely been insisting that Austrian ships with Russian cargoes and soldiers did not sail to the places still held by the Turks but they should be allowed to freely enter the places already occupied by the Russian army. He also immediately sent corresponding instructions to Thom, and after Tatishchev's renewed complaints he dispatched them again a month later. Consequently, the Austrian ships continued to serve the Russians and Thom was soon replaced. Although his withdrawal had already been suggested by Metternich to Francis I in December 1828 and explained by Thom's illness and advanced years, his anti-Russian conduct and Metternich's desire to see a person more suitable for the post of not only economic but also, since the beginning of war, political importance seem to be the most important reasons for Thom's replacement. The fact that Metternich hastened to inform the governor general of New Russia, the southern provinces of the Russian Empire above the Black Sea and the Sea of Azov including Odessa, Prince Mikhail Semyonovich Vorontsov, personally about this change is more than eloquent.[14]

---

[14] Metternich to Thom, Vienna, 3 Jan. and 4 Feb. 1829, HHStA, StK, Konsulate, Odessa 32; Metternich to Francis I, Vienna, 20 Dec. 1828, HHStA, StK, Vorträge 256; Metternich to Francis I, Vienna, 17 July 1829, HHStA, StK, Vorträge 259; Metternich to Esterházy, Vienna, 30 May 1829, HHStA, StA, England 187; Metternich to Vorontsov, Vienna, 8 Feb. 1829, Vorontsov to Metternich, Odessa, 22 March 1829, HHStA, StA, Russland III, 88; Ottenfels to Metternich, Constantinople, 25 Nov. and 10 Dec. 1828, HHStA, StA, Türkei VI, 34; Ottenfels to Metternich, Constantinople, 10 March 1829, HHStA, StA, Türkei VI, 36; Ottenfels to Metternich, Constantinople, 25 May 1829, HHStA, StA, Türkei VI, 37; Tatishchev to Nesselrode, Vienna, 7 Jan., 1 Feb. and 8 March 1829, AVPRI, fond 133, Kantseliariia, opis 468, 11881; Cowley to Aberdeen, Vienna, 21 Jan. 1829, TNA, FO 120/98; Cowley to Aberdeen, Vienna, 30 May 1829, TNA, FO 120/100; Brockhausen to Frederick William III, Vienna, 27 May and 12 June 1829, GStA PK, HA III, MdA I, 6012; Laval to Portalis, Vienna, 11 June 1829, AMAE, CP, Autriche 411; Bourgoing to La Ferronnays, St Petersburg, 27 Dec. 1828, AMAE, CP, Russie 175; the French consul in Odessa to Mortemart, 12 Dec. 1828, AMAE, CP, Russie 176; Ottenfels, *Memoari*, pp. 209–210; Ringhoffer, p. 140.

When the problem concerning navigation in the Black Sea was settled with Russia, an outburst of indignation came from Constantinople where the activities of the Austrian ships later became known. Pertev Effendi had already been offended by Dandolo's recognition of the blockade and had accused Austria of complicity and weakness. Ottenfels' explanation that the admiral could do nothing else at that moment when other European countries had recognised it and when any attempt to get through would inevitably lead to the outbreak of war between Austria and Russia made little impression on the Ottoman foreign minister. Consequently, Pertev's attitude towards Ottenfels was already hostile when the news of the Austrian captains' activities arrived in Constantinople in late April 1829. Although Ottenfels managed to prove that they sailed a good distance away from the war zone, Pertev exploded with anger and anti-Austrian accusations of all kinds, which forced Huszár to leave Pertev's office immediately and Ottenfels to break off contact with him until the moment when Pertev apologised for his undiplomatic behaviour. Metternich reacted with a short response deprecating the conduct of the captains and making the excuse that Austria could do nothing at that moment. This was basically true, but in reality he was also not willing to intervene because he did not want to provoke any new protests from Russia. Although the whole affair soon came to an end, this event definitely contributed to a considerable loss of Austria's influence in Constantinople.[15]

There was one more important reason for the deterioration of Austria's position in the Ottoman capital as well as Pertev Effendi's embitterment: Austria's rejection of the sultan's offer of an offensive and defensive alliance of 7 February 1829 when this proposal was communicated by Pertev to the surprised Huszár. For Austria's consent to its participation in the war, Mahmud II had offered to Francis I two tiny strips of land traversing the Austrian possession of Dalmatia close to Dubrovnik – Klek and Sutorina – and some small and

---

[15] Metternich to Ottenfels, Vienna, 20 May 1829, HHStA, StA, Türkei VI, 39; Pertev to Ottenfels, 11 Feb. 1829, Ottenfels to Pertev, Constantinople, 13 Feb. 1829, Ottenfels to Metternich, Constantinople, 22 Feb. 1829, HHStA, StA, Türkei VI, 36; Huszár to Ottenfels, 28 April and 7 June 1829, Thom to Ottenfels, Odessa, 8 April 1829, Ottenfels to Adelburg, 30 April 1829, Ottenfels to Metternich, Constantinople, 28 April, 14 May, 8 and 25 June 1829, HHStA, StA, Türkei VI, 37; Prokesch-Osten, *Griechen*, II, p. 324.

not clearly defined territorial concessions in Moldavia and Wallachia. For Metternich such an alliance was absolutely unacceptable because Austria could not go to war against Russia and not at all for small territorial concessions, even if Klek and Sutorina had strategic importance for the Danube Monarchy as will be seen later.[16] Metternich gave Constantinople the explanation that Francis I had no territorial desires and in no way wanted to give up the neutrality he had assumed at the beginning of the war. He ended his rejection with the repeated advice to negotiate a peace settlement instead of continuing fighting: "We believe that we know quite precisely what Russia wants. It wants to conserve its right of protectorate over the Principalities; it does not intend to surrender the ports of Anapa and Poti. It wants diplomatic arrangements concerning the transportation of goods from these ports into the Black Sea. We do not believe that its real designs exceed these limits. Why would the Porte not eagerly seize every chance to reconcile itself on these bases with its more powerful neighbour?"[17] What also strengthened Metternich's decisive rejection of the sultan's offer was the Turks' inactivity in military affairs during the winter, which greatly surprised Metternich, who believed that if they took advantage of the problems weighing upon the Russian army, they could easily chase its forces from the right bank of the Danube and take back Varna. Metternich wrote to Ottenfels in December 1828: "The most incomprehensible short-sightedness reduced the Russian forces to such a state that their expulsion would be child's play to any troops other than the Turks."[18] Consequently, he entirely agreed with the internuncio that any military alliance with the Ottoman Empire would mean that the Austrians would assume the burden of war whereas the Turks would remain inactive in the safety of their strongholds. And he also continued to share Ottenfels' scant belief in the victory of the Turks if the war were revived in the spring, in particular when he learnt the name of the new commander of the Russian army in the Balkans, Count Ivan Ivanovich Diebitsch.[19]

---

[16] See Chapter 22.
[17] Metternich to Ottenfels, Vienna, 19 March 1829, HHStA, StA, Türkei VI, 39.
[18] Metternich to Ottenfels, Vienna, 18 Dec. 1828, HHStA, StA, Türkei VI, 35.
[19] Metternich to Esterházy, Vienna, 2 Dec. 1828, HHStA, StA, England 184; Metternich to Ottenfels, Vienna, 3 Jan., 4 Feb., 19 March and 3 April 1829, HHStA, StA, Türkei VI, 39; Huszár to Ottenfels, 7 Feb. 1829, Ottenfels to Metternich, Constantinople, 22 Feb., 26 and 27 March, 12 April 1829, HHStA, StA, Türkei VI,

Metternich and the London Protocol of 22 March 1829

Much as Metternich saw little prospect in a Turkish victory, he also still desired the French and British ambassadors' prompt return to Constantinople because their presence in the Ottoman capital could expedite the settlement of the Greek Question or at least it could not make the sultan's situation worse. He also wanted the Porte to open peace negotiations with Russia. Therefore, Ottenfels continued to prepare the way to the restoration of the diplomatic relations between the two sides in early 1829 and to persuade the Porte to accept the conditions requested by the allies. Nevertheless, no significant change in the Porte's attitude occurred. Mahmud II was willing to talk with the British and French ambassadors, whom he formally invited to return to his capital, but refused to do so with the Russian or Greek agents as demanded by the trilateral Powers. In the same manner, he repeatedly refused to start negotiations with Russia as proved not only by his proposal for the anti-Russian alliance with Austria but also by his earlier refusal to take advantage of a way to open peace talks when a parliamentary Russian brig had arrived in Constantinople in early January 1829 with a proposal for the exchange of war prisoners and for the dispatch of a Turkish plenipotentiary to Akkerman, where peace talks should start. He did not become more conciliatory even later when in early April Ottenfels tried to persuade him to exchange war prisoners and use this event for sending the Turkish negotiators to the tsar; an Austrian ship was even offered by the internuncio for that purpose.[20] Metternich understood that it was difficult for the sultan

---

36.

[20] In early June, some Russian prisoners were finally sent home on an Austrian ship but this manifestation of goodwill was not connected with an attempt for opening peace talks as it had earlier been advised by Ottenfels. Ottenfels to Huszár, 31 Dec. 1828 and 2 Jan. 1829, Huszár to Ottenfels, 3 and 17 Jan. 1829, Pertev to Zuylen, Constantinople, 22 Jan. 1829, Ottenfels to Metternich, Constantinople, 6, 10 and 26 Jan., 10 Feb. and 12 April 1829, HHStA, StA, Türkei VI, 36; Ottenfels to Metternich, Constantinople, 8 June 1829, HHStA, StA, Türkei VI, 37. The Russian proposal for peace negotiations from early January 1829 was veiled with mystery since Nicholas I claimed that it was undertaken in reaction on the Porte's original proposal from the previous year, but the Turks denied that any initiative in this respect had come from them. Metternich did not believe the Russian version that the instigation had come from Constantinople because he saw

to discuss the Greek Question with the agents of the insurgents or the Great Power with whom he was at war. The chancellor criticised the allies for these demands which they must have known the sultan was bound to reject, but he was also convinced that in general Mahmud II, confronted with the overwhelming superiority of the trilateral alliance, had to become considerably more conciliatory.[21]

As the weeks went by, Metternich believed less and less that peace could be restored before the end of the winter because the attitudes of the Great Powers and the Ottoman Empire did not change from the previous year and none of the existing problems seemed any closer to a solution. In mid February, he wrote to Trauttmannsdorff: "Winter is coming to an end. The immense distances which separate the various places where the most important questions of this moment are negotiated also essentially contribute to limiting the advantages that the winter season could offer in favour of a rapprochement between the parties. In the meantime England occupies itself with its interior legislation, France advances on the same pretext towards a revolution in the kingdom and aims for one in Europe; the Russian emperor, completely desirous of peace, is blocking his route to it with new propositions which he passes on to his allies for consideration; the Divan either deliberates or does not know how to get out of its innumerable difficulties. The winter will go by and the season of operations [i.e. the spring] will find the parties engaged without anybody, except

---

no reason for the Porte to conceal it from Austria and Russia to keep it secret until the failure of its flag-bearer. In any case he regarded this step as new proof of the tsar's desire for peace and wanted the sultan to accept the hand offered in reconciliation. Metternich to Esterházy, Vienna, 27 March 1829, HHStA, StA, England 187; Metternich to Ficquelmont, Vienna, 28 March 1829, HHStA, StA, Russland III, 88; Nesselrode to Tatishchev, St Petersburg, 14 Jan. 1829, HHStA, StA, Russland III, 88; Tatishchev to Nesselrode, Vienna, 1 Feb. 1829, AVPRI, fond 133, Kantseliariia, opis 468, 11881; Bray to Ludwig I of Bavaria, Vienna, 4 and 12 Feb. 1829, BHStA, MA, Wien 2402; Maltzan to Frederick William III, Vienna, 20 March 1829, GStA PK, HA III, MdA I, 6012.

[21] Metternich to Ottenfels, Vienna, 10 Dec. 1828, HHStA, StA, Türkei VI, 35; Metternich to Ottenfels, Vienna, 3 Jan. 1829, HHStA, StA, Türkei VI, 39; Metternich to Ficquelmont, Vienna, 23 Jan. 1829, HHStA, StA, Russland III, 88; Metternich to Trauttmannsdorff, Vienna, 27 Jan. and 20 Feb. 1829, HHStA, StK, Preussen 132; Metternich to Apponyi, Vienna, 28 Jan. 1829, HHStA, StA, Frankreich 271; Metternich to Esterházy, Vienna, 1 Feb. 1829, HHStA, StA, England 187; Lerchenfeld to Ludwig I of Bavaria, St Petersburg, 7 March 1829, BHStA, MA, Petersburg 2717.

the French revolutionaries, desiring it. Such is the picture of Europe
and it is not a happy one."[22] His pessimism considerably increased
when he learnt of the signature of a new protocol in London on the
Greek Question on 22 March 1829 fixing the northern frontier of an
autonomous Greece quite far in the mainland between the Gulf of
Arta to the Gulf of Volos and predetermining the administration of it
by a European prince with a hereditary succession. These conditions
were to be conveyed to Mahmud II by French and British ambassadors
who were to return to Constantinople. Metternich regarded only two
conclusions from the March Protocol as positive: the decision to send
the ambassadors back and the replacement of Stratford Canning with
Lord Aberdeen's brother, Sir Robert Gordon. Sir Robert had been
the first secretary of the British embassy for more than ten years and
then the plenipotentiary minister in Vienna, and he was an admirer of
Metternich and on good terms with Ottenfels whom he also personally
knew; the presumption that he would have good relations with both
after his arrival in Constantinople later proved to be well founded.
Otherwise Metternich considered the conditions of the Protocol misguided and in particular the extension of the Greek territory as a bad
way to a prompt settlement and pacification because he was convinced
that the sultan would reject them and he would do so in the peremptory manner as he had often done in the past.[23] According to the
Austrian chancellor, it would not be the ambassadors' negotiations
in Constantinople but the Russo-Ottoman war that would decide the
fate of the Greeks, in other words it would not be the arrival of the
British and French diplomats but the arrival of Russian army in the
Ottoman capital that would terminate the affair: "By undertaking

---

[22] Metternich to Trauttmannsdorff, Vienna, 17 Feb. 1829, HHStA, StK, Preussen
132.

[23] Metternich to Esterházy, Vienna, 25 Feb., 30 April, 19 May and 13 July 1829,
HHStA, StA, England 187; Metternich to Ottenfels, Vienna, 19 March 1829, HH-
StA, StA, Türkei VI, 39; Metternich to Ficquelmont, Vienna, 28 March 1829,
HHStA, StA, Russland III, 88; Tatishchev to Nesselrode, Vienna, 24 Feb. 1826,
AVPRI, fond 133, Kantseliariia, opis 468, 11870; Tatishchev to Nesselrode, Vi-
enna, 17 April 1829, AVPRI, fond 133, Kantseliariia, opis 468, 11881; Maltzan to
Frederick William III, Vienna, 24 Feb., 11 April and 2 May 1829, Brockhausen
to Frederick William III, Vienna, 12 June 1829, GStA PK, HA III, MdA I, 6012;
Laval to Portalis, Vienna, 30 March, 13 and 18 April 1829, AMAE, CP, Autriche
410; Bray to Ludwig I of Bavaria, Vienna, 27 April 1829, BHStA, MA, Wien 2402;
Crawley, *Greek Independence*, p. 154; Dakin, p. 264; Krauter, pp. 238–239.

to convey the conditions of 22 March to Constantinople and enforce them there, the two courts in alliance with Russia have simultaneously determined the limit where the last of these Great Powers will now be entitled to make demands of the sultan in the way of its own methods of war. Regardless of the refusal that the Ottoman monarch will undoubtedly make to the demands of the allies, Russia will certainly not fail to view the propositions of the last Protocol as something well gained for the allies and will enforce them with its coercive means. The minimum of permanent concessions on the part of the Porte will not be found in the hands of the courts of Great Britain and France; they will at the very most be found in the material defeats suffered by the Russian armies."[24]

From the very first moment, Metternich wanted to instruct Ottenfels to abstain from all talks on the Greek Question despite the fact that he had earlier repeatedly expressed his willingness to do the maximum for the restoration of peace in the Ottoman Empire: "We will always support to the best of our ability whatever the three allied courts determine in the spirit of a frank understanding."[25] In his opinion, the trilateral alliance went too far with the March Protocol, and when Tatishchev invited him to contribute to restoring peace more quickly by supporting the territorial enlargement of Greece in Constantinople, the prince regarded this argument as a pure contradiction. Nevertheless, when he was asked for this assistance by the British cabinet, he decided to offer it with respect to most of the conditions of the March Protocol and to press Mahmud II to accept the existence of an autonomous Greece in the Peloponnese and the Cyclades Islands. Nevertheless, he avoided advising him to accept the extension of Greece to include some regions north from the Gulf of Corinth because he knew that this condition would be inadmissible for the sultan almost to the same extent as it was unpopular in Vienna. The chancellor believed that if the Ottoman monarch yielded in all the other clauses and did not reject this one outright, such a compromising response could serve as a good starting point for further negotiations with a prospect for some compromise from the two Maritime Powers, in particular Great Britain where Wellington himself was strongly dissatisfied with the territorial concessions made to

---

[24] Metternich to Esterházy, Vienna, 30 April 1829, HHStA, StA, England 187.
[25] Metternich to Esterházy, Vienna, 28 Jan. 1829, HHStA, StA, England 187.

the Greeks in the March Protocol. Consequently, it was in London
where Metternich saw the last possible rescue for the sultan: "That
the Porte throws itself, so to speak, into the arms of England will
weigh heavily as a burden, but the British cabinet will not be able to
let it fall."[26] If the Ottoman monarch, however, wanted to save not
only what could be saved but also what, in Metternich's opinion, could
not be, he would lose everything in the end. However, this reasoning
had no effect in Constantinople where, despite Ottenfels' considerable
effort, the sultan was not willing to make any sacrifice; and when
Guilleminot and Gordon disembarked in Constantinople on 19 June
1829, the Porte's attitude in the Greek affairs was essentially identical
as when the representatives of the three allied Powers had left the city
in late 1827. On 6 July 1829, Ottenfels made the final and desperate
attempt to overcome this inflexibility with a frank appeal to Pertev
in which he pointed out that Greece was lost and the Porte had to
expect that this truth would also have to be recognised by the states
outside the trilateral alliance. Since Gordon had previously informed
Ottenfels that Metternich's idea of the Porte's acceptance of all conditions except the extension of Greece further into the mainland was
unacceptable for the British government, the internuncio exceeded the
chancellor's instructions and fully supported the demands of the two
ambassadors, but all in vain; Gordon and Guilleminot received the
Porte's absolute rejection of the March Protocol a few days later.[27]

The End of the Russo-Ottoman War

It was thus evident that the settlement of the Greek Question would
not be decided by the negotiations in London or Constantinople but,
as Metternich had well predicted, by the result of the war that had

---

[26] Metternich to Ottenfels, Vienna, 17 April 1829, HHStA, StA, Türkei VI, 39.
[27] Metternich to Ficquelmont, Vienna, 28 March 1829, HHStA, StA, Russland
III, 88; Metternich to Ottenfels, Vienna, 17 April 1829, HHStA, StA, Türkei VI,
39; Gentz to Neumann, Vienna, 26 April 1829, NA, RAM-AC 5, 3; Ottenfels to
Metternich, Constantinople, 25 May, 8, 23 and 25 June, 6 and 10 July 1829, HHStA,
StA, Türkei VI, 37; V. N. Vinogradov, "Les discussions sur la Grèce à Londres
durant la guerre de 1828–1829," *Les relations gréco-russes pendant la domination
turque et la guerre d'indépendance grecque*, Thessaloniki 1983, p. 144; Crawley,
Greek Independence, p. 162; Krauter, p. 248.

been renewed in the spring of 1829. The second campaign proceeded in a very different manner from the previous one. After Diebitsch's decisive victory at Kulevcha on 11 June and his capture of Silistria on 30 June, the Russian army quickly crossed the Balkan Mountains and seized Adrianople on 20 August.[28] The news of the Battle of Kulevcha raised Metternich's hopes that Mahmud II would himself be felt compelled to open peace negotiations as well as yield in the Greek Question, but the sultan surrendered neither after the Battle of Kulevcha and the fall of Silistria in June nor after the loss of Erzurum in eastern Anatolia in July. At that time one of the neutral Powers began a special mission to Constantinople with the aim of convincing the sultan that the tsar did not want to destroy the Ottoman Empire and desired peace. The neutral Power was not Austria as Metternich wished – in May Francis I had told Tatishchev that Russia was to use a third Power for acquainting the Porte with Russia's peace conditions – but Prussia, which enjoyed considerably better relations with Russia. Having met with Nicholas I in early June, Frederick William III sent Lieutenant General Baron Friedrich Carl Ferdinand von Müffling to the Ottoman capital on a mission that was to facilitate the restoration of peace. Metternich approved of this step and was willing to order Ottenfels to support Müffling, who arrived in Constantinople on 4 August. The goal of the Prussian special envoy was exactly the same as that of Metternich: to persuade the sultan to make peace as quickly as possible since the war was lost. On the day of Müffling's arrival the chancellor wrote to Ottenfels: "Advise peace with Russia. The Turks do not know how to wage war."[29] Until the very end of the war, this was the only instruction that Metternich sent to Ottenfels, otherwise he assumed an expectant and rather passive attitude, best characterised with his own words to Gentz from 16 August: "I do not know what I should write to the internuncio. I think I will not write to him at all."[30] When the news arrived in Vienna of the capture of the strategic city of Adrianople only some 270 kilometers north-west from Constantinople, Metternich found the situation so serious that, in the interest of resolving the crisis threatening not only the existence of the Ottoman Empire but also the relations among

---

[28]   Aksan, pp. 354–355; Bitis, pp. 314–315.
[29]   Metternich to Ottenfels, Vienna, 4 Aug. 1829, HHStA, StA, Türkei VI, 39.
[30]   Krauter, p. 251.

the European countries, he even preferred considerably unfavourable peace conditions for the Porte to the continuation of "a situation that leaves Europe in a miserable uncertainty and that is too dangerous for the future."[31]

The Viennese cabinet's desire for peace was augmented by Ottenfels' reports testifying that a prompt end to the war was the only way for Mahmud II, whose situation was becoming rather precarious during the late summer, to avoid disaster. When, for example, the recruitment of 40,000 men was ordered by the Porte on 29 July, the result was a gathering of a quarter of that number, mostly men without experience in fighting. Furthermore, Ottenfels reported that these men had no enthusiasm to fight or even defend the capital and this apathy was generally spread among the Ottomans. It was proved by the fact that 20,000 defenders of Adrianople surrendered the city to Diebitsch without fighting, and a considerable number of them even laid down their weapons and went home. Rather than winning national support, the sultan could expect the growth of general dissatisfaction; the increased number of soldiers in the Constantinople streets was not intended for a clash with the Russians but the supervision of general order. Seeing this disconsolate situation, Ottenfels not only counselled the sending of Turkish plenipotentiaries to Diebitsch's headquarters but also asked the Porte for permission for an Austrian warship to sail to the Golden Horn to take away the employees of the internunciature if a revolution broke out.[32]

---

[31] Maltzan to Frederick William III, Vienna, 8 Sept. 1829, GStA PK, HA III, MdA I, 6013. See also Metternich to Esterházy, Vienna, 24 June 1829, HHStA, StA, England 187; Bernstorff to Brockhausen, Berlin, 5 July 1829, Metternich to Ottenfels, Vienna, 4 and 19 July, 4 Aug. and 16 Sept. 1829, Plass, 30 Aug. 1829, HHStA, StA, Türkei VI, 39; Metternich to Trauttmannsdorff, Vienna, 8 and 20 July, 4 Aug. 1829, HHStA, StK, Preussen 132; Metternich to Ficquelmont, Vienna, 16 July 1829, HHStA, StA, Russland III, 88; Metternich to Francis I, Vienna, 31 Aug. 1829, HHStA, StK, Vorträge 259; Ottenfels to Metternich, Constantinople, 30 July 1829, HHStA, StA, Türkei VI, 37; the record of Tatishchev's conversation with Francis I from 9 May 1829, Tatishchev to Nesselrode, Vienna, 28 July, 22 Aug. and 16 Sept. 1829, AVPRI, fond 133, Kantseliariia, opis 468, 11885; Laval to Portalis, Vienna, 18 July 1829, Laval to Polignac, Vienna, 16 Sept. 1829, AMAE, CP, Autriche 411; Cowley to Aberdeen, Vienna, 16 Sept. 1829, TNA, FO 120/105; K. Pröhl, *Die Bedeutung preussischer Politik in den Phasen der orientalischen Frage: Ein Beitrag zur Entwicklung deutsch-türkischer Beziehungen von 1606 bis 1871*, Frankfurt am Main 1986, p. 173; Baack, p. 159.

[32] Ottenfels to Pertev, 3 Aug. 1829, Ottenfels to Metternich, Constantinople, 7, 8,

In this situation Mahmud II started to be more conciliatory. Whereas he flatly refused Diebitsch's offer for peace at the end of July, in mid August he acceded to the stipulations of the Treaty of London, and although this concession was made for the Peloponnese and Cyclades only, it was a good start. Shortly afterwards, he sent his negotiators to Diebitsch's camp in Adrianople to discuss a peace settlement. He was brought to this step by his fear of not only problems in Constantinople but also of the enemy attacking its walls even though in fact the Russian soldiers were seriously afflicted by disease and in reality unable to attack the metropolis on the Bosphorus. Their number was erroneously estimated by Ottenfels at 60,000 when in fact it did not amount to half of that.[33] Since no one in Constantinople knew of the sorry state of the Russian army, the sultan's situation was generally regarded as hopeless, and the representatives of the Great Powers urged Mahmud II to sign the peace treaty. Furthermore, none of his advisors dared to advise him to refuse Diebitsch's peace terms and thereby "bring down on this capital a catastrophe that could have fatal consequences for the existence of the Ottoman throne."[34] Consequently, the sultan capitulated and admitted that the war was over in Adrianople on 14 September 1829, despite the fact that he found the conditions "exorbitant, onerous, humiliating and unacceptable."[35] They included some Russian territorial gains in the Caucasus and the Danubian Delta with its important trade centre of Sulina; the restitution of six districts to Serbia according to the Treaty of Bucharest and the Akkerman Convention; autonomy for Greece; free passage through the Straits for the ships of all nations trading with Russia; 1.5 million Dutch ducats as a trade indemnity for the financial damage the Ottoman Porte had caused to the Russian Empire from 1806 to 1828, and another 10 million Dutch ducats as a war indemnity for

---

16 and 29 Aug. 1829, HHStA, StA, Türkei VI, 37; Royer to Frederick William III, Pera, 1 Aug. 1829, GStA PK, HA III, MdA I, 7267; Puryear, *France*, p. 73.

[33] The Porte's note to Gordon and Guilleminot, 15 Aug. 1829, Ottenfels to Metternich, Constantinople, 16, 17 and 29 Aug. 1829, HHStA, StA, Türkei VI, 37; Ottenfels to Metternich, Constantinople, 5 and 25 Sept. 1829, HHStA, StA, Türkei VI, 38; Bitis, p. 316.

[34] Ottenfels to Metternich, Constantinople, 11 Sept. 1829, HHStA, StA, Türkei VI, 38.

[35] Ottenfels to Metternich, Constantinople, 10 Sept. 1829, HHStA, StA, Türkei VI, 38.

the damages inflicted during the period 1828–1829. The Principalities and Silistria were to be occupied until the indemnities were paid.[36]

Metternich and the Treaty of Adrianople

According to Alexander Bitis, Metternich's view of the peace conditions was extremely negative.[37] Although this opinion is basically correct, the reality is more complicated. It is true that the chancellor's first reaction was considerably hostile. He made no secret of his opinion that the peace conditions giving considerable autonomy to Serbia, Greece and the Danubian Principalities "seem to severely threaten not only the integrity but also the very existence of the Ottoman Empire."[38] He regarded them as fatal to the independence of the Ottoman Empire and as placing that empire at the mercy of Russia. In his opinion, the sultan ceased to be the sovereign of an independent country. He even declared in the presence of Schwebel that "the fall of the Ottoman Empire is inevitable and imminent, it will give birth to a new political system in Europe, [and] it will lead to complications and incalculable consequences."[39] And he in no way shared Ottenfels' regret about the fact that Austria had been excluded from the peace talks and that the internuncio had not been invited to the negotiations by the representatives of Great Britain,

---

[36] Anderson, *The Great Powers*, pp. 33–35; Bitis, pp. 353–356; Ciachir, pp. 706–707. On the days preceding the peace settlement, Ottenfels was left out the negotiations and was consequently inactive, which led to an accusation from Diebitsch that he instigated the Turks to continue the war. The proof allegedly was found in the absence of his signature under a collective letter of the British, French and Prussian representatives to Diebitsch assuring him about the Porte's desire to make peace. However, from among Guilleminot, Gordon and Müffling and the Turks none of them invited Ottenfels to join this proceeding owing to Russia's scant sympathy for Austria. As explained above, Ottenfels actually did his best to persuade the Porte to conclude peace despite Diebitsch's harsh conditions. Müffling himself admitted in his memoirs that Ottenfels had sincerely advised it. Ottenfels to Metternich, Constantinople, 10 Sept. 1829, HHStA, StA, Türkei VI, 38; Ottenfels, *Memoari*, p. 217; F. C. F. von Müffling, *Aus meinem Leben*, Berlin 1855, p. 272.

[37] Bitis, p. 361.

[38] Maltzan to Frederick William III, Vienna, 26 Sept. 1829, GStA PK, HA III, MdA I, 6013.

[39] Schwebel to Polignac, Vienna, 25 Sept. 1829, AMAE, CP, Autriche 411.

France, Prussia or by the Ottoman dignitaries.[40] On the contrary, Metternich thanked "the heavens for the escape from the necessity to cooperate in a work of destruction."[41] Nevertheless, these statements made on 25 and 26 September cannot be regarded as his final opinion, which over a period of several days became more positive towards the peace settlement. On these initial two days his negative expressions merely represented his first reaction brought about by the proposal of the Treaty in which Diebitsch demanded the 20-year-long Russian occupation of the Danubian Principalities, the condition on which Metternich first thought the peace Treaty had been made. In the final peace settlement the period was reduced to ten years, which was much better for Austria.[42] It is, however, impossible to agree with Sauvigny and regard it as the only factor that lessened Metternich's scepticism and defeatism.[43] In fact this factor was not so important since there were more articles in the final Treaty that caused Metternich's concern. Friedrich von Gentz was a considerably more important source of influence on Metternich's change of attitude towards the peace settlement, having advocated the quick solution of the problems in the Near East owing to those emerging in the West, with the words: "So away with the whole oriental episode!"[44] Gentz regarded the Treaty of Adrianople as considerably less drastic than it could have been: "In comparison with what the Russians could request, and request with impunity, they have demanded little. I do not say that it was in their power to dissolve the Turkish Empire in Europe without exposing themselves to European opposition. I say, however, that they could have demanded the cession of the Principalities and Bulgaria to the Balkan Mountains, and half of Armenia and 50 million instead of 10, without the Porte having possessed either the power or a good friend seriously willing to prevent it."[45] In early October, Gentz wrote

[40] Ottenfels to Metternich, Constantinople, 10 Sept. 1829, HHStA, StA, Türkei VI, 38.

[41] Metternich to Esterházy, Vienna, 26 Sept. 1829, HHStA, StA, England 188.

[42] Pertev's plan of the peace agreement conveyed to Ottenfels in an undated dispatch, attached to Ottenfels to Metternich, Constantinople, 10 Sept. 1829, HHStA, StA, Türkei VI, 38; Royer to Frederick William III, Pera, 9 Sept. 1829, GStA PK, HA III, MdA I, 7267.

[43] Sauvigny, *Metternich et la France*, III, p. 1313.

[44] Krauter, p. 249.

[45] Gentz to [?], [?] Oct. 1829, Prokesch-Osten, *Zur Geschichte der orientalischen Frage*, pp. 193–196. For the same view see also Gentz to Neumann, Vienna, 27 Oct.

to Ottenfels: "Our joy over the end of the war was so great that we would have accepted the peace settlement with a certain patience and resignation even if it had turned out harsher than it actually is. To be able to understand this joy, you would have to know the situation of Europe, the positions of the Great Powers, the sentiments and abilities of the cabinets, the whole political and moral tableau of the period as exactly as we do, for example Prince Metternich and I ... The continuation of this war would have brought an inexpressible misfortune upon Europe. We are spared this danger for the time and I am not ashamed to quote the Roman poet: *Scelera ipsa nefasque hac mercede placent* [the very crimes and unspeakable evils are worth this reward]."[46]

Under Gentz's influence and having contemplated the situation from a wider European point of view, Metternich began to view the peace settlement more favourably on the turn of September and October. With regard to the events accompanying the signing of the Treaty, he was well aware of the fact that the sultan had not been able to obtain better conditions owing to the Porte's hopeless situation, and his original consternation was replaced with relief that "a great disorder has been terminated."[47] The continuation of the war could be beneficial neither to the Porte nor to Austria, and it could cause only a general upheaval welcomed only by the enemies of the preservation of good order: "It is essential to distinguish between two questions: it is necessary to separate the question of the end of the Russo-Turkish war and of the influence that this [end] will have to have on Europe from that of the peace conditions and their effects, both on the respective positions of two reconciled empires and on other European countries. The first of these two matters, the end of the war, must be counted not only among the most fortunate of events, but it must also be welcomed as a *condicio sine qua non*; I do not speak of the triumph of the system of preservation but rather of the possibility that the system of political disorder will be forced to postpone the triumph on which its supporters prided themselves."[48] Consequently,

---

1829, NA, RAM-AC 5, 3.

[46] Krauter, p. 252.

[47] Metternich to Trauttmannsdorff, Vienna, 29 Sept. 1829, HHStA, StK, Preussen 132.

[48] Metternich to Ficquelmont, Vienna, 5 Oct. 1839, HHStA, StA, Russland III, 88.

he did not speak about the peace in such dark tones any more and presented it with more optimism: "Europe had the most urgent need of a return of political peace; the war is over and this fact in itself is an immense boon."[49]

The fact that must be emphasised is that it was in particular Metternich's opinion of the existence of the Treaty, in other words the signing of it, which changed, and not his view of its conditions that even according to his later opinion "ruins the rest of Ottoman independence."[50] He agreed with Ottenfels' extensive analysis of the peace conditions of 25 September which presented them as "the hardest, the most humiliating that had ever been dictated by a victor to a weak enemy."[51] In the prince's opinion, with the territorial gains in Asia, Russia became the factual master of Ottoman Armenia and the moderator of Asia Minor, while the incorporation of six districts into autonomous Serbia and the entire fulfilment of the relevant articles of the Akkerman Convention essentially changed this province into an "independent and powerful country because of the warlike spirit of its people."[52] The delineation of the frontiers of still autonomous Greece according to the Protocol of 22 March created a new power in the Mediterranean. The size of the indemnities was a serious blow to Ottoman finances and the occupation of the Danubian Principalities was highly injurious to the sultan's authority and power in these domains. Their occupation as well as the seizure of the Danubian Delta above all affected Austria's interests.[53] The former was not entirely surprising for Metternich who had expected the possibility of the tsar's occupation of some Ottoman territory until the repayment

---

[49] Ibid. See also Metternich to Ottenfels, Vienna, 2 Oct. 1829, HHStA, StA, Türkei VI, 39; Schwebel to Polignac, Vienna, 1 and 10 Oct. 1829, AMAE, CP, Autriche 411; Bray to Ludwig I of Bavaria, Vienna, 22 Oct. 1829, BHStA, MA, Wien 2402.

[50] Metternich to Ficquelmont, Vienna, 5 Oct. 1839, HHStA, StA, Russland III, 88.

[51] Ottenfels to Metternich, Constantinople, 25 Sept. 1829, HHStA, StA, Türkei VI, 38.

[52] Metternich to Esterházy, Vienna, 26 Sept. 1829, HHStA, StA, England 188.

[53] Metternich to Esterházy, Vienna, 17 Oct. 1829, HHStA, StA, England 188; Metternich to Ottenfels, Vienna, 17 Oct. 1829, HHStA, StA, Türkei VI, 39; Cowley to Aberdeen, Vienna, 26 Sept. 1829, TNA, FO 120/105; Cowley to Aberdeen, Vienna, 17 Oct. 1829, TNA, FO 120/104. For more on Metternich's reaction to the Russian occupation of Moldavia and Wallachia as well as the seizure of the Danubian Delta see Chapter 19.

of indemnities at the beginning of the war: "He does not want its [Ottoman Empire's] death but its ruin. He has no parcels of land to conquer on its territory in Europe; it would be necessary for him to have everything or the major part of everything so that the enterprise would be worth the trouble of the character of an avowed conqueror. Consequently, we are not disposed to believe that at the current time the emperor could aim at material conquests which would scarcely be directed against anything other than the Principalities. He follows another direction that, by right, must appear more lucrative to him. He will inflict on the Porte such pecuniary damages that its utmost resources will be exhausted. It remains to be seen whether this sultan will ever be able to satisfy the requested sum. Therefore, he [the tsar] will retain the securities [read: some Ottoman territories] and he will manage it without having made any conquests at all."[54] The latter, however, was shocking for him because although he expected and even agreed during the war with Russia's acquisition of the locations on the eastern coast of the Black Sea and in the Caucasus, until the very last moment he did not presume that it would aspire to territorial gains in the Balkans. Nicholas I had often promised, and Tatishchev was one of many information channels carrying this protestation to Metternich, that he "had no views of conquest in Europe."[55] However, the assurance of Tatishchev from November 1827 that his sovereign had no material interests beyond the Danube was more exact: the tsar actually did not exceed this limit when he deprived the sultan of the Danubian Delta. However, he did not keep his word when he gained this albeit small territory in the Balkans.[56]

Nicholas I's statement in reaction to the peace terms that "our moderation will reduce to silence the most inveterate back-biters"[57] would hardly have been welcomed in Vienna if it had been known

---

[54] Metternich to Esterházy, Vienna, 31 May 1828, HHStA, StA, England 182.

[55] Cowley to Aberdeen, Vienna, 18 May 1829, TNA, FO 120/100.

[56] Metternich to Esterházy, Vienna, 19 May 1829, HHStA, StA, England 187; Metternich to Trauttmannsdorff, Plass, 25 Aug. 1829, HHStA, StK, Preussen 132; Metternich to Ottenfels, Vienna, 10 Sept. 1829, HDA, 750, OO 38; Metternich to Apponyi, Vienna, 17 Sept. 1829, HHStA, StA, Frankreich 271; Bray to Ludwig I of Bavaria, Vienna, 25 Nov. 1827, BHStA, MA, Wien 2401; Tatishchev to Nesselrode, Vienna, 9 July 1828, AVPRI, fond 133, Kantseliariia, opis 468, 11879; Cowley to Aberdeen, Vienna, 8 and 26 Sept. 1829, TNA, FO 120/105.

[57] Ciachir, p. 705.

there. Metternich had already spoken before the conclusion of peace with some sarcasm about the moderation that the tsar had often proclaimed during the war because the word "moderation" had too wide an interpretation. He regretted that the Prussian cabinet had not moved the tsar to specify the terms of his guarantee when offering him the service of Müffling's mission. He wrote to Trauttmannsdorff on 10 September: "Moderation is always a relative quality; its application is a matter of many variables, as well as of the situations to which it can be applied. Basing a large and joint political enterprise upon only the sole guarantee of moderation is building castles in the air, it is staking the future on one card, it is engaging in a game in which the players are exposed to the most dubious chances of dishonest compromise. Such is the state of things today, it is less a question of whether the Russian emperor will possess the virtue of moderation than whether he will have the strength or the talent to exploit this quality."[58] The surprising seizure of the Danubian Delta did not comply with the hopes that had been nurtured in Vienna as a consequence of the tsar's moderate statements.[59] But considering the situation in Constantinople at the moment of the peace settlement, Metternich's final verdict was a compromise: "The peace Treaty has brought an end to the Russo-Turkish war. Its conditions are moderate or ominous, depending on the point of view of who is judging it. It has saved the Ottoman Empire from its inevitable ruin only to place the existence of the empire in a precarious situation."[60]

The Legend of Metternich's Proposal for the Partition of the Ottoman Empire

At the same time when the European cabinets studied the conditions of the peace Treaty, a new rumour concerning Metternich's secret

---

[58] Metternich to Trauttmannsdorff, Vienna, 10 Sept. 1829, HHStA, StK, Preussen 132.
[59] Metternich to Ficquelmont, Plass, 1 Sept. 1829, HHStA, StA, Russland III, 88; Metternich to Apponyi, Vienna, 17 Sept. 1829, HHStA, StA, Frankreich 271; Cowley to Aberdeen, Vienna, 24 and 26 Sept. 1829, TNA, FO 120/105.
[60] Metternich to Trauttmannsdorff, Vienna, 12 Oct. 1829, HHStA, StK, Preussen 132.

plots spread among them: that the Austrian chancellor, fearing the collapse of the Ottoman Empire, proposed partitioning it at the beginning of September 1829. It appeared later in the same month in Berlin and the first mention was made by the French ambassador to the Prussian court, Count Hector Philippe d'Agoult, who informed the new French premier and, simultaneously, foreign minister, Prince Jules August Armand Marie de Polignac, that Gentz had sent a small pamphlet to Berlin containing the view that the fall of the Ottoman Empire was imminent and, therefore, the proper time for the expulsion of the Turks from Europe and the partition of their provinces in the Continent had arrived. However, Agoult never personally saw the brochure and admitted that "its existence perhaps is fanciful."[61] Nevertheless, despite the fact that its existence was never revealed, the rumour quickly spread among the representatives of German courts and reports with this information also came to Paris at the end of September from Karlsruhe, Darmstadt and Dresden. It was generally believed in Berlin that Austria had made a secret but formal proposal for the partition of the Ottoman Empire to the Prussian cabinet and Ancillon's rejection of it changed little in the widespread suspicion of Metternich.[62] Polignac also took this rumour seriously because it contained the information that in the Austrian plan France was excluded from the division of the spoils and, consequently, he tried to learn more of its existence. In November, his suspicion increased when he obtained this information from Mortemart after an audience with Nicholas I: "He [the tsar] told me that before the peace of Adrianople a project for the partition of Turkey in which France would be excluded had been proposed to him by Austria, that he had not given it serious consideration and that the [French] king could be confident that he [the tsar] would never enter into any scheme of this kind without his loyal and faithful ally."[63]

Some historians have more or less credited this rumour. American historian Vernon John Puryear was inclined to believe the existence of Austria's plan for the partition upon some speculative evidence and supported this with first, Metternich's concern about the change in

---

[61]   Agoult to Polignac, Berlin, 25 Sept. 1829, AMAE, CP, Prusse 272.
[62]   Agoult to Polignac, Berlin, 25 and 30 Sept. 1829, AMAE, CP, Prusse 272; Hammer, p. 162.
[63]   Mortemart to Polignac, St Petersburg, 3 Nov. 1829, AMAE, CP, Russie 178.

the tsar's moderate attitude and the fall of the Ottoman Empire and, second, the existence of the pamphlet that he never saw.[64] Joseph Hajjar introduced this rumour as a proven fact saying that the plan for the destruction of the Ottoman dominion in Europe was prepared at the Viennese Chancellery and formally presented in Berlin and St Petersburg.[65] The credibility of this view seems to be supported by British historian Christopher Montague Woodhouse, who claimed that in early September 1829 Metternich "thought that the Ottoman Empire was doomed."[66] Nevertheless, all these claims and speculations must be resolutely refuted. A proposal for the partition of the Ottoman Empire never originated in Ballhausplatz under Metternich's leadership, not before, during or after 1829. He considered the preservation of the empire as an absolute necessity for the Austrian Empire and any active step in Europe to break it up was unacceptable, in particular when he did not fear its fall in early September when the plan was, according to the rumours, prepared by him. There is no evidence for such anxiety on his part in the studied documents. He was patiently and passively waiting for peace and he did not start to express any concern (see some quotations above) until he received the first draft of the peace conditions in late September – and even at that time his statements seem to be deliberately exaggerated. His concern was most strongly expressed in his statement to Esterházy about the eventual serious consequences resulting from the peace that was to be concluded, but he also declared his opinion that the Ottoman Empire had to be preserved and that "Austria does not strive and never will strive to expand at the expense of its neighbours; the emperor demands nothing from nobody."[67] On 21 September, he wrote again to the same ambassador about the irreparable damage and uncertain future of the sultan's empire but, in the same instructions, he reacted negatively to Wellington's words that "it can be presupposed that, in consequence of the weakening of the Ottoman Empire, the Great

---

[64] Puryear, *France*, pp. 80–83.

[65] J. Hajjar, *L'Europe et les destinées du Proche-Orient (1815–1848)*, Paris 1970, p. 89.

[66] Woodhouse, *Capodistria*, p. 439. The same opinion can also be found in Crawley, *Greek Independence*, p. 171, and Bitis, p. 369.

[67] Metternich to Esterházy, Vienna, 6 Sept. 1829, Prokesch-Osten, *Griechen*, VI, p. 182.

Powers will not be slow to scramble over the pickings,"[68] declaring: "After this judgement, very thoughtlessly expressed and undoubtedly even more thoughtlessly conceived, Austria must necessarily find itself placed, in the duke's opinion, in the first line with the expansionist Powers ... It is then a sad discovery like this which charges me with the necessity to make it clear to the English cabinet that our empire will never aspire to the destruction of what, in consequence of the trilateral business, remains of the Ottoman power!"[69]

The most convincing evidence for the lack of any foundation to the rumour is the absolute non-existence of any mention of the plan either in Metternich's or other diplomats' correspondence from that period. No clear expression, not even the slightest hint of it can be found. The same applies to Gentz's alleged pamphlet never actually seen by his contemporaries or historians. Schwebel wrote to Polignac later in October that "neither before nor after the conclusion of the peace did I hear a single word uttered by Prince Metternich or any of his aides or any member of the diplomatic corps that could arouse or confirm the opinion that the Viennese cabinet had drafted plans for the partition and had communicated them to other cabinets."[70] The tsar's statement that Austria made him a proposal for the usurpation of the Ottoman dominion in Europe without France's participation must be regarded as a fabrication aimed at keeping a rift between the cabinets in Vienna and Paris; the letters of Metternich, Ficquelmont and Tatishchev absolutely lack mention of such an offer. The whole story was confused not only by Nicholas I but also by Polignac, who in early December informed Mortemart that Metternich had written in his instructions to Apponyi that "his court had never thought about a plan of this kind but that one of the employees of his secretariat had indeed taken it upon himself to write a proposal on this subject and that this proposal had, as he [Metternich] believed, come to the knowledge of the court in Berlin and perhaps also some other German courts."[71] Nevertheless, what Metternich actually wrote to his

---

[68] Metternich to Esterházy, Linz, 21 Sept. 1829, HHStA, StA, England 188.

[69] Ibid. The same negative reaction to Wellington's supposition that the Great Powers including Austria would start to think about the partition of the Ottoman Empire can also be found in Metternich to Gentz, Linz, 21 Sept. 1829, Prokesch-Osten, *Zur Geschichte der orientalischen Frage*, p. 193.

[70] Sauvigny, *Metternich et la France*, III, pp. 1314–1315.

[71] Polignac to Mortemart, Paris, 2 Dec. 1829, AMAE, CP, Russie 178.

ambassador in Paris was that no one in Vienna had either thought of or prepared such a plan and he presumed that this rumour had been started by a group of liberals. He was told nothing about a proposal drafted at the Chancellery. Apponyi's reports show that Metternich's answer was immediately communicated to Paris and it was also subsequently accepted by Polignac. What the French premier wrote to Mortemart was thus his own invention.[72]

* * *

The immediate future was to show that some stipulations of the Treaty of Adrianople actually were quite burdensome for the Ottoman Empire and the peace settlement as a whole definitely increased Russia's influence over its monarch as well as some of his territories, in particular the Caucasus and the Balkans. An allegory depicting Victory crowning the head of the tsar and a defeated and begging Turk situated beside the Russian monarch seen in the Russian embassy in Vienna during a banquet prepared for the diplomatic corps on 18 December concisely characterised the given situation.[73] Despite the fact that this outcome of the war represented a serious blow for Austria and a defeat for its chancellor, who was well aware of this, Metternich finally came to terms with it because he saw in the ending of the war an important prerequisite for general stability in Europe and a quick settlement of the Greeks' struggle for independence. Unfortunately for him, the following year was to witness a significant wave of

---

[72] Metternich to Apponyi, Vienna, 28 Oct. 1829, HHStA, StA, Frankreich 271; Metternich to Esterházy, Vienna, 16 Dec. 1829, HHStA, StA, England 188; Apponyi to Metternich, Paris, 13 Oct. and 18 Nov. 1829, HHStA, StA, Frankreich 270; Cowley to Aberdeen, Vienna, 25 Dec. 1829, TNA, FO 120/104. Around 20 November, which means at the moment when he was already acquainted with Metternich's answer, Polignac told the British ambassador in Paris that the rumour had been an absolute invention and its author was a "political speculator." Stuart to Aberdeen, Paris, 23 Nov. 1829, TNA, FO 120/104. The reason why the French premier's explanation to St Petersburg differed from Metternich's own explanation is not difficult to understand when one knows Polignac's desire to cultivate good relations with the tsar which, at the same moment, meant to prevent an Austro-Russian rapprochement – anything that could result in their mutual distrust served this purpose well.

[73] Schwebel to Polignac, Vienna, 19 Dec. 1829, AMAE, CP, Autriche 411.

disturbances in Europe, and the final solution of the Greek Question needed yet more time than he presumed or hoped it would at the end of 1829.

10

The Rise of Independent Greece

The Battle of Navarino signified a turning point in the Greek uprising because after the destruction of the Ottoman fleet it became obvious that the sultan would not be able to restore his previous rule over the insurgents. However, it was still not clear whether Greece would be only autonomous or entirely free. The trilateral alliance finally chose complete independence as the best option and as such the Greek Kingdom came into being in 1832. Metternich stood apart from the process leading to the creation of this new state in the Mediterranean but he easily accepted its existence because, first, he preferred its independence to autonomy for pragmatic reasons and, second, he wanted above all an end to this protracted affair that significantly undermined his position in European politics.

Metternich and the Greek Question during the Russo-Ottoman War

The Greek Question was of secondary importance for Metternich during the Russo-Ottoman war and it was entirely subordinated to his desire for a prompt restoration of peace between the two quarrelling empires; he dealt with the Greek issue when planning practical measures only if it could serve his main goal. On the other hand, he naturally continued to pay attention to the events in Greece and considered its future, and the years 1828 and 1829 were important in this respect because he finally came to the conclusion that under the given conditions the best solution was its complete independence. It is true that he had occasionally considered such a possibility earlier in the decade and there is no reason to disbelieve the frankness of his repeated claims from the beginning of the uprising that the only solutions with any long-term prospects were either the suppression of the Greeks or their independence because an autonomy as proposed in the Russian January *Mémoire* of 1824 or later in the St Petersburg

Protocol and Treaty of London would be a compromise solution satisfying neither of the two contesting parties. Nevertheless, until the late 1820s he personally favoured suppression and was far from wanting or even advocating independence, the idea of which he merely used as a means of thwarting the settlement as presented in the Russian January *Mémoire* of 1824 or of saving peace in the early spring of 1828.[1] With the development of the affair after 1827, when the Greeks' complete submission became totally unfeasible owing to the intervention of the trilateral alliance, he began to regard their absolute political emancipation as the best solution.

The moment when Metternich seriously and sincerely started to tend towards this kind of settlement is difficult to determine accurately, but already in late April 1828 he frankly stated to Lord Cowley that he would prefer independence to autonomy. In July of the same year, he repeated this preference in his instructions to Ottenfels, who was authorised to indicate to the Porte the advantages of Greece's absolute political emancipation. This advice of course did not result from any pro-Greek sentiment that was absolutely foreign to Metternich but from a purely realistic assessment of the given situation. First, the Greeks living in an autonomous state within the Ottoman Empire would continue to be dissatisfied and such a state would certainly cause new disputes between them and the Porte, most likely resulting in another insurrection against the sultan's rule. On the other hand, suzerainty over Greece would not make the sultan stronger than if he had been deprived of it, and his power over a *de jure* autonomous but *de facto* independent Greek province would be rather superficial. Second, an autonomous Greece would certainly become a "wooden horse" through which the European states could interfere with the internal affairs of the Ottoman Empire. This interference would be made possible with the guarantee that the three allied Powers intended to confer upon Greece's existence: "In order to predict what these guarantees are worth and how quickly they turn into formal protectorates, which is what these finally are, it should suffice the Ottoman government to consider the two Principalities

---

[1]   Metternich to Lebzeltern, Vienna, 15 Jan. 1825, HHStA, StA, Russland III, 70; Metternich's memorandum attached to Metternich to Esterházy, Vienna, 15 March 1828, HHStA, StA, England 182. For more see Chapters 3 and 7.

on the Danube!"[2] Metternich's rejection of Russia's plan of January 1824 on the creation of four autonomous Greek principalities had been motivated with this concern as the chancellor had not wanted Russia's influence to increase as had happened due to its new clients in the Balkans. In 1828, the same anxiety was the principal reason for his growing sympathy for the Greeks' complete independence and it must be admitted that Metternich's concern about the conversion of Greece to Russia's protectorate was legitimate since this was exactly what this Great Power wanted to achieve.[3] He explained his opinion of this threat to Cowley later in November 1829: "Were the Emp[ero]r Nicholas disposed to afford to Turkey a chance of recovering from her present difficulties he would declare in favor [sic] of the independence of the new states. If on the contrary it should be his policy to keep down Turkey he could not adopt a better method than that of burthening [sic] her with the suzerainty of those states which could not fail to involve her in perpetual dissensions both with the Greeks and with Russia and from which she could derive no possible advantage."[4]

Some months earlier, on the turn of 1828 and 1829, when Metternich had hoped for an improvement of the sultan's position with a quick settlement of the Greek Question, he had advocated autonomy because at that time he regarded a request for full independence as an insuperable barrier in the forthcoming negotiations between the trilateral alliance and the Porte; moreover, France and Great Britain inclined to the former settlement.[5] For this reason, he had refused to meet Nicholas I's request for Austria's support of full independence in London in early 1829: "The Russian court also demands our support in favour of the full independence of Greece as being in principle an Austrian idea. As to the matter itself, we can only also apply to it the same rule that I have just denounced. As for the suitability of the

---

[2]   Metternich to Ottenfels, Vienna, 22 July 1828, HHStA, StA, Türkei VI, 35.

[3]   Metternich to Esterházy, Vienna, 25 April 1828, HHStA, StA, England 182; Cowley to Dudley, Vienna, 25 April 1828, TNA, FO 120/91; Tatishchev to Nesselrode, Vienna, 3 Aug. 1829, AVPRI, fond 133, Kantseliariia, opis 468, 11885; Bitis, p. 372.

[4]   Cowley to Aberdeen, Vienna, 24 Nov. 1829, TNA, FO 120/104. This quotation can also be found – though with minor mistakes – in Bitis, p. 363.

[5]   Metternich to Ottenfels, Vienna, 10 Dec. 1828, HHStA, StA, Türkei VI, 35; Metternich to Apponyi, Vienna, 12 Dec. 1828, HHStA, StA, Frankreich 268; Cowley to Aberdeen, Vienna, 24 Jan. 1829, TNA, FO 120/98; Tatishchev to Nesselrode, Vienna, 1 Feb. 1829, AVPRI, fond 133, Kantseliariia, opis 468, 11881.

idea, in order [for you] to determine your judgement, it will have to
suffice for me to remind you of the times, the circumstances and the
issue when we put forward this idea in the years 1825 and 1828. The
situations have changed so much since those two times and what was
envisaged by us in those earlier [periods] as a means of preventing
the war must necessarily take on a different character in our eyes the
day its application prevents the conclusion of peace."[6] When, however, the war was renewed in the spring of 1829, Metternich no longer
had any reason to support autonomy and returned to his earlier firm
conviction in the suitability of complete independence because he saw
in this solution "the only way for escape from this labyrinth."[7]

The same pragmatism led Metternich to the opinion during 1828
that the territory of an independent Greek state was to be confined
to only the Peloponnese and some adjacent islands. Their loss would
not considerably harm the power of the sultan, who in any case was
unable to reconquer these regions; the peninsula itself was definitely
lost at the moment when the Egyptian army evacuated. In Metternich's opinion, the Gulf and the Isthmus of Corinth would be a suitable Greco-Ottoman frontier easily defendable for both countries. He
strongly opposed any extension of Greek territory to the north because he did not want to deprive Mahmud II of other territory in
which not only Greeks but also Moslems lived. If this sacrifice were
demanded of him by the trilateral alliance, the sultan's consent would
become rather uncertain. As for the Peloponnese and the adjacent islands, Metternich pointed out that these territories could more easily
be surrendered by the Ottoman monarch since no Moslems lived there
any longer as they had been massacred or forced to flee after 1821. In
late 1828, the extent of Greece was an even more important topic for
Metternich than the problem of its future political status. Whereas
he could easily accept Greece's political independence, he was concerned about its territorial expansion north of the Gulf of Corinth or
to the large island of Euboea. He once even labelled the loss of the
latter as "a death-blow to the Porte."[8] And exactly for this reason he

---

[6]   Metternich to Ficquelmont, Vienna, 30 Jan. 1829, HHStA, StA, Russland III,
88.
[7]   Brockhausen to Frederick William III, Vienna, 4 Aug. 1829, GStA PK, HA III,
MdA I, 6013.
[8]   Metternich to Ottenfels, Vienna, 17 April 1829, HHStA, StA, Türkei VI, 39.

also criticised the conference in Poros where the frontiers of Greece were discussed among the three ambassadors and consulted with the Greeks because it was evident that the latter would only agree to a settlement that was the most advantageous for them but would still regard it as the minimum of what they could get. Consequently, he was not greatly surprised with a pro-Greek outcome of this conference. The Protocol signed in London on 22 March 1829 was more surprising for him because he well knew Wellington's anti-Greek sentiment, but despite its content the chancellor still believed that with regard to the territorial extent of Greece, nothing was definitely lost for the sultan if the Greek troops were not allowed to capture the territories on the mainland above the Gulf of Corinth. In any case, all the places seized by the Greek insurgents could be regarded as lost for the sultan because there was no one who could expel them. This opinion was shared with Capodistrias, who had been released from the Russian diplomatic service by Nicholas I in July 1827 and was functioning in Greece as president from early 1828 and pressing for the fighting to be shifted to the area above the Gulf for the exactly same reason that led Metternich to be afraid of it. When Capodistrias failed in his effort to exploit the French expeditionary corps staying in the Peloponnese for this purpose, which Metternich soon learnt of and feared its eventual success, the president had to rely on his own forces which actually tried to gain as much land as they could on the mainland.[9]

During the Russo-Ottoman war, Metternich was willing to contribute to a rapprochement between the trilateral alliance and the Porte, but he did not want to be dragged into the London negotiations, as, for example, when Russia tried to obtain his support for Greece's

---

[9]   Metternich to Esterházy, Vienna, 25 April 1828, HHStA, StA, England 182; Metternich to Trauttmannsdorff, Vienna, 2 Aug. 1828, HHStA, StK, Preussen 129; Metternich to Ottenfels, Vienna, 10 Dec. 1828, HHStA, StA, Türkei VI, 35; Metternich to Ottenfels, Vienna, 17 Jan. and 19 Feb. 1829, HHStA, StA, Türkei VI, 39; Metternich to Ficquelmont, Vienna, 30 Jan. 1829, HHStA, StA, Russland III, 88; Cowley to Dudley, Vienna, 25 April 1828, TNA, FO 120/91; Maltzan to Frederick William III, Vienna, 8 Oct. 1828, GStA PK, HA III, MdA I, 6011; Laval to Portalis, Vienna, 5 and 17 Jan., 27 Feb. 1829, AMAE, CP, Autriche 410; G. L. Arš, "Capodistria et le gouvernement russe (1826–1827)," *Les relations gréco-russes pendant la domination turque et la guerre d'indépendance grecque,* Thessaloniki 1983, p. 128.

independence in early 1829.[10] The main reason for this restraint was
Metternich's unwillingness to become embroiled in the affair in which
the interests of its main protagonists differed and sometimes were even
not quite clear: "The trilateral affair weighs upon Europe like a thick
fog through which it is rather difficult to recognise the issues and,
consequently, take bearings."[11] By supporting the tsar he could easily harm Austria's relations with Great Britain, and he also did not
want to get entangled in a proceeding full of surprises and contradictions which annoyed him: an assault on the Turks north of the Gulf
of Corinth being considered by officers of the French expeditionary
army in the Peloponnese, the three Powers' desire for the pacification
as well as toleration of the Greeks' offensive in the same direction,
variable conditions of the planned settlement officially formulated in
several protocols during a brief period and, finally, the deterioration
of the sultan's position vis-à-vis Greece in the Protocol of 22 March
1829.[12] What made him even more sceptical about a quick settlement
was the disharmony existing within the trilateral alliance owing to its
members' mutual distrust and different aims: "As long as agreement
among the three Powers is not based upon anything other than those
of isolated political calculations and directly opposed interests, what
good could possibly come of their joint enterprise?"[13] Consequently,
although he tried to accelerate the reaching of a solution by urging the
sultan to yield, he decided to remain inactive towards the negotiations
in London because, as he declared, "we do not know how to engage
ourselves in something that does not make sense to us and does not
in our opinion offer any limits."[14]

---

[10] Metternich to Ficquelmont, Vienna, 30 Jan. 1829, HHStA, StA, Russland III,
88; Maltzan to Frederick William III, Vienna, 31 Jan. 1829, GStA PK, HA III,
MdA I, 6012; Tatishchev to Nesselrode, Vienna, 1 Feb. 1829, AVPRI, fond 133,
Kantseliariia, opis 468, 11881.
[11] Metternich to Trauttmannsdorff, Vienna, 14 Dec. 1828, HHStA, StK, Preussen
129.
[12] Metternich to Ottenfels, Vienna, 19 March 1829, HHStA, StA, Türkei VI, 39;
Metternich to Esterházy, Vienna, 27 March 1829, HHStA, StA, England 187; Laval
to Portalis, Vienna, 21 March and 18 April 1829, AMAE, CP, Autriche 410.
[13] Metternich to Esterházy, Vienna, 28 Feb. 1829, HHStA, StA, England 187.
[14] Metternich to Trauttmannsdorff, Vienna, 9 May 1829, HHStA, StK, Preussen
132.

Metternich and the London Conference 1829–1830

Metternich's passivity did not change during the final phase of the Russo-Ottoman war and actually continued after the conclusion of peace. The only difference in his attitude after mid September 1829 was that he was essentially prepared to welcome any solution. Without mentioning of course his total inability to influence the final outcome, this indifference was particularly due to the fact that his absolute priority was the restoration of unity and harmony between the European Powers, which, however, in his opinion was impossible to achieve before the termination of the trilateral alliance that "had existed too long to the misfortune of Europe,"[15] and the renewal of the Alliance of five, naturally for the support of his conservative policy and its crucial goal of saving Europe from revolutionary violence. Since the end of the trilateral alliance depended upon the solution of the Greek Question, Metternich very much wanted to see this affair which had been preoccupying him for so long settled and he cared little about the conditions of the final solution.[16] He told Schwebel in November 1829: "As for us, we want and we wish for a prompt decision in this affair [and for] the urgency of a unanimous decision to be made clear; for it to be reached quickly, and it is assured that whatever it may be, we will agree to it. It is important for us and it is important for the whole of Europe that there is no longer any serious political question under discussion, that every government would have nothing else to do other than to establish the principles of order and good public policy for assuring tranquillity within its own borders. It is with this aim that we also want the [trilateral] alliance to promptly conclude the Greek affair and for there to be no further delay in coming to an agreement to reach a decision with regard to Portugal."[17] Consequently, he did not interfere in the negotiations between Great Britain, France, and

---

[15] Metternich to Esterházy, Linz, 21 Sept. 1829, HHStA, StA, England 188.

[16] Metternich to Trauttmannsdorff, Vienna, 10 Sept. and 3 Nov. 1829, HHStA, StK, Preussen 132; Metternich to Esterházy, Linz, 21 Sept. 1829, Vienna, 16 Dec. 1829, HHStA, StA, England 188; Metternich to Ottenfels, Vienna, 10 Sept. 1829, HDA, 750, OO 38; Metternich to Ottenfels, Vienna, 17 Oct. 1829, HHStA, StA, Türkei VI, 39; Metternich to Apponyi, Vienna, 28 Oct. 1829, HHStA, StA, Frankreich 271; Schwebel to Polignac, Vienna, 1 Oct. and 14 Nov. 1829, AMAE, CP, Autriche 411; Cowley to Aberdeen, Vienna, 8 Nov. and 25 Dec. 1829, TNA, FO 120/104.

[17] Schwebel to Polignac, Vienna, 17 Nov. 1829, AMAE, CP, Autriche 411.

Russia about the future status of Greece and he remained true to his motto: "Come what may, we will not object to it."[18]

There were three principal problems connected with the creation of a new Greek state: the level of its dependence upon the Ottoman Empire, its territorial borders, and the name of its new ruler. As for the first issue, Metternich continued in his conviction that its complete independence was the only feasible solution in the given situation and was much better with regard to the danger of foreign interference within the Ottoman Empire than an autonomous Greece, which would definitely prove to be burdensome to the sultan and be an ongoing source of frustration to him: "We indeed anticipated the [Porte's] strong objections to every form of government for Greece which would exceed the limits of a local system and administrative independence. But the war has taken place and the Porte has consented to the creation of a Greek state, and we have no option but to consider which kind of political existence for Greece will be the most advantageous or, better said, the least disadvantageous in the interest of the Ottoman Empire as well as the peace of the Levant under the given circumstances ... Suzerainty would never be for the sultans anything other than an eternal source of squabbles, compromising of principles and political tension ... So our opinion is that if Greece is free, the problems for the sultan would have to be smaller, which they would not be for him if the Ottoman monarch had to remain entrusted with its protection."[19] When the trilateral alliance decided on complete independence before the end of 1829, the Austrian chancellor not only raised no protests against this solution, but also fully supported it.[20]

---

[18] Metternich to Ottenfels, Vienna, 19 Dec. 1829, HHStA, StA, Türkei VI, 39. For this passivity see also Crawley, *Greek Independence*, pp. 172–174. It must be explained that though remaining outside the trilateral negotiations in London, Metternich was kept fully informed about their progress due to his friendly relations with Cowley and his and Esterházy's friendship with the Duke of Wellington.

[19] Metternich to Esterházy, Vienna, 24 Nov. 1829, HHStA, StA, England 188.

[20] Metternich to Ottenfels, Vienna, 2 and 19 Dec. 1829, HHStA, StA, Türkei VI, 39; Metternich to Trauttmannsdorff, Vienna, 11 Dec. 1829, HHStA, StK, Preussen 132; Metternich to Esterházy, Vienna, 28 Jan. 1830, HHStA, StA, England 191; Cowley to Aberdeen, Vienna, 27 Oct. and 24 Nov. 1829, TNA, FO 120/104; Schwebel to Polignac, Vienna, 26 Nov. 1829, AMAE, CP, Autriche 411; Rayneval to Polignac, Vienna, 25 Jan. 1830, AMAE, CP, Autriche 412; Maltzan to Frederick William III, Vienna, 28 Nov. 1829, GStA PK, HA III, MdA I, 6013; Bray to Ludwig I of Bavaria, Vienna, 3 Jan. 1830, BHStA, MA, Wien 2403.

The territorial extent of Greece interested Metternich only minimally from late 1829 and he did not hesitate to inform the other courts that he had nothing against the extension of its territory although he personally preferred this to be as little as possible. This indifference resulted from the seizure of a considerable part of land north of the Gulf of Corinth by the Greeks prior to late September 1829 when the fighting between them and the Turks was terminated. Afterwards, the topic for the trilateral discussion was not whether to confine Greece to the Peloponnese and the adjacent islands but how much territory in the mainland the new state was to obtain. Since Metternich did not alter his opinion that the insurgents "will never agree to give up part of the land which they have taken possession of in hand-to-hand combat,"[21] he had no other option than to admit that Greece could not be limited to the peninsula and the islands only and to reconcile himself to Greece's territory being larger than he had originally supposed it to be: "The greater or lesser extension of borderlines, determining them from the Gulf of Volos to Arta or from Zeitoun to Aspropotamos seems to us in the research which we have carried out to be of such little importance that it does not enter into our calculations."[22] The chancellor was convinced that the most important task was that the three allied Powers determined a border that could be presented to Mahmud II, and he promised to support their decision. This was clear proof of Metternich's desire for a prompt settlement to which he was willing to make concessions; he even declared in late January 1830 that extending Greece's boundaries further would ensure better prospects for its independent and materially self-sufficient existence.[23]

This statement, however, in no way signified that he was willing to accept anything and go as far as Wellington and Aberdeen seemed willing to go in late 1829 when they contemplated the substitution of the Ottoman Empire with a Greek one. Their idea did not result from any desire to destroy the former, which they wished to preserve

---

[21] Brockhausen to Frederick William III, Vienna, 9 June 1829, GStA PK, HA III, MdA I, 6012.

[22] Metternich to Esterházy, Vienna, 24 Nov. 1829, HHStA, StA, England 188.

[23] Cowley to Aberdeen, Vienna, 27 Oct. and 15 Nov. 1829, TNA, FO 120/104; Tatishchev to Nesselrode, Vienna, 16 Nov. 1829, AVPRI, fond 133, Kantseliariia, opis 468, 11885; Maltzan to Frederick William III, Vienna, 28 Nov. 1829, GStA PK, HA III, MdA I, 6013; Rayneval to Polignac, Vienna, 25 Jan. 1830, AMAE, CP, Autriche 412.

as much as Metternich, but from their growing apprehension in early October 1829 that the Ottoman Empire was doomed owing to the conditions of the Treaty of Adrianople. Aberdeen wrote to Gordon on 10 November 1829: "In looking at the state of anarchy and disorganization of the Turkish Empire, as well as the total change of national character exhibited in the apathy, the disaffection, or the treachery of a great proportion of the population, we may perhaps be tempted to suspect that the hour long since predicted is about to arrive, and that, independently of all foreign or hostile impulse, this clumsy fabric of barbarous power will speedily crumble into pieces from its own inherent causes of decay ... We cannot reasonably look for any long continuance of its existence."[24] Alarmed at this prospect, Wellington as well as Aberdeen panicked and believed that a successor to the Ottoman Empire had to be found. In their opinion the restoration of a Greek (Byzantine) empire with Constantinople as its capital and a Christian prince at its head was the best option because with this solution the partition of the Ottoman Empire would be avoided and the stability in the eastern Mediterranean preserved. This inheritor of the Ottoman domains would be able to resist Russia's expansionism more successfully than would several small countries and would also have much better prospects for durability and vitality than the Ottoman Empire. With the aim of not destroying the latter but preparing for the moment when it might fall, they acquainted Metternich with their idea and asked him for his opinion. The reaction was peremptory and sharply negative. The chancellor totally disagreed with the two Englishmen's views and regretted that they allowed themselves to be persuaded that the further existence of the Ottoman Empire was incompatible with the stipulations of the latest peace Treaty. He was of the firm belief that it was still viable and though weakened by the outcome of its last war with Russia, there was no reason to believe that its existence was about to come to an end. In his opinion, the sultan's empire had to be supported to the last because the stability and balance of power in Europe, and thereby the general peace and order, depended upon its existence. Metternich saw no better alternative for the Ottoman Empire, and certainly not a Greek one; he differed with Wellington and Aberdeen as much in the estimation of Ottoman decline as in Greek vitality: "No, we do not consider the

---

[24] Puryear, *France*, p. 102.

Ottoman Empire as being about to expire yet and equally as little do we regard the new Greek creation as being capable of succeeding this empire!"[25] He also pointed out, and the future was to soon show that he was absolutely right, that Nicholas I did not want to see an establishment of a powerful empire beyond Russia's southern frontier and that he preferred a weak Ottoman neighbour over which he could exert his influence: "The Duke [of Wellington] is mistaken about everything; the Turks are not dead, they are merely beaten. The Greeks do not exist as a nation and for a long time they will have nothing other than an assumed existence. Russia will never want a Greek empire which will be able to stand up to it successfully … Unless I am entirely mistaken, we could well see Emperor Nicholas playing the protector of the Turks from now on."[26] Metternich advised Wellington and Aberdeen not to talk about the fall of the Ottoman Empire, which was not imminent and, therefore, not a topic for current debate, and to focus on the principle of conservation that offered no danger; there was no reason for discussing the destruction of an empire that still existed and the creation of another one whose ability to survive he doubted; furthermore, there were many dangers connected with such a transition. He also worried that this topic could be discussed by the trilateral alliance which would thus prolong its existence and assume the role of an arbiter not only of the Greek but also Ottoman future. Consequently, he advised that "particularly the British cabinet should carefully avoid allowing the trilateral action to continue and conferring upon it an extension of power that the former Alliance has never recognised, that of arranging the fate of empires … The feeling that every question which goes beyond the pacification of the insurgent Greece, such as the one which was stipulated and limited by the Treaty of London, should no longer be regarded as being of the competence of the trilateral counsel. To extend the remit of this counsel would be extremely dangerous as much for the courts allied with Russia as for those who are neutral and in particular for ours which, without exception, is the most immediately interested in the fate of the Ottoman Empire and the parties within it."[27] Aberdeen was somehow surprised at the strength of Metternich's disapproval

---

[25] Metternich to Esterházy, Vienna, 28 Oct. 1829, HHStA, StA, England 188.
[26] Ibid.
[27] Ibid.

and incorrectly accused the chancellor of having changed his opinion of the viability of the Ottoman Empire since the early autumn of 1829.[28] The foreign secretary continued for some time to maintain the view of the Ottoman Empire's inevitable and imminent demise, but he as well as Wellington finally abandoned this belief under the influence of Gordon's reports confirming Metternich's view that it was still viable and most probably would continue to be so.[29]

The third problem that occupied the trilateral alliance after the termination of the Russo-Ottoman war was the choice of a Greek ruler. In face of the jealousy existing among the European Powers, the cabinets in London, Paris and St Petersburg adopted the precept that the candidates should not be chosen from among their own courts, but despite this agreement the selection was still a rather difficult task owing to the close connections of all European dynasties with the principal five Powers. Metternich abstained from this search and just very cautiously expressed his opinion on this topic when he was asked for it. Austria did not have its own candidate, and when Lord Aberdeen sent Metternich a list of Britain's containing two Austrian archdukes, the latter asked the foreign secretary to remove them. He argued with their unwillingness to govern the Greeks and convert to Orthodoxy; another reason for this refusal was his awareness that every Austrian candidate would be inadmissible for France as well as Russia. When Lord Aberdeen asked the chancellor to recommend any candidate and the prince did so in a very reserved way by mentioning Prince Emil Maximilian Leopold of Hesse-Darmstadt, who was actually promoted by the British government, both Powers opposed his choice. Even Prince Philip of Hesse-Homburg, also suggested by Aberdeen – though in no way promoted by Austria and on good terms with Nicholas I – was unacceptable for the tsar, who feared that any

---

[28] Alexander Bitis shares Aberdeen's criticism of Metternich when writing that "Metternich now retracted his initial view that Turkey was doomed" but as explained in the previous chapter, Metternich never seriously believed that. Bitis, p. 369.

[29] Metternich to Esterházy, Vienna, 28 Oct., 24 Nov. and 16 Dec. 1829, HHStA, StA, England 188; Metternich to Ottenfels, Vienna, 2 Feb. 1830, HHStA, StA, Türkei VI, 51; Esterházy to Metternich, London, 12 Oct. 1829, HHStA, StA, England 186; Aberdeen to Cowley, London, 14 Nov. 1829, Cowley to Aberdeen, Vienna, 27 Oct. 1829, TNA, FO 120/104; Maltzan to Frederick William III, Vienna, 27 Oct. and 7 Nov. 1829, GStA PK, HA III, MdA I, 6013; Bitis, pp. 367–370; Crawley, *Greek Independence*, pp. 167–171; Puryear, *France*, pp. 103–104.

Austrian officer or candidate would be under Metternich's influence. Charles X opposed the Prince of Hesse-Homburg for the same reason. As for the other candidates for the Greek throne, Metternich did not openly criticise any of them on the turn of 1829 with the exception of Prince Bernhard of Saxe-Weimar-Eisenach in his instructions to Esterházy. This attitude was in tune with his desire that any ruler should be found, if possible one capable of managing the difficult situation in Greece – something that Metternich regarded as a gigantic task – and that the whole Greek Question should be concluded.[30]

As the negotiations in London went on, Metternich repeatedly assured the three Great Powers that whatever they decided was all the same to him but it was crucial that they did so quickly. For example, he told Tatishchev in November 1829: "It is above all necessary that the three courts make a decision about what they definitely want. If they want to stop with the suzerainty of the Porte and the borders proposed by the Protocol of 22 March, they should comply with this act; the Porte agreed with it in Adrianople. If they want to find an alternative between the most or the least influence the sultan would have over the future Greek state and the most or the least loss of territory, they should decide quickly and make their proposal to the Porte in the mildest and most dignified manner. The one or the other of these alternatives is all the same to us; what would not be acceptable for us would be if the discussions between the allies in the context of their conference and subsequently those with the Porte had to be prolonged infinitely."[31] This complaisance gradually increased due to his concern about the development of affairs in Western Europe, especially in France, where the internal situation was deteriorating owing to the widespread dissatisfaction with ultraconservative King Charles X and his government. Metternich desperately wanted to see

---

[30] Metternich to Esterházy, Vienna, 15 Nov. 1829, HHStA, StA, England 188; Metternich to Ottenfels, Vienna, 18 Nov. 1829, HHStA, StA, Türkei VI, 39; Metternich to Ficquelmont, Vienna, 19 Nov. 1829, HHStA, StA, Russland III, 88; Mortemart to Polignac, St Petersburg, 10 Nov. 1829, AMAE, CP, Russie 178; Maltzan to Frederick William III, Vienna, 14 Nov. and 4 Dec. 1829, GSta PK, HA III, MdA I, 6013; Tatishchev to Nesselrode, Vienna, 16 Nov. 1829, AVPRI, fond 133, Kantseliariia, opis 468, 11885; Sauvigny, *Metternich et la France*, III, p. 1315; Schroeder, *Transformation*, p. 662.
[31] Metternich to Ficquelmont, Vienna, 19 Nov. 1829, HHStA, StA, Russland III, 88.

an end to the Greek Question and the restoration of the former quintuple Alliance and impatiently waited for any agreement of the three
Powers, which was finally reached on 3 February 1830 when three new
Protocols were signed in London. Their most important stipulations
were the constitution of an independent Greek kingdom with a smaller
territory than had been settled in March of the previous year – the
frontier was moved southwards on the line Zeitoun-Aspropotamos –
and the nomination of Leopold of Saxe-Coburg-Saalfeld, who formally
accepted the crown on 23 February.[32]

Metternich welcomed this outcome that, in his opinion, "will give
impetus to an affair that would be so fortunate to see concluded!"[33]
In compliance with his previous promises, he instructed Ottenfels to
give his utmost support to the acceptance of the February Protocols
by the Porte. The chancellor expected the greatest resistance from
the Porte to the independence of Greece, which was a new request directed by the trilateral alliance to Constantinople and, consequently,
the internuncio was ordered to acquaint the Turks with the hard reality that could not be changed owing to the determination of the three
Powers to finish the whole affair in this way: "That the Porte is under
no illusion as to the real needs of its position; that it concedes to what
rejection on its part will no longer be able to invalidate. A free and
independent Greece will exist and it will never be the protestations of
the Divan that will alter anything in its existence."[34] Consequently,
the Porte had no option other than to accept the conditions submitted by the allied representatives in Constantinople, but Ottenfels was
also to persuade the Turks that the Greek independence was a better
option for them: "In dealing with the Divan, use the double argument
[first] that it recognises the necessity because it cannot escape it; then
that in all truth the total independence of Greece would be better for

---

[32] Metternich to Esterházy, Vienna, 16 Dec. 1829, HHStA, StA, England 188;
Metternich to Ficquelmont, Vienna, 11 Feb. 1830, HHStA, StA, Russland III,
90; Maltzan to Frederick William III, Vienna, 3 Feb. 1830, GSta PK, HA III,
MdA I, 6014; Tatishchev to Nesselrode, Vienna, 10 Feb. 1830, AVPRI, fond 133,
Kantseliariia, opis 469, 1830/275; Cowley to Aberdeen, Vienna, 24 Nov. 1829,
TNA, FO 120/104; Crawley, *Greek Independence*, p. 179; Dakin, p. 277; Holland,
pp. 28–33.
[33] Metternich to Esterházy, Vienna, 12 Feb. 1830, HHStA, StA, England 191.
[34] Metternich to Ottenfels, Vienna, 12 March 1830, HHStA, StA, Türkei VI, 51.

it than any limited submission."[35] In brief, following the instructions delivered to him, Ottenfels informally became "the fourth" member of the trilateral alliance pursuing its own goals but naturally in Austria's own interests. Prince Franz von Dietrichstein quite correctly summed up the internuncio's role when telling Prokesch: "Our internuncio has been given the order to say 'yes' to everything that the three want."[36] Ottenfels, who had been entirely passive in the Greek affairs in the preceding months, began to assist in the common effort to obtain a positive response from the Turks – although in fact merely unofficially through his advice since he was not asked by the three representatives to approach the Divan formally. This joint diplomatic pressure was finally crowned with success in April when the Porte yielded to the ultimatum.[37]

Metternich was not generally interested in the details of the February Protocols with one exception: the final – 11th – paragraph of the first Protocol of 3 February concerning the method of Greece's introduction into the European state system: "The three Courts reserve to themselves to embody the present stipulations in a formal Treaty, which shall be signed at London, be considered as executive of that of the 6th of July, 1827, and be communicated to the other Courts of Europe, with the invitation to accede thereto, should they judge it expedient."[38] Although the chancellor had earlier promised to recognise this state immediately after the sultan's assent, he regarded the proposed method as unacceptable for Austria because Francis I was not willing to accede to the Treaty of London or another following

---

[35] Metternich to Ottenfels, Vienna, 7 March 1830, HHStA, StA, Türkei VI, 51.
[36] A. von Prokesch-Osten, *Aus den Tagebüchern des Grafen Prokesch von Osten*, Wien 1909, p. 13.
[37] Metternich to Ottenfels, Vienna, 17 Feb. 1830, HDA, 750, OO 38; Metternich to Ottenfels, Vienna, 19 Feb. 1830, HHStA, StA, Türkei VI, 51; Metternich to Trauttmannsdorff, Vienna, 12 March 1830, HHStA, StK, Preussen 137; Metternich to Apponyi, Vienna, 25 Feb. 1830, HHStA, StA, Frankreich 276; Metternich to Esterházy, Vienna, 16 March 1830, HHStA, StA, England 191; Ottenfels to Metternich, Constantinople, 24 Dec. 1829, HHStA, StA, Türkei VI, 38; Ottenfels to Metternich, Constantinople, 26 March, 23 and 26 April 1830, HHStA, StA, Türkei VI, 50; Royer to Frederick William III, Pera, 7 and 27 March, 10 April 1830, GStA PK, HA III, MdA I, 7269; Cowley to Aberdeen, Vienna, 25 Feb. and 11 March 1830, TNA, FO 120/108; Maltzan to Frederick William III, Vienna, 9 March 1830, GStA PK, HA III, MdA I, 6014; Tatishchev to Nesselrode, Vienna, 10 and 12 March 1830, AVPRI, fond 133, Kantseliariia, opis 469, 1830/275.
[38] Holland, p. 31.

on from this one: "It can only be a question here of the agreement of the courts which, during the development of the whole affair, observed neutrality. Or why invite them *post factum* to [be party] to an agreement, which, at the time of the conclusion of the first trilateral treaty, had been rejected by them? Would it not create a risk of returning to the discussions over principles which our court, perhaps more than any other, will always find it desirable to avoid?"[39] For Metternich the most simple and most convenient method of recognising Greek independence was the one used for the foundation of the United States of America when, after the British king's formal surrender of his sovereignty over his thirteen American Colonies, the European countries had been invited by him to establish their relations with the new independent country in North America. In Metternich's opinion this precedent was also to be used in the case of Greece. It was even more acceptable for him to recognise its independence as had been done during the establishment of the Netherlands when some European countries had entered into relations with them despite the fact that the mother country, Spain, had still been at war with them. In any case, Austria could only proceed according to the common practice of public law, and its relations were to be established directly with the new kingdom: "It seems to us that it is *for the new state itself* to come to introduce itself to the Great Powers; to those which directly contributed to its emancipation as well as to those which, during the course of events which led to this result, followed a course of absolute neutrality. With such a declaration, the new state gives the first signal of its existence and its independence; everything in this method is useful and honourable for it and saves others from embarrassment."[40] The three allied Powers did not oppose this reasoning and satisfied Metternich's objections by abandoning the idea of an executive treaty. The European countries were to recognise Greek independence on their own at the moment when the Porte acknowledged it itself.[41]

---

[39] Metternich to Ficquelmont, Vienna, 26 Feb. 1830, HHStA, StA, Russland III, 90.

[40] Ibid.

[41] Metternich to Esterházy, Vienna, 16 Dec. 1829, HHStA, StA, England 188; Metternich to Esterházy, Vienna, 25 Feb. 1830, HHStA, StA, England 191; Metternich to Ficquelmont, Vienna, 26 Feb. and 4 May 1830, HHStA, StA, Russland III, 90; Metternich to Trauttmannsdorff, Vienna, 2 March 1830, HHStA, StK, Preussen

This protest was, however, somewhat premature because the long-yearned-for end of the Greek affairs was more remote than Metternich hoped owing to Leopold's disagreement with some of the conditions presented to him by the trilateral alliance, in particular those concerning the extent of the Greek territory and the sum of the loan acknowledged to the Greeks and guaranteed by France, Great Britain and Russia. Encouraged by Capodistrias, Leopold demanded changes to the February Protocols, above all more money and the return to the frontier on the Arta-Volos line. The Austrian chancellor had originally been indifferent to Leopold's candidature and even expressed his agreement with this choice because he was happy that a prince had finally been found, but when he learnt of Leopold's additional requests, he inclined to Esterházy's negative assessment of the young prince and started to express displeasure with the fact that a mere nominee could dictate his own conditions to the three Great Powers. When Leopold, having not obtained what he had demanded, renounced the Greek crown on 21 May 1830, Metternich was not very surprised, but he was frustrated with the fact that the final solution of the Greek Question was postponed again.[42] Being well aware of the deteriorating internal situation of Greece and the growing opposition against Capodistrias' transitory rule, he worried that it would be more difficult to find a new candidate who would be willing to

---

137; Ficquelmont to Metternich, St Petersburg, 24 March 1830, HHStA, StA, Russland III, 89; Tatishchev to Nesselrode, Vienna, 27 Feb. 1830, AVPRI, fond 133, Kantseliariia, opis 469, 1830/275; Rayneval to Polignac, Vienna, 1 March 1830, AMAE, CP, Autriche 412; Bray to Ludwig I of Bavaria, Vienna, 12 March 1830, BHStA, MA, Wien 2403.

[42] Metternich to Trauttmannsdorff, Vienna, 11 Dec. 1829, HHStA, StK, Preussen 132; Metternich to Trauttmannsdorff, Vienna, 16 Jan. and 12 June 1830, HHStA, StK, Preussen 137; Metternich to Esterházy, Johannisberg, 5 June 1830, HHStA, StA, England 191; Metternich to Apponyi, Johannisberg, 5 June, Vienna, 12 July 1830, HHStA, StA, Frankreich 276; Metternich to Ottenfels, Vienna, 19 Dec. 1829, HHStA, StA, Türkei VI, 39; Metternich to Ottenfels, Vienna, 3 March 1830, HHStA, StA, Türkei VI, 51; Esterházy to Metternich, London, 23 Jan., 19, 25 and 28 May 1830, HHStA, StA, England 189; Rayneval to Polignac, Vienna, 25 Jan., 3 March, 18 June and 11 July 1830, AMAE, CP, Autriche 412; Maltzan to Frederick William III, Vienna, 19 July 1830, GStA PK, HA III, MdA I, 6014; Bray to Ludwig I of Bavaria, Vienna, 3 Jan. and 10 Feb. 1830, BHStA, MA, Wien 2403; D. C. Fleming, *John Capodistrias and the Conference of London (1821–1828)*, Thessaloniki 1970, pp. 131–138; W. P. Kaldis, "Leopold and the Greek Crown," *Balkan Studies* 8, 1967, 1, pp. 53–62; Dakin, pp. 278–285.

exchange his tranquil existence in the West for anything but stable
a reign in Greece. Metternich wrote in this respect to Ficquelmont
in July: "The Russian Emperor, in qualifying to us the behaviour of
Prince Leopold of Coburg, used the term shameful desertion. You can
rest assured, Mr Ambassador, that the same term finds an echo here.
But which prince could the Great Powers succeed in persuading to
steer a boat without a bottom and without a possible rudder? I do
not know."[43]

The Birth of the Greek Kingdom

It was not regard for Greece's welfare but a strong desire for the end
of the affair which made Metternich's regret that the Greek throne
prepared by the trilateral alliance still remained vacant. Just a day
before Leopold's abdication and soon after learning of the sultan's
acceptance of the February Protocols, Metternich wrote to Ottenfels
with joy resulting from his belief that the end was near: "We are
ready to congratulate the sultan, not on what has happened, but on
his wisdom in putting an end to rather dangerous negotiations by
accepting painful concessions."[44] His optimism fell considerably with
Leopold's renunciation of the crown, which had significantly reduced
any prospect for a prompt settlement of the Greek affairs. As Metternich was to ascertain very soon, this was not the worst that was
to happen in this respect. At the end of July 1830, a new revolution
in France brought an end to Charles X's reign and initiated a series
of revolutions in Europe. The importance of the Greek Question re-
ceded into the background, and for a considerable period there was
even no discussion on this topic at the conference in London.[45] Metternich, whose primary attention was also turned to the European
revolutions, continued to be absolutely passive and merely waited for
new resolutions of the trilateral alliance on the affair that appeared to
him interminable.[46] In February 1832, when the question was still not

---

[43] Metternich to Ficquelmont, Vienna, 17 July 1830, HHStA, StA, Russland III,
90.
[44] Metternich to Ottenfels, Vienna, 20 May 1830, HHStA, StA, Türkei VI, 51.
[45] Crawley, *Greek Independence*, p. 205; Woodhouse, *Capodistria*, p. 474.
[46] Metternich to Ottenfels, Vienna, 2 Nov. 1830, HHStA, StA, Türkei VI, 51.

settled, he expressed his disillusionment in the incomplete state of affairs in the sarcastic way habitual for him: "We will remain voluntary spectators of the presentation of a performance a description of which is itself difficult. The one which would seem to me to suit it best is that of a tragedy blended with vaudeville and all that written in a romantic and burlesque style. Since this genre has not been yet named, it is natural that no one knows how to define it."[47] His sarcasm was well founded to a certain extent not only due to the inability of the three allied Powers to bring the whole matter to an end but also owing to the situation in Greece that had become extremely precarious. Several more or less significant civil wars had broken out among the Greek insurgents after 1830, and after Capodistrias' murder on 9 October 1831 the country fell into a state of complete anarchy.[48] These events brought no pleasure to the Viennese Chancellery and although Metternich naturally did not regret Capodistrias' assassination as much as the loss of Castlereagh, he was also not as pleased as in the case of Canning's death. His old enmity with Capodistrias had considerably softened since 1822 and he regarded his former adversary as one of the few men capable of administering Greece. In 1830, he even considered a federation according to the pattern of the U.S.A. with a president at its head the best political system for Greece and Capodistrias to be the most suitable person for this post. Regarding this restrained goodwill, it cannot be surprising that Metternich easily replied in the affirmative to Capodistrias' wish to have an Austrian consul in Greece in April 1831.[49]

Metternich's criticism of the slowness of the trilateral alliance's decision-making, on the other hand, did not reflect the fact that the events had started to move again on 26 September 1831 when a new Protocol was signed in London; it shifted the frontier of independent Greece back to the line of Arta-Volos. On 13 February 1832, the three Powers formally offered its crown to Otto of Bavaria, the son of Bavarian King Ludwig I. When both agreed, this appointment was made official in a convention signed in London on 7 May 1832. Only one step

---

[47] Metternich to Ottenfels, Vienna, 18 Feb. 1832, HHStA, StA, Türkei VI, 56.
[48] Woodhouse, *The Greek War*, p. 146.
[49] Metternich to Trauttmannsdorff, Vienna, 14 April 1828, HHStA, StK, Preussen 128; Metternich to Ottenfels, Vienna, 18 Feb. 1832, HDA, 750, OO 38; Prokesch-Osten, *Griechen*, II, pp. 391 and 445.

separated the involved parties from the final settlement: Mahmud II's consent to an independent kingdom with its territory exceeding the limit of the February Protocol. The problem did not lie in the independence itself because Mahmud II had already agreed with it in April 1830 but with the Arta-Volos frontier, which he found unacceptable for some time, in particular when his soldiers still held Athens that was to become a Greek town according to the alliance. Consequently, during the summer of 1832, Constantinople witnessed complicated negotiations between the Porte and the representatives of France, Great Britain and Russia which actually had nothing real to offer for the sultan's eventual concession. What finally decided the situation was the war that Mahmud II was waging at that time with Mohammed Ali. The Egyptian superiority did not enable the sultan to withstand the concentrated diplomatic pressure of the three Powers and finally forced him to surrender the requested territory on 21 July 1832 for a financial compensation of 462,000 pounds sterling. This outcome was included in the last protocol signed in London on 30 August 1832. Otto I arrived in Greece in early February 1833.[50]

Metternich neither opposed the Bavarian candidature nor criticised it because he was satisfied that someone acceptable to all the three Great Powers and willing to accept the Greek crown – for the chancellor symbolising nothing else than a crown of thorns – had been found. When the news of the May convention arrived in Vienna, he instructed Ottenfels to persuade the Porte to accept its conditions. Although the internuncio's role in Mahmud II's capitulation on 21 July cannot be overestimated, this result in itself entirely sufficed to create considerable pleasure and relief in the Austrian capital. What spoiled it somewhat was Ottenfels' report informing the chancellor about the sultan's decision to send the Ottoman chargé d'affaires in Vienna, Jean Mavroyéni, to London to obtain some concessions on the part of the trilateral alliance, one of them touching on the re-delimitation of the Greek-Ottoman frontier. Metternich regarded Mavroyéni's mission as a mistake because it was trying to open something which had already, and for Metternich fortunately, been closed. Moreover, the

[50] H. Gollwitzer, *Ludwig I. von Bayern: Königtum im Vormärz, eine politische Biographie*, München 1986, pp. 475–477; P. W. Petridis, *The Diplomatic Activity of John Capodistrias on behalf of the Greeks*, Thessaloniki 1974, p. 214; Holland, pp. 33–38; Vinogradov, pp. 159–160; Woodhouse, *The Greek War*, p. 149.

prince was of the opinion that there was absolutely no chance for its success and he was in no way willing to support the sultan's demands which actually found no echo in London. The Austrian Empire manifested its agreement with the existing settlement with a prompt recognition of independent Greece on 30 September 1832; Austria was also the first country to sign a commercial convention with the Greek Kingdom in March 1835. In 1834, an Austrian envoy finally arrived in Greece. His name was well known in this part of the Mediterranean: Anton Prokesch von Osten. Metternich had already proposed him for this post in the autumn of 1829 and this choice resulted from the conviction that Prokesch was a capable man who was familiar with the situation in Greece and spoke Greek. This estimation was shared by Francis I, who immediately agreed. Although Prokesch had already accepted this offer in early 1830, he only assumed the post four years later; in the meantime after 1831, as Metternich promised to Capodistrias, Austria was represented by Consul Georg Christian Gropius in Nafplion.[51]

* * *

Metternich's reconciliation with Greek independence and his desire to establish good relations with the new kingdom was a result of his pragmatism and matter-of-factness when in the case of necessity he did not hesitate to dispense with his maxims to "save the whole by

[51] Metternich to Francis I, Vienna, 15 Oct. 1829, HHStA, StK, Vorträge 260; Metternich to Ottenfels, Vienna, 3 June, Baden, 3 and 5 Aug., 5 Sept. 1832, HHStA, StA, Türkei VI, 56; Metternich to Neumann, Vienna, 17 Oct. 1832, HHStA, StA, England 199; Ottenfels to Metternich, Constantinople, 10 May, 9 and 25 June, 21 July 1832, HHStA, StA, Türkei VI, 54; Ottenfels to Metternich, Constantinople, 11 Oct. 1832, HHStA, StA, Türkei VI, 55; Neumann to Metternich, London, 9 Nov. 1832, HHStA, StA, England 198; Maltzan to Frederick William III, Vienna, 26 Jan. 1830, GSta PK, HA III, MdA I, 6014; Brassier to Frederick William III, Büyükdere, 7 Aug. 1832, GSta PK, HA III, MdA I, 7271; A. Cunningham, "Stratford Canning, Mahmud II, and Muhammad Ali," E. Ingram (ed.), *Eastern Questions in the Nineteenth Century: Collected Essays*, II, London 1993, p. 49; Krauter, p. 265; Neumann, *Recueil des traités*, IV, pp. 369–373; Prokesch-Osten, *Aus den Tagebüchern*, pp. 11–14; Sauer, *Österreich und die Levante*, p. 214.

sacrificing one part."[52] He was well able to reconcile himself to defeat and adapt to new circumstances. This important feature of Metternich's character is evident from his steps in the final phase of the Greek Question. Tatishchev had already described this personality trait in his report to Nesselrode in April 1826: "I had, on more than one occasion, to express my opinion to you that this minister, once he submitted to a necessity, one to which he had readily acquiesced, would try to make the best of it, if not for the benefit of political interests, at least for the sake of his own self-respect."[53] In June of the following year, Tatishchev expressed himself to his chief in the same way: "In my long career of negotiations, I have never met a minister who knew how to accept a necessity with such good grace as Prince Metternich."[54] This was also observed by Christopher Montague Woodhouse who correctly assessed the chancellor's attitude in the Greek Question on the turn of the 1820s and 1830s: "Metternich, always realistic, knew how to recognize hard facts in the end."[55]

What definitely mitigated the Austrian chancellor's disillusionment with the outcome of the whole affair was the independence of Greece, an appalling outcome for him a decade earlier, but in the early 1830s, in his opinion the best solution for preventing in that former territory of the Ottoman Empire the establishment of Russia's predominant influence which existed at the same time in the autonomous Danubian Principalities. The correctness of this presumption was immediately proved by developments within the Greek Kingdom, which did not become a Russian protectorate but significantly inclined towards Great Britain. For Metternich this was actually no triumph because in the 1830s he considered the influence of the two liberal Powers, Great Britain and France, a serious threat and, consequently, he cooperated with Russia on reducing their influence in Greece as well as in the Ottoman Empire. The most important outcome of the 1832 settlement was for him that the long crisis significantly affecting

---

[52] H. Rieben, *Prinzipiengrundlage und Diplomatie in Metternichs Europapolitik, 1815–1848*, Bern 1942, pp. 19–20.

[53] Tatishchev to Nesselrode, Vienna, 15 April 1826, AVPRI, fond 133, Kantselariia, opis 468, 11870.

[54] Tatishchev to Nesselrode, Vienna, 11 June 1827, AVPRI, fond 133, Kantselariia, opis 468, 11873.

[55] Woodhouse, *Capodistria*, p. 475.

the relations among the Great Powers ended and that the new country did not give rise to a new crisis until his fall in March 1848.[56]

In the final years of his life, Metternich drafted a document *Die Geschichte des Aufstandes der Griechen* housed now in the Czech National Archives in Prague; in this brief retrospection Metternich assessed the Greek war of independence as one of the most important affairs in his long career with enormous influence upon the political as well as social situation in Europe and the crisis by far most affecting the relations among the European Powers during its time.[57] It cannot therefore be surprising that he longed for an end to it and was extremely pleased when this chapter of the Eastern Question was finally and definitely closed. Unfortunately for him, new ones were to be opened, some of them even before 1832, and he was also condemned to pay further considerable attention to Near Eastern affairs in the 1830s.

---

[56] Bitis, p. 373; Sked, *Metternich*, p. 65. For more on the relations between the Austrian Empire and the Greek Kingdom during Metternich's period see F. Engel-Jánosi, "Österreich und die Anfänge des Königreichs Griechenland," *Geschichte auf dem Ballhausplatz: Essays zur österreichischen Außenpolitik 1830–1945*, Styria 1963, pp. 29–64.

[57] Metternich, *Die Geschichte des Aufstandes der Griechen*, NA, RAM-AC 8, 2.

11

The Constantinople Armenian Catholic Affair

The Greeks' struggle for independence was not the only holdover from the 1820s which had to be settled at the beginning of the following decade; the other was the Constantinople Armenian Catholic Affair. It is definitely true that the former issue was of considerably greater importance for the Great Powers and together with the Russo-Ottoman war overshadowed the persecution of the Armenian Catholics who were forced to leave Constantinople and give up their property in early 1828. It would, however, be a mistake to deny any importance to the latter problem, which was considerable, at least from Austria's point of view, not only due to fact that this central European Power was deeply involved in its solution in the early 1830s but also owing to its influence upon Metternich's further religious policy in the Near East.

The Expulsion of the Armenian Catholics from Constantinople

The affair began not because of Mahmud II's hostility towards the three allied Powers which had destroyed his fleet in Navarino Bay, as Hagop Barsoumian claims,[1] but largely owing to the strong enmity existing between the Catholic and Orthodox Armenians in Constantinople. The two groups were officially joined in one millet (a confessional community) under the rule of an Armenian Orthodox patriarch nominated by the sultan, but in practice they lived apart,

---

[1]   H. Barsoumian, "The Eastern Question and the Tanzimat Era," R. G. Hovannisian (ed.), *The Armenian People from Ancient to Modern Times, Volume II: Foreign Dominion to Statehood: The Fifteenth Century to the Twentieth Century*, New York 1997, p. 186.

the former desiring their own spiritual as well as administrative independence from the latter. The religious differences, however, were
only in part the reason for this state of affairs; the fortunes made by
some of the Armenian Catholics living in Pera and Galata, in 1828
over 20,000 individuals,[2] were envied by the Armenian Orthodox, and
this was also to play a significant role in the entire affair. The driving
force behind the persecutions was not Mahmud II but Orthodox Patriarch Karapet, who fully exploited the sultan's fear of his Christian
subjects' loyalty in late 1827. Mahmud II learnt at that time that the
Russians occupied Persian Armenia with the city Ejmiatsin, the seat
of the Armenian patriarch, and they allegedly planned to create an
autonomous Armenian principality dependent on Russia in the same
way as Moldavia and Wallachia. The Ottoman government was fearful
of the possible creation of such a principality because of the unpredictable attitude of its own Armenian subjects, particularly after the
Ottoman governor of Erzurum had announced the emigration of some
Ottoman Armenians to Ejmiatsin since the city had been in Russian
hands. Consequently, Mahmud II invited the Armenian patriarch of
Constantinople at the end of 1827 to meet him and asked him whether
he was able to guarantee his co-religionists' loyalty. The patriarch declared that he could do so only for the part of the nation of which he
was the spiritual head, but not for the Armenian Catholics, who were
obedient to the pope and in close contact with Europeans living with
them in Pera and Galata.[3]

---

[2]   Ottenfels, *Memoari*, p. 198; Krauter, p. 219. The figure of 20,000 originally
given by Ottenfels and later adopted by Krauter considerably differs from that
given by Anton Prokesch von Osten, who claimed that the real number exceeding
40,000 was concealed from the sultan. Prokesch-Osten, *Griechen*, II, p. 202. Spinola
mentioned 30,000 Armenian Catholics. Spinola to Bernetti, Vienna, 28 Aug. 1828,
ASV, Arch. Nunz. Vienna 256.
[3]   Ottenfels as well as Miltitz reported that the immediate cause that aroused
Mahmud II's attention to the loyalty of the Armenian Catholics was Guilleminot's
mistake made on 24 November 1827 when, wanting to support the thesis that with
the autonomy of Greece its inhabitants would not cease to be the sultan's subjects,
he used the example of the Armenian Catholics which, despite their spiritual subordination to the pope, were good subjects of the Ottoman monarch. The problem
was that the Porte never formally acknowledged any connection between the Armenian Catholics and the Holy See and, in the excited atmosphere after the Battle of
Navarino, Mahmud II easily became suspicious and angry when reading the record
of the talks between his advisors and Guilleminot of 24 November. Nevertheless,
Guilleminot's mistake cannot be proved, and the lack of any relevant information

As the patriarch intended, his words, spoken at the moment when the relations between the three allied Powers and the Porte could hardly be worse, aroused the sultan's suspicions against the Armenian Catholics. The patriarch's retinue further increased those suspicions by spreading a rumour in the Divan that the Catholics desired to achieve their political independence from the Ottoman Empire with the help of the pope and the Catholic Powers. The Ottoman monarch was finally misled to take measures against the Armenian Catholics and he evicted them from the capital; the execution of this order was entrusted to the patriarch.[4] This delegation of power proved to have a devastating effect on the Armenian Catholics' situation because what was originally merely a safety measure caused in no way by religious prejudice changed into a religious persecution motivated by religious hatred and the effort to get the apostolic Armenians back into the womb of the Armenian Orthodox church. The patriarch, who had always been invested with vast powers over the members of his millet and whose "mere word was sufficient for the authorities to send any individual – cleric or layman – into exile,"[5] became almost an absolute master over the lives of the Armenian Catholics in early 1828, and they had many reasons to fear his intentions.

The expulsion of the Armenian Catholics from Constantinople started with the issuance of a firman (decree) on 8 January 1828 ordering the leading members of this religious community to leave the capital and go first to Scutari (Üsküdar) and afterwards to Angora (Ankara). On 10 January, another firman ordered three generations of Catholic Armenians, with origins in Angora, regardless of their state, age or sex, to resettle to Angora in the space of 12 days. The patriarch

---

in the French ambassador's reports from that period naturally also cannot serve as irrefutable evidence for its baselessness. In any case, Metternich and Francis I used the whole affair for drawing the attention of the Holy See to their earlier warnings that France's policy would lead to the Catholics suffering in the Levant. Ottenfels to Metternich, Constantinople, 10 Jan. and 2 Feb. 1828, HHStA, StA, Türkei VI, 32; Miltitz to Frederick William III, Pera, 2 Feb. 1828, GStA PK, HA III, MdA I, 7266; *Mémoire sur la position des Arméniens Catholiques dans le Levant*, attached to Metternich to Lützow, Vienna, 29 Feb. 1828, HHStA, StK, Rom 38 – the author of this analysis was Aristaces Azaria and can also be found in Italian in HHStA, StA, Türkei VI, 45; Spinola to Bernetti, Vienna, 25 March 1828, ASV, Arch. Nunz. Vienna 256.

[4]   Ottenfels, *Memoari*, p. 198.

[5]   Barsoumian, p. 185.

warned them that if they did not obey this order, they would be put on a list prepared by him and presented to the sultan who could punish them according to his will. The patriarch also informed the aggrieved individuals that if they wanted to escape the expulsion, they had to renounce their faith in writing and adopt the Eastern Orthodox religion. Nevertheless, most of them refused to give up their confession and 12,000 chose the painful road to Angora. They started their journey on 22 January 1828, without most of their possessions, which they had to leave along with their homes in the city, and went by road with little money, food or adequate clothing. The journey in the harsh winter conditions with heavy snowstorms could not have lasted less than 40 days; thousands suffered, and approximately four hundred, mostly children, died.[6] One of Baron Miltitz's reports to his king indicates that the Ottoman soldiers escorting them had little understanding for their misery. When pregnant women asked them when they could lie down, they were allegedly told: "Wherever you want, on the snow."[7]

On 22 January, the patriarch ordered the Armenian Catholics who had originated in Constantinople to move from Galata and Pera to inner quarters of the city where the majority of Orthodox population lived and which consequently had mostly Orthodox churches. Since the Catholics were unable to rent homes in the designated quarters and were further obstructed by the patriarch who was willing to permit them to do so only if they converted, which they generally refused to do, the Catholics were ordered to move to the villages on the Bosphorus which were also inhabited by the Orthodox Christians. The clergy of the persecuted Catholics could follow their congregants only in the case of the Angorians, but those born in Constantinople were ordered by the patriarch on 2 February to go to the places of their choice, but not to those places situated in the Ottoman territory already inhabited by the Armenian Catholics. The hatred even turned against the nuns of the Armenian Catholics living in seclusion.

---

[6] Huszár to Ottenfels, 8 Jan. 1828, HHStA, StA, Türkei VI, 32; Ottenfels to Metternich, Constantinople, 10 Jan. 1828, HHStA, StA, Türkei VI, 32; Miltitz to Frederick William III, Pera, 2 Feb. 1828, GStA PK, HA III, MdA I, 7266; Spinola to Bernetti, Vienna, 22 March 1828, ASV, Arch. Nunz. Vienna 256; V. Inglisian, *Hundertfünfzig Jahre Mechitharisten in Wien (1811–1961)*, Wien 1961, pp. 40–41.
[7] Miltitz to Frederick William III, Pera, 2 Feb. 1828, GStA PK, HA III, MdA I, 7266.

On 8 March 1828, they were dragged out from their houses by the Armenian Orthodox and, since some of them were too old to walk, they were carried on bearers' shoulders and scorned by the present patriarch. Over 60 were taken from the city. Moreover, all young unmarried women between 22 and 24 years of age were designated as nuns and expelled from Constantinople. The clergy of the Catholic Armenians also had to leave Smyrna at the same time.[8]

The attitude of Ottenfels was completely clear from the very beginning: he flatly refused to doubt the loyalty of the Armenian Catholics; he considered them to be faithful subjects of the sultan and opposed the patriarch's insinuation that they could be otherwise: "Indeed no spirit of revolt or disorder has ever afflicted this nation; it continues to be humble and loyal; it peaceably occupies itself with increasing its wealth through commerce and industry without exhibiting the disturbing ambition that has constantly been a stumbling block of the Greeks living in Constantinople."[9] It was the fanaticism and jealousy of the patriarch and his fellow Orthodox trying to increase their own power and wealth with their hostile behaviour towards the Armenian Catholics that Ottenfels considered to be the principal cause of the whole affair.[10] As for the Porte, the internuncio did not find any evidence of religious intolerance in its behaviour as in the case of the Armenian Orthodox,[11] but he blamed the sultan for transferring the whole matter to the patriarch and his retinue who had a predominant influence over the Ottoman leaders: "The patriarch heretic had enough influence with the government to persuade it to regard the

---

[8] *Mémoire sur la position des Arméniens Catholiques dans le Levant*, attached to Metternich to Lützow, Vienna, 29 Feb. 1828, HHStA, StK, Rom 38; *Relazioni di Constantinopoli in data 10. Marzo 1828*, HHStA, StA, Türkei VI, 45; Spinola to Bernetti, Vienna, 25 and 27 March, 28 Aug. 1828, ASV, Arch. Nunz. Vienna 256; Inglisian, pp. 42–50.

[9] Ottenfels to Metternich, Constantinople, 10 Jan. 1828, HHStA, StA, Türkei VI, 32.

[10] Ottenfels to Metternich, Constantinople, 10 Jan., 2 and 15 Feb. 1828, HHStA, StA, Türkei VI, 32. Exactly the same view was maintained by Baron Miltitz. Miltitz to Frederick William III, Pera, 2 Feb., 3 and 11 March 1828, GStA PK, HA III, MdA I, 7266.

[11] Ottenfels to Metternich, Constantinople, 10 Jan. 1828, HHStA, StA, Türkei VI, 32. This opinion was also entirely shared by the Prussian diplomat, Baron Karl Wilhelm von Canitz und Dallwitz, who maintained that the relocation was in no way a result of any alleged Moslem fanaticism. Canitz to Frederick William III, Pera, 11 April 1828, GStA PK, HA III, MdA I, 7266.

Armenian Catholics as being entirely loyal to foreign Powers and particularly France."[12] The most influential of the Armenian Orthodox was the banker Kassas Arotin, who had free access to the sultan. He also enjoyed good relations with Ottoman officials, whom he and his companions allegedly bribed. The Armenian Catholics were unable to reverse the situation under the given conditions, particularly when prominent members of the Ottoman community, Moslems as well as non-Moslems, found in their expulsion a favourable opportunity to become rich at their expense: the Armenian Catholics' possessions, houses and shops, quite often built of stone, were auctioned off often for barely a twentieth of their real price. Pertev Effendi even offered such a stone house belonging to an emigrated Armenian Catholic in Pera to Valentin von Huszár, but this offer was immediately and sharply declined. It is, however, true, and it must be emphasised here, that whereas Orthodox Christians and some Moslem dignitaries brutally persecuted the Armenian Catholics, some Moslem inhabitants of the capital and even one pasha from the Asia Minor started to protest against the abuse of the Catholics and, being witness to the inhumane treatment meted out by the Armenian Orthodox, they often criticised them and demanded they moderate their behaviour towards the Catholics.[13]

Metternich entirely shared Ottenfels' views. He talked about "a criminal game of the schismatic patriarch"[14] and believed that the Armenian Orthodox exploited the situation; the religious persecution on their part occurred in what for the Divan was only a political measure. He wrote to Ottenfels on 19 February 1828: "The schismatics [Orthodox] constitute the majority among various Christian groups in the Levant. They have their own patriarchs. The Roman Catholics are a minority represented by no superior authority and the hatred borne them by the schismatics can operate unchallenged. The Greeks and the principal authority of the Armenian creed are under the virtual

---

[12] Ottenfels to Metternich, Constantinople, 15 Feb. 1828, HHStA, StA, Türkei VI, 32.

[13] Miltitz to Frederick William III, Pera, 15 Feb. and 3 March 1828, Canitz to Frederick William III, Pera, 11 April 1828, GStA PK, HA III, MdA I, 7266; *Relazioni di Constantinopoli in data 10. Marzo 1828*, HHStA, StA, Türkei VI, 45; Spinola to Bernetti, Vienna, 27 March 1828, ASV, Arch. Nunz. Vienna 256; Ottenfels, *Memoari*, p. 199.

[14] Metternich to Ottenfels, Vienna, 19 Feb. 1828, HHStA, StA, Türkei VI, 35.

protection of Russia; therefore, it is natural that they support the political interests of this Great Power, and by serving it, they operate in their own personal interests by oppressing those of their countrymen who do not share their mistaken beliefs."[15] He had no illusions about the Armenian Orthodox actions in the given affair from the very beginning, as proved by his laconic reaction to the news of the expulsion of 12,000 Armenian Catholics: "It is the schismatic patriarch who has been charged with the execution of this measure and it is superfluous to say that he will acquit himself of it rigorously."[16] As well as Ottenfels, Metternich also pointed out the entirely mistaken presumption of the Porte that some of the Catholics were dangerous to the Ottoman Empire. He himself did not doubt their loyalty.[17] On the contrary, he saw the threat in the inclination of its Orthodox inhabitants towards Russia: "It will never be those Christians who recognise the religious supremacy of the pope who will support the extension of the power of the Russian tsar who is the head of a Christian church hostile to their own. [Given a choice] between the two [the sultan and the tsar], the Ottoman Catholic subjects will prefer the sultan's rule."[18]

Due to Guilleminot's absence from December 1827, the principle protector of Catholicism in the Levant, France, was unable to help the suffering Armenians and its role fell on Austria as the second Catholic Power. The Viennese cabinet had already anticipated this duty after the Battle of Navarino when the French ambassador's departure from the Ottoman capital had been imminent and had willingly accepted it. Consequently, although Francis I was formally invited to this active protection of the Armenian Catholics by a personal letter from Pope Leo XII of 11 March 1828, Austria's assistance had actually been furnished for humanitarian as well as prestigious reasons after the arrival of the first unhappy news from Constantinople. On February 20 Metternich had instructed Ottenfels to help the Armenian Catholics as much as possible and the methods were left to the internuncio's discretion. In fact, Ottenfels had already been defending

---

[15] Ibid.

[16] Metternich to Trauttmannsdorff, Vienna, 25 Feb. 1828, HHStA, StK, Preussen 128.

[17] Metternich to Lützow, Vienna, 29 Feb. 1828, HHStA, StK, Rom 38; Tatishchev to Nesselrode, Vienna, 15 Feb. 1828, AVPRI, fond 133, Kantseliariia, opis 468, 11877; Metternich to Gentz, Vienna, 13 Feb. 1828, Kronenbitter, p. 315.

[18] Metternich to Ottenfels, Vienna, 19 Feb. 1828, HHStA, StA, Türkei VI, 35.

them from the very beginning; he had dared to assume responsibility for this initiative because he had correctly anticipated the approval of his court since Austria's assistance had already been offered to the persecuted Armenian Catholics living in the Ottoman Empire, for example by Kaunitz in 1781 or later by Metternich himself in 1820, in both cases particularly against the Armenian Orthodox. Nevertheless, neither before the chancellor's instructions came, nor afterwards was he able to have any influence on the decisions made by the Ottoman government and the patriarch; the former was deeply involved in the affair owing to its security concerns and greed, the latter particularly for religious reasons. The only "success" was that the Porte's refusals of his requests on behalf of the suffering Armenians were more polite than those addressed to other European diplomats attempting to help them.[19]

When Ottenfels found he was unable to stop or even mitigate the persecutions, he at least tried to reduce the suffering of the masses as well as that of certain individuals. The problem lay in the fact that the number of exiled Catholics was too large for Ottenfels and other Europeans to be able to effectively relieve them, for example by financial donations, and that the orders of the local authorities were so strict that not even official protests of the representative of a friendly Power against the banishment of the Armenian Catholic employee of the internunciature, Kapioglan Rafael Demirgian, could find a positive response at the Porte. Ottenfels at least succeeded in facilitating the escape of the Armenian Catholic clergy from the Ottoman Empire. Since most of them came from the Melkite monasteries in Venice and Vienna, and since the Melkites had enjoyed Austrian support since the rule of Maria Theresa, it is hardly surprising that when the persecution began, a considerable number of them travelled to Trieste and

---

[19] Metternich to Ottenfels, Vienna, 20 Feb. 1828, HDA, 750, OO 37; *Mémoire sur la position des Arméniens Catholiques dans le Levant,* attached to Metternich to Lützow, Vienna, 29 Feb. 1828, HHStA, StK, Rom 38; Leo XII to Francis I, Rome, 11 March 1828, ASV, Arch. Nunz. Vienna 520; Francis I to Metternich, Vienna, 10 April 1828, HHStA, StK, Vorträge 253; Ottenfels to Metternich, Constantinople, 15 Feb. 1828, HHStA, StA, Türkei VI, 32; Ottenfels to Metternich, Constantinople, 19 and 29 March 1828, HHStA, StA, Türkei VI, 33; Spinola to Somaglia, Vienna, 23 and 27 Nov. 1827, Spinola to Bernetti, Vienna, 12, 16, 21 and 26 Feb. 1828, ASV, Arch. Nunz. Vienna 256; Cowley to Dudley, Vienna, 10 Feb. 1828, TNA, FO 120/90.

Vienna furnished with Austrian passports. Metternich issued orders to ensure their acceptance corresponding to their misery and status.[20]

The Armenian Catholics' situation was pitiful in the early spring of 1828. In Charles A. Frazee's words: "In a period of weeks, the Catholic Armenians, once a strong and wealthy group, were reduced to an impoverished and wandering existence."[21] Ottenfels' effort to help them continued but was doomed to failure because first, the ambassador of the second Catholic Power, France, was not present and the internuncio therefore lost some useful diplomatic support, and, second, the Porte was dragged into a war with Russia and had no interest in solving the affair. Although the intensity of the persecutions considerably diminished during the spring of 1828 and they definitely ended in the autumn of the same year, there was no prospect for any real change as long as the war progressed and the only thing that Ottenfels could do for a long time was to try to reduce the financial need of the Armenian Catholics in cooperation with the Holy See. This situation lasted until the termination of the Russo-Ottoman conflict in mid September 1829, which opened the door not only to peace but also to the redress of the injustice perpetrated on the members of this Catholic community.[22]

The Settlement of the Affair

The Austrian Empire was waiting for an opportune moment to start putting pressure on the Porte to set right the wrongs and agree to a stabile solution assuring a secure future for the Armenian Catholics. Francis I was not deaf to an official request for an Austrian inter-

---

[20] Spinola to Bernetti, Vienna, 11 and 18 March, 1 and 12 April, 1 May 1828, ASV, Arch. Nunz. Vienna 256; A. Breycha-Vauthier, *Österreich in der Levante: Geschichte und Geschichten einer alten Freundschaft*, Wien, München 1972, pp. 45–46; Insiglian, pp. 39–47.

[21] C. A. Frazee, *Catholics and Sultans: The Church and the Ottoman Empire, 1453–1923*, Cambridge, New York, Melbourne 1983, p. 259.

[22] Spinola to Cappellari, Vienna, 16 Oct. 1828, ASV, Arch. Nunz. Vienna 256; Spinola to Bernetti, Vienna, 12 Jan. 1829, Spinola to Albani, Vienna, 13 June 1829, Spinola to Ottenfels, Vienna, 12 Jan. and 14 Feb. 1828, ASV, Arch. Nunz. Vienna 256A; Tatishchev to Nesselrode, Vienna, 16 Jan. 1829, AVPRI, fond 133, Kantseliariia, opis 468, 11881; Ottenfels, *Memoari*, p. 199.

vention on their behalf made to him by Pope Pius VIII on 20 July
1829, and he promised to provide the necessary assistance but only at
the moment when peace among Russia and the Ottoman Empire was
restored. As well as in the previous year, however, the pope's request
was unnecessary since the emperor paid considerable personal attention to this affair and his chancellor, entirely sharing the emperor's
goodwill towards the Armenian Catholics, had already instructed Ottenfels to reopen the question when possible in May 1829. Metternich
based his renewed intervention in Constantinople upon a five-point
plan prepared, at his exhortation, by the abbot of the Melkite congregation in Vienna and the archbishop of Caesarea, Aristaces Azaria.
Its fulfilment was to redress the injustice of 1828 and assure the undisturbed existence of the Armenian Catholics in the Ottoman Empire:
(1) freedom of faith and the creation of the office of an Armenian
Catholic patriarch as the head of this community in Ottoman territories; this official would be entirely independent of the Armenian
Orthodox patriarch; (2) the right to carry out their own religious cere-
monies, build new churches and repair their old ones, the last without
the necessity of asking for a new firman; (3) the return of the individuals expelled from Constantinople; (4) the restoration of confiscated
properties; (5) compensation for the injustices suffered in 1828.[23] The
first point was regarded at the Viennese Chancellery as entirely crucial for the prosperity of the nation. Metternich himself had already
proposed the separation of the two Armenian groups through the creation of an Armenian Catholic patriarchate in early 1828, and he never
abandoned the belief that the absolute religious independence of the
Armenian Catholics was the only way to prevent the recurrent persecutions on the part of the Armenian Orthodox and also that their
union was disadvantageous for the sultan because it was a hotbed of
further problems profitable only for Russia, which could exploit them
as an excuse for interfering with the internal affairs of the Ottoman
Empire. He saw no reason why the Porte should oppose this useful
measure that did not contradict the precepts of Islam and, moreover,
would be all the same to the Turks who actually did not exert their
spiritual power over any group of Ottoman Christians.[24]

---

[23] Azaria's undated proposal for the solution of the Armenian Catholic Affair,
attached to the correspondence from Constantinople on 16 October 1829, HHStA,
StA, Türkei VI, 45.

The representatives of several European countries – Catholic as well as Protestant – attempted to improve the Armenian Catholics' fate after the termination of the Russo-Ottoman war, and the Porte was thus exposed to pressure difficult to ignore. The first demand for the Armenian Catholics' return to Constantinople advocated by Ottenfels shortly after the conclusion of peace was submitted in November 1829, when the sultan started to issue firmans allowing the exiled Catholics to resettle to Constantinople and profess their religion unmolested. Although Gordon, who also supported the Armenian Catholics' cause, was satisfied with the outcome, his Austrian and French colleagues regarded it as insufficient and a mere first step towards the achievement of the greater objective to assure an independent patriarchate for the Armenian Catholics. They continued in the diplomatic offensive with the aim of ensuring the separation of the Armenian Catholics from the Armenian Orthodox by the nomination of a spiritual leader for the former. Pertev Effendi had already verbally promised Ottenfels to meet this request on 25 November 1829, but afterwards the Ottoman government retreated behind a barrier of silence. All attempts of the Austrian and French representatives to break it met with the Ottoman dignitaries' demands for patience.[25]

---

[24] Metternich to Ottenfels, Vienna, 19 May, 2 June and 16 Oct. 1829, HHStA, StA, Türkei VII, 34; Metternich to Ottenfels, Vienna, 2 Jan. 1830, HHStA, StA, Türkei VI, 51; Metternich to Ottenfels, Vienna, 18 Jan. 1831, HHStA, StA, Türkei VIII, 4; Metternich to Lützow, Vienna, 29 Feb. 1828 and 14 Feb. 1830, HHStA, StK, Rom 38; Metternich to Francis I, Vienna, 15 Sept. 1829, HHStA, StK, Vorträge 259; Pius VIII to Francis I, Rome, 20 July 1829, Francis I to Pius VIII, Vienna, 17 Oct. 1829, HHStA, StK, Rom 43; Lützow to Metternich, Rome, 7 Nov. 1829, HHStA, StK, Rom 37; Spinola to Albani, Vienna, 13 June, 11 Aug., 20 Oct., 14 Nov., 3 and 31 Dec. 1829, ASV, Arch. Nunz. Vienna 256A.

[25] Ottenfels to Metternich, Constantinople, 26 Oct. and 10 Nov. 1829, HHStA, StA, Türkei VI, 38. These dispatches were replaced with simple notes consisting of a short summary and the information that the original document had been forwarded to Mr Brennes. It was also the fate of several other documents on the Armenian Catholic Affair that were not found in other collections of the Austrian State Archives. Ottenfels to Metternich, Constantinople, 10 Dec. 1829, HHStA, StA, Türkei VI, 38; Ottenfels to Metternich, Constantinople, 11 and 25 Jan. 1830, HHStA, StA, Türkei VI, 50; Chabert to Gordon, Pera, 16 Jan. 1830, Gordon to Aberdeen, Constantinople, 7 Feb. 1830, TNA, FO 78/189; Spinola to Albani, Vienna, 3 Dec. 1829, ASV, Arch. Nunz. Vienna 256A; Spinola to Albani, Vienna, 3 Jan. 1830, ASV, Arch. Nunz. Vienna 256B.

Ottenfels found himself in a difficult situation because he was ordered to obtain a millet for the Armenian Catholics, but he lacked an
official capacity to protect the Catholics in Constantinople and Asia
Minor. Austrian historian Barbara Haider-Wilson claims that Austria
had the official right of the protection of all Ottoman Catholics upon
certain treaty stipulations.[26] However, the reality was very different.
Austria's respective rights were actually rather limited and in the protection of the Catholics it remained in its rights far behind France,
which actually had such rights on the basis of formerly concluded
treaties with the Ottoman Empire, which were older and considerably more explicit than those of Austria. The best characteristic of
the difference between the two Catholic Powers was that France was
a "protector" and Austria a mere "intercessor." The French ambassador was fully entitled to question the Porte in affairs affecting its
Catholics subjects and Austria acknowledged this by relinquishing the
representation of the Ottoman Catholics to France. During Metternich's period before 1829, an internuncio had at least twice consented
to give up his initiatives on behalf of the Ottoman Catholics to a
French ambassador, during their persecutions in Palestine in 1814 and
1818–1819, in both merely supporting his French colleague.[27] Consequently, with Guilleminot's return to Constantinople in the summer
of 1829, France reassumed the role of the main foreign protector of
the Ottoman Catholics. Ottenfels had to recognise that the most important role was arrogated to France and limited himself to informal
assistance, which he offered and which Guilleminot accepted on 9 October 1829. The reason that this aid was not refused lay in the fact

---

[26] In particular in Article 13 of the peace Treaty of Karlowitz signed on 26 January 1699, the sultan's two firmans of 1700, Article 11 of the peace Treaty of Pas-
sarowitz signed on 21 July 1718, Article 9 of the peace Treaty of Belgrade signed
on 18 September 1739, and Article 12 of the peace Treaty of Sistova signed on
4 August 1791. B. Haider-Wilson, "Das Kultusprotektorat der Habsburgermonarchie im Osmanischen Reich: Zu seinen Rechtsgrundlagen und seiner Instrumentalisierung im 19. Jahrhundert (unter besonderer Berücksichtigung Jerusalems),"
M. Kurz, M. Scheutz, K. Vocelka, T. Winkelbauer (eds.), *Das Osmanische Reich
und die Habsburgermonarchie: Akten des internationalen Kongresses zum 150-
jährigen Bestehen des Instituts für Österreichische Geschichtsforschung Wien, 22.–
25. September 2004*, Vienna 2005, p. 129; A. Schopoff, *Les réformes et la protection
des Chrétiens en Turquie 1673–1904*, Paris 1904, pp. 2–4.
[27] Gürbüz, pp. 241–261; Kargl, pp. 149–152; Sauer, *Österreich und die Levante*,
pp. 53–56.

that both Powers were united in the aim of assuring an independent patriarchate for the Armenian Catholics, but its acceptance changed nothing in the fact that the diplomatic interventions of Austria and France were not formally carried out together because the latter jealously guarded its sole protectorate, and Guilleminot proved to be a true Frenchman with his conduct as well as in his statements: "The right for the protection of Catholicism in the Levant belongs above all to France; the internuncio recognised it by placing himself at my disposal."[28] The legal limitations of a possible Austrian involvement are evident in the steps undertaken by the French ambassador and Ottenfels towards the end of 1829. Whereas the former presented a memorandum to the Porte on 27 December in which he officially clarified all the reasons for the Catholic Powers', and in particular France's, intervention on behalf of the Armenian Catholics with the aim of persuading the Ottoman government to satisfy their demands, Ottenfels only informally referred to the promises made by Pertev earlier.[29]

However, none of these attempts led to the desired success. To accelerate the decision-making of the Ottoman officials, Ottenfels decided to support Guilleminot's official steps with a less spectacular move. On 15 January 1830, he met the sultan's personal secretary, Mustafa Bey. The private meeting with this influential Ottoman took place in the Ramiz-Tschiftlik barracks, where Mustafa at that moment was accompanying Mahmud II. Ottenfels gave the reasons for Austria's interest in the Armenian Catholics' fate in the fact that most of their superior as well as their subordinate clergymen were educated in the Melkite congregations in Venice and Vienna. He promptly added that these institutions indoctrinated their collegians with the principles of loyalty and devotion to their legitimate ruler – the sultan. After this introduction, Ottenfels tried to persuade Mustafa that peace among the Armenians would be best ensured by the nomination of a spiritual leader for these Catholics, who would be subject only to the sultan himself and a deputy appointed by him. This provision would officially divide the Armenians, who in reality were already

---

[28] Guilleminot to Polignac, Constantinople, 12 Oct. 1829, AMAE, CP, Turquie 255.
[29] Ottenfels to Metternich, Constantinople, 11 Jan. 1830, HHStA, StA, Türkei VI, 50; Laval to Portalis, Vienna, 15 July 1829, AMAE, CP, Autriche 411; Guilleminot to Polignac, Constantinople, 12 Oct. 1829, AMAE, CP, Turquie 255.

living not together but side by side, into two separate groups. To facilitate the acceptance of this proposal, Ottenfels employed an example
corresponding, as he claimed, to the way of thinking of the people in
the Levant. The whole of the Armenian affair resembled, as he told
Mustafa, an Oriental story: "A rich villager owned a flock consisting
of sheep and goats that he entrusted to his shepherd. As long as the
flock was small in number, the shepherd was able to drive the flock
to pasture and supervise it. However, the flock increased with time
and finally reached such a size that this single shepherd was hard put
to keep it all together. The sheep went on one side along a stream,
whereas the goats climbed in the opposite direction into rocks and
hills. The shepherd was no longer able to gather the flock together,
much less bring it home. Several animals went the wrong way and got
lost every day. Their owner finally recognised that one shepherd was
no longer enough for such a mixed flock. Consequently, he separated
the sheep from goats; he made the old shepherd responsible for the
goats and chose a new shepherd for the sheep. Since then, everything
has been in good order again and to the owner's satisfaction."[30] According to Ottenfels, the Porte was to proceed exactly as the owner
of the flock did.[31]

Even though Mustafa did not promise Ottenfels anything and
only told him that he understood him well and would convey the
message to the sultan, the internuncio later believed that his intervention had considerably influenced the course of events. Two days
later, Guilleminot met Pertev Effendi and Husrev Pasha, the latter
appointed by the sultan as a plenipotentiary commissioner for the arrangement of the Armenian Catholic Affair, and in several hours he
was able to gain acceptance of the two Catholic Powers' demands.
Guilleminot himself attributed the credit for his success to Ottenfels'
conversation with Mustafa, and he acknowledged Ottenfels personally
for his contribution to the points settled on 17 January 1830. They
basically corresponded to Azaria's, quasi Austria's, demands: (1) the
Armenian Catholics would have their own spiritual leader independent
of the Orthodox patriarch; a leader with the rank of a bishop or arch-

---

[30] Ottenfels, *Memoari*, p. 225.
[31] Ottenfels to Metternich, Constantinople, 11 and 25 Jan. 1830, HHStA, StA,
Türkei VI, 50; Guilleminot to Polignac, Constantinople, 6 and 12 Jan. 1830,
AMAE, CP, Turquie 260; Ottenfels, *Memoari*, pp. 224–225.

bishop would be voted by the leaders of the Armenian Catholic nation and would obtain the approval of the pope; (2) the Porte would nominate a Moslem official to be the only agent between the sultan and the Armenian Catholics in civil affairs; (3) the Armenian Catholics would obtain a certain number of churches sufficient for their needs; (4) they would not be compelled to make use of Orthodox clergymen's services in spiritual matters like christenings, weddings and funerals; (5) the Porte would make every attempt to return to the Armenian Catholics the properties confiscated and sold in the two previous years. In the spring, the Ottomans took certain measures to fulfil these promises. The expelled clerics could return, the construction of the first Armenian Catholic church was permitted, the estates started to be returned to their original owners, and the Moslem official was named. Mahmud II chose Ettem Effendi, and this decision met with absolute approval of Ottenfels as well as the Armenian Catholics. Their prospect for a better future further improved on 16 February 1830 when Mehmed Hamid Bey replaced Pertev Effendi as the Ottoman foreign minister, which meant the removal of the Armenian Catholics' most dangerous enemy.[32]

What remained to be done was the restitution of properties, and by the spring of 1830 a considerable number of houses had already been returned to their original owners,[33] and also the election of the Armenian Catholics' leader and the determination of his rank within the Catholic Church as well as within Ottoman society. Ottenfels called Metternich's attention to the importance of the choice of a suitable person because his abilities could contribute to the welfare of the nation and his eventual partiality for Austria could increase this Central European Power's influence among the Armenian Catholics. In this respect he believed that Austrian diplomacy could take advantage of the clergy educated in Venice and Vienna: "Before the last persecution, there was a considerable number of Armenian priests here educated in the Melkite institutions in Vienna and Venice, and it is

---

[32] Ottenfels to Metternich, Constantinople, 11 and 25 Jan., 6 and 25 Feb., 25 Aug. 1830, HHStA, StA, Türkei VI, 50; Guilleminot to Polignac, Constantinople, 25 Jan. and 4 March 1830, AMAE, CP, Turquie 260; Royer to Frederick William III, Pera, 26 Jan. and 26 May 1830, GStA PK, HA III, MdA I, 7269; Spinola to Albani, Vienna, 13 and 14 Feb., 3 April and 8 July 1830, ASV, Arch. Nunz. Vienna 256B.
[33] Guilleminot to Polignac, Constantinople, 11 May 1830, AMAE, CP, Turquie 260.

these men who have best contributed to the surprising progress that Catholicism has made in last several years among the Armenians in Turkey. At the time of the persecution, the majority of these clerics moved to Italy, and above all to Rome. It is urgent that they return to the Levant and Constantinople. The Holy Congregation of the Propaganda must have received from them specific information on the most suitable individuals for making its choice of the post of the head of the Armenian Catholics."[34]

Metternich was also well aware of the importance of the choice of a skilled and pro-Austrian candidate. Therefore, he let the pope know that a member of the Melkite congregations in Austria would definitely be a suitable person for such a task: "It can be presumed that it will not be difficult to find a person among the Armenian priests graduating from the Melkite monasteries in Vienna and Venice competent in all respects to occupy the seat of Constantinople, and the Holy Congregation of the Propaganda, with the knowledge that it certainly has about their individual qualities, will be able to appropriately determine the choice of His Holiness."[35] Nevertheless, although the Holy See agreed with Metternich on the importance of the choice of a competent candidate, it refused to accept his intercession on behalf of Aristaces Azaria. The session of the Holy Congregation of the Propaganda rejected the idea that this man could be a leader of the Armenian Catholics because he was not only an Austrian citizen but also in close relations with the Austrian government including the emperor, which would certainly meet with resistance from France and the Porte. This question was resolved in the meantime in Constantinople in compliance with the settlement of 17 January when the assembly of the Armenian Catholic leaders chose by a majority of votes on 27 February 1830 Don Antonio Nuridschan (Nourigian). Ottenfels found this decision to be ideal and he recommended the chancellor to support Nuridschan in Rome.[36]

---

[34] Ottenfels to Metternich, Constantinople, 25 Jan. 1830, HHStA, StA, Türkei VI, 50.

[35] Metternich to Lützow, Vienna, 14 Feb. 1830, HHStA, StK, Rom 38.

[36] Ottenfels to Metternich, Constantinople, 3 March 1830, HHStA, StA, Türkei VI, 50; Lützow to Metternich, Rome, 27 Feb. 1830, HHStA, StK, Rom 37; Spinola to Albani, Vienna, 14 and 18 Feb. 1830, ASV, Arch. Nunz. Vienna 256B; Inglisian, p. 66.

The proposed backing was necessary since the determination of Nuridschan's spiritual competence and his canonic consecration were in the pope's hands, and in Rome some clergymen started to plot against Nuridschan's appointment as archbishop or even as patriarch. Metternich always maintained that the leader of the Armenian Catholics was to have the same position, including the title and rights, as the Armenian Orthodox patriarch and he therefore intervened in the holy city with the aim of obtaining for Nuridschan as much prestige and as many rights as possible. At least since the exchange of the letters between Pius VIII and Francis I in the previous year, Metternich had tried to win over the pope to the Austrian point of view, and Austrian influence really seemed to be predominant in Rome in this affair as well as in others during that period. Count Rudolf von Lützow, the Austrian internuncio in Constantinople in 1818–1822 and now the ambassador in the Papal State, together with Azaria who arrived in June, were therefore finally successful in advocating Metternich's standpoint. On 6 July 1830, Pius VIII issued a writ constituting an archiepiscopal and patriarchal seat in Constantinople for the Catholic Armenians living in this city and Asia Minor. On the same day, Antonio Nuridschan was installed into this new office. The reason why Nuridschan obtained two nomination decrees, one as archbishop and one as patriarch, was due to the pope's apprehension of Mahmud II's possible disagreement with the patriarchate; this caution soon proved to be well founded.[37]

In the late summer of 1830, the situation of the Armenian Catholics in Constantinople started to change for the worse. The right of return of the exiles, the restitution of their properties and the permission to build their own churches were all suspended. This seemed to be the result of both the recent French invasion into Algeria, one of the sultan's provinces, and Nuridschan's prolonged absence from the Ottoman capital; both reasons were now used by the Armenian Orthodox to invoke the distrust of the sultan and his advisers against the Catholics and prevent their separation at the last minute. The

---

[37] Albani to Lützow, Vatican City, 29 [?] Jan. 1830, Lützow to Metternich, Rome, 7 Nov. and 5 Dec. 1829, 30 Jan., 5 and 24 June, 17 July 1830, HHStA, StK, Rom 37; Lützow to Metternich, Rome, 27 Feb. 1830, HHStA, StK, Rom 43; Metternich to Ottenfels, Vienna, 17 Feb. and 3 March 1830, HHStA, StA, Türkei VI, 51; A. J. Reinerman, *Austria and the Papacy in the Age of Metternich, Volume I: Between Conflict and Cooperation 1809–1830*, Washington 1979, pp. 160–161.

Orthodox patriarch together with Kassas Arotin and Mustafa Bey accused Catholicism of being hostile to the monarchs because its adherents only recognised the authority of the pope, remonstrated against the hostile conduct of one of the Catholic Powers towards the Ottoman African province and also insinuated that Nuridschan was a man entirely devoted to Austria. Nuridschan's position was also undermined by the opposition of the Armenian Catholics from Angora to his leadership and by accusations of too close a relationship between the Armenian Catholic elites and the two Catholic Powers, particularly between Nuridschan and Austria, which probably was not too difficult to believe when Nuridschan returned to Constantinople via Vienna to express his gratitude for Francis I's and Metternich's support in person. The extensive support given by Austria to the Armenian Catholics proved thus to be counterproductive and Ottenfels therefore increasingly limited his activities from the early autumn, merely trying to explain to the Ottoman dignitaries that in fact Austria in no way wanted to interfere with the affairs of an independent country. He pointed out that the reasons for its concern for the Armenian Catholics differed from those of France, and that the prompt settlement of the protracted affair was above all in the interest of the Ottoman government, and this was to be achieved by the consent of Nuridschan's patriarchate.[38]

When the affair was not moving forward during the autumn 1830, Ottenfels attempted to speed up the settlement on 19 November by addressing a memorandum to the Porte in which he presented strong arguments and Francis I's personal recommendation for the fulfilment of the promises earlier given by the sultan. Ottenfels countered in the memorandum some of the accusations raised against the Armenian Catholics; for example, he defended their obedience, mentioning their loyal behaviour to the sultan during the Greek insurrection as well as with the words from the New Testament: "Nothing is more false and more absurd than this accusation! As the founder of our holy religion said: 'Give unto Caesar what is Caesar's and unto God

---

[38] Metternich to Ottenfels, Vienna, 4 Jan. 1831, HHStA, StA, Türkei VIII, 4; Ottenfels to Metternich, Constantinople, 25 Aug. 1830, HHStA, StA, Türkei VI, 50; Ottenfels to Metternich, Constantinople, 10 Nov. 1830, HHStA, StA, Türkei VI, 51; Lützow to Metternich, Rome, 17 July 1830, HHStA, StK, Rom 37; Spinola to Capellari, Vienna, 4 Jan. 1831, ASV, Arch. Nunz. Vienna 256C; Inglisian, p. 78.

what is God's.'"[39] This step, however, had an entirely different effect from the one Ottenfels had wished and instead of the fulfilment of the Porte's January promises it led to its greater suspicions against Nuridschan and Austria's intentions in the whole affair. After this, in Guilleminot's words "indiscreet interference,"[40] Nuridschan reduced his contacts with the internuncio to a minimum and Ottenfels, having lost any influence over the course of events, ceased in his activities altogether.[41]

Mahmud II finally agreed with the division of the Armenian millet, but he refused to nominate Nuridschan as the head of the new Catholic community in late December 1830 under the pretext that the prelate was a creature of the court in Rome, in other words imposed on the Porte from abroad. This argument, in fact a mere pretext, was rather strange because the election of Nuridschan had occurred in the Ottoman Empire at the assembly of local Armenian Catholic spiritual as well as secular dignitaries summoned by Ettem Effendi and was approved by the sultan long before Nuridschan's appointment in the Eternal City. There was thus no other option than to organise a new election on 28 December 1830 and vote Bishop Giacomo della Valle as Nuridschan's successor. The sultan sanctioned this choice on 5 January 1831. The Armenian Catholics obtained thus their own millet with administrative and spiritual autonomy. However, Giacomo della Valle did not receive the necessary clerical authority which could only be vested by the pope. He consequently assumed authority over the secular domain only and left the spiritual domain to Nuridschan.[42] For Metternich this outcome signified a victory because the measure advocated by the Viennese cabinet since the beginning of the crisis was finally accepted. He regretted the disunity among the Armenian Catholics that negatively contributed to the development of the affair

---

[39] Ottenfels' memorandum to Mehmed Hamid Bey, Constantinople, 18 Nov. 1830, attached to Adelburg to Ottenfels, Constantinople, 19 Nov. 1830, HHStA, StA, Türkei VI, 51.

[40] Guilleminot to Sébastiani, Constantinople, 29 Dec. 1830, AMAE, CP, Turquie 261.

[41] Ottenfels to Metternich, Constantinople, 10 and 25 Nov., 10 and 27 Dec. 1830, HHStA, StA, Türkei VI, 51; Guilleminot to Sébastiani, Constantinople, 29 Dec. 1830, AMAE, CP, Turquie 261.

[42] Ottenfels to Metternich, Constantinople, 10 and 25 Nov., 10, 27 and 31 Dec. 1830, HHStA, StA, Türkei VI, 51; Guilleminot to Sébastiani, Constantinople, 11 Jan. 1831, AMAE, CP, Turquie 262.

but was satisfied with the creation of their millet which was the only measure for preventing new persecutions on the part of the Armenians Orthodox.[43] He accepted the joint administration of Valle and Nurid-schan on condition that the two men cooperated: "Provided that this harmony lasts, there will be no major problems to fear from such a division of authority. It is only desirable that the known as well as the secret enemies of our co-religionists never manage to sow the seeds of discord between the two clergymen."[44] This apprehension proved to be unnecessary because the division of responsibility caused no problems as the two men were on friendly terms and proceeded in agreement with each other; they even lived in the same house in Galata. The Armenian Catholics rejoiced at their leaders' unity as well as at the goodwill of the Porte: the emigrees could return to Constantinople, the churches could be built – the construction of one in Galata was already approved – and, before the year passed, the property auctioned off in 1828 either was returned or the undervalued prices for which some Armenians had had to sell their houses were increased to market prices and the balance refunded. Consequently, Ottenfels reported to Vienna in the spring of 1831 that this Catholic community was content with the existing situation and had no reasons for complaint. The general satisfaction was increased three years later when, after Giacomo della Valle's death, the title of patriarch was bestowed on the new leader of the Armenian Catholics, Artin Vartabet.[45]

---

[43] Metternich to Ottenfels, Vienna, 4 and 18 Jan. 1831, HHStA, StA, Türkei VIII, 4.

[44] Metternich to Ottenfels, Vienna, 19 April 1831, HHStA, StA, Türkei VIII, 4.

[45] Ottenfels to Metternich, Constantinople, 26 Jan., 10 Feb., 11 and 26 March, 28 June 1831, HHStA, StA, Türkei VI, 52; Ottenfels to Metternich, Constantinople, 27 Dec. 1831, HHStA, StA, Türkei VIII, 4; Stürmer to Metternich, Constantinople, 25 March 1834, HHStA, StA, Türkei VI, 60; Brassier to Frederick William III, Therapia, 11 Oct. 1831, GStA PK, HA III, MdA I, 7270; Varenne to Sébastiani, Therapia, 25 Sept. 1831, AMAE, CP, Turquie 262; Roussin to Broglie, Therapia, 25 Feb. and 15 March 1834, AMAE, CP, Turquie 268; Spinola to Capellari, Vienna, 3 Feb. 1831, Spinola to Bernetti, Vienna, 5 July 1831, ASV, Arch. Nunz. Vienna 256C.

The Austro-French Discord

The complications of the last months of 1830 concerning Don Nurid-schan led not only to the loss of Ottenfels' influence over the events but also, logically, to a considerable increase of that of Guilleminot, who exerted extraordinary activity in this matter in late 1830. Although the French ambassador's reports says nothing about any French plots against the internuncio and Nuridschan, it is highly likely that Guille-minot proceeded in this way owing to his disapproval of the close re-lations between Austria and this clergyman chosen for an influential religious office in the Levant. Although there is no reason to believe that Giacomo della Valle was a pro-French candidate, for Guilleminot he was a better option than Nuridschan, and this satisfaction was manifested by a festive Te Deum sung in the French embassy's church on 30 December. It is, however, absolutely certain that a considerable rivalry over the protection of the Armenian Catholics really existed between Austria and France. The former did not want all the credit in this affair to be appropriated by the latter, and the government in Paris did not want to share its exclusive rights with the Viennese cabinet. Ottenfels was involved in the affair from the autumn of 1829 not only owing to Austria's sincere wish to support the persecuted Catholic community in the Levant, but also because of its unwill-ingness to fall behind France in this matter. Metternich, dissatisfied with the French proceeding in the Greek affairs, disliked the idea of a unique French protectorate. Although the two Great Powers did not proceed in late 1829 at variance in the affair in which they were united by a mutual interest and in which they agreed on principal points, and although their representatives in Constantinople coordi-nated their steps until January 1830 – Ottenfels correctly attributed the success achieved in the middle of the month to this cooperation – a considerably reserved attitude towards France prevailed at the Chan-cellery in Vienna. This is clearly visible in Metternich's instructions of 2 January 1830 in which he expressed his wish that Ottenfels proceed in the affair alone or with British support, but not with Guilleminot, or as little as possible with him. The internuncio was also to persuade the Porte that it should particularly listen to him: "The seat of the Armenian Catholics is in fact in our country. The patriarch will have to be chosen among the clergymen educated either in Venice or in Vienna. France has nothing to do with it, and it is certainly not the friendship of this Great Power which should enjoy such great favour

with the Divan today. France cannot claim just a religious interest;
additionally, our policy has always been to try to succeed in a way
entirely compatible with the sultan's interest. Therefore, it is entirely
just that it is we who should voice our opinions and likewise it is
we in whom H[is] [H]ighness should have confidence."[46] As a consequence, from late January 1830 no mention of a coordinated action
of Ottenfels and Guilleminot in this affair can be found in their reports; on the contrary, the former's increasing displeasure at France's
exclusive protectorate over the Ottoman Catholics is evident, and it
became entirely unconcealed in his discussions with some members of
the diplomatic corps before the year passed.[47]

It was the French claim for an exclusive protectorship over the
Ottoman Catholics with which Metternich strongly disagreed and
against which, as well as France's other ambitions in the Levant, he
protested because this Great Power, in his opinion, "covered Europe
and in particular the Levant with its dreams of glory and supremacy.
Turks in Constantinople, Greeks in Nafplion and French in Alexandria, the French government has twenty different policies at this moment and all are a mere smokescreen hiding disorder and disruption."[48] He agreed with Ottenfels, who wrote in March 1830 that
by supporting Catholicism, France tried to obtain a greater influence
in the Ottoman Empire which could have serious consequences for the
Ottoman Catholics: "It [Austria] has never sought to control them,
to exercise any particular influence on them; it has wisely avoided
drawing the attention of the schismatics and consequently that of the
Ottoman government to them and to itself. The policy of the French
government has always been less scrupulous. Its alarming activity, its
insatiable desire to play a role and make itself heard eagerly took advantage of the pretext of the spread of Catholicism in Turkey to try
to obtain greater political influence and replace Russia's dominance
there with its own in the course of time ... These attempts would

---

[46] Metternich to Ottenfels, Vienna, 2 Jan. 1830, HHStA, StA, Türkei VI, 51.
[47] Metternich to Ottenfels, Vienna, 19 May 1829, HHStA, StA, Türkei VII, 34;
Ottenfels to Metternich, Constantinople, 11 and 25 Jan. 1830, HHStA, StA, Türkei
VI, 50; Ottenfels to Metternich, Constantinople, 27, 28 and 31 Dec. 1830, HHStA,
StA, Türkei VI, 51; Brassier to Frederick William III, Pera, 27 Dec. 1830, GStA
PK, HA III, MdA I, 7269; Spinola to Capellari, Vienna, 18 Jan. 1831, ASV, Arch.
Nunz. Vienna 256C; Ottenfels, *Memoari*, p. 224.
[48] Metternich to Ottenfels, Vienna, 2 Jan. 1830, HHStA, StA, Türkei VI, 51.

probably be in vain and useless as other similar endeavours of this kind; but they would be enough to harm the religion by exciting the jealousy and mistrust of the Porte and authorising Russia so to speak to redouble its efforts to stimulate the zeal of its co-religionists and to increase the number of its supporters."[49] Metternich's written comments in this as well as Ottenfels' report of 25 January 1830 testify to the importance that the chancellor attached to the weakening of the French exclusiveness in the protection of the Ottoman Catholics. When the internuncio informed him in his latter report about his decision made ten days earlier to visit Mustafa Bey with the aim "of convincing His Highness and his government that our country does not attach less importance to this affair than the French court,"[50] the chancellor wrote in the margin: "Attached the utmost importance."[51] Metternich also marked off beside the text the information that the sultan "*had already charged Serasker Husrev Pasha with settling it* [the affair] *with the French ambassador; that His Highness has been informed about the steps that I* [Ottenfels] *had undertaken in the same affair, and that the participation of our court and the views that we had expressed in this respect had contributed considerably to shaping his decisions.*"[52] In Ottenfels' report of his successful intervention through Mustafa Bey and the following settlement among Guilleminot, Pertev and Husrev, the chancellor marked off and underlined in red the first part of the sentence: "*France will appear to have done everything because its ambassador, as an avowed protector of the Catholic religion in Turkey, seized the principal role*; but he would have accomplished nothing without our assistance and that of other delegations."[53]

Metternich's animosity towards France definitely increased in early 1830 due to its aggressive plans against Algeria[54] and following Guilleminot's pompous declarations about the French protection of the Ottoman Catholics in the Armenian Catholics affair, which was

---

[49] Ottenfels to Metternich, Constantinople, 10 March 1830, HHStA, StA, Türkei VI, 50.
[50] Ottenfels to Metternich, Constantinople, 25 Jan. 1830, HHStA, StA, Türkei VI, 50.
[51] Ibid.
[52] Ibid.
[53] Ibid.
[54] For more on Metternich's opposition to the French expedition to Algeria see Chapter 13.

in sharp contrast with the modest way in which Ottenfels informed the Chancellery about his success in the matter. Since the beginning of the negotiations with the Porte, Guilleminot made it clear in his reports how crucial it was for him that he – and thus France – played the principal role in the whole affair that he regarded as "essential for our esteem in the Levant,"[55] an opinion obviously shared by his government since this part of his report was marked off by Polignac. This vanity became clearly evident after the Porte yielded in January 1830 when Guilleminot denied Ottenfels any merit and claimed it all for himself, denouncing the internuncio in this report as "short-sighted and poorly skilled."[56] Guilleminot wrote to Polignac that Ottenfels had done nothing until the moment when his, Guilleminot's, victory was close and certain; only then had Ottenfels started to act. Nevertheless, the studied documents convincingly prove that Ottenfels had been active long before 15 January and if his efforts were not as ostentatious as those of his French colleague, this was due to the different legal positions of the two Catholic Powers and Guilleminot's unwillingness to cooperate with Ottenfels and enable him to participate more in the negotiations. Further proof of the usefulness of the internuncio's activity is Guilleminot's public acknowledgement for his personal intervention at the Porte in mid January.[57]

Guilleminot's dispatches intercepted by the Austrians considerably irritated Metternich, in particular that of 26 January 1830 in which the ambassador boasted: "Religion, humanity, the glory of Our Noble Master are matters in whose cause and success I have appointed myself a devoted advocate."[58] In reaction to this and other similar expressions, Metternich wrote to Ottenfels: "I regret the manner in which the French court presents the affair in such a way that it can take all the credit in the eyes of Europe always poorly in-

[55] Guilleminot to Polignac, Constantinople, 6 Jan. 1830, AMAE, CP, Turquie 260.
[56] Guilleminot to Polignac, Constantinople, 4 March 1830, AMAE, CP, Turquie 260.
[57] Guilleminot to Polignac, Constantinople, 12 Dec. 1829, AMAE, CP, Turquie 255; Guilleminot to Polignac, Constantinople, 4 March 1830, AMAE, CP, Turquie 260; Gordon to Aberdeen, Constantinople, 7 Feb. 1830, TNA, FO 78/189; Spinola to Albani, Vienna, 3 Dec. 1829, ASV, Arch. Nunz. Vienna 256A; Spinola to Albani, Vienna, 13 and 14 Feb. 1830, ASV, Arch. Nunz. Vienna 256B.
[58] Guilleminot to La Ferronnays, Constantinople, 26 Jan. 1830, attached to Metternich to Lützow, Vienna, 14 Feb. 1830, HHStA, StK, Rom 38.

formed ... [Guilleminot] depicts the success of the negotiation as being solely his own doing, and as constituting a laurel in the crown of the [M]ost [C]hristian King."[59] Metternich's resentment of France was also demonstrated in Rome when he tried to gain the predominant influence for Austria in the Armenian Catholic Affair with the promotion and overstatement of Austria's important contribution to its settlement. When it was preliminarily achieved in mid January 1830, Lützow was instructed to inform the pope without delay about this "Austrian achievement,"[60] before France could do so. The ambassador then notified the Chancellery about the fulfilment of the task: "Austria was the first to inform the Holy See about the victory gained in the cause of Catholicism in the Levant, and the court in Rome consequently knows to whom it is beholden."[61]

An obvious deterioration in the Austro-French relations resulted from the July Revolution in France in 1830. Metternich extended his mistrust of the new liberal regime to its activities in the Levant, and the controversies of the two Powers in various European affairs were also displayed in this area. The chancellor suspected that the Parisian cabinet would merely try to use the religious banner for its own political aims. Austria could thus play a more important role among the Ottoman Catholics, particularly when the fall of the ultra-conservative French king and his government, who counted on the support of the Catholic church, and the problems of their more liberal successors in internal as well as foreign affairs, created, according to the chancellor, conditions for weakening France's influence over them. He wrote to Ottenfels these eloquent words on 5 September 1830: "This is the moment, Mr Baron, when I engage you to take the path of common sense and do what you can to make progress in the matter of the protection of the sultan's Catholic subjects. One of the main characteristics of the new French government will have to be a profound indifference towards religious interests. The influence that it will want to maintain over the Catholics will be purely political. This influence will be harmful to the Porte and useless for the individuals in favour of whom it will allegedly be exercised; its tendency will necessarily be revolutionary in the end. You are today the only representative of a

---

[59] Metternich to Ottenfels, Vienna, 17 Feb. 1830, HHStA, StA, Türkei VI, 51.
[60] Lützow to Metternich, Rome, 27 Feb. 1830, HHStA, StK, Rom 37.
[61] Ibid.

Catholic Power in the Levant; it will be thus your task to watch over the welfare of our co-religionists."[62]

It would be, however, superfluous to regard these words as proof of any real determination for Austria to assume France's protectorate of the Ottoman Armenian Catholics. It is true that Metternich hoped that they would never forget Austria's considerable contribution to their religious independence, that Austria had tried to play a more independent role in the affair and to obtain more influence in Constantinople and some acclaim in Rome, but in fact there was neither any clearly defined policy in this sense nor plans for anything which could start an offensive against France's exclusive position. Moreover, for the reasons mentioned earlier in the text, from late summer 1830 Austria started to show even greater restraint in its conduct in the Armenian Catholic Affair, and Ottenfels' advice conveyed several times to the Ottoman authorities during the autumn that they should settle the affair in order to prevent the intercession of the European Powers seems to be the result not only of his strategy to persuade the Porte to a quick settlement but also of his personal conviction.[63] He mentioned it in his report of 25 August 1830: "I think that at present the most useful course to take here will be to persuade the Porte that it is in its own interests to do itself and with good grace what should increase the Armenian Catholics' sense of loyalty, in order to render in this way all appeals for foreign intervention superfluous. It is in this sense that I do not cease to explain my position to the reis effendi."[64]

Ten years later, during the so-called Syrian Question concerning the European Powers' diplomatic intervention on behalf of the Christians in Syria, the main goal of the Austrian diplomacy was to stabilise the affairs in this region, strengthen the sultan's power and thus make any European interference unnecessary. This was, according to

---

[62] Metternich to Ottenfels, Vienna, 5 Sept. 1830, HHStA, StA, Türkei VI, 51.

[63] Metternich to Ottenfels, Vienna, 18 Jan. 1831, HHStA, StA, Türkei VIII, 4; Ottenfels to Metternich, Constantinople, 25 Aug. 1830, HHStA, StA, Türkei VI, 50; Ottenfels' memorandum to Mehmed Hamid Bey, Constantinople 18 Nov. 1830, attached to Adelburg to Ottenfels, Constantinople, 19 Nov. 1830, Ottenfels to Metternich, Constantinople, 11 and 25 Nov. 1830, HHStA, StA, Türkei VI, 51; Ottenfels to Metternich, Constantinople, 26 March 1831, HHStA, StA, Türkei VI, 52.

[64] Ottenfels to Metternich, Constantinople, 25 Aug. 1830, HHStA, StA, Türkei VI, 50.

Metternich, the best way to prevent the eruption of new problems in the Near East affecting the relations among the European countries.[65] There is a great deal of evidence that this opinion already prevailed at the Chancellery in Vienna in the early 1830s. At the beginning of January 1830, Metternich voiced his opinion against Austria's protection of the Armenian Catholics because, as he told Spinola, it would provoke the Porte's defiance and violate its sovereignty.[66] On 19 February 1830, he personally stated in his instructions to Turin that protection of Ottoman subjects by foreign Powers, like the Russo-Orthodox or Franco-Catholic, were harmful for the Porte, and Austria did not desire them in general, not even for itself.[67] On 19 April 1831, he finally wrote to Ottenfels: "The special and explicit protection that the Armenian Catholics have been enjoying for the last several years from the internunciature naturally had to cease the moment the nation was placed under a direct leader. Such protection would be pointless and it could even lead to problems of more than one nature. But it does not prevent you, Mr Baron, from furnishing the priests from the monasteries of Vienna and Venice, who rely on the particular support of our government, with the necessary passports for their journeys and from doing all you can to facilitate the passage of young men destined to obtain their education in these praiseworthy institutes. In general, you are to prove to our co-religionists on every occasion the fortunate results of the gracious interest that H[is] M[ajesty] o[ur] A[ugust] M[aster] will not cease to take in their fate."[68] The internuncio, who had already expressed his opinion to the chancellor on 26 March 1831 that the goal of the Austrian policy in the Armenian Catholic Affair was a settlement such that they would have no further reason to demand any assistance from the Great Powers and that this outcome was achieved,[69] reacted to the April instructions with delight that he could act in absolute accordance with them while "refraining from taking any action towards the Porte concerning their [the Armenian Catholics'] affairs."[70] It is clear that Austria tried to obtain some in-

[65] For more on this topic see Chapter 29.
[66] Spinola to Albani, Vienna, 3 Jan. 1830, ASV, Arch. Nunz. Vienna 256B.
[67] Metternich to Pilsach, Vienna, 19 Feb. 1830, HHStA, StA, Sardinien 65.
[68] Metternich to Ottenfels, Vienna, 19 April 1831, HHStA, StA, Türkei VIII, 4.
[69] Ottenfels to Metternich, Constantinople, 26 March 1831, HHStA, StA, Türkei VI, 52.
[70] Ottenfels to Metternich, Constantinople, 28 June 1831, HHStA, StA, Türkei

fluence over the Ottoman Armenian Catholics but in no way planned
to provoke a rivalry with France in this matter and thus cause new
frictions in the Near East.

* * *

Even though the Armenian Catholic Affair did not form an important
chapter in the history of the Eastern Question, it was considerably
important for the further living conditions of the Armenian Catholic
community and for shaping the Viennese cabinet's views of not only
the French religious protectorate and the problems of the European
protection of the Ottoman Christians in general, but also the coexistence between Christians and Moslems and various Christian confessions and the Porte's ability to ensure their peaceful and prosperous
life. Its outcome assured the community independence from the Orthodox patriarch, in other words a religious and administrative autonomy
leading to the remarkable progress of the Catholic Armenian millet in
the following decade.[71] The fact that the Ottoman government was
capable of arranging good living conditions for its Christian subjects,
albeit following pressure from some European Powers – Austria among
them and definitely worthy of considerable merit for the achievement
of the positive and stable settlement – led Metternich to the belief
that sultans were likely to repeat this outcome in the case of other
Christian groups in other Ottoman territories. This essentially shaped
his attitude during the dispute over the Syrian Question. The affair
of 1828–1831 also was important for forming the anti-French basis in
his diplomacy. Although it was entirely revealed during the solving of
problems concerning the Syrian Christians in 1840–1841, Metternich
had already demonstrated ten years earlier that he disagreed with the
exclusive French protectorate over the sultan's Catholic subjects and
he maintained that Austria was entitled, if not *de jure* at least *de facto*,
to concern itself in the religious rights of the Ottomans recognising
the pope as the head of their Church. Nevertheless, he accepted the
idea that the Great Powers' general protection of the Ottoman Chris-

VI, 52.
[71] Frazee, p. 260.

tians, including not only their religious but also their political rights, was not desirable because it opened the way to foreign involvement in the internal affairs of the Ottoman Empire in general, which not only violated the sultan's sovereignty but also went against Austria's own interest in the stabilisation of the situation in the Near East. Consequently, Metternich refused to concede any rights to such protectorates for all Powers including Austria. The attitude he assumed in the early 1830s was also fully revealed in 1840–1841.

Occident against Orient

Metternich's intervention in the Catholic Armenian Affair gives rise to the question whether he was not overly motivated by his own religious or any anti-Islamic feelings. The answer to this question is more important than it might seem to be at first sight because it is crucial for a full understanding of his conduct in other religious affairs in the Ottoman Empire as well as in the Eastern Question in general. Dealing with the religious aspects of Metternich's Near Eastern policy necessarily leads a historian to consider the chancellor's opinion of Islam, in other words his attitude to the coexistence of the Western, Christian, civilisation and the Moslem World. Even during Metternich's period this topic attracted the considerable attention of Europeans and, as is the case today, an insight into their way of thinking in this respect often reveals a picture full of clichés and prejudice against the arcane culture in the Near East, a region more remote to Metternich and his contemporaries than to Europeans today. Their inability to fully understand this strange world sometimes led to its distortion when assessed according to their own rules of Western civilisation or even to markedly hostile designs. The most apparent evidence of this overriding attitude of the Occident often based upon little knowledge of the actual situation in the Orient can be found in the Philhellenic movement which Metternich also confronted.

The Influence of the Oriental Academy in Vienna on the Attitude of Austria's Diplomatic Elites towards the Levant

Metternich's world outlook was founded among other things on tolerance to divergent opinions if he did not find them a threat to the existing order. He tried to stop attempts to destabilise the political situation, but he was generally uninterested in questions of confessional preferences, and his religious tolerance was crucial in the latter. He was a child of 18th century enlightenment and his own Catholicism had no significant influence upon his diplomacy anywhere, and this applies also to the Levant.[1] He showed considerable realism in this respect as well as in the assessment of the conditions, not only religious, of the Ottoman Empire, to which he paid considerable attention. This interest was a result not only of the necessity to protect Austria's political and economic interests in this area but also because it was the chancellor's nature to collect the maximum amount of information possible to be able to analyse foreign policies as well as the internal situations of the major and minor players on the chessboard of European diplomacy. Consequently, his general attitude towards the Levant was not based upon any idealistic preconceptions, but a strict analysis of the information that he gathered in several ways. The first and most important method was the steady stream of reports dispatched not only by Austrian but also other agents residing in the Ottoman territories. The documents of non-Austrian diplomats were obtained either through their voluntary handover or their interception by the Austrian black chambers (*cabinets noirs*). In this respect the fact that Vienna lay on the main postal route between Constantinople and Europe proved to be very important because it enabled the Austrians to intercept a considerable amount of European as well as Ottoman correspondence. Second, Metternich discussed this topic with Austrian as well as foreign diplomats, orientalists and travellers. He did so in the Chancellery as well as in his palace, where, generally after coming home in the evening and because of his dislike for idle gossip, he usually raised topics of practical interest to himself, the situation of the Ottoman Empire among them. Finally, Metternich tried to gain accurate knowledge of the real situation prevailing in the Levant by reading newspaper articles and books on the topic. Some of them with his remarks in the margins can be still found in the library of his chateau in Königswart and they reveal that his interest was mostly focused on Islam – this word as well as relevant expressions like fanaticism, fatalism, or oriental barbarity were most frequently

---

[1]   E. Widmann, *Die religiösen Anschauungen des Fürsten Metternich*, Darmstadt 1914, p. 105.

underlined by him.[2] Metternich also had in his library a French issue of the Koran and his letters show that he knew at least some precepts of this book, but since his own copy has no handwritten comments, there is no proof that he personally read it and that his knowledge was not merely indirect.[3] It can be said in general that Metternich's incredible diligence – he dedicated a considerable part of the day as well as the night to his work – together with his personal interest in the religious as well as the other conditions of the Ottoman Empire made him a well-informed statesman who was used by the members of the diplomatic corps in Vienna as a commentator on Oriental events, and without much exaggeration it can be said that Metternich's Vienna served in this respect as a kind of information bureau for foreign cabinets, although mainly in Central Europe.

As for Metternich's opinions of the religious situation in the Near East, it is necessary to point out the fact that they were primarily based upon information brought to him by his own diplomats personally familiar with the conditions existing in the Levant, which means mostly by men educated in the well-known Oriental Academy in Vienna. Since their influence on Metternich, who never visited the Ottoman Empire, was crucial, the impact of the Oriental Academy on Metternich's views through his diplomats schooled in this institution must be explained here in brief. The Academy was founded by Maria Theresa in 1754 with the primary aim to train diplomats and consular agents for the service in the Levant and it became an important training institution for Austria's diplomatic service; Metternich, not only officially supervising the Academy but also personally well aware of its importance, paid considerable attention to its educational programme and staff and intervened in both when he found it necessary. The institution offered not only an excellent education to its students but also made them more understanding of and sensitive to the considerably different milieu and culture of the Near East: "The impact of the educational program of the Oriental Academy ... had cultural

---

[2] A. von Jochmus, *Der Verfall des Osmanen-Reiches seit 1840*, Frankfurt am Main 1858, book number: 37-D-4/I-IV; F. Schott, *Die orientalische Frage und ihre Lösung aus dem Gesichtspunkte der Zivilisation*, Leipzig 1839, book number: 7-A-70 (4624); G. von Stratimirovics, *Die Reformen in der Türkei*, Wien 1856, book number: II-3830.

[3] *L'Alcoran de Mahomet traduit de l'Arabe par André du Ryer*, I–II, Amsterdam, Leipzig 1770, book number: 25-B-12 (17444).

implications that stretched far beyond the hobbies of diplomats and the intellectual idiosyncracies of linguistically gifted alumni. It encouraged students to criticise and reject traditional and recent stereotypes of the Turks and Muslims and to think hard about assigning the erstwhile enemy a place in the human household that, at the same time, respected their religious, cultural and linguistic singularity."[4] Consequently, the internuncios and their subordinates who graduated from the Academy were fairly tolerant to the Ottomans and their way of life, often even having some sympathy or at least personal interest in the social, political, economic and religious conditions existing in the Ottoman Empire. This is evident not only from the contents of their reports but also from their free time activities like, for example, gathering Oriental manuscripts and books, reading them and translating their parts or preparing dictionaries of the Turkish language. Their knowledge of the Levant and Oriental languages – for example, Ottenfels' generation at the Academy had to learn Arabian, Persian, Turkish and Modern Greek – was developed in their youth when they were sent as trainees to gain experience in one of the diplomatic or consular posts in the Levant. These early years were very demanding because together with civilian duties, the young men had to master local languages, customs and behaviour.[5]

Some of these men were even born in the Levant. This mainly concerned the sons of fathers already serving at the internunciature as interpreters; the young boys were then sent for education to the Oriental Academy and having finished it, they returned to Constantinople and followed in their fathers' footsteps. This was also the case of Bartolomäus von Stürmer, the son of the Austrian internuncio, Baron Ignaz von Stürmer. Bartolomäus was born in Constantinople, where he spent his childhood, graduated from the Oriental Academy, served several years at the internunciature as a junior employee and after a certain period spent in other parts of the world replaced Ottenfels in Constantinople in 1833. It is of course hardly to be expected that he played with local children in the streets of Constantinople, but these "streets" would definitely not have been as strange for him as for those diplomats who arrived in the Ottoman capital without any personal

---

[4]   P. S. Fichtner, *Terror and Toleration: The Habsburg Empire Confronts Islam, 1526–1850*, London 2008, p. 130.
[5]   Kargl, pp. 92–99.

experience of the country or relevant education. How important these were is revealed by the unfortunate nomination of Count Rudolf von Lützow for Constantinople. Lützow was Ottenfels' old friend from the Theresian Military Academy in Wiener Neustadt, but their paths separated after they graduated form the Military Academy, and Lützow, in contrast to Ottenfels, did not go on to continue his education in the Oriental Academy. When he was sent by Metternich to Constantinople in 1818, he had experience from the diplomatic services in Copenhagen and Stuttgart but no experience or even knowledge of the Levant. Consequently, it was an insuperable problem for him to familiarise himself with Oriental customs and the rather specific diplomatic style of dealing with affairs with the Porte. Although he was nominated for a temporary period only, he found the conditions so unbearable that he soon started to apply informally but repeatedly to Metternich to be removed and even sent to a less important diplomatic post. Having witnessed the cruelties in Constantinople's streets in 1821, which made him rather anti-Turkish, his request became official and he was very happy when it was met by the chancellor. His later post of Austria's ambassador in Rome was more suited to his nature and he got on significantly better in the headquarters of Catholicism than previously in the capital of the predominantly Moslem empire.[6]

Several men who graduated from the Oriental Academy and possessed personal experience of the Levant reached high functions at the Chancellery and could thus often shape Metternich's views. Although it is impossible to determine their merits, two men who played an important role in this respect were Ignaz von Stürmer and Franz von Ottenfels, who both served as Metternich's deputies in the Chancellery after their service in Constantinople. Valentin von Huszár, the son-in-law of Ignaz von Stürmer, was the first interpreter of the internunciature in the late 1820s, highly esteemed by the Austrian as well as foreign diplomats for his perfect knowledge of Oriental languages, and after his return to Vienna he functioned in the Chancellery as the first interpreter and an important expert on the Levant. Bartolomäus von Stürmer surely influenced Metternich in this respect through his reports after 1833. Furthermore, there were also men who had not been trained in the Oriental Academy but whose opinions were often

---

[6] Ottenfels, *Memoari*, p. 124; Kargl, pp. 13–18; Sauer, *Österreich und die Levante*, p. 113.

heeded by Metternich. By far the most important – and in certain aspects even more significant than the diplomats mentioned above – was Friederich von Gentz. This was not only due to his friendship and close collaboration with Metternich, but also to the fact that Oriental affairs formed one of his spheres of action and in 1821, he was logically entrusted by the chancellor with supervising the Greek insurrection.[7] Consequently, Gentz occupied himself to a great extent with everything that was related with this issue, naturally including the religious conditions, and he also did it from his own personal interest, about which he wrote to one of his friends in 1821: "I must tell you that my favorite [sic] subjects at the present time are the history and geography of the East. A book like the newly published journey of Jaubert to Persia keeps me awake until four o'clock in the morning."[8] Gentz's protégé, Anton Prokesch von Osten, was also among Metternich's advisors, functioning as an expert on Greek and, later in the 1830s, on the Egyptian Questions.

The reader is probably surprised that the name of the most important graduate from the Oriental Academy in Vienna and active at the given period, Joseph von Hammer-Purgstall, has not been mentioned. The explanation is simple: he did not belong among Metternich's closest advisors. Therefore, he definitely had no significant impact on the chancellor's views concerning the religious or other conditions of the Ottoman Empire and played no role in Austria's diplomatic activities in the 1820s and 1830s. However, it is impossible to see the principle reason for this strained relationship, as explained by Purgstall in his memoirs, in the lack of Purgstall's own servility which was usual for those who formed the circle of the prince's advisors, in particular Ottenfels and Prokesch, to whom Purgstall felt a strong resentment resulting from his own unfulfilled ambitions. The reasoning of a very ambitious man embittered by the fact that a diplomatic career had been denied to him must be taken with a pinch of salt.[9] Although Prokesch definitely owed much of his career to the patronage of Gentz and Ottenfels, he, Ottenfels and the others were

---

[7] J. K. Mayr, *Geschichte der österreichischen Staatskanzlei im Zeitalter des Fürsten Metternich*, Wien 1935, p. 137.

[8] Sweet, p. 242.

[9] J. von Hammer-Purgstall, *Erinnerungen aus meinem Leben 1774–1852*, Wien, Leipzig 1940, p. 263; Fichtner, p. 134.

definitely not mere yea-sayers, as claimed by Purgstall, which is important to know when assessing their role in shaping Metternich's views. The employees of the Chancellery as well as the participants in Metternich's soirees, often the same people, were able to express their own opinions freely and of course did so. Certain evidence was offered by Bray who referred to the fact that these debates sometimes "turn into real disputes because Gentz is very stubborn, very animated and very skilful in debating. The prince [Metternich] is considerably calmer, and his great merit is that he never loses sight of the point to which he wants to arrive and that he always brings the discussion back to its real goal. Gentz, who possesses considerable self-esteem, when telling me about these daily conferences, told me that it was perhaps for the welfare of the Austrian Monarchy and Europe that he was also summoned to discussion every day with the prince because these discussions, where personal opinions can be freely expressed, lead to insights and truths which would otherwise never be imagined."[10] Metternich's correspondence with his junior diplomats also prove that they could express their disapproving opinions, and their disagreement in no way harmed their diplomatic careers, even in consideration of the chancellor's vanity and general unwillingness to recognise his own errors. A fitting example can be offered by pointing out Prokesch's significant and openly outspoken disagreement with some of Metternich's views in the early phase of the First Mohammed Ali Crisis. Metternich naturally was not happy with this criticism and reacted with impassivity but when Prokesch proved to be correct, the chancellor acknowledged his mistake and rewarded Prokesch with an important diplomatic mission to Alexandria in 1833.[11]

---

[10] Bray, *Mémoire sur la politique générale des puissances européennes sur les affaires du Levant et sur le direction qu'il parait le plus convenables de donner à la politique de la Baviere*, Irlbach, 31 July 1828, BHStA, MA, Wien 2402.

[11] Prokesch-Osten, *Aus den Tagebüchern*, pp. 169–174. For more on Prokesch's second mission to Alexandria see Chapter 16.

Metternich's Attitude towards Islam

Metternich's attitude towards Islam[12] and his willingness to listen to his subordinates' opinions can be readily learnt from his reaction to the *Mémoire sur l'avenir de l'Empire Ottoman sous le rapport religieux et politique*, which was written by the Austrian representative in Turin, Count Ludwig Senfft von Pilsach, and sent to the chancellor for deliberation on 14 January 1830 even though it is possible that it had been drawn up in April of the preceding year.[13] In any case, Pilsach wrote it under the influence of the latest events in the Near East, undoubtedly the Armenian Catholic Affair being the most important of them, which led a considerable number of contemporaries to believe that the Ottoman Empire was doomed to an early and inevitable fall. Pilsach seemed to share this view and he claimed that Islam was the reason for its decay and the progress of Western civilisation would logically destroy it, which, in his opinion, was welcomed because "the interests of religion, humanity, civilisation made the fall of Islam desirable."[14] Nevertheless, since the existence of the Ottoman Empire was important for Austria, it was necessary to find another ideological pillar. According to Pilsach, it was to be Catholicism, and he introduced a vision of a union of all Catholics living within the Ottoman territories, their number increased through controlled immigration from the Continent, and finally their effort aimed at the Christianisation of the Ottoman Moslems. The Catholics were to serve then as bearers of civilisation and enlightenment thus giving new vitality to the Ottoman Empire, which could not be offered by "Mohammedans."[15]

Metternich strongly disapproved of Pilsach's *Mémoire* that was, in his opinion, entirely delusionary. This negative evaluation is proved first by his critical comments in the margins of the *Mémoire*,[16] second by his instructions to Pilsach on 19 February and 12 April 1830,[17]

---

[12]   In most of his letters, Metternich actually used the word "Islamism" but the real sense of the word as used by him during the studied period is equivalent to what is termed nowadays as "Islam." Therefore, the latter is used in all translations.

[13]   The date 15 April 1829 was written in pencil on the *Mémoire*, which probably indicates the time of its creation. Pilsach to Metternich, Turin, 14 Jan. 1830, HHStA, StA, Sardinien 64.

[14]   Ibid.

[15]   Ibid.

[16]   Ibid.

[17]   Metternich to Pilsach, Vienna, 19 Feb. and 12 April 1830, HHStA, StA, Sar-

third by his instructions to Ottenfels on 3 February 1830, to which the *Mémoire* was attached for the internuncio's examination,[18] and fourth by his positive comments of Ottenfels' analysis of the *Mémoire* written in its margins, as quoted below.[19] Ottenfels analysed Pilsach's *Mémoire* using his own personal knowledge of the Levant in his essay of 10 March 1830. As well as Metternich, he completely rejected Pilsach's views as being sharply at variance with the real situation existing in the Ottoman Empire. He particularly refused to believe in any possibility of a sincere union of all the Catholic communities living there, divided as they were by origin, language, culture and mutual hatred: "To want to establish any unity among the Catholics of the Ottoman Empire would be as difficult ... as to want to create an association between the Portuguese, Spaniard, French, Italian and German Catholics against European Protestants."[20] The idea of the Moslems' possible conversion to Catholicism was also absolutely rejected by the internuncio, who believed that they could be massacred or expelled from the regions they inhabited by the Catholics, but they would never allow themselves to be Christianised. Moreover, any prospect for their forced conversion was made less likely since Christians formed a minority in the Ottoman Empire. Ottenfels estimated that from the total population the Catholics numbered approximately a million souls. Consequently, in his opinion, any attempts at the Christianisation of Moslems would have to be supported by Catholic countries, which Pilsach had also suggested in his *Mémoire*, but the internuncio strongly warned against Europe's interference in this respect because it would result in the suffering of the Ottoman Catholics; it would definitely invoke the resistance of not only the sultan, but also the Russian tsar and the Moslem inhabitants, who, for example, had reacted against the French missionaries' attempt to Christianise them in Palestine with the persecution of all the Catholics living there.[21]

---

dinien 65.

[18] Metternich to Ottenfels, Vienna, 3 Feb. 1830, HHStA, StA, Türkei VI, 51.

[19] Metternich to Pilsach, Vienna, 12 April 1830, HHStA, StA, Sardinien 65; Ottenfels, *Memoari*, p. 225.

[20] Ottenfels to Metternich, Constantinople, 10 March 1830, HHStA, StA, Türkei VI, 50. Ottenfels' report analysing Pilsach's *Mémoire* can also be found, though without Metternich's comments, in Prokesch-Osten, *Griechen*, VI, pp. 196–203.

[21] Ottenfels to Metternich, Constantinople, 10 March 1830, HHStA, StA, Türkei VI, 50; Ottenfels, *Memoari*, p. 226.

Ottenfels likewise objected to Pilsach's thesis about the Moslems' alleged intolerance. The internuncio argued against this that neither proselytism nor an inclination to religious persecution were inherent in either the character of the Turks or their government. If, from time to time, repressions of the Christians occurred in the Ottoman Empire, then it was not because of their faith but either due to the arbitrariness of some Ottoman nobles or the Christians' rebellions and efforts to achieve their political emancipation, where, however, the religious aspect was but a pretext. As for the situation of the Ottoman Catholics, "if there is any oppression, it originates from the vices of the government or governors, and religion doesn't enter into it. *But if there has been any persecution, it has been the work of the schismatics who have provoked them and not of the Turks who regard all religions* [twice underlined by Metternich and with his added comment: 'precisely!'] other than their own in the same way and who generally do not turn violent against a religious sect unless they are encouraged to do so by its adversaries. The persecution of the Armenian Catholics that recently took place is evidence of the truth of this statement."[22]

Ottenfels also sharply came out against the claim that Islam was incompatible with an attempt on the part of the Porte to proceed on the path of enlightenment and civilisation. The internuncio added to this proposition: "The author [Pilsach] thinks that Islam by its nature and even in its very essence opposes the progress of enlightenment and that its religious system must necessarily collapse with Turkey's progressive movement towards civilisation. This idea is not justified; *the dogmas of the Mohammedan religion are not so absurd, contrary to common sense and inimical to the improvement of the civil life and sciences as to be incompatible with the progress of civilisation and the improvement of the administration of the empire. The history of the Arabs at the times of the Abbasid caliphs and the Moors in Spain furnish us with evidence to the contrary* [marked off and commented on by Metternich: 'bravo!'], even though a more thorough examination of the principal dogmas and precepts of Islam would in no way suffice. Oriental despotism has been confused with Islam too often; they have encountered each other in the Levant but they are not inseparable in

---

[22] Ottenfels to Metternich, Constantinople, 10 March 1830, HHStA, StA, Türkei VI, 50.

their nature."²³ The progress of the Ottoman Empire did not therefore depend on Christianity, as was also recently proved by the rise of predominantly Moslem Egypt with skilful Mohammed Ali who in no way planned to abandon his faith.²⁴ Ottenfels closed his analysis with these words: "*I still persist in the belief that Catholicism alone can never save the Ottoman Empire and that its salvation is in Islam* [twice underlined and written in by Metternich: 'That's right']."²⁵

Ottenfels' above-stated reservations to Pilsach's ideas won the absolute agreement of not only Metternich but also Gentz, who wrote to the internuncio on 17 April 1830: "Your reasoning about Catholicism in the Ottoman Empire with regard to the *Mémoire* from Turin is that of a real statesman and this is also the opinion of Prince Metternich. I entirely share your opinion that there is of course no incompatibility between Islam and the progress and reforms of the populations born and brought up in the Moslem faith."²⁶ It is not without interest that in 1825 similar views of Islam and Arab civilisation were expressed by another close and influential collaborator of Metternich, Lebzeltern, who had not visited the Oriental Academy but ranked among the Austrian diplomats who respected this religion and culture, as it is proved from his letter to Gentz: "As for the opinion of Europe with regard to the ancient and modern Greeks, and the Koran and its adherents, it is false. Europe has never owed to ancient Greece a quarter of the high civilisation and benefits which it [Europe] has obtained from the descendents of Mohammed, that great man, that admirable lawmaker. If only Europe had the wisdom as well as the science it learnt from the ancient Arabs! When anyone in Europe says that the Koran sets up insurmountable obstacles to civilisation with its precepts, it is stupidity. It is because they have not read [or] because they have forgotten the history of the caliphs, of the Ottoman emperors of Constantinople, of the kings of Spain, Cordova and Grenada; in the end it is because everybody wants to speak wrongly and despite their ignorance ... With the exception of several idealistic philanthropists – for the most part empty-headed – the excitement which manifests

---

²³ Ibid.
²⁴ Ibid.
²⁵ Ibid.
²⁶ Ottenfels, *Memoari*, p. 226.

itself in favour of the Greeks is driven by the principle leaders; the common people follow them like ewes follow a ram."[27]

In general, Metternich maintained before as well as after 1830 that Islam was not an intolerant religion oppressing the members of other faiths, as he wrote in March 1841: "Moslem law is not actively intolerant. It is indifferent to non-believers, it does not concern itself with the internal regulations of worship; it does not meddle in the affairs of other faiths, and if, in the course of time, one had to report anything more than a deviation of this rule, it is not at all in the spirit of Islam where the cause would have to be sought."[28] He found the principal dangers for the Christians not in Islam but, firstly, in the mutual malevolence of various Christian Churches whose reciprocal hatred often surpassed the aversion of some Moslems towards them. As for the Catholics, he saw their principal enemies in the Orthodox Christians whom he considered by far more intolerant and inclined to persecution for religious reasons than the Moslems, and his opinion in this matter was intensified by the hostile behaviour of some Greek insurgents against the Ottoman Catholics loyal to the sultan as well as the persecution of the Armenian Catholics by the Orthodox Christians in 1828: "It is not Islam that, in those vast regions, is the real enemy of Catholicism; rather it is the schismatics who are its dangerous and relentless enemies."[29] This was also one of the reasons for his rejection of the plans of some Europeans as well as their governments for the creation of a European protectorate over Jerusalem or a Christian republic in Palestine in 1840–1841; he considered such creations to be in violation of Ottoman sovereignty as well as dangerous for the Catholics owing to the superior number of Orthodox Christians. The Bavarian envoy in Vienna reported in February 1841: "The Prince Chancellor observes that in view of the jealousy between the different confessions of the Christian religion, it is necessary to be on one's guard in order not to provoke the dominant influence of the Greeks, who already predominate due to their

---

[27] Lebzeltern to Gentz, St Petersburg, 28 Oct. 1825, Prokesch-Osten, *Zur Geschichte der orientalischen Frage*, pp. 98–99.

[28] Metternich to Esterházy, Vienna, 7 March 1841, HHStA, StA, England 236.

[29] Metternich to Lützow, Vienna, 14 Feb. 1830, HHStA, StK, Rom 38. See also Metternich's statements in Chapter 11 and Spinola to Bernetti, Vienna, 3 April 1828, ASV, Arch. Nunz. Vienna 256; Altieri to Lambruschini, Vienna, 3 Jan. 1840, ASV, Arch. Nunz. Vienna 280C.

number and their wealth and who have continually tried to gain more land at the expense of the Catholics through the corruption of the Turkish authorities. It is necessary, the prince says, to leave to the Turks the sovereignty over Jerusalem and let them maintain order there."[30] Consequently, Metternich strongly disagreed with the pope, who wanted to liberate the Holy Land, and he also rejected the idea existing among some Europeans of that period of something close to a crusade. Although a whole chapter of this book is dedicated to this problem,[31] it is necessary to emphasise here already that Metternich also showed a greater respect for Islam and Moslems than many of his contemporaries, who forgot, as Metternich rightly remarked, that Jerusalem was a holy city not only for Christians, but together with Mecca and Medina also for Moslems. The latter worshipped in the mosque built on the site of Solomon's Temple much like the former in the Church of the Holy Sepulchre. Consequently, the sultan could never surrender this territory, in particular since he was not only the secular ruler, but as caliph also the head of Islam.[32]

The second danger for the Ottoman Christians, according to Metternich, lay in the deficiencies of the inept Ottoman administration, in particular the ill-natured conduct of some local dignitaries who often behaved wilfully and against their sovereign's wishes, or allowed the people to commit atrocities or at least did not prevent them from doing so: "It is not the intolerance of Moslems which is the cause of Christian suffering in the Orient. This cause is primarily to be found in the disorderly administration of the empire, a logical consequence of which is the tyranny of local authorities."[33] As for Mahmud II, he did not suspect him of any religious hatred or desire to persecute his Christian subjects for religious reasons.[34] The correctness of this

---

[30] Lerchenfeld to Ludwig I of Bavaria, Vienna, 20 Feb. 1841, BHStA, MA, Wien 2410.

[31] See Chapter 29.

[32] Metternich to Stürmer, Vienna, 18 Dec. 1840, HHStA, StA, Türkei VI, 78; Metternich to Esterházy, Vienna, 7 March 1841, HHStA, StA, England 236; Altieri to Lambruschini, Vienna, 6 Nov. 1840, ASV, Arch. Nunz. Vienna 280C; Altieri to Lambruschini, Vienna, 29 Jan. 1841, ASV, Arch. Nunz. Vienna 280D. For more see Chapter 29.

[33] Metternich to Esterházy, Vienna, 3 Feb. 1841, HHStA, StA, England 236.

[34] Metternich to Ohms, Vienna, 7 Nov. 1840, HHStA, StK, Rom 64; Metternich to Stürmer, Vienna, 7 Feb. 1841, HHStA, StA, Türkei VI, 83; Metternich to Esterházy, Vienna, 7 March 1841, HHStA, StA, England 236.

opinion is supported by the outcome of the Constantinople Armenian Catholic Affair as well as the conclusions of a leading expert on Ottoman history, American historian Roderic H. Davison, who maintained that during that period there was no systematic persecution of Christians by Moslems in the Ottoman Empire or indeed any systematic oppression of Christians by the Ottoman government.[35] Moreover, Metternich was certain of the Porte's willingness to remedy the administrative abuses making the life of non-Moslems more difficult, and he saw in the solution of the Armenian Catholic Affair a fitting example.

Metternich's sharp rejection of Pilsach's *Mémoire* as well as his other statements clearly prove that he was not influenced by fervent religious dogma or any hostility towards Islam. As for the followers of Islam, the Moslems, the prince did not consider them a serious problem for the Christians even though he naturally knew that some Moslems were not inclined towards the non-Moslem communities and were not willing to agree with equal rights for the Christians, who suffered under discriminatory regulations. However, Metternich did not regard the Moslems as a bloodthirsty people wanting to commit atrocities and force non-believers to convert to Islam. He also had to note that during the Constantinople Armenian Catholic Affair, a considerable number of them criticised the persecutions as well as the many Christians who supported them. On the other hand, it would be a great mistake to regard Metternich as an admirer of Islam or a friend of its adherents. He was no great supporter of the Levant, which remained mysterious for him, and he even sometimes, although not very often, expressed himself in negative ways about the Turks or their empire.[36] He showed considerable interest in the conditions of the Levant and the coexistence of the Moslems and the Christians not because he wanted to but because he simply felt forced to do so by the Oriental affairs threatening peace and stability in Europe. The

---

[35] R. H. Davison, "Turkish Attitudes concerning Christian-Muslim Equality in the Nineteenth Century," R. H. Davison (ed.), *Essays in Ottoman and Turkish History, 1774–1923: The Impact of the West*, Austin 1990, p. 113.

[36] How Metternich perceived the Orient is also evident from his letter from the Galician town Lemberg (Lviv) written in October 1823: "The city is half beautiful and half ugly. A lot of houses are better constructed than those of Vienna, for they have architecture. Then come stretches, either empty or encumbered with barracks. The Orient begins to reveal itself." Wolff, p. 294.

best description of his attitude is neutrality as he knew well that the Near East was not a simple black and white depiction of allegedly cruel Moslems and good Christians. He personally felt no love of the Ottoman Empire, but he also did not see any reason why he should hate it. He never requested the expulsion of the Moslems from Europe or the partition of their state, which of course he could not desire for geopolitical reasons, but he also did not see any reason why he would desire it. His attitude towards Islam and Ottoman society naturally was interwoven with his wish to preserve the sultan's empire but, as well as his foreign policy on behalf of Austria, this attitude also resulted from his general conservative *Weltanschauung*. His statements regarding the co-existence of various faiths in the Ottoman Empire can be regarded as sincere. What he wanted above all was that they lived in peace and behaved according to the precept which he advocated in general: "Do unto others as ye would they should do unto you."[37]

Metternich's Struggle with Euro-Centric Thinkers

This attitude meant that the prince not only advocated the improvement of the Christians' living conditions in the way it was achieved by the Armenian Catholics, in other words to the extent that would not destabilise the power of the sultan and did not threaten the existence of the Ottoman Empire, but that he also opposed the ideas, held by some of his contemporaries in the West, hostile to Islam and the Moslems. With respect for other cultures and religions and according to his conservative principles he rejected the arrogant behaviour towards the Levant on the part of men with little regard for local conditions, traditions and customs and who spoke, like for example well-known German economist Friedrich List, of the necessity to introduce "European civilisation into the most beautiful regions of the universe."[38] The most well-known representatives of Western arrogance towards the Levant of the studied period were the French writer and minister of foreign affairs from 1822 to 1824, Viscount

---

[37] M. Walker (ed.), *Metternich's Europe*, New York 1968, p. 95.
[38] Hajjar, p. 172.

François-René de Chateaubriand, and the French poet, Alphonse de Lamartine. For both, Islam was the enemy of civilisation, the Levant a dark place and the Moslems a primitive people waiting for Europeanisation which equalled, according to the former, the spread of the Western kind of freedom, and according to the latter a simple conquest.[39] These euro-centric ideas which would have turned the Levant into a political-religious battleground if they had been realised were considered extremely dangerous by Metternich, who wanted to maintain the status quo, and he opposed them for the same reasons that he rejected Pilsach's project for the Christianisation of the Ottoman Moslems; he considered similar plans to be unfeasible, arrogant and intolerant, he thought they ignored the real situation in the Levant, were dangerous for the Christians as well as the stability of the Ottoman Empire whose independence they significantly jeopardised and were often motivated by self-interest. His encounter with such zealots can be well compared with his collision with various Western ideological movements like nationalism or liberalism, but it had a specific connotation in the Levant because Metternich not only opposed the ideologists motivated by liberal ideas or nationalism but also conservative or ultraconservative thinkers particularly motivated by their Christian beliefs. It was not important for him from which ideological background such visionaries originated, he criticised all of them whenever he found their plans to be dangerous and impracticable. His clash with them went across the ideological spectre and touched not only the diplomatic but also the journalistic sphere; he not only read a considerable number of articles attacking the Ottoman Empire for whatever reason but he also often instructed his collaborators, above all Gentz until his death in 1832, to issue negative reactions to those articles he disagreed with in the *Österreichischer Beobachter* or some other newspapers.

Metternich knew the ideas of both, Chateaubriand and Lamartine, and he sharply disagreed with them as well as with many of their fellow citizens advocating similar, in his opinion impractical views: "Everybody wants to govern today and it is particularly in France where this sickness has acquired such an intensity; what this crowd of amateurs lacks is a calm and real knowledge of the conditions of the

---

[39] E. W. Said, *Orientalism*, New York 1994, pp. 172 and 179; Bertsch, pp. 286–292.

regions to which these enthusiasts direct their activities."[40] During the period studied, he paid the greatest attention to another Frenchman who desired to felicitate the Levant through the achievements of the Western world: a former surgeon in Napoleon's army and long time resident in Constantinople, Doctor Barrachin, who arrived in Constantinople in 1838 and served there as a reformatory advisor of the Porte. He also directed an Oriental Committee in Paris where, in the spring of 1841, he started to publish the *Revue orientale* in which he expressed his views about the necessity to emancipate the Christians living in the Ottoman Empire, free the Church of the Holy Sepulchre and create a unified religion including Moslems, Greeks, Armenians, and Jews; he also addressed a letter with some of these demands to the sultan and had an article printed with a picture of a liberal Frenchman leading a Moslem, Greek, Armenian and Jew under a flag of a unified religion. His publications were mailed to the Ottoman Empire on French steamships and distributed by the French post, which raised the Porte's complaints in the summer of 1841.[41]

Metternich distrusted Barrachin's Committee, which in his opinion resembled the Philhellenic committees of the 1820s too much, and he rejected Barrachin's ideas as too radical.[42] The complete equality of the various Ottoman religious communities was unacceptable to him not because he was personally against such equality in general but because it would, in his opinion, lead, first, to the worsening of the Catholics' situation because they would be exposed to the animosity of more numerous Orthodox Christians and, second, to the disintegration and final fall of the sultan's empire, which would not endure such a far-reaching change in the structure of the Ottoman society di-

---

[40] Metternich to Apponyi, Königswart, 28 July 1841, HHStA, StA, Frankreich 322.

[41] Metternich to Apponyi, Vienna, 12 July 1841, HHStA, StA, Frankreich 322; Adelburg to Klezl, 13 June 1838, Klezl to Metternich, Büyükdere, 13 June 1838, HHStA, StA, Türkei VI, 67; Barrachin to Abdülmecid I, Paris, 10 Oct. 1841, HHStA, StA, Türkei VI, 83; Canitz to Frederick William IV, Vienna, 29 Nov. 1841, GStA PK, HA III, MdA I, 7365; Königsmarck to Frederick William III, Büyükdere, 13 June 1838, GStA PK, HA III, MdA I, 7280; Königsmarck to Frederick William IV, Büyükdere, 30 June 1841, GStA PK, HA III, MdA I, 7284; Molé [?] to Roussin, Therapia, 10 Jan. 1838, AMAE, CP, Turquie 275; Pontois to Guizot, Therapia, 17 Aug. 1841, AMAE, CP, Turquie 283; *Revue orientale*, Nr. 1, Paris 1841.

[42] Metternich to Apponyi, Vienna, 12 July 1841, HHStA, StA, Frankreich 322.

vided into different millets. Consequently, he regarded it necessary to reject "a remedy for the internal sickness that will inevitably lead to destruction if this empire is abandoned to the danger and to all those who under the pretext of bringing benefits only work towards political upheaval, as the Oriental Committee in Paris evidently does by inciting the Greeks to revolt and by advocating equality there where it tries to settle the social conditions of different populations, where there is religious inequality everywhere, in origins, nationalities, laws, customs, in fact in everything that comprises the lives of individuals, families and nations. A French doctor, Barrachin, feels it is his vocation to develop his system of liberty founded on the principle of equality in a letter addressed to Sultan Abdülmecid dated the 10th of the past month [October 1841]. This letter, which was published in Paris, contains several indisputable remarks as to the sickness; in making a diagnosis, the doctor is a credit to his profession, but with regard to the means he wants to employ, the charlatanism of the school to which he belongs is clearly evident. In order to improve the situation of the rayahs [non-Moslems], it is essential to guarantee them the foundations of their existence, freedom of worship, the security of their properties, the regulation of taxes, the organisation of their communities, courts and administration. It is necessary to begin with what is the most urgent and the most simple and not with abstract theories. Absolute equality would be nowhere in the world more absurd than there."[43] When Ottenfels wrote in his answer to Pilsach's *Mémoire* that granting equality to all rayahs, in other words the transfer of all civil rights or at least most of those which the Moslems enjoyed to the sultan's non-Moslem subjects, would be a veritable remedy, Metternich wrote in the margin: "I fear that not; it would inevitably cause a revolution from which Russia would derive all the advantage."[44] In this respect Metternich crucially subordinated his attitude to his geopolitical interests, as well as his above-mentioned belief that equal rights for the Ottoman Christians would be advantageous for the Orthodox community owing to its significant numerical superiority and, therefore, disadvantageous for the Catholics. Consequently, he saw

---

[43] Canitz to Frederick William IV, Vienna, 29 Nov. 1841, GStA PK, HA III, MdA I, 7365.

[44] Ottenfels to Metternich, Constantinople, 10 March 1830, HHStA, StA, Türkei VI, 50.

the only possible way to improve the Christians' lives was within the framework of the Ottoman laws, the treaties concluded between the Ottoman Empire and European countries and common sense.[45]

What disgusted Metternich above all were political designs he correctly saw beyond similar plans, in other words their authors' desire to increase France's influence in the Levant with the elevation of the Catholic cross in the regions where the crescent moon dominated.[46] For example, in 1840 Lamartine offered to "take an armed intermediary position, land in Syria, gather those populations entirely belligerent, entirely Christian, entirely disposed to France altogether under the French flag, [and] proclaim the independence of Syria under the suzerainty of the Porte and the guarantee of France."[47] This French protectorate over the Ottoman Catholics was to serve its political and economic goals. Barrachin's picture of a Frenchman – and what was even worse for Metternich, a liberal one, – leading the representatives of the four religions was more than eloquent and more than the chancellor could stomach, and he was scornful of such hypocrisy: "There are some men who are motivated by purely religious reasons; for others, the religious mantle serves to veil political aims ... If they want to apply religious ideas to material interests, they expose themselves to very serious delusions. The politicians rallying around the religious banner will certainly find themselves in opposition to the conservative views of the Ottoman Empire that I submit to the cabinets without reservation."[48]

---

[45] Metternich to Apponyi, Vienna, 12 July 1841, HHStA, StA, Frankreich 322; Altieri to Lambruschini, Vienna, 23 April 1841, ASV, Arch. Nunz. Vienna 280D; Flahaut to Guizot, Vienna, 23 Nov. 1841, AMAE, CP, Autriche 429.

[46] Metternich to Stürmer, Vienna, 16 March, 13 April and 13 July 1841, HHStA, StA, Türkei VI, 83; Altieri to Lambruschini, Vienna, 21 May 1841, ASV, Arch. Nunz. Vienna 280D; O. Schulz, "'This Clumsy Fabric of Barbarous Power': Die europäische Außenpolitik und der außereuropäische Raum am Beispiel des Osmanischen Reiches," W. Pyta (ed.), *Das europäische Mächtekonzert: Friedens- und Sicherheitspolitik vom Wiener Kongreß 1815 bis zum Krimkrieg 1853*, Köln, Weimar, Wien 2009, p. 282.

[47] A. Bruneau, *Traditions et politique de la France au Levant*, Paris 1932, p. 141.

[48] Metternich to Apponyi, Vienna, 12 July 1841, HHStA, StA, Frankreich 322.

Metternich and Philhellenism

The anti-Ottoman and anti-Islamic plans of the 1830s and early 1840s represented the continuance of a trend that started with the sudden increase of pro-Greek sentiments in Western society during the 1820s, the so-called Philhellenism, in Europe as well as in the United States of America, which gave birth to a considerable number of similar articles, pamphlets and books generally based upon a one-sided evaluation of the fight between the Greeks and the Turks in which the former were generally regarded as the innocent and suffering descendents of the great ancient Greek civilisation, whereas the latter were viewed as ignorant, cruel, barbarous and inclined to commit atrocities. This fever affected the partisans of all political movements, the liberals seeing in the Greek insurrection a fight for freedom, the conservatives a war between the cross and the crescent and all of them seeing a clash between civilisation and barbarity.[49] Metternich of course stood on the opposite side of the ideological barricade. His attitude was again not motivated by any personal hatred for the Greeks or personal sympathies with the Turks but was merely a result of his political interests and conservative thinking. Johann Dimakis' definition of anti-Philhellenism applies perfectly to Metternich in this respect: "It must be emphasised here that anti-Philhellenism in no way means a hostile attitude towards Greece. It is not directed against the Greek nation or Greek nature. It also cannot be characterised as a positive attitude towards Turkey because it does not aim to justify the Turks and their actions. Admittedly it is aimed at the Greek revolution – and that is its essential characteristic – but not because of any hostility towards the Greeks or goodwill towards the Turks but for reasons of political expediency: because the Greek revolution shook the Ottoman Empire and rocked the political structure which had been created at the Congress of Vienna, and because it paved the way to revolutionary upheavals in other parts of the world."[50]

---

[49] For more on Philhellenism and the activities of the Philhellenes see W. St Clair, *That Greece Might Still Be Free: The Philhellenes in the War of Independence*, Cambridge 2008; D. Howarth, *The Greek Adventure: Lord Byron and Other Eccentrics in the War of Independence*, London 1976; P. C. Pappas, *The United States and the Greek War for Independence 1821–1828*, New York 1985.

[50] J. Dimakis, "Der politische Philhellenismus und Antiphilhellenismus während der Griechischen Revolution in der französischen und deutschen Presse," E. Kon-

One very important reason for Metternich's anti-Philhellenic sentiment is, however, missing in Dimakis' explanation of its characteristics: a highly realistic evaluation and deep understanding of the events connected with the Greek insurrection. Metternich refused to see the Greeks as favourably as did the Philhellenes, and he correctly viewed the considerable popularity of the Greek insurrection in Western society to be the result of a profound ignorance of the reality.[51] He did not share the perception of the black and white division of the roles, and this was definitely not only due to his own political support of the sultan. First of all, he never considered the modern Greeks to be the inheritors of their ancient predecessors, waiting for their liberation to be able to revive the bygone glory of their ancient civilisation, and he was right because the Greeks of the 19th century were everything but this: most of them were illiterate without any passion for or even knowledge of their ancient history. If they looked to the past at all, then it was not to the pagan ancient Greece but to the Christian Byzantine Empire. Their fractioned and constantly quarrelling leaders, engaged above all in power struggles, were for Metternich no descendants of the ancient heroes and he also saw no reason to consider them to be better than the Turks or even bandits – and in truth many of them had been bandits before the outbreak of the insurrection and they continued in this way during its course; their conduct did not improve the situation of the ordinary Greeks or bring the victory in the war with the Turks, which was only won due to the trilateral alliance's intervention, but led to the outbreak of a series of political and military conflicts among themselves, which were also fed by the animosities among the social classes as well as between various regions. Metternich, seeing the lamentable situation of the Greeks and the disunity among them inclined to the belief that no real Greece, no real Greek nation existed in the real sense of this word.[52] In late April 1824, he briefly commented on the sorrowful situation in the Peloponnese: "The other basic information that we receive by post is limited to the details of the complete anarchy that reigns over Morea.

---

stantinou (ed.), *Europäischer Philhellenismus: Die europäische philhellenische Presse bis zur 1. Hälfte des 19. Jahrhunderts*, Frankfurt am Main, Berlin, Bern, New York, Paris, Wien 1994, p. 41.

[51] Metternich to Vincent, Vienna, 17 Oct. 1824, HHStA, StA, Frankreich 254; Metternich to Esterházy, Vienna, 17 Oct. 1824, HHStA, StA, England 169.

[52] Metternich to Apponyi, Vienna, 16 July 1827, HHStA, StA, Frankreich 264.

The leaders are already in open war among themselves and the people of these unhappy regions are its victims."[53] In the late 1820s, French historian and politician Dominique Georges Frédéric Dufour de Pradt claimed in his book published in 1828 *L'Intervention armée pour la pacification de la Grèce* that *"the Greeks* confined to their almost island of Morea *will be able to provide an oasis of peace and personal and domestic happiness."*[54] Metternich, who owned and read this book, underlined some of the words and wrote a sarcastic remark in the margin: "A small earthly paradise inhabited by the Greeks! How charming."[55] It is true that his opinions were scornful but not at all entirely erroneous: the series of civil wars were not terminated before the arrival of Otto, King of Greece, with his small Bavarian army, and when independent Greece was finally founded, a considerable number of its inhabitants – 60,000 out of 800,000 decided in 1834–1836 to move to the Ottoman Empire, where the Greeks generally enjoyed better living conditions.[56]

Another significant difference between Metternich and the Philhellenes lay in their evaluation of the atrocities which accompanied the insurrection. At its very beginning, approximately 25,000 of 40,000 Moslem men, women and children were slaughtered by the Greeks in the Peloponnese.[57] Most of those who survived in the bastioned cities were killed later when these places were captured by the insurgents. The bloodiest slaughter in this respect was the fall of Tripoli in October 1821 where, in the words of the Greek leader Theodoros Kolokotronis, who witnessed the event, the main road from the city gate to the citadel was so covered with dead bodies that his horse's hoofs not once touched the paving. On the other hand, the Greeks were persecuted in the same way in some parts of the Ottoman Empire where the Moslems were the majority. The best known and the most disastrous in this respect were the massacres of the Christians on the island of Chios in 1822 where about 25,000 people were slaugh-

---

[53] Metternich to Lebzeltern, Vienna, 30 April 1824, Mikhaïlowitch, pp. 281–282.
[54] D. G. F. D. de Pradt, *L'Intervention armée pour la pacification de la Grèce*, Paris 1828, book number: 37-D-6c (20958), p. 91.
[55] Ibid.
[56] L. S. Stavrianos, *The Balkans since 1453*, New York 2002, p. 296. The view that the Greeks were not prepared to govern themselves was not rare and was also shared, for example, by Stratford Canning. Aksan, p. 294.
[57] St Clair, p. 12.

tered and more than 40,000 enslaved.[58] Having learnt of the first of the atrocities, Metternich was struck to the same extent as were the Philhellenes and he wrote with scorn on 6 May 1821: "Beyond our eastern border three to four hundred thousand hanged, garrotted, beheaded do not count for much."[59] And he added three days later: "The Greek affair will cost rivers of blood. God himself only knows how it will end. Constantinople is exposed to the excesses of Mussulman anarchy ... The whole population has taken up arms; it massacres and insults the Christians indiscriminately. Lord Strangford was assaulted in the streets; he was spat on in the face and Lady Strangford was beaten. The Janissaries snipe at our sailors from the shores like at sparrows."[60] Nevertheless, in comparison with the Philhellenes who generally overlooked the cruelties perpetrated by the Orthodox Greeks and were willing to see only those caused by the Turks, Metternich was also well aware of the fact that both nations were guilty of such atrocities: "The newspapers do not bring any pleasant news. The Turks ravage the Greeks and the Greeks behead the Turks."[61] He also knew that the Greeks started the massacres in the Danubian Principalities as well as in the Peloponnese and he therefore sharply denounced the declaration of Ignatius, an Orthodox bishop living in Pisa, that the Turks were the aggressors and the Greeks merely defended themselves, as absolutely untrue: "It is the Turks, who according to him, are the aggressors and the Peloponnese Greeks are only justifiably defending themselves. The style of his letter is sugar-coated, full of hypocrisy and lies."[62] It is also clear from Metternich's correspondence that he was not inclined to regard the casualties on the side of the Greeks as much more numerous, or more numerous at all: "If he [Nesselrode] bothered to count the number of dead in the terrible struggle between two equally barbarous nations, there is no doubt that the scales would not weigh in favour of the Ottomans."[63] In brief, Metternich was able to foresee the battles for Chios as well as Tripoli and he wrote prophetically to Lebzeltern before these two principal

[58] T. Cremer-Swoboda, *Der griechische Unabhängingkeitskrieg*, Augsburg 1974, pp. 91–92; Brewer, p. 162; Woodhouse, *The Greek War*, p. 87.
[59] *NP*, III, p. 438.
[60] Metternich to Esterházy, Ljubljana, 9 May 1821, HHStA, StA, England 166.
[61] *NP*, III, p. 443.
[62] Metternich to Lebzeltern, Vienna, 3 Dec. 1821, HHStA, StA, Russland III, 45.
[63] Metternich to Lebzeltern, Vienna, 6 Oct. 1825, HHStA, StA, Russland III, 71.

disasters took place: "You see that the war in these countries [Morea and Epirus] is pulsating with the opportunities which revolutionary movements normally present, but these will not fail to take on the most barbaric character when they are associated with people such as the Turks and the Greeks in the 19th century. You see a deplorable event in Navarino. The massacre of the Turkish prisoners-of-war will influence the Turks in the same way as the Greeks will be influenced by the excesses which the Janissaries seem to have perpetrated on the religious in the convent that served as an asylum and defense for the Arnauts after the defeat of Iordaky's forces."[64]

Furthermore, Metternich did not link the Greek fight for freedom with the clash of religions or even civilisations, which was something common for the Philhellenes. He himself maintained that even though the mutual hatred of both cultures was significantly influenced by their religious diversity, Christianity or Islam itself could hardly be responsible. Accordingly, the atrocities of the Moslems were not a symptom of the alleged intolerance of their religion but merely incidents caused by their frustration. It follows that he did not regard the war between the Greeks and the Turks as a religious conflict and he never drew a parallel between the Greeks' fight for independence and the cause of Christianity. This naturally helped him to refute another popular rumour of that period that the Turks wanted to wipe out the Greek nation, as Chateaubriand claimed in his book *Note sur la Grèce*, which was published in 1825.[65] Metternich sharply criticised this thesis as well as other false views in the Chateaubriand's text: "For as long as the world has existed, never has one man accumulated so many shallow and fallacious ideas in fewer pages."[66] Metternich's disagreement with the content led him to the sarcastic remark that it would be

---

[64] Metternich to Lebzeltern, Vienna, 8 Oct. 1821, HHStA, StA, Russland III, 45. See also Metternich to Esterházy, Vienna, 18 and 20 July 1821, HHStA, StA, England 166; Metternich to Vincent, Vienna, 5 Aug. 1821, HHStA, StA, Frankreich 244; Krusemark to Frederick William III, Vienna, 28 July 1821, GStA PK, HA III, MdA I, 5995; Caraman to Pasquier, Vienna, 16 Dec. 1821, AMAE, CP, Autriche 402; *NP*, IV, p. 70.

[65] H. Koukkou, "The „Note on Greece" (Note sur la Grèce) by François-René de Chateaubriand," E. Konstantinou (ed.), *Europäischer Philhellenismus: Die europäische philhellenische Literatur bis zur 1. Hälfte des 19. Jahrhunderts*, Frankfurt am Main, Bern, New York, Paris 1992, pp. 54–58.

[66] Metternich to Gentz, Ischl, 1 Aug. 1825, Kronenbitter, p. 223.

extremely useful if the book were published with notes correcting the many fictions contained therein.[67]

What irritated Metternich even more was the opinion that in this alleged struggle between religions and cultures the Great Powers should intervene for the cause of Christianity, civilisation and humanitarianism and expel the Turks (read: Moslems) from the Continent; what was often demanded was nothing other than, in the words of one high ranking Russian officer in 1825, "a war of extermination against the fanaticism and barbarism of the ferocious Ottomans."[68] The above mentioned Dufour de Pradt also preached in his *L'Intervention armée pour la pacification de la Grèce* the expulsion of the Turks from all of Europe with the aim to create "a new and civilised nation."[69] Metternich rightly called attention to the fact that Pradt somewhat disregarded that such an act had little in common with humanitarianism and civilisation, both to which the Frenchman so strongly appealed. When Pradt wrote that the expulsion of the "cruel Turks" would be done "to the acclamation of Europe," Metternich sarcastically wrote behind the word Europe "civilised."[70] That is why Metternich even much later held a deep aversion to the authors of various plans with humanitarian justifications and he often labelled them as "would-be philanthropists"[71] and "demagogues."[72] He had no aversion to humanitarianism in itself but he disliked those who wanted to wage war "in the name of *religion* and *humanitarianism*."[73] In such cases he was convinced that these two words lost their real sense, in particular if their authors concealed behind them their own political designs, as happened, for example, in the case of Ancillon's memorandum of June 1821 mentioned in Chapter 2. Ancillon supported the idea of the evic-

---

[67] Metternich to Lützow, Vienna, 19 Jan. 1822, HHStA, StA, Türkei VI, 14; Metternich to Bombelles, Vienna, 13 Nov. 1826, HHStA, StA, Russland III, 75; Spinola to Somaglia, Vienna, 23 Nov. 1827, ASV, Arch. Nunz. Vienna 256; Metternich to Gentz, Ischl, 1 Aug. 1825, Prokesch-Osten, *Zur Geschichte der orientalischen Frage*, p. 79; Widmann, pp. 67–68.

[68] Bitis, p. 165.

[69] Pradt, p. 20.

[70] Ibid., p. 106.

[71] Metternich to Esterházy, Vienna, 5 Aug. 1821, HHStA, StA, England 166.

[72] Altieri to Lambruschini, Vienna, 26 March 1841, ASV, Arch. Nunz. Vienna 280D.

[73] Metternich to Vincent, Frankfurt am Main, 9 Nov. 1821, HHStA, StA, Frankreich 244.

tion of the Turks from Europe because, as he claimed, they had gained their territories by force and their rule was thus illegal. Therefore, the Greeks were no rebels because the Turkish government was no real authority but merely a despotic power, and the European Powers were thus entitled to wage war on the Ottoman Empire in the name of humanitarianism. For Metternich this thesis was politically extremely dangerous, and he opposed it with the argument that the Ottoman rule in Europe was sanctioned by a considerable number of treaties which the sultans had concluded with European countries in the past. Since European dynasties obtained and sanctioned their dominions in the same way, Metternich saw no reason why he should regard the sultan's power as illegitimate only because he was a Moslem and not a Christian. For Metternich legitimacy had a universal validity and, consequently, he found no principle in the law of nations which could justify the expulsion of the Turks from Europe.[74] He rejected Ancillon's memorandum as "unsound in principle and founded upon an erroneous view of the history of the subject on which it treats."[75]

The sharp criticism of Ancillon's views was due to Metternich's fear that the Great Powers would misuse their humanitarian ideas for their own political aims. In part, this finally happened in the mid 1820s in connection with Ibrahim Pasha's so-called barbarisation project for the depopulation of the Peloponnese and the replacement of local Greeks by Egyptian fellahs (peasants). This accusation later proved to be absolutely false and already at that time it had been regarded in Vienna as entirely unfounded. Ibrahim Pasha and his father were religiously tolerant with no animosity towards the Greeks and although they enslaved some of them, they did so with the aim of assuring order.[76] It also was impossible for Mohammed Ali to send large numbers of Egyptians to Greece because he needed workers for his farms and

---

[74] *Mémoire Confidentiel de Mr. Ancillon à Berlin*, late June 1821, Prokesch-Osten, *Griechen*, III, pp. 342–345; Metternich to Lützow, Vienna, 19 Aug. 1821, HHStA, StA, Türkei VI, 11; Metternich to Esterházy, Vienna, 2 Oct. and 9 Nov. 1821, HHStA, StA, England 166; Metternich to Lebzeltern, Milan, 18 June 1825, HHStA, StA, Russland III, 71; Metternich to Ottenfels, Vienna, 2 March 1828, HHStA, StA, Türkei VI, 35.

[75] Gordon to Londonderry, Vienna, 3 Oct. 1821, TNA, FO 120/49.

[76] Metternich to Esterházy, Vienna, 14 Aug. 1821, HHStA, StA, England 166; Gentz to Ghica, Vienna, 15 May 1826, *DI*, III, p. 135; Lebzeltern to Metternich, St Petersburg, 7 June 1826, Prokesch-Osten, *Griechen*, IV, p. 271; Marlowe, p. 161; Woodhouse, *The Battle of Navarino*, p. 37.

manufacturing and men for his army. Metternich regarded the accusation as "an evil business which uses religion and humanitarianism as a pretext for disrupting the routine order of things,"[77] and Gentz correctly explained the main reason for its baselessness: "Let us leave aside the lies, even more absurd than atrocious, with which the public papers saturate their readers. No sane man would imagine that any government would cheerfully create a project for the destruction of the total population of a country in order to reign over a desert."[78] Nevertheless, the rumour of the barbarisation project was used by the Lievens in late 1825 to persuade Canning to accept a more hostile policy towards the Ottoman Empire and then by Canning himself for the justification of the St Petersburg Protocol.[79] The argument of humanitarianism was also used for justifying the Treaty of London in which the preamble stated that the steps of their signatories were led by "sentiments of humanity."[80] Not by chance has their intervention in the Greek Question leading to the Battle of Navarino been presented by some historians as an example of a "humanitarian intervention."[81] This interpretation is hardly tenable because the real motives of the trilateral alliance were different and what it merely wanted to do was to legitimise the imperialistic action against the Ottoman Empire, in the words of German historian Oliver Schulz, "to cloak political self-interest with the mantle of humanitarianism."[82]

Metternich and the Philhellenes

What Metternich feared most in Philhellenism was its dangerous revolutionary potential. Its adherents were for him revolutionaries not unlike the members of the Italian Carbonari or German Burschen-

---

[77] Metternich to Princess Lieven, 12 June 1826, NA, RAM-AC 6, 1.

[78] Gentz to Gordon, Vienna, 23 July 1826, Prokesch, *Zur Geschichte der orientalischen Frage*, pp. 145–146.

[79] Brewer, p. 254; Temperley, "Princess Lieven," p. 67.

[80] Holland, p. 7.

[81] For example R. Heydenreuter, "Die erträumte Nation: Griechenlands Staatswerdung zwischen Philhellenismus und Militärintervention," R. Heydenreuter, J. Murken, R. Wünsche (eds.), *Die erträumte Nation*, München 1995, p. 60.

[82] Schulz, "This Clumsy Fabric of Barbarous Power," p. 295.

schaften,[83] and he was right from his point of view because a considerable number of the Philhellenes were recruited from those whose hunger for political change in France, Germany, Italy or anywhere in Europe could not be fulfilled, often due to the resistance directly led or at least supervised by the Austrian chancellor; the fact that the insurrection found a strong echo in German universities or among the Decembrists was no coincidence.[84] They found in the Greek struggle for independence a way to disseminate their own ideas, which made Metternich consider this affair another battlefield where he had to cross arms with "subversive" ideas and actions. Therefore, he did not understand how the French regime could tolerate the spread of pro-Greek ideas in the governmental press: "The passion with which the French royalist papers support the Greek revolt is curious. They undoubtedly follow this line because they consider it to be Christian and they forget that these are the radicals who hoisted the standard of the cross in the hope of one day covering it with the red cap."[85]

In his fight with the Philhellenes, Metternich had two weapons at his disposal: the press and political influence. The former particularly concerned the *Österreichischer Beobachter* that became the flagship of anti-Philhellenic press. It was regarded as the most well-informed newspaper for the events in south-eastern Europe, and information issued in the *Beobachter* was often reprinted in foreign papers, mostly within the German Confederation but also, for example, in the *Journal de St.-Pétersbourg politique et littéraire*. Moreover, Gentz, supervising the editing of the articles in the *Beobachter*, also wrote for the *Augsburger Allgemeine Zeitung*; Metternich and Gentz were thus able to speak, naturally incognito, to the readers of other German newspapers. As for the *Beobachter* itself, it did not want to side too obviously with the Turks and, therefore, an effort to maintain formal impartiality and considerable caution are clearly visible in the relevant articles

---

[83] Metternich to Esterházy, Vienna, 14 Aug. 1821, HHStA, StA, England 166; Metternich to Zichy, Vienna, 31 March 1822, HHStA, StK, Preussen 115.

[84] F. Heyer, *Die Orientalische Frage im kirchlichen Lebenskreis: Das Einwirken der Kirchen des Auslands auf die Emanzipation der orthodoxen Nationen Südosteuropas 1804–1912*, Wiesbaden 1991, p. 153; I. S. Dostian, "L'attitude de la société russe face au mouvement de libération national grec," *Les relations gréco-russes pendant la domination turque et la guerre d'indépendance grecque*, Thessaloniki 1983, p. 65; Cremer-Swoboda, pp. 77–79.

[85] Metternich to Vincent, Vienna, 5 Aug. 1821, HHStA, StA, Frankreich 244.

that contained reliable information although a certain pro-Turkish bias never entirely disappeared. For instance, the Turkish atrocities were generally moderated and those committed by the Greeks, for example in Tripoli, were always emphasised. Upon Metternich's order, the *Beobachter* never presented the Greko-Turkish war as a religious conflict between the Christians and the Moslems.[86]

As for political influence, Metternich tried to exploit it for the suppression of the Philhellenic activities in Europe, above all the departure for Greece of European volunteers whose aim was to fight with the insurgents for their freedom. It was of course easy for him to achieve a complete victory in Austria: in April and May 1821, when young Greeks from German universities tried to obtain permission from the Austrian authorities for passage through Austrian territories, Metternich easily forestalled it and permission could be granted only to individuals approved by the Ottoman chargé d'affaires in Vienna, Jean Mavroyéni. In the late summer, at Metternich's request, Francis I forbade entry into the Austrian Empire and passage through its territories to all Europeans who wanted to get to Greece and fight there against the Turks. Nevertheless, outside Austria's territory, even in the parts of Europe over which Metternich exerted some influence, like the German Confederation or the Apennines, his position was considerably more difficult. As for Germany, numerous groups started to go to the French and Italian ports from which they sailed to the Peloponnese soon after the outbreak of the war. For this mania Metternich particularly blamed German university professors, in particular a professor of Greek language from Munich, Friedrich Wilhelm von Thiersch, for not only advocating the Greek cause in the lecture rooms and the press, as Metternich remarked with sarcasm, as a "new Trojan war,"[87] but also for trying to persuade soldiers to desert the armies of

---

[86] A. Fournier, A. Winkler (eds.), *Tagebücher von Friedrich von Gentz (1829–1831)*, Zürich, Leipzig, Wien 1920, p. 4; H.-M. Kirchner, "Joseph Anton v. Pilat, Chefredakteur des "Österreichischen Beobachter" und Korrespondent der Augsburger "Allgemeinen Zeitung" und die Berichterstattung über den griechischen Aufstand in der Augsburger "Allgemeinen Zeitung" von 1821 bis 1827," E. Konstantinou (ed.), *Europäischer Philhellenismus: Die europäische philhellenische Presse bis zur 1. Hälfte des 19. Jahrhunderts*, Frankfurt am Main, Berlin, Bern, New York, Paris, Wien 1994, p. 93; Jahn, p. 33; Dimakis, p. 50; Mühlhauser, p. 111; Widmann, p. 68.

[87] Metternich to Vincent, Vienna, 5 Aug. 1821, HHStA, StA, Frankreich 244.

the German countries and create a German legion that was to be sent to Greece. Metternich saw in Thiersch "another example of a delirium that has affected the heads of most German scholars."[88] Metternich objected to Thiersch's appeal to German citizens to disobey their rulers and to fight beyond the frontier of the German Confederation, which was regarded in Vienna as an activity in sharp contradiction to the rights of the German sovereigns. This criticism was soon extended by referring to the German professors' "cruel game with the giddiness of youth,"[89] an accusation provoked by the fact that the young men departed to Greece with an image indoctrinated by the academics who had often not visited Greece personally and merely knew the country from the texts of ancient authors. The young men arriving with the expectations that they would find the Peloponnese filled with Plutarch's men were promptly brought down to earth by the reality. This happened to a considerable number of Philhellenes regardless of their age, nationality or education, Anton Prokesch himself being one of them.[90] They started to return home in 1821 and report their experience in the Peloponnese that considerably differed from what they had learnt from their professors and other Philhellenes at the universities or in the newspapers. Metternich naturally welcomed their disillusion because he could use it as an argument in dealing with foreign governments about prohibiting the Europeans from fighting in Greece. This ready-made exploitation of the suffering of some Philhellenes, however, does nothing to alter a certain justification of Metternich's criticism: "While the radical hacks everywhere and above all in Germany sing hymns in praise of the Greeks and while French journalists report to us that in countless theatres the Hellenist public loudly applauds the dramatic tragedies of the Peloponnese, the first amateurs of the Greek liberation are starting to return to our ports from their crusades. The picture that they portray of the situation in

---

[88] Metternich to Trauttmannsdorff, 26 Sept. 1821, HHStA, StA, Russland III, 45.
[89] Metternich to Lebzeltern, Vienna, 14 Oct. 1821, HHStA, StA, Russland III, 45.
[90] Metternich to Lebzeltern, Vienna, 12 Sept. 1821, HHStA, StA, Russland III, 45; Metternich to Trauttmannsdorff, 26 Sept. 1821, attached to Metternich to Lebzeltern, Vienna, 14 Oct. 1821, HHStA, StA, Russland III, 45; Piquot to Frederick William III, Vienna, 9 May 1821, GStA PK, HA III, MdA I, 5996; M. Chvojka, *Josef Graf Sedlnitzky als Präsident der Polizei- und Zensurhofstelle in Wien (1817–1848): Ein Beitrag zur Geschichte der Staatspolizei in der Habsburgermonarchie*, Frankfurt am Main 2010, p. 286; Bertsch, pp. 79–84.

the land of Pericles and Themistocles is entirely at variance with the heroic chants of their colleagues, the German professors and students. Far from having made their fortunes in the classical land, they were robbed of the little money that they had brought with them; instead of winning glory all they got was beaten with sticks."[91]

With his diplomatic intervention in Bavaria and Württemberg, Metternich finally achieved his goal of making Thiersch cease his pro-Greek agitation; but, first, this success did nothing to alter the fact that a considerable number of German officers and students had managed to depart for Greece and, second, after some decline, Philhellenism was revived in these two countries as well as in other parts of Germany again in the mid 1820s. In 1826, King Ludwig I of Bavaria, an ardent Philhellene and the father of the first Greek king, even sent several officers of the Bavarian army to Greece, but their disillusionment and failure was similar to that which a considerable number of other Philhellenes had already suffered. The cabinet in Berlin prohibited the participation of Prussians in the Greek cause at the beginning of the war, but in the following years it allowed collections of donations for the insurgent Greeks.[92] In the Apennines where Austria's influence can also be regarded as considerable in the 1820s, Metternich enjoyed similar mixed success. The main sea port of Tuscany, Leghorn, with a numerous Greek diaspora, was an important gateway for the Philhellenes going to Greece. Metternich tried to persuade the government in Florence to stop the departure of ships loaded with am-

---

[91] Metternich to Zichy, Vienna, 4 Sept. 1821, HHStA, StK, Preussen 113.
[92] Metternich to Lebzeltern, Vienna, 12 Sept. 1821, HHStA, StA, Russland III, 45; Metternich to Zichy, Vienna, 16 Sept. 1821, HHStA, StK, Preussen 113; *Rapport de la Direction de police de Venise à Mr le Gouverner de la province*, Venice, 6 April 1822, attached to Metternich to Esterházy, Vienna, 24 April 1822, HHStA, StA, England 166; Metternich to Vincent, Vienna, 11 Oct. 1821, HHStA, StA, Frankreich 244; Metternich to Vincent, Vienna, 24 April 1822, HHStA, StA, Frankreich 247; Metternich to Lebzeltern, Vienna, 2 June 1826, HHStA, StA, Russland III, 75; Metternich to Ottenfels, Vienna, 12 June 1826, HHStA, StA, Türkei VI, 24; Caraman to Pasquier, Vienna, 14 Sept. 1821, AMAE, CP, Autriche 402; Gordon to Londonderry, Vienna, 3 Oct. 1821, TNA, FO 120/49; R.-W. Eustathiades, *Der deutsche Philhellenismus während des griechischen Freiheitskampfes 1821–1827*, München 1984, p. 132; E. Konstantinou, "Trägerschichten des Philhellenismus und Frühliberalismus in Europa," E. Konstantinou, U. Wiedenmann (eds.), *Europäischer Philhellenismus: Ursachen und Wirkungen*, Neuried 1989, p. 63; H. Loewe, *Friedrich Thiersch und die griechische Frage*, München 1913, pp. 14–18; Gollwitzer, p. 474; St Clair, p. 121.

munition, weapons, cannons and adventurers of various nationalities to the Peloponnese, but all in vain. Similar support was offered to the Greeks in the papal port, Ancona, but in this case Metternich finally persuaded the Holy See to terminate pro-Greek activities in this port and also not to consider the insurrection a war between Christianity and Islam but a mere rebellion against a legitimate ruler. The latter was particularly important for him because he had worried about the pope's eventual support of the Christians, though Orthodox, against the Moslems, which could add a significant impetus to the Philhellenic movement as well as invoke pro-Greek policies in some Catholic countries, or even move Alexander I to support his co-religionists because how would he be able to abandon them if the Catholic pope supported them? Metternich's anxiety was not without reason because some members of the curia in Rome actually regarded the Greeks as Christian fighters in a holy war against "infidels."[93]

The anti-Greek attitude of Rome was also important for Metternich in relation to France, where he used the pope's influence on the kings to reduce any pro-Greek feelings. This was a very rare example of the use of a religious card by Metternich in dealing with affairs of a fundamentally political – non-religious – nature. According to Alan J. Reinerman, Metternich had some success with playing this papal card in Paris after 1821, but it is actually impossible to prove any real achievements. In any case, when in 1827, under the pretext of eventual dangers for the Ottoman Catholics resulting from the three Powers' intervention in the Ottoman Empire, Metternich tried to persuade Pope Leo XII to use his influence on Charles X to stop the policies of the trilateral alliance, the Battle of Navarino prevented him from having any success. This setback well characterises Metternich's fruitless attempts to reduce the French and British governments' toleration of

---

[93] Metternich to Zichy, Vienna, 2 Feb. 1822, HHStA, StK, Preussen 115; Metternich to Lützow, Vienna, 3 Feb. and 20 March 1822, HHStA, StA, Türkei VI, 14; Metternich to Lebzeltern, Vienna, 31 March 1822, HHStA, StA, Russland III, 54; Metternich to Lebzeltern, Vienna, 30 March 1823, HHStA, StA, Russland III, 60; Metternich to Ottenfels, Vienna, 18 March 1823, HHStA, StA, Türkei VI, 19; Metternich to Lützow, Vienna, 26 Oct. 1827, HHStA, StA, Rom 38; Lützow to Metternich, Constantinople, 25 Feb. 1822, HHStA, StA, Türkei VI, 13; Ottenfels to Metternich, Constantinople, 25 Feb. 1823, HHStA, StA, Türkei VI, 18; Spinola to Somaglia, Vienna, 30 Oct. and 24 Nov. 1827, ASV, Arch. Nunz. Vienna 256; Reinerman, "Metternich, the Papacy and the Greek Revolution," pp. 180–185.

the Philhellenic activities in France and Great Britain. It is true that the cabinet in Paris closed Marseille at the end of 1822 to the crowds of the Philhellenes from various countries who wanted to embark there on any of the ships sailing into the Levant, but it is not clear whether this governmental measure was caused by Metternich's urgency or the warnings of the Philhellenes already returning from Greece that other volunteers would find there nothing except "misery, death and ingratitude."[94] Moreover, in the mid 1820s Charles X allowed the existence of the Greek Committee in Paris, the issue of pro-Greek articles in the ultraconservative governmental press and personally demonstrated his pro-Greek sentiments, for example with the purchase of the famous picture *Massacre at Chios* from Eugène Delacroix. Metternich criticised this complicity of the government and expressed his incomprehension at how it could allow such hostile conduct towards a third country with which it was at peace: "What difference is there in reality between support for a war given by the subjects of a country (and what is more, by a compact and confessed association of those subjects) to insurgents, against a government with which their own sovereign authority is at peace, and support provided to a country at war with the homeland?"[95] However, his objections were rejected in Paris under the pretext that the government could do nothing against the Philhellenes because to do so could damage public opinion. As for London, Canning's presence at the head of affairs prevented any success of Metternich's objections in advance, and it was considerably annoying for the chancellor to watch British Philhellenes like George Gordon Lord Byron, Frank Abney Hastings, Sir Richard Church or Thomas Lord Cochrane playing a considerable role in the Greek affairs.[96]

---

[94] Brewer, p. 138.
[95] Metternich to Vincent, Vienna, 2 Sept. 1825, HHStA, StA, Frankreich 257.
[96] Metternich to Esterházy, Vienna, 11 Aug. 1823 and 5 March 1824, HHStA, StA, England 169; Metternich to Ottenfels, Vienna, 20 May 1824, HHStA, StA, Türkei VI, 22; Metternich to Vincent, Vienna, 17 Oct. 1824, HHStA, StA, Frankreich 254; Metternich to Vincent, Vienna, 5 Sept. and 10 Dec. 1825, Ischl, 17 Aug. 1825, HHStA, StA, Frankreich 257; Metternich to Zichy, Vienna, 21 Sept. 1825, HHStA, StK, Preussen 121; Metternich to Apponyi, Vienna, 8 June 1826, HHStA, StA, Frankreich 260; Metternich to Lebzeltern, Vienna, 3 March 1825, HHStA, StA, Russland III, 70; Tatishchev to Nesselrode, Vienna, 21 June 1826, AVPRI, fond 133, Kantseliariia, opis 468, 11870; A. Piussi, "The Orient of Paris: The Vanishing of Egypt from Early Nineteenth-Century Paris Salons (1800–1827)," D. Panzac,

Metternich and the Greeks

Metternich's political opposition to the insurrection gave rise to the view that he desired the annihilation of the Greeks. For example, the Prussian Envoy in St Petersburg, Reinhold Otto Friedrich von Schöler, wrote to Berlin after the signature of the St Petersburg Protocol that "for its part Austria certainly must give up the wistful hope of which this treaty robs it, namely, that the Greeks could be entirely exterminated."[97] Russian historian A. L. Narotchnitzki claimed that Metternich tried to forestall Russia's intervention in the insurrection due to his desire to offer more time "to the Ottoman authorities to continue to cut the throats of the Greeks on a massive scale."[98] This opinion must be resolutely refuted because Metternich's anti-Greek policy was not motivated by any personal hatred and he was not a man who wished that people, individuals or masses, were murdered anywhere and he never approved of the massacres of the Greeks in the same way that he never agreed with the massacres of the Moslems. He hastened to warn Mahmud II against the unjust and excessive brutality, fanaticism and eventual extermination of the Greeks, in his opinion a proceeding in contradiction not only with humanity but also the precepts of Islam. He also condemned the murder of the Greek patriarch and advised humane conduct, amnesty and administrative improvements. There is no reason to regard these warnings and counsels as insincere although they naturally were also motivated with regard to Russia as well as public opinion in Europe, which Metternich labelled as the sixth and most powerful power in the Greek affairs. This is proved with his practical deeds: he not only tolerated but also explicitly agreed with the activities of the Austrian agents with the aim of helping the suffering Greeks, as well as in other cases the Moslems. Metternich naturally knew and approved the help which the Austrian agent in Athens, Georg Christian Gropius, offered to the Greeks. During the massacres at Chios, Austrian Consul Georg Stiepovich saved some inhabitants in the building of the consulate although it must be admitted that they were mainly Catholics. Nevertheless, after the

---

A. Raymond (eds.), *La France et l'Égypte à l'époque des vice-rois 1805–1882*, Le Caire 2002, pp. 41–58; Sauvigny, *Metternich et la France*, III, p. 1073.
[97] Schöler to Frederick William III, St Petersburg, 6 April 1826, Ringhoffer, p. 263.
[98] Narotchnitzki, p. 93. For a similar view see H. Ypsilanti, *Metternichs Stellung zum griechischen Freiheitskampf*, unpublished dissertation, Wien 1927, p. 88.

disaster in Chios, Ottenfels and Strangford urged the Porte to more clemency and humanity in its conduct towards all subjects regardless of their faith with the aim of not repeating the same bloody scenes. With regard to humane treatment, the Austrian Levant squadron behaved according to its principles when the captive Greek pirates were not handed over to the Turks, which would have equalled handing them over to their certain execution, but were taken for trial in Trieste. A measure of merit for avoiding the massacres of the Christians in Smyrna after the Battle of Navarino must be accorded Admiral Dandolo. In the spring of 1828, Prokesch assured the exchange of Greek prisoners for captive Egyptians and he was finally able to arrange it at the rate of 172 to 112, which was a considerably better result than the Greeks had been expecting. And when, for example, Rigny ensured the safe withdrawal of the Greek garrison from Acropolis in 1827, Metternich approved the French admiral's conduct.[99]

Furthermore, the numerous Greek diaspora in Vienna, Pest, Venice and Trieste suffered no persecutions from the government in the 1820s and, on the contrary, the Austrian Empire served as a safe haven for the Greeks who had not participated in the insurrection but were forced to leave their homes due to the war and flee to the Austrian territories. They started to arrive at the very beginning of the rebellion from the Danubian Principalities and, with the passage of time, they also came in ever increasing numbers from the areas north of the

---

[99] Metternich to Lützow, Ljubljana, 17 May, 3 June and 17 July 1821, HHStA, StA, Türkei VI, 11; Metternich to Ottenfels, Vienna, 18 Dec. 1825, HHStA, StA, Türkei VI, 24; Metternich to Esterházy, Ljubljana, 21 May 1821, HHStA, StA, England 166; Metternich to Vincent, Vienna, 5 Aug. 1821, HHStA, StA, Frankreich 244; Metternich to Zichy, Vienna, 24 Aug. 1821, HHStA, StK, Preussen 113; Metternich to Esterházy, Vienna, 29 Jan. 1822, HHStA, StA, England 166; Ottenfels to Metternich, Constantinople, 10 May 1823, HHStA, StA, Türkei VI, 18; Miltitz to Frederick William III, Pera, 10 May 1823, GStA PK, HA III, MdA I, 7257; Caraman to Pasquier, Vienna, 1 June 1821, AMAE, CP, Autriche 402; Caraman to Damas, Vienna, 29 June 1827, AMAE, CP, Autriche 408; G. Pfligersdorffer, "Philhellenisches bei Prokesch von Osten," E. Konstantinou (ed.), *Europäischer Philhellenismus: Die europäische philhellenische Literatur bis zur 1. Hälfte des 19. Jahrhunderts*, Frankfurt am Main, Bern, New York, Paris 1992, p. 88; G. Pfligersdorffer, "Österreichs griechenfreundliche Diplomatie in der ersten Hälfte des 19. Jahrhunderts," E. Konstantinou, U. Wiedenmann (eds.), *Europäischer Philhellenismus, Ursachen und Wirkungen*, Neuried 1989, pp. 193–194; Prokesch-Osten, *Griechen*, I, p. 156, *Griechen*, II, p. 180; Sauer, *Österreich und die Levante*, pp. 148–149.

Gulf of Corinth as well as the Peloponnese. In late 1821, when news – although unverified – arrived in Vienna that the British authorities of the Ionian Islands had refused to accept some Greek fugitives, Francis I was recommended by his advisors to offer them an island in the Adriatic Sea and proclaim a sanctuary for these unfortunates. Six years later, Metternich also advised the emperor to accept additional Christian refugees, the Greeks of course not excepted, from the Ottoman domains should war break out between the Ottoman Empire and Russia, and he also supported the acceptance of Greek refugees abroad, for example in the Papal State.[100]

In the spring of 1827, when the representatives of the Greek community in Vienna asked Metternich for permission to make a financial collection on behalf of its suffering co-religionists in Greece, the chancellor agreed on the condition that the raised money would be distributed to the needy by the Austrian consul general in Corfu. He did so despite the fact that he knew that the instigator of this plan was Patriarch Ignatius with whom he ideologically disagreed as mentioned above, and the prince even forwarded the request to Francis I who finally consented. Metternich also willingly helped Jean Mavroyéni, of Greek origin, to save his life when the latter was called by Mahmud II to return to Constantinople shortly after the outbreak of the insurrection. It was certain that had Mavroyéni obeyed this order, he would have lost his head as had recently happened to one of his Greek relatives. Metternich advised him to stay in Austria and move for a while to Pressburg, where Mavroyéni actually stayed undisturbed until the end of the decade. When the war ended, he was reinstalled in his office by the same sultan again in 1832.[101]

Further proof of Metternich's personal neutrality towards the Greeks can also be found in his treatment of Alexander Ypsilantis, who fled to the Austrian Empire in late June 1821 and was imprisoned

---

[100] Metternich to Lebzeltern, Vienna, 8 Oct. 1821, HHStA, StA, Russland III, 45; Metternich to Francis I, Vienna, 21 Dec. 1827, HHStA, StK, Vorträge 252; Gordon to Londonderry, Vienna, 3 and 9 Oct. 1821, TNA, FO 120/49; Caraman to Montmorency, Vienna, 28 Feb. 1822, AMAE, CP, Autriche 403; Chvojka, pp. 284–285; Reinerman, "Metternich, the Papacy and the Greek Revolution," pp. 180–182.
[101] Tatishchev to Nesselrode, Vienna, 12 May 1827, AVPRI, fond 133, Kantseliariia, opis 468, 11873; T. Blancard, *Les Mavroyéni: Histoire d'Orient (de 1700 à nos jours)*, II, Paris 1909, pp. 179–181. For more on Metternich's attitude towards Jean Mavroyéni see Chapter 22.

with his two younger brothers in the fortress of Mukachevo (Munkács). This decision was not taken lightly by the Viennese cabinet because Metternich and Francis I did not want to have these prisoners. Under normal conditions, they would have been transported through Austria's territory and allowed to go, but such conduct would be much too risky for the government in their case. Metternich could not risk an entanglement with the Porte if the Ypsilantis decided to go to Greece and continue fighting against the Turks. On the other hand, they could not be handed over to the Turkish authorities either because this would have been their death sentence, something which could cause displeasure in St Petersburg. Consequently, after an agreement with Alexander I, the Ypsilantis remained in the Austrian jail. Although Mahmud II complained that they were not handed over to him for punishment, there was nothing that he could really object to because the chosen procedure was completely legal: according to the Austro-Ottoman treaties, the brothers could not be given asylum, which imprisonment surely was not.[102]

Since Alexander Ypsilantis found Mukachevo bad for his health, he was transferred with his brothers to Theresienstadt in the summer of 1823. Their imprisonment in Mukachevo had already been quite luxurious and it continued to be so after their removal to Bohemia, and Metternich was significantly responsible for this. He personally allowed them to correspond with their mother, he sent them 45 books, he proposed Theresienstadt owing to Alexander's deteriorating health and he also consented for this reason to Alexander's stay for medical reasons in the spa of Pistyan in Hungary (Pöstyén, today Piešťany in Slovakia) in the mid 1820s. They enjoyed good food and even could walk or ride horses in the neighbourhood of Theresienstadt. The main problem was that all of this cost a considerable amount of money, which was paid for out of the military treasury in Prague and, therefore, the military command sent Metternich repeated requests for the repayment of the bills. The total sum due at the end of the winter of 1827 had reached the incredible amount of 19,620 florins.[103] Met-

[102] Metternich to Lebzeltern, Vienna, 5 July 1821, HHStA, StA, Russland III, 45; Metternich to Esterházy, Vienna, 20 July 1821, HHStA, StA, England 166; Metternich to Lützow, Vienna, 5 and 17 July, 10 Sept. 1821, HHStA, StA, Türkei VI, 11; Krusemark to Frederick William III, Vienna, 14 July 1821, GStA PK, HA III, MdA I, 5995; Gordon to Londonderry, Vienna, 15 July 1821, TNA, FO 120/48.
[103] Metternich to Zichy, attached to Metternich to Bernstorff, Vienna, 3 March

ternich therefore found himself in a precarious situation because he
had to balance the costs from the Chancellery's budget; despite his
numerous urgent demands addressed to the Ypsilantis' mother, he obtained just a fraction of the requested sum, even when he warned her
that if the amount was not paid off in full, her sons would be treated
as normal prisoners, which meant, for example, that they would get
only basic rations instead of poultry, veal and venison in the future.
Metternich even requested the Russian cabinet to persuade Madam
Ypsilantis to pay, but all he finally obtained was the explanation that
she could not do so because of her precarious financial situation. This
led in early 1826 to a certain reduction of the costs, but the brothers'
lives still were considerably better than those of ordinary prisoners.[104]

One cannot be surprised that Metternich sincerely wished to get
rid of the prisoners, not by sending them to their deaths but by proposing to Alexander I in the autumn of 1823 that they should be released
under the condition that they departed for the U.S.A. and never returned to Europe; however, Alexander I rejected such a possibility
and counter-proposed that the Ypsilantis should be transferred to any
province within the Austrian Empire. Metternich willingly passed on
this request to Francis I, but since the emperor's condition that the
Ypsilantis family would promise to pay for the brothers' food was
not obtained, and Alexander I as well as Nicholas I refused to cover
their costs, nothing changed until the spring of 1827 when the latter
started to officially request their release. Metternich recommended to
Francis I that he should agree for financial, political as well as humanitarian reasons. He found the several-year-long imprisonment sufficient
punishment and to end it to be desirable not only due to the tsar's
attitude but also due to the deteriorating health of Alexander Ypsilantis since the early summer of 1827. Francis I finally agreed and

---

1827, A. Moutafidou, "Alexandros Ypsilantis in Theresienstadt 1826–1827,"
SOF 63/64, 2004/2005, p. 242.

[104] Metternich to Lebzeltern, Vienna, 24 Nov. 1823, HHStA, StA, Russland III, 60;
Metternich to Lebzeltern, Vienna, 7 Feb. and 17 April 1824, HHStA, StA, Russ-
land III, 64; Metternich to Lebzeltern, Ischl, 11 Aug. 1824, HHStA, StA, Russland
III, 65; Metternich to Lebzeltern, Vienna, 30 Nov. 1825, HHStA, StA, Russland
III, 71; Stürmer to Lebzeltern, Vienna, 28 April 1825, HHStA, StA, Russland III,
70; Lebzeltern to Metternich, St Petersburg, 10 Jan. 1826, HHStA, StA, Russ-
land III, 73; P. Broucek, "Alexander Ypsilantis' Gefangenschaft in Österreich,"
MÖStA 17/18, 1964/1965, pp. 554–556.

in October ordered that Alexander and his brothers were released on the condition that they went to Verona and lived there under police supervision and at their own expense. However, Alexander Ypsilantis never arrived in this north Italian town because he fell seriously ill on his way and had to stop in Vienna, where he died on 31 January 1828.[105]

It is symptomatic for Metternich that he had willingly and without delay allowed this instigator of the Greek insurrection to stay in the Austrian capital for as long as he needed for his recovery,[106] and although it is definitely true that Metternich's conduct towards Alexander Ypsilantis must be regarded in the wider context of Austria's political interests and its need to maintain good relations with Russia, it proves that the chancellor did not behave cruelly towards the man who caused so much trouble to the chancellor with his revolutionary enterprise in the Principalities. That Metternich supported the brothers' good living conditions was in no way necessary, in particular during the reign of Alexander I, who did not pay any attention to their fate. Consequently, one cannot deny a sense of humanity in the chancellor's behaviour towards the Ypsilantis and the validity of Alan Sked's claim that Metternich in no way wished to imprison people and that he behaved with considerable mercy towards those imprisoned for political crimes.[107]

*   *   *

It would be a serious mistake to consider the measures undertaken by Metternich on behalf of the Ypsilantis and the Greeks in general

---

[105] Metternich to Lebzeltern, Vienna, 24 Nov. 1823, HHStA, StA, Russland III, 60; Metternich to Lebzeltern, Vienna, 19 Jan. 1824, HHStA, StA, Russland III, 64; Metternich to Lebzeltern, Vienna, 22 May 1824, HHStA, StA, Russland III, 65; Metternich to Francis I, Vienna, 3 April 1827, HHStA, StK, Vorträge 250; Metternich to Francis I, Vienna, 19 July and 12 Sept. 1827, HHStA, StK, Vorträge 251; Metternich to Francis I, Vienna, 13 Oct. 1827, HHStA, StK, Vorträge 252; Metternich to Tatishchev, Vienna, 20 Oct. 1827, Tatishchev to Nesselrode, Vienna, 3, 20 and 25 Oct., 24 Nov. 1827, AVPRI, Fond 133, Kantseliariia, opis 468, 11874; Maltzan to Frederick William III, Vienna, 7 Sept. 1827, GStA PK, HA III, MdA I, 6008.

[106] Tatishchev to Nesselrode, Vienna, 28 Dec. 1827, AVPRI, Fond 133, Kantseliariia, opis 468, 11874.

[107] Sked, *Metternich*, pp. 174–177, 244.

as well as his criticism of their slaughter as proof of any hidden pro-
Greek sentiment on his part that allegedly could not be revealed for
political reasons, as Greek historian Kleanthes Nikolaides claimed.[108]
This definitely was not the case. Metternich actually was no friend of
the Greeks in the same way that he was not of the Turks, but he was
also not personally hostile to either of them. His attitude influenced
by the ideas of the 18th century and his in-depth of knowledge of the
conditions of the Turko-Greek war led him to personal neutrality towards the protagonists who massacred each other with the same zeal.
He did not mourn the bloody scenes in the Ottoman Empire, but he
also did not applaud them; he saw no reason why he should attribute
the principal guilt for the atrocities to the religions which were misused by the protagonists of the war, and he also saw no reason why he
should blame Islam only. This attitude as well as his statements concerning this religion and the religious situation existing in the Levant
can be considered as sincere, in other words resulting not only from
Austria's geopolitical needs but also his own *Weltanschauung*, and as
far more sensible and less arrogant than the opinions shared by a considerable number of Western visionaries who were eager to promote
their own world-views but without regard for the actual situation in
the Near East. Metternich never had these ambitions and never behaved disdainfully or adversely towards Islam in spiritual matters. He
did not consider Islam to be dangerous to the European civilisation
built on Christian principles, and even though he personally did not
feel any inclination to the Orient, in his practical policy-making his
own Catholic faith played an extremely insignificant role, if any role
at all. His conduct in the religious affairs of the Levant proves that
he based his steps upon very rational thinking and a good knowledge
of the situation existing beyond Austria's south-eastern border. One
cannot therefore be very surprised when reading the claim of a prominent historian of the Armenian nation that "Metternich, alone among
the European diplomats of that era, embraced and understood the
Sublime Porte wonderfully well."[109]

---

[108] K. Nikolaides, "Die Politik des Fürsten Metternich gegenüber der großen Revolution von 1821," *Oesterreichische Rundschau* 18, 1922, pp. 778–789.
[109] This opinion is quoted in Breycha-Vauthier, p. 48.

13

The French Expedition to Algeria

Metternich's hope in the autumn of 1829 that the difficulties within the Ottoman Empire would be promptly solved soon proved to be unfounded. The discussions over the Greek Question continued and the Ottoman Empire was doomed to become embroiled in yet another crisis concerning its western cape: Algeria. The French king and his cabinet seeking to gain glory on the international scene decided in early 1830 to send the French army against this Ottoman province. Although Austria had no direct interests in this part of North Africa, Metternich immediately raised his voice against France's imperialistic activities directed against the sultan's domain because it could have a negative impact not only on the sultan's prestige but also on the relations among the European Powers and the internal situation in France. The chancellor's criticism was not only quick but also loud, even louder than the discontent of the British government. Even though he later had to accept the French occupation of Algeria, his early opposition clearly proves the extent to which he regarded the position of the Ottoman Empire, including its African territory, as intermingled with the situation in Europe. The fact that the sultan's state had not become a member of the European state system enabled France to direct its imperialistic aims against the Ottoman possession in Africa with impunity.

France's Thirst for Glory and the Drovetti Project

The cause of the French hostile proceeding against Algeria lay in the tensions between this North African Ottoman Province and France which escalated after the end of April 1827 when Algerian Dey Hussein Pasha famously struck the French consul in the face three times with a fly-whisk and from that moment refused to offer satisfaction demanded by France.[1] Since Sultan Mahmud II was not interested in this affair because of his own problems in Greece, France had to proceed on its own. At first, it limited itself to a naval blockade of the Algerian ports. However, this measure was entirely insufficient and the longer it lasted, the more Hussein Pasha came to believe that France would go no further and he began to feel certain that his safety was assured. Consequently, in July 1829, he resolutely rejected the last French offer of conciliation.[2]

It is impossible to fully understand the French government's resulting reaction as well as Metternich's opposition to its decisions concerning Algeria after mid 1829 without an appreciation of France's hunger for political recovery on the international scene after 1815, in other words for the restoration of its influence in the regions where its position had been considerably stronger before the outbreak of the revolution in 1789: namely in Western Europe and the Mediterranean. France of the 1820s was a country where public opinion longed for the revival of its bygone glory, and their kings, Louis XVIII and Charles X, were not deaf to this desire, in particular when they wanted to win the support of the public for the Bourbon Monarchy and thereby strengthen their own power with military adventures abroad. This led the former to send his troops to Spain in 1823 and the latter his to the Peloponnese five years later. However, the glory gained was rather precarious and especially in Greece the French forces achieved very little: they repaired the local communications, in other words they were "devoted to pioneer work instead of to glory."[3] Most of them returned home before the end of 1829. This gave little satisfaction to Charles X, who focused on increasing his own prestige since his ultra-conservative rule was daily becoming more unpopular in France in the late 1820s.

---

[1]   The history leading to this insult had its roots in the 1790s and can only be explained in brief here: Algerian grain was sold to France in the 1790s but the price was never fully repaid. Hussein Pasha in vain addressed reclamations to the French government that regarded the affair as terminated and did not answer them. This silence together with discourteous behaviour of the French consul general, Pierre Deval, caused Hussein's displeasure finally leading to the famous blows, not entirely incomprehensible considering the conduct of France and its agent. G. Esquer, *Histoire de l'Algérie (1830–1960)*, Paris 1960, p. 5. According to Gentz, the strikes were even deserved; Metternich never touched this topic. Gentz to Metternich, Vienna, 13 June 1830, Kronenbitter, p. 345.

[2]   Dodwell, p. 95.

[3]   Crawley, *Greek Independence*, p. 157.

Therefore, he even contemplated in the same year that "perhaps a war against the court of Vienna would be useful to me, in that it would put an end to internal wrangling and bring the nation to act together as it desires."[4] The result of this desire was not a war with Austria but the famous Polignac Plan of early September 1829 in which Polignac, persuaded about the imminent and inevitable fall of the Ottoman Empire, proposed its partition and subsequent significant territorial changes in the whole of Europe, with France particularly seeking to gain Belgium, at that time an integral part of the Dutch Kingdom. The project was approved by Charles X and sent to St Petersburg where, however, the French ambassador did not acquaint Nicholas I with its existence since he knew that the tsar desired to maintain the status quo in the East as well as in the West.[5]

Although never executed, the Polignac Plan is significant because it well reflects France's revisionist ambitions aimed at the modification or even destruction of the 1815 settlement.[6] Metternich did not know of its existence, but if he had been aware of it, he would definitely have labelled it in the same negative way as he did in the case of a very similar project published by Baron Louis-Auguste Camus de Richemont earlier in 1829: "Incomprehensible product of a pen guided by dementia."[7] Metternich was naturally well aware of France's ambitions since it was impossible for him not to hear the voices calling for the shift of its frontier to the Rhine, the seizure of Belgium and the replacement of Austria's influence in the Apennines with France's. At least since the mid 1820s he regarded the French policy as equally ambitious as that of Russia, and as the decade was drawing to an end, his dissatisfaction increased in this respect. The expedition to the Peloponnese was for him an evidential result of this

---

[4]   Sked, *Metternich*, p. 68.
[5]   R. Bullen, "France and Europe, 1815–1848: The Problem of Defeat and Recovery," A. Sked (ed.), *Europe's Balance of Power, 1815–1848*, London 1979, pp. 124–126; A. Debidour, *Histoire diplomatique de l'Europe depuis l'ouverture du Congrès de Vienne jusqu'à la clôture du Congrès de Berlin (1814–1878)*, Paris 1891, pp. 270–271; R. Marcowitz, *Großmacht auf Bewährung: Die Interdependenz französischer Innen- und Außenpolitik und ihre Auswirkungen auf Frankreichs Stellung im europäischen Konzert 1814/15–1851/52*, Stuttgart 2001, p. 101; Droz, p. 306; Hammer, pp. 153–160; Puryear, *France*, pp. 76–79; Schiemann, II, p. 384.
[6]   Schroeder, *Transformation*, p. 659.
[7]   Sauvigny, *Metternich et la France*, III, p. 1311.

"spirit of conquest"[8] and proof of the government's weakness in trying to pander to the self-esteem of the nation with a warlike policy.
Caraman confirmed this view when telling the chancellor that "this
proposed measure was not so much dictated by a desire of expediting
the settlement of the Greek Question as of doing something which
should bring France prominently forward and be agreeable to the liberal party in that country."[9] Metternich briefly characterised the given
situation with this sarcastic remark: "France wants to make its mark
– it wants to proceed, march, be active; it will even be prepared to
attach itself to one chariot or another so long as the government in
Paris can boast that it has driven it."[10] Metternich feared that if the
French cabinet responded to the public call for a more active policy
abroad, their hunger for action would not be satisfied but, on the
contrary, would increase and the king and his ministers would have
to go much further than they actually wanted: "This expedition [to
the Peloponnese] is motivated by the French court, by a compelling
need to come to physical action, by a need that the government itself
declares is the result of the movement that has seized the will of the
people in the kingdom. We will never regard this reason as a good
political reason. Governments which give in to the will of the people
show at the very least proof of a most deplorable weakness."[11] He well
understood that Charles X wanted to remedy domestic problems in
France with successes abroad, but he worried about France's internal
situation and he disagreed with its inclination to rescue it with an adventurous foreign policy: "Weak in their administrative position, the
French ministers have pursued a phantom of political and military
glory for a long time ... This absurdity takes place nowhere but in
France."[12] These critical words were written on 10 December 1829,
which meant just days before the arrival of the first news of France's
seriously prepared designs against Algeria that annoyed Metternich,
but regarding France's previous adventurous plans this latest one in
no way surprised him.[13]

[8] Tatishchev to Nesselrode, Vienna, 14 Aug. 1828, AVPRI, fond 133,
Kantseliariia, opis 468, 11879.
[9] Cowley to Aberdeen, Vienna, 12 July 1828, TNA, FO 120/93.
[10] Metternich to Esterházy, Vienna, 9 July 1828, HHStA, StA, England 183.
[11] Metternich to Trauttmannsdorff, Vienna, 5 Aug. 1828, HHStA, StK, Preussen
129.
[12] Metternich to Ottenfels, Vienna, 10 Dec. 1828, HHStA, StA, Türkei VI, 35.

Hussein Pasha's refusal of any conciliation arrived in Paris at the very moment when Polignac was occupied with his ambitious plan to change the map of Europe, followed later, in the autumn of 1829, by plans for territorial changes in the Rhineland. Consequently, Polignac was not willing to waste French troops on a punitive expedition to North Africa, and he welcomed the proposal of the recently retired French consul general in Egypt, Bernardino Drovetti, who suggested that Mohammed Ali's army not only punish Hussein Pasha but also occupy Tunis and Tripoli. Although France would obtain no territory in Algeria, it would be able to strengthen its influence in North Africa owing to its good relations and close cooperation with the Egyptian governor. The first talks between France and Mohammed Ali occurred in the second half of November 1829. The Egyptian governor regarded the project with favour and was willing to offer 40,000 Egyptian soldiers under Ibrahim Pasha's command. For this help he demanded the loan of 20 million francs and the donation of four French battle ships, each with 80 cannons. This counterproposal was dispatched to the French government.[14]

Although French diplomacy was proving to be successful in Alexandria, the situation was less favourable in Constantinople. In December, Guilleminot acquainted the Porte with information about the proposed Egyptian expedition. At the same time, he warned that if Mahmud II refused to approve the campaign, France would undertake it alone, with all the ensuing consequences. However, the sultan decided not to yield to pressure and he rejected the French proposal because he did not trust the goals of the French government and his own powerful vassal. The most significant reason for the refusal seems to have been the fact that a secret understanding in relation to this

[13] Metternich to Lebzeltern, Ischl, 15 Aug. 1825, HHStA, StA, Russland III, 71; Metternich to Ottenfels, Vienna, 6 Jan., 4 Aug. and 17 Sept. 1828, HHStA, StA, Türkei VI, 35; Metternich to Trauttmannsdorff, Vienna, 13 and 18 Aug. 1828, HHStA, StK, Preussen 129; Metternich to Apponyi, Vienna, 12 Nov. 1828, HHStA, StA, Frankreich 268; Metternich to Esterházy, Linz, 21 Sept. 1829, Vienna, 16 Dec. 1829, HHStA, StA, England 188; Tatishchev to Nesselrode, Vienna, 25 June, 4 and 14 Aug. 1828, AVPRI, fond 133, Kantseliariia, opis 468, 11879; Brockhausen to Frederick William III, Vienna, 16 and 19 Aug. 1828, GStA PK, HA III, MdA I, 6011; Krauter, p. 249.
[14] M. Lamuniére, *Histoire de l'Algérie illustrée: De 1830 à nos jours*, Paris 1962, p. 26; R. T. Ridley, *Napoleon's Proconsul in Egypt: The Life and Times of Bernardino Drovetti*, London 1998, p. 169; Puryear, *France*, pp. 121–122.

subject had already been concluded between the governor of Egypt
and the French court, an act which manifestly undermined the sultan's
interests and rights of supremacy. According to Ottenfels, it was logical that the Porte opposed the French plan, and he sharply denounced
the fact that France had contacted Mohammed Ali before the sultan:
"To invite an Ottoman pasha, without the preliminary agreement of
his sovereign, to engage in a military expedition against another vassal
of the Turkish Empire, is to treat him as an independent power."[15]
After the rejection of the French plan, Mahmud II offered his own
solution, based on a suggestion that he should act as intermediary
between France and the dey. For this purpose, he was willing to send
an extraordinary commissary, Tahir Pasha, to Algiers. The commissary would invite Hussein Pasha to hear the French complaints and
promptly resolve all outstanding disagreements. This was the position
at the end of 1829, a diplomatic outcome which the French cabinet
hoped to keep secret.[16]

Metternich's Criticism of the Drovetti Project

Metternich learnt about Drovetti's idea to make use of the Egyptian
army against Hussein Pasha from the report of the Austrian consul general in Alexandria, Joseph von Acerbi, dated 25 June 1829.
Drovetti was fascinated by his own idea for some time, making no
secret of it. He frequently discussed it with the British consul and at
least once with Acerbi. Drovetti saw in such a "heroic enterprise"[17]
a means of civilising this part of Africa. Drovetti was convinced that
the seizure of the Barbary States (including Morocco) would meet
with the resistance of neither Mahmud II nor the Great Powers. Mohammed Ali would be able to establish free trade in this area, abolish
piracy and end the practice of ransom payments paid by some Euro-

---

[15] Ottenfels to Metternich, Constantinople, 24 Dec. 1829, HHStA, StA, Türkei
VI, 38.
[16] The project presented by Guilleminot to Pertev Effendi, Constantinople, 1 Dec.
1830, attached to Gordon to Aberdeen, Constantinople, 15 Dec. 1829, TNA,
FO 78/181; C. Gaultier-Kurhan, *Mehemet Ali et la France 1805–1849: Histoire
singuliere du Napoleon de l'Orient*, Paris 2005, p. 152.
[17] Acerbi to Metternich, Alexandria, 25 June 1829, HHStA, StA, Türkei VI, 37.

pean states to protect their own ships. In addition, he would be able to introduce civilisation and enlightened government, as was already the case in Egypt. This would replace the situation where brigands were able to rule by force of arms. However, Acerbi did not share his French colleague's optimism. With regard to the system of monopolies in Egypt, he doubted that free trade would be introduced in the seized regions. In addition, he did not believe in the civilising mission of the Egyptian governor, something which he had failed to achieve in the Sudan. One man's domination over North Africa held no advantages for Austria, except in relation to the suppression of piracy: "Today we have to contain four disunited and weak deys; then we would have one strong one instead. They have no navy and no regular army; he would have both."[18] Acerbi's opinion was considerably influenced by his strong mistrust of the Egyptian governor's character: "He [Mohammed Ali] is an ambitious man, insatiable in relation to power, resistant to any kind of control. If he does not respect his sovereign when he is weak, would he respect him any more when he is powerful? If he does not respect the treaties, the conventions or even the consulates and the consuls when he is a servant of the Porte, would he respect them any better as an independent power? I consider Mohammed Ali to be a man of extraordinary intelligence for a Turk; but I do not allow myself be so blinded by my admiration for him that I agree with everything he does; that would be imprudent."[19]

Acerbi's news of Drovetti's project did not cause any concerns in Vienna at the time because it was only the personal idea of one man and, moreover, the attention of the Chancellery was focused on the Balkans where the struggle between the Ottoman Empire and Russia was culminating. The same attitude prevailed in relation to the report of the new French consul general in Egypt, Jean François Mimaut, dated 22 July 1829. This report exposed the intrigues of France and Mohammed Ali against the Porte. Metternich simply instructed Prince Esterházy to familiarise Lord Aberdeen with the report and open the eyes of the British cabinet towards the real goals of French policy in the Near East. However, the chancellor himself saw no reason to take any action and this passivity did not change till the end of the year when he only learnt about plans to put the Drovetti project

---

[18] Ibid.
[19] Ibid.

into effect as a result of acquiring three intercepted letters, written by Guilleminot on 2, 9 and 13 December 1829. Metternich did not hesitate to show them to Lord Cowley and he sent them to London for Aberdeen's use at the beginning of January 1830. It is necessary to point out that the act of forwarding mail to other cabinets, in other words attempting to set one country against another, was typical of Metternich's modus operandi. He was happy to encourage second states to fight on behalf of Austrian interests without having to pursue his own active diplomacy. This tendency is obvious, particularly in situations that were important in relation to the Habsburg Monarchy, but not to the extent that Vienna had to address itself to the problem directly. French activity towards Algeria was a good example of this and Metternich did not miss any opportunity to nurture the aversion of the British cabinet towards the Near Eastern policy of the government in Paris with which he disagreed.[20]

Metternich's attitude towards the Drovetti project was entirely negative. First of all, the chancellor could not remain indifferent to anything that would strengthen France's influence in the Mediterranean. Secondly, he was afraid of possible complications in relations between France and the Porte and also between France and Great Britain. Any deterioration in their relationship would, inevitably, affect the coexistence of all European Powers. Metternich was keen to avoid further complications in the Levant so soon after matters had been resolved. Thirdly, he always regarded French activities in the Levant with great distrust, particularly if they did not correspond with his own principles, and he considered the Algerian project to be another attempt to violate them. He was affected by the negotiations between the French government and Mohammed Ali, undertaken without the sultan's cognizance and approval. By such behaviour, France had attributed an extraordinary stature to one of the Ottoman governors and had, more or less, put him on the same footing as an independent ruler. In particular, Metternich condemned Guilleminot's December note demanding the sultan's approval of the Egyptian cam-

---

[20] Metternich to Esterházy, Vienna, 26 Sept. 1829, and attached Mimaut's dispatch, Alexandria, 22 July 1829, HHStA, StA, England 188; Metternich to Esterházy, Vienna, 4 Jan. 1830, HHStA, StA, England 191; Dodwell, p. 101; Sauvigny, *Metternich et la France*, III, p. 1343.

paign, the note that he found "imperative and disdainful."[21] Fourthly, he entirely agreed with Acerbi's concerns about the excessive power of the Egyptian governor should he be in a position to administer the whole of North Africa.[22] In short, Metternich found the entire Algerian project "risky and fallacious."[23]

Another reason for Metternich's distrust of the project was its anxious dissimulation on the part of the French government. At the beginning of January 1830, Polignac denied that the governor of Egypt had been invited by France to take part in the expedition against Algeria or that he would be supported by the cabinet in Paris during the campaign. After reports from Constantinople and Corfu providing evidence of the existence of the Egyptian expedition project, as well as a union between France and Egypt, Polignac was forced to admit that cooperation had been agreed, but he ascribed the initiative to Mohammed Ali. In the middle of January, he told the British ambassador in Paris, Lord Stuart de Rothesay, that he had learnt about the project only recently. According to the French premier, Mohammed Ali himself suggested to the French government that he would assume the task of seizing Algeria if France would offer naval support. After the occupation of Algeria, Tunis and Tripoli, the Egyptian governor intended to end piracy and restate his loyalty to the sultan. Charles X, Polignac continued, decided to accept the offer after "a long and mature deliberation."[24] Polignac was not informed officially about the king's support for the Mohammed Ali project (*sic*) until 25 January 1830. When Count Apponyi asked Polignac as to whether the cabinet did not fear that through cooperating with the vassal of the Porte, they might not facilitate his declaration of independence, the premier replied that Mohammed Ali's attention and activities would be fixed on the West and not on the East, towards Syria, where Mohammed Ali's primary interests were presumed to lie. Polignac defended the whole plan at other courts by referencing "an official doctrine" that

---

[21] Metternich to Esterházy, Vienna, 3 Jan. 1830, HHStA, StA, England 191.
[22] Metternich to Esterházy, Vienna, 28 Jan. 1830, HHStA, StA, England 191; Metternich to Ottenfels, Vienna, 4 Feb. 1830, HHStA, StA, Türkei VI, 51; Cowley to Aberdeen, Vienna, 28 Jan. 1830, TNA, FO 120/108.
[23] Metternich to Apponyi, Vienna, 5 Feb. 1830, HHStA, StA, Frankreich 276.
[24] Apponyi to Metternich, Paris, 24 Jan. 1830, HHStA, StA, Frankreich 272.

cooperation with Mohammed Ali would be advantageous for the general interests of civilisation and particularly for the Porte.[25]

In Vienna, French Ambassador Count Gérard de Rayneval conveyed Polignac's request that Metternich should use his influence in Constantinople and persuade Mahmud II to order his Egyptian vassal to proceed against the dey of Algeria. Nevertheless, Metternich was in no way prepared to satisfy this request and strongly recommended that France acquiesce to the proposal of the Porte for the dispatch of a commissioner to Algiers. Austria was ready to exert all its influence in order to give effect to such a measure, and Metternich was convinced that the British government would be equally ready to use its influence for the purpose of obtaining full satisfaction for France by amicable means. At the same moment, he called upon the French government not to place more difficulties in the way of the Porte and to avoid anything that could directly or indirectly reduce its authority "among its subordinated population, for fear that the social ties that unite the diverse parts of the [Ottoman] Empire would be severed, resulting in a general collapse which would have the immediate effect of plunging the whole of Europe into the type of difficulties that had not been seen for many years."[26]

Regarding the fact that Mahmud II withheld his consent in relation to Mohammed Ali's participation in the Algerian campaign, Metternich advised Polignac not to support the project (*sic*), since it might result in the Egyptian governor becoming a rebel.[27] Finally, he warned Rayneval that "it will not only be the Porte that will look unfavourably on the submission of the greater part of the northern African coast to the power of the Egyptian pasha; England ... will tolerate the extension of his dominion over these countries ... with almost as much difficulty as if France were to possess them."[28] Metternich was right in attempting to use Great Britain to influence

---

[25] Apponyi to Metternich, Paris, 14, 24 and 25 Jan. 1830, HHStA, StA, Frankreich 272; Esterházy to Metternich, London, 2 Feb. 1830, HHStA, StA, England 189; Stuart to Aberdeen, Paris, 15 Jan. 1830, TNA, FO 120/109.

[26] Rayneval to Polignac, Vienna, 28 Jan. 1830, AMAE, CP, Autriche 412.

[27] Metternich to Esterházy, Vienna, 28 Jan. 1830, HHStA, StA, England 191; Cowley to Aberdeen, Vienna, 28 Jan. 1830, TNA, FO 120/108; Maltzan to Frederick William III, Vienna, 2 Feb. 1830, GStA PK, HA III, MdA I, 6014; Sauvigny, *Metternich et la France*, III, p. 1340.

[28] Rayneval to Polignac, Vienna, 28 Jan. 1830, AMAE, CP, Autriche 412.

Polignac. He instructed Apponyi as follows: "Do not conceal from the minister that we are convinced that the affair will not be brought to a desired and acceptable conclusion other than in ways that can only lead to a further complication of the issues and compromise the attitudes of France or the sultan towards the other Powers."[29] Apponyi also sought to assure the first minister about the Austrian cabinet's desire to see the restoration of friendly relations between France and Algeria as soon as possible. If it were within its power, Austria was prepared to do anything that could contribute to this goal. As regards Polignac's claim that it was Mohammed Ali who had suggested the Egyptian campaign in North Africa, Metternich did not believe this falsehood because he was well informed about the real state of affairs. At the beginning of February 1830, he wrote to Ottenfels: "The rumour that the viceroy of Egypt first made the proposal for the expedition against Algeria and other Barbary States was entirely fabricated. It is the French government which first raised this issue; we know this from reliable sources."[30] Metternich did not hide, even from Rayneval, the view that the first proposition concerning Algeria did not come from Alexandria but from Paris.[31]

Metternich's Opposition to the French Expedition and the Fall of Algiers

Metternich's dissenting attitude towards military intervention in Algeria did not change even after the French government's decision, dated 31 January 1830, to undertake its own expedition against the dey. On the contrary, the abandonment of the Drovetti project, and the decision about its own military operation, was met by the chancellor with less sympathy. Firstly, Mohammed Ali's enterprise would be more acceptable because his occupation of the Ottoman provinces in North Africa would change nothing in relation to the sultan's absolute rights.

---

[29] Metternich to Apponyi, Vienna, 5 Feb. 1830, HHStA, StA, Frankreich 276.
[30] Metternich to Ottenfels, Vienna, 4 Feb. 1830, HHStA, StA, Türkei VI, 51.
[31] Metternich to Esterházy, Vienna, 28 Jan. 1830, HHStA, StA, England 191; Metternich to Apponyi, Vienna, 5 Feb. 1830, HHStA, StA, Frankreich 276; Maltzan to Frederick William III, Vienna, 2 Feb. 1830, GStA PK, HA III, MdA I, 6014.

Secondly, strong resistance from Great Britan had to be expected,
even stronger than in the event of an Egyptian campaign. Later, in
May, when the British opposition had really been aroused, Rayneval
reported to Paris that "Metternich should not be surprised by the dis-
gruntlement of the English ministry; he forecast it from the beginning
and did not hide from us [French] that our expedition against Algeria
was one of the affairs that would immediately cause countless complications and problems."[32] Thirdly, Metternich considered the outcome
of the expedition as uncertain and achievable only with difficulties.[33]
Even if France succeeded in the military campaign, it would have to
face the decision as to whether to withdraw its troops from Algeria
or to change the punitive expedition into a long-lasting occupation.
Both options came with serious problems: "You could limit yourself
to taking and destroying the places occupied by the Berbers without
changing anything regarding the state of the country; and in this case
you would not destroy piracy as sooner or later it would start again;
alternatively you could take advantage of your conquest to establish
a sustainable regime on the coast. However, opposition from England
and political complications would be sure to follow."[34]

Metternich was not only speaking about complications in the
diplomatic field. He was well aware of the real reasons for the French
crusade. The real purpose of Polignac's expedition was not for humanitarian reasons or to avenge injured national feelings but to gain
domestic popularity by military means. The ensuing popularity would
be utilised in elections that were on the verge of being called due to
the tense situation in France. In short, the expedition was intended
to win laurels for the Bourbons and strengthen the king's somewhat
fragile position within the country. Metternich did not share these
hopes that were attached to the campaign and he feared the impact
of its possible failure on domestic affairs even more than the impact of
the possible success of the expedition on relations between the Great
Powers. He even maintained that the expedition, which was intended
to save the king's government, could easily result in its fall if it failed.

---

[32] Rayneval to Polignac, Vienna, 16 May 1830, AMAE, CP, Autriche 412.
[33] Metternich to Ottenfels, Vienna, 17 Feb. 1830, HHStA, StA, Türkei VI, 51;
Apponyi to Metternich, Paris, 2 and 9 Feb. 1830, HHStA, StA, Frankreich 272;
Rayneval to Polignac, Vienna, 1 March 1830, AMAE, CP, Autriche 412.
[34] Rayneval to Polignac, Vienna, 5 Feb. 1830, AMAE, CP, Autriche 412.

In Ottenfels' words, Charles X and his first minister had started to engage in "a gamble,"[35] and Metternich doubted that the assumed risk was outweighed by the potential advantages that would occur if the expedition were successful. He doubted that even a victory would actually produce an increase in popularity for the French king: "The Algerian expedition is going to take place; it is an enterprise that does not concern us directly, and we do not consider it to be a wise or opportune measure. What occupies us above all is the primary cause, the real motive of the expedition. It is evident that it cannot be found in anything other than in the sense of need on the part of the ministry to call to its rescue or to the rescue of the throne (which amounts to the same thing in the overall scheme of things) the military spirit so easily aroused in the nation. It is fortunate that the movement they are trying to influence is directed against an inhospitable coast, and in this fact there probably is some merit on the part of the current administration because the previous one had in no way hesitated to advance the claim so popular in France for the so-called natural frontiers of the kingdom! But what must be the position of a country where for the amusement of the society, for the distraction of political factions, for the creation of some support for itself, the government is reduced to throwing itself into an enterprise full of risks, rich in sacrifices of every kind, an enterprise that, in the event of failure can bring down the throne and that in the opposite case will inevitably give birth to a long series of political complications!"[36] Sauvigny attributed the hostile attitude of Vienna towards the expedition to Metternich's anxiety about the internal affairs in France, and it is clear from the available documents that in the spring of 1830 these concerns were, in all likelihood, the main cause of the chancellor's aversion to the French plan. Although his numerous warnings in this respect were undoubtedly intended as the means to frighten Polignac and his king, there can be no doubt that they were sincere.[37]

---

[35] Ottenfels to Metternich, Constantinople, 10 May 1830, HHStA, StA, Türkei VI, 50.

[36] Metternich to Trauttmannsdorff, Vienna, 27 April 1830, HHStA, StK, Preussen 137.

[37] Metternich to Esterházy, Vienna, 27 March 1830, HHStA, StA, England 191; Metternich to Trauttmannsdorff, Vienna, 27 March and 27 April 1830, HHStA, StA, Preussen 137; Metternich to Ficquelmont, Vienna, 2 April 1830, HHStA, StA, Russland III, 90; Metternich to Ficquelmont, Vienna, 14 April 1830, SOA, RA C-

Metternich saw nothing but problems in relation to the campaign because serious consequences were to be expected whatever the outcome. Success would lead to a growth in tension in British-French relations, while the result of failure would be an internal crisis in France. Therefore, Metternich warned the French cabinet of undertaking a campaign on its own, as he had done in the case of Franco-Egyptian cooperation. Although he recognised that Charles X had the right of satisfaction from Hussein Pasha, and he himself did not hesitate to declare ostentatiously that "the honour of France is the honour of Europe and all of us are interested that it [France] obtains satisfaction,"[38] he believed that the French king ought to choose such means that would cause no complications. In Metternich's opinion, only cooperation with the Porte and other Great Powers could lead to a successful resolution and produce a satisfactory outcome for France. He was also in no doubt that joint action would lead to an acceptable order on the North African coast. Consequently, France ought to halt its unilateral action, support Tahir Pasha's mission, pin its hopes on the success of the mission and rely on the backing of Austria and Great Britain.[39] This continued to be his advice to Rayneval until the end of March, despite the fact that at that time it was obvious that the cabinet in Paris was not to be diverted from the expedition. For all that, the chancellor tried once again, in his instructions to Apponyi on 27 March 1830, to influence Polignac and draw his attention to the dangers resulting from military intervention. Moreover, he counselled him to make use of the armaments in Toulon as a means of lending support to Tahir Pasha's mission, thus assuring the success of his negotiations in Algiers. Nevertheless, Metternich himself did not believe in the success of such a ploy and his instructions to Ottenfels from that time forward, concerning the Algerian Affair, were of

---

A 383; Metternich to Apponyi, Vienna, 27 April 1830, HHStA, StA, Frankreich 276; Metternich to Ottenfels, Vienna, 9 May 1830, HDA, 750, OO 38; Apponyi to Metternich, Paris, 23 March and 2 April 1830, HHStA, StA, Frankreich 272; Sauvigny, *Metternich et la France*, III, p. 1352.

[38] Rayneval to Polignac, Vienna, 5 Feb. 1830, AMAE, CP, Autriche 412.

[39] Metternich to Esterházy, Vienna, 25 Feb. 1830, HHStA, StA, England 191; Metternich to Apponyi, Vienna, 27 March 1830, HHStA, StA, Frankreich 276; Rayneval to Polignac, Vienna, 5 Feb. and 3 March 1830, AMAE, CP, Autriche 412; Cowley to Aberdeen, Vienna, 25 Feb. 1830, TNA, FO 120/108; Maltzan to Frederick William III, Vienna, 26 March 1830, GStA PK, HA III, MdA I, 6014.

a defeatist nature. Should the expedition take place, Ottenfels was instructed only to claim that the views of Austria in relation to this affair had always been "reasonable and correct."[40] This pessimism was proved to be well founded. Already by 2 April 1830, Apponyi was reporting from Paris that the expedition was irrevocably decided upon and that nothing could reverse the French cabinet's decision. When, later in April, he conveyed information about the instructions given in March, Polignac again rejected Metternich's concerns about the possible results of the expedition and his encouragement to rely on the results of Tahir Pasha's negotiations with the dey. According to Polignac, the Porte's initiative came too late and the peace mission in relation to the Algerian Affair could only have been effective if it had been offered in September or October 1829. Now, with the preparations of the French army and navy being so advanced and having cost a considerable amount of money, it was too late. The first minister saw in Tahir Pasha's mission nothing but an attempt to delay the campaign, something which was absolutely unacceptable to the French government.[41]

Austrian diplomacy did not limit itself to warnings addressed to the French cabinet but also supported the British conduct in Constantinople. There was complete agreement between Vienna and London in relation to the Algerian Question, Franco-Egyptian cooperation and the independent French expedition. Lord Aberdeen had opposed the alliance between France and Mohammed Ali from the beginning. Like Metternich, he argued in favour of the sultan's sovereignty: "To enter directly into such engagements with him [Mohammed Ali] and at his own initiative, would seriously affect his relations with the Porte and would really be the equivalent of recognising, at least in practice, his total independence."[42] Moreover, France and Mohammed Ali had no right to attack two other regencies, Tunis and Tripoli, because these provinces had provided no rationale for interference. The British cabinet therefore instructed Sir Robert Gordon to "draw the attention of the Divan to the affair and persuade it to exercise its influence on the viceroy in order to persuade him to refuse to take

[40]   Metternich to Ottenfels, Vienna, 17 April 1830, HHStA, StA, Türkei VI, 51.
[41]   Apponyi to Metternich, Paris, 2 and 26 April 1830, HHStA, StA, Frankreich 272; Cowley to Aberdeen, Vienna, 27 March 1830, TNA, FO 120/108.
[42]   Esterházy to Metternich, London, 18 Feb. 1830, HHStA, StA, England 189.

part in such an enterprise, and particularly to persuade the sultan to follow up on his proposal to send a Turkish agent to Algiers, someone who would serve as a mediator between the dey and France."[43] The British gambled everything on the rejection of the Drovetti project by the Porte and Tahir Pasha's timely and successful action. In Aberdeen's opinion, if Hussein Pasha submitted to the French conditions, military intervention would become superfluous. These views entirely coincided with those advocated in Vienna and it cannot be surprising that the instructions for Gordon were supported by Metternich; he ordered Ottenfels to assist his British colleague in urging the Porte to attempt prompt diplomatic intervention in relation to the dispute between Paris and Algiers. In his opinion, the result would almost certainly have led to the dey's immediate submission and his approval of an arrangement with France. By these means Austria supported the British position in endeavouring to thwart the anti-Algerian project.[44]

The Austro-British attitudes did not change after France's declaration that it would act alone against Algeria. The British ministers agreed with the Austrian chancellor that the war, in this case, was not a means to an end but an end in itself and they sharply denounced the fact that the cabinet in Paris wanted to wage war in order to consolidate its power and popularity. They also agreed with Metternich that a defeat for the French army in North Africa would inevitably lead to the government's fall and, much like him, they were not convinced as to whether success could actually save it. Moreover, geopolitical ambitions in the Mediterranean were of considerable importance in relation to London's reasoning and there were serious concerns that if the expedition actually took place, and the French set foot in Algeria,

---

[43] Esterházy to Metternich, London, 23 Jan. 1830, HHStA, StA, England 189.

[44] Metternich to Ottenfels, Vienna, 4 Feb. 1830, HHStA, StA, Türkei VI, 51; Metternich to Apponyi, Vienna, 5 Feb. 1830, HHStA, StA, Frankreich 276; Metternich to Esterházy, Vienna, 12 Feb. 1830, HHStA, StA, England 191; Maltzan to Frederick William III, Vienna, 5 Feb. 1830, GStA PK, HA III, MdA I, 6014; Cowley to Aberdeen, Vienna, 7 Feb. 1830, TNA, FO 120/108. However, Metternich was not seriously concerned that Mahmud II would yield to French pressure and permit Mohammed Ali to participate in the intervention against Algeria. The accuracy of this judgement was soon proved by the reports from Constantinople. Metternich to Ottenfels, Vienna, 2 Jan. 1830, HHStA, StA, Türkei VI, 51; Ottenfels to Metternich, Constantinople, 25 Feb., 3 March and 10 April 1830, HHStA, StA, Türkei VI, 50.

they might never leave but would be dazzled by their own success and try to gain control over the whole North African coast.[45]

In accordance with their instructions, Ottenfels and Gordon promptly asked the Porte to intervene in Algiers and force the dey to solve the problems with France as quickly as possible in order to avoid more serious complications and misfortunes. They were not supported in their demand by Guilleminot, who declared: "All that is pointless and a waste of time; we have exercised enough patience and we have shown the greatest moderation and indulgence towards the dey of Algeria. The time for negotiation is now over, enormous preparations have been made in order to punish the insolence of this Barbarian and the expedition against Algeria will take place without delay."[46] According to the French ambassador, France was firmly resolved to intervene in Algiers and Tahir Pasha's mission could not change its decision. Despite this statement, Ottenfels and Gordon sought in vain to encourage an acceleration of Tahir Pasha's departure that was also delayed by Ramadan and an unfavourable wind. The Turkish dignitary did not sail from Constantinople until 15 April 1830. Metternich could only deplore the tardiness of the Porte, but it seems to be certain that Tahir Pasha's timely departure would not have changed anything in relation to the French intervention in Algeria. With regard to the real aims of the expedition, Charles X and Polignac could not and did not want to agree to a peaceful resolution of their differences with the dey. They did not want to risk such a possibility and they decided to prevent the Turkish commissioner from arriving in Algeria. Therefore, when Tahir Pasha appeared near the Algerian coast in the second half of May, he was stopped by a French squadron and sent to Toulon, without being able to say a word to Hussein Pasha. On his way to the southern French port, he met a large French fleet, sailing in the opposite direction. The expeditionary forces disembarked 20 kilometers west of Algiers on 14 June 1830. The city was seized on 5 July. The dey was exiled to the Apennines, where he stayed for the rest of his life. Although Lord Stuart expressed his great indignation about

---

[45] Esterházy to Metternich, London, 13 April and 19 May 1830, HHStA, StA, England 189; Aberdeen to Stuart, London, 21 April 1830, TNA, FO 120/109.
[46] Ottenfels to Metternich, Constantinople, 25 Feb. 1830, HHStA, StA, Türkei VI, 50.

the treatment of Tahir Pasha, Great Britain finally resigned itself to the French expedition and took no action.[47]

The British-Austrian conduct in the whole affair was admittedly insufficient. However, Metternich was not to blame for this, as claimed by Rayneval in his report dated 17 May 1830. According to the French ambassador, Great Britain was not prepared to wage war against France over the Algerian situation because Austria was not prepared to do so either. However, this allegation is rather problematic. Metternich considered French diplomacy towards Algeria to be dangerous for two reasons: the possible complications in diplomatic relations and possible internal complications in France. He could not look favourably on the growth of French power in the Mediterranean, but this eventuality did not threaten Austrian interests as much as a Russian expansion in the Balkans. If the cabinet in Vienna had not come out against St Petersburg in the preceding two years, during the Russo-Ottoman war, nobody could expect that it would do so against Paris in the spring of 1830. The planned expedition was important for Metternich because even though designs against Algeria did not lie in the orbit of Austrian interests, it naturally could weaken the Ottoman Empire as a whole. However, Vienna had no means of forestalling the expedition, unless it wished to expose itself to the danger of a war on the Continent, and Algeria of course was not worth this risk. According to Metternich, the only country that could challenge the French plan and which was particularly interested in the distribution of power in the Mediterranean was Great Britain. French intervention in Algeria, and its possible occupation, might be the first step towards the restoration of French influence in the Mediterranean and a change in the balance of power in this area. Although the British government

---

[47] Ibid.; Apponyi to Metternich, Paris, 31 May 1830, HHStA, StA, Frankreich 272; Stuart to Aberdeen, Paris, 31 May 1830, TNA, FO 120/109; Cowley to Aberdeen, Vienna, 19 March 1830, TNA, FO 120/108; Aberdeen to Stuart, London, 31 May 1830, the note presented to Prince Polignac by Lord Stuart de Rothesay dated 3 June 1830, TNA, FO 120/110; Maltzan to Frederick William III, Vienna, 27 April 1830, GStA PK, HA III, MdA I, 6014; Gordon to Aberdeen, Constantinople, 7 Feb., 2 and 26 March, 17 April and 17 Aug. 1830, Chabert to Gordon, 12 Jan. 1830, TNA, FO 78/189; Royer to Frederick William III, Pera, 31 March, 10 and 25 April 1830, GStA PK, HA III, MdA I, 7269; Guilleminot to Polignac, Constantinople, 3 May 1830, AMAE, CP, Turquie 260; O. Eck, *Seeräuberei im Mittelmeer: Dunkle Blätter europäischer Geschichte*, München, Berlin 1940, p. 294; J. B. Wolf, *The Barbary Coast: Algeria under the Turks*, Toronto 1979, p. 336.

was well aware of this fact and, in contrast to Austria, in possession of the type of large fleet necessary for the defence of the North African coast, it took no action. In the beginning, the cabinet in London did nothing more than keep "a careful eye on the intrigues of France in this part of the Mediterranean"[48] and it continued on this course until the end of the affair. In May 1830, its attitude towards France became more challenging but by then it was too late. Metternich was of the opinion that it would have been convenient and useful to come out against France several months earlier. Moreover, the Duke of Wellington's weak and evasive speech on the French expedition delivered in the House of Commons in July finally persuaded Polignac that he did not need to worry about any hostile action on the part of Great Britain. Ergo, it was Wellington's ministry which allowed the French fleet and army to capture Algiers. With Great Britain sitting back even though it considered the situation to be of importance to its national interests,[49] no one could expect that lacking strong naval forces Austria would do more.[50] Consequently, the only thing Metternich could do was to wish Charles X's armies good luck and, after the news of the occupation of Algiers, to congratulate them on their "glorious success."[51]

---

[48] Esterházy to Metternich, London, 23 Jan. 1830, HHStA, StA, England 189.

[49] For this opinion see M. E. Chamberlain, *Lord Aberdeen: A Political Biography,* London, New York 1983, pp. 236–237; H. Temperley, *England and the Near East: The Crimea,* London, New York, Toronto 1936, p. 61.

[50] Metternich to Esterházy, Vienna, 4 Jan. 1830, HHStA, StA, England 191; Metternich to Ficquelmont, Vienna, 22 May 1830, HHStA, StA, Russland III, 90; Metternich to Ottenfels, Vienna, 27 May 1830, HDA, 750, OO 38; Apponyi to Metternich, Paris, 20 July 1830, HHStA, StA, Frankreich 274; Rayneval to Polignac, Vienna, 17 and 29 May 1830, AMAE, CP, Autriche 412; Tatishchev to Nesselrode, Vienna, 22 May 1830, AVPRI, fond 133, Kantseliariia, opis 469, 1830/275.

[51] Rayneval to Polignac, Vienna, 17 July 1830, AMAE, CP, Autriche 412. The point that must be underlined here is that the change in attitude does not mean that during the spring of 1830 a volte-face took place in Vienna and that the Austrian chancellor and the emperor looked positively on the French adventure and started to approve of it. The French historian, Gustave Gautherot, assumes that the attendance of Prince Friedrich von Schwarzenberg in the campaign proves such a claim. G. Gautherot, *La conquête d'Alger 1830,* Paris 1929, p. 29. However, Friedrich's participation cannot serve as proof of Gautherot's opinion. The presence of the young officer, the son of the deceased Marshal Prince Karl von Schwarzenberg, in North Africa was a private action, aimed at gaining military knowledge and experience. There were more interested young nobles in Austria for this enterprise, but Francis I only gave permission to Friedrich. Metternich was not

Discussions over the Future of Algeria and
the Algerian Problem in the 1830s

The capture of Algiers did not terminate the whole issue since the question of Algeria's future remained to be answered. Since early 1830, Polignac assured Apponyi and Stuart that the goal of the French campaign was not the colonisation of the province and that France recognised the sultan's sovereignty: "We recognise, I repeat to you, the sovereignty of the Porte, and all our future projects concerning Algeria will comply with it. After we have conquered the country, we will prolong our military occupation for the time necessary for all the conditions that were the goal and the motivation of our expedition to be completely fulfilled."[52] The forces planned to withdraw as soon as piracy and slavery had been destroyed, the security of French commerce had been ensured and the expenses of the expedition reimbursed. Having achieved these goals, Polignac told Apponyi, "as soon as the order established in Algeria offers to the whole of Europe sufficient guarantees of a stable and consolidated future, our troops will leave this foreign territory and France will never raise any claim to it."[53] However, these assurances were problematic for several reasons. Although for Charles X and his prime minister the main purpose of the campaign was to ensure success in the elections and not the permanent annexation of the Ottoman province, Polignac concealed the fact that France planned to seize a part of the coast from the town of Bone to Cape Roux. As Metternich, not doubting the real French plans for the future of Algeria aptly remarked: "It is not on account of one blow with a fly-whisk that a hundred million are spent and 40,000 men deployed."[54] Furthermore, the temporary occupation

---

pleased about this request, but when the emperor agreed to let the young prince go to Algeria, Metternich had no other option than to secure the consent of the French government. In Paris, the matter was solved quickly and without any problems. Metternich to Apponyi, Vienna, 26 May 1830, HHStA, StA, Frankreich 276; Apponyi to Metternich, Paris, 6 June 1830, HHStA, StA, Frankreich 272; Rayneval to Polignac, Vienna, 26 May 1830, AMAE, CP, Autriche 412; Prokesch-Osten, *Aus den Tagebüchern*, p. 28.

[52] The conversation with Prince Polignac on the Algerian Affair, attached to Apponyi to Metternich, Paris, 19 June 1830, HHStA, StA, Frankreich 272.

[53] Apponyi to Metternich, Paris, 20 July 1830, HHStA, StA, Frankreich 274.

[54] Rayneval to Polignac, Vienna, 27 March 1830, AMAE, CP, Autriche 412.

was not restricted by any fixed date and could be extended for an indefinitely long period. French politicians and diplomats were of a different opinion as to the withdrawal and a considerable number of them expressed an entirely different view from the prime minister. For example, the ministers of the army and navy, Count Louis Auguste Victor de Ghaisne de Bourmont and Baron Charles d'Haussez, and Guilleminot requested a permanent occupation.[55] Moreover, the concept of withdrawal had another important enemy, as Apponyi reported in July: "It is not, however, in line with public opinion on this affair that it would be necessary to take advantage of any success that is achieved. It sees no other outcome in this affair than a permanent conquest, the establishment of a French colony, and this idea is also passionately embraced by the liberals and by the royalists. Any minister who wishes to pursue a fair and enlightened policy will undoubtedly meet with strong opposition. It will be impossible for him to stay faithful to the agreements he has concluded with his allies during the development of this important affair without creating new problems."[56] The cabinets in Vienna and London were also concerned that Polignac's promises were only verbal and their value was thus limited. Stuart's attempts to obtain any written statement were entirely fruitless. He did not hide his frustration from Apponyi: "I would have been perfectly content if Prince Polignac had expressed to me in a written note one tenth of what he declared verbally in relation to the frank and selfless intentions of his government, but however much I tried, I was not able to persuade him to do so. How then can any man not suspect France of ulterior motives in relation to its conduct towards Algeria?"[57] Although Metternich looked on Stuart's effort with understanding, he thought it would be impossible to win from the French cabinet a more satisfactory explanation as to their ulterior intentions. After the great expense of the armaments,

---

[55] Apponyi to Metternich, Paris, 12 July 1830, HHStA, StA, Frankreich 274; Stuart to Aberdeen, Paris, 26 Feb. 1830, TNA, FO 120/110; Polignac to Laval, Paris, 12 May 1830, TNA, FO 120/110; the conversation with Prince Polignac on the Algerian Affair, attached to Apponyi to Metternich, Paris, 19 June 1830, HHStA, StA, Frankreich 272; Gordon to Aberdeen, Constantinople, 17 Aug. 1830, TNA, FO 78/190; J. Serres, *La politique turque en Afrique du Nord sous la Monarchie de Juillet*, Paris 1925, p. 33.
[56] Apponyi to Metternich, Paris, 12 July 1830, HHStA, StA, Frankreich 274.
[57] Apponyi to Metternich, Paris, 20 May 1830, HHStA, StA, Frankreich 272.

for which the ministers were responsible to the Chambers and to the nation, they could hardly venture to declare publicly that they looked to no result beyond a mere redress of grievances. At the same moment, the chancellor regretted that the British government, rightly considering the latter explanations of Prince Polignac as vague and insufficient, had not acted sooner. Had it made its demands several weeks earlier, before public opinion and national pride had taken hold in France, it might have been possible to reach an agreement.[58]

At the moment when the French expedition seemed to be inevitable, the cabinet in Vienna assumed the role of an unconcerned bystander and accepted a fait accompli. This step was alleviated by two facts. Firstly, the chancellor was pleased with the French decision to seek popularity in Algeria, rather than directing its belligerency towards its so-called natural frontiers, namely, the Rhine. Therefore, he did not mind as much as the cabinet in London that the French nation found in North Africa "the outlet for martial energy that had been accumulating since 1815"[59] and he reconciled himself more easily to this fact. Secondly, the French government declared its intention to organise a conference in Paris, seeking the attendance of the representatives of the Great Powers that were in a position to solve the future of Algeria. The French king also stated that if his army were successful, he would take no further action unless it was taken in concurrence with his allies. Metternich agreed to the talks, partly because he considered them as a means of forestalling possible international complications even though he did not expect them to take place owing to Britain's conciliatory attitude and partly because he saw in the conference an opportunity for the restoration of the unity of the five Great Powers which had been destroyed during the Greek insurrection.[60] Regarding the situation in Europe, he believed that it was

---

[58] Apponyi to Metternich, Paris, 20 May 1830, HHStA, StA, Frankreich 272; Cowley to Aberdeen, Vienna, 17 April and 25 May 1830, TNA, FO 120/108; Maltzan to Frederick William III, Vienna, 21 May 1830, GStA PK, HA III, MdA I, 6014.

[59] C. J. Bartlett, *Great Britain and Sea Power 1815–1853*, Oxford 1963, p. 83.

[60] Metternich to Apponyi, Vienna, 27 April and 17 July 1830, HHStA, StA, Frankreich 276; Metternich to Trauttmannsdorff, Vienna, 27 April 1830, HHStA, StA, Preussen 137; Metternich to Esterházy, Johannisberg, 5 June 1830, HHStA, StA, England 191; Cowley to Aberdeen, Vienna, 4 June 1830, TNA, FO 120/108; Maltzan to Frederick William III, Vienna, 12 and 22 June, 14 July 1830, GStA PK, HA III, MdA I, 6014.

important that the Powers "should return to the terrain of the ancient Alliance."[61] Polignac was well aware of this fact and he skilfully used it in managing relations with Vienna, as is obvious from his speech to Apponyi: "I want to see a revival of the Quintuple Alliance; it is my secret and you will soon learn more of it."[62]

It is possible to deduce from available sources that at the planned conference Metternich intended to act together with Great Britain, even if not too forcefully because he did not want to aggravate relations with France on account of distant Algeria. In any case, in July he made preparations, along with Cowley. Firstly, they discussed the possible admission of other Mediterranean states to the Paris talks. The French cabinet had already decided to invite Sardinia and Spain and it was expected that Spain would invite Naples. Whereas Cowley was afraid that France was trying to secure a dominant voice at the conference, Metternich did not share this concern. In his opinion, France could not obtain a dominant voice because none of these courts would actually espouse the interests of France. With regard to Naples, in particular, Metternich was convinced that it would be guided in its opinions by the position taken by Austria and Great Britain. The second subject for discussion between Metternich and Cowley was the plan for solving the future of Algeria, presented in Vienna by the Sardinian representative, Count Carlo Francesco di Pralorme. The government in Turin proposed three options: (1) Algeria would remain in the possession of the Porte; (2) it would become a French colony; (3) it would be administrated by the Order of Malta. Cowley expressed his opinion that his government would never support any solution that deprived the Porte of the sovereignty of Algeria. He argued that the Porte had a clear right and it would be a flagrant act of injustice and a departure from all principles to deprive it of its legitimate claim. He thus clearly declared for the first option. Metternich also considered the first option as the only one which was not liable to serious objections even though he regretted the lack of a guarantee that would ensure that a new dey, appointed by the sultan, would not become too independent and restore piracy and slavery.[63]

---

[61] Maltzan to Frederick William III, Vienna, 3 Feb. 1830, GStA PK, HA III, MdA I, 6014.
[62] Sauvigny, *Metternich et la France*, III, p. 1349.
[63] Metternich to Apponyi, Johannisberg, 5 June 1830, HHStA, StA, Frankreich 276; Cowley to Aberdeen, Vienna, 13 July 1830, TNA, FO 120/108; Rayneval to

Nevertheless, these discussions were entirely overshadowed by the fact that the planned conference did not, in the end, take place owing to the revolution in France that erupted at the end of July 1830. When Metternich congratulated Charles X in mid July on the French success in Algeria, expressing his satisfaction with the swift victory of the invading troops, his greetings were undoubtedly sincere. He was fully aware of the worsening situation in France and he regarded it as being of considerable seriousness because, in his opinion, the weak position of the French king was something that caused difficulties for the whole of Europe. A possible upheaval within the kingdom would inevitably have consequences beyond its frontiers. Polignac did not share these concerns about the course of events in the country and he rejected both Metternich's warnings of the negative impact of the expedition on the internal situation in France as well as the threat of a possibly successful revolution. His optimism was soon challenged. The news of the initial victories of the French forces reached Paris on 23 June on the day of the election, but it altered nothing in relation to the voting, and Charles X and Polignac sustained a crushing defeat. The opposition obtained 270 seats whereas the government only 145. The expedition did not change the hostile attitude of the public towards the king and his cabinet, regardless of the victories in North Africa. Calculations by the ultraconservatives that military glory would secure them wide support proved to be entirely erroneous. In addition, the French obviously did not share the same enthusiasm for the occupation of Algiers as their monarch, who, according to Apponyi, "since the time of the restoration had never been seized with such feelings of happiness and contentment."[64] When, on 11 July 1830, and in the presence of the king, the Te Deum resounded in Notre Dame in celebration of Hussein Pasha's capitulation, the people assembled outside the cathedral were strangely silent. At the end of the month, these French citizens were celebrating the fall of Polignac's cabinet and Charles X's escape into exile. Louis Philippe, of the Orleans dynasty, became the new king. This change in relation to the French throne, as well as the stormy events in the Europe of 1830 and 1831, not only proved the accuracy of Metternich's apprehension, but also allowed France to keep Algeria for more than 130 years because

---

Polignac, Vienna, 20 July 1830, AMAE, CP, Autriche 412.
[64] Apponyi to Metternich, Paris, 12 July 1830, HHStA, StA, Frankreich 274.

although Louis Philippe was no ardent coloniser, he could never leave the North African territory gained by his predecessor due to a wave of national opposition beginning during the summer of 1830 when the French public started to support the maintenance of French presence in Algeria. The cabinets in Vienna and London were well aware of this and since they did not want to endanger the unsteady position of the new royal regime, they let the whole affair die down.[65]

No practical opposition came from Constantinople either because Mahmud II was unable to face the military superiority of France and defend his outlying North African dependency. Although the news of the occupation of Algiers by the French troops caused a "rather painful and even more embarrassing impression"[66] in the Ottoman capital, the sultan could not afford to wage war with France. However, the Porte was never reconciled to the situation and never recognised the occupation. In 1834, Algeria could be still found on the list of Ottoman pashaliks and even at the beginning of the 20th century the offices of high Ottoman dignitaries were decorated with maps entitled *Afrique du Nord Ottomane*, with the sultan's territory extending to Morocco. This attitude was manifested in a practical way soon after the expedition when the Porte formally demanded the return of Algeria in May 1831, and a year later when it sought, according to Ottenfels, to link the Greek Question and its final solution to the outcome of the North African province discussions. The Ottoman dignitaries maintained the view that since France was demanding that the sultan make territorial concessions in Greece, he was now in a

---

[65] Metternich to Apponyi, Vienna, 27 April 1830, HHStA, StA, Frankreich 276; Metternich to Trauttmannsdorff, Vienna, 27 April 1830, HHStA, StA, Preussen 137; *Conversation avec Mr le Prince de Polignac sur la question des élections et des Chambres qui vont s'ouvrir*, Paris, 13 June 1830, attached to Apponyi to Metternich, Paris, 19 June 1830, HHStA, StA, Frankreich 272; Bray to Ludwig I of Bavaria, Vienna, 27 March and 18 May 1830, BHStA, MA, Wien 2403; Maltzan to Frederick William III, Vienna, 24 April and 14 July, 1830, GStA PK, HA III, MdA I, 6014; H. A. C. Collingham, *The July Monarchy: A Political History of France 1830–1848*, London, New York 1988, p. 247; H. L. Hoskins, *British Routes to India*, New York, London, Toronto 1928, p. 141; C.-A. Julien, *Histoire de l'Algérie contemporaine: La conquête et les débuts de la colonisation (1827–1871)*, Paris 1964, p. 62; M. Price, *The Perilous Crown: France between Revolutions 1814–1848*, London 2007, p. 136; P. Renouvin, *Histoire des relations internationales, V: Le XIX(e) siècle I*, Paris 1954, p. 421; Lamuniére, p. 30; Serres, p. 61.
[66] Ottenfels to Metternich, Constantinople, 10 Aug. 1830, HHStA, StA, Türkei VI, 50.

position to ask France for the restitution of a dependency that was
still a part of the Ottoman Empire. However, such speculation was
immediately forbidden by Lord Stratford Canning in the interests of
securing a quick solution of the Greek problem. In the following years,
the Porte tried several times to reopen the Algerian Question but the
cabinet in Paris refused to discuss this topic. In February 1835, the
French ambassador in Constantinople, Baron Albin-Rein Roussin, informed the Porte about "the impossibility of returning Algeria after
the sacrifices of men and money made by France in taking possession
of the colony."[67] When the French army finally captured the Algerian
city of Constantine in October 1837, the whole affair was to all intents
and purposes terminated.[68]

Metternich, realistic as ever, was well aware of the Porte's hopeless situation and the impossibility of regaining the lost province since
the formation of the July Monarchy in 1830. He was convinced that
to ask Louis Philippe to evacuate his troops would be the same as to
request the king to give up his throne. Therefore, Metternich's prime
concern was to forestall any complications in relations between the
Ottoman Empire and France or even the outbreak of war. In his opinion, the sultan could insist on his rights but otherwise he ought to
do nothing.[69] He expressed, on several occasions, the view that "the
Algerian Affair is one of those which will take time to resolve. All the
steps taken by the Porte in relation to this affair up to the present
time, as well as all the approaches it has made either in Constantinople, London or Paris have produced no result so far and they have not
moved any closer to a resolution of the issue. The reason is quite simple: The Porte has no means by which it can force France to abandon
its conquest, and England, the only Great Power that possesses the

[67] Stürmer to Metternich, Constantinople, 11 Feb. 1835, HHStA, StA, Türkei VI,
63.
[68] Metternich to Apponyi, Vienna, 18 Oct. 1834, HHStA, StA, Frankreich 294;
Ottenfels to Metternich, Constantinople, 25 April and 10 May 1832, HHStA, StA,
Türkei VI, 54; Stürmer to Metternich, Büyükdere, 18 June, 9 and 22 July 1834,
HHStA, StA, Türkei VI, 61; Guilleminot to Sébastiani, Constantinople, 14 May
1831, AMAE, CP, Turquie 262; Roussin to Rigny, Therapia, 27 May 1834, AMAE,
CP, Turquie 268; B. Kodaman, *Les Ambassades de Mustapha Réchid Pacha à
Paris*, Ankara 1991, pp. 43–91; Julien, p. 1.
[69] Metternich to Stürmer, Vienna, 16 Aug. 1836, HHStA, StA, Türkei VI, 65;
Lamb to Palmerston, Vienna, 5 Aug. 1836, TNA, FO 120/153; Beauvale to Palmer-
ston, Vienna, 30 July 1839, TNA, FO 120/180.

power to do so, will in no way actively intervene in this affair. In my opinion, there is only one position that the Divan can adopt in this situation: to refrain from every action or approach that could compromise the sultan's sovereign rights over the country."[70] If the sultan thought that a long silence would adversely affect his rights, he would be able to issue a declaration against the French occupation of Algeria: "This measure will not harm the attitude of the Divan towards France and seems to me to be the only convenient approach at the present time, anything more radical would only serve to make things more difficult without actually attaining His Highness's goal."[71] Even though Mahmud II had the right to demand the withdrawal of French soldiers from Algeria, the question was whether it would be wise to do so. Metternich responded in the following manner: "We do not believe that this would be wise. It is a reasonable policy for every Great Power not to expose itself to the possibility of a rejection, particularly when this Great Power has no means of avenging itself. This would be precisely the situation to which the Porte would consign itself if, in the actual and general state of affairs, it were to demand the evacuation of the French forces from the Algerian Regency."[72]

* * *

The French expedition in Algeria is not only a textbook example of Metternich's realism and pragmatism, but also of his foresight. He never readily gave his approval to this adventurous enterprise as American historian David H. Pinkney claims[73] but, analogous to his conduct in the final phase of the Greek Question, he demonstrated his realistic approach at the point when he realised that the course chosen by the French government could not be altered. As the fate of Algeria was not vitally important to Austria and, on the other hand, the French success was vitally important for the future of Polignac's cabinet and France's peace, and since Great Britain refused to ener-

---

[70] Metternich to Stürmer, Vienna, 31 Jan. 1837, HHStA, StA, Türkei VI, 67.
[71] Ibid. For the same opinion see Metternich to Ficquelmont, Vienna, 27 May 1837, HHStA, StA, Russland III, 111.
[72] Metternich to Stürmer, Vienna, 28 March 1837, HHStA, StA, Türkei VI, 67.
[73] D. H. Pinkney, *The French Revolution of 1830*, New Jersey 1972, p. 16.

getically oppose the expedition, the chancellor assumed the role of a spectator. He hoped to use the situation for his own and ever present goal, i.e. the restoration of the Alliance of European Powers and, in all likelihood, the opportunity to assume the role of mediator in the Algerian Affair between France and Great Britain.[74] The July Revolution frustrated these hopes and although the campaign was successful and the July Revolution erupted for different reasons, the 40,000 elite soldiers dispatched to Africa and therefore absent from France considerably contributed to the speedy victory of the revolutionaries.[75] Metternich's warnings in relation to the consequences of the expedition proved to be well founded, in particular his opinion that not even a victory would ensure the king's popularity.

For Austria's Near Eastern policy in the following decade, the whole Algerian Affair was of considerable importance because it signified a turning point in Metternich's analysis of the main threat to the Ottoman Empire. In the 1820s, he saw the principal danger in Russia, not because he would have presumed that the two tsars wished to destroy it but because they represented the most significant danger and because Russo-Ottoman disputes could develop into a war, which finally happened. After 1829, Russo-Ottoman relations significantly improved and there was no threat for the Porte from the North. On the other hand, Metternich realised only too well that with the expedition to Algeria, France started to actively revive its power in the Mediterranean, and he had a number of reasons to regard France after 1830 as the most dangerous Power if not for the very existence of the Ottoman Empire, then certainly for its stability. It was no coincidence that in the 1830s, Metternich's views and steps in the Eastern Question were mostly and markedly anti-French.

---

[74] A similar conclusion see in Sauvigny, *Metternich et la France*, III, pp. 1351–1352.

[75] R. Tombs, *France 1814–1914*, London, New York 1996, p. 351; Sir C. Petrie, *Diplomatic History 1713–1933*, London 1947, p. 177; Price, p. 145.

14

Austria's Economic Interests in the Ottoman Empire and the Early Phase of the First Mohammed Ali Crisis

Metternich was responsible not only for the guardianship of Austria's political but also its economic interests beyond its south-eastern border. Although commercial affairs were generally administered by the Court Chamber (*Hofkammer*), its defence abroad was connected with political affairs and, consequently, the responsibility for this fell to the Chancellery; an internuncio in Constantinople was thus responsible not only for political but also economic affairs and the influence of the Chancellery was also decisive in this respect at the consular level.[1] This naturally leads to the question as to whether Austrian activities in the Ottoman market were reflected by Metternich in the pursuance of his foreign policy and whether he paid any attention to them at all. To be able to answer this question, it is necessary to first pose another one: was the Ottoman market important to Austrian manufacturers, merchants and ship-owners?

Austria's Commercial Relations with the Ottoman Empire

The main problem lies in the distinct lack of hard data, not to mention the contradictions that exist within the very limited source materials. There is no complete set of statistics concerning Austrian trade with

---

[1] A. Brusatti, "Der österreichische Außenhandel um 1820," H. Matis, K. Bachinger, K. Hildegard (eds.), *Betrachtung zur Wirtschafts- und Sozialgeschichte*, Berlin 1979, p. 147; Sauer, *Österreich und die Levante*, pp. 40–41.

adjacent countries, except the one which provides the extract that is offered below (Graph 1). Nevertheless, while the information was

Graph 1

Austrian-Ottoman Trade as a Percentage of Austrian Commerce

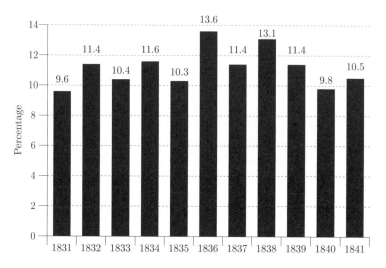

Sources: *Tafeln zur Statistik der österreichischen Monarchie*, I–XIV, Wien 1828–1844; *Ausweise über den Handel von Oesterreich*, Wien 1842.

gathered by the customs administrators and based upon the payment of the duties on exported and imported goods for most parts of the Habsburg Monarchy, this did not include the three free ports: Trieste, Venice and Fiume. No information exists regarding the further movement of the duty-paid goods transported between the interior and the three ports, which is a serious problem since Trieste, in particular, served as the commercial gateway to the Levant and a considerable part of the goods transported between this port and the Austrian Empire had their origin or destination on Ottoman soil. Therefore, one cannot discover the exact value of the trade between the two empires because the existing data for Trieste's sea trade cover all goods that went through the port. This is a problem again because Trieste, particularly in the years after 1815, served as a transshipment point for European trade with the Levant, and a considerable number of the goods loaded on the ships had their origin in France, the German states, Switzerland or even the U.S.A.[2]

Since no credible data for overland commerce between the two empires exist, as well as the fact that the importance of the Danube as a trade route was still insignificant at that time owing to the natural obstacles to navigation on the river, the extent of the trade can best be estimated through reference to trade centring on Trieste (shipping between Venice and Fiume and the Near East was of secondary importance). The Ottoman Empire was an important commercial partner of this port and the most important of all foreign countries, which is confirmed not only by the statistics (Graphs 2 and 3) but also through the recorded views of contemporaries.[3] The trade data for Trieste clearly indicate the importance of the Ottoman market for the Austrians but one must not forget that this interpretation cannot be solely determined through reference to the statistics. Although in terms of the overall volume of the Austrian Empire's trade it remained in third place, behind Germany and Italy, and the trade balance with their south-eastern neighbour was always negative for the Austrians, a great number of the Oriental goods were sold with the profit remaining in Europe. The Ottoman lands served as a source of raw materials, particularly cotton, which were either exported further afield to Switzerland and Germany or processed into manufactured goods in Austrian factories, the Ottoman market then serving as the outlet for their manufactured goods.[4] The significance of the Ottoman market can be also derived from Austria's position in the Levant trade in relation to the other European Powers. Austria was definitely an important trading partner of the Ottoman Empire representing a 24 per cent share of its foreign trade in the 1830s,[5] and it appears to have

---

[2]   R. Owen, *The Middle East in the World Economy 1800–1914*, London, New York 1981, p. 87; [unknown author] *Triest und Oesterreichs Antheil am Welthandel während der lezten* [sic] *zehn Jahre*, Triest 1842, p. 12.

[3]   For example, by J. Springer, *Statistik des österreichischen Kaiserstaates*, II, Wien 1840, p. 500, S. Becher, *Statistische Uebersicht des Handels der österreichischen Monarchie mit dem Auslande während der Jahre 1829 bis 1838*, Stuttgart, Tübingen 1841, p. 270, or the unknown author of *Triest und Oesterreichs Antheil am Welthandel während der lezten* [sic] *zehn Jahre*, Triest 1842, p. 43.

[4]   Springer, p. 502.

[5]   D. Quataert, "An Essay on Economic Relations between the Ottoman and Habsburg Empires, 1800–1914," A. Tietze (ed.), *Habsburgisch-osmanische Beziehun-*

Graph 2

Trade with the Ottoman Empire as a Percentage

of the Commerce of Trieste

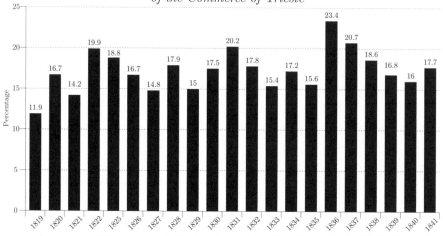

Sources: *Tafeln zur Statistik der österreichischen Monarchie*, I–XIV, Wien
1828–1844; *Ausweise über den Handel von Oesterreich*, Wien 1842.

Graph 3

Trieste Trade Data 1819–1841

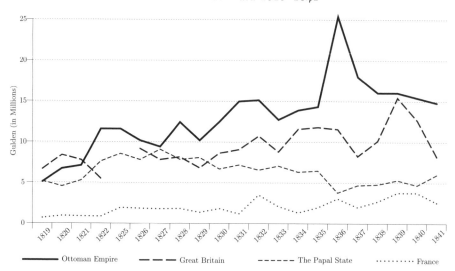

Sources: *Tafeln zur Statistik der österreichischen Monarchie*, I–XIV, Wien
1828–1844; *Ausweise über den Handel von Oesterreich*, Wien 1842; R. Angerlehner, *Österreichischer Schiffsverkehr und Seehandel 1815–1838, Teil II: Statistik*, unpublished dissertation, Wien 1968, p. 74.

gen: Relations Habsbourg-ottomanes, Wien 1985, p. 249.

retained this preeminent position among the Powers during most of the decade, even ahead of France and Great Britain. During the revolutionary and Napoleonic periods, the former lost its clear predominance in the eastern Mediterranean trade, its trade falling in value from approximately 70 million francs with the Ottoman Empire in 1791 to 23 million in 1817, and pre-Revolutionary levels were not achieved again until the 1840s.[6] It was Austria which took most advantage of the decrease in France's commerce with the Levant and gained much of it after 1815.[7] As for Great Britain, Roger Owen estimates the value of its trade with the Ottoman Empire during 1840–1841 at 2.5 million pounds, in comparison with the 2 million shared by France and Austria. However, there was an additional 2 million for the latter from the overland route.[8] If this is the case, as is highly likely and supported by some fragmentary data, one can presume with a great deal of certainty that for most of the two preceding decades Austria had actually been the most significant trading partner of the Ottoman Empire because the British trade did not significantly increase until shortly before the 1840s. According to the Prussian envoy in Vienna, Prince Franz Ludwig von Hatzfeldt-Trachenberg, in the mid 1820s Austria's trade even exceeded the combined British and Russian economic interests in the Near East.[9]

The eastern Mediterranean was not only an important market for the Austrians but also an important theatre for the activities of their merchant navy. Owing to the protectionism of European markets, the Ottoman market provided valuable commercial opportunities for the emerging Austrian industrial base, its merchants and also its shipowners and their crews. Austrian ships not only carried goods to and from their own sea ports but also arranged for the transportation of a considerable part of the Ottoman traffic in goods; their position was extremely advantageous, owing to various Austro-Ottoman treaties

[6] E. Eldem, "Capitulations and Western Trade," S. N. Faroqhi (ed.), *The Cambridge History of Turkey, Volume 3: The Later Ottoman Empire, 1603–1839*, Cambridge 2006, p. 323; H. Inalcık, D. Quataert (eds.), *An Economic and Social History of the Ottoman Empire*, Cambridge 2009, p. 832; Puryear, *France*, p. 53; Owen, p. 86.

[7] Stiepovich [?] to Royer, Pera, 22 June 1829, GStA PK, HA III, MdA I, 7267.

[8] Owen, p. 86.

[9] Hatzfeldt to Frederick William III, Vienna, 26 April 1826, GStA PK, HA III, MdA I, 6006.

and the sultans' firmans, all of which had resulted in the awarding of
vast privileges to the Austrians and had enabled them to enjoy "the
most favoured nation status."[10] In the mid 1820s, the number of Austrian commercial vessels exceeded those of other European nations,
and according to some reports it reached 800 ships, but more likely it
was about 600; in any event, Austria was considered as the most significant shipping power in the Levant at that time.[11] For comparison,
in 1823 more than 600 Austrian ships but only 16 French ships sailed
to Constantinople.[12] In 1838, of the 501 Austrian larger commercial
ships active at least half were operating in the eastern Mediterranean
and the Black Sea.[13] The importance is also clearly visible when one
compares the movement of Austrian ships in Ottoman, other European and world ports, excluding coastal navigation (cabotage), from
1832 to 1841 (Graph 4). The number of visits by Austrian ships to
the ports in the Levant was smaller than in other parts of the world –
13,611 to 24,254, but these figures must be understood in the context
of the fact that the Ottoman Empire covered only a small part of the
area where Austrian ships were active. Even more impressive is the
value of goods transported by Austrian ships in 1841 when the figure
of 73,875,797 gulden for the Levant considerably outweighed that of
42,039,819 for the Occident.[14] It is clear that without the Ottoman
market the Austrian commercial fleet would have been considerably
smaller.

To be able to answer the principle question of this chapter,
whether Metternich was in any way influenced in his decision-making

---

[10] Franz von Ottenfels, *Observation sur le commerce de l'Autriche dans le Lev-
ant et plus parti entièrement sur la navigation du Danube*, attached to Ottenfels,
Memoari, HDA, 750, OO 18, p. a34; Adelburg to Stürmer, Pera, 17 Oct. 1834, attached to Stürmer to Metternich, Büyükdere, 14 Oct. 1835, HHStA, StA, Türkei
VIII, 7.
[11] Hatzfeldt to Frederick William III, Vienna, 2 April 1825, GStA PK, HA III,
MdA I, 6005; Maltzan to Frederick William III, Vienna, 19 Oct. 1826, GStA PK,
HA III, MdA I, 6007; Maltzan to Frederick William III, Vienna, 22 Feb. 1827,
GStA PK, HA III, MdA I, 6008; Stiepovich [?] to Royer, Pera, 22 June 1829,
GStA PK, HA III, MdA I, 7267.
[12] Puryear, *France*, p. 29.
[13] Becher, p. 169.
[14] *Tafeln zur Statistik der österreichischen Monarchie für das Jahr 1841:
Zusammengestellt von der kaiserl. königl. Direction der administrativen Statistik,
Vierzehnter Jahrgang*, Wien 1844.

Graph 4
Austrian Ships in Foreign Ports 1832–1841

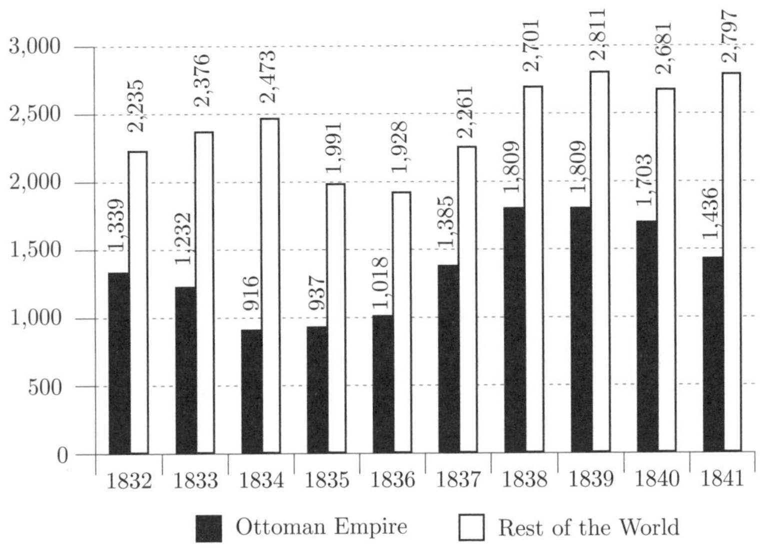

Sources: *Tafeln zur Statistik der österreichischen Monarchie*, I–XIV, Wien 1828–1844; *Ausweise über den Handel von Oesterreich*, Wien 1842.
Note: For the late 1830s the steamships are included.

by the economic interests of the Austrian Empire, it is also necessary to consider the most significant Ottoman destinations where the Austrians' activities were concentrated. By far the greatest number of their ships sailed to Constantinople, which formed a crossroads for Austria's commercial navigation. For example, in 1837 Austria was third from among the European countries in the number of ships arriving at the port but the first from among the Great Powers; with its 732 ships it fell behind the Greeks with 832 and the Sardinians with 778, but exceeded the 700 British (including the Ionians under the British flag) and 555 Russian ships.[15] In 1840, Austria with 869 considerably surpassed Great Britain with 567 ships.[16] The high number was due to the fact that Constantinople was situated on the

---

[15]   V. J. Puryear, *International Economics and Diplomacy in the Near East, 1834–1853*, Stanford 1969, p. 112.

[16]   Owen, p. 97. According to Austrian sources, there were even 890 Austrian ships in Constantinople in 1840. *Tafeln zur Statistik der österreichischen Monarchie für das Jahr 1841: Zusammengestellt von der kaiserl. königl. Direction der administrativen Statistik, Vierzehnter Jahrgang*, Wien 1844.

waterway between the Mediterranean and the Black Sea, which also was a very important area for Austrian commerce and navigation. In the 1820s, the most important carrying power in the Black Sea trade was Austria, and Metternich reflected this fact in his letter to Francis I from late 1828 declaring that navigation in this sea belonged to "the most profitable source of income"[17] for Austria's shipping, and he was absolutely right because the trade in grain from the Black Sea was crucial for the prosperity of the Austrian merchant navy during *Vormärz*. During 1827 at least 300 Austrian ships sailed in the Black Sea, above all for this commodity. Unsurprisingly, when the Russians launched the blockade of the Dardanelles in 1828–1829, Austrian navigation fell into a state of serious crisis.[18] When the Black Sea was opened to the ships of other European nations after 1829, the Austrians obtained some serious competition but despite this, they still played an important role in this area in the 1830s. In the second half of 1836, for example, the Austrian vessels were the second most numerous from among non-Ottoman ships sailing up and down through the Straits; first were the Greeks with 85 up and 181 down, the Austrians second with 101 and 147 respectively, followed by the British and Ionian in the third place with 97 and 130.[19] In Odessa, by far the most important Russian port in the Black Sea, between 1815 and 1826 Austrian vessels were second in tonnage behind those of Russia, but in the 1830s Austrian vessels led all others both in numbers and tonnage, while those of Sardinia and Russia competed for the second place.[20] Not only Austrian navigation but also Trieste itself prospered from the Russian grain which was warehoused in this har-

---

[17]   Metternich to Francis I, Vienna, 20 Dec. 1828, HHStA, StK, Vorträge 256.
[18]   R. Angerlehner, *Österreichischer Schiffsverkehr und Seehandel 1815–1838*, unpublished dissertation, Wien 1968, pp. 144–146.
[19]   Ponsonby to Palmerston, Therapia, 5 Jan. 1837, TNA, FO 78/301.
[20]   V. J. Puryear, "Odessa: Its Rise and International Importance, 1815–50," *Pacific Historical Review* 3, 1934, pp. 197–203. According to French sources, in 1832 the Austrian ships were not first but second in number in Odessa, falling behind the Russians: Of 403 ships which arrived in the port, 135 sailed under Russian, 102 under Austrian, 85 under British, 44 under Sardinian flags. Of 349 ships which departed, 112 sailed under Russian, 85 under Austrian, 75 under British, 41 under Sardinian flags. Irrespective of whether first or second, it is clear that for the Austrians Odessa was a very significant commercial destination. Chattaye to Bourgoing, Odesssa, 18 Nov. 1831, AMAE, Correspondance consulaire et commerciale, Odessa 4.

bour, which, together with Leghorn, Genoa and Marseille, served as a depository for this commodity for Western Europe.[21] It is also necessary to mention the importance of Trabzon, the Ottoman port in the eastern part of the Black Sea, which offered good opportunities for export as well as import and from which an important trade route led to Erzurum and further to Persia, attracting the attention of the merchants of more European countries in the 1830s.[22] Austrian consular and diplomatic agents supported the trade with this area and during this decade, Austria was the most active country in this port: in 1830, the 11 Austrian ships considerably exceeded in number those of 4 Tuscan, 3 British, 3 Russian, 3 Neapolitan, and 2 Sardinian vessels.[23] In 1840, Trabzon was visited by 38 or 40 Austrian, but only 24 Russian and 9 British ships.[24] The significance of this port for Austria is also clearly evident from the fact that from late 1837 an Austrian steamship, incidentally named *Fürst Clemens Metternich*, sailed between Trabzon and Constantinople.[25]

In the eastern Mediterranean, Smyrna played an important role for Austria. This is evident from, first, the number of foreigners living in this city; according to statistics from 1847 also useful for the earlier period, 4,000 Austrians lived there, but only 712 French, 206 British and 180 Russians.[26] Second, the Austrians were represented by 20 commercial houses in the 1820s.[27] Third, in 1840, Smyrna was visited by 216 Austrian, but only 113 British and 40 French ships.[28] Nevertheless, despite its considerable potential, various problems caused the stagnation of Austria's trade in the mid 1830s in this city, whose commercial importance seemed to fall behind that of Alexandria, a gateway to Egypt that, as a result of Mohammed Ali's reformatory ef-

---

[21] Angerlehner, p. 103.

[22] C. Issawi, "The Tabriz-Trabzon Trade, 1830–1900: Rise and Decline of a Route," *IJMES* 1, 1970, 1, pp. 18–27.

[23] Ghersj to Ottenfels, Trabzon, 1 Nov. 1830, attached to Ottenfels to Metternich, Constantinople, 10 Dec. 1830, HHStA, StA, Türkei VIII, 2; Ghersj to Ottenfels, Trabzon, 12 Jan. 1831, attached to Ottenfels to Metternich, Constantinople, 11 March 1831, HHStA, StA, Türkei VIII, 3.

[24] Angerlehner, p. 163; Owen, p. 97.

[25] C. King, *The Black Sea: A History*, Oxford 2004, p. 176; Angerlehner, p. 146.

[26] R. Kasaba, *The Ottoman Empire and the World Economy: Nineteenth Century*, New York 1988, p. 70.

[27] Angerlehner, p. 148.

[28] Owen, p. 97.

forts, experienced immense economic growth and an increase in trade
with Europe.[29] The country profiting considerably from this development was Austria and several main factors contributed to it. The
Egyptian market opened up at the moment when Austria entered
an era of peace after the Napoleonic Wars with its merchant navy
augmented by Venetian commercial vessels. During the Greek war
for independence, Austria's merchant fleet transported goods for the
Turks and also troops and supplies to Ibrahim Pasha's expedition to
the Peloponnese.[30] One of the most important trading routes within
the Ottoman Empire was that between Alexandria and Constantinople, which served as an artery supplying the capital with Egyptian
grain. The Austrians also were highly interested in this trade. Their
commercial interests in Egypt are also evident from the presence of
28 Austrian commercial houses in Cairo and another two in Alexandria in the mid 1820s,[31] the fact that Trieste and Venice were by far
the most important foreign ports for Egyptian trade and that Austrian ships were the most frequent foreign visitors to the Alexandrian
port (Graph 5).[32]

Another important factor that contributed to the considerable increase of Austria's commercial involvement in the land on the Nile was
the volume of the production of long-staple cotton, which was by far
the most important commodity exported from Egypt to Europe from
the 1820s onwards. Cotton was of great significance for Austrian manufacturers and their nascent industry – the technical revolution had
started in the Habsburg Monarchy around 1830 and the most progressive users of steam engines were the textile factories.[33] Consequently,

[29] The unexploited commercial opportunities led an Austrian agent, Heinrich von
Testa, to explain the reasons in *Mémoire sur les causes du décroissement pro-
gressif du commerce de Smyrne*, Smyrna, 15 April 1836, attached to Stürmer to
Metternich, Constantinople, 18 May 1836, HHStA, StA, Türkei VIII, 9.

[30] Miltitz to Frederick William III, Pera, 27 May 1824, GStA PK, HA III, MdA I,
7258; Miltitz to Frederick William III, Pera, 10 Sept. 1824, GStA PK, HA III,
MdA I, 7259.

[31] M. Purkhart, "Österreichs Handel mit Ägypten," I. Lazar, J. Holaubek (eds.),
Egypt and Austria V: Egypt's Heritage in Europe, Koper 2009, p. 186.

[32] Miltitz to Frederick William III, Pera, 15 April 1824, GStA PK, HA III, MdA I,
7258; *Tableau du mouvement dans le port d'Alexandrie en 1826*, attached to Miltitz
to Frederick William III, Pera, 10 May 1827, GStA PK, HA III, MdA I, 7264.

[33] D. F. Good, *The Economic Rise of the Hapsburg Empire 1750–1914*, London,
Berkeley, Los Angeles 1984, pp. 49–50; Becher, p. 119.

Graph 5
The Arrivals of European Ships in Alexandria

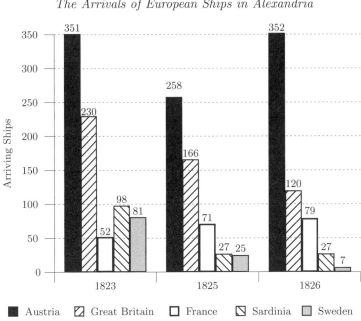

Austria   Great Britain   France   Sardinia   Sweden

Sources: *Prospetto generale dimonstrante la provenienza e destinazione dei bastimenti arrivati e partiti dal porte d'Alessandria d'Egitto dal 1. Gennajo al 31. Decembre 1823*, attached to Miltitz to Frederick William III, Pera, 15 April 1824, GStA PK, HA III, MdA I, 7258; Sir J. Bowring, *Report on Egypt 1823–1838 under the Reign of Mohamed Ali*, London 1998, p. 202.

the increase in production meant that more cotton was needed, and between 1815 and 1839 most of it was imported into Austria from the Levant, probably in the region of three quarters of its needs; of this amount, more than half originated in Egypt. Moreover, not all of the Levant cotton imported through Trieste was consumed by the national industry: a considerable part was further exported from this port to Switzerland and the German states. Although, as Walter Sauer rightly points out, the import of American cotton increased in the 1830s,[34] the amount imported to Austria from the United States was still less than half the total quantity imported in 1839, and its price was still higher than the price of the Levant cotton. The importance

---

[34] W. Sauer, "Schwarz-Gelb in Afrika: Habsburgermonarchie und koloniale Frage," W. Sauer (ed.), *K. u k. colonial: Habsburgermonarchie und europäische Herrschaft in Afrika*, Wien, Köln, Weimar 2002, p. 27.

of Egyptian cotton for Austrian textile production and shipping can
be easily derived from existing data (Graphs 6 and 7).

Graph 6

Export of Cotton from Egypt 1823–1837

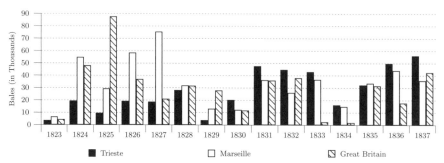

Source: Sir J. Bowring, *Report on Egypt 1823–1838 under the Reign of Mohamed Ali*, London 1998, pp. 181–182.

Graph 7

Austrian Share of the Egyptian Cotton Export Market 1823–1837

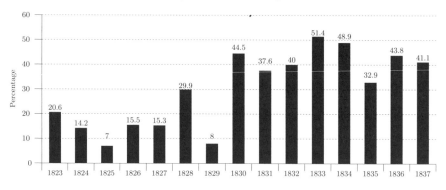

Source: Sir J. Bowring, *Report on Egypt 1823–1838 under the Reign of Mohamed Ali*, London 1998, pp. 181–182.

Cotton was by far Austria's most important trade item in the
Egyptian market but certainly not the only one. Chiefly in the 1830s,
Austria was pre-eminent among all European countries in relation
to the import of a range of commodities from this Ottoman North
African province: coffee, cotton wool, cotton twists, ivory, tortoise-
shell, incense, gum, senneh, tamarind and saffron. Furthermore, Austrian ships carried a variety of goods to Trieste and Venice: for example, corn, mother of pearl, linseed, flax, skins, rice and linen. Iron,
paper, marble, cigars, glassware, woollen hats, crockery and other

commodities were all exported to Egypt.[35] Of special importance for Mohammed Ali was timber from Istria for the construction of his ships.[36] Particularly for Trieste, Egypt was for many years by far the most important province of the Ottoman Empire.[37] In 1836, when trade between the two empires achieved its highest level, the exchange of goods with Egypt constituted more than a third of the total value of the Trieste-Ottoman commerce (Graph 8).

Graph 8
Trieste Trade Data 1819–1841

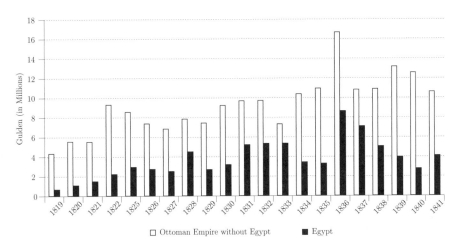

□ Ottoman Empire without Egypt   ■ Egypt

Sources: *Tafeln zur Statistik der österreichischen Monarchie*, I–XIV, Wien 1828–1844; *Ausweise über den Handel von Oesterreich*, Wien 1842; R. Angerlehner, *Österreichischer Schiffsverkehr und Seehandel 1815–1838, Teil II: Statistik*, unpublished dissertation, Wien 1968, p. 74.

---

[35] Metternich to Ottenfels, Vienna, 17 Oct. 1832, HHStA, StA, Türkei VI, 56; Campbell to Palmerston, Alexandria, 3 Nov. 1834, TNA, FO 78/247; A. Haikal, "Die Auswirkung der britischen Kolonialpolitik auf die Wirtschaft Ägyptens," W. Markov (ed.), *Kolonialismus und Neokolonialismus in Nordafrika und Nahost*, Berlin 1964, p. 228; Sir J. Bowring, *Report on Egypt 1823–1838 under the Reign of Mohamed Ali*, London 1998, pp. 200–203; Sauer, *Österreich und die Levante*, p. 280; Sauer, "Schwarz-Gelb in Afrika," p. 23.
[36] Mimaut to Broglie, Alexandria, 30 June 1833, AMAE, CP, Égypte 3.
[37] Miltitz to Frederick William III, Pera, 10 May 1827, GStA PK, HA III, MdA I, 7264; K. R. Greenfield, "Commerce and New Enterprise at Venice, 1830–48," *JMH* 11, 1939, 3, p. 317; Springer, p. 502.

Although completely reliable statistics are lacking, especially for the period before 1830, and one can only work with fragments of the data needed to make an accurate comparison of the European countries' trade with Egypt, Austria appears to have held a pre-eminent position and was its most significant European trading partner of all the European Powers during the late 1820s and most of the 1830s, followed by Tuscany, Great Britain and France.[38] If Austrian vessels were undoubtedly the most frequent visitors to the Alexandrian port during the 1820s, then with regard to trade, Austria seemed to rank in the first place at the end of the same decade, or was slightly behind Tuscany, but significantly ahead of Great Britain and France.[39] One can claim this superiority with a good deal of certainty for 1831 (Graph 9). The British consul general in Alexandria, Colonel Patrick Campbell, reported to his government in late 1834 on the dominant commercial position of Austria in Egypt at that time. The importance

Graph 9
Alexandria Trade Data, 1831

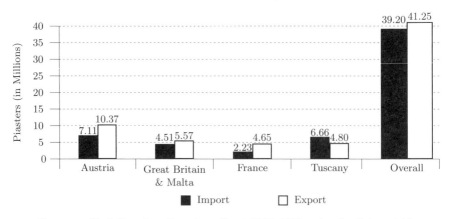

Sources: Sir J. Bowring, *Report on Egypt 1823–1838 under the Reign of Mohamed Ali*, London 1998, p. 201; *British Parliamentary Papers*, XLVI, 1844, pp. 245–246.

---

[38] Austria's first place among the European countries in the trade with Egypt is proved not only by fragmentary statistics but also consular reports. Mimaut to Polignac, Alexandria, 28 Aug. 1829, G. Douin (ed.), *L'Égypte de 1828 à 1830: Correspondance des consuls de France en Égypte*, Roma 1935, p. 370.

[39] Mimaut to Polignac, Alexandria, 10 June 1830, Douin, *L'Égypte de 1828 à 1830*, p. 424.

of this North African region for the Austrians was also evident in their frequent transportation of mail, which was much greater than was undertaken by the British. A year earlier, Campbell had even complained that he had had to make use of Austrian or French warships in order to send and receive his correspondence because the British navy was severely neglecting this task.[40] Although Great Britain was considerably increasing its trade with the Ottoman Empire and was closing in on Austria's lead during the 1830s, it did not succeed in overtaking the Austrian share of trade with Egypt until 1839.[41] France, usually regarded as Mohammed Ali's most ardent supporter, was to continue to lag behind Austria during the entire decade (Graph 10).[42] In brief,

Graph 10
Alexandria Trade Data 1836–1839

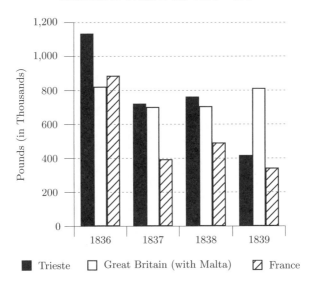

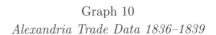

Source: R. Owen, *The Middle East in the World Economy 1800–1914*, London, New York 1981, p. 96.

the existing data offer clear evidence that Egypt was an important overseas trading partner for the Austrian Empire in the period before

[40] Campbell to Palmerston, Alexandria, 28 May 1833, TNA, FO 78/227; Campbell to Palmerston, Alexandria, 3 Nov. 1834, TNA, FO 78/247.
[41] Fahmy, *All the Pasha's Men*, p. 294; Kasaba, p. 47.
[42] For 1840, the situation was similar to the previous year when Great Britain ranked first, Austria second and France third. Haikal, p. 228.

1848, even after 1839 when Great Britain overtook Austria as Egypt's foremost European trading partner. This change was not only a result of Austria's decline in trade with Egypt in 1839 but also the gradual increase of British commercial activities with which Austrians were unable to keep up and which caused them financial losses.[43]

Metternich's Support of Trieste and the Austrian Lloyd

The fact that the Ottoman market was very significant for the Austrian Empire naturally does not explain whether the Viennese Chancellery was aware of this, which is not a superfluous question because Metternich has generally not been depicted as a man with much of a flair for economics and foreign trade, if any at all. This neglect is all the more serious in that it has nothing common with reality. Metternich actually paid considerable attention to economics. Some evidence can be found, for example, through reference to Metternich's interest in the economic situation of Hungary and his enterprises in his Bohemian domain, Plass, where he established a smelting-house and a factory for the manufacture of iron products.[44] As for the Ottoman Empire, it is possible to find in Metternich's correspondence the evidence that Austria's commercial interests were regarded by him as one of the reasons for his involvement in Near Eastern affairs.[45] For example, he wrote in August 1834: "The topographical situation of the Austrian Monarchy, a considerable number of administrative and commercial interests and finally political considerations of the most important nature together do not allow us to remain indifferent to

---

[43] Prokesch to Archduke Johann, Athens, 27 May 1838, A. Schlossar (ed.), *Briefwechsel zwischen Erzherzog Johann Babtist von Österreich und Prokesch-Osten*, Stuttgart 1898, p. 54; Purkhart, pp. 185–190.

[44] J. Hučka, "K historii Metternichovy železárny v Plasích [On the History of Metternich's Ironworks in Plass]," I. Budil, M. Šedivý (eds.), *Metternich a jeho doba: Sborník příspěvků z konference uskutečněné v Plzni ve dnech 23. a 24. dubna 2009 [Metternich and His Time: Memorial Volume of the Conference Held in Pilsen on 23 and 24 April 2009]*, Plzeň 2009, pp. 85–93; Siemann, p. 104.

[45] The interest in the commercial affairs of the Levant at the Viennese Chancellery is also evident from the attention paid to them by Gentz. Mayr, *Staatskanzlei*, p. 137.

what happens in the Levant."[46] All the more significant proof for his awareness of the Ottoman Empire's importance for Austria's trade were his practical steps, like his support of the growth of Austrian commerce on the Danube[47] or the activities of Trieste.[48]

For Metternich, the importance of Trieste lay in the fact that it served as a gateway for commodities imported from the Levant not only into the Danube Monarchy itself but also into Switzerland and Germany, and he could use this in negotiations concerning the German Customs Union, which came into existence in January 1834. For several preceding years, Metternich had tried unsuccessfully to prevent its foundation. When he failed in this, he wanted to change the strong protectionist system of Austria, in other words to carry out a reform of its tariffs, not due to Austria's direct accession to the German Customs Union because he knew well that such a proposal was unacceptable in Austria but with the aim of some legal rapprochement: to open the door to the conclusion of a mutual commercial treaty which would enable Austria to exercise more influence in German economic affairs. When he was promoting the idea of Austria's close cooperation with the Customs Union, he used Trieste in dealing with those German states involved in trade through this port, for example Bavaria. Consequently, he supported Bavaria's wish for a simplified access system to this port or its connection with Bavaria, Württemberg and even with Bohemia and Prussia via railway. The latter project whose realisation he much desired would have facilitated the transport of goods between Trieste and Central Europe, which was separated from the Adriatic by mountains, and would have significantly improved the connection of Austria's economy with foreign markets and partly indentified its economic interests with those of the German Customs Union. However, Metternich failed in both the settlement with Bavaria concerning its access to Trieste and the construction of the railway between the interior and the monarchy's coast. The failure of these projects was largely the result of the inflexibility of Austrian bureaucracy that was too strong to overcome; during *Vormärz*, some bureaucrats led by the Bohemian nobleman and minister of state of the Austrian Empire

---

[46] Metternich to Apponyi, Baden, 3 Aug. 1834, HHStA, StA, Frankreich 294.

[47] For more on Metternich's support of navigation on the Danube see Chapter 19.

[48] D. Winkler, G. Pawlik, *Die Dampfschiffahrtsgesellschaft Österreichischer Lloyd 1836–1918*, Graz 1986, p. 10.

for finance, Count Franz Anton von Kolowrat-Liebsteinsky, who had
personal interests in Bohemia, put through the construction of the
railway leading from Vienna through Moravia to Bohemia at the expense of the construction of the railway to Trieste, which shows how
limited Metternich's influence actually was within Austria.[49]

Metternich's support of the railway between the core of the monarchy and Trieste also resulted from his fascination with new technolo-
gies, in particular with steam engines, which were being implemented
in Europe during his period in transportation overland as well as
transportation by water. This interest in technological progress manifested itself in connection with Trieste in three significant ways: first,
the already mentioned support of the railway;[50] second, the support of
the idea of the creation of the Suez Canal – if realised, the route from
Trieste to Bombay would be shortened by about 61 percent, whereas
from London to Bombay it would be reduced by about only 43 percent, and he was convinced that this advantage would be considerably
beneficial for Austria's navigation as well as for Trieste itself;[51] third,
the concern he attached to the steamship navigation that started to
increase rapidly in the eastern Mediterranean after the mid 1830s, to
which Metternich paid a great deal of attention. He was displeased
with the French government's decision of 1835 to establish two steam
packet lines between Marseille and, respectively, Constantinople and
Alexandria. The reasons for his resentment were more political than
commercial in origin because these pioneering steamships had little

---

[49] A. Beer, *Die Finanzen Oesterreichs im XIX. Jahrhundert*, Prag 1877, pp. 186–
189, 195; W. Drobesch, "Il ruolo di Trieste tra I porti marittimi e fluviali austriaci (1719–1918)," R. Finzi, L. Panariti, G. Panjek (eds.), *Storia economica
e sociale di Trieste, Volume II: La città dei traffici 1719–1918*, Trieste 2003,
p. 365; H.-W. Hahn, *Geschichte des Deutschen Zollvereins*, Göttingen 1984, pp. 70
and 130; W. O. Henderson, *The Zollverein*, Cambridge 1939, p. 137; G. Otruba,
"Der Deutsche Zollverein und Österreich: Nachklang zum 150. Jahrestag der
„Gründung" des Deutschen Zollvereines," *ÖGL* 15, 1971, 3, pp. 127–128; H. Rumpler, "Economia e potere politico: Il ruolo di Trieste nella politica di sviluppo
economico di Vienna," R. Finzi, L. Panariti, G. Panjek (eds.), *Storia economica e
sociale di Trieste, Volume II: La città dei traffici 1719–1918*, Trieste 2003, pp. 78–
79.
[50] Metternich to Gentz, Johannisberg, 22 June 1830, Kronenbitter, p. 348; Woodward, p. 35.
[51] Metternich to Laurin, Vienna, 25 and 28 April 1843, E. Dross (ed.), *Quellen
zur Ära Metternich*, Darmstadt 1999, pp. 288–291; N. Rahimi, *Österreich und der
Suezkanal*, unpublished dissertation, Wien 1968, pp. 13–14.

space for goods and were more valuable for the transportation of people and post than cargo. Metternich was concerned that the potential success of the French steam packets, operating with considerable state financial support, might lead to them taking over the transportation of mail between Western Europe and the Ottoman Empire, until then delivered via the Austrian Empire, which would thus have considerably decreased the income of the Austrian postal service and could have led to Austria's dependence on the French services in this matter. This also was exactly the reason why the French established their own steamship lines: to avoid their own correspondence being read by the Austrians, an absolutely logical decision from the French point of view but a nightmare for Metternich, who made the best of Vienna's central position for the transportation of foreign diplomatic correspondence that he could intercept.[52] His concerns were well founded in many respects, and despite some technical problems at the beginning of French steamship navigation in 1837 and considerably higher prices for carrying the post, the French represented a serious threat to Austria's postal service.[53]

[52] Guilleminot to Sébastiani, Constantinople, 5 April 1831, AMAE, CP, Turquie 262; J. K. Mayr, *Metternichs Geheimer Briefdienst: Postlogen und Postkurse,* Wien 1935, pp. 8–9; A. Patera, "Die Rolle der Habsburgermonarchie für den Postverkehr zwischen dem Balkan und dem übrigen Europa," H. Heppner (ed.), *Der Weg führt über Österreich... Zur Geschichte des Verkehrs- und Nachrichtenwesens von und nach Südosteuropa,* Wien, Köln, Weimar 1996, pp. 49–51; R. Wurth, "Österreichs orientalische Post: Durch Balkan und Levante," *Österreichische Postgeschichte* 16, Klingenbach 1993, p. 43; Tischler, p. 242.

[53] Metternich to Apponyi, Vienna, 10 April 1835, HHStA, StA, Frankreich 297; Stürmer to Metternich, Büyükdere, 21 June 1837, HHStA, StA, Türkei VI, 66; Eyragues to Molé, Therapia, 23 May 1837, AMAE, CP, Turquie 274. In February 1836, Metternich committed himself to the internuncio by assuring him that he was able to control the contents of Ottoman diplomatic correspondence with London and Paris. However, at the end of the decade, the Porte decided to send its correspondence by French steamers, which moved Metternich to recommend to the Porte in May 1840 that they return to using the service of Austria's post as a more "useful" way of communication with its ambassadors in the West. The Porte finally agreed, which enabled Metternich to read through its correspondence again. This story well evidences the importance of this control for the Austrian chancellor. Metternich to Stürmer, Vienna, 3 Feb. 1836, HHStA, StA, Türkei VI, 65; Metternich to Stürmer, Vienna, 19 May 1840, HHStA, StA, Türkei VI, 78; Mustafa Reshid Pasha to Chequib Effendi, Constantinople, 8 July 1840, HHStA, StK, Interiora, Intercepte 28.

In order to save the situation, Metternich supported the development of Austria's own steamship navigation service in the eastern Mediterranean, which led to his considerable patronisation of the Steam Navigation Company of the Austrian Lloyd with its headquarters in Trieste. He fully supported its foundation in 1836, which led to establishing the connection between Trieste and Constantinople, Smyrna, Alexandria and other less important ports in the eastern Mediterranean in 1837, and he soon entrusted it with the transportation of Austrian post, thus giving Lloyd the certainty of income. In addition, he facilitated financial support from the Rothschilds for the company when it faced serious financial problems in 1838–1839. He acted in this manner because he thought that the collapse of the Austrian Lloyd would be a disaster for the monarchy.[54] The company recognised his goodwill towards them by naming one of its steamers after him, the *Principe Metternich*, and awarding him an honorary title, Protector of the Austrian Lloyd, which, according to American historian Ronald E. Coons, should not be mistaken as a purely honorific title but one which recognised the practical support actually provided by Metternich.[55] In addition, his portrait was displayed in the organisation's reading room until March 1848, when Karl Ludwig von Bruck "saved it from destruction at the hands of revolutionaries by speaking to the threatening crowd of the chancellor's many efforts on behalf of Trieste's economic and commercial development."[56] In that revolutionary year, Trieste witnessed demonstrations of hostility towards Metternich, for example the renaming of the steamer originally carrying his name, which Metternich greatly regretted. Later, after his return to Vienna from which he had had to flee in March 1848, his third wife, Princess Melanie, said of his chagrin: "Klemens has forgiven and forgotten all the trials and tribulations he suffered;

---

[54] R. Agstner, "The Austrian Lloyd Steam Navigation Company," M. Wrba (ed.), *Austrian Presence in the Holy Land in the 19th and early 20th Century*, Tel Aviv 1996, pp. 136–140; R. E. Coons, *Steamships, Statesmen, and Bureaucrats: Austrian Policy towards the Steam Navigation Company of the Austrian Lloyd 1836–1848*, Wiesbaden 1975, p. 89; R. E. Coons, "Metternich and the Lloyd Austriaco," *MÖStA* 30, 1977, pp. 49–56; D. Ivanissevich, "L'apertura delle linee del Lloyd Austriaco con l'Impero otomano," G. Pavan (ed.), *Trieste e la Turchia*, Trieste 1996, p. 58; L. Sondhaus, *The Habsburg Empire and the Sea: Austrian Naval Policy 1797–1866*, West Lafayette 1989, pp. 95–96.

[55] Coons, *Steamships*, p. 134.

[56] Ibid.

however, the most painful for him was the ingratitude of the people of Trieste."[57]

Metternich's Protection of Austria's Commercial Interests in the Eastern Mediterranean

Metternich used the Austrian Lloyd company against the French steamship navigation but he was never willing to actively pursue a policy against French competition because he recognised that he had neither the right nor the means to do so.[58] Nevertheless, at the moment he felt that it was necessary to protect Austria's commerce with force, he did not hesitate to do so, as happened during the Greek insurrection when the waters surrounding Greece were full of Greek pirates attacking not only Turkish or Egyptian but also European merchant vessels. Since Austrian ships were more commonly seen in the Archipelago and the Ionian Sea than those of any other nation, they were often attacked by the Greeks. The latter's hostility was also provoked by the fact that Austria diplomatically sided with the Turks and that the Austrian ships sailed for the Turks. It must be emphasised that there was nothing romantic in the pirates' activities and that the incidents of injury or murder of Austrian sailors were not sporadic. The cruelty of the war between the Turks and the Greeks showed itself in the barbarity of the Greek pirates and the ships were sometimes sunk with their crew fastened to a mast. To protect their own ships as well as the sailors, Metternich did not hesitate to advocate to Francis I the employment of the Austrian navy in the dangerous waters on 31 May 1821. The emperor agreed and four warships were sent to the Greek waters in July, forming thus the core of the Austrian Levant squadron whose radius of operation was the whole eastern Mediterranean including the western coast of Greece. It was gradually reinforced in the following years, and in early 1826, it numbered 22 warships. It was not an entirely sufficient number but definitely quite considerable for Austria's small war navy and even more

---

[57] *NP*, VI, p. 292.
[58] Metternich to Apponyi, Vienna, 10 April 1835, HHStA, StA, Frankreich 297.

than possessed by the British in these waters at that time.[59] Metternich, who initiated the use of force at the beginning, continued to supervise the navy's activities against "a war of permanent piracy"[60] and supported its reinforcement. It must be emphasised here that the use of the naval force was due to the welfare of Austria's Levant trade, which in Metternich's own words was "the only considerable trade which she [Austria] possessed."[61] The presence of the sizeable squadron was the only way for Metternich to prevent its complete destruction. He also repeatedly attempted to establish a cooperation of European fleets for a more effective defence of the trade of all nations, in particular the naval solidarity of the British and French, but with little success. With the destruction of the Turko-Egyptian fleet in Navarino Bay, the trilateral alliance negated what Metternich had requested and what the Treaty of London declared as one of its aims, the suppression of piracy, because the absence of Ottoman warships relinquished the sea to the activities of Greek pirates of which Austria was the principle victim. The problem gradually abated when the Greek insurrection was coming to an end, which enabled the Austrian government to first reduce and finally dissolve the Levant squadron.[62]

---

[59] A. von Khuepach, H. von Bayer, *Geschichte der k. u. k. Kriegsmarine, II. Teil: Die K. K. Österreichische Kriegsmarine in dem Zeitraum von 1797 bis 1848, III. Band: Geschichte der k. k. Kriegsmarine während der Jahre 1814–1847: Die österreichisch-venezianische Kriegsmarine*, Graz, Köln 1966, pp. 194–196; H. Putschek, *Die Verwaltung Veneziens 1814–1830 mit besonderer Berücksichtigung von Konterbandwesen und Seeraub*, unpublished dissertation, Wien 1957, pp. 113–115; Bartlett, p. 79; Sauer, *Österreich und die Levante*, pp. 127–143; Sondhaus, pp. 63–72.

[60] *Les observations sur la dépêche de Mr. Canning à S. H. Wellesley du 31. décembre 1824, relative aux droits de guerre reconnus aux Grecs*, attached to Metternich to Lebzeltern, Vienna, 18 Feb. 1825, HHStA, StA, Russland III, 70.

[61] Wellesley to Canning, Vienna, 1 Sept. 1825, TNA, FO 120/71.

[62] Metternich to Lebzeltern, Vienna, 20 June 1822, HHStA, StA, Russland III, 54; Metternich to Lebzeltern, Vienna, 20 Dec. 1824, HHStA, StA, Russland III, 65; Metternich to Lebzeltern, Milan, 18 June 1825, Ischl, 13 Aug. 1825, HHStA, StA, Russland III, 71; Metternich to Esterházy, Vienna, 24 June 1822, HHStA, StA, England 166; Metternich to Esterházy, Vienna, 8 Sept. 1825, HHStA, StA, England 173; Metternich to Esterházy, Vienna, 4 Nov. 1827, HHStA, StA, England 179; Metternich to Esterházy, Vienna, 18 Dec. 1828, HHStA, StA, England 184; Metternich to Esterházy, Vienna, 25 Feb. and 1 March 1829, HHStA, StA, England 187; Metternich to Ottenfels, Vienna, 29 Jan. 1825, HHStA, StA, Türkei VI, 24; Metternich to Ottenfels, Vienna, 19 Feb. 1829, HHStA, StA, Türkei VI, 39; Metternich to Vincent, Vienna, 20 Oct. 1825, HHStA, StA, Frankreich 257; Lützow

The Greek insurrection was an extreme situation that forced Austria to undertake extraordinary measures for the defence of its trade, exceeding the usual diplomatic method of handling its economic affairs with the Ottoman Empire. Metternich also was of course directly involved in these negotiations. For example, when the Straits were opened to the ships of all European countries in the early 1830s, the Chancellery ensured that Austrians obtained the most advantageous conditions and insisted on their enforcement in the following years; when, in the mid 1830s, the Ottoman administration attempted to introduce higher toll charges on Austrian ships than had been settled by treaties, the internunciature immediately intervened and put an end to this arbitrary decision.[63] The Austrian government reacted in the same way whenever Austrian merchants were in danger of being oppressed by the Ottomans through breaking the treaty stipulations like in 1821 when the grain export was prohibited for some time, or the introduction of additional taxes which were at variance with existing Austro-Ottoman treaties.[64] The defence was also assumed with the same zeal in 1832 when a problem arose in relation to the ending of an Austro-Ottoman customs tariff agreement from 1818 and the negotiation of a new one. Metternich was considerably involved in this affair and Ottenfels finally succeeded in retaining the earlier tariff until a new document was signed.[65] Negotiations between Vienna and Constantinople following the signing of the British-Ottoman

to Metternich, Constantinople, 18 Aug. 1821, HHStA, StA, Türkei VI, 12; Lützow to Metternich, Constantinople, 25 June and 10 July 1822, Ottenfels to Metternich, Constantinople, 9 Nov. 1822, HHStA, StA, Türkei VI, 13; Ottenfels to Metternich, Constantinople, 25 Sept., 15 and 25 Oct. 1827, HHStA, StA, Türkei VI, 28; Ottenfels to Metternich, Constantinople, 25 Nov. and 12 Dec. 1828, HHStA, StA, Türkei VI, 34; Ottenfels to Metternich, Constantinople, 10 Feb. 1829, HHStA, StA, Türkei VI, 36; Caraman to Montmorency, Vienna, 22 June 1822, AMAE, CP, Autriche 403; Caraman to Damas, Vienna, 11 April, 6 June and 6 July 1826, AMAE, CP, Autriche 407; Gordon to Londonderry, Vienna, 3 July 1822, TNA, FO 120/53; Tatishchev to Nesselrode, Vienna, 13 March 1826, AVPRI, fond 133, Kantseliariia, opis 468, 11870; Sauer, *Österreich und die Levante*, pp. 229–230; Sondhaus, p. 73.
[63] Metternich to Ottenfels, Vienna, 1 June 1830, HHStA, StA, Türkei VIII, 2; Adelburg to Stürmer, Pera, 17 Oct. 1834, attached to Stürmer to Metternich, Büyükdere, 14 Oct. 1835, HHStA, StA, Türkei VIII, 7.
[64] Lützow's note to the Porte, 20 May 1821, attached to Lützow to Metternich, Constantinople, 25 May 1821, HHStA, StA, Türkei VI, 11.
[65] Metternich to Ottenfels, Vienna, 3 Feb., 18 March, 4 Sept. and 4 Dec. 1832, HHStA, StA, Türkei VIII, 24; Sauer, *Österreich und die Levante*, p. 264.

Commercial Convention in Balta Liman in 1838 were also enthusiastically led by Metternich although he finally decided not to accede to
it.[66]

A fitting example of Metternich's readiness to support Austrian
trade was his reaction to the commercial conditions in Syria in 1836,
at that time under Mohammed Ali's administration. Syria was not the
most important destination of the Austrian merchants and although
they started to be more active in this part of the Ottoman Empire in
the early 1830s and in 1835 their 76 ships visiting the Syrian ports
represented the second place among the European countries, behind
387 Greek ships but ahead of 65 British, 59 Sardinian and 26 French
ships, their activities decreased later in the decade; the number of
their ships in Syrian ports decreased four times from 1835 to 1838
and Austria also significantly fell behind Great Britain and France
in the value of the exchanged goods.[67] In 1836, however, Metternich
exerted great effort in relation to the Syrian silk trade, which was
important for Austria where the government had supported the production of silk goods since the 18th century; the importance of the
Viennese industry in silk products was clearly evident from the fact
that in the factories particularly concentrated around Vienna steam
engines had been widely installed by 1840.[68] Syria under Mohammed
Ali's leadership had originally held a monopoly on silk production,
and this monopoly had then been transferred *de facto* to the British
who managed to obtain its abolition by Mahmud II's decree on 24 December 1835. The problem for Austria lay in the fact that the removal
of this monopoly only applied to the British and this led to a situation
where they were able to hold an economic advantage over other Europeans since the latter were still subject to Mohammed Ali's monopoly.
From the Austrian point of view, the monopoly in the silk trade was
not actually abolished but only transferred to the British, who were

---

[66] Metternich to Stürmer, Vienna, 27 Nov. and 11 Dec. 1838, 15 and 29 Jan., 5,
12 and 19 Feb., 5 and 19 March, 23 April, 7 May, 11 and 25 June, 30 July and
6 Aug. 1839, HHStA, StA, Türkei VIII, 24; Puryear, *International Economics*,
p. 140.
[67] A. von Laurin, *Syrien, Tharsus und Adana in Junius 1836*, attached to Stürmer
to Metternich, Büyükdere, 21 Sept. 1836, HHStA, StA, Türkei VI, 65; Angerlehner,
p. 124; Owen, p. 96.
[68] J. Blum, "Transportation and Industry in Austria, 1815–1848," *JMH* 15, 1943,
1, p. 34.

not only able to buy this commodity for a considerably lower price than other nations but also introduced improved techniques for spinning. As a result of this, British manufacturers were able to produce silk fabric over 30 percent more cheaply than their counterparts in, for example, Austrian Lombardy. Metternich intervened without hesitation in mid 1836 and his argument focused on the Austrian right to be treated as the most privileged nation trading with the whole of the Ottoman Empire. Having established this line of argument, he successfully fought for the right of Austrians to enjoy the same favourable conditions as the citizens of other countries and was able to obtain from the sultan on 17 August 1836 the same advantages for Austrian merchants which were already enjoyed by the British. What is an even more interesting aspect of this intervention is Metternich's attempt to obtain France's support, warning its government of a potential death-blow to the Lyons industry if the issue of the British monopoly were not addressed. Although the French cabinet ignored the warning and decided not to cooperate with Austria in this affair, Metternich's desire to win its support, together with the reports of foreign diplomats residing in Vienna, clearly prove the considerable importance that he paid to this affair.[69]

---

[69] Metternich to Apponyi, Vienna, 5 July 1836, HHStA, StA, Frankreich 303; Metternich to Stürmer, Vienna, 12 July and 9 Aug. 1836, HHStA, StA, Türkei VIII, 9; Mahmud II's firman to Mohammed Ali, 24 Dec. 1835, attached to Laurin to Stürmer, Alexandria, 20 Jan. 1836, HHStA, StA, Ägypten 1; Mahmud II's firman to Mohammed Ali, 11 Aug. 1836, attached to Stürmer to Metternich, Büyükdere, 17 Aug. 1836, HHStA, StA, Türkei VI, 65; Apponyi to Metternich, Paris, 26 July 1836, HHStA, StA, Frankreich 300; Sainte-Aulaire to Broglie, Vienna, 16 June 1836, AMAE, CP, Autriche 423; Roussin to Broglie, Therapia, 10 Jan. 1836, AMAE, CP, Turquie 272; Tatishchev to Nesselrode, Vienna, 17 June 1836, AVPRI, fond 133, Kantselariia, opis 469, 1836/216; Maltzan to Frederick William III, Vienna, 16 June 1836, GStA PK, HA III, MdA I, 6027; Königsmarck to Frederick William III, Büyükdere, 2 Aug. 1836, GStA PK, HA III, MdA I, 7278.

Metternich's Regard for Austrian Commercial Interests from the Example of his Behaviour towards Mohammed Ali before and during the First Turko-Egyptian War

It is possible to conclude that Austria's economic interests in the Near East were significant and that Metternich not only was aware of their existence but also supported them. What still remains to be answered is whether this perspective ever influenced his conduct of predominantly diplomatic affairs. The answer can be found in his attitude towards the first war between Mahmud II and Mohammed Ali, the so-called First Mohammed Ali Crisis, in the early 1830s. However, for a full understanding of Metternich's attitude it is necessary to sketch in brief earlier Austro-Egyptian relations. Before the outbreak of the Greek insurrection, Metternich regarded Mohammed Ali as the most questionable governor that the Porte could install in Egypt, and Count Lützow was warned against the pasha's alleged disloyalty and capriciousness in June 1818: "The present Egyptian governor could really be dangerous to the interests of the Porte. After getting rid of the former rulers of this wealthy province, the so-called Mamluks, by means of a bloody putsch several years ago, he skilfully managed to take advantage of religious unrest among the Wahhabis in Arabia in order to increase his own power through the seizure of this beautiful strip of land at their expense under the brilliant pretext of liberating the holy pilgrimage sites of Mecca and Medina from their yoke. Furthermore, not being satisfied with this success he has placed in Italy, Switzerland, France, and Sweden his own agents, who tirelessly attempt not only to hire artists and craftsmen of whatsoever origin but also to buy ships, cannons, and other military equipment. At the same time, he constantly strives to appropriate increasingly more of the profitable business of his province, and even though he still pretends to be the faithful and loyal subject of the Porte, it seems obvious that his effort is concentrated upon establishing an independent existence."[70] This distrust caused the Viennese cabinet to maintain a restrained attitude towards Mohammed Ali, who, from the end of the Napoleonic Wars, wanted to intensify economic relations with Austria. Consequently,

---

[70] Sauer, *Österreich und die Levante*, p. 94.

when Mohammed Ali wanted to buy some weapons in Austria in the early 1820s, the government refused to permit this trade because it suspected Mohammed Ali of wanting to use the weapons against the sultan.[71]

Mohammed Ali's loyalty to the sultan during the Greek insurrection somewhat changed Austria's attitude and led to its consent to the sale of weapons to the Egyptian governor, but since the French and British had not hesitated to meet Mohammed Ali's requests and sell him the weapons earlier in the 1820s, there was no more interest on the part of the Egyptian pasha.[72] The only significant purchase concerned the construction of an Egyptian frigate in Venice, but although it was completed in mid 1827, technical problems and the international situation caused by the trilateral intervention in the Greek Question significantly postponed its delivery to Mohammed Ali. This most probably saved it from destruction in Navarino Bay,[73] which facilitated Metternich's reply to Mohammed Ali's anger caused by this delay: "I do not have much trouble in offering a response. Our rejoinder is in Navarino."[74] Nevertheless, this laconic remark in no way characterises Metternich's strong conviction that Mohammed Ali deserved "more careful consideration"[75] due to Austria's extensive economic interests in Egypt. This attitude is clearly evident from the chancellor's reaction to the complaints made by two Austrian merchants of alleged non-payment from the pasha for delivered goods. When Francis I asked Metternich in 1828 whether Austria should not support them by diplomatic means, even by confiscation of Egyptian property in Austria, he obtained this decisively disapproving answer: "The case in question is not about a financial matter between two private citizens whereby common law could serve as a measure and manual but about a demand of Austrian subjects to the governor of a

---

[71] Ibid., pp. 93–95; D. McEwan, *Habsburg als Schutzmacht der Katholiken in Ägypten: Verfassung der Studie über das österreichische Kirchenprotektorat von seinen Anfängen bis zu seiner Abschaffung im Jahre 1914*, Kairo, Wiesbaden 1982, p. 70; Gürbüz, pp. 275–279.

[72] Ottenfels to Metternich, Constantinople, 24 Dec. 1824, HHStA, StA, Türkei VI, 21; Sauer, *Österreich und die Levante*, p. 94.

[73] Metternich to Esterházy, Vienna, 31 Dec. 1827, HHStA, StA, England 179; G. Durand-Viel, *Les campagnes navales de Mohammed Aly et d'Ibrahim*, II, Paris 1935, pp. 439–440; Sauer, *Österreich und die Levante*, p. 245.

[74] Metternich to Werner, Vienna, 16 Nov. 1827, HHStA, StK, Preussen, 125.

[75] Metternich to Francis I, Vienna, 24 April 1828, HHStA, StK, Vorträge 253.

friendly independent state, and indeed a man, who, although the vassal of the Ottoman Porte, still possesses enough authority and power himself to be able to act according to his own opinions, especially in cases of local administration, and precisely for this reason to demand a certain degree of personal consideration and tact. Furthermore, the country represented by Mohammed Ali Pasha is rich in the most valuable natural resources and affords an unlimited number of resources to exchange for the products of the Austrian Empire, which, moreover, because of its geographic location is advantageously situated to consider trade with Egypt as one of its most profitable sources of income. These simple observations should be enough to prove that any violent coercive measures against the property of the viceroy in this country are out of the question without costing the court here the most delicate compromises and even exposing Austria's trade with Egypt in general to the most obvious danger."[76]

The good relationship between Austria and Egypt on the turn of the 1820s manifested itself in the exchange of gifts. With Mohammed Ali's donation of a giraffe to Francis I in 1828, Austria became an object of the pasha's famous "giraffe policy," when Ali sent these animals to France, Great Britain and Constantinople as well, and it must be said that this animal, whose transportation Metternich had to personally supervise from his cabinet at the Chancellery, won great popularity in Vienna which reached a real giraffe-mania manifesting itself in food, clothing, jewellery, hairstyles, music and perfumery. Nevertheless, when the animal died in June 1829 despite the attentive care given to it, Mohammed Ali's offer to send another one was politely refused because just the upkeep of the first one in Schönbrunn had cost an incredible 20,000 gulden.[77] One must also add considerable expenses for the presents which Metternich proposed the emperor send the pasha in return for the animal, like 300 bottles of Tokaji and particularly manufactured goods from Austrian factories serving not only as presents but also as promotion of Austrian industry. Gifts were also

---

[76] Metternich to Francis I, Vienna, 9 March 1828, HHStA, StK, Vorträge 253.

[77] Metternich to Francis I, Vienna, 4 Aug. 1829, HHStA, StK, Vorträge 259; Metternich to Francis I, Vienna, 31 Dec. 1829, HHStA, StK, Vorträge 260; Guilleminot to Molé, Constantinople, 11 Nov. 1830, AMAE, CP, Turquie 261; C. Riedl-Dorn, "Tiere auf weiter Fahrt: Expeditionen für Tiergarten und Museum," M. G. Ash, L. Dittrich (eds.), *Menagerie des Kaisers – Zoo der Wiener: 250 Jahre Tiergarten Schönbrunn*, Wien 2002, pp. 353–358; Gaultier-Kurhan, p. 133.

exchanged between Metternich and Mohammed Ali. The former sent several hundred bottles of wine from his domain in Johannisberg, and the latter reciprocated with two Arabian horses, two cashmere scarves, Indian cloth interlaced with gold and mocha coffee.[78]

Despite these ostentatious manifestations of mutual goodwill, doubts about Mohammed Ali's loyalty to the sultan never entirely disappeared but were definitely reduced during the 1820s. It is true that the Austrian consul general in Alexandria after August 1826, Joseph von Acerbi, strongly disliked the pasha and suspected him of various disloyal designs, but Metternich and Ottenfels were placated with Mohammed Ali's declarations of fidelity and trusted him, or they were at least satisfied with his inaction. Consequently, Metternich ordered Acerbi to be on friendly terms with the pasha and meet his wishes whenever it was possible. Mohammed Ali continued to enjoy Metternich's confidence even after the French-Egyptian negotiations on the Algerian conquest as the chancellor did not attribute the initiative to him. However, the prince was not blind, and the news of military preparations in Egypt during 1831 made him believe in November that Mohammed Ali would invade Syria, which was a correct judgement at an appropriate time because in the same month the pasha sent his troops to the north, thereby unleashing a crisis within the Ottoman Empire which was to have serious after-effects in the Levant as well as in the West.[79]

Ottenfels could not understand why the pasha had chosen to conduct his offensive at a moment when Mahmud II, having defeated the rebellious pashas of Baghdad and Scutari earlier in the same year,

---

[78] Acerbi to Metternich, Alexandria, 2 Jan. 1828, attached to Metternich to Francis I, Vienna, 24 April 1828, HHStA, StK, Vorträge 253; Acerbi to Metternich, Trieste, 13 Nov. 1830, NA, RAM-AC 12, 2.

[79] Metternich to Ottenfels, Vienna, 19 June 1827, HHStA, StA, Türkei VII, 34; Metternich to Ottenfels, Vienna, 18 Nov. 1831, HHStA, StA, Türkei VIII, 4; Metternich to Ottenfels, Vienna, 18 July 1830, Ottenfels to Metternich, Constantinople, 25 April, 14 May and 12 July 1831, HHStA, StA, Türkei VI, 51; Ottenfels to Metternich, Constantinople, 25 Nov. and 25 Dec. 1828, HHStA, StA, Türkei VI, 34; Ottenfels to Metternich, Constantinople, 25 May 1829, HHStA, StA, Türkei VI, 37; Ottenfels to Metternich, Constantinople, 10 Dec. 1829, HHStA, StA, Türkei VI, 38; Ottenfels to Metternich, Constantinople, 25 June, 16 Aug. and 10 Sept. 1830, HHStA, StA, Türkei VI, 50; Tatishchev to Nesselrode, Vienna, 28 Feb. 1828, AVPRI, fond 133, Kantselariia, opis 468, 11877; Maltzan to Frederick William III, Vienna, 19 July 1830, GStA PK, HA III, MdA I, 6014.

would be able to concentrate all his forces against him. In fact, Mohammed Ali had longed to annex Syria to his Egyptian domain for many years. Its strategic location and natural and human resources would considerably enhance his power. Since Mahmud II had given him only Crete in return for his assistance in the fight against the Greeks, the pasha regarded this reward as entirely insufficient and he coveted Syria, but without success. The sultan's refusal to give him Syria gave him no alternative but to either reconcile himself to the situation or take Syria by force, the latter option corresponding to his ambition to increase his own prestige and assure his heritage for his descendants. Therefore, he prepared intensively for an incursion in this area but was unable to take advantage of Mahmud II's difficulties with the pashas of Baghdad and Scutari because in the summer of 1831 a major cholera epidemic occurred in Egypt; the beginning of the campaign therefore had to be postponed for several months. Mahmud II refused to collude with his governor's steps and condemned him as a traitor, deposed him and sent an army to Syria in the spring of the following year. However, the Ottoman forces proved to be much less fighting-fit than those of Egypt, which were under Ibrahim Pasha's skilled command again. Ibrahim captured Acre in late May 1832 and managed to rout the Ottoman troops in two battles in July. It was not the enemy but his father who prevented further advances; Mohammed Ali hesitated in taking full advantage of these victories for fear that a march against Constantinople could provoke an intervention by the European Powers in the conflict. He wanted to achieve his objectives through negotiation and for this reason an unannounced suspension of hostilities occurred in the Ottoman Empire in August 1832.[80]

The fact that the Egyptian soldiers stopped far from the capital undoubtedly contributed to the limited attention paid by the Great Powers to the conflict, even after the Ottoman July defeats; Austria

---

[80] Rossetti to Ottenfels, Alexandria, 29 March 1831, Ottenfels to Metternich, Constantinople, 10 and 28 June 1831, HHStA, StA, Türkei VI, 52; Ottenfels to Metternich, Constantinople, 25 Oct. and 25 Nov. 1831, HHStA, StA, Türkei VI, 53; Ottenfels to Metternich, Constantinople, 10 May 1832, and attached the Porte's note to all foreign missions in Constantinople, 4 May 1832, HHStA, StA, Türkei VI, 54; M. H. Kutluoğlu, *The Egyptian Question (1831–1841): The Expansionist Policy of Mehmed Ali Paşa in Syria and Asia Minor and the Reaction of the Sublime Porte*, Istanbul 1998, pp. 56–59; Dodwell, pp. 111–112; Fahmy, *All the Pasha's Men*, pp. 62–65; Puryear, *France*, p. 151.

was no exception. This lack of concern was brought about for two reasons. First, the Austrian diplomats residing in the Near East entirely underestimated the true situation. Ottenfels seemed to believe the assurances of the Ottoman dignitaries in Constantinople in relation to the superiority of the sultan's armed forces, and he did not, therefore, hesitate to advise a prompt showdown with the rebellious vassal in the first months of the crisis. His erroneous judgement was strengthened not only by Ibrahim Pasha's long siege of Acre but also by Acerbi's reports concerning Mohammed Ali's financial problems and the widespread discontent of the inhabitants, both inevitably leading to an imminent collapse of his rule. Acerbi even claimed that the offensive against Syria was an act of mere plunder, undertaken in order to acquire the treasure stored in Acre, a sum, allegedly, of between 20 and 30 million taler.[81] Following on from this news, Ottenfels wrote to Vienna on 10 April 1832 that regarding "the extreme misery and absolute impoverishment to which Mohammed Ali has reduced Egypt by his faulty system of administration and his ruinous measures, one can no longer be uncertain of the final outcome of the fight that he has so imprudently begun."[82] However, all of the information provided by Acerbi, and mentioned above, was entirely incorrect, as was Ottenfels' confidence in Ottoman superiority. Ottenfels was finally forced to admit to his erroneous assessment of the situation when he wrote on 10 August 1832: "It is evident today that the Divan was totally incorrect in its presumption concerning the importance and consistency of Mohammed Ali's enterprise, and we have shared in its mistake in this respect owing to the intelligence we received about the viceroy describing him as reduced to his last taler and to his last man."[83] Nevertheless, even the successes of the Egyptian armed forces caused no change in Austrian passivity because, and this is the second reason for

---

[81] Acerbi to Metternich, Alexandria, 4 Nov. 1831, Ottenfels to Metternich, Constantinople, 16 Dec. 1831, HHStA, StA, Türkei VI, 53; Acerbi to Metternich, Alexandria, 30 April and 6 July 1832, Ottenfels to Metternich, Constantinople, 25 Feb., 26 March, 10 and 25 April, 25 May 1832, HHStA, StA, Türkei VI, 54; Brassier to Frederick William III, Büyükdere, 25 Aug. 1832, GStA PK, HA III, MdA I, 7271; A. J. Rustum, *The Royal Archives of Egypt and the Origins of the Egyptian Expedition to Syria 1831–1841*, Beirut 1936, p. 28.

[82] Ottenfels to Metternich, Constantinople, 10 April 1832, HHStA, StA, Türkei VI, 53.

[83] Ottenfels to Metternich, Constantinople, 10 Aug. 1832, HHStA, StA, Türkei VI, 55.

its lack of interest, as from the beginning of the Turko-Egyptian rupture, Metternich was entirely absorbed with other affairs in Europe,
which he regarded as being of greater importance. In particular he was
concerned with the Belgian Question and, from February 1832, with
the French occupation of Ancona, an event significantly worsening
the relations between France and Austria. Consequently, everything
Metternich undertook in connection with the Syrian crisis until the
late autumn of the same year was an expression of his wish that the
conflict should remain an internal affair of the empire and would soon
be resolved in favour of the legitimate ruler.[84]

The simple desire for his victory was less than Mahmud II actually wanted to obtain from Austria. In the spring of 1832, he pursued
a diplomatic offensive in Europe in an attempt to isolate his disobe-
dient Egyptian vassal. In Vienna, however, his appeals received only
a limited response. Metternich and Francis I naturally sided with him
against Mohammed Ali, whose questionable loyalty they denounced as
a threat to the existing legitimate order and the stability created at the
Congress of Vienna. Moreover, Metternich declared himself opposed
to Mohammed Ali's attempt to conquer Syria, not only for geopolitical
but also for economic reasons: "The immediate and inevitable consequence of the annexation of Syria to Mohammed Ali's domain would
be, furthermore, the introduction of this system of monopoly that
would serve, it is true, to promptly fill the treasuries of the viceroy
but which would, on the other hand, exhaust and drain all of the
country's resources in the long term. The disastrous effects of this
ruinous system have already been severely felt in Egypt as much by
the producers as by foreign trade."[85]

There was one crucial reason precluding Austria's extremely unfriendly behaviour towards Mohammed Ali or even any military intervention, which, it is true, was never seriously considered as an option
in Vienna during the first Turko-Egyptian war: the extensive activities
of Austrian merchants in Egypt. With respect to their interests and
properties in this North African province, the Chancellery could not

[84] Metternich to Ottenfels, Vienna, 18 Dec. 1831, HHStA, StA, Türkei VI, 53;
Metternich to Ottenfels, Vienna, 18 Feb. 1832, HHStA, StA, Türkei VI, 56; Metternich to Neumann, Vienna, 8 April 1832, HHStA, StA, England 199; Sauer,
Österreich und die Levante, p. 274; Puryear, *France*, p. 174.
[85] Metternich to Neumann, Vienna, 17 Oct. 1832, HHStA, StA, England 199.

satisfy the requests of the Porte regarding the prohibition of Austrian ships from entering Egyptian ports or the closing of those which were part of Austrian territory to the Egyptian trade. Neither could the Austrians be prevented from trading with Mohammed Ali. In addition, Austrian vessels were not offered to the sultan in order to help in the transportation of his military equipment to Syria, largely through fear of possible losses suffered at the hands of Egyptian men-o'-war even though none of the Austrian authorities actually forbade Austrian captains from entering Mohammed Ali's service for the same purpose. Another demand raised by Jean Mavroyéni relating to the confiscation of a war brig under construction in a shipyard in Trieste for the Egyptian governor was also rejected. Ottenfels even prevented the publication of the Viennese cabinet's opinions on the conflict in the Ottoman official newspaper, the *Moniteur Ottoman*, so as not to provoke Mohammed Ali's anger against Austrian commerce and navigation. The same leniency towards the pasha was also witnessed in the case of the internment of two Austrian merchant vessels which had tried to sail into a port subject to the Egyptian blockade, a measure which, naturally, was not recognised by the Austrian government. Acerbi raised a protest against their seizure and demanded their immediate release. However, the interested offices in Vienna did not support the complaint, having regard for the trading relationship with Egypt. The affair finally ended peacefully when both ships were set free.[86]

Austrian caution was symptomatic of the whole crisis. Neither Metternich nor Ottenfels was in sympathy with grandiose but ineffective gestures, such as the recall of the Russian consul general in Egypt, Lavison, in the late summer of 1832, undertaken as a means of demonstrating the displeasure of Nicholas I at Mohammed Ali's behaviour. Nevertheless, it was a cheap sacrifice considering Russia's negligible commercial interests in this province; when Lavison's withdrawal was followed by the prohibition of Russian merchants from conducting trade with the pasha, only a few of the tsar's subjects suffered from the measure. For Austria similar steps were entirely

---

[86] Ottenfels to Metternich, Constantinople, 25 Jan., 10 May and 10 Sept. 1832, HHStA, StA, Türkei VI, 54; Acerbi to Ottenfels, Alexandria, 6 July 1832, HHStA, StA, Türkei VI, 55; Brassier to Frederick William III, Büyükdere, 11 May 1832, GStA PK, HA III, MdA I, 7271; Sauer, *Österreich und die Levante*, pp. 280–284.

impracticable; when Acerbi declared his wish to imitate the Russian example and leave Alexandria, Ottenfels' and Metternich's answers were strictly negative. The former wrote to Acerbi "that the position of Austria towards Egypt, together with the Porte, is very different; that our commercial relations and maritime trading with Egypt are of immense importance and that we cannot interrupt them without causing the utmost damage to our industry and our financial interests; that the number of our subjects and the value of their capital in Egypt are such that we could expose them to very serious risks with the withdrawal of our consulate; that the presence of a commercial agent is in no way incompatible with the state of rebellion because the agents of the European Powers continue to reside and discharge their functions in the countries that find themselves at war; that our court is, in any case, under less pressure to recall its consulates from Egypt because the Divan itself has not in any way made such a demand."[87] Metternich even advocated the decision not to recall Acerbi in opposition to Francis I, who was inclined to follow the tsar's decision. However, the chancellor saw no reason for such a move, and he wrote to the emperor in late August 1832: "Finally, concerning Egypt, Austria's relations with this province are of a significantly different nature than those of Russia. Russia's commercial trade with Egypt is insignificant; it can only suffer minimally from a temporary interruption. The case for the Austrian merchant navy is entirely different. Our commercial ships visiting Egyptian ports annually number several hundred and generally exceed half of the total number of all other nations. The capital value of the ships and their cargo is incalculable. In addition to this, without exception, all the valuable products of Egypt are in the hands of the viceroy, he is their only seller, and he always arranges payment to himself of considerable sums of money as advance payments for the delivery of goods. These simple observations suffice for estimating the damage that the suspension of our commercial relations with the province in question would necessarily inflict upon us. Trieste, Venice, Fiume would be brought to ruin by such a measure and the repercussions of this blow on the commercial

---

[87] Ottenfels to Metternich, Constantinople, 25 July 1832, HHStA, StA, Türkei VI, 54.

state of our monarchy in general would have the most detrimental consequences."[88] Unsurprisingly, Acerbi finally remained in Egypt.[89]

Metternich even went as far as instructing Acerbi, who manifested all too obviously his opposition to Mohammed Ali's actions, to desist from making threats in his disapproving statements because the Austrian Empire had no means of realising them and, even if it had kept such threats at its disposal, they could not be used because of the danger posed with regard to its business affairs with Egypt. As the chancellor wrote to Ottenfels in late 1832, the declarations of Austrian agents in the Levant had to simultaneously conform to conservative principles and to economic interests; in other words, it was necessary to find a middle course between two extremes, "imprudent threats and absolute silence."[90] No wonder that the maximum degree of Austrian anti-Egyptian diplomacy was reflected in a formal but not impolite condemnation of the rebellion in the name of the emperor in Alexandria, the refusal to issue exit permits for unreliable persons suspected of trying to sail from Dalmatia to Egypt, the internment of an Egyptian colonel by a Dalmatian governorate and the transmission of valuable information on the strength of the Egyptian army to the Porte, all of which were pitifully limited measures given the prevailing conditions.[91]

* * *

The minister plenipotentiary of the United States in Vienna, Henry Muhlenberg, later claimed after a year-long stay in Vienna that Metternich was "no great friend to anything like a free system of Commer-

---

[88] Metternich to Francis I, Baden, 30 Aug. 1832, HHStA, StK, Vorträge 268.

[89] Ottenfels to Metternich, Constantinople, 25 Sept. 1832, HHStA, StA, Türkei VI, 55; Brassier to Frederick William III, Büyükdere, 7 Aug. 1832, GStA PK, HA III, MdA I, 7271; Schiemann, III, p. 210.

[90] Metternich to Ottenfels, Vienna, 15 Dec. 1832, HHStA, StA, Türkei VI, 56.

[91] Ottenfels to Metternich, Constantinople, 10 Dec. 1831, HHStA, StA, Türkei VI, 53; Ottenfels to Metternich, Constantinople, 25 April 1832, HHStA, StA, Türkei VI, 54; Ottenfels to Metternich, Constantinople, 8 Jan. 1833, Ottenfels to Acerbi, Constantinople, 6 Jan. 1833, HHStA, StA, Türkei VI, 56; Maltzan to Frederick William III, Vienna, 14 and 23 Jan. 1833, GStA PK, HA III, MA I, 6021; Sauer, *Österreich und die Levante*, p. 280.

cial [*sic*] intercourse. Indeed, commerce does not seem ever to have
engaged, or at present to engage much of his attention. There are
other and what are deemed here more important concerns to take up
his time. In those he evidently delights. They are his strong points.
Giving but a casual glance at commerce, as a minor affair, he is ei-
ther not a master of the subject or does not wish to be troubled by it.
Upon the whole, though he does not say so, I would set him down
as opposed to changes in the present system unless the absolute necessity of change should become so evident and be so loudly called
for as to render it irresistible."[92] Ronald E. Coons disagreed with
such an opinion: "Judged on the basis of Metternich's frequent attempts to further the interests of the Steam Navigation Company of
the Austrian Lloyd, Muhlenberg's remarks are both misleading and
unfair. Contrary to the impression the American diplomat conveyed
to his superiors in Washington, Metternich in fact gave far more than
merely a casual glance at economic matters."[93] The information presented in this chapter entirely vindicates the opinion of the latter:
it is evident that Austria's economic interests in the Near East were
taken into account at the Chancellery in Vienna and that Metternich and his subordinates tried to create a good position for Austrian
merchants in the Ottoman dominions and did not hesitate to protect
their interests which, moreover, sometimes limited their freedom to
make decisions because any overtly hostile action against Mohammed
Ali could have resulted in the closure of the Egyptian ports and the
exposure to danger of the properties belonging to Austrians living in
the land on the Nile: in both cases the losses to Francis I's subjects
would have been enormous. The degree of respect which Metternich
had for them is evident from his strict refusal to recall the Austrian
consul general and his cautious behaviour towards the pasha during
the whole crisis.

It is also necessary to agree with Coons' second opinion that for
Metternich the political interests were more important and they determined his Near Eastern policy.[94] Metternich definitely subordinated
economic considerations to political ones, which were manifested in
two levels. First, he was unwilling to support Austrian trade in the

---

[92] Coons, *Steamships*, p. 133.
[93] Ibid.
[94] Ibid., p. 134.

Near East unreservedly and thus provoke a commercial-political conflict. He was never willing to allow commercial considerations to impair the quality of relations between countries; in other words he did not wish to unleash the dangers of international tension purely on the grounds of economic considerations. His support of Austrian economic interests thus had certain limits and he saw no reason why relations between countries needed to deteriorate owing to commercial competition, the Near East region included. He saw it as his duty to protect the already existing treaties with the Sublime Porte, which offered advantages to Austrian merchants in the Ottoman territories. He also sought to obtain better conditions for them whenever possible and defend them against the arbitrariness of Ottoman officials, but he was in no way inclined to turn the Levant into a theatre of commercial war between the European countries. Vernon John Puryear is absolutely right when claiming that Metternich was willing to assist Austrian commercial development, but he was not an adherent of an aggressive commercial policy.[95] Second, when it was necessary for Metternich to make a decision between political and economic interests, he always chose the former, as he did during the Second Mohammed Ali Crisis in 1840 when, after a lengthy hesitation, he actively supported a British-Ottoman military intervention in Syria against the Egyptian forces. At that time, however, the political importance of the crisis in the Near East by far exceeded the economic interests of the Austrian Empire in Egypt. Consequently, Metternich had more regard for political than economic interests. Nevertheless, this does not change the fact that he did not ignore the latter in the Ottoman Empire and Austria's economic interests had a notable degree of importance in the design and execution of his Near Eastern policy.

Metternich's desire to maintain an untroubled trading situation abroad for Austrian merchants was one of the reasons why he always desired to maintain tranquillity in the Levant. At the end of 1832, this was a wish unlikely to be fulfilled because the conflict between the sultan and his Egyptian pasha was in no way settled. Even worse, since Mahmud II did not want to surrender Syria to Mohammed Ali, the latter was so embittered by the failure of his offer for a peace settlement that he decided to renew the campaign. Recent history was repeated once again: Ibrahim Pasha routed the sultan's last army at

---

[95] Puryear, "Odessa," p. 212.

Konya on 21 December 1832 and obtained not only control over Asia
Minor but also an open road to Constantinople, protected only by the
waters of the Bosphorus and an extraordinary quantity of snow. Neither of these natural bulwarks nor the Ottomans were the cause of a
cessation of hostilities, but Mohammed Ali decided to halt his advance
again for fear of the hostile reaction of the Great Powers; not weapons
but talks were to solve the dispute.[96] At that moment, foreign assistance was finally offered to Mahmud II, not by Austria, Great Britain
or France, but by Russia, which surprised a considerable number of
contemporaries although in no way did it surprise Metternich.

---

[96] Ottenfels to Metternich, Constantinople, 25 Aug., 25 Oct., 27 and 31 Dec. 1832,
HHStA, StA, Türkei VI, 55; Kutluoğlu, pp. 78–82.

15

Russia and France from the Treaty of Adrianople to the Settlement of the First Mohammed Ali Crisis

A widespread opinion exists that it was the July Revolution which opened the way to the reconciliation between the Austrian Empire and Russia, whose relations had significantly deteriorated due to the Near Eastern affairs in the previous years. Nevertheless, when at the end of July 1830 revolutionaries took to the streets of Paris, the reconciliation between Austria and Russia was already in progress. This process was facilitated by Russia's more friendly policy towards the Ottoman Empire after the end of war in September 1829. It was not Russia but France whose steps Metternich strongly disliked in the early 1830s, not only in the West but also in the East, and in both areas he diplomatically opposed the designs of the French government as well as those of the French people. His confidence in Russia's policy and disapproval of the French activities were fully revealed during the later phase of the First Mohammed Ali Crisis.

Austro-Russian Rapprochement

As explained earlier in the book, Metternich had decided to improve the relations between Austria and Russia in early 1829, but the restoration of their earlier cordiality was impossible until the end of the Russo-Ottoman war. When this happened in Adrianople on 14 September 1829, the process could start in full, and it was very important for Metternich that it would be met with success because his primary goal in the following months was the restoration of unity and harmony between the European Powers, which, of course, could not be achieved without first improving relations with Russia. He also naturally needed the tsar's support for the fight against liberalism and nationalism, and he did not overlook France's effort to obtain an alliance with Russia during 1829, which would have been extremely dangerous for Austria if it had come into being.[1]

The rapprochement was made considerably easier for Austria by a key event that occurred in St Petersburg two days after the signature of the Treaty of Adrianople: members of a special committee, which was entrusted by Nicholas I to decide upon the further direction of the relations with the "sick man on the Bosphorus," unanimously came to the conclusion that the preservation and not the destruction of the Ottoman Empire was in accordance with Russian interests. The advantages of maintaining the Ottoman presence in Europe were greater than any eventual territorial gains at its expense, especially if these gains were rather uncertain because any Russian expansion to the south would certainly meet with the hostile coalition of Austria, France and Great Britain. The financially weak Russian Empire would not be able to resist such a coalition and assert all its territorial demands. Moreover, the committee concluded that other members of the diplomatic concert would also request their own share in the spoils and Russia, almost certainly, would have three powerful neighbours on its southern frontier instead of one weak one that posed no threat and that enabled Russian dominance in the Black Sea where the tsar's fleet was protected from the stronger navies of the two Maritime Powers. The committee members' decision did not signify any turning point in Russia's Near Eastern policy because after 1815 the tsars did not strive for the destruction of the Ottoman Empire, but it confirmed the correctness of the vision of the Russian statesman and Alexander I's close aide, Viktor Pavlovich Kochubey, of the "weak neighbour policy" from 1802, which now became official policy after Nicholas I accepted the counsel of his advisers and decided to pre-

---

[1] Metternich to Apponyi, Vienna, 28 Oct. and 16 Dec. 1829, HHStA, StA, Frankreich 271; Metternich to Apponyi, Vienna, 25 Feb. 1830, HHStA, StA, Frankreich 276; Metternich to Esterházy, Vienna, 12 and 25 Feb. 1830, HHStA, StA, England 191; Metternich to Ficquelmont, Vienna, 11 Feb. 1830, HHStA, StA, Russland III, 90; Metternich to Trauttmannsdorff, Vienna, 2 March 1830, HHStA, StK, Preussen 137; Metternich to Ottenfels, 10 Sept. 1829, HDA, 750, OO 38; Cowley to Aberdeen, Vienna, 8 and 24 Nov., 25 Dec. 1829, TNA, FO 120/104; Bullen, "France and Europe," p. 135.

vent the fall of the Ottoman Empire that could lead to war among European Powers.[2]

Although nothing indicates that Metternich knew about the secret decision of the special committee, shortly after the end of the war he arrived at the conviction that Nicholas I did not desire another war and the partition of Ottoman territories. Already on 15 September 1829, Metternich wrote to Apponyi: "We believe that H[is] I[mperial] M[ajesty] does not aspire to the expulsion of the Ottoman power from Europe. Russia will not commit such a great mistake ... It will content itself with the benefit that it has already acquired: the structural weakening of its two neighbours in the Levant [the Ottoman Empire and Persia] and the advantage of becoming through certain concessions the sovereign arbiter of the Ottoman Empire's existence in Europe, which is much more important than the acquisition of some desert regions."[3] Nesselrode's and Nicholas I's words about the inextricable difficulties connected with an eventual expulsion of the Ottomans from the Continent and about Russia's desire to maintain the Ottoman Empire conveyed by Ficquelmont to Vienna in October 1829[4] contributed to Metternich's assumption expressed in the instructions to Esterházy: "The truth is that the Russian Emperor did not believe that the moment for the expulsion of the Ottoman power from European soil has arrived. Since then and until the date when this monarch adopts an alternative political system, he will have to be willing to conserve what he did not want to destroy. In this fact, my Prince, lies one of the guarantees of the prolonged existence of European Turkey."[5] In other instructions to Esterházy Metternich added: "It is not rare to see a conquering Power change its mode of conduct

[2] F. F. Martens, *Die russische Politik in der Orientfrage*, St. Petersburg 1877, p. 31; R. J. Kerner, "Russia's New Policy in the Near East after the Peace of Adrianople," *CHJ* 5, 1935–1937, 3, pp. 283–290; M. S. Anderson, "Russia and the Eastern Question, 1821–1841," A. Sked (ed.), *Europe's Balance of Power, 1815–1848*, London 1979, p. 87; M. Rendall, "Restraint or Self-Restraint of Russia: Nicholas I, the Treaty of Unkiar Skelessi, and the Vienna System, 1832–1841," *IHR* 24, 2002, 1, pp. 59–60; Bitis, *Russia*, pp. 358–361.

[3] Metternich to Apponyi, Vienna, 17 Sept. 1829, HHStA, StA, Frankreich 271.

[4] Though these statements of course resulted from the special committee's decision, it is necessary to emphasise the information mentioned above that the very existence of the committee and its resolution remained unknown to Ficquelmont and Metternich.

[5] Metternich to Esterházy, Vienna, 16 Dec. 1829, HHStA, StA, England 188.

towards a state which is a renowned rival when the same state has
no more chance for its existence than the option of subjugation. This
consideration, my Prince, is of utmost importance and worth noting
because from it will necessarily emerge the prospect of the more or less
future peaceful state of the Ottoman Empire, as well as that of the
more or less opposition of Russia to the establishment of a new state
of things in European Turkey."[6] The prince also well understood the
main difficulty which the tsar had to face should he want to destroy
the sultan's empire: "Russia alone can ruin the vast edifice, either by
undermining it silently or by an open attack; it has employed these
two means to reduce it to its current state but it does not want to go
farther for fear of complications the results of which it cannot foresee.
If it wanted to bring down the Ottoman Empire, it would only be with
the idea of a partition; from this moment, its situation is changing. It
no longer finds itself fighting one-to-one against a state considerably
weaker than itself; it is dealing first with Austria, then with England
and undoubtedly also with other Great Powers which will not allow
it [Russia] to dispose of such vast and fertile regions as it pleases."[7]
Until the summer of the following year, Metternich was completely
reassured by his certainty of Nicholas I's benign attitude towards the
Porte because the chancellor could not overlook the moderation in the
tsar's approach; the Russian monarch changed his policy towards the
Porte and was willing to moderate the severity of the conditions contained in the Treaty of Adrianople. The Austrian statesman rightly
regarded this more friendly behaviour as a sign of a turnaround.[8]

From the quoted texts in the previous paragraph, it is also evident that Metternich was not naive and correctly estimated that the
tsar's reversal had not resulted from any sympathetic attitude towards

---

[6] Metternich to Esterházy, Vienna, 24 Nov. 1829, HHStA, StA, England 188.
[7] Rayneval to Polignac, Vienna, 25 Jan. 1830, AMAE, CP, Autriche 412.
[8] Metternich to Esterházy, Vienna, 28 Oct. and 24 Nov. 1829, HHStA, StA,
England 188; Metternich to Esterházy, Vienna, 20 Jan. 1830, HHStA, StA, England
191; Metternich to Ottenfels, Vienna, 19 Dec. 1829, HHStA, StA, Türkei VI, 49;
Metternich to Ottenfels, Vienna, 18 March and 10 April 1830, HHStA, StA, Türkei
VI, 51; Metternich to Apponyi, 29 Jan. and 5 Feb. 1830, HHStA, StA, Frankreich
276; Metternich to Ficquelmont, Vienna, 22 May 1830, HHStA, StA, Russland
III, 90; Ottenfels to Metternich, Constantinople, 10 April, 10 May and 11 June
1830, HHStA, StA, Türkei VI, 50; Cowley to Aberdeen, Vienna, 9 Jan. and 7 Feb.
1830, TNA, FO 120/108; Rayneval to Polignac, Vienna, 25 Jan. 1830, AMAE, CP,
Autriche 412.

the sultan and his subjects but a pragmatic calculation: Russia had achieved everything in the Near East that it wanted to achieve and the existence of a weak neighbour under its influence was the best option at that moment. Despite the fact that Austria and Russia pursued the same goal, the preservation of the Ottoman Empire, for different reasons, Metternich was satisfied because this was the most that he could expect from Nicholas I. And since the chancellor was able to agree with the conditions of the Treaty of Adrianople and no other important difference in opinions existed between the two courts in Vienna and St Petersburg, he presumed in early 1830 the restoration of the cordial relations between the two Powers. To facilitate this, Ottenfels was instructed to express his goodwill to Count Ribeaupierre and special agent Count Alexej Fedorovic Orlov. For the same reason the internuncio also was to recommend to the Porte that it accept the request of Russia, Great Britain and France for the creation of an independent Greece.[9]

In the interest of the renewal of good relations with Russia, Metternich did not show his disconcertion with the Treaty of Adrianople in the presence of Tatishchev and did not come out with any opposition to any of its articles. Austrian official statements relating to the peace were also rather reserved. With respect to the accord existing between Berlin and St Petersburg, Metternich did not hesitate to assure Maltzan at the end of September 1829 that owing to the brilliant success of the tsar's forces, the peace conditions had to be regarded as moderate. The chancellor informed him with the same caution of Ottenfels' strong criticism of the peace conditions as being the opinions of one Austrian diplomat and not the entire Austrian cabinet. Emperor Francis I congratulated Nicholas I on the ending of the war without expressing his opinion of the Treaty. Tatishchev, who read Francis I's letter before its dispatch, noticed that no remark

---

[9]   Metternich to Esterházy, Vienna, 24 Nov. 1829, HHStA, StA, England 188; Metternich to Apponyi, Vienna, 13 Jan. 1830, HHStA, StA, Frankreich 276; Metternich to Ottenfels, Vienna, 21 Jan., 17 and 19 Feb., 3, 7 and 12 March, 17 April 1830, HHStA, StA, Türkei VI, 51; Ficquelmont to Metternich, St Petersburg, 19 Jan. 1830, HHStA, StA, Russland III, 89; Tatishchev to Nesselrode, Vienna, 26 Jan. and 20 March 1830, AVPRI, fond 133, Kantseliariia, opis 469, 1830/275; Cowley to Aberdeen, Vienna, 25 Feb. and 11 March 1830, TNA, FO 120/108; the record of the conversation between Metternich and Prokesch on 4 March 1830, Prokesch-Osten, *Aus den Tagebüchern*, p. 15.

about the tsar's moderation and generosity towards the Porte had been made and expressed his concern that this could be viewed with regret in St Petersburg. Metternich replied: "It is not necessary in a letter of mere congratulation upon the termination of the war to comment on the conditions of the peace, and I think you may be satisfied with our silence upon that text."[10] However, wanting to prevent anything that could worsen its position towards Russia, after this reproach the Viennese cabinet started to show more understanding for the tsar's alleged moderation. On 15 November 1829, during an audience with Tatishchev, Francis I concluded his praise of Nicholas I for not destroying the Ottoman Empire with these words: "Today there remains one concern left to us. It is that of our sincere understanding. To attain this we [Francis I and Nicholas I] do not have to do much. As the Russian Emperor trusts me as I trust him, we have no need of any other basis than that of the simplest confidence. On the day when Europe knows that the monarchs, and particularly Emperor Nicholas and I, are of the same opinion, these troublemakers will find their legs cut out from under their feet. Send these words to Your Master; they are the sincere expressions of my thoughts. You know by experience that I am unable to say what I do not think, and that I also think what I say."[11] On seeing the record of the emperor's statement as noted by the Russian ambassador, Metternich wrote to the latter: "I am entirely convinced that you have perfectly captured the words of the Emperor because I find in them nothing other than the arguments that H[is] I[mperial] M[ajesty] himself personally developed twenty times to me."[12] Tatishchev of course did not miss the point of Francis I's declaration and knew very well that Austria greatly desired the restoration of the union with Russia. It was also impossible to fail to understand it because the chancellor often openly talked about this desire.[13]

---

[10] Cowley to Aberdeen, Vienna, 17 Oct. 1829, TNA, FO 120/104.

[11] Tatishchev to Nesselrode, Vienna, 16 Nov. 1829, AVPRI, fond 133, Kantseliariia, opis 468, 11885.

[12] Metternich to Tatishchev, Vienna, 15 Nov. 1829, AVPRI, fond 133, Kantseliariia, opis 468, 11885.

[13] Ficquelmont to Metternich, St Petersburg, 28 Oct. 1829, HHStA, StA, Russland III, 86; Cowley to Aberdeen, Vienna, 4 Oct. and 8 Nov. 1829, TNA, FO 120/104; Schwebel to Polignac, Vienna, 14 Nov. 1829, AMAE, CP, Autriche 411; Tatishchev to Nesselrode, Vienna, 25 Sept., 6 Oct., 3 and 16 Nov. 1829, AVPRI, fond 133, Kantseliariia, opis 468, 11885; Tatishchev to Nesselrode, Vienna, 26 Jan. and

Metternich considered the reconciliation between Austria and Russia to be urgent, among other reasons, because of the worsening situation in France, where discontent with the regime of Charles X grew from day to day. He had been concerned about this for a long time and, together with Francis I, had been sending warnings about the situation in France to the tsar since early 1828. They both of course used this topic with the aim of diverting Nicholas I from war with the Ottoman Empire, but Metternich's correspondence proves that these warnings were not merely intended with one purpose in mind. Undoubtedly the same apprehensions contributed to the readiness of Russia for the close relations with Austria because Nicholas I shared Metternich's fear of revolution and the situation in France, and the support of conservatism was also the theme of his foreign as well as domestic policy. Moreover, the tsar had received worrisome news from Tatishchev about the good relations developing between Austria and Great Britain with a potential of a political alliance in late 1829. Metternich obviously supported this impression with the aim of persuading the tsar to improve Russia's relations with Austria.[14] When Ficquelmont reported that the suspicion of an Austro-British alliance disquieted the Russian cabinet and made it more inclined to a rapprochement with Austria, Metternich wrote in the margin: "Precisely!"[15]

---

10 Feb. 1830, AVPRI, fond 133, Kantseliariia, opis 469, 1830/275; Maltzan to Frederick William III, Vienna, 29 Sept. and 16 Oct. 1829, GStA PK, HA III, MdA I, 6013; Bray to Ludwig I of Bavaria, Vienna, 22 Oct. 1829, BHStA, MA, Wien 2402.

[14] Metternich to Trauttmannsdorff, Vienna, 22 June 1828, HHStA, StK, Preussen 129; Metternich to Trauttmannsdorff, Vienna, 27 April 1830, HHStA, StK, Preussen 137; Metternich to Esterházy, Linz, 21 Sept. 1829, HHStA, StA, England 188; Francis I to Nicholas I, Laxenburg, 24 May 1828, attached to Tatishchev to Nesselrode, Vienna, 25 May and 13 Sept. 1828, AVPRI, fond 133, Kantselariia, opis 468, 11879; Tatishchev to Nesselrode, Vienna, 7 Jan. and 26 Feb. 1829, AVPRI, fond 133, Kantseliariia, opis 468, 11881; Tatishchev to Nesselrode, Vienna, 18 Oct. and 25 Dec. 1829, AVPRI, fond 133, Kantseliariia, opis 468, 11885; Tatishchev to Nesselrode, Vienna, 17 March and 14 April 1830, AVPRI, fond 133, Kantseliariia, opis 469, 1830/275; Rayneval to Polignac, Vienna, 25 Jan. 1830, AMAE, CP, Autriche 412; Maltzan to Frederick William III, Vienna, 22 and 29 April 1829, GStA PK, HA III, MdA I, 6012; Maltzan to Frederick William III, Vienna, 24 April 1830, GStA PK, HA III, MdA I, 6015; Bray to Ludwig I of Bavaria, Vienna, 22 Oct. and 28 Nov. 1829, BHStA, MA, Wien 2402; Bray to Ludwig I of Bavaria, Vienna, 27 March and 18 May 1830, BHStA, MA, Wien 2403; Schiemann, II, p. 311.

In the spring of 1830, both Powers sharing identical views on the situation in Europe as well as in the Near East were thus on the verge of an entente, and this is proved, among other factors, by Nesselrode's shift in views. Still, in the summer of 1829, during an eight-day-long stay on the tsar's yacht, Nesselrode had been personally hostile towards Austria and he had not spoken a word to Ficquelmont. Now, in 1830, however, he was the driving force of the understanding with Vienna and decided to meet with Metternich in Carlsbad in August, a decision that had naturally been made long before the outbreak of the revolution in France. Consequently, periodic fights in the Parisian streets did not cause any reversal in the Austro-Russian relations, but rather, together with upheavals in other parts of the Continent, only accelerated the process initiated after the Peace of Adrianople, and the cordial relations and close cooperation between three conservative Powers, Austria, Russia and Prussia, were the logical consequence. Metternich's statement from late October 1830 that "the union of the views and decisions between our and the Russian court is *complete*; today, there are no differences between us"[16] can somehow sound too confident, but the opinion that "the union among the three Northern Courts is more intimate than ever"[17] was also generally shared by disinterested observers and confirmed by the measures taken by the three conservative Powers on the international scene. How far Russian diplomacy had advanced towards Austria is evident from the fact that the former arch-enemy of the Danubian Monarchy, Pozzo di Borgo, became the principal advocate of Metternich's policy in the second half of 1830, following Nesselrode earlier in the same year.[18]

[15] Ficquelmont to Metternich, St Petersburg, 19 Jan. 1830, HHStA, StA, Russland III, 89.
[16] Metternich to Ottenfels, Vienna, 20 Oct. 1830, HDA, 750, OO 38.
[17] Report from Vienna, 4 Dec. 1830, SS, HD, SG 10026, Wien 92.
[18] Metternich to Ficquelmont, Vienna, 17 July 1830, SOA, RA C-A 383; Metternich to Ottenfels, Vienna, 18 July 1830, HDA, 750, OO 38; Ficquelmont to Metternich, St Petersburg, 19 Jan., 5 and 24 March, 8 and 10 June 1830, HHStA, StA, Russland III, 89; Tatishchev to Nesselrode, Vienna, 10 Feb. 1830, AVPRI, fond 133, Kantseliariia, opis 469, 1830/275; W. Kantor, *Karl Ludwig Graf Ficquelmont: Ein Lebensbild mit besonderer Rücksicht auf seine diplomatische Mitarbeit bei Metternich*, unpublished dissertation, Wien 1948, pp. 103–104; Molden, p. 93.

Metternich and France after the July Revolution

As for Austro-French relations at the end of the 1820s and in the early 1830s, one must understand that France's actions in the Levant were for Metternich only secondary symptoms of the policy threatening Austrian interests more directly in other parts of Europe. France under the Restoration as well as under Louis Philippe had revisionist ambitions in Europe and hoped that it would finally reverse the order created at the Congress of Vienna and improve its own position in the diplomatic concert. Metternich was not blind to this and he also knew that France chose the Mediterranean as a playground where it could count upon less opposition from other Powers, which was proved in the case of the Algerian conquest. The main difference between the French regimes before and after July 1830 was that the latter was liberal and, trying to strengthen its position at home by means of a seemingly bolder diplomacy than that of the pre-July governments, it accompanied its attempts with revolutionary rhetoric. Consequently, the deeper worsening of the relations between Paris, which was disposed to change the status quo, and Vienna, which was defending it, was inevitable. Both parties disagreed over the events in the areas more important for the Austrian Empire than North Africa: in Belgium, Poland and particularly the Apennines, the traditional sphere of the Habsburgs' influence, where the French effort to weaken Austria's dominance led to their occupation of Ancona in February 1832. These events, of course, further significantly contributed to the improved relationship between Austria and Russia manifested in the joint advance in the above-mentioned affairs and later intensified in those of the Iberian Peninsula and the Near East. The July Revolution had one more important benefit for Metternich: he no longer had to fear a French-Russian alliance because Nicholas I became even more hostile towards France and specifically its monarch; the tsar's strong antipathy towards Louis Philippe was insuperable. The cooperation between St Petersburg and Vienna was thus simplified by their common enemy and the fact that no significant differences in opinion existed between them, even in their views of the continuing existence of the Ottoman Empire, where the tsar did not hesitate to show his goodwill towards the sultan by replacing Ribeaupierre with the more amicable Count Apollinarii Petrovic Butenev and reducing a part of the war indemnity in 1831.[19]

It was a certain paradox that at the same moment when Europe was undergoing a wave of revolutions, the Ottoman Empire, after many years of insecurity and war, was experiencing a period of miraculous calm and order. Ottenfels commented on this situation with these words: "Whereas in the rest of Europe revolutions and political upheavals erupt one by one in horrifyingly rapid succession, Turkey is enjoying absolute peace and a domestic tranquillity of which few examples can be found in the annals of this empire."[20] It is no surprise that Austria as well as other members of the pentarchy lost interest in the course of events in the Near East for some time. Only in the spring of 1831 did Metternich have to pay attention again to the situation at the sultan's court because the Ottoman elites, at other times rather insensitive to events on the Continent, started to speculate about the possibility of taking advantage of the tsar's problems with the repression of the Polish insurrection, which had broken out at the end of November 1830, for the modification of the conditions contained in the Treaty of Adrianople. This revisionist tendency of the Porte did not go unnoticed by Guilleminot who, having demonstrated much support for the July Revolution and being left in his office by the new French regime, declared on 19 March 1831 to the reis effendi that a war between France and Russia was inevitable because of the events in Poland and the time had come for the Porte to take advantage of the Russians' difficulties with their struggle against the Polish insurgents and get revenge on their old enemy for the losses suffered in the last conflict: "In the middle of this unrest, is the Porte going to stay inactive? Does it not have injuries to revenge, losses to put right? Can it delude itself of the consequences of the charges [of the indemnity] to which it was subjected? Does it not know that their final result must be its political annihilation? Finally, would it

---

[19] Ottenfels to Metternich, Constantinople, 10 Nov. 1830, HHStA, StA, Türkei VI, 51; Ottenfels, *Memoari*, pp. 234–235; B. Jelavich, *Russia's Balkan Entanglements, 1806–1914*, Cambridge, New York, Port Chester, Melbourne, Sydney 1991, p. 91; B. Jelavich, *The Habsburg Empire in European Affairs 1814–1918*, Chicago 1969, pp. 36–39; C. Vidal, *Louis-Philippe, Metternich et la crise italienne de 1831–1832*, Paris 1931, pp. 209–222; Droz, pp. 312–313.
[20] Ottenfels to Metternich, Constantinople, 26 March 1831, HHStA, StA, Türkei VI, 52.

prefer to die of misery with certainty than to take advantage of the glorious opportunities that are offered to it?"[21] If Austria allied itself with Russia, Guilleminot continued, France would certainly defeat it. Great Britain ought to stay neutral or support France. The ambassador simultaneously warned the Porte that if it did not join Louis Philippe, the French monarch would not help to avert the losses that the sultan would inevitably suffer in the coming all-European war. He soon repeated this statement in the presence of other prominent Ottoman dignitaries.[22]

Guilleminot actually acted without relevant instructions from his government, only under the impression that a war between France and Russia was highly probable. When his statement to Ottoman dignitaries was revealed, his government denied that it had given such authority to its French ambassador and immediately recalled him from office. Although Guilleminot accepted the disgrace and told Ottenfels that he had been "influenced by the possibility of an early rupture [between France and Russia] and by the conflicting circumstances,"[23] Metternich regarded this as a poor excuse and the French ambassador's statements as a serious threat not only to the Porte but to the whole of Europe and saw in them a reflection of the policy that Louis Philippe, "the king of the street," had pursued since his accession to the throne and that, according to the Austrian chancellor, "offers a sad spectacle to the world."[24] As to the possible impact of the Polish affair on the sultan's attitude, he instructed Ottenfels to confront French intrigues and to urge Mahmud II and his advisers to stay on friendly

---

[21] Guilleminot to Sébastiani, Constantinople, 4 April 1831, AMAE, CP, Turquie 262.

[22] Metternich to Ottenfels, Vienna, 5 and 19 Sept., 2 and 20 Oct. 1830, Ottenfels to Metternich, Constantinople, 10 Oct., 10 and 25 Nov., 10 Dec. 1830, HHStA, StA, Türkei VI, 51; Ottenfels to Metternich, Constantinople, 10 Jan., 25 Feb., 26 March and 28 May 1831, HHStA, StA, Türkei VI, 52; Maltzan to Frederick William III, Vienna, 13, 15 and 29 April 1831, and attached Gordon to Palmerston, Constantinople, 31 March 1831, GStA PK, HA III, MdA I, 6016; Brassier to Frederick William III, Pera, 11 Jan., 26 Feb. and 26 May 1831, GStA PK, HA III, MdA I, 7270; Guilleminot to Jourdan, Constantinople, 9 Sept. 1830, Guilleminot to Molé, Constantinople, 11 Oct. 1830, AMAE, CP, Turquie 261; Guilleminot to Sébastiani, Constantinople, 4 April 1831, AMAE, CP, Turquie 262.

[23] Ottenfels to Metternich, Constantinople, 28 May 1831, HHStA, StA, Türkei VI, 52.

[24] Metternich to Ottenfels, Vienna, 12 May 1831, HHStA, StA, Türkei VI, 52.

terms with all the Great Powers at any price. On 21 April 1831, he wrote to the internuncio: "Stop the Divan by all the means at your disposal. Allow no foolishness!"[25] Luckily for the conservative Powers, the Ottoman ruler did not allow himself to be dragged into a war which he was in no way prepared to wage. Therefore, his advisers hastened with assurances that the Porte would remain neutral and would not provoke war with Russia. Although Ottenfels did not doubt the sincerity of these claims, he was not entirely sure whether the Divan would resist the temptation and, should the Polish insurrection continue, it would not attempt to alter the Treaty of Adrianople in the matters of Serbia, the Principalities and the war indemnity. Consequently, Metternich could not ignore another threat that arose shortly after Guilleminot's speech in the form of the Polish Revolutionary Committee in Paris presided by Marquis Gilbert du Motier de Lafayette, whom the chancellor regarded as the spirit of revolutionary propaganda. The Committee had sent Konstantin Wolicky, well known for his pamphlet against Grand Duke Constantine, Mr Komierowsky and Mr Linowski to Constantinople, where they stayed under the protection of the French embassy. These Poles were charged with the task with which Guilleminot had failed: to persuade the Porte to disregard the obligations arising from the Treaty of Adrianople, to make a military demonstration and to demand the restoration of Poland, which would, under the given conditions, amount to declaration of war on Russia. Nevertheless, it was not difficult for Ottenfels to thwart such a plan and convince the sultan to do nothing, especially when the news of the Russian victories over the Poles crowned with the capture of Warsaw in September 1831 gave the Ottomans no prospect for success in any eventual diplomatic pressure on St Petersburg.[26]

[25] Metternich to Ottenfels, Vienna, 21 April 1831, HHStA, StA, Türkei VI, 52.

[26] Metternich to Ottenfels, Vienna, 3 Feb., 21 April, 4 and 20 May, 28 Sept., 19 Oct. and 2 Nov. 1831, HHStA, StA, Türkei VI, 53; Metternich to Ottenfels, Vienna, 8 June 1831, HDA, 750, OO 38; Metternich to Ficquelmont, Vienna, 18 Oct. 1831, SOA, RA C-A 383; Ottenfels to Metternich, Constantinople, 26 March and 10 June, HHStA, StA, Türkei VI, 52; Ottenfels to Metternich, Constantinople, 10 and 26 Sept., 19 Oct., 2, 11 and 25 Nov. 1831, HHStA, StA, Türkei VI, 53; Guilleminot to Sébastiani, Constantinople, 28 May 1831, AMAE, CP, Turquie 262; Varenne to Sébastiani, Constantinople, 28 July and 20 Aug. 1831, AMAE, CP, Turquie 262; Maltzan to Frederick William III, Vienna, 12 April and 9 June 1831, GStA PK, HA III, MdA I, 6016; report from Vienna, 2 May 1831, SS, HD, SG 10026, Wien 92; Ottenfels, *Memoari*, pp. 233–234; *Memoire des Konstantin*

Metternich's Struggle against the Foundation of the Moniteur Ottoman

With his measures in Constantinople during 1831, Metternich proved his complete support of Russia and considerable animosity towards France. Whereas Austro-Russian relations experienced a total reversal during the two years following the conclusion of peace in Adrianople and both countries were in harmony on the question of the Ottoman Empire, relations between Austria and France in European affairs deteriorated considerably, which also became apparent in the Near East, where France and not Russia represented an imminent threat for Metternich. In addition to the Austro-Russian rapprochement not being just the result of the July Revolution, Metternich's animosity towards France had deeper roots, and he had criticised France's steps in the Levant prior to the summer of 1830. He saw in Guilleminot's provocation and the Poles' activities under French protection the continuation of the adventurous diplomacy of the Restoration aimed at increasing French influence abroad as well as securing support in domestic affairs. The mistrust of governments in Paris regardless of the regime moved Metternich to observe their operations within the Ottoman Empire as well as the activities of the citizens themselves. In early 1830, which means already during the Restoration, he had come out against the idea of the Porte to send young Ottomans to be educated in France, which he labelled as the hotbed of revolution threatening the whole of Europe.[27] In the following year, he attempted to prevent French lawyer and journalist Alexandre Blacque, who was in contact with Lafayette and supported the Polish insurrection, from printing a newspaper in the French language in Constantinople. Since this affair well characterises the chancellor's animosity towards France and even the private activities of the Frenchmen in the Levant, as well as his backing of Russia, it is appropriate here to sketch it in brief.

In July 1831, Blacque arrived in Constantinople and since he was already the editor-in-chief of a newspaper published in Smyrna, the

---

Wolicki über die im Auftrag der polnischen Regierung nach Frankreich und Konstantinopel unternommene Gesandschaft, Prokesch-Osten, *Aus den Tagebüchern,* pp. 232–235.

[27] Metternich to Ottenfels, Vienna, 28 Sept. 1831, HHStA, StA, Türkei VI, 53. For more on Metternich's attempt to forestall sending Ottoman students to France in 1830 see Chapter 21.

Courrier de Smyrne, Ottenfels presumed that his probable goal in the Ottoman capital was to publish another newspaper. Although Blacque denied this as rumour, the internuncio was firm in his suspicion. In Ottenfels' opinion, it was very likely that Blacque would succeed in his plan because he was in favour with high Ottoman dignitaries, who considered him a vocal admirer of the sultan. Ottenfels shared their positive evaluation of Blacque in the late 1820s because the Frenchman was "the most tenacious defender of the rights of the Turks, the Ottoman Empire, and the Moslems in general,"[28] which he openly demonstrated with his journalistic activities during the Greek insurrection and particularly during the Russo-Ottoman war. In September of 1827, when Blacque was editor-in-chief of the *Spectateur Oriental*, Ottenfels recognised him as a man who sometimes got lost in ambiguities and misdiagnosed questions of high policy, but who in essence tried to be truthful and impartial and who possessed much insight and sane and correct judgement. In January 1828, Ottenfels wrote about two issues of the *Spectateur Oriental*: "They contain incontestable truths, reflections on great political questions which are as fair as they are profound and ideas deserving to be appreciated by allied cabinets."[29] In the autumn of the same year, Ottenfels continued to praise Blacque's papers, this time the *Courrier de Smyrne*, which defended "with its opinions and courage the cause of right and common sense."[30] Metternich shared this opinion. Although he felt Blacque sometimes exaggerated, in general he felt the French journalist got things right. Consequently, it was no coincidence that the *Österreichischer Beobachter* often reprinted the articles from the *Spectateur Oriental* and that the Greeks and Philhellenes called Blacque's newspaper the echo of the former. It also is not without interest that Prokesch was Blacque's friend and published his articles in the *Courrier de Smyrne*.[31]

[28] O. Koloğlu, "Alexandre Blacque, défenseur de l'État ottoman par amour des libertés," H. Batu, J.-L. Bacqué-Grammont (eds.), *L'Empire Ottoman, la République de Turquie et la France*, Istanbul 1986, pp. 179–195.

[29] Ottenfels to Metternich, Constantinople, 10 Jan. 1828, HHStA, StA, Türkei VI, 32.

[30] Ottenfels to Metternich, Constantinople, 13 Nov. 1828, HHStA, StA, Türkei VI, 34.

[31] Metternich to Esterházy, Vienna, 12 Feb. 1828, HHStA, StA, England 182; Ottenfels to Metternich, Constantinople, 25 Sept. 1827, HHStA, StA, Türkei VI,

Nevertheless, Metternich's and Ottenfels' attitudes towards Blacque significantly changed after the July Revolution. Blacque did not hesitate to show his support to the political change in his native country in the *Courrier de Smyrne*, which forced Ottenfels to report in October 1830: "The spirit of this newspaper has absolutely changed: from a trusty reporter of the news in the Levant it has become the voice of French revolutionaries. I am of the opinion that its circulation in Austria can no longer be tolerated without restriction as it was in the past."[32] Blacque's support of revolution and the fight for freedom logically increased his already existing negative attitude towards Russia. Although his anti-Russian feeling was also held and, therefore, welcomed in Vienna in the second half of the 1820s, in 1831 this was not the case. Consequently, when the angered Russians requested in early 1831 the suppression of the publication of Blacque's newspaper due to his obvious hostility towards them, Ottenfels was instructed to support their demand.[33] It is also evident from Metternich's later objections, conveyed by Ottenfels to the Porte, that Blacque's anti-Russian attitude was very likely the reason Austria acted against Blacque's plan in 1831: "It is the same man [Blacque], who, in the newspaper he has edited until today, has shown himself to be the enemy of the monarchic governments and a keen partisan of revolutionary principles, who has shown so little regard for foreign courts that he has given several of them cause to address justifiable complaints to the Sublime Porte, and finally who has openly declared himself to be the bitter enemy of the court that the Sublime Porte should most highly respect and on no account provoke [Russia]. The very choice of Mr Blacque will displease the Russian court and it will not find favour among the other courts well disposed to the Ottoman Empire."[34]

27; Ottenfels to Metternich, Constantinople, 12 and 25 July 1831, HHStA, StA, Türkei VI, 52; Bertsch, pp. 107–108; Dimakis, p. 51.

[32] Ottenfels to Metternich, Constantinople, 11 Oct. 1830, HHStA, StA, Türkei VI, 51.

[33] Metternich to Ottenfels, Pressburg, 20 Oct. 1830, HDA, 750, OO 38; Ottenfels to Metternich, Constantinople, 27 Sept. 1830, HHStA, StA, Türkei VI, 50; Ottenfels to Metternich, Constantinople, 27 Dec. 1830, HHStA, StA, Türkei VI, 51; Ottenfels to Metternich, Constantinople, 12 July 1831, HHStA, StA, Türkei VI, 52.

[34] *Observations confidentielles*, Constantinople, 28 Oct. 1831, attached to Ottenfels to Metternich, Constantinople, 10 Nov. 1831, HHStA, StA, Türkei VI, 53.

Ottenfels' concerns about Blacque's desire to publish a newspaper in Constantinople soon proved to be well founded when he discovered evidence for the plan. The internuncio then immediately launched a campaign against the project in conjunction with Butenev, who asked him for assistance. Ottenfels was concerned not only about Blacque's invectives against conservative principles and Russia but also about the growth of French influence in Constantinople. Although the French chargé d'affaires, Baron Jacques-Édouard Burignot de Varenne, denied that he had any connection with Blacque or that he supported the project – which was true, Ottenfels suspected that Varenne would have some influence on the editing of the paper and that the paper would help strengthen links between the French and Husrev Pasha, who was an advocate of Blacque's project. Ottenfels was also not satisfied by assurances from the Porte that, when it came to state affairs, two Ottoman censors would control the content. The internuncio doubted the effectiveness of such censorship.[35]

Metternich naturally shared Ottenfels' opinion of Blacque's project and instructed the internuncio to thwart it. According to Metternich, the sultan had the full right to publish newspapers and it was also desirable that he informed his subjects about his decisions and reforms, but the papers ought to be published in Turkish and under the direct control of Ottoman officials. It was important that the editorial staff printed what the sultan authorised and this would help ensure that. Moreover, the chancellor could not abide the privileging of the French language: "Where does this preference for the French language and nation come from? Would the Porte accord France a status over all other Powers? It is [France] alone from whom [the Porte] would solicit commendation? Is it the French nation that [the Porte] judges to be the apogee of civilisation? To make such a choice and such a declaration publicly denigrates all other nations."[36] Metternich argued that no government had found it appropriate to publish newspapers in foreign languages because doing so would grant foreigners extensive influence and privileges. In the event that Mahmud II wanted

---

[35] Ottenfels to Metternich, Constantinople, 25 Aug. 1831, HHStA, StA, Türkei VI, 52; Ottenfels to Metternich, Constantinople, 16 Sept. and 10 Oct. 1831, HHStA, StA, Türkei VI, 53; Varenne to Sébastiani, Constantinople, [?] Aug. 1831, AMAE, CP, Turquie 262.

[36] *Observations confidentielles*, Constantinople, 28 Oct. 1831, HHStA, StA, Türkei VI, 53.

to familiarise Europe with his decisions, he could do it via Austrian newspapers. Because the sultan felt compelled to publish newspapers in a Christian language, Metternich made the argument that Italian, which was common in the Levant, would be a better option than French. Ottenfels was instructed, among other things, to draw the sultan's attention to the fact that the Austrian emperor "had never allowed the printing of a French newspaper in his lands."[37] Metternich also regarded the choice of the editor as the worst possible because he considered Blacque to be a man "revolutionary to the core; enlightened friends of the Porte will be horrified and radicals will be satisfied [by this choice]."[38] In his campaign against Blacque, the prince did not hesitate to use appropriated correspondence between the editor and Lafayette. The chancellor labelled Blacque Lafayette's agent and warned Mahmud II against entrusting the Frenchman with the editing of the newspaper. In Metternich's opinion, an Italian editor-in-chief would be much better; it would be considerably easy for Austria to offer one or for the sultan to find one among the many Italians living in his capital.[39]

The Ottoman foreign minister denied Metternich's accusation that the Porte wanted to hurt its friends by publishing a French paper and raised well-founded counterarguments. Did Russia prefer the French when a French newspaper was published in St Petersburg? Or did Europe prefer the French when the French language was used generally in diplomatic relations? Metternich was also fighting against the collective force of the Ottoman upper class, which was favourably disposed towards French. The influence of the Romance language dated back to the early European diplomatic missions to the Ottoman Empire. It facilitated communications between Europeans and the Divan; the Ottoman dragomans never spoke with foreign diplomats in any other language. Knowledge of French became necessary for members of upper Ottoman society and a symbol of progressivism. According to the internuncio, it would have been impossible to weaken its influence and replace it with Italian, which was the language of mer-

---

[37] Metternich to Ottenfels, Vienna, 6 Oct. 1831, HHStA, StA, Türkei VI, 53.
[38] Ibid.
[39] Metternich to Ottenfels, Vienna, 6 Oct. 1831, Lafayette to Blacque, Paris, 21 July 1831, attached to Metternich to Ottenfels, Vienna, 19 Oct. 1831, *Observations confidentielles*, Constantinople, 28 Oct. 1831, HHStA, StA, Türkei VI, 53.

chants and workers and considered by diplomats and aristocrats to be
entirely inferior and useless for members of the upper class or any Ottomans attempting to climb the social ladder. Furthermore, Blacque
had concealed his plan long enough that Metternich was unable to
frustrate it; his warnings against the possible consequences of a newspaper edited by a Frenchman came too late because the Porte had
already agreed to the publishing the newspaper in French which pan-
dered to "the self-esteem of the sultan, who is most interested in this
French newspaper because he is eager for the praise of civilised Europe for his reforms and innovations, and the French have been trying
for a long time through the information channels at their disposal
to obtain the sultan's ear [and] to persuade the sovereign that it is
France that leads European civilisation and that their language is the
only one that is generally studied and understood."[40] It was nearly
impossible to undertake anything against the project the moment it
became a personal matter to Mahmud II, who was looking forward
to the first issue of the *Moniteur Ottoman.* The Ottoman ministers
could not oppose their master's wish, in particular when the sultan's
subjects were acquainted with his approval of the project and eagerly
awaited the first issue. If the Porte had changed its opinion owing
to influence from abroad, it would be compromised before its own
inhabitants and in "the eyes of the whole world."[41] The first issue
of the *Moniteur Ottoman* was thus printed in November 1831 and
although Ottenfels found nothing harmful in its content, he did not
refrain from warning that "each child is innocent when they are born
and man cannot presume their character until the moment when they
grow up."[42] Nevertheless, in the following years, the Austrians im-
parted essentially no criticism of the *Moniteur Ottoman,* suggesting
that the cabinet in Vienna did not regard Blacque's newspaper as a
threat and accepted its existence.[43]

---

[40] Ottenfels to Metternich, Constantinople, 25 Oct. 1831, HHStA, StA, Türkei
VI, 53.
[41] Adelburg to Ottenfels, Constantinople, 4 Nov. 1831, HHStA, StA, Türkei VI,
53.
[42] Ottenfels to Metternich, Constantinople, 10 Nov. 1831, HHStA, StA, Türkei
VI, 53.
[43] Adelburg to Ottenfels, Constantinople, 4 Nov. 1831, Ottenfels to Metternich,
Constantinople, 25 Nov. 1831, HHStA, StA, Türkei VI, 53; Stürmer to Metternich,
Constantinople, 25 Nov. 1840, HHStA, StA, Türkei VI, 77. Though the Porte as-

Russia's Military Intervention on the Bosphorus and the Conclusion of the First Mohammed Ali Crisis

Metternich's pro-Russian and anti-French attitudes became fully evident in the Near East during the First Mohammed Ali Crisis. Although he did not offer assistance to Mahmud II, this in no way meant that he objected if such assistance was offered by another Power. Therefore, when defeats in July 1832 forced Mahmud II to ask the British cabinet to send fifteen warships against Mohammed Ali in the autumn, the chancellor supported this request without hesitation even though he did not believe that the government in London would satisfy it. This prediction proved to be well founded because Great Britain refused to commit itself militarily in the eastern Mediterranean. At this for Mahmud II undoubtedly critical moment, however, help arrived from Russia. As early as on the day of the Battle of Konya, Butenev informed the Porte that Nicholas I was prepared to send his naval and ground forces to the Straits if the sultan wanted. This offer was soon repeated by the tsar's special agent Count Nicholas Nikolayevich Muravyov, who afterwards went to Alexandria and in mid January 1833 recommended in a not very diplomatic manner to Mohammed Ali that he reconcile with the Ottoman ruler, albeit without success. This conduct of Russian diplomacy was a logical outcome of the weak neighbour policy accepted in September 1829 because the overthrow of the sultan could have fatal consequences for Russia: either the fall of the Ottoman Empire or the seizure of its throne by the man who seemed able to restore its former glory and transform the empire into a powerful state, or at least one more viable than it was, would thereby create a threat for the Russian domination in the Black Sea. Moreover, the Russian elites disdained, as did Metternich, the activities of the French in Mohammed Ali's service; they regarded the Egyptian governor as a puppet in the hands of the hated Louis Philippe and his rise as the result of the revolutionary spirit spreading from France. For this reason Nicholas I and Nesselrode feared that after the occupation of Constantinople by Egyptian forces, French influence would become

---

sured the Austrians that Blacque would work as the editor-in-chief only temporarily, in reality, he published the newspaper until his death in 1836. Adelburg to Ottenfels, Constantinople, 31 Oct. and 4 Nov. 1831, HHStA, StA, Türkei VI, 53.

predominant in the whole of the Ottoman Empire, which would thus become a tool of French diplomacy hostile towards St Petersburg.[44]

Mahmud II hesitated to accept the assistance offered, but when Mohammed Ali's army approached to a distance of 150 miles from Constantinople at the end of January 1833, he was far too worried about a possible assault on the city to refuse. On 2 February, he formally requested the sending of a Russian expeditionary force. Rear-Admiral Mikhail Lazarev's squadron sailed into the Bosphorus 18 days later and anchored almost under the windows of the French embassy, where only three days before the new French ambassador, Baron Albin-Rein Roussin, had arrived. Seeing the Russian flags on the masts of Lazarev's ships, Roussin's pride was injured. He did not believe in the goodwill of the Russian policy that also threatened to weaken the influence of both Maritime Powers over the sultan's court. It is certainly no exaggeration to say that the Russian presence on Ottoman soil – the tsar's troops camped on the Asiatic coast of the Bosphorus – invoked more serious apprehensions on his part than the military victories of the Egyptian governor. Consequently, Roussin opened a diplomatic offensive with the aim of persuading Mahmud II to ask the Russians to withdraw from the Bosphorus. Having failed in this with his threats first of immediate departure because, as he declared, the arrival of the Russians deprived the Ottoman Empire of its independence and the presence of the French representative in Constantinople was thus unnecessary or secondly with the summoning of the French fleet into the Sea of Marmara if the Russian intervention was not terminated, he changed tactics and presuming that the conclusion of peace with Mohammed Ali would make the presence of the tsar's forces superfluous, he decided to solve the problem by taking an arbitrary step. Without appropriate instructions from his government,

[44] Metternich to Neumann, Vienna, 17 Oct. 1832, HHStA, StA, England 199; Metternich to Ottenfels, Vienna, 5 Dec. 1832, HHStA, StA, Türkei VI, 56; Metternich to Ficquelmont, 8 Dec. 1832, HHStA, StA, Russland III, 97; Neumann to Metternich, London, 9 Nov., 4 and 28 Dec. 1832, HHStA, StA, England 198; Lamb to Palmerston, Vienna, 16 Oct. 1832, TNA, FO 120/124; Ottenfels to Metternich, Constantinople, 11 and 25 Oct. 1832, HHStA, StA, Türkei VI, 54; M. S. Anderson, *The Eastern Question 1774–1923: A Study in International Relations*, London, New York 1966, p. 79; W. B. Lincoln, *Nicholas I: Emperor and Autocrat of All the Russias*, London 1989, p. 203; Bitis, *Russia*, p. 468; Rendall, "Nicholas I," p. 57; Rodkey, *The Turko-Egyptian Question*, p. 16.

Roussin promised in the name of France that the Egyptian governor would accept Mahmud II's peace conditions. This formed the content of the convention concluded between Roussin and the Porte on 21 February 1833. Nevertheless, the action was a total failure because Mohammed Ali refused to renounce any of his territorial demands covering the whole of Syria and Adana. Roussin's recommendation to the Porte of 26 March to accept the settlement with Mohammed Ali on his terms rather than any prolonged encampment of Russian forces before Constantinople produced "a hardly describable consternation"[45] among the members of the Divan and signed the death warrant for the diplomatic intervention that ended with the absolute defeat of France and in no way contributed to the departure of the tsar's army. Quite to the contrary, it prolonged the army's presence close to the Ottoman capital because Butenev, who initially seemed willing to satisfy the sultan's request for their decampment, refused to do so when he learnt that it had been initiated by Roussin. Nicholas I also felt offended by the French ambassador's behaviour and was not willing to recall his soldiers and marines until the Egyptian army withdrew beyond the Taurus. The feeling of the Russians is well characterised by Tatishchev's reaction to France's declaration against the sultan's acceptance of Russia's military assistance: "Such an arrogant tone assumed by a dominant Power would be an abuse of force; on the part of Louis Philippe's government it is an impertinence."[46] Finally, Mahmud II no longer demanded the withdrawal of the Russians because after Roussin's failure they formed the only shield against Mohammed Ali. The Russian influence at his court thus logically increased, which was surely not the outcome that the French ambassador had desired to achieve.[47]

In contrast to Roussin, Metternich confided in Nicholas I and approved of the steps the tsar had undertaken since the beginning of the crisis simply for the reason, as the chancellor wrote in December 1832,

---

[45] Stürmer to Metternich, Constantinople, 27 March 1833, HHStA, StA, Türkei VI, 57.

[46] Tatishchev to Nesselrode, Vienna, 29 Jan. 1833, AVPRI, fond 133, Kantseliariia, opis 469, 1833/211.

[47] Ottenfels to Metternich, Constantinople, 4, 11, 21 and 24 Feb. 1833, HHStA, StA, Türkei VI, 56; Stürmer to Metternich, Constantinople, 24 and 27 March 1833, HHStA, StA, Türkei VI, 57; Bitis, *Russia*, p. 475; Puryear, *France*, pp. 190–196; Rendall, "Nicholas I," pp. 40–41.

that "the attitude that the Russian tsar assumed in this deplorable conflict between the sultan and Mohammed Ali generally corresponds to our principles as well as our opinions."[48] And he added in mid February of the following year: "The Russian Emperor did not offer his moral or even, if necessary, material assistance to the Divan with the aim of annihilating the sultan, or destroying his government, or making material conquests in his domains. What this monarch keeps in mind in the present circumstances is what we also want."[49] The chancellor considered the sultan's request for Russian intervention to be justifiable, foresighted and logical in the circumstances when Great Britain and France had refused to help him. He saw nothing dangerous in the military support for the Porte or other countries; it was merely assistance offered to the legitimate ruler against a rebel and therefore Ottenfels was instructed to support Butenev enthusiastically. Metternich also did not hide his own opinion of the expediency of the tsar's military assistance, which led French representatives at Vienna to suspect Metternich of concealing his fear of the Russian intervention and of immoderate forbearance towards St Petersburg. In March 1833, the French chargé d'affaires, Baron Edmond de Bussierre, reported to Paris that outwardly the chancellor displayed no uneasiness but "it is necessary to be wary of attaching too much confidence in the optimism that Mr Metternich feigns in relation to the Russian intentions, and one should more likely suppose that lately this outward expression of calm masks serious alarm."[50] Nevertheless, this perception was wrong. The military intervention was executed entirely according to Metternich's principles and his objections were unnecessary. He thought, however, that the dispatch of warships would have been sufficient for the defence of Constantinople and the disembarkation of the ground forces therefore superfluous. It is also true that the Austrian chancellor would have preferred the diplomatic action of all Great Powers against Mohammed Ali, which, in his opinion, would have been enough to force his submission to the presence of Russian troops in the heart of the predominantly Moslem empire, but without a united effort of all the Great Powers, he was well aware that such a

---

[48] Metternich to Neumann, Vienna, 11 Dec. 1832, HHStA, StA, England 199.
[49] Metternich to Neumann, Vienna, 15 Feb. 1833, HHStA, StA, England 204.
[50] Bussierre to Broglie, Vienna, 7 March 1833, AMAE, CP, Autriche 418.

proceeding was impossible and Roussin's "pacifistic bravado"[51] could not provide any desirable result; in short, there was no alternative at that moment.[52]

In any case the lack of concern at the Chancellery in Ballhausplatz over the tsar's intervention and possible territorial demands at the expense of the sultan was no misjudgement of the situation but the consequence of real confidence in his intentions resulting from a correct analysis of the Russian Near Eastern policy based on the experience of the previous several years. Consequently, Metternich's confidence in the tsar's conduct was only reinforced by the reports from Constantinople written in October 1832, in which Ottenfels talked about the trustworthy Russian policy striving for the preservation of the Ottoman Empire, and from St Petersburg, where Nicholas I personally assured Ficquelmont on 18 February 1833 of the sincerity of his actions and declared that he had no interest in the downfall of his southern neighbour nor any intent to follow the aggressive plans of his grandmother, Catherine the Great. As to the conversation of 18 February, it is likely that British historian Matthew Smith Anderson somewhat overestimates its significance if he claims that the tsar tried to bring about any joint action between himself and Austria in the Near East. According to the available sources, this was not his objective; he only tried to inform Metternich and Francis I about the Russian military intervention on the Bosphorus and assure them that he wanted no material benefits for the assistance offered to the sultan, trying thus to obtain their diplomatic backing.[53]

---

[51] Report from Vienna, 23 March 1833, SS, HD, SG 10026, Wien 92.

[52] Metternich to Ottenfels, Vienna, 4, 14 and 22 Feb. 1833, HHStA, StA, Türkei VI, 59; Metternich to Neumann, Vienna, 15 Feb. 1833, HHStA, StA, England 204; Metternich to Ficquelmont, Vienna, 4 May 1833, HHStA, StA, Russland III, 99; Metternich to Ficquelmont, Vienna, 5 March 1833, SOA, RA C-A 383; Metternich to Apponyi, 18 March and 21 April 1833, HHStA, StA, Frankreich 289; Stürmer to Metternich, Constantinople, 27 March 1833, HHStA, StA, Türkei VI, 57; Maison to Broglie, Vienna, 13 and 28 Jan., 12 Feb. 1833, Bussierre to Broglie, Vienna, 7 March 1833, Sainte-Aulaire to Broglie, Vienna, 13 May 1833, AMAE, CP, Autriche 418; Sainte-Aulaire to Broglie, Vienna, 5 July 1833, AMAE, CP, Autriche 419; Maltzan to Frederick William III, Vienna, 19 Feb. 1833, GStA PK, HA III, MdA I, 6021; Martens to Frederick William III, 11 April 1833, GStA PK, HA III, MdA I, 7272; Tatishchev to Nesselrode, Vienna, 9 and 19 Jan., 15 Feb. and 11 March 1833, AVPRI, fond 133, Kantseliariia, opis 469, 1833/211; De Loë to Goblet, Vienna, 28 Feb. 1833, ADA, CP, Autriche 1.

[53] Ottenfels to Metternich, Constantinople, 25 Oct. 1832, HHStA, StA, Türkei

On the other hand, an entirely different perspective of French behaviour during the whole of the crisis prevailed at the Viennese Chancellery. Metternich viewed the activities of French diplomats in Constantinople and Alexandria with uneasiness. Although he did not think that France was trying to contribute to the fall of the Ottoman Empire, he could not fail to see its duplicitous policy and goodwill towards Mohammed Ali, whose successes the chancellor also attributed to French "support of all kinds."[54] Metternich suspected the government in Paris of wanting to turn Egypt into a local power, which would officially remain a part of the Ottoman Empire but in reality would be independent enough to serve as a possible ally. The logical outcome would be the growth of French influence in the Levant, which was much more dangerous to Austrian interests than the activities of a conservative Russia with the evident intention to preserve the sultan's power as much as possible. Metternich's suspicion was to a great extent well founded; the cabinet in Paris really favoured the Egyptian governor and his effort to obtain Syrian pashaliks because it saw in the increase of his power a way to strengthen its own influence over the Mediterranean and particularly North Africa, which was, after the Algerian conquest, considered as a primary region for French expansion. Therefore, the French cabinet did not raise any serious objections against the pasha's campaign and advised Mahmud II to show self-restraint and generosity of spirit. As late as in the autumn of 1832, under the pressure of events France raised the objection in Alexandria against a possible overthrow of the sultan that would be unacceptable in Paris. It also offered to mediate between the Ottoman Empire and its vassal state several times before Roussin's convention for the sake of a prompt peace settlement, but the unwillingness of both belligerent men to yield foredoomed this proposal.[55]

VI, 54; Anderson, *Eastern Question*, p. 87; Beer, *Die orientalische Politik*, p. 399; Molden, pp. 86–89; Temperley, *Crimea*, p. 67.

[54] Metternich to Trauttmannsdorff, Vienna, 19 Feb. 1833, HHStA, StK, Preussen 152.

[55] Ottenfels to Metternich, Constantinople, 11 July 1832, HHStA, StA, Türkei VI, 54; Ottenfels to Metternich, Constantinople, 25 Sept., 25 Oct. and 27 Dec. 1832, HHStA, StA, Türkei VI, 55; Ottenfels to Metternich, Constantinople, 10 and 25 Jan. 1833, HHStA, StA, Türkei VI, 56; Brassier to Frederick William III, Büyükdere, 25 Aug. and 25 Sept. 1832, GStA PK, HA III, MdA I, 7271; Bullen, "France and Europe," p. 142; Kutluoğlu, pp. 82, 86 and 89; Puryear, *France*, pp. 154–168.

These attempts at mediation embarrassed Metternich for several reasons. First, peace mediated by France implied the danger that it would be more advantageous for Mohammed Ali. Second, the chancellor regarded the intervention of a third party into a dispute between a monarch and his subject as a flagrant violation of the principle of sovereignty. Third, he objected to the importunity with which France wanted to retain the leading role and simultaneously exclude Russia from participation in the solution of the whole crisis. In his opinion, the present cabinet in Paris continued in the diplomacy of its predecessors who wanted to oversee events under any circumstances and dazzle the public; policies in Navarino, Algiers, Antwerp or Ancona were continued in Constantinople and Alexandria.[56] Metternich entirely agreed with Ottenfels, who wrote on 10 November 1832 that France did not want to admit that anything happened without its active participation: "I have observed for a long time that there is no affair, no problem in Europe in which France would not seek to interfere because it believes that its honour, or better said its self-esteem, would suffer if it [France] had the impression of being excluded."[57]

Although the French government assumed a more hostile attitude towards Mohammed Ali after the Russian intervention on the Bosphorus, Metternich continued to criticise its actions in Constantinople. He considered the incident concerning Roussin to be a pointless dispute, one of many follies of the French diplomacy which Austria encountered in other parts of Europe. Although Roussin had acted without appropriate instructions, the chancellor saw in his action further proof of the egoistic French foreign policy: "The incident created by the convention of 21 February is of the same nature as those that the government of July has provoked in all affairs. This convention has the moral value of the affairs of Ancona and Antwerp; it is similar to the role that France played and still plays in the Dutch-Belgian affair, in that of Switzerland, Spain and Portugal. Everywhere we discover the same principles, the same self-assertion and unconstrained vanity

---

[56] Metternich to Ottenfels, 4 and 14 Feb. 1833, HHStA, StA, Türkei VI, 59; Metternich to Apponyi, 21 April 1833, HHStA, StA, Frankreich 289; Metternich to Neumann, 3 May 1833, HHStA, StA, England 204; Maltzan to Frederick William III, Vienna, 29 Jan. 1833, GStA PK, HA III, MdA I, 6021.

[57] Ottenfels to Metternich, Constantinople, 10 Nov. 1832, HHStA, StA, Türkei VI, 54. See also Ottenfels to Metternich, 10 Jan. 1833, HHStA, StA, Türkei VI, 56.

of the French government to seize at any price the dominant role in the question of the day. Whatever it accomplished yesterday it wants to do in every circumstance tomorrow."[58] Above all, Metternich did not understand the reasons for Roussin's anti-Russian conduct and why the French ambassador obstructed the assistance that the sultan had requested from the tsar and that followed the goal common to all Great Powers: the preservation of the Ottoman Empire. For the chancellor it was not only a matter of principles or geopolitics but also law. In his opinion, the sultan as a sovereign ruler had the right to ask another sovereign monarch for help and he definitely did not diminish his independence in any way as a result of this step, as Roussin claimed. Metternich perceptively pointed to the fact that according to this theory, through Roussin's diplomatic measure of 21 February France also turned the Ottoman Empire into a vassal state. Moreover, nobody would have prevented France and Great Britain from sending military assistance to the sultan against his Egyptian governor and if he had accepted it, nobody in Vienna would have objected to it; Metternich had not only supported Mahmud II's official request in London for the British naval aid but he also later recommended that both Western Powers support the Russian intervention by attaching their own fleets to Lazarev's squadron. Since they did not help the sultan, who was without effective protection against the Egyptian army after the Battle of Konya, the Austrian chancellor entirely approved of the Ottoman ruler's decision not to give in to Roussin's pressure and not to demand the withdrawal of Russian forces.[59]

According to Sir Charles Kingsley Webster, Metternich praised Roussin's intervention when it seemed to be successful but as soon as he learnt of its failure, he started to criticise it.[60] However, Webster's interpretation is rather inaccurate: Metternich applauded the mea-

---

[58] Metternich to Apponyi, Vienna, 18 March 1833, HHStA, StA, Türkei VI, 59.
[59] Metternich to Apponyi, Vienna, 18 March and 6 April 1833, HHStA, StA, Frankreich 289; Metternich to Neumann, Vienna, 18 March and 9 April 1833, HHStA, StA, England 204; Metternich to Ficquelmont, Vienna, 20 March 1833, HHStA, StA, Russland III, 99; Metternich to Ottenfels, Vienna, 21 March 1833, HHStA, StA, Türkei VI, 59; Metternich to Trauttmannsdorff, Vienna, 7 April 1833, HHStA, StK, Preussen, 152; Maltzan to Frederick William III, Vienna, 26 Feb. 1833, GStA PK, HA III, MdA I, 6021; Lamb to Palmerston, Vienna, 17 Jan. 1833, TNA, FO 120/136; Tatishchev to Nesselrode, Vienna, 7 Feb., 11 March and 16 April 1833, AVPRI, fond 133, Kantseliariia, opis 469, 1833/211.
[60] Webster, *Palmerston*, I, p. 293.

sure because he gathered from Bussierre that Roussin had succeeded in concluding peace, which, in the chancellor's words, would naturally have been an act worthy of admiration and praise: he had learnt of a success and not the actual fact that the French ambassador in Constantinople had assumed the role of a mediator and his achievement was more than precarious. Consequently, Metternich actually did initially tell Bussierre that "Roussin could congratulate himself on one of the greatest successes that an ambassador had achieved for a long time."[61] When he learnt of the real truth of the matter, his strong reproof was a logical consequence. When Bussierre asked him why he was dissatisfied when he had previously seemed to have approved of Roussin's action, Metternich briefly replied: "The internuncio informed us about a convention, the admiral [Roussin; actually vice-admiral] notified you that he had signed a peace treaty. There is a big difference between a convention concluded between France and the Porte and a peace treaty signed between Mohammed Ali and the sultan."[62] Metternich also did not conceal from Bussierre his displeasure at Roussin's egoistic and entirely incomprehensible effort to obtain the Russians' departure from Constantinople and deprive the city of the only defence in such a critical moment for the sultan. Instead of supporting the Russian advance and following the same course as France, the preservation of the Ottoman Empire, Roussin made the support of the sultan a secondary goal, and the primary one the removal of the Russians. This action could only have negative results because the tsar's injured pride did not allow the departure of the Russians until the definite solution of the crisis.[63] Metternich angrily commented on the outcome of Roussin's conduct with these words: "When someone shows me a result, when he writes me that peace is secured, I reply without hesitation, so much the better. But if I learn in no time that

---

[61] Bussierre to Broglie, Vienna, 10 March 1833, AMAE, CP, Autriche 418.

[62] Metternich to Ficquelmont, Vienna, 11 March 1833, HHStA, StA, Russland III, 99.

[63] Metternich to Apponyi, Vienna, 18 March and 6 April 1833, HHStA, StA, Frankreich 289; Metternich to Trauttmannsdorff, Vienna, 20 March 1833, HHStA, StA, Preussen 152; Metternich to Stürmer, Vienna, 18 April 1833, HHStA, StA, Türkei VI, 59; Maltzan to Frederick William III, Vienna, 8 March 1833, GStA PK, HA III, MdA I, 6021; Tatishchev to Nesselrode, Vienna, 11 and 20 March 1833, AVPRI, fond 133, Kantseliariia, opis 469, 1833/211; Lamb to Palmerston, Vienna, 13 April 1833, TNA, FO 120/136.

in fact nothing was achieved and only mistrust [of the Russians' presence on the Bosphorus] was expressed, when I learn that in wanting to stipulate this or that condition [the Russians' withdrawal], nothing was done except the prevention of what would have been achieved [the Russians' departure] if nobody had interfered in this affair, then I say, so much the worse! And I can express nothing but regret."[64]

Perhaps if the French activities in Constantinople threatening to worsen the relations among the Great Powers had been successful and had brought peace to the Near East, Metternich could have accepted them, but they had the opposite effect. After the news of Roussin's failure, the chancellor was shocked by the recommendation given to the Divan to give in to Mohammed Ali's demands. He predicted that despite the ineffectiveness of Roussin's initiative, a great diplomatic victory would be celebrated in Paris: "The French nation tends to find favour with everything that assigns to France an active role, regardless whether this role is good or harmful, correct or incorrect in its presumption, effective or dangerous in its results ... If Mohammed Ali had given in to Admiral Roussin's pressure, then France would have boasted that it had saved the sultan. Mohammed Ali did not yield and it is thus the viceroy who was saved by France, and provided its government takes the lead in any action, the [French] people will approve it."[65] This prediction turned out to be prophetic when the overweening pride attributed by Metternich to France was actually revealed in the French press, which did not hesitate to take the credit for the settlement of the conflict which ended with Mahmud II's absolute defeat in a peace settlement negotiated between the Turkish negotiators and Ibrahim Pasha in the Egyptian military camp in Kütahya on 5 May 1833; the sultan, seeing that the Russian army was strong enough to defend his capital but not to expel the Egyptian army from the Asia Minor, finally yielded and granted Mohammed Ali all the required provinces. The French were able to read in the *Journal des débats* on 1 August 1833 this statement: "French influence was so effective during these negotiations, [and] it was so instrumental in its intervention in the events in Asia Minor and their successful resolution that we can heartily congratulate ourselves on

---

[64] Bussierre to Broglie, Vienna, 22 March 1833, AMAE, CP, Autriche 418.
[65] Metternich to Apponyi, Vienna, 13 April 1833, HHStA, StA, Frankreich 289.

the role that France played during this significant affair."[66] The Austrian chancellor's reaction was far less poetic, in particular because when at the very same moment Mahmud II surrendered, Mohammed Ali officially promised to reduce his own demands. The pasha decided to do so after the joint Austro-British diplomatic pressure in Alexandria in which Anton Prokesch von Osten played an active role. His diplomatic mission to Egypt in 1833 clearly shows that the sultan could have been spared some losses and reveals the anti-French basis of Austria's Near Eastern policy.

[66] É. Bourgeois, *Manuel historique de politique étrangère*, Paris 1926, p. 105. It is even more curious that German historian Reiner Marcowitz explains Mahmud II's concession of Syria and Adana to Mohammed Ali as a result of the French mediation, a hardly tenable argument or a very curious understanding of the word "mediation." Marcowitz, p. 154.

16

The Second Mission of Anton Prokesch von Osten to Alexandria

During the First Mohammed Ali Crisis, Metternich did not remain entirely passive. When the affair became more serious in early 1833 owing to Russia's intervention on the Bosphorus, he decided to facilitate the restoration of peace in the Near East by sending Anton Prokesch von Osten to Alexandria. Prokesch was instructed to persuade the Egyptian governor to moderate his territorial demands and thus make the reconciliation with the sultan more feasible. The mission is not significant in itself because it finally did not influence the outcome of the crisis, but it demonstrates the significance that Metternich attributed to Near Eastern affairs as well as his distrust of France, the latter being also indirectly manifested in Anton Prokesch von Osten's contest with French diplomat Baron Boislecomte for "diplomatic glory."

The Origins of Prokesch's Mission

The anti-Russian attitude of the French government from early 1833 revealed itself not only in Constantinople but also in London where the French ambassador and former foreign minister of Napoleon I, Charles Maurice de Talleyrand-Périgord, suggested in accordance with his instructions that France, Great Britain and Austria should act in the whole affair together and mediate between the two quarrelling parties, explicitly omitting Russia with the aim of excluding it from the resolution of the Near Eastern crisis. This was entirely unacceptable for Metternich unwilling to abandon Nicholas I, who had granted the sultan the military aid that could not be given by Austria and had been refused by the two Maritime Powers. Moreover, Talleyrand's idea was totally contradictory to what Metternich actually wanted: to exclude France from the negotiations if it did not want to cooperate with the conservative Powers. He also wanted to obtain British support for Russia's conduct because, as he underlined his own words in red, *"the English cabinet does not desire anything other than what we want."*[1] Consequently, Metternich tried to thwart Talleyrand's plan and bring Great Britain to the conservative camp which was, however, rather difficult due to fact that Wellington's ministry had been replaced in November 1830 by a liberal cabinet in which the post of foreign secretary was assumed by John Henry Temple 3rd Viscount Palmerston, with whom Metternich significantly disagreed on most European affairs in the early 1830s, in particular over Belgium and Portugal. In November 1832, Metternich even labelled Palmerston as "the worst of the bad."[2] Nevertheless, in early 1833, the Austrian chancellor thought that he could succeed and persuade the foreign secretary to cooperate with the conservative Powers instead of with France and thus break up the union of the two liberal Powers in the Oriental field.[3]

Having been upset by Roussin's anti-Russian proceeding in Constantinople and Talleyrand's actions in London, Metternich did his best to persuade Palmerston of the correctness and benevolence of Russia's Near Eastern policy and warn him of France's close relationship with Mohammed Ali and the latter's dangerous designs in the Mediterranean: "France does not want the destruction of the Porte but it aims at establishing a power that under the appearance of a subjugation more nominal than real will be strong enough to be able to offer it [France] the advantages of an ally for its political designs further afield. If in the event and in view of the spirit that was always characteristic of the cabinet of Versailles, as it is today of the cabinet of Tuileries, nothing should surprise us; it is no less true that the views of France are not and will never be accordance with ours; that

---

[1] Metternich to Ottenfels, Vienna, 22 Feb. 1833, HHStA, StA, Türkei VI, 59.
[2] Metternich to Ottenfels, Vienna, 4 Nov. 1832, HHStA, StA, Türkei VI, 56.
[3] Metternich to Ottenfels, Vienna, 14 Feb. 1833, HHStA, StA, Türkei VI, 59; Tatishchev to Nesselrode, Vienna, 27 Jan., 5, 7 and 13 Feb., 11 March 1833, AVPRI, fond 133, Kantseliariia, opis 469, 1833/211; Broglie to Talleyrand, Paris, 21 Jan. 1833, Talleyrand to Broglie, London, 6, 28 and 31 Jan. 1833, Le Duc de Broglie (ed.), *Mémoires du Prince de Talleyrand*, V, Paris 1998, pp. 96, 108–109, 111–113, 115; Prokesch-Osten, *Aus den Tagebüchern*, p. 178.

in the general situation of current affairs they are no less opposed to those of Russia, and that they will always remain in opposition with the primary interests of the court of London. The three courts share the views of France concerning the existence of the sultan, but their opinions differ from those of this Great Power with regard to the extraordinary self-aggrandisement of the viceroy; the four courts could proceed together in the first of these directions, while the natural force of things will have to unite Austria, Russia and Great Britain in the opposite direction to the ambitious views of France. It is on the last basis on which we must concentrate our thinking and base our approach."[4] Baron Philipp von Neumann, temporarily representing Austria in London instead of Prince Esterházy, who was on leave, was instructed to "make it clear to Lord Palmerston that he will do best if he proceeds with Austria instead of with France if he wants to settle the affair."[5]

Metternich finally did not achieve the desired cooperation of Great Britain with the conservative Powers but at least the British cabinet did not accept Talleyrand's proposal. What also pleased the chancellor was Palmerston's decision to name a new consul general in Alexandria, Colonel Patrick Campbell, and to instruct him to object to Mohammed Ali's behaviour and urge him to reduce his territorial demands. These demands consisted of all the Syrian pashaliks, which covered the whole area between the Sinai Peninsula and the Taurus Mountains, some districts in the latter with strategic passes giving whoever possessed them control of the way from Syria to Asia Minor and the town of Adana for the facilitation of the transport of wood for Egyptian shipyards. The pasha did not want to obtain his demands by force with his army waiting inactive in Asia Minor because he feared the escalation of the crisis if it attacked the Ottoman capital, but he also refused to give up his peace conditions. Mahmud II refused to pay such a high cost for peace and decided to resist, but although he obtained through the Russian military aid effective protection of his capital and strong backing for not yielding, he also had no power to destroy his enemy's armed forces. The crisis found itself in deadlock in early 1833, and this gave the European cabinets time to act. How they exploited it in Constantinople was shown in the previous chapter, but

---

[4]   Metternich to Ottenfels, Vienna, 14 Feb. 1833, HHStA, StA, Türkei VI, 59.
[5]   Metternich to Neumann, Vienna, 21 Feb. 1833, HHStA, StA, England 204.

the solution to the Ottoman-Egyptian conflict actually no longer lay in Constantinople but in Alexandria where, according to Metternich, a new diplomatic offensive had to be launched. He was well aware of the fact that in the actual situation where Mohammed Ali dominated land and sea the decision the pasha "takes will determine everything."[6] Therefore, when the chancellor learnt of Campbell's commission, he resolved to follow this step and send to Egypt his own special agent, who would cooperate with the British and thus help to solve the crisis and simultaneously achieve the strengthening of the British-Austrian cooperation for which Metternich eagerly longed.[7]

Such a special agent was needed because due to Joseph von Acerbi's strong antipathy towards Mohammed Ali and the subsequent strained mutual relations it was impossible for top-level negotiations to be entrusted to him; moreover, Metternich did not trust Acerbi's political talent in combating the French intrigues. Consequently, it was necessary to find someone sufficiently skilled and acquainted with the conditions prevailing in Egypt. The choice logically fell on Prokesch, who had already met Mohammed Ali in 1826 and was well known for his admiration of this Oriental despot and his reforms as well as for his considerable knowledge of the Levant. All of this led Metternich to trust in Prokesch's influence over the governor of Egypt. The main reason for his choice was Prokesch's correct assessment of the distribution of power between Mohammed Ali and Mahmud II from the very beginning of the crisis; Prokesch was the only Austrian diplomat who had not shared the generally widespread belief in the sultan's victory and had correctly predicted the defeat of the Ottoman troops, an opinion that had received no echo in the Chancellery for a long time.[8] Metternich thereby admitted his own error and tolerated his

---

[6] Bussierre to Broglie, Vienna, 25 March 1833, AMAE, CP, Autriche 418.

[7] The instructions for Campbell, London, 4 Feb. 1833, Metternich to Ottenfels, Vienna, 4, 14 and 22 Feb. 1833, HHStA, StA, Türkei VI, 59; Metternich to Neumann, Vienna, 15 and 21 Feb. 1833, HHStA, StA, England 204; Metternich to Ficquelmont, Vienna, 1 March 1833, HHStA, StA, Russland III, 99; Ottenfels to Metternich, Constantinople, 8 and 29 Jan., 4, 8 and 21 Feb. 1833, HHStA, StA, Türkei VI, 56; Maltzan to Frederick William III, Vienna, 12 Feb. 1833, GStA PK, HA III, MdA I, 6021; Lamb to Palmerston, Vienna, 14 Feb. 1833, TNA, FO 120/136.

[8] Metternich to Ottenfels, Vienna, 13 Feb. 1833, HDA, 750, OO 38; Metternich to Neumann, Vienna, 15 Feb. 1833, HHStA, StA, England 204; Tatishchev to Nesselrode, Vienna, 13 Feb. and 1 March 1833, AVPRI, fond 133, Kantseliariia,

subordinate's positive attitude towards the Egyptian governor, which is also proved in a relevant passage of Prokesch's book on Mohammed Ali quoting Metternich that, however, cannot be verified and must be accepted with a pinch of salt: "You predicted the course of the war better than the cabinets did. You want in principle the same thing that I want; the preservation of Turkey, though in a different way. I do not rebuke you for that because I value your intentions and even accept that you may have a better perspective on the matter than the cabinets. But I have to take them into account and particularly stress the principle that every insurrection with a weapon in the hand of the vassal against the sultan is reprehensible and that the preservation of the throne for the present dynasty is a political necessity for Europe. Therefore, what must be done is to bring peace between the sultan and his powerful vassal as soon as possible to remove the dangers threatening Europe from this conflict ... We intend to send a delegate to Mohammed Ali ... I have it in mind to choose you. Prepare yourself for the journey."[9]

Prokesch learnt of his mission on 10 February 1833. Its goal was to acquaint Mohammed Ali with the negative attitude of the Austrian Empire towards his rebellious behaviour and urge him to moderate his demands and conclude peace as soon as possible. However, owing to the Egyptian victories on the battlefields, it was impossible to deny Mohammed Ali the acquisition of Syria including Damascus, and Metternich resigned himself to this concession. This realism already manifested itself in the attitude of the prince in the autumn of 1832, even before the Battle of Konya, under the weight of the reports from the Near East. When the sultan's special envoy, Namik Pasha, travelled via Vienna to London to request the British naval support, Metternich warned him against continuing in the war without sufficient resources: "If I were in the place of the sultan, I would ask myself: Do I have means to expel the Egyptians from Syria? If yes, then I would not hesitate even a moment to do so. If not, then I would not endanger the fate of the empire but I would negotiate with Mohammed Ali."[10] "The sultan's nature precludes this," replied Namik

---

opis 469, 1833/211.

[9]   Prokesch-Osten, *Mehmed-Ali*, p. 37.

[10]   Metternich to Ficquelmont, Vienna, 8 Dec. 1832, HHStA, StA, Russland III, 97.

Pasha, "in particular when he believes that he has sufficient means
at his disposal."[11] Nevertheless, the insights provided by Namik did
not dispel Metternich's concerns; with a full sense of the gravity of
the situation, the chancellor came to the conclusion that Mahmud II
should consider carefully the possibility of the surrender of Syria to
his vassal and not risk another defeat that could have fatal consequences for the future existence of the Ottoman Empire. The course
of events thus entirely confirmed Metternich's apprehension, held from
late 1832, regarding the insufficient resources of the Porte to pursue
a successful fight against Mohammed Ali; in the prince's own words,
after the Battle of Konya the Ottoman Empire seemed to be "within
two inches of its ruin."[12] Under the given conditions, the loss of Syria
was for Metternich an inevitable consequence of the course of the war.
What he opposed was the cession of Adana with its strategic passes
in the Taurus Mountains, which, in his opinion, ought to remain under the sultan's direct rule.[13] Its eventual handover to the Egyptian
pasha would significantly strengthen his power and, consequently, future political goals, something that concerned Metternich for the future: "Mohammed Ali's plans are not yet aimed at the overthrow of
the throne in Constantinople. Forced by the events, this rebel has no
regard for Mahmud but his plans follow a more prudent direction.
The viceroy is still occupied with establishing his own power. Once
this purpose is assured, more than from any military successes gained
due to the weakness and ineptitude of his adversaries, he will expand
his political horizons."[14]

German historian Daniel Bertsch claims that Prokesch was to
mediate peace between Mahmud II and Mohammed Ali but this view
is inaccurate.[15] It was all-important for Metternich that the Austrian
diplomatic intervention in favour of Mahmud II did not have the char-

[11]   Ibid.
[12]   Metternich to Trauttmannsdorff, Vienna, 18 Jan. 1833, HHStA, StK, Preussen
152.
[13]   Metternich to Neumann, Vienna, 17 Oct. 1832, HHStA, StA, England 199;
Metternich to Ottenfels, Vienna, 17 Oct. and 15 Dec. 1832, HHStA, StA, Türkei
VI, 56; Metternich to Ottenfels, Vienna, 20 Jan. and 14 Feb. 1833, HHStA, StA,
Türkei VI, 59; Metternich to Ficquelmont, Vienna, 12 Feb. 1833, HHStA, StA,
Russland III, 99; Maltzan to Frederick William III, Vienna, 15 and 18 Dec. 1832,
GStA PK, HA III, MdA I, 6020; Prokesch-Osten, *Aus den Tagebüchern*, p. 174.
[14]   Metternich to Neumann, Vienna, 15 Feb. 1833, HHStA, StA, England 204.
[15]   Bertsch, p. 179.

acter of mediation because Metternich considered such a proceeding to be a serious violation of statehood, and he instructed Prokesch in this respect: "Since the principles recognised by our court would never allow us to assume the right to act as mediators between a legitimate sovereign and his rebellious subjects, powerful reasons founded on a sound and enlightened policy prevent us from choosing this mode of terminating the current conflict ... Avoid rigorously in your conduct everything which could give your actions the appearance of mediation."[16] Prokesch was not to assume the role of a mediator but align himself with the sultan and use this position to oppose Mohammed Ali's demands regarding Adana, a position very different from the character of Roussin's, as Metternich later explained to Apponyi: "The admiral [Roussin, in fact vice-admiral] constantly talks and acts as a mediator; the two imperial courts [Austria and Russia] behave in a manner which supports the sultan's rights. The former is positioned between the sultan and his rebellious vassal, [while] the two imperial courts have taken up a position in support of the sultan."[17] Prokesch was also instructed to act together with Campbell, with whose instructions Metternich was acquainted and of which he entirely approved, and resist the intrigues of the French and prevent the British consul general from falling under their influence.[18] Metternich roundly expressed his strong distrust of France in his instructions: "France regards Egypt as a conquest that, sooner or later, cannot escape from it and the well-known saying of Napoleon 'that the Mediterranean is destined by nature to be a French lake' has not lost anything in its value in the eyes of the present [French] government."[19] What Prokesch actually was to do in Alexandria was summarised by Metternich in this way: "The sultan has indicated he is prepared to make concessions to him [Mohammed Ali]. You must constantly to do all you can to persuade the viceroy not to make overly excessive demands."[20]

---

[16] Metternich to Prokesch, Vienna, 23 Feb. 1833, HHStA, StA, Türkei VI, 59.
[17] Metternich to Apponyi, Vienna, 9 May 1833, HHStA, StA, Frankreich 289.
[18] Metternich to Prokesch, Vienna, 23 Feb. 1833, Metternich to Ottenfels, Vienna, 14 Feb. 1833, HHStA, StA, Türkei VI, 59; Lamb to Campbell, Vienna, 23 Feb. 1833, TNA, FO 78/227; F. Engel-Jánosi, *Die Jugendzeit des Grafen Prokesch von Osten*, Innsbruck 1938, pp. 155–161.
[19] Metternich to Prokesch, Vienna, 23 Feb. 1833, HHStA, StA, Türkei VI, 59.
[20] Ibid.

Prokesch's Arrival in Egypt and the Boislecomte Affair

Prokesch departed from Trieste on 4 March 1833 and arrived in Alexandria after sunset on 2 April after sailing for 29 days on rough seas.[21] On the following day, he met Campbell who had been there since 26 March. Due to their identical instructions it was not difficult for both men to concur in a joint approach to Mohammed Ali, whom Prokesch met for the first time on 5 April. During this audience, the Austrian diplomat denounced the revolt and recommended to the pasha to withdraw his army from Asia Minor and reconcile himself to lesser territorial gains. He repeated this also three days later during another meeting. Nevertheless, Mohammed Ali refused to give in to these demands and declared that he would not conclude peace with his sovereign until he received all the required domains, and he added that no threat would induce him to renounce one inch of the terrain, particularly not that of Adana which he wanted for its strategic position as well as for its wood supplies which he needed for the construction of his fleet. He believed that owing to Mahmud II's "generosity" he would finally get everything he wanted. If, however, his expectation unfortunately turned out to be false, he declared that he was prepared to conform to the will of God and die an honourable death with a sword in his hand and devote his last breath to the welfare of his nation. It was easy for Mohammed Ali to make such theatrical statements because he did not have to fear an attack from the almost unarmed sultan and he did not believe that any European Power would bear the costs of an assault on him for a piece of land in Asia Minor, Austria least of all since, as he told Prokesch: "Austria will not go against me. The destruction of Egypt would lead to the ruin of Trieste, whereas the prosperity of Syria would increase the welfare of that city."[22] This was definitely an exaggeration but not without an element of truth. With regard to this fact and the lack

---

[21] Prokesch visited the Austrian consulate on the day of his arrival. He wrote later in his book on Mohammed Ali that he had arrived in Egypt on 3 April, but this mistake is refuted not only by his own letters and diary but also by Campbell's report. Prokesch to Metternich, Alexandria, 3 April 1833, HHStA, StA, Türkei VI, 59; Campbell to Palmerston, Alexandria, 2 April 1833, TNA, FO 78/227; Prokesch-Osten, *Mehmed-Ali*, p. 37; Prokesch-Osten, *Aus den Tagebüchern*, p. 179.
[22] Prokesch to Metternich, Alexandria, 8 April 1833, HHStA, StA, Türkei VI, 59.

of any coercive means, both Prokesch and Campbell were unable to make any progress during the whole month of April and at the beginning of May they were still unsuccessful. Nothing changed even after the arrival of the French diplomat, Baron Charles Joseph Edmond de Boislecomte,[23] on 29 April 1833, because his primary tasks were to demand the retreat of the Egyptian forces from Asia Minor and remedy Roussin's considerably hostile behaviour towards Mohammed Ali; there was no question of any French pressure or even military intervention against Egypt because of Adana. Moreover, in compliance with his second goal, Boislecomte expressed his opinions much less sharply than his Austrian and British colleagues and did not forget to mention the special regard France felt for its Egyptian protégé.[24]

Whereas the relations between Boislecomte and Campbell were good, between Boislecomte and Prokesch there existed an apparent coolness from the very beginning, which was caused by the anti-French animosity generally widespread in the Austrian diplomatic corps as well as Prokesch's discovery that Boislecomte used the rank of the plenipotentiary without authorisation. What followed was insignificant for the course of events but perfectly represented the attitude of Austria towards France on a small scale. Therefore, the two men's contest for diplomatic glory resulting from Prokesch's careful observation of the distinctions exhibited to his French colleague and his

---

[23] Baron, later Count, Charles Joseph Edmond de Boislecomte (1796–1863), started his diplomatic career as a third secretary at the French embassy in Vienna and later served at the embassies in St Petersburg and Madrid. He participated in the congresses in Troppau, Ljubljana and Verona. In September 1825 he became a deputy head of the Political Department at the French Ministry of Foreign Affairs and was promoted to the director in 1829. He retired after the July Revolution in the following year and he remained out of the diplomatic service until 1833 when he was chosen for the mission in Egypt. After his departure from Alexandria at the beginning of July 1833, he travelled through the Ottoman Empire until 1835. He represented France in various countries until 1848. G. Douin (ed.), *La mission du Baron de Boislecomte, l'Égypte et la Syrie en 1833*, Caire 1927, p. XXXVII.

[24] Prokesch to Metternich, Alexandria, 6 and 11 April, 3 May 1833, and attached *Discours prononcé par M. le Baron Boislecomte, Ministre plénipotentiaire, envoyé en mission en Égypte, à S. A. Méhémet Ali, Vice-roi d'Égypte, dans l'audience du 1ᵉʳ Mai 1833*, HHStA, StA, Türkei VI, 59; Prokesch to Metternich, Alexandria, 8 April 1833, Stürmer to Prokesch, Constantinople, 22 April 1833, Stürmer to Metternich, Büyükdere, 23 April and 5 May 1833, HHStA, StA, Türkei VI, 57; Campbell to Palmerston, Alexandria, 9 April and 2 May 1833, TNA, FO 78/227; Puryear, *France*, p. 198.

jealous defence of his own position in the hierarchy of the diplomatic body should be explained in brief here. The story started on the first day of May in the morning when the French diplomat went ashore for the expected audience with the Egyptian governor. Since a considerable honour had been paid by Mohammed Ali to Muravyov in January of the same year, Boislecomte and the French consul general in Egypt, Jean François Mimaut, requested an even greater honour for the representative of the country which was considered to be Mohammed Ali's protector.[25] When the answer containing the promise of a reception identical to the audience of the Russian general was delivered from the palace to Boislecomte, the Frenchman, as he later wrote in his report, replied that "speaking in the name of France and coming here to give Mohammed Ali the fullest expression of its benevolence and interest, I could not accept being held to a comparison with anybody and I demanded that distinctions were added to the ceremony adopted for Mr Muravyov that would not leave anybody in any doubt about the nature of the feelings held for us by a friend who recognised that he had come into power and grown in stature under our protective influence."[26]

Therefore, as in January on the occasion of Muravyov's arrival, a carriage drawn by four white horses was prepared on the shore. By chance, this coach had been used by Napoleon Bonaparte during his Egyptian campaign and his insignia was still visible. A large escort led by the commanding officer of the palace guard accompanied Boislecomte into the palace where the regiment on parade paid homage to the French diplomat, which, as Boislecomte did not forget to mention, had not happened in Muravyov's case. With the band playing *La Marseillaise*, he approached Mohammed Ali, who stood as he invited Boislecomte. Afterwards, the governor sat down close to the Frenchman, which according to the etiquette of the country meant equality of their ranks. Mohammed Ali paid further compliments to Boislecomte to demonstrate that he treated him as an equal: he offered him a hookah as richly ornamented with gold as his own,

---

[25] Mimaut was treated with the same disaffection by Prokesch and Acerbi as was Boislecomte. Campbell to Palmerston, Alexandria, 31 March 1833, TNA, FO 120/139; Campbell to Palmerston, Alexandria, 8 April 1833, TNA, FO 78/227; Puryear, *France*, p. 201.

[26] Boislecomte to Broglie, Alexandria, 1 May 1833, Douin, *La mission du Baron de Boislecomte*, pp. 3–4.

and coffee was served to both men at the same moment. Nevertheless, Boislecomte forgot to mention in his report to his government
the fact that this grandiose reception was achieved largely due to the
information that he operated in Egypt with the rank of the plenipotentiary (*ministre plénipotentiaire*) charged with the special mission
to Mohammed Ali by the French government. To be exact, Mimaut
introduced his colleague under the even stranger and more ostentatious rank: the ex-director of the department of the French Ministry of
Foreign Affairs and plenipotentiary of the French court (*l'ex-directeur
du département des affaires étrangères et ministre plénipotentiaire de
la Cour de France*). The French consul general informed Campbell of
this fact in a note dated 1 May 1833 and Prokesch on the following
day.[27]

The Austrian diplomat suspected the correctness of Boislecomte's
status from the very first moment because he had received no news
from Constantinople about Boislecomte's mission to Alexandria, to
say nothing of any information about the Frenchman's accreditation
from the Ottoman court. He also viewed with considerable displeasure
the compliments bestowed upon Boislecomte during his audience with
Mohammed Ali. Prokesch undoubtedly saw in Boislecomte's claim to
honours exceeding those awarded to Muravyov a symptom of French
vanity, in particular when he learnt that "on the morning of the audience of that general [Muravyov] there was a heavy rain and that the
pasha [Mohammed Ali] with his usual courtesy, had of his own accord,
sent his carriage for him, and of which chance the French had now
availed themselves."[28] With regard to the expected meeting between
Prokesch and Boislecomte, the former needed to learn the exact rank
of the latter to know the level of respect he was obliged to grant to the
Frenchman. Too little grace would equal impoliteness, while too much
would lead to the humiliation of the Austrian diplomat and thus his
emperor. Therefore, on 2 May 1833, Prokesch provoked the exchange

---

[27] Mimaut to Prokesch, Alexandria, 2 May 1833, Prokesch to Metternich, Alexan-
dria, 4 May 1833, HHStA, StA, Türkei VI, 59; Mimaut to Campbell, Alexandria,
1 May 1833, Campbell to Palmerston, Alexandria, 2 May 1833, TNA, FO 78/227;
Mimaut to Broglie, Alexandria, 9 May 1833, AMAE, CP, Égypte 3; Martens to
Frederick William III, Büyükdere, 26 May 1833, GStA PK, HA III, MdA I, 7272;
Boislecomte to Broglie, Alexandria, 1 May 1833, Douin, *La mission du Baron de
Boislecomte*, p. 3.
[28] Campbell to Palmerston, Alexandria, 2 May 1833, TNA, FO 78/227.

of notes with Mimaut in the matter of Boislecomte's rank. In the first note, the Austrian put the question at which court Boislecomte was accredited as a plenipotentiary.[29] The French consul general's answer contained the invitation to the consulate for a meeting with Boislecomte but no word of the accreditation.[30] Nevertheless, Prokesch was not to be brushed off so easily, and, because Mimaut's note did not contain the desired explanation of the qualification and credentials of the French agent, he repeated his question: "Having an official position with His Highness Mohammed Ali, I am obliged to know the position under which an official of the court on friendly terms with mine presents himself to the vizier in order to be able to offer him the due respect according to the rank under which his government has installed him into the office. For this reason, I am asking you, Sir, that you kindly inform me whether I can consider the envoy as a plenipotentiary to His Highness Mohammed Ali, which could only increase the level of high esteem that I will be delighted to pay to him."[31] At this moment, the French consul general could not claim any longer that Boislecomte held the rank of plenipotentiary. However, Mimaut did not hesitate to assert that his colleague would have required from Mohammed Ali or other diplomats anything other than to be considered the French king's agent on a special mission. Mimaut also added that on the occasion of Boislecomte's arrival in Egypt, only he himself informed Yusuf Boghos Bey about his compatriot's rank used at the French Ministry of Foreign Affairs.[32] Nevertheless, the acknowledgement that in reality Boislecomte did not hold the rank that was officially declared after his arrival and used at the meeting with Mohammed Ali was undoubtedly rather humiliating for Mimaut. Boislecomte's turn to be embarrassed came a day later, on 3 May 1833, when he received a visit from Prokesch. When Prokesch found both doors to the entrance to Mimaut's hall open and unguarded, he entered and immediately encountered Boislecomte, whom he did not know and whom he considered owing to his humble behaviour to be Boislecomte's secretary, Mr Noué. Having introduced himself,

---

[29] Prokesch to Mimaut, Alexandria, 2 May (A) 1833, HHStA, StA, Türkei VI, 59.
[30] Mimaut to Prokesch, Alexandria, 2 May (A) 1833, HHStA, StA, Türkei VI, 59.
[31] Prokesch to Mimaut, Alexandria, 2 May (B) 1833, HHStA, StA, Türkei VI, 59.
[32] Mimaut to Prokesch, Alexandria, 2 May (B) 1833, HHStA, StA, Türkei VI, 59. For more on this exchange of letters between Prokesch and Mimaut see also Campbell to Palmerston, Alexandria, 3 May 1833, TNA, FO 78/227.

Prokesch tacitly waited for an answer. The situation had to be undoubtedly embarrassing for the Frenchman who, after some pause, broke the silence and started to excuse himself for the mistake concerning his rank. As soon as Prokesch realised with whom he was speaking, he interrupted Boislecomte's apologies to end this awkward situation and thus spare him from more serious humiliation.[33]

Prokesch's circumspection regarding Boislecomte's rank spared him from the fate of Colonel Campbell, who had let himself be dragged into the two Frenchmen's game, and, during Boislecomte's visit, had dealt with him as if he were a plenipotentiary. The British consul general was considerably angry when he learnt the truth, and Boghos Bey also did not hide his irritation. Having judged the whole matter retroactively, Prokesch considered the conduct of both French diplomats as a typical example of the ridiculous vanity characteristic of the whole French diplomacy and he did not regret his exposure of what was still remembered in Alexandria as the "fanfaronade" at the end of the decade. In fact, he had definitely acted with the aim of striking this blow at Boislecomte, which was an action entirely corresponding with the strong antipathy of Austrian diplomats and Metternich in particular towards France. It is probably not necessary to add that in the case of a Russian diplomat, Prokesch would have never proceeded in the way he did in the case of Boislecomte, for he would not have wanted to harm the cordial relations between Austria and Russia. As for those between him and Boislecomte, they naturally remained implacable. It is true that the Frenchman wrote at the end of June 1833 that "except for some slight sensibility typical for our positions, our relations were very good,"[34] but their mutual underlying antipathy and jealousy are clearly visible in both diplomats' dispatches on the occasion of the receipt of presents from Mohammed Ali. Boislecomte obtained a snuff-box richly ornamented with diamonds, the price of which was estimated to be 600 pounds sterling, and a sabre embroidered with gold. He did not fail to draw attention to the fact that his Austrian colleague received only a horse. Nevertheless, on this point he was entirely mistaken as it is evidenced in Prokesch's and Campbell's reports: the Austrian diplomat obtained not only two Arabian horses

---

[33] Prokesch to Metternich, Alexandria, 4 May 1833, HHStA, StA, Türkei VI, 59.
[34] Boislecomte to Broglie, Alexandria, 29 June 1833, Douin, *La mission du Baron de Boislecomte*, p. 73.

(and not one as Boislecomte claimed), but also, like Boislecomte, a snuff-box ornamented with diamonds and a sabre and in addition a scarf and some souvenirs for his wife. These luxurious presents proved the considerable honour paid to him by Mohammed Ali, and through other presents – two Arabian horses, two scarves and two pieces of embroidered cloth – to Metternich and his wife as well.[35] According to Prokesch, this fact invoked the envy of Boislecomte and Campbell, saying that the former "was apparently neglected by the viceroy [Mohammed Ali],"[36] whereas the latter was "blinded by jealousy."[37]

The End of Negotiations and Prokesch's Role in the Austro-Egyptian Relations after 1833

At the same time as Boislecomte's arrival came the official confirmation of the earlier rumour that Mahmud II was willing to grant Mohammed Ali the whole of Syria. This news aggravated the position of the Austrian and British diplomats because the sultan's acquiescence gave hope to Mohammed Ali that he would finally obtain everything he desired. Therefore, he refused the settlement offered to him because Adana was not included, which moved Prokesch and Campbell to start a new diplomatic offensive on 5 May with the help of new instructions from British and Austrian representatives in Constantinople and the information from the British government that if Mohammed Ali would not reduce his demands, the British fleet was ordered to blockade the Alexandrian port. Although this threat seemed to have an effect, the negotiations lasted for several more days before the turning point was reached in the evening of 9 May when, after three and a half hours of

---

[35] Prokesch to Metternich, Alexandria, 4 and 8 May, 29 June 1833, Prokesch to Stürmer, Alexandria, 8 May 1833, HHStA, StA, Türkei VI, 59; Stürmer to Metternich, Büyükdere, 26 July 1833, HHStA, StA, Türkei VI, 57; Martens to Frederick William III, Büyükdere, 26 May 1833, GStA PK, HA III, MdA I, 7272; Campbell to Palmerston, Alexandria, 1 July 1833, TNA, FO 78/227; Boislecomte to Broglie, Alexandria, 29 June 1833, Douin, *La mission du Baron de Boislecomte*, pp. 75–76; H. von Pückler-Muskau, *Aus Mehemed Alis Reich: Ägypten und der Sudan um 1840*, Zürich 1985, p. 128.

[36] Prokesch to Metternich, Alexandria, 29 June 1833, HHStA, StA, Türkei VI, 59.

[37] Prokesch-Osten, *Aus den Tagebüchern*, p. 186.

long discussion with Mohammed Ali during which "the same ground was gone over and over and the same arguments enforced in every way which we thought likely to be of use,"[38] Campbell and Prokesch obtained from their counterpart a verbal promise that if the sultan refused to grant him Adana, he would not demand it any more, would reconcile himself with Syria and recall the troops from Asia Minor. On 14 May, at 4 o'clock in the afternoon, he satisfied the request of both diplomats and gave the promise in writing. However, only two hours later, a ship which entered the Alexandrian harbour brought news that Mahmud II had finally acquiesced and surrendered Adana as well as Syria.[39]

Mohammed Ali obtained everything he demanded and the diplomatic victory of both European diplomats was revealed to be entirely worthless. Prokesch reacted to the sultan's weakness with these words: "See how with an inconceivable coincidence the Porte compromises our efforts in ceding with one simple stroke everything that we have just regained."[40] The same disillusion prevailed in Vienna where Metternich, in statements that were full of "sorrow and dejection,"[41] expressed his surprise that Mahmud II had gone as far as he had on 5 May, an act of weakness to which Metternich responded with this laconic statement: "The farce is thus complete!"[42] The chancellor was convinced that the Ottoman ruler could have been spared the excessive losses if he had placed more confidence in the support of the Great Powers, including France, which finally also declared against the cession of Adana. Unfortunately for Mahmud II, he was not aware of their unanimous attitude in this matter at the moment of his capitulation, which was not, however, any sort of justification for Metternich's annoyance: "Nothing was so easy for the Porte as sav-

---

[38] Campbell to Palmerston, Alexandria, 10 May 1833, TNA, FO 78/227.
[39] Yusuf Boghos Bey to Prokesch, Alexandria, 14 May 1833, Prokesch to Metternich, Alexandria, 13 April and 14 May 1833, Prokesch to Stürmer, Alexandria, 10 May 1833, HHStA, StA, Türkei VI, 59; Stürmer to Metternich, Büyükdere, 11 and 28 May 1833, HHStA, StA, Türkei VI, 57; Mandeville to Campbell, Therapia, 22 April 1833, Yusuf Boghos Bey to Campbell, Alexandria, 14 May 1833, Campbell to Palmerston, Alexandria, 16 and 29 April, 7, 8, 9 and 15 May 1833, TNA, FO 78/227.
[40] Prokesch to Metternich, Alexandria, 15 May 1833, HHStA, StA, Türkei VI, 59.
[41] Bussiere to Broglie, Vienna, 17 April 1833, AMAE, CP, Autriche 418.
[42] Metternich to Ficquelmont, Vienna, 25 May 1833, HHStA, StA, Russland III, 97.

ing Adana. Everything was in its favour and it had the means at its
disposal. The intentions of the European Powers were pronounced on
the subject, they were unanimous. The fact that they were not known
in Constantinople on a certain day is not at all a sufficient reason for
justifying the decision taken by the sultan. In Constantinople everything happens slowly, except for those decisions that instead of being
made in haste should be made after careful consideration."[43] Metternich criticised the outcome of the crisis for two other reasons. Firstly,
he was concerned, and the events of the following years were to prove
him right, that Mahmud II would never be reconciled to the loss he
had suffered and would long for revenge. This is why the chancellor
did not talk about the settlement of 5 May 1833 as being a peace settlement but only as the creation of a new order, a development that
promised nothing but trouble for the future.[44] Secondly, he saw in the
extension of Mohammed Ali's power an increase of French influence
over the eastern Mediterranean; the cabinet in Paris was able to obtain
through its protégé something that Napoleon had been unable to gain
by force of arms: "In this way the acquisition of Adana by Mohammed
Ali is completely a question of European policy. It is particularly an
English, Austrian and Russian question. The seas of the Levant will
belong to Egypt from now on, in other words to France. Instead of
becoming a market for all nations engaged in commerce, Egypt will
become a power and this power will form a French outpost against
England and Russia in Asia. The Mediterranean will thus become a
French lake, exactly what Napoleon wanted to achieve."[45]

In connection with the short-lived victory of the diplomats, some
doubts about Prokesch's real merit in the resolution of the negotiations with Mohammed Ali have occurred in the past. Especially Sir
Charles Kingsley Webster with a strong animosity towards Metternich
and Prokesch expressed the opinion that the surrender of the Egyptian governor was achieved mainly by the threat of the naval blockade, that the final pressure was applied by Campbell and Boislecomte,
and that Prokesch took no part in it.[46] One must agree with the first

---

[43] Metternich to Apponyi, Vienna, 20 May 1833, HHStA, StA, Frankreich 289.
[44] Ibid.; Metternich to Stürmer, Vienna, 4 July 1833, HHStA, StA, Türkei VI,
59; Sainte-Aulaire to Broglie, Vienna, 19 and 27 May 1833, AMAE, CP, Autriche
418.
[45] Metternich to Neumann, 8 May 1833, HHStA, StA, England 204.
[46] Webster, *Palmerston*, I, pp. 287–288.

statement because Mohammed Ali's decision had to be significantly influenced by the prospect of the paralysis of Egyptian trade and the transport of troops by sea together with the arrival of additional Russian forces on the Bosphorus and the consequently smaller chance for success of a possible Egyptian assault on the Ottoman capital. Nevertheless, Prokesch definitely participated in the negotiations with the governor and Boghos Bey with the same zeal as his British colleague. Moreover, both men closely cooperated, which is proved by Austrian, British, Prussian and French documents. In any case, the Austrian agent played a more important role than Boislecomte, who, as already mentioned above, had held back since his arrival and exerted no significant pressure on Mohammed Ali in the matter of Adana. The difference in the attitudes of the governments in London and Paris is clearly visible in the fact that while the former was prepared to blockade Alexandria, the latter only threatened to send the French fleet to the eastern Mediterranean without any reference to the blockade of the Egyptian port. This passivity was caused by the pro-Egyptian tendency of France and the desire not to harm French-Egyptian relations more than was necessary for the settlement of the war. Unsurprisingly, Boislecomte decided after his arrival in Alexandria to proceed alone and not to advise Mohammed Ali to give up Adana. Boislecomte later praised himself for this fact because he did not unnecessarily compromise his government at the moment when Mahmud II ceded the province. It is also true that Prokesch ensured that Boislecomte was left out of the negotiations because Campbell could not ask his French colleague to proceed jointly without Prokesch's approval, and he never got it.[47]

This reflection might seem somewhat unnecessary in so far as Campbell's and Prokesch's success in the negotiations with Mohammed Ali was short-term, and it was to all intents and purposes ex-

---

[47] Broglie to Mimaut, Paris, 19 March 1833, Prokesch to Metternich, Alexandria, 6 April and 14 May 1833, Prokesch to Stürmer, Alexandria, 8 May and 16 June 1833, HHStA, StA, Türkei VI, 59; Prokesch to Metternich, Alexandria, 4 May 1838, Stürmer to Metternich, Büyükdere, 26 May 1833, HHStA, StA, Türkei VI, 57; Boislecomte to Yusuf Boghos Bey, Alexandria, 8 May 1833, Campbell to Palmerston, Alexandria, 2, 9 and 13 May 1833, TNA, FO 78/227; Martens to Frederick William III, Büyükdere, 11 June 1833, GStA PK, HA III, MdA I, 7272; Boislecomte to Broglie, Alexandria, 9, 12 and 16 May 1833, Douin, *La mission du Baron de Boislecomte*, pp. 29–49; Puryear, *France*, p. 200.

tremely brief since it lasted only several days or, in the case of the written surrender of Adana, only several hours. Nevertheless, as for the mission itself, it did not lack importance for Prokesch and, thereby, the future of Austro-Egyptian relations as well. For Prokesch, the mission served to increase the esteem in which he was held by the Austrian ruling elites and certainly contributed to his prestige as a prominent expert on the conditions prevailing in the Ottoman Empire. However, this fact altered nothing in Francis I's earlier decision to nominate Prokesch to the post of Austrian envoy in Athens. To all appearances Prokesch seemed to prefer to be sent as consul general to Egypt. During his mission of 1833 terminated on 29 June, the local European community as well as Mohammed Ali presumed that Prokesch would be the man who would replace Acerbi in Egypt and perhaps for this reason the governor gave his guest due consideration and even wrote a letter to Metternich full of praise for Prokesch. Furthermore, Prokesch himself seemed to prepare his own way to the post with his strong support of Acerbi's request to be moved from Egypt and his advice to the Austrian chancellor that the present consul general should be replaced with a more capable man who would be able to solve matters usual for a consular post as well as complicated diplomatic affairs owing to the fact that the Egyptian governor *de facto* became the second ruler of the Ottoman Empire after his victorious fight with the sultan. Metternich was well aware of the fact that Acerbi had to be recalled from Egypt but for this post he finally chose not Prokesch but Anton von Laurin who arrived in Egypt in December 1834.[48]

Metternich acknowledged Prokesch's familiarity with Egypt in a different way: in the autumn of 1834, he ordered that Laurin was subordinated in diplomatic matters to the new Austrian envoy in Athens instead of the representative in Constantinople. The latter still had the right to obtain Laurin's reports, but Prokesch was charged with supervising the political correspondence between Alexandria and Vi-

---

[48] Prokesch to Metternich, Trieste, 8 Aug. 1833, HHStA, StA, Türkei VI, 59; Mohammed Ali to Metternich, Alexandria, 27 June 1833, attached to Campbell to Palmerston, Alexandria, 1 July 1833, TNA, FO 78/227; Maltzan to Frederick William III, Vienna, 26 Jan. 1830, GStA PK, HA III, MdA I, 6014; Prokesch to Metternich, Alexandria, 4 May 1833, Prokesch-Osten, *Aus dem Nachlasse*, p. 135; G. Hamernik, *Anton Ritter von Laurin: Diplomat, Sammler und Ausgräber*, unpublished dissertation, Wien 1986, p. 3; Sauer, *Österreich und die Levante*, pp. 335–337.

enna, commenting on the events in the land on the Nile and instructing Laurin to persuade Mohammed Ali to remain at peace. Metternich explained this measure by way of Mohammed Ali's extraordinary significance and the necessity of receiving the news from Egypt and delivering his own instructions to Laurin as quickly as possible: "The viceroy of Egypt is not, like other pashas, a simple administrator of regions entrusted to his care. He is a very powerful vassal and all the more formidable for his sovereign ... It is thus of the utmost interest for us to observe and anticipate his initiatives, like those other Great Powers who would aspire to exert influence over his designs and resolutions, and predict or eliminate everything in them that could compromise the preservation of the Ottoman Empire and, therefore, the general peace of Europe. The theatre of these actions is not in Constantinople, it is where Mohammed Ali resides."[49] This step produced some surprise among the Ottomans as well as European diplomats, and the Russian consul general in Alexandria, Duhamel, even attacked it as being the utmost impropriety because Egypt formed an integral part of the Ottoman Empire and it was natural and appropriate that the agents in this province were directed by the representatives accredited at the Porte and not the Greek government; for that reason, as he declared, "the pasha of Egypt is very flattered by this arrangement and he regards it as a semi-recognition [of his independence]."[50] Laurin, whose personal relationship with Prokesch was somewhat strained, was also displeased with this modus operandi and openly criticised it after his arrival in Egypt in the presence of other consuls.[51]

The man who objected most to the sending of reports from Egypt to Vienna via Athens was Bartolomäus von Stürmer, who substituted for Ottenfels in Constantinople in mid March 1833. Ottenfels originally was to go to Austria for a long-desired vacation, but after his arrival Metternich offered him employment at the Chancellery where Ottenfels finally became the head of the department dealing with in-

---

[49] Metternich to Stürmer, Vienna, 3 Dec. 1834, HHStA, StA, Türkei VI, 62.
[50] Report from Duhamel, Alexandria, 24 Sept. 1834, attached to Stürmer to Metternich, Büyükdere, 21 Oct. 1834, HHStA, StA, Türkei VI, 61.
[51] Metternich to Prokesch, Vienna, 17 Oct. 1834, HHStA, StK, Griechenland 12; Metternich to Ficquelmont, Vienna, 20 Oct. 1834, HHStA, StA, Russland III, 103; Metternich to Stürmer, Vienna, 3 Dec. 1834, HHStA, StA, Türkei VI, 62; Martens to Frederick William III, Büyükdere, 11 Nov. 1834, GStA PK, HA III, MdA I, 7274; Mimaut to Rigny, Cairo, 15 Jan. 1835, AMAE, CP, Égypte 5.

ternal affairs and an advisor of the state. As for Stürmer, who was functioning as an extraordinary envoy, he was deeply disappointed not to be nominated as internuncio despite Ottenfels' promotion and the fact that other members of the diplomatic corps in Constantinople addressed him in this way by force of habit. He obtained the relevant credentials of an internuncio only in September 1835.[52] With regard to Laurin's political reports, Stürmer joined in this criticism of them because he felt offended by the reduction of part of his responsibilities. In his opinion, the factor of faster delivery of dispatches to Vienna via Athens was not a sufficient reason for such an important change. However, Metternich denied the allegations that the change had been caused by any reasons other than the question of expedience and Prokesch's expertise: "This arrangement is based exclusively on the geographical situation. With the establishment of an Imperial mission in Greece we have obtained an intermediate point placed on the shortest route between Vienna and Alexandria ... It is thus doubly advantageous for us to use this intermediate point lying on the most direct way between Vienna and Alexandria as the most expeditious way of obtaining information and having it dispatched to our new consul general in Egypt (a man otherwise entirely unqualified in the handling of political affairs) through the channel of a diplomatic agent, whose expert knowledge of men and things in the land will enable him to deal more appropriately with the information received."[53] Consequently, Stürmer was unable to influence Metternich's decision and had to accept the fact that Laurin sent his dispatches primarily via Athens and only in some cases by way of Constantinople.[54]

---

[52] Metternich to Francis I, Baden, 1 Aug. 1832 HHStA, StK, Vorträge 268; Stürmer to Metternich, Büyükdere, 7 Sept. 1833, HHStA, StA, Türkei VI, 58; Stürmer to Metternich, Constantinople, 15 Jan. and 30 April 1834, HHStA, StA, Türkei VI, 60; Königsmarck to Frederick William III, Büyükdere, 9 and 16 September 1835, GStA PK, HA III, MdA I, 7276; Ottenfels, *Memoari*, pp. 253–273; Mayr, *Staatskanzlei*, p. 24.
[53] Metternich to Stürmer, Vienna, 18 Feb. 1835, HHStA, StA, Türkei VI, 64.
[54] Stürmer to Metternich, Büyükdere, 21 Oct. 1834, HHStA, StA, Türkei VI, 61; Sauer, *Österreich und die Levante*, p. 349.

*   *   *

This state of affairs corresponded with Metternich's high estimation of Prokesch as well as the importance he attributed to Mohammed Ali after 1833. For the following eight years the European cabinets occupied themselves with the so-called Egyptian Question raised by Mohammed Ali's ambitions and Mahmud II's desire to annihilate his too powerful Egyptian vassal. This problem significantly exceeding the limits of an internal problem of the Ottoman Empire finally led to a new and more serious crisis in 1839 that lasted more than two years. All the time from 1833 to 1841 Prokesch served as Metternich's advisor in this Egyptian Question. Despite the fact that Prokesch was personally sympathetic to Mohammed Ali and did not always share the views of his superior, Metternich was easily able to deal with Prokesch's difference in opinions and use him as a useful and skilled advisor in his effort to preserve the Ottoman Empire. This fact offers further evidence against the allegation that Metternich inclined to assemble around himself mere yea-saying minions.

17

Unkiar-Skelessi and Münchengrätz

Shortly after the termination of the First Mohammed Ali Crisis, two important events occurred in 1833 with crucial impact on the development of the Eastern Question in the following years: the signature of the Russo-Ottoman Treaty in Unkiar-Skelessi and the Austro-Russian negotiations in Münchengrätz. These events intensified the aversion and distrust of the two Maritime Powers towards Russia and also contributed to the deterioration of their relations with Austria, which continued to be Russia's ally. Contemporaries as well as later historians often misunderstood the motivation of Metternich's cooperation with Russia and his opinions on Near Eastern affairs in the second half of 1833. The most significant and harmful myth is that Metternich yielded in Münchengrätz to Nicholas I's interests in the East in return for the tsar's support against the revolutions in the West. Erroneous claims like this fundamentally distort the real picture of not only Metternich's Near Eastern policy but also his general role and aims in European politics.

The Treaty of Unkiar-Skelessi

The Kütahya peace settlement disappointed the Porte and displeased Austria but the other Powers involved reconciled more easily with its conditions. Nicholas I was indifferent to the degree of the weakening of the sultan's authority in the area of the Fertile Crescent where he had no direct interests; his primary target not to allow the fall of the Ottoman Empire and the accession of a capable Egyptian governor to the Ottoman throne had been achieved.[1] In Paris and London the ter-

---

[1] Kutluoğlu, p. 102; Martens, p. 35.

mination of hostilities was welcomed as a precursor to the Russians' departure from the Bosphorus, which was the primary goal of both cabinets and to which they subordinated all their diplomatic steps in Constantinople in the spring of 1833. Although a vision of the Ottoman territory without Russian soldiers was not entirely unattractive for Metternich, in particular after the settlement of the crisis, he refused to support the conduct of the two Maritime Powers because first, he did not find the presence of Lazarev's squadron as dangerous as the subversive behaviour of the French, and second, he trusted the tsar's promise for the immediate withdrawal of his forces at the moment when the Egyptian army retreated behind Taurus. The prince was also well aware of the fact that a diplomatic offensive in the Ottoman capital accompanied by the threat of sending the foreign fleets into the Sea of Marmara could seriously worsen the relations between Russia and other Great Powers. The apprehension prevailing in Vienna of an eventual rupture among the Great Powers is evident from the summoning of all Austrian officers to active service, the conscription of recruits faster than usual and the purchase of a considerable quantity of cloth and 4,000 horses for the army in the early spring of 1833.[2]

The mutual distrust also reduced the already low level of ability of the pentarchy to act, from which Mohammed Ali could and finally also did profit. Metternich had hoped that the joint action of both Western Powers together with Austria and Russia would assure a prompt and successful solution to the Turko-Egyptian war because, as he was firmly convinced, the collective pressure on Mohammed Ali would be enough to make him yield.[3] Consequently, he tried to dispel the suspicions of the cabinets in Paris and London of Nicholas I's sinister intentions by assuring them of the tsar's sincerity and inof-

---

[2] Metternich to Ficquelmont, Vienna, 11 March and 4 June 1833, HHStA, StA, Russland III, 99; Sainte-Aulaire to Broglie, Vienna, 13 May 1833, AMAE, CP, Autriche 418; report from Vienna, 26 March and 7 April 1833, SS, HD, SG 10026, Wien 92.

[3] Mohammed Ali's conciliatory behaviour in May 1833 after learning of the threat of the use of the British fleet, as well as his later cautious conduct towards the Great Powers, prove that Metternich's optimism was extremely well founded. Stratford Canning shared it at that time and believed that just the presence of the British squadron before Alexandria would be enough to assure that the pasha would yield. Crawley, *Greek Independence*, p. 213.

fensive designs because,[4] as he wrote to Apponyi on 18 March 1833, "in advocating the case for a sound policy we are simultaneously advocating both the position of the Russian tsar and our own."[5] Five days later, he told Bussierre: "We assure you that in St Petersburg they want exactly the same as we do ourselves. Accept our guarantee: We will be equally prepared to offer Russia the same guarantee of the sincerity of your intentions."[6] And he continued: "All of us share the same intention, the same impartiality; let us follow the same line of approach and not go against each other. It is mistrust that destroys everything, complicates everything [and] aggravates even the simplest affair."[7]

All the attempts of the Austrian chancellor to calm the troubled waters were futile because the cabinets in London and Paris had little confidence in his and the Russian monarch's assurances and were too concerned about the extent of their own influence over the sultan's court if the tsar's forces were to remain close to the Ottoman capital for too long. In an attempt to achieve their departure, Roussin claimed the right of the French fleet to enter the Sea of Marmara in the first half of April 1833. Although new British Ambassador John Lord Ponsonby did not act as uncompromisingly as his French counterpart, he also contemplated inviting the British fleet to the Golden Horn. In the second half of June, the fleets of both Maritime Powers anchored at the Island of Tenedos in the immediate vicinity of the Dardanelles.[8]

---

[4]   Metternich to Ottenfels, Vienna, 19 Dec. 1832, HHStA, StA, Türkei VI, 56; Metternich to Stürmer, Vienna, 3 June 1833, HHStA, StA, Türkei VI, 57; Metternich to Apponyi, Vienna, 27 Jan., 2 Feb., 6 and 21 April 1833, Metternich to Hügel, Vienna, 9 June 1833, HHStA, StA, Frankreich 289; Metternich to Neumann, Vienna, 15 Feb. and 8 March 1833, HHStA, StA, Türkei VI, 57; Metternich to Trauttmannsdorff, Vienna, 20 March 1833, HHStA, StK, Preussen 152; Lamb to Palmerston, Vienna, 8 Jan., 8 and 22 March, 14 April 1833, TNA, FO 120/136; Maltzan to Frederick William III, Vienna, 23 Jan. and 1 Feb. 1833, GStA PK, HA III, MdA I, 6021; Maison to Broglie, Vienna, 25 Feb. 1833, Bussierre to Broglie, Vienna, 18, 22, 25 and 28 March, 16 June 1833, AMAE, CP, Autriche 418.
[5]   Metternich to Apponyi, Vienna, 18 March 1833, HHStA, StA, Frankreich 289.
[6]   Bussierre to Broglie, Vienna, 22 March 1833, AMAE, CP, Autriche 418.
[7]   Ibid.
[8]   Stürmer to Metternich, Constantinople, 11 and 23 April 1833, HHStA, StA, Türkei VI, 59; Puryear, *France*, pp. 206–207; L. Sainte-Aulaire, *Souvenirs (Vienne 1832–1841)*, Paris 1926, p. 18.

Roussin's request for permission to send the French fleet to Constantinople was regarded in Vienna as another entirely needless measure, a new "attempt to obtain a triumph in the French press for the
national vanity by attributing the departure of the Russians as a consequence of the arrival of the French force."[9] Therefore, at the beginning of June, Metternich not only refused the appeal of both Western
Powers for Austrian support in their effort to dispose of the Russians
still camping on the Bosphorus but also instructed Stürmer to forestall
all Roussin's anti-Russian plans. Stürmer had already sought support
from among the Ottoman dignitaries and foreign diplomats for the
tsar's conduct and the continuance of his soldiers and marines in the
Ottoman Empire until the return of the Egyptian army to Syria, and
he therefore had no problem complying with these latest instructions,
especially when Roussin and Ponsonby changed their strategy and
assumed a passive attitude. They learnt of the Russo-Ottoman offensive and defensive treaty negotiation, whose conclusion they regarded
as a lesser evil than the continuing presence of Russian troops and
warships. They presumed that the Russians would leave immediately
after the signing of this treaty and did not want to do anything that
could prevent such an outcome.[10]

The negotiation between Count Orlov sent again by Nicholas I
to Constantinople and Mahmud II's delegates was finally successful.
After receiving news of the departure of the last Egyptian soldier from
Asia Minor, both sides concluded in the Russian military camp in
Unkiar-Skelessi on 8 July 1833 a defensive treaty consisting of public
and secret clauses. In the first part both countries promised mutual
assistance in the event of an attack from a third party. In the second,
secret, part the sultan was relieved of the obligation to offer military
aid in such a case, but he was obliged to close the Straits to the navies

---

[9] Lamb to Palmerston, Vienna, 9 June 1833, attached to Metternich to Neumann,
Vienna, 9 June 1833, HHStA, StA, England 204.
[10] Metternich to Stürmer, Vienna, 3 June 1833, HHStA, StA, Türkei VI, 57;
Metternich to Ficquelmont, Vienna, 4 June 1833, HHStA, StA, Russland III, 99;
Stürmer to Metternich, Büyükdere, 5 and 25 May 1833, HHStA, StA, Türkei
VI, 57; Sainte-Aulaire to Broglie, Vienna, 19 May and 4 June 1833, AMAE, CP,
Autriche 418; Lamb to Palmerston, Vienna, 3 June 1833, TNA, FO 120/137; Brock-
hausen to Frederick William III, Vienna, 3 and 5 June 1833, GStA PK, HA III,
MdA I, 6021; Tatishchev to Nesselrode, Vienna, 5 June 1833, AVPRI, fond 133,
Kantseliariia, opis 469, 1833/210; V. J. Puryear, "L'opposition de l'Angleterre et
de la France au traité d'Unkiar-Iskelesi en 1833," *RH* 1938, 182, pp. 287–288.

of any states at war with Russia. Two days after the conclusion of the Treaty of Unkiar-Skelessi, the Russians left the Bosphorus. As was customary in the Ottoman Empire, the secrecy did not last long and the wording of the agreement including the secret articles was known to Ponsonby at the latest on 12 July.[11]

When the French and British ambassadors at Vienna, Count Louis de Sainte-Aulaire and Sir Frederick Lamb, learnt of the planned conclusion of the defensive and offensive (*sic*) alliance between Russia and the Porte at the beginning of July, they immediately arranged a meeting with Metternich, who considered the rumour of this alliance to be false and he was sure that it would be disclaimed by the next messenger. In any case he denied that he had been informed in this matter: "You do not know precisely what happened in Constantinople, and I swear to God and people on my honour and conscience that I am completely ignorant of the facts."[12] And he was not lying because he really was entirely ignorant in this matter. In the following weeks he also refused to believe the planned signing of the Treaty for he received no information to that effect and he was convinced that the tsar surely would not have concealed such an intention from his ally; moreover, he did not even receive any reports from Constantinople on the negotiations. The first one containing any mention of the Treaty was that sent on 14 July in which Stürmer notified Metternich of its conclusion but did not mention the secret clause; the secrecy was not revealed to Stürmer from Butenev until 7 August. Ficquelmont came to learn of it from Nesselrode four days later.[13]

It is interesting to note that Orlov and the members of the Russian mission dined in the internunciature on 6 July and on the following day Stürmer was a guest at the banquet arranged by Orlov and Butenev in honour of the tsar's birthday. Although they evi-

---

[11] Stürmer to Metternich, Büyükdere, 10 July 1833, HHStA, StA, Türkei VI, 57; Anderson, *The Great Powers*, pp. 42–44; Webster, *Palmerston*, I, p. 304.

[12] Sainte-Aulaire to Broglie, Vienna, 5 July 1833, AMAE, CP, Autriche 419.

[13] Metternich to Ficquelmont, Vienna, 10 July 1833, HHStA, StA, Russland III, 99; Stürmer to Metternich, Büyükdere, 10 July 1833, HHStA, StA, Türkei VI, 57; Stürmer to Metternich, Büyükdere, 7 Aug. 1833, HHStA, StA, Türkei VI, 58; Lamb to Palmerston, Vienna, 3, 8 and 23 July 1833, TNA, FO 120/137; Sainte-Aulaire to Broglie, Vienna, 5 and 6 July 1833, Baden, 14 July 1833, AMAE, CP, Autriche 419; Brockhausen to Frederick William III, Vienna, 5 and 16 July 1833, GStA PK, HA III, MdA I, 6021; Tatishchev to Nesselrode, Vienna, 10 July 1833, AVPRI, fond 133, Kantseliariia, opis 469, 1833/210; Molden, p. 75.

dently had more than one opportunity, they told him nothing about the planned conclusion of the Treaty despite the cordial relations that existed between them and Stürmer as well as earlier with Ottenfels. Furthermore, Orlov had already experienced Metternich's and Ottenfels' support during his previous diplomatic mission in Constantinople after the termination of the Russo-Ottoman war. Despite this, he did not inform Stürmer of the Treaty until his departure on 12 July. Undoubtedly the situation was of some embarrassment for both Orlov and Stürmer, but in any case the latter was not entirely pleased with the explanations given by the Russian diplomat as to why he had not informed his Austrian colleague sooner: he knew that Stürmer had not been given instructions for such a circumstance, he did not know whether the negotiations would be successful, and he presupposed that the tsar had already informed the Austrian emperor. This deception put Stürmer into an awkward position because he had to face a considerable number of questions on his own opinion of the Treaty although until the autumn he had no instructions on this matter. Finally, he had no choice but to defend the content of the document without knowing his own government's attitude towards it although he naturally knew Metternich's general views and he himself was convinced it contained nothing that could be of concern.[14]

Metternich remained ignorant of the full text of the Treaty until mid August when he was finally confronted with its reality. Although he explained the entire confusion to be the result of Orlov's clumsiness and he tried to show no embarrassment, Sainte-Aulaire did not doubt that Metternich must have felt humiliated as a result of the tsar's conduct. It is impossible to disagree with the French ambassador's opinion because it had to be a rather humiliating situation for Metternich: after his frank and zealous defence of the Russian Near Eastern policy, he was the last man who learnt of the Treaty. He was certainly mortified by the distrust of his ally and this is clearly evident from, first, his reproach to Tatishchev and, second, his later extraordinarily frank comments made in late December 1833 to Lamb when he told him what he had said to Nicholas I in Münchengrätz that September: "I took a guarantee for your conduct which has been fal-

---

[14] Stürmer to Metternich, Büyükdere, 10, 14 and 26 July, 7 and 11 Aug. 1833, HHStA, StA, Türkei VI, 57; Roussin to Broglie, Therapia, 16, 22 and 23 July 1833, AMAE, CP, Turquie 267.

sified [and] I undertook a guarantee for your actions which has proved false. I do not object to the principle of your Treaty, and you have committed no offense which should divide us, but you have weakened my power of serving you in the same way again. Should I ever feel myself called upon hereafter to answer for the conduct of your Govt [government], what can I expect from France and England, but that they should reply: Dupe[d] once, you may be deceived again!"[15] The Russians' silence towards the Austrians also invited the distrust of the cabinets in London and Paris towards Metternich because no one was willing to believe that the chancellor really had not known about the plan to conclude the Russo-Ottoman Treaty: denial of its existence on his part was generally considered to be a lie and only gradually did the opinion that he had been deceived prevail.[16]

Despite his hurt pride and humiliation, Metternich continued to advocate the tsar's policy and the content of the Treaty of Unkiar-Skelessi because, in his opinion, the document in no way weakened the sultan's independence and Russia obtained no advantages threatening the rights of other Great Powers. After 8 July 1833, the Ottoman Empire was no more nor less dependent on its powerful northern neighbour than before and also in the question of the Straits no real change had occurred. As to their being closed during a war between Russia and any other European state or states, he even welcomed it because it ensured the neutralisation of the Black Sea and the preclusion to the creation of a battle zone beyond the Austrian frontiers. On the basis of these arguments he concisely labelled the document as "the Treaty without real value,"[17] which was later confirmed by American historian Philip Edward Mosely's almost identical words ("the self-contradictory and, at bottom, useless treaty") as well as the research of other historians like Jacob Coleman Hurewitz, Maria N. Todorova or Alexander Bitis.[18] And even if Metternich preferred a unilateral

---

[15] Lamb to Palmerston, Vienna, 26 Dec. 1833, TNA, FO 120/137.

[16] Metternich to Esterházy, Königswart, 28 July 1833, Töplitz, 16 Aug. 1833, HH-StA, StA, England 204; Tatishchev to Nesselrode, Töplitz, 13 Aug. 1833, AVPRI, fond 133, Kantseliariia, opis 469, 1833/210; Sainte-Aulaire to Broglie, Vienna, 31 Aug. 1833, AMAE, CP, Autriche 419; Webster, *Palmerston*, I, p. 306.

[17] Sainte-Aulaire to Broglie, Vienna, 30 Nov. 1833, AMAE, CP, Autriche 419.

[18] J. C. Hurewitz, "Russia and the Straits Question: A Reevaluation of the Origins of the Problem," *WRP* 14, 1962, pp. 605–632; P. E. Mosely, *Russian Diplomacy and the Opening of the Eastern Question in 1838 and 1839*, Cambridge 1934, p. 30;

agreement of all Powers ensuring the future existence of the Ottoman Empire, with regard to the impossibility of achieving general consent to this question, he was easily able to accept the existence of a Russo-Ottoman alliance: "The primary task was to save the Ottoman Empire. We would have preferred a method other than the Treaty of 8 July, but owing to England's and France's refusal of assistance, protection offered by Russia is a better option than the isolation of the Porte exposed to the mercy of its very formidable enemy, the viceroy of Egypt. The Treaty of 8 July does not contradict any stipulation in previous contracts. In principle no one has a right to object to it and Austria will defend it if necessary."[19] In short: there was nothing in the document to cause Austria any consternation and that is why it was not difficult for its chancellor to congratulate Mahmud II on its signing.[20]

At this point one must mention Alexander Lyon Macfie's opinion that Metternich had reacted to the conclusion of the Treaty with great displeasure and had angrily informed Sainte-Aulaire: "It would be better for the Empire of Austria to face the risk of a war of extermination rather than to see Russia aggrandised by a single village at the expense of the Turkish Empire."[21] However, this is a total misinterpretation of the sources. First, no evidence of any negative reaction on the part of the chancellor was found in any of the researched correspondence including that housed in the French Ministry for Foreign Affairs. Second, the words Metternich repeated throughout the year of a single village or an inch of soil whose annexation by Russia would have been a reason for Austria to go to war were not an indication of his supposed anger but a way to make the British and French believe in his real confidence in Russia's benign intentions towards the

---

M. N. Todorova, "Mythology of the Eastern Question: The Treaty of Unkiar-Iskelessi," M. N. Todorova (ed.), *Aspects of the Eastern Question: Essays from the First Bulgarian-Dutch Symposium of Historians, Sofia, 6–7 June 1984*, Sofia 1986, p. 25; Bitis, p. 477.

[19] Sainte-Aulaire to Broglie, Vienna, 1 Oct. 1833, AMAE, CP, Autriche 419.

[20] Metternich to Esterházy, Königswart, 28 July 1833, Töplitz, 16 Aug. 1833, HHStA, StA, England 204; Metternich to Hügel, Töplitz, 16 Aug. 1833, HHStA, StA, Frankreich 289; Metternich to Stürmer, Vienna, 3 Oct. 1833, HHStA, StA, Türkei VI, 57; Stürmer to Metternich, Büyükdere, 8 and 11 Aug. 1833, HHStA, StA, Türkei VI, 58; Lamb to Palmerston, Vienna, 3 Sept. 1833, TNA, FO 120/137; Sainte-Aulaire to Broglie, Vienna, 3 Oct. 1833, AMAE, CP, Autriche 419.

[21] A. L. Macfie, *The Eastern Question 1774–1923*, London, New York 1996, p. 22.

Ottoman Empire. His guarantees for the tsar's Near Eastern policy were entirely frank. When Sainte-Aulaire told him that the Treaty was dangerous, the prince asked him: "Would you be prepared to recognise the same danger in a defensive alliance between the Porte and Austria?"[22] After the ambassador's entirely negative answer Metternich continued: "So calm yourself and do not worry any further about the dangers which you attribute to the Russian Treaty. A treaty that Austria approves of is the same as an act signed by it!"[23]

In London and Paris the responses to the Treaty of Unkiar-Skelessi were diametrically opposite to Metternich's and the shock at the news of its conclusion surpassed the reaction to the news of the Russian military intervention on the Bosphorus even though there was really nothing Great Britain and France could object to with any justification. It was particularly the fear of the Russian dominance in the Levant which led both Powers to attempt to forestall the ratification of the Treaty. Nevertheless, the Porte reacted to their representatives' protest notes of 26 August 1833 with the statement that the document contained nothing detrimental for a third party and the sultan as a sovereign monarch was entitled to conclude agreements with other countries. British and French diplomats in St Petersburg received the same response. Metternich's attitude towards the British and French protests was naturally negative because he regarded them as unjustified. He repeated his already expressed opinion that the Treaty was signed by two sovereign rulers and contained nothing disadvantageous to the Ottoman Empire or any other states.[24] He wrote to Stürmer in early October: "The Porte is a sovereign Power and, therefore, absolutely at liberty in its political actions. No third Power that has not been invited to do so has the right to sanction or reject the merit

---

[22] Metternich to Hügel, Vienna, 23 Nov. 1833, HHStA, StA, Frankreich 290.
[23] Ibid.
[24] Metternich to Stürmer, Vienna, 3 Oct. and 24 Dec. 1833, HHStA, StA, Türkei VI, 59; Metternich to Esterházy, Vienna, 10 Dec. 1833, HHStA, StA, England 204; Tatishchev to Nesselrode, Vienna, 2 and 11 Nov. 1833, AVPRI, fond 133, Kantseliariia, opis 469, 1833/210; Sainte-Aulaire to Broglie, Vienna, 4 Nov. 1833, AMAE, CP, Autriche 419; Sainte-Aulaire to Broglie, Vienna, 14 March 1834, AMAE, CP, Autriche 420; Ponsonby's note to the Porte, 26 Aug. 1833, Roussin's note to the Porte, 26 Aug. 1833, the Porte's note to Ponsonby and Roussin, 20 Sept. 1833, Stürmer to Metternich, Büyükdere, 5, 19 and 25 Sept. 1833, HHStA, StA, Türkei VI, 58; Anderson, *Eastern Question*, p. 85; Webster, *Palmerston*, I, p. 305.

of the proceedings of a free and independent Power."[25] When in the autumn of the same year Metternich learnt of the Maritime Powers' declaration that they would behave as though the Treaty did not exist, he found it to be an irrational and unprecedented: "I must admit that every Great Power, if it feels empowered to do so, has the right to protest with the force of arms the conclusion of a transaction between other countries that it regards as prejudicial to its own interests, but if it wants to regard the accomplishment of a reality as not having taken place, this has no precedent, this is absurd."[26] As a practical diplomat, Metternich also did not understand what the two Powers wanted achieve with their protests, the result of which could hardly be other than precisely nothing. In his opinion, the best way to neutralise the Treaty was to avoid the necessity of its conditions being brought into existence, in other words that all the Great Powers united by the same interest in the preservation of the Ottoman Empire would keep a watchful eye on Mohammed Ali's ambitions and Mahmud II's hunger for vengeance and forestall the outbreak of any new war between the two Oriental despots which would force the Russian armed forces to return to the Bosphorus, something that Metternich feared not in itself but due to the highly probable deterioration of the relations among the European Powers that this would cause.[27] He told Sainte-Aulaire: "But the Treaty is a reality even though you do not wish to take its existence into account. So what would you do? In your place I would employ all the means at my disposal to prevent the Treaty from being put into effect, but since you do precisely the opposite, I have given up trying to understand you. It was Roussinades which brought about the Treaty and it will be for everyone to see that it is new Roussinades which will provoke its execution. If this is what is called making policy in Paris, in Vienna we see it rather differently."[28]

---

[25] Metternich to Stürmer, Vienna, 3 Oct. 1833, HHStA, StA, Türkei VI, 59.

[26] Tatishchev to Nesselrode, Vienna, 6 Nov. 1833, AVPRI, fond 133, Kantseliariia, opis 469, 1833/210.

[27] Ibid.; Metternich to Trauttmannsdorff, Vienna, 24 Nov. 1833, HHStA, StK, Preussen 153; Metternich to Esterházy, Vienna, 10 Dec. 1833, HHStA, StA, England 204.

[28] Metternich to Hügel, Vienna, 23 Nov. 1833, HHStA, StA, Frankreich 290.

The Meeting in Münchengrätz

The tension between Russia and the two Maritime Powers intensified the need of a meeting between the monarchs of the conservative Powers. Nicholas I and Francis I had wished to meet since the summer of 1830 and in the following year the latter extended the invitation, but the war in Poland prevented Nicholas I from visiting any place in the Austrian Empire. The two rulers did not finally come face to face until 10 September 1833 when the Russian tsar came to Münchengrätz upon a renewed invitation. For Metternich and his emperor this meeting in the North Bohemian town signified the climax of hitherto cordial relations with Russia. The reunion of the two monarchs and their prominent diplomats occurred, among other reasons, because of the latest events in the Near East, and consequently the Eastern Question was one of the points to be discussed. They quickly agreed on the necessity to preserve the Ottoman Empire with its ruling dynasty and decided to exert all available resources to achieve this goal. If the sultan's empire fell, Austria and Russia agreed to act in unison and consult each other. They also agreed upon an obligation to confront any attempt by Mohammed Ali to extend his power to the European part of the Ottoman Empire although the Egyptian governor had no such aspiration; nevertheless, Metternich and Nicholas I both feared such a prospect, particularly with regard to a possible expansion of French influence over the Balkans through the Egyptian governor. The terms of their agreements were included in a convention consisting of public as well as secret articles and signed on 18 September 1833.[29]

With the outcome of the Münchengrätz meeting there exists a legend, as widespread as it is absurd: that Metternich submitted to Nicholas I's interests in the East in return for his support against the revolutions in the West, and particularly in the Apennines. One of its original propagators, Heinrich von Treitschke, went from the presumption that Russia had been considerably hostile to the Ottoman Empire whereas Metternich had not been, but for Metternich the situation in Europe had been more important than that in the

---

[29] Metternich to Ficquelmont, Vienna, 25 May and 10 July 1833, SOA, RA C-A 383; Metternich to Hügel, Königswart, 30 Aug. 1833, HHStA, StA, Frankreich 289; Tatishchev to Nesselrode, Vienna, 25 May 1833, AVPRI, fond 133, Kantseliariia, opis 469, 1833/211; Lamb to Palmerston, 3 June 1833, TNA, FO 120/137; Molden, pp. 119–123; Schiemann, III, p. 208.

Near East, and therefore, he had agreed to this undertaking.[30] This nationalistic German historian presented this interpretation of events to prove the timidity and lack of credibility of the Austrian chancellor and it was generally accepted by following generations.[31] Whereas historians have changed their views of Nicholas I's alleged desire to destroy his weak southern neighbour since the late 19th century, the legend about Metternich's deal in North Bohemia still persists and has been adopted by a considerable number of historians, lately, for example, by Paul W. Schroeder. The source of this misinterpretation consists, as is clear from Schroeder's work, in the presumption that the Austrians and Russians were united on the danger of the revolutions in the West, but not on the affairs in the Near East, where Metternich allegedly feared Russia's conduct in the early 1830s.[32] Sometimes, however, even the reassessment of Schroeder's conclusion did not lead to the refutation of the "deal theory": although the German historian, Harald Müller, rightly asserts in his paper that during the meeting in Münchengrätz no difference in opinion on the Eastern Question existed between the Austrian chancellor and the tsar, he adds in the same breath that Metternich sacrificed Austrian interests in the Balkans and the whole of the Levant for the tsar's support in other European regions.[33]

Metternich himself predicted a quick arrangement of the meeting in Münchengrätz because, as he claimed in July, in fact there would be nothing to negotiate since the emperor, the tsar and their advisers "want the same thing, and they want it in the same way."[34] After only three days of talks with Nicholas I, the chancellor's expectation became reality: "His [the tsar's] thinking *is in accordance*,

[30] H. von Treitschke, *Deutsche Geschichte im Neunzehnten Jahrhundert, Vierter Theil: Bis zum Tode Friedrich Wilhelms III.*, Leipzig 1889, pp. 329–333.

[31] For this opinion see, for example, R. Albrecht-Carrié, *A Diplomatic History of Europe since the Congress of Vienna*, London 1958, p. 52; D. Southgate, '*The Most English Minister...*' *The Policies and Politics of Palmerston*, London 1966, p. 118; Molden, p. 90; Webster, *Palmerston*, I, pp. 310, 349 and 360.

[32] Schroeder, *Transformation*, pp. 731–732.

[33] H. Müller, "Der Weg nach Münchengrätz: Voraussetzungen, Bedingungen und Grenzen der Reaktivierung des reaktionären Bündnisses der Habsburger und Hohenzollern mit den Romanows im Herbst 1833," *Jahrbuch für Geschichte* 21, 1980, pp. 48 and 53.

[34] Metternich to Ficquelmont, Vienna, 10 July 1833, SOA, RA C-A 383.

I would even say identical *in all points* with ours."[35] Not only these self-confident statements but also the facts support the truth that the document forced none of the signatories to any compromises because their opinions and interests were virtually the same. The tsar had the same views of the situation on the Continent and in the Ottoman Empire as did Metternich. Therefore, Metternich did not have to sacrifice his interests in the East for the tsar's support in the West. The meeting in Münchengrätz also did not signify any important shift in the policy of either conservative Power or their relationship, which had been good long before September 1833; it was only the logical climax of their identical diplomacy in both Europe and the Levant about which Austria and Russia were able to reassure themselves. Metternich commented on the meeting in his instructions to Stürmer of 3 October 1833: "Never has a meeting of monarchs offered such harmony and fewer difficulties of any kind than that which has just taken place. All our expectations of the wisdom and absolute justice of Tsar Nicholas' opinions have become total certainty ... This sincere and intimate understanding of both imperial courts was never more genuine."[36] Consequently, it is impossible to agree with the claim of some historians that the Convention restored good relations between Austria and Russia that had allegedly been shattered by Metternich's concern about a possible Russian expansion in the Near East.[37] As shown above, such a fear had not existed in Ballhausplatz for several years; the Russo-Austrian antagonism over the Eastern Question was a distant memory in 1833. Therefore, the notion of Austrian historian Robert-Tarek Fischer that one of Metternich's successes in North Bohemia was the coercion of Russia to pledge to support the preservation of the Ottoman Empire is also untenable.[38]

Historians have debated for whom the concluded Convention was more advantageous and the first question has been which party conformed its procedure to the other's. With regard to the above-mentioned facts this question loses much of its importance, and yet it is good to pay some attention to Nesselrode's statement from his an-

---

[35] Metternich to Ottenfels, Vienna, 13 Sept. 1833, HDA, 750, OO 38.
[36] Metternich to Stürmer, Vienna, 3 Oct. 1833, HHStA, StA, Türkei VI, 57. See also Metternich to Hügel, Vienna, 22 Oct. 1833, HHStA, StA, Frankreich 290.
[37] For this opinion see Anderson, *Eastern Question*, p. 86; Kutluoğlu, p. 107; Puryear, *France*, p. 203.
[38] Fischer, p. 85. For similar view see also Macfie, p. 23.

nual report on the events of 1833 that "Austria satisfied all the wishes
of Russia: from the Convention of Münchengrätz it can be expected
that in subsequent developments in the Levant [Austria] will proceed
together with Russia and not against it."[39] In other words the Russian vice-chancellor believed that on 18 September Metternich had
moulded his diplomacy to conform to the tsar's concepts. A similar
opinion of Austrian dependence on Russia was also maintained in
Vienna where some members of the traditionally anti-Russian elites
blamed the chancellor for being overly flattered and falling under the
influence of Russian foreign policy. Metternich resolutely and rightfully rejected such views: "When Russia took another route from the
one I chose, I left it to go its own way. Today I am proceeding with
Russia because it is proceeding with me. A few years ago I did not
cooperate with it on the Greek Question and I was criticised for it. Today, when [Russia] wants the preservation of the Turkish Empire, I go
along with it, and I am criticised again. I do not conform to anybody
but I take the path that I consider to be correct. Whoever I find on
the same path I will take along with me."[40] This statement, however,
in no way signified, as wrongly interpreted by Harald Müller, that the
chancellor would have regarded himself as taking the lead while the
tsar merely followed him.[41] There is no evidence that Metternich had
such an ambition at that time. He only wanted to say that he had
not had to give up his own goals because the other party had adopted
them.

The second question is connected with the interpretation of the
stipulation about the joint action in the event of an attack against the
sultan or the fall of his empire. Usually it has been considered as a
great success for Metternich, for example by Barbara Jelavich, Philip
E. Mosely, Paul W. Schroeder, Alan Sked or Maria N. Todorova, who
claimed that this part of the Convention of Münchengrätz greatly
restricted the Russian freedom of action in the Eastern Question because of the tsar's assurance that no moves would be made without a
prior agreement with the Austrian Empire, which thus limited the advantage resulting from the Treaty of Unkiar-Skelessi.[42] Nevertheless,

---

[39] Molden, p. 107.
[40] The record of the conversation between Metternich and Prokesch on 25 Dec.
1833, Prokesch-Osten, *Aus den Tagebüchern*, p. 199.
[41] Müller, p. 60.
[42] Jelavich, *Habsburg Empire*, p. 49; Mosely, p. 26; Schroeder, *Transformation*,

it is difficult to share this conclusion relating at least to the restriction of the 8 July agreement. If the sultan had been attacked, Russia would have still been obliged to offer assistance even if Austria had disagreed, and the only advantage for Metternich in such a case was a greater chance to be informed about the tsar's intervention beforehand, which means that the Treaty of 8 July was not limited by the outcome of Münchengrätz. Consequently, Russia's independence was factually restricted only if it had wanted to intervene in the Ottoman Empire outside the terms of the obligation included in the Treaty of 8 July.

Was Russia really so limited in its freedom of action in the Near Eastern affairs with the Convention of Münchengrätz? And, on the other hand, did Nicholas I achieve success in this North Bohemian town by preventing the reconciliation of Austria with the Maritime Powers – in the words of Theodor Schiemann and Harald Müller, the creation of a coalition between Vienna, Paris and London?[43] To put it another way, to what extent were these two conservative Powers committed to joint action in the Levant in their mutual interest and to not cooperating with other countries? In my opinion, it is difficult to find an irrefutable answer since the text of the Convention seems to be somehow ambiguous in this respect. The explicit prohibition for either of the contracted parties to act independently is stipulated only in the second secret article and is applicable only in the event of the fall of the Ottoman Empire and with the aim of constituting a new order in the Levant. The non-secret parts contain only their pledge to defend both the sultan's independence and throne.[44] It is thus evident that the agreement to act jointly seems to concern how both Powers would proceed in the Near East in the event of the downfall of the Ottoman Empire, and it obliged them to jointly help the sultan in specified cases, but it did not prevent either of them from discussing the Eastern Question or concluding treaties with other countries, at least with the aim of achieving the goals contained in the non-secret part of the Convention of Münchengrätz. Some proof for the view that no prior agreement between Austria and Russia was needed in such cases can be found in the events of 1839: when in the late summer, in reaction

---

p. 632; Sked, *Metternich*, p. 91; Todorova, "Mythology," p. 29.
[43] Müller, p. 54; Schiemann, III, p. 238.
[44] Molden, pp. 119–123.

to a new Turko-Egyptian conflict again bringing the sultan's empire to the verge of collapse, Nicholas I decided to proceed primarily with Great Britain instead of Austria and to settle the Eastern Question within the terms of the stipulations contracted in North Bohemia six years previously, he did not consult Metternich in advance and presented him with a fait accompli.[45]

It is, however, true that Nicholas I succeeded in deepening the gulf between Austria and the Western Powers by forbidding the publication of the Convention, which, in contrast to the Treaty of Unkiar-Skelessi, remained unknown to the British and the French. Consequently, Metternich had no weapon with which he could dispel fears existing in London and Paris of a possible agreement between the two conservative Powers on the division of the Ottoman Empire or of Austrian consent to the Russian annexation of Moldavia and Wallachia. He tried to go with his explanations on the given situation as far as he could, which meant he could assure the Maritime Powers that nothing was agreed in Münchengrätz with which they would not agree; he told Sainte-Aulaire in November: "You have chosen Constantinople for the arena in which you battle with the Russian influence over Near Eastern questions. What can result from a contest in such a badly chosen place? ... I answer for the political thinking of Emperor Nicholas regarding the sultan. He wants what we want – the preservation of the Ottoman throne."[46] And he added in early December: "Your anxiety is based upon false suppositions; you consider us to be either the accomplices of Russia or deceived by it. We have said many times that we are its accomplices, but only for a single goal, that of preserving the Ottoman Empire, and I must believe that you do not seriously accuse us of being deceived. France can do nothing better than to cooperate in the task that the two imperial courts have set themselves instead of expending its energy with false conjectures and alarming the Porte with ill-founded insinuations."[47] His words that the Russian monarch desired neither Constantinople nor a village in the Principalities once again did not appease French and British ministers. On the

---

[45] For more see Chapter 25.
[46] Metternich to Hügel, Vienna, 23 Nov. 1833, HHStA, StA, Frankreich 290.
[47] Brockhausen to Frederick William III, Vienna, 6 Dec. 1833, GStA PK, HA III, MdA I, 6022.

contrary, this zealous defence of the tsar only aroused their suspicion and resentment towards the Austrian chancellor himself as well.[48]

Metternich strongly disapproved of the decision to conceal the content of the Convention because he found transparency to be the best instrument for overcoming prejudices. He wrote on 27 October 1833 to Esterházy: "The principles of this contract are so admirably irreproachable and tie the hands of every kind of Russian intervention so much so that instead of concealing its existence we should divulge it to every corner of Europe."[49] And to Ficquelmont in mid December: "I cannot regret too much that Tsar Nicholas prevented us from communicating even the text of the Convention concluded between the two imperial courts on the 18th of last September to the courts of England and France, as I had proposed in Münchengrätz. It is natural that the monarchs reached an agreement on the Eastern Question, and they certainly accomplished this task in the most dignified and useful way. I recognise that in view of the manner in which the Maritime Powers conducted themselves with regard to Russia, and if I may be permitted to say towards the tsar personally, this monarch found it beneath his dignity and honour, which are fortunately innate, to enter henceforth into any discussion with them, even on matters both good and laudable. Consequently, I restricted myself to proposing that this communication should simply be made from our part; the tsar has not wanted to see that the silence of his cabinet would clearly indicate the estrangement that it is afflicting on the cabinet in St. James, and that the same silence that the Austrian cabinet has also observed in this respect must necessarily leave them to suppose that some kind of sinister agreement exists between the two emperors."[50] Nevertheless, Nicholas I took a different view and did not reconsider his decision at all, which was a rather short-sighted solution, and he was ultimately the man who suffered the most from it; the secrecy of the Convention of Münchengrätz not only deepened the existing doubts concerning

---

[48] Metternich to Esterházy, Vienna, 10 and 26 Dec. 1833, HHStA, StA, England 204; Lamb to Palmerston, Vienna, 19 July 1834, TNA, FO 120/145; G. H. Bolsover, "Palmerston and Metternich on the Eastern Question, 1834," *EHR* 51, 1936, p. 240; C. W. Crawley, "Anglo-Russian Relations, 1815–1840," *CHJ* 3, 1929, p. 57; Bitis, p. 477; Webster, *Palmerston*, I, p. 314.
[49] Molden, p. 108.
[50] Metternich to Ficquelmont, Vienna, 16 Dec. 1833, HHStA, StA, Russland III, 99.

its conditions in London and Paris but also intensified the distrust of
the French and particularly the British public of Russian intentions
in the Near East, which led to the emergence of Russophobia in the
British Isles and a considerable estrangement in the Russo-British relations in the following years, as explained in the following chapter.
With most probability the tsar could have been spared this if he had
listened to Metternich's advice and had made the effort to explain his
policy instead of cloaking his actions in secrecy.[51]

∗   ∗   ∗

In evaluating Metternich's Near Eastern policy from September 1829
to September 1833 his remarkable analytical skills and his consistency
are immediately evident. He came to the conclusion shortly after the
signature of the Treaty of Adrianople that the tsar had adopted a
considerably pro-Ottoman attitude, and even if the chancellor had no
illusions about the real reasons for this change, he guessed correctly
that the Russian monarch was trying to keep the Ottoman Empire
alive because it suited Russian interests.[52] Therefore, he was able to
accept Nicholas I's assurances at face value since he knew well enough
that he did not need to worry about the tsar's real intentions towards
Russia's weak southern neighbour. Consequently, with regard to the
change in the Russian attitude towards the Ottoman Empire, Metternich had no reason to deviate from his own political line that was
much more consistent than his contemporaries as well as historians
supposed, and he was in no way under the influence of the Russian
court for one very simple reason: the aims of Austria and Russia in the
Levant as well as on the Continent were more or less identical, even
before July 1830. The support offered to Russia at the sultan's court

---

[51] Metternich to Esterházy, Vienna, 27 Oct. 1833, HHStA, StA, England 204;
Metternich to Esterházy, Vienna, 21 Jan. 1834, HHStA, StA, England 208; Metternich to Stürmer, Vienna, 5 Dec. 1833, HHStA, StA, Türkei VI, 57; Metternich
to Ficquelmont, Vienna, 16 Dec. 1833, HHStA, StA, Russland III, 99; Brockhausen
to Frederick William III, Vienna, 6 and 14 Dec. 1833, GSta PK, HA III, MdA I,
6022; M. Lamb, "Writing up the Eastern Question in 1835–1836," *IHR* 15, 1993,
2, p. 241; Webster, *Palmerston*, I, p. 317.
[52] Metternich to Neumann, Vienna, 15 Feb. 1833, HHStA, StA, England 204.

after 1830 was thus a sign not only of Metternich's goodwill towards Austria's powerful eastern neighbour but also of his own long-standing diplomatic theories.

It would naturally be naive to suppose that Metternich was pleased at the considerable Russian influence over the sultan's court or at the presence of Russian armed forces on the Bosphorus, but considering the circumstances he could easily reconcile himself with these facts. He was able to accept Russia's influence over Mahmud II owing to the joint action of both conservative Powers in the majority of the affairs within the Ottoman Empire, for example, against Blacque's journalistic activities after 1830. Furthermore, as a realistic statesman, Metternich was well aware of the impossibility of reducing Russian influence at that moment, and the Convention of Münchengrätz would in no way have affected it, as British historian Desmond Seward stated.[53] Moreover, with regard to the events of the First Mohammed Ali Crisis, it is necessary to draw attention to the fact that Russia's influence did not arise in 1833 as a consequence of the Treaty of 8 July but had already existed three years previously and was later naturally augmented by the tsar's willingness to help the sultan against his rebellious Egyptian governor. In this respect one must agree with Maria N. Todorova that the real success of the Russian diplomacy in the Levant was the Treaty of Adrianople in particular.[54] The Russian predominance in Constantinople was thus nothing new for Metternich in 1833, certainly nothing that would have contributed to a change in his policy, and it is clearly not true, as Nicolae Ciachir claims, that the content of the Treaty of Unkiar-Skelessi caused Austrian diplomats "many a sleepless night."[55] It is necessary to refute with the same strength Paul W. Schroeder's claim that Great Britain, France and Austria failed to stop "what they all recognized as the main danger, Russia and its dominant position at the Porte,"[56] because this was not the main danger for Metternich, in fact under the given conditions it was no danger for him at all.

---

[53] D. Seward, *Metternich: Der erste Europäer. Eine Biographie*, Zürich 1993, p. 232.

[54] Todorova, "Mythology," p. 29. For more on the question of foreign influence over the Porte see Chapter 22.

[55] Ciachir, p. 712.

[56] Schroeder, *Transformation*, p. 729.

As to the presence of the Russian soldiers and marines in the immediate vicinity of Constantinople, Metternich did not object to this
for the simple reason that he preferred them to Egyptian soldiers.
And although he favoured the solution to the conflict by means of
joint pressure from all Powers in Alexandria accompanied by a naval
demonstration of some of them before its port and the arrival of additional fleets to the Golden Horn to join forces with the Russian
squadron if necessary, he soon understood that this solution was unrealistic owing to the mistrust prevailing in Paris and London of the
intentions of St Petersburg. For Metternich it must have been, as Frederick Lamb concisely put it in May 1833, "melancholy to see an affair
of this importance unnecessarily spoilt by disunion and ill-timed jealousy."[57] It was not Russia but rather France which Metternich blamed
for this disunity in the spring of 1833, which can be no surprise since
France was Austria's most dangerous enemy after July 1830, ideologically as well as geopolitically. The Austro-Russian alliance was
thus consolidated in 1830–1831 by the existence of a common adversary, and the Near East was only one of the diplomatic battlefields
between the two conservative courts and Paris. Metternich objected
to France's activities in general because of its egoistic goals and its
desire to take the lead in every international affair because, as he declared, the French cabinet "must be able to say that it was it which
did everything, that it is it that is the moderator of the destiny of the
universe, that it is it that is the master of all things."[58] This would
probably have been forgivable if France had pursued the same aims
as other members of the Concert. However, no Power at that time,
including liberal Great Britain, had for the Austrian Empire so diametrically different priorities as France, and the Near East was no
exception. France's affection for Mohammed Ali led to the duplicity
of its diplomacy, and its protests against the Russian presence on the
Bosphorus masked by an array of fears about the sultan's fate in reality resulted from its concerns about its own interests.[59] Consequently,
when Metternich labelled the tsar's conduct as "sincere, honest and
enlightened" and condemned the French behaviour as "duplicitous,

---

[57] Lamb to Palmerston, Vienna, 8 May 1833, TNA, FO 120/136.
[58] Metternich to Stürmer, Vienna, 3 June 1833, HHStA, StA, Türkei VI, 59.
[59] Metternich to Neumann, Vienna, 3 May 1833, HHStA, StA, England 204; Metternich to Stürmer, Vienna, 20 June 1833, HHStA, StA, Türkei VI, 59.

conceited, weak, audacious and in bad faith,"[60] it is impossible to treat it as a blind adulation of Russia but his own opinion also shared by other Austrian diplomats.

Considering these facts, some traditional views are not tenable. First, that represented, for example, by Matthew S. Anderson that the meeting in Münchengrätz was to "re-establish good relations between the two great conservative monarchies of Europe after the uneasiness which the apparent prospect of large-scale Russian expansion in the Near East had caused in Vienna earlier in the year."[61] Second, that of Frederick Lamb who declared that Metternich only had a choice between the fear of Russia and the fear of revolutions.[62] Third, the opinion repeated by many historians that Metternich supported the tsar in the Near East because he supported any stand against revolutions in Europe, particularly in Germany and Italy. As already stated, Metternich did not fear a Russian expansion in the Levant after 1829 and, as Alan Sked accurately stated, he did not fear it at all since the weakness of the Russian Empire became evident during its wars with the Ottoman Empire and with the Poles.[63] And although it is true that he needed Russian assistance in Italy and Germany, one must entirely agree with Alan Sked again that Russia also needed Austrian backing against revolutions.[64] Therefore, Metternich had already had the tsar's support against their common enemy at his disposal long before the reunion in North Bohemia, where he did not need to buy it, especially not by sacrificing Austrian interests in the Levant where both conservative Powers pursued the same goal. Briefly, no deal was made in Münchengrätz; it was merely a personal meeting confirming the already existing cordial relations between the two Powers.

The above arguments lead to the reflection that it was a real misfortune that the cabinets of the Maritime Powers did not believe Metternich's continual assurances of Nicholas I's real goals and uselessly remonstrated against the presence of his troops on the Bosphorus as well as the Treaty of Unkiar-Skelessi, which in fact changed nothing in the status of the Straits and did not turn the Ottoman Empire into

---

[60] Metternich to Apponyi, Vienna, 3 May 1833, HHStA, StA, Frankreich 289.
[61] Anderson, *Great Powers*, p. 44.
[62] Lamb to Palmerston, Vienna, 1 Oct. 1833, TNA, FO 120/137.
[63] Sked, *Metternich*, p. 89.
[64] Ibid., p. 72.

a Russian protectorate (protectorate in terms of a vassal state). With regard to this agreement, Metternich correctly remained calm even though he was offended by his conservative ally's concealment of it from him. This tsar's secretive nature was proved with negative effect by his insistence on the secrecy of the Convention of Münchengrätz, which was again an entirely needless measure contributing to an even greater cooling of the relations among the Great Powers. Metternich cannot, however, be held responsible for this outcome in any way; he tried to secure the cooperation of the pentarchy and was in his declarations much more frank than one has hitherto supposed. He continued to defend Russia's Near Eastern policy in the following years but his assurances on Russia's behalf fell on deaf ears in the cabinets in London and Paris. The only thing which changed was the distribution of their anti-Russian hostility; whereas until mid 1833 it was more considerable in Paris, later London became the capital of Russophobia and the British liberal government the main critic of the tsar's policy in the Near East. In this respect Ponsonby replaced Roussin and it can be said without much exaggeration that in Lord Palmerston Metternich found a new George Canning.

18

Palmerston, Ponsonby and the British Russophobia

On the turn of 1833, Great Britain replaced France as the loudest "guardian" of the Ottoman Empire against Russia's alleged hostile and dangerous intentions. The distrust, jealousy and desire to promote British interests led Palmerston to the pursuance of a considerably defiant anti-Russian policy in the Near East that continuously disturbed the sultan and harmed the relations among the European Powers. Palmerston's egoistic policy won numerous advocates whose similar or even greater dislike of Russia gave rise to a strong wave of Russophobia in British society. Metternich in vain tried to overcome this strong antagonism and induce all Powers to cooperate in the Eastern Question that, in his opinion, actually ceased to exist because of the mutual wish to preserve the existence of the Ottoman Empire and general peace.

The British anti-Russian Activities in the Near East

The close cooperation between Prokesch and Campbell in Alexandria in the spring of 1833 was not accompanied by a similar Austro-British collaboration in Constantinople or indeed anywhere else. Despite Metternich's anti-French warnings and entreaties on behalf of the Russians, Lord Palmerston decided to maintain the union of the two liberal Powers. The tsarist policy during the crisis and the Treaty of Unkiar-Skelessi strengthened his anti-Russian feelings and made him believe that Nicholas I harboured hostile designs against the Ottoman Empire and that the tsar's expansionist policy represented a serious threat to British geopolitical as well as economic interests. This distrust, together with the jealousy of Russia's diplomatic success in Constantinople, motivated Palmerston to strive to replace Russia's considerable influence over the sultan's court with Britain's after

1833, not by war but by means of a strong and determined diplomacy. For this purpose he found an appropriate instrument in the new British ambassador in Constantinople, John Lord Ponsonby, who shared the foreign secretary's distrust of the Russians and saw their plotting around almost every corner. Ponsonby became a dangerous opponent of Russia's influence in Constantinople not only due to his pathological Russophobic hysteria but also his willingness to pursue a contrastive policy, both of which became all too obvious soon after his arrival in Constantinople in May 1833.[1]

Ponsonby's suspicions of Russia were so high that they even led him to seriously think in late 1833 that Nicholas I was waiting for a suitable moment to send his army to the Bosphorus again and was preparing for this reason numerous intervention forces in Sevastopol and Odessa. This suspicion quickly found a positive echo in London and made Palmerston yet more anti-Russian in his statements. The British naval reinforcements in the Mediterranean undertaken during the year therefore seemed to be justified, as did the presence of the British and French fleets in the Archipelago. There was actually no truth in the rumour, and Metternich was well aware of this, but he was unable to persuade Palmerston that Nicholas I did not want to return his troops and ships to Constantinople and that the tsar was prepared to do so only if the Ottoman Empire was threatened again and he was asked for help by the sultan. The chancellor's criticism of the two Maritime Powers' naval presence in the vicinity of the Dardanelles needlessly disquieting the Porte met with similar silence in both London and Paris, but at least the two Powers finally recalled their fleets before the end of the year, which allayed Metternich's anxiety as well as Mahmud II's. How great was the latter's relief when he learnt about the promise to withdraw the fleets is evident from the fact that he immediately had 32 rams sacrificed in honour of the Prophet.[2]

[1]   R. L. Baker, "Palmerston and the Treaty of Unkiar Skelessi," *EHR* 43, 1928, pp. 83–89; G. H. Bolsover, "Lord Ponsonby and the Eastern Question (1833–1839)," *SEER* 13, 1934, 37, p. 106; G. D. Clayton, *Britain and the Eastern Question: Missolonghi to Gallipoli*, London 1971, p. 74; Webster, *Palmerston*, II, p. 525.
[2]   Stürmer to Metternich, Constantinople, 17, 24 and 31 Dec. 1833, HHStA, StA, Türkei VI, 58; Stürmer to Metternich, Constantinople, 7 Jan. 1834, HHStA, StA, Türkei VI, 60; Martens to Frederick William III, Büyükdere, 11 Nov. 1833, GStA PK, HA III, MdA I, 7273; Brockhausen to Frederick William III, Vienna, 3 and

However, the presentation of notes by the British and French ambassadors to the Porte concerning the content of the Treaty of Unkiar-Skelessi continued during 1834, and in particular with regard to the articles concerning navigation of foreign warships through the Straits. Ponsonby soon overshadowed his French colleague and became the driving force of this activity resulting from the fear that the Treaty assured the closure of the Straits to all countries except Russia, which alone could send its fleet to the Mediterranean at the first suitable opportunity. Consequently, Ponsonby attacked the document under the pretext that it was in contradiction with the 11th article of the British-Ottoman Treaty of 1809 forbidding all non-Ottoman warships sailing through the Straits in times of peace. The whole debate was entirely absurd because, first, Nicholas I and Nesselrode did not want to send warships through the Straits and, second, the Treaty of Unkiar-Skelessi did not allow them to do so because it altered nothing in the principle of their closure to all foreign warships in peace time and its relevant stipulations merely confirmed the principle contained in the British-Ottoman Treaty of 1809. This was exactly what the tsar and his vice-chancellor wanted because their priority was not the opening but the firm closure of the Straits since what they feared above all was an eventual attack from the considerably stronger British and French fleets in the Black Sea. On the other hand, the British and French did not want to sail through the Straits to the north. The mutual distrust and fear were entirely unfounded, which Metternich knew very well.[3] He correctly saw in the Treaty of Unkiar-Skelessi simply

---

7 Jan. 1834, GStA PK, HA III, MdA I, 6023; Ponsonby to Palmerston, Therapia, 17 Nov. 1833, TNA, FO 120/139; Lamb to Palmerston, Vienna, 4 Jan. 1834, TNA, FO 120/145; Sainte-Aulaire to Broglie, Vienna, 30 Nov. and 19 Dec. 1833, AMAE, CP, Autriche 419; Rendall, "Nicholas I," p. 50.

[3] Metternich to Ficquelmont, Vienna, 11 Jan. and 24 Feb. 1834, HHStA, StA, Russland III, 102; Metternich to Esterházy, Vienna, 21 Jan. 1834, HHStA, StA, England 208; Metternich to Stürmer, Vienna, 26 Feb. and 5 March 1834, HHStA, StA, Türkei VI, 62; Sainte-Aulaire to Broglie, Vienna, 14 Nov. 1833, AMAE, CP, Autriche 419; Sainte-Aulaire to Broglie, Vienna, 24 Feb. and 14 March 1834, AMAE, CP, Autriche 420; Tatishchev to Nesselrode, Vienna, 28 Feb. 1834, AVPRI, fond 133, Kantseliariia, opis 469, 1834/217. Metternich's detailed analysis of the foreign warships' right to sail through the Straits and the 11th article of the British-Ottoman Treaty of 1809 *Observations sur le passage des batimens de guerre étrangers par les détroits des Dardanelles et du Bosphore; Article XI. du traité de paix entre l'Angleterre et la Porte du 5. janvier 1809*, was attached to Metternich to Stürmer, Vienna, 26 Feb. 1834, HHStA, StA, Türkei VI, 62.

the assurance of the security of the Russian Black Sea coast in the event of a war with France and Great Britain if the Ottoman Empire remained neutral. It was a defensive measure in no way detrimental for other countries and, in his opinion, "the protests of England and France against a purely defensive measure are thus almost a confession of the intention of these Great Powers to attack Russia on its southern coasts."[4] Therefore, Metternich was not concerned that the Porte might have problems countering Ponsonby's unfounded objections, and it really did not, but despite this Ponsonby continued to present his notes for the least significant reason until mid 1834. Simultaneously, he expressed various nonsensical suspicions concerning Russia, for example, one also shared by Palmerston that there was a secret understanding between the tsar and Mohammed Ali against the Porte.[5] Metternich realised the absurdity of the vision "of the kind which can only be invented by an empty brain like that of Lord Ponsonby."[6] When he learnt from Lamb that Ponsonby had expressed the fear "that Austria will allow Russia to obtain that [the Ottoman capital] which will ultimately go near to make an end of Austria,"[7] the chancellor reacted with even more bitter indignation: "A man who is so blindly prejudiced to the point of allowing that it is probable that we would desire to help the Russians to conquer Constantinople even though we should destroy ourselves in the process is devoid of the main faculties of reason."[8]

It was difficult for Metternich to understand why Palmerston could maintain such a strong anti-Russian attitude and did not join Austria and Russia in the Eastern Question during 1833 despite their

[4] Metternich to Esterházy, Vienna, 14 March 1834, HHStA, StA, England 208.
[5] Stürmer to Metternich, Constantinople, 21 and 28 Jan., 5, 11 and 16 Feb., 5 and 19 March, 29 April 1834, HHStA, StA, Türkei VI, 60; Martens to Frederick William III, Büyükdere, 4 and 14 Feb., 8 June 1834, GStA PK, HA III, MdA I, 7274; R. Bullen, *Palmerston, Guizot and the Collapse of the Entente Cordiale*, London 1974, p. 17; H. N. Ingle, *Nesselrode and the Russian Rapprochement with Britain, 1836–1844*, Berkeley, Los Angeles, London 1976, p. 95; R. C. Middleton, "Palmerston, Ponsonby and Mehemet Ali: Some Observations on Ambassadorial Independence in the East, 1838–1840," *EEQ* 15, 1982, p. 413; Bitis, p. 475; Clarke, p. 207; Puryear, "L'opposition," pp. 290–308; Webster, *Palmerston*, I, p. 305.
[6] Metternich to Stürmer, Baden, 11 Aug. 1834, HHStA, StA, Türkei VI, 62.
[7] Ponsonby to Lamb, [?] Aug. 1834, attached to Metternich to Stürmer, Baden, 26 Aug. 1834, HHStA, StA, Türkei VI, 62.
[8] Metternich to Stürmer, Baden, 26 Aug. 1834, HHStA, StA, Türkei VI, 62.

identical desire to preserve the Ottoman Empire. Metternich found even stranger the British cabinet's sharp criticism of the Russian intervention which pursued their common goal, the preservation of this empire, and was proof of the tsar's pro-Turkish policy. He argued that if Great Britain had acted earlier as he had advised and intervened with its fleet against Mohammed Ali, the crisis could have been solved more easily and with the Great Powers acting together instead of Russia acting alone. In his opinion, when Palmerston missed the opportune time to act, he was later led by "untimely anxiety"[9] resulting in pointless complaints against Russia's unilateral proceeding.[10] Metternich was convinced that the British policy in the Near East during the First Mohammed Ali Crisis could be best characterised with Talleyrand's famous expression: "It is worse than a crime; it is a blunder."[11] The prince wrote in early 1834: "If the sultan did not succumb in any way, it is not England who should get the credit for it; similarly it surely is not the action undertaken by this Great Power that would have been appropriate for contesting the views of Russian predominance if they had actually existed. In every circumstance England has expressed itself too late and it has constantly acted at the wrong time. The first ships of this Great Power presented themselves in the seas of the Levant after the signature [*sic*] of the Peace of Kütahya[12] and the second reinforcement that it sent to this area arrived at the moment when the peace had just been restored with great difficulty and could only bring down the Ottoman throne."[13] And he added in April 1835: "If England had assumed a firm and unequivocal attitude during that period [1832], if it had made energetic representations to Mohammed Ali without delay, it would have probably stopped him in his tracks and the Battle of Konya would have

[9] Sainte-Aulaire to Broglie, Vienna, 19 Dec. 1833, AMAE, CP, Autriche 419.
[10] Metternich to Apponyi, Vienna, 13 April 1833, HHStA, StA, Frankreich 289; Metternich to Neumann, Vienna, 13 April and 3 May 1833, Metternich to Esterházy, Königswart, 28 July 1833, HHStA, StA, England 204; Metternich to Ficquelmont, Vienna, 30 May 1833, HHStA, StA, Russland III, 99; Metternich to Stürmer, Vienna, 5 Dec. 1833, HHStA, StA, Türkei VI, 59; Tatishchev to Nesselrode, Vienna, 25 May 1833, AVPRI, fond 133, Kantseliariia, opis 469, 1833/211; Lamb to Palmerston, Vienna, 3 June 1833, TNA, FO 120/136.
[11] Metternich to Neumann, Vienna, 9 June 1833, HHStA, StA, England 204.
[12] Actually the peace settlement of Kütahya could never be signed because it was only verbal.
[13] Metternich to Esterházy, Vienna, 17 Jan. 1834, HHStA, StA, England 208.

been avoided."[14] In the late 1830s, Palmerston accepted this criticism: "What Metternich says of our shirking from helping the Sultan when Mehemet was at Acre and when a word might have stopped the Pasha without a blow is perfectly true, and there is nothing that has happened since I have been in this office which I regret so much as that tremendous blunder of the English Govt."[15] And he later added: "It is true that Russia alone prevented at that time the occupation of Constantinople by Ibrahim or at least some general break up in consequence of his advance: and I humbly venture to think (and in that opinion I have been more and more confirmed by everything that has passed since) that no British Cabinet at any period of the history of England ever made so great a mistake in regard to foreign affairs as did the Cabinet of Lord Grey in refusing to the Sultan the assistance and protection."[16]

At the moment when all the Great Powers, including France, wanted to preserve the status quo in the Near East, Metternich saw no justifiable reason for the animosity existing between the Maritime Powers and Russia in the Eastern Question, and actually he found it non-existent at the time due to the identical interests of the pentarchy as he wrote for example in 1836: "There is no substance for creating a question which could be given the pompous title of an Oriental affair."[17] Consequently, Metternich continued in his efforts to lessen the mutual suspicions of the two parties and he assured the cabinets in London and Paris that Nicholas I did not want to destroy the Ottoman Empire and no real obstacle for the cooperation of the European Powers actually existed: "The two courts [Austria and Russia] are following a simple approach and they are in no way concealing it. They want to conserve the Ottoman Empire. The Maritime Powers give their assurances that they do not want anything else; so what is the dispute about?"[18] Since he had more faith in Great Britain, he directed his efforts more to London than to Paris, and he did so on the turn of 1833 with the same aim that he had failed to achieve earlier in the year: to bring Great Britain, a natural ally of

---

[14] Metternich to Esterházy, Vienna, 10 April 1835, HHStA, StA, England 214.
[15] Webster, *Palmerston*, I, p. 282.
[16] Ibid., p. 283.
[17] Metternich to Esterházy, Vienna, 29 Nov. 1836, HHStA, StA, England 215.
[18] Metternich to Esterházy, Vienna, 10 Dec. 1833, HHStA, StA, England 204.

Austria in the Near East with identical interests, on the side of the conservative Powers, which would isolate France, thereby forcing it to stay alone or to come into the majority. Nevertheless, it remained as impossible as ever for Metternich to overcome Palmerston's distrust of Russia's designs and "divert his thoughts for a moment from the confines of prejudice and transfer them to the realm of truth."[19] The foreign secretary continued to believe in the evil tsarist plans for the Ottoman Empire and was not prepared to accept any assurances whatsoever to the contrary from the man whom he regarded as Russia's minion and whose reliance upon the tsar's good faith as "absurd and childish."[20] This irresistible disbelief was increased by the secrecy shrouding the Münchengrätz meeting; Palmerston for some time even suspected Austria and Russia of planning the destruction of the Ottoman Empire there. Finally, instead of the rapprochement between Austria and Great Britain that Metternich desired, the exact opposite happened when Great Britain and France concluded with Spain and Portugal the so-called Quadruple Alliance in April 1834, officially for defending the liberal regimes in the Pyrenees, but designed by Palmerston as a counterbalance to the close union of the conservative Powers – Austria, Prussia and Russia – anywhere including the Near East.[21]

Witnessing the anti-Russian activities directed by Palmerston and Ponsonby, Metternich was no less disappointed with the British

---

[19] Metternich to Stürmer, Vienna, 3 Oct. 1833, HHStA, StA, Türkei VI, 59.

[20] K. Bourne, *Palmerston: The Early Years 1784–1841*, London 1982, p. 385.

[21] Metternich to Esterházy, Töplitz, 16 Aug. 1833, Vienna, 27 Oct. and 10 Dec. 1833, HHStA, StA, England 204; Metternich to Esterházy, Vienna, 17 Jan. 1834, HHStA, StA, England 208; Metternich to Trauttmannsdorff, Vienna, 18 Dec. 1833, HHStA, StK, Preussen 153; Metternich to Stürmer, Vienna, 8 Jan. 1834, HHStA, StA, Türkei VI, 62; Metternich to Ficquelmont, Vienna, 11 June 1834, SOA, RA C-A 383; Tatishchev to Nesselrode, Vienna, 13 Dec. 1833, AVPRI, fond 133, Kantseliariia, opis 469, 1833/210; Tatishchev to Nesselrode, Vienna, 25 Jan. 1834, AVPRI, fond 133, Kantseliariia, opis 469, 1834/217; Brockhausen to Frederick William III, Vienna, 14, 17 and 23 Dec. 1833, GStA PK, HA III, MdA I, 6022; Maltzan to Frederick William III, Vienna, 29 Feb. 1836, GStA PK, HA III, MdA I, 6027; Sainte-Aulaire to Broglie, Vienna, 24 Feb. 1834, AMAE, CP, Autriche 420; Sainte-Aulaire to Rigny, Vienna, 3 Nov. 1834, AMAE, CP, Autriche 421; Sainte-Aulaire to Broglie, Vienna, 6 Dec. 1835, AMAE, CP, Autriche 422; Sainte-Aulaire to Broglie, Vienna, 17 Jan. 1836, Sainte-Aulaire to Thiers, Vienna, 16 March 1836, AMAE, CP, Autriche 423; Lamb to Palmerston, Vienna, 26 Dec. 1833, TNA, FO 120/137; Bourne, pp. 378–386; Webster, *Palmerston*, I, pp. 307 and 345.

diplomacy in the Ottoman Empire itself during 1834. The old but less significant issue concerned the presentation of notes attacking the Treaty of Unkiar-Skelessi and its compatibility with the Treaty of 1809. This game when Ponsonby was repeating the questions already answered by the Porte was revived at the end of the year without any practical success. A more important problem for the peace in the Near East were the fleets of the British warships sailing from Malta to the eastern Mediterranean, resulting partly from the conviction that naval demonstrations of force were the best means to restore British influence in Constantinople and partly from the fact that Ponsonby obtained in March 1834 the right to call the British Mediterranean fleet to the Ottoman capital if it was threatened, a provision rather dangerous in the hands of a man of Ponsonby's nature. In June, Metternich learnt for the first time that several British warships had left Malta and operated in the Archipelago. He was significantly annoyed with this step for which he saw no reason at the moment when the Ottoman Empire was enjoying peace and Mohammed Ali as well as the Russians remained inactive, and he questioned Lamb why the British government was disturbing the peace existing in the Levant. When the British ambassador tried to explain the manoeuvres of the British fleet by the necessity of training, Metternich did not believe this explanation and saw no reason why the warships had to sail so far from Malta for such a purpose. His doubts soon proved to be entirely well founded when Palmerston stated during a discussion with the Austrian chargé d'affaires in London, Karl von Hummelauer, that in fact it was a demonstration of force that was to show Russia "that she could not attack Turkey or interfere with her internal institutions with impunity."[22] Since there was no reason to suppose Russia had any intention of doing this, Metternich could only express his regret over this erroneous anti-Russian attitude that "assumes the character of a real sickness that threatens Europe like a thunderstorm which keeps to the horizon ready to rage at the first signal."[23] The chancellor condemned the presence of the fleet in the Archipelago because it could lead to countermeasures from the tsar, something that Metternich feared above all: "Demonstrations provoke other demonstrations,

---

[22] Webster, *Palmerston*, I, p. 334.
[23] Brockhausen to Frederick William III, Vienna, 5 July 1834, GStA PK, HA III, MA I, 6024.

and provocations other provocations, what could come of the peace in the Levant?"[24] Nothing, in his opinion, justified such a demonstration of force. Unfortunately for him, this was not the last naval excursion of the British fleet to Ottoman waters. At the end of 1834, suspecting the Russian armed forces of wanting to return to Constantinople, Ponsonby exercised his right and called for the British warships, which finally anchored in Vourla Bay at the beginning of 1835. Since Ponsonby himself soon realised that there was no actual danger from Russia, the fleet left Vourla for Malta in March.[25]

For Metternich, the needless presentation of notes and the naval excursions were evidence of pointless stratagems, the former tiring him and the latter upsetting him considerably. He saw in Ponsonby the main evil in the Near East since early 1834 and deeply resented his presence in Constantinople and his influence over Palmerston. In the late summer of 1834, Metternich finally gave up all hope of persuading the latter about the passivity of Russia's Near Eastern policy and he terminated his discussion with Palmerston over Russia's intentions because he found it useless: "To preach to those who in no way want to understand or to whom an awkward or too advanced position prevents from being able to admit that they understand is always a waste of effort, and a Great Power, rather than taking such pains for nothing, acts more reasonably and invites fewer risks if it keeps silent. Consequently, we will not speak to the British cabinet about the Eastern affair, but that does not mean we will not listen to what it might be able to entrust to us."[26] Usually very calm, the Austrian chancellor was so ill-humoured that "simply the name of

---

[24] Metternich to Hummelauer, Vienna, 14 June 1834, HHStA, StA, England 208.
[25] Metternich to Stürmer, Vienna, 18 June 1834, HHStA, StA, Türkei VI, 62; Metternich to Apponyi, Vienna, 12 June 1834, HHStA, StA, Frankreich 293; Metternich to Apponyi, Baden, 3 Aug. 1834, HHStA, StA, Frankreich 294; Metternich to Ficquelmont, Vienna, 19 June 1834, HHStA, StA, Russland III, 102; Metternich to Hummelauer, Vienna, 14 June 1834, HHStA, StA, England 208; Stürmer to Metternich, Constantinople, 22 Nov., 12, 16, 23 and 30 Dec. 1834, HHStA, StA, Türkei VI, 61; Stürmer to Metternich, Constantinople, 14 and 28 Jan., 4 and 25 Feb., 11 March 1835, Büyükdere, 18 and 25 June 1834, HHStA, StA, Türkei VI, 63; Lamb to Palmerston, Vienna, 14 and 18 June 1834, TNA, FO 120/145; Cetto to Ludwig I of Bavaria, Vienna, 18 and 28 June 1834, BHStA, MA, Wien 2405; O'Sullivan to Merode, Vienna, 15 July 1834, ADA, CP, Autriche 2; Bartlett, pp. 93–94; Puryear, *International Economics*, p. 21.
[26] Metternich to Apponyi, Vienna, 17 Sept. 1834, HHStA, StA, Frankreich 294.

the English minister provoked a new tirade against the system of the British government."[27] He saw a change in the ministry as the only hope whatsoever for any modification in the British conduct, an event he was expecting and looking for since the mid summer of 1834 and which finally happened in November when Sir Robert Peel formed a new cabinet with the Duke of Wellington as foreign secretary.[28]

Metternich was pleased to see his old friend in the Foreign Office, especially after having enjoyed the presence of Palmerston at this post for several years, but he was circumspect in his expectations. The chancellor knew well that British politicians were generally hostile to Russia and that it was difficult to find new ministers willing to pursue a more pro-Russian policy, in particular when the new cabinet's position in the House of Commons was weak and the Tories were similarly as suspicious of Russia's designs as were the Whigs: "The conservative party in England entirely shares the prejudices of the Whigs against the trend of Russian policy in Oriental affairs. As well as the previous government, it attributes to [Russia] plans of conquest in Europe and in Asia, plans which the tsar is saving to carry out one day when the occasion seems favourable to him. The conservatives as well as the Whigs already see the Russian flag raised on the towers of the seraglio."[29] Consequently, when Sainte-Aulaire claimed that an understanding between Great Britain and Russia would be easier with the Tory ministry, Metternich answered: "I do not think so. The Tories will be no less warlike over this question than the Whigs."[30] On the other hand, although Metternich was convinced that the policy of the new cabinet would not be entirely opposed to that of the previous one, he believed that Wellington's cabinet would not be so "propa-

---

[27] La Rochefoucauld to Rigny, Vienna, 31 Aug. 1834, AMAE, CP, Autriche 421.
[28] Metternich to Esterházy, Vienna, 6 Feb. 1834, HHStA, StA, England 208; Metternich to Esterházy, Vienna, 14 March 1835, HHStA, StA, England 214; Metternich to Stürmer, Vienna, 26 Feb., 10 and 24 Dec. 1834, HHStA, StA, Türkei VI, 62; Metternich to Stürmer, Vienna, 18 and 25 March 1835, HHStA, StA, Türkei VI, 64; Metternich to Ficquelmont, Vienna, 15 Sept. and 20 Oct. 1834, HHStA, StA, Russland III, 103; Brockhausen to Frederick William III, 20 Aug. 1834, GStA PK, HA III, MdA I, 6024; La Rochefoucauld to Rigny, Vienna, 22 Aug. 1834, Sainte-Aulaire to Rigny, Vienna, 25 Sept. 1834, 17 March 1835, AMAE, CP, Autriche 421; O'Sullivan to Nothomb, Vienna, 1 Sept. 1834, ADA, CP, Autriche 2.
[29] Metternich to Ficquelmont, Vienna, 9 Dec. 1834, HHStA, StA, Russland III, 103.
[30] Sainte-Aulaire to Rigny, Vienna, 27 Nov. 1834, AMAE, CP, Autriche 421.

gandist, it will be peaceful without being disingenuous at the same time, it will follow the ways of a reasonable policy and it will not lose itself in those of hateful machinations."[31] Therefore, his hope for the British rapprochement with the three conservative Powers and the destruction of the Quadruple Alliance increased and he recommended to the tsar to be on more friendly terms with the new ministry and thereby destroy the prejudices existing in the British Isles against Russia's Near Eastern policy. He also advised Wellington to deprive Ponsonby of the power to call for the British fleet and he suggested the latter's recall, which the prince considered in late March 1835 to be certain. However, Metternich's expectations mostly proved to be too optimistic. Although Wellington deprived Ponsonby of the right to summon the fleet, and he did so even before he received Metternich's request, and even though he personally also wanted to recall Ponsoby from Constantinople, he did not dare to do so due to the cabinet's weak position; Ponsonby was a brother-in-law of the influential Whig, Lord Grey. And while it is true that Wellington brought to the Foreign Office a mind without prejudice and passion, he made no attempt to reorient the British policy towards Russia; he told Esterházy that he could not carry out his wishes and moderate the British policy in the Near East because public opinion did not allow him to do so from day to day.[32] In any case, he had no more time to modify British policy

---

[31] Metternich to Apponyi, Vienna, 14 Dec. 1834, HHStA, StA, Frankreich 294.
[32] Metternich to Hummelauer, Baden, 17 July 1834, Vienna, 11 Sept., 29 Nov. and 25 Dec. 1834, HHStA, StA, England 208; Metternich to Esterházy, Vienna, 14 March 1835, HHStA, StA, England 214; Metternich to Ficquelmont, Baden, 19 July 1834, HHStA, StA, Russland III, 102; Metternich to Ficquelmont, Vienna, 9 Dec. 1834, HHStA, StA, Russland III, 103; Metternich to Apponyi, Vienna, 1 Dec. 1834, HHStA, StA, Frankreich 294; Metternich to Stürmer, Vienna, 7 Jan., 18 and 25 March 1835, HHStA, StA, Türkei VI, 64; Hummelauer to Metternich, London, 6 Feb. 1835, Esterházy to Metternich, London, 11 and 27 March 1835, HHStA, StA, England 209; Brockhausen to Frederick William III, Vienna, 25 Nov. and 5 Dec. 1834, GStA PK, HA III, MdA I, 6024; Sainte-Aulaire to Broglie, Vienna, 27 Nov. 1834, Sainte-Aulaire to Rigny, Vienna, 17 March 1835, AMAE, CP, Autriche 421; Cetto to Ludwig I of Bavaria, Vienna, 26 Nov. and 3 Dec. 1834, BHStA, MA, Wien 2405; O'Sullivan to Meulenaer, Vienna, 1, 9, 14 and 25 Dec. 1834, ADA, CP, Autriche 2; J. H. Gleason, *The Genesis of Russophobia in Great Britain: A Study of the Interaction of Policy and Opinion*, Cambridge 1950, p. 164; Webster, *Palmerston*, I, p. 349, *Palmerston*, II, p. 597. Palmerston later restored Ponsonby's right to call for the British fleet but it was never misused again. Puryear, *International Economics*, p. 44.

because Peel's government fell in April 1835 and in the new liberal one the Foreign Office was entrusted again to Palmerston, which led to Metternich's bitter reaction: "Well, so Lord Palmerston is back in business! What a joke! Or rather what an insult! Since it is a real insult for the European cabinets, and for my part, I feel it strongly."[33]

Metternich's Rapprochement with Louis Philippe

Palmerston's return to the helm of British diplomacy dashed Metternich's hopes for any improvement in the relations between Great Britain and the conservative Powers at that moment and, consequently, intensified the chancellor's effort to destroy the union of the two liberal Powers by winning the support of not Great Britain but France, whose conduct in the Near East had begun to change since the turn of 1833 when it had started to be rather less biased towards Russia than the British government. The French squadron sailed from the Ottoman coast earlier in December 1833 than the British forces and did not return to the Archipelago in the following year. The notes against the Treaty of Unkiar-Skelessi presented by Roussin and Ponsonby in late 1833 were correctly attributed by Metternich to British pressure: "The latest unacceptable declarations of the two Maritime Powers issued in Constantinople and in St Petersburg are the work of the Secretary of the State. The French cabinet has followed the impetus that it has received from London."[34] In 1834, Roussin soon stopped following his British colleague in presenting them to the Porte. It was the activities of the French ambassador in which France's restraint became most visible: Roussin became as passive in early 1834 as he had been active a year previously, something that Metternich naturally perceived and assessed in a rather positive way. Already in January 1834, Metternich compared France and Great Britain to two "volcanos, of which the former blows out old ashes, whereas from the latter violently spews forth a fiery lava."[35] In September 1834,

---

[33] La Rochefoucauld to Broglie, Vienna, 3 May 1835, AMAE, CP, Autriche 422.
[34] Metternich to Ficquelmont, Vienna, 16 Dec. 1833, HHStA, StA, Russland III, 99.
[35] Metternich to Ficquelmont, Vienna, 31 Jan. 1834, HHStA, StA, Russland III, 102.

Metternich finally found his relations with France over the Eastern Question more acceptable than those with Great Britain.[36] Metternich ascribed the French restraint in the Near East to the beneficial influence of King Louis Philippe, whom he started to regard in 1833 as a man of reasonable views and a barrier against a revolution like the one that had brought the king to the throne but which also could deprive him of it and, consequently, Metternich correctly perceived that the king desired to follow a peaceable foreign policy and preserve the status quo in France as well as beyond its frontier. For this reason Metternich decided to establish good personal relations with the king and at least from early 1834 he maintained correspondence with Louis Philippe by which means he wanted to influence the French foreign policy: "I am pursuing with King Louis Philippe a series of direct discussions, if I may be permitted to call them such, not to find out what he wants, because in order to know that I do not need to learn it from his mouth, but because I regard it useful to prepare a way for us to send the truth to this Prince and leave him in no doubt about what we want as well as what we do not want and should neither want nor permit. The more the king recognises the rightness of our thinking and the frankness of our attitude, the more he will have to feel engaged in holding back the forces of an appalling policy."[37] Metternich very soon succeeded in obtaining Louis Philippe's confidence and became sure of the king's intentions. For example, in the summer of 1834, the chancellor even declared that "Louis Philippe would more likely hang himself than allow the squadron to leave Toulon."[38]

---

[36] Metternich to Trauttmannsdorff, Vienna, 18 Dec. 1833, HHStA, StK, Preussen 153; Metternich to Stürmer, Vienna, 24 Dec. 1833, HHStA, StA, Türkei VI, 59; Metternich to Stürmer, Vienna, 19 March 1834, Baden, 26 Aug. 1834, HHStA, StA, Türkei VI, 62; Metternich to Apponyi, Vienna, 21 and 27 Jan., 13 Feb. 1834, HHStA, StA, Frankreich 293; Metternich to Ficquelmont, Vienna, 31 Jan. 1834, HHStA, StA, Russland III, 102; Metternich to Esterházy, Vienna, 17 Jan., 6 Feb. and 14 March 1834, Metternich to Hummelauer, Vienna, 11 Sept. 1834, HHStA, StA, England 208; Sainte-Aulaire to Broglie, Vienna, 5 Jan. 1834, AMAE, CP, Autriche 420; Brockhausen to Frederick William III, Vienna, 18 Jan. 1834, GStA PK, HA III, MdA I, 6023; O'Sullivan to Merode, Vienna, 18 April 1834, ADA, CP, Autriche 2; Cetto to Ludwig I of Bavaria, Vienna, 8 and 12 Nov. 1834, BHStA, MA, Wien 2405; Prokesch-Osten, *Aus den Tagebüchern*, p. 204; Puryear, "L'opposition," p. 308.

[37] Metternich to Apponyi, Vienna, 31 May 1834, HHStA, StA, Frankreich 293.

[38] Metternich to Ficquelmont, Baden, 19 July 1834, HHStA, StA, Russland III, 102.

The accuracy of this judgement was confirmed by intercepted instructions for Roussin in which the presence of the British squadron in the
Archipelago was criticised as needless and inconvenient and the ambassador was informed that the French warships would not sail in the
same direction.[39]

The replacement of Wellington with Palmerston in 1835 logically
forced Metternich to bet everything on the French card and intensify his attempts to entice the king to a closer cooperation with the
continental Powers. This was not an entirely impossible task because
despite the formal continuance of the Quadruple Alliance, the alliance
between France and Great Britain weakened due to their different
views on the situation in Spain, a fact of which Metternich was well
aware and which made Louis Philippe more well disposed towards
a closer cooperation with Austria and less disposed to follow Great
Britain in its significantly anti-Russian activity in the Near East. The
crucial problem lay in the fact that Metternich did not actually desire
an Austro-French alliance but rather France's detachment from Great
Britain and its union with the conservative Powers whose support he
was never willing to sacrifice. At this moment Metternich's effort encountered an insuperable impediment: Nicholas I, who opposed the
cooperation with France because he distrusted it and personally hated
its king.[40]

Metternich found this hatred illogical, in particular as he was convinced that a friendlier attitude towards the French king on the part
of the tsar could significantly dislodge the British-French alliance.[41]

---

[39] Metternich to Apponyi, Baden, 3 Aug. 1834, HHStA, StA, Frankreich 294;
Rigny to Roussin, Paris, 2 Aug. 1834, attached to Metternich to Ficquelmont,
Baden, 22 Aug. 1834, Metternich to Ficquelmont, Vienna, 25 Jan. and 19 June
1834, HHStA, StA, Russland III, 102; Lamb to Palmerston, Vienna, 26 Dec. 1833,
TNA, FO 120/137; Lamb to Palmerston, Vienna, 2 Nov. 1834, TNA, FO 120/145;
O'Sullivan to Nothomb, Vienna, 1 Sept. 1834, ADA, CP, Autriche 2.
[40] Metternich to Apponyi, Vienna, 25 July 1835, HHStA, StA, Frankreich 298;
Metternich to Apponyi, Vienna, 11 March 1836, HHStA, StA, Frankreich 302;
Metternich to Ficquelmont, Vienna, 4 Jan. 1836, HHStA, StA, Russland III, 107;
Verger to Ludwig I of Bavaria, Vienna, 15 Oct. 1835, Lerchenfeld to Ludwig I
of Bavaria, Vienna, 24 Nov. 1835 and 19 April 1836, BHStA, MA, Wien 2406;
P. G. Dwyer, *Talleyrand*, London 2002, pp. 196–199; Bullen, "France and Europe,"
pp. 137–138; Droz, pp. 324–326; Lincoln, p. 211.
[41] Metternich to Ficquelmont, Vienna, 10 Dec. 1835, SOA, RA C-A 383;
Tatishchev to Nesselrode, Vienna, 9 Feb. 1836, AVPRI, fond 133, Kantseliariia,
opis 469, 1836/216.

Consequently, he attempted for years to reduce the tsar's personal animosity towards Louis Philippe. In February 1836, for example, Ficquelmont conveyed to Nesselrode a card with this information: "Every day Louis Philippe comes closer to a decision; it would only take one single word from Emperor Nicholas today to detach him totally from the English alliance. What do you think?"[42] When Ficquelmont met Nicholas I, the tsar asked him what kind of word he had in mind. The Austrian ambassador answered that a word of politeness would suffice to encourage Louis Philippe to join with the conservative Powers. The tsar answered that he had expressed his gratitude to the king for the fact that France had not joined the British anti-Russian proceedings, adding: "Finally, I do not really see the possibility of a greater rapprochement with such a government. You see again what has just happened; one cannot rely on anything there. Louis Philippe is skilful, it is true, but who will come after him? There is no legitimate succession there; it lacks the slightest basis that could assure its duration."[43] Metternich disagreed with this negative opinion: "What we take great care never to lose sight of is the necessity that Louis Philippe does not confuse his personal and governmental position with that of legitimate monarchs. We show ourselves, in a word, prepared to offer him a hand to help him follow a sound and conservative policy, like a Christian can offer [a hand] to a gentile so often that the question of religion does not come into it at all. Louis Philippe would like to be able to be our co-religionist ... The plain truth is that the approach we are taking with regard to King Louis Philippe contains the most effective means for dissolving what is called the Anglo-French alliance, and there is no less positive certainty than of all the trouble that, in the general interest, it is possible to take to prove to the world that this alliance is nothing other than a fiction, having no other value than that of an anchor that cannot reach deep water, is certainly one of the most useful and richest in its consequences."[44] However, Nicholas I's hatred of Louis Philippe was so great that Nesselrode asked Ficquelmont not to convey Metternich's advice about a better understanding

---

[42] Ficquelmont to Metternich, St Petersburg, 23 Feb. 1836, HHStA, StA, Russland III, 106.
[43] Ibid.
[44] Metternich to Ficquelmont, Vienna, 16 March 1836, HHStA, StA, Russland III, 107.

with the king because there was no hope for the change in the tsar's attitude. At the same time Orlov supported this opinion saying to the ambassador: "In this case I am as angry as you. I have fought against this attitude of the Emperor as much as I could, but this is useless. His loathing comes from his heart, he has nothing but disdain for Louis Philippe and does not want to have direct relations with him."[45] The pessimism of the two Russian dignitaries proved to be well founded because although Metternich did not abandon this topic later in 1836 and 1837, the only result was Nicholas I's negative answer to Ficquelmont and irritation with Nesselrode, who supported Austria's point of view of the usefulness of cordial relations with the French king.[46]

The Churchill Affair

Nicholas I's uncompromising attitude towards Louis Philippe finally led Metternich in mid January 1838 to the statement that the tsar's opinion of France and its king lacked any sense of reality,[47] but that was all that the chancellor could do, besides accepting the bitter fact that the tsar's intransigence made any rapprochement between France and the three conservative Powers impossible, something increasingly desirable for Metternich when Palmerston continued in his dislike and suspicions of Russia and still connected the destruction of its influence over the Ottoman Empire with the legitimate goal of what he called British interests. This opinion was entirely shared by Ponsonby, who could breathe more easily at his post after Palmerston's return to

---

[45] Ficquelmont to Metternich, St Petersburg, 6 April 1836, HHStA, StA, Russland III, 106.
[46] Metternich to Apponyi, Vienna, 28 March 1836, HHStA, StA, Frankreich 302; Metternich to Apponyi, Vienna, 2 and 22 Jan. 1837, HHStA, StA, Frankreich 307; Metternich to Ficquelmont, Vienna, 22 June 1836, SOA, RA C-A 383; Metternich to Ficquelmont, Vienna, 22 July and 24 Sept. 1836, HHStA, StA, Russland III, 108; Metternich to Ficquelmont, Vienna, 3 Feb. 1837, HHStA, StA, Russland III, 110; Ficquelmont to Metternich, St Petersburg, 6 April 1836, HHStA, StA, Russland III, 106; Ficquelmont to Metternich, St Petersburg, 11 Feb. and 18 July 1837, HHStA, StA, Russland III, 109; Gorchakov to Nesselrode, Vienna, 28 Jan. and 1 Feb. 1837, AVPRI, fond 133, Kantseliariia, opis 469, 1836/230; Lamb to Palmerston, Vienna, 21 Nov. 1837, TNA, FO 120/161.
[47] Metternich to Ficquelmont, Vienna, 15 Jan. 1838, SOA, RA C-A 383.

office and continue with impunity in his anti-Russian activities, and he did so with extraordinary vigour. He tried to use every opportunity to reduce Russia's influence, and he got one in early May 1836 when close to Scutari on the Asian shore of the Bosphorus, a British citizen, William N. Churchill, shot by accident a young boy instead of a quail and caused him a minor injury. For this he received the punishment of fifty lashes and was put in prison where he was kept for a short time in irons. With this action the Ottomans violated treaties with Great Britain assuring for Churchill the participation of a British ambassador or consul in a court of law. Ponsonby took advantage of this error on the part of the Ottoman officials to come out against the pro-Russian ministers and signatories of the Treaty of Unkiar-Skelessi: Foreign Minister (Reis Effendi) Mehmed Akif and Minister of Interior Ahmed Pasha. By requesting their removal Ponsonby tried to reduce Russia's influence. The Porte excused itself for the injustice to Churchill, released him, recalled the Ottoman official responsible for Churchill's mistreatment from Scutari and promised to recompense Churchill's suffering, but it refused to recall the ministers who were innocent in the whole affair. Ponsonby rejected any compromise and particularly insisted on Akif's withdrawal, which he presented as a *condicio sine qua non* for whatever settlement was agreed upon. His colleagues, including Stürmer, formally denounced the maltreatment of Churchill but refused to support Ponsonby's request for satisfaction for the alleged "insult made to the honour of England"[48] and were shocked by Ponsonby's strong anti-Ottoman remarks, including the alleged threat of the partition of the Ottoman Empire and the British participation in it if his request was not fulfilled.[49]

The strained situation led Mahmud II to ask for Austrian intervention in London with the aim of moderating the British proceedings

---

[48] Ponsonby to Pisani, Constantinople, 25 May 1836, attached to Stürmer to Metternich, Constantinople, 2 June 1836, HHStA, StA, Türkei VI, 65.
[49] Stürmer to Metternich, Constantinople, 13 and 19 May, 2 and 8 June 1836, HHStA, StA, Türkei VI, 65; Pisani to Ponsonby, Pera, 12 May 1836, Ponsonby to Akif Effendi, Therapia, 10 May 1836, Ponsonby to Palmerston, Therapia, 15 May 1836, TNA, FO 78/274; Ponsonby to Palmerston, Therapia, 10 and 28 June 1836, TNA, FO 78/275; Ponsonby to Palmerston, Therapia, 22 and 26 July 1836, TNA, FO 78/276; Roussin to Thiers, Therapia, 12, 15, 25 and 31 May 1836, AMAE, CP, Turquie 272; Königsmarck to Frederick William III, Pera, 18 May, 1 and 8 June 1836, GStA PK, HA III, MdA I, 7277; Webster, *Palmerston*, II, p. 531.

in the affair. Despite the fact that Metternich was convinced that the best way to resolve the situation was the sultan's direct appeal to the British government through his ambassador, he promptly agreed to help and instructed Hummelauer on 8 June to persuade Palmerston to order Ponsonby to act with greater restraint and restore relations with Akif; Great Britain was to be satisfied with the formal excuse and financial compensation for Churchill, both already offered by the Porte. Nevertheless, when the intercession was in progress, Mahmud II replaced Akif with Ahmed Houloussi Pasha in mid June. Although this ministerial change was explained by Akif's poor health, it was clear that the real reason was Ponsonby's pressure. The sultan thus enabled the British ambassador to achieve a great diplomatic victory and seriously harmed Metternich, whose intervention in London proved to be entirely unnecessary. A significant disillusionment prevailed in Vienna, both for the fact that Mahmud II had caused his own humiliation by his weakness and by the diplomatic slight to the Austrian chancellor. Metternich never forgot this and later refused to act in the same way remembering this weakness and ingratitude.[50]

Metternich well understood the goal of Ponsonby's tactic and one cannot deny that with his intervention in London he definitely tried to save the position of a pro-Russian minister, but the driving force behind his action was not so much fear of weakening Russia's influence but of offending the sultan's dignity. The chancellor regretted the violation of the treaties and advised the Porte to keep to the conditions of international agreements, but he also found Ponsonby's demand excessive and in fact having nothing to do with the affair of

---

[50] Metternich to Stürmer, Vienna, 8 June and 6 July 1836, HHStA, StA, Türkei VI, 65; Metternich to Hummelauer, Vienna, 8 June 1836, HHStA, StA, England 215; Metternich to Ficquelmont, Königswart, 16 Aug. 1836, HHStA, StA, Russland III, 108; Stürmer to Metternich, Constantinople, 25 May 1836, Büyükdere, 16 and 22 June, 27 July 1836, HHStA, StA, Türkei VI, 65; Maltzan to Frederick William III, Vienna, 16 June 1836, GStA PK, HA III, MdA I, 6027; Maltzan to Frederick William III, Vienna, 4 July 1836, Bockelberg to Frederick William III, Vienna, 27 July 1836, GStA PK, HA III, MdA I, 6028; Sainte-Aulaire to Thiers, Vienna, 3 and 15 July 1836, AMAE, CP, Autriche 423; Lerchenfeld to Ludwig I of Bavaria, Vienna, 9 and 19 July 1836, BHStA, MA, Wien 2406; Ponsonby to Palmerston, Therapia, 19 June 1836, TNA, FO 78/275; Roussin to Thiers, Therapia, 19 June 1836, AMAE, CP, Turquie 272; Königsmarck to Frederick William III, Pera, 22 June 1836, GStA PK, HA III, MdA I, 7277.

one "passionate hunter."[51] There was no hypocrisy in this criticism because it was not Metternich's style to carry matters to excess and he proved it in other situations similar to those of the Churchill Affair. When a similar crime had been committed in 1826 during the destruction of the Janissaries by an Ottoman policeman who had assaulted an Austrian citizen named Gemini, Metternich had maintained discretion and despite the Porte's reluctance he had finally achieved a resolution: the Porte had apologised and had put the policeman in jail.[52] Another affair of the same nature had happened only several weeks before the Churchill incident when an Austrian doctor in the Ottoman service had been maltreated and imprisoned for twelve days without an appropriate reason by a pasha; he was finally freed without the necessity for Austria to take matters further.[53] Metternich pointed out the fact that Austria often suffered from raids by bandits from the Ottoman territories on its soil, a matter which was often discussed with the Porte, but the Chancellery never allowed these serious infractions to cause any breakdown in the two Powers' relations, despite the pressure of Austrian military authorities.[54] Consequently, having compared the seriousness of these raids with the maltreatment of one British subject, Metternich posed the question what would become of the peace in the Near East if "for every violation of our territory by the Bosnians, Montenegrins or other nations established along a frontier which extends for 200 German miles, or more than 1,000 English miles, for every rifle shot fired at our peaceful inhabitants on the frontier, for every stolen herd, for every house set on fire, we requested compensation similar to what it pleases Lord Ponsonby to impose on the Divan as *condicio sine qua non* of the preservation of peace between England and the Porte, and even of the very existence of the Ottoman Empire?"[55]

It was the news of Ponsonby's threat of partition that evoked Metternich's fury. The chancellor condemned the ambassador as a

---

[51] Metternich to Apponyi, Vienna, 15 June 1836, HHStA, StA, Frankreich 302.
[52] Ottenfels' note to the Porte, 31 July 1826, Ottenfels to Metternich, Constantinople, 10 Aug. 1826, HHStA, StA, Türkei VI, 25; Ottenfels, *Memoari*, p. 174.
[53] Roussin to Thiers, Therapia, 18 April 1836, AMAE, CP, Turquie 272.
[54] Ottenfels, *Memoari*, pp. 239–240; Buchmann, *Militär – Diplomatie – Politik*, pp. 361–374; Gürbüz, pp. 188–217.
[55] Metternich to Hummelauer, Vienna, 15 June 1836, HHStA, StA, England 215.

"madman"[56] and was heard to shout: "What arrogance! This style is clearly from the school of Lord Palmerston!"[57] He resented above all that despite the official declarations of the British government of its wish to preserve the Ottoman Empire, it allowed such hostile conduct from its diplomat, regardless of whether the information about his threat was correct or not because even without it his actions significantly harmed the authority of the Ottoman sultan and his administration.[58] When Lamb told him that Great Britain actually wanted the preservation of the Ottoman Empire, Metternich replied: "What you have told me proves to me that the British cabinet is beginning to recover from some very dangerous errors. You tell me that they only want the preservation of the Ottoman Empire; how can it be then that it is following the most diametrically opposite course towards this goal? It would be impossible to accept that in London they cannot know the real state of affairs in Constantinople; this being so, they should know there that in order to preserve the sultan's throne there is only one way to be followed: that of not unsettling the weak characters who form the Divan with political phantasmagoria."[59] In mid September, Metternich criticised the British actions in his instructions for Esterházy returning at that time to his ambassadorial post in London: "The British cabinet is appearing to wake with a start after a long sleep. It has fixed its sights on a decadent Empire whose current weak state must largely be attributed to a complete lack of activity on the part of the English Power over a long period! What the British government is seeking today in the Levant is less the preservation of the Ottoman Porte than a political game directed against Russia."[60]

After Akif's removal the whole affair found itself in a stalemate because Mahmud II refused to recall his second minister and even though Ponsonby did not give up this request, he also did not press

---

[56] Metternich to Apponyi, Vienna, 15 June 1836, HHStA, StA, Frankreich 302.

[57] O'Sullivan to Meulenaer, Vienna, 4 July 1836, ADA, CP, Autriche 4.

[58] Metternich to Stürmer, Vienna, 24 May and 15 June 1836, HHStA, StA, Türkei VI, 65; Metternich to Hummelauer, Vienna, 15 June 1836, HHStA, StA, England 215; Metternich to Ficquelmont, Vienna, 22 June 1836, HHStA, StA, Russland III, 108; Sainte-Aulaire to Thiers, Vienna, 16 June 1836, AMAE, CP, Autriche 423; Lerchenfeld to Ludwig I of Bavaria, Vienna, 29 June 1836, BHStA, MA, Wien 2406.

[59] Metternich to Ficquelmont, Königswart, 16 Aug. 1836, HHStA, StA, Russland III, 108.

[60] Metternich to Esterházy, Prague, 17 Sept. 1836, HHStA, StA, England 215.

it because he was instructed by Palmerston to moderate his conduct. Unfortunately for Metternich, the affair was soon revived by Nicholas I, who wanted to revenge the diplomatic defeat and desired Akif's restoration to office and Ponsonby's removal from Constantinople. To achieve this, the tsar wanted the two imperial courts to persuade the Porte to restore Akif and to officially demand in London the removal of Ponsoby from Constantinople. When Butenev acted in this respect, Stürmer did not support him because he lacked the appropriate instructions, which Metternich never sent because he found Russia's demands equally as inappropriate as those of Ponsonby. In his opinion, Great Britain and Russia had instigated a situation where "the independence of the Ottoman Empire, which everyone pretends to want to preserve, will be invalidated by everyone just the same."[61] Metternich was convinced that Austria and Russia could inform the British government that Ponsonby's presence in Constantinople was not compatible with peace in the Levant and recommend his withdrawal, but it would be ill-advised to drag the Porte into a game that could deprive it of the rest of its dignity already significantly harmed by Akif's recall.[62]

Metternich behaved exactly in accordance with his own advice. He did not approach the sultan but suggested the expediency of Ponsonby's withdrawal to Lamb who, however, saw this as impossible to achieve: "You have a thousand reasons to regret the presence of Lord Ponsonby in Constantinople, and in this respect you are certainly no more dismayed than they are in London, but what to do? Ponsonby is a brother-in-law of Lord Grey, and the latter would become a very dangerous adversary of the government if he were displeased!"[63] This statement of weakness considerably annoyed Metternich, who told the

---

[61] Sainte-Aulaire to Thiers, Vienna, 3 July 1836, AMAE, CP, Autriche 423.
[62] Metternich to Ficquelmont, Königswart, 16 Aug. 1836, HHStA, StA, Russland III, 108; Metternich to Stürmer, Vienna, 26 Aug. 1836, HHStA, StA, Türkei VI, 65; Ficquelmont to Metternich, St Petersburg, 24 July 1836, HHStA, StA, Russland III, 106; Stürmer to Metternich, Büyükdere, 24 Aug., 14 and 28 Sept. 1836, HHStA, StA, Türkei VI, 65; Bockelberg to Frederick William III, Vienna, 26 Aug. 1836, GStA PK, HA III, MdA I, 6028; Nesserlode to Butenev, St Petersburg, 10 July, 25 Aug. and 15 Sept. 1836, AVPRI, fond 133, Kantseliariia, opis 469, 1836/43; Tatishchev to Nesselrode, Carlsbad, 13 Aug. 1836, AVPRI, fond 133, Kantseliariia, opis 469, 1836/216.
[63] Metternich to Ficquelmont, Königswart, 16 Aug. 1836, HHStA, StA, Russland III, 108.

ambassador: "What you call the government is no longer an authority with whom the Great Powers who are still able to follow their
convictions can deal with. You weigh the salvation of the Sultan on
one side and regard for Lord Grey on the other. You will see where
such a manner of proceeding leads you!"[64] As predicted by Lamb,
to Metternich's dismay Ponsonby remained in office, but at least the
Churchill Affair was finally resolved in early 1837 when the financial
compensation for Churchill was settled.[65]

David Urquhart and the Vixen Affair

Metternich's displeasure with the situation in Great Britain and its
policy was connected not only with the return of Palmerston to the
Foreign Office or the cabinet's toleration of Ponsonby's activities but
also with the considerable increase of Russophobia among the British
public in whom anti-Russian sentiment was stirred up by various
Russophobes sharing and often exceeding the foreign secretary's unfounded fears of the tsar's geopolitical designs. From among them a
new enemy for Metternich's Near Eastern policy arose, a man forming
with Palmerston and Ponsonby the leading trinity of the British Russophobia: David Urquhart, a man with a "monomaniacal hatred of
Russia"[66] and willing to go even further in his anti-Russian proceedings than Lord Ponsonby. Urquhart gained the reputation of an expert
in Eastern affairs with his book *Turkey and Its Resources* published
in 1833 and became famous a year later with another book *England,
France, Russia, and Turkey*, in which he expressed the opinion that
the principle goal of the tsarist diplomacy was the seizure of Constantinople and the Straits and that the main task of the two liberal
Powers was to prevent this. Urquhart's opinions were accepted by an
appreciative public and were advocated by leading journals. Hostility

---

[64] Ibid.

[65] Metternich to Stürmer, Vienna, 31 Jan. 1837, HHStA, StA, Türkei VI, 67;
Stürmer to Metternich, Constantinople, 15 Feb. and 9 March 1837, HHStA, StA,
Türkei VI, 66; Ponsonby to Palmerston, Therapia, 19 Feb. 1837, TNA, FO 78/301;
Maltzan to Frederick William III, Vienna, 24 Jan. 1837, GStA PK, HA III, MdA I,
6029.

[66] Gleason, p. 177.

towards Russia, of course not only due to Urquhart's activities, became a widespread fashion until the end of the 1830s and the British public demanded an offensive anti-Russian policy in the Near as well as Middle East.[67]

Metternich naturally could not overlook the fact that Russophobia was spreading among the British public like an epidemic and he criticised this tendency as nonsensical: "The English are extremely credulous; there is no other country where the people more readily attach to their prejudices a value that should only be accorded the truth. Accordingly, in England public opinion allows itself to be easily misled by a lie that reinforces one or another of the national sentiments. The Oriental affair, this affair that does not exist, is now a delusion of this nature. The Tories as well as the Whigs, the conservatives as well as the radicals, do not ask themselves whether an Oriental affair actually exists, what it is or what it is not. It is of little importance to them; the national mood has appropriated it, the public spirit has taken hold of it; it embraces it passionately and at the same time anxiously, and skilful politicians, as well as the most inept, because extremes come full circle, exploit the public delusion, either in the interests of the party to which they belong, or in interests of their own personal views."[68] He found the British Russophobia so dangerous that he paid considerable attention to anti-Russian publications; for example he read some works by Urquhart, who even sent a letter to Metternich in late August 1835 with apologies for serious mistakes on Austria's policy in his pamphlet *England, France, Russia, and Turkey*, and labelling Metternich "as the only man who understood Europe, as the only one whom Russia had to fear."[69] Despite this flattery Metternich was so upset with Urquhart's propaganda that he did not answer him.[70]

---

[67] Ibid., pp. 153–173; H.-J. Krautheim, *Öffentliche Meinung und imperiale Politik: Das britische Rußlandbild 1815–1854*, Berlin 1977, pp. 142–223; Lamb, p. 243.

[68] Metternich to Ficquelmont, Vienna, 2 Aug. 1835, HHStA, StA, Russland III, 105.

[69] Urquhart to Metternich, London, 30 Aug. 1835, attached to Metternich to Ficquelmont, Vienna, 1 March 1836, HHStA, StA, Russland III, 107.

[70] Metternich to Stürmer, Vienna, 2 Aug. 1835, HHStA, StA, Türkei VI, 64; Metternich to Ficquelmont, Vienna, 1 March 1836, HHStA, StA, Russland III, 107; La Rochefoucauld to Broglie, Vienna, 28 July 1835, AMAE, CP, Autriche 422.

Metternich soon obtained a more significant reason for his anger because in November 1835, Urquhart started to issue a violently anti-Russian journal called *Portfolio*. Its principal purpose was to publish Russian diplomatic correspondence, predominantly copies, seized by the Polish insurgents in Warsaw during the November Uprising and obtained by Urquhart in August 1835. Urquhart wanted to increase the anti-Russian sentiment in British society and damage the good relations between Austria and Russia with the publication of some Russian representatives' reports containing violent accusations of Austria's anti-Russian actions in late 1828. Metternich correctly regarded this activity as an attempt to set the two conservative Powers against each other and considered the *Portfolio* to be "the scandalous and criminal publication of diplomatic documents handed over to disgraceful factions or speculators by betrayal or pillage."[71] However, he was too practical a statesman to allow this to influence him despite the fact that he was offended by the content of some published documents, in particular by some of Pozzo's dispatches of 28 November and 14 December 1828 accusing the chancellor of wanting to create an anti-Russian coalition of four European Powers and a report written by Tatishchev on the possibility of inciting the Hungarians and Gallicians against the Austrian government in the event of the outbreak of a Russo-Austrian war. Tatishchev's situation was so precarious that he even requested his withdrawal from Vienna, which Nicholas I refused to do. Finally, however, the publication of the documents had no impact on the Russo-Austrian relations and their content was willingly disregarded by both parties.[72]

---

[71] Metternich to Ficquelmont, Vienna, 1 March 1836, HHStA, StA, Russland III, 107.

[72] Ibid.; Metternich to Stürmer, Vienna, 9 March 1836, HHStA, StA, Türkei VI, 65; Ficquelmont to Metternich, St Petersburg, 21 March and 3 April 1836, HHStA, StA, Russland III, 106; Sainte-Aulaire to Broglie, Vienna, 22 Feb. 1836, Sainte-Aulaire to Thiers, Vienna, 16 March 1836, AMAE, CP, Autriche 423; Maltzan to Frederick William III, Vienna, 19, 22 and 29 Feb. 1836, GStA PK, HA III, MdA I, 6027; Lerchenfeld to Ludwig I of Bavaria, Vienna, 15 March 1836, BHStA, MA, Wien 2406; Sainte-Aulaire, pp. 240–241; Gleason, pp. 177–178; Lamb, pp. 248–256. Metternich's anger at Pozzo's reports is evident not only from his correspondence but also from a copy of the *Portfolio* with his own irate remarks in the margins housed today in Königswart. See *The Portfolio or a Collection of State Papers Illustrative of the History of our Times*, London 1836, pp. 395–477, book number 4–B–2.

Although Palmerston was not directly involved in the issue of the *Portfolio*, he welcomed its potential to contribute to the spread of Russophobia in Great Britain as well as to the deterioration of the relations between Austria and Russia. He often shared Urquhart's views that were useful for him as ideological support of his foreign policy and he finally appointed Urquhart first secretary of the British embassy in Constantinople in 1835, to the city Urquhart personally knew from his previous visits but to the post in which he failed and from which he was already recalled in March 1837. During his stays in the Ottoman Empire, Urquhart had come into contact with the Circassian tribes fighting against Russia's domination in the so-called Caucasus War and he came to the conclusion that this arena could be used for a more significant drama with Great Britain and Russia as its principal actors. He and his associates deliberately caused a minor crisis by running the British merchant schooner *Vixen* through a Russian blockade which had been established on the eastern coast of the Black Sea in 1831 as an aid to a more effective campaign against the Circassians. Moreover, the ship carried salt – under the Russian regulations a prohibited commodity. Since they needed the ship to be captured by the Russians, they announced its voyage in the *Morning Chronicle* in advance. This plan finally succeeded when the *Vixen* was arrested by a Russian warship in the Bay of Sudjuk Kale on the Circassian coast on 27 November 1836 because the ship anchored outside Anapa and Redout Kale, two ports from where only trade with the Russian eastern coast of the Black Sea was allowed. The *Vixen* and its cargo were confiscated, and the sailors were eventually freed and sent to Constantinople. According to the expectations of the instigators of this ploy, the reaction of the Russian authorities was to attract Britain's attention to Russia's war with the Circassians and deteriorate the Russo-British relations and even provoke a war if possible. Although the consequences were not so serious, this incident led to an anti-Russian campaign in the British press and, in the first months of 1837, also to a minor diplomatic crisis between London and St Petersburg.[73]

[73] D. Gillard, *The Struggle for Asia 1828–1914: A Study in British and Russian Imperialism*, London 1977, p. 60; C. King, "Imagining Circassia: David Urquhart and the Making of North Caucasus Nationalism," *Russian Review* 66, 2007, 2, pp. 248–252; Bolsover, "Lord Ponsonby," p. 107; Gleason, pp. 191–192; Ingle, pp. 64–66; Lamb, p. 246; Puryear, *International Economics*, p. 27; Schiemann,

According to Sir Charles Kingsley Webster, Metternich played a disgraceful role in this affair when he promised to maintain neutrality at the beginning with the prospect of becoming a mediator between Great Britain and Russia but finally yielded to Russia's point of view. Palmerston, the British historian continued, showed great foresight when he did not count on the Austrian chancellor much and avoided stepping into a trap, making from the affair "one of the best examples of Palmerston's good sense and diplomatic skill in handling an awkard position."[74] Nevertheless, the studied documents reveal a different story from how it was presented by Webster, who particularly based his own version on reports from Lamb, who himself incorrectly assessed the situation and believed what he wanted to believe more than what Metternich was actually telling him. It is difficult to avoid an impression that Webster willingly accepted the above-mentioned version based upon the British documents because it enabled him to depict Palmerston's heroism and diplomatic talent in contrast with Metternich's treachery and humiliating role in the whole affair.[75]

According to Webster, during a meeting with Lamb on 27 January 1837, Metternich seemed to agree to preserve neutrality as was requested by the British ambassador with the prospect for future Austrian mediation. In reality Metternich already manifested a considerable partiality to Russia during this meeting. When he was asked by Lamb about his opinion of the seizure of the *Vixen*, the chancellor answered that it was identical to the official explanation offered by the Russian cabinet and he also sharply condemned the voyage of the *Vixen* because he knew well that Urquhart and his Russophobe friends had arranged it with the aim of harming Russo-British relations, in brief it was an act of revolutionary and warlike spirit.[76] Where Metternich remained cautious was only on the question of the law under which the ship was seized: "The affair is divided into two distinctive questions under one point of view and difficult to separate from one another. I, who never confuse two questions of a different nature in one and the same affair, I in no way intend to examine here the issue

---

III, pp. 290–291; Webster, *Palmerston*, II, p. 563.

[74] Webster, *Palmerston*, II, p. 570.

[75] Ibid., pp. 570–576.

[76] Metternich to Ficquelmont, Vienna, 3 Feb. 1837, HHStA, StA, Russland III, 110; Metternich to Esterházy, Vienna, 8 Feb. 1837, HHStA, StA, England 218; Lamb to Palmerston, Vienna, 3 Feb. 1837, TNA, FO 120/161.

concerning the sovereignty of Circassia. As so often when it concerns a question of fact, it is necessary to start doing a thorough examination, and in this case I declare that I do not know the truth of the facts. Whatever the truth of the matter, what is certain is that it is not questions of maritime law which have raised the *Vixen* Affair but an attempt at revolutionary policy. I have determined my position from now on."[77] Lamb agreed and added: "All that I ask is that you do not say it too loudly; I may be so bold as to predict that you could be called on to take on a more useful role."[78] Metternich showed no inclination to the eventual role of a mediator and terminated the discussion with these words: "I understand your thinking but take care not to deceive yourself. The questions of facts are such as they are and a third party can play no role there; as for the moral question, for me it is resolved."[79]

It is evident that Metternich clearly expressed his political support to Russia, and on the same day he hurried to give his assurance to the Russian chargé d'affaires in Vienna substituting for the absent Tatishchev, Prince Alexander Mikhailovich Gorchakov. The only area where he remained passive was on the question of law of which he had no idea. He wrote about this to Esterházy on 8 February: "I freely admit that the real position of Circassia is absolutely unknown to me ... I urge you to never lose sight of the fact that we endeavour above all to maintain an attitude of perfect impartiality with regard to the question of law."[80] Exactly for this reason Metternich did not want to enter into this question during his January meeting with Lamb: "In no way did I want to enter into a discussion with him about the question of the law of sovereignty and this for the following two reasons: first, because the position of Circassia is rather unknown to me, and then because this question is in reality only of secondary importance in the affair under discussion. It is evidently an attempt on the part of the semi-political and semi-revolutionary movement represented by the *Portfolio*."[81] And he expressed his opinion in the same way to Gor-

---

[77] Metternich to Esterházy, Vienna, 8 Feb. 1837, HHStA, StA, England 218.
[78] Ibid.
[79] Ibid. Lamb's version actually is not very different. Lamb to Palmerston, Vienna, 3 Feb. 1837, TNA, FO 120/161.
[80] Metternich to Esterházy, Vienna, 8 Feb. 1837, HHStA, StA, England 218.
[81] Metternich to Ficquelmont, Vienna, 3 Feb. 1837, HHStA, StA, Russland III, 110. See also Lamb to Palmerston, Vienna, 3 Feb. 1837, TNA, FO 120/161.

chakov: "The law is one, it makes no exceptions. It does not change its nature according to the sympathies which one has for the parties involved. Consequently, I would not give an opinion on a question that I have in no way examined and studied in all its details. Besides I have not been asked to do so, [and] I will thus pass on to the second point that, in my opinion, dominates the other, which is to say the origin of the incident. As for that, it has clearly demonstated to me that it is of a revolutionary nature. It is a page of the *Portfolio* put into action; and when it concerns questions which show signs of a similar tendency, the work of two closely allied cabinets is invariably evident. There is not the slightest expression of disapproval either in their action or in their language."[82]

It was precisely this legal aspect which obtained a crucial significance during February when Palmerston based his interrogation of the Russian cabinet on this basis. He took advantage of the mistake that the Russian authorities made themselves when the government explained the seizure of the *Vixen* was due to the vessel's violation of the quarantine and customs cordon, whereas Admiral Lazarev declared that the ship was confiscated as spoils of war on grounds of a violation of a blockade. This raised the question whether Russia actually was the owner of the territory and therefore entitled to establish a cordon or was attempting to conquer it and had thereby established the blockade. Palmerston not only touched on this ambiguity but also called into question Russia's sovereignty over some Circassian coastal regions when he claimed that it was not clear whether the Ottoman Empire had actually possessed the territory before 1829 and, consequently, whether it could transfer it to Russia in the Treaty of Adrianople.[83]

When Metternich learnt of Palmerston's reasoning, he merely renewed his request already directed to St Petersburg at the beginning of February for an explanation of the legal issue in order to be able to oppose the British accusations, and he continued in his neutrality regarding the legal aspect of the affair until the receipt of the answer.[84]

---

[82] Gorchakov to Nesselrode, Vienna, 28 Jan. 1837, AVPRI, fond 133, Kantseliariia, opis 469, 1836/230.

[83] Esterházy to Metternich, London, 17 and 21 Feb. 1837, HHStA, StA, England 216; Ingle, pp. 68–69; Schiemann, III, p. 292.

[84] Metternich to Ficquelmont, Vienna, 3 Feb. 1837, SOA, RA C-A 383; Metternich to Ficquelmont, Vienna, 24 Feb. 1837, HHStA, StA, Russland III, 110; Gorchakov

He considered a prompt answer to be expedient, as he explained to Ficquelmont on 4 March: "What would appear positive to me is that the Russian court has to establish itself on perfectly clear ground. The shores of Abkhazie are or are not, either *de jure* or *de facto*, placed under the sovereignty of the emperor. This is a matter of fact ... The subdued subjects, the Circassians, must obey the customs and quarantine laws of the Empire. Non subjects or rebellious subjects must be captured or brought to heel. In the first of these situations commercial regulations are applicable; in the second one the right of a blockade can be applied ... Such is the realm of law, and it is broad and solid. It is up to the Cabinet of St Petersburg to declare the basis for its action. Once it has adopted this attitude, it will become easy for its friends to choose for themselves the course which, according to their interpretations, they ought to follow."[85] However, he personally maintained an obviously pro-Russian attitude in secret instructions of the same day: "Abkhazie must belong to Russia. The fact is certain because it is natural. It belongs to it [Russia] or it does not belong to it yet; it is a question of fact as I have said in my dispatch of today. In both cases the emperor has the right to prevent anyone from trying to stir up either his subjects or his enemies. However, what is certain is that the seizure of the English ship has to have been prompted on a basis of action: on that of a blockade or that of [a violation of] the customs or quarantine laws; I say 'or' and not 'and,' which makes me go back into the trial of Figaro."[86]

The explanations offered by the Russian diplomats, however, did not offer a clear answer to the source of its sovereignty over Circassia for a long time and, on the contrary, they confused the whole issue even more. On 22 February, Nesselrode wrote to Pozzo that the coast under dispute as well as the adjacent regions had been possessed by the Porte for a long time and relinquished to Russia in the 4th article of the Treaty of Adrianople. However, seeing Metternich's doubts, in early March Gorchakov prepared a very long memorandum on the topic based upon Nikolay Mikhailovich Karamzin's *History of*

---

to Nesselrode, Vienna, 24 Feb. 1837, AVPRI, fond 133, Kantseliariia, opis 469, 1836/230.

[85] Metternich to Ficquelmont, Vienna, 4 March 1837, HHStA, StA, Russland III, 110.

[86] Ibid.

the Russian State, in which he claimed that Russia had possessed the territory since the 11th century. Metternich discovered two principal problems in this memorandum. First, it lacked evidence and offered an inadequate explanation of the problem, and Metternich reacted with these words: "If what you have just read to me is proved, you will undoubtedly be right. But where is your proof?"[87] Second, the explanation was in evident contradiction with what Nesselrode claimed and, therefore, Metternich told Gorchakov: "The Imperial [Russian] Cabinet establishes its rights of possession exclusively upon the Treaty of Adrianople. You infer them from a series of historical events; as you see there is a contradiction between your note and the memorandum of your Court."[88] When Gorchakov insisted on the truth of his version, Metternich merely replied: "I will just wait to see how your Court has resolved the question. I do not intend to impose myself as a judge between its agents, and I believe that the cause of your master will only be able to gain from it."[89] Consequently, they both agreed to wait for the final answer from St Petersburg, which meant that Metternich continued to maintain the attitude adopted after his first meeting with Lamb on the topic.[90] He wrote to Ficquelmont on 21 March: "By positioning our Cabinet on a basis of truth, by declaring our ignorance on the question of sovereignty, and by not hesitating at the same moment to express our disapproval at the sending of the *Vixen*, by going even farther in declaring that the shores of Abkhazie, regardless of whether they belong or do not belong to Russia, must necessarily belong to the sovereign of other trans-Caucassian provinces, I believe we have assumed the only attitude appropriate for us, either due to our respect for our close alliance with Russia or in opposition to the subversive policy of England."[91]

---

[87] Metternich to Ficquelmont, Vienna, 21 March 1837, HHStA, StA, Russland III, 110.

[88] Gorchakov to Nesselrode, Vienna, 11 March 1837, AVPRI, fond 133, Kantseliariia, opis 469, 1836/230.

[89] Metternich to Ficquelmont, Vienna, 21 March 1837, HHStA, StA, Russland III, 110.

[90] Nesselrode to Pozzo di Borgo, St Petersburg, 22 Feb. 1837, HHStA, StA, Russland III, 111; Gorchakov to Nesselrode, Vienna, 9, 11 and 14 March 1837, AVPRI, fond 133, Kantseliariia, opis 469, 1836/230; Sainte-Aulaire to Molé, Vienna, 2 March 1837, AMAE, CP, Autriche 424; Maltzan to Frederick William III, Vienna, 4, 9 and 14 March 1837, GStA PK, HA III, MdA I, 6029; Lerchenfeld to Ludwig I of Bavaria, Vienna, 10 March 1837, BHStA, MA, Wien 2407.

The wish to remain passive until the desired clarification of the legal aspect of the affair placed Metternich in an awkward situation. On the one hand Lamb was going to extraordinary lengths to get the chancellor on the British side. The ambassador even claimed that this partiality already existed and, for example, he assured the Ottoman ambassador in Vienna, Ahmed Fethi Pasha, of Prince Metternich's inclination in favour of England and his alleged statement that "in the event of a rupture between this Power and Russia, Austria would sooner detach itself from its alliance with it [Russia] than sacrifice the interests of England."[92] It is difficult to find any reasonable explanation for Lamb's optimism because Metternich's statements did not offer any justification for it and Lamb's reports also do not contain anything that would evidence anything else. Metternich continued to condemn the *Vixen's* adventure and politically he was on Russia's side, and in the legal question he only answered that he lacked sufficient knowledge. What Lamb regarded as proof of Metternich's pro-British partiality was the publication of British articles in the *Österreichischer Beobachter*, but this is rather weak evidence because, first, Gorchakov himself saw nothing dangerous in their publication regarding their rather inoffensive content and, second, the articles advocating Russia's point of view were also published in the same newspaper. The members of the diplomatic corps in Vienna who discussed the affair with Metternich also did not share Lamb's opinion. Sainte-Aulaire did not understand his British colleague's conviction regarding Metternich's alleged partiality because he not only saw no sign of it himself but rather the clear opposite in the chancellor's statements. The Prussian envoy in Vienna, Count Mortimer von Maltzan,[93] shared this opinion, as is evident from his report from mid March: "If in my turn, Sire, I dare to express an opinion on the subject of this affair, it is that in so far as the efforts of Sir Frederic Lamb to try to make the Court of Vienna understand the British views and interpretations in the

---

[91] Metternich to Ficquelmont, Vienna, 21 March 1837, HHStA, StA, Russland III, 110.

[92] Pertev to Reshid, Constantinople, 15 March 1837, attached to Metternich to Ficquelmont, Vienna, 1 April 1837, HHStA, StA, Russland III, 110.

[93] To spare the reader any confusion, it is necessary to explain the fact that during *Vormärz*, Prussia was represented in Vienna by two envoys named Maltzan: Baron Bogislaw von Maltzan from 1827 to 1833 and, after his death, Count Mortimer von Maltzan from 1833 to 1841.

Vixen Affair have completely failed and that the language of Prince Metternich corresponds, on the one hand, with the real interests of Russia, but on the other hand also with the dignity of the cabinet that His Highness represents, it seems to me that there is no reason for expressing any criticism. Wanting a cabinet to embrace a cause the nature of which it is ignorant and which was indisputably neglected in respect of its form would be absurd and would require its needless humiliation."[94] Gorchakov's reports do not differ in this respect from the dispatches of his French and Prussian colleagues. It is true that he expressed his own inner belief that Metternich secretly nurtured the hope for a more active role in the affair, but more likely that of a moderator than a mediator. However, this impression merely resulted from the fact that Metternich refused to support Russia in the legal discussion until the clarification of the problem. Otherwise Gorchakov was unable to inform his cabinet about any proposal for mediation or even the slightest chance of one in this respect, and he praised the chancellor for his passive attitude with no obvious signs of any desire to mediate.[95] In mid March, he finally stated that there was actually very little that Russia could complain about in the political aspect of the affair: "The attitude of Austria in the *Vixen* Affair has never ceased to be correct as regards its declaration on the role that it would play should this incident lead to a serious complication. If the English cabinet deludes itself with a contrary illusion, it is because it strongly wishes to do so."[96]

Metternich actually did not want to assume the role of either mediator or moderator. As in the Churchill Affair, in this one he also did not want to become involved in the Russo-British conflict that, in his opinion, could never provoke a war between the two contesting parties. Much as in previous years, he found such a situation impossible because Russia could never attack the British Isles and Great Britain could not effectively threaten Russia without France, and the

---

[94] Maltzan to Frederick William III, Vienna, 16 March 1837, GStA PK, HA III, MdA I, 6029.

[95] Gorchakov to Nesselrode, Vienna, 1, 3, 15 and 21 Feb., 9 March 1837, AVPRI, fond 133, Kantseliariia, opis 469, 1836/230; Lamb to Palmerston, Vienna, 25 Feb. 1837, TNA, FO 120/161; Sainte-Aulaire to Molé, Vienna, 11 March and 8 April 1837, AMAE, CP, Autriche 424.

[96] Gorchakov to Nesselrode, Vienna, 14 March 1837, AVPRI, fond 133, Kantseliariia, opis 469, 1836/230.

chancellor knew well in the mid 1830s that France did not want to wage war on Russia: "Could France want a war? No! Could a war between England and Russia be waged without the participation of France? No. Therefore, there will be no war."[97] And it was not the *Vixen* that could change the attitude of the French government. Consequently, Metternich wrote to Ficquelmont: "England will not wage an offensive war owing to the *Vixen* Affair, and for the very simple reason that it cannot wage one."[98] The chancellor was neutral in the question of what was right not because he planned to be a mediator or moderator in the future but because he was absolutely ignorant of the legal aspects of the case and did not want to burn his fingers when dealing with it, in particular when he saw no reason why he should do so when he did not fear any serious consequences. Consequently, he made no attempt to take part in the negotiations and repeatedly told Lamb that the whole dispute was to be directly settled between Russia and Great Britain. If anyone at all showed any support for Austria's mediation, then it was only Lamb and to a certain extent Esterházy, who worried that the affair could finally provoke a war which was to be prevented by some mutual concessions between Great Britain and Russia and Austria's peaceful intercession. Nevertheless, Lamb himself assured Palmerston that Esterházy's apprehension was never shared by Metternich.[99]

The Russian cabinet, the second complication, expected from Metternich exactly the opposite to Lamb: the chancellor's definite defence of its legal point of view. Nicholas I was entirely satisfied

[97] Maltzan to Frederick William III, Vienna, 7 Dec. 1835, GStA PK, HA III, MdA I, 6026.
[98] Metternich to Ficquelmont, Vienna, 21 March 1837, HHStA, StA, Russland III, 110.
[99] Metternich to Esterházy, Vienna, 21 Jan. 1834, HHStA, StA, England 208; Metternich to Hummelauer, Vienna, 9 Jan. 1836, HHStA, StA, England 215; Metternich to Esterházy, Vienna, 28 Jan. 1837, HHStA, StA, England 218; Metternich to Ficquelmont, Vienna, 3 Feb. 1837, SOA, RA C-A 383; Esterházy to Metternich, London, 4 and 17 Feb., 10 March and 12 May 1837, HHStA, StA, England 216; Tatishchev to Nesselrode, Vienna, 3 Jan. 1834, AVPRI, fond 133, Kantseliariia, opis 469, 1834/217; Gorchakov to Nesselrode, Vienna, 21 and 24 Feb. 1837, AVPRI, fond 133, Kantseliariia, opis 469, 1836/230; Sainte-Aulaire to Molé, Vienna, 30 Jan. 1837, AMAE, CP, Autriche 424; Maltzan to Frederick William III, Vienna, 1 and 17 Feb. 1837, GStA PK, HA III, MdA I, 6029; Lamb to Metternich, Vienna, 4 March 1837, TNA, FO 120/170; Lamb to Palmerston, Vienna, 5 March 1837, TNA, FO 120/161.

with the way in which the prince expressed himself in late January to Lamb, but when the tsar learnt of his restraint in the legal aspect of the affair, Lamb's boasting of Metternich's pro-British sympathies and Esterházy's wavering attitude in London, he became, together with Nessselrode, extremely displeased and suspected their Austrian ally of an inclination to betray them. This finally moved the Russian cabinet to send the explanation of the legal aspect of the affair to Vienna on 18 March. According to this document, Russia gained the territory by the Treaty of Adrianople, its sovereignty over Circassia was indisputable and the capture of the *Vixen* was explained by the violation of the quarantine and customs cordon. Nesselrode's instructions to Gorchakov with this answer also expressed extraordinarily frank displeasure at the Viennese cabinet's attitude, which was definitely rather discourteous from a diplomatic point of view, together with great surprise over its hesitation to support Russia's legal standpoint.[100] Ficquelmont wrote to Metternich on the same day from St Petersburg: "It is felt here, and Mr Tatishchev also told me that it was his opinion, Your Highness, that during Your meetings with Sir F. Lamb, and above all in Your instructions addressed to Prince Esterházy on 8 February, You did not express Yourself in a manner explicit enough against the attack that England would seem to want to make *against the sovereign right of Russia* [underlined by Metternich] over the territories inhabited by the Circassian people."[101]

When Metternich received the letters from Ficquelmont and Nesselrode of 18 March, containing the clarification he had been impatiently waiting for, he obtained the necessary knowledge in order to be able to express himself to the British cabinet on behalf of Russia in the legal aspect of the affair. The chancellor rejected Russia's frustration and told Gorchakov: "In order to *strongly* declare my conviction of this right, I needed to know the claims upon which you wish to base it, as well as the basis of support for your action. I was waiting for the hallowed words from St Petersburg in order to comply with

---

[100] Ficquelmont to Metternich, St Petersburg, 24 Feb. 1837, HHStA, StA, Russland III, 109; Gorchakov to Nesselrode, Vienna, 9 March 1837, AVPRI, fond 133, Kantseliariia, opis 469, 1836/230; Nesselrode to Gorchakov, St Petersburg, 18 March 1837, HHStA, StA, Russland III, 111; Sainte-Aulaire to Molé, Vienna, 8 April 1837, AMAE, CP, Autriche 424.
[101] Ficquelmont to Metternich, St Petersburg, 18 March 1837, HHStA, StA, Russland III, 109.

them. Now they are known to me, I do have not the slightest hesitation about the language which it seems to me to contain, and you will see whether Austria understands and can fulfil the obligations of the alliance."[102] The appropriate instructions supporting Russia's view were sent to Esterházy on 8 April 1837; they were written in such a way that they must be regarded as aimed more for the Russian than for the British cabinet – as proof of Austria's support that had earlier been regarded by the former as insufficient. In this respect, they were entirely effective in St Petersburg. As for Lamb, he was considerably displeased with, as he claimed, the sudden and complete change in Metternich's attitude, but as shown above, nothing of the kind had actually happened.[103]

The *Vixen* Affair was terminated during May 1837 when Palmerston satisfied himself with Russia's official response that the ship had been confiscated because it had violated Russian laws when it entered a port having neither customs nor quarantine. It did not directly affect the Ottoman Empire, and the most important incident that happened in Constantinople in connection with this affair was Ponsonby's desire to obtain the sultan's firman with the permission for the British fleet to go through the Straits if necessary, which was refused by the Porte to Metternich's satisfaction.[104] In fact, the Ottoman Empire lost for some time its attraction for British Russophobia, which was redirected

---

[102] Gorchakov to Nesselrode, Vienna, 1 April 1837, AVPRI, fond 133, Kantseliariia, opis 469, 1836/230.

[103] Metternich to Ficquelmont, Vienna, 11 April 1837, HHStA, StA, Russland III, 110; Metternich to Ficquelmont, Vienna, 27 May 1837, HHStA, StA, Russland III, 111; Metternich to Esterházy, Vienna, 8 April 1837, HHStA, StA, England 218; Esterházy to Metternich, London, 29 April 1837, HHStA, StA, England 216; Gorchakov to Nesselrode, Vienna, 4 March 1837, AVPRI, fond 133, Kantseliariia, opis 469, 1836/230; Nesselrode to Tatishchev, St Petersburg, 9 May 1837, HHStA, StA, Russland III, 111; Sainte-Aulaire to Molé, Vienna, 10 April and 9 May 1837, AMAE, CP, Autriche 424; Lamb to Palmerston, Vienna, 21 April 1837, TNA, FO 120/161; Maltzan to Frederick William III, Vienna, 3 April 1837, GStA PK, HA III, MdA I, 6029; Lerchenfeld to Ludwig I of Bavaria, Vienna, 18 April 1837, BHStA, MA, Wien 2407; O'Sullivan to Meylandt, Vienna, 21 April 1837, ADA, CP, Autriche 5.

[104] Metternich to Ficquelmont, Vienna, 1 April 1837, HHStA, StA, Russland III, 110; Metternich to Esterházy, Vienna, 8 April 1837, HHStA, StA, England 218; Esterházy to Metternich, London, 23 March, 14 and 28 April, 12 and 30 May 1837, HHStA, StA, England 216; Ficquelmont to Metternich, St Petersburg, 2 and 8 May 1837, HHStA, StA, Russland III, 109; Ingle, pp. 70–71.

from the Near to the Middle East in 1837 and 1838; the Eastern Question was thus replaced by the so-called Great Game between Russia
and Great Britain for the control over Afghanistan and Persia, where
the British cabinet suspected Russia of a desire for conquest, which
was similarly an unfounded fear as it had also been with regard to
the concern about the tsar's conquest at the expense of the Ottoman
Empire. History repeated itself again, only the scene was different:
during 1838, these suspicions concerning the Middle East led to the
deterioration of Russo-British relations, which in turn led Ponsonby to
a new prediction that a war between them was inevitable and Metternich to the repeated accusation of the British ambassador's madness.
The chancellor continued to think that such a war between just the
two Great Powers, and it had to be limited to just them because no
other Powers desired to join their dispute over the Middle East, was
impossible. As well as in the previous affairs concerning the Ottoman
Empire, he regarded Palmerston in this case as the culprit: "The habit
of characterising the affair as Eastern is in all reality nothing other
than the practical application of the hateful resentment which Lord
Palmerston and several men of his ilk have directed against Russia's
power ... The Dardanelles and Circassia have been abandonned, and
it is Persia that has replaced these two places to which the public attention was previously directed."[105] Metternich correctly considered
Palmerston's fears about Nicholas I's aggressive intentions towards
Persia or even India equally as unfounded as those concerning the Ottoman Empire and he continued to assure the Maritime Powers that
the tsar did not have such intentions. Since Palmerston still distrusted
Metternich as well as Russia, the British apprehension about the increase of Russia's influence over Persia in 1837–1838 finally led the
Albion to a needless war with Afghanistan in early 1839.[106]

---

[105] Metternich to Trauttmannsdorff, Vienna, 17 Nov. 1838, HHStA, StK, Preussen
162.

[106] Metternich to Stürmer, Vienna, 13 Nov. 1838, HHStA, StA, Türkei VI, 67;
Metternich to Kaisersfeld, Vienna, 12 Nov. 1838, Metternich to Ficquelmont, Vi-
enna, 28 Nov. 1838, HHStA, StA, Russland III, 112; Metternich to Hummelauer,
Vienna, 16 Dec. 1838, HHStA, StA, England 219; Stürmer to Metternich, Con-
stantinople, 24 Oct. 1838, HHStA, StA, Türkei VI, 68; Sainte-Aulaire to Molé,
Vienna, 27 Oct. 1838, AMAE, CP, Autriche 426; Milbanke to Palmerston, Vienna,
20 Nov. and 24 Dec. 1838, TNA, FO 120/169; Maltzan to Frederick William III,
Vienna, 7 Nov. 1838, GStA PK, HA III, MdA I, 6031; Lerchenfeld to Ludwig I of
Bavaria, Vienna, 30 Oct., 9 Nov., 2 and 12 Dec. 1838, BHStA, MA, Wien 2407;

*   *   *

British historian David Brown claims that it was Metternich's fault that Austria and Great Britain did not cooperate in the Eastern Question in the 1830s because Metternich's policy was too unreliable: "So long as Metternich failed to give a clear and firm line to Austrian policy, Palmerston could see no way to make Austria a British ally."[107] Nevertheless, this opinion is not tenable. Regarding the facts, the problem was not connected with Metternich, who was definitely right all along in the Near Eastern affairs of that time[108] and totally sincere and consistent in his statements, but with Palmerston and other Russophobes who were mistaken during the whole period and disbelieved the assurances of the Austrian chancellor about the tsar's desire to preserve the Ottoman Empire. They did not see it not only because they were too blinded by their generally incorrect or exaggerated presumptions but also because they longed to replace Russia's influence over the Ottoman Empire with Britain's. The result of both, the needless distrust and hunger for power, contributed to the worsening of relations among these two as well as the other Great Powers and to the anti-Russian sentiment that developed into a real hatred in Great Britain by the end of the 1830s.[109] Metternich knew that this was absolutely nonsensical because the five Powers' desire for the preservation of the Ottoman Empire was identical but, unfortunately, despite this unity of interests, two of them made its further existence more uncertain. He firmly stood on the side of Russia, not only and not particularly due to his need for this conservative ally as historians are generally inclined to claim but simply because he perfectly analysed the situation and correctly saw in Russia not an enemy but the supporter of the political status quo in the Near East. For him it was Palmerston who threatened it with his distrust and jealousy of Russia: "The most reprehensible aspect of the political approach of the Principal Secretary of the State with regard to the Ottoman Empire

---

Lerchenfeld to Ludwig I of Bavaria, Vienna, 26 Jan. 1839, BHStA, MA, Wien 2408; Anderson, "Russia and the Eastern Question," p. 93; Gillard, pp. 38–53.

[107] D. Brown, "Palmerston and Austria," L. Höbelt, T. G. Otte (eds.), *A Living Anachronism? European Diplomacy and the Habsburg Monarchy: Festschrift für Francis Roy Bridge zum 70. Geburtstag*, Wien, Köln, Weimar 2010, p. 40.

[108] Sked, *Metternich*, p. 94.

[109] Gleason, p. 277.

is that he has chosen this Empire as an arena for throwing down the gauntlet to Russia."[110] On the other hand, he was in no way a blind ally of Russia and he was able to see that Nicholas I picked up this gauntlet and played the same game.[111] The Austrian chancellor also was not prepared to support the tsar in any measures which weakened the sultan's authority, like the advice from 1836 that the Porte should restore Akif Effendi to office and officially request Ponsonby's withdrawal in London. In this case Metternich not only remained passive but he also informed the tsar of his disapproval. What he tried to do after 1833 above all was to overcome the mutual distrust and persuade the members of the diplomatic concert that they were all actually pursuing the same goal and that there was no real Eastern Question at that particular moment. It was not his fault that his well-founded defence of the tsar found no echo in the West, above all in the British Foreign Office. There would definitely have been no Eastern Question, or it would have been far less threatening, if the Western cabinets had listened to Metternich.[112]

[110] Metternich to Hummelauer, Vienna, 16 Dec. 1838, HHStA, StA, England 219.
[111] Ibid.
[112] Sked, *Metternich*, p. 93.

19

The Danube and the Danubian Principalities

In the history of the Eastern Question, the Danubian Principalities represented an important focal point in the relations between the Great Powers involved and the Sublime Porte. In particular for Austria the position of Moldavia and Wallachia was of extreme importance and there was hardly another region in the Ottoman Empire, except Serbia, that would have had similar geopolitical value for the Viennese cabinet. Austria's influence over the Principalities considerably decreased after the Treaty of Adrianople, which enabled Russia to achieve their temporary military occupation and the seizure of the mouth of the Danube. Metternich was often criticised by his contemporaries for his too condescending attitude towards Russia in these regions. Nevertheless, his conduct in the issues concerning the Russian occupation, administrative changes in Moldavia and Wallachia implemented by the tsar and navigation on the Danube could hardly be called weak. Always practical and as aware of Austria's power limits as ever, Metternich decided to pursue a cautious, well-calculated and finally, under the given conditions, successful policy instead of risking direct confrontation.

The Russian Occupation of the Principalities

Although the Principalities enjoyed a considerable autonomy, their preservation under the sultan's rule was of the most vital interest to the Habsburg Monarchy beyond its south-eastern border because their annexation by Russia would lead not only to a considerable growth of the latter's influence over the Balkans but also to the extension of the Russo-Austrian frontier, something which would be extremely undesirable to the Austrian supreme command considering the numerical superiority of the tsarist army. Furthermore, the concern existing in

Vienna for Russia's territorial expansion on the western coast of the
Black Sea was motivated not only by geopolitical but also economic
reasons. In terms of trade conventions concluded with the Sublime
Porte and the sultan's firmans, Austria enjoyed a position in the Principalities "akin to those of a colonial power."[1] Austrian merchants
enjoyed vast privileges and their commercial vessels could sail freely
up and down the Danube, even as far as the sea. Consequently, the
Austrian share in the foreign trade of the Principalities during the period under research was far more significant than all other European
countries' trade, and the number of people with Austrian passports
by far exceeded other foreign residents in Moldavia and Wallachia.[2]

Metternich strove to maintain the status quo in the Principalities not merely because of his conservatism but particularly due to the
above-mentioned geopolitical and economic reasons, which naturally
influenced his considerations. He did so in two ways in the 1820s.
First, he hoped to assure Austrian political influence in the Principalities, and he was successful, at least in Wallachia; the Austrian
agent in Bucharest had considerable effect on the administration, and
Hospodar Grigore IV Ghica was pro-Austrian, particularly due to his
correspondence with Friedrich von Gentz, who served with Metternich's approval as a paid advisor of the Wallachian princes from 1813
to 1828.[3] The pro-Austrian inclination also seemed to predominate
among Wallachian boyars. Second, Metternich tried to prevent the
outbreak of war between Russia and the Ottoman Empire because he
was well aware that Austria's significant position in the Principalities
could quickly be lost and its economic supremacy seriously harmed
if they were to be occupied or even annexed by Russia, whose Near
Eastern policy was clearly focused on gaining supremacy over this
part of the Balkan Peninsula. To his displeasure, this effort gained
additional strength after the conclusion of the Akkerman Convention
in 1826 and was naturally intensified after Russia's occupation of the
Principalities following the outbreak of war with the Ottoman Em-

---

[1]   Bitis, p. 457.
[2]   Miltitz to Frederick William III, Pera, 10 July 1824, GStA PK, HA III, MdA I,
7259; J. Hagemeister, *Mémoire sur le commerce des ports de la Nouvelle-Russie, de
la Moldavie et de la Valachie*, Odessa 1835, p. 167; G. Zane, "Die österreichischen
und die deutschen Wirtschaftsbeziehungen zu den rumänischen Fürstentümern
1774–1874," *Weltwirtschaftliches Archiv* 26, 1927, 1, p. 36; Roman, pp. 41–49.
[3]   Sweet, p. 249.

pire in 1828. The removal of the two hospodars cooperating with the Porte, as well as Austria, was only the tip of the iceberg.[4]

It is a question difficult to answer whether on Russia's annexation of the Principalities Austria would have reacted by declaring war when this did not happen. Metternich admitted such a possibility during a talk with the British ambassador in late 1827: "It would pave the way to the destruction of the Austrian Monarchy and although the Emperor has not as yet added a single man to his force upon the frontier, yet the moment it shall appear to be the intention of Russia to take permanent possession of those provinces, His Imperial Majesty will not only protest against such a measure but oppose it if necessary at the head of our hundred thousand men."[5] Despite these strong words and the importance of the Principalities for Austria, Metternich was entirely unable to thwart Russia's actions. The financial and consequent military weakness of the country reduced him to the role of a mere observer and he was only able to watch on as the events destroying Austria's political influence unfolded. This degree of inaction was of course facilitated by Nicholas I's promise that he would not annex any territory in Europe. However, as seen earlier in the book, he broke this promise when he gained the Danube Delta by the Treaty of Adrianople. As for the territory beyond the river, the Principalities were merely to be occupied for a period of ten years until the trade and war indemnities of 11.5 million ducats imposed on the Sublime Porte had been paid. These stipulations concerning the Principalities and the Danube were naturally most burdensome for Austria. The Russian presence at the mouth of the Danube was a shock for Metternich, particularly since he had not expected any Russian territorial gains in Europe. The ten-year occupation of the Principalities was too long for him and he claimed that it was "in fact equivalent to the cession of those Provinces to Russia, and no one acquainted with her policy can alter himself to believe that after so long [an] occupation she will consent to evacuate them."[6] And even if they were eventually evacuated, Metternich believed that after the de-

---

[4]   Metternich to Esterházy, Vienna, 9 Nov. 1827, HHStA, StA, England 179; Kreuchely to Miltitz, Bucharest, 28 Feb. 1827, attached to Miltitz to Frederick William III, Pera, 10 March 1827, GStA PK, HA III, MdA I, 7264; Stiepovich [?] to Royer, Pera, 22 June 1829, GStA PK, HA III, MdA I, 7267; Bitis, p. 436.
[5]   Wellesley to Dudley, Vienna, 16 Dec. 1827, TNA, FO 120/88.
[6]   Cowley to Aberdeen, Vienna, 26 Sept. 1829, TNA, FO 120/105.

struction of several fortresses on the right bank of the Danube and the recognition of their autonomous status, the two Principalities would be *de facto* removed from the sultan's authority and placed under the tsar's rule. The circumstances reminded Metternich of the situation in the Crimea at the time of the reign of Catherine the Great, when the area had obtained autonomy but was later annexed by Russia.[7]

According to Metternich, the presence of Russian soldiers threatened to transform the Principalities into "a perpetual thorn in the side of Austria."[8] Unsurprisingly, the "deplorable duration"[9] of their occupation was for him the most dangerous result of the Russo-Ottoman war. The principal reason for this discontent was the danger that Austria's rights would be violated, which the presence of Russian soldiers indeed implied. This was supported by the report of a French agent, probably somewhat exaggerated but not at all ill-founded: "Where are the privileges guaranteed by former capitulations of the Porte to their [Great Powers'] governments? Did the Treaty of Adrianople abolish them? Where does the audacity of the barbarians [Russians] come from, leading them to violate the homes of the Austrians, French and British, and with the use of force cause havoc there? The Austrian subject Riss [?] has just gained, as his allocation in relation to military lodgings, an officer and two petty officers, each having his own concubine. And if he dares not offer a free dinner, sumptuous enough in the opinion of these gentlemen or their ladies, he will be subjected to military discipline like so many others."[10] The immediate infraction of Austrian rights was not, however, what Metternich feared the most. The tsar decided that, during the occupation, administrative changes advantageous for Russia would be introduced and the Austrian chancellor was well aware of this fact. Already by the summer of 1829 he was alarmed by some of the Russian plans for reforms in

---

[7] Metternich to Ficquelmont, Vienna, 5 Oct. 1829 HHStA, StA, Russland III, 88; Metternich to Ottenfels, Vienna, 17 Oct. 1829, HHStA, StA, Türkei VI, 39; Metternich to Esterházy, Vienna, 17 Oct. 1829, HHStA, StA, England 188; Cowley to Aberdeen, Vienna, 8 Sept. 1829, TNA, FO 120/105.
[8] Cowley to Aberdeen, Vienna, 4 Oct. 1829, TNA, FO 120/104.
[9] Metternich to Ficquelmont, Vienna, 5 Oct. 1829, HHStA, StA, Russland III, 88.
[10] Hugot to Polignac, Bucharest, 13 Nov. 1829, E. de Hurmuzaki, N. Hodoș (eds.), *Documente privitoare la istoria Românilor, Volumul XVII: Corespondență diplomatică și rapoarte consulare franceze (1825–1846)*, București 1913, p. 227.

the Principalities including, as he learnt, even an introduction of a political constitution. Although he did not know the full details at that time, he was correctly convinced that they were aimed at lessening the ties of the two provinces with the sultan. In his opinion, this would eventually lead not only to a growth of Russian influence but also provoke the local leaders into a struggle for independence.[11]

Therefore, even before the end of the war, during talks with Tatishchev, Metternich had begun to object to the creation of a local army or the planned election of hospodars under Russian supervision. After hearing news of the gathering of boyars under the presidency of a Russian diplomat, Matvei Lvovici Minciaky, to discuss the latter innovation, he did not hesitate to challenge Tatishchev on this matter, declaring: "So you wish to make these provinces independent of the Porte and, to this end, from then on establish a new order, which you will then insist on being regarded as the status quo."[12] When Tatishchev replied that he knew nothing about the assembly of the boyars and that this was not a topic for discussion between them, Metternich declared: "But several boyars have approached us to ascertain whether Austria is prepared to recognise the total emancipation of the Principalities; their approach was formal and I am informing you of it."[13] One has only to be aware of Metternich's usual calm and diplomatic caution, particularly when dealing with Russia, to fully appreciate the sharpness of his tone, evidence of his extreme indignation.

---

[11] Metternich to Francis I, Vienna, 14 June 1827, HHStA, StK, Vorträge 251; Metternich to Francis I, Vienna, 3 July 1828, HHStA, StK, Vorträge 254; Metternich to Francis I, Waltersdorf, 8 Aug. 1828, HHStA, StK, Vorträge 255; General P. F. Zheltukhin's note to the Wallachian Divan, 21 June 1829, attached to Metternich to Trauttmannsdorff, Vienna, 4 Aug. 1829, HHStA, StK, Preussen 132; Metternich to Esterházy, Vienna, 13 July 1829, HHStA, StA, England 188; Metternich to Ottenfels, Vienna, 19 July 1829, HDA, 750, OO 38; Metternich to Ottenfels, Vienna, 2 Oct. 1829, HHStA, StA, Türkei VI, 39; Cowley to Aberdeen, Vienna, 19 July 1829, TNA, FO 120/102; Brockhausen to Frederick William III, Vienna, 19 July 1829, GStA PK, HA III, MdA I, 6013; Tatishchev to Nesselrode, Vienna, 3 Aug. and 6 Oct. 1829, AVPRI, fond 133, Kantseliariia, opis 468, 11885; Bray to Ludwig I of Bavaria, Vienna, 5 Nov. 1828, BHStA, MA, Wien 2402.

[12] Tatishchev to Nesselrode, Vienna, 21 July 1829, AVPRI, fond 133, Kantseliariia, opis 468, 11881.

[13] Ibid.

During the months following the Treaty of Adrianople, it became more and more evident in Vienna that the Russian plans for administrative reform in the Principalities would contain provisions extremely harmful to the rights of foreigners, affecting, in particular, the Austrians who enjoyed vast privileges in the Principalities, as mentioned above. The boyars thought that their actual administrative independence from the Porte provided them with an opportunity to modify the treaties between the Ottoman Empire and European countries, with the aim of raising the status of the local inhabitants to that of the foreigners, thus enabling the former to compete from a greater position of strength in economic affairs. The Russian chairman of the Divans of Moldavia and Wallachia (the assemblies of local boyars), Count Pavel Dmitrievich Kiselev, was more than willing to satisfy their desire with the aim of breaking Austria's considerable economic influence that had so far remained undiminished.[14] In late 1829 and early 1830, Metternich received a considerable number of warnings regarding Russia's plans in Moldavia and Wallachia. For example, in April 1830, an Austrian agent in Sibiu dispatched the drafts of nine articles relating to future Organic Statutes (*Règlement organique*) with the agent's analysis clearly demonstrating their negative impact on the Austrians in the spheres of commerce and justice. In early July, the chancellor's apprehension was further deepened following a report from St Petersburg, where Ficquelmont had obtained an ominous response from State Counsellor P. G. Divov, charged with the foreign affairs portfolio during Nesselrode's absence in the capital, to his enquiry regarding the planned changes in the administration of Moldavia and Wallachia and their impact on Austrian prerogatives. He was informed that Austria would be notified at the appropriate moment as to any changes that Austria might find "contradictory to its rights."[15] A month later, Ficquelmont complained about the trials and tribulations of the Austrian citizens in the Principalities.[16]

---

[14] Lippa to Metternich, Czernowitz, 25 Nov. 1829, E. de Hurmuzaki, I. Nistor (eds.), *Documente privitoare la istoria Românilor, Volumul XXI: Corespondenţă diplomatică şi rapoarte consulare austriace (1828–1836)*, Bucureşti 1942, p. 187; Lagan to Sébastiani, Bucharest, 18 March 1831, Hurmuzaki, XVII, p. 246; Lagan to Sébastiani, Bucharest, 25 Nov. 1831, Hurmuzaki, XVII, p. 258; Bitis, p. 456.

[15] Ficquelmont to Metternich, St Petersburg, 2 July 1830, HHStA, StA, Russland III, 89.

[16] Ficquelmont to Metternich, St Petersburg, 14 Aug. 1830, HHStA, StA, Russ-

Since Metternich wanted to frustrate plans for the creation of a political constitution for both lands and safeguard the favoured position of the Austrians, he began to contemplate strategies for hastening the withdrawal of the Russian troops from the Principalities. If successful in this ambition, Russia's direct political control of the Principalities would be terminated, which would also frustrate or at least make more difficult the introduction of the planned reforms. It is true that Metternich did not follow the British lead of objecting to the articles of the Treaty of Adrianople and, in the interest of renewing good relations with Russia, he did not show his annoyance at Tatishchev's presence or even talk with the ambassador about the stipulations concerning the Principalities. But this discretion did not mean that Metternich was entirely passive; it only proved that he was a more skilled and practical diplomat than the British ministers, in particular Wellington, who proceeded to raise objections that were as violent as they were useless to St Petersburg, the only result being a souring of relations between Great Britain and Russia.[17]

The strategy for achieving an early withdrawal of the Russian forces chosen by Metternich in late 1829 was the prompt repayment of the Ottoman indemnities. The Treaty envisaged such a possibility, but the problem lay in the fact that the Porte was unable, after many years of battles with the Greeks and the exhausting war with its powerful northern neighbour, to collect from its provinces the enormous amount required. Any other European Power would have been able to solve such a complicated situation by negotiating a loan, but the sultan did not have access to similar opportunities in his own country. Therefore, Metternich set about exploring the possibility of negotiating a loan of 300 million francs for the Porte, to be provided by European bankers. Even though the chancellor was well aware of the difficulties accompanying such an arrangement, he and Gentz considered its execution to be of considerable significance for Austrian inter-

---

land III, 89; Fleischhackl to Metternich, Sibiu, 21 April 1830, Hurmuzaki, XXI, pp. 264–265.

[17] Ficquelmont to Metternich, St Petersburg, 28 Oct. 1829, HHStA, StA, Russland III, 86; Maltzan to Frederick William III, Vienna, 29 Sept. 1829, GStA PK, HA III, MdA I, 6013; Cowley to Aberdeen, Vienna, 4 and 17 Oct. 1829, TNA, FO 120/104; Tatishchev to Nesselrode, Vienna, 18 Oct. 1829, AVPRI, fond 133, Kantseliariia, opis 468, 11885; Bray to Ludwig I of Bavaria, Vienna, 22 Oct. 1829, BHStA, MA, Wien 2402; Crawley, *Greek Independence*, p. 168; Dakin, p. 274.

ests. It is clearly evident, not only from Metternich's correspondence but also from the reports of foreign diplomats, how much importance he placed on the evacuation of Russian forces from the European part of the Ottoman Empire.[18]

The first challenge was to find bankers who were financially strong enough and willing to offer the loan. A considerable number of prominent bankers and capitalists in Vienna or Paris expressed their willingness to consider the plan, but they insisted on guarantees from the Great Powers. Metternich understood the justification of their demand and turned to the governments in London and Paris for help in this matter. However, Wellington and Aberdeen were opposed to the underwriting of guarantees and the same negative response also came from Polignac. Consequently, Metternich had to proceed alone. Despite this setback, he won over the members of the powerful Rothschild family, in Vienna as well as in London, to the plan. Naturally, they also expected guarantees on the part of the Porte. The proposal that the silver and copper mines in Asia Minor as well as timber for construction could serve this purpose persuaded them to start negotiations. Nevertheless, the Ottomans showed little inclination to accept a loan or even to discuss the topic with Ottenfels, who was instructed by Metternich already in October 1829 to persuade them of its usefulness. It was not until the Porte realised that the tsar would not reduce the debt by more than 2 million ducats in late April 1830 that Mahmud II gave his consent to the beginning of talks. In May, the Rothschilds' agent, Moritz Goldsmith, arrived in the Ottoman capital and entered into negotiations, with Ottenfels' full support. The internuncio was instructed to make the Porte conclude an agreement with the Rothschilds and to draw the sultan's attention to the fact that an eventual contract would hasten the departure of the Russians from the occupied provinces, which would be considerably advantageous for the Porte: it would ensure their tributes were secured for its treasury. Although Metternich seemed confident that the loan could be arranged for the immediate discharge of the indemnities, the protracted discussions were leading nowhere and finally ended in July when the Porte

---

[18] Metternich to Esterházy, Vienna, 4 Oct. 1829, HHStA, StA, England 188; Ottenfels to Metternich, Constantinople, 25 Sept. 1829, HHStA, StA, Türkei VI, 38; Maltzan to Frederick William III, Vienna, 9 Oct. and 14 Nov. 1829, GStA PK, HA III, MdA I, 6013.

officially refused to accept a loan from the Rothschilds. The official reason for the rejection was the Porte's allegedly sufficient supply of money, but this was far from the truth and the real reason for the failure of Metternich's project was the Ottomans' unwillingness to meet Goldsmith's demands regarding the guarantees.[19]

Despite this failure, Metternich still paid close attention to the process of the drafting of the Organic Statutes and did not hesitate to express strong disagreement with the planned changes harmful to Austrian subjects. From the outset, he was prepared not to yield in this affair of the highest importance for the Habsburg Monarchy. On the last day of 1829, he declared in a letter to Nesselrode that he was against any change in the favourable status of the Austrians in the Principalities by the Russo-Ottoman settlement: "We are entirely convinced that it has never been, nor will it become in the future, the intention of Russia to invalidate or even abolish the rights and privileges that have been conferred on us in Wallachia and Moldavia as a result of formal capitulations made to us by the Porte or the concessions, equally formally made to us by the hospodars ... [because] it depends on the pleasure neither of Russia nor of the Ottoman Porte to arbitrarily change anything in relation to the rights obtained by a third Power. It would be necessary to deny all elementary knowledge of public law to contest such an obvious truth."[20] Metternich did not leave the Russian vice-chancellor in any doubt that Austria would not

---

[19] Metternich to Ottenfels, Vienna, 2 and 17 Oct. 1829, HHStA, StA, Türkei VI, 39; Metternich to Ottenfels, Vienna, 17 Feb. and 10 April 1830, HHStA, StA, Türkei VI, 51; Metternich to Esterházy, Vienna, 4 and 28 Oct. 1829, HHStA, StA, England 188; Metternich to Trauttmannsdorff, Vienna, 12 Oct. 1829, HHStA, StK, Preussen 132; Sina to Metternich, Vienna, 15 Oct. 1829, and Salomon Rothschild to Metternich, Paris, 8 Oct. 1829, both attached to Metternich to Ottenfels, Vienna, 17 Oct. 1829, HHStA, StA, Türkei VI, 39; Ottenfels to Metternich, Constantinople, 25 Sept., 26 Oct. and 10 Nov. 1829, HHStA, StA, Türkei VI, 38; Wallenburg to Metternich, Constantinople, 25 May 1830, Mustafa Bey to Salomon Rothschild, Constantinople, 11 July 1830, Ottenfels to Metternich, Constantinople, 25 Jan., 10 March, 25 June, 10 and 26 July 1830, HHStA, StA, Türkei VI, 50; Esterházy to Metternich, London, 12 Oct. and 27 Nov. 1829, HHStA, StA, England 186; Apponyi to Metternich, Paris, 22 and 29 Oct., 23 Dec. 1829, HHStA, StA, Frankreich 270; Cowley to Aberdeen, Vienna, 8 Nov. 1829, TNA, FO 120/104; Cowley to Aberdeen, Vienna, 12 April 1830 TNA, FO 120/108; Royer to Frederick William III, Pera, 11 June 1830, GSta PK, HA III, MdA I, 7269; Bitis, pp. 376–377.

[20] Metternich to Nesselrode, Vienna, 31 Dec. 1829, HHStA, StA, Russland III, 87.

interfere in the Russo-Ottoman negotiations on the internal affairs of the Principalities but would oppose changes directly harming its own interests. This was a fundamental principle of Austrian policy in the affair and Ficquelmont did his best to ensure the protection of Austrian rights in the Principalities through negotiations with Nesselrode in the following two years.[21]

The result of these proceedings was not only Nesselrode's assurance that the Austrian prerogatives would not be adversely affected by the Organic Statutes but also that this status would be maintained since, ultimately, the Russians did not dare to harm Austria's interests. Furthermore, most of the changes which might have led to such negative consequences and which appeared in the draft version of the Organic Statutes were eventually removed from the final version promulgated in July 1831 in Wallachia and January 1832 in Moldavia.[22] The Russians even assured the Austrian agent in Moldavia, Franz von Wallenburg, that if any deprivations to the Austrians had occurred, then not they but the local authorities had been guilty because the Russians recognised these rights based upon Austro-Ottoman treaties and would also recognise them in the future. The main reasons for such compliance were the Polish insurrection, which was in progress when the Statutes were being prepared, and, later, Russia's need of Austria's diplomatic support in the Ottoman Empire against French, and particularly British, Russophobia. In addition, one cannot ignore the likelihood of British and French influence in opposing any infractions of the rights of Europeans.[23] In any case, the outcome of this

---

[21] Ibid.; Metternich to Ottenfels, Vienna, 18 Jan. 1832, HHStA, StA, Türkei VIII, 5; Ficquelmont to Metternich, St Petersburg, 23 Nov. and 24 Dec. 1830, HHStA, StA, Russland III, 89; Ficquelmont's verbal note to Nesselrode, St Petersburg, 18 Sept. 1831, Ficquelmont to Metternich, St Petersburg, 14 Nov. 1831, HHStA, StA, Russland III, 92.

[22] For more on the promulgation of the Organic Statutes see Jelavich, *Russia's Balkan Entanglements*, p. 99.

[23] Ficquelmont to Metternich, St Petersburg, 27 Dec. 1831, HHStA, StA, Russland III, 92; Ottenfels to Metternich, Constantinople, 25 Jan., 10 and 25 Feb. 1832, HHStA, StA, Türkei VI, 54; Wallenburg to Metternich, Jassy, 15 Feb. 1833, Hurmuzaki, XXI, p. 475; Lagan to Sébastiani, Bucharest, 26 Dec. 1831, 5 and 27 Jan. 1832, Hurmuzaki, XVII, pp. 260–261. Alexander Bitis claims that the rights of Austrian merchants were abolished in 1831 and 1832. Bitis, p. 463. In fact, however, most of the originally planned changes in this area were not introduced by the Russians at that time, either on paper or in practice. Nevertheless, as mentioned above in the text, the desire to secure equal rights for foreigners and local

matter was a great success for Austria, irrespective of the degree to which it deserved the credit for it. Metternich could now observe the Russian military occupation with less apprehension and he really did do just that. When, in March 1832, his chronic lack of finances compelled Mahmud II to approach Austria with a plea for assistance in negotiating a three million ducat loan from Viennese bankers in order to pay the instalment to Russia, Metternich was not willing to satisfy the request because the political situation was not as pressing as it had been two years earlier. Consequently, when Mavroyéni tried to persuade the chancellor by insinuating that the Russians planned to stay in the Principalities for ever, he only obtained evasive assurances that it was not true and a profession of confidence in the personal character of Tsar Nicholas I.[24]

---

inhabitants originated from the Wallachians and Moldavians themselves. Austria, as well as other interested Powers, had to face up to this pressure in the following years, but the danger actually came more from the locals and the Porte than from Russia. Metternich anxiously supervised the observance of Austria's rights and when, for example, he learnt of the sultan's cancellation of the foreigners' privileges and immunities in the Principalities in 1834, he sharply opposed them. Austria was prepared to regard them as invalid because it did not recognise the nullification of the patents based upon international treaties by a mere internal administrative regulation: "*We expressly reserve our rights* and we will regard every arbitrary innovation in the treatment of our subjects in the two Principalities as a contravention of the existing treaties between the two empires." Metternich to Stürmer, Vienna, 23 Sept. 1834, HHStA, StA, Türkei VIII, 6. For more see also Lagan to Sébastiani, Bucharest, 3 March 1832, Hurmuzaki, XVII, pp. 262–263; Lagan to Sébastiani, Bucharest, 26 April 1832, Hurmuzaki, XVII, pp. 276–277; Lagan to Broglie, Bucharest, 15 Feb. 1833, Hurmuzaki, XVII, p. 286; Mimaut to Rigny, Bucharest, 19 Oct. 1834, Hurmuzaki, XVII, pp. 423–424; Cochelet to Rigny, Bucharest, 28 Jan. 1835, Hurmuzaki, XVII, p. 450; Mimaut to Rigny, Jassy, 26 March 1835, Hurmuzaki, XVII, p. 487; Cochelet to Thiers, Bucharest, 4 June 1836, Hurmuzaki, XVII, p. 623; Duclos to Molé, Jassy, 20 Nov. 1837, Hurmuzaki, XVII, p. 676.

[24] Metternich to Ottenfels, Vienna, 20 May 1832, HHStA, StA, Türkei VI, 56; Ottenfels to Metternich, Constantinople, 26 March, 25 April, 10 May, 10 and 25 July 1832, HHStA, StA, Türkei VI, 54; Lamb to Palmerston, Vienna, 25 April 1832, TNA, FO 120/124. Another reason for Metternich's restraint in the question of the loan was the fact that the Porte owed money to the Austrian banking house Stametz-Meyer for the purchase of corn in 1829 and since the chancellor, as well as the Rothschilds, had been involved in this affair and saw little readiness of the Ottomans to meet their obligations, they naturally did not want to repeat the mistake by agreeing to a new loan. For more see Chapter 22.

The passive response and the refusal to help the Porte with its financial obligation to Russia in 1832 was partially based upon a sincere feeling of confidence in the tsar's Near Eastern policy during that period, but in no way did it signify that Metternich had given up his desire for a prompt withdrawal of the Russian occupation forces from the Principalities. The problem lay in the fact that when the sultan had been unable to repay the debt in advance, all rights of decision were transferred to Nicholas I and the chancellor did not want to press him on this matter due to his desire to maintain the cordial relationship between Austria and Russia. This is clearly evident from his conversation with Tatishchev in early May 1833 when Metternich was reacting to the tsar's wish to come to a joint position regarding the future of the Ottoman Empire. He recommended that, first of all, there was a need for Russia to evacuate the Principalities because, as the chancellor argued, it was necessary to dispel the assumption existing in Europe, and even in Austria, that Russia wanted to claim them by means of a lengthy occupation. Tatishchev cautioned Metternich not to request this because it could aggravate Austro-Russian relations and the prince decided to follow the advice and keep silent on this matter.[25]

Later, however, Nicholas I himself decided to adopt this step and signed a convention with an Ottoman agent in his capital on 29 January 1834, which settled the administrative and military situation in the Principalities. Russian troops were recalled when new hospodars were nominated by the sultan later in the year. Some troops remained in Silistria and continued to safeguard the roads connecting this fortress with Russian soil until the total closing of the debt, something that was later reduced by the tsar yet again. Although the number of remaining Russian soldiers was still considerable, the St Petersburg Convention was generally regarded as a demonstration of his goodwill. Whereas British and French diplomats considered it to be a success resulting from the intransigent anti-Russian policy of the two Maritime Powers over the previous months, Metternich was already claiming at the end of 1833 that it was a favour to Austria and that Nicholas I had promised to evacuate the Principalities except Silistria during the meeting in Münchengrätz in September of

---

Tatishchev to Nesselrode, Vienna, 5 May 1833, AVPRI, fond 133, Kantseliariia, opis 469, 1833/211.

the same year. Since no detailed summary of the meeting exists, there is no proof in support of Metternich's boast or Alexandre C. Sturdza's claim that the chancellor even persuaded the tsar to conclude the St Petersburg Convention while in this North Bohemian town.[26] If Metternich's affirmation was really well founded, and there is no reason not to believe that the tsar had made some ambiguous statement towards him and Francis I that he would evacuate the Principalities, particularly if he was already resolved to do so, the prince still did not seem to be entirely sure of the alleged promise.[27] This is evident from his instructions to St Petersburg from mid December 1833 onwards by which he tried to persuade the Russian monarch to undertake a prompt evacuation in order to reduce the unwarranted preoccupation of the Maritime Powers, thus exploiting their aggressive policy towards Russia as a means of achieving Austria's goal: "The evacuation of the Principalities would be an immense coup. Will the Emperor [tsar] not render this service? He would crush all prejudices in a single act and even though I am not malicious by nature, I would not be able to prevent myself from feeling great satisfaction if fate allowed me to prove to these foolish adversaries that everything they believe is false!"[28]

The other question relates to whether the withdrawal of the Russian forces was really the result of Nicholas I's goodwill and a gesture of friendship towards Austria, or even a real sacrifice, as claimed, for example, by Alan Sked and Matthew S. Anderson.[29] This could well have been the motivation but, in fact, there was no need for Russia to prolong the occupation after the desired administrative changes had been put into practice and Russian influence seemed to have been secured.[30] Metternich himself regarded the solution of 29 January 1834

---

[26] A. C. Sturdza, *Règne de Michel Sturdza: Prince régnant de Moldavie 1834–1849*, Paris 1907, p. 30.

[27] Lamb to Palmerston, Vienna, 26 Dec. 1833, TNA, FO 120/137; Brockhausen to Frederick William III, Vienna, 21 Jan. 1834, GStA PK, HA III, MdA I, 6023; Cetto to Ludwig I of Bavaria, Vienna, 22 Feb. 1834, BHStA, MA, Wien 2405; H. Seton-Watson, *The Russian Empire 1801–1917*, Oxford 1967, p. 212; Bitis, pp. 376–377.

[28] Metternich to Ficquelmont, Vienna, 16 Dec. 1833, HHStA, StA, Russland III, 99.

[29] Sked, *Metternich*, p. 92; Anderson, "Russia and the Eastern Question," pp. 79–97.

[30] Rendall, "Restraint or Self-Restraint," p. 52; G. Platon, "Le «Problème

as being the result of necessity rather than generosity, and it only delighted him in part for two reasons. First, he viewed the concessions with scepticism because he had been convinced from the very beginning that the military occupation of the Principalities was a burden for the local inhabitants and it was better for Russia to terminate the state of affairs and thus not risk losing their allegiance; the fact that the departure of the Russian troops beyond the Pruth was celebrated as a great event by both Moldavians and Wallachians proved the accuracy of this presumption to a certain extent although their withdrawal also diminished the influence of a generally unpopular Russia in the coming years. Second, Metternich had wanted Silistria to be evacuated at the same time and he had also tried to persuade the tsar to withdraw from this fortress on the turn of 1833. When this did not happen, he regretted the presence of the Russian troops in this location as well as their involvement in communications placements linking it to Russian soil, and he definitely was not persuaded by Tatishchev's arguments that the Russian presence in Silistria was the best guarantee for ensuring the allegiance of the Christians living on the right bank of the Danube to the sultan.[31]

Although there are some indications that the evacuation of Silistria was mentioned during Metternich's meeting with Nicholas I in Töplitz in 1835, an event which finally occurred in the following year to Metternich's great pleasure and which was definitely a result of the tsar's regard for his relations with Austria, Metternich did not seriously dispute this matter or others concerning the Principalities with Russia except for issues relating to navigation on the Danube after 1834. It is true that Austrian agents in Moldavia and Wallachia sometimes complained of the Russian agents' conduct in relation to administrative affairs, but Metternich allowed Russia a free hand in political affairs and ordered his own agents to act in such a way as not to raise complaints from the Russian authorities. These instructions

---

roumain» et le «Problème oriental» dans la première moitié du XIXe siècle: Interférences et implications," *Revue roumaine d'histoire* 2, 1979, p. 377; Bitis, p. 375.

[31] Metternich to Esterházy, Vienna, 15 Nov. 1829, HHStA, StA, England 188; Tatishchev to Nesselrode, Vienna, 10 and 24 Feb. 1834, AVPRI, fond 133, Kantseliariia, opis 469, 1834/217; G. Blottner, "Die antirussische Stimmung in den Donaufürstentümern 1830–1848 vornehmlich aus der Sicht zeitgenössischer österreichischer Quellen," *SOF* 42, 1983, pp. 224–228; Bitis, p. 462.

were indeed strictly obeyed. The silence of the Viennese cabinet in relation to the Russian position after 1834 is obvious; no reference with regard to this matter has been found in Metternich's instructions, personal correspondence or the reports of foreign diplomats residing in Vienna. If he had exhibited a high degree of resignation to the actual Russian protectorate over the two provinces before January 1834, his apathy afterwards was absolute and the British discontent with the Russian predominance had no chance of obtaining his diplomatic support.[32]

Austria's acquiescence of Russian predominance in the Principalities was often sharply denounced by many parties: the Moldavians and Wallachians habitually complained that Austria had given them up to "Russian tyranny,"[33] British, French and Prussian diplomats and agents levelled accusations that Austria had lost its courage in relation to Russia, and even the representatives of some second ranking countries expressed concerns, for example the Bavarian envoy in Vienna, Maximilian Emanuel von Lerchenfeld-Aham, wrote in early April 1840: "The Principalities of Moldavia, Wallachia and Serbia are entirely under Russian influence and obedient to its word. Austria seems to have abandoned all its influence in these adjoining provinces that are of the greatest interest to it. Everywhere one can see the greatest compliancy of the Imperial cabinet in relation to Russia. They

---

[32] Metternich to Ferik Ahmed Pasha, Vienna, 26 April 1836, Metternich to Stürmer, Vienna, 26 April 1836, HHStA, StA, Türkei VI, 65; Wallenburg to Metternich, Jassy, 2 April 1838, HHStA, StA, Moldau-Walachei II, 56; Tatishchev to Nesselrode, Vienna, 25 May 1833, AVPRI, fond 133, Kantseliariia, opis 469, 1833/211; Tatishchev to Nesselrode, Vienna, 8 Jan. and 14 April 1836, AVPRI, fond 133, Kantseliariia, opis 469, 1836/216; Nesselrode to Butenev, St Petersburg, 31 March 1836, AVPRI, fond 133, Kantseliariia, opis 469, 1836/43; Lamb to Palmerston, Vienna, 18 Feb., 13 March and 17 May 1834, TNA, FO 120/145; Cetto to Ludwig I of Bavaria, Vienna, 22 Feb. 1834, BHStA, MA, Wien 2405; Lerchenfeld to Ludwig I of Bavaria, Vienna, 13 March 1836, BHStA, MA, Wien 2406; O'Sullivan to Merod, Vienna, 18 April and 6 Aug. 1834, ADA, CP, Autriche 2; Mimaut to Broglie, Jassy, 20 Nov. 1833, Hurmuzaki, XVII, p. 306; Cochelet to Broglie, Bucharest, 10 Aug. 1835, Hurmuzaki, XVII, p. 503; Cochelet to Thiers, Bucharest, 4 June 1836, Hurmuzaki, XVII, p. 622; Huber to Guizot, Jassy, 14 May 1841, Hurmuzaki, XVII, p. 809; G. Platon, "Romanian Principalities and England in the Period Previous the Revolution of 1848," G. Buzatu (ed.), *Anglo-Romanian Relations after 1821*, Jassy 1983, p. 60; Sauer, "Sulina-Frage, Erster Teil," p. 198.

[33] Duclos to Molé, Bucharest, 9 Aug. 1837, Hurmuzaki, XVII, p. 667.

anxiously avoid doing anything that might cause offence."[34] A year later, he added that the Austrian cabinet "has unfortunately long since abandoned the outlying Turkish provinces to the protectorate and the dominant interests – that is to say Russian dictatorship. It has even neglected to delegate intelligent consuls to the provinces of Serbia, Moldavia and Wallachia in order to keep watch there and maintain relations worthy of a powerful neighbour such as Austria. Whereas England always deploys distinguished persons there, such as Colonel Hodges [in Serbia], Austria only has mediocre persons, simple negotiators, incapable of undertaking political tasks there. The prince chancellor seems to have desired to avoid every potential for antagonising the cabinet in St Petersburg by the choice of these consuls."[35]

Regardless of whether Lerchenfeld's reports were exaggerated or not, there were significant reasons for Austria's self-restraint. They can be summarised in four principal interconnected points. First, Metternich could do nothing about the situation given the prevailing conditions: a war was out of the question, a diplomatic offensive was hardly likely to be successful if it was undertaken alone and any cooperation with the two Maritime Powers was generally rather problematic. Moreover, Austria needed Russian support in Germany and Italy and it did not dare disturb the intimacy existing between the two conservative cabinets. Second, Metternich was well capable of reconciling himself to defeat and adapting to new circumstances, which he had aptly demonstrated in the early 1830s in relation to his conduct surrounding the Greek Question, as well as with regard to the Principalities when he concluded that the best way to secure Austrian interests was through direct cooperation with Russia. Third, the chancellor's awareness of the tsar's desire to maintain the Ottoman Empire contributed to his acceptance of the Russian predominant position in Moldavia and Wallachia. Fourth, over the years, the refusal to engage in any sort of diplomatic or even military confrontation, as well as the adoption of a new strategy aimed at obtaining maximum benefits in the Principalities through friendly relations with St Petersburg, had proved to be not entirely disadvantageous. Whereas Russia dominated

---

[34] Lerchenfeld to Ludwig I of Bavaria, Vienna, 4 April 1840, BHStA, MA, Wien 2409.
[35] Lerchenfeld to Ludwig I of Bavaria, Vienna, 2 May 1841, BHStA, MA, Wien 2410.

politically in this region, Austria did so economically, an achievement that could not have been attained without a certain degree of condescension attitude towards the Russian cabinet.[36] The success of this approach was confirmed in relation to the issue that was to become more and more important for the Austrian Empire, an issue that since the mid 1830s had constituted by far the most significant, and with a little exaggeration almost the exclusive, agenda of the Viennese Chancellery in connection with the Principalities: navigation on the Danube.

Disputes over Navigation on the Danube

It was somehow symbolic that at the same moment that the St Petersburg Convention was signed and the withdrawal of the Russian troops became imminent, Metternich instructed Ottenfels, serving at that time at the Viennese Chancellery, to summarise his opinions in relation to the importance of the river, generally labelled the great artery of the Danube Monarchy. In fact, this was not yet the case but its potential to grow into such was generally recognised.[37] Ottenfels tried to explain in his memorandum why the Danube had not yet become an important outlet for Austrian manufactured goods and agricultural products and how such a goal could be achieved. This document, housed in the Croatian State Archives in Zagreb and entirely forgotten by historians, is significant not only for the information it contained but also for the fact that, on the one hand, it reflected the attitude of the relevant Austrian authorities towards shipping on the Danube and, on the other hand, it laid the foundations of Austria's official policy in relation to this matter.[38]

---

[36] Fox-Strangways to Wellington, Vienna, 19 March 1835, TNA, FO 120/149; Huber to Soult, Jassy, 31 Jan. 1840, Hurmuzaki, XVII, p. 766; J. R. Lampe, M. R. Jackson, *Balkan Economic History, 1550–1950: From Imperial Borderlands to Developing Nations*, Bloomington 1982, p. 99; N. Farca, *Russland und die Donaufürstentümer 1826–1856*, München 1992, pp. 241–243; R. R. Florescu, *The Struggle against Russia in the Romanian Principalities: A Problem in Anglo-Turkish Diplomacy, 1821–1854*, Iaşi 1997, p. 294; Zane, p. 47.

[37] Sauer, "Sulina-Frage, Erster Teil," p. 198.

[38] F. von Ottenfels, *Observation sur le commerce de l'Autriche dans le Levant et plus parti entièrement sur la navigation du Danube*, attached to Ottenfels, *Memo-*

According to Ottenfels, the Ottoman dominion in the Balkan Peninsula offered to the Danube Monarchy the advantages associated with colonies: an outlet for manufactured goods and a source of raw materials. Austria would be able to export the former and import the latter, both important considerations during a period when Austrian industrialisation was taking place.[39] There were three ways of gaining access to these markets. First, overland, which was, however, costly, lengthy and difficult owing to the rather poor state of the Ottoman roads. Second, by sea, but this was impractical because ships sailing from the ports on the northern cape of the Adriatic Sea along the Balkans to the Danube Delta had to cover such a long distance and, moreover, they often had to wait a long time for a favourable wind in the Straits. Consequently, the most suitable was the third, Danubian, option. This route included not only the Danube itself but also its tributaries, forming together a vast river system covering almost all the territories of the Habsburg Monarchy, evoking a picture of a vascular system with vessels leading to one great artery: the Danube. Although Bohemia was not covered, Ottenfels did not fail to point out its connection with the river by the railway (a horse-drawn line) between Linz on the Danube and Budweis on the Vltava River (Moldau), a left-wing tributary of the Elbe, finished in 1832. Goods from the majority of the Habsburg lands including, for example, North Bohemia with its significant glass factories, could thus be quickly and cheaply transported not only to the adjacent Ottoman provinces in the Balkans, including the Principalities, but also to the Black Sea area and, through Trabzon, to the Caucasus and Persia.[40]

Not only the economic but also the geopolitical aspects of shipping on the Danube were stressed by Ottenfels in his memorandum.

---

ari, HDA, 750, OO 18, pp. a31–a46.

[39] When Ottenfels wrote his memorandum, industrialisation in Austria was in progress and there was much reason for optimism. For more on this topic see Good, pp. 39–59.

[40] Ottenfels, *Observation sur le commerce*, HDA, 750, OO 18, pp. a32–a39; Blum, p. 31. The glassware was actually exported from North Bohemia to the Ottoman market when Ottenfels was writing his memorandum, and it went even further: according to the memoirs of a European traveller, the quality glassware in the Tabriz bazaar originated almost exclusively from Bohemia. V. Vomáčková, "Österreich und der deutsche Zollverein," *Historica 5: Historische Wissenschaften in der Tschechoslowakei*, Prag 1963, p. 115; G. G. Gilbar, "The Persian Economy in the Mid-19th Century," *DWI* 19, 1979, 1–4, p. 198.

Its eventual connection with the significant German rivers, the Main and the Rhine, would have given rise to an immense river network, stretching through Europe and connecting the Black Sea with the North Sea. This was not an idle dream since a project to connect the Danube with the Main, a tributary of the Rhine, was already in existence in 1829. The Bavarian diplomat August von Gise was to discuss it in Vienna in January 1834,[41] and only two years later work on the canal between Bamberg and Kelheim began. According to Ottenfels, not only economic but also political advantages would accrue to Austria if the project were to be realised and the water route Rhine-Main-Danube put into operation. At the very same time that Ottenfels was writing his memorandum, the German Customs Union was being established without the participation of Austria. By connecting the two important river networks, which was particularly in the interest of Bavaria and Württemberg, members of the Union since 1834, the Danube Monarchy would have been in control of the most significant trade route from Germany to the Balkan markets. This would have become a persuasive argument for a settlement with the German Customs Union being more advantageous for Austria.[42] Ottenfels concisely stated this opportunity: "The execution of these projects [for the connection of the above-mentioned rivers] cannot fail to create a new relationship between Germany and Austria, based upon the reciprocity of interests."[43] This consideration was not entirely unjustified because other German countries were also interested in the development of this waterway, like Prussia, which was directly involved due to its Rhine provinces. When in June 1836 in Vienna its commissaries negotiated a rapprochement of Austria with the German Customs Union, they were considerably interested in the navigability of the Danube to which they attributed great importance for the transport of Prussian goods to Asia. Sachsen, although it did not have a direct link to the above-mentioned rivers, also had an interest in the development of a waterway because, together with Austria, it had been the most important exporter to the Principalities until the

---

[41] Prokesch-Osten, *Aus den Tagebüchern*, p. 203.
[42] Ottenfels, *Observation sur le commerce*, HDA, 750, OO 18, pp. a38–a42.
[43] Ibid., p. a41.

early 1830s and had therefore been attentively observing the whole
issue during the entire decade.[44]

The reason why the Austrians had not already taken full advantage of the potential of the Danube, even though they had been
attempting to do so since the late 17th century,[45] was, in addition to
the former confrontations with the Ottoman Empire, the natural obstacles presented by the river itself. Unlike the political impediments,
the natural challenges still existed in the early 1830s. The most serious obstacles were between Belgrade and Vidin, where the rocks
narrowed the river bed and caused a series of cataracts through which
boats had great difficulty navigating when the water level was low.
The most troublesome part was a 2.5 kilometre long stretch called
the Iron Gate that literally barred ships with a larger draught for
most of the year, including all the steamships that were being put
into service by the Austrians during the period when Ottenfels was
writing his memorandum. Consequently, it prevented the Habsburg
Monarchy from establishing an important commercial route on the
Danube at that time although hydraulic experts were later persuaded
that the removal of the natural obstacles, including those at the Iron
Gate, was possible, thus making the Danube navigable right down to
the Black Sea.[46]

Ottenfels' memorandum, including his recommendation that the
Viennese cabinet should support any activities leading to the uninterrupted movement of shipping, met with Metternich's absolute approval. This is not at all surprising given that the prince was a man
greatly interested in the economic growth of the Habsburg Monarchy. Evidence for his support of navigation on the Danube can be
found in his instructions to Ottenfels to write the memorandum,
his backing of the creation of the First Austrian Danube Steam-
Navigation Company (*Erste Donaudampfschiffahrtsgesellschaft*, for
short *DDSG*) in 1829 and the fact that he became one of its ini-

---

[44] Tatishchev to Nesselrode, Vienna, 12 June 1836, AVPRI, fond 133,
Kantseliariia, opis 469, 1836/216; report from Vienna, 22 Sept. 1838, SS, HD,
SG 10026, Wien 93; Zane, pp. 273–274.

[45] Fischer, pp. 22–27; Sauer, "Sulina-Frage, Erster Teil," p. 199.

[46] Ottenfels, *Observation sur le commerce*, HDA, 750, OO 18, pp. a36–a38.
This challenge was described in the same way in the following year by Robert
J. Colquhoun's report on navigation of the Danube, addressed to Palmerston,
Bucharest, 25 Oct. 1835, TNA, FO 78/997.

tial share-holders,[47] and finally, which may be surprising information for British historian Robert Evans, who claims that Metternich ignored Stephan Széchenyi's commercial and other plans,[48] in the chancellor's cooperation in this matter with this Hungarian magnate who had sailed down the Danube as far as the delta and then across the Black Sea to Constantinople in 1830 in order to ascertain the best strategies for making the river navigable. The importance that was attributed to commercial navigation on the Danube in the Viennese Chancellery is also evident from the fact that the 17th article of the Austro-Greek commerical and navigation treaty from 1835 was entirely dedicated to this issue.[49] Finally, it was Metternich who arranged the foundation of the *K. k. Zentralkommission für die Donaudampfschiffahrts-Angelegenheiten* in 1836, dealing with all matters concerning the Danube beyond the Austrian frontier. He took this step in response to the slow nature of Austrian bureaucracy and with the aim of providing a facility for quickly resolving matters of importance to the empire.[50]

Metternich was also the person who took responsibility for removing the natural obstacles on the lower Danube since most of cataracts including the Iron Gate was situated in Ottoman territory and the sultan's consent to blowing up the rocks was needed. The preliminary verbal agreement had already been obtained by Ottenfels in 1830, but it was rather vague and Stürmer, instructed by the greatly interested Metternich in this respect, had to make a new request in early 1834,

---

[47] It is not without interest that Metternich was represented at the meetings of the *DDSG* by Ottenfels who, however, was not a share-holder. Some other important personalities from Austrian diplomatic circles with close ties to the chancellor were share-holders, like Apponyi, Esterházy or Lebzeltern. *Sitzungs-Protocoll der General-Versammlung der k. k. priv. ersten Donau-Dampffschiffahrts-Gesellschaft vom 13. Februar 1837*, attached to Gorchakov to Nesselrode, Vienna, 4 March 1837, AVPRI, fond 133, Kantseliariia, opis 469, 1837/230; Sondhaus, p. 95.

[48] R. Evans, "Primat der Außenpolitik? Metternich und das österreichische Staats- und Reichsproblem," *Anzeiger der philosophisch-historischen Klasse* 144, 2009, 2, p. 66.

[49] Neumann, *Recueil des traités*, IV, p. 373.

[50] Ottenfels to Metternich, Constantinople, 16 Aug. 1830, HHStA, StA, Türkei VI, 50; Ottenfels, *Observation sur le commerce*, HDA, 750, OO 18, p. a44; *Instructions secrètes pour le Baron Hauer*, attached to Ottenfels, *Memoari*, HDA, 750, OO 18, p. a52; Ottenfels, *Memoari*, p. 275; M. J. Quin, *A Steam Voyage down the Danube*, I, London 1835, p. 125; K. Waldbrunner, *125 Jahre Erste Donaudampfschiffahrtsgesellschaft*, Wien 1954, p. 21.

arguing that the Austro-Ottoman treaties since the end of the 17th century ensured Austria's free navigation on the river and promising that all relevant costs would be met by the Viennese cabinet. In spite of this, the answer of the Porte was negative.[51] Stürmer did not accept this response and decided to continue: "In this country one lives from day to day and what one does in the morning is reversed in the evening. Whoever speaks last is usually the one who is right; consequently, until one is sure that the discussion has ended, one finds it more difficult than anywhere else to predict the future."[52] Nevertheless, Stürmer's further actions failed to alter the Porte's resistance. The Ottoman officials' arguments focused on two points: they were concerned about the security of the fortified positions that lay further down the river and apprehensive that the destruction of the natural obstacles would open up the way for the introduction of Austrian gunboats; they also had religious concerns, arguing that the rocks had been situated in the river since the creation of the world and that their removal would be in defiance of God's will. As to the first argument, the Ottomans were not only referring to a potential war with Austria but also one with the Maritime Powers. "I could not believe my ears when I heard this reasoning," Stürmer wrote to Metternich, "I answered that I strongly doubted that France and England would have ever sent their armies and fleets to Constantinople by way of the Danube."[53] As to the second argument, even though it appears to be strange and raised with the aim of merely camouflaging political considerations, it actually seemed to be a position held by some members of the Divan, for example the conservative minister of the interior, Pertev Effendi,[54] which led Roussin to make this sharp criti-

---

[51] Metternich to Stürmer, Vienna, 18 Feb. 1834, HHStA, StA, Türkei VIII, 8; Metternich to Ficquelmont, Vienna, 15 April 1834, HHStA, StA, Russland III, 102; Ottenfels to Metternich, Constantinople, 10 April and 25 June 1830, HHStA, StA, Türkei VI, 50; Stürmer to Metternich, Constantinople, 18 Feb. and 12 March 1834, HHStA, StA, Türkei VI, 60; Martens to Frederick William III, Büyükdere, 3 April 1834, GStA PK, HA III, MdA I, 7274; Lamb to Palmerston, Vienna, 22 May 1834, TNA, FO 120/145.

[52] Stürmer to Metternich, Constantinople, 12 March 1834, HHStA, StA, Türkei VI, 60.

[53] Stürmer to Metternich, Constantinople, 29 April 1834, HHStA, StA, Türkei VI, 60.

[54] Adelburg to Stürmer, 12 and 16 March 1834, Stürmer to Metternich, Constantinople, 12, 19 and 25 March, 1 and 29 April 1834, HHStA, StA, Türkei VI,

cism: "One must admit that they are great imbeciles! This navigation, if it were to be established as it must be hoped that it will be, would be beneficial to all and would, in particular, provide incalculable advantages to this country [the Ottoman Empire]."[55]

Metternich refused to retreat in this affair: "The settlement of the [question of] navigation on the Danube is too important for Austria, [and] the interests of our national industry and our internal as well as foreign trade are too deeply connected with it for the Porte's refusal to lead us to abandon our project."[56] The significance paid by the chancellor to this affair was stressed by his successful attempts to obtain the support of the pashas of Vidin and Orşova, as well as some Ottoman officials in Constantinople, some of them most probably by bribery. He also successfully sought consent for the hydraulic works from the Princes of Serbia, Moldavia and Wallachia. However, not even with this backing was Stürmer able to make any impact on the intransigence of the Porte during the spring and summer of 1834. It was at that point that Metternich and his diplomatic staff looked to the tsar for assistance. The Russian chargé d'affaires in the Ottoman capital, Baron Peter Ivanovich Ruckmann, substituting for Butenev who was on holiday in Russia, had offered support from the very beginning, even without the appropriate instructions, and was happy to meet all Stürmer's requests. The Russian authorities in the Principalities pursued the same course. After the first reports from Constantinople, which offered little hope of success, Metternich asked Nicholas I in mid April 1834 for Russia's official support with the aim of breaking the opposition of the Ottomans to the hydraulic works on the Danube. He claimed that it was a lack of awareness and a basic ignorance that had led to their needless doubts, alarm and mistrust. The tsar satisfied the request without hesitation and promised that Butenev, who was about to return to Constantinople at that time, would be furnished with appropriate instructions.[57]

60; Stürmer to Metternich, Büyükdere, 25 June and 1 July 1834, HHStA, StA, Türkei VI, 61.

[55] Stürmer to Metternich, Büyükdere, 1 July 1834, HHStA, StA, Türkei VI, 61.

[56] Metternich to Stürmer, Vienna, 16 April 1834, HHStA, StA, Türkei VI, 62.

[57] Metternich to Ficquelmont, Vienna, 15 April 1834, HHStA, StA, Russland III, 102; Metternich to Stürmer, Vienna, 16 April and 28 May 1834, HHStA, StA, Türkei VI, 62; Adelburg to Stürmer, Constantinople, 26 May 1834, Stürmer to Adelburg, Constantinople, 3, 4 and 8 May 1834, Stürmer to Metternich, Con-

Butenev arrived in the Ottoman capital in late August 1834 and he immediately informed the Porte of Russia's support for the Austrian request, considering there to be nothing harmful in it either from an economic or a military point of view. This assistance soon proved to be crucial because even by September the Ottomans had started to be more flexible and, despite some minor problems in the negotiations that occurred during the autumn, they finally gave in. It is true that the documents do not offer a clear explanation as to whether Mahmud II agreed to the blowing up of the rocks in some parts of the river, which actually took place at that time, or whether he was merely reconciled to it retroactively. However, it is abundantly clear that Russia's support improved Austria's position in Constantinople and that the first Austrian steamship was travelling through the Iron Gate before the end of 1834, which set off a rapid increase in the activities of the *DDSG* on the Danube and in the Black Sea as shown by a considerable increase in the number of its passengers from 17,727 to 211,401 between 1835 and 1842.[58]

Metternich and Francis I were extremely grateful for the tsar's support. Although some contemporaries expressed surprise, it was in

---

stantinople, 12 and 25 March, 8, 15 and 22 April, 7, 16, 17 and 28 May 1834, HHStA, StA, Türkei VI, 60; Stürmer to Metternich, Büyükdere, 10, 18 and 30 June, 9, 16, 22 and 30 July 1834, HHStA, StA, Türkei VI, 61; Lerchenfeld to Ludwig I of Bavaria, St Petersburg, 24 Jan. 1834, BHStA, MA, Petersburg 2722; Martens to Frederick William III, Pera, 13 May 1834, Büyükdere, 8 June and 18 Nov. 1834, GStA PK, HA III, MdA I, 7274; Lamb to Palmerston, Vienna, 25 May 1834, TNA, FO 120/145.

[58] Stürmer to Metternich, Büyükdere, 2, 17, 24 and 30 Sept., 7 and 15 Oct., 23 Dec. 1834, HHStA, StA, Türkei VI, 61; Stürmer to Metternich, Constantinople, 7 Jan. 1835, HHStA, StA, Türkei VI, 63; Martens to Frederick William III, Büyükdere, 28 Oct., 4 and 18 Nov. 1834, GStA PK, HA III, MdA I, 7274; O'Sullivan to Meulenaer, Vienna, 23 May 1836, ADA, CP, Autriche 4; "Extrait de l'ouvrage du docteur Nebenius sur la ligue commerciale de l'Allemagne, Chapitre VII: L'Autriche," *Le Portfolio ou Collection de Documents politiques relatifs à l'histoire contemporaine* 2, Paris 1836, 13, p. 180; C. Ardeleanu, "From Vienna to Constantinople on Board the Vessels of the Austrian Danube Steam-Navigation Company (1834–1842)," *Historical Yearbook* 6, 2009, p. 188; B. von Gonda, *Die ungarische Schiffahrt*, Budapest 1899, pp. 72–77; H. Hajnal, *The Danube: Its Historical, Political and Economic Importance*, The Hague 1920, p. 55; F. Heiderich, *Die Donau als Verkehrstraße*, Wien, Leipzig 1916, p. 28; Springer, p. 515. Despite this success, much remained to be done and the decisive regulations in relation to the navigability of the Iron Gate did not occur, for various reasons, until the 1890s. Lampe, p. 107.

no way an illogical development because the Russian monarch was hardly in a position to refuse support at a time when he urgently needed Austrian backing in the face of the defiant policy of the two Maritime Powers in Constantinople. A rejection of the call for support would have been inopportune owing to the significance that was attributed in Vienna to the hydraulic works. The Russian monarch did not wish to take the risk of causing any cooling in relations with the Central European Power and found it necessary to support its requests concerning both navigation on the Danube and also the right for Austrian steamships to cruise between the Danube Delta and Constantinople, something that the Ottoman government had also tried to prevent. The decision made in St Petersburg was presumably eased by the fact that Russia could always restrict shipping on the Danube in its Delta region, an area that Russia had annexed as part of the Treaty of Adrianople.[59]

The Sulina Question

The ceding of the mouth of the Danube to Russia, as Metternich declared shortly after he learnt of it, was equally detrimental to Austria and the Ottoman Empire, and he described it as depriving the former of its ability to freely navigate the river. For the Danube Monarchy, this territory was in no way simply a tiny and insignificant strip of land, as British historian Alan Palmer claims.[60] Since Metternich had assumed that Russia would not aspire to any territorial gains on the Continent, he was badly surprised by its seizure.[61] Nevertheless, whereas there was a theoretical chance that the chancellor would be able to shorten the Russian troops' presence in the Principalities by the mediation of a loan, in the case of the Delta he could do absolutely

---

[59] Metternich to Ficquelmont, Vienna, 27 May 1834, HHStA, StA, Russland III, 102; Metternich to Ficquelmont, Baden, 3 Sept. 1834, Vienna, 20 Oct. 1834, HHStA, StA, Russland III, 103.

[60] A. Palmer, *Metternich: Councillor of Europe*, London 1972, p. 242.

[61] Metternich to Trauttmannsdorff, Plass, 25 Aug. 1829, HHStA, StK, Preussen 132; Cowley to Aberdeen, Vienna, 17 Oct. 1829, TNA, FO 120/104; Cowley to Aberdeen, Vienna, 8, 24 and 26 Sept. 1829, TNA, FO 120/105; Maltzan to Frederick William III, Vienna, 26 Sept. 1829, GStA PK, HA III, MdA I, 6013.

nothing and had to reconcile himself to the new Russian possession on the Black Sea coast. As in the case of his resignation in relation to the Russian protectorate over the Principalities, his contemporaries found it difficult to understand what they assumed to be his passive attitude. For example, almost eleven years later, Maltzan recalled the non-reaction of the Viennese cabinet and criticised Metternich's "political impotence that can be redressed neither by conferences nor protocols," and he finished his report to the Prussian king with these words: "Hungary can never be prosperous and peaceful, Sire, unless the mouth of the Danube is free!"[62]

Criticism of Austria's connivance with the Russian domination over the Danube Delta with the Sulina Channel, the only navigable branch of the river to the Black Sea, was rather usual for that period and was connected with accusations against the Russian authorities of interposing obstacles to commercial shipping on the Danube. They were allegedly guilty of provocative behaviour towards foreign vessels, the imposition of over-harsh quarantine measures established in 1836 and of neglecting to remove sandbanks at the mouth of the Sulina Channel. The latter failure contributed to the lowering of the water level and, consequently, the inability of steamships to pass through without unloading a part of their cargo. These allegations were automatically appropriated by many historians.[63] For example, Sir Charles Kingsley Webster did not hesitate to use them in vindication of Palmerston's aggressive conduct towards Russia, with the statement that "quarantine regulations were applied by the Russians in such a way as to hamper both Austrian trade and that of the Principalities."[64]

The criticism of the Russian administration in Sulina, however, must be seen in the larger context of the explosion of Russophobia in Great Britain in the 1830s. The above-mentioned accusations were

---

[62] Maltzan to Frederick William IV, Vienna, 13 May 1841, GStA PK, HA III, MdA I, 7364.

[63] A. Hoffmann, "Die Donau und Österreich," *Südosteuropa-Jahrbuch* 5, 1961, p. 41; E. Oberwalder, *Die Rechtsstellung der Donau als Wasserstrasse und die Volkswirtschaftlichen Auswirkungen auf die Donauschiffahrt*, unpublished dissertation, Wien 1947, p. 8; J. LeDonne, "Geopolitics, Logistics, and Grain: Russia's Ambitions in the Black Sea Basin, 1737–1834," *IHR* 28, 2006, 1, p. 37; Farca, pp. 412–414; Heiderich, p. 16.

[64] Webster, *Palmerston*, II, p. 580.

raised after 1836 in particular by people who were either active in the anti-Russian campaign in the British press and the *Portfolio* or by those influenced by these Russophobic attitudes. David Urquhart himself paid considerable attention to the Danube from the very beginning of his anti-Russian campaign and the *Portfolio* frequently mentioned navigation on the river. As well as in the case of Circassia, he wanted to focus the attention of the British government to the Danubian Principalities and engage it in the task of undermining Russia's position in this part of the Balkans. The Sulina Question was an important card in this game and finally a successful one because the establishment of the quarantine regulations in Sulina in 1836 – violently attacked by Urquhart – caused British alarm concerning the tsar's alleged plan of hindering navigation on the Danube. Fearing possible harm to British commerce, Palmerston reacted in June 1836 by sending a strong formal protest to St Petersburg against the establishment of the quarantine.[65] Although the Russian government denied the accusation of impeding shipping in the Sulina Channel, new controversy in Russo-British relations was brought into being and continued to be "an important hot spot in Anglo-Russian diplomatic relations."[66]

The criticism of the Russian agents in the Principalities can also be found in the not always trustworthy and probably over-exaggerated reports of some of the Austrian agents in the Principalities; these reports seem to have been influenced either by the Portfolio or their own ambition to invoke the Chancellery's attention and point out the importance of their mission.[67] There are also other reports which assess the situation in the Delta differently; for example, Prussian officers returning home from Constantinople in 1839 testified during their stopover in Vienna that they were not aware of any grievances

---

[65] C. Ardeleanu, "Russian-British Rivalry regarding Danube Navigation and the Origins of the Crimean War (1846–1853)," *Journal of Mediterranean Studies* 19, 2010, 2, p. 166; C. Ardeleanu, "The Lower Danube, Circassia and the Commercial Dimensions of the British-Russian Diplomatic Rivalry in the Black Sea Basin (1836–1837)," I. Biliarsky, O. Cristea, A. Oroveanu (eds.), *The Balkans and Caucasus: Parallel Processes on the Opposite Sides of the Black Sea*, Newcastle upon Tyne 2012, pp. 42–49; C. Ardeleanu, "The Danube Navigation in the Making of David Urquhart's Russophobia (1833–1837)," *Transylvanian Review* 19, 2010, Supplement Nr. 5:4, pp. 338–345.
[66] Ardeleanu, "The Lower Danube," p. 41.
[67] Sauer, "Sulina-Frage, Erster Teil," pp. 187–88 and 198.

in relation to the conduct of the Russian authorities towards vessels entering the river.[68]

The problem of the sandbanks is too complicated an issue to be able to accept without reservations the accuracy of the reports, often written by authors who were already negatively disposed towards Russia. Austrian historian Manfred Sauer correctly draws our attention to the fact that information about the lowering of the water level was never proved by any measurements during that period – the first one being carried out on the eve of the Crimean War; however, the repeated unverified statements gave it the appearance of truth. It is a similar story with regard to the accusation that the Russians deliberately ignored the silting up of the mouth of the Sulina in order to paralyse navigation on the Danube.[69] As for the quarantine arrangements on the Sulina, concerning ships originating from Ottoman ports, it does not seem to have been as burdensome for the merchants as the British claimed and did not have a serious impact on the development of trade on the river. Moreover, the Russians applied the rules in a more moderate way than was usual in other Russian Black Sea ports.[70]

It is also debatable as to whether those Russians involved in trade in the region were adversely affected by Austrian exports or only by the grain exports from the Principalities. It is obviously the case that if the restrictions had indeed been introduced in the Delta, both would have been affected, but was it Russia's real desire to economically damage Austria? The general opinion prevailing in Austria was that the export of manufactured goods from the monarchy in no way affected Russian commerce in the Black Sea area, based as it was on the export of grain. The same commodity from Hungary was more expensive and only able to compete in the years of poor harvests in Russia when its price increased. Improved navigation on the Danube would thus have caused no serious problems to the Russian merchants and, on the contrary, they could have profited from the increase in trade between the two Powers, something that was extraordinarily low from the Austrian point of view when compared with its annual trade levels

---

[68] Beauvale to Palmerston, Vienna, 16 Nov. 1839, TNA, FO 120/180.
[69] Sauer, "Sulina-Frage, Erster Teil," p. 190.
[70] Ibid., p. 188.

with other European countries.[71] Sir Frederick Lamb wrote in relation to this issue: "The German and Hungarian corn could not in ordinary years compete with that of the Southern Provinces of Russia from its higher price and in the event of the failure of the crop in those provinces it would be a valuable resource even to themselves. The other objects which would descend the Danube such as timber, glass, cloth, hardware and other manufactured goods are not furnished by Russia."[72]

Russian authorities were divided on this point. One attitude, representing in particular the views of the minister of finance, Count Egor Frantsevich Kankrin, and the commercial circles in Odessa, was afraid of the growth of Austrian commerce and transportation in the Black Sea area and strongly desired to use the possession of Sulina as a means of paralysing them as well as the growing export of grain from the Principalities. It is undoubtedly interesting that some merchants in Odessa on the other hand advocated cooperation with Austria. For example, the Russian Steam Company of Odessa collaborated with the *DDSG* and it was definitely much more important for Austrian merchants that a pro-Austrian attitude existed among the most influential personalities of the Russian Empire: Nicholas I and Nesselrode, who, together with Prince Vorontsov, the governor of New Russia, did not share Kankrin's views. They were all well aware of the importance of the Austrian entente and were not disquieted by the increasing commerce on the Danube, unlike the minister of finance, and they did not wish to cause problems for Austrian vessels sailing up and down the river. After their rejection of the calls by the field marshal, Count Ivan Ivanovich Diebitsch-Zabalkanskii, and Kiselev to annex the Principalities in the early 1830s, they also decided to proceed "generously" with Austria in relation to the Sulina Question.[73] Nothing supports

---

[71] Metternich to Ficquelmont, Vienna, 15 April 1834, HHStA, StA, Russland III, 102; Ottenfels, *Observation sur le commerce*, HDA, 750, OO 18, pp. a39–a43; *Ausweise über den Handel von Oesterreich im Verkehr mit dem Auslande und über den Zwischenverkehr von Ungarn und Siebenbürgen, mit den anderen österreichischen Provinzen, im Jahre 1840. Vom Rechnungs-Departement der k. k. allgemeinen Hofkammer. Erster Jahrgang (Erste Abtheilung)*, Wien 1842, pp. 208–209; H. Pavelka, *Englisch-österreichische Wirtschaftsbeziehungen in der ersten Hälfte des 19. Jahrhunderts*, Graz, Wien, Köln 1968, p. 44.

[72] Lamb to Palmerston, Vienna, 25 May 1834, TNA, FO 120/145.

[73] R. R. Florescu, "British Reactions to the Russian Régime in the Danubian Principalities," *JCEA* 31, 1962, p. 38; Kantor, p. 280; Puryear, *International Eco-*

historian Nikolaus Farca's claim that the tsarist court came to a decision to use its position in the Delta as a vehicle for systematically
impeding international navigation on the lower Danube.[74]

The conciliatory attitude towards the conservative ally is clear
from the Russians' conduct in Sulina where, however, it is necessary
to make a distinction between the behaviour of the local subaltern
staff and the above-mentioned Russian elites, in particular Vorontsov,
who tried to redress the misconduct of the former group. The local
officials were often pedantic and corrupt and the logical cause of the
complaints made by the Austrians. Vorontsov definitely had the will
to curb their behaviour but it was not always easy to prevent the
local officials from taking "small favours" from the boat captains.
Even though he strictly forbade this practice and made some personal changes, the fees continued to be paid with a degree of "consent" and they do not appear to have been too onerous or caused
much discontent. More serious were the actions of the public health
staff in prohibiting the debarkation of ship crews on the Bessarabian
bank of the river in emergency situations, which led to the wreck of
an Austrian vessel in the winter of 1835–1836. Vorontsov abolished
this prohibition and he was also keen not to excessively burden the
Austrian ships with quarantine measures. The reports of customs sur-
veyors, who were later sent to the lower Danube by Kankrin and who
were critical of Vorontsov's willingness to compromise and of the inefficiency of the quarantine regime, offer some evidence that European
merchants were not exposed to serious impediments in this area.[75]

The discord between Vorontsov and Kankrin is also clearly visible when one considers the plans for the employment of a steam
dredger in the Sulina branch, which the former advocated but the
latter sharply rejected.[76] Vorontsov even complained during his visit
to Metternich in Königswart in the summer of 1840 about Kankrin's
opposition to the measures to clear the entrance of the river and to
reduce the quarantine restrictions to the lowest possible levels.[77] The
Austrian chancellor had been well aware of the two strands of opin-

---

nomics, pp. 110–111.

[74]   Farca, pp. 161–163 and 412.

[75]   Sauer, "Sulina-Frage, Erster Teil," pp. 224–233.

[76]   Ibid., p. 234.

[77]   Beauvale to Palmerston, Königswart, 25 Aug. 1840, TNA, FO 120/189.

ion that existed among the Russian elite for years, particularly as the tsar had made no secret of it when he had told Ficquelmont: "I have made a decision in line with the wishes of the Emperor [of Austria] in spite of advice to the contrary from some of my ministers; I am of the opinion that we can only benefit from free navigation on the Danube; it will lead to an increase in commerce in the Black Sea, and we will see an increase in profits for us."[78] Metternich regarded the situation in the Russian government with ease and, as he stated in 1834, he was in no way surprised by "opponents in the departments of the interior. In Russia it is the same as in Austria and in all other countries, these departments never want to listen to anything and they do not examine the issues with impartiality until the moment of decision. Then, they discover that their opposition was mistaken."[79] Since Metternich was well aware that the tsar and his retinue were seeking to cooperate with Austria in this respect, he was not willing to be dragged into anti-Russian measures, which was exactly what some of the British were trying to achieve with their references to the insidious designs of the Russian government against European commerce on the Danube. Metternich maintained that Russia's proceedings in affairs concerning the river were moderate and its willingness to yield was a result of the assertive but discreet interventions after 1834 of the Austrian diplomatic and consular representatives, who were campaigning against the legal and administrative restrictions to free navigation. As for the quarantine issue, he officially reacted to the British insinuations in 1840 of the dangers connected with the hygiene measures in a statement that the Russians were entitled to take such measures as long as they did not hinder commerce.[80]

It would be a mistake, however, to presume that Metternich saw no potential dangers in the quarantine restrictions should the measures affecting them became harsher in the future. Similarly, he was

---

[78] Ficquelmont to Metternich, St Petersburg, 2 Jan. 1839, HHStA, StA, Russland III, 114.

[79] Metternich to Ficquelmont, Baden, 3 Sept. 1834, HHStA, StA, Russland III, 103.

[80] Strangways to Wellington, Vienna, 5 Jan. 1835, TNA, FO 120/149; Beauvale to Palmerston, Vienna, 16 Nov. 1839, TNA, FO 120/180; Gardner [?] to Palmerston, Guirgewo Quarantine, 3 Aug. 1836, TNA, FO 120/155; Beauvale to Palmerston, Vienna, 18 July 1840, TNA, FO 120/189; Puryear, *International Economics*, p. 34; Sauer, "Sulina-Frage, Erster Teil," p. 189.

not entirely deaf to the reports regarding the lowering of the water level at the mouth of Danube. On the turn of 1838, he either started to regard the reports as evidence of a current problem or at this time began to consider the silting up of the river as a possible future problem, or both. It was no coincidence that he opened negotiations with Russia in early 1839 regarding free navigation in the Sulina Channel with the aim of dealing with this matter through the development of a contract between the two conservative Powers. He sought an agreement by which Russia would be obliged to safeguard sufficient water levels, build a lighthouse and pledge itself not to delay ships more than was necessary. He was willing to agree that Russia was entitled to collect special fees to cover expenses incurred and he estimated that this would amount to 40,000 roubles (1,800 pounds sterling) for the dredging operations. When the British objected that the levying of a charge was at variance with the settlement of the Congress of Vienna, which had committed each signatory country to ensuring it met its own costs regarding navigability, Metternich countered that the Danube Delta was in poor condition because of Turkish neglect and that Russia would not wish to meet the necessary expenditure from its own budget. In his opinion, principles and practice were sometimes at variance with each other and it was necessary to modify the treaties if one wanted to attain the desired goal.[81]

The request for the conclusion of a treaty concerning the Danube met with an immediate positive echo in St Petersburg, but the outbreak of the second war between Mahmud II and Mohammed Ali in the spring of 1839 delayed the negotiations, which were entirely interrupted after Ficquelmont's sudden departure to Vienna at the end of July. This situation lasted until his return to St Petersburg in May 1840, when his main task was to conclude a treaty regarding navigation on the Danube with the primary aim of preventing the silting up of the Sulina Channel. In the Russian capital, Nicholas I immediately agreed to the Austrian proposals and arguments, saying: "Your request is absolutely correct; I have authorised Nesselrode to negoti-

---

[81] Milbanke to Palmerston, Vienna, 24 Dec. 1838, TNA, FO 120/169; Milbanke to Palmerston, Vienna, 8 Jan., 22 Feb. and 24 March 1839, TNA, FO 120/180; Beauvale to Palmerston, Vienna, 30 April 1840, TNA, FO 120/189.

ate with you; speak to him about it."[82] Since the two parties were in agreement and the tsar was backed on the Russian side not only by Nesselrode but also by Vorontsov, the content of the convention concluded on 25 July 1840 fulfilled all Austrian ambitions. It included the principle of free navigation on the Danube and obliged Russia to begin work as soon as possible on clearing the Sulina branch from the obstructions to navigation and to build a lighthouse. Austrian vessels were not to be stopped at Sulina longer than was necessary for presenting their papers, while Russian ships were given free access to the Austrian part of the Danube. With the exception of the fees to be paid by vessels sailing through the Delta to cover the costs of dredging the riverbed and the construction of the lighthouse, no other charges or customs were permitted.[83]

Even though the stipulation concerning the sufficient level of the water was later not observed by the Russians and the water level of the Danube was considerably low in the early 1850s,[84] at that given moment it was a valuable diplomatic victory for the Viennese cabinet. Whether the tsar had planned from the very beginning that he would not fulfil this commitment, or whether it was the result of the behaviour of his subordinate authorities is difficult to ascertain. In the 1830s, however, when faced with the hostility of the Maritime Powers, Nicholas I was forced to placate Austria by agreeing not to complicate the lives of its citizens in the Principalities and on the Danube. He was definitely aware of the importance the Austrian Empire attributed to its commercial interests in this area, and Ficquelmont did not leave the Russian monarch in any doubt about this when stressing from the very beginning of the negotiations in 1840 the necessity of cement-

---

[82] Ficquelmont to Metternich, St Petersburg, 19 May 1840, HHStA, StA, Russland III, 119.

[83] Metternich to Stürmer, Vienna, 19 May 1840, HHStA, StA, Türkei VI, 78; Tatishchev to Nesselrode, Vienna, 23 Jan. 1839, AVPRI, fond 133, Kantseliariia, opis 469, 1839/213; Tatishchev to Nesselrode, Vienna, 7 May 1840, AVPRI, fond 133, Kantseliariia, opis 469, 1840/177; Beauvale to Palmerston, Vienna, 30 April 1840, TNA, FO 120/189; Kantor, p. 254. The Convention was ratified by the Austrian emperor on 5 September 1840. Neumann, *Recueil des traités*, IV, pp. 460–463; K. Strupp (ed.), *Ausgewählte diplomatische Aktenstücke zur orientalischen Frage*, Gotha 1916, pp. 71–72; Lorenz, p. 123; Puryear, *International Economics*, pp. 144–145.

[84] W. Knorr, *Die Donau und die Meerengenfrage: Ein völkerrechtsgeschichtlicher Rückblick*, Weimar 1917, p. 56; Heiderich, p. 16.

ing the Austro-Russian political alliance with material interests. The
benefits do not seem to have been only on the Austrian side because
the development of steam navigation on the Danube contributed to a
considerable growth of trade between the two Powers, which moved
Tatishchev to suggest in March 1840 that a Russian consulate should
be established in Vienna.[85] Even Sir Charles Kingsley Webster admits
that in the case of the Sulina Question "there was much negotiation
with Russia concerning the freedom of navigation of the Sulina branch,
but on the whole that Power acceded to [Austria's] all demands with a
good grace and the problem caused at this time little friction between
the two countries."[86]

*   *   *

Nicholas I's conciliatory behaviour reconciled Metternich to Russia's
dominance in Moldavia and Wallachia. When the chancellor recognised that he was unable to prevent the Russian annexation of the
Danube Delta and failed to achieve a prompt withdrawal of its forces
from Ottoman soil, he resigned himself to an alternative course of
action. He decided to defend Austrian interests by exerting his influence not in the Principalities but in St Petersburg and to place
the emphasis on the Austro-Russian alliance, in other words to attain
his desired goals by collaboration instead of confrontation. Although
this cooperation was not explicitly articulated and, on the part of
Austria, was more passive than active, it certainly existed in reality:
even Austrian restraint in responding to the conduct of the Russian
agents benefited the tsar. Moreover, Metternich sometimes displayed
more energetic support when he played a supervisory role in relation
to the French and British activities in this region, exhibiting a high
level of distrust and apprehension with regard to their behaviour. As
for the French, he wrote to Stürmer in August 1833 in reaction to
the forthcoming installation of the hospodars: "We do not know, at

---

[85] Ficquelmont to Metternich, St Petersburg, 2 Jan. 1839, HHStA, StA, Russland
III, 114; Ficquelmont to Metternich, St Petersburg, 19 May 1840, HHStA, StA,
Russland III, 119; Tatishchev to Nesselrode, Vienna, 16 March 1840, AVPRI, fond
133, Kantseliariia, opis 469, 1840/177.
[86] Webster, *Palmerston*, II, p. 581.

the moment, as to how far this rumour can be substantiated; what is important for us is that the choice falls to people who are honest and as far as possible independent of all foreign influence, namely that of France whose busy and restless policy would unfortunately not be conducive to the maintenance of public order and tranquillity that we would like to see in these provinces because of their immediate proximity to and multiple relations with our own country."[87] With regard to the British, in 1840 he advised Sir Frederick Lamb, now Lord Beauvale, to recall the anti-Russian British consul in Bucharest, Robert Gilmour Colquhoun, pointing out his poor relationship with Hospodar Alexandru II Ghica.[88]

It was difficult for the British and French to understand Metternich's passivity towards Russian domination in regions of high geopolitical and economic importance for the Austrian Empire and they usually denounced him for his "complicity." One cannot forget, however, that his restrained policy was profitable for Austria and instrumental in obtaining a number of concessions not only from Russia, which was trying to satisfy the complaints and requests of the Viennese cabinet concerning Austria's rights in the Principalities and shipping on the Danube, but also from Great Britain. The British cabinet, in an effort to establish a collaborative relationship with Austria against Russia, had concluded a convention on 3 July 1838 with Austria, which was considerably advantageous for Austrian merchants. Henceforth, they were entitled to carry goods to Great Britain not only from Europe but also Africa and Asia via Austrian sea and river ports and those on the Danube from the Austrian frontier to its mouth, which infringed the British navigation code but was finally sanctioned by the British Parliament. The existence of this agreement probably influenced the tsar's decision to conclude the St Petersburg Convention in 1840 with the aim of not causing an Austro-British rapprochement as a result of his eventual refusal to concur with Austrian demands.[89] Metternich was thus able to take advantage of the British-

---

[87] Metternich to Stürmer, Vienna, 2 Aug. 1833, HHStA, StA, Türkei VIII, 24.
[88] Metternich to Beauvale, Königswart, 3 Sept. 1840, and attached Ghica to Metternich, Bucharest, 16 July 1840, TNA, FO 120/190. For more on the dispute between Colquhoun and Ghica see N. Iorga, *A History of Anglo-Roumanian Relations*, Bucharest 1931, pp. 83–84.
[89] Henderson, p. 134; Pavelka, p. 42; Sauer, "Sulina-Frage, Erster Teil," p. 191, "Sulina-Frage, Zweiter Teil," pp. 74–76.

Russian rivalry in the 1830s in order to advance Austria's economic
interests even though he in no way planned to sacrifice the entente
with his conservative ally. Some time after his fall in March 1848, he
still positively assessed the Austro-Russian cooperation in this area
and pointed out that owing to its existence the Russian predominance
in Moldavia and Wallachia had not become a tragedy for Austria.[90]
The studied documents from the period after 1834 support the truth
of this assessment, as does Barbara Jelavich's appraisal that Austria
and Russia were on excellent terms in the Principalities at that time
and united in the aim of maintaining the status quo.[91]

Paul W. Schroeder has stated his opinion that the conditions
of the Treaty of Adrianople particularly affected Austria and Great
Britain and later caused trouble between Russia and Europe.[92] One
cannot disagree with this, yet one cannot overlook the fact that these
problems did not come into being until the 1850s, in part for the reason
that Metternich refused to follow Wellington's bitter but belated complaints directed to St Petersburg in late 1829 and he never joined the
outburst of French and British Russophobic outcries in the 1830s. The
general and often used explanation for this restraint was Metternich's
need for entente with the tsar against revolutions and liberalism. Although he actually did need this support, there was more beyond this
single reason to explain his attitude. He simply realised that once the
war was over, he could do nothing about its outcome, and if he could,
at what price? Austria could hardly be successful in a diplomatic rift
with Russia over the Principalities, and even joint diplomatic pressure with Great Britain would only lead to uncertain results although
undoubtedly also to a serious deterioration in Austria's relations with
Russia. Another war on the turn of 1829 was out of the question because France and Prussia would never wage one against Russia or
even urge it to modify the Treaty of Adrianople, and Wellington, albeit loud in his declarations, could hardly be expected to be decisive
in his actions as he was not during the Russian military campaigns in
1828 and 1829. Consequently, Metternich decided to keep silent but,

---

[90] *Geheimes Memorandum! Die Verwicklungen im Osmanischen Reiche gegenüber
den Neugestaltungen in Austro-Germanien-betreffend*, 1849, NA, RAM-AC 8, 2.
[91] B. Jelavich, *Russia and the Formation of the Romanian National State 1821–
1878*, London, New York, New Rochelle, Melbourne, Sydney 1984, p. 34.
[92] Schroeder, *Transformation*, p. 660.

at the same time, act in a more practical way than Wellington and try to save what could be saved by cautious diplomacy. It is questionable whether his attempt to ensure the withdrawal of Russian troops from the Principalities with the loan for the Porte could have been successful because, although the tsar admitted such a possibility in early 1830, the administrative changes were far too important for Russia to be threatened with the premature termination of the occupation. In any case, Wellington's refusal to support Metternich's plan contributed to its failure and the prince had to take advantage of the revolutions in 1830, particularly that in Poland considerably stressing the value of alliance with Austria, to move Nicholas I and Nesselrode not to weaken Austrian economic predominance in Moldavia and Wallachia. Since the tsar and his vice-chancellor did not dare to use Russia's influence against their most useful ally in economic affairs, Metternich had no reason to contest Russia's political predominance and, consequently, the Austro-Russian "mariage de convenance" was able to exist and generally harmoniously so in the 1830s. Metternich's attitude towards the Principalities offers other evidence that he took into consideration not only the geopolitical but also the economic interests of the Habsburg Monarchy, and, being well aware of its financial and military limits, he pursued not only a conservative but also realistic and pragmatic foreign policy. And in this case one can hardly deny its success.

20

Mahmud II's Reformatory Effort

In the 1830s all the Great Powers desired the preservation of the Ottoman Empire, which was generally regarded as the necessary condition for the maintenance of the European balance of power. Mahmud II tried to satisfy this wish, and, having destroyed the main opposition to any attempts for the regeneration of the country he governed, the Janissaries, in 1826, he started a new phase of reforms. His reformatory effort naturally attracted the attention of European cabinets; Metternich personally was extremely interested in the internal situation of the Ottoman Empire. Consequently, in their reports their representatives did not limit themselves to the diplomatic relations between the Ottoman Empire and Europe but also described the internal conditions of the former. It is of course true that sometimes the line between the internal and external affairs was not very clear because many of what began as purely internal matters soon became a part of international relations owing to the interference of foreign states which were both curious and anxious to take advantage of the effort to regenerate the Ottoman Empire to increase their own influence over the Near East. This finally led to a mutual struggle for dominance in this regard, and attempts for the regeneration of the Ottoman Empire became thus an integral component of the Eastern Question in the 1830s.

Metternich's Opinions on the Decay and Possible Revival of the Ottoman Empire

Metternich paid as much attention to Mahmud II's reformatory effort as to the religious conditions of the Ottoman Empire, for the same reasons and with the use of the same information channels as introduced in Chapter 12. The two issues, the religious conditions and the effort for the regeneration of the Ottoman state, were often connected topics and, therefore, analysed in the same books, articles and diplomatic reports which Metternich read and used for forming his opinions on these matters. He naturally could not ignore the reforms pursued in this part of the world, an interesting phenomenon to which he assumed a similar attitude as towards reforms in the Austrian Empire or Italian countries.[1] What Alan J. Reinerman wrote about Metternich's attitude towards the changes in the Apennines is basically also applicable to those concerning the Ottoman Empire: "His approach to reform was basically administrative in nature, not political. He hoped that the adoption of the administrative, financial, judicial, and humanitarian innovations of the revolutionary era would be sufficient to satisfy public opinion so that revolutionary political innovations would no longer be demanded. A modern, efficient administration responsive to popular needs, humane and equitable laws, a sound financial system, a paternalistic welfare policy for the poor, governmental encouragement of economic development – these and similar measures which would promote popular contentment without weakening royal authority were the core of Metternich's reform program."[2] Of course it must be pointed out that Metternich's attitude towards the reforms within the sultan's state was shaped by its different internal conditions diverging from those in European, read Christian, countries. As the chancellor himself declared in early 1829, the Ottoman Empire differed so much from European countries that signs of progress there could hardly be evaluated according to European standards: "The vitality of the Ottoman Empire rests on foundations of a unique nature and it is not possible to measure them by any scale used in European civilisation."[3]

The Ottoman Empire offered a deplorable spectacle in the first half of the 19th century and its weakness was becoming more and more obvious during that period, in particular due to the Ottoman defeats in various wars in the 1820s and 1830s. Metternich naturally knew well the weakness of the empire that to him resembled a body suffering from a chronic and incurable illness.[4] The many blows which

---

[1] Reinerman, "Metternich and Reform," pp. 524–548; Siemann, pp. 104–105.
[2] Reinerman, "Metternich and Reform," pp. 526–527.
[3] Metternich to Esterházy, Vienna, 5 Jan. 1829, HHStA, StA, England 187.
[4] Metternich's most important analyses of the internal situation of the Ottoman Empire can be found in Metternich to Stürmer, Vienna, 3 Dec. 1839, HHStA, StA,

it had suffered in the past like wars and upheavals could not seriously harm a healthy person, but they had to have fatal consequences for an incurable man, and consequently, any violent concussion could lead to this patient's death within 24 hours.[5] In the words of a builder, he considered the Ottoman Empire to be an "old and creaky edifice full of leaking entrances and windows that with one blow could come crashing down from one day to the next."[6] This scarcely optimistic judgement of the lamentable situation of the Ottoman Empire was made not only owing to his knowledge of its economic, administrative and military weakness, but also, and in particular, because of the reports from foreign diplomats in Constantinople, the most important being those written by the Austrians and Prussians he read most often, revealing the Ottomans' weak sense of identification with their own state, their negligible willingness to take part in the reformatory process and their reluctance to face difficult challenges, as was proved in times of danger. The Ottomans showed almost no readiness to defend the capital when the Russians or Egyptians were practically knocking at its gates, the former in 1829, and the latter twice in the 1830s. In these difficult situations, a general apathy prevailed among them, between commoners as well as the elite, and Mahmud II could not count upon their patriotism to support his unsteady throne.[7] The sultan was even heard to say in the late summer of 1829 when the war with Russia was approaching its end: "At present I am convinced that the Turks are my greatest enemies and that I must fear them more than the Russians."[8]

Türkei VI, 72, published also in *NP*, VI, pp. 358–366; Metternich to Apponyi, Vienna, 26 May 1841, HHStA, StA, Frankreich 322, dispatched on the same day also to Prince Esterházy, HHStA, StA, England 237, Baron Erberg, HHStA, StK, Preussen III, 178, and Baron Meysenbug, HHStA, StA, Russland III, 123.

[5] Metternich to Stürmer, Vienna, 18 May 1833, HHStA, StA, Türkei VI, 59; Lerchenfeld to Ludwig I of Bavaria, Vienna, 12 Nov. 1839, BHStA, MA, Wien 2408.

[6] Lerchenfeld to Ludwig I of Bavaria, Vienna, 5 June 1839, BHStA, MA, Wien 2408.

[7] Ottenfels to Metternich, Constantinople, 29 Aug. 1829, HHStA, StA, Türkei VI, 37; Ottenfels to Metternich, Constantinople, 10 and 31 Dec. 1832, HHStA, StA, Türkei VI, 55; Stürmer to Metternich, Büyükdere, 21 Aug. 1833, HHStA, StA, Türkei VI, 58; Stürmer to Metternich, Büyükdere, 10 July 1839, HHStA, StA, Türkei VI, 69; Martens to Frederick William III, Büyükdere, 25 and 30 March, 23 April 1833, GStA PK, HA III, MdA I, 7272.

[8] Malaguzziny to Metternich, Vienna, 19 April 1830, HHStA, StA, Türkei VI,

In late March 1833, during the war between Mahmud II and Mohammed Ali, the Prussian envoy in Constantinople, Baron Friedrich von Martens, sent a rather pessimistic report on the sad state of the Ottoman Empire: "The Sultan, the Seraglio, the Divan, the Ministry, the Ulemas, the people – Turkish, Greek and Armenian, nothing hangs together, no one even gives a hand to help each other or understand one another; nobody agrees with anything and a remarkable dissolution exists in all areas, in all elements of the state. One would be inclined to say we are stagnating here in a state of barely organised chaos; nowhere is there any energy, any measures, unity, judgement, resolution. This is an ancient, ruined edifice that hardly stands on its unsteady columns and seems to have lost its base ... Finally, the Ulemas start to say openly that it would be better to see and have Ibrahim here than the Sultan."[9] And he continued in this scepticism a few days later: "When one considers the general situation of the Porte, it is as deplorable as it could be. Humiliation is everywhere, patriotism nowhere; there are no supporters of the government; public opinion is always declaring more against the Russians; there are insufficient preparations in everything and everywhere; there is a total lack of energy in this careless and degenerate nation; there are soldiers without experience and leaders without real courage; there is an enemy who only has to show himself to win the hearts of all; there is scorn for the sovereign; there is a prime minister, a first favourite (the serasker), who, as well as the rest of the prominent employees, wants above all to retain his position, his richness, his influence. What state with such characteristics could save itself?"[10] Stürmer, who generally was more broadminded about the Ottomans and their country, described the situation in the same way at that time: "When one warns the Turks of a revolution that could break out in consequence of the current events, they tell us: so much the better; we doing so badly that we cannot but profit from every kind of change."[11] The same

---

17. This disconsolate internal situation in Constantinople and Adrianople at the end of the Russo-Ottoman war in 1829 is briefly sketched in Chapter 9.

[9] Martens to Frederick William III, Pera, 25 March 1833, GStA PK, HA III, MdA I, 7272.

[10] Martens to Frederick William III, Pera, 30 March 1833, GStA PK, HA III, MdA I, 7272.

[11] Stürmer to Metternich, Constantinople, 27 March 1833, HHStA, StA, Türkei VI, 57.

despair can also be found in the internuncio's reports sent to Vienna in 1839, when the Porte gradually lost its army, monarch and fleet in the fight with Mohammed Ali. In Constantinople a universal desire for peace prevailed although it had to be expected that it would be re-deemed only by extensive concessions; the lower classes wanted it for fear of their existence, the members of the elite in the hope of preserv-ing their positions. In Stürmer's opinion, "never were the Turks more depressed. They are beaten, consternated, humiliated, and they even seem to abandon hope in the salvation of the Ottoman Empire."[12] Ac-cording to him, this little faith in the long duration of the empire was a symptom of the deep crisis in the state system and society and was also wide-spread among its members in peacetime when, for example, it used to happen that some old Ottomans stopped the Europeans in the streets and asked them how many years they gave to its existence, whether six, five or even less.[13]

The sad state of the Ottoman society is underlined by the fact that the government did not try very hard to change this apathy for fear that with an attempt to raise national enthusiasm, it would lose the control over the course of events. The apprehension of its own people's disloyalty was not without foundation because in difficult times doubts about the point of any change at the top of the state apparatus – including the ruler – could be heard in public, even among the conservative bodies (Ulemas). One cannot wonder that even the Ottoman forces enjoyed the scant confidence of their monarch, and sometimes they were not even sent against the enemy for fear they would desert. This anxiety proved to be entirely justifiable in the summer of 1839, when a considerable part of the army did desert and almost the entire fleet defected.[14]

---

[12] Stürmer to Metternich, Büyükdere, 22 July 1839, HHStA, StA, Türkei VI, 69.
[13] Stürmer to Metternich, Büyükdere, 10 and 22 July 1839, HHStA, StA, Türkei VI, 69; Stürmer to Metternich, Büyükdere, 28 Aug. 1839, HHStA, StA, Türkei VI, 70; Bockelberg to Frederick William III, Vienna, 15 Jan. 1839, GStA PK, HA III, MdA I, 6032.
[14] Ottenfels to Metternich, Constantinople, 31 Dec. 1832, HHStA, StA, Türkei VI, 55; Stürmer to Metternich, Constantinople, 27 March 1833, HHStA, StA, Türkei VI, 57; Stürmer to Metternich, Büyükdere, 8 July 1839, HHStA, StA, Türkei VI, 69; Martens to Frederick William III, Büyükdere, 25 March 1833, GStA PK, HA III, MdA I, 7272. For more on the desertion of the sultan's army and the defection of his navy see Chapter 23.

The critical conditions of the Ottoman state system and society left nobody at the Chancellery in Ballhausplatz in any doubt that reforms were necessary, and Metternich was in no way a man to oppose such reforms – he even urged the Porte to adopt them. However, since he believed that the problems of the Ottoman Empire did not lie only in that it had fallen behind the West in technology but also in the general degeneration of the whole of its society, he held the view that the changes could not be only cosmetic and that merely adopting the technical and civilising achievements of the West was insufficient. According to him, the principal goal of reforms was to be the regeneration of Ottoman society. Consistent with his conservative thinking, he maintained that the sultan had to pursue reforms with regard for history and traditions, particularly with regard for the religion that was the ideological basis of his power and the fundamental link between him and his subjects, in other words the crucial bolt holding the empire together.[15] In his opinion, any attempts to intrude upon Ottoman customs, religious principles and practices as determined in the Koran, in other words attempts to intrude on the traditional way of life of the Ottoman society were the chief reason for "the lack of energy in which the Mussulman nation finds itself."[16] Continuing in this way had to end in inevitable ruin because, as the prince declared, "ashes do not catch fire."[17]

Consequently, each serious offence against Ottoman traditions and customs met with Metternich's disagreement. The model example of such an unwelcome event was the occasion of the evening party held by Gordon on the British warship *Blonde* on 4 November 1829, shortly after the end of the Russo-Ottoman war. The soirée passed off under the Ottoman banner and the flags of the European nations at peace with the Ottoman Empire and was attended by more than 200 people: prominent Ottoman dignitaries, the members of the sultan's court and European diplomats with their wives. They behaved in a highly friendly manner and the most prominent and generally elderly Ottomans, trying to demonstrate their goodwill, conformed to

---

[15] Metternich to Ottenfels, Vienna, 22 Feb. 1833, Metternich to Stürmer, Vienna, 3 Oct. 1833, HHStA, StA, Türkei VI, 59; Metternich to Esterházy, Vienna, 26 May 1841, HHStA, StA, England 237.

[16] Metternich to Trauttmannsdorff, Vienna, 19 Feb. 1833, HHStA, StK, Preussen 152.

[17] Ibid.

the habits of Europeans, showing disregard for Moslem habits with their improper behaviour in several ways: they drank too much champagne, played cards and danced the *polka* with European ladies. In particular their drinking of alcohol aroused the attention of the Europeans, who could hardly fail to notice that the Ottomans willingly and very often made toasts to the sultan's as well as European monarchs' health and that some of them sooner or later displayed significant symptoms of drunkenness; for example, Serasker Husrev Pasha was seen embracing the tsar's young adjutant and the two men swearing eternal friendship.[18]

Gordon prided himself for opening the door to European civilisation for the Ottoman Empire through the violation of the precepts of Koran,[19] but Metternich was of entirely different opinion: "The greatest enemies of the Turks could not have done them a worse favour than a friend did them. Mr Gordon's party has certainly produced the most dreadful effect by discrediting the members of a government that, having lost its power in practice, can only sustain itself on opinion and the moral power that lie in the theocratic principle that constitutes it and forms its basis."[20] The chancellor regarded this open violation of prescripts of the Koran by leading representatives of the empire as a primary symptom of the disorganisation of the predominantly theocratic state,[21] and he empathised with the dismay of the Prussian envoy in Constantinople, Camille Royer de Luynes, that with such people close to the sultan "there is no prospect for the salvation of the state."[22] He did not feign his regret of the prominent Ottomans' conduct in his instructions to Ottenfels: "The life of empires is composed of moral and material forces. The latter must conform to the rules of the former, and where the moral force is still intact, hope for regeneration is not lost. Your remark that during that infamous

---

[18] Ottenfels to Metternich, Constantinople, 10 Nov. 1829, HHStA, StA, Türkei VI, 37; Royer to Frederick William III, Pera, 5 Nov. 1829, GStA PK, HA III, MdA I, 7268; Gordon to Aberdeen, Constantinople, 11 Nov. 1829, TNA, FO 78/181; Guilleminot to Polignac, Constantinople, 11 Nov. 1829, AMAE, CP, Turquie 255; Ottenfels, *Memoari*, pp. 218–219.

[19] Krauter, p. 258.

[20] Schwebel to Polignac, Vienna, 3 Dec. 1829, AMAE, CP, Autriche 411.

[21] Maltzan to Frederick William III, Vienna, 4 and 22 Dec. 1829, GStA PK, HA III, MdA I, 6013.

[22] Royer to Frederick William III, Pera, 5 Nov. 1829, GStA PK, HA III, MdA I, 7268.

night the leading personalities of the Empire and the most notable members of the Ulemas openly violated the regulations of the Koran suffices for conferring the most regrettable character to this event. The final power of the Ottoman Empire lies in its theocratic principle; if it is weakened, the Empire is undermined at its very foundations. For various reasons, I believe I have the right to predict that the banquet given by Mr Gordon will have far more serious consequences than the signature of the Treaty of Adrianople had."[23]

Metternich's contemplation about Islam had a more rational cause than might be evident at first sight. It resulted from his opinion that it was the common thread of Islam uniting rather different ethnic groups that bound the Ottomans to the sultan. Without this link, which had been established during the early days of the empire, the sultan would lose his authority to reign over them, particularly when some of his subjects started to lean towards nationalism and liberalism, both seen by Metternich as disastrous. If the role of Islam were significantly weakened, the multi-ethnic state still at the level of European feudalism of the eleventh to the fifteenth centuries would, in the prince's opinion, cease to exist. The main problem of this attitude lay in the fact that this gamble on Islam was intended to serve for some time as a barrier against ideas that Metternich considered to be subversive, but it could not be maintained indefinitely, and the prince was well aware of this fact. Consequently, although he regarded respect for Islam as the crucial condition for the improvement of the predominantly Moslem Empire, he found at the same time in this religion the principal impediment to the entire regeneration of the state and its ability to achieve the status of European countries because it constituted an entirely different structure of society with roots based upon religious law and any attempt to rebuild it completely would lead to its disintegration.[24] He therefore came to the strong conviction: "Some states are like individuals who are never healthy. Turkey is such a state because Islam does not permit the existence of any healthy state organism. From time to time an incurable illness de-

---

[23] Metternich to Ottenfels, Vienna, 2 Dec. 1829, HHStA, StA, Türkei VI, 39.
[24] Ibid.; Metternich to Neumann, Vienna, 24 June 1840, HHStA, StA, England 230; Maltzan to Frederick William III, Vienna, 10 July 1826, GStA PK, HA III, MdA I, 6006; Maltzan to Frederick William III, Vienna, 4 and 22 Dec. 1829, GStA PK, HA III, MdA I, 6013; Lamb to Palmerston, Vienna, 13 March 1834, TNA, FO 120/145.

velops. One can be cured for some time but never fully recovered. A chronic ailment persists and can never be removed from his body."[25] His pessimism never diminished, not even at the end of the second Turko-Egyptian conflict of 1839–1841, when Austria and other Great Powers rescued the sultan's declining state from peril: "Seeking in this end [of the Turko-Egyptian war] the secure conditions for the internal pacification of the Ottoman Empire, its reconstruction on new bases, or even the revival of an old social structure flawed by the very thing on which it is founded, Islam, would be indulging oneself in dreaming of the kind of Utopia which remains inaccessible to us."[26]

Nevertheless, the fact that Islam could not secure the regeneration of the Ottoman Empire for all time was the essential point for Metternich who, seeing no other option if he wanted to preserve the sultan's empire for as long as possible, continued to insist that only placing emphasis on this faith together with the cautious improvement of the empire's ill-functioning government, courts and army could prolong its existence at all, and he was also convinced that the empire possessed resources which could enable its prolonged existence if they were correctly exploited. By "caution" Metternich meant a sensible application of Western models because Ottoman society differed from European society in that fundamental point: religion. He was absolutely certain that the achievements of European countries could not always be in accordance with Moslem customs and that a law functioning well in France or Great Britain would not necessarily be beneficial in a culturally different milieu.[27] This particularly held for eventual attempts to equalise various religious groups which Metternich opposed, as explained in Chapter 12, because he found such a deep intrusion into the legal basis of the empire and the consequent disintegration of the traditional social structure on which the empire was based as incompatible with its further existence.[28]

---

[25] The discussion between Prokesch and Metternich, Vienna, 7 Dec. 1839, Prokesch-Osten, *Aus dem Nachlasse*, p. 183.

[26] Metternich to Apponyi, Vienna, 5 May 1841, HHStA, StA, Frankreich 322.

[27] Metternich to Apponyi, Vienna, 30 Dec. 1833, HHStA, StA, Frankreich 290; Maltzan to Frederick William III, Vienna, 5 Dec. 1839, GStA PK, HA III, MdA I, 7350.

[28] The role of the Christians in Metternich's views on the Ottoman reform movement was never significant, and one could even say that the attention he paid to them in this respect was insufficient. He definitely saw them as an integral part

Indeed, Metternich regarded attempts to reconstruct the Ottoman Empire through the blind copying of the legislative models from the Western countries but without regard to the different traditions of the Levant as a bigger evil than other causes of the decay of the empire like the heterogeneous ethnic composition of its population or the defeats suffered in the wars of the previous 100 years,[29] and he always emphatically warned the Ottomans against such a course of action: "Base your government upon respect for your religious institutions which form the fundamental basis of your existence as a Power and which form the first link between the sultan and his Moslem subjects. Go with the times and consider the requirements that this will bring. Put your administration in order, reform it, but do not overthrow it to replace it with forms which are not useful to you and which expose the monarch to the criticism that he does not know the value of what he attacks nor of what he wants to replace it with ... Do not borrow from European civilisation forms that are incompatible with your institutions because the Western institutions are based on principles different from those serving as fundamental to your Empire. The West is based on Christian law; you practice Islam, and you cannot found a Christian society ... We in no way intend to hinder the Porte in the improvement of its administrative system but we advise it not to look for models for these improvements in examples which have nothing common with the conditions of the Turkish Empire; do not in any way imitate those countries whose fundamental legal systems are contrary to the traditions of the Levant; strenuously resist importing into Moslem regions reforms that cannot work other than disruptively because, under the given conditions, they are devoid of all constructive and organisational power."[30]

---

of the Ottoman society based upon Islam and their future in millets. Though he did not desire any significant change in this social structure, he well knew that the sultan should do everything possible for ensuring their satisfaction and, therefore, he advised the Porte: "Give your Christian subjects the most complete protection. Show them real tolerance, do not allow the pashas and subordinate agents to persecute them, do not meddle with their religious affairs, but rather be the sovereign protector of their privileges." Metternich to Esterházy, Vienna, 26 May 1841, HHStA, StA, England 237.

[29] Metternich to Apponyi, Vienna, 26 May 1841, HHStA, StA, Frankreich 322; Sainte-Aulaire to Guizot, Vienna, 19 May 1841, AMAE, CP, Autriche 429.

[30] Metternich to Esterházy, Vienna, 26 May 1841, HHStA, StA, England 237.

This opposition to the blind copying of European examples, however, did not mean that Metternich was totally against the Sublime Porte's turning to the West for inspiration. He only desired that the application of Western achievements be done cautiously and in particular "in a Turkish way, and not in a French, English, Russian or Austrian style."[31] The Ottoman Empire, as he argued, had to "remain Mussulman."[32] He often presented this opinion to Ottoman diplomats residing in Vienna or travelling through that city, not concealing from Mahmud II that it "would be much better to pursue a more traditional path of progress than to lose the affection of his subjects through a mania of innovations and reforms that are for the most part only bad imitations."[33] This statement from early 1836 contained not only advice but also criticism of Mahmud II's reformatory measures. According to Metternich, this sultan had chosen – unfortunately for his empire – the second approach. This negative attitude was the result of a certain disillusion felt by Metternich as well as his diplomats on this topic after almost a decade of Mahmud II's attempts at reform that started after the dissolution of the Janissaries in June 1826.[34]

Metternich's Criticism of Mahmud II's Reforms

Mahmud II hoped to achieve success through his reforms like Mohammed Ali's accomplishments in the land on the Nile or those of Peter the Great, whom he much admired, in Russia a century earlier. He had in common with them the necessity to overcome the opposition of military elites and, like the former after the destruction of the Mamluks and the latter after the suppression of the Streltsy, Mahmud II, after discharging his own military opposition, turned his attention to Europe, where he wanted to gain inspiration for the reconstruction of his weak empire. Nevertheless, he actually fell behind both the men he admired in the results. He certainly had a sincere aspiration to

---

[31] Metternich to Stürmer, Vienna, 3 Dec. 1839, HHStA, StA, Türkei VI, 72. See also Altieri to Lambruschini, Vienna, 4 June 1841, ASV, Arch. Nunz. Vienna 280D.

[32] Metternich to Stürmer, Vienna, 3 Dec. 1839, HHStA, StA, Türkei VI, 72.

[33] Lerchenfeld to Ludwig I of Bavaria, Vienna, 23 Feb. 1836, BHStA, MA, Wien 2406.

[34] Lamb to Palmerston, Vienna, 18 June 1834, TNA, FO 120/145.

renew the bygone splendour of the Ottoman Empire and he was an intelligent man with an interest in the technological progress of the West, which was manifested, for example, by his greater pleasure at presents like globes, models of fortresses, leather teams for the battery horses or military musical instruments rather than gifts usually sent like luxurious fabrics or porcelain, but he lacked a better knowledge of the situation in Europe, which he had never visited in contrast to Peter the Great. This probably explains why he did not understand the real reasons for the technological and economic superiority of the West over the Levant and he presumed that it would be sufficient to adopt some of the achievements of European countries without regard for the different conditions of Ottoman society in order to overcome the enormous differences between the two worlds. Consequently, his policy of centralisation and modernisation showing itself, for example, in the creation of a new regular army and modernised institutions, printing first newspapers, sending Ottoman youths for studies to Europe and founding new schools, establishing a quarantine and introducing vaccination campaigns can hardly be regarded as a complete success, and some historians doubted whether there was any success at all. For example Josef Matuz, Sir Charles Kingsley Webster or Zahra Zakia regarded Mahmud II's reforms as rather superficial.[35] On the other hand, Dutch historian Erik Jan Zürcher denied that they were only "window-dressing" and stopped at "the doorstep of the Porte."[36] British historian Malcolm Edward Yapp seemed to be somewhere between these different opinions,[37] which seems to be the most acceptable opinion because although Mahmud II laid the foundations important for further changes, his reformatory activities were often cosmetic and finally unsuccessful.

At the very beginning, the destruction of the Janissaries raised hopes at the Viennese Chancellery for the start of significant internal improvements going to the heart of the empire's problems. Ottenfels

---

[35] J. Matuz, *Das Osmanische Reich: Grundlinien seiner Geschichte*, Darmstadt 1996, p. 224; Z. Zakia, "The Reforms of Sultan Mahmud II (1808–1839)," K. Çiçek, *The Great Ottoman-Turkish Civilisation, Vol. 1: Politics*, Ankara 2000, p. 424; Webster, *Palmerston*, I, p. 86.

[36] E. J. Zürcher, *Turkey: A Modern History*, London, New York 1998, p. 47.

[37] M. E. Yapp, *The Making of the Modern Near East*, London, New York 1987, p. 108.

believed in the "enormous beneficial effect"[38] of the so-called Auspicious Event and the introduction of the changes necessary for the modernisation of the country, and Gentz seemed to share this optimistic view. Metternich also welcomed the abolishment of this praetorian guard destabilising the internal situation of the country and hoped this would be the step opening the way to the needed reforms, but he was more pessimistic than his colleagues as to the beneficial effect for the regeneration of the Ottoman Empire, and the reports from Austrian as well as other, particularly Prussian, agents in the Near East reinforced his pessimism.[39] As the Austrian and Prussian diplomats in Constantinople concluded between 1826 and 1839, Mahmud II's headlong Westernisation generally manifested itself through the adoption of entirely unnecessary and pointless measures like the orders concerning the implementation of European-style clothing or the shortening of traditional long male beards, which were regarded by the sultan as old-fashioned.[40] At the end of 1835, Stürmer reported: "Everything in the new institutions is sacrificed to ostentation and to appearances; examined closely, their value is reduced to zero ... It is the same thing in the case of new schools. There are professors and instruments, but that is all. The former, almost all foreigners, cannot get anyone to listen to them, and the latter are there only for show. Mushir [Marshal] Ahmed Pasha, going through one of these schools with me some time ago, wanted to show me an electric machine to prove to me that nothing is lacking in these sorts of institutions. It was

---

[38] Ottenfels to Metternich, Constantinople, 22 June 1826, HHStA, StA, Türkei VI, 25.

[39] Metternich to Ottenfels, Vienna, 5 July 1826, HHStA, StA, Türkei VI, 24; Ottenfels to Metternich, Constantinople, 10 and 26 June 1826, HHStA, StA, Türkei VI, 25; Maltzan to Frederick William III, Vienna, 3 and 10 July 1826, GStA PK, HA III, MdA I, 6006; Ottenfels to Gentz, Constantinople, 26 June 1826, Prokesch-Osten, *Zur Geschichte der orientalischen Frage*, p. 134; Gentz to Metternich, Vienna, 15 Aug. 1826, Kronenbitter, p. 293.

[40] Ottenfels to Metternich, Constantinople, 10 March 1829, HHStA, StA, Türkei VI, 36; Stürmer to Metternich, Constantinople, 18 Jan. 1837, HHStA, StA, Türkei VI, 66; Martens to Frederick William III, Constantinople, 31 Dec. 1832, GStA PK, HA III, MdA I, 7272; Königsmarck to Frederick William III, Büyükdere, 26 Aug. 1835, GStA PK, HA III, MdA I, 7276; Königsmarck to Frederick William III, Büyükdere, 5 Oct. 1836, GStA PK, HA III, MdA I, 7278; Königsmarck to Frederick William III, Büyükdere, 4 and 11 Jan. 1837, GStA PK, HA III, MdA I, 7279; A. von Prokesch-Osten, "Über die dermaligen Reformen im türkischen Reiche, 1832," *Kleine Schriften*, V, Stuttgart 1844, p. 401.

pulled out with difficulty from an old cupboard. It was covered with dust and completely broken. He was embarrassed by this and told me: We will fix it."[41] At the same time Stürmer conveyed to the Prussian Envoy in Constantinople, Count Hans Karl Albert von Königsmarck, his conviction that "all the innovations are superficial and do not get at the root of the problem in any way, and being more child's play than real progress according to European civilisation, they are bound to collapse sooner or later."[42] Königsmarck entirely shared this opinion, which is among other ways demonstrated by his ironical appraisal of the reforms made in 1836: "Everything that has been done during the last year [for the Ottoman Empire] to come closer to Europe and civilise itself is limited more or less to the change of the titles Reis Effendi and Kiaya Bey to those of the ministers of foreign affairs and interior with the elevation of their holders to the rank of pasha; the placement of the sultan's portrait in the barracks and the palaces of the admiralty, the Serasker and the Porte; the nominal division of the Empire into six Mushirates (military commands) with the aim of creating a militia; the construction of a bridge between Constantinople and Galata that had to be designated under the denomination 'benefaction of Sultan Mahmud' in order [for those responsible for it] not to be punished; the permission given to the pashas and the prominent dignitaries to travel in a coach with four horses, and the ministers of the second and third class and Ulemas to travel in a coach with two horses; finally, the mintage of coins with the sultan's portrait but which no one has yet dared to put into circulation and of which several pieces should be distributed among the companions of His Highness to judge through their reaction the effect which would be produced in the public by this innovation contradictory to the religious dogmas that would be pointlessly violated again."[43] Mahmud II's preference for appearances sometimes reached absurd proportions, as Königsmarck continued in his criticism: "The personal vanity of the sultan, his weak character and his superficial knowledge attach more to the form than to the substance of things [and] manifest themselves at every step;

---

[41] Stürmer to Metternich, Constantinople, 16 Dec. 1835, HHStA, StA, Türkei VI, 64.

[42] Königsmarck to Frederick William III, Büyükdere, 25 Nov. 1835, GStA PK, HA III, MdA I, 7276.

[43] Königsmarck to Frederick William III, Büyükdere, 4 Jan. 1837, GStA PK, HA III, MdA I, 7279.

they are revealed in the huge wooden edifices that he [Mahmud II] orders to be constructed and that fall into ruin as soon as they are finished, in the fleet anchored along the Bosphorus, where it rots but responds to salutes when shown in public, an ostentation that [Vice-] Admiral Roussin indicated to me last year [1836] as a luxury that France or England would not be rich enough to afford. It is necessary to say how little Sultan Mahmud comes close to Peter the Great with whom he likes to be compared when one sees that during the repairs to the fortification on the Bosphorus he had the walls whitened and crowned with wooden towers on which an immense flag with the imperial insignia was raised, that the parades of his troops, reported in the official newspaper from time to time, consist of him eating and drinking in the barracks with his favourites, waiting for the soldiers under the windows to fire a quantity of powder to make the maximum noise, and that the visits to the shipyards have no other purpose than for him to enjoy the spectacle which is offered by a ship that is launched for the first time at sea."[44]

In particular the Austrian diplomats familiar with the Oriental milieu could not fail to see the problems which Mahmud II had to face when attempting to reform his decaying empire, above all the lack of skilled and educated men and money, and the series of wars with foreign as well as internal enemies. Nevertheless, they were convinced that Mahmud II significantly contributed to some of these impediments not only because of his ignorance but also due to his negative personality traits, for example his impatience to see the results of his reformatory effort during his lifetime, which led to his headlong pursuance of them. Ottenfels remembered a comic story testifying to this trait on the turn of the 1820s. Mahmud II once saw an Austrian captain in a hussar uniform and expressed his desire due to his mania for uniforms to possess a similar one. Metternich strongly supported this request and even recommended to Francis I to send more uniforms of various origins and ranks, which eventually happened. On receiving them, Mahmud II with his typical impatience wanted to see the uniforms immediately, which led to the opening of all the boxes and the unwrapping of all the uniforms and accessories. Since no Ottoman had any experience with them, when one adjutant tried, upon the sultan's order, to put on one of the uniforms, all the pieces were mixed up.

[44] Ibid.

Not until the arrival of an Austrian captain was everything put back in order.[45]

The Austrians regarded the sultan's taste for alcohol as a more serious deficiency in his personality; in fact, this was nothing new in the Moslem world or among the sultans but a serious problem in the case of Mahmud II, who did little to conceal this habit contrary to the precepts of Islam and drank in excess. When he fell seriously ill in the spring of 1839, it did not go unnoticed that his serious condition was considerably deteriorated by a vice taken from the West: inebriety. This blame of the West was in no way unfounded because for Mahmud II drinking alcohol – wine and champagne – really was a symptom of Westernisation and modernity. Furthermore, according to Ottenfels, an important impetus in Mahmud II's liking for alcohol as well as parties was the soirée on the *Blonde*, and in the following months, the sultan openly asked the internuncio for Tokaji and appeared incognito in a masquerade at the internunciature. Ottenfels concluded that under the influence of these habits, in particular the love of alcohol, the sultan's interest in reforms declined during 1830 and later mostly focused on petty reformatory topics instead of the pursuance of the steps in actually important matters.[46] Furthermore, the expenses for alcohol, soirées and the furnishing of the imperial palaces in the European style contributed to the exhaustion of the state treasury at the moment when the country and the reforms needed each piaster.[47]

---

[45] Metternich to Francis I, Vienna, 17 July 1829, HHStA, StK, Vorträge 259; Metternich to Ottenfels, Vienna, 2 Jan. 1830, HHStA, StA, Türkei VI, 51; Metternich to Ottenfels, Vienna, 18 March 1830, HHStA, StA, Türkei VIII, 2; Ottenfels to Metternich, Constantinople, 11 Jan. 1830, HHStA, StA, Türkei VI, 50; Ottenfels, *Memoari*, p. 220.

[46] Metternich to Ottenfels, Vienna, 4 Feb. 1830, Ottenfels to Metternich, Constantinople, 28 Nov. and 10 Dec. 1830, HHStA, StA, Türkei VI, 51; Ottenfels to Metternich, Constantinople, 26 Nov. 1829, HHStA, StA, Türkei VI, 38; Ottenfels to Metternich, Constantinople, 11 Jan., 26 Feb. and 26 July 1830, HHStA, StA, Türkei VI, 50; Stürmer to Metternich, Constantinople, 18, 20, 24 and 26 June 1839, HHStA, StA, Türkei VI, 69; Bockelberg to Frederick William III, Vienna, 30 June 1839, GSta PK, HA III, MdA I, 7346; Ottenfels, *Memoari*, pp. 219–221; F. Georgeon, "Ottomans and Drinkers: The Consumption of Alcohol in Istanbul in the Nineteenth Century," E. Rogan (ed.), *Outside In: On the Margins of the Middle East*, London, New York 2002, pp. 14–16.

[47] Ottenfels to Metternich, Constantinople, 10 July 1832, HHStA, StA, Türkei VI, 54; Stürmer to Metternich, Constantinople, 16 Dec. 1835, HHStA, StA, Türkei VI, 64. For example, in 1836 during the wedding ceremony of one of the sultan's daugh-

Metternich shared this opinion and wrote in October 1830: "The Sultan drinks in the expectation of toasts and he courts the customs of Europe. He is wrong because empires are not civilised by means of parties."[48] And he added in early November: "The Sultan's parties are nothing other than pure agony for me. It is not through toasts that the caliph can hope to reform his empire – that is taking hold of civilisation from completely the wrong end."[49]

Metternich also shared the verdict of various diplomats that Mahmud II's changes generally met with little success, that the old offices were abolished and new institutions founded but that their efficiency remained basically unchanged. The chancellor was becoming more and more convinced that Mahmud II by far did not take advantage of the given opportunity for the reforms to which he had opened the door in the summer of 1826. When Ottenfels wrote to him in early 1830 that "it should suffice us at the moment to know that the Sultan occupies himself without respite to give his Empire the new institutions more in harmony with the needs of his people and the progress of the civilisation that he would like to bestow upon them,"[50] Metternich added in the margin of the report: "I am far from sharing the satisfaction of the internuncio."[51] In the summer of 1832, Metternich wrote to Ottenfels: "The Sultan has destroyed a great deal up to now but we have yet to see him build anything."[52] He continued to express the same scant confidence in Mahmud II's reforms in the following years, and when the sultan died in mid 1839 and left his Empire on the verge of collapse in consequence of a second unsuccessful war with Mohammed Ali, Metternich made this conclusion: "The most serious mistake that he [Mahmud II] committed was, in my opinion, to attach more importance to the form than to the core of matters and to attribute to the *form* the value that he ought to have actually accorded only to the *substance* of his enterprise ... [Moreover,] instead of taking mea-

---

ters the guests could see the tableware made for the sultan in Paris for 680,000 francs. Stürmer to Metternich, Constantinople, 4 and 11 May 1836, HHStA, StA, Türkei VI, 65.

[48] Metternich to Ottenfels, Vienna, 20 Oct. 1830, HHStA, StA, Türkei VI, 51.

[49] Metternich to Ottenfels, Vienna, 2 Nov. 1830, HHStA, StA, Türkei VI, 51.

[50] Ottenfels to Metternich, Constantinople, 11 Jan. 1830, HHStA, StA, Türkei VI, 50.

[51] Ibid.

[52] Metternich to Ottenfels, Baden, 5 Aug. 1832, HHStA, StA, Türkei VI, 56.

sures that perhaps could have been useful if they had been executed
in conformity with the empire's own national style, Mahmud did not
hesitate to implement them in a way that was completely alien."[53] In
brief, Metternich accused Mahmud II, first, of starting but not fin-
ishing generally superficial reforms, in other words of destroying old
institutions without replacing them with new ones, and second, of setting out in the wrong direction or, more precisely, continuing in the
course wrongly set by Selim III when he imitated conditions of the
Western Powers which were inapplicable in the Moslem state.[54] The
chancellor summarised his opinion in his instructions to Stürmer in
March 1841: "The problems which overwhelm this empire are mostly
derived from the untimely reforms which the last Sultans undertook.
A solid structure must be built with high quality materials and upon
a perfectly rational plan. This has not been the case with the factors which have served the reforms in Turkey. Having borrowed from
abroad only useless ideas, everything had to fail because nothing could
respond to what the creators were resolved to do. Every country exists
under conditions which are suitable to it, and where these conditions
do not exist, strictly speaking there exists no country. The religious
law that must form the backbone of every society plays a predominant role in the political structure of the Levant, but because Islam
is neither a creator nor a civiliser, it will not be through changes in
its name or variations in its forms which could lead an empire subject
to the strictures of Islam to either material or moral well-being. If I
were the Sultan, I would seize the religious law and I would try to
make the best of it as far as possible. This is what Mahmud did not
understand and what the present reformers also will not understand.
Consequently, there is actually nothing of significance really to be
done in Turkey and good and evil will always be so closely connected
that the enterprises will fail, not because those who will embark upon
them will not want to do good but because it is not in the nature of
things that they could achieve it."[55]

---

[53] Metternich to Stürmer, Vienna, 3 Dec. 1839, HHStA, StA, Türkei VI, 72.
[54] Metternich to Apponyi, Vienna, 13 July 1839, HHStA, StA, Frankreich 315;
Metternich to Stürmer, Vienna, 30 July 1839, HHStA, StA, Türkei VI, 71; Metternich to Stürmer, Vienna, 26 March 1841, HHStA, StA, Türkei VI, 83; Lamb to
Palmerston, Vienna, 18 June 1834, TNA, FO 120/145; Beauvale to Palmerston,
Vienna, 19 May 1841, TNA, FO 120/197.
[55] Metternich to Stürmer, Vienna, 26 March 1841, HHStA, StA, Türkei VI, 83.

Metternich's opinion of the importance in preserving the Ottoman-Moslem character of the empire and the inappropriateness of automatically applying European forms of government in a culturally different region was naturally reinforced by his conservatism and his struggle against liberalism, which does not mean, however, that it was not based on a good deal of sense. The basic premise about the need to maintain the specific character of the Ottoman Empire seems to be well founded because of the fact that, as pointed out by Carter Vaughn Findley, the three main sources of legal authority of a traditional Islamic state were the Islamic religious-legal tradition, its customs and the will of the sovereign.[56] Sir Charles Kingsley Webster also emphasised the fact that the sultan's power rested on the faith of Islam because "only that gave him undisputed authority over his people and the ascendancy of his people over the races which they [the sultans] had conquered."[57] As to Metternich's warning against blind copying from the West, one may cite historian Afaf Lufti al-Sayyid Marsot: "One cannot import reforms wholesale without any attempt at adjusting them to the specificity and ethos of a country."[58] It is not without interest that a similar view was at that time held by Mohammed Ali, who transformed Egypt into a local power through his reforms. This admirer of Napoleon was convinced that the innovations borrowed from the West ought to be applied in the Levant in compliance with the Ottoman-Moslem tradition, and he declined to copy blindly the modernisations adopted by European countries, adapting them in conformity with local customs. His opinion was noted by a British traveller, Sir John Bowring: "We cannot proceed as fast as we wish, nor do every thing we desire to do. If I were to put on Colonel Campbell's trousers, (looking at the consul-general, who is six feet high,) would that make me as tall as Colonel Campbell?"[59] The same opinion was also declared by Ibrahim Pasha in 1833: "Turkey still possesses in itself seeds of improvement and strength, but they must be well directed. The Porte have [*sic*] taken civilization by the wrong

---

[56] C. V. Findley, *Bureaucratic Reform in the Ottoman Empire: The Sublime Porte, 1789–1922*, Princeton, New Jersey 1980, p. 166.

[57] Webster, *Palmerston*, I, p. 86.

[58] A. Lufti al-Sayyid Marsot, "What Price Reform?" D. Panzac, A. Raymond (eds.), *La France et l'Égypte à l'époque des vice-rois 1805–1882*, Le Caire 2002, p. 7.

[59] Bowring, p. 378.

side; it is not by giving epaulettes and tight trousers to a nation that you begin the task of regeneration ... dress will never make a straight man of one who is lame."[60]

What is even more interesting in connection with Mohammed Ali is the fact that, although Metternich did not conceal his doubts about the abilities of Mahmud II, whom, as the legitimate monarch, he always supported in political matters, he did not hesitate to accord due recognition to the high intelligence, even "unquestionable genius,"[61] and great organisational abilities of the ambitious and sometimes disloyal Mohammed Ali, whom Metternich opposed politically and once even militarily.[62] Despite this antagonism, the chancellor never challenged the Egyptian governor's merits as the regenerator of Egypt, where, in his own words, "the viceroy had done great work."[63] Metternich was convinced that Egypt made "an extraordinary development"[64] due to Mohammed Ali's reforms, and he did not object to the changes that were aimed at the economic growth and bureaucratic efficiency in Egypt, especially when they resulted in Austrian citizens growing rich and did not adversely affect the customs and the faith of Moslems: "More skilful than Sultan Mahmud, he [Mohammed Ali] was able to appropriate the reforms borrowed in Europe without offending Moslem customs or faith; this cleverness made him more powerful than his sovereign."[65] In this respect one must understand Metternich's remark in the margin of the Pradt book where the author stated that at the moment when Western civilisation entered Egypt, "Egypt will fall, with many others, *into the inevitable trap that* [European] *civilisation sets for those who invoke it because,*

---

[60] F. E. Bailey, *British Policy and the Turkish Reform Movement*, London 1942, p. 172.
[61] Metternich to Trauttmannsdorff, Vienna, 19 Feb. 1833, HHStA, StK, Preussen 152.
[62] Metternich to Esterházy, Vienna, 28 Jan. 1830, HHStA, StA, England 191; Metternich to Trauttmannsdorff, Vienna, 19 Feb. 1833, HHStA, StK, Preussen 152; Metternich to Stürmer, Vienna, 18 May 1839, HHStA, StA, Türkei VI, 70; Metternich to Prokesch, Vienna, 12 Dec. 1840, Prokesch-Osten, *Aus dem Nachlasse*, p. 190; Metternich to Prokesch, Vienna, 2 Jan. 1841, Prokesch-Osten, *Aus dem Nachlasse*, p. 207.
[63] Sainte-Aulaire to Soult, Vienna, 18 May 1839, AMAE, CP, Autriche 426.
[64] Metternich to Laurin, Vienna, 12 April 1834, HHStA, StA, Ägypten 1.
[65] Metternich to Stürmer, Vienna, 12 Nov. 1839, HHStA, StA, Türkei VI, 72.

having once entered in its ways, they can never leave it [underlined and commented on by Metternich: 'An excellent observation!'].[66]

This also proves that Metternich was not simply opposed to changes in the Near East, as supposed by historian Muhammad Sabry, who claimed that the new course of reforms pursued in Egypt and Syria contributed to Metternich's antipathy towards Mohammed Ali; it should have been of concern to Metternich that the Egyptian governor "had introduced a new spirit into all Moslem or Christian provinces placed under his authority."[67] A similar but considerably more absurd opinion was also presented by Pierre Crabitès, who declared that Metternich "was the champion of reaction, and was thus bitterly opposed to the Pasha who impersonated the cause of Liberalism."[68] It was not Mohammed Ali's reforms and certainly not his liberalism, which actually never existed, and indeed Metternich never suspected the pasha of such inclination, but rather his disloyalty towards his sovereign that the chancellor denounced. On the contrary, according to Metternich, the reforms pursued by Mohammed Ali in the land on the Nile might well serve as an example for the sultan's larger reformatory efforts, which in fact they did to a considerable extent because Mahmud II undertook many of his reformatory measures in reaction to similar steps made by his Egyptian governor, from the printing of newspapers or the sending of students to Europe to the creation of a modern regular army. The fact that Mohammed Ali's accomplishments always outshone his sovereign's reformatory efforts intensified Mahmud II's hatred towards his Egyptian vassal as well as Metternich's regret that a man of Mohammed Ali's skills was in power in Alexandria and not in Constantinople. Mohammed Ali's achievements clearly manifested that improving the internal situation of the Ottoman Empire was possible, and despite Metternich's rather pessimistic judgements about its internal situation and his opinion that no complete revitalisation was achievable, the success of Mohammed Ali's reforms in Egypt contributed to the optimism about the further existence of the Ottoman Empire that prevailed in Ballhausplatz,

---

[66] D. G. F. D. de Pradt, *L'Intervention armée pour la pacification de la Grèce*, Paris 1828, book number: 37–D–6c (20958), p. 21.
[67] M. Sabry, *L'Empire Égyptien sous Mohamed-Ali et La Question d'Orient (1811–1849)*, Paris 1930, p. 458.
[68] Crabitès, p. 227.

where Metternich insisted that it was not the lack of resources but the inability to exploit them properly that was hampering the sultan's reformatory attempts and that the empire could continue to exist for decades with correctly applied reforms centred on the improvement of the functioning of the entire state apparatus.[69]

*   *   *

It would be rather difficult, if not entirely impossible, to find in European history a statesman of Metternich's importance who paid so much attention to the internal situation of the Ottoman Empire. The diligence with which the Austrian chancellor gathered the relevant information and the passion with which he commented on the internal conditions of this and other states was unique, and his belief in the need to carry out reforms in the Levant definitely was sincere. No other Austrian minister from any earlier or later period was as interested in the topic as Metternich. Of all the Europeans at his level of significance in the first half of the 19th century, only Lord Palmerston dealt with it to a similar degree – although almost exclusively through practical steps such as, for example, sending British military advisors to the Near East; he did not take to theoretical philosophising as did the Austrian chancellor, which was a predictable difference resulting from the rather distinct characters of the two men.[70] Whether Metternich was right in his contemplation is naturally a different issue open to discussion. It is also true that despite his strong criticism, Metternich offered no truly innovative ideas about what could actually be done to regenerate the Ottoman Empire, but it must be said that this was not his duty and that nobody else at the time really had a viable plan either.

---

[69] Metternich to Stürmer, Vienna, 3 Oct. 1833, HHStA, StA, Türkei VI, 59; Metternich to Esterházy, Vienna, 7 Aug. 1839, HHStA, StA, England 225; Metternich to Esterházy, Vienna, 26 May 1841, HHStA, StA, England 237.

[70] F. S. Rodkey, "Lord Palmerston and the Rejuvenation of Turkey, 1830–41: Part I, 1830–39," *JMH* 1, 1929, 4, pp. 570–593; F. S. Rodkey, "Lord Palmerston and the Rejuvenation of Turkey, 1830–41: Part II, 1839–41," *JMH* 2, 1930, 2, pp. 193–225.

What can be noted without hesitation is a certain difference between Metternich's statements and his actions in the problems of foreign interference into the Ottoman reform movement. On the one hand he advised, and he did so sincerely, that the Great Powers should end their disputes over the Near East, and he particularly meant the British-Russian struggle. He told Lamb in August 1836 that "the greatest service we could render the Sultan would be to turn his attention exclusively to the administration of His internal affairs by removing from him the distraction of external politics. That for this purpose it is necessary that the dispute between England and Russia should cease, for that while the Sultan is occupied with the alternate hopes and alarms arising from it, He is kept in a state of excitement highly unfavourable to the gradual and settled march which is requisite to consolidate the reforms in progress in the Interior of His Empire, upon the perfecting of which His future strength must depend."[71] Metternich was convinced that if the Great Powers wanted the survival of the Ottoman Empire, they were to stop considering it to be an arena for their duels which would continue to hinder the implementation of the sultan's reforms.[72] Nevertheless, although he actually desired the removal of the tensions in the relations between the European countries over the Near East thereby assuring peace to Mahmud II, he personally intervened with the sultan's attempts for reforms, in particular in the military sphere, in this way contributing himself to the transformation of this originally internal problem into an object of interest to the European Powers and an issue for their contention through which they attempted to increase their own influence over the Ottoman Empire.

[71] Lamb to Palmerston, Vienna, 5 Aug. 1836, TNA, FO 120/153.
[72] Metternich to Esterházy, Vienna, 26 May 1841, HHStA, StA, England 237; Lamb to Palmerston, Vienna, 5 Aug. 1836, TNA, FO 120/153; Altieri to Lambruschini, Vienna, 4 June 1841, ASV, Arch. Nunz. Vienna 280D.

Ottoman Military Reforms

The improvement of the sultan's armed forces was by far the most attentively observed part of the Ottoman reform movement by the Great Powers. It was in this sphere where they particularly competed for the increase of their influence in the Near East. Metternich was very active in this contest and exerted great effort for the improvement of Austro-Ottoman relations through a share of Austrian military institutions and officers in the education of Ottoman students. At the same time, he was very active in frustrating France's participation in this training process.

The Education of Ottoman Students in Europe

The Ottoman defeats in the war with the Greek insurgents pointed out the urgent need to reform the Ottoman armed forces. The creation of a strong regular army was the primary aim of Mahmud II's reformatory effort launched with full vigour after the dissolution of the Janissary corps in 1826. As well as other reforms, this process also attracted the attention of Austrian and Prussian diplomats whose reports contained the same scepticism as they expressed towards other attempts at the regeneration of the Ottoman Empire; they pointed out the sultan's lack of knowledge in how to achieve this goal. Mahmud II only vaguely understood the art of warfare because he never led his soldiers in battle, but he compensated for this with a taste for manoeuvres and parades. One can but wonder that he was interested more in uniforms and parades than in the practical skills of his soldiers and, that consequently, the military band seemed to be the best trained part of the army, at least in 1829, but this troop never decides battles.[1] The monarch's inexperience would not have mattered if he had been surrounded by skilful and capable advisers familiar with the European art of war and the reasons for its superiority over Ottoman warfare, but this was not Mahmud II's case. One can have but a poor impression of their capability when reading the statement made by the sultan's prominent military advisor and destroyer of the Janissaries, Hüseyin Pasha, to Ottenfels shortly before his departure to the unsuccessful war with Ibrahim Pasha in 1832: "I tell you my excellent friend that I do not understand very much about strategic movements and military manoeuvres. I know well enough how to fight behind ramparts and fortifications, and I believe that I have demonstrated this. But I fear that I will be unable to hold out against the well-trained troops and the skilful manoeuvres of Ibrahim Pasha, who is supported by so many European officers and engineers. However, with God's help I will do my duty, as a good Moslem and loyal servant of His Sovereign must do."[2]

The low opinion of the Ottoman dignitaries' military capabilities held by Ottenfels, Stürmer, several Prussian envoys in the 1820s and 1830s and, consequently, by Metternich,[3] was not particularly caused by the personality of Hüseyin Pasha but another man, who was responsible for military reforms for a long time: Husrev Pasha. He was no supporter of radical changes in Ottoman society, but he did not oppose the reforms in the army of which he was in charge from 1827 to 1836 as its commander-in-chief (serasker). He was also able to influence its structure from March 1838 when he became president of the Supreme Counsel. The main reason for his active role in the military reforms seemed to be his continuing desire to remain in his monarch's favour, but, like his sovereign, he lacked the relevant knowledge. Consequently, he offered rather dubious assistance in the improvements in the Ottoman armed forces. Not only Ottenfels, Stürmer or the

---

[1] Ottenfels to Metternich, Constantinople, 25 April 1828, HHStA, StA, Türkei VI, 33; Ottenfels to Metternich, Constantinople, 14 May 1829, HHStA, StA, Türkei VI, 37; Ottenfels, *Memoari*, p. 207.

[2] Ottenfels, *Memoari*, p. 244.

[3] For all see Ottenfels to Metternich, Constantinople, 14 May 1829, HHStA, StA, Türkei VI, 37; Malaguzziny to Metternich, Vienna, 19 April 1830, HHStA, StA, Türkei VI, 17; Königsmarck to Frederick William III, Büyükdere, 4 April and 8 Aug. 1838, GStA PK, HA III, MdA I, 7280; Königsmarck to Frederick William III, Büyükdere, 6 Nov. 1839, GStA PK, HA III, MdA I, 7281.

Prussian representatives in Constantinople but also Guilleminot, who was on good terms with this pro-French Ottoman dignitary, depicted Husrev as a servile charlatan and opportunist courting favour with Mahmud II and doing nothing that was useful for the military reforms but only whatever was pleasing to the sultan, supporting in this manner the ostentatious improvements useful during parades but of little value in real combat.[4] According to Ottenfels, "Serasker Husrev Pasha only sees things from the point of view of a courtesan, that is to say, for ways to please his sovereign and increase his own credit. It is he who is the principal reason that since the restoration of peace [in Adrianople], military reforms have been reduced to frequent, often tiny changes in uniforms and equipment, but almost no institution or measure of any real usefulness has been put into effect."[5] Königsmarck described Husrev's character and actions with similarly unflattering words: "In all seasons and in all weathers he [Husrev Pasha] is seen travelling around Constantinople, the Bosphorus and its environs, in a boat, on a horse, in a coach, on foot; he is everywhere and he meddles with everything. But with all this activity he only touches on matters without going any further into any of them; he starts everything but he finishes nothing. A skilful courtier, he would always like to have something new and pleasing to tell his master, to submit some new inventions to him, to propose improvements in military organisation or civil administration, but he abandons his projects, however wise or beneficial they may be, as soon as he notices that they no longer amuse the fickle humour of His Highness. The serasker only

---

[4]   Ottenfels to Metternich, Constantinople, 26 March 1829, HHStA, StA, Türkei VI, 36; Ottenfels to Metternich, Constantinople, 14 May and 5 Sept. 1829, HHStA, StA, Türkei VI, 37; Ottenfels to Metternich, Constantinople, 10 May 1830, HHStA, StA, Türkei VI, 50; Stürmer to Metternich, Constantinople, 30 March 1833, HHStA, StA, Türkei VI, 57; Miltitz to Frederick William III, Pera, 10 May 1823, GStA PK, HA III, MdA I, 7257; Miltitz to Frederick William III, Pera, 10 Feb. 1827, GStA PK, HA III, MdA I, 7264; Stiepovich [?] to Royer, Pera, 22 June 1829, GStA PK, HA III, MdA I, 7267; Königsmarck to Frederick William III, Büyükdere, 28 March 1838, GStA PK, HA III, MdA I, 7279; Königsmarck to Frederick William III, Büyükdere, 26 June 1839, GStA PK, HA III, MdA I, 7281; Guilleminot to Polignac, Constantinople, 25 June 1830, AMAE, CP, Turquie 261.
[5]   Ottenfels to Metternich, Constantinople, 25 Feb. 1830, HHStA, StA, Türkei VI, 50.

takes matters seriously for as long as they flatter the vanity of the Sultan."[6]

The view of Husrev Pasha as a servile opportunist who needed to be seen as an ardent reformer in order to maintain his power was an entirely correct opinion, as has been shown by historians Virginia Aksan, Mesut Uyar or Edward J. Erickson.[7] His negative influence over the pursuance of changes in the Ottoman army, together with the lack of *savoir-faire* of other Ottomans and their liking for intrigues, their ignorance of the real reasons for the technological, economic and military superiority of the West over the Levant, and the monarch's impatience often contributed to the incorrect and insufficient reforms in the Ottoman army. This opinion was not only held by German-speaking diplomats but, for example, also by French General Lieutenant Count Osery, who was a hero of the Napoleonic Wars, in which he lost an arm, and a brother-in-law of Marshal Jean Victor Marie Moreau. In the spring of 1829 Osery had stayed in Constantinople, where Austria had supported his employment in the Ottoman army, which finally did not happen owing to Moreau's family's good relations with the tsar who was waging war with the sultan during that period.[8] Osery discussed the conditions of the Ottoman armed forces with Ottenfels; his views were identical to those of Austrian and Prussian diplomats or those of the Prussian officer serving in the Ottoman army later in the 1830s and achieving splendid glory in the European battlefields later in the century, Helmuth von Moltke.[9] Osery was very critical of reforms and, for example, he could not understand why at that time the excellent Ottoman cavalry had been restructured according to the European model and had thus lost many of the characteristics that had previously made this component of the sultan's army a re-

---

[6] Königsmarck to Frederick William III, Büyükdere, 19 Oct. 1836, GStA PK, HA III, MdA I, 7278.

[7] M. Uyar, E. J. Erickson, *A Military History of the Ottomans: From Osman to Atatürk*, Santa Barbara, Denver, Oxford 2009, p. 134; Aksan, p. 377.

[8] Metternich to Ottenfels, Vienna, 3 April 1829, HHStA, StA, Türkei VI, 39; Ottenfels to Metternich, Constantinople, 25 May 1829, HHStA, StA, Türkei VI, 37; Cowley to Aberdeen, Vienna, 30 May 1829, TNA, FO 120/100; Cowley to Aberdeen, Vienna, 15 June 1829, TNA, FO 120/101.

[9] For all these views see Königsmarck to Frederick William III, Büyükdere, 25 Nov. 1835, GStA PK, HA III, MdA I, 7276; Königsmarck to Frederick William III, Büyükdere, 5 Oct. 1836, GStA PK, HA III, MdA I, 7278; Königsmarck to Frederick William III, Büyükdere, 4 Jan. 1837, GStA PK, HA III, MdA I, 7279.

spected enemy even among the Cossacks: "The Turkish cavalry was one of the best units of the Ottoman Empire; it always was superior to the Russian cavalry; what it lacked was good direction and to be effectively employed. Instead of leaving it as it was and adding brave and intelligent officers who would know how to lead it into combat where it could offer useful and decisive service, attempts have been made to transform it into a European cavalry and to replace their [the Ottomans'] traditional Turkish or Cossack saddles to which they have been accustomed since their childhood with saddles of European style with stirrups in which they do not know how to remain seated."[10] Although these words are hard to believe, their validity were confirmed by Count Orlov staying in Constantinople on the turn of 1829, who, after seeing a military parade of the Ottoman cavalry organised after the European fashion, told Ottenfels that several riders unable to remain in their new saddles had fallen off their horses: "I would desire to know the name of the foreign instructor in charge of the exercises of these troops in order to be able to propose to the emperor [tsar] that he should decorate him with one of his medals because he has taught the Turks to fall off their horses, which would not have happened if they had ridden on their traditional saddles."[11] Metternich agreed with Osery's criticism: "I admit, although with much regret, the correctness of the observations of this general, and I share his fear that the Sultan will waste in futile military trivialities some of the precious time that remains to him for working on the rescue of his Empire."[12] And at the end of the Russo-Ottoman war, the chancellor expressed the opinion that he often stated in connection with the Ottoman reform movement in general: "What the course of military events proves is that the Turks, while having renounced their old system of war, possess neither the time nor knowledge necessary to create a new one."[13]

The foreign training of the Ottoman troops mentioned by Orlov is important because it points to one of the most serious problems concerning the new Ottoman regular army – the lack of well trained

[10] Ottenfels to Metternich, Constantinople, 14 May 1829, HHStA, StA, Türkei VI, 37.

[11] Ottenfels, *Memoari*, p. 222.

[12] Metternich to Esterházy, Vienna, 30 May 1829, HHStA, StA, England 187.

[13] Metternich to Ottenfels, Plass, 30 Aug. 1829, HHStA, StA, Türkei VI, 39.

officers. Mahmud II, who often declared that "one of my eyes is fixed
on my son, the other on my soldiers,"[14] was well aware of this fact.
He had two possibilities with regard to the training of his troops:
to send Ottoman cadets to European military schools or train them
in schools that would be established in his empire and led by European military instructors. He finally decided to adopt both methods,
which, however, attracted the attention of some European Powers.
Austria was fully involved in it from the very beginning in late 1829
when Mahmud II occupied himself with the project to send Ottoman
students to France to obtain a technical and military education. He
was influenced by the news of Egyptian students having been successfully sent to France by Mohammed Ali some years before.[15] With
his characteristic impatience, Mahmud II wanted to follow the example of his powerful Egyptian vassal as soon as possible and was
strongly supported in this plan by Husrev Pasha. Mahmud II took
it a step further, wanting to send the students not only to France
but also to Great Britain and Austria. His Private Secretary Mustafa
Bey discussed this topic with Ottenfels, who readily assured the Ottoman dignitary about the readiness of Austria to satisfy the request.
This was completely true because the Viennese cabinet was more than
willing to welcome Ottoman students. In Metternich's and Ottenfels'
opinion, Vienna was an ideal place for the young Ottomans to obtain
a solid education without the danger of being influenced by what they
considered to be improper ideas. Francis I did not hesitate to offer his
capital for this purpose, and Ottenfels was instructed in early January
1830 to convey the proposal to the sultan's court.[16]

---

[14] Malaguzziny to Metternich, Vienna, 19 April 1830, HHStA, StA, Türkei VI,
17.

[15] A little known fact is that three students were also sent by Mohammed Ali
to Upper Carniola (Oberkrain) in the Austrian Empire, now in Slovenia, in 1831
to learn skills in the textile industry. Ibrahim Pasha's letter, Cairo, 1831, Arhiv
Republike Slovenije, AS 1080, Zbirka muzejskega društva za Kranjsko, š. 1, fasc. 2
Orientalica, učna pisma 7, pismo Ibrahima iz Kaira.

[16] Metternich to Ottenfels, Vienna, 2 Jan. 1830, HHStA, StA, Türkei VI, 51;
Ottenfels to Metternich, Constantinople, 10 Dec. 1829, HHStA, StA, Türkei VI,
49; Ottenfels to Metternich, Constantinople, 25 Jan. 1830, HHStA, StA, Türkei
VI, 50; Malaguzziny to Metternich, Vienna, 19 April 1830, HHStA, StA, Türkei
VI, 17; Royer to Frederick William III, Pera, 12 Jan. 1830, GStA PK, HA III,
MdA I, 7269.

The proposal was sincerely meant, but its main goal undoubtedly was to offer an alternative to the idea of sending Ottoman students to France, which did not please the cabinet in Vienna. Although Metternich supported the idea of acquainting young Ottomans with the sciences as studied and practiced by Europeans, he criticised the choice of the destination and considered it one of the many mistakes frequently committed by the sultan in his effort to reform his declining empire. France was for him the worst possible choice because he was convinced that the French Revolution of 1789 had dealt a deep blow to French society and had precipitated a state of moral anarchy from which it never fully recovered. To the contrary, perfidious theories again gained strength in this "unfortunate country"[17] that he considered as "a lost land (as far as lands can be) and a ceaseless source of misfortune for the whole of Europe."[18] It is not surprising that he regarded French diplomacy as revolutionary and its principle goal "to introduce disorder, disorganisation and to facilitate disruption in all parts of the civilised world!"[19] Consequently, he considered France to be the enemy not only of Austria but also of all conservative Europe and that it was necessary for him to watch it vigilantly and steadily, and he did so not only in the troubled waters of the German Confederation and the Apennines but also in the Ottoman Empire, where he scrutinised French activity and worked to diffuse its influence in the region, at least in the 1830s. Although he was unable to reduce French influence in Mohammed Ali's Egypt, he tried to achieve this in Constantinople where he could expect better results due to his own prestige.[20]

---

[17] Metternich to Apponyi, Königswart, 31 Dec. 1827, HHStA, StA, Frankreich 265.

[18] Rodkey, *Turco-Egyptian Question*, p. 132.

[19] Metternich to Apponyi, Vienna, 9 March 1834, HHStA, StA, Frankreich 293.

[20] From a considerable number of documents containing Metternich's negative opinion of France and its society see Metternich to Apponyi, Vienna, 16 Dec. 1829, HHStA, StA, Frankreich 271; Metternich to Apponyi, Vienna, 8 Jan. 1833, HHStA, StA, Frankreich 289; Metternich to Apponyi, Vienna, 17 Sept. 1834, HHStA, StA, Frankreich 294; Metternich to Apponyi, Vienna, 9 July 1838, HHStA, StA, Frankreich 311; Metternich to Esterházy, Vienna, 10 Dec. 1833, HHStA, StA, England 204; Metternich to Esterházy, Vienna, 5 Dec. 1840, HHStA, StA, England 231; Metternich to Ficquelmont, Vienna, 14 June 1840, HHStA, StA, Russland III, 120; Maltzan to Frederick William IV, Vienna, 28 April 1841, GStA PK, HA III, MdA I, 6034.

Because of the revolution and because of Napoleon himself, Metternich considered France to be a country corrupted by dubious ideas, which, if brought back to Constantinople by students influenced by those ideas, could disrupt the government and society and potentially damage the Ottoman Empire, which could become a theatre of revolution. The earlier sending of young men by Mohammed Ali was already regarded in Vienna as such a threat. Consequently, the chancellor instructed Ottenfels in early January 1830 to forestall the French aspect of the project and did not forget to mention a month later that "sending men to us will always be less dangerous for the Porte than dispatching them to other places. The young Turks, like the officers, will find in our country a useful direction or, what is equal, a Mohammedan direction."[21] In this respect, Ottenfels skilfully acquitted his task. He had often opposed the sultan's intention to send young Ottomans to France for training before the arrival of Metternich's January instructions, and these provided him with the additional needed support for his objections. Consequently, he succeeded in persuading the Porte not to send Ottoman students to France. Nevertheless, this was merely a short-term diplomatic success because the young Ottomans were finally sent to France, Great Britain and Prussia in 1835. Furthermore, Husrev manifested his pro-French inclinations with his own private initiative when sending several young Turks from his own household to France in the early 1830s.[22]

As for sending the young men to Austria, the emperor's offer was accepted positively by the sultan and his retinue but it was not put into effect until the mid 1830s when five Ottoman cadets were sent to Vienna for training in the Technical Military Academy (*K. k. Ingenieurakademie*) situated in the building of the Savoy Riding Academy (*Laimgrube*). They formed, in Metternich's words, some-

---

[21] Metternich to Ottenfels, Vienna, 3 Feb. 1830, HHStA, StA, Türkei VI, 51.
[22] Metternich to Ottenfels, Vienna, 2 Jan. 1830, HHStA, StA, Türkei VI, 51; Ottenfels to Metternich, Constantinople, 25 Jan. 1830, HHStA, StA, Türkei VI, 50; Guilleminot to Maison, Constantinople, 16 and 24 Dec. 1830, AMAE, CP, Turquie 261; Varenne to Sébastiani, Therapia, 10 Nov. 1831, AMAE, CP, Turquie 262; Gentz to Metternich, Vienna, 12 Aug. 1826, Kronenbitter, p. 284; K. Kreiser, "Türkische Studenten in Europa," G. Höpp (ed.), *Fremde Erfahrungen: Asiaten und Afrikaner in Deutschland, Österreich und in der Schweiz bis 1945*, Berlin 1996, pp. 385–400; N. Berkes, *The Development of Secularism in Turkey*, Montreal 1964, p. 128; Uyar, Erickson, p. 146.

thing like an "Ottoman Military Academy"[23] under the direction of Captain Franz von Hauslab, an extraordinarily learned absolvent of the same Academy, who was an instructor at this institute and who had also been the personal educator of Archduke Charles' children since 1833 and the next emperor, Francis Joseph I, after 1843. Hauslab had lived in Constantinople for two years, learnt Turkish and later visited the city to personally bring the students to the Austrian capital. The young men arriving in the city on the Danube in the years 1834 and 1837 finally graduated from the Academy and, moreover, demonstrated many skills and abilities.[24] This is proved by their very good school work and exam results as well as the report about their education written some months after Mahmud II's death by Lerchenfeld, in late November 1839: "Of all the measures that the late sultan [Mahmud II] undertook for the civilisation of his nation, the sending of young people abroad for their studies and to learn the military sciences has been the most successful. Many young Turks sent by their

[23] Metternich to Mustafa Reshid Pasha, Vienna, 10 Nov. 1840, HHStA, StA, Türkei VIII, 20. This denomination or a similar one used by Stürmer in 1841, the "Turkish Military School in Vienna," was found in more studied sources. However, it is difficult to say whether such a school or, better said, something like a department in the Technical Military Academy was actually established in Vienna. Stürmer to Metternich, Constantinople, 12 May 1841, HHStA, StA, Türkei VIII, 16.

[24] The arrival of the first group seems to be in 1834 because already at the very beginning of 1835, the first results of their education were received by Mahmud II. Ottenfels to Metternich, Constantinople, 11 Jan. 1830, HHStA, StA, Türkei VI, 50; Metternich to Stürmer, Vienna, 17 Sept. 1834, HHStA, StA, Türkei VIII, 24; Stürmer to Metternich, Constantinople, 11 Feb. 1835, HHStA, StA, Türkei VIII, 8; Stürmer to Metternich, Büyükdere, 5 July 1837, HHStA, StA, Türkei VI, 66; Mavroyéni to Metternich, Vienna, 23 Oct. 1837, HHStA, StA, Türkei VIII, 10; Königsmarck to Frederick William III, Büyükdere, 21 July 1835, GStA PK, HA III, MdA I, 7275; Königsmarck to Frederick William III, Pera, 30 Dec. 1835, GStA PK, HA III, MdA I, 7276; Königsmarck to Frederick William III, Pera, 17 Feb. 1836, GStA PK, HA III, MdA I, 7277; Lerchenfeld to Ludwig I of Bavaria, Vienna, 29 Nov. 1839, BHStA, MA, Wien 2408; Ottenfels, *Memoari*, p. 224. Just a few words on the topic of the Ottoman students' military studies in Vienna can be found in these books, unfortunately with some factual errors: M. Brunner, H. Kerchnawe, *225 Jahre Technische Militärakademie 1717 bis 1942*, Wien 1942, p. 44; F. Gatti, *Geschichte der k. u. k. Technischen Militär-Akademie, Band I: Geschichte der k. k. Ingenieur- und k. k. Genie-Akademie 1717–1869*, Wien 1901, p. 554; H. Schalk, *250 Jahre militärtechnische Ausbildung in Österreich*, Wien 1968, p. 101.

government are here to experience military service and master the art of war. These young men do the service together with the troops. They ride in the ranks, command the drills of their platoons in Turkish uniforms, and distinguish themselves with their zeal and their diligence. Last autumn during an artillery exercise these young Turks operated their cannon and fired with such an accuracy that assured them the praise of all the senior officers. In the examination at the school of artillery, the professor of astronomy, Mr Littrow, invited to assist, gave them some very difficult problems, which they solved perfectly. There are some students among them who are attending the technical school and who are making very good progress. All these students speak German and French and they can be often seen at the theatre."[25] Lerchenfeld's favourable evaluation reflected the positive attitude of the Austrian elites involved in the project towards the practice of sending Ottoman students to the Austrian Empire. For example, Archduke Johann told the same Bavarian envoy in late 1837: "If thirty military cadets are sent to Vienna for training, they will be sufficient in number in a few years to organise and discipline several exemplary battalions. These in their turn would instruct other officers and non-commissioned officers, who could be later deployed in different regiments. The adoption of this system will lead to good results. The young Turkish officers who stay here for their education for a couple of years effectively display the best motivation and natural abilities. They take part in the training of the troops, they even command the platoons, in a word they seek to educate themselves, and some of them already speak German well enough to be able to enjoy theatrical performances."[26]

There is no reason to doubt that this view was sincere, but the effort to bring more students under Austria's supervision was undoubtedly increased by the opportunity this would give Austria to have the influence that it could later exert through them in the Ottoman

[25] Lerchenfeld to Ludwig I of Bavaria, Vienna, 29 Nov. 1839, BHStA, MA, Wien 2408.
[26] Lerchenfeld to Ludwig I of Bavaria, Vienna, 31 Dec. 1837, BHStA, MA, Wien 2407. The improvement in German was also due to the fact that the Ottoman students frequently met with the scholars from the Oriental Academy, both groups improving their knowledge of foreign, German and Turkish languages. V. W. E. von Starkenfels, *Die kaiserlich-königliche Orientalische Akademie zu Wien: Ihre Gründung, Fortbildung und Gegewärtige Einrichtung*, Wien 1839, p. 37.

Empire. Leopold von Haan, who accompanied Archduke Johann to Constantinople in October 1837, explained the reasons for such an expectation: "There have to be future political benefits for the state where such people are trained because next to the love for one's native country there also remains the affection for the country where one was educated."[27] Metternich was naturally well aware of this fact, which is evident in the attention he paid to the presence of the Ottoman cadets in Vienna and the supervising role of Hauslab, who was the man who deserved the greatest merit for the cadets' swift progress. Unsurprisingly, Mahmud II rewarded him in early 1835 with words of praise and a box ornamented with diamonds, and when Hauslab was promoted to a squadron leader and his duties were to take him away from Vienna, Metternich intervened and ensured his continued tutorial role at the Academy with a higher rank because Hauslab was in a position to play an important role in the Porte's decision-making whether to send more cadets to Austria. Consequently, when Johann announced during his stay in Constantinople in 1837 that Austria was prepared to receive further Ottoman cadets, Hauslab was already a member of the archduke's retinue and probably contributed to Mahmud II's decision to send another group of six young Ottomans to Vienna for a military education. Hauslab personally escorted them from Constantinople on 27 November. This perfectly dovetailed into the policy pursued by Metternich, who continued to attach importance to the presence of Ottoman students, paid personal attention to their studies and encouraged the increase in their number in following years. He repeatedly advised the Porte to take advantage of the functional "institution" producing capable officers.[28] He repeated

---

[27] V. von Haan (ed.), *Erzherzog Johann von Österreich, Leopold von Haan: Eine russisch-türkische Reise im Jahre 1837*, Wien 1998, p. 184.
[28] Metternich to Stürmer, Vienna, 3 March 1835, Stürmer to Metternich, Constantinople, 11 Feb. 1835, HHStA, StA, Türkei VIII, 8; Metternich to Rifaat Bey, Vienna, 28 July 1838, HHStA, StA, Türkei VIII, 24; Metternich to Mustafa Reshid Pasha, Vienna, 10 Nov. 1840, HHStA, StA, Türkei VIII, 20; Metternich to Stürmer, Vienna, 10 Nov. 1840, Ahmed Fethi Pasha to Metternich, Constantinople, 8 Dec. 1840, HHStA, StA, Türkei VIII, 15; Stürmer to Metternich, Constantinople, 11 Oct. 1837, HHStA, StA, Türkei VI, 66; Mavroyéni to Metternich, Vienna, 23 Oct. 1837, Stürmer to Metternich, Constantinople, 29 Nov. 1837 HHStA, StA, Türkei VIII, 10; Stürmer to Metternich, Constantinople, 1 July, 23 Sept. and 25 Nov. 1840, HHStA, StA, Türkei VIII, 14; Königsmarck to Frederick William III, Büyükdere, 29 Nov. 1837, GStA PK, HA III, MdA I, 7279;

in 1840 what he had stated ten years earlier, namely that the cadets sent to Vienna would return home "as good Moslems, well-trained and competent in all kinds of service that one would want to assign them. They will not introduce into their homeland fantastic ideas incompatible with the spirit and customs of the country. These men will know what is useful and practical and nothing in their way of thinking will be altered."[29]

The Employment of European Officers in the Ottoman Army

According to Metternich, Archduke Johann and most of other Austrians involved in the project, the Ottoman students' studies abroad were much more useful than the employment of foreigners in the Ottoman army. This view was also shared by Moltke and Prince August of Prussia, the latter staying in Constantinople for a while at the same time as Johann. Prince August stated in his essay on the Ottoman army written in late 1837 or early 1838 that the Prussian officers functioning in the sultan's service at that time were entirely insufficient for the implementation of useful reforms, that increasing the number of foreign officers would not prove more successful, for example owing to the language barrier, and that sending young Ottomans to Europe was far more reasonable.[30] However, Mahmud II was of a different opinion and he also wished to improve his army through the knowledge and skills of European officers employed in his service; the hiring of foreigners was to compensate for his shortage of educated experts. As well as in the case of the plan to send young Ottomans to Europe, the idea of a foreign military mission in the Ottoman Empire also had its Egyptian example. The employment of French officers by Mohammed

---

B. Sutter, "Die Reise Erzherzog Johanns 1837 nach Russland, Konstantinopel und Athen," W. Koschatzky (ed.), *Thomas Ender (1793–1875)*, Wien 1964, p. 38; Haan, pp. 201–202.

[29] Metternich to Mustafa Reshid Pasha, Vienna, 10 Nov. 1840, HHStA, StA, Türkei VIII, 20.

[30] August Prince of Prussia, *Mémoire sur l'organisation de l'armée Ottomane*, attached to Klezl to Metternich, Büyükdere, 30 May 1838, HHStA, StA, Türkei VI, 67; E. Kessel, *Moltke*, Stuttgart 1957, p. 120.

Ali had proved itself to be beneficial and the Egyptian troops trained by them demonstrated their superiority over the Turkish troops in the battles in 1832. Although some French and Italian officers, particularly those of lower ranks without the knowledge necessary for the vast reforms, had already been employed in the Ottoman army, their impact on the troops to which they were detached with limited powers was extremely questionable. Consequently, in the mid 1830s, Mahmud II decided to follow Mohammed Ali's example again, this time in hiring a larger number of French officers. He planned to send them to the Turkish Military Academy in Constantinople established in 1834, in other words to ask for a French military mission. The Ottoman plenipotentiary in Paris, Mustafa Reshid Bey, was instructed to discuss this matter with the French government. This was the revival of a project of the former French ambassador in Constantinople, Count Guilleminot, from 1830 known to Metternich. In that year, the high costs of the proposed academy for 200–300 students and the counterarguments of Count Orlov seemed to lead the Porte to put the plan on hold. Four years later, Husrev Pasha revived the idea, attaching great importance to it. As Metternich learnt, the Porte planned to hire thirty French officers: fifteen for the training of the regular army and fifteen for training the imperial guard.[31]

Metternich was naturally not indifferent to this project. He had no objection to the Porte seeking such assistance if it was well considered. If it were not, however, it could pose a serious problem because it was important not only which reforms were carried out but also by whom; and according to Metternich, many changes harmful to Ottoman society had been blindly copied from the West simply for the reason that they were advised by a "crowd of adventurers,"[32] to whom Sultan Mahmud II imprudently opened the door in his reformatory enthusiasm and whom he allowed to infiltrate the machinery of the Ottoman administration.[33] Metternich expressed strong criticism re-

---

[31] Metternich to Stürmer, Vienna, 7 Jan. and 13 March 1835, HHStA, StA, Türkei VI, 64; Nesselrode to Butenev, St Petersburg, 3 Feb. 1835, HHStA, StA, Türkei VI, 63; Guilleminot to Polignac, Constantinople, 24 July 1830, AMAE, CP, Turquie 261; A. Levy, "The Officer Corps in Sultan Mahmud II's New Ottoman Army, 1826–1839," *IJMES* 2, 1971, 1, p. 24; Findley, *Bureaucratic Reform*, p. 134.
[32] Metternich to Stürmer, Vienna, 16 March 1841, HHStA, StA, Türkei VI, 83.
[33] Ibid.; Beauvale to Palmerston, Vienna, 13 April and 7 Aug. 1841, TNA, FO 120/197.

garding the unsystematic nature of the employment of Europeans; he disliked the fact that people of various opinions had been assembled to work on one objective, which had negative consequences particularly in the creation of a new regular army that lacked homogeneity because it was trained by Prussians, French and Italians: "The Porte has soldiers and officers kitted out more or less in the European style, but it no longer has an army because having destroyed the old Ottoman army, it had no idea how to replace it with a new one."[34] The fate of Ottoman troops in the wars of the studied period as well as later research on this topic gave some validity to Metternich's criticism.[35]

The commitment of the French officers only to the creation of a regular and disciplined army found little favour with Metternich, namely for two principal reasons. First, it would considerably strengthen France's influence in the Bosphorus. Something similar had already happened in Egypt, where France increased its influence by placing French personnel in Mohammed Ali's service. Metternich worried that France could achieve similar success in Constantinople. This concern was often intensified by his diplomats like Ottenfels in 1831 writing about some foreign officers of lesser ranks in the Ottoman service: "A considerable number of French and Italian officers, who have wormed their way into the Turkish troops as instructors and of whom almost all are members of Napoleon's party, already form a kind of advance guard of spies which could be soon followed by others more capable of doing harm. These individuals will offer to lead the Turks against the Russians, the Austrians or any other Great Power hostile to France."[36] Second, Metternich complained of the foreigners' problematic character, in other words their liberal thinking with little respect for the specifics of the Levant, which could have fatal consequences for the sultan's empire. He considered the ambition of some of them to gain the fortune they were unable to secure at home to be as dangerous as their desire to spread the world-saving visions inapplicable in a culturally different milieu.[37] He maintained that the ruin of the Ottoman Empire would be inevitable if it were to be left to "all

---

[34] Metternich to Stürmer, Vienna, 3 Dec. 1839, HHStA, StA, Türkei VI, 72.
[35] Levy, pp. 21–39.
[36] Ottenfels to Metternich, Constantinople, 26 March 1831, HHStA, StA, Türkei VI, 52.
[37] Metternich to Stürmer, Vienna, 3 Dec. 1839, HHStA, StA, Türkei VI, 72; Metternich to Stürmer, Vienna, 16 March 1841, HHStA, StA, Türkei VI, 83.

who under the pretext of bringing benefits worked in fact only towards its disruption,"[38] and the French were those whom he feared above all in this respect. He was concerned that the uniforms of the French instructors concealed individuals propagating revolutionary ideas and subversive dogmas: "The peace and tranquillity of the capital of the Ottoman Empire could be jeopardised due to such a large number of French officers among whom, one must admit, there will be some who, in the guise of instructors, will try to spread revolutionary ideas and beliefs subversive to the existing order in Turkey."[39]

From his conservative point of view, Metternich had some reasons for apprehension because the foreigners in the Ottoman Empire, actually the French above all, like Dr. Barrachin and Alexandre Blacque in Constantinople and most of the French in Alexandria, were among the supporters of the intellectual thoughts he opposed. Historian Raouf Abbas wrote about the latter: "Most of the French personnel recruited by Muhammad Aly [*sic*] were servants of the First Empire, trained and influenced by the traditions of the French Revolution and the epoch of Napoleon,"[40] a fact known to Metternich and which he could only view unfavourably. There were not only the liberals he disliked, but also, for example, the adherents of Saint-Simonianism, mostly the French again, who went to the Near East to spread their visions of utopian socialism. Whereas their group was promptly expelled by Mahmud II from Constantinople in 1833 due to their offensive behaviour, they found better conditions for their activities in Mohammed Ali's Egypt, where altogether 81 of them came in the period 1833–1834.[41] Metternich was displeased with their presence in the land on the Nile but there was nothing he could do about it. However, he did not want to allow the spread of various ideas threatening the order and tranquillity of the Ottoman Empire at its very heart and, therefore, he

---

[38] Canitz to Frederick William IV, Vienna, 29 Nov. 1841, GStA PK, HA III, MdA I, 7363.
[39] Metternich to Esterházy, Vienna, 14 March 1835, HHStA, StA, England 214.
[40] R. Abbas, "French Impact on the Egyptian Educational System under Muhammad Aly and Ismail," D. Panzac, A. Raymond (eds.), *La France et l'Égypte à l'époque des vice-rois 1805–1882*, Le Caire 2002, p. 92.
[41] Stürmer to Metternich, Constantinople, 25 April 1833, HHStA, StA, Türkei VIII, 5; S. Moussa, "Les saint-simoniens en Égypte: le cas d'Ismayl Urban," D. Panzac, A. Raymond (eds.), *La France et l'Égypte à l'époque des vice-rois 1805–1882*, Le Caire 2002, pp. 225–233; Fargette, p. 93; Gaultier-Kurhan, pp. 157–162.

extended his own struggle against the "perfidious theories" and those who brought them from the West to Constantinople and he ordered Stürmer to forestall the employment of the French officers in the Military Academy in early January 1835. At the same time, he informed the Russian cabinet about this plan with the goal of securing its support, which was not too difficult given Nicholas I's shared antipathy towards France. In a letter to Butenev, Nesselrode opposed the employment of the French in the Military Academy and presumed that the Russian ambassador had surely cooperated with Stürmer "over the best measures to employ for preventing the execution of a project with which we disagree with the same force and for the same reason as the court in Vienna."[42] Metternich's determination to forestall the project was strengthened on learning of the identical attitude of the tsar's court, and he even asked for the support of conservative British Prime Minister the Duke of Wellington, who expressed his regret of the Porte's one-sided pro-French orientation in this affair even though nothing indicates that he wished to become involved with the matter.[43]

Husrev Pasha and some other Ottoman dignitaries denied the existence of the project and assured Stürmer that they understood the danger in young Ottomans being instructed in the Academy led by French officers. In contrast, Akif Effendi recognised its existence but declared he was against it. Akif was in good relations with Stürmer and Butenev and it was he who helped them to persuade the Divan at the beginning of March 1835 to devise new instructions for Mustafa Reshid Bey. According to these instructions, if Reshid still had not made any arrangement concerning the delegation of the French professors and officers to Constantinople, he was to quietly abandon the plan. In the event that a preliminary agreement had been arranged,

---

[42] Nesselrode to Butenev, St Petersburg, 3 Feb. 1835, HHStA, StA, Türkei VI, 63.

[43] Metternich to Stürmer, Vienna, 7 Jan. and 13 March 1835, HHStA, StA, Türkei VI, 64; Metternich to Ficquelmont, Vienna, 10 Jan. and 13 March 1835, HHStA, StA, Russland III, 105; Metternich to Ficquelmont, Vienna, 16 April 1836, SOA, RA C-A 383; Metternich to Esterházy, Vienna, 14 March 1835, HHStA, StA, England 214; Esterházy to Metternich, London, 27 March 1835, HHStA, StA, England 209; Ficquelmont to Metternich, St Petersburg, 6 April 1835, HHStA, StA, Russland III, 104; Nesselrode to Butenev, St Petersburg, 3 Feb. 1835, HHStA, StA, Türkei VI, 63.

he was to take no further steps and conclude nothing definitive. If the whole affair had already been settled beyond recall, the French were to be allowed to come to the Ottoman capital but not be employed in the army. The sultan gave his full consent to the instructions and they were immediately sent to Paris. In April 1835, the tensions arising from the planned employment of the French in the Military Academy were finally averted. Mustafa Reshid Bey received instructions before he had a definite settlement with the Parisian cabinet and abandoned the project without any difficulty. No French officers were employed in the Turkish Military Academy during Mahmud II's lifetime, including the two or three French officers who were signed on by Resid before he obtained his counter-order and who arrived in Constantinople in March 1836.[44]

Stürmer and Butenev undoubtedly deserved the lion's share of the credit for preventing the employment of the French in the Turkish Military Academy but Metternich's vigilance was also important. In addition, he continued to observe the employment of foreign officers by the Ottomans and he did not hesitate to oppose other French assistance if and when it was necessary. As to other French officers serving in the Ottoman army from earlier periods, their sacking *en masse* in late 1836 can be hardly ascribed to anything other than the concentrated Austro-Russian diplomatic pressure. In the mid 1830s, Metternich also supported the Russian effort against Palmerston's attempt to deploy British officers in the Ottoman army and navy and particularly against Polish General Wojciech Chrzanowski during two stays after 1836. Chrzanowski was sent by the leader of the Polish emigrants in Paris, Prince Adam Czartoryski. Unsurprisingly, Chrzanowski was supported by the pro-French Husrev Pasha and, therefore, he won Mahmud II's favour. Later, due to his ties with the British, he served more as Palmerston's agent. In both cases he represented a danger for Metternich. As with the French military instructors and officers, Metternich was also successful in the case of Chrzanowski and the British

---

[44] Metternich to Stürmer, Vienna, 8 April 1835, HHStA, StA, Türkei VI, 64; Stürmer to Metternich, Constantinople, 28 Jan., 25 Feb., 4 March and 22 April 1835, HHStA, StA, Türkei VI, 63; Stürmer to Metternich, Constantinople, 30 March 1836, HHStA, StA, Türkei VI, 64; Königsmarck to Frederick William III, Büyükdere, 21 July 1835, GStA PK, HA III, MdA I, 7275; Königsmarck to Frederick William III, Pera, 30 March 1836, GStA PK, HA III, MdA I, 7277; Berkes, pp. 111–112; Uyar, Erickson, pp. 147–151.

officers: the former had no significant influence on the Ottoman army and mostly stayed in eastern Anatolia, and the latter were never employed by the sultan, at least not in any significant number.[45]

Mahmud II's acquiescence under the Austro-Russian pressure did not mean that he gave up his plan for the employment of foreign military advisers, but rather that he only planned to modify his choice. Already in July 1835, Husrev Pasha informed Königsmarck about the sultan's wish to employ several Prussian artillerymen, but since Königsmarck obtained no answer from his king, he thought that Frederick William III was unwilling to grant the request and did not discuss the affair any more. However, the Porte itself raised the issue again at the end of the year and made a formal request at the beginning of 1836. It asked for fifteen Prussian instructors – eleven officers and four non-commissioned officers – to be sent to Constantinople for three years. This switch to Prussia was generally explained by historians by, first, Prussia's limited activity in the Eastern Question being more palatable to the sultan than the other Powers' active struggle for the predominant influence over his court, second, Moltke's presence in the Ottoman Empire since October 1835, and third, the arrival of Marquis Caraman's work *Essai sur l'organisation militaire de la Prusse* of 1831 of which the Turkish translation gripped Mahmud II because it described the effective Prussian military reform carried out at the minimum possible expense. One must add, however, that par-

---

[45] Metternich to Stürmer, Vienna, 26 and 27 Jan. 1836, HHStA, StA, Türkei VI, 65; Stürmer to Metternich, Constantinople, 10 Feb. 1836, HHStA, StA, Türkei VI, 64; Stürmer to Metternich, Büyükdere, 6 July and 14 Dec. 1836, Adelburg to Stürmer, Pera, 6 July 1836, HHStA, StA, Türkei VI, 65; Ficquelmont to Metternich, St Petersburg, 5 Jan. 1836, HHStA, StA, Russland III, 106; Königsmarck to Frederick William III, Pera, 27 Jan. and 17 Feb. 1836, GStA PK, HA III, MdA I, 7277; Roussin to Molé, Therapia, 12 Nov. 1837, AMAE, CP, Turquie 275; Ponsonby to Palmerston, Therapia, 28 Dec. 1836, TNA, FO 78/278; R. A. Berry, "Czartoryski's Hôtel Lambert and the Great Powers in the Balkans, 1832–1848," *IHR* 8, 1985, 1, pp. 46–49; H. H. Hahn, *Außenpolitik in der Emigration: Die Exildiplomatie Adam Jerzy Czartoryskis 1830–1840*, München, Wien 1978, pp. 211–212; L. Maier, "Reformwille und Beharrung: Das Osmanische Reich 1835–1839 aus der Sicht Helmuth von Moltkes," J. Matešić, K. Heitmann (eds.), *Südosteuropa in der Wahrnehmung der deutschen Öffentlichkeit vom Wiener Kongreß (1815) bis zum Pariser Frieden (1856)*, München 1990, p. 44; M. N. Todorova, "British and Russian Policy towards the Reform Movement in the Ottoman Empire (30-ies – 50-ies of the 19th c.)," *Études Balkaniques* 13, 1977, p. 19; Rodkey, "Lord Palmerston and the Rejuvenation of Turkey, Part I," p. 578.

ticularly the second and third factors merely increased the already existing reputation of excellence of the Prussian army held by the Ottomans; it was no accident that they were so interested in Prussian artillerymen because they believed in the superiority of Prussia's artillery and nicknamed all Prussians "those artillerymen."[46] Mahmud II himself thought a great deal not only of Peter the Great or Napoleon Bonaparte but also Frederick the Great, and after 1835 Husrev was as much pro-Prussian in this respect as he had been earlier pro-French. Stürmer even attributed the project of the employment of the Prussian officers to him: "The demand for the Prussians is above all the work of the serasker, who is not especially partial to us and has always had a particular preference for the Prussian army."[47] Despite Stürmer's complaint about the preference for Prussia, the Porte also asked Austria for its officers in the beginning. The internuncio was informed about this plan in January 1836 by Akif Effendi, who declared that his monarch would like to obtain some professors and instructors from the country where the Ottoman students had made such great progress in their studies in such a short time. The formal request for six military experts was delivered to Stürmer in February; Mahmud II desired to employ one professor of geometry, one professor of fortification and relevant sciences, one instructor for the organisation of the military academy, one instructor of the horse artillery, one instructor of the foot artillery and one hussar for the organisation of a hussar regiment that the sultan had long wished for.[48]

---

[46] The Ottomans also seemed to use such nicknames for other nations: the French were "the people without religion;" the British "those without faith;" the Austrians "those who like fur coats," and the Russians "the fishermen." Königsmarck to Frederick William III, Pera, 20 April 1836, GStA PK, HA III, MdA I, 7277.

[47] Stürmer to Metternich, Constantinople, 10 Feb. 1836, HHStA, StA, Türkei VI, 64.

[48] Adelburg to Stürmer, Pera, 24 Jan. 1836, Akif Effendi's note to Stürmer, 8 Feb. 1836, Stürmer to Metternich, Constantinople, 27 Jan., 4, 10 and 24 Feb., 10 March 1836, HHStA, StA, Türkei VI, 64; Stürmer to Metternich, Constantinople, 11 May 1836, Büyükdere, 24 Aug. 1836, HHStA, StA, Türkei VI, 65; Stürmer to Metternich, Büyükdere, 19 July 1837, HHStA, StA, Türkei VI, 66; Trauttmannsdorff to Metternich, Berlin, 15 March 1836, HHStA, StK, Preussen 162; Ahmed Fethi Pasha to Metternich, Constantinople, 4 April 1836, Stürmer to Metternich, Constantinople, 16 March 1836, HHStA, StA, Türkei VIII, 9; Königsmarck to Frederick William III, Büyükdere, 21 July 1835, GStA PK, HA III, MdA I, 7275; Königsmarck to Frederick William III, Pera, 30 Dec. 1835, GStA PK, HA III, MdA I, 7276; Königsmarck to Frederick William III, Pera, 6 and 27 Jan., 16 March

The two German Powers agreed with the sultan's request, and they did so for a simple principal reason: there was no alternative for the cabinets in Berlin and Vienna in early 1836 other than to satisfy it because when Mahmud II had been prevented from employing French and British military advisers, a refusal would undoubtedly have moved him to turn again to the two liberal Powers, turning the victory of conservatism into defeat. Nevertheless, there was one significant difference in their agreements. Whereas the Prussian king was convinced by the tsar to agree, Metternich did not need persuading since he was the prominent player in this matter and more than willing to send Austrian officers to Constantinople. His desire is evident from the fact that while firstly Prussia was not only absolutely passive during the other Powers' struggle for the employment of their own officers in the Ottoman service but also rather restrained towards the Porte's original attempt to obtain Prussian artillerymen and, secondly, it did not agree to the sending of the officers until the moment the king realised that the tsar really wanted them, Metternich had tried since the very beginning to influence the sultan's choice for the most suitable country to contribute to his military reforms.[49] According to Königsmarck, and there is no reason to disbelieve him, when Austria and Russia succeeded in preventing the project of the Turkish Military Academy led by the French, they recommended that the Porte appeal in this matter to the governments "whose citizens' morality and the principles of order in which they have been brought up would offer better guarantees of reliability."[50]

The different roles played by the two German Powers in the affair also are clearly evident in the speed of Austria's answer to the request, the enthusiastic style of this answer and finally its willingness to cover almost all the expenses of its own officers, which was in sharp contrast to the expenses incurred by the Prussians, which were to be

---

and 27 April 1836, GStA PK, HA III, MdA I, 7277; R. Wagner, *Moltke und Mühlbach zusammen unter dem Halbmonde 1837–1839*, Berlin 1893, p. 15; Hajjar, p. 174; Kessel, p. 115.

[49] Stürmer to Metternich, Constantinople, 10 Feb. 1836, HHStA, StA, Türkei VI, 64; Königsmarck to Frederick William III, Pera, 30 Dec. 1835, GStA PK, HA III, MdA I, 7276; J. L. Wallach, *Anatomie einer Militärhilfe: Die preußisch-deutschen Militärmissionen in der Türkei 1835–1919*, Düsseldorf 1976, p. 19.

[50] Königsmarck to Frederick William III, Pera, 30 Dec. 1835, GStA PK, HA III, MdA I, 7276.

completely paid by the Porte. Other evidence that Austria insisted on the success of this project much more so than Prussia can also be found in the behaviour of the Viennese court and Chancellery towards the extraordinary Ottoman ambassador, Ahmed Fethi Pasha, sent in the summer of 1835 to congratulate new Emperor Ferdinand I on his accession to the throne. This influential dignitary and general of the imperial guard (ferik), about whom Mahmud II once said that "he is my Orlov,"[51] was welcomed with exceptional warmth, was accommodated in a hotel from July to September at the expense of Ferdinand I and was favoured with attention far above that required by protocol. As for the honours accorded to Ahmed, for example, a military parade took place in his honour on 14 August, during which a command and the rank of marshal was conferred on him. When Ahmed expressed his desire to visit a considerable number of military places including the fortification of Linz or the Military Academy in Wiener-Neustadt, it was immediately granted and one can hardly suppose that the Austrians did so without ulterior motives.[52] More than eloquent are the words from a notice on Ahmed's stay in Austria published in the *Österreichischer Beobachter* that his mission would not only strengthen the friendly relations of the two countries but also "contribute considerably to the foundation of more helpful institutions and useful facilities in the Ottoman Empire."[53]

Although the exact content of discussions between Austrian dignitaries and Ahmed Fethi Pasha is not known, the former undoubtedly desired to increase Austria's influence in Constantinople by entering into friendly relations with the latter, which could be particularly advantageous in military affairs. The first goal was definitely achieved

---

[51] Stürmer to Metternich, Büyükdere, 27 July 1835, NA, RAM-AC 2, 6.

[52] Stürmer to Metternich, Constantinople, 21 May 1835, HHStA, StA, Türkei VI, 63; Stürmer's note to the Porte, Constantinople, 7 April 1836, Stürmer to Metternich, Constantinople, 6 and 13 April 1836, HHStA, StA, Türkei VI, 64; the Porte's memorandum to Königsmarck, 6 Dec. 1836, HHStA, StA, Türkei VI, 65; Königsmarck to Frederick William III, Pera, 19 May and 24 June 1835, GStA PK, HA III, MdA I, 7275; Königsmarck to Frederick William III, Pera, 23 March 1836, GStA PK, HA III, MdA I, 7277; Maltzan to Frederick William III, Vienna, 31 July and 7 Aug. 1835, GStA PK, HA III, MdA I, 6026; O'Sullivan to Meulenaer, Vienna, 3 and 15 Aug. 1835, ADA, CP, Autriche 3; Verger to Ludwig I of Bavaria, Vienna, 19 and 27 Sept. 1835, BHStA, MA, Wien 2406; report from Vienna, 22 July, 8 and 19 Aug. 1835, SS, HD, SG 10026, Wien 93.

[53] *Österreichischer Beobachter*, Nr. 270, 27 Sept. 1835.

because after his return to the Ottoman capital in early November 1835, Ahmed demonstrated warm pro-Austrian sentiment. He was very pleased with the way he had been welcomed and treated by the emperor and his court, in particular by the chancellor and his wife. Metternich purposely stayed in contact with Ahmed to a degree exceeding that of usual diplomatic correspondence, proving that the prince tried to maintain very cordial relations with this dignitary and use him as a pro-Austrian member of the Ottoman government, in particular for the support of the employment of Austrian officers.[54] This effort was undoubtedly successful because Ahmed, pleased with this approach of the prominent European statesman, really did provide practical support in the sultan's project for the employment of foreign officers and sided with Austria in this affair. Unfortunately for Metternich, Ahmed's activities finally did not help Austria to succeed in supplying military assistance to Mahmud II and this was finally provided only by Prussia.[55] The reason for this shift in the Porte's attitude is not clear. German historian Georg Rosen claimed that it was due to Russia's secret opposition to the presence of Austrian officers in the Levant.[56] Nevertheless, he did so without quoting any relevant documents and this view seems to be rather precarious. Although Nicholas I undoubtedly preferred the Prussian military mission, the Austrians were still a much better choice than the French or British and, moreover, he urgently needed the support of the Austrian Empire in the Near East; any plots against the employment of its citizens could have had serious consequences if they had been revealed, which was almost certain in the conditions of the sultan's court crowded with corruptible and devious people. If this had happened, it could have had serious consequences for the Russian position in Constantinople where the British zealously tried to undermine it.[57]

---

[54] For more on Metternich's desire to exploit his contacts with Ahmed Fethi Pasha for the increase of Austria's influence in Constantinople see Chapter 22.

[55] Metternich to Ahmed Fethi Pasha, 22 Feb. 1836, Metternich to Stürmer, Vienna, 23 Feb. 1836 HHStA, StA, Türkei VI, 65; Stürmer to Metternich, Constantinople, 11 Nov. 1835 and 9 March 1836, HHStA, StA, Türkei VI, 64; Stürmer to Metternich, Constantinople, 20 April 1836, NA, RAM-AC 2, 6; Königsmarck to Frederick William III, Pera, 17 Feb. 1836, GStA PK, HA III, MdA I, 7277.

[56] Rosen, p. 234.

[57] In early 1836, the Russian cabinet even feared an early British-Ottoman rapprochement and asked Metternich for support, but this fear was baseless. Metternich to Stürmer, Vienna, 3 Feb. 1836, HHStA, StA, Türkei VI, 65.

The studied diplomatic correspondence offers no evidence for Rosen's theory, and the instructions to Butenev of 2 February 1836 in which Nesselrode conveyed the tsar's pleasure at the Porte's decision to hire Prussian and Austrian military instructors instead of those from Great Britain and France even prove the opposite. As for Austria, Nesselrode called Butenev's attention to the necessity of maintaining a close alliance between St Petersburg and Vienna at the very moment Palmerston was trying to weaken it or at least give the impression that this entente was crumbling. Consequently, there was only one possible order for Butenev from Nesselrode in the case of Austrian instructors: "Particularly in the matter of the choice of the Austrian officers, convey to the Porte that sending them will arouse neither the envy nor the suspicion of the emperor [tsar]. You can even stamp this declaration with the sincerity and frankness that always accompany assurances that come directly from our Noble Master."[58] Butenev dealt then according to this instruction with the Ottomans, which means that there had to be a different external or internal reason for the withdrawal of the request for the Austrian officers. As for the former, it is entirely possible that the formerly unsuccessful Western Powers in return frustrated Austrian ambitions. On the other hand, Ottoman documents could throw more light onto the attitude of the Porte that can be only guessed here. One cannot hide the fact that a considerable number of the sultan's advisers were not favourably inclined to Austria, in particular Husrev Pasha.[59] Stürmer already reported in February 1836 on anti-Austrian intrigues at the sultan's court: "They have worked from various angles to frustrate everything that could give Austria excessive influence over the affairs of this country. As I know from Mr Butenev, at one moment there was even a question of demanding only Prussian instructors. I said that it was all the same to us, considering that it was beneath our dignity to assert ourselves to render an unwanted service to the Porte."[60]

---

[58] Nesserlode to Butenev, St Petersburg, 2 Feb. 1836, AVPRI, fond 133, Kantseliariia, opis 469, 1836/43.

[59] Stürmer to Metternich, Constantinople, 10 and 24 Feb., 9 March 1836, HHStA, StA, Türkei VI, 64; Stürmer to Metternich, Constantinople, 11 May 1836, HHStA, StA, Türkei VI, 65; Königsmarck to Frederick William III, Pera, 17 Feb. 1836, GStA PK, HA III, MdA I, 7277.

[60] Stürmer to Metternich, Constantinople, 10 Feb. 1836, HHStA, StA, Türkei VI, 64.

Although the personal sentiments of the Ottoman dignitaries might have played an important role in the fact that only Prussian officers were finally hired, Ottoman leaders could also have abandoned the idea of employing the Austrians because they planned to reform the army according to the Prussian model, and for this purpose the Prussians were a logical choice.[61] Moreover, European officers were to deal with Ottoman batteries on the frontier with Austria and it would be illogical for Austrian soldiers to train the recruits that would serve against them in the event of an Austro-Ottoman war. The Austrians could also have been refused for the simple reason that the Porte did not know to which purpose they were really to serve because the plans for the use of the "German" officers were changed in the course of 1836; a few Europeans were to be delegated to various Ottoman commanders as advisers. Consequently, four officers instead of fifteen from Prussia and none from the Austrian Empire were to be hired. This was announced to Königsmarck in September 1836 and the official request was dispatched to Berlin in December.[62]

Here it is necessary to refute the claim raised by German historian Jehuda L. Wallach that the reduction from fifteen to four was caused by Austrian intrigues resulting from envy; there is no sign of such plots in the studied documents.[63] Austria did not oppose Prussia's military assistance and although the two Great Powers' negotiations with the Porte proceeded separately, Metternich supported the

---

[61] In early 1841, the Porte rejected the proposal of a British ambassador to employ six British artillerymen with the explanation that the Ottoman artillery had been reformed after the Prussian fashion. Stürmer to Metternich, Constantinople, 4 March 1841, HHStA, StA, Türkei VI, 80. It is not, however, the purpose of this book to deal with the degree to which the Ottomans reformed their army after the Prussian model, which is, moreover, very difficult to do owing to the lack of sources. T. Heinzelmann, *Heiliger Kampf oder Landesverteidigung: Die Diskussion um die Einführung der allgemeinen Militärpflicht im Osmanischen Reich 1826–1856*, Frankfurt am Main 2004, pp. 105–108. Probably the work of the Ottoman interpreter in Berlin, Carabed, archived in Vienna could serve as research material on the topic: *Observations sur l'organisation militaire en Prusse et sur son application à l'Empire Ottoman*, attached to Nourri Efendi to Mustafa Reshid Pasha, Berlin, 1 Jan. 1840, HHStA, StK, Interiora, Intercepte 28.

[62] Stürmer to Metternich, Constantinople, 23 Nov. 1836, the Porte's memorandum to Königsmarck, 6 Dec. 1836, HHStA, StA, Türkei VI, 65; Königsmarck to Frederick William III, Pera, 20 April 1836, GStA PK, HA III, MdA I, 7277; Hajjar, p. 176; Pröhl, p. 182.

[63] Wallach, p. 19.

Prussians against the hostility of the British cabinet, who opposed their forthcoming presence in the Levant, as is evident from its instructions to Ponsonby, who was ordered to tell the Porte that the officers coming from Berlin could be regarded "as sent by the Russian government, and for purposes unfriendly to England and injurious to Turkey."[64] However, when Lord Russel asked the Austrian envoy in Berlin, Count Joseph von Trauttmannsdorff-Weinsberg, whether Austria did not fear that the Prussian officers could be the long arm of Russia, the latter did not hesitate to defend the usefulness of their presence in the Ottoman Empire.[65]

The way in which the Porte informed the Viennese cabinet that it would not employ its officers was typical for Ottoman diplomacy: it did so with complete silence. After the settlement of negotiations between the Porte and Stürmer about the status of the Austrians who were to reside in the Ottoman Empire, the internuncio was informed in late April 1836 that the discussions would continue in Vienna. For this purpose Ahmed Fethi Pasha was named a permanent Ottoman ambassador. However, the Ottomans never actually reopened negotiations on the subject in either the Austrian or Ottoman capital. The delay resulting from Ahmed's journey to Vienna, where he did not arrive until the last day of September, already indicated such a strategy, and the members of the Divan maintained their silence towards the internuncio much as did Ahmed towards Metternich. Since Metternich as well as Stürmer was not inclined to speak out in this affair, it came to nothing.[66] The cabinet in Vienna adopted the passive attitude as outlined by the internuncio earlier when he had learnt that the talks would continue in Vienna: "The matter regarding the instructors is suspended at the moment like all the others. I have decided not to talk about it with anybody any more but to wait until the moment is deemed opportune to reopen the discussion on the topic with me. I

---

[64] Rodkey, "Lord Palmerston and the Rejuvenation of Turkey, Part I," p. 585.
[65] Trauttmannsdorff to Metternich, Berlin, 1 July 1837, HHStA, StK, Preussen 165.
[66] Stürmer to Metternich, Constantinople, 10 Feb., 20 and 27 April 1836, HHStA, StA, Türkei VI, 64; Königsmarck to Frederick William III, Pera, 6 April 1836, GStA PK, HA III, MdA I, 7277; Ponsonby to Palmerston, Therapia, 16 April 1836, TNA, FO 78/274; report from Vienna, 1 Oct. 1836, SS, HD, SG 10026, Wien 93; Bockelberg to Frederick William III, Vienna, 4 Oct. 1836, GStA PK, HA III, MdA I, 6028.

find this attitude to be the only one appropriate to the dignity of the imperial court; any over-eagerness [on our part] would cause another disadvantage, that would, among others, lead the Porte, by nature so distrustful, to believe that we are interested in hastening the dispatch of these instructors and claiming for ourselves the credit for a service that it [the Porte] has to request and acknowledge."[67]

Austria's assumed passivity could not of course escape the attention of the second German Power whose envoy in Vienna wrote in late December 1836 to Berlin: "Three months have passed since the arrival of the Turkish ambassador in Vienna without a word being said about the affair in question; the way in which it stops and starts will depend on the moves initiated by the Porte, the imperial cabinet having firmly decided not to take the initiative in any way."[68] Consequently, only three Prussian officers, Vincke, Fischer and Mühlbach, arrived in Constantinople in late August 1837 and joined Moltke, the fourth chosen by the king. The story of their two-year activity in the Levant is not the goal of this book and, moreover, is too well known to be repeated here. What can be briefly said, however, is that their observations on the Ottoman reform movement and its army, and particularly the views of Moltke, entirely confirmed the criticism contained in the Prussian and Austrian diplomats' reports from previous years. The service of Moltke and his colleagues had no really positive effect on the army because the Ottomans simply did not know how to take advantage of their qualities. Moreover, the Prussians exercised no real power or authority and the soldiers had no reason to listen to them. Moltke, Mühlbach and Vincke were finally deployed in 1838 at army headquarters, where military commanders were often deaf to their advice. This proved to be fatal for the Turkish commander, Hafiz Pasha, who did not listen to Moltke's warnings before the Battle of Nezib with the Egyptian army in June 1839, in which he was completely defeated. At that time the two-year period assigned to the Prussians was about to terminate and Frederick William III decided to recall them. Moltke, Mühlbach and Vincke followed Fischer who had departed earlier for home.[69] Although their presence in the

---

[67] Stürmer to Metternich, Constantinople, 11 May 1836, HHStA, StA, Türkei VI, 65.

[68] Maltzan to Frederick William III, Vienna, 21 Dec. 1836, GStA PK, HA III, MdA I, 6028.

[69] Stürmer to Metternich, Büyükdere, 30 Aug. 1837, HHStA, StA, Türkei VI, 66;

sultan's service was insignificant for Ottoman military reforms, their reports, and especially those of Moltke, sent to Berlin and read in Vienna, were a valuable source of information for Metternich on important Near Eastern events, in particular in early 1838 when a war between Mahmud II and Mohammed Ali seemed to be imminent, or a year later when it actually broke out. Already in September 1836, when Moltke was the only Prussian officer in the sultan's service, Stürmer drew attention to the great informative value of his reports and recommended that Metternich have his own Austrian officer in the Ottoman Empire regularly reporting to Vienna, which finally did not happen.[70]

Although the decision concerning the non-employment of the Austrian officers had to be the cause of some disappointment in Vienna, hiring the Prussians instead of the French and British was regarded as a triumph of conservative diplomacy and definitely offered some consolation. It also did not prevent Austria from continuing to think about cementing its good relations with the Ottoman Empire

---

Königsmarck to Frederick William III, Büyükdere, 30 Aug. and 6 Sept. 1837, GStA PK, HA III, MdA I, 7279; Pröhl, pp. 182–184; Wallach, pp. 23–28.

[70] Stürmer to Metternich, Büyükdere, 7 Sept. 1836, HHStA, StA, Türkei VI, 65. Metternich gained a certain compensation in this respect in the presence of the two physicians in Constantinople, whom Mahmud II requested in 1838. Austrian doctors Jakob Neuner and Karl Ambros Bernard, recommended by Metternich's personal physician Friedrich Jäger whom the chancellor had entrusted with the task of finding doctors for the Ottoman service, arrived in Constantinople in early December of the same year. The former soon became Mahmud II's personal physician and through his reports Metternich was the first European statesman in the spring of 1839 to learn of the sultan's imminent death. The latter became a director of the Imperial Medical School in Galata-Serai and informed Metternich about the events in the Ottoman Empire in the following years. Königsmarck to Frederick William III, Büyükdere, 12 Oct. 1838, GStA PK, HA III, MdA I, 7280; M. Chahrour, "'A Civilizing Mission'? Austrian Medicine and the Reform of Medical Structures in the Ottoman Empire, 1838–1850," *Studies in History and Philosophy of Biological and Biomedical Sciences* 38, 2007, 4, pp. 689–692; A. Kernbauer, "Die österreichischen Ärzte in Istanbul und die Großmachtdiplomatie," M. Skopec, A. Kernbauer (eds.), *Österreichisch-türkische medizinische Beziehungen historisch und modern (Mitteilungen der österreichischen Gesellschaft für Geschichte der Naturwissenschaften 10/1990)*, Wien 1990, pp. 11–14; A. Terzioğlu, "Ein kurzer Blick auf die österreichisch-türkischen medizinischen Beziehungen von Anbeginn bis heute," A. Terzioğlu, E. Lucius (eds.), *Österreichisch-türkische medizinische Beziehungen: Berichte des Symposions vom 28. und 29. April 1986 in Istanbul*, Istanbul 1987, pp. 46–48.

through its own military assistance to the sultan's military reforms. It is clearly evident from the above-mentioned Archduke Johann's visit to Constantinople in October 1837 that resulted in the sending of several Ottoman cadets to Vienna and in the presenting of Austria's gifts of the total value of 4,872 florins to Mahmud II by Hauslab on 4 November 1837. These gifts were generally of a military nature or were intended for the use by the army: military material and equipment, models of military tools, geometrical instruments for the measurement and completion of military maps, books and maps of military character. Stürmer accompanied the presentation of these items with speeches characterised by the usual diplomatic courtesy and with an evident intimation that Mahmud II enjoyed the greatest confidence in Austria's participation in Ottoman military reforms.[71] The internuncio started with these words: "His Majesty the emperor, my most gracious master, knows the active interest which Your Majesty ceaselessly pays to the creation of Your army. He takes a sincere pleasure in it because he sees in this glorious effort an important assurance for the security of the Ottoman Empire. Always ready to contribute to the accomplishment of the useful intentions of Your Majesty, as much as it is in his power, the emperor has had a selection of models, military tools and geometrical instruments made by the best craftsmen in Vienna, which, in addition to several maps and military equipment, seemed to complete the collection Your Majesty already possesses in this respect."[72]

---

[71] Metternich to Stürmer, Vienna, 25 July 1837, HHStA, StA, Türkei VI, 67; Metternich to Stürmer, Vienna, 5 Sept. 1837, HHStA, StA, Türkei VIII, 10. The presents for military purposes were often sent by the Viennese cabinet to Constantinople. Metternich wanted in this way not only to flatter the sultan but also, as well as in the case of the presents for Mohammed Ali, to promote Austria's industry. Metternich to Francis I, Vienna, 17 July 1829, HHStA, StK, Vorträge 259; Metternich to Ottenfels, Vienna, 4 Feb. 1830, HHStA, StA, Türkei VI, 51; Metternich to Ottenfels, Vienna, 2 Oct. 1830, Ottenfels to Metternich, Constantinople, 10 Dec. 1830, HHStA, StA, Türkei VIII, 2; Metternich to Ottenfels, Vienna, 18 March, 1 and 19 April 1831, HHStA, StA, Türkei VIII, 4; Metternich to Stürmer, Vienna, 4 July 1837, HHStA, StA, Türkei VI, 67; Ottenfels to Metternich, Constantinople, 10 Sept. 1830, HHStA, StA, Türkei VI, 50; Ottenfels to Metternich, Constantinople, 10 and 25 Nov. 1830, HHStA, StA, Türkei VI, 51; Stürmer to Metternich, Constantinople, 1 March 1837, HHStA, StA, Türkei VI, 66; Stürmer to Metternich, Constantinople, 29 July 1840, HHStA, StA, Türkei VIII, 14; Ottenfels, *Memoari*, p. 220.

[72] Stürmer to Metternich, Constantinople, 8 Nov. 1837, HHStA, StA, Türkei VIII,

Flattery and patience were the only means that Austria had to achieve the employment of its own officers in the Ottoman Empire. It finally saw this happen during the second war between Constantinople and Alexandria when Austria and Great Britain assisted the Turkish forces in the Syrian campaign against Mohammed Ali in 1840–1841. In addition to the Austrian expeditionary forces fighting on the Syrian coast under Austria's banner,[73] four officers were employed directly by the Porte at its own expense. In November 1840, Stürmer introduced them to Sultan Abdülmecid I: Lieutenant-Colonel Philippovich, Major Trattner, Major Pott and Captain Platzer. However, what had happened to the Prussian officers happened to them too: the Porte in fact did not know how to employ them. It had originally requested them with the aim of employing them to build fortification works but this plan was abandoned. Therefore, they asked to be sent to Syria for where they actually departed in early December, but when they arrived at their destination, they realised that they had nothing to do there either, and they were happy when they were recalled home in February 1841.[74] The same fate met Austrian military doctors sent to Syria when the Viennese cabinet learnt in early November 1840 of an absolute lack of capable physicians and surgeons in the Turkish army waging war in Syria. Metternich immediately initiated the sending of ten doctors chosen by the Court Council of War (four senior officers and six junior officers). They arrived in Syria in late February 1841, where they were to be employed in the Ottoman military hospitals. It is certain that they really were active in hospitals in Beirut, Jaffa, Acre, Damascus and Sidon, but their service was frustrated by many difficulties, for example, the problematic conduct of the Turks in de-

---

10.
[73] For more on Austria's participation in the Syrian campaign see Chapter 27.
[74] Stürmer to Metternich, Constantinople, 21 Oct., 18 Nov. and 9 Dec. 1840, HHStA, StA, Türkei VIII, 14; Metternich to Stürmer, Vienna, 22 Sept. and 30 Oct. 1840, HHStA, StA, Türkei VI, 78; Metternich to Stürmer, Vienna, 6, 19 and 20 Oct., 13 Nov. 1840, Metternich to Mavroyéni, Vienna, 6 Oct. 1840, Stürmer to Metternich, Constantinople, 30 April 1841, HHStA, StA, Türkei VIII, 15; Königsmarck to Frederick William IV, Büyükdere, 26 Aug. 1840, GStA PK, HA III, MdA I, 7282; Königsmarck to Frederick William IV, Büyükdere, 18 Nov. and 2 Dec. 1840, GStA PK, HA III, MdA I, 7283; Königsmarck to Frederick William IV, Büyükdere, 30 March 1841, GStA PK, HA III, MdA I, 7284; Basili to Titov, Beirut, 23 Feb. 1841, Titov to Nesselrode, Pera, 2 Feb. and 13 March 1841, AVPRI, fond 133, Kantseliariia, opis 469, 1841/41.

laying the payment of the agreed salaries and paying little interest in the doctors' work in the disastrous hospital organisation, which was in fact non-existent, and which was something that Moltke had also criticised in the Ottoman army some years earlier. To improve the existing state of affairs it was necessary to make an enormous effort, but the conditions did not permit it, and in mid April 1841 Stürmer recommended to Metternich the withdrawal of the doctors. Most of those who survived the plague which afflicted the region in early 1841 left Syria in June.[75]

*   *   *

With the return of the Austrian officers who had been intended to support the fortification works and supply medical treatment from Syria back to the Danube Monarchy, the chapter of Austria's military assistance to the Ottoman Empire during the period under examination closed although a few Ottoman students still remained in Vienna in the 1840s. From the military point of view one cannot overestimate its significance: the presence of Austrian officers and military doctors in Syria had no distinct benefit, in fact it was an absolute fiasco, and the impact of the Austrian military educational system on Ottoman military reforms through the Turkish students is impossible to ascertain from available sources. From the diplomatic point of view Metternich achieved his main victory in preventing any significant military cooperation between the Porte and the Maritime Powers but definitely not in the presence of Ottoman students in Vienna or Austrian officers in the Ottoman Empire because the numbers of both were extremely low. Consequently, they could hardly make the relations between Austria and the Porte more cordial and in this way significantly increase Austria's influence over the sultan's court. This of course gives rise to

---

[75] Metternich to Stürmer, Vienna, 10 Nov. 1840, Stürmer to Metternich, Constantinople, 14 and 30 April 1841, HHStA, StA, Türkei VIII, 15; Stürmer to Metternich, Constantinople, 7 July 1841, HHStA, StA, Türkei VIII, 16; Maltzan to Frederick William IV, Vienna, 13 Nov. 1840, GStA PK, HA III, MdA I, 7359; Maltzan to Frederick William IV, Vienna, 10 Dec. 1840, GStA PK, HA III, MdA I, 7360; Königsmarck to Frederick William IV, Büyükdere, 18 Nov. 1840, GStA PK, HA III, MdA I, 7283.

the question of how great its influence over the Porte actually was, not an entirely unimportant one considering the fact that it was influence and not territories for which the Great Powers were vying in the Near East during the 1830s.

The Extent of Austria's Influence in Constantinople

It was not the sultan's territory but rather influence over his decision-making for which the Great Powers competed in the 1830s. Austria took part in this contest, but despite its good relations with the Ottoman Empire during the period under research, its influence often fell behind expectations. It was thus often very difficult or entirely impossible for Metternich to obtain agreement from the Porte even in affairs of vital importance for Austria but not particularly significant for the Porte like navigation on the Danube, to say nothing of his limited chances of affecting its steps on the highest diplomatic level.

The Klek, Sutorina and Stametz Affairs

The good relations existing between Austria and the Ottoman Empire could create the impression that the influence of the former over the latter's decision-making was significant. The declarations of the Ottoman elites seemingly support such a presumption. For example in 1823, Mahmud II claimed that he regarded Prince Metternich as the greatest European statesman as well as a friend of the Porte, and that he had "the greatest confidence in him."[1] At the end of 1831, the sultan even expressed his satisfaction with Austria's conduct in Greek affairs in a special decree: "Whereas the events of last forty years led the courts and nations in Europe to take all kinds of engagements and form all kinds of alliances, His Imperial Majesty always demonstrated inviolable goodwill to Our Sublime Porte. Moreover, from the beginning to the end of the Greek revolution, the Austrian Emperor as well

---

[1] Hatzfeldt to Frederick William III, Vienna, 19 July 1823, GStA PK, HA III, MdA I, 6002.

as His Foreign Minister, Prince von Metternich, refrained from interfering in this affair and have until this moment recognised the rights
of Our Sublime Porte. We sincerely acknowledge the value of these
favourable proceedings of the Austrian Court, and, in truth, these
proceedings increase from day to day the level of satisfaction and the
genuine contentment that We feel. It is thus a necessary consequence
for Our dignity and for Our Imperial justice that in reciprocating from
Our part, the ministers of Our Sublime Porte take into consideration
the ouvertures and the requests addressed to them by the representative of the above-mentioned Court."[2] His foreign ministers often
declared themselves in the same way. Mehmed Hamid Bey assured
Ottenfels in 1830 that "the Porte has always had such irrefutable
proof of the friendship and goodwill of the Austrian Imperial Court,
which has given it so many occasions to admire and appreciate the
great wisdom of the political system followed by the Viennese cabinet that the Ottoman ministry will always regard it in its interest
to follow the counsel of Your Highness [Metternich] and plan its approach in important political questions according to the example of
Austria."[3] In 1836, Akif told Stürmer: "Everybody knows that Prince
von Metternich is a great statesman, and furthermore we know that
he is truly our friend."[4] These declarations of respect for Metternich were accompanied by presents like the sultan's portrait and a
snuff-box with diamonds in 1836, and even with the conferment of
the Ottoman Order of Glory (*Nichan Iftikhar*) in the following year.[5]
Stürmer wrote about the first gift formally presented to Metternich
for his friendship and counsel given to the Porte: "Indeed, a portrait
sent by the Sultan in such a way is a distinction without precedence

[2]   The sultan's hatt-i sharif communicated to Ottenfels on 25 December 1831,
attached to Ottenfels to Metternich, Constantinople, 27 Dec. 1831, HHStA, StA,
Türkei VI, 53.
[3]   Ottenfels to Metternich, Constantinople, 25 Oct. 1830, HHStA, StA, Türkei
VI, 51.
[4]   Stürmer to Metternich, Constantinople, 23 March 1836, HHStA, StA, Türkei
VI, 64.
[5]   Stürmer to Metternich, Constantinople, 6 April 1836, HHStA, StA, Türkei VI,
64; Stürmer to Metternich, Constantinople, 13 Sept. and 1 Nov. 1837, HHStA,
StA, Türkei VI, 66; Stürmer to Metternich, Constantinople, 7 Feb. 1838, HHStA,
StA, Türkei VI, 67; Königsmarck to Frederick William III, Pera, 6 April 1836,
GSta PK, HA III, MdA I, 7277.

and demonstrates the extent of the consideration of which, with justification, Your Highness enjoys in this country."[6]

There is no reason to doubt that Metternich enjoyed a good deal of respect at the sultan's court and that his advice was taken into consideration as is clear from the intercepted and translated Ottoman diplomatic correspondence,[7] but the principle question is whether it was also followed because this would amount to real influence of any practical value. Actually it mostly was not and Austria's influence was generally quite insignificant for most of the studied period covering the two decades from 1821 to 1841, and it also definitely did not correspond with the level of Austro-Ottoman friendship often manifested in mutual grandiose declarations and numerous presents. This conclusion is naturally easy to present but rather difficult to prove because the level of influence is always hard to measure, particularly in the unstable milieu of the Ottoman politics. The views of contemporary foreign diplomats can help to reveal it, but their own ambitions and mutual animosities make such a source of information rather precarious. In fact, it can be ascertained only according to the ability of Austria's various representatives to affect the decision-making of the Ottoman dignitaries, and that is why it is necessary to know in detail their activities and to what extent they were successful in enforcing their wishes so that a historian is able to determine their real influence and avoid superficial conclusions.

Consequently, for a full understanding of the extent of Austrian influence over the Ottoman court, it is necessary to choose examples showing the effort of the Viennese cabinet to carry through its own proposals in Constantinople. A good example was already offered in Chapter 19 when explaining Austria's effort to make the Danube navigable to the Black Sea in 1834 and the reluctance of the Ottomans that was finally overcome only with Russia's assistance. Nevertheless, although the ineffectiveness of Austria's influence is clearly evident from this affair, it is better to limit the choice only to those disputes that were not affected by the intervention of a third party because in

---

[6] Stürmer to Metternich, Constantinople, 6 April 1836, HHStA, StA, Türkei VI, 64.
[7] For all of this see Pertev Pasha to Mustafa Reshid Bey, Constantinople, 15 March 1837, attached to Metternich to Ficquelmont, Vienna, 1 April 1837, HHStA, StA, Russland III, 110.

those cases a negative or positive result cannot be determined simply by Austria's position in Constantinople and it is not necessary to deal with other factors or to contemplate whether Austrian diplomacy would not finally have succeeded without foreign, or in the question of the Danube Russia's, help. The ability of the Austrians to overcome various obstructions and enforce their wishes, as well as the limits of their efforts, can be best demonstrated in two affairs of minor significance within the sphere of the Eastern Question but still interesting as proof of Austria's influence and Metternich's personal involvement in Near Eastern affairs: first, Austria's desire to obtain two Ottoman strips of land, Klek and Sutorina, in the proximity of Dubrovnik, and second the desire of the Viennese banking house J. H. Stametz and Company to get back its money owed by the Porte. In both cases Austria had to proceed alone, in other words without the support of other Great Powers, and the achievement of these goals thus depended upon the effectiveness and finesse of its diplomats residing in the Ottoman capital and the support of their superior.

The first affair concerned two small strips of land, Klek and Sutorina, intersecting Austria's territory above and below Dubrovnik. When the city was seized by France during the Napoleonic Wars, these Ottoman territories were also occupied by the French but the Porte did not dare protest. At the Congress of Vienna, the city was formally adjudged to Austria, but the small territories, occupied by the Austrian army at that time, were returned by Francis I to Mahmud II despite the fact that they would cut off the Austrian domain in Dalmatia from not only Dubrovnik but also the Bay of Kotor, which was inconvenient for financial, quarantine and military reasons. For several years, however, the Viennese cabinet did not pay much attention to this problem, in particular because Mahmud II allowed free movement over these strips. This passivity changed in the early 1830s due to the deterioration of Austro-French relations, in particular after the French occupation of Ancona in February 1832. The French fleet cruising in the Adriatic Sea together with a rumour that the French were contemplating the occupation of Klek and Sutorina made Metternich fear such a possibility, or their seizure by any European Power in the future, and moved him to instruct Ottenfels to open negotiations with the Porte about their purchase or at least their temporary occupation by Austrian troops.[8]

Ottenfels started the talks in early April 1832, but the proposal for a temporary occupation was immediately refused and the request to purchase was merely taken ad referendum. Despite Ottenfels' repeated requests, nothing happened for a long time, which made Metternich, originally expecting a quick and positive solution, rather impatient, writing in December: "It is an affirmative clearly stated in writing that we believe we may expect due to our friendship with the Porte."[9] This optimism was based upon the information that Klek and Sutorina were uninhabited and infertile, and thus without any real value for the sultan. However, Pertev Effendi, the minister of interior at that time and entrusted with the negotiations, argued that they contained seven villages and several mosques; the correctness of Pertev's statement was confirmed by Austria's own investigation. This fact prevented Mahmud II from surrendering these territories or exchanging them for another one neighbouring the Bay of Kotor and offered by Ottenfels with Metternich's approval on 18 February 1833. After the sultan's refusal, Metternich was easily able to abandon the affair because the activities of the French in the Adriatic Sea became less threatening and the fear of their seizure of Klek and Sutorina disappeared.[10]

The history of the Stametz Affair began during the Russo-Ottoman war in late October 1828 when the Porte had problems with the food supply to its starving garrisons in the fortresses on the Danube

---

[8] Metternich to Ottenfels, Vienna, 18 Nov. 1831 and 2 Jan. 1832, HHStA, StA, Türkei III, 17; Metternich to Ottenfels, Vienna, 16 March 1832, HHStA, StA, Türkei VI, 56.

[9] Metternich to Ottenfels, Vienna, 5 Dec. 1832, HHStA, StA, Türkei VI, 56.

[10] Metternich to Ottenfels, Baden, 3 Aug. 1832, Vienna, 5 Dec. 1832, HHStA, StA, Türkei VI, 56; Ottenfels to Nedjib Effendi, 3 April 1832, Ottenfels to Akif Effendi, 8 May 1832, Ottenfels' note to the Porte, 22 July 1832, Ottenfels to Metternich, Constantinople, 10 April, 10 and 25 May, 25 July 1832, HHStA, StA, Türkei VI, 54; Ottenfels to Metternich, Constantinople, 25 Sept. and 10 Nov. 1832, HHStA, StA, Türkei VI, 55; Ottenfels' note to the Porte, Constantinople, 18 Feb. 1833, Ottenfels to Metternich, Constantinople, 11 Jan., 15 and 25 Feb., 11 March 1833, HHStA, StA, Türkei VI, 56; Caboga to Metternich, Dubrovnik, 13 June and 17 July 1832, HHStA, StA, Türkei III, 17; Maltzan to Frederick William III, Vienna, 16 March 1833, GStA PK, HA III, MdA I, 6021; Ottenfels, *Memoari*, pp. 248–249; Gürbüz, pp. 218–229; Krauter, pp. 265–269.

and therefore addressed a request to Metternich whether Austria would permit the transport of cereals from its provinces neighbouring the Ottoman Empire because the Danubian Principalities suffered from a considerable lack of food. The answer from Vienna was prompt and positive: the Ottomans could buy the cereals in Hungary and the Austrians promised to take steps to facilitate the whole transaction; the only condition was the strict secrecy of the whole operation because of Russia. The importance of this purchase for the Ottoman Empire is evident not only from the relief of the Ottoman dignitaries after the receipt of Metternich's consent but also from their monarch's official decree in which he expressed his deep gratitude for this support.[11]

Metternich paid considerable attention to the affair and he engaged the Viennese banker, Baron Salomon Mayer von Rothschild, who, as well as the rest of his extensive family, wished to preserve the status quo in the Near East and who maintained a pro-Ottoman and anti-Russian attitude. The participation of the Rothschilds in the arrangement was camouflaged by the name of the banking house Stametz, which was to ensure the purchase of cereals for the Ottomans because the activities of this company would attract less attention and would not lead to the speculations in the prices of this commodity. An agent of the Viennese company, Mr Glavany, was sent to Constantinople to negotiate the agreement. Finally, a contract was signed on 22 February 1829 by which Stametz was obliged to supply the Danubian fortresses with a needed quantity of cereals. The Porte pledged in return to pay the cost of this commodity and the expenses resulting from its delivery without delay. The Austrian diplomatic corps itself was not officially involved in the negotiations because it regarded them purely as a business transaction, but it is at most evident that Ottenfels facilitated Glavany's task. The supplies were under way from 19 May to 15 August 1829, and 348,169 1/2 bushels of cereals overall were sold for 557,149 gulden 6 kreutzer. Their transport on the Danube was expedited on the Austrian side by the direct intervention of the cabinet. Moreover, the agents of the Stametz Company lent

---

[11] Metternich to Ottenfels, Vienna, 20 Nov. 1828, HHStA, StA, Türkei VI, 35; Ottenfels to Pertev Effendi, 10 Dec. 1828, Ottenfels to Metternich, Constantinople, 29 Oct. and 18 Dec. 1828, HHStA, StA, Türkei VI, 34.

10,000 gulden to the Ottoman commissary, Ali Aga, entrusted to take deliveries, and paid the transport costs.[12]

The duty of the banking house was thus discharged and the Porte now had its turn to fulfil its obligations. After several instalments, the poor state of the treasury resulted in the protraction and finally the suspension of the repayments under the pretext of the need of the Porte to control its bills. In this situation, the internunciature in Constantinople started to act and summoned a meeting of a committee for the discussion on the debt. Its members met several times between 12 and 23 November 1830 and finally recognised the debt in the full amount of 557,149 gulden 6 kreutzer as well as the loan to Ali Aga of 10,000 gulden, but they refused to pay the required extras covering the delivery cost and taxes, which had been paid in Austrian territory but had not been included in the prices of the cereals, and Aga Ali had not been informed about them when he had overdrawn the shipments. The committee members designated these extras as exaggerated, abnormal and at variance with the conditions of the contract. They argued that the agreement with Stametz had been signed in Constantinople and only transport through Ottoman and not Austrian territory had been stipulated. Consequently, the costs that had arisen in the Habsburg Monarchy had to be shared by the suppliers and not the buyer. An agent of the banking house attending the discussions protested against this decision, but his objections fell on deaf ears despite the fact that they were supported by the first dragoman of the internunciature, Eduard von Adelburg. The latter at least managed to persuade the Ottomans to repay the acknowledged sum, which was done by the end of 1830.[13]

The outstanding debt demanded by the Stametz Company ran to 225,079 gulden and 17 kreutzer at the beginning of 1831, partly owing

---

[12] Metternich to Ottenfels, Vienna, 16 Jan. and 19 March 1829, HHStA, StA, Türkei VI, 39; Metternich to Ottenfels, Vienna, 3 April 1829, HDA, 750, OO 38; Glavany to Stametz, Constantinople, 21 Feb. 1829, Ottenfels to Metternich, Constantinople, 10, 22 and 25 Feb., 26 March and 12 April 1829, HHStA, StA, Türkei VI, 36. For the details of the whole affair from the very beginning to November 1834 see the overview of the first dragoman of the Austrian internunciature in Constantinople, Eduard von Adelburg, to Stürmer, Pera, 23 Nov. 1834, attached to Stürmer to Metternich, Constantinople, 3 Dec. 1834, HHStA, StA, Türkei VI, 61 [hereafter: Adelburg, *Overview*, HHStA, StA, Türkei VI, 61].

[13] Adelburg, *Overview*, HHStA, StA, Türkei VI, 61; Brassier to Frederick William III, Pera, 27 Dec. 1830, GStA PK, HA III, MdA I, 7269.

to the interest of 6 percent. Consequently, Adelburg called for a session of a new committee in January of the same year that admitted secondary costs of 543,427 1/2 piaster (approximately a quarter of the demanded sum) but nothing more because Pertev Effendi considered the interest claimed for the delayed payment to be unacceptable. Another agent of the Viennese banking house, Mr Autran, still regarded this decision as insufficient and together with the Austrian dragoman protested against the decision of the Ottoman dignitaries. Metternich supported the Stametz Company, declared they were entitled to the interest and pressed the continuance of negotiations but, particularly owing to Pertev's resistance, the Austrian grievances were doomed to failure and their only result was, after many months, the official note from the Porte dated 21 September 1831 confirming the original verdict. Although Ottenfels refused to terminate the dispute and countered with the note of 15 November 1831, he did not break the silence prevailing in Constantinople on this matter because the Ottomans considered it to be solved and, moreover, they did not want to pay at the same time they became obliged to pay the indemnities to Russia and punish Mohammed Ali's invasion to Syria of which they learnt at that very moment. Nothing could change their intransigence and Ottenfels' only achievement was the acquittance of the expenses recognised in January 1831.[14]

The battle was lost but the war was in no way regarded in Vienna as over. The banking house did not view the affair as settled and in the meantime the sum they demanded was further increasing due to the accruing interest. Metternich continued to side with the Stametz Company and regard the behaviour of the Porte as "blatant ingratitude."[15] Nevertheless, despite his personal interest in the affair, nothing happened until May 1834 when Count Apponyi appealed to the head of the Parisian branch of the Rothschild family, Baron James de Rothschild, to confiscate the corresponding sum of 800,000 francs

---

[14] Metternich to Ottenfels, Vienna, 3 June, 2 Nov. and 16 Dec. 1831, Ottenfels' note to the Porte, 15 Nov. 1831, HHStA, StA, Türkei VIII, 4; Ottenfels to Metternich, Constantinople, 10 Feb. and 25 April 1831, HHStA, StA, Türkei VIII, 3; Ottenfels to Metternich, Constantinople, 27 Dec. 1831, HHStA, StA, Türkei VIII, 4; Ottenfels to Metternich, Constantinople, 25 Aug. and 25 Sept. 1832, HHStA, StA, Türkei VI, 55; Adelburg, *Overview*, HHStA, StA, Türkei VI, 61; Brassier to Frederick William III, Pera, 26 Jan. 1831, GStA PK, HA III, MdA I, 7270.
[15] Metternich to Ottenfels, Vienna, 5 Sept. 1832, HHStA, StA, Türkei VI, 54.

on behalf of the Stametz Company, quasi in favour of his own syndicate, from the debt that the Greeks were obliged to pay on behalf of the sultan for their independence. The money for this purpose had been earlier granted by the Rothschilds and it was therefore not difficult for them to recoup the sum for the repayment of another obligation. Metternich supported this step and instructed Stürmer to take advantage of it and persuade the Porte to acquiesce, but this measure merely infuriated Mahmud II, who was shorter of money than usual owing to his daughter's wedding. When the Greek representative in Constantinople, Konstantinos Zografos, refused to condemn Rothschild's step as illegal, the sultan's anger turned against Greece. He had the Greek ships detained, applied an embargo on Greek goods and threatened the interruption of diplomatic relations; in late June the Porte actually broke its contact with Zografos. The Ottoman-Greek relations improved only when Zografos promised to write to his government and recommend it insist on the original obligation towards the Porte and not accept the intervention of the Rothschilds. The controversy between both countries was finally solved during July 1834 by the intervention of Russia, France and Great Britain, who, as the protectors of the Greek Kingdom, opposed the action of Apponyi and James Rothschild and insisted that the Greek debt had to remain unaltered. The Parisian banker was thus forced to withdraw and Apponyi's attempt to solve the Stametz Affair failed.[16]

Somewhat surprisingly, Mahmud II did not react to the Austrian mission until late August 1834 and probably nothing would have changed in his attitude if Stürmer had not undertaken a new "diplomatic offensive" ordered by Metternich, who wanted to end the dispute as soon as possible. The banking house supported this effort with a compromise offer: the debt could be redeemed by goods, for example opium, and the company was willing to write off 40,000 gulden

---

[16] Metternich to Stürmer, Vienna, 19 Oct. 1833 and 8 July 1834, Baden, 5 Aug. 1834, HHStA, StA, Türkei VIII, 6; Stürmer to Metternich, Constantinople, 28 May 1834, HHStA, StA, Türkei VI, 60; Apponyi to James Rothschild, Paris, 16 May 1834, Stürmer to Metternich, Büyükdere, 18 and 25 June, 22 July 1834, HHStA, StA, Türkei VI, 61; Roussin to Rigny, Therapia, 27 May, 17 June, 1 and 31 July 1834, AMAE, CP, Turquie 268; Roussin to Rigny, Therapia, 26 Aug. 1834, AMAE, CP, Turquie 269; Martens to Frederick William III, Büyükdere, 1, 8 and 15 July, 26 Aug., 25 Nov. 1834, GStA PK, HA III, MdA I, 7274; N. Ferguson, *The House of Rothschild: Money's Prophets 1798–1848*, London 2000, p. 456; Holland, p. 19.

from the whole amount that had compounded owing to the interest to 175,562 gulden 2 kreutzer on 31 October 1834. Nevertheless, the new negotiation with the Porte led to no result. Reis Effendi Mehmed Akif said to Adelburg in September 1834 that he doubted whether a decision made by a new committee would be any different from those made in January 1831. He saw the only chance for an agreement in a second discount of 40,000 gulden by the Viennese banking house, which would result in the reduction of the debt to less than 100,000 gulden. Although Stametz was willing to accommodate this proposal, no progress was made owing to the opposition of Pertev, who rejected any compromise settlement. Consequently, Akif informed the Austrian dragoman on 14 October 1834 that the Porte considered the affair to be solved and only due to its special regard for the imperial court in Vienna was it prepared to offer any settlement to the Stametz Company at all. The amount of this settlement was to be decided by the Ottomans themselves. Adelburg rejected this proposal because, as he stated, it was a question of law and not a favour and the amount of the debt, moreover, would be left to the arbitrariness of the sultan. Although Akif was still ready to continue in discussion, all goodwill ended at the threshold of the ministry of interior. Pertev declared again on 12 November 1834 that the cereals and all secondary costs had already been paid in full and all other demands for payment were groundless. Furthermore, the quality of some of the supplies had been so bad that the corn had been inedible. The repayment of the debt by an amount determined by the Porte was the only possible way to settlement and if the company refused it, the negotiation was over. This result undoubtedly signified the failure of Austrian diplomacy, but the offer of the settlement was a certain indication for the future that the Porte was still prepared to negotiate.[17]

It is evident from the above-mentioned facts that the main obstruction to a possible understanding was Pertev's presence at the helm of the state affairs. Pertev considered the Stametz Affair to be a question of honour because he had been personally deeply involved in it since the very beginning and a possible fulfilment of any financial obligations would mean his personal failure. Already in 1831, he was

---

[17] Stürmer's note to the Porte, Büyükdere, 20 Aug. 1832, Stürmer to Metternich, Büyükdere, 30 July, 19 and 27 Aug., 10 Sept., 7 and 14 Oct., 3 Dec. 1834, HHStA, StA, Türkei VI, 61; Adelburg, *Overview*, HHStA, StA, Türkei VI, 61.

the most influential member of the committee as well as the greatest opponent of the repayment to the Viennese banking house and he told Mahmud II in January 1833 that the whole dispute was over; unsurprisingly, he felt offended by Apponyi's step the following year. Stürmer was therefore pessimistic in December 1834 with regard to a positive solution to the Stametz requirements as long as Pertev remained in power: "Would Mr Stametz and Company like to reconcile themselves to the payment of their debt with a sum probably much more modest than they are demanding from the Divan? I do not believe so. However, I must admit that I hardly see any other way to restore any glimmer of a negotiation. I have tried all means, even bribery in letting the Reis Effendi know through round-about ways that his efforts would not go unrewarded; everything has been in vain and will also be in the future, and we can no longer doubt it if Pertev Effendi continues to oppose us."[18]

Stürmer did not change his opinion throughout the following three years during which the whole affair stagnated, and it was not by accident that Metternich started a new phase of discussions in November 1837, immediately after the receipt of the news of Pertev's death. He believed that not only the death of this powerful opponent but also the presence of Mustafa Reshid Bey at the head of the Ottoman foreign ministry would change the course of events because the chancellor had talked with Reshid on this issue during the latter's short stay in Vienna, which gave hope for a prompt and positive settlement. Consequently, Stürmer logically addressed his new note of 5 December 1837 relating to the Stametz Affair to Reshid and expressed his regret that he would start his sixth year in Constantinople without obtaining settlement of the justifiable claim of the Austrian company, which had saved the starving Ottoman garrison in Vidin from inevitable death, and he required an immediate and satisfactory solution. Adelburg conveyed the content of this note to Reshid with a statement that the Austrian cabinet strongly recommended satisfication of the Viennese banking house's demands because it was the Austrian emperor and his chancellor who had convinced this company to involve itself in the business and sell the cereals to the Ottomans in the first place. If the Porte objected to the existence of the interest,

---

[18] Stürmer to Metternich, Constantinople, 3 Dec. 1834, HHStA, StA, Türkei VI, 61.

it had to realise that it originated from the fault of Pertev, who had ignored the claims of the company and thus delayed the settlement of the Ottomans' debt. The interest was regarded in Vienna as entirely legitimate and in conformity with the regulations used in the West; therefore, the Stametz Company was not demanding anything else from the Porte that it would not have demanded from another debtor. On 18 December 1837, Stürmer paid a personal visit to Reshid and repeated the arguments raised by Adelburg. The Ottoman foreign minister was somehow shocked by the size of the outstanding debt that had reached 200,000 gulden by that time, but he did not challenge it and the negotiation moved quickly towards a definitive settlement, partly due to Reshid's complaisant attitude, partly because both sides were prepared to make concessions. During March 1838 they reached a compromise agreement: the banking house would obtain 100,000 gulden, partly in money and partly in goods. This decision was formally announced by the Ottoman government in a note addressed to the internuncio on 2 April 1838, and the bill of change was handed over at the beginning of June. Austrian diplomacy thus helped the Viennese company to discharge its claims albeit after making a reduction of 106,000 gulden.[19]

It is difficult to say who the winner of the dispute was. If it was the Porte, then it was a Pyrrhic victory: not because it had to pay more than it wanted, but because the trust of Austrian bankers in its credibility was in ruins. The chronic lack of finances and the need to redeem the compensation to Russia from the late 1820s after the lost war compelled Mahmud II to approach Austria with a request for the mediation of a loan in 1832. However, already at this time

---

[19] Metternich to Stürmer, Vienna, 14 Nov. 1837, HHStA, StA, Türkei VIII, 10; Stürmer to Metternich, Büyükdere, 25 June 1834, HHStA, StA, Türkei VI, 61; Stürmer to Metternich, Constantinople, 8 April 1835, HHStA, StA, Türkei VI, 63; Stürmer to Metternich, Constantinople, 27 Jan. 1836, HHStA, StA, Türkei VI, 64; Stürmer's note to Mustafa Reshid Bey, Constantinople, 5 Dec. 1837, Stürmer to Adelburg, Constantinople, 7 Dec. 1837, Stürmer to Metternich, Büyükdere, 30 Aug. 1837, Constantinople, 29 Nov., 6, 13 and 20 Dec. 1837, HHStA, StA, Türkei VI, 66; the Porte's note to Stürmer, Constantinople, 2 April 1838, Stürmer to Metternich, Constantinople, 18 Jan., 21 Feb., 28 March and 4 April 1838, HHStA, StA, Türkei VI, 67; Stürmer to Metternich, Constantinople, 20 Dec. 1837, HHStA, StA, Türkei VIII, 10; Stürmer to Metternich, Constantinople, 21 March 1838, Adelburg to Klezl, 1 June 1838, Klezl to Metternich, Büyükdere, 2 May and 6 June 1838, HHStA, StA, Türkei VIII, 11.

when the affair of the Viennese banking house was still not resolved, the Austrian bankers were not willing to lend money to the sultan. The behaviour of the Ottoman Empire towards the Stametz Company left such a bad impression that no bank was prepared to enter into negotiations on the question of a loan. Metternich asked the Rothschilds for assistance but they were not willing to do anything until their, formally Stametz, Affair was solved to their satisfaction. Metternich, who himself did not incline to engage Austria in negotiating the loan,[20] commented on this situation with these laconic words: "With the refusal to discharge a debit of several hundred thousand gulden the Divan has deprived itself of the possibility of getting [i.e. borrowing] millions."[21] In 1840, with the full experience of the long and not entirely successful settlement of the claim of the Stametz Company, the Viennese bankers were naturally even more reluctant to meet the Porte's new request for a loan although they did not entirely refuse it. Nevertheless, they required guarantees, for example, diamonds or the production of copper mines, or the guarantee of a third party, namely Austria, which Metternich entirely understood after the previous bad experience: "What they demand is security and no real financial deal is possible without this factor."[22] However, the bankers received none from Austria because Metternich was not willing to enter the same territory again and spend time over another financial dispute. It is true that he was prepared, as he conveyed to Beauvale in January 1840, to accept the risk and offer Austria's guarantee of the loan with other four or three Powers, but there was no chance to obtain their consent.[23] And since the Porte was not willing to offer its precious

---

[20] Metternich to Ottenfels, Vienna, 20 May 1832, HHStA, StA, Türkei VI, 56; Metternich to Ottenfels, Vienna, 19 June 1832, HHStA, StA, Türkei VIII, 5; Ottenfels' note to the Porte, Constantinople, 22 July 1832, Ottenfels to Metternich, Constantinople, 26 March, 25 April, 10 May, 10 and 25 July 1832, HHStA, StA, Türkei VI, 54.
[21] Metternich to Ottenfels, Vienna, 3 June 1832, HHStA, StA, Türkei VI, 56.
[22] Metternich to Stürmer, Vienna, 19 May 1840, HHStA, StA, Türkei VI, 74.
[23] Sina to Metternich, Vienna, [?] 1840, Arnstein and Eskeles, Rothschild and Simon G. Sina to Metternich, Vienna, 26 May 1840, Metternich to Stürmer, Vienna, 17 March and 19 May 1840, HHStA, StA, Türkei VI, 78; Stürmer to Metternich, Constantinople, 1 and 15 April 1840, HHStA, StA, Türkei VI, 74; Stürmer to Metternich, Constantinople, 17 and 22 Aug. 1840, HHStA, StA, Türkei VI, 75; Pontois to Thiers, Therapia, 7 June 1840, AMAE, CP, Turquie 280; Salomon Rothschild to Metternich, [June or July] 1840, N. M. Gelber, "Oesterreich und die Damaskusaf-

stones or the production of copper mines, nobody now came from Austria with assistance. Unhappy Mustafa Reshid, now Pasha, was so disappointed that he even shouted: "It would seem that Prince von Metternich himself scarcely counts on the lasting existence of this [Ottoman] Empire!"[24] Stürmer rejected this accusation and put an end to the question of a loan with a remark on the fact that, as for the Rothschilds, "the memory of the Stametz Affair is still too painful for them to enter new relations with the Porte."[25]

Austria's Fluctuating Level of Influence in the 1820s and 1830s

The failure of the attempt to get Klek and Sutorina and the protraction of the Stametz Affair as well as its final settlement clearly indicate the limit of Austrian influence as well as the reasons for it, as explained in more detail later in the chapter. It would, however, be a mistake to make a far-reaching conclusion concerning this influence during all of the two decades from 1821 to 1841 because it naturally fluctuated. In the early 1820s, Great Britain enjoyed the greatest influence due to Strangford's pro-Turkish activities, leading the Ottomans to regard Great Britain as anti-Russian and even prepared to give military support to the Sublime Porte in the event of a war with its formidable northern neighbour. On the other hand, Metternich's mediating policy and Lützow's restraint made them suspicious of Austria as being too pro-Russian. With George Canning in London, Ottenfels in Constantinople and pro-Austrian Seida Effendi's presence at the helm of Ottoman diplomacy from 1823 to 1827, the balance started to swing to the side of Austria in the mid 1820s. Austria's influence was almost exclusive later in this period due to the support it offered to Mahmud II in the Greek Question, but this happened only because no other Great Power sided with the Ottoman

---

faire im Jahre 1840," *Jahrbuch der Jüdisch-Literarischen Gesellschaft* 18, 1927, p. 257.
[24] Stürmer to Metternich, Constantinople, 10 June 1840, HHStA, StA, Türkei VI, 74.
[25] Ibid.

Empire and there was no competition that Austria had to overcome. Moreover, although this influence was exclusive, it was also rather problematic because, as seen earlier in the book, the Porte listened to Metternich's advice but usually did not follow it.[26] In reaction to the difficulties in persuading the Porte to remove all its troops from the Danubian Principalities, Metternich lamented: "They consider us to be sincere and real friends of the Porte. But then they should believe us!"[27] What Seida Effendi once declared in the mid 1820s was therefore actually far from the truth: "When our most sincere friend, the Austrian Emperor, raises his voice, there can be no further doubt about the decision of my Master, the Sultan."[28]

After the termination of the Russo-Ottoman war in September 1829, the predominant influence was seized by Sir Robert Gordon but only to be handed over to the Russians during the first months of 1830. The position of Austria in the early 1830s considerably differed from that of Russia which had enjoyed almost exclusive influence three years before the signature of the Treaty of Unkiar-Skelessi, strange findings at first sight considering the fact that the former had been the best friend and the latter the most formidable enemy of the Porte during the 1820s.[29] After a more detailed investigation, this situation was quite logical. The cabinet in St Petersburg secured a decisive influence in the Ottoman capital at the beginning of the following

---

[26] Lützow to Metternich, Constantinople, 26 Nov. 1821, HHStA, StA, Türkei VI, 12; Lützow to Metternich, Constantinople, 25 Sept. 1822, HHStA, StA, Türkei VI, 13; Ottenfels to Metternich, Constantinople, 4 Jan. and 4 March 1825, HHStA, StA, Türkei VI, 22; Ottenfels to Metternich, Constantinople, 23 Aug. and 10 Nov. 1825, HHStA, StA, Türkei VI, 23; Miltitz to Frederick William III, Pera, 10 Oct. 1825, GStA PK, HA III, MdA I, 7261; Tatishchev to Nesselrode, Carlsbad, 3 Aug. 1826, AVPRI, fond 133, Kantseliariia, opis 468, 11870; Stiepovich [?] to Royer, Pera, 22 June 1829, GStA PK, HA III, MdA I, 7267; Kargl, p. 189; Krauter, p. 125.

[27] Krauter, p. 130.

[28] Ibid., p. 165.

[29] Ottenfels to Metternich, Constantinople, 30 Oct. and 10 Nov. 1829, HHStA, StA, Türkei VI, 38; Ottenfels to Metternich, Constantinople, 10, 23 and 26 April, 10 May, 11 June, 10 Aug. and 10 Sept. 1830, HHStA, StA, Türkei VI, 50; Ottenfels to Metternich, Constantinople, 11 Oct. 1830, HHStA, StA, Türkei VI, 51; Gordon to Aberdeen, Constantinople, 16 June 1830, TNA, FO 78/190; Gordon to Palmerston, Constantinople, 29 Jan. 1831, TNA, FO 120/114; Cowley to Aberdeen, Vienna, 23 June 1830, TNA, FO 120/108; Ottenfels, *Memoari*, pp. 222 and 235.

decade because of the victory in the above-mentioned conflict and its willingness to reduce the war indemnity imposed on the Porte. In other words, not gratitude but fear and mercenariness were the logical motivation for the behaviour of the sultan and his court. The mortified Ottenfels was not surprised so much by the positive attitude of the Porte towards Russia but by its reserve towards Austria: "It is undoubtedly not appropriate at this time for Austria to seek the predominant influence in Constantinople and desire to be consulted in preference to others in discussions on great political questions. But at least the Porte could remember the countless instances of genuine concern for the welfare of this Empire and the sincere and impartial conduct of Austria so strongly in contrast with the policies followed by other cabinets which called themselves its friends. This conduct should earn the unlimited confidence of the Ottoman government for the Court of Vienna for ever. However, that is not the case. It has never been more reserved towards us; it has never been more absolutely silent over everything concerning political affairs."[30]

The reason the Ottomans attributed so little value to their relations with Austria was the fact that they regarded the support given to them during the war with Russia from 1828 to 1829 as insufficient, and they were particularly dissatisfied by the Austrian refusal to conclude an alliance with them against the tsar. Pertev Effendi complained to Gordon that Austria's friendship had no effect when Turkey stood most in need of it: "What boots it us [sic] that Austria has inveighed against Greek independence, and the Russian war, if she has not interposed a hand; but has calmly suffered her best neighbour to be torn to pieces and trampled under foot, at one and the same time, by two common enemies."[31] Consequently, since the Habsburg Monarchy offered no practical help to the Porte, the Porte came to regard it as a useless ally and, therefore, it lost its consideration and influence at the Porte after 1829. As Jean Mavroyéni declared, the sultan and his advisors trusted its friendship but they also felt that it had left the Porte to its own devices in more than one crisis when it ought to have come to its aid.[32] Ottenfels knew well the Ottomans' at-

---

[30] Ottenfels to Metternich, Constantinople, 26 July 1830, HHStA, StA, Türkei VI, 50.
[31] Gordon to Palmerston, Constantinople, 29 Jan. 1831, TNA, FO 120/114.
[32] Ottenfels to Metternich, Constantinople, 25 Feb. 1829, HHStA, StA, Türkei VI, 36; Metternich to Ottenfels, Vienna, 19 March 1829, HHStA, StA, Türkei VI,

titude on this issue: "In the current situation [when Russian influence dominates in Constantinople] we should not be surprised at seeing the Porte take into no account the many demonstrations of the constant and genuine interest that we have had in it in an era when so many other Powers have worked and are still working towards its ruin. All of that is forgotten and we are so far from being able to expect any sign of confidence on its part that it does not even seem to appreciate those that we would like to give to it. Such a lack of communication like the silence of the Reis Effendi does not say anything other than: Of what use were Austria's declarations of friendship; did this Great Power succeed in parrying just one of the blows that were dealt to us? There is no difference between not having friends and having those who are of no use to us."[33]

The confidence in Austria's sincere friendship, in other words the Ottomans' recognition of the fact that Metternich considered the preservation of their empire to be one of the principle goals of his foreign policy and he supported it whenever it was necessary, was another factor undermining Austria's influence in Constantinople. They appreciated Metternich's goodwill and took his advice into account, but since they did not have to be suspicious of his intentions nor fear his foreign policy, they had no reason to satisfy his wishes as often as they did in the case of Russia, which did not hesitate to accompany its demands with threats if it found it necessary. In reaction to the Porte's unwillingness to meet Austria's request concerning Klek and Sutorina, Ottenfels wrote in June 1832: "All favours are given to those whom it [the Divan] fears; and if one day we want to obtain from it the slightest thing, it will be necessary, if I am not too mistaken, to use a different language from the one we are used to using towards the Porte as a friend."[34] At the end of the same year, Ottenfels added: "The Porte is full of the idea that Austria will remain its friend regardless of what it does. Forty years of peace [and] of an unchanging friendship have convinced it of this. Such a long period during which we have never let it hear so much as a single threat here has reassured

---

39; Gordon to Palmerston, Constantinople, 29 Jan. 1831, TNA, FO 120/114; Lamb to Palmerston, Vienna, 18 June 1834, TNA, FO 120/145; Gürbüz, p. 422.

[33] Ottenfels to Metternich, Constantinople, 10 Aug. 1830, HHStA, StA, Türkei VI, 50.

[34] Ottenfels to Metternich, Constantinople, 26 June 1832, HHStA, StA, Türkei VI, 54.

it to such an extent that it has lost any sense of its weakness towards us."[35] Consequently, there was no reason for the Ottomans to accompany their expressions of friendship or trust in Austria with tangible proof, as seen in the two above-mentioned affairs or in the case of the hydraulic works on the Danube; after the first refusal of the Porte to allow the hydraulic project, Metternich expressed his strong displeasure at the reluctance of the Divan to satisfy more frequently the requests of the Viennese Chancellery: "It is not for the first time that we have had occasion to see the little value of the Ottoman ministers' protestations of friendship and confidence uttered always when they need the help or support of Austria. Yet when we ask them for the slightest regard, the slightest concession, we always find them rigid, suspicious and unwilling."[36]

Metternich strongly regretted the alleged ingratitude of the Ottomans to Austria, but he did not allow himself to be discouraged owing to Russia's predominant position in the years after 1830 because he was able to reconcile himself to the given situation owing to the identical interests of the two empires.[37] Furthermore, Russia used its influence in support of Austria's needs as shown in the question of navigation on the Danube in 1834. The French reports from Constantinople of that period prove the very low level of Austria's influence and, consequently, its need to rely on the support of Russia: "As for Austria's influence, it is completely non-existent, not only with regard to foreign matters but also in relation to its own interests. Its negotiation regarding the works for clearing the earth from the Danube with the aim of establishing a line of steamships there, and the other one for obtaining compensation for the death of an Austrian agent in Cyprus, both of which date back to almost a year ago, have made no progress and will not do so for a long time. By sacrificing itself to Russia in the Levant, Austria's policy has resulted in the Porte totally denying it any influence in matters it [the Porte] otherwise concerns itself."[38] Two years later, the French diplomatic

---

[35] Ottenfels to Metternich, Constantinople, 27 Dec. 1832, HHStA, StA, Türkei VI, 55.

[36] Metternich to Stürmer, Vienna, 16 April 1834, HHStA, StA, Türkei VI, 62.

[37] Metternich to Ficquelmont, Vienna, 22 May 1830, HHStA, StA, Russland III, 90; Metternich to Ottenfels, Vienna, 27 May 1830, HDA, 750, OO 38; Metternich to Francis I, Vienna, 26 June 1830, HHStA, StK, Vorträge 262.

[38] Roussin to Rigny, Therapia, 11 Dec. 1834, AMAE, CP, Turquie 269. See also

correspondence reported: "Austria keeps itself at a distance, and its representative, in order to be able to play any role to which he aspires, has placed himself behind the Russian legation from which he sometimes borrows – and at this moment – precarious influence."[39] Consequently, Metternich was also not upset with the existence of the Treaty of Unkiar-Skelessi because with regard to Russia's influence over the Ottoman Empire, the Treaty definitely strengthened it but was not its cause and, moreover, there was nothing detrimental for Austria in this respect.[40] Metternich also did not share the liberal British cabinet's opinion that the Treaty established "a protectorate of the first of these Great Powers over the other, which in reality only exists as it would have existed without this Treaty because of the geographical proximity of the two [empires], because of their respective strength and weakness, because of the ability to give support, and finally, for indelible reasons, because it is in the nature of things for them to be this way."[41]

Austrian historian Berthold Sutter claims that Austria's friendship in the mid 1830s was important to Mahmud II because it signified a counterbalance to Russia's predominant influence.[42] However, this opinion is entirely false because Metternich not only did not regard Russia's influence in Constantinople to be particularly dangerous but he also did nothing that could challenge it. On the contrary, he regarded with suspicion Ponsonby's attempts after 1834 to replace Russia's predominance with Britain's: "Everything that Lord Ponsonby is saying about the necessity to free the Sultan from Russian influence is an illusion, and will turn into an immense danger for the Ottoman Empire."[43] Unfortunately for Russia as well as Austria, the ambassador finally achieved his goal until 1838.[44]

Roussin to Rigny, Therapia, 20 July 1834, AMAE, CP, Turquie 269.

[39] Eyragues to Molé, Therapia, 12 Nov. 1836, AMAE, CP, Turquie 273.

[40] Martens to Frederick William III, Pera, 13 May 1834, GStA PK, HA III, MdA I, 7274; Roussin to Rigny, Therapia, 11 Dec. 1834, AMAE, CP, Turquie 269.

[41] Metternich to Esterházy, Vienna, 14 March 1834, HHStA, StA, England 208.

[42] Sutter, p. 39.

[43] Metternich to Hummelauer, Vienna, 16 Dec. 1838, HHStA, StA, England 219.

[44] Klezl to Metternich, Büyükdere, 26 Sept. 1838, Stürmer to Metternich, Constantinople, 24 Oct. 1838, HHStA, StA, Türkei VI, 68; Webster, *Palmerston*, II, p. 527.

There were various reasons for Ponsonby's success and it is impossible to deny that one of them was his skill and activity, which enabled him to obtain considerable pro-British sympathy and support from among the sultan's advisors. This raises the question of how much the European representatives could contribute to gaining influence and, in particular, why Ottenfels and Stürmer were not as successful as Ponsonby, especially when they had the potential to build a network of contacts among the Ottoman dignitaries due to their service in Constantinople during their youth when, as was proved in their later diplomatic correspondence, they made friendly contact with some Ottomans who later played a significant role at the top of the administration or still maintained some influence over it. For example, Ottenfels wrote about the use of such a contact from his earlier years in the summer of 1823 when he tried to persuade the Porte of the correctness of Austria's point of view. On 7 August, he visited an influential dignitary, Ghanib Effendi, introducing the conversation with these words: "You do not see before you the internuncio of the Austrian Imperial Court but an old friend or, better said, a son who came to his father to place his sorrows and his woes upon his father's breast. I call you my father because it was you who occupied the post of Reis Effendi when, sixteen years ago, I attended the Porte as an interpreter. It was under your ministry that I began my political career, that I learnt the approach and the manner of dealing with the affairs at the Porte."[45]

Furthermore, the knowledge of language and customs also made such a task easier for the internucios during their service. Of course they did not generally deal directly with the ministers but through their dragomans, but still their skills facilitated their penetration into local society. His knowledge of Turkish also helped Ottenfels to make a good first impression, something very important for the Ottomans, during his first meeting with Mahmud II on 15 October 1822. The initial audience at the Ottoman court significantly differed from those in Europe. It was very long and rather lacking in the usual etiquette for a foreign diplomat used to the European courts. Lützow, not accustomed to Oriental habits, was deeply offended by such a proceeding and particularly with the sultan's lack of concern when saying to the

---

[45] Ottenfels to Metternich, Constantinople, 11 Aug. 1823, HHStA, StA, Türkei VI, 19.

internuncio only one sentence expressing the wish for the preservation of good relations between the two empires. In fact it was actually not a rude reception because Mahmud II sometimes did not say anything or even favour a diplomat with a glance. All the more successful was Ottenfels when he entered his post in the Ottoman capital. On his way on the Danube, he sent a letter in Turkish to the pasha of Vidin. When Mahmud II learnt of this, he expressed the desire to hear Ottenfels make his opening speech in Turkish, which Ottenfels promised to do. Therefore, when he entered the audience chamber, Mahmud II told him: "Come closer, Monsieur Minister, come even closer."[46] Ottenfels came much closer to the throne than was customary and when he finished his speech in Turkish two or three steps from the sultan, Mahmud II expressed himself in a cordial manner. This manifestation of favour was entirely exceptional and for Ottenfels a good start. Mahmud II was so pleased that Ottenfels spoke to him in Turkish that he ordered this fact written down by an Ottoman historiographer into the annals of the empire.[47]

Favours like this one well indicate the potential of the internuncios educated in the Viennese Oriental Academy but of course say nothing about their real influence. Moreover, sometimes these favours were all very well on the surface but rather problematic after a more detailed investigation, like the one granted by Mahmud II to Ottenfels on 10 March 1833 during the latter's last audience with the sultan before his departure from Constantinople. Ottenfels was invited by Mahmud II and lavished with praise and presented with an ornate medallion studded with diamonds and the sultan's monogram that was worn by the grand vizier but never given to a foreigner. However, it is debatable whether the sultan's medallion was such a great expression of his regard as was interpreted by Ottenfels himself. It is evident from the reports of other European representatives in Constantinople that the diplomatic corps was surprised that after his period of more

---

[46] Ottenfels, *Memoari*, p. 134. According to Miltitz, Mahmud II addressed Ottenfels with the Turkish expression "Elgi Bey," which was also a considerable expression of favour because the sultan never used the title "bey" for a foreign diplomat. Miltitz to Frederick William III, Pera, 25 Oct. 1822, GStA PK, HA III, MdA I, 7256.

[47] Ottenfels to Metternich, Pera, 10 and 25 Oct. 1822, HHStA, StA, Türkei VI, 13; Miltitz to Frederick William III, Pera, 10 and 25 Oct. 1822, GStA PK, HA III, MdA I, 7256; Ottenfels, *Memoari*, pp. 130–135; Kargl, pp. 16–18.

than ten years in the Ottoman Empire, during which he always maintained a strictly pro-Ottoman attitude, the internuncio had received only this decoration and not the painting of the Ottoman ruler which he was said to desire. It is probably not necessary to recall the fact that at the very same moment Ottenfels was having to swallow a bitter pill following the sultan's refusal to sell Klek and Sutorina to Austria, something which Ottenfels strongly desired to solve before leaving his post.[48]

The unexploited potential of Austrian diplomats raises another question concerning the capabilities of Ottenfels as well as Stürmer. It is true that evelutions of them by their contemporaries were not entirely positive. Ottenfels was generally described as an intelligent and polite but weak man. This weakness, however, must be attributed to his friendly and mild character, which led to his unwillingness to provoke conflicts. He was a man of an entirely different nature from the British ambassadors in Constantinople like Strangford, Stratford Canning or Ponsonby and probably more suited to an administrative than a diplomatic post in the period and in the location where the restrained character peculiar to him gave no advantage.[49] Metternich himself wrote about Ottenfels that he was "shy and reserved by nature."[50] Ottenfels' successor, Baron Bartolomäus von Stürmer, was not considered by his contemporaries to be any more skilled and suitable for his post. Moreover, the Prussian envoy, Baron Friedrich von Martens, depicted his character as reputedly jealous and irritable and filled with a hunger to achieve a predominant influence over the sultan's court: "Mr Stürmer, who is clever enough but excessively jealous

---

[48] Ottenfels to Metternich, Constantinople, 11 March 1833, HHStA, StA, Türkei VI, 56; Martens to Frederick William III, Büyükdere, 12 and 22 March 1833, GStA PK, HA III, MdA I, 7272; Maltzan to Frederick William III, Vienna, 29 March 1833, GStA PK, HA III, MdA I, 6021; Mandeville to Lamb, Therapia, 11 Nov. 1832, attached to Metternich to Ottenfels, Vienna, 5 Dec. 1832, HHStA, StA, Türkei VI, 56.

[49] Hatzfeldt to Frederick William III, Vienna, 4 Dec. 1824, GStA PK, HA III, MdA I, 6004; Caraman to Damas, Vienna, 30 April 1827, AMAE, CP, Autriche 408; Küpfer to Bernstorff, Pera, 6 Nov. 1829, attached to Guilleminot to Damas, Constantinople, 23 Nov. 1827, AMAE, CP, Turquie 248; Bray to Ludwig I of Bavaria, Vienna, 25 Feb. and 7 Nov. 1828, BHStA, MA, Wien 2402; Gordon to Palmerston, Constantinople, 29 Jan. 1831, TNA, FO 120/114.

[50] Metternich to Trauttmannsdorff, Vienna, 22 Feb. 1828, HHStA, StK, Preussen 128.

and sensitive, never deals honestly with anybody at any time but tries to obtain an exclusive influence with the Porte ... Mr Stürmer has exactly the same character as his late father, which is well known: tiresome, jealous and sensitive about even the tiniest little thing. He [Stürmer Jr.] is upset for not having and not having been able to obtain more significant influence over the resolutions of the Porte: so suspicious of everything, narrow-minded and distrustful, he only strives to play the role of a dictator like his father did for a long time."[51] This led Martens to the scathing verdict that Austria's influence in Constantinople "will remain non-existent as long as the [Austrian] court does not change its minister."[52] On the other hand, it is necessary to add that Martens' criticism is not entirely reliable owing to his problematic relations with Stürmer.[53]

The characters of Ottenfels and Stürmer and the events themselves prove that the criticism of the Austrian diplomats as hardly being capable of ensuring a greater influence of the Danube Monarchy within the Ottoman Empire is not entirely unfounded. Nevertheless, it would be a serious mistake to ascribe the principal blame for this to them. Some of the main reasons undermining Austria's position have already been mentioned above: the lack of fear on the part of the Ottoman dignitaries of any hostility from the friendly Central European Power and their conviction that Austria would offer little practical assistance when necessary.[54] A third but no less important reason was Austria's low financial investment in the highest servants of the Ottoman Empire. Ottenfels even claimed in his memoirs that the Viennese cabinet was not accustomed to bribery in dealing with the Porte and that he personally never used this method of facilitating procedures during his long service in Constantinople from 1822

---

[51] Martens to Frederick William III, Büyükdere, 26 June 1833, GStA PK, HA III, MdA I, 7272.

[52] Martens to Frederick William III, Büyükdere, 10 Feb. 1835, GStA PK, HA III, MdA I, 7274.

[53] Stiepovich [?] to Royer, Pera, 22 June 1829, GStA PK, HA III, MdA I, 7267; Martens to Frederick William III, Büyükdere, 26 June 1833, GStA PK, HA III, MdA I, 7272; Martens to Frederick William III, Pera, 13 May 1834, GStA PK, HA III, MdA I, 7274.

[54] In early 1831, Sir Robert Gordon advocated Ottenfels' skills and conduct and explicitly ascribed the reasons for Austria's low level of influence to these two general factors only. Gordon to Palmerston, Constantinople, 29 Jan. 1831, TNA, FO 120/114.

to 1833.[55] This statement, however, is hard to believe. First, bribery was a very usual way to attain desired goals in Constantinople and another Austrian internuncio, Baron Ignaz von Stürmer, had done so often simply because he had found it necessary. Unsurprisingly, the representatives of all the Great Powers in Constantinople tried to win the decisive influence over the administrative machinery of the state with bribery and one can hardly imagine that Austria did not play this game for so long. Second, in early 1833 before his departure from Constantinople, Ottenfels prepared for the Chancellery a list of presents with corresponding values, not higher than 350 florins a piece, given to Ottoman dignitaries since 1824, some of them being given, as explained in the list, for "assistance" or "intercession."[56] For example, in late 1832, Ottenfels presented the grand vizier with a snuff-box richly ornamented with diamonds to facilitate the settlement of the Klek and Sutorina Affair. Metternich himself advocated the use of bribery. In 1828, he requested Francis I's consent to present a snuff-box ornamented with precious stones to Pertev and make him thus more well disposed to Austria's counsels. In 1836, during Stürmer's presence in Constantinople, Metternich sent Akif a snuff-box ornamented with precious stones as an expression of satisfaction for Akif's pro-Austrian attitude. What supports a certain truth to Ottenfels' claim is the fact that similar presentations of gifts were quite usual in the Ottoman Empire and not regarded as classical bribes. As for giving money, no proof was actually found in the studied documents that Austria would have used cash for bribes in the Ottoman Empire although such a thing is always difficult to prove. Nevertheless, what can be taken for granted is the fact that the Viennese cabinet did not spend much money on bribery or "presents," and this lack of generosity could hardly find much favour among the Ottoman dignitaries generally considerably inclined to corruption, in particular when, for example, Russia seemed to be very generous in this respect.[57]

[55] Ottenfels, *Memoari*, p. 249.
[56] Ottenfels to Metternich, Constantinople, 25 Feb. 1833, HHStA, StA, Türkei VIII, 5.
[57] Metternich to Francis I, Vienna, 20 Oct. 1828, HHStA, StK, Vorträge 255; Metternich to Stürmer, Vienna, 2 Feb. 1836, HHStA, StA, Türkei VIII, 9; Ottenfels to Metternich, Constantinople, 25 Oct. 1832, HHStA, StA, Türkei VI, 55; Kargl, pp. 250–256; Webster, *Palmerston*, II, p. 527.

It was thus difficult for Ottenfels and Stürmer to find someone in the highest circle who would support Austrian requests, something necessary at the sultan's court where competition between various cliques took place. The members of the court cabals were crucial for the gain or loss of influence of foreign countries, and therefore their representatives strove for the support of the most powerful Ottomans, who were surrounded by numerous partisans due to an extensive client system reaching into the administration to its lowermost levels. To get such a party on one's side was the best and probably also the only possible way to assure the most advantageous decision of the Porte. However, if the state apparatus was controlled by men without any attachment for a certain country, it was extremely difficult to accomplish anything. The internuncios obviously failed to get greater support in this field because the leading Ottomans of this period usually did not often feel much rapport with Austria.

Such an attitude was also held by the two top leaders, Husrev Pasha and Pertev Effendi (Pasha after 1836). In the early 1830s, Husrev was well known for his pro-French bias manifested by his support of Blacque's plan to print the French newspaper in Constantinople in 1831 or of the military cooperation between the Ottoman Empire and France, despite the French support of the Greek insurgents, their expedition to Algeria and inclination to Mohammed Ali. This popularity of France was not unusual among the members of the Ottoman higher society and it is possible that it was even greater than their affection to a considerably more amicable Austria. Later in the decade Husrev was said to become pro-Russian, but definitely without becoming pro-Austrian because he always disliked and distrusted this Central European Power. The only man who could compete in power with Husrev was Pertev, in the mid 1830s the most powerful Ottoman dignitary of the empire. Pertev actually was not ill disposed to Austria but neither was he favourably inclined towards it, partly because of its entente with Russia to which Pertev was considerably hostile.[58]

---

[58] Ottenfels to Metternich, Constantinople, 28 April 1829, HHStA, StA, Türkei VI, 37; Ottenfels to Metternich, Constantinople, 25 Aug. 1831, HHStA, StA, Türkei VI, 52; Stürmer to Metternich, Constantinople, 30 March 1833, HHStA, StA, Türkei VI, 57; Stürmer to Metternich, Constantinople, 18 Feb. 1834, HHStA, StA, Türkei VI, 60; Stürmer to Metternich, Constantinople, 9 March 1837, HHStA, StA, Türkei VI, 66; Stürmer to Metternich, Constantinople, 25 Nov. 1840, HHStA, StA, Türkei VI, 77; Malaguzziny to Metternich, Vienna, 19 April 1830,

It was unfortunate for the Viennese cabinet that it was Pertev who represented the Porte in negotiations over the affairs concerning the Stametz Company, Klek and Sutorina. As explained above, he was personally involved in the former and, therefore, unwilling to yield. As for the two strips of land, the problem with Pertev lay in the fact that he did not forget Austria's rejection of the Ottoman offer for an anti-Russian alliance from 1829. It was Pertev who communicated this idea to Ottenfels, as well as the offer of Klek and Sutorina that went with it as a reward for this alliance.[59] Ottenfels commented on the situation later in his memoirs with the use of Vergil's words: "I do not know any nation where the *'manet alta mente repostum'* [it remains stored deep in the mind], in other words the rancour, would be so deeply rooted as with the Turks. And Pertev Effendi was a Turk in every sense of the word."[60] If it is possible to believe Baron Martens, then in 1834 Stürmer fawned on those pro-Russian dignitaries at the sultan's court who were in opposition to Pertev and his clients and thus antagonised this powerful official and closed the door to his support.[61]

The internunciature was only one of two principal ways Metternich could influence the Porte's decision-making, the second being the Ottoman representation in Vienna. During the studied period, however, the latter only existed after 1832 because between 1821 and 1832 its activities were suspended by Mahmud II. Consequently, what remained to Metternich for most of the 1820s besides the internucniature was Gentz's correspondence with the Wallachian hospodars, also

---

HHStA, StA, Türkei VI, 17; Roussin to Rigny, Therapia, 20 July 1834, AMAE, CP, Turquie 269; Roussin to Broglie, Therapia, 18 Aug. 1835, AMAE, CP, Turquie 271; Achart to Meylandt, Pera, 3 July 1839, ADA, CP, Turquie 1; Stiepovich [?] to Royer, Pera, 22 June 1829, GStA PK, HA III, MdA I, 7267; Königsmarck to Frederick William III, Büyükdere, 19 Oct. 1836, GStA PK, HA III, MdA I, 7278; Königsmarck to Frederick William III, Büyükdere, 13 May 1840, GStA PK, HA III, MdA I, 7282.

[59] Ottenfels to Metternich, Constantinople, 25 April 1832, HHStA, StA, Türkei VI, 54; Ottenfels, *Memoari*, p. 249. For more on the sultan's offer of the alliance between Austria and the Ottoman Empire in 1829 see Chapter 9.

[60] Ottenfels, *Memoari*, p. 249.

[61] Martens to Frederick William III, Büyükdere, 23 Sept. 1834, GStA PK, HA III, MdA I, 7274; Stürmer to Metternich, Constantinople, 8 April 1835, HHStA, StA, Türkei VI, 63; Stürmer to Metternich, Büyükdere, 19 April and 26 July 1837, HHStA, StA, Türkei VI, 66.

known in Constantinople where Metternich could use it for influencing the Divan, for example in his unsuccessful effort to persuade it to send an Ottoman negotiator to the Congress of Vienna. The Russo-Ottoman war put an end to Gentz's correspondence and, consequently, deprived Gentz of an annual income of 400 ducats (approximately 46,000 francs) and Metternich of an instrument for influencing the Porte, but in 1831, the well-connected Ottoman dignitary Stephanos Vogorides wanted to use Gentz for the same purpose for the Porte, in other words as the sultan's paid political advisor. Metternich willingly agreed partly due to his friend always being in financial need, partly owing to his own desire to increase Austria's influence in Constantinople. Nevertheless, Gentz's death in June 1832 precluded such a possibility, and Vogorides did not become a defender of Austrian interests in the Ottoman Empire, which had unfortunate consequences for the level of Austria's, and particularly Russia's, influence over the Sublime Porte. Although Vogorides held the unimportant post of the prince of Samos from the end of 1832, he exerted great influence in Constantinople which was later used by Ponsonby for the destruction of Russia's predominant position.[62]

At the same moment when Vogorides wished to use Gentz as an Ottoman correspondent, Mahmud II decided to restore his representation in Vienna and renominate Jean Mavroyéni to the office of the Ottoman chargé d'affaires, the post that this man had already held from 1811 to 1821. Although at that time the Viennese cabinet had wanted an Ottoman representative of Turkish and not of Greek origin, Mavroyéni gradually won considerable respect for his character and qualities from Metternich, the court as well as the diplomatic corps in Vienna. Therefore, when the chancellor learnt in the summer of 1831 that the sultan intended to restore his agency in Vienna, he welcomed this possibility and strongly recommended the choice of Mavroyéni. This support seemed to be an important factor in Mavroyéni's final appointment at the end of 1831 to the post he assumed in the following year. His relations with Metternich continued to be friendly and the chancellor's goodwill even went so far that when

---

[62] Ottenfels to Metternich, Constantinople, 28 Dec. 1831, HHStA, StA, Türkei VI, 53; Ottenfels to Metternich, Constantinople, 11 and 25 Feb. 1832, HHStA, StA, Türkei VI, 54; Ottenfels to Metternich, Constantinople, 31 Dec. 1832, HHStA, StA, Türkei VI, 55; Ottenfels, *Memoari*, p. 251; Tischler, p. 237.

he learnt of Mavroyéni's monthly income of 6,000 piasters (approximately 700 florins), he confidentially interceded in Constantinople for this amount to be increased as it was in his opinion insufficient to afford Mavroyéni a comfortable lifestyle in Vienna. When Ahmed Fethi Pasha was appointed to be the Ottoman ambassador to Austria in 1836, Metternich advocated the preservation of Mavroyéni's position and, therefore, the respect the Ottoman chargé d'affaires was enjoying by that time. This finally happened independently of Metternich's intercession when Mavroyéni was appointed a counsellor of the embassy and he continued to fulfil in this role the duties of a chargé d'affaires.[63]

Metternich tried to use his good relations with Mavroyéni for obtaining a better position for Austria in Constantinople, but the European documents offer little information on their talks or the impact of Mavroyéni's reports in Constantinople. More can be said in this respect about the relevant significance of Ahmed Fethi Pasha who represented Mahmud II in Vienna on a special mission in 1835 and then served as permanent ambassador during 1836–1837. Ahmed got credit for his gallant and friendly behaviour but was not considered to be particularly clever or proficient in diplomatic affairs. Stürmer wrote about him to Metternich before Ahmed's first journey to Vienna in 1835: "He is an excellent and easy-going man with whom my relations could never be more amicable. He understands nothing of diplomatic affairs and he is the first one to admit it, but he lacks neither shrewdness nor powers of observation and sometimes he is ready with a positive response. I dare to hope that Your Highness

---

[63] Metternich to Ottenfels, Vienna, 19 July 1831, HHStA, StA, Türkei VIII, 4; Metternich to Ottenfels, Vienna, 17 Jan. and 3 Feb. 1832, HHStA, StA, Türkei VIII, 5; Metternich to Stürmer, Vienna, 30 March and 3 May 1836, HHStA, StA, Türkei VIII, 9; Metternich to Stürmer, Vienna, 11 Jan. 1840, HHStA, StA, Türkei VIII, 15; Ottenfels to Metternich, Constantinople, 28 June 1831, HHStA, StA, Türkei VI, 52; the Porte's note to Ottenfels, 26 Dec. 1831, Ottenfels to Metternich, Constantinople, 16, 27 and 28 Dec. 1831, HHStA, StA, Türkei VI, 53; Stürmer to Metternich, Constantinople, 20 April 1836, NA, RAM-AC 2, 6; Stürmer to Metternich, Constantinople, 19 May 1836, HHStA, StA, Türkei VI, 65; report from Vienna, 3 April 1841, SS, HD, SG, Wien 94; O'Sullivan to Meulenaer, Vienna, 23 May 1836, ADA, CP, Autriche 4; Tatishchev to Nesselrode, Vienna, 11 Jan. 1839, AVPRI, fond 133, Kantseliariia, opis 469, 1839/213; R. H. Davison, "Vienna as a Major Ottoman Diplomatic Post in the Nineteenth Century," A. Tietze (ed.), *Habsburgisch-osmanische Beziehungen: Relations Habsbourg-ottomanes*, Wien 1985, pp. 252–263; Blancard, p. 149; Gürbüz, pp. 321–322.

will be pleased with this choice."[64] During his stay in Vienna as permanent ambassador, Ahmed lived up to this reputation spending his time more on wasting money on his residence with which he impressed the diplomatic corps than on other more practical tasks, which were mostly undertaken by Mavroyéni.[65]

This situation proved the validity of Stürmer's reservation about the establishment of the Ottoman embassy in Vienna in 1836. He reacted to Ahmed's appointment with the comment "a waste of money,"[66] explaining this in his report to Metternich: "I do not know to what extent the establishment of a permanent embassy could be favourable to the Imperial court, but it is certain that the Porte could save itself a considerable new expense at a time when its finances require the most severe economising."[67] The chancellor agreed with the internuncio because he also largely found the measure pointless and not desirable due to the Porte's shortage of money. Nevertheless, most likely it was not the embassy itself but Ahmed's return that he actually objected to, not because he would have had bad relations with him but, rather the opposite, because they had become quite friendly during Ahmed's first stay in Vienna and continued to be so after his return to Constantinople, as it is shown from their correspondence. When, for instance, Ahmed sent Metternich a gift from Mahmud II,

---

[64] Stürmer to Metternich, Constantinople, 21 May 1835, HHStA, StA, Türkei VI, 63.

[65] Stürmer to Metternich, Büyükdere, 27 July 1835, NA, RAM-AC 2, 6; Königsmarck to Frederick William III, Büyükdere, 19 Oct. 1836, GStA PK, HA III, MdA I, 7278; Wagner to Frederick William III, Pera, 5 April 1837, GStA PK, HA III, MdA I, 7279; Maltzan to Frederick William III, Vienna, 2 Dec. 1836, GStA PK, HA III, MdA I, 6028; Maltzan to Frederick William III, Vienna, 3 June 1840, GStA PK, HA III, MdA I, 7354; Sainte-Aulaire to Molé, Vienna, 2 Dec. 1836, AMAE, CP, Autriche 424; Verger to Ludwig I of Bavaria, Vienna, 28 Nov. 1836, BHStA, MA, Wien 2406; Lerchenfeld to Ludwig I of Bavaria, Vienna, 3 July, 12 Aug. and 31 Dec. 1837, BHStA, MA, Wien 2407. When Ahmed served as permanent ambassador in Vienna, the Ottoman embassy was located in Mariahilfer-straße 42. In the 1830s, the Ottoman agency moved several times and was also located during the decade in Minoritenplatz 21, which means in the immediate vicinity of the Chancellery, and Bürgerspitalgasse 1100. Davison, "Vienna as a Major Ottoman Diplomatic Post," p. 275.

[66] Königsmarck to Frederick William III, Pera, 20 April 1836, GStA PK, HA III, MdA I, 7277.

[67] Stürmer to Metternich, Constantinople, 20 April 1836, HHStA, StA, Türkei VI, 64.

the sultan's portrait, in early April 1836, he accompanied it with a letter with this *post-scriptum*: "I beg of Y[our] H[ighness] to remember me kindly to Madam the Princess and present her with my humble respects."[68] Metternich's answer was no less amicable as is seen in his own *post-scriptum* of his letter from late April: "My wife charges me to extend her greetings to you. She is very well and since husbands are always obedient to their wives, I had to allow mine to take possession of His Highness's portrait. She has placed it in her study with the expectation that one day it will become part of my beloved son's inheritance and he will convey it in due course to his own son."[69] Ahmed was pleased with this approach of the prominent European statesman and generally replied to the chancellor's letters or the messages conveyed by the internuncio with much warmth and affection. In late April 1836, for example, he wrote to Metternich: "As for me, My Prince, every hour that rings reminds me of your goodness, your kindness and your constant friendship of which Y[our] H[ighness] has furnished me with so much evidence, and I eagerly wait to be informed about the state of your good health always hoping that Y[our] H[ighness] will never want to remove me from the top of the list of your good servants and friends."[70] A month later, he explained an "order" to the chancellor expressed earlier as a joke "because there is no ceremony between us and, consequently, we believe we can speak openly to one another."[71] Besides the cordial attitude towards Metternich accompanied by these almost curious expressions of friendship and affection, Ahmed also was in direct contact with Metternich's third wife, Melanie, to whom he sent personal greetings on the birth of their daughter Maria von Metternich-Winneburg together with a bracelet as a present. Metternich used Ahmed's partiality towards him to further Austria's interests at the sultan's court, not only on the question of the employment of Austria's officers in the Ottoman army as explained in the previous chapter but also in the Stametz Affair in which

---

68 Ahmed Fethi Pasha to Metternich, Constantinople, 4 April 1836, HHStA, StA, Türkei VIII, 9.
69 Metternich to Ahmed Fethi Pasha, Vienna, 26 April 1836, attached to Metternich to Stürmer, Vienna, 26 April 1836, HHStA, StA, Türkei VI, 65.
70 Ahmed Fethi Pasha to Metternich, Constantinople, 27 April 1836, HHStA, StA, Türkei VIII, 20.
71 Ahmed Fethi Pasha to Metternich, Constantinople, 30 May 1836, HHStA, StA, Türkei VIII, 20.

Ahmed actually also interceded with the sultan but also without success, in the latter case due to Pertev's strong opposition. In any event, Ahmed was of some use to Metternich in Constantinople but not in Vienna, where the Ottoman dignitary finally spent only a little time with no important results worthy of note.[72]

Considerably more significant for Austria's influence in Constantinople was Ahmed's successor, Sadık Rifat Bey, representing the Porte in Austria in 1838–1839. He was not judged more positively than Ahmed; although regarded as similarly good-natured and more skilled in the task he assumed because he was an assistant to the undersecretary of state for foreign affairs from 1834 to 1838, he was also considered to be superstitious, indecisive, of low intelligence and to possess few diplomatic skills.[73] His strong critic, Joseph von Hammer-Purgstall, considered him to be "stupid, greedy and ignorant."[74] Nevertheless, even though Metternich was not impressed with Rifat's intelligence, he assessed him more positively than some contemporaries and his relations with Rifat were cordial.[75] When Rifat returned to Constantinople in late 1839, he became, as well as Ahmed Fethi earlier, a pro-Austrian man at the top of the Ottoman administration and remained in contact with Metternich, for example writing to him in May 1840: "To the personal reasons which make my memory of Vienna so precious, the close union that exists between [our] two govern-

---

[72] Metternich to Stürmer, Vienna, 17 Feb. 1835, HHStA, StA, Türkei VIII, 8; Metternich to Stürmer, Vienna, 5 Jan. 1836, HHStA, StA, Türkei VIII, 9; Metternich to Stürmer, Vienna, 23 Feb., 3 and 4 May 1836, HHStA, StA, Türkei VI, 65; Metternich to Stürmer, Vienna, 24 Jan. 1837, HHStA, StA, Türkei VI, 67; Stürmer to Metternich, Constantinople, 11 Nov. 1835, HHStA, StA, Türkei VI, 64; Stürmer to Metternich, Constantinople, 7 June 1837, HHStA, StA, Türkei VIII, 10; Ahmed Fethi Pasha to Metternich, Constantinople, 4 April 1836, HHStA, StA, Türkei VIII, 9; Ahmed Fethi Pasha to Melanie von Metternich-Winneburg, Constantinople, 13 April 1836, NA, RAM 388, 2551; Tatishchev to Nesselrode, Vienna, 10 May 1836, AVPRI, fond 133, Kantseliariia, opis 469, 1836/216; Bockelberg to Frederick William III, Vienna, 4 Oct. 1836, GStA PK, HA III, MdA I, 6028.

[73] Lerchenfeld to Ludwig I of Bavaria, Vienna, 2 May 1838, BHStA, MA, Wien 2407; Lerchenfeld to Ludwig I of Bavaria, Vienna, 10 April 1841, BHStA, MA, Wien 2410; Königsmarck to Frederick William IV, Büyükdere, 31 March 1841, GStA PK, HA III, MdA I, 7284; Ş. Mardin, *The Genesis of Young Ottoman Thought: A Study in the Modernization of Turkish Political Ideas*, Syracuse 2000, p. 176.

[74] Hammer-Purgstall, p. 322.

[75] Metternich to Stürmer, Vienna, 11 and 21 Jan. 1840, HHStA, StA, Türkei VIII, 15.

ments has further added political rapport and bound us more closely. We know how much the superior wisdom of Your Highness weighs upon the balance of Europe and that it has contributed significantly to preserving and strengthening this union and I, for my part, hope with all sincerity that the heavens preserve You for the peace and happiness of Europe."[76]

It was no accident that during 1840–1841, Austria's influence in Constantinople was not only quite high but also at its greatest during the studied period and with time it became the most significant of all the European Powers. Rifat, who was even labelled by Stratford Canning as "Metternich's pet,"[77] definitely contributed to this situation, in particular after his appointment to the Ottoman foreign ministry in late March 1841, but the same merit must be ascribed to the preceding foreign minister, Mustafa Reshid Pasha, who was Pertev's protégé and was generally regarded as an admirer of the Western liberal Powers, but who did not behave adversely towards Austria and was sympathetic towards Metternich, as will be shown in Chapter 30. It was not a coincidence that the Stametz Affair was settled when Reshid assumed the reins of the Ottoman foreign ministry; Eduard von Klezl explicitly pointed out that it was only solved due to Reshid's help.[78] The French support to Mohammed Ali during the Second Mohammed Ali Crisis from 1839 to 1841 and Ponsonby's growing aversion to Reshid made the minister even more pro-Austrian and finally enabled Stürmer to increase his own influence in Constantinople during 1840 and boast that "Reshid placed the highest confidence in the counsel of Austria, and under his ministry our influence in this country achieved its highest point."[79] The facts as well as the reports of other European diplomats support this immodest statement.[80]

[76] Rifat to Metternich, Constantinople, 4 May 1840, HHStA, StA, Türkei VIII, 20.

[77] A. Cunningham, "Stratford Canning and the Tanzimat," E. Ingram (ed.), *Eastern Questions in the Nineteenth Century: Collected Essays*, II, London 1993, p. 120.

[78] Klezl to Metternich, Büyükdere, 6 June 1838, HHStA, StA, Türkei VIII, 11.

[79] Stürmer to Metternich, Constantinople, 29 March 1841, HHStA, StA, Türkei VI, 80.

[80] Stürmer to Metternich, Constantinople, 8 Jan. 1840, HHStA, StA, Türkei VI, 73; Stürmer to Metternich, Constantinople, 29 March 1841, HHStA, StA, Türkei VI, 80; Maltzan to Frederick William III, Vienna, 1 Jan. 1840, GStA PK, HA III, MdA I, 7351; Pontois to Guizot, Therapia, 27 Nov. 1840, AMAE, CP, Turquie 281.

Rifat's pro-Austrian attitude can also be perfectly demonstrated with his choice of the Ottoman representative in Vienna after Mavroyéni's death on 31 March 1841. Since Rifat had a problem finding a suitable person for the vacated post quickly, he made a strange decision when he conferred the protection of Ottoman interests in Austria upon Valentin von Huszár, who had earlier served for years at the internunciature in Constantinople, finally as its first dragoman from 1827 to 1829. Huszár was generally appreciated for his great knowledge of Oriental languages, and according to Baron Miltitz, he was the best dragoman in Constantinople, speaking Turkish better than many Turks and being fully appreciative of the Koran and Oriental çustoms.[81] The Prussian envoy wrote about Huszár in 1827: "His eloquence in Turkish has become a legend among the Moslems themselves, who marvel at seeing an infidel so well-versed in their language, laws and customs."[82] Rifat had a good opportunity to ascertain Huszár's qualities during his ambassadorial stay in Vienna where he often dealt with this first interpreter and advisor for Oriental affairs at the Chancellery. Huszár's abilities and his good relations with Rifat finally led to the unusual decision in the spring of 1841 to make an Austrian citizen, who was simultaneously a high official in diplomatic affairs, an Ottoman agent. Metternich consented to this because Huszár's appointment promised to ensure him greater influence over Ottoman politics and for Huszár it meant greater income, as he was being paid simultaneously by the two governments. Although this was a temporary measure only, it showed the high level of confidence shown by the Porte to the Viennese cabinet at that time.[83]

[81] Ottenfels to Metternich, Constantinople, 25 Feb. 1829, HHStA, StA, Türkei VI, 36; Ottenfels to Metternich, Constantinople, 28 April 1829, HHStA, StA, Türkei VI, 37; Miltitz to Frederick William III, Pera, 25 Oct. 1821, GStA PK, HA III, MdA I, 7255; Miltitz to Frederick William III, Pera, 5 Nov. 1827, GStA PK, HA III, MdA I, 7265; Hatzfeldt to Frederick William III, Vienna, 4 Aug. 1823, GStA PK, HA III, MdA I, 6002; O'Sullivan to Meylandt, Vienna, 5 Aug. 1839, ADA, CP, Autriche 6; report from Vienna, 3 April 1841, SS, HD, SG, Wien 94.
[82] Miltitz to Frederick William III, Pera, 17 May 1827, GStA PK, HA III, MdA I, 7264.
[83] Report from Vienna, 26 May 1841, SS, HD, SG, Wien 94; O'Sullivan to Meulenaer, Vienna, 26 May 1841, ADA, CP, Autriche 8; Lerchenfeld to Ludwig I of Bavaria, Vienna, 5 June 1841, BHStA, MA, Wien 2410; Altieri to Lambruschini, Vienna, 4 June 1841, ASV, Arch. Nunz. Vienna 280D.

* * *

Despite its considerable increase during 1840–1841, Austria's real influence at the sultan's court was much less significant in the whole period under research from 1821 to 1841 than one could suppose regarding the generally good Ottoman-Austrian relations. The weak position undermined Austria's requests in affairs insignificant from a diplomatic point of view like the navigability of the Danube, Stametz or Klek and Sutorina, as well as in affairs of the highest political significance, for example, during the Greek insurrection when Metternich's influence over the Sublime Porte was assessed by European diplomats as very high, in particular in the late 1820s, but on closer inspection it is clear that the Ottomans scarcely listened to his advice. Although they respected him during the 1820s as well as in the following decade, his means for influencing their decision-making were extremely limited. In the 1830s, Austria's influence in Constantinople consisted of merely supporting that of Russia, which definitely was not without importance in the development of the Eastern Question because Austria's sincere pro-Ottoman attitude, well known to the Ottomans, made them more trustful of the tsar's designs; if Metternich had decided to destroy Russia's position by joining the Maritime Powers, the results would definitely have been devastating for the tsar. However, even Austria's support of Russia finally did not prevent Ponsonby's victory when eliminating Russia's predominance in 1838, and this can be considered as further proof of Austria's weak influence in Constantinople.

The Egyptian Question and the Beginning of the Second Mohammed Ali Crisis

The preservation of the political status quo in the Ottoman Empire was a desire shared by all the Great Powers after 1833; they all feared the far-reaching consequences of a new war between Mohammed Ali and Mahmud II on the very existence of the empire as well as peace on the Continent. Consequently, Metternich went to considerable lengths to keep the antagonism in the relations between the sultan and his pasha at a tolerable level. When a new war finally broke out in the Levant in the spring of 1839, he assumed the lead and provoked the diplomatic intervention of all European Powers into the conflict in late July. From that moment the Second Mohammed Ali Crisis ceased to be an internal affair of the Ottoman Empire and became a serious problem for European politics.

The Development of the Egyptian Question before 1838

After the end of the first Turko-Egyptian war in May 1833, the Ottoman Empire was actually governed from two centres: Constantinople and Alexandria. Sultan Mahmud II was still its only formal head of state, but half of his domains were administered by Mohammed Ali, who extended his power over Egypt, Sudan, Syria, Adana, Crete and a considerable part of the Arabian Peninsula. The sultan's authority in these territories was only nominal. This was a result of the Agreement of Kütahya that did not lead to an enduring peace but merely to a provisional cessation of hostilities. Mahmud II lost too much of his power to be able to reconcile himself to the situation and he looked forward to the time when he could exact revenge. He wanted to regain his lost provinces and ruin his too powerful and disloyal vassal. Obviously this was not in line with the wishes of Mohammed Ali who wanted to obtain hereditary possession of all the provinces under his administration thereby securing these holdings for his descendants. Whether he desired complete independence, as was often said of him by his contemporaries, is still open to discussion, but most likely he primarily wanted just autonomy within the Ottoman Empire to which he was closely attached by political, cultural and religious roots. When he openly threatened with independence in 1834 and 1838, he obviously did so for fear about the future of his family's rule over the provinces he had gained and with the aim of obtaining their hereditary possession from the sultan with this ruse.[1] Consequently, as well as the Eastern Question concerning the future of the Ottoman Empire there was simultaneously the Egyptian Question relating to the future of Mohammed Ali and his family.

In Vienna the Agreement of Kütahya was regarded as what it exactly was: a breathing space before a new encounter. Metternich was rather sceptical that peace would be preserved in view of the animosity existing between the sultan and the pasha, whose ambitions the chancellor feared. Metternich's misgivings were shaped by the views of Prokesch, who was regarded as Austria's leading expert on Mohammed Ali and, therefore, invited to Münchengrätz in September 1833. Although Prokesch arrived after the signature of the Convention on 18 September, he took part in further talks on the situation of the Ottoman Empire and was asked for a written report on Mohammed Ali's designs and power, which gave rise to two analyses: *Report on the Egyptian Question* and *Report on the Actual Egyptian Forces Compared with Those of the Sublime Porte*. These two documents undoubtedly influenced Austria's policy in the Egyptian Question in the following years. In the former, Prokesch maintained the position that Mohammed Ali never aspired to obtain control over the entire Ottoman Empire; rather Prokesch felt Mohammed Ali wanted to establish one of his own that extended from the Taurus Mountains to the deserts of the Sudan and the Arabian Peninsula.[2]

---

[1] A. Abdel-Malek, "Moh'ammad ʿAlî et les fondements de l'Égypte indépendante," *Les Africains* 58, Paris 1977, p. 238; Gaultier-Kurhan, p. 178; Kutluoğlu, pp. 118 and 128; Rustum, *The Royal Archives*, p. 61.

[2] A. von Prokesch-Osten, *The Report on the Actual Egyptian Forces Compared with Those of the Sublime Porte*, September 1833, and *The Report on the Egyp-*

Even though Prokesch changed his view a year later and regarded Mohammed Ali's eventual declaration of independence mainly as a consequence of the sultan's attack, Metternich suspected that until early 1839 the pasha endeavoured to found an independent Arab empire from provinces under his administration, of course an unacceptable step for the chancellor, who saw no advantage in the existence of such a new state in the Near East, not only because it raised questions of legitimacy but also, and in particular, because the loss of such a great territory to the Ottoman Empire would inevitably destabilise the whole region. It could lead to the collapse of the relatively fragile Ottoman Empire, and even if it survived such a loss, its limited extent and weakened power base would have made it essentially defenceless against economic or even territorial expansion by another state. If Mohammed Ali declared his independence and successfully established his own empire, this new state would be connected with the fate of its founder, and it could not survive his death for long: "The Egyptian power is called Mohammed Ali; it is possible that tomorrow it will be called Ibrahim Pasha but it will never become the inheritance of his [Mohammed Ali's] family."[3] In Metternich's opinion, the fact that Mohammed Ali created a regular army, navy, and industry was not a guarantee of the durability of his power in the world of Arabs where tribal loyalties were the primary political force and Mohammed Ali did not belong to an Arab tribe. The natural consequence of his personal ambitions would inevitably lead to an Arab empire that "would become a source of trouble and general disruption such as can occur only in political entities deprived of any foundation of sustainability."[4] The result of Metternich's consideration on this matter was the unwavering opinion that the existence of an Arab empire in part or in all of the area controlled by the Ottoman Empire did not guarantee that it would last longer than the sultan's, even despite

---

tian Question, Münchengrätz, 18 Sept. 1833, attached to Metternich to Esterházy, Vienna, 27 Oct. 1833, HHStA, StA, England 204; Metternich to Apponyi, Vienna, 20 May 1833, HHStA, StA, Frankreich 289; Metternich to Ficquelmont, Vienna, 30 Oct. 1833, HHStA, StA, Russland III, 99; Prokesch-Osten, *Aus den Tagebüchern*, pp. 192–195.
[3]   Metternich to Apponyi, Vienna, 26 June 1838, HHStA, StA, Türkei VI, 67.
[4]   Ibid.

Mohammed Ali's reformatory skills which Metternich well knew and appreciated.[5]

The most imminent danger resulting from Mohammed Ali's possible declaration of independence, and another reason for Metternich to forestall it, was Mahmud II's guaranteed hostile reaction and the outbreak of a new Turko-Egyptian war. It was taken for granted that the sultan would never willingly surrender his provinces and it was also well known in Vienna that he desired to wage a new war against the pasha when the moment was found to be opportune in Constantinople. Unfortunately for the Ottoman monarch, given the superiority of the Egyptian army over his own forces, the pasha's victory in a conflict was generally presumed, as was also stated by Prokesch in his second report comparing the pasha's and sultan's forces. Mahmud II could naturally be saved by a new Russian military intervention in the Straits, but the principal problem with this lay in the fact that France and Great Britain refused to allow a unilateral Russian intervention in the Ottoman Empire. They declared that if the tsar's armed forces appeared on the Bosphorus, they would send their fleets into the Sea of Marmara, something considered by Nicholas I as a casus belli for Russia. Consequently, a war between the sultan and the pasha could have serious consequences not only for the Levant but also Europe.[6]

For Metternich the best way to prevent the outbreak of war among the European Powers was to prevent the situation arising where the tsar found it necessary to send his troops to the Bosphorus again. Exactly for this reason the fundamental objective of Austria's Near Eastern policy after 1833 was the preservation of status quo created by the Agreement of Kütahya in which Metternich focused his effort on diverting Mahmud II from thoughts of revenge and persuading him to be patient and Mohammed Ali from disloyalty to-

---

[5] Metternich to Esterházy, Vienna, 14 March 1834, Metternich to Hummelauer, Vienna, 31 Oct. 1834, HHStA, StA, England 208; Metternich to Stürmer, Baden, 26 Aug. 1834, HHStA, StA, Türkei VI, 62; Metternich to Esterházy, Vienna, 26 June 1838, Königswart, 27 July 1838, HHStA, StA, England 219; Metternich to Stürmer, Vienna, 18 Feb. 1835, HHStA, StA, Türkei VI, 64; Lamb to Palmerston, Vienna, 13 March 1834, TNA, FO 120/145; Langsdorff to Molé, Vienna, 25 June 1838, AMAE, CP, Autriche 425; K. Lachmayer, *Mehmed Ali und Österreich*, unpublished dissertation, Wien 1952, p. 35; Bertsch, p. 191.
[6] A. von Prokesch-Osten, *The Report on the Actual Egyptian Forces Compared with Those of the Sublime Porte*, September 1833, attached to Metternich to Esterházy, Vienna, 27 Oct. 1833, HHStA, StA, England 204; Kutluoğlu, p. 110.

wards his sovereign. Metternich was convinced that this task was not impossible to achieve if the Great Powers cooperated in the Egyptian Question, which they actually did because all of them wished to maintain the status quo in the Near East.[7] Russia continued to see in Mohammed Ali a threat for the same reasons which had provoked its military intervention in early 1833. The tsar's fear of any increase in the pasha's power is clearly evident from the Münchengrätz Convention in which he, together with Francis I, pledged to prevent any limitation of the sultan's power or his possible overthrow, nominally by Mohammed Ali, who was considered to be the primary threat to the sultan's state. Both Russia and Austria accepted an obligation to oppose any attempt by the pasha to extend his authority over the European part of the Ottoman Empire. The third conservative Power, Prussia, played a marginal role in the Eastern Question and all it actually wanted was the preclusion of everything that could negatively influence the affairs in the West. Therefore, the attitude of the cabinet in Berlin towards Mohammed Ali was entirely in agreement with that shared by Austria and Russia. Great Britain was even more hostile to the Egyptian governor because it regarded his ambitions as a direct threat to its interests in the Near and Middle East: the system of monopolies preventing the penetration of cheaper British goods in Egypt and Syria, the control of the overland route to India over Suez or Syria, Egypt's expansion in the Arabian Peninsula, its victories over the Ottoman forces in 1832 bringing the Russians into the Golden Horn and strengthening thus their influence over the Sublime Porte. All of these caused considerable hostility on the part of Palmerston, who became the fiercest and most dangerous opponent of Mohammed Ali after 1833.[8]

Another reason for Palmerston's aversion to Mohammed Ali and which Metternich purposely encouraged in the British foreign secretary was the widespread belief about the pasha's close friendship with

---

[7] Metternich to Esterházy, Vienna, 10 Dec. 1833, HHStA, StA, England 204; Metternich to Esterházy, Vienna, 17 Jan. 1834, HHStA, StA, England 208; Metternich to Laurin, Vienna, 12 April 1834, HHStA, StA, Ägypten 1; Stürmer to Metternich, Constantinople, 13 Nov. 1834, HHStA, StA, Türkei VI, 61; Lamb to Palmerston, Vienna, 26 Dec. 1833, TNA, FO 120/137.

[8] E. Lengyel, *Egypt's Role in World Affairs*, Washington 1957, p. 12; J. Ridley, *Lord Palmerston*, London 1970, p. 212; Clayton, p. 70; Hoskins, pp. 266–269; Molden, pp. 119–123.

France. In fact, the French governments primarily wished to preserve the status quo in the Near East as did the other Great Powers despite the fact that French relations with Mohammed Ali were the friendliest from among all the Powers and strong affection actually existed for him among the French, including the members of the most influential circles, who considered Mohammed Ali to be the successor of the traditions that Napoleon left in Egypt with his military expedition and who claimed the credit for the regeneration of Egypt on behalf of France due to numerous French advisors in Mohammed Ali's service. The expansion of Egypt was thus tolerated only as far as it did not threaten the very existence of the Ottoman Empire. Therefore, the principal goal of the French diplomacy was that Mohammed Ali remained loyal to Mahmud II, and the maximum that it was willing to allow was the hereditary rule of his family over Egypt and some other provinces. This attitude led France to pursue an ambivalent policy simultaneously flirting with the sultan as well as his powerful vassal, a political line that was to cause France's serious diplomatic defeat during the Second Mohammed Ali Crisis.[9]

The mutual desire of the Great Powers to preserve the situation as established in Kütahya was already proved in the summer of 1834 when relations between Constantinople and Alexandria seriously deteriorated again. When an uprising in Syria erupted against Egyptian supremacy at the beginning of May, Mahmud II watched in the hope that it would succeed and considered helping the rebels. At the end of July, Stürmer wrote to Vienna: "It is no longer Mohammed Ali who is looking for a fight with the Porte; it is the sultan who, in his weakness, wants to attack his powerful and formidable vassal and profit from his [Mohammed Ali's] assumed problems in order to bring him down."[10] Some of the elite Ottoman dignitaries exhibited the same aggressive attitude, like Akif Effendi who said to Stürmer in early August: "Should we now sit with our arms crossed? Peace in Syria has been destroyed. We should act in accordance with the circumstances."[11] Evidence of the gravity of the situation can be found in

---

[9]   F. Charles-Roux, *Thiers et Méhémet-Ali: La grande crise orientale et européenne de 1840–1841*, Paris 1951, p. 14; Kutluoğlu, p. 110; Puryear, *France*, p. 208.

[10]   Stürmer to Metternich, Büyükdere, 28 July 1834, HHStA, StA, Türkei VI, 61.

[11]   Stürmer to Metternich, Büyükdere, 8 Aug. 1834, HHStA, StA, Türkei VI, 61.

the views of more members of the diplomatic corps in Constantinople who considered a new war to be inevitable.[12]

Mahmud II's provocative behaviour found no supporters in Vienna. Metternich strongly opposed a possible infraction of the Agreement of 5 May 1833 and in his instructions to Stürmer he expressed his opinion that the sultan had made peace and therefore he ought to respect it, particularly since the uprising in Syria did not justify a new war in which the defeat of the Turks was absolutely certain. Therefore, temporisation was, in Metternich's opinion, the best decision for Mahmud II whom he criticised for his impatience: "There is nothing as impatient as weak people, and the greatest of their faults is always the one of being weak when they could and should be strong and of having notions of power and energy when they should remain calm."[13] Stürmer was instructed to clearly state that Austria would not approve of any military action and would provide no support. He was also told to work with other representatives of the European Powers in a common effort to save the peace. Their joint approach and particularly the suppression of the rebellion in Syria by the Egyptian army in July 1834 finally led the Porte to moderation. From the beginning of September, Stürmer was announcing to Vienna that the threat of Ottoman aggression had been definitely averted.[14]

Nevertheless, the Porte's retreat did not ease the tension in the Ottoman Empire. The sultan's belligerency was known in Alexandria and in mid August 1834, Mohammed Ali reacted with anger by announcing that at the first sign of hostility on the part of the Porte he would not feel bound by loyalty to his sovereign and he would use

---

[12] Stürmer to Metternich, Büyükdere, 13 Aug. 1834, HHStA, StA, Türkei VI, 61; Martens to Frederick William III, Büyükdere, 12 Aug. 1834, GStA PK, HA III, MdA I, 7274; Kutluoğlu, pp. 114–115.

[13] Metternich to Stürmer, Baden, 2 Sept. 1834, HHStA, StA, Türkei VI, 62.

[14] Metternich to Stürmer, Baden, 11 and 26 Aug. 1834, HHStA, StA, Türkei VI, 62; Metternich to Ficquelmont, Baden, 14 Aug. 1834, HHStA, StA, Russland III, 102; Metternich to Ficquelmont, Baden, 3 Sept. 1834, HHStA, StA, Russland III, 103; Metternich to Hummelauer, Vienna, 11 Sept. 1834, HHStA, StA, England 208; Stürmer to Metternich, Büyükdere, 19 and 27 Aug., 2 and 17 Sept. 1834, HHStA, StA, Türkei VI, 61; Sainte-Aulaire to Rigny, Vienna, 9 Aug. 1834, La Rochefoucauld to Rigny, Vienna, 28 and 31 Aug., 5, 13 and 16 Sept. 1834, AMAE, CP, Autriche 421; Brockhausen to Frederick William III, Vienna, 12 Aug. and 16 Sept. 1834, GStA PK, HA III, MdA I, 6024; Martens to Frederick William III, Büyükdere, 1 Sept. 1834, GStA PK, HA III, MdA I, 7274.

all his forces to achieve complete independence. In Stürmer's opinion, it was possible that Mohammed Ali could carry out this threat particularly because he often discussed it and accompanied it with extensive armament; the pasha went so far as to ask Metternich for support for his plan for independence. In a letter formally addressed to Prokesch on 3 September, Yusuf Boghos Bey announced that the pasha had never desired independence but at the moment was forced by circumstances to declare it: "The influence of Austria would be of the greatest significance to the success of such a bold plan, particularly for the direct or indirect impetus which it could give to other Great Powers that also have real interests in maintaining the stability of Europe. The viceroy [Mohammed Ali] hopes that this reason combined with the important commercial relations existing between Austria and Egypt will be a sufficiently effective reason for the decision of His Excellence [Metternich] to look favourably on this proposal and give it His influential support."[15] The Austrian chancellor was surprised by the fact that the pasha addressed to him the request for assistance against the sultan. He saw the most probable explanation for it in some French journals, in particular *Le Temps* and the *Journal des débats*, which had some time earlier printed articles claiming that Austria had abandoned Russia and joined the Maritime Powers with the aim of opposing the tsar's designs in the Near East. Since Mohammed Ali was interested in the contents of European journals relating to the Ottoman Empire and Egypt, he addressed his letters not only to France and Great Britain but also to Austria, trying to obtain their support with strong anti-Russian rhetoric declaring that the tsar was trying to provoke a new Turko-Egyptian war and use the weakening of the Ottoman Empire for its new military intervention at its heart. In any case, Metternich refused to offer his support and expressed his regret that Mohammed Ali supported the ideas expressed in Boghos' letter. According to the chancellor, a declaration of independence would only cause great harm and would be met with the opposition of the Powers. He also rejected the allegations raised against Russia. Since France and Great Britain answered Mohammed Ali in the same way, the pasha gave up his ambitions for the time being and decided to remain in subjection to the Porte. At the end

---

[15] Yusuf Boghos Bey to Prokesch, Alexandria, 3 Sept. 1834, HHStA, StA, Türkei VI, 62.

of 1834, his statements became increasingly moderate and he finally informed Laurin of his desire to live with Mahmud II in peace and to assure him that he would never attack his sovereign. The end of the year brought relief to Metternich as well as the confirmation of his belief that if the Great Powers cooperated, it was quite possible to prevent even the greatest calamity. This opinion significantly shaped his later proceedings in the Egyptian Question.[16]

The whole affair had one unpleasant consequence for Austria. Its negative answer to the request for support for his separatist plans displeased Mohammed Ali to such an extent that he even took revenge by making a serious accusation against Prokesch: the Austrian diplomat was said to have instigated the pasha's hunger for independence during his last mission in Egypt in 1833. Boghos informed the European consuls that he possessed Prokesch's letters proving this accusation. This assertion can be found in the reports of the Russian consul general in Egypt, Duhamel, who at the end of 1834 accused Prokesch of being the first one who inspired Mohammed Ali to create an independent Arab empire, and also in Campbell's later dispatch from 1838 in which the British consul general wrote about Prokesch's putative letter (memorandum) to Mohammed Ali dated 17 May 1833, in which the idea of Egyptian independence had been encouraged.[17] Their claims were

---

[16] Metternich to Apponyi, Vienna, 18 Oct. and 2 Nov. 1834, HHStA, StA, Frankreich 294; Metternich to Hummelauer, Vienna, 18 and 31 Oct. 1834, HHStA, StA, England 208; Metternich to Ficquelmont, Vienna, 20 Oct. and 10 Nov. 1834, HHStA, StA, Russland III, 103; Metternich to Stürmer, Vienna, 7 Nov. and 31 Dec. 1834, Prokesch to Yusuf Boghos Bey, Vienna, 18 Oct. 1834, HHStA, StA, Türkei VI, 62; Metternich to Stürmer, Vienna, 23 Feb. 1836, HHStA, StA, Türkei VI, 65; Metternich to Prokesch, Vienna, 10 Dec. 1835, HHStA, StK, Griechenland 12; Champion to Metternich, Alexandria, 17 and 23 Aug., 24 Sept. 1834, Antonelli to Stürmer, Alexandria, 30 Sept. 1834, Stürmer to Metternich, Büyükdere, 30 Sept., 7 and 29 Oct. 1834, Constantinople, 12, 16, 17 and 20 Dec. 1834, HHStA, StA, Türkei VI, 61; Laurin to Stürmer, Cairo, 14 Jan. 1835, Stürmer to Metternich, Constantinople, 11 March 1835, HHStA, StA, Türkei VI, 63; Duhamel to Nesselrode, Alexandria, 26 Aug. 1834, Duhamel to Butenev, Alexandria, 15 Nov. 1834, HHStA, StA, Türkei VI, 61; Brockhausen to Frederick William III, Vienna, 18 Oct. 1834, GStA PK, HA III, MdA I, 6024; Brockhausen to Frederick William III, Vienna, 3 Jan. 1835, GStA PK, HA III, MdA I, 6025; Campbell to Palmerston, Alexandria, 12 Oct. 1834, TNA, FO 78/247; Lamb to Palmerston, Vienna, 2 Nov. 1834, TNA, FO 120/145; Sainte-Aulaire to Rigny, Vienna, 18 and 25 Oct., 7 Nov. 1834, AMAE, CP, Autriche 421; Cetto to Ludwig I of Bavaria, Vienna, 22 Oct. 1834, BHStA, MA, Wien 2405.

[17] Duhamel to Butenev, 31 Dec. 1834, attached to Stürmer to Metternich, Con-

adopted by several historians who were of the opinion that Prokesch's alleged sedition led the Egyptian governor to believe that a declaration of independence would meet with much sympathy and support from some European Powers and, consequently, to his request addressed to Paris, London and Vienna in September 1834.[18] Muhammad Sabry went in his speculation so far that he was convinced that Prokesch, in his admiration for Mohammed Ali, advised the foundation of an Arab empire extending to the Persian Gulf because he wanted to remove the governor from France's influence and alienate him from Great Britain, which would have considered the creation of such an empire to be a threat to its dominion in India.[19] On the other hand, Austrian historian Friedrich Engel-Jánosi familiar with Prokesch rejected the validity of the accusation raised against the diplomat.[20]

Prokesch naturally denied that he would have incited the Egyptian governor to establish an Arab empire and Metternich did not believe the "absurd and mendacious rumours"[21] because he was convinced that his agent knew too well the invariable principles of Austrian foreign policy and he would have never dared to encourage Mohammed Ali in his plans for independence. The chancellor ordered his diplomats to come out against the accusation, particularly Stürmer, who himself considered it to be entirely groundless. Metternich's rather fierce and hostile reaction is easily understandable if one realises that the allegation impeached not only the honour of one diplomat but also the whole Austrian diplomacy in the Near East because it was not clear to contemporaries whether Prokesch had acted wilfully or in accordance with the instructions of his court; the chancellor thus defended in this matter not only his subordinate but also himself.[22]

---

stantinople, 18 Feb. 1835, HHStA, StA, Türkei VI, 63; Sabry, pp. 271–272.

[18] Kutluoğlu, p. 118; Webster, *Palmerston*, I, p. 340.

[19] Sabry, pp. 270–271.

[20] Engel-Jánosi, *Die Jugendzeit*, p. 161.

[21] Metternich to Stürmer, Vienna, 18 March 1835, HHStA, StA, Türkei VI, 64.

[22] Metternich to Stürmer, Vienna, 31 Dec. 1834, HHStA, StA, Türkei VI, 62; Metternich to Stürmer, Vienna, 18 Feb. and 18 March 1835, HHStA, StA, Türkei VI, 64; Metternich to Prokesch, Vienna, 31 Dec. 1834 and 24 Feb. 1835, HHStA, StK, Griechenland 12; Metternich to Ficquelmont, Vienna, 27 Feb. 1835, HHStA, StA, Russland III, 105; Metternich to Esterházy, Vienna, 21 March 1835, HHStA, StA, England 214; Stürmer to Metternich, Constantinople, 28 Jan. and 11 March 1835, HHStA, StA, Türkei VI, 63; Strangways to Wellington, Vienna, 5 Jan. 1835,

If the second possibility must be entirely rejected, the former should be analysed. Prokesch's rejection of the allegation and Metternich's hostile attitude to it naturally do not necessarily signify its lack of any foundation; the former had to deny the accusation because his career was at stake, and the latter had to repudiate it even if he had known it to be true, at least with regard to maintaining good relations with the sultan, who certainly would have been resentful if the charge had proved to be well founded. Although there is no document which would clearly refute Duhamel's and Campbell's claim, it can be regarded as fabricated with almost absolute certainty. First of all, Prokesch had no reason to do what he was accused of. Second, if Prokesch had counselled Mohammed Ali to declare independence, he would have acted not only at absolute variance with his instructions but also against the wishes of his emperor, which was an act equal to high treason, and Prokesch, as a diplomat and officer of the Austrian army, had to be well aware of this fact. Despite the unlikelihood that he would have been brought to court if the charge had proved to be true, his career in the diplomatic service certainly would have ended and he would have been excluded from Austrian higher society where the emperor's mere wish was seen as an order. Prokesch himself had to know this very well because several decades later the desire of Emperor Francis Joseph I to replace Prokesch with someone else in a certain function led to Prokesch's immediate offer of resignation.[23] Third, Mohammed Ali was well known for his cunning in dealing with European countries and his undoubted dissatisfaction with the refusal of the Viennese cabinet to assist him in breaking away from the Ottoman Empire cannot be omitted in judging the accusation raised by him against Prokesch. Metternich saw exactly this malice as the source of the rumour: "Is it not evident that Mohammed Ali, seeing the fading of his ambitious dreams and finally recognising the miscalculations following from his mistaken belief that Austria could support his projects of independence, finds it very simple to put into the mouths of the Austrian agent the ideas that existed only in his own heart?"[24] What supports this view is the fact that when Metternich entrusted his envoy in Athens to ask Boghos Bey, who had spread

---

TNA, FO 120/149.
[23] Bertsch, p. 425.
[24] Metternich to Stürmer, Vienna, 18 Feb. 1835, HHStA, StA, Türkei VI, 64.

the accusation among the Europeans, when and how Prokesch was supposed to have instigated Mohammed Ali's bid for independence, no answer came from Egypt and no letters were offered as evidence of Prokesch's alleged incitement in 1833. By this silence the whole affair was also terminated.[25]

In the mid 1830s, the relations between Mahmud II and Mohammed Ali were relatively good and neither of them did anything that could threaten the fragile stability of the region. Metternich supported this peace with his advice for the Porte to be patient, to do nothing against the elderly Mohammed Ali and to wait for his death, and he continued to carefully observe the pasha's statements and deeds. Hand in hand with this détente, the relations of the Viennese cabinet with the Egyptian governor were good, something that Metternich strongly desired for political as well as economic reasons. The chancellor cemented the good relations whenever it was possible. For example, when the pasha asked Austria for mining experts, Metternich supported the accomplishment of this request and in March 1836, several Austrians led by Joseph Russegger arrived in Egypt; they prospected for gold in some provinces administered by the pasha until mid 1838, although without success. Mohammed Ali similarly wished to be on friendly terms with Austria and proof of this can be also found in the new presents he sent to Metternich after 1833, for example an antique statue.[26]

---

[25] Metternich to Apponyi, Vienna, 18 Oct. 1834, HHStA, StA, Frankreich 294; Metternich to Stürmer, Vienna, 18 March 1835, HHStA, StA, Türkei VI, 64; Metternich to Esterházy, Vienna, 21 March 1835, HHStA, StA, England 214; Metternich to Ficquelmont, Vienna, 21 March 1835, and attached Prokesch to Yusuf Boghos Bey, Athens, 14 Feb. 1835, HHStA, StA, Russland III, 105.

[26] Metternich to Stürmer, Vienna, 24 and 26 Nov., 3 Dec. 1834, HHStA, StA, Türkei VI, 62; Metternich to Prokesch, Vienna, 26 Nov. 1834, HHStA, StK, Griechenland 12; Metternich to Laurin, Vienna, 12 April 1834, Metternich to Lobkowitz, Vienna, 11 April and 19 Dec. 1835, Lobkowitz to Metternich, Vienna, 2 April and 4 Dec. 1835, HHStA, StA, Ägypten 1; Stürmer to Metternich, Constantinople, 18 March, 14 May and 10 June 1835, HHStA, StA, Türkei VI, 63; Stürmer to Metternich, Büyükdere, 5 and 28 Oct. 1835, HHStA, StA, Türkei VI, 64; Nourri Bey to Akif Effendi, Vienna, 1 Nov. 1836, HHStA, StA, Türkei VI, 65; Königsmarck to Frederick William III, Büyükdere, 28 Oct. 1835, GStA PK, HA III, MdA I, 7276; Königsmarck to Frederick William III, Pera, 23 and 30 March 1836, GStA PK, HA III, MdA I, 7277; Campbell to Palmerston, Alexandria, 9 Oct. 1834, TNA, FO 78/247; Hamernik, p. 4; Mayr, *Geschichte der österreichischen Staatskanzlei*, p. 143; Sauer, *Österreich und die Levante*, pp. 439–448.

Despite the apparent tranquillity, hidden tension and animosity between Constantinople and Alexandria continued to exist. Stürmer was convinced that Mahmud II would never sincerely reconcile with the extensive power of his vassal, which was confirmed in the instructions to Reshid Bey from late 1836 and intercepted by the Austrians, stating that "there is no hope for peace or security so long as such a treasonous and intractable vassal is not removed and his power reduced."[27] Owing to his military weakness, Mahmud II decided at the same time to achieve this goal through negotiations. In November 1836, he sent Sarim Effendi to Egypt to solve the question of tribute and offer Mohammed Ali hereditary possession of Egypt. In return, the pasha was to reduce the number of his troops and ships and return occupied provinces to the sultan's control. It was no coincidence that at the same moment Husrev Pasha, Mohammed Ali's mortal enemy, was recalled from his post of the serasker. However, Mohammed Ali rejected the offer because he did not want to reduce his armed forces or give up any province under his administration. In March 1837, the Porte declared that it would offer Mohammed Ali Egypt, Saida and Acre with Egypt going to Ibrahim Pasha after his father's death. For this concession, the Egyptian governor was to return all other provinces. Perhaps in an attempt to save face, the Ottoman dignitaries pretended that the initiative in this affair came from Mohammed Ali.[28]

Metternich was utterly convinced that the Porte had made a mistake because the affair inevitably had to end in its diplomatic defeat since Mahmud II offered too much from his point of view but still too little for Mohammed Ali, and, consequently, the pasha's rejection of the compromise had to be expected. The chancellor considered thus the entire affair as useless and misguided, especially in light of the

---

[27] Instructions for Mustafa Reshid Bey, Constantinople, the autumn of 1836, HHStA, StA, Türkei VI, 65.

[28] Stürmer to Metternich, Constantinople, 13 Jan. 1836, HHStA, StA, Türkei VI, 64; Laurin to Stürmer, Cairo, 17 Jan. 1837, Stürmer to Metternich, Constantinople, 9 and 11 Nov. 1836, HHStA, StA, Türkei VI, 65; Stürmer to Metternich, Constantinople, 4 Jan., 22 and 23 Feb., 1, 9, 15 and 22 March, 26 April 1837, HHStA, StA, Türkei VI, 66; Königsmarck to Frederick William III, Büyükdere, 15 Nov. 1836, GStA PK, HA III, MdA I, 7278; Königsmarck to Frederick William III, Pera, 28 Feb. 1837, GStA PK, HA III, MdA I, 7279; Eyragues to Molé, Therapia, 18 Nov. 1836, AMAE, CP, Turquie 273; Kutluoğlu, pp. 121–122.

fact that the internal situation of the Ottoman Empire was stabilised
and relations with Egypt on solid footing. In his opinion, by making
hasty offers similar to those proffered by Sarim Effendi and through
direct negotiations, Mahmud II only encouraged the ambitions of his
powerful vassal, something he would truly regret in the future. Metternich wrote to Ficquelmont: "There is a lack of skill in the conduct
of the Divan in this new situation, which is one of the usual fail-
ings of the Turks. Why did the Porte undertake the initiative in new
concessions towards a man with the nature of the pasha of Egypt
who will never be content with the concessions that the sultan offers
him? ... Since the peace [Agreement] of Kütahya, we have continually advised patience to the Porte and the sultan. Let Mohammed
Ali be satisfied with the concessions that have been granted to him
by this peace."[29] Metternich openly told Ahmed Fethi Pasha that
the sultan ought to have done nothing except wait for the moment
when Mohammed Ali himself would have asked for Ibrahim Pasha's
appointment as his successor. Then Mahmud II could have offered
Egypt and if Mohammed Ali had not been satisfied and had provoked
a quarrel, the sultan would have been able to rely on the help of the
Great Powers.[30] Metternich correctly maintained that the initiative
most likely arose from Constantinople: "From Laurin's report and the
news from Constantinople I cannot doubt that it was Sarim Effendi
who was instructed to initiate the proposals on behalf of the viceroy.
The idea of such an approach is worthy in all points of the inept
course of action that characterises the policy of the Porte. To take the
initiative of making proposals in a situation where His Highness has
to find his salvation in gaining time and the given circumstances is to
make a mistake of which, I believe, only the Turks are capable. What

---

[29] Metternich to Apponyi, Vienna, 25 March 1837, HHStA, StA, Frankreich 307.
[30] Metternich to Stürmer, Vienna, 14 March and 6 June 1837, HHStA, StA, Türkei
VI, 67; Metternich to Apponyi, Vienna, 25 March 1837, HHStA, StA, Frankreich
307; Metternich to Esterházy, Vienna, 25 March 1837, HHStA, StA, England 218;
Metternich to Prokesch, Vienna, 27 May 1837, HHStA, StK, Griechenland 12;
Sainte-Aulaire to Molé, Vienna, 21 and 30 March 1837, AMAE, CP, Autriche 424;
Lerchenfeld to Ludwig I of Bavaria, Vienna, 26 March 1837, BHStA, MA, Wien
2407; Maltzan to Frederick William III, Vienna, 27 and 29 March 1837, GStA PK,
HA III, MdA I, 6029; O'Sullivan to Meylandt, Vienna, 12 April 1837, ADA, CP,
Autriche 5.

will be necessary to do today will be to let the whole affair sink into oblivion."[31]

Metternich's expectation that the offer would be rejected was validated in Alexandria in April 1837. Mohammed Ali showed little satisfaction with the extent of territorial concessions and he decided to maintain the status quo. Although his rejection led to no immediate crisis, the animosity existing between him and his monarch slowly started to reveal itself again, for example by Mahmud II's renewed goodwill to Husrev Pasha who finally became president of the Supreme Counsel in March 1838. At the same time both sides were developing new armaments. Mohammed Ali did so because at the end of the previous year another uprising broke out in Syria and the Egyptian troops suffered serious losses. The pasha had to reinforce them but he also feared that the Porte would like to take advantage of his own problems as it had planned in 1834 and attack him. Eduard von Klezl, substituting for the absent Baron Stürmer from April to October 1838, shared the pasha's anxiety of Mahmud II's further conduct and claimed that a quick victory over the rebels would be desirable because "if it does not happen, one would always have to fear that the sultan would sooner or later give in to some ill-considered advice and try to re-conquer this province [Syria] by some rash action which would expose him to the most serious of dangers."[32] Klezl's alarm was entirely shared by Metternich, who was concerned less about Mohammed Ali's zeal than the military preparations of the Turks in eastern Anatolia. The chancellor did not presume that the Egyptian governor would attempt to provoke a conflict in which he would have to face not only his sovereign but also the European Powers. However, in the case of the sultan and his ministers, Metternich was of an entirely different opinion. He found them belligerent and short-sighted. He therefore warned the Porte against starting a new war to which Austria would be ill disposed. This may have been unnecessary as the fear of a possible Turkish intervention in Syria was at that moment unfounded. Mahmud II did not intend to attack his vassal, something confirmed by Moltke in mid April 1838 when reporting from eastern

---

[31] Metternich to Esterházy, Vienna, 12 May 1837, HHStA, StA, England 218.
[32] Klezl to Metternich, Constantinople, 11 April 1838, HHStA, StA, Türkei VI, 67.

Anatolia that the Turkish armament was this time directed against the Kurds.[33]

The Tensions between Alexandria and Constantinople in 1838

Although neither side wanted to attack the other, Mohammed Ali distrusted the sultan so much that he revived his separatism. On 23 March 1838, he informed Laurin that he saw in his independence the only guarantee of his safety. On 6 May, he even told Laurin that he would be glad to see Austria assume the role of a mediator in negotiations about his independence with the Porte. He talked long about the significant influence of the Austrian chancellor in the Ottoman capital and expressed his hope that Metternich would advise him on how to achieve independence without the use of arms. Laurin did not refuse this request immediately, playing for time instead in order to further uncover the governor's true intentions. He did not have to wait long. The pasha appeared to be attempting to ascertain the attitudes of European cabinets, bringing the situation to a head on 25 May when he told the French and British consuls about his intent to declare independence. Having done this, he was still willing to await statements from the European Powers before executing his threat. He justified it with fears about the future of his family and reforms. In his opinion, it was better to declare independence, be attacked by the sultan and risk everything than to endure any longer a situation which had become untenable for him.[34]

---

[33] Laurin to Stürmer and Prokesch, Cairo, 12 April 1837, Laurin to Metternich, Alexandria, 26 Sept. 1837, Stürmer to Metternich, Constantinople, 18 Jan., 15 Feb. and 19 April 1837, HHStA, StA, Türkei VI, 66; Metternich to Stürmer, Vienna, 20 March 1838, Laurin to Stürmer, Cairo, 6 Jan. 1838, Stürmer to Metternich, Constantinople, 18 Jan., 21 Feb., 7, 14, 21 and 28 March 1838, Klezl to Metternich, Constantinople, 2 May 1838, Medem to Nesselrode, Cairo, 2 March and 1 April 1838, HHStA, StA, Türkei VI, 67; Kutluoğlu, p. 124; Sauer, *Österreich und die Levante*, p. 388.

[34] Klezl to Metternich, Büyükdere, 18 April 1838, HHStA, StA, Türkei VI, 67; Klezl to Metternich, Büyükdere, 11 July 1838, HHStA, StA, Türkei VI, 68; Dodwell, p. 171; Sauer, *Österreich und die Levante*, p. 392.

Metternich considered the impending crisis much less dangerous than one might expect. Although he did not doubt Mohammed Ali's desire to satisfy his ambitious desires to be the founder of an empire and simultaneously assure the succession of this creation to his descendants, and although the chancellor believed that Mohammed Ali would not hesitate to attempt to fulfil this dream if he could do so without endangering his present existence, he had faith in the caution and intelligence of the Egyptian governor who was a skilled diplomat but not a warrior,[35] as explained by the illegitimate son of Napoleon Bonaparte, Count Alexandre Walewski, who visited Egypt in 1840 and wrote about Mohammed Ali's character: "At first sight one could believe that vanity and calculation alternately influence the decisions of Mohammed Ali, but this would be a huge mistake. His first step can sometimes be directed by vanity, self-esteem, pride. His decisions are always based on a very thorough analysis ... He is endowed with shrewdness and insight. His is strong-willed and persevering, he is above all very clever ... To summarise my opinion of Mohammed Ali with one example, I would say that if he had been born into our civilisation, he would more likely have become a Metternich or a Talleyrand rather than a Napoleon."[36] This comparison is quite fitting and although Metternich himself expressed nothing similar, his statements concerning Mohammed Ali show if not admiration then definitely the respect he felt for the "old fox."[37] As with his attitude towards the pasha in the sphere of reforms, Metternich's opinion of him in the diplomatic sphere was also unaffected by the disloyalty of the Egyptian governor and it never reached the level of personal animosity expressed by Palmerston who labelled Mohammed Ali as "an ignorant barbarian," "a robber,"[38] and "a waiter in a coffee shop."[39] Such severe and abusive condemnations cannot be found in the correspondence of the Austrian chancellor who, on the contrary, never denied the diplomatic talent and foresight of the

---

[35] Metternich to Esterházy, Königswart, 27 July 1838, HHStA, StA, England 219.

[36] Cattaui, p. 201.

[37] Metternich to Ficquelmont, Vienna, 20 Oct. 1834, HHStA, StA, Russland III, 103.

[38] Temperley, *Crimea*, p. 89.

[39] Lufti al-Sayyid Marsot, *Muhammad Ali*, p. 244.

pasha.[40] Metternich often talked about Mohammed Ali's "real skill"[41] and "sound analysis."[42] And as in reformatory efforts, in diplomatic activities as well the chancellor regarded him as more competent than Mahmud II: "Mohammed Ali is indeed shrewder and wiser than the sultan who, though not lacking intelligence, is ignorant of the affairs of this world."[43]

Metternich considered Mohammed Ali to be too experienced, capable, and astute in the art of diplomacy to act so unwisely and jeopardise his own and his family's future by making a risky move at that time. As for his plans for independence, Metternich was convinced that the question was not what the old pasha wanted but what he was actually able to do, and the prince maintained the position that the pasha knew that he could not go as far as he was threatening to do. In the prince's opinion Mohammed Ali was merely probing into the attitudes of the European Powers: "He [Mohammed Ali] is playing a political game with the Great Powers in true oriental style. His aim is to throw confusion among the cabinets and sound them out. If they become divided, he will take advantage of the breach caused by the lack of cohesion on their part. If they oppose him with moral unanimity, he will do nothing."[44] It would suffice for them to tell Mohammed Ali categorically that they insisted he observe the Agreement of Kütahya and that they would never recognise his independence. In such a case there was no need to worry that war would break out "because Mohammed Ali has too much experience to act against the clearly pronounced will of the Great Powers, which could do him harm."[45] Metternich therefore remained optimistic throughout the entire affair and considered a war nothing but a fantasy. His strong belief in Mohammed Ali's good sense undoubtedly contributed to his rejection of Palmerston's proposal that the Austrian army intervene in Syria. Metternich regarded this idea as entirely absurd, "an idle dream"[46] that was incompatible both with the seriousness of

---

40 Metternich to Neumann, Vienna, 21 June 1833, HHStA, StA, England 204.
41 Metternich to Esterházy, Königswart, 28 July 1833, HHStA, StA, England 204.
42 Ibid.
43 Metternich to Apponyi, Vienna, 21 May 1839, HHStA, StA, Frankreich 315.
44 Metternich to Apponyi, Vienna, 20 June 1838, HHStA, StA, Frankreich 311.
45 Metternich to Esterházy, Vienna, 25 June 1838, HHStA, StA, England 219.
46 Metternich to Nesselrode, Vienna, 3 Aug. 1838, HHStA, StA, Russland III, 112.

the affair and the practical potential of Austria: "If Lord Palmerston thinks that Syria is a province bordering the Austrian Empire, he can be surely be excused on account of ignorance, like some men, allegedly statesmen, who are sometimes engaged at the helm of affairs in England!"[47] Metternich regarded an eventual blockade of Egyptian ports by the British and French navies as an entirely sufficient measure if Mohammed Ali did not want to submit to the verbal warnings of the European Powers.[48]

As with the threat of independence, the chancellor reacted with similar calm to Mohammed Ali's wish that Austria should assume the role of mediator in negotiations between Alexandria and Constantinople and support the Egyptian governor in Constantinople: "The viceroy's wish that I intercede with the Porte on behalf of his project and expressed to Mr Laurin is not of a nature that I could comply with. In such cases, silence is the best policy."[49] Unfortunately for Metternich, in this respect Austrian diplomacy committed a faux pas when Mohammed Ali succeeded in enlisting the services of a senior-ranking Austrian officer for his plan. At the end of July, the Egyptian governor learnt from his source in Constantinople that the chief of the Ottoman navy, Vice-Admiral Ahmed Fevzi Pasha, was charged to negotiate the heredity title of Mohammed Ali's territorial possessions. At that time, the chief of the Austrian squadron, Rear-Admiral Francesco Bandiera, was in Alexandria. Since Laurin was instructed to support the reconciliation of Egypt and the Porte, he considered it wise to offer Mohammed Ali Bandiera's assistance in contacting Fevzi Pasha. Although this help was accepted, Bandiera's mission was unsuccessful. In fact, the Ottoman ministers were not ready to begin talks with the Egyptian vassal, and Fevzi Pasha therefore refused to

---

[47] Ibid.

[48] Metternich to Apponyi, Vienna, 26 June 1838, HHStA, StA, Türkei VI, 67; Metternich to Esterházy, Vienna, 25 and 26 June, 3 and 27 July 1838, HHStA, StA, England 219; Metternich to Ficquelmont, Vienna, 28 April 1838, SOA, RA C-A 383; Langsdorff to Molé, Vienna, 19 and 25 June, 4 July, 1 and 7 Aug. 1838, AMAE, CP, Autriche 425; Maltzan to Frederick William III, Vienna, 23 June 1838, GStA PK, HA III, MdA I, 6031; Maltzan to Frederick William III, Vienna, 2 July 1838, GStA PK, HA III, MdA I, 7344; Lamb to Palmerston, Vienna, 3 July 1838, TNA, FO 120/169; Verger to Ludwig I of Bavaria, Vienna, 3 July 1838, BHStA, MA, Wien 2407.

[49] Metternich to Prokesch, Vienna, 11 June 1838, Prokesch-Osten, *Aus dem Nachlasse*, p. 173.

oblige Mohammed Ali and comply with his wish to "embrace him in Alexandria."[50] Klezl regretted Laurin's initiative because first it was a fundamental principle of the Austrian diplomacy not to mediate between a sovereign ruler and his subject, which suggested a negation of the sovereign rights of the former, and second because Laurin/Bandiera's action had no chance for success and could only needlessly discredit the Austrian emperor. Although there is no direct evidence of Metternich's reaction to this indiscretion, the correspondence of other Austrian diplomats strongly indicates that the chancellor shared Klezl's objections.[51]

Metternich took his time to issue a definitive reply to Mohammed Ali's May declaration because he wanted to acquaint himself with the views of the other Powers. The British and French cabinets had to issue positions that did not differ from those dispatched from Berlin and St Petersburg. Thus he could not be sure of the unity of opinions until the arrival of dispatches from London and Paris and before he had a chance to meet with the Russian and Prussian monarchs in Töplitz in Bohemia. Once he knew the positions of the Great Powers, which were in general agreement in their opposition to Mohammed Ali's plan, on 5 and 6 August Metternich sent instructions to Laurin in which he stated that he would not tolerate a possible separation of Egypt and its associated territories from the Ottoman Empire. If Mohammed Ali was determined to attempt this, despite strong warnings against such a step, Austria would never acknowledge it and was prepared to provide the sultan with moral and material support. However, things never progressed this far. As a result of the categorical opposition of the Great Powers, Mohammed Ali realised that he had not chosen a good time to declare independence and he abandoned the plan in mid August, before the arrival of the Austrian statement. Entirely according to Metternich's expectations, Mohammed Ali did not want to face the European coalition and proved that he was a clever and circumspect politician. He abandoned the idea of independence and started to talk about hereditary rule over the provinces under his administration, which actually became his preferred solu-

---

[50] Bandiera to Klezl, Smyrna, 10 Aug. 1838, HHStA, StA, Türkei VI, 68.
[51] Ottenfels to Klezl, Vienna, 28 Aug. 1838, HHStA, StA, Türkei VI, 67; Klezl to Metternich, Büyükdere, 15 Aug. 1838, Constantinople, 12 Sept. 1838, HHStA, StA, Türkei VI, 68; Sauer, Österreich und die Levante, p. 397.

tion, and he pledged not to change the status quo for the time being. He expressed his change of heart by dispatching the annual tribute to Constantinople accompanied by a rather respectful letter and by informing the Porte about a trip he planned to Senaar. The sending of money coupled with Mohammed Ali's absence in Egypt was a powerful indication that he did not plan to wage war in the near future, and it was thus interpreted in Vienna. This complete withdrawal confirmed that Metternich's appraisal of the situation was correct.[52]

What Metternich continued to fear from the spring of 1838 onwards was any hasty reaction by the Sublime Porte to Mohammed Ali's threat. Therefore, he advised it to take no measures against the powerful vassal and instead rely on the diplomacy of the European Powers: "In any case, the best and in my opinion the only useful course of action for him [the sultan] and one which he can follow without any danger is to remain inactive and with his calm attitude prove his confidence in the interest that the Great Powers have in him. Every unconsidered measure on his part . . . would have unpredictable results."[53] Mahmud II followed this advice during the summer, but Mohammed Ali's disloyal behaviour irritated him to such an extent that he started to prepare for revenge. The first attempt was made only in the diplomatic field when Adelburg was asked at the end of August whether the Great Powers would unite to depose Mohammed Ali, whom the sultan "would forgive for his past transgressions and to whom he would give money and a palace in the capital where . . . he would continue to live peacefully under the protection of the munificent sovereign."[54] Klezl saw in this bizarre suggestion the "blindness and arrogance that surpassed everything that one had previously seen

---

[52] Metternich to Nesselrode, Vienna, 2/3 and 7 Aug. 1838, HHStA, StA, Russland III, 112; Metternich to Trauttmannsdorff, Vienna, 4 and 7 Aug. 1838, HHStA, StK, Preussen 162; Metternich to Laurin, Vienna, 5 and 6 Aug. 1838, Metternich to Klezl, Vienna, 6 Aug. 1838, HHStA, StA, Türkei VI, 67; Metternich to Apponyi, Vienna, 8 Aug. 1838, HHStA, StA, Frankreich 311; Ottenfels to Klezl, Vienna, 9 Oct. 1838, HHStA, StA, Türkei VI, 67; Klezl to Metternich, Büyükdere, 22 Aug. and 26 Sept. 1838, HHStA, StA, Türkei VI, 68; Laurin to Metternich, Alexandria, 31 Aug. 1838, HHStA, StA, Ägypten 1; Bockelberg to Frederick William III, Vienna, 8 Aug. 1838, GStA PK, HA III, MdA I, 7344; Fahmy, *Ruler of Egypt*, pp. 86–91; Kutluoğlu, p. 128.
[53] Metternich to Klezl, Vienna, 3 July 1838, HHStA, StA, Türkei VI, 67.
[54] Adelburg to Klezl, Constantinople, 29 Aug. 1838, HHStA, StA, Türkei VI, 68.

in the pomp of the Mohammedan diplomacy."[55] Metternich was of the same opinion; he considered the new Ottoman plan to be "further evidence of the stupidity of the Porte ... [The Great Powers] do not do well in proposing to M[ohammed] Ali that he [Mohammed Ali] be pensioned off by the sultan. He would be offered, as the last pasha of Baghdad, a good hotel in Constantinople with meals provided!"[56] Since no Power supported this curious plan, it was soon abandoned by the Porte.[57]

The Outbreak of the Second Mohammed Ali Crisis and the Intervention of the European Powers

Even though the tensions between the sultan and his pasha did not lead to war during 1838, nothing could mitigate Mahmud II's anger at Mohammed Ali, whose ruin became a fixed goal of the old and sick monarch. With the aim of obtaining foreign support, Mahmud II allowed the conclusion of the British-Ottoman Commercial Convention of Balta Liman on 16 August 1838 although it was disadvantageous to his own empire. He hoped to win the active support of Great Britain against the Egyptian governor through commercial concessions, but this did not happen because Palmerston wanted to preserve peace in the Near East as much as Metternich did. The expectation that the pasha would not accept the Convention abolishing the monopolies and significantly reducing the level of internal duties throughout the empire and that the British would compel him to do so by force also did not occur since Mohammed Ali finally declared his willingness to comply with its conditions. This outcome was welcomed by Metternich who disliked the existence of the Convention from the political point of view and he was pleased that it finally remained harmless in this respect. The danger of a new war in the Levant, however, did not diminish because Mahmud II had clearly decided to wage one and

---

[55] Klezl to Metternich, Büyükdere, 29 Aug. 1838, HHStA, StA, Türkei VI, 68.
[56] Metternich to Lamb, Pavia, 15 Sept. 1838, HHStA, StA, Türkei VI, 68.
[57] Metternich to Klezl, Vienna, 6 Aug. 1838, Klezl to Metternich, Büyükdere, 20 June 1838, HHStA, StA, Türkei VI, 67; Adelburg to Klezl, Constantinople, 24 July 1838, Klezl to Metternich, Büyükdere, 25 July 1838, HHStA, StA, Türkei VI, 68.

was preparing his armed forces for a new conflict with his rival. In late 1838, Metternich considered the outbreak of a new war as merely postponed and anxiously anticipated the following year that continued to offer a picture of the Porte's feverish armament. Although the Ottoman dignitaries did not openly reveal the sultan's desire for war, they did not hide the fact that their master considered the maintenance of the status quo to be impossible. Stürmer thought that they wanted to provoke a war and blame Mohammed Ali for causing it, a rather dangerous step since the internuncio regarded the Turkish army as inferior in number, discipline and fighting power and he feared that such a war would end in disaster for the Porte.[58]

Metternich shared this apprehension and strongly warned the Turks against taking up arms because, first, their defeat was more than probable and, second, their open hostility could lead to Mohammed Ali's declaration of independence. He instructed Stürmer to let it be understood at the sultan's court that Austria was against a new war and "would regard itself as free of any obligations to the Porte if it made the mistake of becoming the aggressor."[59] In Constantinople Stürmer communicated these warnings to Mahmud II and advised him to preserve the peace, but to no effect. The expressions of the Ottoman dignitaries as well as Moltke's letters from the Turkish camp, known to Metternich, confirmed the seriousness of the situation and the scant prospect for the preservation of peace, which became more and more fragile during the spring of 1839. In April, Metternich obtained clear proof of the sultan's actual hostile intentions from the intercepted instructions for Reshid Pasha, residing at that time in London.[60] At the end of the month, Metternich was so embittered

---

[58] Ottenfels to Klezl, Vienna, 4 Sept. 1838, Metternich to Stürmer, Vienna, 13 Nov. 1838, HHStA, StA, Türkei VI, 67; Laurin to Klezl, Alexandria, 15 Sept. 1838, Klezl to Metternich, Büyükdere, 22 Aug., 19 and 26 Sept., 3 and 17 Oct. 1838, Stürmer to Metternich, Constantinople, 14 Oct. and 14 Nov. 1838, 16 and 30 Jan., 6, 20 and 27 Feb. 1839, HHStA, StA, Türkei VI, 68; Ottenfels to Prokesch, Vienna, 11 Sept. 1838, HHStA, StK, Griechenland 12; Sainte-Aulaire to Molé, Venice, 9 Oct. 1838, AMAE, CP, Autriche 426; Maltzan to Frederick William III, Venice, 9 Oct. 1838, GStA PK, HA III, MdA I, 7344; J. B. Williams, *British Commercial Policy and Trade Expansion 1750–1850*, Oxford 1972, p. 296; Owen, p. 91; Webster, *Palmerston*, II, p. 615.
[59] Metternich to Stürmer, Vienna, 6 April 1839, HHStA, StA, Türkei VI, 71.
[60] Metternich to Stürmer, Vienna, 26 Feb., 6 and 30 April 1839, HHStA, StA, Türkei VI, 71; Nourri Effendi to Mustafa Reshid Pasha, Constantinople, 10 April

that he openly criticised the warlike spirit of the Porte in the presence of Rifat Bey, declaring that if Mahmud II followed bad advice, no one would be able to save him "because neither princes nor common people were ever saved from a sickness called suicide."[61]

By referring to bad advice Metternich had in mind the expressions of Lord Ponsonby who was inconsistent with the common effort of his colleagues in deterring the Porte in the appropriate manner. He did not openly counsel the Porte to wage war because this would have meant disobeying Palmerston's explicit instructions, but he unofficially encouraged Mahmud II in his warlike plans. He assured the sultan that in the event of a Turkish attack and consequent defeat, Great Britain and Russia would have no choice other than to enter the conflict on his side to prevent the collapse of the Ottoman Empire. When Metternich learnt of this, he became extremely irritated and had a new reason to regret Ponsonby's presence in Constantinople. In late March 1839, he asked Palmerston to instruct Ponsonby to act on behalf of peace, which the foreign secretary did, but for Metternich the new instructions came too late and could not entirely remedy the unfortunate consequences of Ponsonby's activity.[62] The British ambassador was the person, according to the chancellor, who was responsible for the eagerness for war predominating in the Ottoman

1839, attached to Metternich to Ficquelmont, Vienna, 27 April 1839, HHStA, StA, Russland III, 115; Stürmer to Metternich, Constantinople, 13 and 20 March, 3 April 1839, HHStA, StA, Türkei VI, 68; Stürmer to Metternich, Constantinople, 17 April 1839, HHStA, StA, Türkei VI, 69; Königsmarck to Frederick William III, Büyükdere, 13 March 1839, GStA PK, HA III, MdA I, 7281; Maltzan to Frederick William III, Vienna, 29 April 1839, GStA PK, HA III, MdA I, 7345; Lerchenfeld to Ludwig I of Bavaria, Vienna, 1 April 1839, BHStA, MA, Wien 2408; Tatishchev to Nesselrode, Vienna, 3 and 29 April 1839, AVPRI, fond 133, Kantseliariia, opis 469, 1839/213.

61 Metternich to Ficquelmont, Vienna, 27 April 1839, HHStA, StA, Russland III, 115.

62 Metternich to Hummelauer, Vienna, 28 March 1839, HHStA, StA, England 225; Metternich to Ficquelmont, Vienna, 7 April and 14 June 1839, HHStA, StA, Russland III, 115; Metternich to Trauttmannsdorff, Vienna, 14 June 1839, HHStA, StK, Preussen 172; Metternich to Apponyi, Vienna, 14 June 1839, HHStA, StA, Frankreich 315; Milbanke to Palmerston, Vienna, 28 March 1839, TNA, FO 120/180; Sainte-Aulaire to Molé, Vienna, 29 March 1839, AMAE, CP, Autriche 426; Tatishchev to Nesselrode, Vienna, 29 April 1839, AVPRI, fond 133, Kantseliariia, opis 469, 1839/213; Maltzan to Frederick William III, Vienna, 11 June 1839, GStA PK, HA III, MdA I, 7345; Ridley, *Palmerston*, p. 219; Bolsover, "Lord Ponsonby and the Eastern Question," p. 112.

capital: "It is this man (and he is mad) who has arranged matters since lately it has no longer been possible for him to disrupt them. It is he who advised the sultan to abandon the status quo in order to later recommend to him to maintain it after the explicit order of his court. With policies pursued in such a manner, the peace of the whole world will be destroyed!"[63]

Metternich did his best to preserve peace in the Near East. When Mahmud II asked him via Stürmer in late April for advice on how to proceed against Mohammed Ali, the chancellor drew up instructions on 18 May with the aim of averting the sultan from war despite the fact that he expected his advice to be rejected, as is also evident from the fact that Stürmer was instructed to offer this advice on behalf of himself and not in the name of the Viennese cabinet and thereby prevent a diplomatic defeat. Metternich summarised his arguments from the previous years against a war that could have unpredictable and serious consequences for the Ottoman Empire. Since he did not believe in the possibility of Mahmud II's victory due to Mohammed Ali's military superiority, it was essential for the Porte not to jeopardise its future with a rash action now. Therefore, it was to remain at peace and act according to the agreement made in Kütahya for the time being. As for the future, it was to assure the hereditary tenure of Egypt to Mohammed Ali's family, something that Metternich regarded as absolutely necessary due to the distribution of power between Constantinople and Alexandria. Such a compromise solution was realistic because Metternich trusted the pasha's intelligence and matter-of-factness, as he wrote to Apponyi two days later: "It is nevertheless possible to count on the shrewd character of this man, his talent to grasp the truth of matters and the huge amount of experience that he has acquired. From my part I do not believe any more that he still dreams of founding an Arab empire. What undoubtedly interests him above all is the continuing existence of what he has established, but the part that confines itself to Egypt and what is beyond it [Sudan]. He has created nothing in Syria nor elsewhere, he has merely caused destruction. Will he ever consent to the reduction of his power and strength during his lifetime? I strongly doubt it. Would he prefer the chance to assure his son a part of what he possesses to that of abandoning everything to the perils of war? If he is wise, he must prefer

---

[63] Metternich to Apponyi, Vienna, 21 May 1839, HHStA, StA, Frankreich 315.

certainty to uncertainty, and should he in the final analysis not want it, matters will remain as they are as if no one had tried to settle them. This is our opinion and our entire opinion."[64] If Mohammed Ali did not want to accept a compromise offer, the united intervention of the European Powers could easily overcome his opposition.[65]

Metternich's discretion in communicating his counsel was well founded because Mahmud II ignored the chancellor's help to the same extent as he had done before in the Churchill Affair. Soon after dispatching his May instructions, Metternich obtained from Stürmer as well as Laurin information about the Turkish army's movement to the Syrian frontier; its advanced guard crossed the Euphrates on 21 April. However, even at the beginning of June when the first skirmishes with Egyptian troops took place in Syria, the Porte still denied that it had ordered an attack on the Egyptian vassal and it explained the movement of its own troops by the necessity to react against Mohammed Ali's provocations. This blatant lie angered Metternich, leading him to this sharp statement in late May: "If a government does not know whether it is at war or at peace with an enemy and it is four or five days away from the theatre where these events are taking place, it can only happen in Turkey."[66] It was not until 9 June that the Porte officially declared war on Mohammed Ali. Metternich could do nothing other than accept this fact and declare that not the pasha but the sultan was the aggressor.[67]

[64] Metternich to Apponyi, Vienna, 20 May 1839, HHStA, StA, Frankreich 315.

[65] Metternich to Hummelauer, Vienna, 9 and 20 May 1839, HHStA, StA, England 225; Metternich to Stürmer, Vienna, 18 May 1839, Rifat Bey to Nourri Effendi, 18 May 1839, HHStA, StA, Türkei VI, 71; Stürmer to Metternich, Constantinople, 24 April 1839, HHStA, StA, Türkei VI, 69; Beauvale to Palmerston, Vienna, 1 June 1839, TNA, FO 120/180; Lerchenfeld to Ludwig I of Bavaria, Vienna, 2 June 1839, BHStA, MA, Wien 2408.

[66] Metternich to Stürmer, Vienna, 28 May 1839, HHStA, StA, Türkei VI, 71.

[67] Metternich to Hummelauer, Vienna, 21 May 1839, HHStA, StA, England 225; Metternich to Stürmer, Vienna, 28 May and 4 June 1839, HHStA, StA, Türkei VI, 71; Metternich to Apponyi, Vienna, 4 June 1839, HHStA, StA, Frankreich 315; Metternich to Ficquelmont, Vienna, 22 June 1839, HHStA, StA, Russland III, 115; Stürmer to Metternich, Constantinople, 8, 15 and 22 May 1839, HHStA, StA, Türkei VI, 69; report from Laurin, Alexandria, 16 May 1839, HHStA, StA, Ägypten 1; Maltzan to Frederick William III, Vienna, 22 May 1839, GStA PK, HA III, MdA I, 7345; Lerchenfeld to Ludwig I of Bavaria, Vienna, 2 June 1839, BHStA, MA, Wien 2408; Sainte-Aulaire to Soult, Vienna, 12 June 1839, AMAE, CP, Autriche 426; Kutluoğlu, p. 136.

In the meantime, Mohammed Ali, well aware of his sovereign's hostile intentions, prepared for war with the same resolution. Nevertheless, the situation in Alexandria was different from that in Constantinople because the pasha wanted to maintain peace and did not stop expressing this wish during his numerous sessions with the consuls. On 16 May 1839, he told Laurin that "he would organise the retreat of his army and recall his son Ibrahim Pasha to Damascus if the sultan's troops that had crossed the Euphrates at the town of Bir would withdraw to the far bank of the river."[68] Moreover, he was prepared to withdraw a part of his regiments from Syria if the Great Powers would guarantee his tenure of all the provinces previously under his administration and agree with their being placed under the hereditary possession of his family. With this ostentatious offer he of course wanted the sultan to bear the responsibility for unleashing a new war, but it is also true that he sincerely tried to avoid the conflict until the last moment. Metternich correctly observed the situation in Alexandria with less apprehension than the events in the Ottoman capital, as he wrote in early May to Ficquelmont: "It is in Constantinople where we see this spirit of resentment, hatred and giddiness that, deaf to the voice of reason and prudence, burns with impatience to abandon the status quo at any price ... On the contrary we consider Mohammed Ali to be too clear-sighted and we recognise in him enough common sense and shrewdness to be sure that he will evaluate his position correctly."[69] When Metternich was asked by Tatishchev at the same time to order Laurin to support the Russian consul in Alexandria in his effort to dissuade Mohammed Ali from opening hostilities, out of respect for his Russian ally he complied with this request despite the fact that he well knew that there was little to fear from the pasha. Nevertheless, even Mohammed Ali's patience had its limits. When he learnt in early June of an encounter between his Arabic militia and a Turkish cavalry regiment and the subsequent occupation of Syrian villages by the Turks, he ordered Ibrahim Pasha on 10 June to attack the enemy. The decisive battle took place near Nezib on 24 June where the sultan's army, in accordance with the assumptions of Metternich and other Austrian diplomats, was routed. In the wake of this disaster,

---

[68] Laurin to Stürmer, Alexandria, 16 May 1839, HHStA, StA, Ägypten 1.
[69] Metternich to Ficquelmont, Vienna, 5 May 1839, HHStA, StA, Russland III, 115.

two armies in Asia Minor deserted and left the way to Constantinople open. The city was now at the mercy of the Egyptian commander, who was determined to bring the campaign to a triumphant end, appear before the sultan and present peace conditions. As had happened during the first Turko-Egyptian war, at this point Ibrahim Pasha's advance was again halted by his father, who did not want to risk the European Powers' military intervention that was to be expected if the Egyptian troops attacked the Ottoman capital. Instead of pursuing the campaign, Mohammed Ali planned to force the Porte to accept his conditions through negotiations.[70]

The achievement of the pasha's goal seemed to be significantly facilitated by Mahmud II's death at the end of June,[71] an event for some time anticipated by Metternich, who had been well informed about the sultan's deteriorating health by the latter's personal physician Dr. Neuner. This created a new problem for the empire concerning the successor, Abdülmecid I, who only was 16 years old and without the appropriate education or abilities. Metternich had been seriously concerned about the impact of Mahmud II's death on the internal situation of the empire, and he had even feared political disturbances in its capital: "To tell the truth, the Ottoman Empire has never been in a crisis like the current one ... The Sultan's illness puts this sovereign's life in imminent danger and with it the whole future and perhaps also the very existence of this empire."[72] The chancellor's fears regarding the takeover of power by Abdülmecid I finally

---

[70] Metternich to Prokesch, Vienna, 13 May 1839, HHStA, StK, Griechenland 12; Metternich to Laurin, Vienna, 13 May 1839, Laurin to Metternich, Alexandria, 6, 10 and 17 June 1839, Mohammed Ali to Ibrahim Pasha, Alexandria, 10 June 1839, Nesselrode to Medem, St Petersburg, 29 March 1839, HHStA, StA, Ägypten 1; Laurin to Stürmer, Alexandria, 2 April 1839, Stürmer to Metternich, Constantinople, 17 April 1839, HHStA, StA, Türkei VI, 69; Tatishchev to Nesselrode, Vienna, 8 May 1839, AVPRI, fond 133, Kantseliariia, opis 469, 1839/213; L. W. Ufford, *The Pasha: How Mehemet Ali Defied the West, 1839–1841*, Jefferson, London 2007, pp. 38–46.

[71] The date of Mahmud II's death slightly differs in the literature. Metternich was convinced that Mahmud II died on 29 June and his death was kept secret by the Ottoman dignitaries for some time for them to be able to decide the method of solving the conflict with Mohammed Ali. Metternich to Apponyi, Vienna, 13 July 1839, HHStA, StA, Frankreich 315; Beauvale to Palmerston, Vienna, 11 July 1839, TNA, FO 120/180; Lerchenfeld to Ludwig I of Bavaria, Vienna, 12 July 1839, BHStA, MA, Wien 2408.

[72] Metternich to Stürmer, Vienna, 2 July 1839, HHStA, StA, Türkei VI, 71.

proved to be unfounded, in particular due to the fact that the reins of government were assumed by Husrev Pasha who became grand vizier. Despite his unsympathetic attitude towards Austria, Metternich welcomed Husrev's presence at the head of the administration since it helped to assure peace and order in the capital. Husrev also tried to end the war with Mohammed Ali. At the beginning of July, the representatives of the Great Powers were informed about the Divan's intention to declare an armistice and grant Mohammed Ali the hereditary tenure of Egypt. Nevertheless, the subsequent negotiations in Alexandria produced no result because the Egyptian governor found the concessions insufficient. He demanded the hereditary possession of all provinces under his administration and Husrev's removal from office.[73]

Mohammed Ali's unwillingness to yield was not only due to the triumph at Nezib and Mahmud II's death but also because of the defection of the Turkish fleet that set sail from the Dardanelles to Alexandria on 5 July. The gain of almost all the enemy's entire navy changed the balance of power in favour of the Egyptian governor to such an extent that his demands could be hardly refused by the Porte. Consequently, he found the offer of hereditary Egypt only to be entirely ridiculous and he had no reason to relinquish any of his peace conditions, including the removal of the grand vizier who, as Mohammed Ali told Laurin, "is detested by the whole nation and for whom all means are admissible for achieving his objective, including a knife and poison."[74] The situation with the new Ottoman monarch

---

[73] Metternich to Ficquelmont, Vienna, 29 June 1839, HHStA, StA, Russland III, 115; Metternich to Ficquelmont, Vienna, 8 and 9 July 1839, HHStA, StA, Russland III, 116; Metternich to Stürmer, Vienna, 2 July 1839, HHStA, StA, Türkei VI, 71; Metternich to Esterházy, Vienna, 3 July 1839, HHStA, StA, England 225; Metternich to Apponyi, Vienna, 3 July 1839, HHStA, StA, Frankreich 315; Stürmer to Metternich, Constantinople, 5, 12, 18, 20, 24 and 26 June 1839, Büyükdere, 1, 3 and 8 July 1839, HHStA, StA, Türkei VI, 69; Sainte-Aulaire to Soult, Vienna, 29 June 1839, AMAE, CP, Autriche 426; Königsmarck to Frederick William III, Büyükdere, 5 and 26 June 1839, GStA PK, HA III, MdA I, 7281; Bockelberg to Frederick William III, Vienna, 18 June 1839, GStA PK, HA III, MdA I, 7345; Bockelberg to Frederick William III, Vienna, 27 and 30 June, 2 and 8 July 1839, GStA PK, HA III, MdA I, 7346; Bockelberg to Frederick William III, Vienna, 16 July 1839, GStA PK, HA III, MdA I, 6032; Lerchenfeld to Ludwig I of Bavaria, Vienna, 19 June, 8 and 11 July 1839, BHStA, MA, Wien 2408.
[74] Laurin to Stürmer, Alexandria, 16 July 1839, HHStA, StA, Türkei VI, 69.

seemed to be so hopeless that Stürmer even proposed in his mid July report that the two quarrelling parties settle matters directly without the participation of the Great Powers.[75] With regard to the course of events, he did not regard the pasha's demands as too excessive: "Fortunately, Mohammed Ali's requirements are more modest than we originally feared. He demands neither sovereignty nor independence ... but he is satisfied with the status quo and the heredity. I see there nothing other than the Agreement of Kütahya that Your Highness wanted to adopt as the solution. The heredity in addition to it, that is the whole concession, but it seems moderate to me when I consider it as the outcome of the events that providence saw fit to determine in all respects in favour of Mohammed Ali."[76]

Metternich in no way shared the internuncio's opinion and strongly opposed any direct settlement between the pasha and the sultan without the cognizance of the Great Powers. On 13 July, the chancellor already knew of Mahmud II's death but lacked knowledge of the two other disasters. Already at this moment he instructed Stürmer to demand from the Porte its complete and unreserved confidence in the Great Powers' support and consultations with their representatives on every important step. Three days later, he informed Stürmer that the Great Powers were to assist the young sultan in establishing a lasting settlement of the Egyptian Question, which meant that it had to differ from the Agreement of Kütahya and "would be compatible with the internal peace of the Ottoman Empire and would contain a guarantee of its stability."[77] Their assistance was necessary since Mohammed Ali's hereditary rule was to be limited, according to the chancellor, to Egypt only, which was an outcome with which the pasha could hardly agree without the constraint of Europe. On 17 July, Metternich finally learnt of the Turkish army's defeat and the fleet's defection. His concerns about a direct settlement between the Porte and the pasha considerably increased and he therefore immediately ordered Stürmer to prevent it and assure the former and warn the latter of the unanimous readiness of the Great Powers to offer their support to the legitimate monarch. A week later, Metternich explicitly instructed the internun-

---

[75] Stürmer to Metternich, Büyükdere, 17 July 1839, HHStA, StA, Türkei VI, 69.
[76] Stürmer to Metternich, Constantinople, 24 July 1839, HHStA, StA, Türkei VI, 69.
[77] Metternich to Stürmer, Vienna, 16 July 1839, HHStA, StA, Türkei VI, 71.

cio to act with his colleagues and together prevent the new sultan from responding to Mohammed Ali's ultimatum until the receipt of the Powers' advice: "The Porte does not actually live its own life at the moment; it lives the life that its formidable enemy allows it to live and with the support that the Great Powers will give it should Mohammed Ali choose to entirely overthrow the throne of the legitimate sovereign. Surely a Great Power reduced to such an extreme should not negotiate on the ways and means of the rescue which may still remain to it? Yet the only means available to the Porte today are provided by the interest that Europe takes in its preservation."[78] When Metternich learnt on the turn of July about the Turks' willingness to negotiate the entente with Mohammed Ali without the Great Powers' participation, he became extremely displeased. Stürmer's preference for a direct settlement and lack of action to prevent one was even said to make him furious. Therefore, Metternich instructed the internuncio to take the position of Ponsonby and Roussin, both advocating the European intervention and the limitation of Mohammed Ali's power to a minimum.[79]

Metternich did not know that at the very moment when he was bitterly criticising the internuncio there was no longer any reason for it because Stürmer had already remedied his sharp deviation from the policy of his court. Without knowledge of the precise instructions of 24 July but having received those from mid July in the morning of the 27th of the month, he immediately proposed to his colleagues the presentation of a collective note to the Divan intended to forestall its direct agreement with Mohammed Ali, a rather probable outcome because its members had decided on the previous day to meet almost all conditions of the pasha and send a negotiator to Alexandria. After

---

[78] Metternich to Stürmer, Vienna, 24 July 1839, HHStA, StA, Türkei VI, 71.
[79] Metternich to Stürmer, Vienna, 13, 16, 17 and 30 July 1839, HHStA, StA, Türkei VI, 71; Metternich to Stürmer, Vienna, 1 Aug. 1839, HHStA, StA, Türkei VI, 72; Metternich to Apponyi, Vienna, 13 and 14 July 1839, HHStA, StA, Frankreich 315; Metternich to Esterházy, Vienna, 13 July, 2 and 7 Aug. 1839, HHStA, StA, England 225; Rifat Bey to Nourri Effendi, Vienna, 16 July 1839, HHStA, StA, Türkei VI, 71; Beauvale to Palmerston, Vienna, 18 and 19 July, 1 Aug. 1839, TNA, FO 120/180; Struve to Nesselrode, Vienna, 23 July 1839, AVPRI, fond 133, Kantseliariia, opis 469, 1839/214; Bockelberg to Frederick William III, Vienna, 23 and 31 July 1839, GStA PK, HA III, MdA I, 7346; Lerchenfeld to Ludwig I of Bavaria, Vienna, 5 Aug. 1839, BHStA, MA, Wien 2408; O'Sullivan to Meylandt, Vienna, 8 Aug. 1839, ADA, CP, Autriche 6.

Stürmer's intervention on 27 July, the negotiator's departure was prevented and the representatives of the Great Powers therefore obtained
time to prepare their note. They quickly agreed on its text edited by
Stürmer and Roussin: "The undersigned [Stürmer, Ponsonby, Roussin,
Königsmarck, Butenev] have received, this morning, from their respective Governments instructions, in virtue whereof they have the honour
to inform the Sublime Porte, that agreement among the Five Great
Powers on the Question of the East is secured, and to invite it to
suspend any definitive resolution without their concurrence, waiting
for the effect of the interest which these Powers feel for it."[80] On the
following day, 28 July, the dragomans of the five Powers presented the
Collective Note in the assembly hall of the Divan headed by Husrev
Pasha. The document was accepted, the concessions to Mohammed
Ali forgotten and the negotiator's departure definitely cancelled. The
Porte pledged to proceed together with the five Powers and not to conclude a direct agreement with Mohammed Ali. The pasha was disappointed with the foreign intervention and did not lessen his demands,
but he also did not dare to reopen the campaign and risk a war with
the European countries. When Metternich learnt of Stürmer's initiative leading to the Collective Note of 27 July, he was full of praise for
him as well as his colleagues.[81] He declared: "The representatives of
the five Great Powers can congratulate themselves for having rendered
a great service to the Porte and Europe with their agreement!"[82] And
he later did not fail to congratulate himself on being its author, sometimes in a rather boastful manner: "The collective approach of the
Great Powers' plenipotentiaries in Constantinople that resulted from
my efforts is undoubtedly one of the most fortunate achievements that

[80] J. C. Hurewitz, *The Middle East and North Africa in World Politics: A Documentary Record, Volume 1: European Expansion, 1535–1914*, New Haven, London
1975, p. 113.
[81] Metternich to Esterházy, Vienna, 23 Aug. 1839, HHStA, StA, England 225;
Stürmer to Adelburg, 27 July 1839, Adelburg to Stürmer, 27 and 28 July 1839,
Stürmer to Metternich, Büyükdere, 29 July 1839, HHStA, StA, Türkei VI, 69; Laurin to Stürmer, Alexandria, 6 Aug. 1839, HHStA, StA, Türkei VI, 70; Königsmarck
to Frederick William III, Büyükdere, 29 July 1839, GStA PK, HA III, MdA I,
7281; Ponsonby to Palmerston, Therapia, 29 July 1839, TNA, FO 78/357; Ufford,
pp. 75–76.
[82] Metternich to Stürmer, Vienna, 13 Aug. 1839, HHStA, StA, Türkei VI, 72.

destiny has afforded me during my long political career because it is this event that has saved the Ottoman Empire."[83]

* * *

Metternich's opposition to Mohammed Ali's ambitions after 1833 stemmed not only from a possible violation of the principle of legitimacy but also from his understanding of the negative consequences they would have on the geopolitical situation in the Levant. It was not important for the chancellor whether the pasha's real aim was merely a heredity claim under Ottoman sovereignty or full independence because the outcome of either goal would have been identical: a factual division of the Ottoman Empire. Furthermore, a war between the sultan and his vassal and the expected defeat of the former could seriously affect the relations among the European Powers, which was another reason for Metternich's effort to prevent the outbreak of such a war. When he failed in 1839, he continued to oppose Mohammed Ali's ambitions regardless of whether they were clearly directed towards heredity within the legal frame of the Ottoman Empire. The Turkish defeat changed nothing in his determination to limit the pasha's hereditary tenure to Egypt alone if possible. This attitude towards Mohammed Ali before as well as after 1833 is clearly consistent. Therefore, it is necessary to dispute the opinion of Austrian historian Walter Sauer that in the Habsburg Monarchy two opposite tendencies existed during the studied period: one pro-Egyptian supporting the modernisation of this Ottoman province and seeing in Mohammed Ali's reforms an economic opportunity for the Austrian Empire and the other aimed against the changes in the land on the Nile regarding them as dangerous for Austria's economic interests. According to Walter Sauer, the first tendency dominated Austria's diplomacy in the early 1830s and the proof was to be Anton Prokesch's second mission to Egypt in 1833 where he was to negotiate with the pasha instead of Acerbi, whereas the latter prevailed at the end the decade and the proof could

---

[83] Maltzan to Frederick William III, Vienna, 1 Jan. 1840, GStA PK, HA III, MdA I, 7351. For Metternich's similar statement see also Lerchenfeld to Ludwig I of Bavaria, Vienna, 12 Nov. 1839, BHStA, MA, Wien 2408.

be found in Austria's military intervention against Mohammed Ali in Syria in 1840.[84]

This, however, is an unhistorical interpretation because actually there were never two tendencies in Austria's diplomacy. As evidenced in Chapter 20, Metternich regarded the changes in Egypt positively and not as dangerous for Austria. Of course Mohammed Ali's protective system of monopolies was sometimes criticised by the Austrians, but they could cope with it. Metternich was also able to see the advantages of the presence of a strong governor assuring the stability, order and economic growth in Egypt from which foreigners could profit. During the first Turko-Egyptian conflict, Metternich even expressed the opinion that even if Mohammed Ali were defeated, the Ottoman Empire would lose because "Egypt would become so to speak nothing and the clowns who would be prepared to seize it would be easily found."[85] As seen in Chapter 16, Prokesch's mission to Alexandria in 1833 was in no way a manifestation of Metternich's goodwill towards Mohammed Ali. In brief, the attitude of the Chancellery was always the same: as long as Mohammed Ali remained loyal to the sultan, there was a strong inclination to maintain good relations with him and profit from the economic growth of Egypt caused by the pasha's reforms. Whenever he became disloyal and with his personal ambitions threatened the stability of the Ottoman Empire and thus peace among the European Powers, he had to be stopped, which is exactly what happened in 1839.

The only difference with the first Turko-Egyptian conflict lay in the fact that Metternich considered the consequences of the second war as more serious due to the development of the Eastern Question in the preceding years and he was consequently far more active in 1839 than he was in 1832. This activity led to the Collective Note of 27 July with which he achieved an undeniable diplomatic success because it crucially strengthened the position of the young sultan and dashed the hopes of the Egyptian governor for a victory achieved through direct negotiations with the Porte, which would have led most probably to the factual division of the empire into two parts. It was now the Euro-

---

[84] W. Sauer, "Ein Jesuitenstaat in Afrika? Habsburgische Kolonialpolitik in Ägypten, dem Sudan und Äthiopien in der ersten Hälfte des 19. Jahrhunderts," ÖGL 55, 2011, 1, pp. 10–12.

[85] Metternich to Ottenfels, Vienna, 18 Dec. 1831, HHStA, StA, Türkei VI, 53.

pean Powers which assumed responsibility for resolution of the crisis, whereas the sultan and the pasha were merely assigned secondary roles in this performance. Consequently, from the end of July 1839, the solution of the crisis could not be found on the Bosphorus or on the Nile but at the five most significant European courts. Metternich hoped that it would be settled in the same way as the less threatening one from the previous year: through their common understanding and cooperation which would take advantage of Mohammed Ali's caution and move him by means of their diplomatic pressure to yield and give up his excessive demands. The Collective Note offered time to prepare this joint proceeding and the only thing that remained to secure was the unity of the Great Powers itself, something which Metternich had been trying to achieve since the spring of 1839.

24

The Plan for a Viennese Conference on the Eastern Question

Metternich hoped that the Collective Note of 27 July would not be the only success of his diplomatic activities in 1839. He had long desired to summon in Vienna a ministerial conference on the Eastern Question that would enable him to control events and become once more the leading diplomat of Europe. He seemed to be very close to the realisation of his dream in the summer of 1839, but Russia's refusal to participate in the Viennese negotiations was a deathblow to the plan and a crushing shock for him. Historians have sometimes claimed that he wanted to use the Viennese negotiations as a tool to limit Russia's independence of action, but a more correct explanation is that he wanted to bind Russia as well as the Maritime Powers, in other words to exploit the negotiations in order to attain the goal he had in vain tried to achieve since 1833: to overcome the dangerously egoistical and uselessly distrustful policies of Russia as well as the Maritime Powers and ensure their cooperation in the Near East.

Metternich's Dream of Summoning a Viennese Conference on the Eastern Question

Metternich's effort to prevent the outbreak of the second Turko-Egyptian war was not confined only to Constantinople but was also directed to the European cabinets. He particularly wanted to bridge the gulf still existing between Russia and the Maritime Powers making the solution of the forthcoming crisis more difficult. Great Britain and France continued to distrust Russia and were not willing to join in the proceedings with this Great Power in the Near East despite Metternich's firm assurances of the tsar's peaceful aims. On the other

hand, Nicholas I continued to consider the Eastern Question to be his
private affair and he expressed his opinion several times in this respect
to Ficquelmont: "I do not interfere with the Spanish and Portuguese
affairs; they concern France and England. Italy is your affair, and I
am only there to support you. It is the same thing in Germany; it concerns Prussia and you. But as for Turkey, it is my affair!"[1] Metternich
strongly disagreed with this opinion because he regarded the future
of the Ottoman Empire as a matter concerning the whole of Europe
and not just Russia. He always maintained this point of view, saying,
for example, in mid 1835: "To want to establish in favour of the two
imperial courts a kind of exclusive right regarding this subject would
mean to support an absurd thesis. The affairs of the Levant, as all
other questions of high policy, are the general domain of the Great
Powers. Due to their position as bordering nations, the two imperial
courts have a special interest in dealing carefully with [Turkey]; in
the same way they also have the means to act against Turkey which
the more distant Powers do not. Anything which goes beyond these
two facts has no other value than that of insupportable claims in theory and practice ... What, in the second case, the imperial courts
would not be able to prevent would be the other Great Powers having the same as well as conflicting interests. Eastern affairs do not
contain anything that cannot be found, more or less, in other political questions towards which every Great Power can, at its own risk
and cost, assume an attitude that it finds suitable ... Something to
which I would not only have no objections but would even regard as
extremely desirable would be a frank and sincere agreement between
the two imperial courts and the two Maritime Powers, the objective of
which would be for them to declare before the eyes of the Porte as well
as the whole of Europe their sincere determination to contribute, each
for its own part and by all the means at the disposal of each court, to
the conservation of the Ottoman Empire."[2] However, Metternich had
little success with his conciliatory arguments in St Petersburg as he
had also had in London and Paris.[3]

---

[1] Ficquelmont to Metternich, St Petersburg, 10 June 1839, HHStA, StA, Russland III, 114.
[2] Metternich to Ficquelmont, Baden, 29 July 1835, HHStA, StA, Russland III,
104.
[3] Kantor, p. 199; Lorenz, p. 99; Rendall, "Restraint or Self-Restraint," p. 49.

It undoubtedly grieved the elderly chancellor to see the relations among the Great Powers spoiled by unreasonable jealousies and misunderstandings. To remove them, he not only used simple persuasion but also attempted to assume the role of mediator at a conference. Remembering the period of 1814–1822 filled with conferences and congresses making him the "coachman of Europe," he regarded this method to be the most suitable for assuring peace on the Continent and he argued that if, for example, the conference in Carlsbad eased the tension over the situation within the German Confederation, there was no reason why another one would not have a similar effect in the Levant. Therefore, in the spring of 1833, he proposed a conference in Vienna that would solve the complicated situation of the Ottoman Empire and its relations with the European Powers. Unfortunately for him, the July Revolution of 1830 had created a gulf between the liberal and conservative Powers, so that neither the willingness of the five Powers to cooperate under his leadership nor the necessary conditions for his leadership existed in the 1830s. The most serious impediment to his ambitions was Palmerston, who rejected the idea of a conference in Vienna and assumed the same negative attitude towards Metternich's proposal of the following year that the Great Powers' representatives in Vienna should be charged with supervising the affairs in the Near East. Metternich therefore had no option other than to abandon his project for making Vienna a centre of discussions over the Eastern Question, the project that had preoccupied him for eighteen long months.[4]

---

[4] Metternich to Apponyi, Vienna, 6 April 1833, HHStA, StA, Frankreich 289; Metternich to Neumann, Vienna, 3 May 1833, HHStA, StA, England 204; Lamb to Palmerston, Vienna, 13 April, 8 and 21 May 1833, TNA, FO 120/136; Lamb to Palmerston, Vienna, 18 Feb., 19 July, 31 Oct. and 2 Nov. 1834, TNA, FO 120/145; Maltzan to Frederick William III, Vienna, 23 April 1833, GStA PK, HA III, MdA I, 6021; Brockhausen to Frederick William III, Vienna, 22 July and 20 Aug. 1834, GStA PK, HA III, MdA I, 6024; Sainte-Aulaire to Broglie, Vienna, 19 and 27 May 1833, AMAE, CP, Autriche 418; Sainte-Aulaire to Broglie, Vienna, 14 July 1833, AMAE, CP, Autriche 419; La Rochefoucauld to Rigny, Vienna, 19 July, 22 and 31 Aug. 1834, Sainte-Aulaire to Rigny, Vienna, 25 Sept. 1834, AMAE, CP, Autriche 421; Tatishchev to Nesselrode, Vienna, 10 May 1833, AVPRI, fond 133, Kantseliariia, opis 469, 1833/211; Tatishchev to Nesselrode, Vienna, 3 Jan. 1834, AVPRI, fond 133, Kantseliariia, opis 469, 1834/217; K. Kraus, *Politisches Gleichgewicht und Europagedanke bei Metternich*, Frankfurt am Main 1993, p. 82; F. S. Rodkey, "The Views of Palmerston and Metternich on the Eastern Question in 1834," *EHR* 45, 1930, 180, p. 627.

Palmerston's attitude resulted, first, from his strong distrust of Metternich, whom he even labelled a "slave of Russia,"[5] and second, from the fact that he himself wanted to lead the events and direct the discussions concerning the future of the Ottoman Empire. Therefore, he proposed at the same time as Metternich his own plan, which was basically identical to the Austrian one, only with a different location for the conference: London. Now the objection came from Vienna because Metternich had no reason to satisfy the wish that Palmerston had twice denied him. Moreover, the chancellor feared that the city on the Thames might become a permanent centre of European affairs, which is what Palmerston actually desired.[6] After the experience with the London conferences on the Greek and Belgian Questions, Metternich voiced his opposition to the possibility of "granting any kind of permanency to the London conference; of gradually elevating it to the status of a political institution, and thus attributing to it the significance and the influence of an Areopagus [a Court of Appeal] in which the representatives of the three continental Powers would be reduced to the role of accomplices in the reformatory policy of the two Maritime Courts."[7]

The two statesmen's contest for power and prestige deepened their mutual animosity. Sir Charles Kingsley Webster explained their unwillingness to agree to a conference in the other's capital by the incompatibility of their characters and opinions as well as the same desire each man had for his own prestige and control of affairs. This opinion is undoubtedly correct, and particularly in the case of Metternich, the question of prestige was rather important, as shown in Prussian Envoy Count Mortimer Maltzan's words from August 1839 regarding Metternich's wish to "close his long and distinguished political career with an act crowning his high reputation."[8] Nevertheless, Webster did not point out another difference between the motives each of the two men had to hold a conference in his own capital. Palmerston maintained a distinctly anti-Russian attitude, and the discussions he planned on the Eastern Question were intended to prevent

---

[5]   Sir C. K. Webster, *Palmerston, Metternich and the European System, 1830–41*, London 1934, p. 12.
[6]   M. E. Chamberlain, *Lord Palmerston*, Cardiff 1987, p. 51.
[7]   Metternich to Neumann, Vienna, 9 June 1833, HHStA, StA, England 204.
[8]   Maltzan to Frederick William III, Vienna, 15 Aug. 1839, GStA PK, HA III, MdA I, 7347.

the conservative Power from military intervention in the Ottoman Empire owing to the "great jealousy it would excite in the West."[9] This strong partiality, however, made him an unsuitable person to lead the talks proposed for an agreement to be reached between the Maritime Powers and Russia. In contrast, Metternich actually stood between both quarrelling parties when he rightly advocated a peaceful Russian policy in the Near East while simultaneously being well aware that a second Russian unilateral military intervention in the Straits was impossible due to the strong opposition of Great Britain and France.

The most important difference between holding a conference in London or in Vienna thus lay in the fact that in the capital on the Danube the discussions would be led by a man who could really fulfil the role of mediator, whereas in London, the British foreign secretary would represent only one position and, despite the fact that Great Britain and Russia pursued the same goal in the Levant – the preservation of the Ottoman Empire – their mutual distrust and ill will could make any agreement unattainable. This undoubtedly was another reason that Metternich constantly rejected the idea of a conference on the Eastern Question under Palmerston's leadership. The one exception came in the summer of 1838, when the chancellor himself suggested that the Great Powers gather at the seat of the British Government to arrange a joint action against Mohammed Ali who was threatening to declare his independence at that time. Metternich was able to make this concession because he correctly predicted that Mohammed Ali's separatism was not a serious problem. The chancellor also knew that there was consensus among the Great Powers in this matter as none of them wanted to see the foundation of an Arab empire in the Levant. Russia and Great Britain would definitely coordinate their navies' actions more easily before the port of Alexandria than Constantinople, and the discussions in London about the former were unlikely to be long and complicated. The talks ultimately did not take place because Nicholas I saw no reason to agree to them after Mohammed Ali's retreat. Metternich accepted this position and also refused to negotiate in London, where Palmerston altered the chancellor's original proposal when he tried to link the talks about Mohammed Ali with the question of the Straits and therefore make the proposed conference

9 Sked, *Metternich*, p. 93.

an instrument for his own anti-Russian policy instead of a setting for general agreement.[10]

Metternich's Proposal for Negotiations in Vienna

Palmerston's failure in 1838 could hardly cause Metternich any consternation particularly when it still gave the chancellor hope for his own conference on the Eastern Question. Although he formally abandoned this project in 1834, in fact he never entirely gave it up. This ambition resurfaced in the spring of 1839 due to the worsening relations between Mahmud II and Mohammed Ali. Because the former's defeat was generally expected in European cabinets, they once again presumed the possibility of their own intervention on his behalf, with the accompanying risk of a clash between the Maritime Powers and Russia in the Straits. Metternich believed that this outcome could be avoided either by the sultan's unlikely victory or, in the event of the Ottoman forces' defeat, by uniting the Great Powers prior to their intervention. The crucial problem lay in the fact that there was no consensus among the leading European states. According to Metternich, the best way to create the desired union and find a way out of the deteriorating Near Eastern crisis was, unsurprisingly, negotiation among the Powers involved. As he declared in early June 1839: "It is absolutely necessary for the four Great Powers to come to agreement among themselves on the joint measures that will be undertaken in the event of the Porte being threatened by a catastrophe."[11] In his opinion, the solution had to be found quickly to avoid the outbreak of war between Mahmud II and Mohammed Ali or, if the Powers came together too late, to end any such war as soon as possible. Once the

---

[10] Metternich to Stürmer, Vienna, 13 Nov. 1838, HHStA, StA, Türkei VI, 67; Maltzan to Frederick William III, Milan, 9 Sept. 1838, GStA PK, HA III, MdA I, 7344; Lamb to Palmerston, Venice, 25 Oct. 1838, TNA, FO 120/169; Mosely, pp. 72–83; Webster, *The European System*, p. 27.

[11] Lerchenfeld to Ludwig I of Bavaria, Vienna, 5 June 1839, BHStA, MA, Wien 2408. Metternich mentioned only four Great Powers because the fifth, Prussia, was nominal in this affair. Later, he brought this German Power into the negotiations and talked about the discussions of the five Powers. Lerchenfeld to Ludwig I of Bavaria, Vienna, 24 July 1839, BHStA, MA, Wien 2408.

threat of war had been removed, the long-term peaceful coexistence between the sultan and his Egyptian vassal had to be arranged.[12]

Unsurprisingly again, Metternich was convinced that this goal was to be attained in Vienna, which would become the diplomatic capital of Europe once more with the chancellor at the head of affairs mediating between the liberal Powers and Russia. Consequently, his plan fulfilled his dream of his mastery over Europe and the frank belief that a well-functioning pentarchy unhampered by needless distrust and jealousy was necessary at a time when Mohammed Ali could overthrow the Ottoman Empire. As he wrote: "In an urgent matter of this nature, we see no separate Austria, no separate Russia, no separate France. On the contrary, we are, to our way of thinking, uniting the Great Powers into a coalition, and the good [read: effective intervention] that will be done by the abilities of the one or the other will be in our eyes of advantage not only to the sultan but to the whole of Europe as well."[13] To be able to create this union, Metternich had to persuade the Great Powers to agree to participate in the Viennese negotiations. He defended the venue for the meeting by its geographical position; among the capitals of the Great Powers, Vienna was situated the shortest distance from Constantinople, which meant closest to the developing crisis, and on the way to Paris, London, and Berlin. For this reason the diplomats in Vienna were able to react promptly to the changes in the Ottoman Empire. Metternich hoped that this argument would facilitate the acceptance of the plan. He was convinced that the tsar would easily consent to it and would not refuse the assistance of the man who closely stood by him during the 1830s. He also did not doubt the support of his second conservative ally, Prussia. This German Power had no interests in the Levant and did not pursue any active policy of its own in this region. Frederick William III in fact considered Vienna to be the most suitable city for the achievement of a general consensus and supported the idea.[14]

---

[12] Metternich to Stürmer, Vienna, 6 and 30 April 1839, HHStA, StA, Türkei VI, 71; Metternich to Hummelauer, Vienna, 20 May 1839, HHStA, StA, England 225; Metternich to Apponyi, Vienna, 4 June 1839, HHStA, StA, Frankreich 315; Sainte-Aulaire to Soult, Vienna, 18 May 1834, AMAE, CP, Autriche 426.

[13] Metternich to Apponyi, Vienna, 14 June 1839, HHStA, StA, Frankreich 315.

[14] Ibid.; Metternich to Trauttmannsdorff, Vienna, 22 May 1839, HHStA, StK, Preussen 172; Metternich to Ficquelmont, Vienna, 29 June 1839, HHStA, StA, Russland III, 115; Metternich to Esterházy, Vienna, 2 Aug. 1839, HHStA, StA,

In contrast to both Eastern courts, Metternich considered the acceptance of his project in Paris and particularly in London to be less certain. The basic impediment for close cooperation with the two Maritime Powers was their continual distrust of Russia. It was still difficult for Metternich to dispel their fears about the tsar's aims in the Near East, and nothing indicated in early 1839 that the bad relations between the British lion and the Russian bear were likely to become more cordial. The relations between St Petersburg and Paris were even worse, being seriously affected by Nicholas I's personal aversion towards the "king of the barricades."[15] The antipathy existing between the tsar and the French king was in sharp contrast to the good relations prevailing between Ballhausplatz and the Tuileries. As seen in Chapter 18, unlike Nicholas I, Metternich did not regard Louis Philippe as a threat to conservative values and assessed, although never accepted, the king's proposals for cooperation in European affairs. Since the two men's relations were friendly, the king trusted Metternich's abilities and influence in St Petersburg more than Palmerston's and was definitely more willing to recognise the chancellor as the leader in the solution of the Near Eastern crisis. Metternich was well aware of this compliancy and decided to take advantage of it; he tried to use Louis Philippe to persuade Palmerston to agree to the ministerial conference in Vienna. The chancellor tried in this way to use France as a "wooden horse" in dealing with London because he believed that the French intercession would placate Her Majesty's cabinet. Therefore, in his instructions to the Austrian ambassador in Paris as well as in meetings with the French representative in Vienna between 18 and 20 May, he drew attention to the necessity for general consent over the Eastern Question because only the close cooperation of the Great Powers could assure a reasonable solution to the forthcoming crisis. He suggested creating this union in Vienna.[16]

England 225; A. Hasenclever, *Die Orientalische Frage in den Jahren 1838–1841: Ursprung des Meerengenvertrages vom 13. Juli 1841*, Leipzig 1914, p. 87; Webster, *Palmerston*, II, p. 626.

[15] Ingle, p. 140.

[16] Metternich to Apponyi, Vienna, 20 May, 4 and 14 June 1839, HHStA, StA, Frankreich 315; Metternich to Hummelauer, Vienna, 20 May 1839, HHStA, StA, England 225; Sainte-Aulaire to Soult, Vienna, 18 May and 3 June 1839, AMAE, CP, Autriche 426; Maltzan to Frederick William III, Vienna, 5 June 1839, GStA PK, HA III, MdA I, 7345.

The French premier, Marshal Nicolas Jean-de-Dieu Soult, preferred London or Constantinople to be the centre of negotiations, but Metternich knew that he could count on the king, and this belief proved to be well founded when France accepted the Austrian proposal on 4 June. This assistance, however, was not disinterested. The king believed that he would detach Austria from Russia in the event of the latter's refusal to participate in the proposed ministerial conference.[17] He expected in such an event the deterioration of Austro-Russian relations and the creation of a union between Vienna and Paris. This prospect was to be proved lacking in any foundation in the near future; even at the moment of his utmost personal humiliation, Metternich put reason before emotion and did not sacrifice the vital alliance with conservative Russia for an entente with liberal France.

Having won in Paris in early June 1839, Metternich turned his attention to London, where he had to overcome the more difficult obstacle to his plan. He had already made the same proposal to Palmerston as he had to Paris with the offer of the rapprochement between Austria and Great Britain and the warning that a successful intervention in the Levant that would not threaten the general peace was possible only if it were undertaken in the name of the Alliance and not by one Power alone. Palmerston was not pleased to relinquish the leadership of the Eastern affairs to Metternich, but he was aware of the fact that a chance for a conference to be held in London was negligible; he well remembered the Russian refusal of the previous year, and nothing indicated that Nicholas I would behave any differently in the summer of 1839. Moreover, the situation in the Ottoman Empire was deteriorating considerably. Therefore, albeit reluctantly and with reservation, Palmerston finally accepted Metternich's offer. His words written to the British ambassador in Vienna on 20 June prove how difficult the concession was for him: "We do not know what to say about a conference at Vienna. Metternich is so feeble and timid and tricky and so much swayed by Russia, and by nature so prone to crooked paths and to playing off one party against the other. And so fond of staving off difficulties and putting off the evil day, that I greatly doubt whether a Vienna conference would lead to anything

---

[17] E. Guichen, *La crise d'Orient de 1839 à 1841 et l'Europe*, Paris 1921, p. 31; Webster, *Palmerston*, II, p. 630.

good."[18] He ascribed the concession to the fact that the consent of France had been ensured, which confirms the correctness of the chancellor's chosen tactic towards the Western Powers.[19]

When Metternich opened the door to the round table meeting, he paid great attention to its form. He carefully avoided calling it a "conference" or even "congress," and whenever he found these words in diplomatic correspondence, "a malaise seized him."[20] He claimed that Vienna was to witness a series of informal discussions between himself and the representatives of the Great Powers, who would be informed about the attitudes of their respective governments and empowered by a certain freedom of action, which would enable them to arrive at a plan for the pacification of the Levant. The assumed solution would be sanctioned by the governments and put to the sultan and his vassal for consideration. Metternich had several reasons for taking a stand on the form of the Viennese meeting. First, he did not want the Ottoman Empire to take part in the discussions, which would have been inevitable if the representatives had been summoned to a formal conference; at the congress in Aix-la-Chapelle in 1818, the principle had been adopted that the interests of a third country could not be discussed at a conference or congress without its participation.[21] Metternich distrusted the ability of the Ottoman diplomacy too much and was too familiar with the sultan's uncompromising attitude to be willing to face them in Vienna. He was also not sure whether Mahmud II would give his representative in the Austrian capital sufficient authority to negotiate over the internal affairs of his own empire.[22]

---

[18] Webster, *The European System*, p. 28.

[19] Metternich to Esterházy, Vienna, 1 June 1839, HHStA, StA, England 225; Beauvale to Palmerston, Vienna, 1 June 1839, TNA, FO 120/180; Cetto to Ludwig I of Bavaria, London, 28 June 1839, BHStA, MA, London 2234; Struve to Nesselrode, Vienna, 9 July 1839, AVPRI, fond 133, Kantseliariia, opis 469, 1839/214; Webster, *Palmerston*, II, p. 631.

[20] Sainte-Aulaire to Soult, Vienna, 8 July 1839, AMAE, CP, Autriche 426.

[21] For more details on this issue see Chapter 5.

[22] Metternich to Apponyi, Vienna, 13 and 14 June, 13 July 1839, HHStA, StA, France 315; Sainte-Aulaire to Soult, Vienna, 3 June and 8 July 1834, AMAE, CP, Autriche 426; Beauvale to Palmerston, Vienna, 14 June 1839, TNA, FO 120/180; Struve to Nesselrode, Vienna, 10 July 1839, AVPRI, fond 133, Kantseliariia, opis 469, 1839/214; Bockelberg to Frederick William III, Vienna, 16 July 1839, GStA PK, HA III, MdA I, 6032.

Moreover, according to Metternich, an unofficial gathering of diplomats would enable them to achieve their objective faster than more formal summits attracting more general attention. The memory of the negotiations over the Belgian Question at the London conference that had lasted for eight long years was too fresh, as is evident from his words written in mid June: "It is not in a similar way that any good can be done because such a conference offers to the two Maritime Powers a great opportunity to extend the discussions in ways that could cause immense political embarrassment to the more reliable cabinets that will take part in it, as well as to the whole of Europe. The example of the London conference is certainly a case that proves what dangers and Anglo-French absurdities can result from diplomacy structured in this form."[23] Metternich also thought that he could control an informal meeting more easily than a summit.[24]

The most important reason for his reluctance to use the term "conference" for the forthcoming negotiations was Metternich's conviction that Nicholas I was better disposed to consent to talks of a less formal kind, which seems to indicate that Metternich was not absolutely sure of the tsar's agreement to the plan and that the chancellor, like Palmerston, remembered the Russian rejection of the London conference the previous year. Regardless of how Metternich designated the meeting, however, in practice it would have been a "ministerial conference" if it had ever taken place, which is also shown by the chancellor's words to the French ambassador: "For God's sake, let us say nothing of the kind, let us avoid the word [conference] to be sure of having the event; we will have one [a conference] sooner or later, but, to start with, it is important that we appear modest."[25]

Metternich's actions created an illusory harmony among the Great Powers and, on the turn of June and July 1839, his ambitions seemed as though they would soon be fulfilled. He was pleased by the course of events, and he worked very hard, as much as fifteen hours a day, on the preparation for the meeting. The only thing detract-

---

[23] Metternich to Trauttmannsdorff, Vienna, 14 June 1839, HHStA, StK, Preussen 172.

[24] Metternich to Apponyi, Vienna, 14 June 1839, HHStA, StA, Frankreich 315; Metternich to Ficquelmont, Vienna, 14 June 1839, HHStA, StA, Russland III, 115; Metternich to Trauttmannsdorff, Vienna, 14 June 1839, HHStA, StK, Preussen 172.

[25] Sainte-Aulaire to Soult, Vienna, 8 July 1839, AMAE, CP, Autriche 426.

ing from Metternich's satisfaction was the fact that even at the end of July he had still not received an answer from St Petersburg on his proposal. Tatishchev was residing at that time at the tsar's court and Chargé d'Affaires Friedrich Georg Wilhelm von Struve had no instructions concerning the Russian participation in the Viennese negotiations. Nevertheless, Metternich showed no apparent concern that Nicholas I would reject the plan, and he explained the delay in the tsar's answer by the fact that the invitation had been sent to St Petersburg later than to Paris and London.[26] He also presumed that it would be accepted without reservation: "What we have so far done is only preparation, but to complete it, we still have to obtain the Russian word of approval, and I am expecting this approval with absolute confidence."[27]

The question of the degree of Metternich's confidence in the tsar's positive attitude cannot be satisfactorily answered, but it definitely existed to a great extent and was certainly strengthened by the course of events in the Ottoman Empire from June and early July. According to Metternich, the negative outcome of the crisis for the Porte only underlined the necessity of a union among the Great Powers and it was in their interest to agree to the talks in Vienna. The meeting's immediate result was intended to prevent the Ottoman ministers from making overly excessive concessions and to discourage Mohammed Ali from demanding too much. Later, a settlement for the pacification for the Levant was to be addressed first to Constantinople and if approved there, then to Alexandria for unconditional acceptance. On the other hand, the Ottoman losses raised the problem of European military intervention in the Straits. Although the cabinets in Paris and London agreed to discussions with Russia in Vienna, they still did not believe its intentions and they still demanded reciprocity with regard to the military power engaged in the Straits if it was the only means to prevent Mohammed Ali from seizing Constantinople. At the beginning of June, Metternich had already faced the Maritime

---

[26] Metternich to Stürmer, Vienna, 2 July 1839, HHStA, StA, Türkei VI, 71; Metternich to Ficquelmont, Vienna, 14 and 21 June 1839, HHStA, StA, Russland III, 115; Lerchenfeld to Ludwig I of Bavaria, Vienna, 24 July 1839, BHStA, MA, Wien 2408; Lerchenfeld to Ludwig I of Bavaria, St Petersburg, 9 Aug. 1839, BHStA, MA, Petersburg 2727; Webster, *The European System*, p. 30.

[27] Metternich to Ficquelmont, Vienna, 21 June 1839, HHStA, StA, Russland III, 115.

Powers' demands on the collective defence of the Ottoman capital against a possible Egyptian attack, with British, French, and even several Austrian warships assisting the Russian squadron in the Sea of Marmara.[28]

Metternich considered this request to be unnecessary because he believed that Russian forces were sufficient to protect Constantinople, and the fleets of the Maritime Powers would be more useful in Alexandria, but he could not flatly refuse it with respect to the British and French ambassadors' participation in the forthcoming talks. It is also true that he did not see any risk in this cooperation either for Russia or the Porte if it was undertaken in union with other Great Powers, and it was in line with his opinion that the Eastern Question was to be solved by all of them rather than just Russia because every Great Power desired the preservation of the Ottoman Empire and no single country was to be its sole protector. Therefore, much as he had previously defended the Russian right to intervene on the Bosphorus, he openly started to restate his old view that the tsar had no right as well as no power to prevent the other European Powers from taking part in the task in which they were also concerned.[29] He suggested to Nicholas I on 21 June that he should agree to the military intervention of France and Great Britain in the Straits if the Egyptian army approached: "They want to cooperate so that the Russian power should not be the only one to which the sultan and his empire should owe their existence. They keep at their disposal naval forces only to maintain a balance of power, and they want their flags to be seen in the Sea of Marmara. Can they be prevented from doing so? I do not believe so and therefore it will be necessary to invite them and turn a unilateral operation into a joint action. To give it explicitly the

---

[28] Metternich to Apponyi, Vienna, 13 July 1839, HHStA, StA, Frankreich 315; Sainte-Aulaire to Soult, Vienna, 4 June 1834, AMAE, CP, Austria 426; Lerchenfeld to Ludwig I of Bavaria, Vienna, 12 July 1839, BHStA, MA, Wien 2408.

[29] Metternich to Ficquelmont, Vienna, 21 and 29 June 1839, HHStA, StA, Russland III, 115; Metternich to Esterházy, Vienna, 3 July 1839, HHStA, StA, England 225; Metternich to Apponyi, Vienna, 3 July 1839, HHStA, StA, Frankreich 315; Sainte-Aulaire to Soult, Vienna, 4, 27 and 29 June 1834, AMAE, CP, Autriche 426; Sainte-Aulaire to Soult, Vienna, 21 July 1834, AMAE, CP, Autriche 427; Beauvale to Palmerston, Vienna, 30 June, 1, 11 and 14 July 1839, TNA, FO 120/180; Lerchenfeld to Ludwig I of Bavaria, Vienna, 8, 12, 16 and 24 July 1839, BHStA, MA, Wien 2408; Struve to Nesselrode, Vienna, 29 June 1839, AVPRI, fond 133, Kantseliariia, opis 469, 1839/214.

character [of a joint action], several Austrian ships could take part in it."[30] He repeated this proposal eight days later, when again he clearly advocated the possible operation of a small Austrian squadron on the Golden Horn and its unifying role: "With the Maritime Powers demanding its presence, and Russia making the same request to us, even if our fleet were to be ineffective, it would actually prove the benefit of uniting the Great Powers in a cause common to all of Europe."[31]

With hindsight, this concession to the Maritime Powers proved to be a mistake that contributed considerably to the tsar's distrust of the goal of the Viennese talks. As Ficquelmont reported on 29 June, Nicholas I still regarded the closure of the Dardanelles to the British and French fleets as a question of honour, and he instructed Butenev to leave Constantinople if the sultan permitted them to enter the Sea of Marmara. The problem escalated during July when the request of the two Maritime Powers almost became an ultimatum and Soult and Palmerston started to insist on permission for their warships to pass through the Dardanelles if the Russians were called upon to defend Constantinople. This pressure was intensified by the presence of the French and British fleets in the vicinity of the Dardanelles, together numbering sixteen line-of-battleships, four corvettes, five brigs, and two steamships in early August.[32]

The Austrian chancellor was indignant at the resulting aggressive conduct of the two Western cabinets, which he regarded not only as entirely unnecessary but also dangerous for the success of the Viennese negotiations. He labelled their behaviour in the Straits Question as a "French fury" and a "bad English game."[33] He would agree with the presence of their fleets before the port of Constantinople if necessary, but such a need did not arise, and to make demands in such a manner was an unnecessary provocation of Russia. Moreover, he saw the cooperation of the Western Powers with Russia in the matter of the Straits as a way to save the sultan's throne and assure stability in

---

[30] Metternich to Ficquelmont, Vienna, 21 June 1839, HHStA, StA, Russland III, 115.

[31] Metternich to Ficquelmont, Vienna, 29 June 1839, HHStA, StA, Russland III, 115.

[32] Ficquelmont to Metternich, St Petersburg, 15 July 1839, HHStA, StA, Russland III, 114; Stürmer to Metternich, Büyükdere, 14 Aug. 1839, HHStA, StA, Turkey VI, 70; Kutluoğlu, p. 146.

[33] Metternich to Stürmer, Vienna, 24 July 1839, HHStA, StA, Türkei VI, 71.

the Near East. Nevertheless, the steps of the Maritime Powers' representatives, particularly Roussin who was very active in this matter, could destabilise the relations among the Great Powers. Therefore, Stürmer was instructed to refrain from participating in the action of his British and French colleagues and to keep the Austrian squadron in Smyrna apart from the two fleets.[34] Metternich refused to agree with their close cooperation because, as he wrote in late July, "our presence will be wherever it will be able to serve to confirm the existence of the union of the Great Powers, and it will not take place where exactly the opposite will occur."[35] On the other hand, he definitely disagreed, naturally not very strongly, with the tsar's refusal to cooperate with them. Metternich wrote about the conduct of Russia and the two Maritime Powers: "Where both parties are mistaken is that each is seeking something in the matter that cannot be found in it, and this is the most dangerous element that could lead to an equally grave affair."[36]

On 7 August 1839, Metternich summarised in his instructions to Apponyi the behaviour of the cabinets in London and Paris as "an inopportune folly of the two maritime courts concerning a question that should not be posed."[37] It was particularly France that he found to blame, not only for Roussin's activities in Constantinople but also for announcing through another French representative in Berlin that Roussin had raised the request regarding the presence of the British and French warships in the Sea of Marmara with Metternich's approval. This statement clearly was not true, but its lack of substance could hardly be known in St Petersburg.[38] Metternich reacted sharply in his instructions to Paris on 7 August: "The French cabinet is full of *intrigues*, and it is simultaneously unbelievably *clumsy*. With these two characteristics, it is impossible to advance in the affair success-

---

[34] Metternich to Stürmer, Vienna, 21 and 24 July 1839, HHStA, StA, Türkei VI, 71; Metternich to Ficquelmont, Vienna, 2 Aug. 1839, HHStA, StA, Russland III, 115; Stürmer to Bandiera, Büyükdere, 13 Aug. 1839, Stürmer to Metternich, Büyükdere, 10 and 14 Aug. 1839, HHStA, StA, Türkei VI, 70; Beauvale to Palmerston, Vienna, 30 July 1839, TNA, FO 120/180; Struve to Nesselrode, Vienna, 19 and 23 July 1839, AVPRI, fond 133, Kantseliariia, opis 469, 1839/214.
[35] Metternich to Stürmer, Vienna, 24 July 1839, HHStA, StA, Türkei VI, 71.
[36] Ibid.
[37] Metternich to Apponyi, Vienna, 7 Aug. 1839, *NP*, VI, p. 353.
[38] Beauvale to Palmerston, Vienna, 2 Aug. 1839, TNA, FO 120/180.

fully, or even advance at all. This is a regression ... They see only *themselves* in Paris ... *All for and by France* is a phrase that sounds good to French ears but grates on the ears of others."[39] He declared that Soult should "brandish a sabre" less in the interest of solving the conflict, and he posed this rhetorical question to Apponyi: "What do the Dardanelles have in common with the breakdown in relations between Mohammed Ali and the Porte?"[40]

Nicholas I's Rejection of Metternich's Plan

Metternich's growing displeasure at the conduct of both Maritime Powers was connected with the disquiet increasing in Vienna since mid July owing to the silence prevailing in St Petersburg about a meeting. Some diplomats residing in the Austrian capital even regarded the tsar's refusal to take part in it for granted. The sharp tone of Metternich's instructions of 7 August was caused by the unfavourable news that had just arrived from St Petersburg. What they had suspected was true: Nicholas I informed Ficquelmont at a ball on 22 July that the Near Eastern crisis was to be solved directly between the two quarrelling parties. Mahmud II's death was not the tragedy for him that it was for Metternich because it could open the way to the settlement between the Porte and Mohammed Ali. Because the Russian monarch considered such a development of the affair to be a certainty, he saw no topic for discussions in Vienna where, as he expected, the other Great Powers would have united against him and forced him to cooperate in the Straits. He feared that Austria would take the side of Great Britain and France, and this assumption was particularly based upon Metternich's advice to him in June to cooperate with the Maritime Powers in the Sea of Marmara and the prince's willingness to send the Austrian squadron there. Metternich can be easily criticised for this basic mistake, but he had some reason to believe in the Russian approval because Beauvale had discussed the possibility of naval cooperation in the Straits with Nesselrode

---

[39] Metternich to Apponyi, Vienna, 7 Aug. 1839, *NP*, VI, p. 353.
[40] Ibid., p. 374.

in the autumn of the previous year and he had not received a negative reaction, all of which Metternich knew.[41]

Nevertheless, the Straits Question was only the tip of the iceberg. The tsar and his vice-chancellor also feared that the Powers would demand a guarantee of the independence and territorial integrity of the Ottoman Empire, something that Soult had actually suggested in the summer of 1839. Since Nicholas I was not prepared to guarantee the latter, it led to the possibility of Russia being isolated in this matter. Although there is no proof that Metternich planned to promote this idea, it signified little at the time when the Russian monarch and his vice-chancellor were not generally disposed to the solution of the Eastern Question in Vienna. They did not believe Metternich and were not prepared to make him the mediator between Russia and the Maritime Powers.[42]

German historian Adolf Hasenclever wondered how Metternich could presume that Russia would agree for Vienna to be the centre of negotiations on the Eastern Question when Count Orlov told Maltzan during his stay in this city in March 1839 that the tsar opposed such a plan.[43] The problem lies in the fact that Orlov as well as Grand Duke Alexander, who was in Vienna at the same time, told the chancellor nothing of the tsar's opposition, and Maltzan also withheld from

---

[41] Metternich to Ficquelmont, Vienna, 2 Aug. 1839, HHStA, StA, Russland III, 115; Ficquelmont to Metternich, St Petersburg, 25 July 1839, HHStA, StA, Russland III, 114; Nesselrode to Butenev, St Petersburg, 28 Aug. 1839, HHStA, StA, Türkei VI, 70; Beauvale to Palmerston, Vienna, 30 June 1839, TNA, FO 120/180; Lerchenfeld to Ludwig I of Bavaria, Vienna, 24 and 26 July, 2, 5 and 11 Aug. 1839, BHStA, MA, Wien 2408; Sainte-Aulaire to Soult, Vienna, 24 July and 8 Aug. 1834, AMAE, CP, Autriche 427; Bockelberg to Frederick William III, Vienna, 26 July 1839, GStA PK, HA III, MdA I, 7346; Maltzan to Frederick William III, Vienna, 7 and 9 Aug. 1839, GStA PK, HA III, MdA I, 7347; Struve to Nesselrode, Vienna, 2 Aug. 1839, AVPRI, fond 133, Kantseliariia, opis 469, 1839/214; O'Sullivan to Meylandt, Vienna, 8 Aug. 1839, ADA, CP, Autriche 6; Sir Frederick Lamb's conversation with Count Nesselrode and Prince Metternich at Milan on 3 September 1838: An enclosure with Lamb to Palmerston, 8 September 1838, F. S. Rodkey, "Conversations on Anglo-Russian Relations in 1838," *EHR* 50, 1935, pp. 122–123; Guichen, p. 110; Lorenz, p. 102; Sainte-Aulaire, *Souvenirs*, p. 258.

[42] S. Gorīanov, *Le Bosphore et les Dardanelles: Étude sur la Question des Détroits*, Paris 1910, p. 59; Ingle, p. 110; Martens, p. 36; Rendall, "Restraint or Self-Restraint," p. 52; Rodkey, *The Turko-Egyptian Question*, p. 99; Schiemann, III, p. 386.

[43] Hasenclever, *Die Orientalische Frage*, p. 45.

Metternich the information he had obtained from Orlov.[44] Sainte-Aulaire, who had reservations about the tsar's consent in July, also said nothing to Metternich about his doubts.[45] Even Struve explained matters in such a way in early July that the Belgian representative in Vienna believed that the answer from St Petersburg would be positive.[46] Nesselrode also informed Ficquelmont on 10 June that Russia remained open to solutions other than solely bilateral cooperation between Russia and the Porte, and on 13 July, Nicholas I assured the Austrian ambassador during a military parade that he did not want to solve the Egyptian Question without the consent of Europe.[47]

At the same time, however, the tsar complained several times that the invitation to the Viennese talks had been dispatched to Paris and London before being sent to St Petersburg. Metternich explained this procedure due to the necessity of first ensuring the participation of the Maritime Powers. Having succeeded, he sent a letter full of flattery that was, however, really nothing other than an announcement of a fait accompli. Although from the very beginning Metternich did not conceal his plan from Struve, one cannot be surprised that the tsar was displeased with the way the talks were being called to action. This was undoubtedly Metternich's other mistake that further contributed to Nicholas I's unwillingness to agree to Russian participation in the meeting, expressed in late July. Having heard the tsar's refusal, Ficquelmont personally went to Vienna to convey the information, and, despite a delay due to a minor accident involving his coach, he arrived in only eight days, on 5 August. Three days later, the Russian messenger confirmed what Metternich had heard from his ambassador. The chancellor deeply regretted the tsar's decision as well as Ficquelmont's vacation of his post at such an important moment, but he did not give up and worked with Ficquelmont towards the goal of saving his dream by changing the tsar's attitude.[48]

---

[44] Metternich to Ficquelmont, Vienna, 12 March 1839, HHStA, StA, Russland III, 115; Sainte-Aulaire to Molé, Vienna, 9 March 1839, AMAE, CP, Autriche 426; Maltzan to Frederick William III, Vienna, 10 March 1839, GStA PK, HA III, MdA I, 6032; Lerchenfeld to Ludwig I of Bavaria, Vienna, 12 March 1839, BHStA, MA, Wien 2408.

[45] Sainte-Aulaire to Soult, Vienna, 8 July 1839, AMAE, CP, Autriche 426.

[46] O'Sullivan to Meylandt, Vienna, 8 July 1839, ADA, CP, Autriche 6.

[47] Lorenz, pp. 98–101.

[48] Metternich to Kaisersfeld, Vienna, 13 Aug. 1839, HHStA, StA, Russland III,

The result of the discussions between Metternich and Ficquelmont was a personal letter that the count sent to Nesselrode on 7 August in which he advocated the chancellor's plan aimed at securing the cooperation of the pentarchy in the Near East because it was still needed. The crisis was in no way averted and the future of the Ottoman Empire was still uncertain, which also meant that the question of the Straits could complicate the relations among the Great Powers. The two problems were not simply Russo-Austrian affairs because these two Powers did not have the authority to solve them alone and the other members of the pentarchy also had the right to participate in the preservation of the Ottoman Empire. France and Great Britain not only had their own interests in this region but were also strong maritime powers on the other side of the Straits, and any attempt to exclude them from the affair would have definitely ended in a conflict: "To divide the four Powers into two different camps is to cut the Turkish Empire in half; it is to destroy it, so to speak; it is to put a cause of an inevitable war into the centre of its ruins; it is to assume our position on the side of the weakest, the least intelligent, the poorest; it is to abandon to our adversaries the richest, the strongest, and the most intelligent part. This division, [which will be] the inevitable result of the principle of abandoning an entente of the five Great Powers, proves that it is an affair that can only be resolved by negotiation."[49] Because the disagreement existed in particular between the two Maritime Powers and Russia, and Austria stood between them, Metternich had suggested Vienna as the venue for reaching an understanding. He now asked the tsar and his vice-chancellor to recognise that the preservation of the Ottoman Empire was not a question that could be resolved only by the two imperial courts because it was a European problem that could be solved only by all the prominent European cabinets. The solution was entirely necessary because, as Ficquelmont stated, "it is a question of general peace or general war."[50]

116; Ficquelmont to Nesselrode, Vienna, 7 Aug. 1839, SOA, RA C-A 385; Maltzan to Frederick William III, Vienna, 6 and 9 Aug. 1839, GStA PK, HA III, MdA I, 7347; Struve to Nesselrode, Vienna, 4 June 1839, AVPRI, fond 133, Kantseliariia, opis 469, 1839/214; Hasenclever, *Die Orientalische Frage*, p. 45.

[49] Ficquelmont to Nesselrode, Vienna, 7 Aug. 1839, SOA, RA C-A 385.
[50] Ibid.

These arguments had no effect in St Petersburg, and the only consequence of the chancellor's extraordinary assignment was his exhaustion due to overwork, that, together with a fever, led to the gradual worsening of his health between 11 and 13 August, and finally to a breakdown. A rumour of a heart attack immediately spread through Vienna, but fortunately for the old prince, the disease was not that serious. He had to remain in bed till 25 August, and the members of the thereby paralysed diplomatic corps could do nothing but wait for reports about the chancellor's condition. After treatment, he departed on 10 September to his chateau in Johannisberg in the Rhineland where he spent six weeks recovering. Baron Ottenfels assumed the leadership of the Chancellery as he usually did during Metternich's absence, but Ficquelmont, who had to return quickly from his vacation in Savoy, took control over the Near Eastern crisis. His temporary presence as the head of Austrian diplomacy was a clear signal to St Petersburg about the uninterrupted support of the Danube Monarchy for its conservative Eastern ally because Ficquelmont was the most pro-Russian of all Austrian diplomats. This was soon shown when he tried to placate Russia by insisting that the British and French fleets be removed further from the Dardanelles. The fact that must be emphasised is that Ficquelmont followed the course already begun by Metternich before his departure from Vienna. In late August, the chancellor had ordered the Austrian squadron to sail from Smyrna to Rhodes, and he had persuaded Beauvale and Sainte-Aulaire to instruct their ambassadors in Constantinople not to insist on the fleets entering into the Sea of Marmara. Austria definitely could not afford to lose its Russian ally, and the above-mentioned steps prove that the Austrian diplomatic elites were well aware of it.[51]

---

[51] Metternich to Stürmer, Vienna, 23 and 27 Aug. 1839, HHStA, StA, Türkei VI, 71; Metternich to Esterházy, Vienna, 26 Aug. 1839, HHStA, StA, England 225; Metternich to Koller, Vienna, 6 Sept. 1839, HHStA, StK, Preussen 172; Metternich to Apponyi, Vienna, 10 Sept. 1839, HHStA, StA, Frankreich 315; Metternich to Ficquelmont, Vienna, 6/10 Sept. 1839, HHStA, StA, Russland III, 115; Ficquelmont to Trauttmannsdorff, Vienna, 14 Sept. 1839, HHStA, StK, Preussen 172; Ficquelmont to Stürmer, Vienna, 19 Sept. 1839, HHStA, StA, Türkei VI, 71; Ferdinand I to Ficquelmont, Schönbrunn, 20 Aug. 1839, SOA, RA C-A 375; Metternich to Maltzan, Vienna, 9 Sept. 1839, Maltzan to Frederick William III, Vienna, 15 and 18 Aug., 10 and 13 Sept. 1839, GStA PK, HA III, MdA I, 6032; Verger to Ludwig I of Bavaria, Vienna, 31 Aug., 9 and 14 Sept. 1839, BHStA, MA, Vienna 2408; Lerchenfeld to Ludwig I of Bavaria, Vienna, 17 Aug. 1839,

On the other hand, Nicholas I also did not want Russia's relations with Austria to deteriorate, and therefore Nesselrode showed great favour to Austria's chargé d'affaires and the tsar made the best of the anniversary of the Battle of Borodino when he named Archduke Albert of Habsburg a colonel of the Uhlan Regiment of the Duke of Nassau. Moreover, the tsar sent a letter to Metternich with best wishes for his recovery and complimentary words about his good qualities. This flattery could not be as successful as Nicholas I probably hoped because his refusal to consent to the Russian participation in the meeting, which led to its failure, was far too painful for Metternich. The chancellor did not conceal his disappointment in his discussions with foreign diplomats. After his sincere defence of the Russian Near Eastern policy, he felt betrayed. The humiliation was all the more poignant because he himself had assured the diplomatic corps in Vienna all along that the tsar would accept the project with pleasure, that he would agree entirely with its views and that foreign diplomats could count on Russia's participation in the meeting on the Eastern Question because Russia, as the chancellor had declared many times, desired a joint solution.[52] He had told Beauvale that Russia's agreement to the negotiations was a mere formality and he answered for the tsar;[53] he assured the government in Paris that an absolute conformity in views and desires existed between Vienna and St Petersburg;[54] and he said to Lerchenfeld that "the tsar entirely agrees with us and certainly also wants to proceed with us."[55]

Geheimes Hausarchiv München, Nachlass König Ludwig I., I-XVI 301; O'Sullivan to Meylandt, Vienna, 18 and 23 Aug. 1839, Louvencourt to Meylandt, Vienna, 11 Sept. and 3 Oct. 1839, ADA, CP, Autriche 6; Struve to Nesselrode, Vienna, 17 and 23 Aug. 1839, Tatishchev to Nesselrode, Vienna, 10 and 14 Sept. 1839, AVPRI, fond 133, Kantseliariia, opis 469, 1839/214; Beauvale to Palmerston, Vienna, 3 Sept. 1839, TNA, FO 120/180; Sainte-Aulaire to Soult, Vienna, 9 Sept. 1834, AMAE, CP, Autriche 427; "Aus dem Tagebuche der Fürstin Melanie," *NP*, VI, pp. 309–312; Sainte-Aulaire, *Souvenirs*, p. 258.

[52] Kaisersfeld to Metternich, St Petersburg, 14 Sept. 1839, HHStA, StA, Russland III, 114; Lerchenfeld to Ludwig I of Bavaria, Vienna, 5 and 22 Aug. 1839, BHStA, MA, Wien 2408; Maltzan to Frederick William III, Vienna, 13 Sept. 1839, GStA PK, HA III, MA I, 7348; Maltzan to Frederick William III, Vienna, 24 Nov. 1839, GStA PK, HA III, MA I, 7350; Guichen, p. 133.

[53] Beauvale to Palmerston, Vienna, 11 and 12 July, 12 Aug. 1839, TNA, FO 120/180.

[54] Metternich to Apponyi, Vienna, 3 July 1839, HHStA, StA, Frankreich 315.

[55] Lerchenfeld to Ludwig I of Bavaria, Vienna, 12 July 1839, BHStA, MA, Wien

Metternich was as offended after the tsar's refusal as he had been self-confident before it, and his bitterness was visible long after the failure of the planned talks.[56] During a meeting with Prokesch on 7 December 1839, Metternich explained the Russian refusal this way: "Europe is composed of three national tribes: Germanic, Romance, and Slavic. In the Germanic one, the word 'honour' is very powerful; in the Romance one, it has degenerated into a question of honour; in the Slavic language, the word does not even exist at all. The Germanic and Slavic tribes are represented in the Russian cabinet, and the policy is determined according to whichever one prevails. Both principles live in the tsar, but he inclines towards the Slavic one."[57] Seven days later, Maltzan wrote to Berlin that "the relations between the two imperial cabinets will not regain the sincere and cordial character that they enjoyed in previous times. The blow struck by the Russian cabinet to Mr Chancellor of the Court and the State is too profound and sensitive for it ever to heal. The thorn will remain in the wound, and I fear that the bad memories will exist forever between the two Great Powers."[58] The Prussian envoy was largely correct because Metternich definitely displayed considerable coolness toward Russia at least during the Near Eastern crisis of 1839–1841.

Metternich's irritation was caused not only because his project failed, but also because the tsar's actions pushed him aside in solving the Near Eastern crisis. Even before Metternich's departure to Johannisberg, Nicholas I had decided to join forces with Great Britain directly, and his attempt found a positive echo in London. Consequently, when the chancellor returned to Vienna on 30 October 1839, he found the situation in international affairs entirely changed. The Russo-British rapprochement was in progress and, after Christmas, London rather than Vienna became the centre of discussions about the Eastern Question. The initiative was thus given to Palmerston,

---

2408.
[56] Maltzan to Frederick William III, Vienna, 14 Dec. 1839 and 1 Jan. 1840, GStA PK, HA III, MdA I, 7351; Sainte-Aulaire to Soult, Vienna, 10 Sept. 1839, AMAE, CP, Autriche 427.
[57] The record of the discussion between Prokesch and Metternich, Vienna, 7 Dec. 1839, Prokesch-Osten, *Aus dem Nachlasse*, p. 181.
[58] Maltzan to Frederick William III, Vienna, 14 Dec. 1839, GStA PK, HA III, MdA I, 7351.

and Metternich could only assist in the effort to reach a settlement of the Turko-Egyptian conflict.[59]

The idea of the ministerial conference in Vienna therefore failed and Metternich did not experience a time of glory but a confrontation with a painful reality; his self-confidence was weakened, his nerves were on edge, and his face allegedly showed signs of his having aged a great deal.[60] One can agree with Webster's claim that "the blow was undoubtedly the most severe which Metternich experienced before the Revolution of 1848."[61] The transfer of the centre of negotiations to London was an unquestionable defeat for the chancellor, who had relied too much on the tsar's willingness to see the Near Eastern affairs settled in Vienna. Nicholas I acted in a way unexpected by Metternich, and with his decision to transfer leadership to Palmerston, he disappointed Metternich for the second time in Near Eastern affairs in the 1830s. The first time had been in 1833 when his conservative ally did not inform him about the planned signing of the Russo-Ottoman Treaty of Unkiar-Skelessi and the ignorance of its existence put Metternich into an awkward position and caused him great embarrassment. In 1839 his frustration was much greater because he believed that he had sufficiently proved his goodwill towards Russia with his loyalty in preceding years.

This was unfortunately not the case, and strong fears of Metternich's possible anti-Russian conduct prevailed in St Petersburg. Nicholas I and Nesselrode worried that the chancellor would join the two Maritime Powers if Russia did not proceed in compliance with his wishes.[62] Beauvale seems to confirm the validity of this concern when he wrote in late July 1839 that Metternich's action was similar to the time when he had distanced himself from Napoleon and allied himself with the anti-French alliance: "I have been in this trade long enough to have seen Prince Metternich separate himself from Napoleon, and the

---

[59] Metternich to Stürmer, Vienna, 5 Nov. 1839, HHStA, StA, Türkei VI, 72; Metternich to Kaisersfeld, Vienna, 25 Nov. 1839, HHStA, StA, Russland III, 116; Sainte-Aulaire to Soult, Vienna, 31 Oct. 1839, AMAE, CP, Autriche 427; Maltzan to Frederick William III, Vienna, 2 Nov. 1839, GStA PK, HA III, MdA I, 6032; Louvencourt to Meylandt, Vienna, 30 Oct. 1839, ADA, CP, Autriche 6; Schroeder, *Transformation*, pp. 736–737.
[60] Louvencourt to Meylandt, Vienna, 3 Sept. 1839, ADA, CP, Autriche 6.
[61] Webster, *The European System*, pp. 30–31.
[62] Puryear, *International Economics*, p. 165.

process was precisely similar to that which is taking place at present.
He will do his best to avoid a separation, he will try to the end to
keep Russia with him, but at every failure he will advance a step toward us."[63] This opinion was also held by Russian historian Serge
Gorianov and to a certain extent by other historians,[64] for example,
Matthew S. Anderson, who claimed that "Austria's wavering attitude
now [in the summer of 1839] made her seem a very uncertain ally."[65]
The studied correspondence from not only 1839 but also from previous years, however, shows that Metternich never planned to proceed
without Russia and such an eventuality was entirely impossible for
two reasons: first, Austria could not break the alliance with its conservative ally; second, the isolation of Russia, in other words a rupture
among the Powers, was exactly what Metternich tried to prevent and
the eventual exclusion of this Great Power from the Viennese negotiations would inevitably have had such a result. The tsar's refusal
was so painful for Metternich for precisely this reason, and it was
also for this reason that he refused to open the discussions without
Russian participation and tried to change the tsar's attitude. It was
therefore due to this refusal that the conference did not take place because, at least for Metternich, it made no sense without the presence
of the Russian ambassador. The discussions without his participation
were compatible with Palmerston's aims at that time but not with
Metternich's. The prince defended Russian policy in the Near East
entirely in conformity with his notion of peace management even after Russia's rejection of his plan.[66] He told Beauvale and Maltzan on
6 September 1839: "I answer even at this hour for the good intentions
of Russia, and I have never ceased to believe that it will support us
in the objective we are trying to attain."[67]

The tsar and his vice-chancellor also feared that the main goal
of Metternich's proceeding in this affair was to restrict Russia and
subordinate its actions to the control of other Great Powers.[68] Met-

---

[63] Beauvale to Palmerston, Vienna, 30 July 1839, TNA, FO 120/180.
[64] Gorianov, p. 53.
[65] Anderson, "Russia and the Eastern Question," p. 93.
[66] Beauvale to Palmerston, Vienna, 2 Aug. 1839, TNA, FO 120/180.
[67] Maltzan to Frederick William III, Vienna, 6 Sept. 1839, GStA PK, HA III,
MdA I, 7348.
[68] Nesselrode to Meyendorff, St Petersburg, 24 July 1839, A. de Nesselrode (ed.),
Lettres et papiers du Chancelier Comte de Nesselrode, 1760–1850, VII, Paris 1908,

ternich had more reasons to be anxious about the unpredictable and aggressive policy of the Maritime Powers, however, and he definitely wanted to restrict them to the same extent as Russia to prevent dangerous conduct by either side, requesting certain concessions from all parties to bridge the differences among them: namely, an end of the Maritime Powers' distrust towards Russia and their willingness to cooperate with it, and the tsar's renunciation of an exclusive role in solving Ottoman affairs. In this way Metternich wished to stabilise the situation in the Near East and prevent any further deterioration in the relations among the Great Powers. This effort was correctly assessed by the representative of the United States in Vienna in early October 1839: "Austria, in fact, appears to act the part of a mediator in the whole business and to use her influence to calm the jealousies and suspicion known to exist, in all matters relating to Turkey, between the English, French, and Russian Governments. It is this character which gives to Austria the great weight she possesses in the conferences and which has enabled her to make the Powers less distrustful of each other and to induce them to act with a certain degree of unity in the important and over-agitated question."[69]

*   *   *

Metternich proposed to save the Porte by eliciting the cooperation of the Great Powers, even in the Straits, which he found to be a necessary concession to France and Great Britain, but which finally proved to be the main reason for the Russian refusal to participate in the Viennese talks. Nevertheless, in late 1839, Great Britain and Russia decided to cooperate, and Nicholas I agreed with the naval presence of other Powers' fleets in the Sea of Marmara, which was exactly what Metternich had advocated in the summer of the same year. The motivation for the tsar's conduct is well known to historians today: he preferred to deal with Great Britain directly without the control of another Power, and, moreover, to isolate France through

---

p. 287.
[69] Clay to Forsyth, 1 Oct. 1839, Rodkey, *The Turko-Egyptian Question*, Appendix, p. 251.

this manoeuvre, in which he finally succeeded.[70] Nothing was illogical in this approach, but one can also understand the consternation at the Chancellery in Ballhausplatz at the Russian consent to the presence of the Western fleets in the Straits, which had previously been declared to be incompatible with the tsar's honour and the principle reason for the condemnation of Metternich's conference plan. There was, moreover, another shift in Russian policy in late 1839: Nicholas I originally rejected the negotiations in Vienna, explaining that they were unnecessary when the sultan was prepared to accede to considerable losses in a direct settlement with his Egyptian vassal, which was not only acceptable for the tsar but also recommended by him to the Porte. Later, however, owing to the improvement of the Russo-British relations and with the aim of separating France, which was supporting Mohammed Ali, Nicholas I became a zealous supporter of the sultan. This was exactly what Metternich had requested from the other Powers in the spring and summer of 1839.

Due to Nicholas I's conduct, it was Palmerston who controlled the path to the solution of the Near Eastern affairs on the turn of the 1830s and 1840s. It was a certain paradox because it was the British foreign secretary, whose Russophobia had significantly contributed to the tension in the relations among the Great Powers, particularly in the Levant, who had made the settlement of the Near Eastern affairs almost impossible for such a long time. One must understand that the struggle between Palmerston and Metternich for leadership over diplomatic affairs was not only a contest between these two ambitious men but also a conflict between two different ways of thinking. Whereas for Palmerston a conference was a tool to separate Austria and Russia and to obtain the latter's submission to the will of the liberal Powers, for Metternich it was a way to unite the two quarrelling parties on the basis of their sincere and common wish to preserve the Ottoman Empire.

---

[70] Rendall, "Restraint or Self-Restraint," p. 53.

En route to the London Convention for the Pacification of the Levant

The failure of Metternich's peace management efforts in the summer of 1839 had serious consequences for the further involvement of the European Powers in the Second Mohammed Ali Crisis. Their cooperation was not achieved and the disharmony in the views on the solution of the conflict in the Near East that arose between France and other Great Powers protracted the crisis. Metternich, deeply convinced that Mohammed Ali's power had to be limited as far as possible, firmly maintained a pro-Turkish attitude, but his conviction of the necessity of gaining France's support against Mohammed Ali made him cautious about proceeding without its concurrence. Tired of the month-long refusal of the French to meet any of the compromise proposals presented by the other Powers, Metternich finally agreed to limit Mohammed Ali's power in a coalition of four instead of five Powers. In mid July 1840, almost a year after the presentation of the Collective Note of 27 July to the Divan, the crisis reached its new phase when Austria, Great Britain, Russia and Prussia decided to act against the pasha without France.

The Russo-British Rapprochement and the Secession of France

The Collective Note of 27 July 1839 made the Great Powers responsible for the solution of the crisis, but the failure of the plan for the Viennese conference made finding such a solution more difficult. The crucial question in the late summer of 1839 was whether Mohammed Ali would grant them time to do this or whether he would try to terminate the affair himself by sending his army against Constantinople.

Fortunately for the young sultan, although the pasha threatened with
the latter in September, he did not go beyond verbal sabre-rattling.
His fear of the Great Powers' military intervention discouraged him
from making any aggressive moves and limited him to the fortification
of some strategic points along the coast during the following months.
He did nothing to endanger the sultan's position, while at the same
time doing nothing that would satisfy him either; he did not return
the Turkish fleet despite the diplomatic pressure from the European
consuls and he did not significantly reduce his territorial demands; he
was merely prepared to return Crete.[1]

Metternich correctly regarded Mohammed Ali's defensive measures as clear proof that the pasha would not dare to renew the military operations. The chancellor reconciled himself to this as the maximum one could expect from the old pasha and advised the Porte to
do nothing that could provoke him to abandon his assumed passivity;
temporisation was the best option for the Turks. This advice was easy
to follow since they had no means for breaking the undeclared truce.
Their most significant step for the remainder of 1839 was the issue of
a note on 22 August inviting the Great Powers to find a solution and
informing them that the sultan was prepared to grant Mohammed Ali
Egypt in hereditary tenure, but nothing else.[2]

[1]   Laurin to Stürmer, Alexandria, 16 Aug. 1839, HHStA, StA, Türkei VI, 70;
Laurin to Stürmer, Alexandria, 13 and 16 Sept., 15 and 27 Oct. 1839, HHStA, StA,
Ägypten 1; Laurin to Stürmer, Alexandria, 6 Nov. and 14 Dec. 1839, Stürmer to
Metternich, Constantinople, 6 Nov. and 31 Dec. 1839, HHStA, StA, Türkei VI, 71;
Laurin to Stürmer, Alexandria, 6 March 1840, HHStA, StA, Türkei VI, 73; Laurin
to Stürmer, Alexandria, 6 May 1840, HHStA, StA, Türkei VI, 74; Königsmarck to
Frederick William III, Büyükdere, 30 Oct. 1839, GStA PK, HA III, MdA I, 7281;
Cochelet to Soult, Alexandria, 15 Oct. 1839, É. Driault (ed.), L'Égypte et l'Europe:
La crise de 1839–1841, I, Caire 1930, p. 336; Kutluoğlu, p. 150.
[2]   Metternich to Stürmer, Vienna, 20 Aug. and 24 Dec. 1839, Ficquelmont to
Stürmer, Vienna, 19 Sept. and 8 Oct. 1839, HHStA, StA, Türkei VI, 72; Metternich to Stürmer, Vienna, 17 March 1840, HHStA, StA, Türkei VI, 78; Metternich
to Neumann, Vienna, 17 March and 25 April 1840, HHStA, StA, England 230; Metternich to Apponyi, Vienna, 16 Jan. 1840, HHStA, StA, Frankreich 319; Stürmer
to Metternich, Büyükdere, 31 July 1839, HHStA, StA, Türkei VI, 69; the Porte's
note to Stürmer, 22 Aug. 1839, Laurin to Stürmer, Alexandria, 26 Aug., 6 and
16 Sept., 6 and 19 Oct. 1839, Stürmer to Metternich, Büyükdere, 7, 10, 14, 19, 20,
23 and 28 Aug., 5, 12, 18, 25 and 26 Sept., 1, 2, 9, 16 and 29 Oct. 1839, HHStA,
StA, Türkei VI, 70; Lerchenfeld to Ludwig I of Bavaria, Vienna, 12 Nov. 1839,
BHStA, MA, Wien 2408; Maltzan to Frederick William III, Vienna, 15 Nov. 1839,
GStA PK, HA III, MdA I, 7350; Maltzan to Frederick William III, Vienna, 17 Jan.

With this note instigated by Stürmer and approved by Metternich the Porte formally accepted the Collective Note of 27 July. The crucial problem lay in the fact that there was no prospect for a prompt fulfilment of the Great Powers' engagement to solve the crisis due to their disunion. However, it was no longer caused by the animosity between Great Britain and Russia which had lasted for some years because relations between the two countries began to improve in the late summer of 1839. Having rejected the idea of the Viennese talks, Nicholas I decided to approach Great Britain directly. In mid September, his prominent diplomat, Count Philipp Ivanovich Brunnov, arrived in London with an offer of Russia's cooperation with the other Great Powers in the Eastern Question. The tsar promised not to renew the Treaty of Unkiar-Skelessi which was due to expire in 1841, but he requested the closure of the Straits for all European warships in times of war and peace with the only special exception for a Russian squadron that would be entitled to enter the Sea of Marmara in the event of an Egyptian assault on Constantinople. Palmerston welcomed these proposals and he objected only to Russia's unilateral intervention on the Golden Horn. For such a case he demanded the right for the participation of the British and French fleets. With this counter-proposal Brunnov left the British capital. As already mentioned in the previous chapter, Nicholas I agreed with the naval presence of the Maritime Powers in the Sea of Marmara and decided to send Brunnov to London for the second time to finish the negotiations on the Straits Question as well as the settlement of the Turko-Egyptian conflict.[3]

Nicholas I's action was definitely an insult to Metternich. What the tsar refused to approve in Vienna he was now prepared to accept in London, but the Austrian chancellor proved again to be a pragmatic and rational statesman and since the Russo-British rapprochement was based upon principles with which he could agree, he did not hesitate to support it. In his opinion, such mutual understanding was a necessary premise for solving the Near Eastern crisis. During his first stay in London, Brunnov had been supported by Esterházy. On his way from London, the Russian diplomat personally visited Metternich and spent time with him from 19 to 24 October in Johannisberg

---

1840, GStA PK, HA III, MdA I, 7352.
[3] Metternich to Stürmer, Vienna, 10 Sept. 1839, HHStA, StA, Türkei VI, 72; Temperley, *Crimea*, p. 111; Ingle, pp. 124–127.

and Frankfurt am Main. The chancellor was satisfied with the result of Brunnov's mission and optimistic about the outcome; he correctly predicted that the tsar would accept Palmerston's counterproposal. When Metternich was later invited by Nicholas I for Austria's participation in the forthcoming talks in London, he agreed, but he made Austria's participation conditional upon the closure of the Straits to foreign warships only in times of peace because, as he argued, the sultan could not be deprived of calling on foreign support in times of war. Furthermore, the principle of their closure was to be based upon an ancient Ottoman right,[4] which would preserve the sultan's sovereignty: "The real principle, according to us, is in the closed sea that is a sovereign right for the Porte. It is this Great Power whose right to take initiative in this matter must be recognised, it is it that must be permitted to express the principle and declare its willingness to apply it, whereas the role of the [other] Great Powers is to recognise this right and accept the fact. However, the Porte may only discuss its state of peace, with either Russia or the Great Powers which possess naval forces. At time of war, it has the morally and materially imprescriptible right to summon its friends to its aid and repel its enemies."[5]

As in the case of Palmerston's objections, Nicholas I also submitted to those of Metternich. From that moment therefore, nothing hindered the sending of the Austrian diplomat, Baron Philipp von Neumann, on a special mission to London. Neumann knew the British capital well, having once served there, and he was also familiar

[4]   Metternich to Esterházy, Vienna, 10 and 30 Sept. 1839, Johannisberg, 21 Oct. 1839, HHStA, StA, England 225; Metternich to Trauttmannsdorff, Vienna, 13 Oct. 1839, HHStA, StK, Preussen 172; Metternich to Apponyi, Vienna, 9 Dec. 1839, HHStA, StA, Frankreich 316; Metternich to Stürmer, Vienna, 24 Dec. 1839, Ficquelmont to Stürmer, Vienna, 11 Oct. 1839, HHStA, StA, Türkei VI, 72; Metternich to Kaisersfeld, Vienna, 25 Nov. 1839, HHStA, StA, Russland III, 116; Esterházy to Metternich, London, 25 Sept., 1, 8 and 14 Oct. 1839, HHStA, StA, England 223; Verger to Ludwig I of Bavaria, Vienna, 14 Oct. 1839, Lerchenfeld to Ludwig I of Bavaria, Vienna, 28 Dec. 1839, BHStA, MA, Wien 2408; Tatishchev to Nesselrode, Vienna, 9 Nov. and 20 Dec. 1839, AVPRI, fond 133, Kantseliariia, opis 469, 1839/215; Tatishchev to Nesselrode, Vienna, 2 and 8 Jan. 1840, Tatishchev to Brunnov, Vienna, 1 Jan. 1840, AVPRI, fond 133, Kantseliariia, opis 469, 1840/177; Beauvale to Palmerston, Vienna, 16 Nov. 1839, TNA, FO 120/180; Ingle, p. 127; Webster, *Palmerston*, II, pp. 650–657.
[5]   Metternich to Esterházy, Johannisberg, 30 Sept. 1839, HHStA, StA, England 225.

with the Near Eastern crisis since he had assisted in this question at the Chancellery during the previous months. At the end of 1839, he was to take part in the negotiations instead of Esterházy, who had temporarily left Great Britain to solve his own affairs at home. The talks between Palmerston, Brunnov and Neumann started during the Christmas celebrations in Palmerston's country house in Broadlands and then continued in London. The discussed topics were the status of the Straits and the future of Mohammed Ali.[6] The three men settled the former in the way that Russia, Great Britain and France would cooperate with their navies in the Sea of Marmara if Ibrahim Pasha marched against Constantinople, and Austria was to send several ships pro forma as well. The Straits were to be closed to foreign warships in times of peace only and as a result of the sultan's ancient right, as Metternich desired. Mohammed Ali was to be confined to Egypt and obtain hereditary rule over it. The use of coercive measures if he refused to submit to the will of the European Powers was approved. All the conditions complied with Metternich's long-held opinions, and in mid January 1840 Neumann obtained full power to sign a convention solving the two affairs in the arranged way. Since the same consent was dispatched for a Prussian representative from Berlin at almost the same moment, Austria, Great Britain, Prussia and Russia were able to sign a convention concerning the Straits and the Egyptian Question in early 1840 and all they were waiting for was for the French to declare their position.[7]

---

[6] Neumann was not authorised to discuss Mohammed Ali's future until the receipt of Metternich's instructions of 1 January 1840 because the chancellor had originally been informed by the tsar that Brunnov would negotiate only the Straits Question. Metternich to Neumann, Vienna, 1 Jan. 1840, HHStA, StA, England 230; Metternich to Kaisersfeld, Vienna, 2 and 31 Jan. 1840, HHStA, StA, Russland III, 120; Metternich to Stürmer, Vienna, 8 Jan. 1840, HHStA, StA, Türkei VI, 78; Maltzan to Frederick William III, Vienna, 1 Jan. 1840, GStA PK, HA III, MdA I, 7351.

[7] Metternich to Trauttmannsdorff, Vienna, 4 Jan. 1840, HHStA, StK, Preussen 175; Metternich to Kaisersfeld, Vienna, 10 Dec. 1839, HHStA, StA, Russland III, 116; Metternich to Stürmer, Vienna, 24 Dec. 1839, HHStA, StA, Türkei VI, 72; Tatishchev to Nesselrode, Vienna, 10 Dec. 1839, AVPRI, fond 133, Kantseliariia, opis 469, 1839/215; Maltzan to Frederick William III, Vienna, 5 Dec. 1839, GStA PK, HA III, MdA I, 7350; Maltzan to Frederick William III, Vienna, 14 Dec. 1839, GStA PK, HA III, MdA I, 7351; Lerchenfeld to Ludwig I of Bavaria, Vienna, 19 Dec. 1839, BHStA, MA, Wien 2408; Nesselrode to Meyendorff, St Petersburg, 27 Nov. 1839, Nesselrode, pp. 294–295; Hasenclever, *Die Orientalische*

Simultaneously with the British-Russian rapprochement went the dissension of France from the position maintained by other Powers in the Egyptian Question. During July 1839 French public opinion started to support Mohammed Ali, who was regarded after the Battle of Nezib as "the Napoleon of the East,"[8] a French ally who had to be protected by France. In the attitude of the French public, traditional revolutionary and Napoleonic nostalgia combined with actual political and economic interests, and the public pressure finally moved the Parisian cabinet to assume a more pro-Egyptian attitude. This was proved in two ways. First, the king as well as his government became unwilling to intervene militarily against the pasha. In early August, Palmerston prepared instructions for the British Mediterranean fleet to sail to Alexandria and gain control over the Turkish warships, even by force if necessary. However, the French cabinet refused to cooperate in this measure, which was finally abandoned by Palmerston as well. Owing to France's resistance, the Turkish fleet held by Mohammed Ali could not be returned to the sultan for the time being. Metternich immediately noticed this difference in the British and French attitudes and disagreed with the French mindset as incompatible with the internal peace of the Ottoman Empire. He originally wanted to send Austria's naval squadron with the fleets of the Maritime Powers to Alexandria, but seeing the disunion between them in this respect, he finally had to state that any demonstration of force was pointless under the given conditions.[9] Second, the French government did not want to considerably limit Mohammed Ali's territorial possessions and also in this respect it was in no way willing to use coercive mea-

---

Frage, p. 109; Ingle, pp. 128–130; Webster, *Palmerston*, II, pp. 660–662.

[8]   P. Guiral, *Adolphe Thiers ou de la nécessité en politiques*, Paris 1986, p. 171.

[9]   Metternich to Esterházy, Vienna, 13 July 1839, HHStA, StA, England 225; Metternich to Stürmer, Vienna, 23 and 27 Aug. 1839, HHStA, StA, Türkei VI, 72; Metternich to Apponyi, Vienna, 10 Sept. 1839, HHStA, StA, Frankreich 316; Ficquelmont to Stürmer, Vienna, 19 Sept. 1839, HHStA, StA, Türkei VI, 72; Ficquelmont to Esterházy, Vienna, 26 Sept. 1839, HHStA, StA, England 225; Stürmer to Metternich, Büyükdere, 4, 5 and 11 Sept. 1839, HHStA, StA, Türkei VI, 70; Sainte-Aulaire to Soult, Vienna, 12 Sept., 8 Oct. and 13 Nov. 1839, AMAE, CP, Autriche 427; Beauvale to Palmerston, Vienna, 21 Sept. 1839, TNA, FO 120/180; R. de Castries, *Louis-Philippe*, Paris 1980, p. 290; S. Charléty, "La Monarchie de Juillet (1830–1848)," E. Lavisse (ed.), *Histoire de France contemporaine: Depuis la révolution jusqu'à la paix de 1919*, V, Paris 1922, p. 167; Guichen, pp. 71–84; Hasenclever, *Die Orientalische Frage*, p. 72; Kutluoğlu, p. 147; Marcowitz, p. 153.

sures against him. The king and his first minister wanted the pasha to retain more provinces under his family's hereditary administration than the other Powers were willing to allow: in particular Egypt, Syria and Arabia. This attitude frustrated Metternich and Palmerston, who agreed that the territorial concessions to Mohammed Ali were to be as few as possible, at best the hereditary tenure of Egypt alone, because only such a solution could preserve a durable peace in the Ottoman Empire.[10] According to Matthias Schulz, Metternich assumed this attitude after the first negotiations between Palmerston and Brunnov,[11] but the chancellor's opinion, as seen in Chapter 23, had actually already been formed at the beginning of the crisis and he continued to maintain it during the whole of its course: "We are convinced that the greater the extension of the portions of this empire placed under the hereditary government of Mohammed Ali and his descendants, the less possible it will be to attain the proposed goal. Consequently, we desire that the concession of heredity is limited solely to the pashalik of Egypt. Should Austria remain isolated in its support for this concession restricted to Egypt, it will side with the opinion that could result from an entente of the Great Powers, but in any case it would prefer the minimum of concessions on the part of the Porte."[12]

It definitely is not true, as Paul W. Schroeder claims, that Metternich wished to divide France and Great Britain later in 1839 much as Nicholas I also wanted.[13] This was dangerous and counterproductive for the chancellor in the given situation. He did not mind the coolness in their relations, but he wanted to prevent France's isolation to the extent desired by the tsar and thus a serious rupture that would make the settlement of the crisis more difficult. Metternich was still convinced that a peaceful solution, in other words Mohammed Ali's surrender of the Turkish fleet and his acceptance of hereditary rule

---

[10] Metternich to Stürmer, Vienna, 13 Aug. and 12 Nov. 1839, HHStA, StA, Türkei VI, 72; Metternich to Apponyi, Johannisberg, 25 Sept. and 1 Oct. 1839, Vienna, 19 Nov. 1839, HHStA, StA, Frankreich 316; Sainte-Aulaire to Soult, Vienna, 8 July 1839, AMAE, CP, Autriche 426; Struve to Nesselrode, Vienna, 19 July 1839, AVPRI, fond 133, Kantseliariia, opis 469, 1839/214; Beauvale to Palmerston, Vienna, 8 Sept. 1839, TNA, FO 120/180; Hall, p. 250; Kutluoğlu, p. 151; Rodkey, *The Turko-Egyptian Question*, p. 128; Webster, *Palmerston*, II, pp. 641–643.
[11] Schulz, *Normen und Praxis*, p. 119.
[12] Metternich to Koller, Vienna, 7 Aug. 1839, HHStA, StK, Preussen 172.
[13] Schroeder, *Transformation*, p. 740.

limited to Egypt without the need to use coercive measures against him, was still possible if France exerted its influence over the pasha to persuade him to accept the less advantageous conditions which would be offered to him by the sultan and backed by all Great Powers. As well as in previous years, he continued to trust the pasha's foresight and apprehension of the European Powers' hostile attitude: "Mohammed Ali is too closely connected with Europe because of everything that he does in Egypt and he has learnt enough to understand the relations between the states and the actions of some on the others not to understand as well that a political position that does not have the sanction of Europe contains no guarantee of durability."[14] With France isolated, Metternich saw no prospect for any success of diplomatic pressure: "Our firm conviction is that Mohammed Ali will agree with everything only when he knows that the courts are in agreement about what they want, whereas nothing will move him to abandon a refusal, which is easy to understand, as long as he knows that this accord does not exist."[15] If the chancellor's faith in the success of the five Powers' diplomatic pressure had proved to be false, then their military intervention was necessary, but in this case Metternich regarded France's cooperation as even more vital because only France and Great Britain had at their disposal the considerable forces in the Mediterranean for such a task and, therefore, the burden of such an action lay upon them. If the former abstained, such a measure would become more problematic or even impossible. Consequently, Metternich claimed that the understanding of the two Maritime Powers on the further proceedings against the pasha was crucial: "It is when France and England understand each other that the affair will be able to proceed."[16] Afterwards, the three conservative Powers, possessing no considerable forces in the Mediterranean, would join them.[17] In any

---

[14] Metternich to Apponyi, Vienna, 10 Sept. 1839, HHStA, StA, Frankreich 316.
[15] Metternich to Apponyi, Johannisberg, 1 Oct. 1839, HHStA, StA, Frankreich 316.
[16] Metternich to Apponyi, Johannisberg, 13 Oct. 1839, HHStA, StA, Frankreich 316.
[17] Metternich to Ficquelmont, Vienna, 10 Sept. 1839, HHStA, StA, Russland III, 116; Metternich to Esterházy, Johannisberg, 25 Sept. and 21 Oct. 1839, Vienna, 19 Nov. 1839, HHStA, StA, England 225; Metternich to Apponyi, Johannisberg, 21 Oct. 1839, Vienna, 19 Nov. 1839, HHStA, StA, Frankreich 316; Metternich to Neumann, Vienna, 1 Feb. 1840, HHStA, StA, England 230; Ficquelmont to Trauttmannsdorff, Vienna, 6 Oct. 1839, HHStA, StK, Preussen 172; Sainte-Aulaire

case, with either the diplomatic pressure or the military intervention, Metternich regarded the unity of the five Powers as urgently needed, as he wrote to Esterházy on 10 September: "A positive action against Mohammed Ali is very difficult. This convinces me of the necessity to establish a close and sincere coalition of the five Great Powers. Work as hard as you can in this respect: that England, towards whom Russia is making such progress, keeps silent for the moment on all questions except the one regarding Egypt, and that it sincerely aligns itself with Russia; that the English cabinet simultaneously tries to reconcile itself with that of France and that it exercises its influence over Paris in persuading the ministry of the necessity of not following at the same time in the Levant two objectives which are so obviously opposed to each other ... We, from our point of view, we keep two objectives in view; the first, that is to say the most immediate, to save the existence of the Porte as best we can; the second, not to ignite a general war in Europe because of the Porte because then everything would be lost. We would have the war without saving the Porte."[18]

Metternich definitely desired the success of the British-Russian rapprochement, something he had sincerely wanted for years, but in no way at the expense of the French in 1839. Therefore, he assumed a cautious attitude towards France and tried to prevent its isolation by weakening its pro-Egyptian bias and ensuring Prussia's assistance in his effort in bringing France and Great Britain together. He also welcomed a concession made in October by Palmerston, who proposed Mohammed Ali should keep Egypt as hereditary tenure with the southern part of Syria without Acre for his lifetime. However, all these attempts failed. Louis Philippe maintained a strong pro-Egyptian attitude and Metternich could not count on him in this affair; his considerable influence over the the French king from the previous years now significantly diminished. The Bavarian diplomat, Franz Gabriel von Bray-Steinburg, reported from Paris at the beginning of February 1840: "The relations between France and Austria, until recently so close, have considerably cooled off and the salutary influence that the Viennese cabinet exerted through the king on the affairs of France is entirely destroyed. King Louis Philippe suspects Prince Metternich

---

to Soult, Vienna, 10 Sept. and 31 Oct. 1839, AMAE, CP, Autriche 427; Maltzan to Frederick William III, Vienna, 3 Nov. 1839, GStA PK, HA III, MdA I, 7349.
[18] Metternich to Esterházy, Vienna, 10 Sept. 1839, HHStA, StA, England 225.

of having secretly provoked the missions of Mr Brunnov, and he accuses him of having toyed with him by abusing the unlimited trust with which he favoured him. Count Apponyi is feeling the significant effects of this change with regard to his position here, and he has lost the royal confidence that until now kept him informed of every important affair."[19] As for Palmerston's offer regarded by the chancellor as a mark of conciliation, Soult rejected it as insufficient and requested for the pasha not only Egypt but also the whole of Syria as hereditary tenure. For Palmerston as well as Metternich such a solution was unacceptable. The chancellor was frustrated by France's attitude and what irritated him even more was its isolated approach in Constantinople, which was at sharp variance with the attitudes of the other signatories of the Collective Note and the sultan's interests. Roussin, who was known for his animosity to Mohammed Ali, was replaced on 23 October 1839 by an extraordinary envoy, Count Eduard Pontois, who started, upon Soult's instructions, to advise the Porte to settle its dispute with Mohammed Ali directly and without the participation of the other Great Powers. According to the French plan, the sultan as well as the pasha was to make some concessions with the aim of restoring peace. However, this attempt was doomed because Stürmer and Ponsonby successfully opposed Pontois' intrigues and easily persuaded Reshid Pasha, who had returned to Constantinople at the beginning of September and resumed his post of foreign minister, to await the decision of all the Powers. Since Mohammed Ali was not willing to give up more than Crete, the French initiative failed in Egypt as well.[20]

---

[19] Bray to Ludwig I of Bavaria, Paris, 1 Feb. 1840, BHStA, MA, Paris 2102/1.
[20] Metternich to Apponyi, Johannisberg, 25 Sept. 1839, Vienna, 19 Nov. 1839, Ficquelmont to Apponyi, Vienna, 26 Sept. 1839, HHStA, StA, Frankreich 316; Metternich to Esterházy, Johannisberg, 30 Sept. 1839, HHStA, StA, England 225; Metternich to Kaisersfeld, Vienna, 25 Nov. and 19 Dec. 1839, HHStA, StA, Russland III, 116; Metternich to Stürmer, Vienna, 24 Dec. 1839, HHStA, StA, Türkei VI, 72; Ficquelmont to Trauttmannsdorff, Vienna, 14 and 27 Sept., 6 Oct. 1839, HHStA, StK, Preussen 172; Stürmer to Metternich, Constantinople, 13 and 21 Nov., 1, 11 and 20 Dec. 1839, Pontois to Sainte-Aulaire, Therapia, 19 Nov. 1839, Laurin to Stürmer, Alexandria, 17 Nov., 3 and 6 Dec. 1839, HHStA, StA, Türkei VI, 71; Stürmer to Metternich, Constantinople, 8 Jan. 1840, HHStA, StA, Türkei VI, 73; Apponyi to Metternich, Paris, 11, 14 and 27 Jan., 23 Feb., 10 and 12 March 1840, HHStA, StA, Frankreich 317; Maltzan to Frederick William III, Vienna, 15 Oct. 1839, GStA PK, HA III, MdA I, 7349; Königsmarck to Frederick William III,

Pontois' encouragement of the Porte to make a direct settlement did not unduly worry Metternich, who trusted Reshid enough not to fear its success. Nevertheless, France's opposition to both the use of coercive measures as well as Palmerston's compromise proposal regarding territorial gains for Mohammed Ali together with its intrigues in Constantinople and Alexandria hardened the chancellor's attitude towards the Parisian cabinet, whose pro-Egyptian attitude he regarded as the most serious impediment for the solution of the crisis. In late September 1839 such an accusation appeared in his correspondence: "The four cabinets are pro-Turkish, the Tuileries cabinet is pro-Egyptian, and it is about the sultan and Mohammed Ali that the question is concerned. Since the five cabinets are divided, the difficulty for them to arrive at any agreement over the modus operandi is a totally natural consequence of their division. If the four courts did not encounter the opposition of France, or if this Great Power sincerely shared the opinion of other four courts, the Turko-Egyptian affair would be settled very quickly. Mohammed Ali would submit with perfect grace to the declared will of Europe."[21] The level of his embitterment from the same period is also easily recognisable from his letters: "The French policy is malicious, dishonest, underhand, ambitious, and just one of these traits would be enough to make it dangerous; combined, these traits turn into a European disaster."[22] As for Pontois, Metternich angrily commented on his conduct in December: "The role of Mr Pontois is a wretched role. It reflects precisely the attitude adopted by the French cabinet itself."[23] In the same month, he also openly warned Sainte-Aulaire that if he had to make a choice between the pro-Egyptian attitude of France and the strong anti-Egyptian attitude of Great Britain, he would not hesitate to support the latter.[24] Although he was still convinced that the British-French

---

Büyükdere, 27 Nov. and 18 Dec. 1839, GStA PK, HA III, MdA I, 7281; Ponsonby to Palmerston, Therapia, 13 Nov. and 11 Dec. 1839, TNA, FO 78/360; Pontois to Soult, Therapia, 17 Nov. 1839, AMAE, CP, Turquie 279; Kutluoğlu, p. 152; Marlowe, p. 251.

[21] Metternich to Apponyi, Johannisberg, 25 Sept. 1839, HHStA, StA, Frankreich 316.

[22] Ibid.

[23] Metternich to Stürmer, Vienna, 24 Dec. 1839, HHStA, StA, Türkei VI, 72.

[24] Metternich to Stürmer, Vienna, 12 Nov. 1839, HHStA, StA, Türkei VI, 72; Metternich to Esterházy, Vienna, 19 Nov. 1839, HHStA, StA, England 225; Lerchenfeld to Ludwig I of Bavaria, Vienna, 29 Nov. 1839, BHStA, MA, Wien 2408; Sainte-

cooperation was necessary to solve the crisis, he was not prepared to agree with their harmony coming at the expense of the sultan: "It is after all in the sense of the principle of conserving the Ottoman Empire that England assumed, as well as ourselves, the basis of its policy in the Levant and that I tried to bring the two cabinets of Paris and London together."[25]

At the end of 1839, it was becoming more and more evident that if France did not change its attitude, it would become isolated. Metternich pertinently assessed the situation when stating that France was "headed in a direction where nobody else could follow."[26] The difference in opinion between Austria and France was so considerable that Metternich almost ceased talking with Sainte-Aulaire about the Eastern Question after the beginning of 1840 saying that "our discussions on this subject can only have the value of gossip, it would be better to refrain from them."[27] The French ambassador finally left Vienna in March for vacation because he considered staying any longer in the Austrian capital to be pointless.[28]

The London Conference and the Signing of the Convention of 15 July 1840

The isolated attitude of France made Metternich desire even more a prompt and successful termination of the negotiations in London. He was rather optimistic after achieving a quick agreement between Palmerston, Neumann and Brunnov in early January 1840, but disap-

Aulaire to Soult, Vienna, 2 Dec. 1839, AMAE, CP, Autriche 427; Maltzan to Frederick William III, Vienna, 27 Nov. 1839, GStA PK, HA III, MdA I, 7350; Maltzan to Frederick William III, Vienna, 25 Dec. 1839, GStA PK, HA III, MdA I, 7351; Maltzan to Frederick William III, Vienna, 1 Jan. 1840, GStA PK, Rep. 81 Gesandschaften (Residenturen) u. (General-) Konsulate nach 1807, Gesandschaft Wien II, 201/1.

[25] Metternich to Esterházy, Johannisberg, 19 Nov. 1839, HHStA, StA, England 225.

[26] Metternich to Stürmer, Vienna, 24 Dec. 1839, HHStA, StA, Türkei VI, 72.

[27] Sainte-Aulaire to Soult, Vienna, 31 Jan. 1840, AMAE, CP, Autriche 428.

[28] Metternich to Stürmer, Vienna, 8 Jan. 1840, HHStA, StA, Türkei VI, 78; Metternich to Apponyi, Vienna, 9 March 1840, HHStA, StA, Frankreich 319; Sainte-Aulaire, *Souvenirs*, pp. 284–285.

pointment was quick to follow. Although France abstained from the talks, it had considerable influence on their progress through some pro-French members of the British government who did not want to proceed without France. When Palmerston presented the cabinet the conditions for solving the issues of the Straits and the Turko-Egyptian conflict as settled with Neumann and Brunnov, they were rejected. For some time the future of the negotiations in London seemed to be rather uncertain and the irritated Metternich even at first considered them to be at an end. He instructed Neumann to stay in the British capital but to abandon it if Brunnov decided to leave.[29] The prince objected to the French influence on the discussions and the weak attitude of the British cabinet: "It is clear that it was a mistake to choose this capital for the meeting of the cabinets. A country whose governmental authority is itself unstable and, consequently, weak and awkward can never be regarded as the most suitable place for serving as a centre of any negotiation."[30]

This complaint shows how much Metternich regretted the fact that the British and not the Austrian capital was the centre of negotiations over the Eastern Question. According to Adolf Hasenclever and Heinrich von Srbik, he never entirely abandoned hope for the failure of the London negotiations and their transfer to Vienna.[31] Count Maltzan claimed that the problems accompanying the negotiations in London were "at the bottom of his heart rather satisfactory. For the Imperial Chancellor it was always a kind of nightmare to see the conclusion of this affair in London and under the supreme direction of Russia and England. Necessity compelled him to pretend otherwise and forced him to direct his efforts to the goal of conciliation, but his views on the success of this affair under the given conditions are not, I suppose, sincere. Today when the breakdown of these negotiations

---

[29] Metternich to Neumann, Vienna, 12 and 22 Jan., 7 and 21 Feb. 1840, HHStA, StA, England 230; Metternich to Kaisersfeld, Vienna, 9 Feb. 1840, HHStA, StA, Russland III, 120; Metternich to Stürmer, Vienna, 26 Feb. 1840, HHStA, StA, Türkei VI, 78; Maltzan to Frederick William III, Vienna, 3, 6, 8 and 28 Feb. 1840, GStA PK, HA III, MdA I, 7352; Lerchenfeld to Ludwig I of Bavaria, Vienna, 20 and 27 Feb. 1840, BHStA, MA, Wien 2409; Cetto to Ludwig I of Bavaria, London, 28 Jan. and 21 Feb. 1840, BHStA, MA, London 2235; Webster, *Palmerston*, II, p. 667.

[30] Metternich to Stürmer, Vienna, 12 Feb. 1840, HHStA, StA, Türkei VI, 78.

[31] Hasenclever, *Die Orientalische Frage*, p. 124; Srbik, *Metternich*, II, p. 70.

is more than probable, the Chancellor evidently appears to breathe more easily and nurtures the hope that the moment approaches when he will be able to seize control of this great affair once again and prove that those who snatched it from him made a false calculation and that it is only he who can cut the new Gordian knot."[32] Maltzan was convinced that Metternich wanted to take over the leadership of negotiations over the Egyptian Question, leaving the discussion over the Straits to negotiators in London.[33] Similar presumptions are, however, exaggerated because despite his injured pride, Metternich never tried to destroy the London negotiations nor did anything that could endanger their progress simply because his desire to terminate the affair as soon as possible and his sense for reality did not allow such destructive actions.[34] As he wrote to Apponyi in early May: "It was in Vienna where, from the beginning I believed the most useful agreement over the serious affair of the Levant could be reached most advantageously. Events decided otherwise and they were mistaken, but once the issue has been set aside, it is necessary to remain loyal to the principle."[35]

On the other hand, Metternich also wanted to keep as much influence as he already had over the development of affairs. This was one of the reasons why he was displeased with Palmerston's request for the arrival of a Turkish negotiator to London. The foreign secretary took this step to gain time and support against the pro-French members in his own cabinet. Metternich knew that very well, but he still was against this measure because, first, he feared that the disunion among the Great Powers would become more evident in Constantinople and, second, he was convinced that the Powers should solve their disunion in London and then present their support to the sultan. He therefore found the presence of a Turkish agent in the British capital

---

[32] Maltzan to Frederick William III, Vienna, 11 Feb. 1840, GStA PK, HA III, MdA I, 7352.
[33] Ibid.
[34] Metternich to Neumann, Vienna, 22 and 27 Jan. 1840, HHStA, StA, England 230; Metternich to Stürmer, Vienna, 12 and 26 Feb. 1840, HHStA, StA, Türkei VI, 78; Metternich to Apponyi, Vienna, 1 May 1840, HHStA, StA, Frankreich 319; Tatishchev to Nesselrode, Vienna, 2 Jan. 1840, AVPRI, fond 133, Kantseliariia, opis 469, 1840/177; Lerchenfeld to Ludwig I of Bavaria, Vienna, 7 Feb. 1840, BHStA, MA, Wien 2409; Langsdorff to Thiers, Vienna, 26 March 1840, AMAE, CP, Autriche 428.
[35] Metternich to Apponyi, Vienna, 6 May 1840, HHStA, StA, Frankreich 319.

superfluous: "They want to continue in the negotiations between the cabinets and even admit a representative of the Porte! My intuition tells me that if the natural order of the established entente is abandoned, there will be no possibility of success. It will become impossible for the Porte, in the present situation, to be represented anywhere other than in Constantinople because to speak to the Turks about the conditions of the arrangement between the Porte and Mohammed Ali before the cabinets themselves are in agreement on this subject would not be the way to settle the Turko-Egyptian affair at all but would make the Divan and the Egyptian pasha both witnesses and judges of the differences which exist among the Christian courts [and] because in this approach time must necessarily be deemed unimportant and would provide the Egyptian pasha with powers difficult to evaluate in his further resistance."[36] There was another reason for his displeasure: Metternich objected to Palmerston trying to make a conference from the talks and the chancellor also worried that the direct involvement of the Porte in the negotiations would decrease his own influence over Constantinople. The fact that the Turkish agent, Nourri Effendi, who arrived in London at the end of March 1840, was instructed to listen to Neumann's advice did much to ease the chancellor's disquiet. Metternich was finally satisfied with Nourri's proceeding under Neumann's direction aimed at overcoming the opposition of France and some pro-French British ministers. Nourri's first step in London was a note of 7 April addressed to the Great Powers reminding them of their pledge contained in the Collective Note of 27 July 1839 to help the sultan. The text was actually edited by Neumann. In late May, Nourri was replaced by a new Turkish plenipotentiary, Chekib Effendi, who continued in pressing the Powers for a quick settlement. In a note of 31 May, he repeated the request for a quick solution of the crisis.[37]

---

[36] Metternich to Beauvale, Vienna, 14 Feb. 1840, HHStA, StA, Türkei VI, 78.

[37] Metternich to Neumann, Vienna, 21 Feb., 4 and 17 March, 16 April 1840, HHStA, StA, England 230; Metternich to Stürmer, Vienna, 26 Feb., 14 and 16 April 1840, HHStA, StA, Türkei VI, 78; Metternich to Trauttmannsdorff, Vienna, 7 March 1840, HHStA, StK, Preussen 175; Metternich to Kaisersfeld, Vienna, 8 March 1840, HHStA, StA, Russland III, 120; Neumann to Metternich, London, 8 Feb. 1840, HHStA, StA, England 228; Maltzan to Frederick William III, Vienna, 12 and 18 Feb., 11 March 1840, GStA PK, HA III, MdA I, 7352; Tatishchev to Nesselrode, Vienna, 15 Feb. and 11 March 1840, AVPRI, fond 133, Kantseliariia, opis 469, 1840/177; E. B. Chancellor (ed.), *The Diary of Philipp von Neumann, 1819 to 1850*, London 1928, p. 142; Kutluoğlu, p. 157.

Neither Nourri's nor Chekib's invitations to join the intervention of the Great Powers on behalf of the sultan changed anything
in France's pro-Egyptian attitude, which was also maintained by the
new ministry that formed under Adolphe Thiers on 1 March 1840.
This ministerial change did not in the least please Metternich, who
regarded Thiers as a dangerous revolutionary and despot. He referred
to Thiers as a "new consul" and his accession to the ministry as "a
revolution within the [July] revolution."[38] The new French minister
would probably have agreed with this evaluation because he not only
admired Napoleon Bonaparte but also once said of himself: "I love the
revolution; I am a child of the revolution. I love it more than anyone
else. I would be nothing without the revolution."[39] In the Egyptian
Question, however, he was personally more moderate, but due to the
pro-Egyptian attitude of the French public, he could do nothing but
continue in Soult's policy, which he had inherited: reject the use of
coercive measures against Mohammed Ali and ensure him the hereditary tenure of not only Egypt but also Syria at least. Although a
supporter of the alliance with Great Britain, he could not sacrifice
Mohammed Ali and, therefore, he was willing to negotiate with other
Powers in London only under these conditions.[40]

Despite his strong criticism of France's pro-Egyptian attitude,
Metternich became less willing to proceed without its participation
in the whole affair during the spring of 1840. He was still convinced
that only the Maritime Powers possessed useful means for coercing
Mohammed Ali to yield, but seeing France in opposition to the other
Great Powers and the British cabinet divided in this question, he
doubted that a successful way out of the crisis could be found under
the given conditions. He pointed out the fact that Palmerston had led
Great Britain into four serious affairs which dangerously overextended

[38] Metternich to Kaisersfeld, Vienna, 6 April 1840, HHStA, StA, Russland III,
120.
[39] Guichen, p. 255.
[40] Metternich to Ficquelmont, Königswart, 5 Sept. 1836, SOA, RA C-A 383; Metternich to Ficquelmont, Vienna, 6 Jan. 1837, HHStA, StA, Russland III, 110; Metternich to Stürmer, Vienna, 10 March 1840, HHStA, StA, Türkei VI, 78; Metternich to Nesselrode, Vienna, 9 March 1840, HHStA, StA, England 230; Metternich
to Kaisersfeld, Vienna, 21 March 1840, HHStA, StA, Russland III, 120; Apponyi
to Metternich, Paris, 10, 18 and 22 April, 11, 14, 18 and 29 May, 16 June 1840,
HHStA, StA, Frankreich 317; Lerchenfeld to Ludwig I of Bavaria, Vienna, 4 April
1840, BHStA, MA, Wien 2409.

British power: the wars in Afghanistan and with China and serious disputes with the U.S.A. and with the Kingdom of Naples.[41] The chancellor was not sure whether the British cabinet would follow the foreign secretary in the Egyptian affair without France: "Lord Palmerston is waging four potential wars at the same time; that against China, that in Central Asia, that against Naples and that against Egypt. Does the cabinet share the opinion of its political director?"[42] Consequently, he found it necessary to restore the diplomatic concert and proceed in a coalition of five. Maltzan reported on 23 April: "Metternich puts the question simply: 'Can the question of pacification be resolved with five or with four?' He answers: 'With five easily, with four not and never.'"[43]

The cooperation of France could only be ensured by making territorial concessions to Mohammed Ali. Already in mid March, Metternich contemplated in his instructions to Neumann the possibility of granting Mohammed Ali Egypt as a hereditary state and the whole of Syria for life. However, Neumann was forbidden to make any proposal in this respect. On 25 April 1840, Metternich informed Neumann about a similar idea according to which Mohammed Ali could obtain Egypt and the Arabian Peninsula as a hereditary state and some of the five Syrian pashaliks for his lifetime with the right to nominate his descendants to administer them after his death. Adana, the rest of Syria and Crete would be returned to the sultan. This was also not a proposal that Neumann was authorised to communicate to Palmerston, but was only an eventuality, as Metternich wrote, "a measure in extremis."[44] However, Neumann went further than he was instructed and introduced these instructions to Palmerston, who initiated a new compromise proposal to France, conveyed by Neumann to the French ambassador in London, François Pierre Guillaume Guizot, on 5 May

[41] Metternich to Neumann, Vienna, 25 April 1840, HHStA, StA, England 230; Metternich to Apponyi, Vienna, 1 May 1840, HHStA, StA, Frankreich 319; M. E. Chamberlain, *'Pax Britannica?' British Foreign Policy 1789–1914*, London, New York 1988, pp. 75–76. For more on Metternich's attitude to the Neapolitan Sulphur Crisis see M. Šedivý, "Metternich and the Anglo-Neapolitan Sulphur Crisis of 1840," *Journal of Modern Italian Studies* 16, 2011, 1, pp. 1–18.

[42] Metternich to Neumann, Vienna, 25 April 1840, HHStA, StA, England 230.

[43] Maltzan to Frederick William III, Vienna, 23 April 1840, GStA PK, Rep. 81 Gesandschaften (Residenturen) u. (General-) Konsulate nach 1807, Gesandschaft Wien II, 201/1.

[44] Metternich to Neumann, Vienna, 25 April 1840, HHStA, StA, England 230.

1840: Mohammed Ali was to obtain hereditary rule over Egypt and
the southern part of Syria with Acre for his lifetime. This offer was
based upon the content of Metternich's instructions from 25 April but
not their result as historian John Marlowe incorrectly claimed.[45]

Metternich criticised Neumann for his independent action because the instructions merely contained an idea for discussion among
the four Powers and not an offer to France, but one can hardly believe
that he really was so disappointed with Neumann's conciliatory step,
which he probably hoped would meet some positive echo in Paris.
His criticism actually was not that strong and what he actually objected to was the fact that the offer was met with the same negative
response in Paris because Thiers was not willing to agree with this,
from his point of view insufficient, concession although it was more
generous than the one made by Palmerston to Soult in October 1839.
Thiers expected that the four Powers would make a new and better
offer and he regarded the proposal of 5 May not as an end but as a
beginning.[46] Nevertheless, Metternich was not willing to go too far in
his concession to France and grant Syria to Mohammed Ali as hereditary tenure because it would be the equivalent of dividing the sultan's
empire into two parts and, as he wrote in early June, "every arrangement which would lead this empire to be divided into two parts placed
under hereditary authorities would be, in our opinion, a mortal blow
delivered to the Ottoman Empire."[47]

As well as in the case of Soult, Metternich also had to face
Thiers' attempts to achieve a direct settlement between the sultan
and the pasha without the cognizance of other Great Powers, which
actually was the only thing the French prime minister could do if
he did not want to join the conference in London. According to Paul
W. Schroeder, Metternich also was "encouraging the Turks and Egyp-

---

[45] Metternich to Neumann, Vienna, 17 March and 25 April 1840, HHStA, StA,
England 230; Neumann to Metternich, London, 8 May 1840, HHStA, StA, England
228; Beauvale to Palmerston, Vienna, 24 April and 9 May 1840, TNA, FO 120/189;
Charles-Roux, *Thiers*, p. 68; Marlowe, p. 258; Webster, *Palmerston*, II, p. 683.
[46] Metternich to Neumann, Vienna, 24 June and 10 July 1840, HHStA, StA,
England 230; Metternich to Ficquelmont, Vienna, 1 July 1840, HHStA, StA, Russland III, 120; Maltzan to Frederick William IV, Vienna, 21 June 1840, GStA PK,
HA III, MdA I, 7354; Struve to Tatishchev, Vienna, 30 June 1840, AVPRI, fond
133, Kantseliariia, opis 469, 1840/178; C. H. Pouthas, "La Politique de Thiers
pendant la crise orientale de 1840," *RH* 182, 1938, p. 88.
[47] Metternich to Stürmer, Vienna, 2 June 1840, HHStA, StA, Türkei VI, 78.

tians to negotiate,"[48] but this simply is not true. Metternich was against a direct settlement between the sultan and the pasha in 1840 as much as he had been during the previous year. It is true that he was prepared to sanction any direct settlement if it was not too disadvanteagous for the former, but he did not believe in such an outcome because, in his opinion, any direct settlement between the two men, in particular when arranged by France, could be hardly advantageous for the sultan. Therefore, the chancellor always strongly urged the Porte to remain calm and patient and not to start direct negotiations with Mohammed Ali: "We reserve the right to demand of the Divan that it continues to accord us the confidence that it demonstrates to us daily and, furthermore, we demand that it continues to maintain itself in an expectant attitude with calmness and firmness."[49] Thiers' attempts to assure a direct settlement between Alexandria and Constantinople and become a mediator between the two parties as well as between Mohammed Ali and the European Powers naturally annoyed Metternich to the same extent as those of Soult. The chancellor knew about this effort not only from the reports he received from the Ottoman capital but also from an intercepted letter written by Thiers' close friend, the French journalist Jacques Coste, to Ahmed Fethi Pasha in early May. Coste warned Ahmed in the name of the French prime minister that Russia, Great Britain and Austria wanted to divide the Ottoman Empire and that France was the only real friend of the Porte. Therefore, the sultan was to listen to France only. Finally, he recommended a quick solution with Mohammed Ali.[50] Metternich angrily wrote to Ficquelmont in mid June: "There you see, Mr Ambassador, the policy that offers us a wonderfully realistic portrait of a great man [Thiers] who believes himself to be the civilian successor of the military Napoleon."[51]

---

[48] Schroeder, *Transformation*, p. 743.
[49] Metternich to Stürmer, Vienna, 8 Jan. 1840, HHStA, StA, Türkei VI, 78.
[50] Metternich to Stürmer, Vienna, 8 Jan., 12 and 26 Feb., 17 March and 18 July 1840, HHStA, StA, Türkei VI, 78; Metternich to Neumann, Vienna, 12 and 22 Jan., 25 April and 24 June 1840, HHStA, StA, England 230; Metternich to Ficquelmont, Vienna, 14 June 1840, HHStA, StA, Russland III, 120; Langsdorff to Thiers, Vienna, 30 June 1840, AMAE, CP, Autriche 428; H. Malo, *Thiers 1797–1877*, Paris 1932, p. 296; C. H. Pouthas, *La Politique étrangère de la France sous la monarchie consitutionnelle*, Paris 1948, p. 75.
[51] Metternich to Ficquelmont, Vienna, 14 June 1840, HHStA, StA, Russland III, 120.

Fortunately for the Powers involved in the London negotiations, Thiers' encouragement of the Egyptian governor had no prospect for success because in Constantinople Reshid and Fethi held firm and were waiting patiently for the outcome, and Pontois, who was named ambassador in March 1840, in vain tried to change their minds. In Alexandria Mohammed Ali was still ill disposed to make any significant concessions which could open the door to a direct settlement with the Porte, as Thiers advised him. Although Metternich sent instructions to Stürmer to prevent any French intrigues, he was not concerned about the Porte's attitude due to his belief in Reshid. This confidence in no way changed after Husrev Pasha's removal from the office of grand vizier in early June, which gave the impression that the Porte was more willing to negotiate with the pasha, but as Metternich correctly presumed, this was not the case. Mohammed Ali, who himself saw the fall of his old enemy as a way of opening the door to a direct settlement, was soon disappointed when his agent, Sami Bey, arrived in Constantinople to open peace negotiations but Reshid, loyal to the Porte's cooperation with the Great Powers and hostile to a direct settlement with the pasha, refused.[52]

---

[52] Metternich to Stürmer, Vienna, 2 June 1840, HHStA, StA, Türkei VI, 78; Metternich to Trauttmannsdorff, Vienna, 18 June 1840, HHStA, StK, Preussen 175; Stürmer to Metternich, Constantinople, 29 Jan., 5, 12 and 19 Feb., 4, 11, 18 and 25 March 1840, HHStA, StA, Türkei VI, 73; Laurin to Stürmer, Alexandria, 16 June 1840, Stürmer to Metternich, Constantinople, 1, 8, 15, 22 and 26 April, 6 and 13 May, 10, 17 and 24 June, 8, 9, 16 and 22 July 1840, HHStA, StA, Türkei VI, 74; Maltzan to Frederick William IV, Vienna, 14 June 1840, GStA PK, HA III, MdA I, 7354; Königsmarck to Frederick William IV, Büyükdere, 1 and 16 July 1840, GStA PK, HA III, MdA I, 7282; Langsdorff to Thiers, Vienna, 4 June 1840, AMAE, CP, Autriche 428; F. R. Chesney, C. Molbech, E. H. Michelsen, *Das Türkische Reich*, Leipzig 1974, p. 224; Charles-Roux, *Thiers*, pp. 40–50; Guichen, p. 225; Kutluoğlu, pp. 156–159; Marlowe, pp. 256–257. In the late spring of 1840, Reshid complained about the prolongation of the crisis due to the inability of the Great Powers to reach any conclusion. He, as well as other Ottoman dignitaries, wanted to see the end of the affair and they were becoming impatient. Consequently, in July, Reshid himself started to prepare a plan for the pacification that seemed to him to be acceptable for Mohammed Ali. Stürmer helped him to edit it during the night from 13 to 14 July and the sultan agreed with it. The plan was to be kept secret until the moment when Metternich gave his opinion of it. According to this plan, Mohammed Ali was to obtain Egypt as a hereditary state. The pashaliks of Acre, Saida and Tripolis would also be granted to him, and after his death they would be inherited by his sons and grandsons under the condition that no inheritor could accumulate more of these pashaliks or any of them

During the spring of 1840, the opposition of France to the anti-Egyptian attitude generally shared by the other Great Powers proved to be insuperable. It was similarly difficult for Palmerston to overcome the pro-French opposition in his own cabinet at the same time. To improve his own position towards his colleagues, he wanted to obtain from Metternich the engagement of Austria's military assistance against Mohammed Ali if necessary. This was also desired by the ministers and would be rather useful due to the unpopularity of the limited Russo-British cooperation with the British public. If Austria, as popular in the British Isles as Russia was unpopular, promised to cooperate in coercive measures, it would be easier for Palmerston to get the cabinet on his side. Neumann entirely supported this request and reported that Austria's promise to participate in this respect would entirely change the situation in favour of the foreign secretary, who came up with two projects for Austria's military participation. First, 4,000 Austrian soldiers would assist in an attack against Crete, but Metternich regarded such a step as entirely void of any strategic value: "The seizure of Crete could in no way contribute to bringing about the submission of Mohammed Ali. The loss of this island, even supposing that he lost the Egyptian corps which is situated there, would not diminish his means of resistance. Everything concerning Crete does not add up, in a word, to a coercive measure. An attack against Crete made with the aim of replacing it under Turkish domination, and without having stipulated the relevant conditions in advance, could excite the sizeable Greek population to resist. 4,000 men could not then suffice for the enterprise, which moreover would change its nature because it would be a matter of the Powers bringing an end to a civil war between the Mussulmans, and Austria would not want to occupy itself with an enterprise that could incite a new revolt among

---

and Egypt as well. After the death of the sons and grandsons, the Syrian pashaliks would be returned to the Porte. If Mohammed Ali refused this offer, then the Porte was prepared to add Crete or the pashalik of Damascus for his lifetime. Although the plan was prepared upon Metternich's instructions for Neumann of 25 April known to Reshid through Stürmer, Metternich in no way initiated the plan that finally was not executed due to the settlement that was reached in London at the same time. Consequently, having received the plan from Stürmer, Metternich merely replied that his answer was the London Convention of 15 July. Metternich to Neumann, Königswart, 31 July 1840, HHStA, StA, England 230; Stürmer to Metternich, Constantinople, 20 and 27 May, 16 July 1840, HHStA, StA, Türkei VI, 74.

the Greek population."[53] Since Palmerston did not insist on this plan, it was soon entirely abandoned.[54]

According to Palmerston's second idea, 12,000–15,000 Austrian soldiers would be sent to Syria on British ships and paid by the Porte.[55] However, such a number was not feasible for Austria, and Metternich did not want to drag Austria into an enterprise that, in his opinion, had little chance for success without France's active participation because Great Britain had the naval but not the necessary land forces in the Mediterranean and Russia had both in the Black Sea but it was questionable whether it would apply them in the Mediterranean. Additionally, Prussia had no vessels at its disposal and Austria's naval forces were few and its land forces could be hardly sent to Syria in any large number. Nevertheless, Palmerston did not give up. Austria's direct assistance in coercive measures was for him so important that he finally asked for the participation of just two Austrian ships for the blockade of the Alexandrian port because their moral effect on the British public would be enormous and would enable the British cabinet to proceed without France. Metternich raised his objections even against this proposal because he regarded the blockade as an insufficient measure for coercing Mohammed Ali to surrender. This restraint was not merely due to his regard for France but also to the negative attitude of some senior-ranking Austrian dignitaries to Austria's military involvement in the Levant; for example Count Kolowrat was for a direct settlement between the sultan and the pasha and against the expense of a military intervention. Nevertheless, the chancellor personally was not against coercive measures and never explicitly refused Austria's participation in them, and this was soon revealed and proved to have an important effect on the development of affairs.[56]

[53] Metternich to Stürmer, Vienna, 2 June 1840, HHStA, StA, Türkei VI, 78.
[54] Metternich to Neumann, Vienna, 25 April 1840, HHStA, StA, England 230; Metternich to Trauttmannsdorff, Vienna, 29 April 1840, HHStA, StK, Preussen 175; Neumann to Metternich, London, 11, 16 and 17 March 1840, HHStA, StA, England 228; Maltzan to Frederick William III, Vienna, 28 March and 11 April 1840, GStA PK, HA III, MdA I, 7353; Beauvale to Palmerston, Vienna, 12 April 1840, TNA, FO 120/189; Tatishchev to Nesselrode, Vienna, 12 April 1840, AVPRI, fond 133, Kantseliariia, opis 469, 1840/177; Webster, *Palmerston*, II, pp. 675–677.
[55] Neumann to Metternich, London, 9 Feb. 1840, HHStA, StA, England 228.
[56] Metternich to Neumann, Vienna, 25 April and 9 June 1840, HHStA, StA, England 230; Metternich to Stürmer, Vienna, 2 June 1840, HHStA, StA, Türkei

In mid June, Metternich still regarded any proceeding against Mohammed Ali without France's direct participation or at least its consent as dangerous. As he declared at the beginning of the month: "A convention signed in London without France could become a question of war for Europe."[57] The wish to terminate the whole Oriental affair together with Thiers' encouragement of the Porte to a direct settlement with Mohammed Ali and his refusal of Neumann's offer of 5 May finally moved the chancellor to change his mind and explicitly offer Austria's naval assistance for coercive measures against the pasha. This decision was for the first time contained in his instructions to Trauttmannsdorff on 18 June and more importantly to Neumann on 24 June. He decided to proceed as a coalition of four Powers because he realised that there was no possibility to do so as five and he was convinced that it was necessary to proceed in some way. This promise of Austria's military support was crucial for Palmerston to overcome the pro-French opposition in the British cabinet. The foreign secretary told Neumann in the morning of 9 July that with this pledge "Austria had decided the question in the cabinet"[58] that had finally resolved to proceed as a coalition of four on the previous day. The most decisive impetus for the British government's decision, however, was Palmerston's threat of resignation, which would definitely have led to its fall.[59]

It was thus possible for Austria, Great Britain, Prussia, Russia and the Ottoman Empire to conclude the Convention for the Pacification of the Levant on 15 July 1840. According to this agreement

---

VI, 78; Metternich to Ficquelmont, Vienna, 14 June 1840, HHStA, StA, Russland III, 120; Neumann to Metternich, London, 9, 12 and 22 May 1840, HHStA, StA, England 228; Beauvale to Palmerston, Vienna, 24 April 1840, TNA, FO 120/189; Langsdorff to Thiers, Vienna, 2 and 10 July 1840, AMAE, CP, Autriche 428; O'Sullivan to Lebeau, Vienna, 3 July 1840, ADA, CP, Autriche 7.

[57] Metternich to Stürmer, Vienna, 2 June 1840, HHStA, StA, Türkei VI, 78.

[58] Neumann to Metternich, London, 9 July 1840, HHStA, StA, England 228.

[59] Metternich to Trauttmannsdorff, Vienna, 18 June 1840, HHStA, StK, Preussen 175; Metternich to Neumann, Vienna, 24 and 27 June 1840, HHStA, StA, England 230; Metternich to Ficquelmont, Vienna, 1 July 1840, HHStA, StA, Russland III, 120; Neumann to Metternich, London, 9 July 1840, HHStA, StA, England 228; Maltzan to Frederick William IV, Vienna, 30 June 1840, GStA PK, HA III, MdA I, 7354; Struve to Tatishchev, Vienna, 30 June 1840, Struve to Nesselrode, Vienna, 1 July 1840, AVPRI, fond 133, Kantseliariia, opis 469, 1840/178; Webster, *Palmerston*, II, p. 690.

signed in London, the Straits were to be closed in times of peace and it was stated that this closure resulted from the sultan's ancient right. Furthermore, it solved the question of Mohammed Ali's future. Egypt was granted as a hereditary state to his family and he was granted the southern part of Syria with the fortress of Acre for the rest of his life, under the condition that he would accept this offer within the space of ten days from the moment it was presented to him by the sultan's agent. If he did not accept it, his sovereign would withdraw the offer of the southern Syria. If he refused the second, reduced settlement after another ten days, his future would be decided by the sultan together with the signatories of the Convention. In the Reserved Protocol, the signatories assumed the right to coerce the pasha to accept the conditions by force. The military intervention would take place even before its ratification.[60] Metternich was satisfied with the settlement of the status of the Straits as well as the reduction of Mohammed Ali's power. What diminished his satisfaction was his fear of the reaction of France, which had remained outside the settlement. He expected that it would be displeased, and he was right, but the degree of the French rage definitely surpassed his expectation and led to a serious European crisis in the second half of 1840.[61]

---

[60] Hurewitz, *The Middle East*, pp. 116–120.

[61] Metternich to Stürmer, Vienna, 18 July 1840, HHStA, StA, Türkei VI, 78; Metternich to Ficquelmont, Vienna, 18 July 1840, HHStA, StA, Russland III, 120; Metternich to Neumann, Plass, 25 July 1840, HHStA, StA, England 230; Beauvale to Ponsonby, Vienna, 17 July 1840, HHStA, StA, Türkei VI, 78; Maltzan to Frederick William IV, Vienna, 17 July 1840, GStA PK, HA III, MdA I, 7355; Struve to Nesselrode, Vienna, 19 July 1840, AVPRI, fond 133, Kantseliariia, opis 469, 1840/178.

26

The Rhine Crisis

The exclusion of France from the London Convention provoked a sharp reaction of the French public as well as the government, the latter trying to change the anti-Egyptian policy of the four allied Powers through ostentatious warlike rhetoric and preparations. This gamble failed in its principle aim to prevent the military intervention against Mohammed Ali but it provoked a serious crisis on the Continent. The French threats caused not only a general war scare but also indignation in the German Confederation. Metternich did not suppose that the French king and his cabinet would risk war against the other Powers, but he feared that the events would get out of their control and lead to social and political upheaval with unpredictable consequences. Therefore, although firm in his determination to defeat Mohammed Ali and unwilling to make excessive concessions, he fully employed his peace management with the aim of improving relations between France and the signatories of the London Convention. He had to deal not only with the aggressive conduct of the French administration but also Prussia's attempt to take advantage of the provoked nationalism in Germany in order to improve its own power within the Confederation and above all with the opposition in the Austrian governmental circles temporarily weakening his position in the administration of the state.

Metternich's Reaction to the Outburst of Indignation in France

The London Convention was signed not only without France's participation but also without its knowledge. When the French learnt of its existence later in July 1840, they felt insulted and humiliated by the decision of the other Great Powers to force Mohammed Ali to accept the conditions regardless of the Parisian cabinet's opinion and because they had not invited France to its signature. Soult branded

the Convention as a "new treaty of Chaumont" and a considerable
number of his fellow-citizens agreed with this evaluation and believed
that this national insult "must be wiped out in blood."[1] The press
displayed unusual accord in its negative view of the Convention and
warmongering articles appeared in journals regardless of political affiliation. They also cited a speech given by Duke Paul de Noailles to
the Chamber of Deputies in February in which the duke laid claim
to compensation for France on the Rhine instead of the Levant if the
Ottoman Empire was destroyed and its territory divided among the
Great Powers. The French public was influenced by this opinion and
intended to restore France's reputedly aggrieved honour on the Rhine
by ensuring the natural frontier.[2]

Thiers and Louis Philippe did not desire in any way to wage
a war against the signatories of the Convention, and not at all for
Mohammed Ali, but they also wanted to avoid a serious diplomatic
defeat. They finally decided to display strength and courage and they
therefore launched an ostentatious armament: military classes from
the years 1836–1839 were called to arms, the immediate construction
of a considerable number of warships was ordered and the idea of con-
structing the Parisian fortification was revived. These measures were
accompanied with the king's and his first minister's sharp criticism of
the conduct of the other Powers, who had allegedly isolated France.
Thiers talked about desiring peace but simultaneously indicated the
possibility of war, saying, for example, to Apponyi on 10 August:
"I would regard myself as the most unfortunate man if war were to
break out under my ministry, but I will not refuse to serve to my country in such an extreme situation!"[3] British historian John Hall even
described a situation when this "civilian Napoleon," as Metternich
named the French prime minister, was "lying on the floor, with his
maps spread out before him, like the great man about whom he had

---

[1]   J. Hall, *England and the Orleans Monarchy*, London 1912, p. 280.
[2]   Werther to Frederick William IV, Paris, 30 July 1840, GStA PK, HA III, MdA I,
7355; Luxbourg to Ludwig I of Bavaria, Paris, 31 July 1840, BHStA, MA, Paris
2102/1; I. Backouche, *La monarchie parlamentaire, 1815–1848: De Louis XVIII à
Louis-Philippe*, Paris 2000, p. 284; J. P. T. Bury, R. Tombs, *Thiers, 1797–1877: A
Political Life*, London, Boston, Sydney 1986, p. 70; C. Ledré, *La presse à l'assaut
de la monarchie 1815–1848*, Paris 1960, p. 174; Guichen, p. 227; Hasenclever, *Die
Orientalische Frage*, p. 184.
[3]   Apponyi to Metternich, Paris, 11 Aug. 1840, HHStA, StA, Frankreich 318.

written so much [Napoleon], he planned vast military and diplomatic combinations."[4] Louis Philippe was sometimes even more indignant in his verbal reactions to the Convention than his first minister and, as well as Thiers, he used surprisingly revolutionary rhetoric when talking with the representatives of Austria and Prussia: "You are total ingrates. But this time, do not think I will detach myself from my minister and my country. You want war and you shall have it; and if it is necessary, I will set the tiger [of revolution] free. He knows me and I can play with him. We will see whether he will respect you as much as me."[5] In reality, however, neither Louis Philippe nor Thiers seriously thought of war and revolution. Their daring rhetoric and threats were only a bluff chiefly designed to gain popularity at home and deter Austria and Prussia from the ratification of the Convention and, when the latter failed, to detach them from Great Britain and Russia and force them to make some concessions to France.[6]

The news of the French fervour found Metternich strong and calm at his chateau in Königswart for where he left from Vienna for several weeks on 18 July. He saw no reasonable grounds for such a hostile reaction and strongly advocated the conclusion of the Convention. He also sharply denounced the accusation that its signatories isolated France because, in his opinion, it had been this Power that had refused to cooperate even after repeated exhortations. He wrote to Apponyi on 4 August: "Count, neither Austria nor any other court wanted to engage in a group of four. It is France that refused to participate in the collective joint action of the five courts."[7] Two days later, he expressed himself in the same manner in his instructions to Stürmer: "The cries which are heard in France today would be justified if Europe had united against the country, but what sense do these cries have when they are about nothing other than to prevent the Ottoman Empire from becoming the prey of one of its vassals? Is it not a different question, and is France not striving to be regarded as the natural

---

[4] Hall, p. 293.

[5] Cattaui, p. 199.

[6] Apponyi to Metternich, Paris, 25, 26, 27 and 30 July, 1, 2 and 22 Aug. 1840, HHStA, StA, Frankreich 318; Luxbourg to Ludwig I of Bavaria, Paris, 8 Aug. 1840, BHStA, MA, Paris 2102/1; T. E. B. Howarth, *Citizen King: The Life of Louis-Philippe, King of French*, London 1961, p. 264; Charles-Roux, *Thiers*, p. 188; Hall, p. 283.

[7] Metternich to Apponyi, Königswart, 4 Aug. 1840, HHStA, StA, Frankreich 319.

protector of the Porte? Everything in this is devoid of sense and it is very French."[8] The warlike statements of the French king and his first minister did not unduly concern him simply for the reason that he was completely sure that Louis Philippe would never go to war and absolutely certain that Thiers also did not desire war over a question of a few Syrian pashaliks for Mohammed Ali. He knew, and he was entirely correct, that the former was not a gambler and he would never let himself or his country be dragged into such a dangerous game and would never declare war against the whole of Europe for little apparent reason. This conviction was strengthened by the king's secret and repeated assurances to Apponyi of his pacifism and readiness to oppose his first minister if he wanted to go too far in this respect.[9] As for Thiers, Metternich also correctly supposed that he was not actually willing to follow in Napoleon's footsteps. On 20 August, the chancellor expressed his hope for the minister's prudence: "Purely destructive actions will not make anyone laugh except maniacs, and I do Mr Thiers the honour of not counting him as one of them."[10]

The position that Metternich assumed at the beginning of August against France was simple. First, he was not willing to change anything in the proceedings as settled in the London Convention. The signatories were to show their determination to fulfil their obligations and stand united and firm against France's threatening attitude. It was not Metternich but the new Prussian king, Frederick William IV, who feared being dragged into a conflict on the Rhine over the sultan's interests, and he therefore reacted to the French threats by insisting on the addition of another protocol to the London Convention in which the Great Powers would promise that Prussia would not have to help them against France. Only under this condition was he prepared to ratify the document. In no case did Metternich, who ratified the Con-

[8] Metternich to Stürmer, Königswart, 6 Aug. 1840, HHStA, StA, Türkei VI, 78.
[9] Metternich to Neumann, Königswart, 31 July 1840, HHStA, StA, England 230; Metternich to Stürmer, Königswart, 28 Aug. 1840, HHStA, StA, Türkei VI, 78; Apponyi to Metternich, Paris, 5 Aug. and 9 Sept. 1840, HHStA, StA, Frankreich 317; Langsdorff to Thiers, Vienna, 20 July 1840, AMAE, CP, Autriche 428; Maltzan to Frederick William IV, Königswart, 8 Aug. 1840, GStA PK, Rep. 81 Gesandschaften (Residenturen) u. (General-) Konsulate nach 1807, Gesandschaft Wien II, 201/2.
[10] Metternich to Apponyi, Königswart, 20 Aug. 1840, HHStA, StA, Frankreich 319.

vention without hesitation, accept the Prussian request for signature of the additional protocol that would definitely be interpreted in Paris as a rupture between the allies. He feared that in such a case Thiers, under the impression that intimidation would move the Great Powers to give in, would even increase his threats and the armament of France. The additional protocol could thus increase the chance of what it was designed to prevent: war. The chancellor's apprehension was intensified by the fact that he had not yet met Frederick William IV and had had no opportunity to get acquainted with him and his views in person. To change this, he decided to discuss the matter with the king personally. Both men met in Pilnitz near Dresden on 13 August 1840. Metternich succeeded in persuading the king to withdraw the demand for the additional protocol. However, it was only a Pyrrhic victory because the protocol was concluded in London two days after the meeting in Pilnitz. Baron Neumann did not know the chancellor's attitude towards this matter and was persuaded by other diplomats to add his signature to the protocol that accommodated the demands of the Prussian monarch. In the event of a war, the protocol conferred the right to Prussia to maintain its "absolute freedom of action and particularly to adopt a position of strict neutrality."[11] Metternich regretted the existence of the protocol, but, despite this defeat, the meeting in Pilnitz cannot be considered as a complete failure on his part. He was satisfied when he learnt that Prussian foreign policy remained unchanged and that Frederick William IV, as well as his father Frederick William III, regarded cooperation with Austria as essential to Prussia. Metternich's influence in Berlin did not weaken at this time, and during 1840 both German Powers acted in close accord.[12]

---

[11] A. Hasenclever, "König Friedrich Wilhelm IV. und die Londoner Konvention vom 15. Juli 1840," *Forschungen zur brandenburgischen und preußischen Geschichte* 25, 1913, p. 156.

[12] Metternich to Neumann, Königswart, 10 and 23 Aug. 1840, HHStA, StA, England 231; Ottenfels to Stürmer, Vienna, 25 Aug. 1840, HHStA, StA, Türkei VI, 78; Maltzan to Frederick William IV, Königswart, 10 Aug. 1840, Werther to Bülow, Berlin, 14 Aug. 1840, GStA PK, Rep. 81 Gesandschaften (Residenturen) u. (General-) Konsulate nach 1807, Gesandschaft Wien II, 201/2; Tatishchev to Nesselrode, Dresden, 15 Aug. 1840, AVPRI, fond 133, Kantseliariia, opis 469, 1840/178; Lerchenfeld to Ludwig I of Bavaria, Vienna, 20 Aug. 1840, BHStA, MA, Wien 2409; W. Bußmann, *Zwischen Preußen und Deutschland: Friedrich Wilhelm IV.*, Berlin 1990, p. 143; Hasenclever, "König Friedrich Wilhelm IV.," pp. 147–151.

The second factor guiding Metternich's conduct towards France was the emphasis laid upon the preservation of good relations regardless of its threats and the preclusion of the escalation of tensions that could develop into an all-European war. He urged Apponyi to stay calm and show the utmost placability towards Thiers. The ambassador was not to be led astray by the minister's warlike statements. Other Austrian diplomats had to assume the same moderation and they actually behaved according to this instruction. For example, Neumann assured the French chargé d'affaires in London, Count François Adolphe Bourqueney, that "as far as we are concerned, we will show proof of the innocence of our intentions. We will conscript no soldiers, we will buy no horses, we will cast no cannons. The situation in Prussia will be the same. If you attack us ... you will find us defenceless."[13] Since Metternich knew well that Louis Philippe and Thiers desired to get out of the difficult situation in which they found themselves with their refusal to cooperate with the other Powers, he tried to offer them some way out that would enable them to save face with regard to the French public. At the beginning of August, Metternich proposed that France should take advantage of its influence over Mohammed Ali and persuade him to accept the conditions of the London Convention. In such a case the credit for the settlement could be ascribed to France: "What means does King Louis Philippe have for getting out of the position as bad as it is dangerous in which his government finds itself to be involved? It is rather simple. By using his influence over the pasha of Egypt to persuade him to agree with what will be able to provide his descendants with a future compatible with the existence of the Ottoman Empire. It will thus be France which will have pacified the Levant."[14] During a talk with Sainte-Aulaire who returned to Austria in early August and followed Metternich to Königswart, the chancellor promised that in such a case the *Österreichischer Beobachter* would publish an article ascribing all credit for the pacification to France. On 23 August, he repeated that with his plan he was offering "to French vanity the chance to cry from the rooftops of the French Foreign Ministry on la Rue des Capucines to all France and Europe 'it is here and not in London where the Levant was pacified!'"[15] In the end,

[13] Guichen, p. 349.
[14] Metternich to Apponyi, Königswart, 4 Aug. 1840, HHStA, StA, Frankreich 319.
[15] Metternich to Neumann, Königswart, 23 Aug. 1840, HHStA, StA, England 231.

the offer with which he wanted to find a way for France to extricate itself from isolation met with no success because Louis Philippe and Thiers wanted to obtain more – a complete annulment of the London Convention, something absolutely unacceptable for Metternich, who strongly insisted on the enforcement of its conditions in practice.[16] As he wrote on 24 August: "We strongly reject any idea to consider the conclusion of the treaty of 15 July as invalid and to subordinate our approach to that of France, but on the other hand we are inclined more than ever to facilitate to this Great Power the ways in which it could coordinate its approach with ours."[17]

Metternich's Project for the League to Preserve Peace

Metternich's effort to overcome the gulf that occurred between France and other Powers was accompanied with an attempt to create a bulwark against the former's eventual hostile conduct against the latter. The desire to be prepared for any eventuality and in particular to take advantage of the given situation and strengthen the pillars of the European state system materialised later in August when Metternich, with the assistance of Ficquelmont and Beauvale, came up with a project for a defensive alliance of four Powers against France and a considerably more interesting and far-reaching project for the league to preserve peace in Europe. The former was a simple defensive

---

[16] Metternich to Erberg, Königswart, 3 Aug. 1840, HHStA, StK, Preussen 176; Metternich to Apponyi, Königswart, 4 Aug. 1840, HHStA, StA, Frankreich 319; Metternich to Neumann, Königswart, 22 and 23 Aug. 1840, HHStA, StA, England 231; Apponyi to Metternich, Paris, 25 Aug. 1840, HHStA, StA, Frankreich 318; Lerchenfeld to Ludwig I of Bavaria, Vienna, 5 Aug. 1840, BHStA, MA, Wien 2409; Sainte-Aulaire to Thiers, Vienna, 6 Aug. 1840, Marienbad, 31 Aug. 1840, AMAE, CP, Autriche 428; Maltzan to Frederick William IV, Königswart, 10 and 24 Aug. 1840, GStA PK, Rep. 81 Gesandschaften (Residenturen) u. (General-) Konsulate nach 1807, Gesandschaft Wien II, 201/2; Maltzan to Frederick William IV, Königswart, 21 Aug. 1840, GStA PK, HA III, MdA I, 7356; Tatishchev to Nesselrode, Dresden, 14 Aug. 1840, AVPRI, fond 133, Kantseliariia, opis 469, 1840/178; Altieri to Lambruschini, Königswart, 22 Aug. 1840, ASV, Arch. Nunz. Vienna 280C.

[17] Metternich to Erberg, Königswart, 24 Aug. 1840, HHStA, StK, Preussen 176.

measure reacting to the current war scare. The latter, much preferred
by Metternich to the mere defensive alliance, had a long-term character and was to forestall the outbreak of any war in Europe regardless
of the aggressor. It was a reaction to the absurd situation when war
threatened to break out in the heart of the Continent due to an unre-
lated affair in distant Syria. Metternich found it necessary to assure
peace through a more complex measure than was the settlement of
the Congress of Vienna. The project of the league of which eventual
acceptance would significantly change European public law consisted
of six articles. The first one obliged its members to solve the problems
peacefully. According to the second one, if a problem arose between
some members, it was to be solved at a conference. If a conciliatory
approach failed, the third article committed the member states to defend with all the means at their disposal any country or countries
attacked. The fourth article clearly stated that the obligation contained in the third one held true even in the case where an aggressor
was a member country of the league. The fifth article stipulated that if
no one asked for help but peace in Europe was endangered, the Great
Powers were to negotiate the problem as well and act if necessary for
the preservation of general peace. The sixth and last article made it
clear that all countries had the right to enter this association but that
the Great Powers would retain exclusive rights to negotiate and act
as was stipulated in the previous articles.[18]

   According to German historian Irmline Veit-Brause, the project
for the league was an association of conservative Powers against revolutionary France and certainly a reversion to the Holy Alliance.[19]
Veit-Brause, who actually did not know the details of the project
published by Frederick Stanley Rodkey in the *American Historical
Review* in 1930, is completely mistaken in this respect. It was not a
union of conservative Powers only and not a Holy Alliance at all. The
difference between the Holy Alliance and Metternich's project for the
league is clearly visible at first sight; the latter was a rather practical
security measure attempting to strengthen the peaceful coexistence of

---

[18] Beauvale to Palmerston, Königswart, 29 Aug. 1840, Vienna, 30 Sept. 1840,
TNA, FO 120/189; F. S. Rodkey, "Suggestions during the Crisis of 1840 for a
'League' to Preserve Peace," *AHR* 35, 1930, 2, pp. 308–316; Lorenz, pp. 118–122.
[19] I. Veit-Brause, *Die deutsch-französische Krise von 1840: Studien zur deutschen
Einheitsbewegung*, Köln 1967, pp. 44–45.

European countries. In contrast to the Holy Alliance and the Troppau Protocol, it was not a weapon of conservative or reactionary policy. Of course the fifth article enabling the member Powers to solve the threats to peace without being invited to do so by a threatened country or countries seems to entail a germ of interventional principle, but since Metternich based the realisation of the idea on the acceptance of Great Britain, telling Beauvale that he was even prepared to sign it without the participation of Russia and France, the project could hardly be intended to be the second Troppau Protocol simply because neither Palmerston nor other British minister would accept it. Beauvale wrote to Palmerston about the league in this respect on 29 August: "Its direction however would be exclusively against aggression from without, neither interfering with the independence of nations nor with their efforts for internal improvement. This is so much in accordance not only with the material interests of nations, but with the opinions and speculative reasonings of the age, it is so peculiarly consonant to the ideas and feelings of England, and if practicable, would be considered as so great a benefit to humanity at large, that I entertain no doubt of its receiving the favourable consideration of Her Majesty's Government."[20] The league was thus designed as a barrier against war and not revolution although for Metternich these dangers went hand in hand. The chancellor explained the purpose of the league during a conversation with Maltzan on 10 September: "My treaty proposal is the opposite of the Holy Alliance, so to speak in regard to what it covers. The Holy Alliance was essentially moral; my project is essentially material and practical. It is about building a bullwark against the usurpations of French boasting and against the whims of men like Mr Thiers who can be brought onto the political stage by constitutional reforms at any moment and who can easily obtain the power to shake the foundations of European politics. Consequently, it is about creating solid guarantees against possibilities of this kind. I see these guarantees in a treaty of a defensive nature that would be concluded not only among the four Powers but also all European governments which would want to participate in them. The nature of this defensive treaty would be practical ... The governments would commit themselves to the preservation of peace, and they would become guarantors of the integrity and independence of

---

[20] Rodkey, "A 'League' to Preserve Peace," p. 310.

every member state of the alliance."[21] The project finally fell into oblivion when Palmerston refused to sanction it because he considered it to be useless.[22] Although it became a small and insignificant episode during the Rhine Crisis, it remains an important testament of Metternich's political rationale having little in common with moral theorisation; it is not the Holy Alliance but the project for the league to preserve peace that stands as a symbol for Metternich.

The Rhine Crisis at Its Peak

The idea for the league resulted not only from Metternich's general political attitudes but also from the talks on the Eastern Question that filled Metternich's summer days at Königswart. Besides Ficquelmont and Beauvale participating in the project, there were more diplomats creating together a sort of informal conference after Metternich's return from his short stay in Saxony: Tatishchev, Sainte-Aulaire, Maltzan, Esterházy, Lützow and the papal nuncio in Vienna, Lodovico Altieri. As time went by, they noticed Metternich's apparent confidence in the preservation of peace. From late August, when the poor relations with France continued and the tension in no way decreased, they generally did not share his peace of mind. At that time Metternich was actually not particularly concerned about the situation and his own correspondence proves that although he regarded it as serious, he was convinced that a war was unlikely. This confidence was also shown in his practical steps like his refusals to deal with Thiers about new concessions to Mohammed Ali as well as to accept the proposal of the Belgian king, Leopold I, for the removal of the centre of negotiations from London to Vienna. The king wanted to facilitate the reconciliation between the signatories of the Convention and France by taking the whole affair from Palmerston's hands. This idea was supported by Guizot, British Prime Minister Lord Melbourne, Frederick William IV, and the Prussian ambassador in London, Baron Heinrich von Bülow, who even wanted to replace

---

[21] Maltzan to Frederick William IV, Königswart, 11 Sept. 1840, GStA PK, Rep. 81 Gesandschaften (Residenturen) u. (General-) Konsulate nach 1807, Gesandschaft Wien II, 201/3.

[22] Rodkey, "A 'League' to Preserve Peace," p. 308.

the London Convention with another one with France also as a signatory. Metternich opposed the possibility of any modification of the Convention at the time as well as the idea of negotiating with France in the Austrian capital. He well remembered Nicholas I's rejection of the talks in Vienna from the previous year and did not want to burn his fingers and risk the tsar's annoyance again, in particular when the chancellor did not believe in the success of his mediation between the signatories of the Convention and France led by a man like Thiers.[23]

With the arrival of September, Metternich's continued to maintain a confident attitude, but his assurances that no one need fear war and that the French government had no reason to wage one were increasingly regarded as too optimistic. As Maltzan reported, for him and Beauvale Metternich's "security was a kind of nightmare."[24] Both of them tried to persuade the chancellor to promptly return to Vienna and take more decisive steps for the case of an outbreak of war. The absence of any armament in the Austrian Empire made the foreign diplomats, and particularly the representatives of German and Italian countries, rather nervous. They criticised this passivity that gave them little prospect for Austria's effective protection in the event of a French attack. Their apprehension was increased by the fact that the Austrian army, after its augmentation in reaction to the revolu-

[23] Metternich to Lebzeltern, Königswart, 17 Aug. 1840, HHStA, StA, Neapel 94; Metternich to Erberg, Königswart, 24 Aug. 1840, HHStA, StK, Preussen 176; Metternich to Neumann, Königswart, 25 Aug. and 2 Sept. 1840, Vienna, 8 Oct. 1840, Metternich to Leopold I, Königswart, 2 Sept. 1840, HHStA, StA, England 231; Metternich to Apponyi, Königswart, 1 Sept. 1840, HHStA, StA, Frankreich 319; Metternich to Schwarzenberg, Vienna, 4 Sept. 1840, HHStA, StA, Sardinien 77; Dietrichstein to Metternich, Brussels, 21 July 1840, HHStA, Gesandschaftsarchiv, Brüssel 2; Leopold I to Metternich, Claremont, 13 Aug. 1840, HHStA, StA, Frankreich 319; Maltzan to Frederick William IV, Königswart, 18, 21 and 22 Aug. 1840, GStA PK, HA III, MdA I, 7356; Maltzan to Frederick William IV, Königswart, 2 Sept. 1840, GStA PK, HA III, MdA I, 7357; Altieri to Lambruschini, Königswart, 22 Aug. 1840, ASV, Arch. Nunz. Vienna 280C; Tatishchev to Nesselrode, Prague, 25 Aug. 1840, AVPRI, fond 133, Kantseliariia, opis 469, 1840/178; Beauvale to Palmerston, Königswart, 31 Aug. 1840, TNA, FO 120/189; Struve to Nesselrode, Königswart, 3 Sept. 1840, AVPRI, fond 133, Kantseliariia, opis 469, 1840/178; A. Stern, "König Leopold I. von Belgien und die Krise von 1840," *Historische Vierteljahrschrift* 22, 1923, pp. 312–318; E. C. Corti, *Leopold I of Belgium: Secret Pages of European History*, London 1923, pp. 128–130; Sainte-Aulaire, *Souvenirs*, p. 301.
[24] Maltzan to Frederick William IV, Königswart, 11 Sept. 1840, GStA PK, HA III, MdA I, 7357.

tions of 1830 and 1831, was reduced after the death of Francis I. In 1836, the number of soldiers was decreased by more than a quarter and the annual military budget was reduced from 48 million in 1835 to 40 million in the following years. Metternich reacted to the foreign diplomats' reproaches with the explanation that Austria did not want to give France any pretext for distrusting Austria's intentions in its own preparations for war, and he also used this argument when dealing with Austrian authorities.[25] When, for example, in August 1840 Marshal Radetzky asked the governor of Milan, Count Franz von Hartig, to reinforce the Austrian army in Italy, Metternich answered that he did not find this request unjustified but that "I must oppose every preventative measure on our part that would lead to public opinion that Austria believes in the danger [of war]. Military measures are not the appropriate means for avoiding the danger, but rather would give rise to it."[26]

Although this argument of not alarming France with preparations for war was not entirely insincere, the principal reason for this restraint must be sought in the internal situation of the Austrian Empire and Metternich's very limited influence on its domestic affairs in which he encountered Count Kolowrat, the advocate of the army's reduction in the 1830s. Kolowrat was significantly supported in this respect by his client, Baron Peter Joseph Eichhoff, who was named the president of the Chamber of Finance in the mid 1830s. Their position strength-

---

[25] Metternich to Apponyi, Königswart, 18 Sept. 1840, HHStA, StA, Frankreich 319; Lamb to Palmerston, Vienna, 15 May 1832, TNA, FO 120/124; Sainte-Aulaire to Thiers, Vienna, 13 April and 4 May 1836, Sainte-Aulaire to Molé, Vienna, 28 Sept. 1836, AMAE, CP, Autriche 423; Tatishchev to Nesselrode, Vienna, 19 April 1836, AVPRI, fond 133, Kantseliariia, opis 469, 1836/216; Lerchenfeld to Ludwig I of Bavaria, Vienna, 14 Aug., 1 and 8 Sept. 1840, BHStA, MA, Wien 2409; Verges to Ludwig I of Bavaria, Dresden, 16 Aug. 1840, BHStA, MA, Dresden 2820; O'Sullivan to Lebeau, Vienna, 23 Aug. and 2 Sept. 1840, ADA, CP, Autriche 7; Bockelberg to Frederick William IV, Vienna, 26 Aug. 1840, GStA PK, Rep. 81 Gesandschaften (Residenturen) u. (General-) Konsulate nach 1807, Gesandschaft Wien II, 201/2; Maltzan to Frederick William IV, Königswart, 29 Aug. and 11 Sept. 1840, GStA PK, HA III, MdA I, 7357; Beauvale to Palmerston, Königswart, 27 and 29 Aug. 1840, TNA, FO 120/189; Struve to Nesselrode, Königswart, 31 Aug. 1840, Tatishchev to Nesselrode, Vienna, 29 Sept. and 3 Oct. 1840, AVPRI, fond 133, Kantseliariia, opis 469, 1840/178; report from Vienna, 2 Oct. 1840, SS, HD, SG, Wien 94.
[26] A. Novotny, *Oesterreich-Preussen in den Jahren 1840–1848*, unpublished dissertation, Wien 1928, p. 29.

ened in early 1840 when Metternich's loyal and influential supporter, General Count Karl von Clam-Martinitz, died in January. Ficquelmont's appointment as a State and Conference Minister in the same year did not entirely counterbalance this loss. After the signature of the London Convention, the position of Kolowrat and his adherents further improved due to the opposition existing in Vienna against Austria's too active Near Eastern policy, in other words participation in the coercive measures against Mohammed Ali which exposed Austria to the danger of war with France. The crisis found Austria in a difficult economic situation when the empire experienced financial problems due to the fact that the market was overpriced. When the news of the signature of the London Convention arrived in Vienna, the bourse reacted with a drop in value and suffered several days of chaotic trading. The confusion negatively impacted not only government securities but also industrial prices. The fear of war provoked by the subsequent news of the French armament caused real panic that kept stock prices down for some time and this was repeated several times during the Rhine Crisis. The consequent financial difficulties of Austrian companies and shareholders led not only to some bankruptcies but also several suicides, and the government would have found it difficult under the given conditions to get a loan for the armament if it had asked for one.[27] Lerchenfeld reported on 7 August: "The treaty is regarded here as a very serious event which still cannot be judged in all its dimensions ... It is feared that it [France] will bring war to Italy and to the Rhine and that the king, even with the most pacifist

---

[27] O'Sullivan to Meulenaer, Vienna, 15 Nov. 1834, ADA, CP, Autriche 2; O'Sullivan to Meulenaer, Vienna, 28 Sept. 1836, ADA, CP, Autriche 4; O'Sullivan to Meylandt, Vienna, 6 June 1837 and 2 Feb. 1838, ADA, CP, Autriche 5; O'Sullivan to Lebeau, Vienna, 3 Aug. and 7 Oct. 1840, ADA, CP, Autriche 7; Tatishchev to Nesselrode, Vienna, 31 Jan. 1840, AVPRI, fond 133, Kantseliariia, opis 469, 1840/177; Langsdorff to Thiers, Vienna, 1 Aug. 1840, Sainte-Aulaire to Thiers, Vienna, 6 Aug. and 21 Sept. 1840, AMAE, CP, Autriche 428; report from Vienna, 5, 8, 12 and 15 Aug., 22 and 26 Sept., 7 and 9 Oct. 1840, SS, HD, SG, Wien 94; Lerchenfeld to Ludwig I of Bavaria, Vienna, 5, 7, 14, 23 and 26 Aug., 28 Sept., 1, 6, 10 and 14 Oct. 1840, BHStA, MA, Wien 2409; Maltzan to Frederick William IV, Vienna, 3 Oct. 1840, GStA PK, HA III, MdA I, 6033; Nesselrode to Meyendorff, St Petersburg, 14 Feb. 1840, Nesselrode, VIII, p. 13; Meyendorff to Nesselrode, Berlin, 16 Nov. 1839, Hoetzsch, p. 82; E. Herzog, *Graf Franz Anton Kolowrat-Liebsteinsky: Seine politische Tätigkeit in Wien (1826–1848)*, unpublished dissertation, Wien 1968, pp. 42 and 121; Beer, *Die Finanzen Oesterreichs*, p. 145; Lorenz, p. 124.

sentiments, could not hold back the general eagerness [for war] without risking the fall of the throne and causing a revolution ... Public opinion in Vienna declares itself against the treaty of 15 July. No one wants to embark on a war because of the Eastern Question that could only be in the interests of Russia and England. The directors of great banking houses say that loans for arming and waging war will not be given."[28]

A war with France would be rather unpopular in Austria and the Viennese, generally little interested in foreign affairs, asked themselves what Austria had in common with Syria and what they had in common with the Turks? If a strong government led by a capable emperor had existed, all of this might have signified little for Metternich, but Ferdinand I was not only an incapable but also an incompetent monarch and the State Conference actually directing internal affairs instead of the feeble-minded emperor was itself also rather weak. Maltzan described on 11 September "a rather strange spectacle to see the Conference on holiday and taking recreation while the political horizon laden with thunderclouds threatens the tranquillity of Europe. For almost two months, the Chancellor has been on holiday in a corner of Bohemia at a very great distance from the centre of the affairs of the monarchy; the small valleys of Ischl have been serving as promenades for Count Kolowrat for the same period of time; Mr Ficquelmont is with his family in Töplitz; Archduke Francis Charles is on holiday; Archduke Louis, the only member of this areopagus who did not leave Vienna, is bitterly complaining of the desolateness into which he has been plunged, but his weakness does not allow him to do anything about this singular state of affairs ... While events impose on governments the obligation to adopt a serious and appropriate attitude towards resisting actual and future dangers, the Imperial Conference removes itself from the scene and even dares to boast ... that the Imperial Government finds itself so secure with regard to the question of peace and war that it has not yet spent a single kreutzer on any precautionary measures."[29] Nothing changed with Metternich's return to Vienna on 23 September because Kolowrat stayed in Bohemia

---

[28] Lerchenfeld to Ludwig I of Bavaria, Vienna, 7 Aug. 1840, BHStA, MA, Wien 2409.
[29] Maltzan to Frederick William IV, Königswart, 11 Sept. 1840, GStA PK, HA III, MdA I, 7357.

and outside the capital, from where he continued, with the help of Eichhoff also absent from the capital, in undermining the chancellor's position. They claimed that if Metternich wanted to lead Austria into war, then it would be without financial means. When Eichhoff presented the proposal for the state budget for 1841 in September, he supported the view that war against France was out of the question, and he was even heard to say to his friends that Metternich was to be removed. Kolowrat even sent a memorandum to Archduke Louis in which he openly criticised Metternich's conduct in the Near Eastern crisis, and Louis was said to agree with this criticism.[30] Lerchenfeld reported to the Bavarian king on 14 October about the situation of the empire: "There seems to exist a state of real paralysis. The Austrian Government, Sire, makes a rather distressing impression in the current crisis. The ministry is incomplete: Count Kolowrat, instead of hastening to his post to defend his opinion at the Conference in such a crisis, is not coming back. He was expected on the 12th, but he is in Prague and is not moving. He has explained himself in writing: he maintains that Austria cannot wage war, that it should not wage one, [and] that he does not believe that it could avoid one. He says that he depends upon the Austrian cabinet reuniting with that of Prussia to declare that England has gone too far and that the two courts would distance themselves from it [England] if England is unwilling to proceed with more moderation. Count Kolowrat does not have the energy to come and discuss the situation and can only sulk. He says if Prince Metternich started the affair, if he has allowed himself to become so involved with England through his carelessness, then he knows how to extricate the state from it. Is this a conduct of a great statesman? But Count Kolowrat has already shown several times that he is cast from such a mould."[31]

---

[30] O'Sullivan to Lebeau, Vienna, 23 Aug., 15 and 20 Oct. 1840, ADA, CP, Autriche 7; Maltzan to Frederick William IV, Königswart, 29 Aug. 1840, GStA PK, HA III, MdA I, 7357; Maltzan to Frederick William IV, Vienna, 3 and 11 Oct. 1840, GStA PK, HA III, MdA I, 6033; Lerchenfeld to Ludwig I of Bavaria, Vienna, 23 Sept., 1, 6 and 10 Oct. 1840, BHStA, MA, Wien 2409; report from Vienna, 24 Sept. 1840, SS, HD, SG, Wien 94; Tatishchev to Nesselrode, Vienna, 3 and 10 Oct. 1840, AVPRI, fond 133, Kantseliariia, opis 469, 1840/178; Beauvale to Palmerston, Vienna, 8 and 14 Oct. 1840, TNA, FO 120/189; Altieri to Lambruschini, Vienna, 9 Oct. 1840, ASV, Arch. Nunz. Vienna 280C.

[31] Lerchenfeld to Ludwig I of Bavaria, Vienna, 14 Oct. 1840, BHStA, MA, Wien 2409.

Metternich was unable to enforce any measures concerning the strengthening of the army even if he had wanted to, which led Maltzan to a categorical conclusion on the turn of September that the chancellor's influence on the internal affairs was non-existent, and Tatishchev expressed the same opinion at the same moment: "From everything that has happened there manifests a sad truth: that the position of Prince Metternich in internal affairs has weakened so much that he is no longer in the position to give weight to his opinion. Therefore, he must hold back his opinions and engage in trial and error. Outflanked by the influence of Count Kolowrat, he is reduced today to the simple role of a foreign minister and he needs all his skilfulness to conceal the progressive decline of his influence that could end up damaging the political credit of Austria abroad. There is thus no need to attribute the conduct of Prince Metternich in the current crisis to a personal lack of energy as he would certainly like nothing better than to point out, but rather to the state of finances in Austria on the one hand and to the narrow-minded opinions of those who are in reality at the helm of affairs on the other."[32] Beauvale shared this opinion and, as well as the Russian ambassador, feared that if a war with France broke out, Metternich could fall from power.[33] Metternich himself was heard to say to a confidente: "If I do not succeed in bringing this affair to good end, I will be chased out of here."[34]

The financial problems and internal opposition did not allow Metternich to let the situation get out of control. The country he tried to lead through this dangerous time without detrimental effect could not be driven into the vortex of war. Austria would gain nothing and could only lose in a possible conflict. Not only the fate of the Ottoman Empire but also the Austrian domain in the northern Apennines and its influence in the German Confederation were at stake. Metternich had no weapon except the pen he used for writing his considerable number of dispatches and advice and his insistence in having faith in the maintenance of peace. He definitely deeply believed in his own assurances during his stay in Königswart, but his confidence started to

---

[32] Tatishchev to Nesselrode, Vienna, 29 Sept. 1840, AVPRI, fond 133, Kantseliariia, opis 469, 1840/178.

[33] Beauvale to Palmerston, Vienna, 30 Sept. 1840, TNA, FO 120/189; Maltzan to Frederick William IV, Vienna, 1 Oct. 1840, GStA PK, HA III, MdA I, 6033.

[34] Bockelberg to Frederick William IV, Vienna, 20 Oct. 1840, GStA PK, HA III, MdA I, 6033.

fade and he became concerned soon after his return to Vienna when the crisis significantly deteriorated and its new phase began. Simultaneously with his return, the news arrived in the Austrian capital that Mohammed Ali refused all the conditions of the London Convention, which made the use of coercive measures against him necessary. On the turn of September, the news of Mohammed Ali's deposal by the sultan and the bombardment of Beirut by the allied forces were delivered to Vienna and with a short delay to Paris. In France, the reaction to these measures was even sharper than it had been in the case of the London Convention and the situation now appeared to be more serious than ever. The cannon of Beirut, in Heinrich Heine's words, "re-echoes painfully in the heart of every Frenchman"[35] and considerably strengthened the warlike sentiment of the French. Not the year 1830 but 1789 was remembered in the French press, young men enthusiastically offered their services at recruitment offices, audiences in operas and theatres insisted on singing *La Marseillaise*, English students were driven from lectures at the Sorbonne and the press printed bellicose articles; for example, *Le National* appealed to the heroism of the children of the revolution on 4 October: "Do you know what a dignified government of a country would have done? Mobilisation; an army of one hundred thousand men would be searching its battlefield on the Rhine. Ancona would be in our hands. Fifty thousand men would be camping in the Alps ... Revolution, it is our national character and it is that which should be invoked today ... It is its principles which must be spread. It is its faith which must be preached."[36] The answer of the French government was less aggressive but still intimidating; according to its official statement, France would have a regular army of 639,000 men and 300,000 men in the national guard in the spring of the following year.[37]

This latest development in the crisis definitely disturbed Metternich, who saw the French reaction as equally unjustified as in the summer: "In no period of history has Europe offered a more extraordi-

[35] Hall, p. 302.

[36] Guichen, p. 382.

[37] Sainte-Aulaire to Thiers, Vienna, 21 Sept. 1840, AMAE, CP, Autriche 428; report from Paris, 6 Oct. 1840, SS, HD, SG, Paris 19; Le Hon to Lebeau, Paris, 6 Oct. 1840, ADA, CP, France 10; Luxbourg to Ludwig I of Bavaria, Paris, 9 and 16 Oct. 1840, BHStA, MA, Paris 2102/1; Charles-Roux, *Thiers*, p. 231; Mansel, p. 363.

nary spectacle than the one it offers under the present circumstances. In its midst a great state [France] is becoming agitated and pronouncing itself to be in danger. From where are these dangers threatening it? Where are the enemies prepared to attack? No soldiers are marching beyond the frontiers of this state, not even at a great distance and not in [France's] direction; no arsenal is at the ready; no idea of war has taken hold of anybody! Where is the enemy? This is the country that calls for war, that covers itself with soldiers, that makes appeals to warlike ideas, that threatens its peaceful neighbours and that proclaims its peaceful intentions at the same time! This country claims it has been insulted!"[38] As in the preceding two and half months, the chancellor trusted Louis Philippe and Thiers and did not believe that they would seriously contemplate waging war against the other Powers, a belief which he continued to repeat to sceptical foreign diplomats. He based his opinion upon the peaceful character of the king and the rationality of his first minister. This conviction was reassured with Apponyi's report of 5 October stating that the king was promising him that he would do whatsoever in his power to prevent a conflict and the first minister was talking about war without any sincere desire to wage one, something Metternich believed as he told Lerchenfeld: "Thiers is no madman. He is a wise and astute man, a man of great intellect, who carefully considers what he wants to do and who is conservative but wears the cap of liberty on his head."[39] What actually worried Metternich was Thiers' effort to win popularity by means of nationalistic and threatening measures which could seriously deteriorate the whole situation and lead to the point when, in Apponyi's words from the end of July, "a negligible and unexpected incident could suffice to start a war,"[40] regardless of whether the first minister wanted one or not. Since the very beginning of the crisis, Metternich disliked Thiers' play with words like war and revolution in a country with a rich revolutionary history and political instability such as France had and with so volatile a people as the French were.[41] At the end of August, Metternich wrote to Stürmer:

---

[38] Metternich to Apponyi, Vienna, 23 Oct. 1840, HHStA, StA, Frankreich 319.
[39] Lerchenfeld to Ludwig I of Bavaria, Vienna, 1 Oct. 1840, BHStA, MA, Wien 2409.
[40] Apponyi to Metternich, Paris, 30 July 1840, HHStA, StA, Frankreich 318.
[41] Apponyi to Metternich, Paris, 5 Oct. 1840, HHStA, StA, Frankreich 318; report from Vienna, 25 Sept. 1840, SS, HD, SG, Wien 94; Lerchenfeld to Lud-

"Mr Thiers, for his part, should rather fear than desire a conflagration of which the repercussions on the natural order of things in France cannot be predicted. But by stirring up popular passions, he is taking on that natural order, and a man who himself has no backbone, how could he suppose that he could halt the floods caused by the storm, regardless of whether this would be his work or that of a superior force to which he had to submit."[42]

Thiers' activities were all the more dangerous for Metternich because they did not only affect France but were also pursued beyond its frontier. Since late August Metternich had been receiving news from other parts of the Continent that could not leave him undisturbed: Thiers' attempts in Turin for an alliance with the Kingdom of Sardinia, his identical attempts in Naples full of pro-French sentiments owing to the aggressive British conduct during the Sulphur Crisis from the previous months, the pro-French and anti-Austrian and anti-Prussian articles in the Belgian press and the news of the armament in Belgium, all of which disconcerted the signatories of the London Convention who worried about Belgium's attitude in the event of war in Europe. Although the monarchs of all three kingdoms finally declared their complete neutrality in such a case, the spread of the crisis through the Continent could not leave Metternich unaffected, in particular when he saw the revolutionary potential in the background. In this respect he considered the Apennines as the most serious troublespot in Europe and feared the influence of the French policy over the peninsula in 1840 to the same extent as he had done ten years earlier after the outbreak of the July Revolution. He had already written to Neumann in August: "I ask Lord Palmerston to attach some value to the reports which you will show him and which will prove to him the effect that the current situation is having in Switzerland and Italy. That is where the power of the French cabinet raising the flag of propaganda lies. It has the anarchists in these lands on its side and certainly there is a large number of them in Switzerland. What is even more to be feared in Italy than the anarchists is the weakness

---

wig I of Bavaria, Vienna, 25 Sept., 1, 6 and 21 Oct. 1840, BHStA, MA, Wien 2409; O'Sullivan to Lebeau, Vienna, 9 and 20 Oct. 1840, ADA, CP, Autriche 7; Bockelberg to Frederick William IV, Vienna, 14 Oct. 1840, GStA PK, HA III, MdA I, 7358; J. L. Richardson, *Crisis Diplomacy: The Great Powers since the Mid-Nineteenth Century*, Cambridge 1994, p. 60; Cattaui, p. 187.

[42] Metternich to Stürmer, Königswart, 28 Aug. 1840, HHStA, StA, Türkei VI, 78.

of the governments, and I cannot tell you which of them could be more dangerous in its consequences, the number of individuals lost to radicalism or the weakness of the princes."[43] It was therefore not the suspicion of Thiers' wanting to wage war but his threatening activities with consequences difficult to predict which alarmed Metternich and had led him since the very beginning of the crisis to deal directly with Louis Philippe and by depicting the fatal consequences of war for France and of revolution for the July Monarchy to reduce Thiers' influence over the king.[44] The chancellor later wrote: "I bet everything on one card: on the hope for conflict between the king and Thiers."[45]

This effort brought no immediate success and Metternich had to find another way to reduce the tensions in early October. More than ever he regarded it necessary to open to France "a small door by which it could re-enter the affair; a door that no one is more disposed to open to it than I am."[46] First of all, he condemned the removal of Mohammed Ali as dangerous with respect to the explosive situation in

---

[43] Metternich to Neumann, Königswart, 23 Aug. 1840, HHStA, StA, England 231.

[44] Metternich to Apponyi, Königswart, 4 and 20 Aug. 1840, HHStA, StA, Frankreich 319; Metternich's circular, Königswart, 27 Aug. 1840, HHStA, StA, Türkei VI, 78; Metternich to Neumann, Königswart, 2 Sept. 1840, HHStA, StA, England 231; Metternich to Trauttmannsdorff, Vienna, 13 and 27 Oct. 1840, HHStA, StK, Preussen 176; Metternich to Schwarzenberg, Vienna, 12 Nov. 1840, HHStA, StA, Sardinien 77; Apponyi to Metternich, Paris, 25, 29 and 31 Aug., 8 Sept. 1840, HHStA, StA, Frankreich 318; Dietrichstein to Metternich, Brussels, 17 and 25 Aug., 4 Sept. and 9 Oct. 1840, HHStA, Gesandschaftsarchiv, Brüssel 2; Lebzeltern to Metternich, Naples, 28 Aug., 11 Sept. and 23 Oct. 1840, HHStA, StA, Neapel 92; Schwarzenberg to Metternich, Turin, 30 Sept. and 26 Oct. 1840, HHStA, StA, Sardinien 77; Serkendorff to Frederick William IV, Brussels, 4 Aug., 5 Sept., 9, 24 and 28 Oct. 1841, GStA PK, HA III, MdA I, 4522; Sambuy to Solaro, Turin, 12 Aug. 1840, HHStA, StA, Sardinien 77; Tatishchev to Nesselrode, Königswart, 20 Aug. 1840, AVPRI, fond 133, Kantseliariia, opis 469, 1840/178; Altieri to Lambruschini, Königswart, 22 Aug. 1840, Vienna, 23 Oct. 1840, ASV, Arch. Nunz. Vienna 280C; Bernstoff to Frederick William IV, Naples, 27 Aug. 1840, GStA PK, HA III, MdA I, 5596; O'Sullivan to Metternich, Vienna, 4 Sept. 1841, Metternich to O'Sullivan, Königswart, 11 Sept. 1840, ADA, CP, Autriche 7; Vilain to Lebeau, Berlin, 9 Sept. and 6 Nov. 1840, Willmar to Lebeau, Berlin, 20 Oct. 1840, ADA, CP, Prusse 5; H. T. Deschamps, *La Belgique devant la France de Juillet: L'opinion et l'attitude francaises de 1839 à 1848*, Paris 1956, pp. 49–102; A. J. Reinerman, "Metternich, the Powers, and the 1831 Italian Crisis," *Central European History* 10, 1977, 3, p. 208; Pouthas, *La Politique étrangère*, p. 280.

[45] Malo, p. 322.

[46] Metternich to Neumann, Vienna, 28 Sept. 1840, HHStA, StA, England 231.

Europe and informed the French government that Austria would not support this step and that Austrian forces fighting in Syria against the pasha would not attack him in Egypt itself. Second, Metternich contemplated in his instructions to Neumann of 5 and 15 October some territorial concessions to Mohammed Ali in Syria for his lifetime, namely granting the pashalik of Acre, which was nothing other than a return to the first proposal of the London Convention. Third, Metternich proposed on 7 October to summon a conference to Wiesbaden, a small town in the Rhineland close to Frankfurt am Main. He desired talks with France in which the representatives of the four Powers would question France about its intentions and simultaneously assure it of their own non-belligerence. This project failed owing to the decisive opposition of Nicholas I and Palmerston. The tsar was pleased with the isolation of France and when he had to choose between concessions to France and war, he clearly favoured the latter. The foreign secretary did not desire the latter but was not willing to make any compromise steps. Both of them were united in their contempt for Metternich's placability that actually existed but was somehow exaggerated by some diplomats, in particular by Beauvale who inaccurately reported in late September Metternich's inclination to separate Austria from other signatories of the Convention, which actually was not the case.[47]

Palmerston's desire for peace without concessions to France finally materialised. This happened, however, because the warlike attitudes of some French people remained under the control of the king and his first minister, both behaving much in conformity with Metternich's expectation. Thiers actually did not desire war but wanted to vindicate himself with an honourable retreat. The first was manifested

---

[47] Metternich to Stürmer, Vienna, 29 Sept. and 18 Oct. 1840, HHStA, StA, Türkei VI, 78; Metternich to Trauttmannsdorff, Vienna, 9 and 18 Oct. 1840, HHStA, StK, Preussen 176; Metternich to Neumann, Vienna, 5, 8 and 15 Oct. 1840, HHStA, StA, England 231; Meysenbug to Metternich, St Petersburg, 7 Nov. 1840, HHStA, StA, Russland III, 119; Metternich to Ficquelmont, Vienna, 11 Oct. 1840, HHStA, StA, Russland III, 120; Beauvale to Palmerston, Vienna, 25 and 30 Sept., 8 Oct. 1840, TNA, FO 120/189; Maltzan to Frederick William IV, Vienna, 29 Sept. 1840, GStA PK, HA III, MdA I, 7358; Tatishchev to Nesselrode, Vienna, 10 and 27 Oct. 1840, AVPRI, fond 133, Kantseliariia, opis 469, 1840/178; Sainte-Aulaire to Thiers, Vienna, 19 and 20 Oct. 1840, AMAE, CP, Autriche 428; Lerchenfeld to Ludwig I of Bavaria, Vienna, 23 Oct. 1840, BHStA, MA, Wien 2409; Ingle, p. 140; Webster, *Palmerston*, II, p. 714.

in his memorandum addressed to the Great Powers on 8 October in response to the removal of Mohammed Ali. Thiers stated that the future of the pasha's rule in Syria depended on the result of the allied intervention but he had to retain Egypt; France could not allow him to be expelled from the land on the Nile, which the allied Powers actually did not intend to do. Metternich noticed the conciliatory spirit of the memorandum indiciating that France would not wage war owing to Mohammed Ali's possession of Syria and informed Sainte-Aulaire that he regarded peace in Europe as assured. Thiers' second desire, an honourable retreat, was contained in his proposal for the king's opening speech for the Chamber of Deputies that was to meet at the end of the month; its text contained bold and somehow threatening statements which were to mask the retreat of 8 October from the French public. At that moment, a tired Louis Philippe refused to continue in Thiers' intimidating foreign policy and rejected the threatening parts of the speech. Thiers and his colleagues used this opposition as the reason for their resignation on 21 October. A new French cabinet was constituted eight days later, with Marshal Soult as the prime minister again. In reality, the government was led by Guizot who became the minister of foreign affairs.[48]

The governmental change in France represented the turning point in the development of the Rhine Crisis and fundamentally contributed to the easing of the tension in Europe although not to its end. Guizot immediately informed French diplomats abroad that his aim was to preserve peace and he avoided the provocative declarations of his predecessor, but he continued in his policy of armed neutrality and neither acceded to the London Convention nor cooperated with its signatories. Like Thiers, Guizot also wanted to spare himself and his country from a too humiliating retreat and he therefore refused to

---

[48] Metternich to Trauttmannsdorff, Vienna, 18 Oct. 1840, HHStA, StK, Preussen 176; Metternich to Neumann, Vienna, 19 Oct. 1840, HHStA, StA, England 231; Metternich to Sainte-Aulaire, Vienna, 20 Oct. 1840, Metternich to Apponyi, Vienna, 23 Oct. 1840, HHStA, StA, Frankreich 319; Apponyi to Metternich, Paris, 23 Oct. 1840, HHStA, StA, Frankreich 318; Bockelberg to Frederick William IV, Vienna, 19 Oct. 1840, GStA PK, HA III, MdA I, 7358; Lerchenfeld to Ludwig I of Bavaria, Vienna, 23 Oct. 1840, BHStA, MA, Wien 2409; Altieri to Lambruschini, Vienna, 23 Oct. 1840, ASV, Arch. Nunz. Vienna 280C; G. Antonetti, *Louis-Philippe*, Paris 1994, p. 825; Cattaui, p. 188; Charles-Roux, *Thiers*, pp. 225–233 and 263–264; Malo, p. 318.

discuss the cessation of armament before the termination of the crisis; this determined attitude was to coerce the other Powers to make some concessions to Mohammed Ali and thereby to France. He proposed in early November that the pasha obtain Crete for his lifetime instead of Syria, which was to be returned to the sultan. This calculation was forestalled when news arrived in Paris that the allied forces had captured Acre at the beginning of November and that Mohammed Ali had given it up in exchange for the promise of hereditary Egypt at the end of the month. Even after these important events, Guizot did not stop preparations for a war that neither he nor his king was willing to wage. On 1 December, the French army numbered 465,023 men and continued to increase. On 12 December, the Parisian cabinet received 140 million Francs in credit for the construction of the fortification of the capital. The state of the "armed peace" (*la paix armée*), as Guizot called the attitude of France, was to continue until the moment when Mohammed Ali's future in Egypt was assured and the Turko-Egyptian conflict definitely over.[49] On 10 December, he wrote to Sainte-Aulaire: "I have always fought to maintain peace. In my mind, the restoration of the European concert always represented the preservation of peace. But we are still waiting. And it is in order to wait with a sense of security and advantage that we have built our armaments ... As for the size of our army, we must keep it at the present level as long as the current situation lasts."[50]

Metternich welcomed Thiers' fall and the accession of Soult/Guizot's ministry because he knew well the characters and peaceful aims of its two leaders. And since he was well aware of their and the king's difficult situation and the force of public opinion in France, he understood their effort to extricate themselves from the crisis with the reputation of the French cabinet intact. Consequently, he continued to maintain the conciliatory attitude he had assumed in August and regarded it as necessary that the French government would be able

---

[49] Apponyi to Metternich, Paris, 6 and 23 Nov., 6 Dec. 1840, HHStA, StA, Frankreich 318; Guizot's circular, Paris, 2 Nov. 1840, AMAE, CP, Autriche 428; Arnim to Frederick William IV, Paris, 6 Nov. 1840, GStA PK, Rep. 81 Gesandschaften (Residenturen) u. (General-) Konsulate nach 1807, Gesandschaft Wien II, 201/4; P. O'Brien, "L'Embastillement de Paris: The Fortification of Paris during the July Monarchy," *French Historical Studies* 9, 1975, 1, pp. 63–82; Hasenclever, *Die Orientalische Frage*, p. 235.

[50] F. Guizot, *Mémoires pour servir à l'histoire de mon temps*, Paris 1971, p. 413.

to proclaim: "It is I who saved the pasha of Egypt."[51] He personally had no objection to this if it would contribute to the ease of tension in Europe: "The whole world will join in with this claim and we will be the first."[52] As in previous months, he exhorted Apponyi to moderation and even to "caution"[53] if the ambassador found it necessary. Nevertheless, the unchanged intensity of armament and the disinclination to terminate the crisis as soon as possible disquieted the Austrian chancellor. It was not the construction of the fortification of Paris that he objected to because he correctly regarded this effort as a measure aimed at strengthening the king's position in the country. It was the size of the French army and the national guard that he sharply criticised. He wrote to Apponyi on 24 November: "This number [in Metternich's correspondence 420,000–480,000], Mr Ambassador, would not be that of a state at peace, either for France or for any other empire ... Any country that could send 200,000 men over its borders any day would not be at peace with its neighbours; it would be at war with them because peace is not a word, it is a fact."[54] For this reason he strongly disliked the term "armed peace" that was for him nothing other than "nonsense,"[55] "a prepared-for war."[56] The position assumed by France necessarily had to disquiet its neighbours and force them to react with their own preparations for an unwanted war, making the situation in the Continent rather insecure. Metternich particularly pointed out the reaction of the German countries as well as the German people alarmed by the French belligerency.[57]

[51] Metternich to Apponyi, Vienna, 8 Nov. 1840, HHStA, StA, Frankreich 319.
[52] Ibid.
[53] Ibid.
[54] Metternich to Apponyi, Vienna, 24 Nov. 1840, HHStA, StA, Frankreich 319.
[55] Metternich to Esterházy, Vienna, 5 Dec. 1840, HHStA, StA, England 231.
[56] Metternich to Apponyi, Vienna, 2 Jan. 1841, HHStA, StA, Frankreich 322.
[57] Metternich to Apponyi, Vienna, 24 Nov. 1840, HHStA, StA, Frankreich 319; Metternich to Esterházy, Vienna, 5 and 18 Dec. 1840, HHStA, StA, England 231; Metternich to Erberg, Vienna, 19 Dec. 1840, HHStA, StK, Preussen 176; Apponyi to Metternich, Paris, 10 and 29 Sept. 1840, HHStA, StA, Frankreich 318; Lerchenfeld to Ludwig I of Bavaria, Vienna, 1 Oct. and 10 Dec. 1840, BHStA, MA, Wien 2409; Maltzan to Frederick William IV, Vienna, 13 Dec. 1840, GStA PK, HA III, MdA I, 6033; Maltzan to Frederick William IV, Vienna, 14 Dec. 1840, GStA PK, HA III, MdA I, 7360; Tatishchev to Nesselrode, Vienna, 19 Dec. 1840, AVPRI, fond 133, Kantseliariia, opis 469, 1840/178.

The Rise of the German Confederation

It was the German aspect of the crisis to which Metternich also had to pay particular attention in the autumn of 1840. The warlike articles in *Le National* and other French journals, the French appeals for revolution and for the march to the Rhine, the concentration of troops on France's eastern frontier, all this caused a somewhat surprising and unexpectedly violent reaction among the Germans. What Metternich had feared when he was criticising the French press in early September is precisely what happened: "The inflammatory and dangerous speeches used to heighten passions – the insane abuses that the French press exaggerates and that it hurls like torches into the interior of its own country and in all directions abroad."[58] But what the Bonapartist *Le Capitole* presumed on 2 August proved to be entirely incorrect: "If tomorrow our banner is unfurled on the bank of the Rhine, then tomorrow Prussia will be nothing more than an old electorate of Brandenburg ... Almost the whole of Germany is waiting for us in order to be able to proclaim Germania and get rid of the small despots which dishonour it."[59] The author of these words, as well as many other Frenchmen, forgot that the year 1840 was neither 1792 nor 1830, which they had expected to see revisited. Their words about revolution and their desire for the Rhine provoked no sympathies among the Germans but rekindled with full force their anti-French sentiment of the wars of liberation from 1813. Passions were whipped up to the maximum. The German-language press answered threatening and provocative articles in French papers with similar zeal. A proclamation was delivered for the affiliation of Alsace to the German Confederation. In particular the Rhineland was increasingly in a mood for war. It was no accident that at that time Nikolaus Becker composed *Das Rheinlied*, Max Schneckenburger *Die Wacht am Rhein* and, with a certain delay in 1841 but under the influence of the events of the previous year, August Heinrich Hoffman von Fallersleben *Deutschland, Deutschland über Alles*.[60]

---

[58] Metternich to Leopold I, Königswart, 2 Sept. 1840, HHStA, StA, England 231.
[59] J. Binoche, *Histoire des relations franco-allemandes de 1789 à nos jours*, Paris 1996, p. 22.
[60] A. Geisthövel, *Restauration und Vormärz 1815–1847*, München, Wien, Zürich 2008, p. 46; O. J. Hamenn, "The Failure of an Attempted Franco-German Liberal Rapprochement 1830–1840," *AHR* 52, 1946, 1, p. 64; H. A. Winkler, *Germany:*

The surge of nationalism in the German Confederation did not exclude Vienna, as Maltzan reported in December: "The great German alliance has indeed gained a high degree of popularity. Indignant cries against the French conceit resound on the shores of the Danube as well as the Spree and Rhine. The new national song *Sie sollen ihn nicht haben den Rhein* is chanted in Vienna as much as in the whole of Germany and, I repeat that I believe I can confirm that pro-German sympathies, rather weak in Austria until now, have recently made such progress that would seem to ensure them lasting for a long time."[61] Metternich was not blind to this patriotic upheaval and maintained that "the national sentiment in Germany reached the same level as in 1813 and 1814,"[62] which was not far from truth. In his opinion, Thiers "likes to be compared to Napoleon; well, with respect to Germany, the comparison is perfect, and Mr Thiers might even surpass him. In only a short period of time he has achieved in Germany what took the Emperor ten years of oppression!"[63] This situation did not worry him a great deal because he had nothing against the German patriotism and its poetry, and Becker's song was published in Austria and sung in the Viennese streets with his consent. He also appreciated the fact that the Germans were willing to unite in defence against a common enemy.[64]

The willingness to defend the Confederation also affected the German monarchs, some of them influenced not only by fear of an attack from France but also by the wave of German nationalism. In October the members of the German Customs Union prohibited the export of horses needed by the French army, a measure agreed by Metternich and followed by Austria in late October. Some German states

---

The Long Road West, Volume 1: 1789–1933, Oxford 2006, pp. 78–79; Marcowitz, p. 168.

[61] Maltzan to Frederick William IV, Vienna, 13 Dec. 1840, GStA PK, HA III, MdA I, 7360.

[62] Metternich to Apponyi, Vienna, 24 Nov. 1840, HHStA, StA, Frankreich 319.

[63] Metternich to Apponyi, Vienna, 8 Nov. 1840, HHStA, StA, Frankreich 319.

[64] Guichen, p. 419. It actually was more bearable for Metternich to hear the German songs in Vienna than *La Marseillaise* in Pest, as happened in a theatre where the orchestra played and sang the French anthem upon the request of the audience. This considerably embittered the chancellor. O'Sullivan to Lebeau, Vienna, 10 Nov. 1840, ADA, CP, Autriche 7; Maltzan to Frederick William IV, Vienna, 13 Nov. 1840, GStA PK, HA III, MdA I, 6033; Lerchenfeld to Ludwig I of Bavaria, Vienna, 30 Oct. and 25 Nov. 1840, BHStA, MA, Wien 2409.

undertook certain steps for the improvements of their armies, but the defence of the Confederation of course rested upon the shoulders of Austria and Prussia to whom the eyes of the princes turned with hope for protection against France. The absence of military preparations in Austria giving them little hope for effective protection from its part increased the significance of Prussia and thereby its influence among the other members of the Confederation. Frederick William IV, personally much affected by the wave of nationalism, was generally considered to be its main protector.[65] The letters of German diplomats were full of praise for the Prussian king and they generally contained what the Bavarian representative in Saxony wrote at the end of October: "Intelligent people in this country are looking with anxiety towards the Rhine and with confidence towards its powerful ally in the North. It is generally understood that in the event of war the armed forces of the sovereigns of southern Germany would primarily have to defend their own frontiers, which are at the same time those of the German Confedaration, and that consequently an invasion into the Saxon lands could not be repulsed without Prussian assistance. People are confidently relying on the personnel qualities and federal sentiments of King Frederick William."[66]

Austria's passivity led to a considerable decrease of its prestige and the king of Württemberg even said of Metternich in the first half of October: "He no longer has influence among us."[67] At the same time, however, no division occurred between the two German Powers, which needed each other for a successful defence against France's eventual aggression. The cabinets in Berlin and Vienna continued to cooperate in the diplomatic field and simultaneously tried to develop together

---

[65] Lerchenfeld to Ludwig I of Bavaria, Vienna, 17 Oct. 1840, BHStA, MA, Wien 2409; report from Vienna, 19 and 31 Oct. 1840, SS, HD, SG, Wien 94; O'Sullivan to Lebeau, Vienna, 27 Oct. 1840, ADA, CP, Autriche 7; Bockelberg to Frederick William IV, Vienna, 3 Nov. 1840, GStA PK, HA III, MdA I, 6033; Dönkoff to Frederick William IV, Munich, 10 Nov. 1840, GStA PK, HA III, MdA I, 2487; Willmar to Lebeau, Berlin, 17 Nov. 1840, ADA, CP, Prusse 5; F. L. Müller, *Britain and the German Question: Perceptions of Nationalism and Political Reform, 1830–63*, Basingstoke 2002, pp. 43–46; H. Schulze, *Der Weg zum Nationalstaat: Die deutsche Nationalbewegung vom 18. Jahrhundert bis zur Reichsgründung*, München 1985, p. 82.

[66] Verges to Ludwig I of Bavaria, Dresden, 30 Oct. 1840, BHStA, MA, Dresden 2820.

[67] Guichen, p. 420.

militarily. For Metternich, Prussia's diplomatic and military backing was very important either for preventing war or for fighting side by side if war broke out. In the latter case, the Austrian diplomatic and military elites feared above all an isolated war in which Austria had to face France in the Apennines.[68] Consequently, Metternich wrote to Frederick William IV on 9 October: "At the present time, everything depends on the close unity of Austria and Prussia because these two Powers form the central power in Europe and this surely results from the geographical position of both states, their independence and their roles as leading members of the German Confederation. The attitude taken by these two Powers must be aimed at suppressing cries for war and ensuring that the Turko-Egyptian conflict reaches a quick settlement."[69] Metternich was also convinced that "the active and close relationship between Austria and Prussia is the first condition for the preparedness of all Germany for defence."[70] The ministerial change in France changed nothing in his conviction of the "absolute urgency with which the two German Powers determine their attitudes and actions with regard to the eventualities of the future."[71]

Frederick William IV was of the same opinion and promptly accommodated Metternich's request. In mid November, the Prussian king sent General Karl von Grolmann with Colonel Joseph Maria von Radowitz to Vienna to agree on terms for the defence of the German Confederation. The former arrived on 16 November, the latter, spending some time on the way in Dresden, on 20 November. Metternich deputised Austrian State Minister Count Karl Ludwig von Ficquelmont and President of the Court Council of War General Count Ignaz von Hardegg to attend the negotiations with the Prussian officers on military affairs, and on political issues he dealt with the Prussians personally. The Austro-Prussian military negotiations came to a quick conclusion and an agreement was signed on 28 November 1840. According to the contract, both Powers were obliged to defend the German Confederation, particularly the Rhineland, where

---

[68] Metternich to Trauttmannsdorff, Vienna, 9 Oct. 1840, HHStA, StK, Preussen 176.
[69] Metternich to Frederick William IV, Vienna, 9 Oct. 1840, *NP*, VI, p. 470.
[70] W. Deutsch, "Die Mission von Heß und Radowitz, 1840," *Gesamtdeutsche Vergangenheit, Festschrift für Heinrich von Srbik*, München 1938, p. 257.
[71] Maltzan to Frederick William IV, Vienna, 5 Nov. 1840, GStA PK, HA III, MdA I, 6033.

Austria promised to send its troops in the event of a French attack. In return, Frederick William IV was obliged to "regard an isolated assault on Austria in Italy as an attack against the entire Confederation."[72] This was a crucial gain for the Viennese cabinet, something that Metternich had already tried to achieve in his project for the defensive league against France in August. Consequently, the chancellor commented on the outcome of 28 November in a very positive way: "The important result that has arisen from this negotiation is the idea expressed in the name of the Prussian king to be prepared to regard any attack by France against Austrian possessions in Italy as against himself; and [the second result is] the obligation undertaken afterwards by this prince [Frederick William IV] to propose at an opportune moment to the Confederation complete solidarity in this matter. It is inasmuch an important concession on the part of Prussia in the interest of the Austrian state, a concession that nobody could have foreseen until recently and that in our opinion must itself be viewed as an important result arising from General Grolmann's journey."[73] With Prussian aid, the courts of Bavaria, Württemberg, Hanover, and Baden were persuaded to accede to the agreement and to pledge to defend Austrian dominions in the Apennines. The Treaty of 28 November 1840 definitely represented a great success for Metternich because it significantly strengthened Austria's security and this diplomatic victory is changed little by the fact that, when the war scare was over and the improvement of the military organisation was approved by all members of the German Confederation in March 1841 as mentioned later in this chapter, Austria finally refused to ratify it.[74]

---

[72] Deutsch, p. 258.

[73] Metternich to Münch, Vienna, 28 Nov. 1840, *NP*, VI, p. 481.

[74] Metternich to Esterházy, Vienna, 14 Nov. 1840, HHStA, StA, England 231; Bockelberg to Frederick William IV, Vienna, 3 Nov. 1840, Maltzan to Frederick William IV, Vienna, 17 and 24 Nov. 1840, GStA PK, HA III, MdA I, 6033; Grolman to Frederick William IV, Vienna, 19 Nov. 1840, Radowitz to Frederick William IV, Vienna, 26 Nov. and 4 Dec. 1840, Maltzan to Frederick William IV, Vienna, 27 May 1841, GStA PK, HA III, MdA I, 6094; Tatishchev to Nesselrode, Vienna, 18 and 30 Nov. 1840, AVPRI, fond 133, Kantseliariia, opis 469, 1840/178; O'Sullivan to Lebeau, Vienna, 30 Nov. 1840, ADA, CP, Autriche 7; Beauvale to Palmerston, Vienna, 2 Dec. 1840, TNA, FO 120/189; W. D. Gruner, "Der deutsche Bund, die deutschen Verfassungstaaten und die Rheinkrise von 1840," *Zeitschrift für bayerische Landesgeschichte* 53, 1990, 1, p. 60; Deutsch, p. 260; Rodkey, "A 'League' to Preserve Peace," p. 310; Veit-Brause, p. 61.

The Rhine Crisis in Germany was not, however, terminated with the Treaty of 28 November and the subsequent accession of some other members of the Confederation. There were two other problems for Metternich to solve, both of them caused by Frederick William IV. The first one originated in early November when the Prussian king proposed to raise a formal request to France for an explanation of the purpose of its armament; this request was to be made jointly by Austria, Prussia and the German Confederation "as one European Power."[75] Metternich disagreed with the participation of the Confederation because the resulting voice would be too loud and, consequently, too irritating and provocative for France and unsuitable at the moment when its new cabinet had firmly decided for peace despite the continuous preparations for the opposite. In his opinion, the measures undertaken for strengthening the armies of the German states were to be carried out cautiously and without affected declarations because it was important that "the Confederation has given the French government neither an incentive nor a pretext to take action. The necessity for France to regain the frontier on the Rhine, the necessity alleged by the French press as the reason for the armament directed particularly against Germany, will certainly never be given by a reasonable government as justification for a war that is motivated by nothing else."[76] Metternich himself acted according to this advice when, simultaneously with the Austro-Prussian military negotiations in Vienna, he constantly assured Sainte-Aulaire that they were not aimed against France and that "the German Confederation is an entirely pacifist entity; it will never take the initiative in aggression. Armament on its part is absolutely defensive and nobody should be offended by it."[77] Therefore, at the end of November the chancellor persuaded the Prussian king to communicate the request in Paris in a more confidential and friendly way through the Austrian and Prussian ambassadors only, which happened on 6 December. The answer that France would continue its armament until the end of the crisis

---

[75] Frederick William IV, *Bestimmungen für die Sendung nach Wien*, Berlin, 5 Nov. 1840, GStA PK, HA III, MdA I, 6094.
[76] Metternich to Trauttmannsdorff, Vienna, 24 Nov. 1840, HHStA, StK, Preussen 176.
[77] Sainte-Aulaire to Guizot, Vienna, 27 Nov. 1840, AMAE, CP, Autriche 428.

but would maintain peace was accepted by the two German Powers as sufficient and terminated the whole question.[78]

Metternich wanted to use the patriotic wave among the German monarchs in late 1840 to ensure their unity and improve the state of the federal defence: "I hope to finish the great work of Mr Thiers. He has excited the German national sentiment; it is necessary to know how to make the best use of this fact for the German homeland to enter the ranks of effectively respectable powers. Mr Thiers will have thus contributed to a great and useful deed."[79] In February 1841, he similarly explained himself on the same topic: "The events of the previous year have had a positive effect in Germany. They have revealed their neighbour's true colours to German eyes; they have awakened the sense of German nationality and have shown the members of the common fatherland that its power to secure the independence of the whole can only be found in a close cooperation of its parts. One can but wish that this opportunity will be exploited to strengthen the Confederation."[80] Here arose the second problem that Metternich had to solve; the differing opinions on how to reform the federal military structure between Austria and Prussia. Soon after the military negotiations in Vienna, Frederick William IV came to the decision that his popularity among the German states enabled him to obtain military leadership in the Confederation through such a reform. The changes he proposed in January 1841 would thus significantly change not only the character of the federal army but also the Confederation itself. The resulting increase of Prussia's influence at Austria's expense was something that Metternich naturally could not permit and he finally managed to persuade the king to give up most of his ideas. The chancellor was backed by the southern German states which feared the

---

[78] Metternich to Apponyi, Vienna, 29 Nov. 1840, HHStA, StA, Frankreich 319; Metternich to Schwarzenberg, Vienna, 7 Dec. 1840, HHStA, StA, Sardinien 77; Apponyi to Metternich, Paris, 6, 9 and 16 Dec. 1840, HHStA, StA, Frankreich 318; Grolman to Frederick William IV, Vienna, 19 Nov. 1840, GStA PK, HA III, MdA I, 6094; Tatishchev to Nesselrode, Vienna, 18 Nov. and 19 Dec. 1840, AVPRI, fond 133, Kantseliariia, opis 469, 1840/178; Lerchenfeld to Ludwig I of Bavaria, Vienna, 19 Nov. 1840, BHStA, MA, Wien 2409; O'Sullivan to Lebeau, Vienna, 30 Nov. and 21 Dec. 1840, ADA, CP, Autriche 7; Sainte-Aulaire to Guizot, Vienna, 27 Nov. and 1 Dec. 1840, AMAE, CP, Autriche 428; Beauvale to Palmerston, Vienna, 2 Dec. 1840, TNA, FO 120/189.

[79] Metternich to Esterházy, Vienna, 26 Dec. 1840, HHStA, StA, England 231.

[80] Novotny, p. 42.

diminishing of their own independence due to the proposed reforms; their distrust of Prussia's ambitions finally brought them to Austria's camp. An excellent example of this shift was the Bavarian king, Ludwig I of Bavaria, who had originally expressed a strong inclination towards Frederick William IV in late 1840, but in the following year, he did not support Prussia's plan for the reform and sided with Austria. Consequently, Metternich's viewpoint eventually prevailed. The dispute between Berlin and Vienna was finally arranged without doing any harm and the measures they jointly proposed for the more efficient military organisation of the federal forces in March 1841 in Frankfurt am Main were easily accepted by other members of the Confederation. By this victory Metternich won the duel with Frederick William IV that concerned not only the military but also political, federal, character of the German Confederation that was menaced by Prussia's aggressive and militarised nationalism.[81]

Metternich was satisfied with this outcome and wrote at the end of the month to Prince Esterházy: "The character that it [Confederation] has recently displayed towards France assigns to the German Confederation a role in the great conflicts of Europe that for a long time it had traditionally not been thought capable of. This role can only grow if it is nurtured carefully and it is on this that we intend to focus ... Two factors have contributed considerably to bringing Germany back to life; the first (and this was the most effective) was the arrogance of the claims of the French ministry of the first of March; the other cause of Germany's reawakening must be sought in the Russian and English inconsistencies that so onerously complicated the essentially so simple Turko-Egyptian affair. The German Confederation has become aware of itself and it has left the torpor of its early infancy. The protocol of the Diet [in Frankfurt am Main] of 13 March

---

[81] Dönkoff to Frederick William IV, Munich, 15 Dec. 1840, GStA PK, HA III, MdA I, 2487; Beauvale to Palmerston, Vienna, 3 Jan. and 9 March 1841, TNA, FO 120/197; J. Angelow, *Von Wien nach Königgrätz: Die Sicherheitspolitik des Deutschen Bundes im europäischen Gleichgewicht (1815–1866)*, München 1996, p. 112; R. D. Billinger Jr., "They Sing the Best Songs Badly: Metternich, Frederick William IV, and the German Confederation during the War Scare of 1840–41," H. Rumpler (ed.), *Deutscher Bund und deutsche Frage 1815–1866*, München 1990, pp. 95–111; J. Honsell, *Bayern und die Rheinkrise von 1840*, unpublished thesis, München 2002, pp. 59–68; L. Höbelt, "Zur Militärpolitik des deutschen Bundes," H. Rumpler (ed.), *Deutscher Bund und deutsche Frage 1815–1866*, München 1990, pp. 130–134; Novotny, p. 14.

that Count Münch[82] will not have delayed sending you signals, in my opinion, great progress in the political education of the federal body."[83] Similar statements as well as practical steps prove that Metternich sincerely wished to improve the striking power of the German Confederation. Consequently, it is difficult to agree with his frequent critic, Paul W. Schroeder, who labelled the end of the Rhine Crisis as "a typical Metternichian victory" when peace in Europe was preserved and Austria's interests were secured but the fundamental problem of the German Confederation's more effective ability to defend itself was not "solved or even confronted."[84] Leaving aside the malicious term of "a typical Metternichian victory," it is necessary to point out the fact that Metternich actually confronted the problem with the aim of solving it but that it is difficult to say how exactly and why the result was not better than it probably could have been because the state of research on this topic is rather incomplete, and it definitely does not allow typically Schroederian far-reaching conclusions.

The absence of any steps to improve the Austrian army in the late summer and early autumn should be explained not only by Metternich's desire not to provoke France but also by the opposition of Kolowrat to additional expenditure for war preparations. The implementation of some measures for the reinforcement of the army after late November resulted from the significant improvement of Metternich's position in internal affairs.[85] The military victories of the al-

---

[82] Eduard von Münch-Bellinghausen was the Austrian envoy to the German Confederation.

[83] Metternich to Esterházy, Vienna, 29 March 1841, HHStA, StA, England 236.

[84] Schroeder, *Transformation*, p. 749.

[85] The issue of the German Confederation's ability to defend itself raised the question of the fighting capacity of the Austrian army. It was a popular habit for German-speaking diplomats to depict it as low, and Heinrich Treitschke willingly claimed that it in no way was prepared for war with France. American historian Gunther Erich Rothenberg offered a rather negative picture of Austrian armed forces and claimed that only the Austrian army in Italy commanded by Marshal Radetzky was able to compete with that of France and that the rest of Austria's troops were not prepared for challenging operations. These negative evaluations are rather precarious because the Austrian documents containing information about insufficiencies in the army applied to the functioning of the highest levels of military administration, not the actual capability of the troops. The content of non-Austrian documents is also problematic because foreign diplomats and officers often tended to depict the states of armies of other countries in dark colours, probably darker than they actually were. From the turn of 1840, such criticism applied to not only

lied forces in Syria and Thiers' pacifistic memorandum of 8 October reduced the Austrian elites' criticism of the chancellor, and the intervention of Archduchess Sophie and Archduke Charles on his behalf helped improve his relations with Archduke Louis in mid October. The support of the Habsburg family, the ministerial change in Paris, Mohammed Ali's submission and successful military negotiations with Grolmann and Radowitz made his position unshakeable in November. The preceding criticism was forgotten and the chancellor was now praised for his policy which had averted war on the Continent and brought laurels to the Austrian expeditionary forces in Syria. Even Kolowrat who returned to Vienna at the end of October 1840 was heard to compliment his old rival. This flattery, however,

---

the Austrian but also Bavarian, Saxon or Württemberg armies, and even the French army, which definitely was not in an ideal position at the beginning of the crisis, and the French themselves claimed that their armament was to remedy the deficiencies from the previous years when it had been neglected. In the Prussian army some deficiencies were also revealed during a later federal inspection. However, when the same federal inspection was undertaken in Austria in the autumn of 1841, its verdict was highly satisfactory. If foreigners criticised anything in the Austrian armed forces in the autumn of 1840, it was particularly the non-redeployment of the forces on the empire's western frontier and the insufficient number of 257,252 men actually prepared for war (out of 413,995 men constituting the Austrian army at that time owing to 156,743 men on leave; the number the state prescribed for war was 400,537 men), not the army's low combat efficiency. And when some steps were undertaken by the Austrian authorities to improve the position of the army at the end of 1840, then it was ascertained that the provisions in the magazines were quite sufficient. Some deficiencies also were remedied at that time, together with the purchase of 8,000 horses. Maltzan to Frederick William IV, Vienna, 3 Oct. 1840, GStA PK, Rep. 81 Gesandschaften (Residenturen) u. (General-) Konsulate nach 1807, Gesandschaft Wien II, 201/3; Sainte-Aulaire to Guizot, Vienna, 11 Oct. 1841, AMAE, CP, Autriche 429; Lerchenfeld to Ludwig I of Bavaria, Vienna, 6 and 14 Oct., 8 Nov., 10 and 19 Dec. 1840, BHStA, MA, Wien 2409; Altieri to Lambruschini, Vienna, 9 and 23 Oct. 1840, ASV, Arch. Nunz. Vienna 280C; Beauvale to Palmerston, Vienna, 14 Oct. 1840, TNA, FO 120/189; report from Vienna, 14 and 21 Oct. 1840, SS, HD, SG, Wien 94; Bockelberg to Frederick William, Vienna, 3 Nov. 1840, Maltzan to Frederick William IV, Vienna, 19 Dec. 1840, GStA PK, HA III, MdA I, 6033; Dönkoff to Frederick William IV, Munich, 30 Nov. 1840, GStA PK, HA III, MdA I, 2487; O'Sullivan to Lebeau, Vienna, 9 Oct., 17 and 30 Nov., 26 Dec. 1840, ADA, CP, Autriche 7; Willmar to Lebeau, Weimar, 8 Feb. 1841, ADA, CP, Prusse 6; S. Krauss, *Die politischen Beziehungen zwischen Bayern und Frankreich 1814/1815–1840*, München 1987, p. 385; G. E. Rothenberg, "The Austrian Army in the Age of Metternich," *JMH* 40, 1968, 2, pp. 162–164; Hall, p. 283; Novotny, pp. 18–23.

did not dispel the old hostility between the two men and Metternich did not hesitate to take advantage of the given situation to further reduce Kolowrat's influence by the removal of Kolowrat's important ally, Baron Eichhoff, who sealed his own fate on 18 November with a memorandum on the negative impact of the London Convention on Austrian finances, in particular its banking sector, containing strong criticism of Metternich's foreign policy. This was a mistake at the moment when Metternich was enjoying general confidence and was supported by Archduke Louis. On 25 November, Eichhoff was replaced at the head of the Chamber of Finance by Baron Carl Friedrich von Kübeck. It is not clear whether Kübeck was Metternich's close ally at that time but he definitely was not his enemy. The chancellor's influence also increased with the appointment of Count Hartig to a high administrative function of the head of the Political Section of the State Council. Kolowrat was beaten, he even made no attempt to save Eichhoff, and he himself – suffering from problems with his eyes – resigned in November from the supervision of Austrian finances.[86]

* * *

Metternich's influence on Austria's internal affairs was stronger at the end of 1840 than it had been for a period of several years. At the same time, the Rhine Crisis was virtually at an end. Metternich's actions during the crisis offered a good example of his peace management and

[86] Bockelberg to Frederick William IV, Vienna, 30 Oct., 1 and 3 Nov. 1840, Maltzan to Frederick William IV, Vienna, 13, 20 and 27 Nov., 13 Dec. 1840, GStA PK, HA III, MdA I, 6033; Maltzan to Frederick William IV, Vienna, 30 Nov. 1840, GStA PK, HA III, MdA I, 7360; Tatishchev to Nesselrode, Vienna, 21 Oct., 4, 12 and 30 Nov. 1840, AVPRI, fond 133, Kantseliariia, opis 469, 1840/178; O'Sullivan to Lebeau, Vienna, 30 Oct. and 30 Nov. 1840, ADA, CP, Autriche 7; report from Vienna, 31 Oct., 25 and 28 Nov., 19 Dec. 1840, SS, HD, SG, Wien 94; Lerchenfeld to Ludwig I of Bavaria, Vienna, 13 and 25 Nov., 4 Dec. 1840, BHStA, MA, Wien 2409; F. Hartig (ed.), *Metternich-Hartig: Ein Briefwechsel des Staatskanzlers aus dem Exil 1848–1851*, Wien, Leipzig 1923, p. 11; M. Freiherr von Kübeck (ed.), *Tagebücher des Carl Friedrich Freiherrn von Kübeck von Kübau*, II, Wien 1909, p. 5; H. Meynert, *Peter Joseph Freiherr von Eichhoff, früherer k. k. Hofkammerpräsident, sein Leben und ämtliches Wirken*, Wien 1849, pp. 22–23; Beer, *Die Finanzen Oesterreichs*, p. 150; Hammer-Purgstall, pp. 331–332; Herzog, p. 45.

adroit analytical skills. It is difficult to entirely agree with the assessment of historian James L. Richardson that although the chancellor "misjudged the outcome, his was the most acute perception of the nature of the risk of war in autumn 1840."[87] The second part is correct because Metternich's alarm resulted from the instability of French politics that could lead, directly or indirectly, to a more serious European crisis or conflagration, and this actually was the only danger for European peace because there never was a serious threat of war since the king and his two first ministers never seriously intended to wage one. However, Metternich also knew this and he never claimed that a war on the Continent was inevitable or probable. Therefore, the first part of Richardson's evaluation is more than problematic and it significantly exaggerates Metternich's apprehension of a possible war between France and the signatories of the London Convention.

Metternich also enjoyed some diplomatic success when he prevented the increase of Prussia's influence over the military and political affairs of the German Confederation, ensured the help of the Confederation for an eventual French attack in the Apennines and prevented any provocative measures of the Confederation against France.[88] He was thus able to strengthen Austria's position against an eventual French attack and simultaneously forestall further growth of passionate bellicosity and hostility. However, despite his continuous attempts to persuade Guizot to end France's isolation and cooperate with the other Powers, the French foreign minister refused to do so and also to stop France's armament until the Turko-Egyptian conflict was settled and Mohammed Ali's position in Egypt secured.[89] Consequently, the crisis was not in fact entirely terminated with the arrival of the year 1841, and the restoration of the European concert depended on the course of events in the Ottoman Empire where, at

---

[87] Richardson, p. 60.
[88] Schroeder, *Transformation*, pp. 748–749.
[89] Metternich to Erberg, Vienna, 19 Dec. 1840, HHStA, StK, Preussen 176; Metternich to Apponyi, Vienna, 2 and 4 Jan. 1841, HHStA, StA, Frankreich 322; Metternich to Trauttmannsdorff, Vienna, 21 Feb. 1841, HHStA, StK, Preussen 178; Apponyi to Metternich, Paris, 6, 9, 16 and 23 Dec. 1840, HHStA, StA, Frankreich 318; Apponyi to Metternich, Paris, 7, 14 and 21 Jan., 14 Feb. 1841, HHStA, StA, Frankreich 320; Tatishchev to Nesselrode, Vienna, 7 Jan. 1841, AVPRI, fond 133, Kantseliariia, opis 469, 1841/191; Maltzan to Frederick William IV, Vienna, 26 Jan. 1841, GStA PK, HA III, MdA I, 7361; Metternich to Sainte-Aulaire, Vienna, 30 Dec. 1840, *NP*, VI, pp. 427–428.

the end of 1840, the situation was considerably changed due to the successful allied military intervention in Syria.

The Syrian Campaign

In the autumn of 1840, Austrian armed forces took part in a military intervention in Syria with the aim of driving Mohammed Ali's army back to Egypt and forcing the pasha to yield to the conditions of the London Convention of 15 July. Although their participation was few in number, the Austrians fought with courage and gained merit for the successful outcome of the campaign. Metternich attentively observed the operations from his office in Ballhausplatz and despite his fears about the negative impact of the attack against Mohammed Ali on the hypersentive French public, he was convinced that once the operations were launched, they had to be brought to an early and victorious close because the war in Syria was to decide both, the Egyptian Question as well as the dispute between France and the signatories of the London Convention.

Mohammed Ali's Unyieldingness and Deposal

The hostile reaction of France to the existence of the London Convention was felt not only in the West but also in the East. Pontois was quick to resort to threats and he informed Reshid Pasha through the French dragoman on 16 August that "the French government, the king and the nation regard the conclusion of the treaty that was signed in London as an insult to France made by the Ottoman representative."[1] Pontois informed the Ottoman foreign minister that the Convention was "directed against the interests of Islam"[2] and, according to Reshid's version of his discussion with the dragoman, the ambassador threatened that if the Porte ratified it, France would ac-

---

[1] Stürmer to Metternich, Constantinople, 17 Aug. 1840, HHStA, StA, Türkei VI, 75.

[2] Ibid.

tively support the pasha and "unite its effort with his in inciting the populations in Asia and Europe to revolt against the present Turkish rule."[3] These words about possible sedition and revolt against a legitimate sovereign incensed Metternich, and his reaction condemning the statement that, as he declared, deserved "a place among the greatest scandals of all time,"[4] was not long in coming. He requested from the French government "its explanations for this seditious language and believed that he could hope that these explanations would pave the way to a more moderate tone in French declarations."[5] Louis Philippe and Thiers refused to believe that Pontois could utter such a "hideous and absurd tirade,"[6] and they distanced themselves from their ambassador and denied that they would have instructed him to make such threatening statements. Pontois defended himself with the explanation that he had been misunderstood and that he had become a victim of intrigue because although the core of his declaration had been correct, Reshid had added much of his own. Metternich in no way believed Pontois' version and saw the French government as an accomplice in this affair; however, he considered the French explanations to be satisfactory and set the matter aside.[7]

Unlike Metternich, the Porte did not respond to the French ultimatum. It ratified the London Convention regardless of Pontois'

---

[3] Ibid.
[4] Metternich to Neumann, Königswart, 2 Sept. 1840, HHStA, StA, England 230.
[5] Ottenfels to Stürmer, Vienna, 8 Sept. 1840, HHStA, StA, Türkei VI, 78.
[6] Apponyi to Metternich, Paris, 10 Sept. 1840, HHStA, StA, Frankreich 318.
[7] Metternich to Neumann, Königswart, 31 Aug. 1840, HHStA, StA, England 231; Metternich to Apponyi, Königswart, 1 and 18 Sept. 1840, HHStA, StA, Frankreich 319; Metternich to Meysenbug, Vienna, 29 Sept. 1840, HHStA, StA, Russland III, 120; Stürmer to Metternich, Constantinople, 17, 19 and 22 Aug. 1840, HHStA, StA, Türkei VI, 75; Apponyi to Metternich, Paris, 6, 10 and 14 Sept. 1840, HHStA, StA, Frankreich 318; Königsmarck to Frederick William IV, Büyükdere, 17 and 21 Aug. 1840, GStA PK, HA III, MdA I, 7282; Pontois to Thiers, Therapia, 19, 22 and 25 Aug., 27 Sept. 1840, AMAE, CP, Turquie 281; Struve to Nesselrode, Königswart, 31 Aug. 1840, Tatishchev to Nesselrode, Vienna, 19 Sept. 1840, AVPRI, fond 133, Kantseliariia, opis 469, 1840/178; Beauvale to Palmerston, Königswart, 31 Aug. 1840, TNA, FO 120/189; Sainte-Aulaire to Thiers, Marienbad, 1 Sept. 1840, AMAE, CP, Autriche 428; Maltzan to Frederick William IV, Königswart, 30 Aug. 1840, GStA PK, HA III, MdA I, 7357; Maltzan to Frederick William IV, Königswart, 7 Sept. 1840, GStA PK, Rep. 81 Gesandschaften (Residenturen) u. (General-) Konsulate nach 1807, Gesandschaft Wien II, 201/3; Lerchenfeld to Ludwig I of Bavaria, Vienna, 8 Sept. 1840, BHStA, MA, Wien 2409; Kutluoğlu, p. 163.

threats and the sultan's advisors did not even tell the ambassador that they had already informally recognised the July Convention on 7 August when the former Ottoman ambassador in Vienna, Rifat Bey, was sent to Alexandria to inform Mohammed Ali of the wording of the agreement and obtain his answer. During their meeting on 16 August, the Egyptian governor refused to submit to its conditions and declared that he would prefer to die than to accept them. On the following day, he met the consuls of the signatory Powers and rejected the ultimatum with the statement that he was prepared to fight against them. Nor did he change his opinion after the first ten-day period given by the Convention. This attitude was the result of Thiers' exhortation to unyieldingness and the promise of French support. The first minister maintained the hope that he would become the mediator between Mohammed Ali and the other Great Powers and that the French policy of armed neutrality would discourage the latter from a military intervention in the Levant and force it to moderate the anti-Egyptian conditions of the Convention. To increase France's influence over Mohammed Ali, Thiers sent Count Alexander Walewski to Egypt in early August. He was to inform the pasha about the French armament and persuade him not to attack the sultan but also not to yield to the allies' pressure.[8] Stürmer correctly reflected Mohammed Ali's point of view and the reason for his firmness when he wrote to Metternich that the Egyptian governor "is too clever to have any illusions about the dangers he faces. But it seems that he still hopes that France will not refuse to play the role of mediator and he also hopes that if he succeeds in maintaining the status quo until spring, there will be dissension among the allies letting him triumph in this matter."[9]

Metternich was convinced that Mohammed Ali would submit to the London Convention if France did not oppose it. Walewski entirely shared this opinion and claimed that the pasha would have accepted its conditions even at the moment when France abstained from the signature if he had been instructed to persuade the pasha to conform to them. Since Thiers told him to do the opposite, when the sec-

---

[8]   Stürmer to Metternich, Constantinople, 26 Aug. and 1 Sept. 1840, Laurin to Stürmer, Alexandria, 25 and 26 Aug. 1840, HHStA, StA, Türkei VI, 75; Charles-Roux, *Thiers*, pp. 98–108; Guichen, pp. 359–360; Temperley, *Crimea*, p. 119.
[9]   Stürmer to Metternich, Constantinople, 10 Sept. 1840, HHStA, StA, Türkei VI, 75.

ond deadline went by on 5 September, Mohammed Ali unsurprisingly showed little willingness to moderate his unyielding attitude. He even declined to meet Rifat and the consuls personally and had them informed through Boghos Bey that he was only willing to accept some of the conditions, saying that he was prepared to return to the sultan all the provinces he held except Egypt and Syria, which he wanted to retain as hereditary tenure in "recognition of the long-lasting and useful services he had provided to the Sublime Porte."[10] In a letter written the next day, he assured Reshid Pasha that he wanted to administer Syria for the sultan's welfare: "As long as I live, I will spare no effort in raising Syria to a higher level of civilisation and prosperity, which no other administration could achieve, so that its inhabitants [can] enjoy total peace and so that through my actions I can show my gratitude to my Noble Ruler."[11] The partial acceptance of the conditions equalled, according to Rifat, a final refusal and he sailed on the same day back to Constantinople. Shortly thereafter, the consuls of Austria, Russia and Great Britain and the Prussian agent followed his example and at the 14 September request of the Porte left Egypt on 23 September for Beirut, where they stayed until their departure to the Ottoman capital on 24 October.[12]

When Rifat returned to Constantinople and Mohammed Ali's rejection of the London Convention became known, Ponsonby demanded Mohammed Ali's deposal as governor of Egypt. He turned to his colleagues for support. Stürmer and Königsmarck immediately gave theirs while Russian Chargé d'Affaires Vladimir Titov, on behalf of the absent Butenev, resolutely refused his. Titov argued that such a strong measure could never be successful if the Porte lacked the power to take action and the attempt to depose Mohammed Ali could cause more harm than good. He was finally persuaded, however, and he accompanied the other diplomats to Reshid Pasha with whom the

---

[10] Laurin to Stürmer, Alexandria, 5 Sept. 1840, HHStA, StA, Türkei VI, 75.

[11] Mohammed Ali to Mustafa Reshid Pasha, Alexandria, 6 Sept. 1840, HHStA, StA, Türkei VI, 75.

[12] Laurin to Stürmer, Alexandria, 5 Sept. 1840, Stürmer to Metternich, Constantinople, 10 Sept. 1840, the Porte's note to Stürmer, Constantinople, 14 Sept. 1840, HHStA, StA, Türkei VI, 75; Stürmer to Laurin, Constantinople, 16 Sept. 1840, HHStA, StA, Türkei VI, 76; Cattaui, p. 199; Charles-Roux, *Thiers*, p. 246; Kutluoğlu, pp. 164–167.

details of Mohammed Ali's deposal were arranged and then officially proclaimed on 14 September.[13]

The eagerness of the European diplomats did not find sympathy with the signatory governments of the London Convention. Ponsonby in particular faced harsh criticism; in London his action was qualified as "highly criminal"[14] and in St Petersburg Nesselrode even demanded his recall. Metternich also disapproved of the resolution for the Egyptian governor's deposal and this unpleasantly surprising resolution renewed his old displeasure at Ponsonby: "It is a real calamity that this man lacking restraint and judgement is found at this post during such serious times only because of his relationship with Lord Grey. In Constantinople they calculate what moral effect the deposal of Mohammed Ali will have on Syria and Egypt, but they are mistaken; in these countries one cannot calculate the moral effect but only the practical means. What madness to pronounce a death sentence on someone whom one does not yet have firmly in one's grasp."[15] The fact that the declaration of deposal could not be immediately enforced led the chancellor to the opinion that the sultan's decision was a useless, short-sighted and unwise measure: "A declaration of deposal is nothing but empty words if it is not immediately supported by the available material power. Naval forces alone are insufficient to destroy a man in Mohammed Ali's position, someone who, although he was never the legitimate overlord of the provinces in the possession of His Highness [the sultan], was nonetheless no less the real master of the land that he controls with the sword."[16] Furthermore, this step exceeded the stipulations of the London Convention that stated nothing nor included anything in the document that had also been signed by the sultan's representative about Mohammed Ali's removal from the governorship of Egypt. If the pasha refused its conditions, as he actually did on 5 September, the sultan could at most withdraw the offer of hereditary title to Egypt. In the event the sultan wanted to

---

[13] Stürmer to Metternich, Constantinople, 10 and 14 Sept. 1840, Ponsonby to Stürmer, Therapia, 10 Sept. 1840, the Porte's note to Stürmer, Constantinople, 14 Sept. 1840, HHStA, StA, Türkei VI, 78; Königsmarck to Frederick William IV, Büyükdere, 14 Sept. 1840, GStA PK, HA III, MdA I, 7283.

[14] Bolsover, "Lord Ponsonby and the Eastern Question," p. 113.

[15] Lerchenfeld to Ludwig I of Bavaria, Vienna, 1 Oct. 1840, BHStA, MA, Wien 2409.

[16] Metternich to Stürmer, Vienna, 28 Sept. 1840, HHStA, StA, Türkei VI, 78.

act more energetically and punish his vassal, he could do so only after consultation with the allies.[17]

What increased Metternich's criticism was his fear of the hostile reaction of France to the deposal for which, moreover, Austria was fully responsible due to Stürmer's complicity. Metternich sharply criticised him for the abuse of power and recommended that he literally obey the wording of the Convention and the instructions of his government: "Lord Ponsonby is a man of vivid imagination, perhaps a madman. Lord Ponsonby listens to no one's advice but his own and he cannot take into account the way things are but the way he would like them to be; he lives in a world where illusions become reality ... Never again follow Lord Ponsonby into such misguided stupidity."[18] He regretted that Stürmer had not accepted Titov's position, and he did not hesitate to assure Sainte-Aulaire that the whole affair was "an entirely senseless measure and he [Metternich] regretted the weakness of Mr Stürmer, who had been misguided in this affair by Lord Ponsonby."[19] To temper the violent reaction of the French public in October, the chancellor promised the French ambassador that Austria would advocate the restoration of Egypt to Mohammed Ali, namely to his hereditary possession. Neither Austria nor Great Britain was actually willing to enforce Mohammed Ali's deposal; they formally rejected the action of the Porte, having in mind the preservation of peaceful relations with France and also the insufficiency of their military power for a possible intervention in Egypt.[20]

---

[17] Metternich to Neumann, Vienna, 25 and 28 Sept. 1840, HHStA, StA, England 231; Metternich to Erberg, Vienna, 26 Sept. 1840, HHStA, StK, Preussen 176; Metternich to Stürmer, Vienna, 28 Sept. 1840, HHStA, StA, Türkei VI, 78; Beauvale to Palmerston, Vienna, 25 Sept. 1840, TNA, FO 120/189; Lerchenfeld to Ludwig I of Bavaria, Vienna, 28 Sept. 1840, BHStA, MA, Wien 2409; Ingle, p. 136.
[18] Metternich to Stürmer, Vienna, 28 Sept. 1840, HHStA, StA, Türkei VI, 78.
[19] Sainte-Aulaire to Thiers, Vienna, 19 Oct. 1840, AMAE, CP, Autriche 428.
[20] Metternich to Neumann, Vienna, 25 Sept. and 5 Oct. 1840, HHStA, StA, England 231; Metternich to Meysenbug, Vienna, 29 Sept. and 1 Nov. 1840, HHStA, StA, Russland III, 120; Metternich to Erberg, Vienna, 3 Oct. 1840, HHStA, StK, Preussen 176; Metternich to Stürmer, Vienna, 29 Sept. 1840, Palmerston to Ponsonby, London, 15 Oct. 1840, HHStA, StA, Türkei VI, 78; Tatishchev to Nesselrode, Vienna, 29 Sept. 1840, AVPRI, fond 133, Kantseliariia, opis 469, 1840/178; O'Sullivan to Lebeau, Vienna, 29 Sept. 1840, ADA, CP, Autriche 7; Lerchenfeld to Ludwig I of Bavaria, Vienna, 6 Oct. 1840, BHStA, MA, Wien 2409; Bockelberg to Frederick William IV, Vienna, 13 Oct. 1840, GStA PK, HA III, MdA I, 7358; Sainte-Aulaire to Thiers, Vienna, 20 Oct. 1840, AMAE, CP, Autriche 428; Ridley,

The Military Intervention in Syria

At the moment when Mohammed Ali was deposed, the military intervention against him was already in progress. It was not directed against Egypt itself but Syria with the aim to push Ibrahim Pasha back to the Nile Delta. If the forces were successful, Mohammed Ali's power would be destroyed not only in Syria but also in the Arabian Peninsula and the way to Constantinople would be blocked for his army. The allies also expected the support of the local inhabitants and, in Metternich's opinion, this was actually crucial for the success of the intervention, an opinion which proved to be completely justified. As for Egypt, only some ports were to be blocked from the sea. The main burden of fighting was to be borne by the British and the Turks, the former dominating the sea, the latter offering most of the land forces. British Admiral Sir Robert Stopford was appointed commander-in-chief, and the total number of the allied forces did not exceed 33,000 men during the campaign. The enemy forces consisted of approximately 85,000 soldiers. Austria's involvement in the intervention was small and never exceeded the level of a representative participation. The commander of the Austrian naval squadron was Rear-Admiral Francesco Bandiera, and an important role was to be played by the nineteen-year-old Archduke Frederick Ferdinand Leopold of Austria, the third son of Archduke Charles and a pupil of Major Hauslab. The Austrian squadron numbered four warships at the beginning: the frigates *Medea* and *Guerriera*, the latter commanded by Archduke Frederick, and the corvettes *Clemenza* and *Lipsia*. The armed steamship *Marianne* later arrived on the war scene. The figure concerning the Austrians who could be deployed in the land battles increased during the autumn due to reinforcements but never exceeded 400. Their most important unit for fighting on land was the rocket battery that enjoyed a good reputation. When reporting about the Austrian army, Cowley had written to Aberdeen in August 1828: "The rocket artillery (Congreve rockets) surpasses in utility and accuracy everything of this kind in Europe."[21] The rocket battery proved its usefulness during the Syrian campaign, also for the reason that

---

Palmerston, pp. 238–240.

[21] Cowley to Aberdeen, Vienna, 19 Aug. 1828, TNA, FO 120/93. For more on the Austrian rocket artillery see Buchmann, *Militär – Diplomatie – Politik*, pp. 99–102.

it demoralised enemy troops who were not familiar with this weapon and regarded it as an instrument of the devil.[22]

From Austria's point of view the history of the military intervention against Mohammed Ali had already begun on 17 July 1840 when the Court Council of War ordered Bandiera to join the British fleet, subordinate to Stopford's command and sail with him to the Syrian coast. Instead of Syria, Bandiera anchored in the Alexandrian harbour first at Stopford's request so that the Austrian and British warships might motivate Mohammed Ali with their presence to accept the conditions of the London Convention. They were also to prevent the pasha from sending his warships to the open sea. Together with Bandiera, Archduke Frederick remained in the port and he was even invited by Mohammed Ali for supper but he had to decline this invitation for political reasons and remain on his ship under the pretext of indisposition. When the pasha refused to yield without fighting, several British warships and the Austrian corvette *Clemenza* were left off the coast of Alexandria to preserve the blockade whereas Bandiera and Frederick sailed with Stopford to Beirut, joining on the way the sultan's squadron led by the British captain in Turkish service, Baldwin Walker, carrying Turkish landing troops. On 10 September, 5,000 Turks, 1,500 British and 200 Austrians went ashore north of Beirut. At the same time the allied fleet started to bombard the town. Since the allies did not dare to attack it, they operated on the coast under the command of the skilful and active British commodore, Sir Charles Napier, who won several clashes with the Egyptians in open terrain.[23]

These victories in small skirmishes and the support of local inhabitants who rose against the Egyptian rule could not bring about the final triumph of the allies. The forthcoming winter forced them

---

[22] Metternich to Neumann, Königswart, 15 and 18 Sept. 1840, HHStA, StA, England 231; Stürmer to Metternich, Constantinople, 12 Aug. 1840, HHStA, StA, Türkei VI, 75; H. Scholl, *Abriß der Geschichte des Krieges 1840–41 in Syrien*, Wien 1866, pp. 11–29; Fischer, p. 105; Khuepach, p. 248; Sabry, p. 518.

[23] Metternich to Stürmer, Vienna, 18 July 1840, Ottenfels to Stürmer, Vienna, 4 Aug. 1840, HHStA, StA, Türkei VI, 78; the instructions for Bandiera, Vienna, 17 July 1840, HHStA, StA, Türkei VI, 78; Stürmer to Metternich, Constantinople, 12 and 17 Aug., 10 Sept. 1840, Stopford to Stürmer, Mytilene, 10 Aug. 1840, Stürmer to Bandiera, Constantinople, 4 Aug. 1840, HHStA, StA, Türkei VI, 75; Beauvale to Ponsonby, Vienna, 17 July 1840, HHStA, StA, Türkei VI, 78; R. L. Dauber, *Erzherzog Friedrich von Österreich*, Graz, Wien 1993, p. 88; Khuepach, p. 247.

to capture the fortress towns on the coast to win strongholds for the over-wintering and protection of their troops. Stopford, an elderly and cautious man, originally had little faith that the attacks against the towns could be successful and contemplated the withdrawal of his forces to Cyprus and the termination of operations until the spring of 1841, but Bandiera, Frederick and Napier persuaded him to continue fighting and to give the order to attack Sidon. The responsibility for its capture was assumed by Napier and Frederick, who sailed on 26 September and decided to attack the town on the same day. The fortification of Sidon was weak and did not seem likely to withstand attack for long. At noon, the allies started to bombard it and within an hour the coastal batteries were silenced. The allies went ashore and attacked the town from three directions and forced the defenders to retreat into the citadel. Here the offensive got stuck. When Archduke Frederick noticed this, he exceeded the duties of a naval officer and landed with Austrian reinforcements, joined the first Austrian landing force in the house of the Austrian consulate and, followed by his men, stormed the citadel through a breach in its wall. The citadel was captured despite strong resistance before sunset. Frederick won general acclaim and decorations from fifteen European courts for his courageous conduct, which delighted his father, who became more well disposed towards Metternich, something very helpful for the chancellor in his contest with Kolowrat.[24]

On 10 October, Beirut was taken by the allies and six days later Tripoli on the Lebanese coast was placed under their control. Whereas in Beirut the role of the Austrians was marginal, the credit for winning Tripoli was due to just the Austrian marines and happenstance. On 15 October, the *Clemenza*, which had been recalled from Alexandria to the Syrian coast, was forced by a storm to find a safe harbour in Tripoli. On the following morning, the town experienced a deafening explosion. The Egyptian garrison had feared an assault against the town and had fled, and their absence had been used by the inhabitants for plundering. Owing to a misfortune, a powder magazine had

---

[24] Tatishchev to Nesselrode, Vienna, 27 Oct. 1840, AVPRI, fond 133, Kantseliariia, opis 469, 1840/178; J. Bergmann, *Erzherzog Friedrich von Österreich und sein Antheil am Kriegszuge in Syrien im Jahre 1840*, Wien 1857, pp. 31–36; C. Vimercati, *Die kaiserlich königliche österreichische Marine im Oriente: Geschichtlicher Rückblick auf das Jahr 1840*, Wien 1845, p. 97; Dauber, p. 96; Fischer, p. 110.

exploded. After the request of the Austrian consul, the captain of the
Clemenza sent 30 men with two rocket guns to the town to keep order. The citadel was garrisoned by the Austrians and their flag hoisted
above the town. They remained there until 17 November 1840 when
the *Clemenza* set sail. During their presence peace and order actually
were preserved.[25]

Despite the continuous victories of the allies, Stopford regarded
the situation as disadvantageous in late October and again contemplated a withdrawal to Cyprus. Napier opposed this idea and advocated the assault against the key stronghold on the coast, Acre.
Bandiera and Frederick supported the British commodore, and although unaware of it, they were fulfilling Metternich's desire for a
bolder approach and the achievement of a prompt and decisive victory
that would terminate the campaign in the East and prevent France
from continuing in its threatening and gambling policy in the West.
The chancellor was satisfied when he learnt of the beginning of the military intervention despite the irritation it provoked in France. At that
moment he was convinced that it was necessary to vigorously pursue
the operations and what he feared above all was that they would not
be accomplished by the time winter arrived. Then it would not be possible to maintain contact with the disembarked troops, which would
lead either to their evacuation or defeat, both signifying a victory for
Mohammed Ali and a triumph for France. He also did not forget the
fate of the insurgents whose useful assistance gave good prospects for
the allies' final success. As Beauvale wrote to Palmerston: "The idea
of leaving it [Syria] after raising the inhabitants in insurrection had
struck him with dismay."[26] Consequently, Metternich was greatly annoyed when he learnt of Stopford's plan to abandon Syria in early
October and equally as pleased when he learnt mid month that it
would not be deserted: "We are completely satisfied that Admiral
Stopford has changed his mind. The enterprises in Syria seem to meet
with success; consequently it is necessary to give them as solid a base
as possible; a retreat would be a huge mistake."[27] In late October,
his optimism was considerably increased by the news of the allies'
victories and in early November he became firmly convinced that the

---

[25]　Khuepach, p. 254; Kutluoğlu, p. 170.
[26]　Beauvale to Palmerston, Vienna, 14 Oct. 1840, TNA, FO 120/189.
[27]　Metternich to Neumann, Vienna, 15 Oct. 1840, HHStA, StA, England 231.

poor situation of the Egyptian armed forces in Syria would force Mohammed Ali to withdraw them to Egypt before the end of the year. He
also believed in the fall of Acre due to the low moral of the Egyptian
soldiers.[28] Therefore, in mid November he regretted that the fortress
had not been captured yet due to Stopford's vacillation: "It is deeply
regrettable that he did not push his advance to Acre, the capture of
which would have offered a certain end to the conflict, even in the context of the overall political situation. If Commodore Napier made an
enormous effort when making his last and glorious operations against
Ibrahim Pasha, he [Stopford] had no reason for reducing him to the
state of inactivity as he seems to have done!"[29]

When Metternich was writing this criticism of the British commander-in-chief, he did not know that Acre had already been taken.
This was due to the orders from London which finally forced the hesitating Stopford to attack the fortress. Since Bandiera's and Frederick's
intransigence moved him to agree with the Austrians' participation in
this enterprise, three Austrian warships – the *Medea*, *Guerriera*, and
Lipsia – appeared together with one Turkish and seventeen British
warships off the coast of Acre on 2 November. The allied fleet started
the bombardment of the town in the afternoon of the following day.
In two hours, a powder magazine close to the entrance of the town
harbour exploded. The number of casualties was enormous, but since
the disaster had more impact on the defenders' moral than on the
fortification itself, the bombardment continued until the evening. In
the following night from 3 to 4 November, an Austrian returned to
the *Guerriera* from his probing mission with the information that
the Egyptians had left a part of the town's coastal fortification unguarded. Soon afterwards, Walker arrived and confirmed the accuracy
of this information; in his opinion, a good chance for capturing the

---

[28] Metternich to Neumann, Vienna, 8 Oct. 1840, Metternich to Esterházy, Vienna, 11 and 14 Nov. 1840, HHStA, StA, England 231; Metternich to Ficquelmont,
Vienna, 11 Oct. 1840, HHStA, StA, Russland III, 120; Metternich to Erberg, Vienna, 11 Nov. 1840, HHStA, StK, Preussen 176; Metternich to Stürmer, Vienna,
13 Nov. 1840, HHStA, StA, Türkei VI, 78; Beauvale to Palmerston, Vienna, 8 Oct.
and 14 Nov. 1840, TNA, FO 120/189; Maltzan to Frederick William IV, Vienna,
9 Oct. 1840, GStA PK, HA III, MdA I, 6033; Tatishchev to Nesselrode, Vienna,
10 Oct. 1840, AVPRI, fond 133, Kantseliariia, opis 469, 1840/178; Lerchenfeld to
Ludwig I of Bavaria, Vienna, 10, 17, 19, 28 and 30 Oct., 13 Nov. 1840, BHStA,
MA, Wien 2409.
[29] Metternich to Stürmer, Vienna, 13 Nov. 1840, HHStA, StA, Türkei VI, 78.

town by means of an unexpected attack had arisen and he asked Frederick for cooperation. The archduke immediately agreed and, having obtained Bandiera's consent, joined the action. Under the cover of darkness, he disembarked with approximately 112 Austrians in the same place where Duke Leopold V of Austria had distinguished himself with an attack against the Tour des Mouches in 1191 during the third crusade; Walker went ashore farther westward. The wall before the Austrians had actually been abandoned by the defenders but the gate remained closed. Fortunately for the attackers, a window next to the gate serving now as an embrasure for artillery remained opened. First Frederick with his retinue behind him got through the window into the town, and, making their way through the tortuous backstreets among sleeping Egyptian soldiers, arrived at the main part of the citadel which they occupied without resistance. When the preparations for defence against an eventual counterattack were made, the archduke ordered the Ottoman flag to be raised with the Austrian flag on the right and the British flag on the left. The scene was lit up at dawn and celebrated with 21 salutatory cannon shots from the *Guerriera* and soon afterwards from other ships of the allied fleet. At that time Walker's British-Ottoman detachment arrived. When the Egyptians learnt of the capture during the night, they immediately capitulated. Their losses were considerable – 2,000 dead or wounded owing to the bombardment and the explosion of the powder magazine from the previous day and 3,000 captive, whereas the allies only had 21 dead and 41 wounded, of whom the Austrians lost but two dead and six wounded. The fact that Acre was captured on 4 November when Archduke Charles celebrated his name day was a symbolic accomplishment of the Austrian squadron's successful actions on the Syrian coast and a fitting tribute of the brave son to his famous father. The Austrian warships sailed for Beirut on 6 November and in the first week of December the whole allied fleet left the Syrian coast where 300 British and 200 Austrian sailors were left to garrison duty in selected forts. The participation of the Austrian squadron therefore ended in practice; officially it was terminated on 15 March 1841 when Bandiera obtained the order to terminate his subordinated position to Stopford.[30]

---

[30] Stürmer to Metternich, Constantinople, 11 Nov. 1840, HHStA, StA, Türkei VI, 77; R. Basch-Ritter, *Österreich auf allen Meeren: Geschichte der k. (u.) k. Kriegs-*

As already mentioned above, Austria's participation in the Syrian campaign was symbolic and it is not possible to ascribe to its squadron the victory that was mainly achieved due to the large British fleet and the numerous Ottoman land troops and the active support of the Syrian insurgents. The second extreme would be an absolute omission of its positive contribution to the final success as is usual among a considerable number of historians, in particular English-speaking ones, who are prone to forget Frederick's bravery in Acre. This seems to be caused by their considerable reliance on Sir Charles Napier's book *The War in Syria* upon which they based their own work. Despite the fact that Napier was on very cordial terms with Bandiera and Frederick, he entirely concealed the latter's heroic deed during the night of 3 to 4 November.[31] Consequently, for example, British historian John Arthur Ransome Marriot ascribed the fall of the fortress to the bombardment from the sea and placed it on 3 November.[32] American scholar Letitia W. Ufford mentioned Frederick's night-time exploit, but in her opinion, without offering any evidence for her claim, the British were the first who reached the citadel and raised the flag, whereas Frederick arrived and raised his flag later "in his carefully orchestrated role."[33] However, regarding the high number of persuasive sources, there can be no doubt that the story praising the young archduke is entirely warranted and there is no reason to deny it. Although not decisive for the result of the campaign, the bravery of Frederick and other Austrians was admirable and rightfully became a glorious chapter of Austria's military history. Metternich wrote to Bandiera on 25 November: "It is not only your sovereign and your country that are pleased to acclaim your extraordinary merits. England applauds them no less. It acknowledges that it is not the power of the Austrian squadron in terms of numbers but the valour and the courage of its men, the wisdom of its commander and its sincere and loyal coopera-

---

marine von 1382 bis 1918, Graz, Wien, Köln 1987, p. 50; A. von Jochmus, *Der Verfall des Osmanen-Reiches seit 1840*, Frankfurt am Main 1858, p. 31; J. B. Schels, "Saint Jean d'Acre 1291–1840," *Österreichische Militärische Zeitschrift* 5, 1841, pp. 158–161; Bergmann, pp. 37–42; Dauber, p. 106; Fischer, p. 116; Khuepach, pp. 255–265; Scholl, p. 54; Vimercati, p. 46.

[31] Sir C. Napier, *The War in Syria*, I, London 1842, pp. 204–211.

[32] J. A. R. Marriot, *The Eastern Question: An Historical Study in European Diplomacy*, Oxford 1924, p. 243.

[33] Ufford, p. 179.

tion that significantly contributed to the success of a campaign equally as glorious for the united forces."[34] Great Britain's recognition of the squadron's conduct mentioned by Metternich came on 5 November from Stopford[35] who also communicated to Bandiera the praise from the British Admiralty in December: "I have great pleasure in conveying to Your Excellency by desire of the Lords Commissioners of the Admiralty, their Lordships' warmest thanks and high gratification for the services the Squadron under Your orders have [*sic*] performed, and Your cordial cooperation in the various operations on the coast of the Syria, more especially at the capture of St. Jean d'Acre, and their Lordships desire their best acknowledgments for the manner in which Your Excellency and His Royal Imperial Highness the Archduke Frederick and the Officers performed the Services allotted to You."[36] The courage of the archduke and other Austrian marines found a positive echo among young men from aristocratic as well as middle-class families in the transalpine provinces of the Habsburg Monarchy; they started to enter the naval service in considerably higher numbers after 1840 and balanced the by then predominating Italian character of the Austrian navy.[37] Metternich was aware of the significance of its deployment on the Syrian coast in attracting recruits: "The Austrian navy has a limited existence. The opportunity to show itself to be worthy of its flag was a stroke of good fortune for this branch of the armed forces. By satisfying the wishes of His Imperial Majesty through its services it could not have obtained more a flattering testimony of its abilities and one of which it could be more proud than the British navy of its own."[38]

When Frederick returned to Vienna and appeared on 9 March 1841 in the imperial box of the Hofburg theatre accompanied by his father and the emperor, the audience rewarded his chivalrous deeds from the previous autumn with a spontaneous, rousing and long ovation.[39] Metternich himself was pleased with Frederick's conduct and

34 Metternich to Bandiera, Vienna, 25 Nov. 1840, HHStA, StA, Türkei VI, 78.
35 Stopford to Bandiera, Acre, 5 Nov. 1840, HHStA, StA, Türkei VI, 83.
36 Stopford to Bandiera, [?], 17 Dec. 1840, HHStA, StA, Türkei VI, 83.
37 Basch-Ritter, p. 48.
38 Metternich to Esterházy, Vienna, 15 Feb. 1841, HHStA, StA, England 236.
39 Report from Vienna, 10 March 1841, SS, HD, SG, Wien 94; Lerchenfeld to Ludwig I of Bavaria, Vienna, 12 March 1841, BHStA, MA, Wien 2410; Maltzan to Frederick William IV, Vienna, 12 March 1841, GStA PK, HA III, MdA I, 6034;

particularly his exploits in Acre because the chancellor correctly understood the significance of its seizure: "After the fall of Acre, the object of which was Syria, the enterprise is, in our opinion concluded. This province is thereby returned to the sultan. There is no one in France who could dispute this and they will have to regret the illusions they had about the Egyptian forces."[40] Metternich also noticed Frederick's forgiving gesture when raising the British flag together with the Austrian one, which was a reaction to the dispute between Leopold V of Austria and King Richard I of England in 1191. When the former had demanded the same position as the English and French kings, he had been rejected and his flag torn down from the ramparts of Acre on Richard I's order. When Richard I had been returning home through Austria, Leopold V imprisoned him and one of the charges was the insult of throwing down his banner at Acre. Archduke Frederick thus put an end to an old grievance between Austria and England in a chivalrous manner with flags on either side of the Ottoman flag. This fact increased Metternich's satisfaction with the result of the campaign, most probably because it symbolised the Austro-British amity always desirable and useful for him in the Eastern Question.[41] The chancellor, with reference to the story of the third crusade, stated with some exaggeration: "Young Frederick had good fortune; it only remains to him now to conquer the Holy Sepulchre."[42]

O'Sullivan to Lebeau, Vienna, 15 March 1841, ADA, CP, Autriche 8.

[40] Metternich to Stürmer, Vienna, 25 Nov. 1840, HHStA, StA, Türkei VI, 78.

[41] Metternich to Apponyi, Vienna, 21 Nov. 1840, HHStA, StA, Frankreich 319; Metternich to Esterházy, Vienna, 21 Nov. 1840, HHStA, StA, England 231; Metternich to Erberg, Vienna, 24 Nov. 1840, HHStA, StK, Preussen 176; Metternich to [?], Vienna, 24 Nov. 1840, NA, RAM-AC 12, 5; Lerchenfeld to Ludwig I of Bavaria, Vienna, 25 Nov. 1840, BHStA, MA, Wien 2409; Maltzan to Frederick William IV, Vienna, 30 Nov. 1840, GStA PK, Rep. 81 Gesandschaften (Residenturen) u. (General-) Konsulate nach 1807, Gesandschaft Wien II, 201/4; J. Eschler, "Die Syrische Expedition im Jahre 1840 und Österreichs Beteiligung daran," *Jahres-Bericht der n.-ö. Landes-Oberrealschule und der mit ihr verbundenen Wiener-Neustadt*, Wiener Neustadt 1915, p. 66.

[42] Metternich to [?], Vienna, 24 Nov. 1840, NA, RAM-AC 12, 5.

Mohammed Ali Surrenders

As Metternich predicted, the capture of Acre destroyed Mohammed Ali's power in Syria and caused his defeat. The surprising allied victory forced Ibrahim Pasha to withdraw his forces from Jaffa, Jerusalem and Aleppo to Damascus by the end of November, and the continuing pressure of the allied troops and the hostile actions of the insurgents finally caused him to retreat from Syria to Egypt, which started at the end of December. In this case Ibrahim Pasha proved his military talent when he escaped his pursuers and returned to Egypt with the rest of his army in February 1841. Mohammed Ali was of the same opinion as Metternich of the consequences of the fall of Acre, and when he received this news, together with that of the resignation of Thiers' ministry, he realised only too well that his fighting was at an end and he willingly concluded a convention with Napier in Alexandria on 27 November 1840 in which he pledged to withdraw his troops from Syria and return the sultan's fleet. In exchange, Napier promised the recognition of Mohammed Ali's hereditary tenure of Egypt by the Porte, the suspension of military operations against the retreating Egyptian army and the provision of several ships for the transport of wounded Egyptian soldiers.[43]

Napier acted in this matter on his own account and the Convention he signed met with stout resistance from Ponsonby, Stopford, Stürmer and Reshid, all of them criticising the commodore for usurping the right which belonged to the sultan alone when he promised to the pasha the hereditary tenure of Egypt. Stopford immediately invalidated it and Reshid refused to recognise it or agree to the cessation of hostilities with Mohammed Ali. Metternich also disagreed with Napier's conduct in Alexandria for the very same reason. He considered the Convention to be a mistake in principle because only an Ottoman officer commissioned by the sultan could discuss and settle the matter with the Egyptian governor. If the pasha submitted to the sultan's will in presence of the Ottoman officer, then he could obtain a pardon and the Great Powers could recommend the hereditary

---

[43] *Convention passée entre le commodore Napier, commandant les forces navales de S. M. Britannique devant Alexandrie et S. Exc. Boghos Bey, chargé d'affaires spécial de S. A. le Vice-Roi d'Égypte, signée à Alexandrie le 27 novembre 1840*, N. Bordeano, *L'Égypte d'aprés les Traités de 1840-41*, Constantinople 1869, pp. 40–41; Kutluoğlu, p. 173; Napier, I, pp. 282–283.

tenure of Egypt for him and his descendants. Since October, when the victory in Syria seemed to be more and more probable, Metternich had maintained that Mohammed Ali and not Abdülmecid I had to make the first step in this respect. Therefore, he did not support Palmerston's instructions to Ponsonby of 15 October recommending the sultan to pardon the pasha and give him Egypt in hereditary tenure. He agreed with the objective but not the form, and the only correct way was to await Mohammed Ali's compliance and then say a good word in Constantinople for the sultan's concessions. British historians Sir Charles Kingsley Webster and John Marlowe saw beyond this attitude the alleged instability of Metternich's opinions turning like a weathervane according to the situation in international affairs.[44] In this case, however, one must see in this attitude more Metternich's former emphasis on the sultan's sovereign rights as, for example, a year before in the Straits Question. After Mohammed Ali's deposal on 14 September, the chancellor did not change his attitude in the question of the method of his reinstatement in Egypt. Precisely for this continuing regard for the sovereignty of the Ottoman Empire, Metternich considered the rejection of this agreement by the Porte as entirely justified,[45] called Napier an "amateur diplomat"[46] and condemned his conduct as an "inconceivable stupidity"[47] and an "act of

---

[44] Marlowe, pp. 280–281; Webster, *Palmerston*, II, p. 729.

[45] Metternich to Neumann, Vienna, 19 and 30 Oct. 1840, Metternich to Esterházy, Vienna, 31 Oct. and 21 Dec. 1840, HHStA, StA, England 231; Metternich to Apponyi, Vienna, 23 Oct. and 8 Nov. 1840, HHStA, StA, Frankreich 319; Metternich to Trauttmannsdorff, Vienna, 27 Oct. 1840, Metternich to Erberg, Vienna, 1 Nov. and 22 Dec. 1840, HHStA, StK, Preussen 176; Palmerston to Ponsonby, London, 15 Oct. 1840, Metternich to Stürmer, Vienna, 30 Oct. 1840, HHStA, StA, Türkei VI, 78; Ponsonby to Stürmer, Constantinople, 6 Dec. 1840, Ponsonby to Napier, Therapia, 7 Dec. 1840, the Porte to Stürmer, Therapia, 8 Dec. 1840, Stürmer to Metternich, Constantinople, 8 and 10 Dec. 1840, HHStA, StA, Türkei VI, 77; Beauvale to Palmerston, Vienna, 28 Oct. 1840, TNA, FO 120/189; Bockelberg to Frederick William IV, Vienna, 31 Oct. and 4 Nov. 1840, GStA PK, HA III, MdA I, 7359; Maltzan to Frederick William IV, Vienna, 18 Dec. 1840, GStA PK, Rep. 81 Gesandschaften (Residenturen) u. (General-) Konsulate nach 1807, Gesandschaft Wien II, 201/4; Tatishchev to Nesselrode, Vienna, 4 and 30 Nov. 1840, AVPRI, fond 133, Kantseliariia, opis 469, 1840/178; Lerchenfeld to Ludwig I of Bavaria, Vienna, 13 Nov. and 25 Dec. 1840, BHStA, MA, Wien 2409; O'Sullivan to Lebeau, Vienna, 16 Nov. 1840, ADA, CP, Autriche 7; Sainte-Aulaire to Guizot, Vienna, 26 and 30 Dec. 1840, AMAE, CP, Autriche 428.

[46] Metternich to Apponyi, Vienna, 21 Dec. 1840, HHStA, StA, Frankreich 319.

[47] Metternich to Stürmer, Vienna, 23 Dec. 1840, HHStA, StA, Türkei VI, 78.

insanity."[48] He wrote to Stürmer: "Commodore Napier's stupidity is a new and illustrious example of the risks to which men of action are exposed when they allow themselves to be carried away by a spirit of adventure, and he is consequently unable to apply good judgement, which a sense of discipline imposes on more capable individuals."[49]

Although Metternich disagreed with the way Napier's Convention was created, he was satisfied with most of its terms and did not object to Mohammed Ali's submission itself, which he regarded as a sign of the desired restoration of peace in the Near East and good relations among the European Powers. What remained was to find an appropriate form, which happened on 14 November when the diplomats negotiating in London agreed upon the conditions under which Mohammed Ali could preserve his rule over Egypt. They were in essence identical to those mentioned in the Convention concluded in Alexandria. The initiator of this action was Baron Neumann, who saw in this step a potential way out of the crisis. On the same day, Palmerston instructed Stopford to send an officer to the pasha with the assurance that if he submitted at once and proved it with the restoration of the sultan's fleet and the evacuation of his army from all the provinces except Egypt, the four Powers would secure in Constantinople his reinstatement as Egyptian governor. Regarding his heredity title, the officer was instructed not to refuse it but also not to discuss it, as it was under the sultan's jurisdiction. This was an evident concession to Metternich, which is also shown in the end of Palmerston's instructions: "Nevertheless, in order to make still more apparent the just respect which is due to the rights of His Highness, the Cabinet in Vienna is of the opinion that the advice which the representatives of the Four Powers should be called upon to address to the Divan, relative to the reinstatement of Mehemet Ali [sic] in the pachalic [sic] of Egypt, ought not to be put forth at Constantinople until after Mehemet Ali [sic] has taken the preliminary step of applying to his sovereign for pardon, submitting himself to the determination of His Highness. Taking into consideration that this opinion of the Cabinet of Vienna serves as fresh proof of the respect with which the Courts, parties to the Convention of July 15, have for the inviolability of the

[48] Ibid.
[49] Ibid.

sultan's rights of sovereignty and independence."[50] In Alexandria on 8 December 1840, Mohammed Ali agreed to the terms presented by the British officer, Captain Edward Fanshawe. Three days later, the pasha sent a letter to the grand vizier in which he assured the Porte of his loyalty, Ibrahim Pasha's withdrawal from Syria and the actual preparations in the Alexandrian port for the departure of the Turkish fleet. Metternich was fully satisfied with this course of events during which Mohammed Ali yielded and the sultan's sovereignty remained preserved.[51]

* * *

Austria's military participation in the war in Syria in 1840 proves that Metternich attributed to the Second Mohammed Ali Crisis and its outcome such considerable importance for Austria's interests that he allowed the deployment of the Austrian naval squadron against the easternmost part of the Mediterranean. It is true that he hesitated at the very beginning to meet Palmerston's request and offer assistance to the British and Turkish armed forces because he was convinced of the superiority of Mohammed Ali's army and the impossibility of crushing it without France's participation. Additionally, he worried about France's negative reaction to the use of coercive measures without its consent. One also cannot overlook the opposition to a military adventure in the Near East among some Austrians themselves led by Kolowrat, an opposition that already existed in the spring of 1840 and later developed into an open attack against Metter-

---

[50] Napier, II, p. 15.

[51] Metternich to Stürmer, Vienna, 18 Dec. 1840, HHStA, StA, Türkei VI, 78; Metternich to Esterházy, Vienna, 18 Dec. 1840, HHStA, StA, England 231; Metternich to Erberg, Vienna, 22 Dec. 1840, HHStA, StK, Preussen 176; Mohammed Ali to Rauf Pasha, Alexandria, 11 Dec. 1840, Stürmer to Metternich, Constantinople, 16 and 23 Dec. 1840, HHStA, StA, Türkei VI, 77; Maltzan to Frederick William IV, Vienna, 22 Dec. 1840, GStA PK, HA III, MdA I, 6033; Cetto to Ludwig I of Bavaria, London, 17 Nov. 1840, BHStA, MA, London 2235; Lerchenfeld to Ludwig I of Bavaria, Vienna, 25 Dec. 1840, BHStA, MA, Wien 2409; Sainte-Aulaire to Guizot, Vienna, 26 Dec. 1840, AMAE, CP, Autriche 428; Maltzan to Frederick William IV, Vienna, 30 Dec. 1840, GStA PK, HA III, MdA I, 7361; Metternich to Sainte-Aulaire, Vienna, 30 Dec. 1840, AMAE, CP, Autriche 428; Kutluoğlu, p. 174.

nich's Near Eastern policy in general. Nevertheless, when Metternich realised that France would not cooperate in pursuing the goal that he regarded as necessary for the maintenance of a stable and peaceful situation in the Levant, one could even say the very preservation of the Ottoman Empire, he decided to take part in the military intervention because it was in the interest not only of the Porte but also of Austria to do so. And although he did not agree with the measures like the deposal of Mohammed Ali which were impracticable, inexecutable and threatening to the situation in Europe, he was faint-hearted neither before nor after the outbreak of the Rhine Crisis and advocated the quick accomplishment of the military intervention because it offered a way out of the crises in the Near East as well as the West. Moreover, he realised that such a military intervention could increase Austria's influence in the Ottoman Empire, and for this reason, as explained in Chapter 21, he pressed for the employment of Austrian officers and doctors in the Levant, although finally without the expected success. On the other hand, he could be satisfied with the operation of the Austrian naval squadron and Archduke Frederick in particular on the Syrian coast, and he fully realised the significance of the courage of Austrian marines and the chivalrous prince to public opinion in Europe as well as in Austria itself. Above all, he could be content with the result of the military intervention that moved Mohammed Ali to submission and France to moderation. At the end of 1840, the crisis entered thus its final phase.

The Damascus Affair

The conflict between Alexandria and Constantinople from 1839 to 1841 became an important episode in the history of the Eastern Question not only for its political consequences in both the East and the West but also because it led to the European Powers paying considerably more attention to the religious affairs of the Levant and the various religious-humanitarian-political plans concerning the future of the Ottoman non-Moslem communities in Western society spreading with similar force as had happened during the Greek fight for independence. The primary concern was for the Syrian Christians and was mainly provoked by Syria's return to the sultan's direct rule on the turn of 1840. The first wave of interest, however, had arisen earlier in the year in connection with the persecution of the Jews in Damascus. Their misfortune provoked various reactions in Europe, sympathetic as well as anti-Semitic. Metternich not only ranked among those sympathetic to the plight of the Jews, but he was also fully involved in the affair from the very beginning and actively tried to save the persecuted Jews from injustice and oppression.

Metternich, the Jews and the Damascus Blood Libel

The history of the Damascus Affair began shortly after the disappearance of the Capuchin friar, Tommaso, and his servant, Ibrahim Amara, on 5 February 1840, allegedly in the Jewish quarter of this city. The Jewish inhabitants were accused of murdering both men for their blood for the bread for the Jewish Passover. Anti-Jewish attitudes led to riots, sacking, imprisonment and extremely brutal questioning with the use of torture that resulted in forced confessions, conversion to Islam and even death. When the blood of Tommaso and his servant, this crucial proof of guilt, was not found in any house in the Jewish quarter, around 63 Jewish children were arrested with the aim of forcing their mothers to reveal the hiding place. The mistake of local authorities, however, was the seizure of the Jewish merchant and Austrian citizen, Isaac Picciotto, on 7 March, which marked a new phase of the affair because the Ottomans were not entitled to take such a measure since the Austro-Ottoman agreements excluded Austrian citizens from Ottoman jurisdiction.[1]

This step prompted the immediate intervention of Laurin in aid of not only Picciotto but also other persecuted inhabitants of Damascus. Observing the whole affair from Alexandria, he did so because of his duty to protect Austrian citizens as well as his personal opinion of the inconclusiveness of forced confessions. His intervention from March until April 1840 was extremely important because he was the only European diplomat in the Levant who decidedly intervened on the side of the accused Jews at that time; he never hesitated and never waited, and he did not demand a pardon but justice. His effort was finally rewarded with partial success when he moved Mohammed Ali to stop the brutal questioning. At the end of May a considerable number of those held were set free, but nine Jews still remained in prison. Laurin's other important move was the dispatch of reports from Damascus to the Austrian consul general in Paris, Baron James de Rothschild, who decided to publish them in newspapers and thus draw attention to the atrocities committed within the Ottoman territory. The importance of this step lay in the fact that Austrian reports offered Europeans a new insight into the events in Damascus because until then, particularly in France, the source of information had been French diplomatic correspondence supporting the charge against the Jewish inhabitants.[2]

---

[1] J. Frankel, *The Damascus Affair: "Ritual Murder," Politics, and the Jews in 1840*, Cambridge, New York, Melbourne 1997, pp. 19–91.

[2] Laurin to Stürmer, Alexandria, 27 March 1840, Gelber, p. 229; Laurin to James Rothschild, Alexandria, 5 April 1840, Gelber, pp. 232–233; Laurin to Stürmer, Alexandria, 3 and 6 May 1840, Gelber, pp. 239–249; James Rothschild to Salomon Rothschild, Paris, 7 May 1840, Gelber, pp. 241–242; Laurin to Carl Meyer Rothschild, Alexandria, 6 May 1840, J. Frankel, "A Historiographical Oversight: The Austrian Consul-General and the Damascus Blood Libel (with the Laurin-Rothschild Correspondence, 1840)," A. Rapoport-Albert, S. J. Zipperstein (eds.), *Jewish History: Essays in Honour of Chimen Abramsky*, London 1988, p. 301; R. Erb, "Die »Damaskus-Affäre« 1840 und die Bedeutung des Hauses Rothschild für die Mobilisierung der öffentlichen Meinung," G. Henberges (ed.), *Die Rothschilds: Beiträge zur Geschichte einer europäischen Familie*, Sigmaringen 1994, p. 107.

Laurin's goal was not only to stop the torture and have the prisoners released but also to prove that the whole accusation was groundless. Therefore, his next step was his advice of 5 May to James Rothschild to send an agent to the Ottoman Empire with the aim of helping to investigate the alleged crime, which is exactly what happened when Adolphe Crémieux, a member of the Jewish Consistory of France, and Sir Moses Montefiore, the president of the Board of Deputies of British Jews, decided to go to the Levant to act on behalf of the Damascus Jews, in other words to demand the release of the last nine prisoners and the opening of a fair trial. They arrived in Alexandria on 8 August 1840 where, in the meantime, the Austrian consul general had obtained consent from Mohammed Ali for their involvement.[3]

Until early May, Laurin certainly acted of his own accord because Metternich's first instructions on the matter were not sent from Vienna before 10 April 1840 when the Austrian chancellor personally interceded on the behalf of the suffering Jews. To be able to correctly understand Metternich's motivation, it is necessary to put his involvement in the Damascus Affair into a wider context of his personal attitude towards the Jews. The prevailing opinion is that Metternich was on good terms with them and generally did not express anti-Jewish sentiments. The single known negative statement was that of "a Jewish criminal" concerning a Moravian Jew, the writer, journalist and revolutionary Hermann Jellinek, who contributed to a radical newspaper in Vienna, *Der Radikale*, and after the defeat of the uprising in Vienna in 1848 was executed with the verbal approval of Metternich, who resided at that time as an emigré in London. This, however, does not mean that Metternich was hostile towards all Jews in general. First, he approved of the execution because Jellinek was a revolutionary, not because he was a Jew. Second, Metternich often added to men of revolutionary spirit information of their origin and therefore, expressions like "French revolutionaries" or "Italian criminals" can

---

[3] Laurin to Salomon Rothschild, Alexandria, 5 May 1840, Frankel, "A Historiographical Oversight," pp. 300–301; Laurin to Carl Meyer Rothschild, Alexandria, 25 May 1840, Frankel, "A Historiographical Oversight," pp. 302–303; H. Graetz, *Geschichte der Juden vom Beginn der Mendelssohnschen Zeit (1750) bis in die neueste Zeit (1848)*, XI, Leipzig 1900, p. 507; R. S. Simon, M. M. Laskier, S. Reguer, *The Jews of the Middle East and North Africa in Modern Times*, New York 2003, p. 22.

be found in his correspondence, in fact not indicating much about his attitude towards these nations as a whole. Any prejudices he may have had against the Jews were merely those that were also characteristically held by some Jews from higher social classes against some members of their own race.[4]

Metternich's disinterested attitude towards the members of the Jewish religion is more evident from his practical behaviour towards them, although not in the Austrian Empire itself where their affairs were entirely in the emperor's hands, and neither Francis I nor Ferdinand I were well disposed to them. Therefore, Metternich did not often dare to intervene on behalf of the Austrian Jews, for which he has later been criticised. Although this criticism is not unjustified, it is necessary to understand that the position of the Austrian chancellor entirely depended on the goodwill of his monarch, and when both above-mentioned emperors resolutely opposed a crucial change in the legal constraints concerning their Jewish subjects, Metternich generally did not want to risk his own future for an already lost cause that, frankly speaking, was not the most important part of his agenda. More useful could be the investigation of the situation of a Jewish community in his own domain in Königswart where in 1847 46 Jewish families lived, but the state of research on this topic is rather weak and the only fact which seems to be certain is that they were in no way oppressed.[5]

Considerably more on Metternich's attitude towards the Jews can be revealed from his conduct in regions beyond the limits of the Austrian Empire. In the diplomatic field, Metternich started to support Jews soon after his accession to the helm of Austrian diplomacy, particularly in Germany where he could take advantage of Austria's considerable influence. During the Napoleonic Wars, the Jews obtained civil rights equal to those of other citizens due to the French occupation of German states, and they naturally wanted to retain them also

---

[4]   Metternich to Laurin, Vienna, 10 April 1840, Gelber, pp. 233–234; Metternich to Stürmer, Vienna, 10 April 1840, Gelber, pp. 234–235; M. Grunwald, Vienna, Philadelphia 1936, p. 287; B. F. Pauley, *From Prejudice to Persecution: A History of Austrian Anti-Semitism*, Chapel Hill, London 1992, p. 20.

[5]   S. Dubnow, *Die neueste Geschichte des jüdischen Volkes: Das Zeitalter der ersten Reaktion und der zweiten Emanzipation (1815–1881)*, Berlin 1929, pp. 135–143; R. Švandrlík, *Historie Židů v Mariánských Lázních* [*The History of the Jews in Marienbad*], Mariánské Lázně 2005, p. 73.

after the fall of Napoleon. Metternich agreed with their request, but his support of their political emancipation often met with strong resistance from local administrations, for example in the former Hanseatic cities Hamburg, Lübeck and Bremen, which finally proved to be invincible. Consequently, during the Congress of Vienna in 1814–1815, the Congress of Aachen three years later and the ministerial conference in Vienna in 1820, the prince achieved no significant improvement in the legal status of the Jews.[6]

To the contrary, their demand for better civil rights evoked a strong resistance in academic circles and nationalist student associations (*Burschenschaften*) supporting anti-Semitic feelings throughout the German Confederation; just as a historical reminder: the members of these associations were militarily organised, carried daggers, burnt books and sometimes attacked peaceful inhabitants. In consequence of their activities and a deep-rooted prejudice as well as for economic reasons, an anti-Jewish outburst occurred in Würzburg at the beginning of August 1819. It is not surprising that the affair began at a local university where an elderly professor recently advocating the emancipation of the Jews saved his own life by running away from hostile students. Other pogroms followed soon in other German cities and even in Prague, Copenhagen, Cracow and Riga. These persecutions went down in history as the "Hep! Hep! Riots" after a widespread derogatory rallying cry against the Jews in Germany.[7] Metternich made a stand for the victimised Jewish citizens and demanded that the authorities responsible immediately put an end to the disgraceful situation that had got out of their control. The passivity of local police forces and city guards to the persecutions caused Metternich to become extremely concerned, and in the case of Frankfurt am Main he even threatened to send a confederate military garrison from Mainz into the city if its senate did not immediately stop the riots with its

---

[6] S. Baron, *Die Judenfrage auf dem Wiener Kongreß*, Wien, Berlin 1920, pp. 79–180; I. Kracauer, *Geschichte der Juden in Frankfurt a. M. (1150–1824)*, II, Frankfurt a. M. 1927, pp. 455–461 and 498–501; E. Sterling, *Judenhaß: Die Anfänge des politischen Antisemitismus in Deutschland (1815–1850)*, Frankfurt am Main 1969, p. 27; E. Timms, "The Pernicious Rift: Metternich and the Debate about Jewish Emancipation at the Congress of Vienna," *Year Book* (Leo Baeck Institute, Oxford) 46, 2001, pp. 8–16.
[7] "Hep! Hep! Jude verreck!" means in English "Death to all Jews!" A. Elon, *The Pity of It All: A Portrait of German Jews 1743–1933*, London 2002, p. 102.

own force, which the senates finally did in Frankfurt as well as other cities.[8] He also tried to help the Jews in the Apennines, namely in the Papal State where, in 1824, he put a great deal of energy into attempts to secure more humane treatment for the Jews, and in 1832 and 1833, he frustrated the plan for the separation of the Jews from the Christian population,[9] which led Salomon Rothschild to express this appreciation: "May God bestow his blessing upon Your Highness for the goodness You have shown to thousands."[10]

In the Ottoman Empire Metternich had no reason to intervene on behalf of the Jews before 1840, and his only active involvement in this respect was an annual remittance by mail of the amount of 580–595 florins gathered in Vienna in the form of a bill of exchange to a Jerusalem Jewish foundation taking care of poor Jews in the 1830s.[11] This passivity changed with the persecution of the Damascus Jews, which moved Metternich to intervene on their behalf. With the exception of the forwarding of the Austrian consular correspondence to Paris for the reason explained later in the chapter, he entirely approved of Laurin's conduct. He regarded the accusation of the ritual murder as completely absurd and although he did not know who had assassinated Father Tommaso and his servant, he found the whole investigation based upon forced confessions to be misguided and resulting from medieval preconceptions, religious fanaticism and attempts to seize the properties of the rich members of the Jewish community.[12] He wrote Laurin on 10 April: "The accusation of intentionally

---

[8] Ibid., pp. 101–103; P. Viereck, "Bulwark Against Potential Fascism," E. E. Kraehe (ed.), *The Metternich Controversy*, New York, Chicago, San Francisco, Atlanta, Dallas, Montreal, Toronto, London, Sydney 1971, pp. 89–93; Sterling, p. 164.

[9] Metternich to Lützow, Vienna, 13 July 1832, HHStA, StK, Rom 46; Reinerman, "Metternich and Reform," p. 541.

[10] E. C. Corti, *Der Aufstieg des Hauses Rothschild*, Wien 1954, p. 319.

[11] Metternich to Ottenfels, Vienna, 16 Nov. 1830, HHStA, StA, Türkei VIII, 2; Metternich to Ottenfels, Vienna, 2 Nov. 1831, HHStA, StA, Türkei VIII, 4; Metternich to Ottenfels, Vienna, 16 Nov. 1832, HHStA, StA, Türkei VIII, 5; Metternich to Stürmer, Vienna, 3 Dec. 1833 and 18 Nov. 1834, HHStA, StA, Türkei VIII, 6; Metternich to Stürmer, Vienna, 28 June and 13 Dec. 1836, HHStA, StA, Türkei VIII, 9; Metternich to Stürmer, Vienna, 13 Nov. 1838 and 12 Nov. 1839, HHStA, StA, Türkei VIII, 12; Metternich to Stürmer, Vienna, 1 Dec. 1840, HHStA, StA, Türkei VIII, 15.

[12] Metternich to Laurin, Vienna, 10 April 1840, Gelber, pp. 233–234; Metternich to Stürmer, Vienna, 10 April 1840, Gelber, pp. 234–235; Metternich to Laurin,

murdering Christians for the Passover blood ritual is so absurd in its nature, and the methods adopted by the governor of Damascus to prove such an unnatural crime were definitely so badly chosen, that nobody will be surprised if the actual guilty parties are not found and consequently the Egyptian local authorities are seen to be tainted with the accusation of pointless brutality."[13] On the same day he expressed himself in the same way in his instructions to Stürmer: "Like diseases, prejudices recur from time to time and break out here and there. So the news is reaching me right now simultaneously from Damascus and Rhodes[14] of atrocities which were committed by the authorities and people against the Israelites and probably are still being committed because of the old myth according to which they have been accused of seeking Christian blood for the forthcoming Jewish Passover and therefore murdered a Catholic priest here and a Greek boy there. Whether the murder was actually committed by them is naturally for me beside the question, but it is clear that it makes a poor impression when the authorities let themselves be carried away by the frenzy of such prejudices to such an extent that they exceed the limits of justice to the persecution of whole families and communities."[15] In his opinion it was "a duty for all governments to dispel the false rumours which people have spread attacking Jews and to forestall the revival of the hatred and persecution of Jews that reappeared in Germany in clashes in Würzburg and Frankfurt less than 25 years ago."[16]

Metternich was the first European statesman who intervened on the behalf of the Damascus Jews: he instructed Laurin to continue in the "rescue mission" and he himself tried to help them from his office at the Chancellery in Vienna. When Salomon Rothschild wrote to him in June 1840 that, three days before his disappearance, Father Tommaso had allegedly had a sharp dispute with some Moslems and shortly afterwards had been seen leaving the city with his servant,

---

Vienna, 27 May 1840, Gelber, pp. 243–244.

[13] Metternich to Laurin, Vienna, 10 April 1840, Gelber, p. 234.

[14] Simultaneously with the pogrom in Damascus, the persecution of the Jews occurred in Rhodes for identical reasons when a Greek Orthodox boy disappeared. Metternich also intervened on their behalf. Metternich to Stürmer, Vienna, 10 April 1840, Gelber, pp. 234–235; Frankel, *The Damascus Affair*, pp. 69–70.

[15] Metternich to Stürmer, Vienna, 10 April 1840, Gelber, pp. 234–235.

[16] Lerchenfeld to Ludwig I of Bavaria, Vienna, 22 May 1840, BHStA, MA, Wien 2409.

probably for fear of the Moslems' revenge, Metternich immediately requested the Vatican to find out whether both men were not hiding in any of the Syrian monasteries. However, this rumour later proved to be false. Soon afterwards, the Austrian chancellor intervened again in the Eternal City against the propagation of an anti-Jewish pamphlet published in Damascus by Greco-Catholic Patriarch Maximus that, according to Laurin, contained "the most obscure opinions of Christianity from the distant past."[17] Unfortunately, Austrian diplomacy encountered with both requests a rather reserved attitude from the Catholic Church; instead of any assistance came only criticism of Laurin's report containing information different from that in both the French diplomatic correspondence and the Catholic anti-Semitic press.[18]

Metternich ignored the reproof from the Vatican, did not hesitate to openly disagree with anti-Semite texts during talks with the Papal nuncio in Vienna and continued to publish news favourable to the Jews in the *Österreichischer Beobachter* and to influence the attitude of other newspapers within the Austrian Empire as well as beyond its frontiers in their favour. He also sent 4,000 florins from Salomon Rothschild to Damascus where they were distributed by the Austrian consul, Caspar Giovanne Merlato, to the afflicted Jews. Laurin was also instructed to offer every possible assistance and protection to Crémieux and Montefiore because Metternich was convinced that the solution of the murder was necessary for the vindication of the accused Jews in the eyes of public opinion. Although a fair trial was never held and the crime remained unresolved, the mission of both Jewish commissaries contributed to the release of the last Jewish prisoners on 6 September 1840. Montefiore's subsequent visit to Constantinople moved the sultan to issue a firman on 6 November denouncing the accusation of a ritual murder as gross libel and confirming the Ottoman Jews' security of life and property and the freedom of their faith. The credit for this decree and another in the summer of the following year against the harassment and oppression of the Jews in Syria can also

---

[17] Laurin to Metternich, Alexandria, 16 Aug. 1840, Gelber, p. 262.

[18] Salomon Rothschild to Metternich, Vienna, 12 June 1840, Gelber, p. 249; Metternich to Lützow, Vienna, 19 June 1840, Gelber, pp. 254–255; Merlato to Laurin, Damascus, 3 Aug. 1840, Gelber, p. 264; Erb, p. 108; Ferguson, *The House of Rothschild*, p. 397; Frankel, *The Damascus Affair*, p. 229.

be ascribed to Austrian diplomacy backing Montefiore in 1840 and trying to improve the living conditions of non-Moslems in the Levant in 1841.[19]

The Religious and European Context of the Damascus Affair

The Catholic Church's unwillingness to help the suffering Jews was in no way surprising in the context of the religious relations in the Near East. Although anti-Jewish incidents were not rare among the Moslems, they were not filled with dislike for the Jews for whom the animosity of the Ottoman Christians, Catholic as well as Orthodox, was considerably stronger. This strong aversion reaching the level of real hatred was confirmed by a considerable number of diplomats and travellers, who reported that a Jew in peril sought refuge in a Moslem's house rather than in that of a Christian. According to the British vice consul in Jerusalem, William Tanner Young, if a Jew dared to cross the threshold of the Church of the Holy Sepulchre, it would most probably cost him his life. A fitting summary of the relations among various confessions was offered by one European traveller when writing: "Moslem boys do not generally play with Christians and even the Christian children are divided among themselves. Those belonging to the Greek Church have their street games apart from those who belong to the Latin Church and they only unite to persecute the poor little Jew."[20] The Moslem authorities usually constrained the animosity of the Christians against the Jews and whenever this protective barrier

---

[19] Metternich to Stürmer, Vienna, 6 May 1840, HHStA, StA, Türkei VIII, 15; Merlato to Stürmer, Damascus, 20 July 1840, Stürmer to Metternich, Constantinople, 5 Aug. 1840, HHStA, StA, Türkei VIII, 14; Altieri to Lambruschini, Vienna, 22 May and 18 Dec. 1840, ASV, Arch. Nunz. Vienna 280C; the sultan's firman addressed to Tahir Pasha, the governor of Jerusalem, and the Jews of Jerusalem, attached to Königsmarck to Frederick William IV, Büyükdere, 7 July 1841, GStA PK, HA III, MdA I, 7284; Metternich to Laurin, Vienna, 27 May 1840, Gelber, pp. 243–244; Metternich to Laurin, Vienna, 11 July 1840, Gelber, pp. 260–261; C. Roth, *A Short History of the Jewish People*, Hartford 1969, p. 380; Dubnow, p. 313; Frankel, *The Damascus Affair*, pp. 137–139; Graetz, p. 492.

[20] T. Parfitt, *The Jews in Palestine 1800–1882*, Woodbridge, Wolfeboro 1987, p. 186.

disappeared, as for example in the Peloponnese and adjacent regions during the Greek insurrection, the consequences could be disastrous. The rebelling Greeks deliberately massacred not only Moslems but also Jews, both owing to religious and profit-seeking reasons. A number of Jews were even burnt to death after the fall of Tripoli in October 1821 into Greek hands. Metternich knew this very well, as it is evident from his instructions to Esterházy from January 1822: "It seems to be certain that several Jewish families were impaled and also burnt to death by these [Greek] brigands."[21] These poor relations among the Christians and the Jews further proved the validity of Metternich's thesis that the mutual dislike of the Ottoman non-Moslem communities made them more dangerous to each other than the Moslems actually were to them.[22]

Unsurprisingly, not Moslems but Christians, local as well as European foreigners, were the impetus of the anti-Jewish persecutions in Damascus. Their anti-Semitism could materialise exactly for the reason mentioned above: the failure of the Moslem administration. The governor of the city and Mohammed Ali's son-in-law, Sherif Pasha, did not want to alienate the Christians by assuring impartial treatment to the Jews and offend thus the outspoken protector of Catholicism in the Ottoman Empire, France, that had been directly involved in the persecutions since the very beginning due to the active participation of its consul in Damascus, Count Benoît Ulysse-Laurent-François Ratti-Menton. While Sherif Pasha acted merely according to duty, followed the practices usual for this region and did not seem to be motivated in his behaviour by any aversion to the Jews but rather by his desire not

---

[21] Metternich to Esterházy, Vienna, 29 Jan. 1822, HHStA, StA, England 166.
[22] Young to Palmerston, Jerusalem, 25 May 1839, A. M. Hyamson (ed.), *The British Consulate in Jerusalem in Relation to the Jews of Palestine 1838–1914, Part I: 1838–1861*, London 1939, p. 6; M. Ma'oz, "Changes in the Position of the Jewish Communities of Palestine and Syria in Mid-Nineteenth Century," M. Ma'oz (ed.), *Studies on Palestine during the Ottoman Period*, Jerusalem 1975, p. 147; M. Ma'oz, "Changing Relations between Jews, Muslims, and Christians during the Nineteenth Century, with Special Reference to Ottoman Syria and Palestine," A. Levy (ed.), *Jews, Turks, Ottomans: A Shared History, Fifteenth through the Twentieth Century*, New York 2002, pp. 108–119; M. Rozen, "The Ottoman Jews," S. N. Faroqhi (ed.), *The Cambridge History of Turkey, Volume 3: The Later Ottoman Empire, 1603–1839*, Cambridge 2006, pp. 256–271; Chamberlain, *Aberdeen*, p. 200; Douwes, pp. 193–203; Dubnow, p. 306; Frankel, *The Damascus Affair*, p. 65; Parfitt, p. 182.

to harm the good relations between Egypt and France so vital for Mohammed Ali at that time, Ratti-Menton on the other hand controlled the persecution from the very beginning and supported the brutal investigation pursued, as he said, with "an appropriate degree of severity."[23] He did so probably because of his own prejudice but certainly owing to his wish to assume the role of the protector of the Christians and increase the prestige of France among the local Catholics through this "witch-hunt."[24] It also was Ratti-Menton, who in early March initiated Picciotto's arrest, ransacked his house and accused Laurin and Merlato of taking money from the Jews for the support of their persecuted co-religionists. Laurin was thus forced to ask the French consul general in Egypt, Adrien-Louis Jules Cochelet, to stop Ratti-Menton's brutal, and in the case of Picciotto also illegal, actions and force him to respect the rights of the Austrian consulate for the protection of Austrian citizens. Moreover, in the case of Picciotto, Laurin was able to produce a decisive alibi. Cochelet, however, refused to satisfy this request and he also did not support Laurin's other pro-Jewish steps because, as he stated, the affair had already been solved and terminated. Therefore, Laurin in cooperation with Stürmer directed the same demand for the reprehension of Ratti-Menton to Pontois and the cabinet in Paris.[25]

Neither Pontois nor the French government were willing to censure anything in Ratti-Menton's behaviour and offer help to the Jews suffering in the Damascus prison. On the contrary, the latter even supported its consul's conduct and contributed to the seditious anti-Jewish campaign in the French Catholic as well as liberal press, thus playing a despicable role in the whole matter. Adolphe Thiers declared in the Chamber of Deputies that he himself believed that "the Jews

---

[23] Frankel, *The Damascus Affair*, p. 38.

[24] Ibid., pp. 57–60.

[25] Stürmer to Metternich, Constantinople, 13 May 1840, HHStA, StA, Türkei VI, 74; Cochelet to Laurin, Alexandria, 7 May 1840, attached to Königsmarck to Frederick William III, Büyükdere, 17 June 1840, GStA PK, HA III, MdA I, 1840, 7282; Pontois to Thiers, Therapia, 27 May 1840, AMAE, CP, Turquie 280; Laurin to Stürmer, Alexandria, 31 March 1840, Gelber, p. 230; Laurin to James Rothschild, Alexandria, 31 March 1840, Gelber, p. 231; Laurin to James Rothschild, Alexandria, 16 April 1840, Gelber, p. 235; Laurin to Stürmer, Alexandria, 3 May 1840, Gelber, p. 238; Stürmer to Pontois, Constantinople, 24 April 1840, Stürmer to Metternich, Constantinople, 29 April 1840, Gelber, p. 237; Erb, p. 106, Frankel, *The Damascus Affair*, p. 173.

committed a murder because of Christian blood for the Jewish religious ceremony"[26] and when James Rothschild and Adolphe Crémieux asked him for help, he replied that the motives for the Damascus persecution were justifiable and the Jews would do better if they let the matter die down. In late June 1840, Salomon Rothschild reacted bitterly to Thiers' address: "I blame the French minister in the face of civilised Europe for a lack of humanity."[27] The piteous behaviour of the French prime minister undoubtedly changed the whole affair into a prolonged dispute of major proportions. He assumed this attitude first because he really did seem to believe the anti-Semitic slander and second because he felt obliged to defend his own diplomat's conduct and not to admit his mistake. Thiers declared in the Chamber: "Until there is proof to the contrary, the cause of this agent [Ratti-Menton] is the cause of justice, the cause of France."[28] In other words the alleged national honour was preferred to justice, and the sentencing of the Jews became the cause of France, something which would be repeated several decades later in connection with the unfortunate Alfred Dreyfus.[29]

Even if it is unclear to what extent Thiers' obstinacy was caused by the publication of the Austrian reports from Damascus by James Rothschild, Metternich seemed to be correct in his criticism when he warned that such obduracy would prevent France from assuming a different position in silence, it would alienate this Power and Austria and make the solution of the affair more difficult. He personally remarked on the affair with the secretary of the French embassy in Vienna, Baron Émile de Langsdorff, but in a very diplomatic manner, declaring in early June: "It is impossible for me, and I believe that it also is impossible for every rational man, to decide from the distance in which we find ourselves by whom and how this unfortunate priest was assassinated. What all of us undoubtedly want is that the assassins are brought to justice and that the innocent, Jews or oth-

---

[26] Ferguson, *The House of Rothschild*, p. 397.
[27] Graetz, p. 501.
[28] Frankel, *The Damascus Affair*, p. 199.
[29] James Rothschild to Salomon Rothschild [?], Paris, 12 May 1840, Gelber, p. 243; J. Kalman, "Sensuality, Depravity, and Ritual Murder: The Damascus Blood Libel and Jews in France," *Jewish Social Studies* 13, 2007, 3, p. 37; Frankel, *The Damascus Affair*, pp. 188–190; Graetz, p. 490; Webster, *Palmerston*, II, p. 762.

erwise, are no longer tortured."[30] The documents reveal no sharper criticism of the French conduct and it is obvious that Metternich did not want to harm the Austro-French relations in any way owing to the Damascus Jews. Nevertheless, it is not true, as Jonathan Frankel claims, that the moderation of Metternich's criticism pronounced in the spring of 1840 was influenced by any fear of an existing threat of war between France and the German states;[31] the threat of war over Europe, the Rhine Crisis, appeared later in the year. In any case, Metternich was not deterred by Thiers' contradictory attitude and did not withdraw his protection of the Jews in any phase of the Damascus Affair, which was finally settled in compliance with most of his wishes, also for the reason that Laurin had succeeded in frustrating French intrigues against the mission of Crémieux and Montefiore in the Levant. Unsurprisingly, when Mohammed Ali's order to release the last prisoners came to Damascus, the French in this city were considerably displeased.[32]

The fact that must be emphasised is that Metternich's general pro-Jewish activities had their limits. If in the interest of humanity and justice he did not hesitate to come into conflict not only with the imperfections of the Ottoman administration but also, and in particular, the arbitrariness of the French king's diplomats, he nevertheless refused to support the dreams of a Palestinian autonomy or even the foundation of a Jewish state in Palestine, a Syrian-Palestinian kingdom, which were expressed during 1840 in British as well as continental newspapers as a result of both the Damascus Affair and the existing Near East crisis. The briefly sketched plans mostly from Evangelical circles met with minimal echo at the courts of European Powers with the certain exception of London where Lord Ashley, a passionate Evangelical with close contacts with the Foreign Office, "had since 1838 been crusading for the return of the Jews to Palestine under some Great Power protection."[33] Palmerston was briefly occupied with the support of Jewish immigration to Palestine and British protection of the Ottoman Jews. In the second half of 1840, he instructed Lord

---

[30] Langsdorff to Thiers, Vienna, 4 June 1840, AMAE, CP, Autriche 428.
[31] Frankel, *The Damascus Affair*, p. 123.
[32] Langsdorff to Thiers, Vienna, 27 May and 4 June 1840, AMAE, CP, Autriche 428; Laurin to Carl Meyer Rothschild, Alexandria, 17 July 1840, Frankel, "A Historiographical Oversight," p. 306; Erb, p. 108.
[33] Webster, *Palmerston*, II, p. 761.

Ponsonby to advise Abdülmecid I to support Jewish immigration to his provinces and obtain his consent to British protection of the Jews in Palestine. In Palmerston's opinion, the coming of rich Jews to the backward Ottoman Empire and their undisturbed existence assured by British protection would contribute to its regeneration. Nevertheless, the sultan was entirely uninterested in the benefits of Jewish immigration and did not support it; the possibility of a British protectorate over the Ottoman Jews was firmly refused. Abdülmecid I saw with reason in this proposal the danger of future British interference into the internal affairs of his empire. This was also the reason why Metternich disagreed with the idea of British protection as well as all other plans weakening the Ottoman administration or even totally ruining it. He justly pointed out that the foundation of an autonomous or even independent Jewish state in Palestine would invoke the resentment of local Christians and Moslems, who also considered Jerusalem to be their holy city and whose number in this place and adjacent regions was considerably greater; the Jews formed only a minority there.[34] In his opinion, similar plans were not feasible and, moreover, threatened the stability of the whole of the Ottoman Empire, the very opposite of the aim of the signatories of the London Convention and the reason why the Austrians and British were fighting in Syria against Mohammed Ali. Therefore, he made a stand against the aspirations of some dreamers and insisted on the preservation of the sultan's sovereignty over all of Syria including Jerusalem. Palmerston compromised with this view and gave up his plans for British protection because despite his sympathetic attitude towards Jews his primary goal was to maintain the integrity of the Ottoman Empire. Finally, owing to Metternich's and Palmerston's attitudes, the topic of the at that time chimerical idea of the foundation of a Jewish state in Palestine thus never became a subject of negotiation among the Great Powers in 1840–1841, and one must admit that no serious concern on this topic existed among the Jewish leaders themselves; their attitudes towards these speculations were rather reserved and most

---

[34] According to Austrian sources, there were 175,000 Jews in the whole of Syria in 1840, which was approximately 10 percent of total population. Laurin's report with the census of the Christian population in Syria, attached to Stürmer to Metternich, Constantinople, 18 Nov. 1840, HHStA, StA, Türkei VI, 77. However, only around 10,000 Jews lived in Palestine. Young to Palmerston, Jerusalem, 25 May 1839, Hyamson, p. 5.

of them were indifferent to the eventual international intervention in favour of the Palestinian Question. Neither in 1840 nor in the following year was a voice raised among them for the recovery of their biblical land.[35]

The Motivation behind Metternich's Assistance to the Persecuted Jews

Metternich's refusal to support these scarcely feasible plans do nothing to change the fact that Austria was the first Power that came out against the persecutions of the Damascus Jews, as was later proved by Crémieux's statement: "Austria was the first that offered a helping hand to the oppressed."[36] This definitely praiseworthy and effective defence, however, caused some historians to face the difficult question as to why the Austrian Empire, in whose own territory the Jews were discriminated, intervened in their favour in the Near East. They were also surprised at how such a "reactionary chancellor" could pay favourable attention to the Jewish population when, in contrast, the liberal-minded Adolphe Thiers expressed strongly anti-Jewish sentiments. Although they never denied the existence of humanitarian reasons, the same historians also did not settle for this explanation only and tried to find another one, for example that Metternich attempted to take advantage of the Damascus Affair to challenge the French claim to defend the interests of Catholics in Syria or to satisfy the

---

[35] Metternich to Guizot, Vienna, 8 Feb. 1841, Metternich to Lützow, Vienna, 14 Feb. 1841, HHStA, StK, Rom 67; Palmerston to Ponsonby, London, 11 Aug., 24 Nov. and 21 April 1840, Hyamson, pp. 33–35 and 40; Ponsonby to Palmerston, Constantinople, 21 Jan. and 1 Feb. 1841, Hyamson, pp. 35–37; H. Laurens, *La Question de Palestine, tome premier 1799–1922: L'intervention de la Terre Sainte*, Paris 1999, pp. 54–58; A. Schölch, "Europa und Palästina 1838–1917," H. Mejcher, A. Schölch (eds.), *Die Palästina-Frage 1917–1948*, München, Wien, Zürich 1993, p. 20; B. Tuchman, *Bible and Sword: England and Palestine from the Bronze Age to Balfour*, London 1988, p. 198; Dubnow, p. 315; Frankel, *The Damascus Affair*, pp. 392–393; Hajjar, p. 333; Webster, *Palmerston*, II, pp. 761–763.
[36] M. Eliav, "Das österreichische Konsulat in Jerusalem und die jüdische Bevölkerung," A. M. Drabek, M. Eliav, G. Stourzh (eds.), *Prag – Czernowitz – Jerusalem: Der österreichische Staat und die Juden vom Zeitalter des Absolutismus bis zum Ende der Monarchie*, Eisenstadt 1984, p. 37.

Rothschilds' request for help due to his close association with these Jewish bankers.[37]

To be able to apply unbiased judgement to the reasons for the Austrian assistance offered to the Jews in Damascus as well as other corners of the world, it is necessary to emphasise the fact that the credit does not belong to Austria as a whole but only to Metternich and his subordinated diplomats; the chancellor was the unrestricted author of Austrian foreign policy and his pro-Jewish measures were his private business. Therefore, although the mentally retarded Emperor Ferdinand I had no desire to improve the situation of his own Jewish subjects, he displayed no interest in those living beyond the frontiers of his empire and left their requests to Metternich's deliberation.

The opinion that Metternich tried to take advantage of the Damascus Affair for the struggle with France for influence over the Syrian Christians is erroneous. Although Metternich really did try to deprive France of its exclusive protection of the Syrian Catholics in 1840 and 1841 as will be explained in the following chapter, the intervention on behalf of the Jews cannot be associated with this matter. The reason is rather simple: the shouts in the Jewish quarter of Damascus after the release of last Jewish prisoners "up with Austria! Down with France! ... Hurrah for the Ottomans! Down with the Cross!"[38] surely could not move the Catholics to be sympathetic towards Austrian diplomats because, as mentioned above, the Christians regardless of their confessions disliked the Jews and were a driving force in their persecution in the Near East in 1840. Support of the Jews was thus entirely counter-productive for any attempt to obtain the support of the Syrian Christians, and Metternich never connected his attempt to deprive France of its position as sole protector of the Catholics with its prior misconduct towards the Damascus Jews, an attempt that he launched later in 1840 when the Damascus Affair already was over.

The connection between Metternich and the Rothschilds naturally was important in the whole affair, as well as in other matters relating to Jews. The chancellor cooperated closely with Salomon Roth-

---

[37] Ibid., p. 38; N. Ferguson, "Metternich and the Rothschilds: "A Dance with Torches on Powder Kegs"?" *Year Book* (Oxford, Leo Baeck Institute) 46, 2001, p. 49; Frankel, "A Historiographical Oversight," pp. 289 and 296–298; Graetz, p. 492.

[38] Frankel, *The Damascus Affair*, p. 361.

schild, who represented his influential family in Vienna after 1816 and performed the function of an informal financial advisor to the Viennese cabinet in internal as well as foreign affairs, including those concerning the Ottoman Empire as already seen in the case of the Stametz Affair or the deliberations about the loans for the Porte after 1829. This cooperation went far beyond the frame of mere formal contacts since the relations between Metternich and the family were rather cordial, a well-known fact leading even to the rumour in Rome in the autumn of 1829 that Salomon strived with the chancellor's approval for the sovereignty of Palestine, which the latter rightfully repudiated as entirely false. These close contacts as well as Metternich's support of the Jews abroad also led his contemporaries to the accusation that he accepted money from the Rothschilds. In fact, it was Friedrich von Gentz who obtained from these Jewish financiers substantial financial donations for his support of their co-religionists. Metternich himself, however, only borrowed from them and he paid back all the loans and sometimes he did so long before they fell due. Leaving aside the question of the conditions of these loans, a topic unresearched until this time, one must admit that Metternich and the members of his family occasionally received some gifts from the Rothschilds, but apparently not of any value that could influence any possible refusal on his part to intervene in the affairs of the Jews.[39]

While the imputation of bribery is without foundation, the extent of the Rothschilds' influence on the Austrian chancellor's pro-Jewish steps abroad, in other words whether he supported the Jews only because of the requests of this well-connected family is a more complicated problem to solve. A number of his interventions on behalf of Jews were certainly initiated and supported by the Rothschilds' appeals to the man whom they called "Uncle,"[40] as for example in the above-mentioned affairs within the German Confederation or the Papal State. Such requests were also important during the Damascus Affair but they were not a dominant factor in Metternich's decision-making. British historian Jonathan Frankel posed the

---

[39] Metternich to Lützow, Vienna, 14 Nov. 1829, HHStA, StK, Rom 38; Lützow to Metternich, Rome, 5 Dec. 1829, HHStA, StK, Rom 37; Spinola to Albani, Vienna, 14 Nov. 1829, ASV, Arch. Nunz. Vienna 256A; Ferguson, "Metternich and the Rothschilds," pp. 24–26; Grunwald, pp. 227–228; Timms, p. 13.

[40] R. Florence, *Blood Libel: The Damascus Affair of 1840*, Madison 2004, p. 136.

question whether Laurin so forcefully favoured the persecuted inhabitants of Damascus because of Metternich's relations with the Jewish bankers, naturally known to the Austrian consul general who could thus expect the approval of his conduct from the Chancellery in Vienna.[41] Undoubtedly ambition could also be a motive for Laurin's behaviour, but one should not underestimate a sense of humanity and compassion as a motivation to protect the accused Austrian citizen and halt an inhumane proceeding. Exactly for these reasons Metternich also intervened, but his unselfish motivation resulting from his dislike for law-breaking and inhuman treatment has always been underestimated because of the rather negative reputation of this statesman. Moreover, one cannot forget that Metternich was a rational man without prejudice in religious matters. Consequently, he had no antipathy towards the Jews and their faith, and he regarded as entirely ludicrous any prejudices such as the Jews' need for blood for the Passover bread. That is why he had no reason not to comply with the Rothschilds' request for assistance to the persecuted Jews abroad, and this family was thus easily able to obtain his agreement to do so. Close personal relations obviously played an important role but one must not forget three facts: First, there is no proof that he would have helped the suffering Jews for mercenary reasons; second, there is no sign that Metternich wrote his sympathetic instructions of 10 April 1840 due to Salomon's intervention and one can thus suppose that he did it of his own accord; third, if he had not wanted to help, that is if it had not been in accordance with his principles or interests to help the persecuted Jews, he would never have done so, and surely not in order to simply cooperate with the Jewish bankers in the economic affairs of the Habsburg Monarchy; in any case, any such cooperation could hardly have been affected by his eventual refusal to help because the Rothschilds took great pains to preserve good relations with Metternich at that time since the cooperation was also advantageous for them.[42] In short, the Rothschilds in themselves were not the only reason for Metternich's aid to their co-religionists in Damascus.

---

[41] Frankel, "A Historiographical Oversight," p. 297.

[42] Corti, pp. 263 and 315.

*   *   *

Metternich's personal views as well as his practical steps in matters concerning the Jews including the Damascus Affair clearly prove that he was not an anti-Semite. It is, however, necessary not to treat him as a pro-Jewish statesman with any special affection for this nation. This was not the case; his actions were not motivated by any extraordinary pro-Jewish sentiments but were due to a simple personal conviction that people of various confessions and nations ought to enjoy identical civil rights and freedoms, naturally limited in line with his conservative thinking, and he saw no reason why the Jews should be excluded from this presumption. In connection with the Ottoman Empire, Metternich's agreement with the emancipation of the Jews of course was different from what he advocated in Germany. His regard for the different structure of the Ottoman society and his belief that it was necessary to preserve its traditional composition in millets, as explained in Chapters 12 and 20, was also applied by him in their case. Furthermore, his respect for Ottoman sovereignty and independence made him view unfavourably any ideas of a Jewish autonomous or independent state or European protection of the Jews in Palestine. Such plans, however, were not very serious at that time and far less topical than similar projects concerning the Syrian Christians, which not only appeared on the turn of 1840 in the European public but were also discussed by the European cabinets, a problem that therefore occupied Metternich's attention considerably more than the future of the Syrian Jews.

29

The Syrian Question

The considerable increase in the Great Powers' interest in the future of the Christians in Syria gave rise to the so-called Syrian Question in late 1840. The reasons for their involvement were both humanitarian and political. The former resulted from the fact that Mohammed Ali and Ibrahim Pasha had introduced a regime of religious toleration and security for all Syrians irrespective of their religious affiliation, including the unprecedented equality of the Christians with local Moslems, but when the Egyptian rule over Syria was approaching its end due to the allied military intervention, the European cabinets started to worry about the Porte's ability to ensure the same living conditions to the local Christians that they had enjoyed for several preceding years. The political reason for the Great Powers' intervention resulted from their desire to increase their own influence by supporting various religious groups. As in the Damascus Affair, Austria was fully involved from the very beginning in the Syrian Question. Metternich tried to settle it in such a way that the Ottoman administration would be fully capable of ensuring the undisturbed existence of its Christian subjects on its own and that foreign interference in its religious affairs would thus be unnecessary. Although Metternich also wished to increase Austria's influence through its support of the Syrian Christians and of those in Mount Lebanon in particular, his approach was based upon his respect for Ottoman sovereignty and his dislike of the misuse of the religious card by European countries for their own self-interested goals, and furthermore, his extensive knowledge of the religious situation of the Levant resulted in a different approach from that of other Great Powers, which were led more by their selfish interests or, as in the case of Prussia, even religious fervour.

Austria's Interest in the Welfare of the Maronites

The beginning of Austrian diplomatic activities on behalf of the Christians in Syria was not in February 1840 as Mordechai Eliav incorrectly asserted[1] because there is no reference to the Syrian Christians in Metternich's letters or discussions with foreign diplomats until July 1840, with the one exception from the beginning of the year when he briefly discussed the issue with Altieri but with no real desire to support the Syrian Catholics at that time.[2]

Metternich's desire to help the Syrian Christians was not of course caused simply by his concern for their plight, but it should be recognised that this did help to motivate his first steps during the crisis. Although Mohammed Ali and Ibrahim Pasha were renowned for their tolerance and the situation of the Christians in the provinces under their rule had improved considerably, nevertheless, the construction of a large army and fleet gave rise to high taxes, forced conscriptions and forced labour that provoked numerous rebellions in the Syrian dominion.[3] These rebellions before 1840 had one thing in common: they were all suppressed by Ibrahim Pasha. The revolt in Mount Lebanon that lasted from May to July 1840 was no different, but it was distinguished by the fact that the Druze, whose religion had its roots in Islam and who had been a motivating force of the previous insurrections against Egyptian rule, did not participate in large numbers. In-

---

[1]   According to Mordechai Eliav, the topic should be contained in Metternich's alleged instructions to Stürmer and Meysenbug (not Meysenbuch as stated by Eliav) dated 6 February 1840. However, no instructions with such content exist. Eliav, p. 35.

[2]   Altieri to Lambruschini, Vienna, 3 Jan. 1840, ASV, Arch. Nunz. Vienna 280C.

[3]   Basic information on the Egyptian administration in Syria and the situation of the Christians in this region can be found in Y. Ben-Arieh, *Jerusalem in the 19th Century: The Old City*, Jerusalem 1984, pp. 107–109; G. Krämer, *Geschichte Palästinas: Von der osmanischen Eroberung bis zur Gründung des Staates Israel*, München 2003, p. 85; I. F. Harik, *Politics and Change in a Traditional Society Lebanon, 1711–1845*, Princeton, New Jersey 1968, pp. 244–245; P. K. Hitti, *Lebanon in History: From the Earliest Times to the Present*, London, New York 1957, pp. 428–432; M. Ma'oz, *Ottoman Reform in Syria and Palestine 1840–1861: The Impact of the Tanzimat on Politics and Society*, Oxford 1968, pp. 17–20; A. J. Rustum, "Syria under Mehemet Ali," *The American Journal of Semitic Languages and Literatures* 41, 1924, 1, pp. 41–49; Dodwell, pp. 248–258; Douwes, pp. 193–203.

stead, the Catholic Maronites had assumed the lead.[4] The displeased Egyptian governor made hostile statements about the latter, which was surprising because with respect to the Great Powers his words regarding the Christians had always been positive and conciliatory. Moreover, his declarations of rigorous measures against the rebels were accompanied by such a massive engagement of force in Lebanon that rumour spread among the Europeans in Alexandria that Mohammed Ali planned a war of extermination against the Maronites.[5]

Having heard this, Anton von Laurin visited the Egyptian governor on 23 June 1840, hoping to moderate his intentions against the insurgents. Mohammed Ali refused to temper his resolve, however, because, as he resolutely stated, the time for negotiating was over and it was time to take action. He declared that the Maronites were surrounded both by Egyptian forces and the Druze and would not escape their fate[6] and furthermore that the Druze would take advantage of victory to establish their own dominance in Lebanon. Alarmed by these threats of severity against the Maronites and given the long-lasting enmity between the Maronites and the Druze, Laurin feared that the former would be massacred and no one would be able to distinguish the innocent from the guilty. This prognosis was supported by the existing state of affairs in Lebanon where the Egyptian troops wilfully slaughtered a certain number of its innocent inhabitants when suppressing the revolt. As Laurin reported to Metternich, "in the country the Bedouins and Albanians [from the Egyptian army] operate and commit various outrages from cutting the fruit trees, ruining the plant and silk plantations to brutal seizures of men able to carry arms. The vast plains and valleys of Pekka and Esdraelon have

---

[4] The insurrection was caused by Mohammed Ali's attempt to deprive the Maronites of weapons given to them some time before for the fight against the Druze. The Egyptian governor later denied this accusation and declared that his order was misunderstood by Ibrahim Pasha who, however, did in fact request the delivery of the weapons from the Christians. Catafago to Laurin, Sidon, 2 June 1840, Laurin to Stürmer, Alexandria, 9 June 1840, HHStA, StA, Türkei VI, 74; H. Cobban, *The Making of Modern Lebanon*, London 1987, pp. 43–44.

[5] Laurin to Stürmer, Alexandria, 26 June 1840, HHStA, StA, Türkei VI, 74; Laurin to Metternich, Alexandria, 26 June 1840, HHStA, StA, Türkei VI, 78.

[6] According to Laurin's report from the autumn of 1840, there were 170,000 Maronites in Syria, most of them in Mount Lebanon. Laurin's report with the census of the Christian population in Syria, attached to Stürmer to Metternich, Constantinople, 18 Nov. 1840, HHStA, StA, Türkei VI, 77.

been without hands that could cultivate them for a long time, there
are no people or animals any more as all of them were hunted, shot
or slaughtered. The Maronites' peaceful settlements are attacked in
the same way."[7] Although Laurin did not presume Mohammed Ali
himself planned the destruction of this Catholic group for fear of Europe's response, his reports nevertheless produced exactly the same
rumour in Vienna as that already circulating in Alexandria. The Egyptian governor was said to want to annihilate all Christians, most of
them Maronites, and the prompt intervention of the Great Powers
was considered to be entirely necessary to avoid such a slaughter. It
is not clear whether Metternich actually believed this rumour but he
was surely aware of the serious situation of the Maronites. Moreover,
his interest in their future was increased by Reshid Pasha's question
addressed to the chancellor in mid July concerning the attitude the
Porte ought to assume towards them. Metternich advised the sultan
to promise clemency to the inhabitants of Mount Lebanon who would
rise up against the Egyptian oppression and to guarantee their ancient
privileges and relieve them of tax obligations for several years.[8] In his
opinion, nothing could prevent the acceptance of this recommendation made only with a view to "win over to its legitimate sovereign a
nation of interest due to its faith and loyalty and at the same time to
give to these people guarantees of their further peaceful existence."[9]

    This was the first step in Metternich's effort to achieve a better
future for the Maronites and for all Christians in Syria. At end of
August, he took a second step when he instructed Stürmer to send an
emissary to Lebanon to ascertain what demands the spiritual leader of
the Catholic nation, Patriarch Yusuf Hubeich, might require from the
Porte. Simultaneously, the emissary was to assure the patriarch that
if the Maronites expressed their loyalty to the Ottoman monarch, the
Austrian emperor would work to gain the sultan's assurance for their

---

[7]   The extract of Laurin's reports written on 18 and 19 June 1840, attached to
Metternich to Neumann, Vienna, 11 July 1840, HHStA, StA, England 230.
[8]   Metternich to Neumann, Vienna, 11 July 1840, Königswart, 31 July 1840, HH-
StA, StA, England 230; Stürmer to Metternich, Constantinople, 16 July 1840,
HHStA, StA, Türkei VI, 74; Lerchenfeld to Ludwig I of Bavaria, Vienna, 19 July
1840, BHStA, MA, Wien 2409; Struve to Nesselrode, Vienna, 19 July 1840, AVPRI,
fond 133, Kantseliariia, opis 469, 1840/178; Pontois to Thiers, Therapia, 7 Aug.
1840, AMAE, CP, Turquie 281.
[9]   Metternich to Stürmer, Königswart, 28 Aug. 1840, HHStA, StA, Türkei VI, 78.

privileges, autonomy and property, in short their future life in peace. By "loyalty" Metternich meant the military assistance required from the Christian inhabitants for the planned invasion of Syria by the British, Austrian and Turkish forces. The Maronite mountain tribesmen in Lebanon together with the Albanians were considered to be the best warriors in the Ottoman Empire, and an alliance with them would be very advantageous. To win them onto his side, Metternich did not hesitate to utilise the groundless rumour about their imminent extermination: "The Maronites are a very peaceful mountain people if they are not tormented, but they are fully resolved to rise against oppression. Moh[ammed] Ali has decided to exterminate these people; it is necessary to let them know, and they will be [informed]."[10] The Porte assented to the mission both because of its pro-Ottoman character and because of the previous discussions on the topic Stürmer had held with Reshid.[11]

Metternich's order was successfully carried out. On 16 September, Stürmer sent an adjutant dragoman, Anton Steindl von Plessenet, whose mother was a Maronite, to Lebanon to learn "the Maronites' wishes and to assure them that the Porte is prepared to grant them privileges, immunities, autonomy and everything that will be able to assure their peace and happiness."[12] He was instructed to ask the patriarch for a written report containing the privileges and prerogatives that the inhabitants of Lebanon desired to obtain from the Porte. On 26 September, Steindl arrived at the Bay of Djounie, 18 kilometers north of Beirut and soon visited Yusuf Hubeich, who by chance lived only two hours away from the anchorage. The Austrian agent informed Yusuf about the emperor's wish to support the threatened Catholic nation and asked him what his people desired from the government in Constantinople. The patriarch required the confirmation of ancient privileges, among them the demand not to be subordinate to any other patriarch, the right to found churches, convents and schools without

---

[10] Metternich to Neumann, Königswart, 25 Aug. 1840, HHStA, StA, England 230.
[11] Metternich to Erberg, Königswart, 26 Aug. 1840, HHStA, StK, Preussen 176; Metternich to Stürmer, Königswart, 28 Aug. 1840, HHStA, StA, Türkei VI, 78; Maltzan to Frederick William IV, Königswart, 7 Sept. 1840, GStA PK, Rep. 81 Gesandschaften (Residenturen) u. (General-) Konsulate nach 1807, Gesandschaft Wien II, 201/3.
[12] Stürmer to Metternich, Constantinople, 17 Sept. 1840, HHStA, StA, Türkei VI, 76.

restraint or the need to ask the sultan for a firman. Moreover, the patriarch raised a new claim that the prince of Lebanon be chosen only from among the Maronite leaders and not from the Greeks, Armenians, Druze or other nations. Furthermore, the Hatt-i Sharif of Gülhane (the Edict of the Rose Garden) prepared by Mustafa Reshid Pasha and promulgated by Abdülmecid I on 3 November 1839 that promised the establishment of guarantees for the security, honour and property of all the sultan's subjects whatever their religion, a new orderly system of taxation and a new system of conscription for the army[13] was to be activated and the existing taxes were to be abolished or reduced for several years to compensate for alleged suffering in previous years. All of these requests were made only verbally because Yusuf asked Steindl for time to prepare a written document. This document was not delivered until the end of October. Yusuf's claims were supported in Vienna since Metternich considered most of them to be just and reasonable, partly because the patriarch wanted only the confirmation of existing rights.[14]

With regard to the second goal of the mission, obtaining the Maronites' support for the war against the Egyptian forces, Steindl was also successful. Immediately after his visit, Yusuf called on the Catholic inhabitants to take up arms and he threatened anyone who would not obey with excommunication. The Maronites joined forces with the allies in their war against the Egyptians and significantly helped the sultan to regain Syria. The main reasons for the Maronites' support, however, were attributable in part to the aversion the mountain tribesmen felt to Ibrahim Pasha's rule and particularly to the activities of the British agent, Richard Wood, who had been sent

---

[13] Anderson, *The Great Powers*, pp. 59–62.
[14] Metternich to Ohms, Vienna, 7 Nov. 1840, HHStA, StK, Rom 64; Metternich to Stürmer, Vienna, 3 Nov. and 18 Dec. 1840, HHStA, StA, Türkei VI, 78; Steindl to Stürmer, Djounie, 7 Oct. 1840, HHStA, StK, Rom 64; Steindl to Stürmer, Beirut, 31 Oct. 1840, HHStA, StA, Türkei VI, 77; Stürmer to Metternich, Constantinople, 18 and 21 Oct. 1840, HHStA, StA, Türkei VI, 76; Stürmer to Metternich, Constantinople, 18 Nov. 1840, HHStA, StA, Türkei VI, 77; Altieri to Lambruschini, Vienna, 6 Nov. and 4 Dec. 1840, ASV, Arch. Nunz. Vienna 280C; Steindl to Wood, Djounie, 3 Oct. 1840, A. B. Cunningham (ed.), *The Early Correspondence of Richard Wood 1831–1841*, London 1966, p. 172; Wood to Ponsonby, Beirut, 29 Oct. 1840, Cunningham, *The Early Correspondence*, p. 179; A. Wandruszka, "Anton Steindl Ritter von Plessenet: Ein österreichischer Diplomat in der Levante," *MÖStA* 25, 1972, p. 452.

by Ponsonby to Lebanon to instigate the uprising of its inhabitants against the Egyptian administration and with whom Steindl was acquainted and had good relations. Consequently, it was not difficult for both men to act together for the desired result and provoke the Maronite uprising in the autumn of 1840.[15]

The Anti-French Bias Underlying Metternich's Religious Policy in the Levant

There was another important outcome of Steindl's mission. During the meeting, Yusuf complained that France as a Great Power had assumed the right of exclusive protectorate over Catholics not only in Lebanon, but also in the whole of Syria, yet it had done nothing for the Maronites recently except to advise them, in the patriarch's words, "not to return force with force, not to take arms, but to suffer peacefully."[16] Since Austria had sent ships to the Syrian coast and as a Catholic country desired the Maronites' prosperity, Yusuf suggested that after three centuries of French protection of the Lebanese Catholics, Austria should now assume the role of protector. He conveyed this desire also to Laurin, who had accompanied Steindl but had negotiated with the patriarch separately. Neither Austrian agent was instructed to discuss Austrian protectorship, however, so they answered evasively, sending the proposal to their superiors.[17]

The patriarch's offer was supported by the British who longed for an end to French influence in Syria and to be thus rid of their greatest rival. Austrian influence in this area was for them much more acceptable than that of the French. Therefore, Wood eagerly advised

---

[15] Stürmer to Metternich, Constantinople, 17 Sept. 1840, HHStA, StA, Türkei VI, 76; Steindl to Stürmer, Beirut, 31 Oct. 1840, HHStA, StA, Türkei VI, 77; Stürmer to Metternich, Constantinople, 2 and 18 Nov. 1840, HHStA, StA, Türkei VI, 77; Ponsonby to Wood, 16 Sept. 1840, Cunningham, *The Early Correspondence*, p. 163; Farah, *The Politics of Interventionism*, p. 37. A share in the achievement was accredited to Steindl also by Wood who stated that Steindl showed "the greatest zeal and anxiety to carry through the instructions of H. Exc. M. le Baron de Stürmer." Wood to Ponsonby, Djounie, 11 Oct. 1840, HHStA, StA, Türkei VI, 76.

[16] Steindl to Stürmer, Djounie, 7 Oct. 1840, HHStA, StK, Rom 64.

[17] Ibid.

Stürmer to accept the proposal by which the Austrian Empire would "gain an immense influence in Syria, an object not unworthy of the serious consideration of a great nation."[18] Lord Ponsonby also expressed the opinion of other British when he declared: "We are *intimately and firmly* united with Austria. It will be a good thing to establish Austrian influence over the Christians instead of that of the French."[19] Nevertheless, Stürmer's attitude towards the matter was reserved. In his opinion, Austria had no right to intervene at the Porte in favour of the Maronites and if it wanted to obtain such a right, the sultan would have to officially agree to Austrian protection, which would inevitably arouse the hostility of the French government. The internuncio maintained that Austria was currently the Maronites' intercessor in Constantinople and had actually become their protector instead of France, who had sacrificed them for Mohammed Ali's sake. In other words, Austria was their patron in practice and it was not necessary to hold this position officially. Moreover, once the Viennese cabinet had fulfilled the patriarch's wishes concerning his nation in the Ottoman capital, one could expect that the Maronites' situation would improve considerably and no foreign Power would need to be involved. As well as Laurin and Steindl, Stürmer also had no instructions enabling him to deal with Yusuf's proposal and he had to transmit Yusuf's question to Vienna. He refused to respond to the patriarch and only assured him that Austria would always support his requests at the Divan.[20] Metternich completely approved of this decision and wrote in the margin of Stürmer's report: "This is the correct form."[21]

Some historians who have generally paid too little attention to Austrian diplomatic correspondence and have relied too much on the French diplomats' reports have claimed that the main goal of Metternich's Syrian policy was to deprive France of its protection of the Syrian Catholics to the benefit of Austria.[22] Nevertheless, this assertion

---

[18] Wood to Ponsonby, Djounie, 11 Oct. 1840, HHStA, StA, Türkei VI, 76.

[19] Ponsonby to Wood, 1 Oct. 1840, Cunningham, *The Early Correspondence*, p. 171.

[20] Stürmer to Metternich, Constantinople, 21 Oct. 1840, HHStA, StA, Türkei VI, 76; Stürmer to Metternich, Constantinople, 18 Nov. 1840, HHStA, StA, Türkei VI, 77.

[21] Stürmer to Metternich, Constantinople, 21 Oct. 1840, HHStA, StA, Türkei VI, 76.

[22] This opinion can be found among others in K. Fattal, J. A. Nohra, *L'Autriche*

is absolutely erroneous because the chancellor believed that Austria's exclusive influence over the Syrian Catholics could only lead to a serious rivalry with France and the other Great Powers, which would endanger stability in the already restless region. Protectorship would not only contradict Metternich's respect for the inviolability of the Ottoman monarch's sovereignty but also the hope to remove areas of friction within the Ottoman Empire that had caused several crises in the Near East for twenty long years. Therefore, Metternich repudiated the idea of an exclusive protectorate over both the political and religious affairs of the Syrian Christians as well as Christians elsewhere in the Ottoman Empire. As for the civil affairs of the Ottoman citizens, not only did Metternich not demand this right for Austria, but he was also of the opinion that no country was entitled to interfere in them because "the sovereign of the country is the only competent and natural defender of the civil and politic rights of his subjects, and foreign courts would violate these rights of the sovereign by competing for the protection of his subjects' rights against his will."[23] Somehow more complicated was Metternich's opinion of the right of all European Powers to protect the Ottoman Christians' freedom to practice their religion, which, according to the prince, "in no way injures the rights of the sovereign."[24] This, however, did not only mean that Metternich wanted to replace France's exclusive protectorate over the Catholics or Russia's over the Orthodox Christians with a general protectorate but also that the chancellor wished to change its form: it was not to be a right of protection but of intercession on behalf of the Ottoman Christians, and as such the word "protection" as used by him must be understood; on the other hand he well knew that owing to the prerogatives that the sultans had imprudently given to France and Russia to intervene in Ottoman internal affairs in this respect, foreign interference could never be entirely removed.[25]

---

et le Liban: Esquisse historique et promenade à travers les petites histoires d'une vieille amitié, Paris 1996, p. 24; S. Khalaf, "Communal Conflict in Nineteenth-Century Lebanon," B. Braude, B. Lewis (eds.), *Christians and Jews in the Ottoman Empire: The Functioning of a Plural Society*, II, New York 1982, p. 117; K. S. Salibi, *The Modern History of Lebanon*, London 1965, p. 42.

[23] Metternich to Ohms, Vienna, 7 Nov. 1840, HHStA, StK, Rom 64.
[24] Ibid.
[25] Ibid.; Metternich to Stürmer, Vienna, 3 Nov. 1840, HHStA, StA, Türkei VI, 78.

These considerations meant that one of Metternich's principal goals in his Syrian policy was not to deprive the French of their protection of the Catholic faith but to share it with them and best upon a basis less detrimental to the sultan's sovereignty. He wanted to share the right for intercession with other Catholic countries since, as he stated, this privilege belonged to all Catholic courts and could not be usurped by only one of them: "We do not deny this right to France; exercising it ourselves, we do not claim it as an exclusive privilege."[26] His aim was clearly pronounced in his instructions to Stürmer on 3 November 1840: "I find it necessary above all to rectify the error that attaches itself to the use of the word protection. In our opinion, no independent sovereign could permit the claim of another foreign sovereign to offer protection to his [the former's] subjects in his own country and usurp thus the right inherent to sovereignty. If the Porte inadvertently or by ill-considered tolerance has still permitted similar protections in religious affairs until now, its self-interest should be aimed towards liberating itself from these protections. According to this, it could not be the intention of the Imperial Court to take the protection of the Catholics in Syria away from France in order to appropriate it for ourselves. What we demand is that the Porte recognises the benevolent interest that Austria takes in the Maronites, its co-religionists, and that it kindly accepts the entreaties and complaints of this nation demanding through the intermediary of the representatives of the H. I. and R. M. [His Imperial and Royal Majesty] the opportunity to transmit them to His Highness; that the Porte declares that in the current circumstance of the Maronites having shown undeniable proof of their attachment and loyalty and having made extraordinary efforts to rid themselves of the yoke of the Egyptian domination, they have acquired the right to claim His Highness's particular benevolence, and considering this, His Highness is determined to bestow upon them favours as the reward for their devotion, and that He consents to Austria, as a Catholic court and as a country, which has aided and assisted in their efforts, being the instrument by which they will be able to send their wishes to the cognizance of the Sublime Porte; that moreover the Porte is ready to consider Austria to be the guarantor of the concessions that will be made to the Maronites

---

[26] Metternich to Ohms, Vienna, 7 Nov. 1840, HHStA, StK, Rom 64.

and to be thus committed to their accomplishment."[27] Consequently, Metternich repeatedly assured Altieri that Austria in no way wanted to assume any protectorship over the sultan's subjects and, therefore, the chancellor refused to meet Yusuf's request for Austria's protection in the exclusive style of France's. In his opinion, it would be a mistake if the Ottoman Christians sought protection abroad, regardless of whether from Austria or France. All that the Great Powers could do was offer occasional assistance in case of need. The ideal situation would be if the Ottoman Christians did not have to seek protection from European countries and their security was assured by the sultan.[28] The truth of Metternich's statements is supported by the above-mentioned fact that neither Steindl nor Laurin were given instructions in case Yusuf should ask to replace the French protectorship with Austria's.[29] However, not even Metternich had to assume a formal attitude towards this demand because when the patriarch handed over the written list of his nation's wishes at the end of October 1840, to Steindl's surprise he no longer required Austrian protection. Yusuf explained the shift in his opinion by the uncertainty over Austrian willingness to satisfy this request.[30]

Metternich's moderate ambitions in no way signified that he was well disposed to France and its activities in the Near East. On the contrary, his policy in Syria as well as the entire Levant in the 1830s was significantly anti-French and also in the Syrian Question his conduct was influenced by his strong aversion to France. He rejected France's exclusive role as protector of the Christians, jealously guarded by French governments regardless of the regime and, as he complained to Altieri, actively enhanced at the expense of the innocent Jews after the murder of Father Tommaso. What he particularly criticised was the fact that for the French this protectorate was only an instrument to gain support for their political and economic goals, and in this

---

[27] Metternich to Stürmer, Vienna, 3 Nov. 1840, HHStA, StA, Türkei VI, 78.
[28] Altieri to Lambruschini, Vienna, 6 Nov., 4 and 18 Dec. 1840, ASV, Arch. Nunz. Vienna 280C.
[29] Stürmer's instructions for Steindl were only verbal and therefore no written document exists. Nevertheless, it is evident from Steindl's and Laurin's statements to Yusuf that they really were not prepared to solve the matter of Austrian protection. For more on the absence of written instructions see also Steindl to Wood, Djounie, 3 Oct. 1840, Cunningham, *The Early Correspondence*, p. 172.
[30] Steindl to Stürmer, Beirut, 31 Oct. 1840, HHStA, StA, Türkei VI, 77.

he was not completely mistaken. He clearly stated his opinion in the instructions to Esterházy on 7 March 1841: "One of the particular defects of the French is that they mix national policy with everything. The French Kings, who made so many sacrifices in the support of religion in the Levant, thereby obtained the right to protect the Christians, which was sanctioned by treaties. If France limited the exploitation of these rights only to religious protection, nobody could complain, but it is not the case. The French governments, regardless of their origin or beliefs, constantly mix their political interests and views with religious protection and the history of past years is rich with new evidence of this fact, which has a double disadvantage: first, of discrediting the foreign protection of the Christian population in Syria, and second, of invoking the distrust of the Porte leading to its condemnation of all Christian courts."[31] Consequently, Metternich's rejection of the idea to replace the French protectorate must be understood as a demonstration of his respect for international law, his desire for general peace and his realistic assessment of Austria's limitations. Moreover, although French influence in Syria was paralysed in 1840, Metternich, as a rational statesman, did not believe in its entire elimination. Nevertheless, even mere participation in the protection of the Syrian Catholics or in an Austro-French cooperation would deliver a blow to France because it would break the by then so jealously guarded French privilege. The prince pursued this goal from the very beginning. Already in the initiation of Steindl's mission there appears a clear desire to weaken French influence over Syrian affairs and to discard the mask of "the French charlatanism that shrouded the Levant with religious colours as well as all other hues."[32] At the end of August 1840, he instructed the internuncio to draw the sultan's attention to the minimal value of friendship with France, which sought only its own profit and rivalry with other Great Powers. He instructed Steindl to inform all Catholics in Lebanon about the particular interest of the Austrian court in their situation and raise their doubts about the positive value of the sole protection of France.[33]

---

[31] Metternich to Esterházy, Vienna, 7 March 1841, HHStA, StA, England 236.
[32] Metternich to Neumann, Königswart, 25 Aug. 1840, HHStA, StA, England 230.
[33] Metternich to Stürmer, Königswart, 28 Aug. 1840, HHStA, StA, Türkei VI, 78; Metternich to Lützow, Vienna, 21 Nov. 1840, HHStA, StK, Rom 64; Altieri to Lambruschini, Vienna, 6 and 20 Nov. 1840, ASV, Arch. Nunz. Vienna 280C; J. A. Nohra, "L'Autriche et la question du Liban (1840–1865)," A. Ti-

Austria's activities in Syria naturally did not escape the attention of the French operating in the Near East. Cochelet accused the Austrian agents of trying to persuade local Christians that only the Austrian Empire could serve as a natural protector of the faith. He wrote to Paris on 18 October 1840: "The aim of the cabinet in Vienna is without any doubt to replace the influence of France, of which it is so jealous and which it would like to destroy. To pursue these aims it has superbly disciplined agents, who use all the means at their disposal to convince uneducated inhabitants [of Syria] that France is an atheistic land where all bonds with Christianity have been broken."[34] At the same time, Pontois was alarmed by Austria's policy, which he also accused of being aimed at the complete destruction of France's protectorate over the Ottoman Catholics and advocated a French counteroffensive.[35] In the capital on the Seine, reports like these caused considerable concern, in particular when in the autumn of 1840 not only the protectorate over the Catholic inhabitants, but also the very future of France's ally, Mohammed Ali, was in jeopardy. Consequently, whereas Austria and Great Britain urged the Maronites to rebel against Egyptian rule, Adolphe Thiers sent the superior of the Lazarists, Father Jean Baptiste Étienne, to Lebanon in September to use his influence over the Maronite clergy to prevent a war between the mountain tribesmen and the Egyptian forces. Father Étienne arrived in Sidon on 24 September, shortly before the allies launched an attack against the city. Owing to the insecure situation in the interior, where the roads were controlled by brigands, Father Étienne did not consider it appropriate to take risks en route to the Maronites, whose discontent was so great that their uprising against the Egyptian forces was imminent. He preferred to end his mission and leave for Alexandria. Attempts by other French agents led by the consuls in Damascus and Beirut, Count Ratti-Menton and Mr Desmeloizes, to persuade the patriarch and other Maronite clerics to forbid the people to take up the sultan's banner also entirely failed in the autumn of 1840. Threats to withdraw French protection of the Catholic Church proved to be useless. British and Austrian influence apparently predominated in Syria.

---

etze (ed.), *Habsburgisch-osmanische Beziehungen: Relations Habsbourg-ottomanes*, Wien 1985, pp. 293–323.
[34] Guichen, p. 391.
[35] Pontois to Guizot, Therapia, 27 Nov. 1840, AMAE, CP, Turquie 281.

Nevertheless, one cannot resist the impression that the withdrawal of Yusuf's suggestion that the Maronites be placed under Austrian protection was a consequence of the French efforts.[36]

As for Cochelet's mention of the Austrian schemes in Syria, they undoubtedly existed, but it seems that the French consul general and his colleagues somewhat exaggerated their importance. The Austrian correspondence offers very few examples of anti-French activity although the Austrian consular network was relatively large. Besides Steindl's mission that accomplished everything the Austrian cabinet had originally wished for, there was only the intervention of Rear-Admiral Bandiera on behalf of Melkite Bishop Agapios Riashi, who had been seized by mountain tribesmen and taken to the camp of allied British, Austrian and Ottoman forces. Agapios faced the accusation that several months previously he had cleverly extradited several emirs and sheikhs into the hands of Mohammed Ali's ally and the emir (prince) of Mount Lebanon, Bashir II Shehab, thus causing their exile to Sennar. Furthermore, he was said to be extremely devoted to Ibrahim Pasha and to have forbidden the people in his parish, under threat of excommunication, to join the uprising against Egyptian rule. The commander of the Ottoman forces in Syria, Mehmed Izzet Pasha, was ordered to take Agapios and two other captured Melkite priests on board a Turkish warship. As soon as Bandiera learnt this, he immediately asked Izzet to surrender the three men and to allow their internment on an Austrian vessel while they awaited trial. Izzet immediately satisfied this request, and this undoubtedly contributed to Austrian prestige in Syria. Although Agapios was regarded as Ibrahim Pasha's spy and was unpopular among the majority of the Christians, at the same time he was a member of the Catholic clergy and considered by the strongly devout members of this religion to be untouchable. The actions of the Austrian rear-admiral contributed to the belief, already

---

[36] Stürmer to Metternich, Constantinople, 7 and 18 Oct. 1840, HHStA, StA, Türkei VI, 76; Steindl to Stürmer, Beirut, 21 Oct. 1840, the report of an unnamed Frenchman settled in Alexandria, Alexandria, 5 Oct. 1840, attached to Stürmer to Metternich, Constantinople, 18 Oct. 1840, HHStA, StA, Türkei VI, 76; Ohms to Metternich, Rome, 24 Oct. 1840, HHStA, StK, Rom 63; Bockelberg to Frederick William IV, Vienna, 31 Oct. 1840, GStA PK, HA III, MdA I, 7359; A. Schlicht, "The Role of Foreign Powers in the History of Lebanon and Syria from 1799 to 1861," *Journal of Asian History* 14, 1980, 2, p. 110; Charles-Roux, *Thiers*, p. 160; Hajjar, p. 519.

widespread among the Lebanese, that in this campaign the Austrian Empire sought specifically to protect the Catholic Church and faith. There were some other activities on the part of Austria explained by some historians as assistance to the Christians, like the sending of several thousand muskets and ten doctors to Syria.[37] This was definitely true at least for the muskets which the British government had already requested in Vienna for the mountain tribesmen at the end of July 1840, but Metternich did not satisfy this demand until a month later, and the weapons left Trieste only at the beginning of November. As for the mission of Austrian doctors already mentioned in Chapter 21, they were to be employed in the Ottoman military hospitals and it is not possible to say whether they were instructed to treat only wounded soldiers or also civilians and thus to increase Austrian influence in the country. Although the latter possibility cannot be entirely refuted, no relevant evidence for this assertion has been found.[38]

The Dispute over the Future of the Syrian Christians and the Plans for the Internationalisation of Jerusalem

When the allies captured the strategic stronghold of Acre on 4 November, the fate of Egyptian hegemony over Syria was sealed. Ibrahim

---

[37] The opinion that the doctors were offered with regard to the Christians is maintained by Joseph Abou Nohra in "L'Autriche et la question du Liban," p. 315, and Joseph Hajjar in *L'Europe et les destinées du Proche-Orient*, p. 522.

[38] Metternich to Neumann, Königswart, 31 July 1840, HHStA, StA, England 230; Metternich to Stürmer, Vienna, 30 Oct. 1840, HHStA, StA, Türkei VI, 78; Steindl's unpublished diary, part II, 3 Oct. 1840, attached to Stürmer to Metternich, Constantinople, 18 Oct. 1840, HHStA, StA, Türkei VI, 76; Stürmer to Metternich, Constantinople, 2 Nov. 1840, HHStA, StA, Türkei VI, 77; Stürmer to Metternich, Constantinople, 14 April 1841, HHStA, StA, Türkei VIII, 15; Stürmer to Metternich, Constantinople, 7 July 1841, HHStA, StA, Türkei VIII, 16; Beauvale to Palmerston, Königswart, 27 Aug. 1840, Vienna, 28 Oct. 1840, TNA, FO 120/189; Bockelberg to Frederick William IV, Vienna, 31 Oct. 1840, Maltzan to Frederick William IV, Vienna, 13 Nov. 1840, GStA PK, HA III, MdA I, 7359; Maltzan to Frederick William IV, Vienna, 10 Dec. 1840, GStA PK, HA III, MdA I, 7360; Königsmarck to Frederick William IV, Büyükdere, 18 Nov. 1840, GStA PK, HA III, MdA I, 7283.

Pasha concentrated on saving the rest of his army and getting to Egypt with as many of his men as possible. Once the main phase of the war in Syria had ended, the question of the future of the Syrian Christians started to gain strength, and in several weeks it became one of the most important parts of the diplomatic agenda of the European cabinets. The situation at the Chancellery in Ballhausplatz was not different, and in the fall of 1840, Metternich contemplated the future of all Syrian Christians regardless of their creed. His interest, originally intended as support for the Maronites and somewhat later for all Catholics, transformed into a concern to ensure conditions that would enable security for all Christians in Syria and thus contribute to the consolidation of a renewed Ottoman administration in the re-conquered region. This approach was to give birth to the co-operation of all European Powers, facilitating the acceptance of their useful proposals at the sultan's court and at the same time preventing suspicions and rivalry between the same Powers that could hamper the achievement of desired results. Metternich was particularly concerned about Nicholas I, who regarded himself as the defender of the Ortho-dox Christians in the Near East and might be offended if Metternich referred only to the members of the Catholic Church.[39] This caution was explained by the prince in his instructions to the Austrian ambas-sador in Rome, Count Rudolf von Lützow, later on 14 February 1841: "The general denomination 'Christians' is the term prudence makes me use when I intend to say 'Catholics,' and you know very well in the state of affairs [in the Levant] that the Moslems are less hostile to the latter than to the Greek and Armenian schismatics. Where it concerns legislation, it would be dangerous to talk of 'Catholics' be-cause Russia would claim for its co-religionists more privileges than would be demanded for the Latin Church."[40]

Metternich assumed that the Great Powers had a right to advise the sultan in Syrian affairs because, with the exception of France, they had helped him to recover this province. The chancellor himself conveyed as much to the Porte on 18 December 1840 in his instruc-tions to Stürmer concerning the future of the Syrian Christians. In his opinion, a considerable number of firmans, hatt-i sharifs and other regulations on behalf of the Ottoman Christians and Churches already

---

[39] Altieri to Lambruschini, Vienna, 18 Dec. 1840, ASV, Arch. Nunz. Vienna 280C.
[40] Metternich to Lützow, Vienna, 14 Feb. 1841, HHStA, StK, Rom 67.

guaranteed their freedoms and untroubled existence. Unfortunately, however, most of these decrees were not being properly executed owing to the disorder of the administrative apparatus that, according to Metternich, led to the tyranny of local authorities and caused the suffering of Ottoman Christians. Therefore, it was not necessary to create new laws or to rebuild the administrative system of the Syrian pashaliks but rather to help the Porte to enforce existing regulations. At the moment when the Porte regained Syria, in places where the Christians formed a considerable proportion of the inhabitants, the most reasonable policy compatible with the sultan's interests was to apply the stipulations of the Hatt-i Sharif of Gülhane in Syria and to establish an administration capable of granting the security of civil and religious rights to people of all creeds. The Ottoman monarch's conduct with regard to the Christians was to be based upon eight fundamental principles: (1) the freedom of religious conviction; (2) each confession could solve its own religious matters; (3) a register of Christians should exist in each district; (4) all existing Churches in Syria including Palestine had to be confirmed; (5) the Christian Holy Places should enjoy the sultan's special protection; (6) the Ottoman monarch should protect pilgrims travelling to Palestine to visit the Holy Places; (7) every pilgrim was obliged to pay a special fee to the Ottoman treasury in exchange for a permit enabling him to visit the Holy Places; afterwards no other charges could be levied upon him; (8) non-Moslem foreigners would continue to be under their consuls' jurisdiction while local Christians would be under Ottoman jurisdiction, except in matters related to their faith. The sultan should assure impartial judgements in both criminal as well as civil cases involving Ottoman citizens regardless of their religion.[41]

These principles were naturally influenced by conservative values, in particular the respect for the state sovereignty represented by the monarch. Although other countries could advise the sultan, they had no inherent right to interfere in his affairs. For this reason Metternich made a distinction between the foreigners living within the Ottoman

---

[41] Metternich to Stürmer, Vienna, 18 Dec. 1840, HHStA, StA, Türkei VI, 78; Metternich to Esterházy, Vienna, 3 Feb. 1841, HHStA, StA, England 236; Altieri to Lambruschini, Vienna, 18 Dec. 1840, ASV, Arch. Nunz. Vienna 280C; Stürmer to Testa, Constantinople, [?] Jan. 1841, attached to Ponsonby to Palmerston, Therapia, 1 Feb. 1841, TNA, FO 78/430.

Empire and professing the Christian faith, who could be protected by their native countries on the basis of relevant agreements, and the sultan's Christian subjects whose civil and political rights could not be protected by other countries because it would be an infraction of the sultan's sovereignty. When it came to religious affairs, however, the Powers should be entitled to express their opinions, and this right had to be shared by all of them and not constitute a privilege of one of them. Every Church in the Near East could choose the Great Power to which it would address grievances concerning problems of faith. With this measure Metternich hoped to forestall French or Russian dominance in the religious affairs of the region. He also tried to weaken the French position when he proposed that while all European Powers including France should discuss the fate of all Ottoman Christians in the following months, the Maronites' future ought to be resolved only by the signatories of the London Convention since this nation had requested help only from the other four Powers, and from Austria in particular. Both matters should be discussed in Constantinople and not in London which had served as a centre of negotiations on the Eastern Question since December 1839. The significance of this proposal lay in Metternich's ambition to control the course of events through his considerable personal influence at the sultan's court at that time and its proximity to Vienna. In addition, this would weaken the position of Palmerston. The chancellor had also been frustrated by the protracted discussions in London and believed his goals could be achieved more quickly in Constantinople, while preserving the appearance of the sultan's sovereignty. At the moment when the accord was achieved, the sultan could then issue a firman in favour of the Syrian Christians.[42]

Metternich's Near Eastern policy sought to encourage peaceful development within the Ottoman Empire. If he could accomplish this end, then the "sick man on the Bosphorus" would no longer attract the attention of the other Powers and would not cause serious crises with their unfortunate repercussions for the rest of the Continent, as had happened in the autumn of 1840 in connection with the Rhine Crisis. At the same time, Metternich did not hesitate to oppose projects that lacked his pragmatism. One of these was a French plan elaborated

---

[42] Metternich to Stürmer, Vienna, 18 Dec. 1840, HHStA, StA, Türkei VI, 78; Sainte-Aulaire to Guizot, Vienna, 26 Jan. 1841, AMAE, CP, Autriche 429.

by Guizot, who transmitted his own proposal regarding the Syrian Christians to the Austrian chancellor for his examination in January 1841. Guizot proposed that Jerusalem be declared a free city like the Republic of Cracow, exempt from Ottoman control and placed under the protection of the Great Powers. It was unclear how just he thought this goal could be achieved since he outlined no practical steps in his correspondence. In any case, Metternich regarded this proposal as dangerous because it attacked the Ottoman sovereignty over Jerusalem and its environs, and was impracticable for two reasons. First, Jerusalem was a holy city not only for Christians, but for Moslems as well. The sultan could never surrender his sovereignty over this territory, especially since he was not only the secular ruler, but as caliph also the head of Islam. Second, if Jerusalem were left to the Christians to govern themselves, the Catholics would undoubtedly be oppressed by the Orthodox Christians, who were numerically and materially superior and whose relations with the Catholic community were hostile.[43] The Austrian chancellor considered the Orthodox believers in the Levant to be far less tolerant than the Ottomans, who were at least uninterested in the particular religious affairs of the Christians. Under the given conditions, Ottoman rule was far more advantageous for the Catholic Church.[44]

The establishment of a free city would also create a new centre of tension and rivalry for the Great Powers, which was exactly what Metternich opposed. Guizot's comparison of a free [city of] Jerusalem

---

[43] The annual fighting between the Catholics and Orthodox Christians in the Church of the Holy Sepulchre during Easter was only the most visible tip of the iceberg. F. Egerton, *Journal of a Tour in the Holy Land, in May and June, 1840*, London 1841, p. 19; Frazee, p. 305. According to Laurin's report, there were more Orthodox Christians than all members of the Churches recognising the pope's primacy in Syria combined: 290,000 against 284,700. In Jerusalem and its environs the majority of the former was overwhelming. Laurin's report with the census of the Christian population in Syria, attached to Stürmer to Metternich, Constantinople, 18 Nov. 1840, HHStA, StA, Türkei VI, 77. According to Muhammad Sabry, out of 1,844,000 inhabitants of Syria there were 345,000 Orthodox Christians, 260,000 Catholics and 977,000 Moslems. Sabry, p. 345.

[44] Metternich to Apponyi, Vienna, 12 July 1841, HHStA, StA, Frankreich 322; Apponyi to Metternich, Paris, 5 and 7 Jan. 1841, HHStA, StA, Frankreich 320; Altieri to Lambruschini, Vienna, 29 Jan. 1841, ASV, Arch. Nunz. Vienna 280D; M. Vereté, "A Plan for the Internationalization of Jerusalem, 1840–1841," N. Rose (ed.), *From Palmerston to Balfour: Collected Essays of Mayir Vereté*, London 1992, pp. 142–149.

with the situation of Cracow could in no way find favour with the chancellor who had regarded the creation of the Free City of Cracow as a mistake. Austria had experienced only problems with Cracow and in Metternich's words, "the courts upon whom weigh the burden of protecting this unhappy creation have enough trouble from the existence of one [place like] Cracow to ever consent to the creation of a second one."[45] Metternich clearly and vigorously objected to the French minister over the proposal, despite the fact that Guizot tempted him with the possibility that France might return to the diplomatic concert from which it had excluded itself with its refusal to cooperate with other Great Powers against Mohammed Ali. The Austrian chancellor asked the French foreign minister to support feasible designs and "not to be distracted by proposals that under the appearance of humanitarian or religious interests deviate from a practical direction, which is probably the only direction that can assure what should be accomplished."[46] According to the report of Count Apponyi dated 16 February, Guizot seemed to accept Metternich's arguments. It is questionable to what extent the French minister was actually influenced by them, but he did renounce this project. The key reason for the French retreat must be seen in the fact that Guizot did not have the support of any other Power and therefore no hope for the enforcement of his idea at the sultan's court where French influence was minimal given its pro-Egyptian policy.[47]

Metternich also repudiated a plan prepared by some Prussians with the consent of Frederick William IV, a man of "politico-clerical *Weltanschauung*,"[48] who, like Guizot, had decided to take advantage of the situation in favour of the Christian inhabitants in Syria against the alleged "fanaticism of the Mussulmans."[49] The Prussian plan was sent to Vienna on 24 February 1841 and intended to place Jerusalem, Bethlehem and Nazareth under the protectorate of the five Powers.

---

[45] Metternich to Guizot, Vienna, 8 Feb. 1841, HHStA, StA, Rom 67.

[46] Metternich to Apponyi, Vienna, 26 Jan. 1841, HHStA, StA, Frankreich 322.

[47] Metternich to Esterházy, Vienna, 7 March 1841, HHStA, StA, England 236; Apponyi to Metternich, Paris, 5 Jan. and 16 Feb. 1841, HHStA, StA, Frankreich 320; Baumgart, p. 306; Vereté, pp. 152–153.

[48] A.-R. Sinno, *Deutsche Interessen in Syrien und Palästina 1841–1898*, Berlin 1982, p. 17.

[49] Werther to Maltzan, Berlin, 24 Feb. 1841, GStA PK, Rep. 81 Gesandschaften (Residenturen) u. (General-) Konsulate nach 1807, Gesandschaft Wien II, 204/2.

The religious communities in those towns would be entrusted to three residents who would supervise the affairs of Christians, Europeans as well as the sultan's subjects. The resident for the Catholics would be nominated by Austria and France, the resident for the Orthodox Christians by Russia and the third one for the Protestants together by Great Britain and Prussia. Each of these Powers would provide its own resident with 60 soldiers for his security. Some selected places would be fortified. The estates owned by the Roman Catholic, Greek and Armenian Churches in the Holy Places would become the common property of the Great Powers.[50] Metternich did not express his objections openly to this plan because he did not want to harm the good Austro-Prussian relations. Instead, he decided to employ Palmerston for this purpose. During a discussion with Lord Beauvale on 2 March 1841 and through copious instructions sent to London five days later, Metternich tried to convince the British foreign secretary of the ineptitude of the Prussian proposal for the solution of the Syrian Christians' future. He himself was not prepared to answer Frederick William IV until after Palmerston and the tsar had replied.[51]

Metternich's reasoning against this real plan for the internationalisation of Jerusalem was similar to the objections he had addressed to the Parisian cabinet. He regarded the Prussian idea as equally impracticable as the French one. The institution of three residents would lead to the factual autonomy of the city and its surroundings, thus weakening Ottoman supremacy over Jerusalem. As he had in February, Metternich expressed apprehension at the proposed removal of the Ottoman government because of the mutual resentment between the Christian creeds and the importance of Jerusalem for the Moslems: "The distributive justice of the Turkish government knows how to deal with the difficulties and sometimes even the suffering that the oppression of the local authorities imposes upon the Christians of all three confessions. The Moslem law is not intolerant. It is indifferent to the non-believers, it in no way cares about the internal regulations

---

[50] The Prussian king's memorandum for Metternich, undated, attached to Werther to Maltzan, Berlin, 24 Feb. 1841, GStA PK, Rep. 81 Gesandschaften (Residenturen) u. (General-) Konsulate nach 1807, Gesandschaft Wien II, 204/2.
[51] Metternich to Esterházy, Vienna, 7 March 1841, HHStA, StA, England 236; Beauvale to Palmerston, Vienna, 2 March 1841, TNA, FO 120/197; Maltzan to Frederick William IV, Vienna, 17 March 1841, GStA PK, Rep. 81 Gesandschaften (Residenturen) u. (General-) Konsulate nach 1807, Gesandschaft Wien II, 204/2.

of the confessions, it does not meddle in the affairs of the foreign religious practices, and if in the course of time one had to regret more than a deviation from this rule, it is not at all in the spirit of Islam where the cause must be sought, but rather on the one hand in the rivalry and excitations of the adherents of the various Christian confessions and on the other hand in the abuse of power by the governors and their subordinates."[52] The destruction of the Ottoman presence in Jerusalem would arouse the animosity of the Moslems as would the presence of European forces that could be used by the various Christian confessions as instruments for solving mutual disputes.[53] In short, as Metternich told Beauvale, the realisation of the Prussian plan would "throw that country into inextricable confusion."[54]

According to the Austrian statesman, there was one important difference between the French and Prussian projects that resulted from the different confessions predominant in those countries. What he disliked in the latter was an excessive promotion of Protestant interests, not because of his own Catholic faith, but owing to the fact that the number of Protestants living in Palestine was small, and their Church owned almost no estates there; a re-allocation of the property of other Churches in the region would require the donation of their property to the Protestants by other confessions who were not willing to share it. In his instructions to Esterházy dated 7 May 1841 Metternich expressed this opinion: "Two ideas evidently predominate in the Prussian plan; the first is to obtain a representation in the Holy Places for the Church designated as Evangelical; the second is to let this Church participate in the property in these regions owned by the Roman Catholic, Orthodox and Armenian Churches. If the first of these claims is devoid of sane moral application, the second one encounters practical considerations that make its admission impossible. This concept is cloudy; it aims to create a state of affairs for which all required elements are missing; it has neither a well-founded point of departure nor a possible point of arrival."[55] Metternich was in this respect correct because there actually existed no real Protestant interest

---

[52] Metternich to Esterházy, Vienna, 7 March 1841, HHStA, StA, England 236.

[53] Lerchenfeld to Ludwig I of Bavaria, Vienna, 30 March 1841, BHStA, MA, Wien 2410; Altieri to Lambruschini, Vienna, 7 April 1841, ASV, Arch. Nunz. Vienna 280D.

[54] Beauvale to Palmerston, Vienna, 2 March 1841, TNA, FO 120/197.

[55] Metternich to Esterházy, Vienna, 7 March 1841, HHStA, StA, England 236.

in the Holy Land at that time and, therefore, he hoped that Palmerston would also view the Prussian plan as "stillborn."[56] The British foreign secretary completely shared the Austrian chancellor's attitude towards the sultan's sovereignty and the solution of the Syrian Christians' future and agreed with Metternich's arguments. The British answer to the Prussian project was therefore negative and since no support came from St Petersburg as well, the plan was removed from the agenda.[57]

In part, the two above-mentioned projects reflect the fact that this period saw many discussions of various plans that might improve the Christians' situation in Syria and particularly in Palestine. At the end of 1840 and the beginning of 1841 some newspapers and pamphlets in Europe produced many such plans. Their authors were individuals as well as various associations whose increased concerns for the future of Syria resulted from the fact that ownership of this region had changed with the aid of the Great Powers. Various fantastic projects like the foundation of a Christian republic or kingdom in Palestine, or making from this part of the world a destination for the surplus of people from some European states were in Metternich's view as impractical and harmful as the plans of the French foreign minister and Prussian king because they were motivated by passion and they ignored the real situation prevailing in the Levant and were thus entirely unfeasible.[58] Metternich naturally opposed them because the emancipation of the Ottoman Christians would inevitably lead to the weakening of the fragile structure of the empire and the political

---

[56] Ibid.

[57] Metternich to Esterházy, Vienna, 7 March 1841, HHStA, StA, England 236; Lerchenfeld to Ludwig I of Bavaria, Vienna, 30 March 1841, BHStA, MA, Wien 2410; Palmerston to Beauvale, London, 11 March 1841, L. Wolf (ed.), *Notes on the Diplomatic History of the Jewish Question: With Texts of Protocols, Treaty Stipulations and other Public Acts and Official Documents*, London 1919, p. 117; R. W. Greaves, "The Jerusalem Bishopric, 1841," *EHR* 64, 1949, 252, p. 336; Hajjar, p. 360; Sinno, p. 20.

[58] Metternich to Lützow, Vienna, 14 Feb. and 12 July 1841, HHStA, StK, Rom 67; Metternich to Guizot, Vienna, 8 Feb. 1841, HHStA, StK, Rom 67; Metternich to Apponyi, Vienna, 12 July 1841, HHStA, StA, Frankreich 322; Apponyi to Metternich, Paris, 16 Feb. 1841, HHStA, StA, Frankreich 320; Altieri to Lambruschini, Vienna, 6 Nov. 1840, ASV, Arch. Nunz. Vienna 280C; Altieri to Lambruschini, Vienna, 26 March and 9 April 1841, ASV, Arch. Nunz. Vienna 280D; Laurens, p. 58; Degeorg, p. 130; Schölch, "Jerusalem in the 19th Century," p. 230.

predominance of the Orthodox believers: "Committees are being established in France to support the Christians' interests in the Holy
Places; some of them are preaching a new crusade, while others would
like to achieve the liberation of the Christian population in different
ways ... In our manner of thinking, there can be no question of the
emancipation of the Christian communities in Syria from the Sultan's
sovereignty because we are firmly resolved to remain loyal to the principle of the preservation of the Ottoman Empire and because we are
absolutely convinced of the most grievous consequences for the Latin
Church following the mass political emancipation of the Christians in
the regions where the schismatic Churches have material wealth and
resources at their disposal."[59]

The prince did not confine himself only to criticism of others'
projects but also prepared his own plan for the solution of the Syrian
Question based upon the conviction that the only practicable way to
stabilise the situation in this part of the Ottoman Empire was the
implementation of the conditions of the Hatt-i Sharif of Gülhane and
the improvement of the Ottoman administration. He discussed his
own plan briefly with Altieri and Sainte-Aulaire at the end of January 1841 and circulated it at the beginning of the following month.[60]
He was particularly motivated by his often stated opinion that the
hitherto maltreatment of the Christians did not result from the intolerance of the sultan and his dignitaries but from the violation of
rights accorded to the Christian inhabitants and from the arbitrary
behaviour of the local pashas. As he wrote to Stürmer on 7 February
1841, "it is not a question of doing anything radically new; it is a
question of maintaining privileges and re-establishing those practices
which existed previously and have lapsed in the course of centuries."[61]
On this account he advocated the appointment of an extraordinary

---

[59] Metternich to Apponyi, Vienna, 12 July 1841, HHStA, StA, Frankreich 322.
[60] Also in this case Mordechai Eliav was incorrect with his dating when he claimed
that Metternich presented his project in the instructions to London on 5 October
1840. Eliav, p. 36. No mention was found in them. Metternich to Neumann, Vienna,
5 Oct. 1840, HHStA, StA, England 231. The same mistake was made by Lucien
Wolf when he dated the *Memorandum Delivered by the Austrian Government to
the Prussian Government* back to October 1840. Wolf, *Notes on the Diplomatic
History*, pp. 111–113. No such document from October was found in any of visited
archives.
[61] Metternich to Stürmer, Vienna, 7 Feb. 1841, HHStA, StA, Türkei VI, 83.

Ottoman emissary in Jerusalem who would occupy himself with the situation of the Christians, the local residents as well as Europeans, with individuals as well as with the Churches in the city and in Bethlehem, and protect them from the abuses of Syrian leaders. Such an emissary would answer only to the sultan and be completely independent of the local pashas. The confessions would be entitled to send their deputies to him to deal with their problems and simultaneously to appeal to the representatives of the Great Powers in Constantinople in purely religious affairs. This measure would assure the security of the Christians without affecting the sultan's reign over Jerusalem. According to Metternich, it was a simple but satisfactory solution and above all, in contrast to the ambitious and chimerical projects, easily feasible because, among other reasons, it rested upon existing legal rules and did not harm the sovereignty of the Ottoman Empire.[62] In late March 1841, the prince wrote to Stürmer: "My work is based only upon two principles, namely these: first, on the respect for the privileges and guarantees accorded from time immemorial to the Christians as well as their religious establishments in these regions, and second, on the institution of a Moslem functionary delegated by the sultan himself to protect the security of the Christians in the Holy Places. I cannot imagine what could prevent the Porte from agreeing to this demand or what could prevent it from accepting it willingly. Everything in our idea is consistent with the well-known interests of the Ottoman monarch and his wish to increase his authority in the eyes of Europe."[63]

Although Metternich's plan was not at variance with the fundamental attitudes of the Porte, and although his influence at the Ottoman court was considerable, he also sought the support of the other Great Powers for the expected negotiations in Constantinople.

---

[62] Metternich to Apponyi, Vienna, 26 Jan. 1841, HHStA, StA, Frankreich 322; Metternich to Esterházy, Vienna, 3 Feb. 1841, HHStA, StA, England 236; Metternich to Stürmer, Vienna, 7 Feb. 1841, HHStA, StA, Türkei VI, 83; Metternich to Lützow, Vienna, 14 Feb. 1841, Vienna, HHStA, StK, Rom 67; Sainte-Aulaire to Guizot, Vienna, 26 Jan. 1841, AMAE, CP, Autriche 429; Altieri to Lambruschini, Vienna, 29 Jan., 12 and 26 Feb., 7 April 1841, ASV, Arch. Nunz. Vienna 280D; Maltzan to Frederick William IV, Vienna, 2 Feb. and 17 March 1841, GStA PK, Rep. 81 Gesandschaften (Residenturen) u. (General-) Konsulate nach 1807, Gesandschaft Wien II, 204/2; Lerchenfeld to Ludwig I of Bavaria, Vienna, 20 Feb. 1841, BHStA, MA, Wien 4010.
[63] Metternich to Stürmer, Vienna, 26 March 1841, HHStA, StA, Türkei VI, 83.

Despite the proclaimed motto that he did "not aspire to create new political contentions but to alleviate them,"[64] the chancellor was only half successful. The first Power he addressed was France; its support would be valuable to him for two reasons. First, Austro-French cooperation would strengthen the Catholics' position in the Levant. He lured Guizot with assurances that both Powers ought to defend the Catholic faith together in terms of their "special and intimate cooperation."[65] Second, joint action with France would eliminate the danger of mutual rivalry, which was a matter of crucial significance for Metternich.[66] In February the chancellor tried to persuade Guizot that the Austrian proposal was practical and should be preferred: "In the project as we are presenting it, a feasible benefit is achieved; wanting to go further is to get lost on paths leading to an abyss. The direct and practical intellect of Mr Guizot forces him to admit, I do not doubt, that our plan offers a remedy for an ill whose source is completely different from that assigned by people undoubtedly motivated by the best intentions who seek the source of that ill where it does not exist. The Christians in Syria do more harm to each other than the Moslems want to do or in fact do to them. The presence of a representative of a sovereign authority motivated by the *esprit de corps* of a central government that is perfectly tolerant will be sufficient to bring into effect the welfare that we want to ensure to the Christian population in general and the Catholics in particular."[67]

Discussion between the two countries did not survive the end of February. Although Metternich boasted that Guizot had agreed to his arguments and declared his willingness to satisfy the chancellor's wish for closer cooperation between Austria and France in the Syrian Question, his claim was not demonstrated in practice. Anyone in Vienna could hardly suppose that after the Austrian intervention with the Maronites and its refusal of the French project, Austria's religious policy would achieve the Parisian cabinet's support. Guizot could not

---

[64] Metternich to Lützow, Vienna, 14 Feb. 1841, HHStA, StK, Rom 67.
[65] Sainte-Aulaire to Guizot, Vienna, 8 Feb. 1841, AMAE, CP, Autriche 429.
[66] Sainte-Aulaire to Guizot, Vienna, 23 Jan. 1841, AMAE, CP, Autriche 429; Altieri to Lambruschini, Vienna, 12 Feb. 1841, ASV, Arch. Nunz. Vienna 280D; C. E. Farah, "Austrian Diplomacy and the Mt. Lebanon Crisis in the Age of Metternich," A. Tietze (ed.), *Habsburgisch-osmanische Beziehungen: Relations Habsbourg-ottomanes*, Wien 1985, p. 330.
[67] Metternich to Guizot, Vienna, 8 Feb. 1841, HHStA, StK, Rom 67.

and did not want to surrender the French dominance in this region that had lasted 300 years and was now seriously threatened by Metternich's diplomacy. Moreover, although himself a protestant, Guizot held both Catholic circles and the nationalist public in France in high regard. The former advocated intervention for religious reasons and the latter for reasons of national glory. Louis Philippe also took a personal interest in the matter and was evidently aggrieved by the Austrian attitude towards the French proposal. Frederick William IV's lack of cooperation can also be most probably ascribed to the disillusionment caused by the failure of the Prussian project. Although Metternich had avoided expressing Austria's open rejection in Prussia's case, nobody in Berlin had any illusions about the attitude of the cabinet in Vienna. Königsmarck's reports from January and the first half of February 1841 show that he assisted Stürmer in the Syrian Question, but this cooperation obviously broke down and was not revived. The explanation for this fact is simple: Königsmarck was not instructed to proceed with his Austrian colleague in this affair any more.[68]

The third influential power that refused to support Austria was the Holy See. Already in the autumn of 1840, Metternich had tried to obtain the recognition of Pope Gregory XVI for his policy towards the Maronites and Catholics in Syria. To achieve this objective, he had roundly criticised France and its Egyptian protégé. He had accused the government in Paris of offering protection to the Christians only to promote its political goals and claimed that it had no real interest in the fate of the Catholics because otherwise Paris would have had no reason to try to claim all the rights for their protection. The Austrian Empire on the other hand sincerely wanted to protect the rights of Syrian Catholics and did not claim an exclusive protection after the fashion of France: "As to the right of protecting the religious interests of the Catholics in Syria, far from wanting to deprive France of it, we will always recognise its [right], not as an exclusive privilege but as a general right belonging to all Catholic Powers. On the other

---

[68] Metternich to Esterházy, Vienna, 7 March 1841, HHStA, StA, England 236; Apponyi to Metternich, Paris, 16, 19 and 20 Feb. 1841, HHStA, StA, Frankreich 320; Königsmarck to Frederick William IV, Büyükdere, 5 Jan., 10 Feb. and 23 June 1841, GStA PK, HA III, MdA I, 7284; Königsmarck to Stiepovich, Büyükdere, 8 Feb. 1841, GStA PK, HA III, MdA I, 7284; M. Jouplain, *La Question du Liban*, Paris 1908, p. 260.

hand, if one wants to see in this protectorate the right to take sides
for the civil and political interests of our co-religionists against their
sovereign, it is an unjustifiable extension [of the right], a so-called right
that would undermine those of the sovereign authority, finally a right
that we recognise for no one and that we ourselves do not want to appropriate ... We will not create a protectorate, [but] we will intercede
for the Sultan's Catholic subjects with the sovereign."[69] He went even
further in his attack against Mohammed Ali: "I cannot believe that in
Rome anyone is deceived by the charlatanism with which Mohammed
Ali is passed off as a benevolent ruler, the hope for civilisation in the
Levant, the protector of the Christians. This vulpine man has created
only what could serve his own personal interest, he is humane only
to the extent it serves him to maintain the resources of his power,
and his toleration for the Christians exists only in the phrases by
which he amuses European travellers. A heavy yoke imposed on Syria
would soon change it into a region as unfortunate as Egypt, and the
repeated insurrections prior to the current crisis must be attributed
to the barbarous measures that the pasha tried to introduce in these
provinces."[70] Although Metternich was entirely right when claiming
that Mohammed Ali was an oppressor acting only in his own interests
and exploiting his own subjects with high taxes, forced labour and
brutal conscriptions, both in Egypt and Syria,[71] his attack against
the pasha's tolerance was unfounded and it is questionable whether
the chancellor really believed his own words in this respect since it is
evident from other documents that he was well aware of Mohammed
Ali's contribution to the security of the European as well as of the
local Christians.[72] At that moment, however, he had not hesitated
to exaggerate in order to convince the representatives of the Papal
State that the Ottoman government would not actually be any less

---

[69] Metternich to Lützow, Vienna, 21 Nov. 1840, HHStA, StK, Rom 64.

[70] Metternich to Ohms, Vienna, 7 Nov. 1840, HHStA, StK, Rom 64.

[71] The opinion that Mohammed Ali's measures caused the impoverishment, suffering and misery of the inhabitants in question is maintained by prominent historians on Mohammed Ali, Khaled Fahmy and Afaf Lufti al-Sayyid Marsot. Fahmy,
Mehmed Ali, pp. 105–107; Lufti al-Sayyid Marsot, "What Price Reform," p. 4.

[72] Metternich to Stürmer, Vienna, 18 Dec. 1840, HHStA, StA, Türkei VI, 78;
Metternich to Stürmer, Vienna, 7 Feb. 1841, HHStA, StA, Türkei VI, 83; Metter-
nich to Ohms, Vienna, 7 Nov. 1840, HHStA, StK, Rom 64; Metternich to Lützow,
Vienna, 21 Nov. 1840, HHStA, StK, Rom 64.

tolerant than the Egyptian regime: "Compared [to Mohammed Ali], the Porte embarked upon a new course during Sultan Mahmud II's rule, the Mohammedan fanaticism disappeared and gave place to real tolerance. Since the new reign [of Abdülmecid I] even greater progress has been made; the Edict of Gülhane has given to the rayahs [non-Moslems] guaranties that they have never had, and it has sanctioned principles that are the safeguard of human rights. Returning to the authority of the Sultan, Syria would have a real chance to improve its fate."[73]

To all appearances Metternich's effort was doomed to failure also in Rome. Lützow and his subordinate, Austrian Chargé d'Affaires Ohms, were convinced of the prevailing pro-French tendency of most of the Catholic clergy in the Vatican City, which was intensified by fear of the war preparations in France and the threat of an eventual French campaign in the Apennines in the autumn of 1840. Cardinal Secretary of State Luigi Lambruschini acknowledged the Austrian endeavour to help the Syrian Catholics and Metternich's project as the most practical, but that was all that the chancellor obtained from the pope. Stürmer's reports from the Ottoman Empire also imply that the pro-French party really did dominate in Rome, something that Metternich was inclined to agree with. Nevertheless, these complaints must be accepted with reserve. It is most likely that the Holy See actually supported neither Austria nor France and wanted to assume a neutral attitude and obtain the support of both Catholic Powers. This seems to be obvious, first, from the fact that Pontois also criticised the Holy See, but for supporting Austria in Lebanon at the expense of France and, second, from the complaints of the two Catholic Powers of the conduct of the patriarchal Latin vicar apostolic in Constantinople and archbishop of Petra, Julian Maria Hillereau. Whereas Metternich accused him of being pro-French in early November and asked the pope to replace him with someone less pro-French, Pontois accused Hillereau of being pro-Austrian.[74] The French ambassador

---

[73] Metternich to Ohms, Vienna, 7 Nov. 1840, HHStA, StK, Rom 64.

[74] Lützow to Metternich, Rome, 20 June and 18 Nov. 1840, Ohms to Metternich, Rome, 10 Oct. 1840, HHStA, StK, Rom 63; Lützow to Metternich, Rome, 28 March 1841, HHStA, StK, Rom 66; Stürmer to Metternich, Constantinople, 16 June 1841, HHStA, StA, Türkei VI, 81; Altieri to Lambruschini, Vienna, 6 Nov. 1840, ASV, Arch. Nunz. Vienna 280C; Altieri to Lambruschini, Vienna, 12 April and 4 June 1841, ASV, Arch. Nunz. Vienna 280D; Lambruschini to Altieri, Rome,

wrote about the need to replace Hillereau: "It would be necessary for us to have here a bishop who not only would not want to prevent the intervention of the [French] embassy into religious affairs but who would actually elicit it, someone who, like the Lazarists here, would see the progress of the Catholic religion in the progress of the French influence and who, understanding that these two interests are completely united, would work for the former as well as for the latter. It is not enough that the Latin bishop is not hostile to the French government, it is necessary that he offers [it] patriotic and enlightened assistance ... The relations between the Catholic populations and the Turkish government and those of various Catholic confessions among themselves must not be settled without France."[75]

The absence of support from Rome, Berlin and Paris proved to be unimportant because of the attitudes of Russia and Great Britain. Despite the fact that Russia wanted to strengthen its own influence over the Orthodox Christians and in the early spring of 1841 prepared its own project for this purpose, which was not in entire compliance with Metternich's, and despite the fact that Nesselrode's first reaction to Metternich's activities in the affair was negative, the tsar decided after some hesitation to support the Austrian plan and he wrote expressing his support to the sultan on 1 May 1841. Metternich also won the backing of London, where Palmerston completely shared the chancellor's views on the Syrian Question. This was not the case for Ponsonby, who both mistrusted Metternich's aims and considered him to be ignorant on this subject. He refused to participate in the affair until he received explicit instructions to do so from London.[76]

Ponsonby was wrong about Metternich's alleged ignorance. According to the testimonies of Altieri, Lerchenfeld and Sainte-Aulaire, Metternich came to his conclusions after a careful study of a considerable number of relevant documents including the former decrees of the Ottoman sultans and discussions with the experts on the topic, which

---

12 Feb. 1841, ASV, Arch. Nunz. Vienna 281I; Pontois to Guizot, Pera, 27 Jan. 1841, AMAE, CP, Turquie 282.

[75] Pontois to Guizot, Therapia, 24 Nov. 1840, AMAE, CP, Turquie 281.

[76] Ponsonby to Palmerston, Therapia, 25 Feb. 1841, TNA, FO 78/432; Beauvale to Palmerston, Vienna, 2 March 1841, TNA, FO 120/197; Altieri to Lambruschini, Vienna, 9 April 1841, ASV, Arch. Nunz. Vienna 280D; Clanricarde to Palmerston, St Petersburg, 23 Feb. 1841, Wolf, *Notes on the Diplomatic History*, p. 113; Guichen, pp. 469–471; Hajjar, pp. 364–366; Webster, *Palmerston*, II, p. 764.

entirely corresponded to his approach to the issues concerning the internal situation of the Ottoman Empire as already explained in Chapter 12.[77] Nevertheless, Stürmer was left until May without British or Russian support and, despite his original optimism, Metternich was not able to persuade the Porte of the practicality of the Austrian plan presented by the internuncio in Constantinople on 18 February 1841. Reshid Pasha expressed his agreement with the position of the cabinet in Vienna but expected some obstructions in the Divan. In the second half of March, he expressed his concern that the Porte had no suitable candidate for the function of an emissary in Jerusalem acceptable to all Christian factions: "We will never find a man whose disinterest and impartiality will be of a nature that could satisfy all parties."[78] Reshid sincerely desired to settle the affair but his position was quickly deteriorating owing to an increasing opposition towards him in the Divan that finally caused his removal from the office of foreign minister at the end of March. Although it is impossible to explain the basis for the Ottomans' protractions from the studied documents, the fact remains that Ponsonby's lack of cooperation was an important reason why the sultan's reserve was not overcome until the end of May. In mid April, Stürmer could only complain that much more could have been done in the matter of the Syrian Christians if the British ambassador had wanted it.[79]

The Setback in Syria and the June 1841 Settlement

The internuncio's dismay corresponded to the seriousness of the situation. In the spring of 1841, the situation in Syria deteriorated considerably in consequence of the harsh treatment meted out by the new Ottoman administration. Although the Porte ordered its forces

---

[77] Sainte-Aulaire to Guizot, Vienna, 26 Jan. 1841, AMAE, CP, Autriche 429; Altieri to Lambruschini, Vienna, 29 Jan. 1841, ASV, Arch. Nunz. Vienna 280D; Lerchenfeld to Ludwig I of Bavaria, Vienna, 20 Feb. 1841, BHStA, MA, Wien 2410.
[78] Stürmer to Metternich, Constantinople, 24 March 1841, HHStA, StA, Türkei VI, 80.
[79] Stürmer to Metternich, Constantinople, 21 and 24 Feb., 14 April 1841, HHStA, StA, Türkei VI, 79; Titov to Nesselrode, Pera, 5 and 13 March, 1 April 1841, AVPRI, fond 133, Kantseliariia, opis 469, 1841/41.

not to maltreat the inhabitants regardless of their creed, the news of the offences committed by the sultan's soldiers against the Syrians had already been reported in the autumn of 1840. Not intolerance but laziness and greed seem to have been their cause. The Ottoman soldiers demanded the same heavy labour from the mountain tribesmen in Lebanon that their own officers ordered them to carry out even though they knew that forced labour was explicitly forbidden. The inhabitants suffered financial losses not only because of the services demanded by the Ottomans, but also because of the bribes that Ottoman troops often required from the peasants coming to Beirut. At the gates they were stopped by the soldiers refusing to let them continue to the market without the payment of an "appropriate tax." Moreover, in the same city the soldiers were billeted only in Christian houses; no Moslem residence was requisitioned for that purpose, and this could not have remained unnoticed.[80]

The Ottomans' vital mistake proved to be the delivery of this territory into the hands of the commander of the Ottoman forces in Syria, Izzet Mehmed Pasha, who was incompetent, cruel to the local inhabitants and who refused to keep the promises made by Wood in the name of the sultan; Napier called Izzet "the worst man in the world."[81] No wonder that Izzet was unpopular with the Europeans and hated by the Syrians; his conduct hardly contributed to the sultan's popularity. Although Ponsonby and Stürmer had achieved his recall by the end of November 1840, no considerable improvement took place. To the contrary, the situation in Syria continued to deteriorate after the new year. The sultan's soldiers continually maltreated the people and Syria was ravaged from all sides. The main offenders were in particular the Albanian troops who were well known in the Near East in this period for their insubordination. They regarded the locals as enemies and treated them accordingly. Some Syrians even felt compelled to take up arms to defend their villages from the Ottoman Albanians. After the intervention of British and Austrian agents, the Albanians were gradually removed from Syria. Nevertheless, neither

---

[80] Steindl to Stürmer, Beirut, 28 Oct. 1840, Stürmer to Metternich, Constantinople, 25 Nov. 1840, HHStA, StA, Türkei VI, 77; Königsmarck to Frederick William IV, Büyükdere, 23 Dec. 1840, GStA PK, HA III, MdA I, 7283.
[81] M. Chebli, *Une histoire du Liban a l'époque des émirs (1635–1841)*, Beyrouth 1984, p. 336.

this measure, nor the sultan's order to protect the Christians and to punish the offenders nor the issue of a firman establishing in Syria an administrative system conforming to the Hatt-i Sharif of Gülhane led to the desired easing of tensions for two main reasons. First, the irregular behaviour of some Ottoman troops and officials did not change. The most obvious example of such misconduct was the governor of Damascus, Hadji Nejib Pasha, who openly demonstrated his disdain for the Christians. He forbade them to enter the city on horseback or to wear brightly coloured clothes. He ordered them to dress in black according to prescriptions that predated the rule of Mohammed Ali and Ibrahim Pasha, who had abolished these degrading regulations that were now unacceptable to the local Christians. Second, the Ottoman administration needed money and that is why the sultan's promise from the previous year concerning the abolition of the tax burden borne by the Syrians of all professions was not kept. After the losses suffered during the war and the outbreak of a plague in the first months of 1841, the violation of this promise was particularly painful. Furthermore, the greed of the pashas made the Christians' situation worse. For example, Assad Pasha in Aleppo ordered the closure of a church with the explanation that it was built under Mohammed Ali's rule without the Porte's permission, and the order was only revoked when the Christians paid a considerable sum to Assad Pasha.[82]

---

[82] Stürmer to Metternich, Constantinople, 10 Sept. 1840, HHStA, StA, Türkei VI, 75; Steindl to Stürmer, Beirut, 21 Oct. 1840, Stürmer to Metternich, Constantinople, 2 and 25 Nov. 1840, HHStA, StA, Türkei VI, 77; the order for the serasker of the Ottoman army in Syria, 28 Jan. 1841, attached to Stürmer to Metternich, Constantinople, 24 Feb. 1841, HHStA, StA, Türkei VI, 79; Stürmer to Metternich, Constantinople, 24 March 1841, HHStA, StA, Türkei VIII, 15; Steindl to Stürmer, Beirut, 17 April 1841, Stürmer to Metternich, Constantinople, 30 April 1841, HHStA, StA, Türkei VI, 80; Königsmarck to Frederick William IV, Büyükdere, 21 and 25 Nov. 1840, GStA PK, HA III, MdA I, 7283; Königsmarck to Frederick William IV, Büyükdere, 3 March and 26 May 1841, GStA PK, HA III, MdA I, 7284; Basili to Titov, Beirut, 1 and 21 Jan., 23 Feb. 1841, Titov to Nesselrode, Pera, 12 Jan., 10 Feb., 5 and 13 March 1841, AVPRI, fond 133, Kantseliariia, opis 469, 1841/41; Beauvale to Palmerston, Vienna, 1 Nov. 1840, TNA, FO 120/189; Wood to Ponsonby, Beirut, 22 Feb. 1841, Wood to Ponsonby, Beirut, 10 Nov. 1840, Ponsonby to Palmerston, Therapia, 30 Nov. 1840, TNA, FO 78/399; Ponsonby to Palmerston, Therapia, 22 Feb. and 3 March 1841, TNA, FO 78/432; Ponsonby to Palmerston, Therapia, 23 May 1841, TNA, FO 78/434; Wood to Rifat Pasha, Therapia, 23 May 1841, TNA, FO 78/435; Wood to Ponsonby, Beirut, 22 Feb. 1841, Cunningham, *The Early Correspondence*, p. 217; Jouplain, pp. 257–259; Farah,

This situation led Stürmer to the conclusion in early June 1841 that there was almost no Ottoman dignitary in Syria who was not greedy for money and the complaint that "with such individuals the regeneration of the empire is impossible, and even its preservation must become more problematic every day."[83]

Not surprisingly, in the spring of 1841, general discontent was widespread throughout Syria. Disillusionment with the Ottoman government was so great that, in the words of Caspar Merlato, if Ibrahim Pasha "appeared in this state of affairs with a few men on the frontier, he would certainly become the master of the province as rapidly as he was expelled."[84] Steindl, who shortly after his return from the first mission was sent again to Syria to observe the internal situation, wrote to Vienna of the serious threat of insurrection against the Ottomans. Even the most determined opponents of Mohammed Ali and his son were now muttering that Egyptian rule had been better. When one of the Ottoman officials warned the discontented inhabitants that he would put them under the authority of Ibrahim Pasha, they answered with the threat: "More likely we would recall Ibrahim to this country if the government of the Porte does not revise its demands."[85] Particularly serious was the situation in Lebanon where the Ottomans controlled only the coast. The interior fell increasingly into a state of anarchy caused by worsening relations between the Maronites and Druze. Steindl was convinced that since the expulsion of the old Prince of Lebanon, Emir Bashir II, and his replacement by his nephew Bashir Qasim III in October 1840, a weak, and among the people, unpopular governor, there was a lack of any central authority.[86]

The Politics of Interventionism, p. 55.

[83] Stürmer to Metternich, Constantinople, 2 June 1841, HHStA, StA, Türkei VI, 83.

[84] Merlato to Stürmer, Damascus, 6 May 1841, HHStA, StA, Türkei VI, 81.

[85] Steindl to Stürmer, Beirut, 14 May 1841, HHStA, StA, Türkei VI, 81.

[86] Metternich to Stürmer, Vienna, 13 Nov. 1840, HHStA, StA, Türkei VI, 78; Laurin's report, [?], 16 Oct. 1840, Stürmer to Metternich, Constantinople, 2 Nov. 1840, HHStA, StA, Türkei VI, 77; Steindl to Stürmer, Beirut, 29 March and 17 April 1841, Stürmer to Metternich, Constantinople, 14 and 30 April 1841, HHStA, StA, Türkei VI, 80; Steindl to Stürmer, Beirut, 10 May 1841, Stürmer to Metternich, Constantinople, 2 June 1841, HHStA, StA, Türkei VI, 81; Titov to Nesselrode, Pera, 20 April 1841, AVPRI, fond 133, Kantseliariia, opis 469, 1841/41; A. Abraham, *Maronite-Druze Relations in Lebanon 1840–1860: A Prelude to Arab Nationalism*, New York 1975, p. 47.

This "extremely sad news from Syria"[87] caused considerable apprehension in Vienna. Metternich considered Ibrahim Pasha's regime to have been tyrannical, but at least stable. In his opinion, the Ottoman administration in Syria was in no way stable and inclined to be more and more tyrannical. It affected the interests of the Porte as well as the Great Powers who had helped the sultan to regain this region and were thus responsible for its future. The only court benefiting from the worsening situation in Syria was France, which really was not the goal for which the allies had sacrificed their soldiers. The chancellor's warning was well founded because the French did not hesitate to take advantage of the Ottomans' difficulties to recover their former influence. They employed priests to agitate among Catholics on behalf of France, declaring that only this Great Power was entitled to protect the Christian religion, its clergy and convents. The French also used another effective weapon: charity. Desmeloizes distributed 10,000 francs among the Maronites in the spring of 1841 as compensation for the damages suffered in the war. The donations continued during the summer and autumn. The French government's goal was nothing other than the exclusive protection of the Syrian Catholics, which was confirmed by the effort of Desmeloizes and Ratti-Menton to prevent the Austrian consuls from granting help to the Christians and Pontois' firm recommendation to Stürmer that the Austrians not interfere in the Maronites' affairs but relinquish them to the French agents. Whenever the Austrians did not comply, the French immediately showed their indignation. For example, Pontois complained in early March when the Maronites communicated their wishes directly to the Porte and not through France and obtained Austria's intercession. Later in the spring, Ratti-Menton provoked a dispute with Merlato in Damascus because the vicar of the Maronite patriarch was accompanied to the pasha by the dragoman and the guard of the Austrian consulate. When Stürmer told Pontois that the dispute could have negative consequences for the Catholics, the ambassador agreed but added that in such a case Merlato would be guilty because protecting them was France's duty and Merlato was to refrain from doing everything that Ratti-Menton himself was entitled to do.[88]

---

[87] Lerchenfeld to Ludwig I of Bavaria, Vienna, 26 Jan. 1841, BHStA, MA, Wien 2410.
[88] Metternich to Esterházy, Vienna, 15 June 1841, HHStA, StA, England 237;

Metternich was annoyed with the French agents in Syria seeking, in his opinion, more political than religious interests by their egoistic conduct and, therefore, the Austrian Empire was not unresponsive to the French activities and tried to neutralise them by sending its own financial support to Syria. Stürmer forwarded sums from various sources in the Austrian Empire, either 1,000 florins (over 11,000 piasters) from the emperor himself, or a considerably greater sum resulting from the collection within the monarchy ordered by the emperor upon the request of the pope. This sum gathered in its various lands and from various classes including the Hungarian magnates was delivered to the Maronites in several payments during the spring and the summer of 1841. Stürmer reported that only between 20 April and 27 July he transmitted 1,130,502 piasters to the Maronites, but since sums of money had also arrived earlier and later, the total amount granted by Austria in 1841 was considerably greater. It is obvious that the reasons behind these donations were not only humanitarian as is evident from the fact that for the sake of preserving friendly relations the Austrians gave money directly to Yusuf as well as gifts to him and the Maronite clergymen.[89]

Metternich to Stürmer, Vienna, 22 June 1841, HHStA, StA, Türkei VI, 83; Steindl to Stürmer, Beirut, 29 March and 17 April 1841, Stürmer to Metternich, Constantinople, 30 April 1841, HHStA, StA, Türkei VI, 80; Merlato to Stürmer, Damascus, 6 May 1841, Stürmer to Metternich, Constantinople, 20 and 26 May, 2 June 1841, HHStA, StA, Türkei VI, 81; Ponsonby to Palmerston, Therapia, 22 Feb. 1841, TNA, FO 78/432; Titov to Nesselrode, Pera, 13 March 1841, AVPRI, fond 133, Kantseliariia, opis 469, 1841/41; Königsmarck to Frederick William IV, Büyükdere, 31 March 1841, GStA PK, HA III, MdA I, 7284; Pontois to Guizot, Pera, 27 Jan. and 7 March 1841, AMAE, CP, Turquie 282; Pontois to Guizot, Therapia, 27 May and 7 June 1841, AMAE, CP, Turquie 283; D. Chevallier, *La société du Mont Liban à l'époque de la révolution industrielle en Europe*, Paris 1971, p. 161; A. Laurent, *Relations historique des affaires de Syrie, depuis 1840 jusqu'en 1842*, I, Paris 1846, p. 267.
[89] Stürmer to Metternich, Constantinople, 24 March, 14, 21 and 30 April 1841, HHStA, StA, Türkei VIII, 15; Stürmer to Metternich, Constantinople, 12, 19 and 26 May, 2 June, 7 and 28 July, 11 and 25 Aug., 1 and 28 Sept. 1841, HHStA, StA, Türkei VIII, 16; Stürmer to Metternich, Constantinople, 26 May, 9 and 30 June 1841, HHStA, StA, Türkei VI, 81; Altieri to Lambruschini, Vienna, 26 Feb., 26 March, 7 and 23 April, 7 May 1841, ASV, Arch. Nunz. Vienna 280D; Metternich to Altieri, Vienna, 26 April and 31 May 1841, Lambruschini to Altieri, Rome, 3 and 8 May 1841, ASV, Arch. Nunz. Vienna 281I; Wood to Ponsonby, Pera, 8 June 1841, TNA, FO 78/434; Timoni to Wood, 5 July 1841, attached to Ponsonby to Palmerston, Therapia, 31 July 1841, TNA, FO 78/436.

Nevertheless, it does not seem that Austrian activities in Syria equalled the energy of the French agents. As Caesar E. Farah pointed out, "Austrian consular officials reacted as good Catholics whenever a situation merited it, but made no real effort to elbow past their French colleagues in this delicate area."[90] Evidence can also be found in Steindl's lament concerning his country's limited involvement: "As to our August Court, it enjoys the greatest sympathies of all Catholic nations in Syria. We would only have to desire it and we would obtain, particularly in Lebanon, more influence than all the other governments."[91] Although Metternich was deliberating at the same moment about possibly instructing the Austrians to intensify their effort,[92] in the end whatever he did was not sufficient because the emperor's agents still did not know the exact intentions of the cabinet in Vienna and were poorly instructed in the affair of the Syrian Catholics. On 2 June 1841 Stürmer asked the chancellor to be advised of the imperial interests in the Syrian Question to be able to "precisely outline to our consuls the boundaries within which they should proceed."[93] However, no definite instruction addressing this problem ever came from Vienna and even though there lacks a clear explanation for this inaction, it is evident that Metternich did not want to go too far and start a serious quarrel with France over the Syrian Christians causing thus additional problems to the Ottoman administration. A reliable explanation can also be found in Stürmer's report of 21 April 1841 in which the internuncio pointed out the difficult situation of altogether eleven Austrian consuls and consular agents in Syria, who were more merchants than diplomats, not always native Austrians and all of them unpaid by the Austrian government and "buried" under a considerable agenda, which leads to the assumption that their work load resulting from their service to Austria as well as their private business prevented them from being active in the struggle with the French on behalf of the local Christians.[94]

---

[90] Farah, *The Politics of Interventionism*, p. 74.

[91] Steindl to Stürmer, Beirut, 10 April 1841, HHStA, StA, Türkei VI, 80.

[92] Beauvale to Palmerston, Vienna, 14 April 1841, TNA, FO 120/197.

[93] Stürmer to Metternich, Constantinople, 2 June 1841, HHStA, StA, Türkei VI, 81.

[94] Stürmer to Metternich, Constantinople, 21 April 1841, HHStA, StA, Türkei VIII, 15.

Owing to the difficulties in Syria, the need to assure the Christians' safety became increasingly urgent. Metternich began to occupy himself with the future character of the Ottoman rule in this region purely from the administrative point of view only at the beginning of December 1840, but he never paid much attention in his correspondence to this topic, at least in comparison with the purely religious problems, although he certainly understood that the welfare of the Syrian inhabitants depended on the efficiency of the state apparatus. The reason for his limited concern about the Ottoman admistration of Syria consisted partly in Metternich's exhaustion with the protracted Near Eastern crisis and partly from his belief that no radical changes had to be made in Syria to attain desired goals. In his opinion, the province ought to return to the situation before the Egyptian invasion and be again divided into four pashaliks in which governors able to enforce the Ottoman laws would be appointed. As for Lebanon, Metternich did not adopt any firm attitude towards Yusuf's request addressed to Constantinople and Vienna that the prince of Lebanon be chosen from among the Maronite leaders because he did not know whether the grounds on which this demand was founded were valid or not. Nevertheless, he found it better that the authority held by a single prince was divided among a greater number of leaders, giving to each of the tribes a chief chosen from among its own members. Various tribes would thus be governed exclusively by their own chiefs paying a very small tribute to the sultan but being responsible for maintaining strict order and peace within their territories.[95] However, Metternich

---

[95] Metternich to Esterházy, Vienna, 26 Dec. 1840, HHStA, StA, England 231; Metternich to Stürmer, Vienna, 7 Feb. 1841, HHStA, StA, Türkei VI, 83. With the deterioration of the internal situation in Lebanon after 1840 Metternich increasingly desired the nomination of a strong prince, namely the exiled Emir Bashir II. Metternich's sympathetic attitude towards the old emir was clearly visible already at the end of 1840 when he criticised Stopford's expulsion of Bashir II from Syria to Malta and was willing to ensure his asylum in Austria or support his move to Constantinople. Already in the late summer of the following year, the critical situation in Syria moved Metternich to advise the Porte to reinstate Bashir II to the post of the prince of Lebanon, but without success. In the mid 1840s, Metternich was supported in this idea by Guizot but this plan was finally thwarted by the opposition of Great Britain. Metternich to Stürmer, Vienna, 29 Dec. 1840, HHStA, StA, Türkei VIII, 15; Ottenfels to Stürmer, Vienna, 24 Aug. 1841, HHStA, StA, Türkei VI, 83; M. Hametner, *Orientpolitik Österreichs in den Jahren 1841–1853*, unpublished dissertation, Wien 1934, p. 25; Farah, "Austrian Diplomacy and the Mt. Lebanon Crisis," p. 330.

only submitted this idea "as one which may be worth examination in conjunction with the ministers of the Porte, not as one on which his mind is made up."[96]

As noted above, Metternich's views of the future administration of Syria as well as the security of Christians living there were motivated by his respect for the sultan's sovereignty and simultaneously by his desire to weaken the French influence. For these reasons he proposed to exclude Acre from the local administration and place it into the hands of a governor installed by the sultan and subordinate only to him. Its garrison was to be composed of Turkish soldiers. The chancellor also opposed the idea that some cities on the Lebanese coast, such as Beirut and Latakia, should be governed directly by Emir Bashir III because it would considerably strengthen the influence of the Maronites over this area. According to Metternich, there was no certainty that the prestige Austria enjoyed among them would prevail forever and if France were to recover its former interest with this Catholic nation, it would strengthen its influence in the seaports and contribute to its political and economic supremacy. Metternich discussed his designs for Acre and the Lebanese sea ports with Palmerston, whose opinions were affirmative, and no opposition came from other cabinets.[97]

The worsening situation in Syria, the French activities and the Ottomans' maltreatment of the Christian population in Bulgaria that

---

[96] Beauvale to Palmerston, Vienna, 2 Dec. 1840, TNA, FO 120/189. At this point it is necessary to mention the proposition that Stürmer allegedly discussed with the Porte for the creation of an autonomous Lebanese principality in 1840, a thesis that historians Khalil Fattal and Joseph Abou Nohra based only on Pontois' three reports. Fattal and Nohra, *L'Autriche et le Liban*, p. 32; Nohra, "L'Autriche et la question du Liban," p. 303. If it was so, and it is very improbable, it had to be only a private matter because there is no corresponding reference in the Austrian or other researched diplomatic correspondence.

[97] Metternich to Esterházy, Vienna, 3 Feb. 1841, HHStA, StA, England 236; Beauvale to Palmerston, Vienna, 2 Dec. 1840, TNA, FO 120/189; Beauvale to Palmerston, Vienna, 3 Jan. and 4 April 1841, TNA, FO 120/197; Tatishchev to Nesselrode, Vienna, 19 Dec. 1840, AVPRI, fond 133, Kantseliariia, opis 469, 1840/178; Tatishchev to Nesselrode, Vienna, 6 Feb. 1841, AVPRI, fond 133, Kantseliariia, opis 469, 1841/191; Titov to Nesselrode, Pera, 5 March 1841, AVPRI, fond 133, Kantseliariia, opis 469, 1841/41; Maltzan to Frederick William IV, Vienna, 26 Dec. 1840, GStA PK, HA III, MdA I, 7360; Maltzan to Frederick William IV, Vienna, 2 Feb. 1841, GStA PK, HA III, MdA I, 6034; Sainte-Aulaire to Guizot, Vienna, 13 Jan. 1841, AMAE, CP, Autriche 429.

rose up against the pasha of Vidin in the spring of 1841 moved Russia and Great Britain to greater activity in the Syrian Question and contributed thus to the greater support on the part of Ponsonby and Titov for Stürmer's negotiation with the Porte. On 31 May 1841, the internuncio visited the sultan and began a new series of discussions with the Porte on Syrian affairs. Pontois was left out, which annoyed him because although he saw nothing harmful for France in Metternich's project, the mere fact that France was excluded was considered by the ambassador as detrimental to its interests. However, he did not seem to oppose his colleagues' activities. The joint effort of Austrian, British and Russian representatives led to a quick solution which complied with Metternich's wishes. On 20 June 1841, Abdülmecid I issued a firman in favour of the Christians in Syria. Division General Tahir Pasha, a former chairman of the Ottoman Military Council, was appointed governor of Jerusalem and Gaza subordinate only to the sultan and given great power to protect the safety of the Christian minorities. The existing rights of non-Moslems were confirmed and new privileges were granted in several letters addressed to Tahir Pasha and other Syrian dignitaries. Moreover, the sultan kept his promises made in the previous year to the benefit of the Syrian population such as the reduction of taxes or granting money to the local chiefs assisting in the fight against the Egyptians.[98]

With this, Austrian diplomacy achieved a success in which Stürmer had "not even dared to hope."[99] Metternich was completely satisfied with the result of his effort to secure a better future for the

---

[98] Metternich to Stürmer, Vienna, 22 June 1841, HHStA, StA, Türkei VI, 83; Stürmer to Metternich, Constantinople, 6, 16, 23 and 30 June 1841, HHStA, StA, Türkei VI, 81; Altieri to Lambruschini, Vienna, 28 April and 7 May 1841, ASV, Arch. Nunz. Vienna 280D; Titov to Nesselrode, Pera, 18 May 1841, AVPRI, fond 133, Kantseliariia, opis 469, 1841/41; Königsmarck to Frederick William IV, Büyükdere, 2, 23 and 30 June 1841, GStA PK, HA III, MdA I, 7284; Bockelberg to Frederick William IV, Vienna, 15 and 30 June, 3 July 1841, GStA PK, HA III, MdA I, 7364; Ponsonby to Palmerston, Therapia, 8 June 1841, TNA, FO 78/434; the firman addressed to Feriq Mehmed Tahir Pasha, 20 June 1841, the grand vizier's letter to the pashas of Damascus, Aleppo, Sidon and feriqs of Tripoli in Syria and Jerusalem, Ponsonby to Palmerston, Therapia, 20 June 1841, TNA, FO 78/435; Pontois to Guizot, Therapia, 17 June 1841, AMAE, CP, Turquie 283.
[99] Stürmer to Metternich, Constantinople, 30 June 1841, HHStA, StA, Türkei VI, 81.

Syrian Christians in a practicable way.[100] He evaluated the benefit of the European intervention in this self-confident way: "We are absolutely convinced that the results of our efforts in the Divan are the only ones which were attainable and the only really practical ones and that they otherwise suffice to fulfil all the hitherto neglected desires of the [Christian] religion, or at least to secure a tolerable and much improved existence than before for the Christians in Syria."[101] This statement was, however, only half true. From a short-term view, Austrian diplomacy had undoubtedly been successful. The chancellor had achieved all of his goals relating to the future of the Syrian Christians, and he had been the driving force of the negotiations that had been successful in June 1841. As to the administrative system, here the Porte also accepted many of Metternich's recommendations because they best served the sultan's own objectives in Syria; the future of Acre and the Lebanese coast was settled according to Metternich's advice when at the beginning of March 1841 Selim Pasha was constituted as an independent governor of Acre; only the number of pashaliks was reduced from four to three but nothing indicates that this fact would be regretted by Metternich. Above all, in cooperation with Great Britain Metternich reduced French dominance over the Syrian Christians. Although Austria's influence over Syria did not approach British influence in the summer of 1841, the Habsburg Monarchy was largely popular among the Catholic population.[102]

From a long-term view, however, Metternich's victory was considerably less spectacular. The arrangements undertaken by the Porte

---

[100] Metternich to Stürmer, Vienna, 29 June 1841, HHStA, StA, Türkei VI, 83; Uditore to Lambruschini, Vienna, 2 and 17 July 1841, ASV, Arch. Nunz. Vienna 280D; Bockelberg to Frederick William IV, Vienna, 7 July 1841, GStA PK, HA III, MdA I, 6034.

[101] Metternich to Lützow, Vienna, 12 July 1841, HHStA, StK, Rom 67. Pontois was of the same opinion when he stated that the firmans had nothing in common with the "impatient desires of the speculative reformers of the Levant but with everything that practical men could reasonably demand at the given moment on behalf of the interests of Christian rayahs and in the cause of humanity!" Pontois to Guizot, Therapia, 27 June 1841, AMAE, CP, Turquie 283.

[102] Stürmer to Metternich, Constantinople, 3 March 1841, Steindl to Stürmer, Beirut, 10 April 1841, HHStA, StA, Türkei VI, 80; C. E. Farah, "The Quadruple Alliance and Proposed Ottoman Reforms in Syria, 1839–1841," *International Journal of Turkish Studies* 2, 1981, 1, p. 102; Farah, *The Politics of Interventionism*, pp. 52, 58, 71 and 81; Hajjar, p. 365.

in June under pressure from three of the Great Powers did not lead to
any significant improvement of the internal situation in Syria because
the problems of this province were too complicated and the discontent of its inhabitants too widespread to be removed by the Porte's
several firmans. The animosity between the Maronites and the Druze
escalated and civil war broke out in Lebanon in the autumn of 1841.
The privileges recognised or newly bestowed upon the Christians such
as their *de facto* equality with the Moslem majority in terms of the
Hatt-i Sharif of Gülhane contributed to an increased animosity on the
part of local Moslems who saw in this an act of blasphemy. Even the
changes in the system of taxation affecting all inhabitants were generally regarded as concessions to the Christians. Consequently, mutual
relations in Syria deteriorated, thanks in part to the intervention of
European countries in aid of the Christian Churches. This was Metternich's biggest failure. His proposals for religious and administrative
affairs had sought to improve the living conditions of the Christians
in Syria and to remove any cause for the interference of the Great
Powers in the internal affairs of the Ottoman Empire. Ultimately he
had hoped to consolidate the sultan's power. Thanks to the persistent
conflict in Syria, however, the situation produced a different outcome
and Lebanon became a centre of tension that continued to attract the
attention of the other European Powers. France played an important
role again and Metternich's fear that it would take advantage of the
unsettled situation in Syria finally proved to be the case. The government in Paris actually restored its temporarily lost influence, particularly among the Maronites. Although Metternich had only sought to
weaken the French protectorate and not to replace it with Austria's
own, and although Austria enjoyed greater respect in this region after 1841, the French come-back must also be regarded as a defeat for
Metternich, in particular owing to France's disinclination to cooperate with Austria in the affairs concerning Catholicism in the Levant.
Consequently, Metternich's offer of July 1841 for Austro-French cooperation in Syria and his recommendation to leave the protection of the
Ottoman Catholics to an apostolic vicar without political ambitions
unsurprisingly received no response from the French, and Metternich's
warning to Sainte-Aulaire in August that to "complicate the interests of the Christians in the Levant with a political question seemed
to him the most certain means for frustrating every improvement of

their fate,"[103] was unable to change in any way the French attitude solicitously guarding its privileged position.[104]

* * *

To be able to summarise Metternich's role in the outcome of the Syrian Question in 1841, some other queries must be raised. First, should Metternich also be held responsible for the social upheaval in Syria and Lebanon after 1841? In fact he could be simply because he was among those who failed to find a long-term solution to the Syrian Question. On closer investigation, however, Metternich's views and actions in the complicated affair did not lack correctness and goodwill and they rested on a realistic assessment of the situation.

Second, was Metternich entirely ignorant as Ponsonby claimed regarding the Syrian Question? He seemed not to be and definitely nobody else offered a better solution at that time. Metternich has been criticised by historians for his reluctance to allow changes in the political and social status quo. In terms of Europe this criticism is well founded. Given the complexities of confessional issues in the Near East, however, his circumspection is understandable. His actions resulted not merely from his conservatism but also from geopolitics and a realistic appraisal of the situation. French and Prussian plans for Jerusalem, for example, would have had a devastating impact on the relations among the various religious communities in this city as well as in other parts of the Ottoman Empire. The annexation of

---

[103] Sainte-Aulaire to Guizot, Vienna, 15 Aug. 1841, AMAE, CP, Autriche 429.

[104] Metternich to Apponyi, Vienna, 28 July 1841, HHStA, StA, Frankreich 322; Stürmer to Metternich, Constantinople, 14 July 1841, HHStA, StA, Türkei VI, 81; Stürmer to Metternich, Constantinople, 11 Aug., 10 and 24 Nov. 1841, HHStA, StA, Türkei VI, 82; Lerchenfeld to Ludwig I of Bavaria, Vienna, 20 June 1841, BHStA, MA, Wien 2410; Königsmarck to Frederick William IV, Büyükdere, 7 July 1841, GStA PK, HA III, MdA I, 7284; Uditore to Lambruschini, Vienna, 17 July 1841, ASV, Arch. Nunz. Vienna 280D; W. Jahrmann, *Frankreich und die orientalische Frage 1875/78*, Berlin 1936, p. 13; A. Schlicht, *Frankreich und die syrischen Christen 1799–1861: Minoritäten und europäischer Imperialismus im Vorderen Orient*, Berlin 1981, p. 39; Farah, *The Politics of Interventionism*, p. 77; Farah, "The Quadruple Alliance," p. 126; Hajjar, p. 515; Schlicht, "The Role of Foreign Powers," p. 111.

Holy Places by European countries would have offended Moslems, weakened the sultan's power and caused a new problem for European diplomacy since no one could presume that the Catholic, Orthodox and Protestant Powers would have been able to achieve harmony. The well-known French-Russian dispute before the Crimean War offers clear proof of this.

Third, was Metternich too optimistic when he counted on the improvement of the Ottoman administration in Syria? In this case, he had no other choice. If the Great Powers finally declared that they wanted to preserve the sultan's sovereignty over Syria, there was no other prospect for the Syrian Christians than to live within the boundaries of the Ottoman Empire. The only way to improve their living conditions was to convince the Porte to maintain a functioning administrative apparatus. Past experience had already proved that the Ottomans were capable of assuring Christians an undisturbed and prosperous life: ten years earlier, with Austrian and French assistance, the life of Catholic Armenians in the Ottoman Empire had been considerably improved by several decrees issued by the Porte.[105] Metternich also tried to assure the same for the Maronites, at least in religious matters. It was not his fault that the Ottomans failed entirely in their takeover of Syria and that the Maronites could not come to an agreement with the Druze over the distribution of political power in Mount Lebanon.[106]

Fourth, did Metternich's involvement in the Syrian Question in 1840 and 1841 contribute to an increased interest of the other European Powers in the religious and political affairs of this region in the following decades? The answer is positive but such an outcome would certainly also have occurred without any Austrian measures taken on behalf of first the Maronites and later all Christians in the same years. Already in the autumn of 1840, a minor dispute between France and Russia over religious affairs occurred and the British in-

---

[105] For more see Chapter 11.

[106] Metternich also had to direct his attention to the situation of Lebanon after 1841. He attempted to solve the crisis when he proposed a division of Lebanon into two parts, Druze and Maronite, and thereby solve the complicated relations between the two antagonised ethnic groups. The Porte accepted this solution and proclaimed the division in early 1843. F. Traboulsi, *A History of Modern Lebanon*, London 2007, p. 24; Hametner, pp. 9–28.

tervened in the internal situation of Syria earlier in the same year.[107] What must be assessed positively in Metternich's case is the fact that the aim of his policy was to create conditions that would make the interference of European Powers into the internal affairs of the Ottoman Empire unnecessary. Although he tried to weaken the French influence over the Maronites at the beginning, particularly because he wanted to use them in the fight against the French protégé Mohammed Ali, Metternich never seriously thought of preventing France from protecting the Catholics and did not permit himself to carry the banner of religion, either before June 1841 nor in the second half of that year when, in the name of Catholicism, the pope tried to drag him into a diplomatic conflict with Prussia and Russia. In mid July 1841, Lambruschini alleged the tsar's hostility towards the Catholic Church and referred to the subversive activities of Russian agents in the Near East. He expressed a wish that Austria would undertake countermeasures.[108] Metternich replied that he could do nothing in this matter and that the only practical measure was to "ensure that the episcopal seats were always occupied by priests of pure doctrine and firm and prudent character."[109] This answer clearly illustrates not only Metternich's scepticism with regard to the activities of Churches in the Levant but also the importance for Austria of the partnership with Russia. Several months later, Lambruschini criticised the Prussian struggle to establish a Protestant bishopric in Palestine with British aid. The pope exhorted Austria and France to protect the Catholic faith from "an outrage hitherto unheard."[110] Metternich had opposed this Protestant institution since the very beginning because he saw no practical reason for its creation since there were almost no Protestants in Syria and, therefore, he saw the measure as absurd: "It is to place a shepherd where no flock exists."[111] He expressed his opinion against this measure in Berlin as well as in London but he did not find the new religious establishment critically dangerous to other confessions.[112] Therefore, he refused to comply with the pope's wish and

---

[107] Stürmer to Metternich, Constantinople, 21 Oct. 1840, HHStA, StA, Türkei VI, 76; Pontois to Thiers, Therapia, 17 Oct. 1840, AMAE, CP, Turquie 281.

[108] Lützow to Metternich, Rome, 17 July 1841, HHStA, StK, Rom 65.

[109] Metternich to Lützow, Königswart, 29 July 1841, HHStA, StK, Rom 67.

[110] Lützow to Metternich, Rome, 13 Nov. 1841, HHStA, StK, Rom 65.

[111] Flahaut to Guizot, Vienna, 23 Nov. 1841, AMAE, CP, Autriche 429.

[112] Altieri to Lambruschini, Vienna, 31 Dec. 1841, ASV, Arch. Nunz. Vienna 280D.

contest the Prussian-British plan because "what could the Catholic courts obtain by opposing the establishment of a Protestant bishopric in Jerusalem? It is not the creation of [such an institution] that could ever threaten the interests of our religion in the Holy Land."[113]

It is evident that Metternich objected more to the French than the Russian, British or Prussian activities in the religious affairs of the Ottoman Empire. His animosity to the French endeavour for the exclusive protectorate was so great that he even recommended to the pope that he send only Italian clericals to the Levant because, in the chancellor's opinion, the French above all sought to propagate the political influence of their nation. The Holy See was also advised to ask not only France but also Austria for assistance if any problems in relation to Ottoman Catholics arose in the future.[114] In any case, even in relation to France, Metternich was resolved to proceed with great restraint because neither before nor after 1841 did he want to transform the eastern Mediterranean into a battlefield of religious-political interests.

---

[113] Metternich to Lützow, Vienna, 30 Nov. 1841, HHStA, StK, Rom 67.
[114] Metternich to Lützow, Vienna, 12 July 1841, HHStA, StK, Rom 67; Lützow to Metternich, Rome, 31 July 1841, Vienna, HHStA, StK, Rom 65; Altieri to Lambruschini, Vienna, 31 Dec. 1841, ASV, Arch. Nunz. Vienna 280D.

Mustafa Reshid Pasha and the Tanzimat

As already explained earlier, Metternich was not an opponent of the Ottoman reform movement and, on the contrary, he wanted crucial and beneficial changes to be carried out in the Ottoman Empire and its decay retarded. The best proof can be found in his attitude towards the leading reformer of the era, Mustafa Reshid Pasha, who is generally called the father of the Tanzimat – the reform period started by the promulgation of the Hatt-i Sharif of Gülhane on 3 November 1839. Metternich not only agreed with the content of this reform edict but he also personally liked and supported its author despite the fact that he did not always agree with Reshid's reformatory views, which he sometimes regarded as somewhat impractical. Metternich's inclination towards Reshid went so far that he even exerted extreme effort to keep him in his post as Ottoman foreign minister in early 1841 even though he knew of Reshid's plan to use the Great Powers to force the sultan to carry out necessary reforms in his empire, a plan amounting to high treason. The history of Metternich's relationship with Reshid offers clear evidence not only of his strong personal belief that reforms had to be carried out but also that he was not a narrow-minded reactionary desperately fighting against any change and everyone with different views.

Metternich's Attitude towards Mustafa Reshid Pasha

One of the crucial obstacles to the Ottoman reform movement at the time of Sultan Mahmud II's reign was the lack of capable men who could assist him in his effort to revive his decaying empire.[1]

---

[1]   Zürcher, p. 47.

The Austrian and Prussian representatives in Constantinople often marked the absence of such advisors as the crucial impediment for its successful regeneration. For example, Ottenfels remarked in the summer of 1832: "This is not at all the time when Sultan Mahmud can hope to realise the project [of reforms]. His intentions are certainly laudable and one cannot praise enough the determination and perseverance with which he follows his goal. But this sovereign himself is largely inerudite and surrounded by advisors who are too ignorant and too interested in flattering him and hiding the truth to know which proper means he ought to choose for implementing his ideas."[2] The rise of talented men was hampered by corruption and the struggle for power, and when someone competent was finally found despite these obstructions, he inevitably became a part of the contest for power taking place between different interest groups, and he sooner or later fell into disfavour with his monarch, who was thus cutting the tree on which he tried to climb.[3] This situation was accurately described by Königsmarck whose dispatches were usually read by Metternich: "They [reforms] do not pursue a fixed and determined aim but change direction at any moment according to the personal ideas and views of the individual advisors. And exactly at the moment when a minister seizes the reins of the government with any force, a hundred people try to discredit him in the eyes of the sovereign whose suspicion can be aroused very easily if one of his servants gains any influence. The sultan's favour substitutes for merit and with this favour his subject obtains or loses a position, fortune or consideration. Therefore, there are intrigues to obtain and keep his favour and that is why mistrust and jealousy dominate between the employees; a smile of the master suffices for making an adversary of a so-called friend."[4]

---

[2] Ottenfels to Metternich, Constantinople, 10 July 1832, HHStA, StA, Türkei VI, 54.

[3] Ottenfels to Metternich, Constantinople, 25 Feb. 1830, HHStA, StA, Türkei VI, 50; Ottenfels to Metternich, Constantinople, 10 Sept. 1832, HHStA, StA, Türkei VI, 54; Ottenfels to Metternich, Constantinople, 8 Jan. 1833, HHStA, StA, Türkei VI, 56; Martens, *Quelques idées sur l'état actuel de la Turquie, ses ressources et le parti qu'on pourrait en tirer*, Büyükdere, 10 June 1834, GStA PK, HA III, MdA I, 7274; Königsmarck to Frederick William III, Büyükdere, 8 Aug. 1838, GStA PK, HA III, MdA I, 7280.

[4] Königsmarck to Frederick William III, Büyükdere, 4 April 1838, GStA PK, HA III, MdA I, 7280.

Metternich was well aware of the fact that Mahmud II was usually surrounded by inefficient minions, who made any advance in his reformative efforts almost impossible: "It is unfortunate that in Turkey, during the reign of Mahmud, his counsellors very often mistook words for actions and forms for the substance that should have served them as a basis."[5] Metternich regretted the absence of competent, educated and incorruptible personalities at the top of the social hierarchy so much that, as explained in Chapter 20, he did not even conceal that he missed a man of Mohammed Ali's skills in Constantinople functioning as the sultan's advisor. Consequently, the chancellor welcomed the new hope for the improvement of the internal conditions of the Ottoman Empire that arose at the end of Mahmud II's reign in the person of Mustafa Reshid Bey (Pasha since January 1838), an Ottoman official and diplomat who was nominated the minister of foreign affairs in July 1837.[6]

Metternich himself had three opportunities to meet personally with Reshid in the 1830s, in Vienna in August 1834 and October 1837, and in Venice in October 1838, and he was then able to make his own opinion of the young Ottoman. The chancellor considered Reshid to be extraordinarily intelligent, incorruptible and devoted to his native country with a sincere wish to regenerate it. He suspected Reshid of being influenced in his reformatory efforts by his admiration for the West and consequently being willing to go further in the changes than was considered in Vienna to be useful for the Ottoman Empire; he was well aware of the fact that Reshid did not lean towards Russia and courted better relations with Great Britain after his appointment to the leadership of the Ottoman foreign ministry, but Reshid's pro-Western tendencies did not seem to give rise to any undue animosity or antipathy on Metternich's part, albeit he regretted them.[7]

[5]   Metternich to Stürmer, Vienna, 26 May 1840, HHStA, StA, Türkei VI, 78.
[6]   Metternich to Esterházy, Vienna, 7 Aug. 1839, HHStA, StA, England 225; Kodaman, p. 21.
[7]   Metternich to Stürmer, Baden, 2 Sept. 1834, HHStA, StA, Türkei VIII, 6; Metternich to Stürmer, Vienna, 27 June 1837, HHStA, StA, Türkei VI, 66; Metternich to Stürmer, Vienna, 24 Oct. 1837, HHStA, StA, Türkei VIII, 10; Metternich to Stürmer, Vienna, 13 Nov. 1838, HHStA, StA, Türkei VI, 67; Metternich to Neumann, Königswart, 31 July 1840, HHStA, StA, England 230; Metternich to Neumann, Königswart, 5 Sept. 1840, HHStA, StA, England 231; La Rochefoucauld to Rigny, Vienna, 28 and 31 Aug. 1834, AMAE, CP, Autriche 421; O'Sullivan to Nothomb, Vienna, 1 Sept. 1834, ADA, CP, Autriche 2; report from Vienna,

It was all-important that Metternich always held the view expressed at the beginning of 1836: "Reshid Bey is one of the most capable men in the Ottoman ministry [read government], who combines much tact and finesse, sane judgement and correct knowledge of the relations between different European cabinets."[8] A little known but rather distinct trait of Metternich's character proved itself in his attitude towards Reshid: in his personal estimations of people and events the prince manifested an extraordinary objectiveness that was not influenced to any extent by personal prejudices or differences in opinions, which means that even if Metternich strongly disliked someone for various reasons or if someone thwarted him, he did not deny his merits or good personality traits. When, for example, Cardinal Secretary of State Ercole Consalvi frustrated Metternich's political designs for the Italian states in early 1820s, he was still regarded by the prince as the only man capable of improving the administration of the Papal State, and Metternich did not cease acknowledging his personal qualities or cooperating with him.[9] And as well as in the case of Mohammed Ali, whose remarkable administrative results in Egypt Metternich never dared to override and with whom he never condescended to making personal assaults because of the Egyptian governor's disloyalty, an occasional disagreement with Reshid Pasha likewise never led to the Austrian chancellor's hostility towards the man in whose skills he saw one of the few chances for the improvement of the situation of the Ottoman Empire and the desired stability of its administration; and although Metternich did not hesitate to enumerate Reshid's mistakes when he found it necessary, his deep affection for this reformer is obvious from the studied correspondence.

The prince seemed to believe that he would be able to influence Reshid's views and decisions, particularly those concerning reforms. He definitely tried to do so during the 1830s, and although the topics

---

27 and 30 Aug. 1834, SS, HD, SG, Wien 93; report from Vienna, 2 Oct. 1838, SS, HD, SG, Wien 93; Maltzan to Frederick William III, Vienna, 28 June 1837, GStA PK, HA III, MdA I, 6029; Maltzan to Frederick William III, Vienna, 19 Oct. 1838, GStA PK, HA III, MdA I, 6031; Maltzan to Frederick William III, Vienna, 1 Jan. 1840, GStA PK, HA III, MdA I, 7351; Bockelberg to Frederick William IV, Vienna, 25 Aug. 1840, GStA PK, HA III, MdA I, 7356; Davison, "Foreign and Environmental Contributions," p. 78.

[8] Metternich to Hummelauer, Vienna, 9 Jan. 1836, HHStA, StA, England 125.

[9] Reinerman, "Metternich and Reform," p. 540.

of their conversations are not entirely known, it can be regarded as certain that the disconsolate situation of the Ottoman Empire was among them; the two men seemed to share the same opinion of the unsatisfactory results of Mahmud II's reforms which were labelled by Reshid as "mere pretensions."[10] When Reshid intensified the Ottoman reformatory efforts in the late 1830s, and particularly after Mahmud II's death, he still consulted with the chancellor at a distance through Baron Stürmer. The studied correspondence proves this claim sufficiently, but there are also two documents in the Haus-, Hof-und Staatsarchiv in Vienna that offer more direct evidence. During the period when the Hatt-i Sharif of Gülhane was promulgated on 3 November 1839, Reshid Pasha asked Metternich for advice in reformatory matters. That the request came from Reshid is proved, first, by the studied Austrian and Russian diplomatic correspondence reflecting Reshid's desire to consult with Metternich on the reorganisation of the Ottoman administration[11] and, second, by the words of Maltzan: "Metternich found the demand, as one might expect, rather considerable and unusual, and despite not wanting to assume such a task and the responsibility associated with it, Metternich nevertheless made an effort to develop in a dispatch some governmental guidelines and a list of recommendations of which the Turkish government would be well advised to never lose sight."[12] The result was the chancellor's broad analysis of 3 December 1839, well known owing to the fact that it was later published by Prince Richard von Metternich-Winneburg,[13] which enabled some historians to use it for a brief reference to Met-

---

[10] Bailey, p. 171.

[11] Metternich to Stürmer, Vienna, 3 Dec. 1839, HHStA, StA, Türkei VI, 72; Tatishchev to Nesselrode, Vienna, 3 Oct. 1839, AVPRI, fond 133, Kantseliariia, opis 469, 1839/214.

[12] Maltzan to Frederick William III, Vienna, 5 Dec. 1839, GStA PK, HA III, MdA I, 7350.

[13] Metternich to Stürmer, Vienna, 3 Dec. 1839, HHStA, StA, Türkei VI, 72, published also by Prince Richard von Metternich-Winneburg in the sixth volume of *NP*, pp. 358–366. The published and abbreviated version lacks, in comparison with the original, the information that it was written upon Reshid's request. However, it still contains the important mention that, earlier in 1839, Metternich had explained his views on how to direct the reforms in the Ottoman Empire to Rifat Bey, departing at that time for Constantinople, as the chancellor wanted to influence Reshid in this way.

ternich's attitude towards the Hatt-i Sharif and the Ottoman reform movement.[14]

There is, however, a second document, more precisely a collection of several documents put together, that the Ottoman minister sent to Metternich not long before his fall in March 1841: three proposals for the internal organisation of the Ottoman administration already rejected by the sultan and a *Mémoire sur la situation actuelle de l'Empire Ottoman* (*Memorandum on the Current Situation of the Ottoman Empire*).[15] This work was instigated by Stürmer, who suggested that Reshid put down his reformatory views in writing and ask the chancellor for their examination. Although Metternich was sceptical as to the contribution of his advice on the Ottoman reform movement, as proved by his words on the margin of the dispatch "useless effort,"[16] he accepted the documents sent in absolute secrecy together with Austrian correspondence on 10 March 1841. The most important one, the Memorandum, started with the explanation of the reasons that had led to the promulgation of the Hatt-i Sharif of Gülhane and the principal aims of the document. It continued to warn against fatal consequences if the principles of the reformatory edict were not called into action, which was very likely to happen owing to the attitude of Abdülmecid I who, under the influence of his retinue, had begun to turn away from the path traced in the Hatt-i Sharif. Reshid was convinced that the sultan's return to an incalculable and oppressive form of government could hardly be tolerated any longer by the Ottoman population and particular by the Christians, who had already started to free themselves from Ottoman rule. The eventual disintegration of the Ottoman Empire would have fatal consequences for the Euro-

---

[14] Berkes, pp. 148–149; Kornrumpf, p. 115.

[15] *Mémoire sur la situation actuelle de l'Empire Ottoman; Projet de réglement concernant la marche des affaires dans les divers bureaux de la Porte; Projet d'un réglement pour le Conseil de justice, ou conseil suprême de l'Etat; Projet concernant l'organisation des Ministéres et des principaux emploise de la Sublime Porte,* attached to Stürmer to Metternich, Constantinople, 10 March 1841, HHStA, StA, Türkei VI, 80.

[16] Stürmer to Metternich, Constantinople, 3 March 1841, HHStA, StA, Türkei VI, 80. This expression of scepticism was not a reaction to Reshid's reformatory effort in itself but to the problems which it had to face and about which Reshid also complained in the Memorandum and during meetings with Stürmer and other European diplomants, namely the increasing opposition of some highly-placed conservative Ottomans, something which Metternich knew. For more see below.

pean Powers and, consequently, they were to pay greater interest to the improvement of its internal situation because this would serve not only humanitarianism, but also geopolitical goals. The most necessary reforms were enumerated by Reshid, who suggested that the Powers' active intervention should take place at a conference in Constantinople between their commissaries and the agents of the Porte, who would arrange the reforms. In his opinion, the form of Austria's government and its legal and administrative principles were to serve as a fitting model because they were the most suitable for the sultan's lands and subjects.[17] Afterwards, the Powers would factually warrant their execution and would force the Ottoman ruler, even with the threat of the division of his empire if necessary, to carry out the changes needed to improve the living conditions of his subjects. Reshid did not doubt that such a threat would force the young sultan to succumb, but he also suggested that the agencies of the Great Powers supervise all relevant details and place one or two battleships on the Bosphorus in order to secure their influence until the entire consolidation of the new institutions came into being.[18]

The confidentiality of this affair was absolutely necessary for Reshid, who in this way proved his absolute trust in Metternich; in particular the content of the *Memorandum on the Current Situation of the Ottoman Empire*, had it been revealed to the sultan, would definitely have caused Reshid's immediate execution. The minister,

---

[17] Reshid did not mention the possibility of Austria serving as an example for some Ottoman reforms for the first time in this Memorandum. Already in March 1838, he had asked Stürmer to convey to Metternich a request for basic information on the Austrian state counsel, the system of taxes and the police system. However, no evidence of an answer to this demand has been found. Stürmer to Metternich, Constantinople, 28 March 1838, HHStA, StA, Türkei VI, 67. Reshid also expressed himself in this sense to Ponsonby in September 1839, as proved at the end of this chapter. T. Subaşi, "British Support for Mustafa Reşid Pasha and his Reforms according to British Sources at the Public Records Office," K. Çiçek (ed.), *The Great Ottoman-Turkish Civilisation, Vol. 1: Politics*, Ankara 2000, p. 428.

[18] Mustafa Reshid Pasha's *Mémoire sur la situation actuelle de l'Empire Ottoman* [*Memorandum on the Current Situation of the Ottoman Empire*], translated into French by Baron Heinrich von Testa, attached to Stürmer to Metternich, Constantinople, 10 March 1841 (N472E), HHStA, StA, Türkei VI, 80. The whole document in French can be found in M. Šedivý, "Metternich and Mustafa Reshid Pasha's Fall in 1841," *British Journal of Middle Eastern Studies* 39, 2012, 2, pp. 277–282. It was also introduced by Nicolas Milev in "Réchid pacha et la réforme ottomane," *Zeitschrift für Osteuropäische Geschichte* 2, 1912, 3, pp. 388–396.

clearly frustrated by the growing conservative opposition in the Divan making the enforcement of reforms increasingly difficult, obviously went much further in his criticism in March 1841 than he had done in his memorandum on the situation of the Ottoman Empire for Palmerston in August 1839, published in 1930.[19] If his words conveyed to the British foreign secretary could have strongly displeased the sultan if he had become aware of them, those of March 1841 were a clear betrayal, and if Metternich had wanted to destroy their author, the handover of the document to the Ottoman officials would have been the best and easiest way; something that Metternich naturally did not plan and did not do. The chancellor promised in his secret instructions to Constantinople of 26 March 1841 to prepare the answer when he had time, but he called Reshid's attention to the fact that his knowledge of the internal situation of the Ottoman Empire was insufficient and his comments could therefore hardly be regarded as conclusive advice.[20] Some evaluation of the situation was already included in the instructions of that day, repeating the views against hasty Westernisation, but no in-depth analysis has been found in the archives in Vienna, probably for the reasons that, first of all, Metternich lacked the enthusiasm to pay attention to a problem he was not very interested in at the moment when other more important affairs connected with the Near Eastern crisis had to be solved, second, the *Mémoire* contained rather extravagant proposals and third, there was finally no need to answer it since Reshid was recalled from office before a month had passed.

Mustafa Reshid Pasha's Fall in 1841

Already from the summer of 1840, the gathering clouds foreboded a coming storm. Intelligence from Constantinople informed Metternich of a growing opposition among the conservative Ottomans to Reshid and his effort to regenerate the empire[21] making the foreign minis-

---

[19] F. S. Rodkey, "Reshid Pasha's Memorandum of August 12, 1839," *JMH* 2, 1930, 2, pp. 251–257.
[20] Metternich to Stürmer, Vienna, 26 March 1841, HHStA, StA, Türkei VI, 83.
[21] Stürmer to Metternich, Constantinople, 16 July 1840, HHStA, StA, Türkei VI, 74; O'Sullivan to Lebeau, Vienna, 16 Dec. 1840, ADA, CP, Autriche 7.

ter's position "more and more uncertain every day."[22] In reaction to the intrigues in the Divan, Reshid sadly declared to Stürmer: "It is necessary to live in the centre of this world to be able to understand what is it like: there is no honour, no conscience, no equity, no common sense; patriotism and a sense of public welfare are unheard of there, and it is he who intrigues more skilfully and who best deceives others [who succeeds]; this unfortunately is the situation of our society."[23] On 29 March 1841, he was finally removed from the foreign ministry and replaced by the former Ottoman representative in Austria, Sadık Rifat Bey, who now became pasha. Rifat's accession to power intensified the existing suspicion that Metternich was behind Reshid's fall. The premise was based upon the presumption that the chancellor considered Reshid Pasha to be the obstacle to the solution of the Turko-Egyptian conflict owing to the latter's hostility towards Mohammed Ali and his alleged close relations with Ponsonby. Metternich had been said to bet on the former ambassador in Vienna, who had been expected to satisfy more easily the wishes of the Austrian cabinet.

One can sometimes be surprised at how easily historians accept rumours and groundless assertions as verified facts, which other researchers then adopt without further investigation because the validity of these so-called facts was never doubted. Some historians of the first half of the 20th century, for example Sébastien Charléty, Frederick Stanley Rodkey and Muhammad Sabry, claimed that Metternich had instigated the change at the head of Ottoman affairs in March 1841 for the above-mentioned reason.[24] The main problem lies in the fact that this statement was always based only on second-hand information and the assumption of the alleged hostility of the conservative statesman towards the Ottoman leading reformer. Count Sainte-Aulaire reported this suspicion to Paris, where a rumour soon spread that Reshid fell owing to Austrian intrigues and this rumour was later repeated by François Guizot in his memoirs.[25] However, Sainte-Aulaire offered no

---

[22] Stürmer to Metternich, Constantinople, 3 March 1841, HHStA, StA, Türkei VI, 80.

[23] Stürmer to Metternich, Constantinople, 4 March 1841, HHStA, StA, Türkei VI, 80.

[24] Charléty, p. 294; Rodkey, *The Turko-Egyptian Question*, p. 226; Sabry, p. 535.

[25] F. Guizot, *Memoirs of a Minister of State, from the Year 1840*, London 1864, p. 105.

evidence and stated that he had not spoken with Metternich on the topic.[26] American historian Frederick Stanley Rodkey, whose findings were recently adopted by Muhammed H. Kutluoğlu, derived his claim from a report of an American representative in Berlin where the same rumour spread in the diplomatic corps.[27] This myth still lives on despite the facts that first, no direct proof has ever been offered and second, it was already rejected by Sir Charles Kingsley Webster more than 60 years ago, although with the use of a limited quantity of British diplomatic correspondence, which, however, was still more evidence than any other historian presented.[28] Despite Webster's findings, historians, lately Bayram Kodaman and Kutluoğlu, mentioned above, have continued to repeat the allegation made earlier.[29]

The accusation against Metternich of plots against Reshid Pasha is in no way tenable. First, none of the Great Powers took part in this plotting and least of all Austria. It is not the aim of this book, and even cannot be, to describe the exact reasons for Reshid's fall, but the studied documents of the European Powers' residents in Constantinople clearly prove that not one of them took an active part in it. The reasons were purely internal and Reshid fell victim to the power game of court cabals. He had to face criticism for his reformatory actions, and Abdülmecid I increasingly listened to those who opposed Reshid for fear that the minister's reforms were undermining the sultan's authority. Stürmer strongly disapproved of the sultan's little faith in his most talented advisor's conduct because he regarded this distrust and the tendency towards making false accusations as a lasting problem preventing skilled men from working long term at the highest levels of the Ottoman administration.[30] He expressed this opinion in a re-

---

[26] Sainte-Aulaire to Guizot, Vienna, 10 April 1841, AMAE, CP, Autriche 429; Apponyi to Metternich, Paris, 26 April 1841, HHStA, StA, Frankreich 320.
[27] Rodkey, *The Turko-Egyptian Question*, p. 226. The same rumour obviously also spread in London because Palmerston asked Lord Beauvale whether he had heard that the Austrians had contributed to Reshid's fall through their influence in Constantinople. Beauvale's answer was entirely negative and he refused to believe the allegation. Beauvale to Palmerston, Vienna, 7 Aug. 1841, TNA, FO 120/197.
[28] Webster, *Palmerston*, II, pp. 766–767.
[29] Kodaman, p. 150; Kutluoğlu, p. 185.
[30] Stürmer to Metternich, Constantinople, 30 Dec. 1840, HHStA, StA, Türkei VI, 77; Stürmer to Metternich, Constantinople, 17 Feb. 1841, HHStA, StA, Türkei VI, 79; Stürmer to Metternich, Constantinople, 3 and 29 March 1841, HHStA, StA, Türkei VI, 80; Stürmer to Metternich, Constantinople, 1 April 1841, HHStA, StA,

port to Metternich several weeks before Reshid's fall: "I still cannot believe in the imminent fall of this minister that would unnecessarily deprive the sultan of the only captain capable of leading the ship of state through the reefs in which it is drifting ... But nothing is impossible in a country where everything is temporary except intrigues and corruption, which dominate all social classes, of which the sultan himself serves as an example, and which frustrate all honest and prudent calculations."[31]

Second, Reshid Pasha was not blamed in Vienna for prolonging the crisis. Although nobody doubted his personal desire to get rid of Mohammed Ali, he always sooner or later compromised with Metternich's moderate counsels. Not Reshid but Ponsonby was considered to be the main originator of the Porte's unwillingness to withdraw and terminate the conflict with Egypt, as it will be explained in the following chapter. The Austrians knew that when Reshid sometimes did not meet their desires at once, it was mainly due to the attitude of other Ottoman dignitaries and the sultan himself, who blamed Reshid for acquiescing too easily to the European Powers and thus Mohammed Ali.[32] Metternich's own words from April 1841 illustrate his confidence in the foreign minister's goodwill: "Reshid tried to finish the age old conflict peaceably; there are some men who want something else, and Reshid was a victim of this divergence of views."[33] Moreover, it was Stürmer with whom Reshid cooperated increasingly during the crisis, and a good understanding had definitely existed between the two sides since September 1839 when Reshid returned to Constantinople from Europe to assume the charge of the foreign ministry; his presence at the head of Ottoman affairs was welcomed in Vienna where his realistic evaluation of the distribution of power between the sultan and Mohammed Ali and his willingness to collaborate with Austria and be on good terms with Russia were highly appreciated. Furthermore, Stürmer was personally extremely sympathetic to Reshid whom he

---

Türkei VI, 83; Königsmarck to Frederick William IV, Büyükdere, 31 March 1841, GSta PK, HA III, MdA I, 7284; Beauvale to Palmerston, Vienna, 13 April 1841, TNA, FO 120/197; Lerchenfeld to Ludwig I of Bavaria, Vienna, 20 Feb., 3 March and 19 April 1841, BHStA, MA, Wien 2410.

[31] Stürmer to Metternich, Constantinople, 3 March 1841, HHStA, StA, Türkei VI, 80.

[32] For more details see Chapter 31.

[33] Metternich to Esterházy, Vienna, 9 April 1841, HHStA, StA, England 237.

considered to be not only intelligent and capable but also incorruptible, and "too honest a man to sacrifice the interests of the country
to which he is devoted for any advantage whatsoever."[34] It is no surprise therefore that already in early 1840, Maltzan considered Reshid
to be "completely the man for Austria"[35] and, in early 1841, Pontois
regarded Stürmer as Reshid's protector.[36]

Third, there is no reason to believe that Lord Ponsonby was
among Reshid's supporters, at least not from the beginning of 1841.
On the contrary, relations between the two men were rather cold. The
ambassador was offended that the Ottoman minister had not consulted with him at every stage, and he blamed him for the refusal of
the British demands for the employment of British artillerymen in the
Ottoman army and the Jewish immigration to Palestine. Ponsonby let
people know at every opportunity about his animosity towards Reshid,
he refused to back a collective intervention of the representatives in
favour of Reshid initiated by Stürmer and finally rejoiced at his fall.
According to Pontois, the British ambassador even openly stated that
his government "takes no particular interest in the ministerial existence of the author of the reforms from Gülhane."[37] It is most likely
that Ponsonby's passivity hastened Reshid's removal because the latter's enemies believed that the minister's withdrawal would please
Great Britain.[38]

[34] Stürmer to Metternich, Constantinople, 24 Feb. 1841, HHStA, StA, Türkei VI,
79.
[35] Maltzan to Frederick William III, Vienna, 1 Jan. 1840, GStA PK, HA III,
MdA I, 7351.
[36] Metternich to Stürmer, Vienna, 16 and 23 March 1841, HHStA, StA, Türkei
VI, 83; Ficquelmont to Stürmer, Vienna, 24 Sept. and 1 Oct. 1839, HHStA, StA,
Türkei VI, 72; Stürmer to Metternich, Constantinople, 20 Dec. 1839, HHStA, StA,
Türkei VI, 71; Stürmer to Metternich, Constantinople, 18 Nov. 1840, HHStA, StA,
Türkei VI, 77; Stürmer to Metternich, Constantinople, 29 March 1841, HHStA,
StA, Türkei VI, 80; Pontois to Guizot, Pera, 20 Jan. 1841, AMAE, CP, Turquie 282;
Lerchenfeld to Ludwig I of Bavaria, Vienna, 16 March, 7 and 10 April 1841, BHStA,
MA, Wien 2410; Königsmarck to Frederick William IV, Büyükdere, 10 March 1841,
GStA PK, HA III, MdA I, 7284; Maltzan to Frederick William IV, Vienna, 2 April
1841, GStA PK, HA III, MdA I, 7363.
[37] Pontois to Guizot, Pera, 7 April 1841, AMAE, CP, Turquie 282.
[38] Stürmer to Metternich, Constantinople, 17 Feb. 1841, HHStA, StA, Türkei VI,
79; Stürmer to Metternich, Constantinople, 3, 4 and 29 March 1841, HHStA, StA,
Türkei VI, 80; Reshid Pasha to Stürmer, received on 9 April 1841, attached to

Consequently, Metternich had no reason to alter his sympathetic attitude towards Reshid Pasha in any way in the spring of 1841, and there can be no doubt that the Ottoman minister still enjoyed his favour. The Austrian chancellor still regarded Reshid as by far the most intelligent and capable of all sultan's advisors, as he declared in mid March: "Reshid Pasha knows of the great interest that I have in his personal survival because I am convinced that he possesses great insights and qualities of intellect and character which, rare in every country, are probably even more needed in his homeland than in other countries differently [read "better"] organised."[39] The good relations between Reshid and Metternich are demonstated not only by these statements or by the already mentioned mutual correspondence but also by Reshid's attachment to Austria and apparent forbearance towards Russia, Austria's key ally. Consequently, it was Metternich who exerted immense effort to save Reshid from deposal. Already in the autumn of 1840, Stürmer was instructed to offer all possible assistance to the foreign minister and to leave the sultan and his retinue in no doubt that in Ballhausplatz the hope for success in the war with Mohammed Ali was connected with Reshid's qualities. How important it was for Metternich to keep Reshid in his office is evident from the fact that Stürmer was to act to the benefit of the minister even in the event that other European diplomats would refuse to cooperate. The prince usually decided for such a "bold" proceeding only in matters important for Austria. Stürmer acted upon his instructions zealously, exerting considerable effort to save the minister.[40]

Stürmer to Metternich, Constantinople, 14 April 1841, HHStA, StA, Türkei VI, 80; Königsmarck to Frederick William IV, Constantinople, 24 Feb. 1841, GStA PK, Rep. 81 Gesandschaften (Residenturen) u. (General-) Konsulate nach 1807, Gesandschaft Wien II, 204/2; Königsmarck to Frederick William IV, Büyükdere, 10 and 31 March 1841, GStA PK, HA III, MdA I, 7284; Titov to Nesselrode, Pera, 5, 13 and 29 March 1841, AVPRI, fond 133, Kantseliariia, opis 469, 1841/41; Pontois to Guizot, Pera, 17 March 1841, AMAE, CP, Turquie 282; Rodkey, "Lord Palmerston and the Rejuvenation of Turkey, Part II," p. 210; Temperley, *Crimea*, p. 158.

[39] Metternich to Stürmer, Vienna, 16 March 1841, HHStA, StA, Türkei VI, 83. In another set of instructions for Stürmer of the same day, Metternich added: "Reshid Pasha undoubtedly is a man of character and more enlightened than all other former, present and future ministers of the Porte."

[40] Metternich to Stürmer, Vienna, 30 Oct. 1840, HHStA, StA, Türkei VI, 78; Stürmer to Metternich, Constantinople, 4 March 1841, HHStA, StA, Türkei VI, 80; Stürmer to Metternich, Constantinople, 1 April 1841, HHStA, StA, Türkei VI,

In March 1841, Metternich warned Reshid against an article in
the *Gazette universelle* of the 11th of that month, reporting that several members of the Ottoman reform party residing in Paris, Europeans as well as Ottomans, of which Reshid was said to be the head,
had decided to publish the *Revue orientale* in the French capital and
distribute it in the sultan's dominions; the first issue had already appeared in March. The aim of the journal edited by Barrachin was
to propagate European-style reforms like civil and political equality,
absolute freedom of conscience, separation of spiritual and temporal
power, or allowing foreigners, that is, non-Moslems, to own land.[41]
Metternich feared that Reshid's opponents in the Divan would misuse
the existence of the journal containing views necessarily invoking the
sultan's anger in the plot to overthrow Reshid, in particular when the
Ottoman embassy in Paris was involved with issuing it, and he immediately offered his assistance to Reshid if needed. The chancellor later
labelled the existence of the *Revue orientale* as one of the reasons for
Reshid's fall, but no proof for this claim has been found in the studied
correspondence.[42]

In the second half of March, Metternich went even further in his
attempt to save Reshid when he asked Palmerston for help with a sincere expression of fear that only the Ottoman reformer could carry out
the conditions of Hatt-i Sharif of Gülhane and that he was a barrier
against "the fanatical party" which would endeavour to prevent all reform and perpetuate the abuses of the ancient system of government.
He accompanied his request with these words: "We would regard his
[Reshid's] departure from the ministry as a disaster. If this minister
perhaps does not possess all the qualities necessary for successfully
resisting the internal evils that overwhelm the Ottoman Empire and
for overcoming all the defects that afflict it, he is, nevertheless, we are
absolutely convinced, the most suitable man for the post he occupies.

83; Beauvale to Palmerston, Vienna, 28 Oct. 1840, TNA, FO 120/189; Maltzan to
Frederick William IV, Vienna, 19 March 1841, GSta PK, Rep. 81 Gesandschaften
(Residenturen) u. (General-) Konsulate nach 1807, Gesandschaft Wien II, 204/2.
[41] For more on Barrachin and the *Revue orientale* see also Chapter 12.
[42] Metternich to Stürmer, Vienna, 16 March, 2 and 6 April 1841, HHStA, StA,
Türkei VI, 83; Altieri to Lambruschini, Vienna, 26 March 1841, ASV, Arch. Nunz.
Vienna 280D; Lerchenfeld to Ludwig I of Bavaria, Vienna, 19 April 1841, BHSta,
MA, Wien 2410; report from Vienna, 24 April 1841, SS, HD, SG, Wien 94; Beauvale
to Palmerston, Vienna, 7 Aug. 1841, TNA, FO 120/197.

Exactly for these reasons the Great Powers should support him; to be successful, the union of their representatives is necessary. If they fail in this, the fanatic Mussulman party stands a great chance of getting rid of this man whose activities are beneficial for the welfare of the empire."[43] Lord Palmerston satisfied this wish, but his relevant instructions to Ponsonby were not dispatched until 1 April, which was obviously too late.[44]

In early April, still unaware of the changed situation at the Ottoman ministry, Metternich undertook his final attempt to save Reshid, and everyone familiar with diplomatic habits of that period must acknowledge that he really was ready to go far to save the minister. He took advantage of the sultan's formal expression of gratitude of 11 March for Austria's assistance in the Turko-Egyptian conflict to improve Reshid's position in Constantinople. Metternich concluded his own answer formally addressed to the foreign minister, who was to convey its content to the sultan according to diplomatic protocol with these words: "If the cause of justice has triumphed, much of the credit belongs to Y[our] E[xcellency] who has never been discouraged by countless difficulties accompanying this salutary task. No one can be praised more than You for the cooperation with the allied monarchs that brought it to its felicitous conclusion. Sultan Abdülmecid I openly recognised it and I am hastening to offer my most sincere felicitations to Y[our] E[xcellency] on this subject, as well as the expression of my considerable respect."[45] It is true that such a complimentary formula was not unusual in diplomatic correspondence but it definitely had a specific reason in this case, which was to show the sultan the Viennese cabinet's partiality for Reshid. Since it was dispatched too late, it is impossible to ascertain whether this letter and Palmerston's in-

---

[43] Metternich to Esterházy, Vienna, 18 March 1841, HHStA, StA, England 236. How dependent Metternich was on Reshid's salvation is also proved by the chancellor's order contained in his instructions to London of the same day that the relevant request for the British support had to be made by Esterházy to Palmerston as soon as possible.

[44] Metternich to Esterházy, Vienna, 18 March 1841, HHStA, StA, England 236; Beauvale to Palmerston, Vienna, 5 March 1841, TNA, FO 120/197; Sainte-Aulaire to Guizot, Vienna, 18 March 1841, AMAE, CP, Autriche 429; Maltzan to Frederick William IV, Vienna, 19 March 1841, GStA PK, HA III, MdA I, 7362; Palmerston to Ponsonby, London, 1 April 1841, TNA, FO 120/194.

[45] Metternich to Reshid, Vienna, 6 April 1841, HHStA, StA, Türkei VIII, 20.

structions might have had some prospect of reversing the situation on behalf of Reshid if they had been delivered before the end of March.

When Metternich learnt about the fall of the Ottoman foreign minister, he did not hide his sorrow: "The high esteem I had for Reshid Pasha's superior skills and character only magnify the real grief I feel over the news of his removal from the post he held so faithfully during the most difficult circumstances when he was in loyal service to his monarch and country and which gave me irrefutable evidence of his credibility and loyalty."[46] Stürmer naturally shared this chagrin and he did not conceal that this event "deeply afflicted him."[47] Ponsonby even reported to Palmerston that the internuncio "wept over his [Reshid Pasha's] removal as if it had been the advent of the day of judgement."[48] Stürmer's sorrow was intensified with his fear for Reshid's life because the internuncio well remembered the unfortunate fate of Pertev Pasha, who had lost his power and his life in 1837 on Mahmud II's order. Therefore, shortly after Reshid's recall, Stürmer asked the new Ottoman foreign minister to ensure that his predecessor would suffer no harm and would be treated better than Pertev Pasha. He also proposed to Metternich the way for rescuing Reshid if necessary: "The recollection of the perfidious and atrocious conduct that was undertaken against the unfortunate Pertev Pasha is still too present in the minds of all for the most serious apprehensions in respect of Reshid not to be aroused. A sure way of saving him would be if the Imperial Court were to request that the sultan send him as an ambassador. It remains to Your Highness alone to judge whether it is expedient to pursue this idea which I dare to submit to You, and which I have in no way communicated to Reshid, and which only occurred to me due to my desire to save from a possibly ominous fate a man so worthy of interest and who is above all so deserving of it from our noble court."[49] Metternich entirely approved Stürmer's conduct because he himself worried about the fallen reformer's safety, as it is proved by his statement from mid April: "I hope that Reshid Pasha will not be exposed to risks to his life and as he has more spirit

---

[46] Metternich to Stürmer, Vienna, 13 April 1841, HHStA, StA, Türkei VI, 83.
[47] Stürmer to Metternich, Constantinople, 1 April 1841, HHStA, StA, Türkei VI, 83.
[48] Webster, *Palmerston*, II, p. 767.
[49] Stürmer to Metternich, Constantinople, 29 March 1841, HHStA, StA, Türkei VI, 80.

and virtues than all his colleagues, he will be able to get back on his feet, but for this it is necessary that he survives."[50] Consequently, the chancellor promptly expressed his wish to welcome Reshid as the sultan's ambassador in Vienna, making thus the best from the fact that Jean Mavroyéni died at the same time when Reshid was recalled and the Ottoman agency in Vienna was empty. Moreover, he also appealed to Palmerston again with a request to help safeguard Reshid's life, which met with the complete agreement of the British foreign secretary.[51] Afterwards, Metternich wrote to Stürmer: "Lord Palmerston instructs Lord Ponsonby to see to it that no disaster happens to Reshid. Since this order corresponds with the one I have already sent to you, you are kindly requested to synchronise your approach in this direction with that of your English colleague."[52]

Nevertheless, Stürmer's and Metternich's apprehension proved to be unnecessary because Abdülmecid I did not plan to harm Reshid in any way, and Reshid was able to live untroubled with his family in the country and finally was not exiled to the outermost part of the empire but to Paris as the Ottoman ambassador. Reshid's Parisian mission did not please Metternich, and Lord Beauvale presumed that the chancellor would exert all his influence on preventing Reshid being sent to the capital of revolution. Metternich finally did not go so far, but he wanted to see Reshid before he assumed the new post and asked him to travel through Vienna, and although he did not mention why he desired this meeting so much, it was surely with the aim of influencing the new Ottoman ambassador's views and steps. Reshid was willing to satisfy this request, but problems with transportation over the Black Sea and on the Danube finally caused him to go to Paris by the traditional way via Marseille.[53]

---

[50] Metternich to Esterházy, Vienna, 15 April 1841, HHStA, StA, England 237.

[51] Metternich to Stürmer, Vienna, 13 and 30 April 1841, HHStA, StA, Türkei VI, 83; Metternich to Esterházy, Vienna, 15 April 1841, HHStA, StA, England 237; Stürmer to Metternich, Constantinople, 29 March and 7 April 1841, HHStA, StA, Türkei VI, 80; Palmerston to Ponsonby, London, 21 April 1841, TNA, FO 120/194; Beauvale to Palmerston, Vienna, 9 April and 3 May 1841, TNA, FO 120/197.

[52] Metternich to Stürmer, Vienna, 30 April 1841, HHStA, StA, Türkei VI, 83.

[53] Metternich to Stürmer, Königswart, 7 Aug. 1841, HHStA, StA, Türkei VI, 83; Stürmer to Metternich, Constantinople, 29 and 31 March, 7 April 1841, HHStA, StA, Türkei VI, 80; Reshid Pasha to Stürmer, 3 June 1841, Stürmer to Metternich, Constantinople, 9 June and 14 July 1841, HHStA, StA, Türkei VI, 81; Stürmer to Metternich, Constantinople, 28 Sept., 6 and 12 Oct. 1841, HHStA, StA, Türkei VI,

At this point it is also necessary to counter the contention that Metternich desired the replacement of the foreign minister because he favoured Sadık Rifat Bey. Nothing indicates that anyone in Ballhausplatz seriously anticipated that Reshid Pasha would be replaced by the former Ottoman representative in Vienna. On the other hand, it is true that thanks to their prior meetings, Rifat also enjoyed Metternich's goodwill and the fact that he was the man who took over the reins of Ottoman foreign policy undoubtedly eased the prince's regret about Reshid's fall, particularly because he saw in Rifat a guarantee that the return to the old Ottoman system of misrule and intolerance after Reshid's removal would not occur. Metternich considered Rifat to be an honest and agreeable man though not as intelligent as Reshid; compared to the latter, the prince attributed to Rifat better forethought in assuming reforms; in other words, he found Reshid more Western in his outlook and Rifat more Mussulman, which in no case meant that the latter was an adversary of the reform movement.[54] The prince compared both men in his instructions for Prince Esterházy: "Both of them are conscientious servants of their master. Reshid is sharper than his successor; the latter is more conventional. Reshid was overly influenced by ideas of reforms in the European way; Rifat understands only Mussulman reforms. I know in this respect all his thoughts, which he has often outlined to me; I also knew those of his predecessor and between these two I have found those of Rifat more practical."[55]

82; Maltzan to Frederick William IV, Vienna, 10 April 1841, GStA PK, HA III, MdA I, 7363; Königsmarck to Frederick William IV, Büyükdere, 14 July 1841, GStA PK, HA III, MdA I, 7284; Ponsonby to Palmerston, Therapia, 13 July 1841, TNA, FO 78/436; Beauvale to Palmerston, Vienna, 7 Aug. 1841, TNA, FO 120/197.

[54] Metternich to Ficquelmont, Vienna, 27 April 1839, HHStA, StA, Russland III, 115; Metternich to Neumann, Königswart, 22 Aug. 1840, HHStA, StA, England 231; Metternich to Esterházy, Vienna, 9 April 1841, HHStA, StA, England 237; Metternich to Stürmer, Vienna, 11 April 1841, HHStA, StA, Türkei VI, 83; Stürmer to Metternich, Constantinople, 7 April 1841, HHStA, StA, Türkei VI, 80; Beauvale to Palmerston, Vienna, 7 Aug. 1841, TNA, FO 120/197; Berkes, pp. 130–132.

[55] Metternich to Esterházy, Vienna, 9 April 1841, HHStA, StA, England 237. Exactly the same opinion was expressed by Pontois. Pontois to Guizot, Therapia, 6 July 1841, AMAE, CP, Turquie 283. The correctness of this comparison was confirmed by Turkish historian and sociologist Şerif Mardin who wrote: "Rifat has usually been labeled [*sic*] a 'reactionary' by European publicists. In reality Rifat was only more cautious than Reşid in his stand toward reform but was in the main

Can one find in this statement any indication that Metternich desired to remove Reshid Pasha from his office in 1841 because of certain differences in opinion of the Ottoman reforms? The answer must be negative, and to add to the information mentioned earlier in the chapter, although the two statesmen's visions really differed to a certain extent, Reshid's more "progressive" outlook was in no way a well-founded or necessary reason to weaken the position of the minister, who, in many ways, acted completely in accordance with Austrian interests, even within the Ottoman reform movement. This also holds for the most important reformatory step during that period, the promulgation of the Hatt-i Sharif of Gülhane, the content of which has always attracted considerable attention of historians who in the past sometimes claimed that it was influenced by liberal ideas brought to Constantinople by the pro-British and pro-French Reshid Pasha.[56] One could thus ask why Metternich was entirely satisfied with a document allegedly written under the impact of the liberal West, but the answer is simple: the chancellor held an entirely different view, he was convinced that its character was conservative – in conformity with Islam and the Ottoman traditions – and the document was simply a declaration of fundamental principles, in other words a Magna Carta of the Ottoman Empire, rather than a constitution as some of his contemporaries believed. Simultaneously, it guaranteed basic civil rights and improved the Ottomans' living conditions. For both its conservative roots as well as its reformatory potential Metternich entirely welcomed the existence of the edict of 3 November 1839.[57] As he wrote to Stürmer: "The step that Sultan Abdülmecid has taken is both correct and wise. He has declared principles that will serve as the pillars of his rule. These principles are just and founded on religious law, which is the supreme law for the entire state."[58] This led Turk-

---

tradition of Turkish reform." Mardin, *The Genesis of Young Ottoman Thought*, p. 177.

[56] S. J. Shaw, E. K. Shaw, *History of the Ottoman Empire and Modern Turkey, Vol. 2: Reform, Revolution and Republic – The Rise of Modern Turkey, 1808–1975*, Cambridge 1977, p. 61; Berkes, p. 144.

[57] Metternich to Stürmer, Vienna, 3 Dec. 1839, HHStA, StA, Türkei VI, 72; Metternich to Esterházy, Johannisberg, 19 Nov. 1839, HHStA, StA, England 219; Maltzan to Frederick William III, Vienna, 20 Nov. 1839, GStA PK, HA III, MdA I, 7350; Lerchenfeld to Ludwig I of Bavaria, Vienna, 20 Nov. 1839, BHStA, MA, Wien 2408.

[58] Metternich to Stürmer, Vienna, 3 Dec. 1839, HHStA, StA, Türkei VI, 72.

ish Cypriot historian and sociologist Niyazi Berkes, one of those who
supported the Western view, to the claim that Metternich as well as
other Europeans had misunderstood the Hatt-i Sharif.[59] Nevertheless,
later research proved that Metternich was correct in his assessment of
the document and that the subsequent Tanzimat reforms were "essentially Turkish in origin."[60] Butrus Abu-Manneh pointed out the fact
that the document showed no influence of Western political theory
and he offers credible evidence that its roots were in Moslem thought
and political concepts.[61] Roderic H. Davison supported this conclusion: "Much of the Hatt-i Sherif had a profoundly Muslim ring. It laid
the decline of the empire directly to the non-observance of the precepts of the glorious Kuran. In the next breath it then attempted to
reconcile Muslim tradition and progress, promising new institutions
which should not contravene Muslim law but should conform to its
demands."[62]

Consequently, Metternich had no reason to oppose Reshid's further activities aimed at the improvement of the state apparatus, and
he really did not do so, in particular when they were sometimes undertaken after direct consultations with Stürmer. According to Metternich, the most problematical aspect of the Hatt-i Sharif of Gülhane
was the ability of the Ottoman administration to put it into effect.
Even here, however, he was fairly optimistic: "His Highness might
encounter certain difficulties in the application of the principles under question; but which governmental measure is not exposed to such
practical problems?"[63] He based his optimism upon Reshid's presence
at the head of affairs, and in fact by the New Year promising reports
on the activities aimed at the improvement of the state apparatus as
well as life in the empire and positive responses of the Ottoman inhabitants started to arrive in Vienna. Metternich personally tried to
help Reshid when he was asked for assistance. This had already happened in late 1839 when Reshid requested Metternich's opinion not
only concerning the Ottoman reforms but also the reorganisation of

---

[59] Berkes, p. 148.
[60] Bailey, p. 228. See also W. Hale, *Turkish Foreign Policy 1774–2000*, London,
Portland 2002, p. 26.
[61] B. Abu-Manneh, "The Islamic Roots of the Gülhane Rescript," *DWI* 34, 1994,
2, pp. 173–203.
[62] Davison, "Turkish Attitudes concerning Christian-Muslim Equality," p. 114.
[63] Metternich to Stürmer, Vienna, 3 Dec. 1839, HHStA, StA, Türkei VI, 72.

Ottoman finances. Metternich offered his assistance in early January 1840. At the same time he also tried to help Reshid obtain a loan in Europe despite Austria's negative experience with the Porte's conduct in the Stametz Affair. When Metternich asked the Viennese bankers for their opinions and Beauvale for eventual assistance from Britain, he obviously did so with regard for Reshid, as he openly stated to the British ambassador, and with the aim of helping the Ottoman foreign minister in his reformatory effort. Metternich was urged in this matter by Stürmer, who strongly advocated Reshid's cause, but their readiness to help encountered insuperable difficulties: the British passivity, the bankers' reluctance to cooperate after their experience with the Stametz Affair and Kolowrat's firm opposition to Austria's participation in the project.[64] All that Metternich could finally do was to let Stürmer and Reshid know that he had actually tried to help but that "there is a big difference between committing oneself to something and being able to do it."[65]

Another financial problem concerning which Reshid consulted with Metternich was the printing of paper money. In 1840, the Porte suffered from serious financial difficulties. It needed money for a new army in the war with Mohammed Ali and for the reforms promised in the Hatt-i Sharif of Gülhane. The idea of issuing paper money already appeared in the Divan at the beginning of the year and was apparently supported by the French financier settled in Constantinople and serving the Porte, Jacques Alléon. Stürmer regarded the printing of paper money in the Ottoman Empire as potentially destructive, "the way to more or less ensure eventual bankruptcy that would complete the ruin of the country."[66] Metternich entirely agreed and, after a consultation with Austrian bankers, he gave an unequivocal opinion against

---

[64] Metternich to Stürmer, Vienna, 8 Jan. and 17 March 1840, HHStA, StA, Türkei VI, 78; Metternich to Neumann, Königswart, 31 July 1840, HHStA, StA, England 230; Stürmer to Metternich, Constantinople, 13 Nov. 1839, HHStA, StA, Türkei VI, 71; Stürmer to Metternich, Constantinople, 8 Jan. 1840, HHStA, StA, Türkei VI, 73; Stürmer to Metternich, Constantinople, 6 Aug. 1840, HHStA, StA, Türkei VI, 75; Beauvale to Palmerston, Vienna, 5 Jan. 1840, TNA, FO 120/189; Lerchenfeld to Ludwig I of Bavaria, Vienna, 9 Jan. 1840, BHStA, MA, Wien 2409; O'Sullivan to Lebeau, Vienna, 3 July 1840, ADA, CP, Autriche 7; Langsdorff to Thiers, Vienna, 10 July 1840, AMAE, CP, Autriche 428.

[65] Metternich to Stürmer, Königswart, 6 Aug. 1840, HHStA, StA, Türkei VI, 78.

[66] Stürmer to Metternich, Constantinople, 28 Feb. 1840, HHStA, StA, Türkei VI, 73.

the measure. Consequently, the internuncio opposed the plan, even personally quarrelled with Alléon, and finally persuaded Reshid to stop it in March. Nevertheless, this success was only temporary. The financial situation of the Porte was so stressed that when it failed to obtain the loan in Europe, it returned to the plan to issue paper money called *kaime*, strictly speaking a hybrid of paper money and treasury notes (government bonds) bearing interest at a rate of 12.5 percent. The first series was issued at the end of August 1840. Despite Metternich's and Stürmer's warnings against its negative impact, the Porte undertook additional issuances over the next months and years. The total value of this paper money printed until the end of 1840 alone reached about 360,000 pounds sterling.[67] Although in the short-term the paper money helped the Porte to avoid a financial crisis, the mid- and long-term consequences more or less confirmed Metternich's and Stürmer's concerns because paper money led to a major wave of inflation and eventually became "hated by many Ottoman subjects and when all of it was retired from circulation in 1862 there was public rejoicing."[68]

Not even Reshid's inclination to employ the French in Ottoman service could force Metternich to act against him. Although the chancellor expressed his willingness to take advantage of the reduced influence of France over the sultan's court in the replacement of the French in Ottoman service in the autumn of 1840 because of France's support of Mohammed Ali, and although he was not excited by Reshid's affection for France, he did not share Ponsonby's conviction that the Ottoman foreign minister was entirely controlled by the French employed in his vicinity and had sold out to France. Stürmer, closely

---

[67] Metternich to Stürmer, Vienna, 17 March 1840, HHStA, StA, Türkei VI, 78; Stürmer to Metternich, Constantinople, 1 April 1840, HHStA, StA, Türkei VI, 74; Stürmer to Metternich, Constantinople, 30 Sept. 1840, HHStA, StA, Türkei VI, 76; Beauvale to Palmerston, Vienna, 17 March 1840, TNA, FO 120/189; Königsmarck to Frederick William III, Büyükdere, 1 and 14 March 1840, GStA PK, HA III, MdA I, 7282; Königsmarck to Frederick William III, Büyükdere, 30 Sept. 1840, GStA PK, HA III, MdA I, 7283; Pontois to Thiers, Therapia, 17 Sept. 1840, AMAE, CP, Turquie 281; Lerchenfeld to Ludwig I of Bavaria, Vienna, 14 Oct. 1840, BHStA, MA, Wien 2409; R. H. Davison, "The First Ottoman Experiment with Paper Money," R. H. Davison (ed.), *Essays in Ottoman and Turkish History, 1774–1923: The Impact of the West*, Austin 1990, p. 62; Ş. Pamuk, *A Monetary History of the Ottoman Empire*, Cambridge 2000, p. 210.

[68] Davison, "The First Ottoman Experiment with Paper Money," p. 60.

cooperating with Reshid, maintained during 1840–1841 that the real influence of the French on the Ottoman state apparatus was non-existent, and many indications prove that if this claim was somewhat exaggerated, then not by much. The French support of Mohammed Ali during that period definitely harmed France's position in Constantinople and had to lessen its influence over Reshid, who was the confirmed enemy of the Egyptian governor. Stürmer, who was actively combating the activities of the French aimed at increasing their influence at the Porte, even maintained in 1840 that Reshid was not well disposed towards Adolphe Thiers because the French prime minister had opposed Reshid's being decorated with the Legion of Honour, which had been, however, finally awarded to him by Louis Philippe in October 1836. Reshid also told Stürmer about Thiers on the turn of July 1840: "He is a real child of the revolution and a man on whom one can never rely."[69] In any case, the French ambassador's delight at the Ottoman minister's fall seems to prove sufficiently that Reshid Pasha really was not an instrument in the hands of the French.[70]

In the same instructions of 9 April as quoted above, Metternich assured Esterházy that the positive evaluation of Rifat did not mean that he would no longer regret Reshid's recall. With hindsight he saw in Reshid's fall a forewarning of the same fate for Rifat, who would have to face the same intrigues of the court cabals. The two men were connected not only by a willingness to reform the Ottoman Empire, but also by an aspiration for a just government and religious toleration, a desire shared by Metternich, who suspected the sultan's followers to be lacking these virtues and who feared that Rifat would meet the same opposition as his predecessor.[71] Reshid himself contributed to this anxiety with his secret Memorandum of March 1841 as well

[69] Stürmer to Metternich, Constantinople, 5 Aug. 1840, HHStA, StA, Türkei VI, 75.
[70] Stürmer to Metternich, Constantinople, 1 July 1840, HHStA, StA, Türkei VI, 74; Stürmer to Metternich, Constantinople, 12 and 25 Nov. 1840, HHStA, StA, Türkei VI, 77; Stürmer to Metternich, Constantinople, 10 and 29 March 1841, HHStA, StA, Türkei VI, 80; Beauvale to Palmerston, Vienna, 1 Nov. 1840, TNA, FO 120/189; Beauvale to Palmerston, Vienna, 13 April and 7 Aug. 1841, TNA, FO 120/197; Kodaman, p. 87.
[71] Metternich to Esterházy, Vienna, 9 April 1841, HHStA, StA, England 237; Beauvale to Palmerston, Vienna, 9 and 13 April, 7 Aug. 1841, TNA, FO 120/197; Lerchenfeld to Ludwig I of Bavaria, Vienna, 19 April 1841, BHStA, MA, Wien 2410.

as open complaints to Austrian and Russian diplomats revealed to
Metternich of the counter-reformatory conduct of Abdülmecid I and
his retinue. He told Titov in early February 1841: "Not long ago, Europe and America were moved to intervene on behalf of the Israelites
persecuted in Damascus. Do we not deserve the same mercy, and is it
not fair that the enlightened and benevolent cabinets concur in saving from disaster the numerous Christian and Moslem populations
innocent of the acts of those who rule over them?"[72] Reshid often
expressed his hope that the Great Powers would "open the sultan's
eyes,"[73] which led Titov to the belief that Reshid wanted to obtain the
assistance of the allied Powers "to oblige the young monarch irrevocably to develop and preserve the reforms established since November
1839."[74] The validity of this assumption is entirely proved by Reshid's
secret Memorandum in March of that year as well as Pontois' reports
also containing Reshid's pessimism regarding the possibility of reform-
ing the Ottoman Empire under the given establishment. As Reshid
allegedly told a Frenchman employed at the Porte: "There are only
two things to do: it is necessary that either the London Conference,
that is to say the *five* Great Powers agree to impose their will on the
Sultan and hold him strictly to the internal reforms which he must
follow, or that *they consider the question of partition*, making Constantinople a free city like Cracow placed under the protection of the
five Courts."[75] It is questionable how seriously Reshid meant the second possibility, but he actually told Pontois in August 1841 that the
Great Powers were to intervene in the Ottoman Empire and force the
sultan to initiate reforms, in other words he repeated his words contained in his March Memorandum sent to Vienna.[76] Nevertheless, the
fact that Reshid conveyed this vision in writing to Metternich proves
the extraordinary personal significance of the Austrian statesman for
the Ottoman reformer.

Metternich had good reason to believe Reshid's warnings in consideration of the incompetent and sometimes oppressive Ottoman ad-

---

[72] Titov to Nesselrode, Pera, 10 Feb. 1841, AVPRI, fond 133, Kantseliariia, opis
469, 1841/41.
[73] Ibid.
[74] Ibid. See also Titov to Nesselrode, Pera, 5 March 1841, AVPRI, fond 133,
Kantselariia, opis 469, 1841/41.
[75] Pontois to Guizot, Pera, 7 Feb. 1841, AMAE, CP, Turquie 282.
[76] Pontois to Guizot, Therapia, 17 Aug. 1841, AMAE, CP, Turquie 283.

ministration newly restored in Syria and the violent behaviour of Ottoman forces against an insurrection in Bulgaria in the spring of 1841. The restless situation in the two Ottoman regions raised the chancellor's doubts whether the government without skilled men would be capable of improving the situation of the Ottoman Empire. Lord Beauvale described the prince's attitude rather precisely: "Metternich is in some degree consoled for Reshid's fall and would be entirely so if he thought Rifat Pacha's [sic] tenure of place a good one, but he fears that in the fall of one minister after another the system of those who have adopted ideas of improvement will ultimately fall with them, and this he would consider as the loss of all present chance for the regeneration of the Ottoman Empire."[77] Therefore, Metternich supported Rifat in the same way as he had previously supported Reshid, and he did not spare him from the same advice: to have regard in his reformatory steps for the real character of the predominantly Moslem empire differing in many aspects from the European, Christian, countries, and not to listen to foreign adventurers, in particular the French, with extreme ambitions as well as self-interest.[78] This was no news for Rifat who told Stürmer that "Prince Metternich always recommended to me that above all we must remain Turks, which should not prevent us from adopting useful reforms."[79] Metternich actually continued to advise the Ottomans to introduce reforms, in particular those outlined in the Hatt-i Sharif of Gülhane: "Keep the promises which you have made in the Edict of Gülhane. The principles which it has proclaimed are applicable to your needs, and by applying them the empire will thrive."[80]

$$* \quad * \quad *$$

Since the preservation of the Ottoman Empire became a fundamental aspect of Metternich's Near Eastern policy, he welcomed everybody

---

[77] Beauvale to Palmerston, Vienna, 13 April 1841, TNA, FO 120/197.
[78] Metternich to Stürmer, Vienna, 13 April 1841, HHStA, StA, Türkei VI, 83; Sainte-Aulaire to Guizot, Vienna, 17 April 1841, AMAE, CP, Autriche 429.
[79] Stürmer to Metternich, Constantinople, 7 April 1841, HHStA, StA, Türkei VI, 80.
[80] Metternich to Apponyi, Vienna, 26 May 1841, HHStA, StA, Frankreich 322.

who could slow down its decay, and for this reason he supported Ottoman reformers of the early Tanzimat period like Mustafa Reshid Pasha and Sadık Rifat Pasha because he was convinced that they sincerely wished to strengthen the pillars of the weak state structure. And although he did not always agree with the steps undertaken by the former, he saw nobody who would be more suitable for this task. Some differences in the two men's views were, under the given conditions, unimportant for Metternich, particularly if Reshid Pasha manifested his goodwill towards Austria in practical affairs like the Stametz Affair before 1838 or in other affairs during the Second Mohammed Ali Crisis when Reshid often cooperated with Stürmer, especially after the worsening of his relations with Ponsonby during 1840. If he did not meet Metternich's requests without delay, the reason lay in his precarious personal situation in the Divan and the growing opposition among more conservative Ottomans accusing Reshid of excessive submission to Europe. Consequently, Metternich had neither long-term nor short-term reasons for wanting Reshid's political destruction. The documents clearly prove that the chancellor, contrary to the allegation that he was behind the intrigues that caused Reshid's fall, actually did his best to save him, and he even worried about threats to Reshid's life and was prepared to take pains to avert the worst if necessary. Moreover, Reshid's earliest return to office was desired by those in the Chancellery in Ballhausplatz; as Stürmer wrote in July 1841: "Reshid's accession to the helm of affairs would certainly be highly desirable for us. He is, I am convinced, the only living Turk who under the given conditions can set the machine in motion reasonably well."[81]

Metternich's affection for Reshid offers further important evidence of a still much neglected phenomenon: that not only the two liberal Powers but also Austria supported the efforts of some Ottomans to regenerate their country although the conservatism of the man leading its foreign policy naturally influenced the character of this assistance. Metternich's opinions of the Ottoman reforms entirely support the conclusion made by Alan J. Reinerman in 1970 after his analysis of the chancellor's attitude towards the possibility of reforms

---

[81] Stürmer to Metternich, Constantinople, 28 July 1841, HHStA, StA, Türkei VI, 83. When Stürmer lost hope in Reshid's revival, he did not conceal his chagrin. Stürmer to Metternich, Constantinople, 8 Sept. 1841, HHStA, StA, Türkei VI, 83.

in the Papal State: "Further proof – if any is needed at this late date – is thus provided that he was by no means the benighted reactionary of nineteenth-century legend, but an intelligent and perceptive conservative who realized that the Restoration settlement could survive only if so reformed as to adapt it to the needs and expectations of a new era."[82] It seemed, however, that Metternich's conservative attitudes were more convenient to the Ottoman elites, who were actually much less liberal and much more conservative in their views than some historians claimed in the 20th century. If this is the case, then Vienna and not Paris or London was the most natural centre for the reformatory ideas of the great Ottoman reformers around 1840: Mustafa Reshid Pasha, who discussed the problem with Metternich personally during his visits to the Danube Monarchy on his travels to the Western capitals, or Sadık Rifat Pasha, who lived in Vienna in 1838-1839 and wrote there his two long reports *Essay concerning European Affairs* and *On the Reform of Conditions in the Ottoman State*[83] and who is now considered in Turkey to be one of the pioneers of modernisation.[84] The idea of Vienna as a focal point for Ottoman reformatory ideas was entirely supported by Roderic H. Davison when he stated that Vienna had a prominent position in the spread of new ideas into the Ottoman Empire at that time,[85] as well as by Turkish historian and sociologist Şerif Mardin who pointed out that Rifat's ideas contained in the dispatches he sent from Vienna to Reshid are very similar to the principles contained in the Hatt-i Sharif of Gülhane.[86]

The studied documents prove that Reshid and Rifat not only discussed their reformatory ideas during their personal meetings with Metternich or through their continuing correspondence with him after their return to Constantinople in the second half of 1839 but also that they requested Metternich's advice and that they undertook some reformatory measures in compliance with it, or at least after listening to it. The most striking example of Metternich's influence is that concerning the religious and administrative settlement of the Syrian Question in June 1841; the acceptance of his suggestions cannot be

---

[82] Reinerman, "Metternich and Reform," p. 546.
[83] Berkes, p. 130.
[84] Findley, p. 138.
[85] Davison, "Vienna as a Major Ottoman Diplomatic Post," p. 254.
[86] Mardin, *The Genesis of Young Ottoman Thought*, p. 177.

surprising since they were simply the ones most in conformity with the sultan's sovereignty and authority and the most realistic of the relevant projects conceived in Europe, and they were thus the most admissible for the Sublime Porte. A certain level of trust in Metternich's advice is clearly evident on the part of Reshid Pasha, who had already expressed as much during a conversation with Ponsonby in September 1839 when he had told the British ambassador that he had complete confidence in the friendship of Great Britain and Austria, but as for the application of reforms, he had "thought of applying to Austria to take the lead, as that power would not be suspected of aiming at revolution."[87]

To what extent Metternich's conservative opinions were really accepted by Reshid, Rifat or other Ottomans is, however, a topic for further research, naturally based upon documents housed in Turkish archives. That his opinions were well received is nevertheless supported by the above-stated facts as well as by Şerif Mardin's conclusions, also adopted by Austrian historian Karl Vocelka,[88] about the influence of Metternich's thoughts on the Tanzimat in its early phase, in other words on Sadık Rifat Pasha's reformatory ideas "deriving from a type of enlightened despotism – possibly more enlightened than despotic – which had characterized the governing of Austria for decades,"[89] and also by Mustafa Reshid Pasha's views incorporated in the Hatt-i Sharif of Gülhane containing "the theories of cameralism or enlightened despotism."[90]

---

[87] Subaşi, p. 428.
[88] K. Vocelka, "Die Beurteilung der Tanzimatzeit in Österreich," *MIÖG* 100, 1992, p. 416; Ş. Mardin, "The Influence of the French Revolution on the Ottoman Empire," *International Social Science Journal* 41, 1989, 119, p. 25.
[89] Mardin, "The Influence of the French Revolution," p. 25.
[90] Ibid.

The End of the Second Mohammed Ali Crisis

After Mohammed Ali yielded, it was the Porte's turn: his submission had to be accepted by the sultan and a final peace settlement arranged between him and the pasha and sanctioned by the Great Powers. Although the crisis thus entered its final phase at the end of 1840, it took more than half a year before it was finally settled owing to the Porte's desire to exploit from the victory more than the pasha was prepared to agree to and to Ponsonby's wilful steps hampering the efforts of the Great Powers to bring about a swift conclusion to the affair. Metternich vied with the Porte as well as with Ponsonby and urged all the Powers to a formal conclusion of the affair that in practical terms was already over. With his usual realism and peace management, he worked on solving the Second Mohammed Ali Crisis as well as the Eastern Question in itself.

The Porte's Hesitation to End the War

Mohammed Ali's submission to Captain Fanshawe gave rise to hope in Vienna for a prompt settlement of the Near Eastern crisis. The days immediately following Fanshawe's return to Constantinople on 16 December 1840 saw, however, another serious impediment to this desired goal: the wish of the sultan and his advisors to take advantage of their military triumph in Syria for the complete destruction of Mohammed Ali's power in Egypt as well. They were unwilling to reverse the pasha's deposal and terminate military operations because they were well aware of his weakness and the existing chance to get rid of him once and for all. They were strongly supported in their warlike attitude by Ponsonby, who became as equally anti-French and anti-Egyptian during the Second Mohammed Ali Crisis as he had been earlier anti-Russian, and he personally also desired the pasha's expul-

sion from Egypt. He had advocated this goal during the autumn and
he continued to do so even in late December 1840 when Mohammed
Ali's surrender became known in Constantinople. The ambassador
urged Reshid Pasha to refuse to have Mohammed Ali reinstalled in
Egypt and to continue fighting against the Egyptian troops retreating
from Syria.[1]

Since the Porte could not decide this matter alone without a previous agreement with the allied courts, Reshid summoned a meeting
with the representatives of Austria, Prussia, Russia and Great Britain
on 20 December where he officially acquainted them with Mohammed
Ali's letter to the grand vizier containing the pledge of submission.
He raised the question whether the submission corresponded to the
wishes expressed in Palmerston's 14 November instructions to Stopford and could be regarded as sufficient. Stürmer found nothing wrong
in Mohammed Ali's letter and simultaneously warned the members of
the Divan against the desire to destroy their enemy, which was an endeavour that the Powers would never assist. Titov and Königsmarck
agreed with the internuncio and together with him urged Reshid Pasha
to proceed with caution and to accelerate fulfilment of the measures
for ending the war. However, Ponsonby stood against his colleagues
and Mohammed Ali's reprieve and claimed that the submission was
incomplete. Abdülmecid I took advantage of this disunion and although he finally accepted the submission of his vassal at the end of
December and promised to restore Mohammed Ali's rule over Egypt
after regaining his own fleet and the complete withdrawal of Egyptian
forces from Syria, he said nothing about hereditary rule and his emis-
saries sent to Egypt on 6 January 1841 to convey his "graciousness"
were not authorised to raise this topic.[2]

The Turks' belligerence aggravated Stürmer, who reacted in his
report of 30 December 1840 with sharp criticism of their actions and
censured them for their pursuit of the complete destruction of the
withdrawing Egyptian army and for inciting rebellion on the Nile:

---

[1]   Pisani to Ponsonby, Pera, 18 Dec. 1840, Stürmer to Metternich, Constantinople,
23 Dec. 1840, HHStA, StA, Türkei VI, 77; Königsmarck to Frederick William IV,
Büyükdere, 23 Dec. 1840, GStA PK, HA III, MdA I, 7283; Kutluoğlu, pp. 176–177.
[2]   Protocol of the conference of 20 December 1840, Stürmer to Metternich, Constantinople, 2, 10, 16, 23 and 30 Dec. 1840, HHStA, StA, Türkei VI, 77; Stürmer to
Metternich, Constantinople, 5 Jan. 1841, HHStA, StA, Türkei VI, 79; Kutluoğlu,
p. 178.

"It [the Porte] cannot abandon hope that the discontent prevailing in Egypt, of which it receives evidence every day, will finally break into insurrection and it would not want to later regret having prevented such an event because of a hasty peace."[3] Stürmer justly claimed that most of the Divan's members did not heed the advice of the Powers, doubted their accord and listened only to Ponsonby, who ostensibly followed instructions from London but in practice advised firmness towards the Egyptian governor. The British ambassador did not abandon hope that Mohammed Ali would be brought to ruin before a peaceful settlement could be reached.[4]

The latest news from Constantinople caused Metternich's indignation: "What occupies Constantinople today is an intrigue, an intrigue doubly dangerous because it damages the good faith of the Great Powers and it exposes Europe to a conflict the eventual consequences of which would have much greater impact than the complex situation that the courts had the good fortune to see through to its practical end could not have had by any reasonable estimation. The conflict between Mohammed Ali and the Porte evidently came to an end, if not formally, then at least in reality, at the moment when Mohammed Ali unconditionally submitted to Admiral Stopford's invitation in the name of the four courts, and when His Highness [the sultan] accepted this submission."[5] The chancellor never intended to attack Mohammed Ali in Egypt and argued that such a step was not included in the London Convention and it would be at sharp variance with the allied Powers' latest decision of 14 November. Austria would never take part in it and Metternich let this be clearly known when he instructed Bandiera in late November to remain under Stopford's command on the Syrian coast but never to follow him in the event of a British attack against Egypt.[6]

---

[3]   Stürmer to Metternich, Constantinople, 30 Dec. 1840, HHStA, StA, Türkei VI, 77.

[4]   Ibid.

[5]   Metternich to Stürmer, Vienna, 18 Jan. 1841, HHStA, StA, Türkei VI, 83.

[6]   Metternich to Stürmer, Vienna, 25 Nov. and 23 Dec. 1840, HHStA, StA, Türkei VI, 78; Metternich to Neumann, Vienna, 29 Nov. 1840, Metternich to Esterházy, Vienna, 2 and 18 Dec. 1840, HHStA, StA, England 231; Metternich to Apponyi, Vienna, 1 Dec. 1840, HHStA, StA, Frankreich 319; Stürmer to Bandiera, Constantinople, 8 Dec. 1840, HHStA, StA, Türkei VI, 77; Sainte-Aulaire to Guizot, Vienna, 1 Dec. 1840, AMAE, CP, Autriche 428; Tatishchev to Nesselrode, Vienna, 19 and 23 Dec. 1840, AVPRI, fond 133, Kantseliariia, opis 469, 1840/178; Maltzan

This restraint was principally caused by the situation on the Continent that made Metternich keen to settle promptly the crisis in the Near East and in no way was he willing to provoke or agree with any measures that could seriously upset France. There also were other reasons for his cautious attitude. He was convinced that the allies did not have sufficient forces in Syria to expel Mohammed Ali from Egypt, and he feared an eventual defeat of the Turks, who should realise that the Egyptian soldiers were "demoralised but still alive."[7] Furthermore, he wanted to introduce a lasting stability as well as peace in the Near East and for this purpose, he regarded Mohammed Ali's hereditary rule as acceptable. The want of a long-lasting settlement was proved by the chancellor's desire for ensuring hereditary rule in the mode of primogeniture that, in his opinion, would assure the future of Mohammed Ali's descendants in the best way and prevent their mutual struggle for power when the line of succession was clear, ensuring the system not common among Moslems but practiced in Europe and useful to substantiate the desire of a father to deflect the distant connections of elder claimants to succession.[8] Consequently, Metternich insisted that "the survival of Mohammed Ali and his descendants was well ensured,"[9] and that this was done as soon as possible. When he learnt of Mohammed Ali's submission to Napier, he wrote to Stürmer: "The moment has come when the Turko-Egyptian affair can and must be brought to a final conclusion that is desirable not only for the welfare of the Ottoman Empire but for the general situation in Europe."[10]

Understandably therefore, Metternich reacted to the Porte's abhorrence to grant hereditary rule and to end the war on the turn of 1840 with sharp condemnation. He saw no reason for an assault on Ibrahim Pasha after his father's submission and the withdrawal of his forces from Syria. Any such attack and uprising against him would be denounced by Austria. If the Porte did not accept this fact and attacked the Egyptian vassal, "we would consider it," as Metter-

---

to Frederick William IV, Vienna, 15 Jan. 1841, GStA PK, Rep. 81 Gesandschaften (Residenturen) u. (General-) Konsulate nach 1807, Gesandschaft Wien II, 204/1.
[7] Metternich to Esterházy, Vienna, 14 Jan. 1841, HHStA, StA, England 236.
[8] Metternich to Stürmer, Vienna, 29 Dec. 1840, HHStA, StA, Türkei VI, 78; Metternich to Esterházy, Vienna, 7 Jan. 1841, HHStA, StA, England 236; Maltzan to Frederick William IV, Vienna, 31 Jan. 1841, GStA PK, HA III, MdA I, 7362.
[9] Metternich to Stürmer, Vienna, 25 Nov. 1840, HHStA, StA, Türkei VI, 78.
[10] Metternich to Stürmer, Vienna, 18 Dec. 1840, HHStA, StA, Türkei VI, 78.

nich wrote on 18 January 1841, "as an infringement of human rights and for the same reason condemn the military action which Ottoman troops may have already undertaken or will still undertake against the remaining parts of the Egyptian army in Syria after the sultan's acceptance of Mohammed Ali's unconditional submission."[11] If the campaign was not halted and the question of hereditary rule was not immediately settled, Metternich threatened that "this hesitation will induce our court to adopt an attitude not entirely favourable to the Porte."[12] This meant that Austria would withdraw its diplomatic and military support of the sultan. Stürmer was ordered to warn Reshid of this, and the courts in Berlin and St Petersburg instructed their representatives in Constantinople in the same way.[13]

Metternich was embittered not only by the attitude of Abdül-mecid I and his advisors but also by Ponsonby's. The chancellor criticised the ambassador for his desire to destroy Mohammed Ali despite the opposite wish of all Great Powers, displaying in this manner little interest for the situation on the Continent.[14] Metternich already wrote in mid November 1840: "Single-minded men like Lord Ponsonby can be fortuitous instruments to employ in the sole direction in which they know how to progress, but it is necessary not to allow them go off course. Lord Ponsonby dreams today only of the destruction of Mohammed Ali, and who would not agree with him when looking at the question in an abstract way? We also keep in mind the punishment of

---

[11] Metternich to Stürmer, Vienna, 18 Jan. 1841, HHStA, StA, Türkei VI, 83.

[12] Ibid.

[13] Metternich to Esterházy, Vienna, 14 and 22 Jan. 1841, HHStA, StA, England 236; Metternich to Stürmer, Vienna, 18 Jan. and 7 Feb. 1841, HHStA, StA, Türkei VI, 83; Maltzan to Frederick William IV, Vienna, 16 Jan. 1841, Werther to Maltzan, Berlin, 16 Jan. 1841, GStA PK, Rep. 81 Gesandschaften (Residenturen) u. (General-) Konsulate nach 1807, Gesandschaft Wien II, 204/1; Tatishchev to Nesselrode, Vienna, 16 Jan. 1841, AVPRI, fond 133, Kantseliariia, opis 469, 1841/191; Beauvale to Palmerston, Vienna, 17 Jan. 1841, TNA, FO 120/197; Hasenclever, *Die Orientalische Frage*, p. 247.

[14] Metternich to Esterházy, Vienna, 26 Dec. 1840, HHStA, StA, England 231; Metternich to Esterházy, Vienna, 7 Jan. 1841, HHStA, StA, England 236; Metternich to Trauttmannsdorff, Vienna, 8 Jan. 1841, HHStA, StK, Preussen 178; Lerchenfeld to Ludwig I of Bavaria, Vienna, 4 and 17 Jan. 1841, BHStA, MA, Wien 2410; Maltzan to Frederick William IV, Vienna, 7 Jan. 1841, GStA PK, HA III, MdA I, 7361; Tatishchev to Nesselrode, Vienna, 20 Jan. 1841, AVPRI, fond 133, Kantseliariia, opis 469, 1841/191; Sainte-Aulaire to Guizot, Vienna, 23 Jan. 1841, AMAE, CP, Autriche 429.

the rebel but at the same time we also understand that besides Mohammed Ali and Egypt there are other issues in the world deserving
our solicitude and our efforts."[15] As Ponsonby continued to frustrate
the settlement between the sultan and the pasha in 1841, Metternich's
criticism was harsh: "Lord Ponsonby presses for the destruction of the
Egyptian army; this is the system of a bandit."[16]

When Metternich was reading Stürmer's report of 30 December,
the situation in Constantinople had already changed in favour of the
peace settlement between the two quarrelling parties. On 7 January,
the internuncio visited Reshid Pasha and insisted on the suspension
of hostilities and the granting of hereditary rule. He was backed by
Titov and Königsmarck, but since Ponsonby still stood in opposition
under the pretext that he lacked instructions which would enable him
to support his colleagues, the attitude of the Porte did not change.
When, however, the British ambassador received on 10 January the
instructions from Palmerston forcing him to advise the Porte to grant
hereditary rule, he had to change his stubborn attitude and support
his colleagues. Their common effort met with success two days later
when Abdülmecid I promised in writing to grant hereditary rule when
Mohammed Ali's submission was confirmed with the return of the
Turkish fleet, which had in fact already happened on 11 January when
it was formally delivered in the Alexandrian port to Baldwin Walker,
and it sailed to Constantinople ten days later. At the same time,
Ibrahim Pasha's army was in full retreat back to Egypt.[17]

From the February Protocol to the Second London Convention

After the restitution of the fleet and the acceptance of all the conditions of the London Convention by the pasha, Abdülmecid I was

[15] Metternich to Stürmer, Vienna, 13 Nov. 1840, HHStA, StA, Türkei VI, 78.
[16] Metternich to Esterházy, Vienna, 14 Jan. 1841, HHStA, StA, England 236.
[17] Palmerston to Ponsonby, 17 Dec. 1840, Metternich to Stürmer, Vienna, 29 Dec.
1840, HHStA, StA, Türkei VI, 78; Stürmer to Metternich, Constantinople, 5, 9,
11, 13, 21 and 28 Jan. 1840, HHStA, StA, Türkei VI, 79; Königsmarck to Frederick
William IV, Büyükdere, 13 Jan. 1841, GStA PK, HA III, MdA I, 7284; Kutluoğlu,
p. 179; Ufford, p. 195.

not able to ignore the hand offered in peace any longer or postpone clemency. On 13 February, he therefore issued a firman that granted hereditary title of Egypt to Mohammed Ali's family. In the document, the sultan nevertheless maintained the right to appoint officers in the Egyptian army and navy for the rank of colonel and above and to choose a new Egyptian governor from Mohammed Ali's male offspring. In addition, the firman gave the sultan one-fourth of the gross income of the province, with the tax collection to be controlled by an Ottoman official.[18] These harsh conditions were either intended to force Mohammed Ali to reject the decree and offer thus a suitable pretext for the invasion of Egypt or to strengthen the sultan's control over Egypt if the pasha accepted it. The representatives of the allied Powers carried a certain responsibility for its text because they had participated in its preparation from the end of January, and Stürmer and Ponsonby had played the most important role. In the European courts the decree was later called "firman Stürmer"[19] because it was presumed that the restrictive conditions were prepared upon the internuncio's advice whereas Ponsonby claimed that he had not at all cooperated in this task. The truth lies somewhere in the middle. Ponsonby desired a less specific text without details of the conditions of Mohammed Ali's rule over Egypt which were to be settled later, whereas Reshid wanted to include the details in the firman. Stürmer supported the latter and, also for this reason, Reshid mostly cooperated with the internuncio, who agreed with some anti-Egyptian conditions because they could help to improve Reshid's position against his enemies circling the sultan. Moreover, Stürmer personally had nothing against greater restriction of Mohammed Ali's power. On the other hand, despite the fact that his idea of a more vague text was not accepted, Ponsonby continued to take part in the discussions over the firman with his colleagues and the members of the Divan, and he significantly influenced some of the conditions contained in it, in particular the method of succession leaving to the sultan the decision of the pasha's successor and the appointment of the sultan's official for controlling the

---

[18] Hurewitz, *The Middle East*, p. 120.

[19] Metternich to Stürmer, Vienna, 30 April 1841, HHStA, StA, Türkei VI, 83; Maltzan to Frederick William IV, Vienna, 2 May 1841, GStA PK, Rep. 81 Gesandschaften (Residenturen) u. (General-) Konsulate nach 1807, Gesandschaft Wien II, 204/3.

collection of tax revenue. Nevertheless, Ponsonby did not participate in the preparation of the final draft because Stürmer recommended to Reshid that he avoid including Ponsonby before the final decision was irrevocably taken since one could presume that "a preliminary communication made to this ambassador could evoke new discussions of interminable length."[20] This was actually what the British ambassador objected to: the fact that he had less influence on the editing of the firman than he wanted, that he did not see its final text before it was promulgated and that, in his opinion, it still was too moderate towards Mohammed Ali.[21]

For Metternich, Stürmer's co-responsibility for the firman was as painful as the internuncio's participation in Mohammed Ali's deposal on 14 September 1840 because also in this case Metternich was significantly dissatisfied with the outcome that, in his opinion, did not solve anything and merely injected a regrettable confusion into the whole affair since it contained conditions difficult or impossible to implement. Prior to the promulgation of the firman, he considered succession under the rule of primogeniture as the most convenient and advised the Divan to accept it over succession by seniority that was more typical of Moslems. In fact, he was able to accept the system of seniority as well since it was not a crucial question for him and later did so when he learnt that Mohammed Ali preferred it, but the method of succession chosen by the Porte was the worst possible for him since it could launch Egypt back into the instability and civil war that had characterised the region in the days before Mohammed Ali's accession to power. The chancellor told Lerchenfeld: "The third method that Lord Ponsonby advised the Porte is the most disastrous. Instead of terminating the question between the Great Lord and the Pasha of Egypt and settling hereditary rule for the future, it calls the

---

[20] Stürmer to Metternich, Constantinople, 17 Feb. 1841, HHStA, StA, Türkei VI, 79.
[21] Ponsonby to Reshid Pasha, 15 Feb. 1841, Stürmer to Metternich, Constantinople, 28 Jan., 1, 3, 5, 15, 17 and 24 Feb. 1841, HHStA, StA, Türkei VI, 79; Ponsonby to Stürmer, Therapia, 28 Jan. 1841, Stürmer to Ponsonby, 29 Jan. 1841, Titov to Nesselrode, Pera, 2, 10, 18 and 19 Feb. 1841, AVPRI, fond 133, Kantseliariia, opis 469, 1841/41; Königsmarck to Frederick William IV, Büyükdere, 3, 5 and 24 Feb. 1841, GStA PK, HA III, MdA I, 7284; Ponsonby to Palmerston, Therapia, 4, 14 and 15 Feb. 1841, TNA, FO 78/430; *Documents diplomatiques: L'Égypte de Mehemet-Ali jusqu'en 1920*, Paris 1920, pp. 10–14; Kodaman, p. 149.

whole problem again into question. It opens all doors to intrigue, even the disunion among the members of the [pasha's] family, and exhausts the country."[22] Metternich criticised Stürmer for consenting not only to the method of succession but also the size of the tribute and the method of its payment. He found the amount "preposterous"[23] and proclaimed that it would be better if the annual tribute was fixed and an exact amount sent to Constantinople. He also pointed out that with regard to the venality of Ottoman clerks and the lack of transparency of the local administration, granting complete control of the province's revenue to the sultan's official was absolutely out of question. His criticism was also directed against the commission of officers since he presumed that "it is not dangerous if the Sultan invests the Pasha with the right to raise officers to the rank of colonel, for the army and hence all its parts serve the Sultan. To be an Egyptian means to be His Highness's subject and to be a soldier in Egypt means to be a Turkish soldier."[24] Moreover, Mohammed Ali surely knew the officer candidates better than his sovereign, which, according to the chancellor, was important to the quality of the Egyptian and thus the Ottoman army.[25]

When the firman's conditions were also found by other signatories of the London Convention, in Metternich's words, to be "improper, unnecessarily persecutory and contrary to the views which guided the four courts in their effort to pacify the Levant,"[26] the chancellor questioned whether it would be possible to treat Mohammed Ali's eventual rejection of the firman as a revolt if this decree was also unacceptable to the Great Powers. He answered this for himself when he not only forbade Bandiera to participate in an enforcement action against the Egyptian vassal but also terminated the rear admiral's

---

[22] Lerchenfeld to Ludwig I of Bavaria, Vienna, 3 March 1841, BHStA, MA, Wien 2410.
[23] Metternich to Stürmer, Vienna, 26 March 1841, HHStA, StA, Türkei VI, 83.
[24] Ibid.
[25] Metternich to Stürmer, Vienna, 12 Feb., 16 and 26 March 1841, HHStA, StA, Türkei VI, 83; Metternich to Esterházy, Vienna, 19 and 28 Feb., 7, 9 and 29 March 1841, HHStA, StA, England 236; Tatishchev to Nesselrode, Vienna, 28 Feb. 1841, AVPRI, fond 133, Kantseliariia, opis 469, 1841/191; Sainte-Aulaire to Guizot, Vienna, 28 Feb. and 18 March 1841, AMAE, CP, Autriche 429; Lerchenfeld to Ludwig I of Bavaria, Vienna, 3 and 30 March 1841, BHStA, MA, Wien 2410; Maltzan to Frederick William IV, Vienna, 5 March 1841, GStA PK, HA III, MdA I, 7362.
[26] Metternich to Stürmer, Vienna, 23 March 1841, HHStA, StA, Türkei VI, 83.

subordination to Stopford. In doing so, he demonstrated that Austria would not consider Mohammed Ali's rejection of the firman as an act of rebellion and in no way would offer its forces for a new military campaign against him.[27]

The fear that Mohammed Ali would not accept the firman was entirely justified. When it was delivered to him on 20 February, he refused to discuss finance, hereditary succession and the appointment of officers and demanded a revision of the document in these points. Since the Great Powers also regarded its conditions as exorbitant, the pasha's disagreement did not anger them and, therefore, the term "positive refusal"[28] was used by their diplomats.[29] Metternich wrote to Stürmer that "the restrictions, which I opposed the day I learnt about His Highness's decree, were judged in London just as I judged them. They were found improper, unnecessarily harsh, and incompatible with the opinions of the four courts in their effort to pacify the Levant."[30] Consequently, Metternich agreed with the pasha's refusal of the firman and supported its modification: "For my part I completely approve it [the refusal]. It is certain that the firman is absolutely unfeasible and I do not doubt that the Porte will satisfy Mohammed Ali's demands."[31]

The firman displeased Metternich because it postponed not only the final settlement of the conflict in the Near East but also France's return to the concert. Guizot was determined to maintain France's isolation and armament until the moment when Mohammed Ali was reinstalled in Egypt and obtained the right to hereditary rule. Although in Vienna no one feared the possibility of war with France in 1841 any more, Metternich, in particular due to the prevailing unrest among the German countries, was considerably annoyed with the protraction of the crisis and tired of Guizot's ongoing "armed peace" that moved the chancellor to this exaggerated exclamation: "On one side is

---

[27] Metternich to Esterházy, Vienna, 28 Feb. and 7 March 1841, HHStA, StA, England 236; Tatishchev to Nesselrode, Vienna, 28 Feb. 1841, AVPRI, fond 133, Kantseliariia, opis 469, 1841/191; Maltzan to Frederick William IV, Vienna, 1 March 1841, GStA PK, HA III, MdA I, 7362.

[28] Sainte-Aulaire to Guizot, Vienna, 8 April 1841, AMAE, CP, Autriche 429.

[29] Metternich to Esterházy, Vienna, 18 March 1841, HHStA, StA, England 236; Fahmy, *Mehmed Ali*, p. 97.

[30] Metternich to Stürmer, Vienna, 23 March 1841, HHStA, StA, Türkei VI, 83.

[31] Sainte-Aulaire to Guizot, Vienna, 18 March 1841, AMAE, CP, Autriche 429.

peace, and this is where we stand. On the other is war. In the middle
is a political monstrosity called an armed peace or a prepared-for war
and is of little consequence to us: We want to know if we are at peace
or at war!"[32] Nothing, however, could move Guizot to change his attitude before the settlement of the Turko-Egyptian conflict, and he
declared in February: "We have, for our part, no proposal to offer. We
are alone, we are at peace and we are waiting ... We accept the fait
accompli."[33] All he was prepared to do for the time being was to agree
with the method of France's return to the diplomatic concert arranged
on the turn of February in London upon the proposal of Esterházy and
Bülow. A text of a protocol was prepared by which the allied Powers
and the Ottoman Empire would formally declare the Turko-Egyptian
affair as ended when this actually happened. Afterwards, a text of a
new Straits Convention would be signed by the Ottoman Empire and
all Powers including France. Since Palmerston and Nicholas I also
agreed with this method to end the crisis, its conclusion depended
only on the successful solution of the dispute between Alexandria and
Constantinople. Since the February firman did not bring it to a close,
neither the protocol nor the new convention could be signed. Although
Metternich tried to persuade Guizot to regard the settlement of the
controversy between the sultan and his pasha as merely a matter of
time, the French minister was not willing to say that the crisis was
over when it still continued. He told Apponyi in March: "Before agreeing to sign the convention, it is necessary that the affair that we have
been told is terminated is really and completely so, which means in
the manner that no foreign intervention whatsoever into it would be
necessary in the future and that no [Power] could interfere in it any
longer. It is necessary to establish such a state of affairs for us to be
able to return to the European concert, and it is this starting point
that must be clear and assured before we can consider abandoning
our current position of isolation."[34] To show goodwill and a desire to
sign the convention in the future, Guizot agreed with the initialisa-
tion of the convention, which was done by all parties in London on
16 March.[35]

---

[32] Metternich to Esterházy, Vienna, 30 Jan. 1841, HHStA, StA, England 236.

[33] Guichen, p. 485.

[34] Apponyi to Metternich, Paris, 11 March 1841, HHStA, StA, Frankreich 320.

[35] Metternich to Trauttmannsdorff, Vienna, 20 Jan. and 21 Feb. 1841, HHStA,
StK, Preussen 178; Metternich to Esterházy, Vienna, 22 Jan. 1841, HHStA, StA,

Metternich finally accepted this result as the maximum achievable at the given moment and did not object to Guizot's decision not to sign the new convention since he laid the blame for the protracting crisis not in Paris but in Constantinople where the solution to the crisis ultimately lay. Consequently, the prince aimed his effort at persuading the Porte to modify the firman in the disputed points. Stürmer was instructed to inform the Porte that the sultan naturally possessed freedom of action and no one could force him to act against his will but he had to understand that the Great Powers were also free in their decision-making. As had been the case in previous months, in March Stürmer's steps were again frustrated by Ponsonby, who still maintained his anti-Egyptian attitude and advised Reshid to change nothing in the firman. The British ambassador's continuous intransigence placed Reshid in an awkward situation where it was difficult for him to satisfy the wishes of the representatives of the allied Powers disunited in their opinion on the final settlement, making thus the whole issue rather confusing for the Turks. The Ottoman foreign minister was caught between the diplomats of three conservative courts led by Stürmer and advocating concessions and Ponsonby and the majority of the Divan desiring to impose the most severe conditions on Mohammed Ali. The Ottoman dignitaries were also plotting against Reshid and blaming him for taking a course altogether too compromising. Therefore, Reshid hesitated to make any important decisions on his own and he often chose the mid-course resulting, for example, in the February firman that could have been even more severe if he had not restrained his warlike colleagues in the Divan. Stürmer defended Reshid's actions in his reports to Metternich, pointing out that the Ottoman foreign minister always ceded to Austria's wishes and that sometimes he would have done so even faster if he had not had to face domestic opposition. The sultan was also said to agree

---

England 236; Metternich to Stürmer, Vienna, 13 Feb. 1841, HHStA, StA, Türkei VI, 83; Metternich to Apponyi, Vienna, 24 Feb. 1841, HHStA, StA, Frankreich 322; Cetto to Ludwig I of Bavaria, London, 19 Jan. and 16 March 1841, BHStA, MA, London 2236; Maltzan to Frederick William IV, Vienna, 19 Feb. 1841, GStA PK, Rep. 81 Gesandtschaften (Residenturen) u. (General-) Konsulate nach 1807, Gesandtschaft Wien II, 204/2; Maltzan to Frederick William IV, Vienna, 19 March 1841, GStA PK, HA III, MdA I, 7362; Tatishchev to Nesselrode, Vienna, 24 Feb. 1841, AVPRI, fond 133, Kantseliariia, opis 469, 1841/191; Hasenclever, *Die Orientalische Frage*, p. 279; Ingle, p. 141; Kutluoğlu, pp. 183–184.

with the Egyptian governor's demand for hereditary rule at Reshid's insistence and assurance that this concession would end the conflict. Metternich knew well Reshid's difficult situation and he did not blame the Ottoman minister for the severe conditions of the February firman exactly for this reason, as he told Lerchenfeld: "Reshid Pasha only acceded to the extremely onerous conditions of the firman out of fear of losing his position since a very strong party in the Divan reproaches him for having made concessions to the Great Powers that are too great and for not defending the interests of the Sublime Porte enough."[36] Consequently, Metternich did not doubt Reshid's willingness to discuss and satisfy the objections to the firman, but Reshid did not get enough time to fulfil this expectation because the refusal of the decree by Mohammed Ali as well as the Great Powers contributed to his fall.[37]

Not Reshid's delicate dance but Ponsonby's recalcitrance evoked Metternich's anger once again. The chancellor was considerably annoyed with the ambassador's conduct in sharp and obvious contrast with the desire of the allied Powers, which they made clear in a note on 30 January 1841 from London requesting the sultan "to revoke the deposal of Mohammed Ali and assure him that his descendants, in direct line, will be successively appointed by the sultan to the Egyp-

---

[36] Lerchenfeld to Ludwig I of Bavaria, Vienna, 16 March 1841, BHStA, MA, Wien 2410.

[37] Metternich to Stürmer, Vienna, 23 and 26 March, 2, 20 and 21 April 1841, HHStA, StA, Türkei VI, 83; Metternich to Esterházy, Vienna, 7 Jan., 9, 21 and 31 March 1841, HHStA, StA, England 236; Stürmer to Metternich, Constantinople, 30 Dec. 1840, HHStA, StA, Türkei VI, 77; Testa to Stürmer, 10 Jan. 1841, Stürmer to Metternich, Constantinople, 11 Jan. 1841, HHStA, StA, Türkei VI, 79; Stürmer's note to Reshid Pasha, 18 March 1841, Stürmer to Metternich, Constantinople, 24 and 31 March 1841, HHStA, StA, Türkei VI, 80; Tatishchev to Nesselrode, Vienna, 24 Feb. 1841, AVPRI, fond 133, Kantseliariia, opis 469, 1841/191; Titov to Nesselrode, Pera, 29 March 1841, AVPRI, fond 133, Kantseliariia, opis 469, 1841/41; Sainte-Aulaire to Guizot, Vienna, 18 March 1841, AMAE, CP, Autriche 429; Königsmarck to Frederick William IV, Büyükdere, 10 March 1841, GStA PK, HA III, MdA I, 7284; Maltzan to Frederick William IV, Vienna, 19 March 1841, GStA PK, HA III, MdA I, 7362; Maltzan to Frederick William IV, Vienna, 22 March 1841, GStA PK, Rep. 81 Gesandschaften (Residenturen) u. (General-) Konsulate nach 1807, Gesandschaft Wien II, 204/2; Maltzan to Frederick William IV, Vienna, 2 April 1841, GStA PK, HA III, MdA I, 7363; Lerchenfeld to Ludwig I of Bavaria, Vienna, 3 March and 2 May 1841, BHStA, MA, Wien 2410; Kutluoğlu, p. 177.

tian pashalik."[38] When Metternich learnt that Ponsonby had refused in mid March to join his colleagues in their attempt to persuade the Porte to modify the method of succession according to this note, he became so upset that he told Sainte-Aulaire: "Lord Ponsonby seems to have no regard for his instructions and only wants to behave as he chooses. He is a madman who would be able to make peace or declare war without the relevant instructions of his court."[39] The chancellor, annoyed with the British ambassador's conduct and the Porte's complicity, felt forced to repeat in early April his January threat about the termination of Austria's support if the sultan did not modify his attitude: "[In such a case] His Imperial Highness would regard himself as relieved of the obligation which he accepted in the agreement of 15 July 1840 and therefore as having complete freedom of position and action."[40] He explained the reason for this threat to Stürmer in this way: "Everything, even the most enduring patience comes to an end, and that of our court has arrived today. In no way do we intend to continue to be engaged in a labyrinth of intrigues, and yet it is to this that the undisciplined and extravagant spirit of Lord Ponsonby has reduced the greatest and the most difficult political enterprise of our time. The ideas of Lord Ponsonby are aimed at causing a second Nezib, and the Porte surely must have had enough of the first attempt. It should devote itself to the improvement of its internal situation and understand what can be left to time; but time does not offer many resources to an adversary of 74 or 75 years, today beaten and in decline. Defeat is a bad basis for reconstructing a fallen power and yet it is on this that Mohammed Ali must rebuild his. The power of the pasha will thus not re-establish itself if the Porte is wise, and it will be if it takes advantage of the victories of its allies and remains in accord with them."[41]

Metternich sent his complaints about "the agony of the Near Eastern affair"[42] not only to Constantinople but also to London and urged Palmerston to rectify his ambassador's behaviour. Although earlier in the year Metternich had incorrectly suspected the foreign

---

[38] *Ordre chronologique de l'affaire Turco-égyptienne*, HHStA, StA, Türkei VI, 72.
[39] Sainte-Aulaire to Guizot, Vienna, 8 April 1841, AMAE, CP, Autriche 429.
[40] Metternich to Stürmer, Vienna, 2 April 1841, HHStA, StA, Türkei VI, 83.
[41] Ibid.
[42] Metternich to Esterházy, Vienna, 15 April 1841, HHStA, StA, England 237.

secretary of secretly trying to expel Mohammed Ali from Egypt owing to British interests, now in March and April the chancellor correctly saw beyond Ponsonby's steps mere insubordination. Palmerston actually agreed with Metternich's arguments concerning the firman and gradually sent several instructions to Constantinople during the next two months with the aim of inducing Ponsonby to cooperate with his colleagues and persuade the Porte to modify the February decree, but nothing significant changed in the latter's conduct until early May when he received Palmerston's strict instructions of 24 April consenting to Metternich's threat of withdrawing Austrian support and announcing that "H[er] Maj[esty's] Government entirely concurs in the view of this matter taken by the Austrian government and are prepared to take the same course."[43] Already before the arrival of these instructions, Abdülmecid I accepted the proposed changes in the firman on behalf of Mohammed Ali. On 19 April, most likely under the influence of Metternich's threat from the beginning of the month, Stürmer was informed that the sultan had agreed to grant Mohammed Ali hereditary rule for his family without his interference, decrease the amount of the annual tribute and allow the appointment of the colonels by the pasha. The issue of a new firman was, however, under the condition of the approval of the allied Powers.[44]

When Metternich learnt about the sultan's decision, he was convinced that the satisfactory end of the affair was assured and that there was no further need for the isolation of France because he re-

---

[43] Palmerston to Ponsonby, London, 21 April 1841, HHStA, StA, Türkei, VI, 83, attached to Metternich to Stürmer, Vienna, 30 April 1841, HHStA, StA, Türkei VI, 83.

[44] Metternich to Esterházy, Vienna, 7, 18 and 31 March, 7 and 15 April 1841, HHStA, StA, England 236; Palmerston to Ponsonby, London, 16 March 1841, Metternich to Stürmer, Vienna, 26 March and 20 April 1841, HHStA, StA, Türkei VI, 83; Metternich to Trauttmannsdorff, Vienna, 9 May 1841, HHStA, StK, Preussen 178; Stürmer to Rifat Pasha, 9 and 13 April 1841, the Porte's memorandum to Stürmer, 19 April 1841, Testa to Stürmer, 19 April 1841, Stürmer to Metternich, Constantinople, 7, 14, 19, 21 and 30 April 1841, HHStA, StA, Türkei VI, 80; Stürmer to Metternich, Constantinople, 4 May 1841, HHStA, StA, Türkei VI, 81; Struve to Nesselrode, Vienna, 3 April 1841, AVPRI, fond 133, Kantseliariia, opis 469, 1841/191; Maltzan to Frederick William IV, Vienna, 6 April 1841, GStA PK, Rep. 81 Gesandschaften (Residenturen) u. (General-) Konsulate nach 1807, Gesandschaft Wien II, 204/3; Beauvale to Palmerston, Vienna, 9 April 1841, TNA, FO 120/197; Königsmarck to Frederick William IV, Büyükdere, 21 April 1841, GStA PK, HA III, MdA I, 7284; Marlowe, p. 289.

garded the acceptance of the modifications by the Egyptian governor as certain: "There is no occasion to ask or wait [for] what Mehemet Ali [sic] may say to the new concessions of the Porte. They are those he has asked for. The answer he will return to the Sultan can be dilatory, but must be good."[45] He promptly asked Guizot to sign the new convention and the French foreign minister agreed and wrote on 16 May to Count Bourqueney: "We have no longer any grounds for refusal [to come out of isolation]. The modifications granted are, for the most part, what Mehemet Ali demands. What still remains in debate is evidently of an internal nature, and ought to be settled between the sultan and the pacha [sic] alone. We have therefore determined to sign when required. Your full powers are ready and will be forwarded without delay."[46] However, Guizot conditioned his signature with the formal declaration of the four Powers and the Ottoman Empire in the protocol that the Turko-Egyptian conflict was indeed over, and it was Palmerston who was now not willing to consider the crisis as terminated until receipt of Mohammed Ali's formal agreement with the new conditions from late April, which were finally enclosed in a new firman prepared by the Porte a month later.[47] It was more favourable for Mohammed Ali: Egypt (including the Sudan) was in hereditary tenure of the pasha's family and the sultan would not choose the successor, and the governor was also granted the right to appoint officers up to the rank of colonel; for higher ranks he had to apply for permission of the sultan. In peacetime, the size of the Egyptian army was not to exceed 18,000 men. The building of vessels of war was forbidden without the sultan's permission. The amount of the annual tribute was fixed at 80,000 purses. When the Porte realised at the

---

[45] Guizot, *Memoirs of a Minister of State*, p. 111.
[46] Ibid., p. 112.
[47] Metternich to Stürmer, Vienna, 20 April 1841, HHStA, StA, Türkei VI, 83; Metternich to Apponyi, Vienna, 26 April, 5 May and 15 June 1841, HHStA, StA, Frankreich 322; Metternich to Esterházy, Vienna, 5 May, 5, 15 and 30 June 1841, HHStA, StA, England 237; Apponyi to Metternich, Paris, 25 June 1841, HHStA, StA, Frankreich 320; Maltzan to Frederick William IV, Vienna, 24 April and 5 May 1841, GStA PK, HA III, MdA I, 7363; Bockelberg to Frederick William IV, Vienna, 15 June and 3 July 1841, GStA PK, HA III, MdA I, 7364; Lerchenfeld to Ludwig I of Bavaria, Vienna, 2 May, 14 and 20 June 1841, BHStA, MA, Wien 2410; Sainte-Aulaire to Guizot, Vienna, 6 May 1841, AMAE, CP, Autriche 429; Cetto to Ludwig I of Bavaria, London, 29 June 1841, BHStA, MA, London 2236; Webster, *Palmerston*, II, pp. 770–771.

end of May that the Great Powers agreed with the new conditions, the firman was dispatched to Egypt on 1 June.[48]

Having learnt of the firman, Metternich considered the whole affair to be settled and Palmerston's attitude pointless, in particular when Mohammed Ali's agreement could be regarded as certain. He wrote to Esterházy on 30 June: "But what does Lord Palmerston want? He wants to let France feel the power of England by proving to it that the Egyptian affair will only end when it [England] wants and regardless of France's attitude. He wants to prove to the two German Powers that he does not need them, that the support of Russia is sufficient for England. He wants to keep Russia in check and have it follow the same course [as England] using the concern that [Russia] always has to see the rapprochement of England and France in a system that would be hostile to it. The Great Powers are thus instruments in his hands with which he likes to play as he pleases. He finds in this his personal satisfaction, and England allows him to do it because it sees in it the proof of its strength."[49] Since Palmerston proved to be unwavering in this issue, it was necessary to wait for the acceptance of the new firman by Mohammed Ali. Completely unthinkable before 1839, these conditions were accepted by the Egyptian governor without hesitation on 10 June. Thereby, the dispute between the sultan and his vassal became a thing of the past in the Levant, and Palmerston was finally willing to declare this fact formally. The entire conflict ended on 13 July 1841 with official signatures from Austria, Prussia, Russia, Great Britain, and the Ottoman Empire affixed to the final protocol formally declaring the crisis as over and with the conclusion of the Second London Convention regarding the Straits, signed on the same day by representatives of the states just mentioned and France.[50] This

---

[48] Hurewitz, *The Middle East*, p. 121. Mohammed Ali had originally submitted to this amount but he also expressed his wish that it be reduced, and the tribute was finally fixed after the summer negotiations in Constantinople to 60,000 purses (3 million florins). This happened with the help of Laurin's reports about the financial situation of Egypt and to Metternich's satisfaction. Ottenfels to Stürmer, Vienna, 10 Aug. 1841, Metternich to Stürmer, Königswart, 10 Aug. 1841, HHStA, StA, Türkei VI, 83; Stürmer to Metternich, Constantinople, 30 April 1841, HHStA, StA, Türkei VI, 80; Stürmer to Metternich, Constantinople, 2 and 23 June, 7, 14 and 28 July 1841, HHStA, StA, Türkei VI, 81; Stürmer to Metternich, Constantinople, 28 Sept. 1841, HHStA, StA, Türkei VI, 82.

[49] Hasenclever, *Die Orientalische Frage*, p. 303.

[50] The protocol was dated retrospectively to 10 July 1841.

Convention, signed for Austria by Neumann and Esterházy, confirmed the closure of the Straits to all foreign warships at time of peace.[51]

Metternich was content with the turn of events[52] and in reaction to the solution of the crisis he claimed that "he had not enjoyed such feelings of tranquillity and peace of mind in the last thirty-three years."[53] Since he wanted to prevent any repetition of the conflict that had eventually ended relatively happily, he warned Laurin, before his return to Alexandria in mid August, that the principal aim of his actions in Egypt would be to secure Mohammed Ali's real submission in the following years, for "Europe wants an Egypt that is a genuine province of the Ottoman Empire and not an Egypt that under the pretext of submission forms an independent state and brings instability to the Empire."[54] Stürmer added in his own instructions for Laurin that the consul general was to urge Mohammed Ali to remove the monopolies hampering European trade: "Mohammed Ali undoubtedly hopes to maintain the monopolies and avoid the last commercial treaty between Great Britain and the Porte to which almost all Great Powers have acceded. However, none of them can tolerate such a state of things and the strongest objections from their part will be the consequence [of his doing so]. Since Austria is significantly interested in this question owing to the extent of our commerce with Egypt, you will dedicate all your energies to it and you will join if need be the consuls of the Great Powers who find themselves in the same situation as we do to take measures which seem opportune to you in agreement with them."[55] Both wishes, that Mohammed Ali should remain loyal and open Egypt's market to European merchants, were satisfied. The pasha appeased himself with his accomplishments and remained

---

[51] Metternich to Stürmer, Vienna, 15 June 1841, HHStA, StA, Türkei VI, 83; Metternich to Apponyi, Vienna, 25 June 1841, HHStA, StA, Frankreich 322; Stürmer to Metternich, Constantinople, 20 and 23 May 1841, HHStA, StA, Türkei VI, 81; Titov to Nesselrode, Pera, 18 May 1841, AVPRI, fond 133, Kantseliariia, opis 469, 1841/41; Maltzan to Frederick William IV, Vienna, 1 June 1841, GStA PK, HA III, MdA I, 7364; Königsmarck to Frederick William IV, Büyükdere, 20 and 23 May 1841, GStA PK, HA III, MdA I, 7284; Anderson, *The Great Powers*, pp. 51–52; Hurewitz, *The Middle East*, p. 123.

[52] Metternich to Stürmer, Vienna, 20 July 1840, HHStA, StA, Türkei VI, 83.

[53] Guichen, p. 530.

[54] Metternich to Stürmer, Vienna, 15 June 1841, HHStA, StA, Türkei VI, 83.

[55] Stürmer to Laurin, Constantinople, 26 July 1841, attached to Stürmer to Metternich, Constantinople, 28 July 1841, HHStA, StA, Türkei VI, 81.

peaceable, and he abolished, although after some resistance as expected by Stürmer and after strong European pressure, the system of monopolies until the mid 1840s.[56]

Metternich's Plan for a Permanent Solution to the Eastern Question

When the Second Mohammed Ali Crisis was drawing to its end, Metternich expressed a desire to assure that the Eastern Question did not harm the relations among the European Powers in the future in the way it had done during the latest crisis, in other words he wanted to ensure peace in the Levant. This goal he intended to achieve in two ways. First, he contemplated making Vienna a permanent centre from which the situation in the Near East was to be supervised and from which the unified reports were to be sent to Constantinople in the case of need; Metternich again argued with Vienna's proximity to the Ottoman capital, which would enable a prompt and, what was also important, unified reaction of Europe to new problems in the Ottoman Empire. Metternich's conceit and hunger for control over the Eastern Question were reflected in this plan that was very similar to the one for the Viennese conference in 1839: "A place can be considered as the most fitting for conducting an affair without it being necessary to establish it as an official and recognised centre of deliberations for that purpose; the courts may therefore regard Vienna as the place to which it will be important to direct the opinions which every court views as the most useful in support of the common cause; it should be there [Vienna] and, if so desired, under my direct control where the exchange of these views can take place among the cabinets. For giving really practical value to such a proceeding, two conditions are urgently necessary; it is above all indispensable that a representative, charged with the important task of being the voice of the sentiment of his court, should be invested with all its confidence; further, it is

---

[56] A. A.-R. Mustafa, "The Breakdown of the Monopoly System in Egypt after 1840," P. M. Holt (ed.), *Political and Social Change in Modern Egypt: Historical Studies from the Ottoman Conquest to the United Arab Republic*, London, New York, Toronto 1968, pp. 291–307.

necessary that in a pressing situation, a representative of the court in Constantinople should be provided with necessary orders for responding to the urgency that, in such situations, he would have to obtain from his colleague in Vienna. These conditions which would be requisite for all officially established centres are above all indispensable in this case from the practical point of view if one wants to take advantage of the short distance [from Constantinople] offered by the geographical position of our capital. These [conditions] are prompted by our proposal from 1839 and we do not believe that the difficulties that occurred were of a nature to diminish the value of our original idea."[57] It would, however, be a mistake to see exclusively beyond this plan Metternich's long desire to lead European affairs. Regarding his idea to include the Ottoman Empire into the European state system at the Congress of Vienna a quarter of a century earlier, it is necessary to understand the whole plan in the wider context of his wish to create a framework of international law protecting the Ottoman Empire from the ambitions of European Powers thereby contributing to the greater stability of European politics as a whole. This goal is also evident from the second idea contemplated by him in 1841 that the Great Powers would formally undertake not to acquire any Ottoman territory in the future. Since his relations with Russia had chilled during the latest crisis, he addressed his ideas to London where, however, they were rejected by Palmerston, who found them useless and unfeasible at the moment when the crisis was over.[58] The foreign secretary particularly objected to the idea of Metternich's supervision of Near Eastern affairs: "For the course pursued during the last two years by Austria in regard to the Turco-Egyptian question has not on the whole been so steady and consistent, nor marked with such firmness and energy as to inspire Her Majesty's Government with that degree of confidence in the policy of the Austrian Cabinet, which an acquiescence in such a scheme would imply; and in fact when the temporary engagements of the Treaty of July shall have been fully worked out and fulfilled,

---

[57] Metternich to Apponyi, Johannisberg, 2 Sept. 1841, HHStA, StA, Frankreich 322.
[58] Beauvale to Palmerston, Vienna, 19 May 1841, TNA, FO 120/197; Maltzan to Frederick William IV, Vienna, 25 May 1841, GStA PK, HA III, MdA I, 7364; Sainte-Aulaire to Guizot, Vienna, 10 July 1841, AMAE, CP, Autriche 429; Webster, *Palmerston*, II, p. 775.

perhaps the best thing will be that the five Powers and Turkey should fall back into their usual state of reciprocal relations."[59]

Another reason for Palmerston's rejection of Metternich's proposals was his conviction that Nicholas I would immediately oppose both ideas if he learnt of them. This presumption was entirely correct. Besides the tsar's well-known unwillingness to restrict himself in the Eastern Question, an important role was played, as well as in the case of Palmerston, by the negative opinion prevailing in St Petersburg of Metternich's timidity during the crisis, in particular since late 1840. When Nesselrode learnt of the chancellor's January threat to withdraw Austria's assistance if the Porte did not accord hereditary rule to Mohammed Ali and did not terminate the Syrian campaign, he reacted with these deprecatory words: "I no longer understand Metternich; he has lost all energy. Such faintheartedness throws a regrettable reflection on the last days of his political life."[60] And in March, Nesselrode accused Metternich of displaying "clumsiness, inconceivable cowardice."[61] In the meantime, the British ambassador in St Petersburg reported that "the Emperor [the tsar] and his ministers seem to think that age, and a great sense of the responsibility that is upon him, have of late much increased Prince Metternich's natural caution and timidity."[62] This criticism is, however, at least considerably exaggerated and to a great extent influenced by the interests and actions of its authors. During the Rhine Crisis, above all in October 1840, Metternich definitely showed a considerable restraint resulting from his apprehension of France, but during the final stage of the Turko-Egyptian conflict from December 1840 he feared neither France nor the other Great Powers and his threats to end Austria's participation in the affair resulted from his strong dissatisfaction with the behaviour of some British and Russian diplomats unnecessarily protracting it and were aimed at forcing the Porte to yield. The chancellor simply did not want to follow Ponsonby in his desire to destroy Mohammed Ali completely, something at sharp variance with the interests of Austria and the whole of German Confederation as well as

---

[59] Webster, *The European System*, p. 35.

[60] Nesselrode to Meyendorff, St Petersburg, 13 Feb. 1841, *Nesselrode*, VIII, p. 124.

[61] Nesselrode to Meyendorff, St Petersburg, 13 March 1841, *Nesselrode*, VIII, p. 132.

[62] Clanricarde to Palmerston, St Petersburg, 23 Feb. 1841, TNA, FO 65/271.

with the preservation of peace on the Continent. For the same reason he was similarly dissatisfied with Nicholas I's personal hostility
towards Louis Philippe leading to the tsar's secret proposal to the
British cabinet for an anti-French quadruple alliance in early 1841
and clearly evident in Brunnov's conduct in London aimed until mid
March against the appeasement with France.[63] Metternich was not
afraid but simply tired and dissatisfied with the protraction of the
conflict that was essentially over at the end of 1840. In his old age he
continued to be cautious but he did not start to be cowardly.[64]

*   *   *

Palmerston's expectation of the tsar's rejection of Vienna as a centre
of diplomatic supervision of the Eastern Question as well as his refusal
to renounce the right to further territorial expansion on his part at
the expense of the Ottoman Empire was definitely correct. What he
failed to predict was the need for such a renunciation of the right to
territorial gains for the termination of the Eastern Question as a topic
of European politics seriously weakening the relations of its principal

---

[63] Metternich to Esterházy, Vienna, 22 Jan., 9 March and 23 April 1841, HHStA,
StA, England 236; Maltzan to Frederick William IV, Vienna, 22 March 1841, GStA
PK, Rep. 81 Gesandschaften (Residenturen) u. (General-) Konsulate nach 1807,
Gesandschaft Wien II, 204/2; F. S. Rodkey, "Anglo-Russian Negotiations about a
'Permanent' Quadruple Alliance, 1840–1841," *AHR* 36, 1931, pp. 343–349; Web-
ster, *Palmerston*, II, p. 769.

[64] In connection with Metternich's 68th birthday on 15 May 1841, it is just interesting – although not actually helpful in the support or rejection of Palmerston's
and Nesselrode's accusations of his timidity – to read Lerchenfeld's evaluation
of Metternich's good health and "the vigour of his spirit. It is a pleasure to see
the clarity of his expositions, the soundness of his logic and the profundity of his
judgement. It is amazing how at his age he is engaged from morning to night (he
often does not leave his cabinet before 11 o'clock, talking about the affairs with
the people who wait for him in the salon until midnight) as he personally edits
memoranda and important dispatches, as he takes care of private correspondence.
He has expedited 104 couriers since 14 July [1840]: his correspondence in this Near
Eastern affair would amount to volumes. Despite all his occupations, he is much
more accessible than any foreign minister of a German court. He often finds extra
time for reading us his dispatches as well as the reports he receives. He is commu-
nicative and enters into every subject with pleasure." Lerchenfeld to Ludwig I of
Bavaria, Vienna, 15 May 1841, BHStA, MA, Wien 2410.

protagonists. The fact that the Ottoman Empire remained, according to Metternich's fitting expression of December 1828, "placed rather under the protection of rival passions than that of the public law,"[65] later led to new crises and wars in the Near East with serious consequences for the situation on the Continent. Unsurprisingly, the long period of peace restored after the Napoleonic Wars was buried in the Crimean War in the 1850s owing to the self-interest of each of the Great Powers involved and their mutual distrust. By that time Metternich was no longer in office because of his political fall in March 1848. During the last seven years of his presence at the Chancellery, however, no affair as serious as those of the preceding 20 years occurred in the Ottoman Empire. Of course, there were the continuous disturbances in the Lebanon and a problem with a Serbian prince in 1842–1843, and with both Metternich had to occupy himself, but none of these incidents caused serious conflicts in the relations among European countries and therefore did not cause the Austrian chancellor undue concern.[66] Consequently, when Metternich departed from Vienna for Bohemia on 17 July 1841, he was taking leave not only of the Austrian capital for the summer but also his active participation in the Eastern Question for ever.

[65] Metternich to Ficquelmont, Vienna, 30 Dec. 1828, SOA, RA C-A 382.
[66] Hametner, pp. 9–51.

Conclusion

Metternich paid considerable attention to events beyond Austria's south-eastern frontier. His voluminous correspondence on Near Eastern affairs related to not only politics at the highest level but also to economics, religion and social matters, his frequent discussions about these topics with Austrian as well as foreign diplomats, monarchs, military officers, travellers and orientalists, his reading of numerous books and newspaper articles on the same topics and, finally, his practical steps prove that he considered not only Germany and Italy but also the Ottoman Empire as areas of enormous importance for the Austrian Empire. Consequently, it is necessary to refute the widespread claim that his perception of the world was merely directed to the West and that he was not interested in the situation in the Near East.[1] One could admit that Metternich was culturally inclined to the West and not at all to the East and this would be entirely correct because he had no personal sympathy for the Levant, but this had no significant influence on his diplomacy, and he still attentively observed events in the Balkans to a similar extent as he did in other European regions bordering on Austria.

Alan Palmer claims that Metternich disliked dealing with the affairs of the Ottoman Empire because Austria had nothing to gain in this area,[2] and with the exception of the sphere of commercial enterprise, which was of extreme importance to Austria, he is right, but one must realise that first, despite this fact Metternich felt obliged to deal with this issue and he therefore paid considerable attention to affairs relating to it, and second, the prince would have definitely been happy if he had not had to solve any problems, including those in the Apennines, the German Confederation or in any other part of the more or less distant world. He also dealt with problems in

---

[1] The correct opinion that Metternich was very interested in Near Eastern affairs, and of course those concerning the Balkans in particular, was already stated by Ulrike Tischler, p. 107.

[2] Palmer, p. 258.

Italy or Germany not because he wanted to or because he could gain much there but because he had to, and this also holds for the Near East. It is also true that both areas in the West were regarded as traditional spheres of Austria's interests, but so were the Balkans, which were of crucial geopolitical and economic importance for the Danube Monarchy. Metternich of course did not actively intervene in the Near East as often as in the West, but this was due to the fact that nations in the former were governed by one monarch usually not requesting foreign assistance in his internal affairs, whereas the latter was full of small independent states whose rulers often asked for Austria's diplomatic or even military support against revolutionary threats. Moreover, when Metternich found it necessary to intervene in the Ottoman Empire, he did so. For example, he contemplated Austria's military intervention in Serbia in 1810 and he sent Austrian forces into the eastern Mediterranean to protect Austria's economic interests against Greek piracy in the 1820s or to assist the sultan against Mohammed Ali in 1840.

It is thus possible to say that Austria followed a more active policy in the German Confederation and Italy than in the Balkans as well as the Near East in general, but it is hardly possible to maintain that it remained inactive in the affairs of the latter as, for example, did French historian René Albrecht-Carrié: "It will be noted, in the case of the Greek episode, that Austria played a surprisingly inactive role despite her major interest in Ottoman affairs. This tendency on Austria's part to remain in the background where Eastern affairs were concerned and to let others take the initiative, leaving them to court her assistance in the uncertainty of what she might elect to do, is characteristic of her Eastern policy; it will appear on more than one occasion, generally to the annoyance of all. The reason for it lay in part at least in the fact that the East held second priority of interest for Austria who looked upon Central Europe as the prime concern of her policy. Not until her eviction from Italy and from Germany was she to put first emphasis on the Near East."[3] This opinion results more from the fact that an enormous number of documents proving the contrary have generally remained unexplored than the actual circumstances. Metternich not only did not consider the Near East to be of secondary importance, but he was also in no way inclined to leave the initiative regarding

---

[3]   Albrecht-Carrié, p. 48.

the region to others. He never surrendered the Balkans to Russia's exclusive supremacy and was certainly not willing to do so voluntarily; he never regarded the Ottoman Empire as Russia's exclusive zone of influence and he did not consider the Eastern Question to be the personal affair of one Great Power only. Finally, above all, his Austria was not passive in the Eastern Question but rather its actions were simply different from those of the other Great Powers directly involved in it: France, Russia, and Great Britain.

Austria's approach towards the Ottoman Empire during *Vormärz* was directed not only by the firm conviction of Francis I and Metternich of the crucial necessity to preserve its existence and without any territorial claims on their part, but also by the characters of these two men who were not inclined to pursue an ambitious and pompous foreign policy. Consequently, their attitudes towards the Ottoman Empire were always friendly and they never threatened it with war even if they had the right to do so due to the harassment of Austria's merchant navy owing to piracy from the Ottoman North African domains or of Austrian citizens tormented by frequent cross-border incursions of bandits from the Ottoman Balkan territories. Francis I and Metternich also never undertook any measure seriously violating the standards of the public law of Europe or at the expense of the sultan even though at least the seizure of Klek and Sutorina would have been advantageous for the Austrian Empire and easily feasible during the studied period when the Porte faced dangerous crises making any seriously hostile reaction from its part had Austria indeed occupied these two small strips of land highly unlikely. The observance of law was also typical for Metternich's approach in economic affairs; he defended Austria's economic privileges whenever he found it necessary to do so – even though he well knew that sometimes they were burdensome for the Porte – but he did not agree with any abuse of these privileges by the Austrians. He always wanted to solve existing problems and not pointlessly cause new ones, which is also evident in his religious policy in the Near East through which he wanted to prevent the European Powers from misusing the religious problems of the Ottoman Empire for their own egoistic interests; his approach to the religious affairs of the East clearly differed from the more imperialistic aims of France and Russia. In brief, Metternich's Near Eastern policy was based upon his respect for the existing international law, the sovereignty of the state and its independence, that is to say upon the desire to maintain order as created at the Congress of Vienna. All of this characterised his approach in Near Eastern affairs, an approach that was in no way passive but was definitely less aggressive, menacing, egoistic and acquisitive, in other words less destabilising for the crumbling structure of the sultan's state as well as for the European state system than the policies of France, Russia and Great Britain.

More or less obvious imperialistic aims are particularly evident in the case of the former two, France and Russia. The French governments during the Restoration as well as the July Monarchy desired to improve France's position in European politics as well as the government's position within the country. Consequently, they often pursued a vainglorious policy that was also clearly aggressive. In the 1820s, various projects of conquest at the expense of the Ottoman Empire were contemplated in French society including governmental circles, of which the famous Polignac Plan is the most striking example but not the only one. France took part in the trilateral alliance not only in an effort to control its allies but also to win the popularity of the French public, and for the latter reason it also sent its armies to the Peloponnese in 1828 and Algeria two years later. After the July Revolution in the 1830s, French governments spread proclamations about friendship towards the Ottoman Empire but simultaneously worked against its interests when, motivated by jealousy, they attempted to forestall Russia's aid offered to the sultan in 1833, courted Mohammed Ali and tried to take advantage of the religious affairs of the Ottoman Empire to increase French influence over the Levant. The Rhine Crisis was a logical consequence of this ambitious policy and desire of the French cabinets to win domestic popularity. Unsurprisingly, it was France that Metternich significantly distrusted for most of the 1820s and whose actions he disagreed with in the Greek Question. In the 1830s, he even regarded France as his principal opponent in the Near East and he disliked or even opposed its activities in most of the relevant affairs of this period: the Algerian Affair, the Constantinople Armenian Catholic Affair, the Damascus Affair, the Syrian Question, the two Mohammed Ali Crises, the Rhine Crisis and the issue of Ottoman reforms. Consequently, Paul W. Schroeder's claim that after 1815 "France and Austria usually cooperated in the Near East"[4] is entirely mistaken.

---

[4] P. W. Schroeder, "The Transformation of European Politics: Some Reflections,"

Russia under both tsars, Alexander I and Nicholas I, did not desire the destruction of the Ottoman Empire but wanted to keep it weak and under their indirect control, and their steps were directed towards this aim and met with success when the Porte was burdened with high indemnities after the lost war with Russia and deprived of both its formal control of Greece and factual control of the Danubian Principalities and Serbia. As shown in the book, justice was in no way always on Russia's side but then legality was also not the leitmotiv of its Near Eastern policy. It was a simple power struggle and neither laws nor alleged regard for the European concert were important factors which would have restrained Russia; what the two tsars regarded to a certain extent was the danger of revolution and above all their fear of the creation of a powerful alliance of other Great Powers if Russia overstepped the limits of greed tolerable for other members of the concert. Due to its financial weakness, in particular in the 1830s, Russia was completely unable to successfully confront such a coalition. It was not as strong as some contemporaries presumed and it was far from being capable of acting independently because to do so would have meant being able to act against the will of the other four Powers, which Russia definitely was not. When it celebrated military or diplomatic victories in the Near East, it was not because of its invincible strength but because of the ineptness of its opponents. The fact that Russia could fight out a victorious war with the Ottoman Empire in the late 1820s was not a result, as Paul W. Schroeder claims, of the fact that "when Russia took the lead resolutely in the Near East, Europe could not unite to stop it,"[5] but because the other Powers quite simply did not unite. Russia entered the war only when Nicholas I neutralised his possible opponents either by binding them with the Treaty of London, as with France and Great Britain, or by depriving them of any possible allies, as was the case of Austria, which would have been isolated if it had decided to wage war against Russia in the late 1820s. In the 1830s, despite the fact that Nicholas I claimed that the Eastern Question was his own private affair, he had to take into consideration the attitudes of the other Powers and secure an ally.

W. Pyta (ed.), *Das europäische Mächtekonzert: Friedens- und Sicherheitspolitik vom Wiener Kongreß 1815 bis zum Krimkrieg 1853*, Köln, Weimar, Wien 2009, p. 32.

[5] Schroeder, *Transformation*, p. 660.

In brief, it is difficult to find in him or Alexander I much sense of a common European identity.

Great Britain was much more interested in the preservation of the Ottoman Empire than were France and Russia, but its conduct in the Eastern Question also did not entirely reflect such a desire. In the 1820s Canning's policy weakened the Ottoman Empire by supporting Greek political emancipation and was motivated by a variety of reasons but definitely not by any for the benefit of Europe or in the interests of the Alliance that he disliked; Palmerston in his Near Eastern policy was particularly motivated by his desire to promote British interests and extreme Russophobia resulting from his jealousy and incorrect judgement of Russia's real intentions in the Near East; his pointlessly hostile anti-Russian policy did not contribute to the peace and stability of the Levant but unsettled the Porte and destabilised the functioning of the concert. The fact that Great Britain did not wage war against Russia after 1833 was caused by Palmerston's sincere desire to avoid one, but it must be also emphasised that Great Britain could not effectively wage a war without allies in the Continent because it lacked the land forces necessary for a decisive victory over Russia. This proves that Great Britain also could not act independently because it did not have the force to do so.[6]

On closer investigation of the conduct of France, Russia and Great Britain in the Eastern Question during the studied period, it is difficult to see their policies being motivated by anything other than selfish ambitions, unilateral goals, national interests, jealousy and mutual distrust and restrained more by the limits of their power than by much respect for the public law of Europe, respect that was allegedly, according to Richard B. Elrod, characteristic of European politics during the era of concert diplomacy.[7] Although the Ottoman Empire was not regarded as a member of the European state system protected by the Viennese settlement, there was no reason why the

---

[6]   Even Prussia, generally uninterested in the affairs of the East, attempted to take advantage of the situation whenever it found it possible to do so, as happened during the Rhine Crisis when Frederick William IV tried to change the balance of power in the German Confederation in his favour. As explained in Chapter 26, this manoeuvre motivated by personal ambition did not meet with its members' approval and was finally forestalled by Metternich defending the interests of Austria as well as those of other German princes.

[7]   Elrod, p. 170.

European countries could not apply the same legal rules towards it as generally accepted among themselves, for example, respect for its sovereignty and territorial integrity. The motivation for such conduct would be logical if they wanted to maintain the stability of the European state system that could be harmed by their competition in the Levant. However, they applied a different set of self-serving rules and sometimes took advantage of the fact that the Ottoman Empire remained beyond the boundaries of Europe, in particular when France took possession of Algeria or when the trilateral alliance intervened in the Greek affairs. Matthias Schulz regarded the latter as an "arbitrational interference"[8] of the concert that assumed the right to force the quarrelling parties into a compromise settlement even by coercive means, and he saw in this evidence of "a certain arbitrational power and peacekeeping power of the Concert."[9] It is, however, difficult to see in this intervention motivated by self-interest and scarcely any humanitarian sentiment and not leading to any compromise settlement but rather a one-sided verdict on behalf of the Greeks anything other than a unilateral dictation of force because the three European Powers involved proceeded beyond any legal limits generally recognised by themselves when they infringed the sovereignty of another country in a manner that they would never have allowed to be used against themselves in a similar case.

The fact that the Ottoman Empire remained unprotected by the public law of Europe while at the same time its vast territories of high economic and geopolitical importance were often situated in Europe's backyard made it a perfect playground for the ambitious games of Great Powers. This was a dangerous situation when their competition for power in the Near East could have considerably negative consequences on the Continent itself, in other words it could destroy the peace restored in Europe after the Napoleonic Wars. Metternich was well aware of this danger and he attempted to remove or at least reduce it by, first, introducing the Ottoman Empire into the family of European countries with rights identical to its members, an idea he advocated in 1814–1815 and most probably also in 1840 because there is no reason to doubt that Metternich also wanted to include the Ottoman Empire in his project for the league to preserve peace in

---

[8] Schulz, *Normen und Praxis*, p. 572.
[9] Ibid.

Europe and, second, by strengthening its security with the Great Powers' formal pledge not to compete for Ottoman regions, proposed in 1841. Neither of these ideas materialised because of the unwillingness of France, Great Britain and Russia to limit their hunger for political predominance over the Levant and subordinate their self-interest to any self-restricting legal regulations.

Metternich was often scorned for his insistence on his conservative principles and his allegedly anachronistic approach to international relations and the problems of the period when, for example, opposing the political emancipation of nations. However, in this respect his Austria did not differ from the other Great Powers actually not pursuing any modern pro-nationalist policies but simply using double standards in domestic and foreign affairs when it suited their own interests to do so, Russia being the most striking example with its support of the Greeks and suppression of the Poles. The difference could be found in the fact that Metternich was not hypocritical in this respect and was extremely consistent in his principles, which can be viewed as legal guidelines for regulating international relations, and he actually behaved in compliance with them at least within the Eastern Question. He was convinced that if the principles of public law were not obeyed, the result would be the destabilisation of the whole structure of European politics. This attitude could be labelled by some as wrong and old-fashioned but its sincerity can hardly be denied. Consequently, if the preservation of peace was in Europe's interests, then Metternich manifested a considerably European outlook in a generally egoistic world, and he did so not only because the interests of Europe in this respect coincided with those of the Austrian Empire but also because such an outlook was deep-rooted in Metternich's *Weltanschauung*.

Metternich also served the general peace with his peace management when first, he insisted on the preservation of its legal framework, the limits of which the Great Powers were not to exceed and second, when he attempted to blunt the edges of the ambitious policies of the other Powers. It is not illogical that his peace management often clashed with their unilateral interests and his views were often unacceptable to or misunderstood by men like Canning, Palmerston, Polignac, Charles X, Thiers, Alexander I, Nicholas I, Pozzo di Borgo, and even Nesselrode, all of whom showed little sense of a common European identity. Metternich was sometimes criticised by some of these men for not supporting their interests or even for deceiving them. The ingrained negative image of the Austrian chancellor as a generally dishonest man hiding his real thoughts even from his colleagues and deceiving his enemies as well as his allies has been often accepted by historians and is firmly rooted in European collective memory.[10] Some of this criticism was well founded, and Metternich of course was not a saint: he often used very diplomatic, that is to say ambiguous language, he tried to employ one state against another and he used other "diplomatic" weapons at his disposal to attain the desired goal. Nevertheless, the studied documents offer clear evidence that much of the criticism raised against him is baseless or at least exaggerated. The fact that must be emphasised is that despite his often sophisticated and subtle diplomatic manoeuvres his foreign policy as a whole was broad and consistent; he generally expressed his views to anybody who wanted to listen and his opinions were definitely much more frank than has generally been supposed. Consequently, his contemporaries often unreasonably distrusted him or saw deception behind his attitudes simply because they did not correspond with their own ambitious plans. The history of the Eastern Question offers a considerable number of examples. For instance, when Alexander I changed his originally hostile attitude towards the Greek insurgents and expected the same from Austria, which did not comply with this expectation, he complained that Metternich had deceived him despite the fact that the chancellor had never concealed that he would not agree with any settlement exceeding the limits of international law respecting the sultan's sovereignty; or when the same tsar at the end of his life was also displeased with the level of Austria's support in the Russo-Ottoman disputes despite the fact that Metternich usually exerted great pains to move the Ottomans to yield, sometimes even in cases when the Russians' requests exceeded the limits of legal validity; Nicholas I was sometimes dissatisfied with Metternich's support in his disputes with France and Great Britain when confronting their Russophobia although in fact this support was quite considerable, but simultaneously he entirely misunderstood the fact that his own actions were often egoistic and that his demand for the recognition of the Near Eastern area as exclusively Russia's affair was not acceptable for the other Powers; Palmerston regarded Metternich as an accomplice of Russia's alleged hostile designs against the Ottoman Empire

---

[10] For all these negative opinions see Schroeder, *Transformation*, p. 460; Webster, *The European System*, p. 36.

and accused him of deceiving the British cabinet when defending Russia's policy towards the Ottoman Empire and of doing little to defend the Ottoman Empire against Russia's influence, yet Metternich was entirely sincere and correct in his defence of Russia's peaceful policy in the Near East, and when the prince did not want to clash with Russia, it was not due to his alleged timidity but to the fact that he saw no reason to do so because he did not want to create new conflicts and because he was also able to obtain concessions from the tsar by amicable means in the same way as he had managed to do so in the Danubian Principalities.

Regarding Metternich's personality, his opinions and steps relating to the Eastern Question reveal that he was a conservative statesman whose policy was based upon rational and generally remarkably correct analyses often leading to unbelievably accurate prognoses. The last resulted not only from his extraordinary analytical skills but also from his profound knowledge of facts resulting from his intensive study of the state of affairs in the Ottoman Empire. Consequently, although he pursued his Near Eastern policy according to his conservative principles, in other words in conformity with his broad politico-legal strategy, his policy can in no way be labelled as purely dogmatic. He very often showed remarkable realism, pragmatism and toleration towards different religions and cultures even though he had no personal attachment to them. What, above all, the studied documents disclose is the fact that Metternich's character and deeds need further in-depth and impartial research before any tenable far-reaching evaluation not only of this man and his activities but also of his period can be made.

Bibliography

Manuscripts

Haus-, Hof- und Staatsarchiv, Vienna

Staatenabteilungen

Türkei III: 17
Türkei VI: 10–15, 17–30, 32–39, 45, 50–83
Türkei VII: 25, 34
Türkei VIII: 2–12, 14–16, 20, 24
England: 166, 169, 173, 175, 177–179, 181–184, 186–189, 191, 198, 199, 204, 208, 209, 214–216, 218, 219, 223, 225, 227, 228, 230, 231, 236, 237
Frankreich: 244, 247, 250, 254, 257, 260, 261, 264, 265, 267, 268, 270–272, 274, 276, 280, 289, 290, 293, 294, 297, 298, 300, 302, 303, 307, 311, 312, 315–320, 322
Russland III: 45, 52, 54, 60, 64, 65, 70, 71, 73, 75, 78, 81, 84, 86–90, 92, 97, 99, 102–105, 107–112, 114–116, 119, 120, 123
Neapel: 92–94
Sardinien: 64, 65, 77
Ägypten: 1
Moldau-Walachei II: 56

Staatskanzlei

Preussen: 113, 115, 117, 121, 125, 128, 129, 132, 137, 152, 153, 162, 165, 169, 172, 175, 176, 178
Rom: 37, 38, 43, 46, 63–67
Griechenland: 12
Interiora/Intercepte: 27, 28, 32
Konsulate/Odessa: 32
Vorträge: 250–260, 262, 268, 272, 274, 287

Gesandschaftsarchiv

Brüssel: 2, 14
Konstantinopel: II/56

Geheimes Staatsarchiv Preussischer Kulturbesitz, Berlin

Ministerium des Auswärtigen I, HA III
Österreich: 5995–5998, 6000–6014, 6016, 6020–6029, 6031–6034, 6093,
  6094
Türkei: 7255–7284
Frankreich: 4906
Bayern: 2487
Sachsen: 3840
Neapel: 5596
Belgien: 4522
Orientalische Angelegenheiten: 7344–7365

*Rep. 81 Gesandschaften (Residenturen) u. (General-) Konsulate nach
1807*
Gesandschaft Wien II: 201/1–4, 204/1–3

The National Archives of the United Kingdom, London

Foreign Office
65 (Russia): 271
78 (Turkey): 181, 189, 190, 226–228, 247, 274–278, 301–303, 357, 360,
  398, 399, 430–436, 997
120 (Austria): 47–49, 51–53, 60, 62, 63, 66–73, 75, 76, 82–88, 90–95,
  97–102, 104, 105, 108–110, 113, 114, 124, 136–139, 145, 147, 149,
  153, 155, 161, 169, 170, 180, 189, 190, 194, 197
195 (France): 116
352 (Stratford Canning Papers): 59
881 (The Affairs of Syria): 181

Arkhiv vneshnei politiki Rossiiskoi Imperii, Moscow

Fond 133, Kantseliariia, opis 468
Vienna: 11870, 11873, 11874, 11877, 11879, 11881, 11885

Fond 133, Kantseliariia, opis 469
Vienna: 1830/275, 1833/210–211, 1834/217, 1836/216, 1837/230,
  1839/213–215, 1840/177–178, 1841/191
Constantinople: 1836/43, 1841/41

Archives du Ministère des affaires étrangères, Paris

Correspondance politique
Autriche: 402–412, 416–429
Prusse: 271, 272
Russie: 175–178
Turquie: 247, 248, 255, 260–262, 267–275, 279–283
Égypte: 3, 5

Correspondance consulaire et commerciale
Odessa: 4

Bayerisches Hauptstaatsarchiv, Munich

Ministerium des Äußern
Wien: 2401–2403, 2405–2410
Berlin: 2618, 2619
Dresden: 2820, 2821
London: 2221–2224, 2228–2230, 2234–2236
Petersburg: 2713–2718, 2721, 2722, 2725, 2727
Paris: 2096/1, 2097/2, 2102/1, 2102/2
Päpstlicher Stuhl: 2498
Varia: 435, 83993

Gesandtschaften
Wien: 1522, 1880

Geheimes Hausarchiv
Nachlass König Ludwig I.: I–XVI 293i, I–XVI 301

Sächsisches Staatsarchiv, Dresden

Hauptstaatsarchiv, Sächsische Gesandschaften
Wien: 92–94
Paris: 19

Archivio Segreto Vaticano, Vatican City

Archivio della Nunziature Apostolica in Vienna: 256, 256A–C, 280C, 280D, 281H, 281I, 520

Archives diplomatiques et africaines, Brussels

Correspondances politiques
Autriche: 1–8
France: 10
Prusse: 5, 6
Turquie: 1, 2

Hrvatski državni arhiv, Zagreb

750/Obitelj Ottenfels: 18, 37, 38

Arhiv Republike Slovenije, Ljubljana

AS 1080, Zbirka muzejskega društva za Kranjsko 1, fasc. 2 Orientalica, učna pisma 7, pismo Ibrahima iz Kaira

Národní archiv, Prague

Rodinný archiv Metternichů, Starý archiv: 388
Rodinný archiv Metternichů, Acta Clementina: 2/4, 2/6, 4/3, 5/2, 5/3, 6/1, 8/2, 12/2, 12/3, 12/5, 13/3

Státní oblastní archiv v Litoměřicích (Leitmeritz), pobočka Děčín (Tetschen)

Rodinný archiv Clary-Aldringenů: 375, 376, 382, 383, 385, 386

Národní památkový ústav, Zámek Kynžvart (Chateau Königswart)

Chancellor Metternich's Library

L'Alcoran de Mahomet traduit de l'Arabe par André du Ryer, I–II, Amsterdam, Leipzig 1770, book number 25-B-12 (17444).

The Portfolio or a Collection of State Papers Illustrative of the History of our Times, London 1836, book number 4-B-2 (1869–1874).

Jochmus, August von, *Der Verfall des Osmanen-Reiches seit 1840*, Frankfurt am Main 1858, book number 37-D-4/I-IV.

Pradt, Dominique Georges Frédéric Dufour de, *L'Intervention armée pour la pacification de la Grèce*, Paris 1828, book number 37-D-6c (20958).

Schott, Friedrich, *Die orientalische Frage und ihre Lösung aus dem Gesichtspunkte der Zivilisation*, Leipzig 1839, book number 7-A-70 (4624).

Stratimirovics, Georg von, *Die Reformen in der Türkei*, Wien 1856, book number II-3830.

Published Correspondence

Anderson, M. S. (ed.), *The Great Powers and the Near East 1774–1923*, London 1970.

Bordeano, N., *L'Égypte d'aprés les Traités de 1840–41*, Constantinople 1869.

British Parliamentary Papers XLVI, 1844.

Broglie, Le Duc de (ed.), *Mémoires du Prince de Talleyrand*, V, Paris 1998.

Chancellor, E. B. (ed.), *The Diary of Philipp von Neumann, 1819 to 1850*, London 1928.

Cunningham, A. B. (ed.), *The Early Correspondence of Richard Wood 1831–1841*, London 1966.

Documents diplomatiques: L'Égypte de Mehemet-Ali jusqu'en 1920, Paris 1920.

Douin, G. (ed.), *L'Égypte de 1828 à 1830: Correspondance des consuls de France en Égypte*, Roma 1935.

Douin, G. (ed.), *La mission du Baron de Boislecomte, l'Égypte et la Syrie en 1833*, Caire 1927.

Driault, É. (ed.), *L'Égypte et l'Europe: La crise de 1839–1841*, I, Caire 1930.

Dross, E. (ed.), *Quellen zur Ära Metternich*, Darmstadt 1999.

Hartig, F. (ed.), *Metternich-Hartig: Ein Briefwechsel des Staatskanzlers aus dem Exil 1848–1851*, Wien, Leipzig 1923.

Hoetzsch, O. (ed.), *Peter von Meyendorff: Ein russischer Diplomat an den Höfen von Berlin und Wien. Politischer und privater Briefwechsel, 1826–1863*, I, Berlin 1923.

Holland, T. E. (ed.), *The European Concert in the Eastern Question: A Collection of Treaties and Other Public Acts Edited with Introduction and Notes*, Aalen 1979.

Hurewitz, J. C. (ed.), *The Middle East and North Africa in World Politics: A Documentary Record, Volume 1: European Expansion, 1535–1914*, New Haven, London 1975.

Hurmuzaki, E. de, Hodoş, N. (eds.), *Documente privitoare la istoria Românilor, Volumul XVII: Corespondenţă diplomatică şi rapoarte consulare franceze (1825–1846)*, Bucureşti 1913.

Hurmuzaki, E. de, Nistor, I. (eds.), *Documente privitoare la istoria Românilor, Volumul XXI: Corespondenţă diplomatică şi rapoarte consulare austriace (1828–1836)*, Bucureşti 1942.

Hyamson, A. M. (ed.), *The British Consulate in Jerusalem in Relation to the Jews of Palestine 1838–1914, Part I: 1838–1861*, London 1939.

Kronenbitter, G. (ed.), *Friedrich Gentz: Gesammelte Schriften, Band XI.4: Briefe von und an Friedrich von Gentz. Schriftwechsel mit Metternich. Zweiter Teil: 1820–1832*, Hildesheim, Zürich, New York 2002.

Metternich-Winneburg, R. von (ed.), *Aus Metternichs nachgelassenen Papieren*, III, IV and VI, Wien 1882–1883.

Mikhaïlowitch, N. (ed.), *Les rapports diplomatiques de Lebzeltern, ministre d'Autriche à la cour de Russie (1816–1826)*, St. Petersburg 1913.

Nesselrode, A. de (ed.), *Lettres et papiers du Chancelier Comte de Nesselrode, 1760–1850*, VII–VIII, Paris 1908.

Neumann, L. von (ed.), *Recueil des traités et conventions conclus par l'Autriche avec les Puissances étrangères 1763–1856*, III–IV, Leipzig 1857.

Prokesch-Osten, A. von (ed.), *Aus dem Nachlasse des Grafen Prokesch-Osten: Briefwechsel mit Herrn von Gentz und Fürsten Metternich*, I–II, Wien 1881.

Prokesch-Osten, A. von (ed.), *Dépêches inédites du chevalier de Gentz aux hospodars de Valachie pour servir à l'histoire de la politique européenne (1813 à 1828)*, I and III, Paris 1877.

Prokesch-Osten, A. von (ed.), *Geschichte des Abfalls der Griechen vom türkischen Reiche im Jahre 1821 und der Gründung des hellenischen Königreiches: Aus diplomatischem Standpuncte*, III–VI, Wien 1867.

Prokesch-Osten, A. von (ed.), *Zur Geschichte der orientalischen Frage: Briefe aus dem Nachlasse Friedrichs von Gentz 1823–1829*, Wien 1877.

Robech, E. de L.-M. de (ed.), *Un collaborateur de Metternich: Mémoires et papiers de Lebzeltern*, Paris 1949.

Schlossar, A. (ed.), *Briefwechsel zwischen Erzherzog Johann Babtist von Österreich und Prokesch-Osten*, Stuttgart 1898.

Strupp, K. (ed.), *Ausgewählte diplomatische Aktenstücke zur orientalischen Frage*, Gotha 1916.

Walker, M. (ed.), *Metternich's Europe*, New York 1968.

Wolf, L. (ed.), *Notes on the Diplomatic History of the Jewish Question: With Texts of Protocols, Treaty Stipulations and other Public Acts and Official Documents*, London 1919.

Diaries, Memoirs, Statistics

Ausweise über den Handel von Oesterreich im Verkehr mit dem Auslande und über den Zwischenverkehr von Ungarn und Siebenbürgen, mit den anderen österreichischen Provinzen, im Jahre 1840. Vom Rechnungs-Departement der k. k. allgemeinen Hofkammer. Erster Jahrgang (Erste Abtheilung), Wien 1842.

Becher, S., *Statistische Uebersicht des Handels der österreichischen Monarchie mit dem Auslande während der Jahre 1829 bis 1838*, Stuttgart, Tübingen 1841.

Bowring, Sir J., *Report on Egypt 1823–1838 under the Reign of Mohamed Ali*, London 1998.

Egerton, F., *Journal of a Tour in the Holy Land, in May and June, 1840*, London 1841.

Fournier, A., Winkler, A. (eds.), *Tagebücher von Friedrich von Gentz (1829–1831)*, Zürich, Leipzig, Wien 1920.

Guizot, F., *Memoirs of a Minister of State, from the Year 1840*, London 1864.

Guizot, F., *Mémoires pour servir à l'histoire de mon temps*, Paris 1971.

Haan, V. von (ed.), *Erzherzog Johann von Österreich, Leopold von Haan: Eine russisch-türkische Reise im Jahre 1837*, Wien 1998.

Hagemeister, J., *Mémoire sur le commerce des ports de la Nouvelle-Russie, de la Moldavie et de la Valachie*, Odessa 1835.

Hammer-Purgstall, J. von, *Erinnerungen aus meinem Leben 1774–1852*, Wien, Leipzig 1940.

Kübeck, M. von (ed.), *Tagebücher des Carl Friedrich Freiherrn von Kübeck von Kübau*, II, Wien 1909.

Müffling, F. C. F. von, *Aus meinem Leben*, Berlin 1855.

Prokesch-Osten, A. von, *Aus den Tagebüchern des Grafen Prokesch von Osten*, Wien 1909.

Pückler-Muskau, H. von, *Aus Mehemed Alis Reich: Ägypten und der Sudan um 1840*, Zürich 1985.

Quin, M. J., *A Steam Voyage down the Danube*, I, London 1835.

Sainte-Aulaire, L., *Souvenirs (Vienne 1832–1841)*, Paris 1926.

Springer, J., *Statistik des österreichischen Kaiserstaates*, II, Wien 1840.

Tafeln zur Statistik der oesterreichischen Monarchie, I–XIV, Wien 1828–1844.

Temperley, H. (ed.), *Das Tagebuch der Fürstin Lieven: Mit politischen Skizzen und einigen Briefen*, Berlin 1926.

Newspapers and Contemporary Periodicals

Österreichischer Beobachter, Nr. 270, Wien 1835.

Revue orientale, Nr. 1, Paris 1841.

Secondary Sources

Abbas, R., "French Impact on the Egyptian Educational System under Muhammad Aly and Ismail," D. Panzac, A. Raymond (eds.),

La France et l'Égypte à l'époque des vice-rois 1805–1882, Le Caire 2002, pp. 91–99.

Abdel-Malek, A., "Moh'ammad ᶜAlî et les fondements de l'Égypte indépendante," *Les Africains* 58, Paris 1977, pp. 235–259.

Abraham, A., *Maronite-Druze Relations in Lebanon 1840–1860: A Prelude to Arab Nationalism*, New York 1975.

Abu-Manneh, B., "The Islamic Roots of the Gülhane Rescript," *DWI* 34, 1994, 2, pp. 173–203.

Agstner, R., "The Austrian Lloyd Steam Navigation Company," M. Wrba (ed.), *Austrian Presence in the Holy Land in the 19ᵗʰ and early 20ᵗʰ Century*, Tel Aviv 1996, pp. 136–157.

Agstner, R., *Von k. k. Konsularagentie zum Österreichischen General-konsulat: Österreich (-Ungarn) und Alexandrien 1763–1993*, Kairo 1993.

Aksan, V. H., *Ottoman Wars 1700–1870: An Empire Besieged*, Harlow 2007.

Albrecht-Carrié, R., *A Diplomatic History of Europe since the Congress of Vienna*, London 1958.

Anderson, M. S., "Russia and the Eastern Question, 1821–1841," A. Sked (ed.), *Europe's Balance of Power, 1815–1848*, London 1979, pp. 79–97.

Angelow, J., *Von Wien nach Königgrätz: Die Sicherheitspolitik des Deutschen Bundes im europäischen Gleichgewicht (1815–1866)*, München 1996.

Angerlehner, R., *Österreichischer Schiffsverkehr und Seehandel 1815–1838*, unpublished dissertation, Wien 1968.

Antonetti, G., *Louis-Philippe*, Paris 1994.

Ardeleanu, C., "From Vienna to Constantinople on Board the Vessels of the Austrian Danube Steam-Navigation Company (1834–1842)," *Historical Yearbook* 6, 2009, pp. 187–202.

Ardeleanu, C., "Russian-British Rivalry regarding Danube Navigation and the Origins of the Crimean War (1846–1853)," *Journal of Mediterranean Studies* 19, 2010, 2, pp. 165–186.

Ardeleanu, C., "The Danube Navigation in the Making of David Urquhart's Russophobia (1833-1837)," *Transylvanian Review* 19, 2010, Supplement Nr. 5:4, pp. 337–352.

Ardeleanu, C., "The Lower Danube, Circassia and the Commercial Dimensions of the British-Russian Diplomatic Rivalry in the Black Sea Basin (1836–1837)," I. Biliarsky, O. Cristea, A. Oroveanu (eds.), *The Balkans and Caucasus: Parallel Processes on the Oppo-*

site Sides of the Black Sea, Newcastle upon Tyne 2012, pp. 39–56.

Arš, G. L., "Capodistria et le gouvernement russe (1826–1827)," *Les relations gréco-russes pendant la domination turque et la guerre d'indépendance grecque*, Thessaloniki 1983, pp. 119–132.

Baack, L. J., *Christian Bernstorff and Prussia: Diplomacy and Reform Conservatism 1818–1832*, New Jersey 1980.

Backouche, I., *La monarchie parlamentaire, 1815–1848: De Louis XVIII à Louis-Philippe*, Paris 2000.

Baggally, J. W., *Ali Pasha and Great Britain*, Oxford 1938.

Bailey, F. E., *British Policy and the Turkish Reform Movement*, London 1942.

Baker, R. L., "Palmerston and the Treaty of Unkiar Skelessi," *EHR* 43, 1928, pp. 83–89.

Baron, S., *Die Judenfrage auf dem Wiener Kongreß*, Wien, Berlin 1920.

Barsoumian, H., "The Eastern Question and the Tanzimat Era," R. G. Hovannisian (ed.), *The Armenian People from Ancient to Modern Times, Volume II: Foreign Dominion to Statehood: The Fifteenth Century to the Twentieth Century*, New York 1997, pp. 175–201.

Bartlett, C. J., *Great Britain and Sea Power 1815–1853*, Oxford 1963.

Basch-Ritter, R., *Österreich auf allen Meeren: Geschichte der k. (u.) k. Kriegsmarine von 1382 bis 1918*, Graz, Wien, Köln 1987.

Baumgart, W., *Europäisches Konzert und nationale Bewegung: Internationale Beziehungen 1830–1878*, München, Wien, Zürich 1999.

Bayrak, M., "The Attitude of the European States during the Greek (Rum) Revolt," K. Çiçek (ed.), *The Great Ottoman-Turkish Civilisation, Vol. 1: Politics*, Ankara 2000, pp. 441–457.

Beer, A., *Die Finanzen Oesterreichs im XIX. Jahrhundert*, Prag 1877.

Beer, A., *Die orientalische Politik Österreichs seit 1773*, Prag, Leipzig 1883.

Ben-Arieh, Y., *Jerusalem in the 19th Century: The Old City*, Jerusalem 1984.

Bergmann, J., *Erzherzog Friedrich von Österreich und sein Antheil am Kriegszuge in Syrien im Jahre 1840*, Wien 1857.

Berkes, N., *The Development of Secularism in Turkey*, Montreal 1964.

Berry, R. A., "Czartoryski's Hôtel Lambert and the Great Powers in the Balkans, 1832–1848," *IHR* 8, 1985, 1, pp. 45–67.

Bertsch, D., *Anton Prokesch von Osten (1795–1876): Ein Diplomat Österreichs in Athen und an der Hohen Pforte. Beiträge zur Wahrnehmung des Orients im Europa des 19. Jahrhunderts*, München

2005.

Bibl, V., *Metternich in neuer Beleuchtung*, Wien 1928.

Billinger, R. D. Jr., "They Sing the Best Songs Badly: Metternich, Frederick William IV, and the German Confederation during the War Scare of 1840–41," H. Rumpler (ed.), *Deutscher Bund und deutsche Frage 1815–1866*, München 1990, pp. 94–113.

Binoche, J., *Histoire des relations franco-allemandes de 1789 à nos jours*, Paris 1996.

Bitis, A., *Russia and the Eastern Question: Army, Government, and Society 1815–1833*, Oxford, New York 2006.

Blancard, T., *Les Mavroyéni: Histoire d'Orient (de 1700 à nos jours)*, II, Paris 1909.

Blottner, G., "Die antirussische Stimmung in den Donaufürstentümern 1830–1848 vornehmlich aus der Sicht zeitgenössischer österreichischer Quellen," *SOF* 42, 1983, pp. 223–230.

Blum, J., "Transportation and Industry in Austria, 1815–1848," *JMH* 15, 1943, 1, pp. 24–38.

Bolsover, G. H., "Lord Ponsonby and the Eastern Question (1833–1839)," *SEER* 13, 1934, 37, pp. 98–118.

Bolsover, G. H., "Palmerston and Metternich on the Eastern Question, 1834," *EHR* 51, 1936, pp. 237–256.

Bourgeois, É., *Manuel historique de politique étrangère*, Paris 1926.

Bourne, K., *Palmerston: The Early Years 1784–1841*, London 1982.

Brewer, D., *The Greek War of Independence: The Struggle for Freedom from Ottoman Oppression and the Birth of the Modern Greek Nation*, Woodstock, New York 2003.

Breycha-Vauthier, A., *Österreich in der Levante: Geschichte und Geschichten einer alten Freundschaft*, Wien, München 1972.

Bridge, F. R., *The Habsburg Monarchy among the Great Powers, 1815–1918*, New York, Oxford, Munich 1990.

Broucek, P., "Alexander Ypsilantis' Gefangenschaft in Österreich," *MÖStA* 17/18, 1964/1965, pp. 550–559.

Brown, D., "Palmerston and Austria," L. Höbelt, T. G. Otte (eds.), *A Living Anachronism? European Diplomacy and the Habsburg Monarchy: Festschrift für Francis Roy Bridge zum 70. Geburtstag*, Wien, Köln, Weimar 2010, pp. 29–48.

Bruneau, A., *Traditions et politique de la France au Levant*, Paris 1932.

Brunner, M., Kerchnawe, H., *225 Jahre Technische Militärakademie 1717 bis 1942*, Wien 1942.

Brusatti, A., "Der österreichische Außenhandel um 1820," H. Matis, K. Bachinger, K. Hildegard (ed.), *Betrachtung zur Wirtschafts- und Sozialgeschichte*, Berlin 1979, pp. 141–153.

Buchmann, B. M., *Militär – Diplomatie – Politik: Österreich und Europa von 1815 bis 1835*, Frankfurt am Main, Bern, New York, Paris 1991.

Buchmann, B. M., *Österreich und das Osmanische Reich: Eine bilaterale Geschichte*, Wien 1999.

Bullen, R. "France and Europe, 1815–1848: The Problem of Defeat and Recovery," A. Sked (ed.), *Europe's Balance of Power, 1815–1848*, London 1979, pp. 122–144.

Bullen, R., *Palmerston, Guizot and the Collapse of the Entente Cordiale*, London 1974.

Bury, J. P. T., Tombs, R., *Thiers, 1797–1877: A Political Life*, London, Boston, Sydney 1986.

Bußmann, W., *Zwischen Preußen und Deutschland: Friedrich Wilhelm IV.*, Berlin 1990.

Castries, R. de, *Louis-Philippe*, Paris 1980.

Cattaui, R., Cattaui, G., *Mohamed-Aly et l'Europe*, Paris 1950.

Chahrour, M., "'A Civilizing Mission'? Austrian Medicine and the Reform of Medical Structures in the Ottoman Empire, 1838–1850," *Studies in History and Philosophy of Biological and Biomedical Sciences* 38, 2007, 4, pp. 687–705.

Chamberlain, M. E., *Lord Aberdeen: A Political Biography*, London, New York 1983.

Chamberlain, M. E., *Lord Palmerston*, Cardiff 1987.

Chamberlain, M. E., *'Pax Britannica?' British Foreign Policy 1789–1914*, London, New York 1988.

Charles-Roux, F., *L'Égypte de 1801 à 1882: Mohamed Aly et sa dynastie jusqu'à l'occupation anglaise*, Paris 1936.

Charles-Roux, F., *Thiers et Méhémet-Ali: La grande crise orientale et européenne de 1840–1841*, Paris 1951.

Charléty, S., "La Monarchie de Juillet (1830–1848)," E. Lavisse (ed.), *Histoire de France contemporaine: Depuis la révolution jusqu'à la paix de 1919*, V, Paris 1922.

Chebli, M., *Une histoire du Liban à l'époque des émirs (1635–1841)*, Beyrouth 1984.

Chesney, F. R., Molbech, C., Michelsen, E. H., *Das Türkische Reich*, Leipzig 1974.

Chevallier, D., *La société du Mont Liban à l'époque de la révolution industrielle en Europe*, Paris 1971.

Chvojka, M., *Josef Graf Sedlnitzky als Präsident der Polizei- und Zensurhofstelle in Wien (1817–1848): Ein Beitrag zur Geschichte der Staatspolizei in der Habsburgermonarchie*, Frankfurt am Main 2010.

Ciachir, N., "The Adrianople Treaty (1829) and its European Implications," *Revue des études sud-est européennes* 17, 1979, pp. 695–713.

Clarke, J., *British Diplomacy and Foreign Policy 1782–1865: The National Interest*, London, Boston, Sydney, Wellington 1989.

Clayton, G. D., *Britain and the Eastern Question: Missolonghi to Gallipoli*, London 1971.

Cobban, H., *The Making of Modern Lebanon*, London 1987.

Cognasso, F., *Storia della questione d'Oriente*, Torino 1946.

Collingham, H. A. C., *The July Monarchy: A Political History of France 1830–1848*, London, New York 1988.

Coons, R. E., *Steamships, Statesmen, and Bureaucrats: Austrian Policy towards the Steam Navigation Company of the Austrian Lloyd 1836–1848*, Wiesbaden 1975.

Coons, R. E., "Metternich and the Lloyd Austriaco," *MÖStA* 30, 1977, pp. 49–66.

Corti, E. C., *Der Aufstieg des Hauses Rothschild*, Wien 1954.

Corti, E. C., *Leopold I of Belgium: Secret Pages of European History*, London 1923.

Cowles, L., "The Failure to Restrain Russia: Canning, Nesselrode, and the Greek Question, 1825–27," *IHR* 12, 1990, 4, pp. 688–720.

Crabitès, P., *Ibrahim of Egypt*, London 1935.

Crawley, C. W., "Anglo-Russian Relations, 1815–1840," *CHJ* 3, 1929, pp. 47–73.

Crawley, C. W., *The Question of Greek Independence: A Study of British Policy in the Near East, 1821–1833*, Cambridge 1930.

Cremer-Swoboda, T., *Der griechische Unabhängingkeitskrieg*, Augsburg 1974.

Cunningham, A., "Stratford Canning and the Tanzimat," E. Ingram (ed.), *Eastern Questions in the Nineteenth Century: Collected Essays*, II, London 1993, pp. 108–129.

Cunningham, A., "Stratford Canning, Mahmud II, and Muhammad Ali," E. Ingram (ed.), *Eastern Questions in the Nineteenth Century: Collected Essays*, II, London 1993, pp. 23–71.

Dakin, D., *The Greek Struggle for Independence*, 1821–1833, London

1973.

Dauber, R. L., *Erzherzog Friedrich von Österreich*, Graz, Wien 1993.

Davison, R. H., "Foreign and Environmental Contributions to the Political Modernization of Turkey," R. H. Davison (ed.), *Essays in Ottoman and Turkish History, 1774–1923: The Impact of the West*, Austin 1990, pp. 73–95.

Davison, R. H., "Russian Skill and Turkish Imbecility: The Treaty of Kuchuk Kainardji Reconsidered," *SR* 35, 1976, 3, pp. 463–483.

Davison, R. H., "Turkish Attitudes concerning Christian-Muslim Equality in the Nineteenth Century," R. H. Davison (ed.), *Essays in Ottoman and Turkish History, 1774–1923: The Impact of the West*, Austin 1990, pp. 112–132.

Davison, R. H., "The 'Dosografa' Church in the Treaty of Küçük Kaynarca," R. H. Davison (ed.), *Essays in Ottoman and Turkish History, 1774–1923: The Impact of the West*, Austin 1990, pp. 51–59.

Davison, R. H., "The First Ottoman Experiment with Paper Money," R. H. Davison (ed.), *Essays in Ottoman and Turkish History, 1774–1923: The Impact of the West*, Austin 1990, pp. 60–72.

Davison, R. H., "Vienna as a Major Ottoman Diplomatic Post in the Nineteenth Century," A. Tietze (ed.), *Habsburgisch-osmanische Beziehungen: Relations Habsbourg-ottomanes*, Wien 1985, pp. 252–263.

Debidour, A., *Histoire diplomatique de l'Europe depuis l'ouverture du Congrés de Vienne jusqu'à la clôture du Congrès de Berlin (1814–1878)*, Paris 1891.

Degeorg, G., *Damaskus von den Ottomanen bis zur Gegenwart*, Wien 2006.

Demelitsch, F. von, *Metternich und seine auswärtige Politik*, Stuttgart 1898.

Deschamps, H. T., *La Belgique devant la France de Juillet: L'opinion et l'attitude francaises de 1839 à 1848*, Paris 1956.

Deutsch, W., "Die Mission von Heß und Radowitz, 1840," *Gesamtdeutsche Vergangenheit, Festschrift für Heinrich von Srbik*, München 1938, pp. 255–265.

Dimakis, J., "Der politische Philhellenismus und Antiphilhellenismus während der Griechischen Revolution in der französischen und deutschen Presse," E. Konstantinou (ed.), *Europäischer Philhellenismus: Die europäische philhellenische Presse bis zur 1. Hälfte des 19. Jahrhunderts*, Frankfurt am Main, Berlin, Bern, New York, Paris, Wien 1994, pp. 41–54.

Dodwell, H., *The Founder of Modern Egypt: A Study of Muhammad Ali*, London 1931.

Doering-Manteuffel, A., *Vom Wiener Kongreß zur Pariser Konferenz: England, die deutsche Frage und das Mächtesystem 1815–1856*, Göttingen 1991.

Douin, G., *Navarin, 6 Juillet – 20 Octobre 1827*, Caire 1927.

Dostian, I. S., "L'attitude de la société russe face au mouvement de libération national grec," *Les relations gréco-russes pendant la domination turque et la guerre d'indépendance grecque*, Thessaloniki 1983, pp. 63–86.

Dostjan, I. J., "Rußland, Österreich und der erste serbische Aufstand 1804–1813," A. M. Drabek, R. G. Plaschka (eds.), *Rußland und Österreich zur Zeit der Napoleonischen Kriege*, Wien 1989, pp. 95–111.

Douwes, D., *The Ottomans in Syria: A History of Justice and Oppression*, London, New York 2000.

Dubnow, S., *Die neueste Geschichte des jüdischen Volkes: Das Zeitalter der ersten Reaktion und der zweiten Emanzipation (1815–1881)*, Berlin 1929.

Drobesch, W., "Il ruolo di Trieste tra I porti marittimi e fluviali austriaci (1719–1918)," R. Finzi, L. Panariti, G. Panjek (eds.), *Storia economica e sociale di Trieste, Volume II: La città dei traffici 1719–1918*, Trieste 2003, pp. 349–367.

Droz, J., *Histoire diplomatique de 1648 à 1919*, Paris 2005.

Durand-Viel, G., *Les campagnes navales de Mohammed Aly et d'Ibrahim*, II, Paris 1935.

Dwyer, P. G., *Talleyrand*, London 2002.

Eck, O., *Seeräuberei im Mittelmeer: Dunkle Blätter europäischer Geschichte*, München, Berlin 1940.

Eldem, E., "Capitulations and Western Trade," S. N. Faroqhi (ed.), *The Cambridge History of Turkey, Volume 3: The Later Ottoman Empire, 1603–1839*, Cambridge 2006, pp. 283–335.

Eliav, M., "Das österreichische Konsulat in Jerusalem und die jüdische Bevölkerung," A. M. Drabek, M. Eliav, G. Stourzh (eds.), *Prag – Czernowitz – Jerusalem: Der österreichische Staat und die Juden vom Zeitalter des Absolutismus bis zum Ende der Monarchie*, Eisenstadt 1984, pp. 31–72.

Elon, A., *The Pity of It All: A Portrait of German Jews 1743–1933*, London 2002.

Elrod, R. B., "The Concert of Europe: A Fresh Look at an International System," *WRP* 28, 1976, 2, pp. 159–174.

Engel-Jánosi, F., *Die Jugendzeit des Grafen Prokesch von Osten*, Innsbruck 1938.

Engel-Jánosi, F., "Österreich und die Anfänge des Königreichs Griechenland," *Geschichte auf dem Ballhausplatz: Essays zur österreichischen Außenpolitik 1830–1945*, Styria 1963.

Erb, R., "Die »Damaskus-Affäre« 1840 und die Bedeutung des Hauses Rothschild für die Mobilisierung der öffentlichen Meinung," G. Henberges (ed.), *Die Rothschilds: Beiträge zur Geschichte einer europäischen Familie*, Sigmaringen 1994, pp. 101–115.

Eschler, J., "Die Syrische Expedition im Jahre 1840 und Österreichs Beteiligung daran," *Jahres-Bericht der n.-ö. Landes-Oberrealschule und der mit ihr verbundeten Wiener-Neustadt*, Wiener Neustadt 1915, pp. 1–83.

Esquer, G., *Histoire de l'Algérie (1830–1960)*, Paris 1960.

Eustathiades, R.-W., *Der deutsche Philhellenismus während des griechischen Freiheitskampfes 1821–1827*, München 1984.

Evans, R., "Primat der Außenpolitik? Metternich und das österreichische Staats- und Reichsproblem," *Anzeiger der philosophisch-historischen Klasse* 144, 2009, 2, pp. 61–76.

Fahmy, K., *All the Pasha's Men: Mehmed Ali, His Army and the Making of Modern Egypt*, Cambridge 1997.

Fahmy, K., *Mehmed Ali: From Ottoman Governor to Ruler of Egypt*, Oxford 2009.

Farah, C. E., "Austrian Diplomacy and the Mt. Lebanon Crisis in the Age of Metternich," A. Tietze (ed.), *Habsburgisch-osmanische Beziehungen: Relations Habsbourg-ottomanes*, Wien 1985, pp. 325–343.

Farah, C. E., *The Politics of Interventionism in Ottoman Lebanon, 1830–1861*, London, New York 2000.

Farah, C. E., "The Quadruple Alliance and Proposed Ottoman Reforms in Syria, 1839–1841," *International Journal of Turkish Studies* 2, 1981, 1, pp. 101–130.

Farca, N., *Russland und die Donaufürstentümer 1826–1856*, München 1992.

Fargette, G., *Mehemet Ali: Le fondateur de l'Égypte moderne*, Paris 1996.

Fattal, K., Nohra, J. A., *L'Autriche et le Liban: Esquisse historique et promenade à travers les petites histoires d'une vieille amitié*, Paris 1996.

Ferguson, N., *The House of Rothschild: Money's Prophets 1798–1848*, London 2000.

Ferguson, N., "Metternich and the Rothschilds: "A Dance with Torches on Powder Kegs"?" *Year Book* (Oxford, Leo Baeck Institute) 46, 2001, pp. 19–54.

Fichtner, P. S., *Terror and Toleration: The Habsburg Empire Confronts Islam, 1526–1850*, London 2008.

Findley, C. V., *Bureaucratic Reform in the Ottoman Empire: The Sublime Porte, 1789–1922*, Princeton, New Jersey 1980.

Fischer, R.-T., *Österreich im Nahen Osten: Die Großmachtpolitik der Habsburgermonarchie im Arabischen Orient 1633–1918*, Wien, Köln, Weimar 2006.

Fleming, D. C., *John Capodistrias and the Conference of London (1821–1828)*, Thessaloniki 1970.

Florence, R., *Blood Libel: The Damascus Affair of 1840*, Madison 2004.

Florescu, R. R., "British Reactions to the Russian Régime in the Danubian Principalities," *JCEA* 31, 1962, pp. 27–42.

Florescu, R. R., "Lord Strangford and the Problem of the Danubian Principalities, 1821–24," *SEER* 39, 1961, 93, pp. 472–488.

Florescu, R. R., *The Struggle against Russia in the Romanian Principalities: A Problem in Anglo-Turkish Diplomacy, 1821–1854*, Iaşi 1997.

Frankel, J., "A Historiographical Oversight: The Austrian Consul-General and the Damascus Blood Libel (with the Laurin-Rothschild Correspondence, 1840)," A. Rapoport-Albert, S. J. Zipperstein (eds.), *Jewish History: Essays in Honour of Chimen Abramsky*, London 1988, pp. 285–317.

Frankel, J., *The Damascus Affair: "Ritual Murder," Politics, and the Jews in 1840*, Cambridge, New York, Melbourne 1997.

Frazee, C. A., *Catholics and Sultans: The Church and the Ottoman Empire, 1453–1923*, Cambridge, New York, Melbourne 1983.

Gatti, F., *Geschichte der k. u. k. Technischen Militär-Akademie, Band I: Geschichte der k. k. Ingenieur- und k. k. Genie-Akademie 1717–1869*, Wien 1901.

Gaultier-Kurhan, C., *Mehemet Ali et la France 1805–1849: Histoire singuliere du Napoleon de l'Orient*, Paris 2005.

Gautherot, G., *La conquête d'Alger 1830*, Paris 1929.

Geisthövel, A., *Restauration und Vormärz 1815–1847*, München, Wien, Zürich 2008.

Gelber, N. M., "Oesterreich und die Damaskusaffaire im Jahre 1840," *Jahrbuch der Jüdisch-Literarischen Gesellschaft* 18, 1927, pp. 217–264.

Georgeon, F., "Ottomans and Drinkers: The Consumption of Alcohol in Istanbul in the Nineteenth Century," E. Rogan (ed.), *Outside In: On the Margins of the Middle East*, London, New York 2002, pp. 7–30.

Gilbar, G. G., "The Persian Economy in the Mid-19th Century," *DWI* 19, 1979, 1–4, pp. 177–211.

Gleason, J. H., *The Genesis of Russophobia in Great Britain: A Study of the Interaction of Policy and Opinion*, Cambridge 1950.

Gollwitzer, H., *Ludwig I. von Bayern: Königtum im Vormärz, eine politische Biographie*, München 1986.

Gonda, B. von, *Die ungarische Schiffahrt*, Budapest 1899.

Good, D. F., *The Economic Rise of the Hapsburg Empire 1750–1914*, London, Berkeley, Los Angeles 1984.

Gorïanov, S., *Le Bosphore et les Dardanelles: Étude sur la Question des Détroits*, Paris 1910.

Graetz, H., *Geschichte der Juden vom Beginn der Mendelssohnschen Zeit (1750) bis in die neueste Zeit (1848)*, XI, Leipzig 1900.

Greaves, R. W., "The Jerusalem Bishopric, 1841," *EHR* 64, 1949, 252, pp. 328–352.

Greenfield, K. R., "Commerce and New Enterprise at Venice, 1830–48," *JMH* 11, 1939, 3, pp. 313–333.

Grimsted, P. K., *The Foreign Ministers of Alexander I: Political Attitudes and the Conduct of Russian Diplomacy, 1801–1825*, Berkeley 1969.

Gruner, W. D., "Der deutsche Bund, die deutschen Verfassungstaaten und die Rheinkrise von 1840," *Zeitschrift für bayerische Landesgeschichte* 53, 1990, 1, pp. 51–78.

Grunwald, M., *Vienna*, Philadelphia 1936.

Günther, M., *Das Verhalten Englands und Österreichs zum griechischen Aufstand in den Jahren 1821–1827*, unpublished dissertation, Wien 1957.

Gürbüz, N., *Die österreichisch-türkischen Beziehungen vom Wiener Kongreß (1814–1815) bis zum Tod des Zaren Alexander I. (1825): Mit besonderer Beachtung der österreischischen Quellen*, unpublished dissertation, Wien 1983.

Guichen, E., *La crise d'Orient de 1839 à 1841 et l'Europe*, Paris 1921.

Guiral, P., *Adolphe Thiers ou de la nécessité en politiques*, Paris 1986.

Haas, A. G., "Metternich and the Slavs," *AHY* 4/5, 1968–1969, pp. 120–150.

Hahn, H. H., *Außenpolitik in der Emigration: Die Exildiplomatie Adam Jerzy Czartoryskis 1830–1840*, München, Wien 1978.

Hahn, H.-W., *Geschichte des Deutschen Zollvereins*, Göttingen 1984.

Haider-Wilson, B., "Das Kultusprotektorat der Habsburgermonarchie im Osmanischen Reich: Zu seinen Rechtsgrundlagen und seiner Instrumentalisierung im 19. Jahrhundert (unter besonderer Berücksichtigung Jerusalems)," M. Kurz, M. Scheutz, K. Vocelka, T. Winkelbauer (eds.), *Das Osmanische Reich und die Habsburgermonarchie: Akten des internationalen Kongresses zum 150-jährigen Bestehen des Instituts für Österreichische Geschichtsforschung Wien, 22.–25. September 2004*, Wien 2005, pp. 121–147.

Haikal, A., "Die Auswirkung der britischen Kolonialpolitik auf die Wirtschaft Ägyptens," W. Markov (ed.), *Kolonialismus und Neokolonialismus in Nordafrika und Nahost*, Berlin 1964, pp. 226–248.

Hajjar, J., *L'Europe et les destinées du Proche-Orient (1815–1848)*, Paris 1970.

Hajnal, H., *The Danube: Its Historical, Political and Economic Importance*, The Hague 1920.

Hale, W., *Turkish Foreign Policy 1774–2000*, London, Portland 2002.

Hall, J., *England and the Orleans Monarchy*, London 1912.

Hamernik, G., *Anton Ritter von Laurin: Diplomat, Sammler und Ausgräber*, unpublished dissertation, Wien 1986.

Hamenn, O. J., "The Failure of an Attempted Franco-German Liberal Rapprochement 1830–1840," *AHR* 52, 1946, 1, pp. 54–67.

Hametner, M., *Orientpolitik Österreichs in den Jahren 1841–1853*, unpublished dissertation, Wien 1934.

Hammer, K., *Die französische Diplomatie der Restauration und Deutschland 1814–1830*, Stuttgart 1963.

Harik, I. F., *Politics and Change in a Traditional Society Lebanon, 1711–1845*, Princeton, New Jersey 1968.

Hartley, J. M., *Alexander I*, London 1994.

Hasenclever, A., *Die Orientalische Frage in den Jahren 1838–1841: Ursprung des Meerengenvertrages vom 13. Juli 1841*, Leipzig 1914.

Hasenclever, A., "König Friedrich Wilhelm IV. und die Londoner Konvention vom 15. Juli 1840," *Forschungen zur brandenburgischen und preußischen Geschichte* 25, 1913, pp. 143–158.

Heiderich, F., *Die Donau als Verkehrstraße*, Wien, Leipzig 1916.

Heinzelmann, T., *Heiliger Kampf oder Landesverteidigung: Die Dis-*

kussion um die Einführung der allgemeinen Militärpflicht im Osmanischen Reich 1826–1856, Frankfurt am Main 2004.

Henderson, W. O., *The Zollverein,* Cambridge 1939.

Herzog, E., *Graf Franz Anton Kolowrat-Liebsteinsky: Seine politische Tätigkeit in Wien (1826–1848),* unpublished dissertation, Wien 1968.

Heydenreuter, R., "Die erträumte Nation: Griechenlands Staatswerdung zwischen Philhellenismus und Militärintervention," R. Heydenreuter, J. Murken, R. Wünsche (eds.), *Die erträumte Nation,* München 1995, pp. 47–77.

Heyer, F., *Die Orientalische Frage im kirchlichen Lebenskreis: Das Einwirken der Kirchen des Auslands auf die Emanzipation der orthodoxen Nationen Südosteuropas 1804–1912,* Wiesbaden 1991.

Hitti, P. K., *Lebanon in History: From the Earliest Times to the Present,* London, New York 1957.

Histoire de la diplomatie française, Paris 2005.

Höbelt, L., "Zur Militärpolitik des deutschen Bundes," H. Rumpler (ed.), *Deutscher Bund und deutsche Frage 1815–1866,* München 1990, pp. 114–135.

Hoffmann, A., "Die Donau und Österreich," *Südosteuropa-Jahrbuch* 5, 1961, pp. 28–42.

Holbraad, C., *The Concert of Europe: A Study in German and British International Theory 1815–1914,* London, Southampton 1970.

Honsell, J., *Bayern und die Rheinkrise von 1840,* unpublished thesis, München 2002.

Hoskins, H. L., *British Routes to India,* New York, London, Toronto 1928.

Howarth, D., *The Greek Adventure: Lord Byron and Other Eccentrics in the War of Independence,* London 1976.

Howarth, T. E. B., *Citizen King: The Life of Louis-Philippe, King of French,* London 1961.

Hučka, J., "K historii Metternichovy železárny v Plasích [On the History of Metternich's Ironworks in Plass]," I. Budil, M. Šedivý (eds.), *Metternich a jeho doba: Sborník příspěvků z konference uskutečněné v Plzni ve dnech 23. a 24. dubna 2009 [Metternich and His Time: Memorial Volume of the Conference Held in Pilsen on 23 and 24 April 2009],* Plzeň 2009, pp. 85–93.

Hurewitz, J. C., "Russia and the Straits Question: A Reevaluation of the Origins of the Problem," *WRP* 14, 1962, pp. 605–632.

Inalcık, H., Quataert, D. (eds.), *An Economic and Social History of the Ottoman Empire*, Cambridge 2009.

Ingle, H. N., *Nesselrode and the Russian Rapprochement with Britain, 1836–1844*, Berkeley, Los Angeles, London 1976.

Inglisian, V., *Hundertfünfzig Jahre Mechitharisten in Wien (1811–1961)*, Wien 1961.

Iorga, N., *A History of Anglo-Roumanian Relations*, Bucharest 1931.

Isambert, G., *L'indépendence grecque et l'Europe*, Paris 1900.

Issawi, C., "The Tabriz-Trabzon Trade, 1830–1900: Rise and Decline of a Route," *IJMES* 1, 1970, 1, pp. 18–27.

Ivanissevich, D., "L'apertura delle linee del Lloyd Austriaco con l'Impero otomano," G. Pavan (ed.), *Trieste e la Turchia*, Trieste 1996, pp. 58–64.

Jahn, H., *Das "Journal de St.-Pétersbourg politique et littéraire" und "The Courier". Die Berichterstattung zweier offiziöser Zeitungen zur "Orientalischen Frage" in den Jahren 1827–1833*, München 1984.

Jahrmann, W., *Frankreich und die orientalische Frage 1875/78*, Berlin 1936.

Jelavich, B., *Modern Austria: Empire and Republic, 1815–1986*, London, New York 1987.

Jelavich, B., *Russia and the Formation of the Romanian National State 1821–1878*, London, New York, New Rochelle, Melbourne, Sydney 1984.

Jelavich, B., *Russia's Balkan Entanglements, 1806–1914*, Cambridge, New York, Port Chester, Melbourne, Sydney 1991.

Jelavich, B., *St. Petersburg and Moscow: Tsarist and Soviet Foreign Policy, 1814–1974*, Bloomington, London 1974.

Jelavich, B., Jelavich, C., *The Establishment of the Balkan National States 1804–1920*, Seattle, London 1977.

Jelavich, B., *The Habsburg Empire in European Affairs 1814–1918*, Chicago 1969.

Jochmus, A. von, *Der Verfall des Osmanen-Reiches seit 1840*, Frankfurt am Main 1858.

Johnson, P., *A History of the Jews*, New York 1988.

Jouplain, M., *La Question du Liban*, Paris 1908.

Julien, C.-A., *Histoire de l'Algérie contemporaine: La conquête et les débuts de la colonisation (1827–1871)*, Paris 1964.

Kagan, K., "The Myth of the European Concert: The Realist-Institutionalist Debate and Great Power Behaviour in the Eastern Question, 1821–41," *Security Studies* 7, 1997/98, 2, pp. 1–57.

Kaldis, W. P., "Leopold and the Greek Crown," *Balkan Studies* 8, 1967, 1, pp. 53–64.

Kalman, J., "Sensuality, Depravity, and Ritual Murder: The Damascus Blood Libel and Jews in France," *Jewish Social Studies* 13, 2007, 3, pp. 35–59.

Kammerhofer, L., "Das Konsularwerk der Habsburgermonarchie (1752–1918): Ein Überblick mit Schwerpunkt auf Südosteuropa," H. Heppner (ed.), *Der Weg führt über Österreich... Zur Geschichte des Verkehrs- und Nachrichtenwesens von und nach Südosteuropa*, Wien, Köln, Weimar 1996, pp. 7–31.

Kargl, A., *Studien zur österreichischen Internuntiatur in Konstantinopel 1802–1818*, unpublished dissertation, Wien 1974.

Kantor, W., *Karl Ludwig Graf Ficquelmont: Ein Lebensbild mit besonderer Rücksicht auf seine diplomatische Mitarbeit bei Metternich*, unpublished dissertation, Wien 1948.

Kasaba, R., *The Ottoman Empire and the World Economy: Nineteenth Century*, New York 1988.

Kernbauer, A., "Die österreichischen Ärzte in Istanbul und die Großmachtdiplomatie," M. Skopec, A. Kernbauer (eds.), *Österreichisch-türkische medizinische Beziehungen historisch und modern, (Mitteilungen der österreichischen Gesellschaft für Geschichte der Naturwissenschaften 10/1990)*, Wien 1990, pp. 7–17.

Kerner, R. J., "Russia's New Policy in the Near East after the Peace of Adrianople," *CHJ* 5, 1935–1937, 3, pp. 280–290.

Kessel, E., *Moltke*, Stuttgart 1957.

Khalaf, S., "Communal Conflict in Nineteenth-Century Lebanon," B. Braude, B. Lewis (eds.), *Christians and Jews in the Ottoman Empire: The Functioning of a Plural Society*, II, New York 1982, pp. 108–134.

Khuepach, A. von, Bayer, H. von, *Geschichte der k. u. k. Kriegsmarine, II. Teil: Die K. K. Österreichische Kriegsmarine in dem Zeitraum von 1797 bis 1848, III. Band: Geschichte der k. k. Kriegsmarine während der Jahre 1814–1847: Die österreichisch-venezianische Kriegsmarine*, Graz, Köln 1966.

King, C., "Imagining Circassia: David Urquhart and the Making of North Caucasus Nationalism," *Russian Review* 66, 2007, 2, pp. 238–255.

King, C., *The Black Sea: A History*, Oxford 2004.

Kirchner, H.-M., "Joseph Anton v. Pilat, Chefredakteur des "Österreichischen Beobachter" und Korrespondent der Augsburger "Allgemeinen Zeitung" und die Berichterstattung über den griechischen Aufstand in der Augsburger "Allgemeinen Zeitung" von 1821 bis 1827," E. Konstantinou (ed.), *Europäischer Philhellenismus: Die europäische philhellenische Presse bis zur 1. Hälfte des 19. Jahrhunderts*, Frankfurt am Main, Berlin, Bern, New York, Paris, Wien 1994, pp. 93–108.

Kissinger, H. A., *A World Restored: Metternich, Castlereagh and the Problems of Peace 1812–22*, London 1957.

Knorr, W., *Die Donau und die Meerengenfrage: Ein völkerrechtsgeschichtlicher Rückblick*, Weimar 1917.

Kodaman, B., *Les Ambassades de Mustapha Réchid Pacha à Paris*, Ankara 1991.

Koloğlu, O., "Alexandre Blacque, défenseur de l'État ottoman par amour des libertés," H. Batu, J.-L. Bacqué-Grammont (eds.), *L'Empire Ottoman, la République de Turquie et la France*, Istanbul 1986, pp. 179–195.

Kondis, B., "Aspects of Anglo-Russian Rivalry during the Greek Revolution," *Les relations gréco-russes pendant la domination turque et la guerre d'indépendance grecque*, Thessaloniki 1983, pp. 109–118.

Konstantinou, E., "Trägerschichten des Philhellenismus und Frühliberalismus in Europa," E. Konstantinou, U. Wiedenmann (eds.), *Europäischer Philhellenismus: Ursachen und Wirkungen*, Neuried 1989, pp. 53–84.

Kornrumpf, H.-J., "Die türkischen Reformdekrete von 1839 und 1856 und ihre Bewertung in zeitgenössischen Akten und Presseerzeugnissen," J. Matešić, K. Heitmann (eds.), *Südosteuropa in der Wahrnehmung der deutschen Öffentlichkeit vom Wiener Kongreß (1815) bis zum Pariser Frieden (1856)*, München 1990, pp. 113–121.

Koukkou, H., "The "Note on Greece" (Note sur la Grèce) by François-René de Chateaubriand," E. Konstantinou (ed.), *Europäischer Philhellenismus: Die europäische philhellenische Literatur bis zur 1. Hälfte des 19. Jahrhunderts*, Frankfurt am Main, Bern, New York, Paris 1992, pp. 53–62.

Kracauer, I., *Geschichte der Juden in Frankfurt a. M. (1150–1824)*, II, Frankfurt a. M. 1927.

Krämer, G., *Geschichte Palästinas: Von der osmanischen Eroberung bis zur Gründung des Staates Israel*, München 2003.

Kraus, K., *Politisches Gleichgewicht und Europagedanke bei Metternich*, Frankfurt am Main 1993.

Krauss, S., *Die politischen Beziehungen zwischen Bayern und Frankreich 1814/1815–1840*, München 1987.

Krauter, J., *Franz Freiherr von Ottenfels: Beiträge zur Politik Metternichs im griechischen Freiheitskampfe 1822–1832*, Salzburg 1913.

Krautheim, H.-J., *Öffentliche Meinung und imperiale Politik: Das britische Rußlandbild 1815–1854*, Berlin 1977.

Kreiser, K., "Türkische Studenten in Europa," G. Höpp (ed.), *Fremde Erfahrungen: Asiaten und Afrikaner in Deutschland, Österreich und in der Schweiz bis 1945*, Berlin 1996, pp. 385–400.

Kutluoğlu, M. H., *The Egyptian Question (1831–1841): The Expansionist Policy of Mehmed Ali Paşa in Syria and Asia Minor and the Reaction of the Sublime Porte*, Istanbul 1998.

Lachmayer, K., *Mehmed Ali und Österreich*, unpublished dissertation, Wien 1952.

Lamb, M., "Writing up the Eastern Question in 1835–1836," *IHR* 15, 1993, 2, pp. 239–268.

Lampe, J. R., Jackson, M. R., *Balkan Economic History, 1550–1950: From Imperial Borderlands to Developing Nations*, Bloomington 1982.

Lamunière, M., *Histoire de l'Algérie illustrée: De 1830 à nos jours*, Paris 1962.

Laurens, H., *La Question de Palestine, tome premier 1799–1922: L'intervention de la Terre Sainte*, Paris 1999.

Laurent, A., *Relations historique des affaires de Syrie, depuis 1840 jusqu'en 1842*, I, Paris 1846.

LeDonne, J., "Geopolitics, Logistics, and Grain: Russia's Ambitions in the Black Sea Basin, 1737–1834," *IHR* 28, 2006, 1, pp. 1–41.

Ledré, C., *La presse à l'assaut de la monarchie 1815–1848*, Paris 1960.

Lengyel, E., *Egypt's Role in World Affairs*, Washington 1957.

Levy, A., "The Officer Corps in Sultan Mahmud II's New Ottoman Army, 1826–1839," *IJMES* 2, 1971, 1, pp. 21–39.

Lincoln, W. B., *Nicholas I: Emperor and Autocrat of All the Russias*, London 1989.

Loewe, H., *Friedrich Thiersch und die griechische Frage*, München 1913.

Lorenz, F., *Karl Ludwig Graf Ficquelmont als Diplomat und Staatsmann*, unpublished dissertation, Wien 1966.

Lufti al-Sayyid Marsot, A., *Egypt in the Reign of Muhammad Ali*, Cambridge 1984.

Lufti al-Sayyid Marsot, A., "What Price Reform?" D. Panzac, A. Raymond (eds.), *La France et l'Égypte à l'époque des vice-rois 1805–1882*, Le Caire 2002, pp. 3–11.

Maier, L., "Reformwille und Beharrung: Das Osmanische Reich 1835-1839 aus der Sicht Helmuth von Moltkes," J. Matešić, K. Heitmann (eds.), *Südosteuropa in der Wahrnehmung der deutschen Öffentlichkeit vom Wiener Kongreß (1815) bis zum Pariser Frieden (1856)*, München 1990, pp. 43–56.

Malo, H., *Thiers 1797–1877*, Paris 1932.

Ma'oz, M., "Changes in the Position of the Jewish Communities of Palestine and Syria in Mid-Nineteenth Century," M. Ma'oz (ed.), *Studies on Palestine during the Ottoman Period*, Jerusalem 1975, pp. 142–163.

Ma'oz, M., "Changing Relations between Jews, Muslims, and Christians during the Nineteenth Century, with Special Reference to Ottoman Syria and Palestine," A. Levy (ed.), *Jews, Turks, Ottomans: A Shared History, Fifteenth through the Twentieth Century*, New York 2002, pp. 108–119.

Ma'oz, M., *Ottoman Reform in Syria and Palestine 1840–1861: The Impact of the Tanzimat on Politics and Society*, Oxford 1968.

Marlowe, J., *Perfidious Albion: The Origins of Anglo-French Rivalry in the Levant*, London 1971.

Marcowitz, R., *Großmacht auf Bewährung: Die Interdependenz französischer Innen- und Außenpolitik und ihre Auswirkungen auf Frankreichs Stellung im europäischen Konzert 1814/15–1851/52*, Stuttgart 2001.

Mardin, Ş., *The Genesis of Young Ottoman Thought: A Study in the Modernization of Turkish Political Ideas*, Syracuse 2000.

Mardin, Ş., "The Influence of the French Revolution on the Ottoman Empire," *International Social Science Journal* 41, 1989, 119, pp. 17–31.

Marriot, J. A. R., *The Eastern Question: An Historical Study in European Diplomacy*, Oxford 1924.

Martens, F. F., *Die russische Politik in der Orientfrage*, St. Petersburg 1877.

Matuz, J., *Das Osmanische Reich: Grundlinien seiner Geschichte*, Darmstadt 1996.

Mayr, J. K., *Geschichte der österreichischen Staatskanzlei im Zeitalter des Fürsten Metternich*, Wien 1935.

Mayr, J. K., *Metternichs Geheimer Briefdienst: Postlogen und Postkurse*, Wien 1935.

McEwan, D., *Habsburg als Schutzmacht der Katholiken in Ägypten: Verfassung der Studie über das österreichische Kirchenprotektorat von seinen Anfängen bis zu seiner Abschaffung im Jahre 1914*, Kairo, Wiesbaden 1982.

Macfie, A. L., *The Eastern Question 1774–1923*, London, New York 1996.

Meriage, L. P., "The First Serbian Uprising (1804–1813) and the Nineteenth-Century Origins of the Eastern Question," *SR* 37, 1978, 3, pp. 421–439.

Meynert, H., *Peter Joseph Freiherr von Eichhoff, früherer k. k. Hofkammerpräsident, sein Leben und ämtliches Wirken*, Wien 1849.

Middleton, R. C., "Palmerston, Ponsonby and Mehemet Ali: Some Observations on Ambassadorial Independence in the East, 1838–1840," *EEQ* 15, 1982, pp. 409–424.

Milev, N., "Réchid pacha et la réforme ottomane," *Zeitschrift für Osteuropäische Geschichte* 2, 1912, 3, pp. 382–398.

Molden, E., *Die Orientpolitik des Fürsten Metternich, 1829–1833*, Wien, Leipzig 1913.

Mosely, P. E., *Russian Diplomacy and the Opening of the Eastern Question in 1838 and 1839*, Cambridge 1934.

Moussa, S., "Les saint-simoniens en Égypte: le cas d'Ismayl Urban," D. Panzac, A. Raymond (eds.), *La France et l'Égypte à l'époque des vice-rois 1805–1882*, Le Caire 2002, pp. 225–233.

Moutafidou, A., "Alexandros Ypsilantis in Theresienstadt 1826–1827," *SOF* 63/64, 2004/2005, pp. 232–244.

Mühlhauser, J., *Die Geschichte des "Österreichischer Beobachter" von der Gründung bis zum Tode Friedrich von Gentz 1810–1832*, unpublished dissertation, Wien 1948.

Müller, F. L., *Britain and the German Question: Perceptions of Nationalism and Political Reform, 1830–63*, Basingstoke 2002.

Müller, H., "Der Weg nach Münchengrätz: Voraussetzungen, Bedingungen und Grenzen der Reaktivierung des reaktionären Bündnisses der Habsburger und Hohenzollern mit den Romanows im Herbst 1833," *Jahrbuch für Geschichte* 21, 1980, pp. 7–62.

Mustafa, A. A.-R., "The Breakdown of the Monopoly System in Egypt after 1840," P. M. Holt (ed.), *Political and Social Change in Modern Egypt: Historical Studies from the Ottoman Conquest to the United Arab Republic*, London, New York, Toronto 1968, pp. 291–307.

Napier, Sir C., *The War in Syria*, I–II, London 1842.

Narotchnitzki, A. L., "La diplomatie russe et la préparation de la conférance de Saint-Pétersbourg sur la Grèce en 1824," *Les relations gréco-russes pendant la domination turque et la guerre d'indépendance grecque*, Thessaloniki 1983, pp. 87–97.

Nichols, I. C., "The Eastern Question and the Vienna Conference, September 1822," *JCEA* 21, 1961, 1, pp. 53–66.

Nichols, I. C., *The European Pentarchy and the Congress of Verona 1822*, The Hague 1971.

Nichols, I. C., "Tsar Alexander I: Pacifist, Aggressor, or Vacillator?" *EEQ* 16, 1982, 1, pp. 33–44.

Nikolaides, K., "Die Politik des Fürsten Metternich gegenüber der großen Revolution von 1821," *Oesterreichische Rundschau* 18, 1922, pp. 778–789.

Nohra, J. A., "L'Autriche et la question du Liban (1840–1865)," A. Tietze (ed.), *Habsburgisch-osmanische Beziehungen: Relations Habsbourg-ottomanes*, Wien 1985, pp. 293–323.

Novotny, A., *Oesterreich-Preussen in den Jahren 1840–1848*, unpublished dissertation, Wien 1928.

O'Brien, P., "L'Embastillement de Paris: The Fortification of Paris during the July Monarchy," *French Historical Studies* 9, 1975, 1, pp. 63–82.

Oberwalder, E., *Die Rechtsstellung der Donau als Wasserstrasse und die Volkswirtschaftlichen Auswirkungen auf die Donauschiffahrt*, unpublished dissertation, Wien 1947.

Otruba, G., "Der Deutsche Zollverein und Österreich: Nachklang zum 150. Jahrestag der "Gründung" des Deutschen Zollvereines," *ÖGL* 15, 1971, 3, pp. 121–134.

Owen, R., *The Middle East in the World Economy 1800–1914*, London, New York 1981.

Palmer, A., *Metternich: Councillor of Europe*, London 1972.

Pamuk, Ş., *A Monetary History of the Ottoman Empire*, Cambridge 2000.

Pappas, P. C., *The United States and the Greek War for Independence 1821–1828*, New York 1985.

Parfitt, T., *The Jews in Palestine 1800–1882*, Woodbridge, Wolfeboro 1987.

Patera, A., "Die Rolle der Habsburgermonarchie für den Postverkehr zwischen dem Balkan und dem übrigen Europa," H. Heppner (ed.), *Der Weg führt über Österreich... Zur Geschichte des Verkehrs- und Nachrichtenwesens von und nach Südosteuropa*, Wien, Köln, Weimar 1996, pp. 37–89.

Pauley, B. F., *From Prejudice to Persecution: A History of Austrian Anti-Semitism*, Chapel Hill, London 1992.

Pavelka, H., *Englisch-Österreichische Wirtschaftsbeziehungen in der ersten Hälfte des 19. Jahrhunderts*, Graz, Wien, Köln 1968.

Petridis, P. W., *The Diplomatic Activity of John Capodistrias on behalf of the Greeks*, Thessaloniki 1974.

Petrie, C., *Diplomatic History 1713–1933*, London 1947.

Petrovich, M. B., *A History of Modern Serbia 1804–1918*, I, New York, London 1976.

Pfligersdorffer, G., "Philhellenisches bei Prokesch von Osten," E. Konstantinou (ed.), *Europäischer Philhellenismus: Die europäische philhellenische Literatur bis zur 1. Hälfte des 19. Jahrhunderts*, Frankfurt am Main, Bern, New York, Paris 1992, pp. 73–90.

Pfligersdorffer, G., "Österreichs griechenfreundliche Diplomatie in der ersten Hälfte des 19. Jahrhunderts," E. Konstantinou, U. Wiedenmann (eds.), *Europäischer Philhellenismus, Ursachen und Wirkungen*, Neuried 1989, pp. 191–209.

Pinkney, D. H., *The French Revolution of 1830*, New Jersey 1972.

Piussi, A., "The Orient of Paris: The Vanishing of Egypt from Early Nineteenth-Century Paris Salons (1800–1827)," D. Panzac, A. Raymond (eds.), *La France et l'Égypte à l'époque des vice-rois 1805–1882*, Le Caire 2002, pp. 41–58.

Platon, G., "Le «Problème roumain» et le «Problème oriental» dans la première moitié du XIXe siècle: Interférences et implications," *Revue roumaine d'histoire* 2, 1979, pp. 373–380.

Platon, G., "Romanian Principalities and England in the Period Previous the Revolution of 1848," G. Buzatu (ed.), *Anglo-Romanian Relations after 1821*, Jassy 1983, pp. 53–61.

Politis, A. G., *L'Hellénisme et l'Égypte moderne*, I, Paris 1929.

Pouthas, C. H., "La Politique de Thiers pendant la crise orientale de 1840," *RH* 182, 1938, pp. 72–96.

Pouthas, C. H., *La Politique étrangère de la France sous la monarchie constitutionnelle*, Paris 1948.

Price, M., *The Perilious Crown: France between Revolutions 1814–1848*, London 2007.

Priestley, H. I., *France Overseas: A Study of Modern Imperialism*, New York, London 1938.

Pröhl, K., *Die Bedeutung preussischer Politik in den Phasen der orientalischen Frage: Ein Beitrag zur Entwicklung deutsch-türkischer Beziehungen von 1606 bis 1871*, Frankfurt am Main 1986.

Prokesch-Osten, A. von, *Mehmed-Ali, Vize-König von Aegypten: Aus meinem Tagebuche 1826–1841*, Wien 1877.

Prokesch-Osten, A. von, *Geschichte des Abfalls der Griechen vom türkischen Reiche im Jahre 1821 und der Gründung des hellenischen Königreiches: Aus diplomatischem Standpuncte*, I-II, Wien 1867.

Prokesch-Osten, A. von, "Über die dermaligen Reformen im türkischen Reiche, 1832," *Kleine Schriften*, V, Stuttgart 1844, pp. 397–407.

Purkhart, M., "Österreichs Handel mit Ägypten," I. Lazar, J. Holaubek (eds.), *Egypt and Austria V: Egypt's Heritage in Europe*, Koper 2009, pp. 185–190.

Puryear, V. J., *France and the Levant from the Bourbon Restauration to the Peace of Kutiah*, Berkeley 1941.

Puryear, V. J., *International Economics and Diplomacy in the Near East, 1834–1853*, Stanford 1969.

Puryear, V. J., "L'opposition de l'Angleterre et de la France au traité d'Unkiar-Iskelesi en 1833," *RH* 1938, 182, pp. 283–310.

Puryear, V. J., "Odessa: Its Rise and International Importance, 1815–50," *Pacific Historical Review* 3, 1934, pp. 192–215.

Putschek, H., *Die Verwaltung Veneziens 1814-1830 mit besonderer Berücksichtigung von Konterbandwesen und Seeraub*, unpublished dissertation, Wien 1957.

Pyta, W., "Idee und Wirklichkeit der „Heiligen Allianz"," F.-L. Kroll (ed.), *Neue Wege der Ideengeschichte: Festschrift für Kurt Kluxen zum 85. Geburtstag*, Paderborn, München, Wien, Zürich 1996, pp. 315–359.

Quataert, D., "An Essay on Economic Relations between the Ottoman and Habsburg Empires, 1800–1914," A. Tietze (ed.), *Habsburgisch-osmanische Beziehungen: Relations Habsbourg-ottomanes*, Wien 1985, pp. 243–250.

Rahimi, N., *Österreich und der Suezkanal*, unpublished dissertation, Wien 1968.

Ransel, D. L., *The Politics of Catherinian Russia: The Panin Party*, New Haven, London 1975.

Rautsi, I., *The Eastern Question Revisited: Case Studies in Ottoman Balance of Power*, Helsinki 1993.

Régnier, P., *Les Saint-Simoniens en Égypte, 1833–1851*, Le Caire 1989.

Reinerman, A. J., *Austria and the Papacy in the Age of Metternich*,

Volume I: Between Conflict and Cooperation 1809–1830, Washington 1979.

Reinerman, A. J., "Metternich and Reform: The Case of the Papal State, 1814–1848," *JMH* 42, 1970, 4, pp. 526–527.

Reinerman, A. J., "Metternich, the Papacy and the Greek Revolution," *EEQ* 12, 1978, 2, pp. 177–188.

Reinerman, A. J., "Metternich, the Powers, and the 1831 Italian Crisis," *CEH* 10, 1977, 3, pp. 206–219.

Rendall, M., "Cosmopolitanism and Russian Near Eastern Policy, 1821–41: Debunking a Historical Canard," W. Pyta (ed.), *Das europäische Mächtekonzert: Friedens- und Sicherheitspolitik vom Wiener Kongreß 1815 bis zum Krimkrieg 1853*, Köln, Weimar, Wien 2009, pp. 237–255.

Rendall, M., "Restraint or Self-Restraint of Russia: Nicholas I, the Treaty of Unkiar Skelessi, and the Vienna System, 1832–1841," *IHR* 24, 2002, 1, pp. 37–63.

Renouvin, P., *Histoire des relations internationales, V: Le XIX(e) siècle I*, Paris 1954.

Richardson, J. L., *Crisis Diplomacy: The Great Powers since the Mid-Nineteenth Century*, Cambridge 1994.

Ridley, J., *Lord Palmerston*, London 1970.

Ridley, R. T., *Napoleon's Proconsul in Egypt: The Life and Times of Bernardino Drovetti*, London 1998.

Rieben, H., *Prinzipiengrundlage und Diplomatie in Metternichs Europapolitik, 1815–1848*, Bern 1942.

Riedl-Dorn, C., "Tiere auf weiter Fahrt: Expeditionen für Tiergarten und Museum," M. G. Ash, L. Dittrich (eds.), *Menagerie des Kaisers – Zoo der Wiener: 250 Jahre Tiergarten Schönbrunn*, Wien 2002, pp. 353–358.

Rodkey, F. S., "Anglo-Russian Negotiations about a 'Permanent' Quadruple Alliance, 1840–1841," *AHR* 36, 1931, pp. 343–349.

Rodkey, F. S., "Conversations on Anglo-Russian Relations in 1838," *EHR* 50, 1935, pp. 120–123.

Rodkey, F. S., "Lord Palmerston and the Rejuvenation of Turkey, 1830–41: Part I, 1830–39," *JMH* 1, 1929, 4, pp. 570–593.

Rodkey, F. S., "Lord Palmerston and the Rejuvenation of Turkey, 1830–41: Part II, 1839–41," *JMH* 2, 1930, 2, pp. 193–225.

Rodkey, F. S., "Reshid Pasha's Memorandum of August 12, 1839," *JMH* 2, 1930, 2, pp. 251–257.

Rodkey, F. S., "Suggestions during the Crisis of 1840 for a 'League' to

Preserve Peace," *AHR* 35, 1930, 2, pp. 308–316.

Rodkey, F. S., *The Turko-Egyptian Question in the Relations of England, France and Russia 1832–1841*, Urbana 1924.

Rodkey, F. S., "The Views of Palmerston and Metternich on the Eastern Question in 1834," *EHR* 45, 1930, 180, pp. 627–640.

Roider, K. A., "Kaunitz, Joseph II and the Turkish War," *SEER* 54, 1976, 4, pp. 538–556.

Roider, K. A., *Austria's Eastern Question, 1700–1790*, Princeton 1982.

Roloff, G., "Fürst Metternich über die slavische und magyarische Gefahr im Jahre 1839," *MIÖG* 52, 1938, pp. 69–70.

Roman, V., *Rumänien im Spannungsfeld der Grossmächte 1774–1878: Die Donaufürstertümer vom osmanischen Vasallentum zur europäischen Peripherie*, Offenbach 1987.

Rosen, G., *Geschichte der Türkei von dem Siege der Reform im Jahre 1826 bis zum Pariser Tractat vom Jahre 1856*, Leipzig 1866.

Roth, C., *A Short History of the Jewish People*, Hartford 1969.

Rothenberg, G. E., "The Austrian Army in the Age of Metternich," *JMH* 40, 1968, 2, pp. 155–165.

Rozen, M., "The Ottoman Jews," S. N. Faroqhi (ed.), *The Cambridge History of Turkey, Volume 3: The Later Ottoman Empire, 1603–1839*, Cambridge 2006, pp. 256–271.

Rumpler, H., "Economia e potere politico: Il ruolo di Trieste nella politica di sviluppo economico di Vienna," R. Finzi, L. Panariti, G. Panjek (eds.), *Storia economica e sociale di Trieste, Volume II: La città dei traffici 1719–1918*, Trieste 2003, pp. 55–124.

Rustum, A. J., "Syria under Mehemet Ali," *The American Journal of Semitic Languages and Literatures* 41, 1924, 1, pp. 34–57.

Rustum, A. J., *The Royal Archives of Egypt and the Origins of the Egyptian Expedition to Syria 1831–1841*, Beirut 1936.

Sabry, M., *L'Empire Égyptien sous Mohamed-Ali et La Question d'Orient (1811–1849)*, Paris 1930.

Said, E. W., *Orientalism*, New York 1994.

Salibi, K. S., *The Modern History of Lebanon*, London 1965.

Sauer, M., *Österreich und die Levante 1814–1838*, unpublished dissertation, Wien 1971.

Sauer, M., "Österreich und die Sulina-Frage 1829–1854, Erster Teil," *MÖStA* 40, 1987, pp. 184–236.

Sauer, M., "Österreich und die Sulina-Frage 1829–1854, Zweiter Teil," *MÖStA* 41, 1990, pp. 72–137.

Sauer, M., "Zur Reform der österreichischen Levante-Konsulate im Vormärz," *MÖStA* 27, 1974, pp. 195–237.

Sauer, W., "Ein Jesuitenstaat in Afrika? Habsburgische Kolonialpolitik in Ägypten, dem Sudan und Äthiopien in der ersten Hälfte des 19. Jahrhunderts," *ÖGL* 55, 2011, 1, pp. 7–27.

Sauer, W., "Schwarz-Gelb in Afrika: Habsburgermonarchie und koloniale Frage," W. Sauer (ed.), *K. u k. colonial: Habsburgermonarchie und europäische Herrschaft in Afrika*, Wien, Köln, Weimar 2002, pp. 17–78.

Sauvigny, G. de B. de, "Sainte Alliance et Alliance dans les conceptions de Metternich," *RH* 223, 1960, pp. 249–274.

Sauvigny, G. de B. de, *Metternich: Staatsmann und Diplomat für Österreich und den Frieden*, Gernsbach 1988.

Sauvigny, G. de B. de, *Metternich et la France après le congrès de Vienne*, II–III, Paris 1970.

Schalk, H., *250 Jahre militärtechnische Ausbildung in Österreich*, Wien 1968.

Schamesberger, H., *Canning und die Politik Metternichs*, unpublished dissertation, Wien 1972.

Schels, J. B., "Saint Jean d'Acre 1291–1840," *Österreichische Militärische Zeitschrift* 5, 1841, pp. 137–164.

Schiemann, T., *Geschichte Russlands unter Nikolaus I.*, I–III, Berlin 1904–1913.

Schlicht, A., *Frankreich und die syrischen Christen 1799–1861: Minoritäten und europäischer Imperialismus im Vorderen Orient*, Berlin 1981.

Schlicht, A., "The Role of Foreign Powers in the History of Lebanon and Syria from 1799 to 1861," *Journal of Asian History* 14, 1980, 2, pp. 97–126.

Schölch, A., "Europa und Palästina 1838–1917," H. Mejcher, A. Schölch (eds.), *Die Palästina-Frage 1917–1948*, München, Wien, Zürich 1993, pp. 11–46.

Schölch, A., "Jerusalem in the 19th Century (1831–1917 AD)," K. J. Asali (ed.), *Jerusalem in History*, Buckhurst Hill 1989, pp. 228–248.

Scholl, H., *Abriß der Geschichte des Krieges 1840–41 in Syrien*, Wien 1866.

Schroeder, P. W., *Metternich's Diplomacy at Its Zenith, 1820–1823*, New York 1962.

Schroeder, P. W., *The Transformation of European Politics 1763–*

1848, Oxford 1996.

Schroeder, P. W., "The Transformation of European Politics: Some Reflections," W. Pyta (ed.), *Das europäische Mächtekonzert: Friedens- und Sicherheitspolitik vom Wiener Kongreß 1815 bis zum Krimkrieg 1853*, Köln, Weimar, Wien 2009, pp. 25–40.

Schütz, E., *Die europäische Allianzpolitik Alexanders I. und der griechische Unabhängigkeitskampf 1820–1830*, Wiesbaden 1975.

Schulz, M., *Normen und Praxis: Das Europäische Konzert der Großmächte als Sicherheitsrat, 1815–1860*, München 2009.

Schulz, O., "'This Clumsy Fabric of Barbarous Power': Die europäische Außenpolitik und der außereuropäische Raum am Beispiel des Osmanischen Reiches," W. Pyta (ed.), *Das europäische Mächtekonzert: Friedens- und Sicherheitspolitik vom Wiener Kongreß 1815 bis zum Krimkrieg 1853*, Köln, Weimar, Wien 2009, pp. 273–298.

Schulze, H., *Der Weg zum Nationalstaat: Die deutsche Nationalbewegung vom 18. Jahrhundert bis zur Reichsgründung*, München 1985.

Sédouy, J.-A. de, *Le congrès de Vienne: L'Europe contre la France 1812–1815*, Paris 2003.

Serres, J., *La politique turque en Afrique du Nord sous la Monarchie de Juillet*, Paris 1925.

Seton-Watson, H., *The Russian Empire 1801–1917*, Oxford 1967.

Seward, D., *Metternich: Der erste Europäer. Eine Biographie*, Zürich 1993.

Shaw, S. J., Shaw, E. K., *History of the Ottoman Empire and Modern Turkey, Vol. 2: Reform, Revolution and Republic – The Rise of Modern Turkey, 1808–1975*, Cambridge 1977.

Siemann, W., *Metternich: Staatsmann zwischen Restauration und Moderne*, München 2010.

Simon, R. S., Laskier, M. M., Reguer, S., *The Jews of the Middle East and North Africa in Modern Times*, New York 2003.

Sinno, A.-R., *Deutsche Interessen in Syrien und Palästina 1841–1898*, Berlin 1982.

Sinoué, G., *Le dernier Pharaon: Méhémet Ali (1770–1849)*, Paris 1997.

Sked, A., *Europe's Balance of Power, 1815–1848*, London 1979.

Sked, A., *Metternich and Austria: An Evaluation*, New York 2008.

Sked, A., "The Metternich System, 1815–48," A. Sked (ed.), *Europe's Balance of Power, 1815–1848*, London 1979, pp. 98–121.

Skiotis, D. N., "The Greek Revolution: Ali Pasha's Last Gamble,"

N. P. Diamandouros, J. P. Anton, J. A. Petropulos, P. Topping (eds.), *Hellenism and the First Greek War of Liberation (1821–1830): Continuity and Change*, Thessaloniki 1976, pp. 97–109.

Sofka, J. R., "Metternich's Theory of European Order: A Political Agenda for 'Perpetual Peace'," *The Review of Politics* 60, 1998, 1, pp. 115–149.

Sondhaus, L., *The Habsburg Empire and the Sea: Austrian Naval Policy 1797–1866*, West Lafayette 1989.

Southgate, D., *'The Most English Minister ... ' The Policies and Politics of Palmerston*, London 1966.

Srbik, H. von, *Metternich: Der Staatsmann und der Mensch*, I–II, München 1925.

Srbik, H. von, "Statesman of Philosophical Principles," E. E. Kraehe (ed.), *The Metternich Controversy*, New York, Chicago, San Francisco, Atlanta, Dallas, Montreal, Toronto, London, Sydney 1971, pp. 33–47.

St Clair, W., *That Greece Might Still Be Free: The Philhellenes in the War of Independence*, Cambridge 2008.

Starkenfels, V. W. E. von, *Die kaiserlich-königliche Orientalische Akademie zu Wien: Ihre Gründung, Fortbildung und Gegewärtige Einrichtung*, Wien 1839.

Stavrianos, L. S., *The Balkans since 1453*, New York 2002.

Sterling, E., *Judenhaß: Die Anfänge des politischen Antisemitismus in Deutschland (1815–1850)*, Frankfurt am Main 1969.

Stern, A., "König Leopold I. von Belgien und die Krise von 1840," *Historische Vierteljahrschrift* 22, 1923, pp. 312–318.

Sturdza, A. C., *Règne de Michel Sturdza: Prince régnant de Moldavie 1834–1849*, Paris 1907.

Subaşi, T., "British Support for Mustafa Reşid Pasha and his Reforms according to British Sources at the Public Records Office," K. Çiçek (ed.), *The Great Ottoman-Turkish Civilisation, Vol. 1: Politics*, Ankara 2000, pp. 427–432.

Sutter, B., "Die Reise Erzherzog Johanns 1837 nach Russland, Konstantinopel und Athen," W. Koschatzky (ed.), *Thomas Ender (1793–1875)*, Wien 1964, pp. 35–41.

Sweet, P. R., *Friedrich von Gentz: Defender of the Old Order*, Madison 1941.

Šedivý, M., "Austria's Role in the Constantinople Armenian Catholics Affair in 1828–31," *Middle Eastern Studies* 48, 2012, 1, pp. 51–71.

Šedivý, M., "From Adrianople to Münchengrätz: Metternich, Russia and the Eastern Question 1829–33," *IHR* 33, 2011, 2, pp. 205–233.

Šedivý, M., "From Hostility to Cooperation? Austria, Russia and the Danubian Principalities 1829–1840," *SEER* 89, 2011, 4, pp. 630–661.

Šedivý, M., "Metternich and Mustafa Reshid Pasha's Fall in 1841," *British Journal of Middle Eastern Studies* 39, 2012, 2, pp. 259–282.

Šedivý, M., "Metternich and the Anglo-Neapolitan Sulphur Crisis of 1840," *Journal of Modern Italian Studies* 16, 2011, 1, pp. 1–18.

Šedivý, M., "Metternich and the Ottoman Reform Movement," *European Review of History/Revue européenne d'histoire* 18, 2011, 4, pp. 427–441.

Šedivý, M., "Metternich and the Syrian Question 1840–1841," *AHY* 41, 2010, pp. 88–116.

Šedivý, M., "Metternich's Plan for a Viennese Conference in 1839," *CEH* 44, 2011, 3, pp. 397–419.

Švandrlík, R., *Historie Židů v Mariánských Lázních [The History of the Jews in Marienbad]*, Mariánské Lázně 2005.

Tappe, E. D., "The 1821 Revolution in the Rumanian Principalities," R. Clogg (ed.), *The Struggle for Greek Independence: Essays to Mark the 150th Anniversary of the Greek War of Independence*, London, Basingstoke 1973, pp. 135–155.

Taylor, A. J. P., "Perceptive but Superficial Tinkerer," E. E. Kraehe (ed.), *The Metternich Controversy*, New York, Chicago, San Francisco, Atlanta, Dallas, Montreal, Toronto, London, Sydney 1971, pp. 101–109.

Temperley, H., *England and the Near East: The Crimea*, London, New York, Toronto 1936.

Temperley, H., "Princess Lieven and the Protocol of 4 April 1826," *EHR* 39, 1924, pp. 55–78.

Temperley, H., *The Foreign Policy of Canning, 1822–27: England, the Neo-Holy Alliance, and the New World*, London 1966.

Terzioğlu, A., "Ein kurzer Blick auf die österreichisch-türkischen medizinischen Beziehungen von Anbeginn bis heute," A. Terzioğlu, E. Lucius (eds.), *Österreichisch-türkische medizinische Beziehungen: Berichte des Symposions vom 28. und 29. April 1986 in Istanbul*, Istanbul 1987, pp. 34–48.

Timms, E., "The Pernicious Rift: Metternich and the Debate about Jewish Emancipation at the Congress of Vienna," *Year Book* (Leo Baeck Institute, Oxford) 46, 2001, pp. 3–18.

Tischler, U., *Die habsburgische Politik gegenüber den Serben und Mon-*

tenegrinern 1791–1822, München 2000.

Todorova, M. N., "British and Russian Policy towards the Reform Movement in the Ottoman Empire (30-ies – 50-ies of the 19th c.)," *Études Balkaniques* 13, 1977, pp. 17–41.

Todorova, M. N., "Mythology of the Eastern Question: The Treaty of Unkiar-Iskelessi," M. N. Todorova (ed.), *Aspects of the Eastern Question: Essays from the First Bulgarian-Dutch Symposium of Historians, Sofia, 6–7 June 1984*, Sofia 1986, pp. 23–31.

Tombs, R., *France 1814–1914*, London, New York 1996.

Traboulsi, F., *A History of Modern Lebanon*, London 2007.

Treitschke, H. von, *Treitschke's History of Germany in the Nineteenth Century*, VI, London 1919.

Treitschke, H. von, *Deutsche Geschichte im Neunzehnten Jahrhundert, Vierter Theil: Bis zum Tode Friedrich Wilhelms III.*, Leipzig 1889.

Triest und Oesterreichs Antheil am Welthandel während der lezten [sic] *zehn Jahre*, Triest 1842.

Tuchman, B., *Bible and Sword: England and Palestine from the Bronze Age to Balfour*, London 1988.

Ufford, L. W., *The Pasha: How Mehemet Ali Defied the West, 1839–1841*, Jefferson, London 2007.

Uyar, M., Erickson, E. J., *A Military History of the Ottomans: From Osman to Atatürk*, Santa Barbara, Denver, Oxford 2009.

Veit-Brause, I., *Die deutsch-französische Krise von 1840: Studien zur deutschen Einheitsbewebung*, Köln 1967.

Vereté, M., "A Plan for the Internationalization of Jerusalem, 1840–1841," N. Rose (ed.), *From Palmerston to Balfour: Collected Essays of Mayir Vereté*, London 1992, pp. 141–157.

Vidal, C., *Louis-Philippe, Metternich et la crise italienne de 1831–1832*, Paris 1931.

Viereck, P., "Bulwark Against Potential Fascism," E. E. Kraehe (ed.), *The Metternich Controversy*, New York, Chicago, San Francisco, Atlanta, Dallas, Montreal, Toronto, London, Sydney 1971, pp. 89–93.

Vimercati, C., *Die kaiserlich königliche österreichische Marine im Oriente: Geschichtlicher Rückblick auf das Jahr 1840*, Wien 1845.

Vinogradov, V. N., "Les discussions sur la Grèce à Londres durant la guerre de 1828–1829," *Les relations gréco-russes pendant la domination turque et la guerre d'indépendance grecque*, Thessaloniki 1983, pp. 133–160.

Vocelka, K., "Die Beurteilung der Tanzimatzeit in Österreich," *MIÖG* 100, 1992, pp. 410–431.

Vomáčková, V., "Österreich und der deutsche Zollverein," *Historica 5: Historische Wissenschaften in der Tschechoslowakei*, Prag 1963, pp. 109–146.

Wagner, R., *Moltke und Mühlbach zusammen unter dem Halbmonde 1837–1839*, Berlin 1893.

Waldbrunner, K., *125 Jahre Erste Donaudampfschiffahrtsgesellschaft*, Wien 1954.

Wallach, J. L., *Anatomie einer Militärhilfe: Die preußisch-deutschen Militärmissionen in der Türkei 1835–1919*, Düsseldorf 1976.

Wandruszka, A., "Anton Steindl Ritter von Plessenet: Ein österreichischer Diplomat in der Levante," *MÖStA* 25, 1972, pp. 449–464.

Webster, Sir C. K., *Palmerston, Metternich and the European System, 1830–41*, London 1934.

Webster, Sir C. K., *The Foreign Policy of Castlereagh, 1815–1822: Britain and the European Alliance*, London 1947.

Webster, Sir C. K., *The Foreign Policy of Palmerston 1830-1841: Britain, the Liberal Movement and the Eastern Question*, I–II, London 1951.

Widmann, E., *Die religiösen Anschauungen des Fürsten Metternich*, Darmstadt 1914.

Williams, J. B., *British Commercial Policy and Trade Expansion 1750–1850*, Oxford 1972.

Winkler, D., Pawlik, G., *Die Dampfschiffahrtsgesellschaft Österreichischer Lloyd 1836–1918*, Graz 1986.

Winkler, H. A., *Germany: The Long Road West, Volume 1: 1789–1933*, Oxford 2006.

Wolf, J. B., *The Barbary Coast: Algeria under the Turks*, Toronto 1979.

Wolff, L., "'Kennst du das Land?' The Uncertainty of Galicia in the Age of Metternich and Fredro," *SR* 67, 2008, 2, pp. 277–300.

Woodhouse, C. M., *Capodistria: The Founder of Greek Independence*, London 1973.

Woodhouse, C. M., *The Battle of Navarino*, London 1965.

Woodhouse, C. M., *The Greek War of Independence*, London 1952.

Woodhouse, C. M., "Kapodistrias and the Philiki Etairia, 1814–21," R. Clogg (ed.), *The Struggle for Greek Independence: Essays to Mark the 150th Anniversary of the Greek War of Independence*, London, Basingstoke 1973, pp. 104–134.

Woodward, E. L., *Three Studies in European Conservatism: Metternich, Guizot, the Catholic Church in the Nineteenth Century,* London 1963.

Wurth, R., "Österreichs orientalische Post: Durch Balkan und Levante," *Österreichische Postgeschichte* 16, Klingenbach 1993, pp. 112–122.

Yapp, M. E., *The Making of the Modern Near East,* London, New York 1987.

Ypsilanti, H., *Metternichs Stellung zum griechischen Freiheitskampf,* unpublished dissertation, Wien 1927.

Zakia, Z., "The Reforms of Sultan Mahmud II (1808–1839)," K. Çiçek, *The Great Ottoman-Turkish Civilisation, Vol. 1: Politics,* Ankara 2000, pp. 418–426.

Zamoyski, A., *Rites of Peace: The Fall of Napoleon and the Congress of Vienna,* London 2007.

Zane, G., "Die österreichischen und die deutschen Wirtschaftsbeziehungen zu den rumänischen Fürstentümern 1774–1874," *Weltwirtschaftliches Archiv* 26, 1927, 1, pp. 30–47.

Zierer, O., *Gouverneure und Rebellen: Geschichte Indiens und des Islam 1760 bis zur Gegenwart 1955,* Murnau, München, Innsbruck, Olten 1956.

Zürcher, E. J., *Turkey: A Modern History,* London, New York 1998.

Index

Miroslav Šedivý (*1980) is a Czech historian and lecturer in history at the University of West Bohemia in Pilsen. His research deals with the diplomatic, economic, military, religious and social history of Europe and the Near East in the first half of the 19th century, strictly speaking with Prince Metternich's foreign policy, Austro-Ottoman relations, the Eastern Question, the July Monarchy in France and German nationalism. He is a co-editor of the memorial volume *Metternich and His Time* (in Czech original: *Metternich a jeho doba*, Pilsen 2009), co-author of the monograph *Egypt during Mohammed Ali's Period* (in Czech original: *Egypt v době Muhammada Alího*, Prague 2010) and author of the book *The Bloody Odyssey: The Greek Struggle for Independence 1821–1832* (in Czech original: *Krvavá odyssea: Řecký boj za nezávislost 1821–1832*, Prague 2011). Additionally, he has written over 60 scholarly papers and articles in Czech, English and German. The most significant results of his research have been published in the journals *Austrian History Yearbook*, *British Journal of Middle Eastern Studies*, *Central European History*, *European Review of History/Revue européenne d'histoire*, *International History Review*, *Journal of Modern Italian Studies*, *Middle Eastern Studies* and *Slavonic and East European Review*.